# Van de Walle Continues to Set the Standard!

## Chapter-by-Chapter Highlights and New Features

### Chapter 1

details the newest *NCTM Principles and Standards* document and gives students a clear understanding of the issues behind the reform movement in mathematics education. Included are discussions of national and international studies, pressures of state standards, and a description of the NSF-supported reform curricula.

### Chapter 2

is thoroughly revised. The theme that "math makes sense" has been added.

### Chapter 3

is reorganized and rewritten to make critical ideas more clear–a tighter and more cohesive presentation of the material has evolved in the fourth edition.

### Chapter 4

now carefully lays out a structure for teaching mathematics through problem solving with the emphasis on "making mathematics problematic." The main focus is on the development of a general framework for instruction. The "before, during, after" structure of a lesson is strengthened in this chapter and is referred to throughout the book. Adapting tradition lessons, teaching tips and FAQs about teaching through problem solving are new to this edition.

### Chapter 5

includes more thorough coverage of combining instruction and assessment as well as new sections on dealing with high-stakes testing.

### Chapter 6

sections have been rearranged and streamlined. New activities and problems have been added, including several calculator activities. Two *Technology Notes* sections focus on software programs that can assist with early number development: using programs to create sets and using software programs to create part-part-whole activities.

### Chapter 7

has a new section on *Teaching Symbolism for the Operations* and includes two *Technology Notes* sections on using software programs for story problems in real context and word problems.

### Chapter 8

includes a more student-centered approach to fact strategies including the use of story problems for strategy development. There is a revised coverage of effective drill and practice. The *Technology Notes* section discusses software programs for fact drill.

### Chapter 9

emphasizes that "computational fluency," an idea found in *Principles and Standards*, is intimately connected with place-value understanding. *Technology Notes* focus on using technology for grouping activities and hundreds charts.

### Chapter 10

is completely new and designed to help teachers develop computational procedures beginning with direct modeling and invented strategies. Numerous examples of student strategies are included, along with ideas for helping students record their work. For each operation, adequate development of the traditional algorithms is included. This chapter makes it clear that invented strategies, mental computation, and traditional methods are not incompatible.

### Chapter 11

deals separately with number sense related to computation and provides an updated view of computational estimation. Specific strategies for estimation skills are included, as is a collection of activities for multi-digit number sense development. Two *Technology Notes* sections discuss software programs that help develop estimation skills.

### Chapter 12

remains the most detailed and thorough discussion of fraction concept development available. *Technology Notes* sections show software for fraction development and models to illustrate equivalent fractions.

## Chapter 13

offers an updated view of fraction computation, with explicit references to computer technology and/or graphing calculators. There is greater emphasis on student-invented methods and estimation. *Technology Notes* section discusses software programs that address the four operations with fractions.

## Chapter 14

continues the emphasis on fraction/decimal connections. It provides more coverage of using graphing calculators for decimal and percent concepts and separate. *Technology Notes* section discusses software that has decimal component and that provides useful practice of decimal-fraction equivalence.

## Chapter 15

reflects the idea that time must be given for the development of proportional reasoning through intuitive activities. This chapter has been trimmed and updated with new activities, including the use of calculators and dynamic geometry software. *Technology Notes* sections discuss spreadsheets for investigating proportions in table form and using dynamic geometry programs to study similarity and proportion.

## Chapter 16

maintains the thorough development of measurement skills and concepts, reflecting the emphasis placed on measurement in the Principles and Standards document. *Technology Notes* section shows how dynamic geometry can help illustrate the relationship between the areas of rectangles, parallelograms, and triangles.

## Chapter 17

offers a detailed description of the development of geometric reasoning and continues to provide a wealth of activities. *Technology Notes* sections are included in each of the three Van Hiele levels address dynamic geometry software programs and other electronic tools for activities at each.

## Chapter 18

explores the concepts of Probability and Data Analysis. New attention is paid to the idea that data is gathered in order to answer questions. Attribute activities have been moved into this chapter since classification is a form of data analysis. The *Technology Notes* sections discuss software for exploring probability concepts and probability with calculators.

## Chapter 19

is a new chapter that begins with a broad discussion of algebraic thinking and goes on to cover the development of repeating patterns, growing patterns, variables, and equations. The discussion of variables has been moved from Ch.21 of the third edition since variables play such a large role in algebraic reasoning.

## Chapter 20

continues the focus on algebraic reasoning with a complete development of fractions, a revision of Ch.21 in the third edition. New activities have been added but the main idea of integrating five different representations of functions, especially with technology, prevails.

## Chapter 21

is a revised and re-titled Chapter 20 from the third edition, completing the development of middle-school concepts. Here the topics of exponents, integers, and real numbers are discussed in depth.

## Chapter 22

offers specific information about topics such as forming cooperative learning groups, designing homework, working in a diverse classroom, using drill and practice, incorporating writing in mathematics, and using the textbook. It includes a section on adapting the three-part lesson format described in Chapter 4.

## Chapter 23

discusses the NCTM vision that all children can learn mathematics. It includes an up-to-date view of multicultural, socioeconomic, and gender equity issues. This chapter provides more information on working with children with learning disabilities, children with mental handicaps, and new sections discussing research on mathematically promising students.

## Chapter 24

is completely revised and updated, and addresses current use of technology (calculators and computers) in the classroom. Suggestions for using technology include guidelines for selecting software, tips for using the Internet, updated, annotated web resources for students and teachers.

0-801-33254-0

# The Addison Wesley Longman Advantage…
## … the ETA/Cuisenaire® Manipulative Starter Kit™

The most powerful mix of hands-on and overhead materials designed to get teaching mathematics off to a great start!

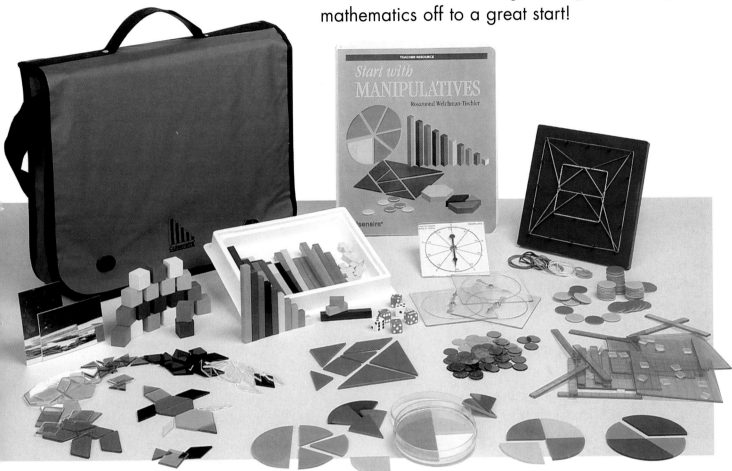

## Manipulative Starter Kit Includes:

24 hardwood color cubes
50 plastic 2-color counters
24-piece plastic fraction circle set
1 Set of 74 Cuisenaire Rods®
4 transparent overhead spinners
50 colorful overhead counters
96-piece overhead pattern block set
1 pair each red, green, and white dice set
2 flexible plastic mirrors
7-piece plastic tangram set
1 25-piece plastic geoboard

**ETA® Cuisenaire**

EXPANDING THE UNIVERSE OF LEARNING™

T eaching mathematics today means using a variety of manipulative materials to help children understand math concepts. The ETA/Cuisenaire Manipulative Starter Kit offers a selection of the most widely used manipulatives and overhead projector materials in classrooms today, and at a huge savings!

The Manipulative Starter Kit is your opportunity to learn how eleven different materials are used to introduce math concepts from kindergarten to eighth grade. A 92-page resource book, *Start with Manipulatives*, by Rosamond Welchman-Tischler, comes complete with a handsome three-ring binder to encourage the addition of classroom notes and information from other resources. This clearly written concise guide begins with an overview of each manipulative and then focuses on its pedagogical usefulness, indicating which math concepts are most appropriately taught with each model.

Equipped with this excellent resource and using the manipulatives from the kit, you will have everything needed to teach mathematics with methods and materials that support the standards set by the National Council of Teachers of Mathematics.

## What makes the Manipulative Starter Kit so popular?

*"The Manipulative Starter Kit gives pre-service teachers the tools to accurately model math concepts. The kit also allows them to study at home and allows for individual investigation."*

Dr. Steven Wilkinson
Assistant Professor of Mathematics
Northeastern State University

*"This kit has become a critical component of our mathematics methods and materials courses fo early childhood and elementary pre-service teachers. In many instances students truly understand mathematical concep for the first time."*

Dr. Claire Graham
Framingham State College

www.etacuisenaire.com

### ETA/Cuisenaire® Manipulative Starter Kit Order Form

☐ I am a teacher education student.

☐ I am a college/university professor.

Name _____

College _____

Address _____

City_____State_____Zip _____

Phone _____FAX _____e-mail _____

Please send me _____ Manipulative Starter Kits (Item No. AI-011324) at $39.95 each, plus 10% shipping and handling, for a total of $ _____. *Please mention code 000603DPAI when ordering*

Charge this order to (check one) ☐ VISA ☐ MasterCard

☐☐☐☐ ☐☐☐☐ ☐☐☐☐ ☐☐☐☐

Exp. Date_____Phone ( )_____

Signature _____

☐ My check for $ _____ is enclosed.

Make check payable to **ETA/Cuisenaire.**

Please mail this order form to:

**ETA/Cuisenaire
500 Greenview Court
Vernon Hills, IL 60061-1862**

☐ Please send me a FREE Mathematics Catalog.

My permanent address, if different from above is:

_____

_____

Prices subject to change without notice.

000603DPA

# Elementary and Middle School Mathematics
## Teaching Developmentally

### FOURTH EDITION

■ ● ▲

## JOHN A. VAN DE WALLE
### Virginia Commonwealth University

Longman

New York Boston San Francisco
London Toronto Sydney Tokyo Singapore Madrid
Mexico City Munich Paris Cape Town Hong Kong Montreal

Publisher: Priscilla McGeehon
Senior Acquisitions Editor: Virginia L. Blanford
Development Manager: Lisa Pinto
Development Editor: Karen Helfrich
Marketing Manager: Marilyn Borysek
Supplements Editor: Jennifer Ackerman
Production Manager: Ellen MacElree
Project Coordination, Text Design, and Electronic Page Makeup: Electronic Publishing Services Inc., NYC
Cover Design Manager: John Callahan
Cover Designer: Kay Petronio
Senior Manufacturing Buyer: Dennis J. Para
Printer and Binder: Quebecor World/Dubuque
Cover Printer: Coral Graphic Services, Inc.

For permission to use copyrighted material, grateful acknowledgment is made to the copyright holders listed throughout this book, which are hereby made part of this copyright page.

**Library of Congress Cataloging-in-Publication Data**
Van de Walle, John A.
    Elementary and middle school mathematics : teaching developmentally / John A.
Van de Walle.—4th ed.
        p.   cm.
    Includes bibliographical references and index.
    ISBN 0-8013-3253-2 (pbk.)
    1. Mathematics--Study and teaching (Elementary) 2. Mathematics--Study and teaching
(Middle school) I. Title.

QA135.5.V335 2000
510'.7'12—dc21
                                                                        00-023003

Please visit our website at http://www.awl.com

ISBN 0-8013-3253-2
12345678910—QUD—03020100

# BRIEF CONTENTS

# DETAILED CONTENTS

# PREFACE

*Children will become confident "doers" of mathematics only if mathematics makes sense to them and if they believe in their ability to make sense of it.*

*Trafton and Claus (1994, p. 21)*

Every child should come to believe that mathematics makes sense and, even more important, that she or he is capable of making sense of mathematics. In working on this fourth edition, these goals for students were foremost in my mind, as I hope they are for every teacher of mathematics. *Elementary and Middle School Mathematics* is more than a textbook. It is designed to be an instructional resource to assist you with the challenging and rewarding task of helping all children become confident "doers of mathematics."

We are in a critical period for the mathematics education of our students. On the one hand, there are wonderful teachers and programs everywhere who are proving that children can do exciting mathematics, develop important skills with real understanding, and enjoy with confidence their ability to do so. On the other hand, there are those who would return children to an era of drill and practice with an emphasis on memorization at the expense of understanding, an approach that has for decades been proved to fail. We cannot let the pendulum of change swing backward.

The fourth edition of this book reflects the continuing growth and change in mathematics education. It is designed to help you be the most important part of that growth—one who helps children develop confidence and understanding as they do mathematics.

## WHAT YOU WILL FIND IN THIS BOOK

Each of the three sections of the book plays an important role in helping you become an effective teacher. Together they form both a resource and a reference for teaching mathematics.

## Section 1: Foundations

The more I work with teachers, the more I find that at every grade level, the teachers with the best understanding of how children learn and the best sense of how to orchestrate a problem-solving environment are the ones who are most effective. In addition, if students are to "do mathematics," teachers themselves must have had real experiences with doing mathematics. Assessment techniques are also an integral part of instruction that good teachers use to enhance learning. And all of this is best understood in the context of current directions in mathematics education. These issues are addressed in the first five chapters. I have worked hard to make them as informative as possible and reflective of current research and practice. Furthermore, I have made every effort to implement these ideas throughout the rest of the text.

## Section 2: Concepts and Procedures

Chapters 6 through 21 focus on the specific mathematics topics encountered in grades K–8. Every major topic of the K–8 curriculum is addressed in depth. Each chapter provides a perspective on the mathematical content and on how children best learn that content, as well as numerous suggestions for activities to engage children in the process of doing mathematics. This book is unique in its treatment of so many topics in such a thorough manner.

Many classroom teachers use this text as a resource and consult it as they plan each new unit. Beyond the numerous activities, the chapters in Section 2 provide details on the development of specific content. The numerous boxed activities for children are integrated with the discussion that surrounds them. Reflecting on the activities as you read can help you think about the mathematics from the perspective of the child. Every activity requires that students be mentally engaged: to figure something out, to search for a pattern, to explain a reason for an idea—in short, to do mathematics as a problem-solving endeavor.

The activities are also there for you. Read them along with the text, not as an aside. After all, you are constructing new knowledge yourself—knowledge about teaching mathematics to children. Like your students, you must become actively engaged in *your own learning* about *children learning* mathematics. By actually doing the activities as you read through the book, you can get an idea of how children might react to or learn from each activity.

## Section 3: Issues and Perspectives

As the foundational chapters of Section 1 provide a framework for the teaching of mathematics, the ideas in this section offer perspective on overarching issues that also build on that foundation. These chapters, or portions of them, can be read at any time, depending on your needs and interests.

Although general principles for the design of effective lessons are developed in Chapter 4, Chapter 22 offers specific information about topics such as forming cooperative learning groups, designing homework, working in a diverse classroom, using drill and practice, incorporating writing in mathematics, and using the textbook.

In Chapter 23, you will read about working with children with learning disabilities, children with mental handicaps, and gifted children. In addition, the chapter provides an up-to-date view of multicultural, socioeconomic, and gender equity issues. Though no easy answers are offered, the information is current, research-based, and thought-provoking, in keeping with the main ideas of the book.

Chapter 24 looks at the role of the calculator and the computer in teaching mathematics. Suggestions for using technology are included throughout the text. This chapter offers perspective and guidance. Tips for using the Internet are also included.

# SPECIAL FEATURES OF THIS TEXT

This fourth edition of *Elementary and Middle School Mathematics* retains all of the features that I believe have helped make the previous three editions so successful. The overall intent is to make the book as useful for you as possible. Here are 11 things to look for.

## Big Ideas

A constructivist perspective calls teachers to plan activities around big ideas rather than tiny skills and concepts. To help you develop an understanding of what is meant by "big ideas," each chapter in Section 2 begins with a brief overview and a listing of the big conceptual ideas related to that chapter. Teachers pressured by state standards will find these short lists useful for identifying the large mathematical ideas that tie seemingly discrete skills together.

## Activities

More than a textbook, this book is a resource for teachers. Activities are suggested for every important concept. Most of these are clearly framed in a box with a title. Other ideas are described directly in the text or in the illustrations. For this edition, every activity has been edited to be a problematic task as described in Chapter 4. Some new activities have been added and some discarded, but each is designed to engage students in doing mathematics.

## Assessment Notes

Near the end of most chapters in Section 2, you will find a short discussion headed "Assessment Notes." These sections are designed to point to special assessment ideas that build on the general themes of the full chapter on assessment, Chapter 5. It is worth noting that most activities in the book are also appropriate as assessment activities. There is no need to have a special reference book for assessment tasks.

## Literature Connections

Children's literature is one of the most inviting ways to get children actively involved in doing mathematics. Many of the chapters in Section 2 contain a feature titled "Literature Connections." In most of these sections, at least three children's literature titles are suggested, with a brief description of how the mathematics of the chapter can be profitably built on the stories. Though certainly not a comprehensive listing of potential literature, these sections will get you started using this exciting vehicle for teaching mathematics. Each work featured under this heading appears in a separate reference list at the back of the book.

## Calculators

Calculator activities are found in every appropriate chapter. They are identified with a small calculator icon so that you can find them easily. Special efforts have been made to expand the use of graphing calculators for middle school activities.

## Technology Notes (NEW!)

In each chapter, look for one or more sections titled "Technology Note." There you will find a general discussion of how computer software may be used profitably (or not) to help with the content that has just been discussed. Specific software titles are usually mentioned, with brief descriptions of how they reflect the general comments. Even if you do not have the same software, the comments will help you look at similar software with an objective eye to judge its potential effectiveness. I have tried to sample the best of the hundreds of titles available. At the same time, I have tried to be candid about the value of certain categories or software titles. Inclusion of any software title in these sections should not be taken as an endorsement.

The "Technology Note" sections are marked with a computer icon, as are certain activities and appropriate paragraphs in the text to identify each discussion or use of computer technology.

## Writing to Learn

To help you home in on the important pedagogical ideas, a list of focusing questions are found at the end of every chapter under the heading "Writing to Learn." These questions are designed to help you reflect on the main points of the chapter. Actually writing out the answers to these questions in your own words is one of the best ways for you to develop your understanding of each chapter's main ideas.

## Explorations

Following the "Writing to Learn" list are a few additional questions that ask you to explore an issue, reflect on observations in a classroom, compare text ideas with those found in traditional curriculum materials, or perhaps take a position on a controversial issue. There are rarely "right" answers to these questions, but they will certainly stimulate thought or provoke spirited conversations. Discuss these with your peer group or with teachers in the classroom.

## Recommendations for Further Reading

The end of each chapter contains a bibliography of useful articles and books to augment the information found in the chapter. Usually these are taken from NCTM journals, yearbooks, and other professional resources that are targeted for the classroom teacher. Three or four of the selections that I feel are especially important or useful are featured, with a short annotation, under the heading "Highly Recommended." It would have been nice to annotate the whole list, but space does not permit. (Note that all sources *cited in the text proper* appear in the References at the back of the book.)

## NCTM *Principles and Standards* (NEW!)

NCTM's *Principles and Standards for School Mathematics* is described in depth in Chapter 1 and is reflected in spirit throughout the book. In Appendix A, you will find a list of the five content standards and specific expectations for grade bands pre-K–2, 3–5, 6–8, and 9–12.

Appendix B contains the six Standards for Teaching Mathematics from *Professional Standards for Teaching Mathematics.* The six Assessment Standards and the four Purposes of Assessment from *Assessment Standards for School Mathematics* are presented in Chapter 5.

## Blackline Masters

The Blackline Masters section at the end of the book offers an extensive collection of masters and directions for making important instructional materials. Many of these masters are unique to this book and support especially interesting activities. Suggestions for the use of these materials are found throughout the book. You are encouraged to copy these pages and duplicate them for your classroom or for activities with children. (Permission to copy these pages is granted on the copyright page.)

# NEW OR DIFFERENT IN THIS EDITION

I've never been able to settle for a "light revision," as was suggested by my editors. This edition represents the most comprehensive revision to date and the one of which I am most proud. In addition to the items highlighted here, every line of text was reconsidered. A wonderful editor helped me make the text more readable and often less wordy. A lot of new text was added, and outdated material was omitted. Every activity underwent review; all are now in keeping with the spirit of teaching through problem solving. They are designed to engage children in a problematic manner. Beyond these global edits, I've made some more obvious changes that I think bring the book completely up to date.

## The Foundations Chapters

Section 1 of the text is, as it should be, I think, a continuous work in progress. Chapter 1 describes in much more detail than before the issues behind the reform movement in mathematics education and concerns related to the pressures of state standards. The discussion of NCTM's *Principles and Standards* was written shortly after its release, to give readers a clear and accurate understanding of that important new publication.

Chapter 3, "Developing Understanding in Mathematics," was reorganized and partly rewritten, primarily to make the critical ideas it contains more clear. I continue to learn and grow, and I hope that is reflected in this chapter especially.

In the third edition, I made a unique stand among texts of this type by suggesting that all mathematics can be taught in a problem-solving environment. I strongly believed this was the right direction and believe it even more strongly today. In this edition, I have sharpened and clarified that theme. The main focus of Chapter 4, "Teaching Through Problem Solving," is on the development of a general framework for instruction. The "before, during, after" structure of a lesson is strengthened and is referred to throughout the book.

## Whole-Number Computation

At the K–6 level, perhaps no issue dominates the discussion of reform more than the development of computational skills with whole numbers. Chapter 10, "Strategies for Whole-Number Computation," is completely new. Based on current research, this chapter is designed to help the teacher develop computational procedures beginning with direct modeling and invented strategies. Numerous examples of student strategies are included, along with ideas for helping students record their work. These invented methods are shown to be the foundation for mental computational procedures. For each operation, adequate development of the traditional algorithms is also included. This chapter is a major departure from the algorithm chapter found in the earlier editions.

Chapter 11, "Number Sense and Estimation with Whole Numbers," provides a collection of activities for multidigit number sense development. Specific strategies for computational estimation skills are included here. Thus in these two chapters, mental computation is shown to develop naturally from regular use of by-hand computational strategies invented by students. Computational estimation is shown to be a result of flexibility with numbers.

## Algebraic Reasoning and Functions

In *Principles and Standards,* Algebra is one of the five content standards for all grades, pre-K to 12. To address this issue, I included a new Chapter 19, titled "Algebraic Reasoning." It begins with a discussion of algebraic thinking in general and goes on to cover the development of repeating patterns, growing patterns, variables, and equations. New in the third edition, Chapter 20, "Exploring Functions," is slightly revised with some new content. Chapter 21 is now titled "Developing Concepts of Exponents, Integers, and Real Numbers." Together these three chapters offer more in-depth coverage of these topics than any other book.

## Attribute Activities and Data Analysis

It is important that process skills not be seen as separate strands in the curriculum. Rather, they should be infused throughout all instructional activities. With this in mind, I could no longer defend a separate chapter on logical reasoning. Therefore, as just noted, I moved the pattern activities to the algebraic think-

ing chapter. Attribute activities are now included with the data analysis discussion in Chapter 18. A primary component of analyzing data is classification. This follows the lead of the Used Numbers Project (Russell & Corwin, 1990).

## Color

It was the publisher's decision to produce this book in full color. All I can say is, "Wow!" I believe it adds more than eye appeal. Hope you like it.

## Companion Web site (www.awl.com/vandewalle)

This online course companion provides a wealth of resources for both students and instructors. Students will find chapter summaries, interactive Web activities, a complete guide to conducting research on the Internet, and more. Instructors will have protected access to the *Instructor's Manual* and teaching links and can also take advantage of Syllabus Builder, our comprehensive course management system.

# NOTES TO THE INSTRUCTOR

No other text offers your students as much as this one does. Even more important, it provides a strong theoretical perspective on children learning mathematics—not a casual overview. That perspective is reflected consistently throughout the book. Second, no other book of this type develops so clearly the strong position articulated by Hiebert and colleagues (1996, 1997) that the best approach to teaching mathematics is to teach with problematic tasks. Third, teachers find the book to be a valuable resource that almost all carry into the classroom rather than sell back to the bookstore. Many school divisions, principals, and classroom teachers buy the book for the same purpose. It has become a standard reference for K–8 teachers. Teachers and supervisors continually tell me how readable and valuable they find the book.

It is a large book! It is not a book to "cover" but a book to use. I have never attempted to teach the content of the entire book in a single semester and would never expect you to. In fact, I tend to cover fewer topics now than in the past. I find it more important to develop a firm understanding of what good instruction is than to attempt to cover strategies for every topic. By providing your students with the detail and information found in this book, you send with them into the classroom the specifics you were unable to cover in class. And you can be assured that the spirit of what you do cover will also be evident in the chapters you skipped.

One suggestion is to spend a significant portion of your course on developing the key ideas about teaching children, especially Chapters 3 and 4. Use an even smaller list of content topics than you may have before. As you develop the content topics you select, allow your class to be a model of the instruction you want for all topics. Teaching through problematic tasks and classroom discourse is a complete shift from the experiences of most teachers. They need the big ideas of teaching more than a lot of detailed methods. Many chapters can be read without instructor input. With a top-quality resource and reference in your hands, your focus can be on how students learn and what good student-oriented teaching is all about. The book will take care of the rest.

As with the previous editions of this book, I have written an *Instructor's Manual* for professors which reflects my own approach to teaching from *Elementary and Middle School Mathematics*. In addition to sample course designs reflecting different emphases and grade ranges, the *Manual* also includes Main Ideas, Suggested Activities, Possible Assignments, and Suggested Test Questions for each chapter of the book.

I am always amazed at how many different styles of methods courses are possible. All who have used this book seem to find their own best strategies for their class. I am hesitant, therefore, to dictate a course, but I am proud to offer this text. I wish you and your students much success and excitement as you explore good mathematics with kids.

# ACKNOWLEDGMENTS

It has been 12 years since I wrote the first edition of *Elementary and Middle School Mathematics*. With each revision, I struggle to keep the text as current as possible, and much has changed over the years. However, were it not for the success of the first edition, you would not be reading this page today. Regardless of how many subsequent editions this text may see, I will always be most sincerely indebted to Warren Crown of Rutgers University, John Dossey of Illinois State University, Bob Gilbert of Florida International University, and Steven Willoughby of the University of Arizona, who gave time and great care in offering detailed comments on the original manuscript. Few mathematics educators of their stature would take the time and effort that they gave to that endeavor.

In preparing this fourth edition, I have received thoughtful input from the following educators, who offered comments on the third edition or on the manuscript for the fourth:

Thomasenia Lott Adams, University of Florida

Lillie Albert, Boston College

Rudie Alec, Wayne State University

Kevin M. Anderson, Southeast Missouri State University

Frank Gardella, Hunter College

Anna Graeber, University of Maryland

Jonathan Knaupp, Arizona State University

Winifred Mallam, Texas Woman's University

Michael Mikusa, Kent State University

Eula Monroe, Brigham Young University

Daniel Orey, California State University / Sacramento

Emma Owens, Clemson University

Donald Ploger, Florida Atlantic University

Edna Schack, Morehead State University

Lynn Stallings, Georgia State University

Marilyn Strutchens, University of Maryland

Tim Whiteford, Trinity College of Vermont

Each of these professionals has challenged me to think through issues and rewarded me with their helpful input.

A special thank-you goes to LaRay Mason, an elementary mathematics specialist in Chesterfield County, Virginia, who helped immensely with information for the new "Technology Note" feature. LaRay helped search for and identify software and provided many useful suggestions.

Special thanks are due to Karen Helfrich, development editor, who ably coordinated a myriad of details throughout the revision process of the fourth edition. I am also indebted to Ann Torbert, an editor who carefully read each line of the third edition and helped me with clarity and brevity.

It seems that with each edition, even more people are involved with production of the book, and it is impossible to mention them all. However, recognition for outstanding work is again due Ellen MacElree, my tireless, friendly project editor at Longman; Bruce Emmer, my thoughtful and meticulous copyeditor; and Judy Kiviat, the most careful and conscientious proofreader imaginable. Each has worked on the last two editions, providing superior attention to detail and keeping in constant communication with me at all times. Without their good spirit and professional skills, this book would never have made it into print. To each of you, I am truly grateful.

## A Personal Note

Many people contribute to the countless details that go into the production of this book. However, my wife is the one who continues to give the most. In a real sense, she is a part of this book. Her belief in me and her daily support and encouragement with each edition make this effort possible. She helps me believe and persevere. She has always been my strongest ally and my closest friend. I love you, Sharon.

On November 12, 1998, a new joy entered our lives when my daughter, Bridget, gave birth to a beautiful baby girl. Maggie, this one's for you!

**John A. Van de Walle**

# Foundations of Teaching Mathematics

Doing Mathematics
The nature of knowing and doing mathematics

Learning
Constructivist views of how children learn

EFFECTIVE MATHEMATICS TEACHING

Teaching Through Problem Solving
Teaching in a problem-solving environment

Assessment
Integrating assessment with teaching to improve both

For teachers of mathematics to be truly effective involves bringing together four basic components: (1) an appreciation of the discipline of mathematics itself—what it means to "do mathematics," (2) an understanding of how students learn and construct ideas, (3) an ability to design and select tasks so that students learn mathematics in a problem-solving environment, and (4) the ability to integrate assessment with the teaching process in order to enhance learning and improve daily instruction.

These four ideas are best understood in the context of the reform movement in mathematics education, a revolution in school mathematics begun in 1989, when the National Council of Teachers of Mathematics published its first *Standards* document. It continues into the twenty-first century with the publication of *Principles and Standards for School Mathematics,* the update to the original *Standards.* This reform movement is discussed in Chapter 1.

Chapters 2 through 5 each develop one of the four components of effective teaching. In many ways, these are the most important chapters of the book. They lay out the foundational ideas on which effective teaching at any grade level is built.

# Chapter 1

# Teaching Mathematics in the Context of the Reform Movement

*In this changing world, those who understand and can do mathematics will have significantly enhanced opportunities and options for shaping their futures. Mathematical competence opens doors to productive futures. A lack of mathematical competence keeps those doors closed. . . . All students should have the opportunity and the support necessary to learn significant mathematics with depth and understanding. There is no conflict between equity and excellence.*

—NCTM (2000, p. 50)

You are reading this book because you are interested in learning how to teach mathematics—to help children learn mathematics. What images and emotions does that thought bring to mind?

Pause now and reflect on your own ideas about the *topic* of mathematics. What does mathematics mean to you? What does it mean to "do mathematics"? What parts of the subject seem most important? Where do calculators and computers fit in? Write down three or four of your strongest thoughts about mathematics. Compare your thoughts with those of others.

Next focus on the teaching part. Someday soon you will find yourself in front of a class of students, or perhaps you are already teaching. What general ideas will guide the way you will teach mathematics? Do children learn mathematics differently from other topics? How can you make it interesting and enjoyable? If mathematics is not exactly your favorite subject, do you think that had anything to do with the way you were taught? How can you help children like the subject more than you do? Add your written thoughts on these questions to those about mathematics.

It is very likely that the general ideas found in the next four chapters will challenge some of your beliefs and cause you to rethink what you have just written. Save these ideas and revisit them after you have finished the first five chapters of this text.

This is an important, perhaps pivotal moment in the history of mathematics education, and you, the teachers who help children learn, will ultimately be the ones who shape mathematics for the children you touch.

This chapter explores the ongoing revolution in mathematics education and thus provides a window through which you can best understand the four components of effective mathematics teaching as discussed in the opening to this section of the book.

## THE REFORM MOVEMENT AND THE NATIONAL COUNCIL OF TEACHERS OF MATHEMATICS

There have been several notable shifts in the direction of mathematics education in our schools. It is useful to place these shifts and movements in the context of the forces that have shaped them.

### A Brief History of Reforms

At its annual conference in April 2000, the National Council of Teachers of Mathematics (NCTM) released *Principles and Standards for School Mathematics*. With this most important document, the council continues to guide a revolutionary reform movement in mathematics education, not just in the United States and Canada but throughout the world.

The momentum for reform in mathematics education began in the early 1980s. Educators were responding to a "back to basics" cry, a reaction to the "new math" of the 1960s and 1970s. There was a growing interest in making problem solving a focus of the mathematics curriculum. The work of Piaget and other developmental psychologists was shifting the focus of mathematics educators from mathematics content to how children can best learn mathematics.

This momentum came to a head in 1989, when NCTM published *Curriculum and Evaluation Standards for School Mathematics*. Since then, we have been caught up in a revolution in mathematics education, a revolution that is more positive, more pervasive, and more widely accepted than any change previously experienced. It is worth noting that in the same year as the release of the *Curriculum Standards* by NCTM, the Mathematical Sciences Education Board (MSEB) released *Everybody Counts: A Report to the Nation on the Future of School Mathematics*. This very readable document outlined the nature of mathematics, the needs of our changing society, and the problems with our past efforts in mathematics education, and it echoed the directions for mathematics suggested by the *Curriculum Standards*. These two publications provided a clearly articulated vision of where we should be heading.

As we begin a new century, indeed a new millennium, it must be admitted that the vision of the 1989 *Curriculum Standards* has not been realized. Progress has been made. Change is visible, albeit slow and incremental. The political naysayers are becoming more and more influential in a bid to return again to "basics." But despite the slow pace of change in long-held beliefs about school mathematics, the revolution continues. This is not a pendulum that we can permit to swing backward.

## Leadership Provided by NCTM

The National Council of Teachers of Mathematics is a professional, nonprofit organization. With over 125,000 members in the United States and Canada, it is the primary professional organization for teachers of mathematics K–12. NCTM provides leadership through its various journals for teachers, national and regional conferences, and numerous high-quality publications.

As noted, NCTM's release of the *Curriculum and Evaluation Standards for School Mathematics* in 1989 was a benchmark event in school mathematics. No other document has ever had such an enormous effect on school mathematics or on any other area of the curriculum. In 1991, NCTM published *Professional Standards for Teaching Mathematics*. The *Professional Standards* articulates a vision of teaching mathematics and builds on the notion found in the *Curriculum Standards* that good and significant mathematics is a vision for all children, not just a few. NCTM completed the package with the *Assessment Standards for School Mathematics* in 1995. The *Assessment Standards* shows clearly the necessity of integrating assessment with instruction and indicates the key role that assessment plays in implementing change. From 1989 to 2000, these three documents have guided the reform movement in mathematics education around the world. In

fact, many countries have done a much better job of implementing the NCTM *Standards* than the United States has.

The NCTM leadership has always recognized the ongoing need to examine its standards and to make adjustments in light of new knowledge from research and practice, new demands of a changing society, and the continued impact of improved and more readily available technology. In 1998, a draft of an updated version of the *Standards* was released for a full year of discussion and feedback. Reviews of the draft were secured from various professional organizations, from a range of selected experts, and from the membership of the NCTM. The review effort was designed not to achieve consensus but to be sure that the writers were aware of all important viewpoints as they articulated an updated vision of the direction of mathematics. In April 2000, NCTM released the new updated *Standards* document, *Principles and Standards for School Mathematics*.

## PRINCIPLES AND STANDARDS FOR SCHOOL MATHEMATICS

The new *Principles and Standards for School Mathematics* should be regarded as a replacement for the 1989 *Curriculum and Evaluation Standards* in that it updates what was written 11 years earlier. It also builds on the major elements of the other two documents. As such, *Principles and Standards* addresses issues of teaching and assessment, advancing the ideas found in the *Professional Standards* and the *Assessment Standards*. It is useful to think of these as a coordinated trio of NCTM *Standards* documents, the main document being the new *Principles and Standards for School Mathematics,* which, along with the two supporting documents, clearly articulates the best vision for teaching and assessment in mathematics.

## Goals For Students

*Principles and Standards* begins with an ambitious vision of a mathematics classroom, one we have barely begun to realize. At the heart of this vision are the same five goals set forth in the 1989 *Standards*. These goals state that *all* students should

1. Learn to value mathematics
2. Become confident in their ability to do mathematics
3. Become mathematical problem solvers
4. Learn to communicate mathematics
5. Learn to reason mathematically

Virtually every job in today's society requires mathematics and, more important, mathematical thinking and reasoning. Today's employers are searching for the ability as well as the confidence to solve problems that have never been encountered before. Children need to see themselves learning to reason and learning to solve problems, not just learning skills.

Taking pride in one's mathematical thinking power is all-important. It can no longer be fashionable to announce, "I never was any good at math." Children must, from the earliest grades and throughout their school experiences, be made to feel the importance of personal success in solving problems, figuring things out, and making sense of mathematics. It is difficult to develop confidence in your mathematical abilities if all you do in that domain is follow unfathomable rules that seem handed down arbitrarily from on high.

In the last chapter of *Principles and Standards,* the authors describe the necessary support required at every level to bring the vision of Chapter 1 to reality. To do so will require effort and responsible actions by teachers, students, supervisors and principals, administrators at the state or province level, teacher educators, and also families and other caregivers.

## A Pre-K-To-12 Perspective

As shown in Figure 1.1, *Principles and Standards* is designed to help teachers and other leaders see the development of mathematics content and processes over the pre-K–12 span. The largest portion of the document is devoted to a discussion of ten standards: five content standards and five process standards. Chapter 3 provides an overview of these ten standards, showing how they are developed across the 14 years of schooling.

Chapters 4 through 7 examine the standards more specifically for each of the four grade bands: pre-K–2, 3–5, 6–8, and 9–12. These four chapters provide specific "expectations" for each of the five content standards (see Appendix A). Here you will find examples of activities and student work to help you envision how the standards might look if enacted in your own classroom. You should understand, however, that *Principles and Standards* was never intended as a curriculum or a resource guide.

## Six Principles Of High-Quality Mathematics Programs

One of the most important features of *Principles and Standards for School Mathematics* is the articulation of six principles fundamental to high-quality mathematics education:

- Equity
- Curriculum
- Teaching
- Learning
- Assessment
- Technology

According to *Principles and Standards,* these principles must be "deeply intertwined with school mathematics programs.

### Principles and Standards for School Mathematics

Chapter 1: **A Vision for School Mathematics**

Chapter 2: **Principles for School Mathematics**

Chapter 3: **Standards for Mathematics Education, Pre-Kindergarten Through Grade Twelve**

| Chapter 4 **Standards for Grades Pre-K–2** | Chapter 5 **Standards for Grades 3–5** | Chapter 6 **Standards for Grades 6–8** | Chapter 7 **Standards for Grades 9–12** |

Chapter 8: **Working Together to Achieve the Vision**

**Figure 1.1** The structure of the *Principles and Standards for School Mathematics* emphasizes the continuity of mathematics across all 14 years of school.

They can influence the development of curriculum frameworks, the selection of curriculum materials, the planning of instructional units or lessons, the design of assessments, the assignment of teachers and students to classes, instructional decisions in the classroom, and the establishment of supportive professional development programs for teachers" (NCTM, 2000, p. 12). The principles make it clear that excellence in mathematics education involves much more than simply listing content objectives.

### The Equity Principle

*Excellence in mathematics education requires equity—high expectations and strong support for all students. (NCTM, 2000, p. 12)*

The strong message of the Equity Principle is high expectations for all students. All students must have the opportunity and adequate support to learn mathematics "regardless of personal characteristics, backgrounds, or physical challenges" (p. 12). The message of high expectations for all is intertwined with every other principle and the document as a whole.

In contrast with expectations for reading and writing, it is quite common in this country to accept that some children will not be able to learn mathematics. Teachers and schools must communicate in their every action that they believe in the ability of *all* students to learn mathematics. Tracking, for example, can have a serious negative effect on expectations and opportunity to learn. High expectations for all must be accompanied by adequate support for both high- and low-achieving students. Teachers must be given the training and the resources to provide the best mathematics for every child.

## The Curriculum Principle

*A curriculum is more than a collection of activities: it must be coherent, focused on important mathematics, and well articulated across the grades. (NCTM, 2000, p. 14)*

Coherence speaks to the importance of building instruction around "big ideas" both in the curriculum and in daily classroom instruction. Students must be helped to see that mathematics is an integrated whole, not a list of isolated bits and pieces.

Mathematical ideas are "important" if they are useful in the development of other ideas, link ideas one to another, or serve to illustrate the discipline of mathematics as a human endeavor. This does not imply a single "best" configuration of the curriculum or a curriculum that is unchanging over time.

Articulation across the grades is not only explicit in this principle but also a significant feature of the entire *Principles and Standards* document. It is important that teachers and curriculum developers alike see how each of the strands of mathematics builds over the years. Without careful articulation across grades, duplication and gaps are inevitable.

## The Teaching Principle

*Effective mathematics teaching requires understanding what students know and need to learn and then challenging and supporting them to learn it well. (NCTM, 2000, p. 16)*

What students learn is almost entirely dependent on the experiences that teachers provide every day in the classroom. To provide high-quality mathematics education, teachers must (1) understand deeply the mathematics they are teaching; (2) understand how children learn mathematics, including a keen awareness of the individual mathematical development of their own students; and (3) select instructional tasks and strategies that will enhance learning. "Teachers' actions are what encourage students to think, question, solve problems, and discuss their ideas, strategies, and solutions" (p. 18).

Teachers and school districts must be committed to the continual development of teaching. Teachers must have an ongoing opportunity to reflect on their practice and improve their understanding of pedagogical strategies, student learning, and mathematics content. Professional development cannot end with the preservice training program.

## The Learning Principle

*Students must learn mathematics with understanding, actively building new knowledge from experience and prior knowledge. (NCTM, 2000, p. 20)*

This principle is based on two fundamental ideas. First, learning mathematics with understanding is essential. Mathematics today requires not only computational skills but also the ability to think and reason mathematically in order to solve the new problems and learn the new ideas that students will face in the future.

Second, the principle states quite clearly that students *can* learn mathematics with understanding. Learning is enhanced in classrooms where students are required to evaluate their own ideas and those of others, are encouraged to make mathematical conjectures and test them, and develop their reasoning skills. Learning, as envisioned in this principle, is clearly an active endeavor of students that takes place best in an environment that stresses problem solving, reasoning, and thoughtful interaction among students.

## The Assessment Principle

*Assessment should support the learning of important mathematics and furnish useful information to both teachers and students. (NCTM, 2000, p. 22)*

In the authors' words, "Assessment should not merely be done *to* students, rather, it should also be done *for* students, to guide and enhance their learning" (p. 22). Ongoing assessment conveys to students what mathematics is important. Assessment that includes ongoing observation and student interaction encourages students to articulate and thus clarify their ideas. Feedback from daily assessment helps students establish goals and become more independent learners.

Assessment should also be a major factor in making instructional decisions. By continuously gathering information about student growth and understanding, teachers can better make the daily decisions that support student learning. For assessment to be effective, teachers must use a variety of assessment techniques, understand their mathematical goals deeply, and have a good idea of how their students may be thinking about the mathematics that is being developed.

## The Technology Principle

*Technology is essential in teaching and learning mathematics; it influences the mathematics that is taught and enhances students' learning. (NCTM, 2000, p. 24)*

Calculators and computers should be seen as essential tools for doing and learning mathematics in the classroom. Technology permits students to focus on mathematical ideas, to reason, and to solve problems in ways that are often impossible without these tools. Technology enhances the learning of mathematics by allowing for increased exploration and enhanced representation of ideas. It extends the range of problems that can be accessed. It also allows students with special needs to bypass less important procedures so that important mathematics can be considered.

Far from being a crutch, technology actually enhances active involvement in the learning process. Students can explore ideas in a variety of modes—numeric, graphical, symbolic—and the teacher is better able to see how students are thinking about new ideas.

Technology is not a substitute for teaching, nor is it a replacement for important by-hand and mental skills. Rather, technology makes it possible to add to the curriculum important ideas that were previously unavailable to students. Realistic numbers and data sets are accessible by young children. Geometric software allows for the manipulation of figures and investigations of relationships impossible even with physical objects. Graphing technologies make realistic exploration of significant algebraic concepts possible.

# The Five Content Standards

The *Principles and Standards* document describes five content standards or strands of mathematics:

- Number and Operations
- Algebra
- Geometry
- Measurement
- Data Analysis and Probability

(See Appendix A for the statement of the standards and the grade-band elaboration for grades pre-K–2, 3–5, 6–8 and 9–12.)

The *Standards* authors never intended that the five content strands would have equal weight or value across the four grade bands. Number and Operations is the largest strand from pre-K to grade 5 and continues to be important in middle school. That emphasis is reflected in this text, with Chapters 6 through 15 addressing content found in the Number and Operations standard.

The emphasis on Number and Operations should not diminish the importance of the other strands. Note that Geometry and Measurement are separate strands, suggesting the unique importance of each of these two areas.

*Principles and Standards* clearly defines Algebra as a strand for all grades. Almost certainly this was not the case when you were in school. This strand is increasingly found in state-level objective lists. We can hope that *Principles and Standards* will help bring consensus to this area and thus have an influence on how algebraic thinking appears in traditional textbooks. In this text, Chapters 19, 20, and 21 address this strand.

# The Five Process Standards

Following the five content standards, *Principles and Standards* lists five process standards:

- Problem Solving
- Reasoning and Proof
- Communication
- Connections
- Representation

Although never labeled or set apart in any way, the 1989 *Standards* began each grade band with the same four standards, the first four of the standards just listed. Those four standards have been cited in countless speeches and articles, used to define state objectives and to guide performance assessments, and held up as a goal for all instruction. In short, they defined the original *Standards* document and the reform movement it heralded.

In *Principles and Standards for School Mathematics*, the writers updated those original four process standards, added Representation, and officially labeled them "process standards," referring to the mathematical process through which students should acquire and use mathematical knowledge. The statement of the five process standards can be found in Table 1.1 (p. 8).

The five process standards should not be regarded as separate strands in the mathematics curriculum. Rather, they direct the methods or processes of doing all mathematics and therefore should be seen as integral components of all mathematics learning and teaching.

To teach in a way that reflects these process standards is one of the best definitions of what it means to teach "according to the *Standards*."

## Problem Solving

Problem solving has been the focus of school mathematics for more than two decades. Problem solving is much more than finding answers to word problems and exercises labeled "problem solving." The Problem Solving standard says that all students should "build new mathematical knowledge through problem solving" (NCTM, 2000, p. 52). This statement clearly indicates that problem solving is to be viewed as the vehicle through which children develop mathematical ideas. Learning and doing mathematics *as you solve problems* is probably the most significant difference in what the *Standards* indicate and the way you most likely experienced mathematics. As will be discussed in depth in Chapter 4, problem solving requires that students be mentally active and that they reflect on the ideas they already possess to build new ideas and increase understanding.

The Problem Solving standard also talks about developing students' disposition to work with problematic situations, to develop various strategies for solving problems, and to learn to monitor and reflect on their mathematical thinking (metacognition).

## Reasoning and Proof

Reasoning is at the heart of the shift from memorizing rules to doing mathematics. Without reasoning, mathematics is reduced to mindless skills that seem mysterious and useless in the real world. If problem solving is the focus of mathematics, reasoning is the logical thinking that helps us solve problems and decide if and why our answers make sense. Students need to develop the habit of providing an argument or a rationale as an integral part of every answer.

## Table 1.1
**The Five Process Standards from *Principles and Standards for School Mathematics***

**Problem Solving Standard**
*Instructional programs from prekindergarten through grade 12 should enable all students to—*

- Build new mathematical knowledge through problem solving
- Solve problems that arise in mathematics and in other contexts
- Apply and adapt a variety of appropriate strategies to solve problems
- Monitor and reflect on the process of mathematical problem solving

**Reasoning and Proof Standard**
*Instructional programs from prekindergarten through grade 12 should enable all students to—*

- Recognize reasoning and proof as fundamental aspects of mathematics
- Make and investigate mathematical conjectures
- Develop and evaluate mathematical arguments and proofs
- Select and use various types of reasoning and methods of proof

**Communication Standard**
*Instructional programs from prekindergarten through grade 12 should enable all students to—*

- Organize and consolidate their mathematical thinking through communication
- Communicate their mathematical thinking coherently and clearly to peers, teachers, and others
- Analyze and evaluate the mathematical thinking and strategies of others
- Use the language of mathematics to express mathematical ideas precisely

**Connections Standard**
*Instructional programs from prekindergarten through grade 12 should enable all students to—*

- Recognize and use connections among mathematical ideas
- Understand how mathematical ideas interconnect and build on one another to produce a coherent whole
- Recognize and apply mathematics in contexts outside of mathematics

**Representation Standard**
*Instructional programs from prekindergarten through grade 12 should enable all students to—*

- Create and use representations to organize, record, and communicate mathematical ideas
- Select, apply, and translate among mathematical representations to solve problems
- Use representations to model and interpret physical, social, and mathematical phenomena

*Source:* Reprinted with permission from *Principles and Standards for School Mathematics.* Copyright ©2000 by the National Council of Teachers of Mathematics. All rights reserved.

Children can and do learn that the reasons for their answers are at least as important as the answers themselves. The habit of providing reasons for answers is best started in kindergarten. However, it is never too late to learn the satisfaction and the value of defending ideas through logical argument.

## Communication
The Communication standard points to the importance of being able to talk about, write about, describe, and explain mathematical ideas. Learning to communicate in mathematics fosters interaction and exploration of ideas in the classroom as students learn in an active, verbal environment. It also makes accessible the world of mathematics beyond the classroom. Each day should include discussion or writing about the mathematical thinking that is going on in the classroom. No better way exists for wrestling with an idea than to attempt to articulate it to others. Mathematical expression, therefore, is part of the process and not an end in itself.

## Connections
The Connections standard has two separate thrusts. First, the standard refers to connections within and among mathematical ideas. For example, addition and subtraction are intimately related; fractional parts of a whole are connected to concepts of decimals and percents. Students should be helped to see how mathematical ideas build on one another

in a useful network of connected ideas. Mathematics is not a laundry list of isolated rules and formulas.

Second, mathematics should be connected to the real world and to other disciplines. Children should see that mathematics plays a significant role in art, science, and social studies. This suggests that mathematics should frequently be integrated with other discipline areas and that applications of mathematics in the real world should be explored.

## Representation
One of the reasons mathematics is so powerful is the way ideas can be expressed with symbols, charts, graphs, and diagrams. Symbolism in mathematics, along with visual aids such as charts and graphs, should be understood by students as ways of communicating mathematical ideas to other people. Symbols, graphs, and charts, as well as physical representations such as counters or fraction "pie pieces," are also powerful learning tools. They permit students to manipulate abstract ideas in visual form. Moving from one representation to another is an important way to add understanding to an idea. For example, an algebraic equation leads to a chart of values and to a graph, both of which add a new dimension to the relationship. A story problem is often better understood when modeled with simple counters. As teachers help develop flexibility with a variety of representations for mathematical ideas, students not only add to their own understanding but also acquire skill in applying mathematical ideas to new areas and communicating ideas to others.

# THE *PROFESSIONAL STANDARDS FOR TEACHING MATHEMATICS*

Although *Principles and Standards* incorporates principles of teaching and assessment, the emphasis is curriculum. The *Professional Standards for Teaching Mathematics* focuses on teaching and is as important today as when it was released in 1991. The *Professional Standards* asserts that teachers are the key agents of change in the classroom. If the revolution is to continue, teachers must shift from a teacher-centered to a child-centered approach in their instruction. Research in cognitive psychology and mathematics education suggests that students actively construct their own meanings through mentally engaging experiences. They do not simply absorb knowledge delivered to them by the teacher or text. The *Professional Standards* describes teaching in ways that are reflective of this constructivist approach. Through extended vignettes of real teachers, the document articulates the careful reflective work that must go into teaching. Effective teaching engages students in problem solving and promotes valuable reflective student discourse about important mathematical ideas.

## Five Shifts in Classroom Environment

The introduction to the *Professional Standards* lists five major shifts in the environment of the mathematics classroom that are necessary to allow students to develop mathematical power. Teachers need to shift

- Toward classrooms as mathematics communities and away from classrooms as simply a collection of individuals

- Toward logic and mathematical evidence as verification and away from the teacher as the sole authority for right answers

- Toward mathematical reasoning and away from mere memorizing procedures

- Toward conjecturing, inventing, and problem solving and away from an emphasis on the mechanistic finding of answers

- Toward connecting mathematics, its ideas, and its applications and away from treating mathematics as a body of isolated concepts and procedures

## The Teaching Standards

The *Professional Standards for Teaching Mathematics* contains chapters on teaching, the evaluation of teaching, professional development, and necessary support for teaching. The teaching section is extraordinarily useful. It offers six standards for

the teaching of mathematics, arranged in four categories: providing worthwhile mathematical tasks, encouraging discourse among students and between students and teacher, providing for an environment in which learning will be enhanced, and analyzing continually both teaching and learning. Chapter 4 of this text describes teaching through problem solving—a process involving these very same ideas. A listing of the six teaching standards can be found in Appendix B.

# THE *ASSESSMENT STANDARDS FOR SCHOOL MATHEMATICS*

The *Assessment Standards for School Mathematics* was published in 1995. It rounds out the trio of NCTM standards documents and is important reading for anyone interested in understanding the reform movement in mathematics education.

The *Assessment Standards* is not a how-to guide but a statement of philosophy and purpose, a book to provide guidance without prescription. It consists of six standards for assessment: Mathematics, Learning, Equity, Openness, Inferences, and Coherence. Further, it describes in some detail four purposes of assessment: to monitor the progress of students, to help make instructional decisions, to evaluate students' achievement, and to evaluate programs. All are aimed at the improvement of student learning.

The inescapable message of the *Assessment Standards* is that assessment and instruction are not separate activities but are intimately intertwined in improving the learning of mathematics. Chapter 5 of this text describes the six assessment standards and discusses the four purposes. There you will find suggestions for making assessment an integral component of instruction, an absolutely essential factor in being a *Standards*-oriented teacher.

# INFLUENCES AND PRESSURES ON REFORM

NCTM has provided the major leadership and vision for the reform movement in mathematics education. However, at least three other forces interact to push and pull at the mathematics classroom in ways that are often more powerful than NCTM. National and international comparisons of student performances make headlines and provoke public reaction. This outcry adds pressure on state boards of education to show that their schools are all "above average." The most direct classroom influence is the textbook. Mainstream publishers are primarily influenced by the classroom teacher and state standards. No single factor controls the direction of change.

# National and International Studies

Large studies that tell the American public how the nation's children are doing in mathematics receive a lot of attention. They influence political decisions as well as provide useful data for mathematics education researchers. Two such studies were conducted in 1995 and 1996.

## The National Assessment of Educational Progress

Since 1969, the National Assessment of Educational Progress (NAEP), a congressionally mandated program, has been assessing what students know and can do in various curriculum areas. To date, there have been eight mathematics assessments based on samples of students 9, 13, and 17 years of age or in grades 4, 8, and 12. The results are often published as "The Nation's Report Card." NAEP is a criterion-referenced study, telling us what percentages of American students know various mathematics concepts and skills. Much of the test is designed to reflect current curriculum.

NAEP provides us with both good and bad news. The good news is that on a small core of items that have been used consistently since 1973 to produce trend data, U.S. students clearly do things better now than in 1973 (Reese, Miller, Mazzeo, & Dossey, 1997). This is in stark contrast to observers who contend that current mathematics reform is producing students who don't know "good old basic mathematics."

The bad news is that even though performance on these traditional items is increasing steadily, the overall performance of our students remains dismal. NAEP reports three levels of achievement: basic, proficient, and advanced. In 1996, only 21 percent of students at fourth grade, 24 percent at eighth grade, and 16 percent at 12th grade were at or above the proficient level, a performance indicating "solid academic performance" (Reese et al., 1997). At fourth and eighth grades, 36 percent and 38 percent, respectively, were found to be below the basic level.

## The Third International Mathematics and Science Study

In 1995 and 1996, 41 nations participated in the Third International Mathematics and Science Study (TIMSS), the largest study of mathematics and science education ever conducted. Data were gathered in grades 4, 8, and 12 from 500,000 students, and from teachers. A video study was conducted at the eighth grade. The most widely reported results are that U.S. fourth-grade students are above the average of the TIMSS countries, below the international average at the eighth grade, and significantly below average at the 12th grade (U.S. Department of Education, 1997a).

Even though the rank ordering for fourth grade places the United States above the average for 26 countries, seven countries (Singapore, Korea, Japan, Hong Kong, Netherlands, Czech Republic, and Austria) had significantly higher scores. Canada and Ireland were similar to the United States. Only 9 percent of U.S. fourth graders would fall in the top 10 percent of all students in the TIMSS study. This is in stark contrast with Japan (32 percent) and Singapore (39 percent) (U.S. Department of Education, 1997c).

The "back to basics" cry in the United States is not supported by the TIMSS data any more than by NAEP data. In fact, the data suggest that there is a widespread emphasis in the United States in both instructional practices and in curricula that must be questioned given the disappointing performance of American students (Babcock, 1998). Curriculum and instructional approaches in the United States are "less in line with cross-national commonalties than are the demanding curricula and classroom practices found in many high-achieving countries" (p. 6). Furthermore, TIMSS does not support a number of other popular "basics" demands: more homework (U.S. students do more than students in most countries), less TV watching (Japanese students watch as much), and more time spent on mathematics (U.S. students have more hours of mathematics instruction than students in Japan or Germany). Tracking prior to high school, common in the United States, is not practiced in most TIMSS nations.

One of the most interesting components of TIMSS is the eighth-grade video study that was conducted in the United States, Germany, and Japan. The results indicate stark contrasts between instructional practices in Japan and the United States. "The typical goal of a U.S. eighth-grade mathematics teacher is to teach students how to do something. The typical goal of a Japanese teacher is to help students understand mathematical concepts" (U.S. Department of Education, 1997a, p. 33). Although 95 percent of U.S. teachers in the study said they were aware of the current reform ideas, in responses to questions about what constituted reform teaching, over 80 percent referred to something other than a focus on thinking. Rather, they pointed to cooperative learning or hands-on activities, which are strategies that can and do go on without any emphasis on thinking. In Japan, researchers found that 83 percent of the topics in eighth-grade lessons were developed rather than stated. By contrast, in the United States, only 22 percent of the topics were developed; 78 percent were stated (U.S. Department of Education, 1996). "The videotape study found that, in many ways, Japanese teaching resembled the recommendations of the U.S. reform movement more closely than did American teaching" (p. 47).

The TIMSS data and the many reports and documents that have been produced about the study provide much more information than can be summarized easily on these pages. A wealth of information, including the U.S. Department of Education's TIMSS Resource Kit, TIMSS test items, and numerous reports, can be found on the Web at http://ustimss.msu.edu.

# State Standards

A major finding of the TIMSS curriculum analysis is that U.S. curriculum is unfocused, contains many more topics than most countries, and involves much more repetition than is found in most countries. We attempt to do everything and as a consequence rarely do it in depth, making reteaching all too common (Schmidt, McKnight, & Raizen, 1996). The proliferation of topics is largely a result of local or state control of curriculum. The United States is the only major TIMSS country that does not possess a national curriculum.

The term *standards* was popularized by NCTM in 1989. Today it is used by nearly every state in the nation to refer to a grade-by-grade listing of very specific mathematics objectives. These state standards or objectives vary considerably from state to state in the degree to which they reflect the reform movement. Most states have had to be very cautious in embracing mathematics reform, especially in the current climate of antireform sentiment in the public sector. Cries for "accountability" and "basics" put serious pressure on states. Even for the states and local districts that encourage reform, the huge cost of teacher retraining and in-service with reform-oriented curricula has made change slow and difficult on any large scale.

Associated with every set of state standards is some form of testing program. Publicly reported test scores place pressure on superintendents, then on principals, and ultimately on teachers. Teachers feel enormous pressure to raise test scores at all costs (Schmidt et al., 1996). For a teacher who has little or no experience with the spirit of the *Standards,* it is very difficult to adopt the student-centered approach to mathematics and the teaching of mathematics espoused by reformers. Unfortunately for children, this often results in endless drill, review, and practice tests.

Are these state standards incompatible with reform? In general, the answer is no. Reform is about helping children understand mathematics and become confident in their abilities to do mathematics and solve problems. There are many wonderful examples of teaching in the spirit of reform. Children in these classrooms achieve quite well, even on the most traditional of standardized tests. These stories need better publicity, and teachers need much more support than is often available. Basic skills can be taught with understanding—and they must be.

# Curriculum

In most classrooms, the textbook is the single most influential factor in determining what actually gets taught and how. What is becoming increasingly complicated is how teachers and school systems attempt to blend the textbook or other curriculum materials with the mandated state standards and the professional directions of NCTM.

Though possibly an oversimplification, mathematics curriculum materials that are used in K–8 classrooms can be categorized as either traditional or reform. Traditional texts are usually developed by large commercial publishers. Reform programs have been initially developed with funding from the National Science Foundation (NSF) and other outside sources by teams of teachers, educational researchers, and mathematicians.

## Traditional Curricula

The publishers of traditional textbooks employ author teams that always include excellent mathematics researchers and educators as well as teachers and supervisors. The tendency is to produce very large textbooks so that they can attend to a wide variety of state and professional agendas (Schmidt et al., 1996). Often publisher statements of NCTM compliance are misleading. NCTM does not approve or sanction any commercial products, so publishers are free to make whatever claims they feel they can support. You should remember that by its very nature, the publishing industry is market-driven. The market—the individuals who make the decisions concerning which programs to purchase for the school systems—is composed largely of experienced teachers. As just noted, these teachers are enormously pressured by state tests. Most of these decision makers have only a cursory understanding of the NCTM *Standards.* The result is that the market requires publishers to stick fairly close to the show-and-explain approach to teaching. Traditional books currently account for well over 80 percent of the textbooks used in schools.

## Reform Curricula

At present, there are three elementary and five middle school programs commonly recognized as reform curricula.* Originally developed with NSF funds, each is now commercially available. A hallmark of these reform programs is student engagement. Children are challenged to make sense of new mathematical ideas through explorations and projects, often in real contexts. Written and oral communication is strongly encouraged. Most programs do not have textbooks but are supported with activity guides, teacher resources, and consumable materials for students. Teacher training is generally seen as important if not essential for districtwide implementation, a fact that adds to the already high cost of most reform programs.

Data concerning the effectiveness of reform curricula as measured by traditional testing programs continue to be gathered. It is safe to say that students in reform programs perform much better on problem-solving measures and at least as well on traditional skills as students in traditional programs (Bell, 1998; Boaler, 1998; Reys, Robinson, Sconiers, & Mark, 1999; Stein, Grover, & Henningsen, 1996; Stein & Lane, 1996; Wood & Sellers, 1996, 1997).

Comparing any of these with a corresponding traditional textbook would be an effective way to understand what reform or *Standards*-based mathematics is all about.

---

*A listing of the eight reform curricula—the developers, publishers, and Internet contacts—can be found at the end of this chapter.

# AN INVITATION TO LEARN AND GROW

The mathematics education described in the *Standards* is almost certainly not the same as the mathematics and the mathematics teaching you experienced in grades K through 8. Along the way, you may have had some excellent teachers who really did reflect the current reform spirit. Examples of good reform curriculum have been around since the early 1990s, and you may have benefited from one of those. But for the most part, with the reform movement well into its second decade, its goals have yet to be realized in the large majority of school districts in North America.

As a practicing or prospective teacher facing the challenge of the three *Standards* documents, you may need to confront some of your personal beliefs—about what it means to *do mathematics*, how one goes about *learning mathematics*, how to *teach mathematics through problem solving*, and what it means to *assess mathematics* integrated with instruction. The next four chapters of this book help you develop these four foundational ideas for teaching.

Section 2 of the book examines the teaching and learning of specific topics in mathematics. The chapters in the second section are designed not only as text material but also as a source of instructional tasks for your future or current teaching. Section 3 covers other topics that influence mathematics teaching across all strands and grade levels: planning and related classroom issues, reaching all children in mathematics, and the role of technology. The chapters in this last section are appropriate to be read at any time.

New directions in mathematics education have opened a world of exciting investigations and opportunities to all students. Mathematics can no longer be equated with mundane computational skills. Teaching mathematics can be an exciting adventure. Perhaps the most exciting part is that you will grow and learn along with your students. Enjoy the journey!

# REFLECTIONS ON CHAPTER 1

## Writing to Learn

At the end of each chapter of this book, you will find a series of questions under this same heading. The questions are designed to help you reflect on the most important ideas of the chapter. Writing (or talking aloud with a peer) is an excellent way to explore new ideas and incorporate them into your own knowledge base. The writing (or discussion) will help make the ideas your own. After you have written your responses in your own words, return to the text to compare what you have written with the book. Make changes, if necessary, or discuss differences with your instructor.

1. How is the new NCTM document, *Principles and Standards for School Mathematics*, related to the 1989 document, *Curriculum and Evaluation Standards for School Mathematics*?

2. What are the five goals for all students that were described originally in the 1989 *Curriculum Standards* and reflected again in the *Principles and Standards* document? Pick two of these goals that you think are the most important, and explain what they mean to you.

3. Give a brief description of each of the six principles in *Principles and Standards* (Equity, Curriculum, Teaching, Learning, Assessment, and Technology). Explain the importance of each principle to the teaching and learning of mathematics.

4. What are the five content strands (standards) defined by *Principles and Standards*?

5. What is meant by a *process* as referred to in the *Principles and Standards* process standards? Give a brief description of each of the five process standards.

6. Among the ideas in the *Professional Standards* are five shifts in the classroom environment, from traditional approaches to a *Standards*-oriented approach. Examine these five shifts, and describe in a few sentences what aspects of each shift seem most significant to you.

7. Describe at least two results derived from NAEP data. What are the implications?

8. Describe at least two results derived from TIMSS data. What are the implications?

9. Describe the influences of state-level standards on classroom mathematics education.

10. Discuss the difference between traditional textbooks and reform curricula.

## For Discussion and Exploration

1. As the last decade of the century ended, the outcry for "basics" was again being heard from a loud and very political minority. The debate over reform or the basics is both important and interesting. For an engaging discussion of the reform movement in light of the "back to basics" outcry, read one or more of the first five articles in the February 1999 edition of the *Phi Delta Kappan*. Where do you stand on the issue of reform versus the basics?

2. Examine a traditional textbook at any grade level of your choice. If possible, use a teacher's edition. Page through any chapter, and look for signs of the five process standards. To what extent are children who are being taught from this book likely to be doing and learning mathematics in ways described by those processes? What would you have to do to change the general approach to this text?

3. Examine a unit from any one of the eight reform curriculum programs, and see how it reflects the NCTM vision of reform, especially the five process standards. How do these curriculum programs differ from traditional textbook programs?

4. Review the sample video from the eighth-grade TIMSS video study. It shows a geometry lesson and an algebra lesson from a typical eighth-grade classroom in each country. What elements of the reform movement do you see in each of these lessons? Caution: You will be very surprised at the U.S. lessons, especially in comparison to the others on the tape.

# Recommendations for Further Reading

## Highly Recommended

Mathematical Sciences Education Board, National Research Council. (1989). *Everybody counts: A report to the nation on the future of mathematics education.* Washington, DC: National Academy Press.
This little booklet, readable in a single evening, provides a compelling rationale for reform in both the mathematics we teach and how it is taught. Here you will find the description of mathematics as "the science of pattern and order" used throughout this text. Myths concerning the nature of mathematics, how it is learned, and by whom are challenged from an angle that is difficult to dispute. More than a decade after its publication, this remains a must read for anyone who wishes to understand why reform is so necessary.

National Council of Teachers of Mathematics. (2000). *Principles and standards for school mathematics.* Reston, VA: Author.
This update to the 1989 document that signaled the beginning of the revolution in mathematics education is one of the most important books that you could read in order to understand the current directions in mathematics education. Every teacher and preservice teacher should read the sections on Principles (Chapter 2), the K–12 overview (Chapter 3), and the standards for his or her grade band of interest. If you can, add this book to your professional library.

Stigler, J. W., & Hiebert, J. C. (1999). *The teaching gap: Best ideas from the world's teachers for improving education in the classroom.* New York: Free Press.
Certainly you have heard how U.S. students are constantly being compared to students in other countries, most notably Japan. The authors of this book have looked carefully at teaching practices in Japan, Germany, and the United States through the lens of the TIMSS video study. Their purpose was to improve education in this country by providing a thoughtful study in contrasts of teaching in three distinctly different cultures.

Teppo, A. R. (Ed.). (1999). *Reflecting on practice in elementary school mathematics: Readings from NCTM's school-based journals and other publications.* Reston, VA: National Council of Teachers of Mathematics.
Frequently, NCTM publishes books of selected readings from its journals. In this instance, more than 60 articles provide perspective on the reform movement, organized according to major areas of the curriculum. If you seek to establish a resource of short, easily read articles on a wide variety of topics, this is an excellent book with which to begin.

Trafton, P. R., & Claus, A. S. (1994). A changing curriculum for a changing age. In C. A. Thornton & N. S. Bley (Eds.), *Windows of opportunity: Mathematics for students with special needs* (pp. 19–39). Reston, VA: National Council of Teachers of Mathematics.
Paul Trafton has long been a recognized leader in mathematics education, especially in the area of reform. With Claus, he describes in one chapter the vision of the 1989 *Standards* and the challenges that vision presents to teachers. The chapter ends with a vignette from a second-grade classroom that vividly brings home the meaning of reform.

## Other Suggestions

Battista, M. T. (1999). The mathematical miseducation of America's youth: Ignoring research and scientific study in education. *Phi Delta Kappan, 80,* 424–433.

Bay, J. M., Reys, B. J., & Reys, R. E. (1999). The top 10 elements that must be in place to implement standards-based mathematics curricula. *Phi Delta Kappan, 80,* 503–506.

Billstein, R. (1998). Middle grades math thematics: The STEM project— a look at developing a middle school mathematics curriculum. In L. Leutzinger (Ed.), *Mathematics in the middle* (pp. 93–106). Reston, VA: National Council of Teachers of Mathematics.

Boaler, J. (1998). Open and closed mathematics: Student experiences and understandings. *Journal for Research in Mathematics Education, 29,* 41–62.

Burns, M. (1998). *Math: Facing an American phobia.* Sausalito, CA: Math Solutions Publications.

Burrill, G. (1998). Changes in your classroom: From the past to the present to the future. *Teaching Children Mathematics, 5,* 202–209.

Curcio, F. R. (1999). Dispelling myths about reform in school mathematics. *Mathematics Teaching in the Middle School, 4,* 282–284.

Ferrini-Mundy, J., Graham, K., Johnson, L., & Mills, G. (Eds.). (1998). *Making change in mathematics education: Learning from the field.* Reston, VA: National Council of Teachers of Mathematics.

Goldsmith, L. T., & Mark, J. (1999). What is a standards-based mathematics curriculum? *Educational Leadership, 57*(3), 40–44.

Jones, M. G., Jones, B. D., Hardin, B., Chapman, L., Yarbrough, T., & Davis, M. (1999). The impact of high-stakes testing on teachers and students in North Carolina. *Phi Delta Kappan, 81,* 199–203.

Lappan, G. (1999). Revitalizing and refocusing our efforts. *Teaching Children Mathematics, 6,* 104–109.

Lappan, G., & Phillips, E. (1998). Teaching and learning in the Connected Mathematics Project. In L. Leutzinger (Ed.), *Mathematics in the middle* (pp. 83–92). Reston, VA: National Council of Teachers of Mathematics.

National Council of Teachers of Mathematics. (1991). *Professional standards for teaching mathematics.* Reston, VA: Author.

National Council of Teachers of Mathematics. (1995). *Assessment standards for school mathematics.* Reston, VA: Author.

O'Brien, T. C. (1999). Parrot math. *Phi Delta Kappan, 80,* 434–438.

Popham, W. J. (1999). Why standardized tests don't measure educational quality. *Educational Leadership, 56*(6), 8–15.

Reese, C. M., Miller, K. E., Mazzeo, J., & Dossey, J. A. (1997). *NAEP 1996 mathematics report card for the nation and the states: Findings from the National Assessment of Educational Progress.* Washington, DC: National Center for Education Statistics.

Reys, B. J., Robinson, E., Sconiers, S., & Mark, J. (1999). Mathematics curricula based on rigorous national standards: What, why, and how? *Phi Delta Kappan, 80,* 454–456.

Reys, R. E., Reys, B. J., Barnes, D. E., Beem, J. K., Lapan, R. T., & Papick, I. J. (1998). Standards-based middle school mathematics curricula: What do students think? In L. P. Leutzinger (Ed.),

*Mathematics in the middle* (pp. 153–157). Reston, VA: National Council of Teachers of Mathematics.

Schoen, H. L., Fey, J. T., Hirsch, C. R., & Coxford, A. F. (1999). Issues and options in the math wars. *Phi Delta Kappan, 80,* 444–453.

Stigler, J. W., & Hiebert, J. C.(1997). Understanding and improving classroom mathematics instruction: An overview of the TIMSS video study. *Phi Delta Kappan, 79,* 14–21.

Tsuruda, G. (1998). Middle school mathematics reform: Form versus spirit. In L. Leutzinger (Ed.), *Mathematics in the middle* (pp. 3–9). Reston, VA: National Council of Teachers of Mathematics.

Van Boening, L. (1999). Growth through change. *Mathematics Teaching in the Middle School, 5,* 27–33.

Willoughby, S. S. (1996). The *Standards:* Some second thoughts. *Mathematics Teaching in the Middle School, 2,* 8–11.

# Reform Curricula

## Elementary Programs

Information about the elementary programs can be obtained from the ARC Center:

E-mail: arccenter@mail.comap.com
URL: www.arccenter.comap.com

*UCSMP Elementary: Everyday Mathematics* (K–6)
Developer: University of Chicago School Mathematics Project
Publisher: Everyday Learning
E-mail: aisaacs@midway.uchicago.edu

*Investigations in Number, Data, and Space* (K–5)
Developer: TERC
Publisher: Scott, Foresman
URL: www.terc.edu/investigations/index.html

*Math Trailblazers: A Mathematical Journey Using Science and Language Arts* (K–5)
Developer: Institute for Math and Science Education, University of Illinois, Chicago
Publisher: Kendall/Hunt
URL: www.math.uic.edu/IMSE

## Middle School Programs

Information about the middle school programs can be obtained from the Show-Me Center:

E-mail: Center@showme.missouri.edu
URL: www.showmecenter.missouri.edu

*Connected Mathematics* (CMP) (6–8)
Developer: Michigan State University
Publisher: Prentice Hall
URL: www.msu.edu/cmp

*Mathematics in Context* (MIC) (5–8)
Developer: University of Wisconsin—Madison
Publisher: Encyclopaedia Britannica
URL: www.ebmic.com

*MathScape* (6–8)
Developer: Educational Development Center
Publisher: Creative Publications
URL: www.edc.org/mathscape

*Middle School Mathematics Through Applications Project* (MMAP) (6–8)
Developer: Institute for Research on Learning
Publisher: Voyager Expanded Learning
URL: www.imvoyager.com

*Middle Grades Math Thematics* (STEM) (6–8)
Developer: University of Montana
Publisher: McDougal/Littell
URL: www.mlmath.com

# Chapter 2
# Exploring What It Means to Do Mathematics

*As a practical matter, mathematics is a science of pattern and order. Its domain is not molecules or cells, but numbers, chance, form, algorithms, and change. As a science of abstract objects, mathematics relies on logic rather than on observation as its standard of truth, yet employs observation, simulation, and even experimentation as means of discovering truth.*

*Mathematical Sciences Education Board (1989, p. 31)*

How would you describe what you are doing when you are *doing mathematics*? Stop for a moment and write a few sentences about what it means to know and do mathematics, based on your own experiences. Then put your paper aside until you have finished this chapter.

The description of doing mathematics you will read about here may not match your personal experiences. That's OK! It is OK to come to this point with whatever beliefs were developed in your previous mathematics experiences. However, it is not OK to accept outdated ideas about mathematics and expect to be a quality teacher. Your obligation and your challenge as you read this chapter and this book are to reconceptualize your own understanding of what it means to know and do mathematics so that the children with whom you work will have an exciting and accurate vision of mathematics.

## CHANGING PERCEPTIONS OF SCHOOL MATHEMATICS

Much change has taken place since 1989 when NCTM set a vision for change in mathematics classrooms. More teachers are beginning to use what might be called a "*Standards* approach": more cooperative learning, more emphasis on concepts and problem solving, and a greater tolerance for and

use of calculators. Often these changes are superficial and are not really changing the nature of what children do and how they think in the mathematics classroom. Furthermore, as noted in Chapter 1, the pressures of state test scores have a tendency to bring out "drill-and-kill" approaches even though such methods have consistently proved ineffective. Fortunately, wonderful exceptions are to be found everywhere.

## Traditional Views of School Mathematics

In the traditional classroom, the teacher represents the source of all that is to be known in mathematics. After reviewing material covered the day before or checking homework, the teacher typically moves on to an explanation of whatever idea is on the next page of the text. Instruction generally consists of showing the children how they are to do the assigned exercises. Even with a hands-on activity using some form of manipulative, the traditional teacher is guiding the children, telling them exactly how to use the materials in a prescribed way. In this environment, the students' attention is necessarily on the teacher's directions, not on mathematical ideas. The focus of the lesson is primarily on getting answers. The students rely on the teacher to determine if their answers are correct.

Children emerge from these experiences with a view that mathematics is a series of arbitrary rules, handed down by the teacher, who in turn got them from some very smart source. The students' role in this exercise is largely passive. They are to accept what they are told and attempt to master each new rule. It is no wonder that students feel they must check with the teacher to see if an answer is correct.

When children are neither asked nor required to understand rules or evaluate their own answers, they are being told loudly and clearly, "You are not capable of understanding these ideas." By the fifth or sixth grade, many children simply refuse to attempt a problem that has not first been explained: "You haven't shown us how to do this." Children accept that every problem must have a predetermined solution, that there is only one way to solve any problem, and that they should not even expect to solve a problem unless they have been given a solution method ahead of time.

This follow-the-rules, computation-dominated, answer-oriented view of mathematics is a gross distortion of what mathematics is really about. It cannot be very exciting. A few children are good at learning rules and thrive on the ensuing good grades. But these are not necessarily the best thinkers in the room. The traditional system rewards the learning of rules but offers little opportunity actually to do mathematics.

## Mathematics as a Science of Pattern and Order

*Mathematics is the science of pattern and order.* This wonderfully simple description of mathematics is found in the thought-provoking publication *Everybody Counts* (MSEB, 1989; see also Schoenfeld, 1992). This definition challenges the popular social view of mathematics as a discipline dominated by computation and rules without reasons. Science is a process of figuring things out or making sense of things. It begins with problematic situations. Although you may never have thought of it in quite this way, mathematics is a science of things that have a pattern of regularity and logical order. Finding and exploring this regularity or order and then making sense of it is what doing mathematics is all about.

Even the youngest schoolchildren can and should be involved in the science of pattern and order. Have you ever noticed that 6 + 7 is the same as 5 + 8 and 4 + 9? What is the pattern? What are the relationships? When two odd numbers are multiplied, the result is also odd, but if the same numbers are added or subtracted, the result is even. There is a logic behind simple results such as these, an order, a pattern.

Consider the study of algebra. One can learn to graph the equation of a parabola by simply following rules and plotting points. Now calculators are readily available to do that as well, and with a speed and precision we could never hope to achieve. But understanding why certain forms of equations always produce parabolic graphs involves a search for patterns in the way numbers behave. Discovering what types of real-world relationships are represented by parabolic graphs (for example, a pendulum swing related to the length of the pendulum) is even more interesting and scientific—and infinitely more valuable—than the ability to plot the curve when someone else provides the equation.

And pattern is not just in numbers and equations but in everything around us. The world is full of pattern and order: in nature, in art, in buildings, in music. Pattern and order are found in commerce, science, medicine, manufacturing, and sociology. Mathematics discovers this order, makes sense of

it, and uses it in a multitude of fascinating ways, improving our lives and expanding our knowledge. School must begin to help children with this process of discovery.

# WHAT DOES IT MEAN TO DO MATHEMATICS?

Engaging in the science of pattern and order—in doing mathematics—is effortful and often takes time. There are lots of ideas to learn. Often these ideas show up on lists of "basic skills." For example, children should be able to count accurately, know their basic facts for addition and multiplication, have efficient methods of computing whole numbers, fractions, and decimals, know measurement facts such as the number of inches in a foot or quarts in a gallon, know the names of geometric shapes, and so on. But to master these bits and pieces is no more doing mathematics than playing scales on the piano is making music.

The *Principles and Standards* document makes it very clear that there is a time and a place for drill and practice but that drill should *never* come before understanding. Repetitive drill of the bits and pieces is not doing mathematics and will never result in understanding. Drill may produce short-term results on traditional tests, but the long-term effects have produced a nation of citizens happy to admit they can't do mathematics. Rather, the bits and pieces that are important are the result of actually doing mathematics. Mere mastery of skills is not doing mathematics.

## The Verbs of Doing Mathematics

Envision for a moment an elementary mathematics class where students are doing mathematics. What verbs would you use to describe the activity in this classroom? Stop for a moment and make a short list before reading further.

Children in traditional mathematics classes often describe mathematics as "work" or "getting answers." They talk about "plussing" and "doing times" (multiplication). In contrast, the following collection of verbs can be found in most of the literature describing the reform in mathematics education, and all are used in *Principles and Standards:*

| | | |
|---|---|---|
| explore | represent | explain |
| investigate | formulate | predict |
| conjecture | discover | develop |
| solve | construct | describe |
| justify | verify | use |

These are science verbs, verbs indicating the process of "making sense" and "figuring out." When children are engaged in the kinds of activities suggested by this list, it is virtually impossible for them to be passive observers. They will necessarily be actively thinking about the mathematical ideas that are involved.

In classrooms where doing mathematics this way is a daily occurrence, the students are getting an empowering message: "You are capable of making sense of this—you are capable of *doing mathematics!*"

## What Is Basic in Mathematics?

In a climate where "basics" or "back to basics" is once again a matter of public discussion, it is useful to ask, what is basic in mathematics? The position of this text is as follows:

> **The most basic idea in mathematics is that <u>mathematics makes sense!</u>**
> - *Every day, students must experience that mathematics makes sense.*
> - *Students must come to believe that they are capable of making sense of mathematics.*
> - *Teachers must stop teaching by telling and start letting students make sense of the mathematics they are learning.*
> - *To this end, teachers must believe in their students—all of them!*

*Every* idea introduced in the mathematics classroom can and should be completely understood by *every* child. *There are no exceptions!* There is absolutely no excuse for children learning any aspect of mathematics without completely understanding it. All children are capable of learning all of the mathematics we want them to learn, and they can learn it in a meaningful manner, a way that makes sense to them.

## An Environment for Doing Mathematics

Look again at the verbs of doing mathematics. They are action verbs. They require reaching out, taking risks, placing ideas out where others can see. Contrast these with the verbs that might reflect the traditional mathematics classroom: *listen, copy, memorize, drill.* These are passive activities. They involve no risks and little initiative. Doing mathematics takes effort and initiative.

Though thinking, reasoning, and sense making can be fun, it can nevertheless be a bit frightening to stick out your neck when no one tells you exactly what to do. The classroom must be an environment where doing mathematics is not threatening, where every student is respected for his or her ideas. Students should feel comfortable taking risks, knowing that they will not be ridiculed.

The teacher's role is to create this spirit of inquiry, trust, and expectation. Within that environment, students are invited to do mathematics. Problems are posed; students wrestle toward solutions. The focus is on students actively figuring things out, testing ideas and making conjectures, developing reasons and offering explanations. Students work in groups, in pairs, or individually, but they are always sharing and discussing. Reasoning is celebrated as students defend their methods and justify their solutions.

# AN INVITATION TO DO MATHEMATICS

If you are to create a classroom environment where children are truly doing mathematics, it is important that you have a personal feel for doing mathematics in this manner. It is quite likely that your experiences in mathematics classes have been quite different. The purpose of this portion of the chapter is to provide you with opportunities to engage in the science of pattern and order—to do some mathematics. Although the tasks or problems are appropriate for students in the intermediate and middle grades, you should not be at all concerned now with how children might approach these problems. Rather, get personally involved in the problems as an adult and discover as much as you can in the process. If possible, find one or two friends to work together with you. Get some paper to scribble ideas on. Try not to be shy about your ideas. Respect and listen to the ideas of your friends. You can and should challenge their ideas, but don't belittle them.

The text will provide hints and suggestions in a poor substitution for the interaction of a teacher. Don't read too much at once. Stop and do as much as you can until you and your group are stuck—really stuck; then read a bit more.

## Let's Do Some Mathematics!

We will explore four different problems. Each is independent of the others. None requires any sophisticated mathematics, not even algebra. Don't be passive! Try your ideas out. Have fun!

**START AND JUMP NUMBERS: SEARCHING FOR PATTERNS**

You will need to make a list of numbers that begin with a "start number" and increase by a fixed amount we will call the "jump number." First try 3 as the start number and 5 as the jump number. Write the start number at the top of your list, then 8, 13, and so on, "jumping" by 5 each time until your list extends to about 130.

Your task is to examine this list of numbers and find as many patterns as you possibly can. Share your ideas with the group, and write down every pattern you agree really is a pattern.

 Get to work before reading further. Keep looking for patterns until you simply cannot think of any more.

***A Few Ideas.*** Here are some kinds of things you may already have thought of:

- There is at least one alternating pattern.

- Have you looked at odd and even numbers?

- What can you say about the number in the tens place? How did you think about the first two numbers with no tens-place digits?
  What happens when the numbers reach above 100? (There are two ways to think about that.)

- Have you tried doing any adding of numbers? Numbers in the list? Digits in the numbers?

 If there is an idea in this list you haven't tried, try that now.

Don't forget to think about what happens to your patterns after the numbers go over 100. How are you thinking about 113? One way is as 1 hundred, 1 ten, and 3 ones. But of course it could also be "eleventy-three," where the tens digit has gone from 9 to 10 to 11. How do these different perspectives affect your patterns? What would happen after 999?

When you added the *digits* in the numbers, the sums are 3, 8, 4, 9, 5, 10, 6, 11, 7, 12, 8, . . . Did you look at every other number in this string? And what is the sum for 113? Is it 5 or is it 14? (There is no "right" answer here. But it is interesting to consider different possibilities.)

***Next Steps.*** Sometimes when you have discovered some patterns in mathematics, it is a good idea to make some changes and see how the changes affect the patterns. What changes might you make in this problem?

 Try some ideas now before going on.

Your changes may be even more interesting than the following suggestions. But here are some ideas that seem a bit more obvious than others:

- Change the start number but keep the jump number equal to 5. What is the same and what is different?

- Try keeping the start number the same, and examine different jump numbers. You will find out that changing jump numbers really "messes things up" a lot compared to changing the start numbers.

- If you have patterns for several different jump numbers, what can you figure out about how a jump number affects the patterns? For example, when the jump number was 5, the ones-digit pattern repeated every two numbers—it had a "pattern length" of two. But when the jump number is 3, the length of the ones-digit pattern is ten! Do other jump numbers create different lengths?

- For a jump number of 3, how is the ones-digit pattern related to the circle of numbers in Figure 2.1? Are there other circles of numbers for other jump numbers?

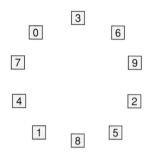

**Figure 2.1** **For jumps of 3, the cycle of digits will occur in the ones place.**

***Looking Back.*** You may want to explore this idea even further—or perhaps you've had enough of jump numbers. There are more ideas than have been suggested here.

A calculator can be used to make the list generation easy for young children or to work with big jump numbers, like 25 or 36. Most simple calculators have an automatic constant feature that will add the same number successively. For example, if you press 3 ➕ 5 🟰 and then keep pressing 🟰, you will get the first sequence of numbers you wrote. (The calculator "stores" the last operation of +5 and repeats the operation on the display for each press of 🟰. This also works for the other three operations.)

---

### TWO MACHINES, ONE JOB

**Ron's Recycle Shop was started when Ron bought a used paper-shredding machine. Business was good, so Ron bought a new shredding machine. The old machine could shred a truckload of paper in 4 hours. The new machine could shred the same truckload in only 2 hours. How long will it take to shred a truckload of paper if Ron runs both shredders at the same time?**

---

***Get Started.*** Sometimes you just have to jump in and do something. Before reading any of the ideas that follow, go ahead and work on this until you either get an answer or get stuck. If you get an answer, try to decide how you can establish that it is correct. If you get stuck, be absolutely certain you are stuck. Write down everything you know, and examine every idea you have had.

 Work before reading on.

***Stuck?*** Are you overlooking any assumptions made in the problem? Do the machines run simultaneously? The problem says "at the same time." Do they run just as fast when working together as when they work alone?

 If this gives you an idea, pursue it before reading more.

Have you tried to predict approximately how much time you think it should take the two machines? Just make an estimate in round numbers. For example, will it be closer to 1 hour or closer to 4 hours? What causes you to answer as you have? Can you tell if your "guestimate" makes sense or is at least in the ballpark? Checking a guess in this way sometimes leads to a new insight.

Some people draw pictures to solve problems. Others like to use something they can move or change. For example, you might draw a rectangle or a line segment to stand for the truckload of paper, or you might get some counters (chips, plastic cubes, pennies) and make a collection that stands for the truckload.

 Go back and try some more.

***Consider Solutions of Others.*** Here are solutions of three elementary school teachers who worked on this problem. (The examples are adapted from Schifter & Fosnot, 1993, pp. 24–27.) Betsy teaches sixth grade. Here is Betsy's solution:

> Betsy holds up a bar of plastic cubes. "Let's say these 16 cubes are the truckload of paper. In 1 hour, the new machine shreds 8 cubes and the old machine 4 cubes." Betsy breaks off 8 cubes and then 4 cubes. "That leaves these 4 cubes. If the new machine did 8 cubes' worth in 1 hour, it can do 2 cubes' worth in 15 minutes. The old machine does half as much, or 1 cube." As she says this, she breaks off 3 more cubes. "That is 1 hour and 15 minutes, and we still have 1 cube left." Long pause. "Well, the new machine did 2 cubes in 15 minutes, so it will do this cube in $7\frac{1}{2}$ minutes. Add that onto the 1 hour and 15 minutes. The total time will be 1 hour $22\frac{1}{2}$ minutes." (See Figure 2.2.)

Cora teaches fourth grade. She disagrees with Betsy. Here is Cora's proposal:

> "This rectangle [see Figure 2.3] stands for the whole truckload. In 1 hour, the new machine will do half of this." The rectangle is divided in half. "In 1 hour, the old machine could do $\frac{1}{4}$ of the paper." The rectangle is divided accordingly. "So in 1 hour, the two machines have done $\frac{3}{4}$ of the truck, and there is $\frac{1}{4}$ left. What is left is one-third as much as what they already did, so it should take the two machines one-third as long to do that part as it took to do the first part. One-third of an hour is 20 minutes. That means it takes 1 hour and 20 minutes to do it all."

Sylvia teaches third grade. She and her partner have these thoughts:

> At first, we solved the problem by averaging. We decided that it would take 3 hours because that's the average. Then Deborah asked how we knew to average. We thought we had a reason, but then Deborah asked how Ron would feel if his two machines together took longer than just the new one that could do the job in only 2 hours. So we can see that 3 hours doesn't make sense. So we still don't know whether it's 1 hour and 20 minutes or 1 hour and $22\frac{1}{2}$ minutes.

At the SummerMath institute where these teachers were participants, they were not told the solution to this problem. That in itself caused some disturbance. But there is little value in seeing a solution from a book or from a teacher. You end up feeling that the teacher is very smart and you are not so smart. No solution is provided here either.

If you have a solution, a good thing to do is see first why you think you are correct and try to articulate that. Then see if you can find a different way to solve the problem than the

New machine does this work in 1 hour.  Old machine does this work in 1 hour.  Both do this in 15 minutes.  New machine does this in $7\frac{1}{2}$ minutes.

**Figure 2.2** Betsy's solution to the paper-shredding problem.

Entire truckload

New machine in 1 hour  Old machine in 1 hour  Both machines together

60 minutes  20 minutes

**Figure 2.3** Cora's solution to the paper-shredding problem.

way you did it the first time. (What would be the value of two different solutions that both lead to the same answer?)

### WHAT CAN YOU FIND OUT ABOUT THIS?

An excellent exploration for young children to help them begin to see how facts are related is to confront them with this observation:

When you make the first number 1 more and the second number 1 less, you get the same answer:

⇑ ⇓
7 + 7 = 14   is the same as   8 + 6 = 14

It works for 5 + 5 too

⇑ ⇓
5 + 5 = 10   is the same as   6 + 4 = 10

What can you find out about this?

Your task here is to examine *what happens when you change addition to multiplication in this exploration. What can you find out about that?* (7 × 7 = 49 and 8 × 6 = 48)? *What other products should you examine?*

Explore until you have developed some ideas. Write down whatever ideas you discover.

***Try Using a Physical Model.*** You have probably found some interesting patterns. Can you tell why these patterns work? In the case of addition, it is fairly easy to see that when you take from one number and give to the other, the total stays the same. That is not exactly the way multiplication works. One way to explore this is to make rectangles for each product and see how they change when you adjust one factor up and the other down (see Figure 2.4a).

You may prefer to think of multiplication as equal sets. For example, 7 × 7 means seven sets with seven things in

each. You increase the number of sets and decrease the number in each set (or the other way around; see Figure 2.4b).

**STOP** Work with one or both of these approaches to see if you get any insights.

***Things to Examine.*** There are a few different ways to go with this exploration. Here are a couple of suggestions. You may be pursuing something a bit different than these ideas. That is fine! The idea in this problem is to conduct your own exploration—to see what you can find out.

■ Have you looked at how the first two numbers are related? For example, 7 × 7, 5 × 5, and 9 × 9 are all products with like factors. How do those results differ when the two factors are 1 apart (7 × 8 or 12 × 13)? What about when the factors differ by 2 or by 3?

■ Maybe you have adjusted the factors up and down by 1. What if you go from 7 × 7 to 9 × 5? Try making adjustments by other numbers.

■ Does it make any difference in the results if you use big numbers instead of small ones?

■ What if *both* factors increase?

This exploration has lots of answers, but the questions to answer are the ones *you* ask. When the problem is really yours and it is not clear that the teacher already knows the answer, students feel more ownership and interest. Rather than "What do you want me to do?" problem ownership shifts the situation to "I think I am going to . . ." (Baker & Baker, 1990). The suggested questions offered here were presented as a list because this is a textbook. In a classroom, the teacher can select challenges and make suggestions when necessary. The teacher can also help students make their own conjectures and observations. Frequently, children will pursue a completely different tack than the one anticipated. Scientists explore new ideas that strike them as interesting and promising rather than blindly following the direction of others. Mathematics is a science.

**Figure 2.4** **Two physical ways to think about multiplication that might help in the exploration.**

This is 7 × 7 as
7 rows of 7.

(a)

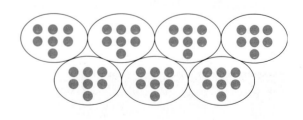

This is 7 × 7 as
7 sets of 7.

(b)

What happens when you change one of these to show 6 × 8?

## THE BEST CHANCE OF PURPLE

Three students are spinning to "get purple" with two spinners (either by spinning first red and then blue or first blue and then red; see Figure 2.5). They may choose to spin each spinner once or one of the spinners twice. Mary chooses to spin twice on spinner A; John chooses to spin twice on spinner B; and Susan chooses to spin first on spinner A and then on spinner B. Who has the best chance of getting a red and a blue? (Lappan & Even, 1989, p. 17)

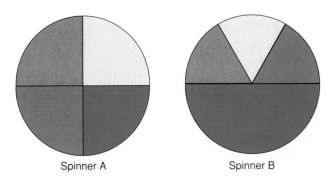

Spinner A                    Spinner B

**Figure 2.5** You may spin A twice, B twice, or A then B. Which option gives you the best chance of spinning a red and a blue?

 As with the other problems, the first thing is to think about the problem and what you know and then to try something that gives you some help. Before reading the suggestions, see what you can come up with.

***Try It Out.*** Sometimes it is tough to get a feel for problems that seem too abstract to think about. One thing that can be done in situations involving chance is to find a way to create the chance and see what happens. For this problem, you can easily make spinners using a freehand drawing on paper, a paper clip, and a pencil. Put your pencil point through the loop of the clip and on the center of your spinner. Now you can flip the paper clip "pointer." Try at least 20 pairs of spins for each choice, and keep track of what happens.

- For Susan's choice (A then B), would it matter if she spun B first and then A? Why or why not?
- Try to describe why you think purple is more or less likely in one of the three cases compared to the other two. It sometimes helps to talk through what you have observed to come up with a way to apply some more precise reasoning.

 Try these suggestions before reading on.

***Try Tree Diagrams.*** On spinner A, the four colors each have the same chance of coming up. You could make a tree diagram for A with four branches, and all the branches would have the same chance (see Figure 2.6). On spinner B, what is the relationship between the blue region and each of the others? How could you make a tree diagram for B with each branch having the same chance?

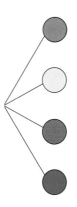

**Figure 2.6** A tree diagram for spinner A in Figure 2.5.

How can you add to the diagram for spinner A so that it represents spinning A twice in succession? Why does your tree diagram make sense? What branches on your diagram represent getting purple?

How could you make tree diagrams for John's and Susan's choices? Why do they make sense?

Whatever idea you come up with on paper should be tested by actually spinning the spinner or spinners.

 Tree diagrams are only one way to approach this. You may have a different way. As long as your way seems to be getting you somewhere, stick with that way. There is one more suggestion to follow, but don't read further if you have an idea to work on.

***Using Grids.*** Suppose that you had a square that represented all the possible outcomes for spinner A and a similar square for spinner B. There are many ways to divide a square in four equal parts, but someone figured out that if you use lines going all in the same direction, you can make comparisons of all the outcomes of one event (one whole square) with the outcomes of another event (drawn on a different square). When the second event (here the second spin) follows the first event, make the lines on the second square go the opposite way from the lines on the first. Make a tracing of one square in Figure 2.7 (p. 22), and place it on the other. You end up with 24 little sections.

Why are there six subdivisions for the spinner B square? What does each of the 24 little rectangles stand for? What sections would represent purple? In any other method you have been trying, did 24 come into play when you were looking at spinner A followed by B?

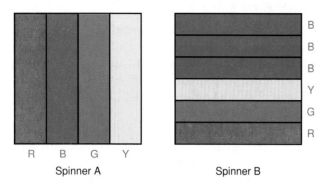

**Figure 2.7** A square shows the chance of obtaining each color for the spinners in Figure 2.5.

## No Answer Book

If you have worked hard on any or all of the four tasks just presented, you still may not have answers or found all of the patterns and ideas that someone else found. If you really gave it some effort and took some risks in sharing whatever ideas you had, you are on the right track. The science of pattern and order sometimes takes a little time and nearly always requires effort.

No answers or solutions are given in this text. How do you feel about that? What about the "right" answers? Are your answers correct? What makes the solution to any investigation "correct"?

In the classroom, the ready availability of the answer book or the teacher's providing the solution or verifying that an answer is correct sends a clear message to children about doing mathematics: "Your job is to find the answers that the teacher already has." In the real world of problem solving outside the classroom, there are no teachers with answers and no answer books. Doing mathematics includes deciding if an answer is correct and why.

## Some More Explorations

Here are four more explorations. For these tasks, there are no hints or discussions, only the problems. The first two you could try with fourth- or fifth-grade children. All four would be useful in the middle grades. The main purpose of presenting them here is to give you an opportunity to do some more mathematics and to begin to experience what that means and feels like.

### FOUR CONSECUTIVE NUMBERS

Some people say that to add four consecutive numbers, you add the first and the last numbers and multiply by 2. What can you find out about that?

Here is an example: 4, 5, 6, and 7 are four consecutive numbers. The sum is 22. Also $4 + 7 = 11$ and $11 \times 2 = 22$. The problem is taken from *Natural Learning and Mathematics* (Stoessiger & Edmunds, 1992). The authors use this task to provide a wonderful illustration of how 11- and 12-year-olds can generate ideas and make them grow. The book is highly recommended.

### ACROBATS, GRANDMAS, AND IVAN

The problem is to use the information given to figure out who will win the third round of tug-of-war.

> *Round 1: On one side are four acrobats, each of equal strength. On the other side are five neighborhood grandmas, each of equal strength. The result is dead even.*
> *Round 2: On one side is Ivan, a dog. Ivan is pitted against two of the grandmas and one acrobat. Again, it's a draw.*
> *Round 3: Ivan and three of the grandmas are on one side, and the four acrobats are on the other.*

**Who will win the third round?**

This problem was originally called "A Mathematical Tug-of-War" and is found in *Math for Smarty Pants* by Marilyn Burns (1982). For a discussion of how fifth graders approached the problem, see *50 Problem-Solving Lessons: Grades 1–6* (Burns, 1996). Silver, Smith, and Nelson (1995) discuss solutions offered by eighth graders.

### PIZZAS: SMALL, MEDIUM, AND LARGE

Pizzas are often sold in small, medium, and large sizes—usually measured by the diameter of the circular pie. Of course, the prices are different for the three sizes. Do you think a large pizza is usually the best buy?

The Sole D'Italia Pizzeria sells small, medium, and large pies. The small pie is 9 inches in diameter, the medium pie is 12 inches in diameter, and the large pie is 15 inches in diameter. For a plain cheese small pizza, Sole D'Italia charges $6; for a medium pizza, it charges $9; for a large pizza, it charges $12. Are these fair prices?

- *Which measures should be most closely related to the prices charged—circumference, area, radius, or diameter? Why?*
- *Use your results to write a report on the fairness of Sole D'Italia's pizza prices.*

This problem (Lappan & Briars, 1995, p. 139) has a number of characteristics worth noting. First, it is contextual;

it is a very realistic problem that might interest middle grade students. Second, the teacher can predict with some certainty what mathematics students will encounter in this problem (measurement and relationships in the geometry of circles). There are lots of ideas about circle measurement involved. This would be a good problem to use *before* the children have developed a collection of formulas. Students have many ways to get at the circle measures, including measuring some actual circles. Formulas are not necessary. There is also a nice opportunity to discuss rate as a type of ratio in this problem.

### TRAPEZOIDS

**A trapezoid is a four-sided figure with one pair of opposite sides parallel. Draw a trapezoid that has an area of 36.**

If a teacher or a text gives you a formula for the area of a trapezoid, this is not a very interesting task. But there are some nice possibilities for discovering patterns and learning about area and perhaps even developing a formula that can come from this. One suggestion is to get some grid paper and draw some trapezoids. (Blackline Masters are provided at the back of the book.)

# HELPING STUDENTS DO MATHEMATICS

Assuming that you have worked on some of the problems in this chapter, you have most likely been trying to make sense of the situations or tasks that you confronted. You were involved in the science of pattern and order. You were *doing mathematics.*

In the best of situations, you did this science, this mathematics, with others. Perhaps you shared your ideas, right or wrong, and tried to defend them. You listened to your peers and tried to make sense of their ideas. Together you tried to come up with a solution. And then you had to decide if your answer was correct without looking in an answer book or asking the teacher.

When students do mathematics like this on a daily basis in an environment that encourages risk and expects participation, it becomes an exciting endeavor. Individuals who are uncomfortable in an answer-oriented, teacher-directed environment begin to develop confidence. Students talk more, share more ideas, offer suggestions, and challenge or defend the solutions of others.

Being the teacher responsible for creating this environment may sound overwhelming. You may have envisioned teaching mathematics as relatively easy—just demonstrate the rules and manage practice. Creating a classroom culture and environment in which children are doing mathematics is not easy. There is no reason to believe that you will be an expert from the start.

NCTM's *Professional Standards for Teaching Mathematics* (1991) offers important guidelines and examples of teachers making changes toward this vision of doing mathematics. As noted in Chapter 1, the first of the major shifts envisioned by the *Professional Standards* is "toward classrooms as mathematical communities" and "away from classrooms as simply a collection of individuals" (p. 3). So that you can create this mathematical community, you next need to understand how children develop mathematical ideas. That is what you will encounter in Chapter 3. In Chapter 4, we will build on the vision of what it means to do mathematics and an understanding of how children learn. There you will find strategies for teaching with tasks or problems. It is an exciting venture!

# REFLECTIONS ON CHAPTER 2

## Writing to Learn

1. Explain what is meant by "Mathematics is a science of pattern and order." Contrast this view with traditional school mathematics.

2. How would you describe what it means to "do mathematics"?

3. Why is doing pencil-and-paper computation not "doing mathematics"?

4. What features of a classroom environment are important for students to be engaged in doing mathematics?

5. How can students come to believe that they are capable of making sense of mathematics?

## For Discussion and Exploration

1. Explore the teacher's edition of any current basal textbook series for any grade level of your interest. Pick one chapter, and identify lessons or activities that promote doing mathematics as a science of pattern and order. In general, would you say that the flavor of the chapter you selected is in the spirit of mathematics as a science of pattern and order? Examine any of the reform curricula (see listing on p. 14). Is the approach there any closer to doing mathematics?

2. In the *Professional Standards,* read the first vignette (pp. 11–15), in which a sixth-grade teacher who has taught for 5

years confronts her own realization that she needs to change. In reaction to this vignette you might

   a. Try her lesson with fifth- to seventh-grade children

   b. Design a lesson on a topic of your own choice that would serve the same purpose of getting children actively involved in real mathematics

   c. Take a lesson out of a fifth- to seventh-grade book and discuss how this teacher might now decide to teach the lesson

# Recommendations for Further Reading

## Highly Recommended

Lampert, M. (1990). When the problem is not the question and the solution is not the answer: Mathematical knowing and teaching. *American Educational Research Journal, 27,* 29–63.

Magdalene Lampert is one of mathematics education's most articulate voices for making shifts toward classrooms as communities where children do mathematics. In this article, she clearly articulates the spirit of the traditional classroom and how it adversely affects the concept of mathematics held by children and teachers.

Malloy, C. E. (1999). Developing mathematical reasoning in the middle grades. In L. V. Stiff (Ed.), *Developing mathematical reasoning in grades K–12* (pp. 13–21). Reston, VA: National Council of Teachers of Mathematics.

Russell, S. J. (1999). Mathematical reasoning in the elementary grades. In L. V. Stiff (Ed.), *Developing mathematical reasoning in grades K–12* (pp. 1–12). Reston, VA: National Council of Teachers of Mathematics.

These two articles are the lead chapters in the 1999 NCTM yearbook on reasoning. Both authors provide excellent perspectives on the importance of helping children engage in the logical solution of problems. Russell's chapter begins with this: "Mathematical reasoning must stand at the center of mathematics learning." Malloy makes the point that even in a diverse classroom, different reasoning styles can be engaged to make learning happen.

Mokros, J., Russell, S. J., & Economopoulos, K. (1995). *Beyond arithmetic: Changing mathematics in the elementary classroom.* White Plains, NY: Cuisenaire–Dale Seymour.

These three author-researchers from TERC use numerous examples from the elementary classroom to develop a realistic image of teaching mathematics from a problem-solving perspective. In looking at teaching, curriculum, and assessment, the importance of problem solving as a way of learning mathematics is quite clear. If you want a realistic look at reform mathematics and children solving problems, this is a useful, accessible book to consider.

National Council of Teachers of Mathematics. (2000). Children as Mathematicians [Focus Issue]. *Teaching Children Mathematics, 6*(6). Can young children do mathematics in the same spirit as described in this chapter? This focus issue of *TCM* provides ample evidence that children really can be engaged in doing mathematics. The articles provide numerous examples and suggest activities. A variety of content areas are explored, including counting, place value, geoemtry, measurement, and computa-

tion. Authors also address issues of developing a community of learners and tips for engaging students in discussion. This is a worthwhile focus issue.

Schifter, D., & Fosnot, C. T. (1993). *Reconstructing mathematics education: Stories of teachers meeting the challenge of reform.* New York: Teachers College Press.

The authors describe real teachers confronting their own concept of mathematics by doing real mathematics themselves. There are also many insights into the classrooms to which these teachers return. It is in this book that Betsy and Cora solve the paper shredder problem (the context was changed). If you feel a bit threatened by the call for change, this is a book that can make you realize you are not alone.

## Other Suggestions

Artzt, A. F., & Yaloz-Femia, S. (1999). Mathematical reasoning during small-group problem solving. In L. V. Stiff (Ed.), *Developing mathematical reasoning in grades K–12* (pp. 115–126). Reston, VA: National Council of Teachers of Mathematics.

Backhouse, J., Haggarty, L., Pirie, S., & Stratton, J. (1992). *Improving the learning of mathematics.* Portsmouth, NH: Heinemann.

Baker, D., Semple, C., & Stead, T. (1990). *How big is the moon?* Portsmouth, NH: Heinemann.

Baker, J., & Baker, A. (1990). *Mathematics in process.* Portsmouth, NH: Heinemann.

Ball, D. L. (1991). Improving, not standardizing, teaching. *Arithmetic Teacher, 39*(1), 18–22.

Ball, D. L. (1991). What's all this talk about discourse? *Arithmetic Teacher, 39*(2), 44–48.

Borasi, R. (1990). The invisible hand operating in mathematics instruction: Students' conceptions and expectations. In T. J. Cooney (Ed.), *Teaching and learning mathematics in the 1990s* (pp. 174–182). Reston, VA: National Council of Teachers of Mathematics.

Bosangue, M. V., Gannon, G. E., & Watson, K. L. (2000). The wonderful world of digital sums. *Teaching Children Mathematics, 6,* 310–313, 318–320.

Cantlon, D. (1998). Kids + conjecture = mathematics power. *Teaching Children Mathematics, 5,* 108–112.

Cobb, P., & Merkel, B. (1989). Thinking strategies: Teaching arithmetic through problem solving. In P. R. Trafton (Ed.), *New directions for elementary school mathematics* (pp. 70–81). Reston, VA: National Council of Teachers of Mathematics.

Corwin, R. B. (1993). Doing mathematics together: Creating a mathematical culture. *Arithmetic Teacher, 40,* 338–341.

Curcio, F. R., & Schwartz, S. L. (1998). There are no algorithms for teaching algorithms. *Teaching Children Mathematics, 5,* 26–30.

Garofalo, J., & Durant, K. (1991). Where did that come from? A frequent response to mathematics instruction. *School Science and Mathematics, 91,* 318–321.

Karp, K. S., & Niemi, R. C. (2000). The math club for girls and other problem solvers. *Mathematics Teaching in the Middle Grades, 5,* 426–432.

Koehler, M. S., & Prior, M. (1993). Classroom interactions: The heartbeat of the teaching/learning process. In D. T. Owens (Ed.),

*Research ideas for the classroom: Middle grades mathematics* (pp. 280–298). Old Tappan, NJ: Macmillan.

Schoenfeld, A. H. (1989). Problem solving in context(s). In R. I. Charles & E. A. Silver (Eds.), *The teaching and assessing of mathematical problem solving* (pp. 82–92). Reston, VA: National Council of Teachers of Mathematics.

Smith, S. Z., Smith, M. E., & Romberg, T. A. (1993). What the NCTM standards look like in one classroom. *Educational Leadership, 50*(8), 4–7.

Steele, D. F. (2000). Enthusiastic voices from young mathematicians. *Teaching Children Mathematics, 6,* 464–468.

Stoessiger, R., & Edmunds, J. (1992). *Natural learning and mathematics.* Portsmouth, NH: Heinemann.

Whitin, D. J. (1989). The power of mathematical investigations. In P. R. Trafton (Ed.), *New directions for elementary school mathematics* (pp. 183–195). Reston, VA: National Council of Teachers of Mathematics.

# Chapter 3

# Developing Understanding in Mathematics

*If the creation of the conceptual networks that constitute each individual's map of reality—including her mathematical understanding—is the product of constructive and interpretive activity, then it follows that no matter how lucidly and patiently teachers explain to their students, they cannot understand for their students.*

*Schifter and Fosnot (1993, p. 9)*

It is a commonly accepted goal among mathematics educators that students should understand mathematics (Hiebert & Carpenter, 1992). The most widely accepted theory, known as *constructivism,* suggests that children must be active participants in the development of their own understanding. Constructivism provides us with insights concerning how children learn mathematics and guides us to use instructional strategies that begin with children rather than with ourselves.

## A CONSTRUCTIVIST VIEW OF LEARNING

Constructivism is firmly rooted in the cognitive school of psychology and the theories of Piaget dating back at least as far as 1960. Constructivism rejects the notion that children are blank slates. They do not absorb ideas as teachers present them. Rather, children are creators of their own knowledge.

### The Construction of Ideas

The basic tenet of constructivism is simply this: *Children construct their own knowledge.* In fact, not just children, but all people, all of the time, construct or give meaning to things they perceive or think about. As you read these words, you are giving meaning to them. You are constructing ideas.

To construct or build something in the physical world requires tools, materials, and effort. How we construct ideas can be viewed in an analogous manner. The tools we use to build understanding are our existing ideas, the knowledge that we already possess. The materials we act on to build understanding may be things we see, hear, or touch—elements of our physical surroundings. Sometimes the materials are our own thoughts and ideas. The effort that must be supplied is active and reflective thought. If minds are not actively thinking, nothing happens.

The diagram in Figure 3.1 is meant as a metaphor for the construction of ideas. Consider the picture to be a small section of our cognitive makeup. The blue dots represent existing ideas. The lines joining the ideas represent our logical connections or relationships that have developed between and among ideas. The red dot is an emerging idea, one that is being constructed. Whatever existing ideas (dots) are used in the construction will necessarily be connected to the new idea because those were the ideas that gave meaning to it. If a potentially relevant idea that would add better meaning to the new idea is either not present in the learner's mind or is not actively engaged, then that potential connection to the new idea simply will not be made. Obviously, learners will vary in the number of connections between a new idea and existing ideas. Different learners will use different ideas to give meaning to the same new idea. What is significant is that the construction of an idea is almost certainly going to be different for every learner, even within the same environment or classroom.

Constructing knowledge is an extremely active endeavor on the part of the learner (Baroody, 1987; Cobb, 1988; von Glasersfeld, 1990). To construct and understand a new idea requires actively thinking about it. "How does this fit with what I already know?" "How can I understand this in the face of my current understanding of this idea?" Mathematical ideas cannot be "poured into" a passive learner. Children must be

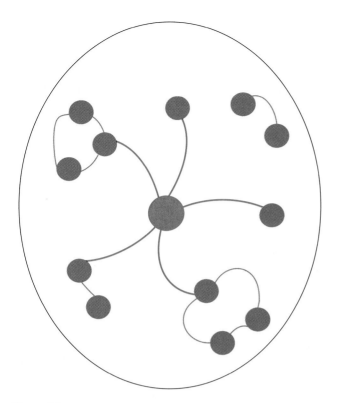

**Figure 3.1** We use the ideas we already have (blue dots) to construct a new idea (red dot), developing in the process a network of connections between ideas. The more ideas used and the more connections made, the better we understand.

mentally active for learning to take place. In classrooms, children must be encouraged to wrestle with new ideas, to work at fitting them into existing networks, and to challenge their own ideas and those of others. Put simply, constructing knowledge requires *reflective thought,* actively thinking about or mentally working on an idea. Reflective thought means sifting through existing ideas to find those that seem to be the most useful in giving meaning to the new idea.

Integrated networks, or *cognitive schemas,* are both the product of constructing knowledge and the tools with which additional new knowledge can be constructed. As learning occurs, the networks are rearranged, added to, or otherwise modified. When there is active, reflective thought, schemas are constantly being modified or changed so that ideas fit better with what is known.

## Examples of Constructed Learning

Consider the solution methods of two fourth-grade children who had been taught the meanings of the operations and had developed a good understanding of place-value concepts, some of the "dots" the children had at their disposal. Both children were from predominantly urban schools where a highly constructivist approach to mathematics had been in place for several years. They were asked to solve the following problem: "Four children had 3 bags of M&M's. They decided to open all 3 bags of candy and share the M&M's fairly. There were 52 M&M candies in each bag. How many M&M candies did each child get?" (Campbell & Johnson, 1995, pp. 35–36). Their solutions are shown in Figure 3.2.

Both children were able to determine the product $3 \times 52$ mentally. The two children used different cognitive tools to solve the problem of $156 \div 4$. Marlena interpreted the task as "How many sets of 4 can be made from 156?" She first used facts that were either easy or available to her: $10 \times 4$ and $4 \times 4$. These totals she subtracted from 156 until she got to 100. This seemed to cue her to use 25 fours. Marlena made no hesitation in adding the number of sets of 4 that she found in 156 and knew the answer was 39 candies for each child.

Darrell's approach was more directly related to the sharing context of the problem. He formed four columns and distributed amounts to each, accumulating the amounts mentally and orally as he wrote the numbers. Like Marlena, Darrell used numbers that were either easy or available to him; first 20 to each, then 5, then 10, and then a series of ones. He added one of the columns without hesitation (Rowan, 1995).

Marlena's Solution

Darrell's Solution

**Figure 3.2** Two fourth-grade children construct unique solutions to a computation.
*Source:* Campbell & Johnson (1995). Used with permission.

If computational speed and proficiency were your goal, you might be tempted to argue that the children need further instruction. But both children clearly constructed ideas about the computation that had meaning to them. They demonstrated confidence, understanding, and a belief that they could solve the problem.

In contrast to these two children, consider a third-grade child in a traditional classroom. She has made a quite common error in subtraction, as shown in Figure 3.3. The problem appeared on a mathematics worksheet, it was subtraction, and the class had been doing subtraction with borrowing. This context narrowed the choices of ways to give meaning to the situation (the "dots" she would likely use). But this problem was a little different from the child's existing ideas about borrowing. The next column contained a 0. How could she take 1 from the 0? That part was different, creating a situation that for her was problematic. The child decided that "the next column" must mean the next one that has something in it. She therefore borrowed from the 6 and ignored the 0. This child used her existing ideas and gave her own meaning to the rule "borrow from the next column."

$$
\begin{array}{r}
^{5}\phantom{0}^{13} \\
6\,0\,3 \\
-\,2\,5\,7 \\
\hline
6
\end{array}
$$

There is nothing in this next column, so I'll borrow from the 6.

**Figure 3.3** **Children sometimes invent incorrect meanings by extending poorly understood rules.**

Children rarely give random responses (Ginsburg, 1977; Labinowicz, 1985). Their answers tend to make sense in terms of their personal perspective or in terms of the knowledge they are using to give meaning to the situation. In many instances, children's existing knowledge is incomplete or inaccurate, or perhaps the knowledge we assume to be there simply is not. In such situations, as in the present example, new knowledge may be constructed inaccurately.

## Construction in Rote Learning

Constructivism is a theory about how we learn. If it is correct, then that is how *all* learning takes place, regardless of how we teach. We cannot choose to have children learn constructively on some days and not others. Even rote learning is a construction. But what tools or ideas are used for construction in rote learning? To what is rotely learned knowledge connected?

Children searching for a way to remember 7 × 8 = 56 might note that the numbers 5, 6 and 7, 8 go in order. Or they may connect the number 56 to that "hard fact" since 56

is unique in the multiplication table. (But then so is 54.) Repetition of a routine procedure may be connected to some mantra-type recitation of the rule, as in "Divide, multiply, subtract, and bring down." This sequence has even been related to the mnemonic "Dirty monkeys smell bad." New ideas learned like this are connected to things that can hardly be called mathematical. Nor are they part of networks of ideas. Each newly learned bit is essentially isolated. Rote knowledge will almost never contribute to a useful network of ideas. Rote learning can be thought of as a "weak construction" (Noddings, 1993).

When mathematical ideas are used to create new mathematical ideas, useful cognitive networks are formed. Returning to 7 × 8, imagine a class where children discuss and share clever ways to figure out the product. One child might think of 5 eights and then 2 more eights. Another may have learned 7 × 7 and noted that this is just one more seven. Still another might look at a list of 8 sevens and take half of them (4 × 7) and double that. This may lead to the notion that double 7 is 14, and double that is 28, and double that is 56. Not every child will construct 7 × 8 using all of these approaches. However, the class discussion brings to the fore a wide range of useful mathematical "dots" so that the potential is there for profitable constructions.

## Understanding

It is possible to say that we know something or we do not. In other words, knowledge is something that we either have or don't have. Understanding is another matter. For example, how did you learn 7 × 8? If you learned it by rote, as most adults did, you may never have thought about the other ideas just discussed. Is your understanding of 7 × 8 just the same as that of a person who has connected some of these other ideas to that fact?

*Understanding* can be defined as a measure of the quality and quantity of connections that an idea has with existing ideas. Understanding depends on the existence of appropriate ideas and on the creation of new connections (Backhouse, Haggarty, Pirie, & Stratton, 1992; Davis, 1986; Hiebert & Carpenter, 1992; Janvier, 1987; Schroeder & Lester, 1989). Understanding is never an all-or-nothing proposition.

One way that we can think about an individual's understanding is that it exists along a continuum (see Figure 3.4). At one extreme is a very rich set of connections. The understood idea is associated with many other existing ideas in a meaningful network of concepts and procedures. Hiebert and Carpenter (1992) refer to "webs" of interrelated ideas. Understanding at this rich interconnected end of the continuum will be referred to as *relational understanding*, borrowing a term made popular by Skemp (1978). At the other end of the continuum, ideas are completely isolated or nearly so. At this end, we have what we will call *instrumental understanding*, again borrowing from Skemp. Rotely learned knowledge is almost always understood instrumentally.

**Figure 3.4** **Understanding is a measure of the quality and quantity of connections that a new idea has with existing ideas. The greater the number of connections to a network of ideas, the better the understanding.**

# Examples of Understanding

If we accept the notion that understanding has both qualitative and quantitative differences, the question "Does she know it?" must be replaced with "How does she understand it? What ideas does she connect with it?" In the following examples, you will see how different children may well develop different ideas about the same knowledge and thus have different understandings.

## Computation in Two Classrooms

Schifter and Fosnot (1993) describe a third-grade class where several children are discussing the problem of sharing 90 jelly beans among four children. They decide to use base-ten models (ones and tens). They share 2 tens to each group and trade a ten for 10 ones.

They next share 2 ones to each group. There is then a discussion of what to do with the 2 leftover ones and how to write down what they have done. One child suggests "$22\frac{1}{2}$" and another "22 R 2." They decide that the best answer for any division depends on the situation and what you want to do with the leftovers.

In a more traditional class, another third grader was quite confident in her ability to do long divisions such as 24,682 ÷ 5. When asked what the "R 2" meant when she

computed 32 ÷ 5, she could only identify 2 as the remainder. Asked to demonstrate 32 ÷ 5 with blocks, she began but then decided it couldn't be done. The child was at a loss to explain "R 2" in terms of the leftover counters (Schifter & Fosnot, 1993). These children all have different understandings of division. Some are very rich understandings; some are very limited. All are different.

## Connections with Early Number Concepts

Consider the concept of "seven" as constructed by a child in the first grade. Seven for a first grader is most likely connected to the counting procedure and the construct of "more than" and is probably understood as less than 10 and more than 2. What else will this child eventually connect to the concept of seven as it now exists? Seven is 1 more than 6; it is 2 less than 9; it is the combination of 3 and 4 or 2 and 5; it is odd; it is small compared to 73 and large compared to one-tenth; it is the number of days in a week; it is "lucky"; it is prime; and on and on. The web of potential ideas connected to a number can grow large and involved.

## A Web of Ideas Involving Ratio

A clear example of the potential for rich relational understanding is found in the many ideas that can be associated with the concept of "ratio" (see Figure 3.5). Unfortunately, many

---

**Division:** *The ratio 3 is to 4 is the same as 3 ÷ 4.*

**Scale:** *The scale on the map shows 1 inch per 50 miles.*

**Figure 3.5** **Potential web of associations that could contribute to the understanding of "ratio."**

**Trigonometry:** *All trig functions are ratios.*

**Slopes of lines (algebra) and slopes of roofs (carpentry):** *The ratio of the rise to the run is $\frac{1}{8}$.*

**Comparisons:** *The ratio of sunny days to rainy days is greater in the south than in the north.*

**RATIO**

**Geometry:** *The ratio of circumference to diameter is always π or about 22 to 7. Any two similar figures have corresponding measurements that are proportional (in the same ratio).*

**Unit prices:** *12 oz. / $1.79 That's about 60¢ for 4 oz. or $2.40 for a pound.*

**Business:** *Profit and loss are figured as ratios of income to total cost.*

children learn only meaningless rules connected with ratio, such as "given one ratio, how do you find an equivalent ratio?"

# Benefits of Relational Understanding

To teach for a rich or relational understanding requires a lot of work and effort. Concepts and connections develop over time, not in a day. Tasks must be selected. Instructional materials must be made. The classroom must be organized for group work and maximum interaction with and among the children. The important benefits to be derived from relational understanding make the effort not only worthwhile but also essential.

## It Is Intrinsically Rewarding

Nearly all people, and certainly children, enjoy learning. This is especially true when new information connects with ideas already possessed. The new knowledge makes sense; it fits; it feels good. Children who learn by rote must be motivated by external means: for the sake of a test, to please a parent, from fear of failure, or to receive some reward. Such learning is distasteful. Rewards of an extra recess or a star on a chart may be effective in the short run but do nothing to encourage a love of the subject when the rewards are removed.

## It Enhances Memory

Memory is a process of retrieving information. When mathematics is learned relationally, there is much less chance that the information will deteriorate; connected information is simply more likely than disconnected information to be retained over time. Retrieval of the information is also easier. Connected information provides an entire web of ideas to reach for. If what you need to recall seems distant, reflecting on ideas that are related can usually lead you to the desired idea eventually. Retrieving disconnected information is more like finding a needle in a haystack.

A large portion of instructional time in American schools is devoted to reteaching and review. If ideas were learned relationally instead of instrumentally, much less time would need to be spent on review.

## There Is Less to Remember

Traditional approaches have tended to fragment mathematics into seemingly endless lists of isolated skills, concepts, rules, and symbols. The lists are so lengthy that teachers and students become overwhelmed. Constructivists, for their part, talk about teaching "big ideas" (Brooks & Brooks, 1993; Hiebert et al., 1996; Schifter & Fosnot, 1993). Big ideas are really just large networks of interrelated concepts. Ideas are learned relationally when they are integrated into a larger web of information, a big idea. Frequently, the network is so well constructed that whole chunks of information are stored and retrieved as single entities rather than isolated bits. For exam-

ple, knowledge of place value subsumes rules about lining up decimal points, ordering decimal numbers, moving decimal points to the right or left in decimal-percent conversions, rounding and estimating, and a host of other ideas. Similarly, knowledge of equivalent fractions ties together rules concerning common denominators, reducing fractions, and changing between mixed numbers and whole numbers.

## It Helps with Learning New Concepts and Procedures

An idea fully understood in mathematics is more easily extended to learn a new idea. Number concepts and relationships help in the mastery of basic facts, fraction knowledge and place-value knowledge come together to make decimal learning easier, and decimal concepts directly enhance an understanding of percentage concepts and procedures. Many of the ideas of elementary arithmetic become the model for understanding ideas in algebra. Reducing fractions by finding common prime factors is the same thing as canceling out common factors.

Without these connections, children will need to learn each new piece of information they encounter as a separate, unrelated idea.

## It Improves Problem-Solving Abilities

The solution of novel problems requires transferring ideas learned in one context to new situations. When concepts are embedded in a rich network, transferability is significantly enhanced and thus so is problem solving (Schoenfeld, 1992). NAEP data for 1990, 1992, and 1996 suggest a slow but significant growth each year in the percentage of U.S. students achieving at or above the basic and proficient levels (Reese, Miller, Mazzeo, & Dossey, 1997), reflecting the increased emphasis on understanding over that same period.

## It Is Self-Generative

"Inventions that operate on understandings can generate new understandings, suggesting a kind of snowball effect. As networks grow and become more structured, they increase the potential for invention" (Hiebert & Carpenter, 1992, p. 74). Skemp (1978) noted that when gaining knowledge is found to be pleasurable, people who have had that experience of pleasure are likely to seek or invent new ideas on their own, especially when confronting problematic situations.

## It Improves Attitudes and Beliefs

Relational understanding has an affective effect as well as a cognitive effect. When learning relationally, the learner tends to develop a positive self-concept about his or her ability to learn and understand mathematics. There is a definite sense of "I can do this! I understand!" There is no reason to fear or to be in awe of knowledge learned relationally. Mathematics then makes sense. It is not some mysterious world that only "smart people" dare enter. At the other end of the continuum, instrumental understanding has the potential of producing mathematics anxiety, a real phenomenon that involves fear and avoidance behavior.

Relational understanding also promotes a positive view about mathematics itself. Sensing the connectedness and logic of mathematics, students are more likely to gravitate toward it or to describe the discipline in positive terms.

# TYPES OF MATHEMATICAL KNOWLEDGE

All knowledge, mathematical or otherwise, consists of internal or mental representations of ideas that the mind has constructed. For some time now, mathematics educators have found it useful to distinguish between two types of mathematical knowledge: conceptual knowledge and procedural knowledge (Hiebert & Lindquist, 1990).

## Conceptual Knowledge of Mathematics

*Conceptual knowledge of mathematics* consists of logical relationships constructed internally and existing in the mind as a part of a network of ideas. It is the type of knowledge Piaget referred to as logico-mathematical knowledge (Kamii, 1985, 1989; Labinowicz, 1985). By its very nature, conceptual knowledge is knowledge that is understood (Hiebert & Carpenter, 1992).

Ideas such as seven, rectangle, ones/tens/hundreds (as in place value), sum, product, equivalent, ratio, and negative are all examples of mathematical relationships or concepts.

Figure 3.6 shows three blocks commonly used to represent ones, tens, and hundreds. By the middle of second grade,

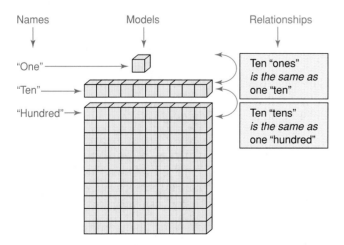

**Figure 3.6**  **Objects and names of objects are not the same as relationships between objects.**

most children have seen pictures of these or have used the actual blocks. It is quite common for these children to be able to identify the rod as the "ten" piece and the large square block as the "hundred" piece. Does this mean that they have constructed the concepts of ten and hundred? All that is known for sure is that they have learned the names for these objects, the conventional names of the blocks. The mathematical concept of a ten is that *a ten is the same as ten ones.* Ten is not a rod. The concept is the relationship between the rod and the small cube. It is not the rod or a bundle of ten sticks or any other model of a ten. This relationship called "ten" must be created by children in their own minds.

In Figure 3.7, the shape labeled A is a rectangle. But if we call shape B "one" or a "whole," then we might refer to shape A as "one-half." The idea of "half" is the *relationship* between shapes A and B, a relationship that must be constructed in our mind. It is not in either rectangle. In fact, if we decide to call shape C the whole, shape A becomes "one-fourth." The physical rectangle did not change in any way. The concepts of "half" and "fourth" are not in rectangle A; we construct them in our mind. The rectangles help us "see" the relationships, but what we see are rectangles, not concepts.

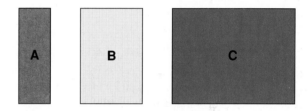

**Figure 3.7**  **Three shapes, different relationships.**

## Procedural Knowledge of Mathematics

*Procedural knowledge of mathematics* is knowledge of the rules and the procedures that one uses in carrying out routine mathematical tasks and also the symbolism that is used to represent mathematics. Knowledge of mathematics consists of more than concepts. Step-by-step procedures exist for performing tasks such as multiplying 47 × 68. Concepts are represented by special words and mathematical symbols. These procedures and symbols can be connected to or supported by concepts, but very few cognitive relationships are needed to have knowledge of a procedure.

Procedures are the step-by-step routines learned to accomplish some task. "To add two three-digit numbers, first add the numbers in the right-hand column. If the answer is 10 or more, put the 1 above the second column, and write the other digit under the first column. Proceed in a similar manner for the next two columns in order." We can say that someone who can accomplish a task such as this has knowledge of that procedure. Again, the conceptual understanding that may or may not support the procedural knowledge can vary considerably from one student to the next.

Some procedures are very simple and may even be confused with conceptual knowledge. For example, seventh-grade children may be shown how to add the integers ⁻7 and ⁺4 by combining 7 red "negative" checkers with 4 yellow "positive" checkers. Pairs consisting of 1 red and 1 yellow checker are removed, and the result is noted. In this example, there would be 3 red negative checkers remaining, and the students would record ⁻3 as the sum. This might be called a manipulative or physical procedure. Notice that it is conceivable that a student could master a procedure such as this with very little understanding, or it could be integrated with a conceptual web related to integers and thus be well understood.

Symbolism includes expressions such as $(9 - 5) \times 2 = 8$, $\pi$, $<$, and $\neq$. What meaning is attached to this symbolic knowledge depends on how it is understood—what concepts and other ideas the individual connects to the symbols. Symbolism is part of procedural knowledge whether it is understood or not.

## Procedural Knowledge and Doing Mathematics

Procedural knowledge of mathematics plays a very important role both in learning and in doing mathematics. Algorithmic procedures help us do routine tasks easily and thus free our minds to concentrate on more important tasks. Symbolism is a powerful mechanism for conveying mathematical ideas to others and for "doodling around" with an idea as we do mathematics. But even the most skillful use of a procedure will not help develop conceptual knowledge that is related to that procedure (Hiebert, 1990). Doing endless long-division exercises will not help a child understand what division means. In fact, students who are skillful with a particular procedure are very reluctant to attach meanings to it after the fact.

From the vantage of learning mathematics, the question of how procedures and conceptual ideas can be linked is much more important than the usefulness of the procedure itself (Hiebert & Carpenter, 1992). Recall the two children who used their own invented procedure to solve $156 \div 4$ (see Figure 3.2, p. 27). Clearly, there was an active and useful interaction between the procedures the children invented and the ideas they were constructing about division.

It is generally accepted that procedural rules should never be learned in the absence of a concept, although, unfortunately, that happens far too often.

## THE ROLE OF MODELS IN DEVELOPING UNDERSTANDING

It has become a cliché that good teachers use a "hands-on approach" to teach mathematics. Manipulatives, or physical materials to model mathematical concepts, are certainly important tools available for helping children learn mathematics. But they are not the panacea that some educators seem to believe them to be. It is important that you have a good perspective on how manipulatives can help or fail to help children construct ideas.

## Models for Mathematical Concepts

Return for a moment to the idea of a mathematical concept as a relationship, a logical idea. There are no physical examples of mathematical concepts in the physical world. The concept of "hundred," for example, is a quantity relationship that a group of 100 items has with a single item of the same type. We can talk of 100 people, 100 dollars, or 100 acts of kindness. None of those sets *is* a hundred. Hundred is only a relationship that the group has with one thing like those in the group. It is impossible to imagine "hundred" without first understanding "one."

A *model for a mathematical concept* refers to any object, picture, or drawing that represents the concept or onto which the relationship for that concept can be imposed. In this sense, any group of 100 objects can be a model of the concept "hundred" because we can impose the 100-to-1 relationship on the group and a single element of the group.

It is incorrect to say that a model "illustrates" a concept. To illustrate implies showing. That would mean that when you looked at the model, you would see an example of the concept. Technically, all that you actually see with your eyes is the physical object; only your mind can impose the mathematical relationship on the object (Thompson, 1994). For a person who does not yet have the relationship, the model does not illustrate the concept *for that person*.

### Examples of Models

As noted, physical materials have become enormously popular as tools for teaching mathematics. They can run the gamut from common objects such as lima beans for counters to commercially produced materials such as wooden rods or plastic geometric shapes. Figure 3.8 shows six common examples of models for six different concepts. Consider each of the concepts and the corresponding model. Try to separate the physical model from the relationship that you must impose on the model in order to "see" the concept.

For the examples in Figure 3.8:

(a) The concept of "six" is a relationship between sets that can be matched to the words *one, two, three, four, five, six.* Changing a set of counters by adding one changes the relationship. The difference between the set of 6 and the set of 7 is the relationship "one more than."

(b) The concept of "length" could not be developed without making comparisons of the length attribute of different objects. The length measure of an object is a comparison relationship of the length of the object to the length of the unit.

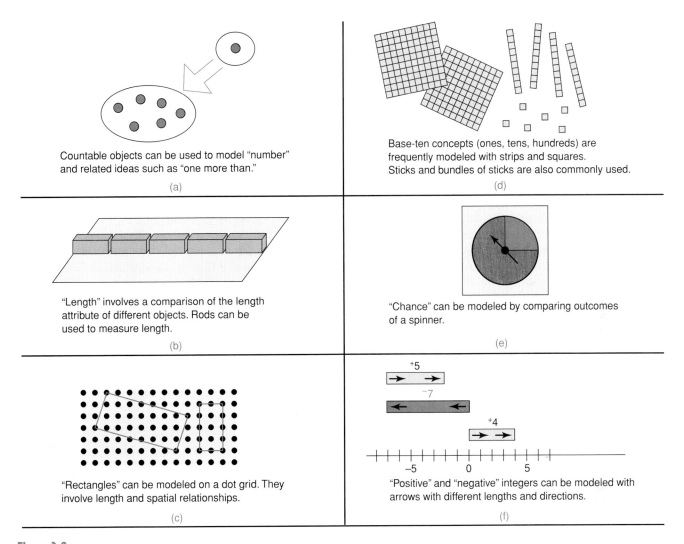

**Figure 3.8** **Examples of models to illustrate mathematics concepts.**

(c) The concept of "rectangle" is a combination of spatial and length relationships. By drawing on dot paper, the relationships of the opposite sides' being of equal length and parallel and the adjacent sides' meeting at right angles can be illustrated.

(d) The concept of "hundred" is not in the larger square but in the relationship of that square to the strip ("ten") and to the little square ("one").

(e) "Chance" is a relationship between the frequency of an event's happening compared with all possible outcomes. The spinner can be used to create relative frequencies. These can be predicted by observing relationships of sectors of the spinner. Note how chance and probability are integrated with ideas of fractions and ratio.

(f) The concept of a "negative integer" is based on the relationship "is the opposite of." Negative quantities exist only in relation to positive quantities. Arrows on the number line are not themselves negative quantities but

model the "opposite of" relationship in terms of direction and size or magnitude relationship in terms of length.

Staying with integers for a moment, this concept is often modeled with counters in two colors, perhaps red for negative quantities and yellow for positive. The "opposite" aspect of integers can be imposed on the two colors. The "magnitude" aspect is found in the quantities of red and yellow counters. Although colored counters and arrows are physically very different, the same relationships can be imposed on each. Children must construct relationships in order to "see" positive and negative integers in either model.

It is important to include calculators in any list of common models. The calculator models a wide variety of numeric relationships by quickly and easily demonstrating the effects of these ideas. For example, if the calculator is made to count by increments of 0.01 (press ⊞ 0.01 ⊜), the relationship of one-hundredth to one whole is illustrated. Press 3 ⊞ 0.01. How many presses of ⊜ are required to get from 3 to 4? Doing the required 100 presses and observing how the display changes along the way is quite impressive. Especially note what happens after 3.19, 3.29, and so on.

## Models and Constructing Mathematics

To "see" in a model the concept that it represents, you must already have that concept—that relationship—in your mind. If you did not, then you would have no relationship to impose on the model. This is precisely why models are often more meaningful to the teacher than to students. The teacher already has the concept and can see it in the model. A student without the concept sees only the physical object.

Thus a child needs to know the relationship before imposing it on the model. If the concept does not come *from* the model—and it does not—how does the model help the child get it?

Mathematical concepts that children are in the process of constructing are not the well-formed ideas conceived by adults. New ideas are formulated little by little over time. As children actively reflect on their new ideas, they test them out through as many different avenues as we might provide. For example, this is where the value of student discussions and group work comes in. Talking through an idea, arguing for a viewpoint, listening to others, and describing and explaining are all mentally active ways of testing an emerging idea against external reality. As this testing process goes on, the developing idea gets modified and elaborated and further integrated with existing ideas. When there is a good fit with external reality, the likelihood of a correct concept's having been formed is good.

Models can play this same role, that of a testing ground for emerging ideas. Models can be thought of as "thinker toys," "tester toys," and "talker toys."* It is difficult for students (of all ages) to talk about and test out abstract relationships using words alone. Models give learners something to think about, explore with, talk about, and reason with.

## Expanding the Idea of a Model

Lesh, Post, and Behr (1987) talk about five "representations" for concepts, two of which are manipulative models and pictures (see Figure 3.9). In their research, they also consider written symbolism, oral language, and real-world situations to be representations or models of concepts. Their research has found that children who have difficulty translating a concept from one representation to another are the same children who have difficulty solving problems and understanding computations. Strengthening the ability to move between and among these representations improves the growth of children's concepts.

The five representations illustrated in Figure 3.9 are simply an expansion of the model concept. The more ways that children are given to think about and test out an emerging idea, the better chance it has of being formed correctly and integrated into a rich web of ideas and relational understanding.

---

*The term *thinker toy* is taken from Seymour Papert's book *Mindstorms* (1980), in which the inventor of the Logo computer language describes the computer as a powerful and flexible device that encourages learners to play with ideas and work through problems. "Tester toys" and "talker toys" were suggested in the current context by Laura Domalik, a first-grade teacher.

**Figure 3.9    Five different representations of mathematical ideas. Translations between and within each can help develop new concepts.**

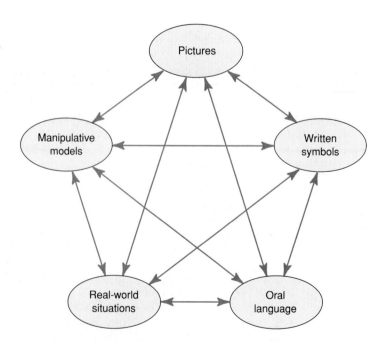

# Using Models in the Classroom

If we think of models as thinker toys or talker toys, we can identify three related uses for them in a developmental approach to teaching:

1. To help children develop new concepts or relationships
2. To help children make connections between concepts and symbols
3. To assess children's understanding

## Developing New Concepts

Models help children think and reflect on new ideas. To that end, they should always be accessible for students to select and use freely. A variety of models should be available to help with an important idea. Students should be encouraged to select and use materials to help them work through a problem or explain an idea to their group. They should select models that make sense to them. Do not force students to use a particular model.

You will undoubtedly encounter situations in which you use a model that you think clearly illustrates an idea but the child just doesn't get it. Remember that you already possess the well-formed concept, so you are able to impose it on the model. The child, however, is in the process of creating the concept and is using the model to test an emerging idea. Your job is to get children to think with models, to work actively at the test-revise-test-revise process until the new concept fits with the physical model you have offered. It is not possible to show mathematics with models. You can only provide models on which mathematical relationships or concepts can be imposed. When the child's concept fits the model, the child sees the concept. When the concept does not seem to fit, the child cannot see it in the model. The child's concept is different from the one that you can impose on the model and so must undergo further construction or revision.

## Connecting Symbols and Concepts

Teachers will say, "But when they try to do it without manipulatives, they can't." Yet it is unrealistic to expect children automatically to transfer newly formed ideas to symbolic procedures without some guidance. Models can serve as a link between concepts and symbols as well as a means of developing concepts.

A general approach is to have students write down what they have done with models. "Write an equation to tell what you just did." "I see how you did that problem with the blocks. How would you go about recording what you did?" When children see written mathematics as expressions or recordings of ideas that they have already developed, the written or symbolic form is more likely to make sense.

## Assessing Children's Understanding

When children in the classroom are using models in ways that make sense to them (rather than following your direc-

tions), how they use the physical models is a wonderful window into their minds. This allows classroom observation of your students to become a student-by-student assessment.

If you want more detailed information about the understanding children have constructed, a good suggestion is to have them explain ideas with manipulative materials. The models give the child something to talk with when their abstract ideas prove difficult for them to explain. This might be done in a diagnostic setting, where you sit down, one on one, with a child and try to find out what he or she is thinking. Remember that drawings are also models. When students write explanations for their answers or describe their ideas in writing, always encourage them to draw pictures to help them show what they are thinking. (Assessment is discussed in depth in Chapter 5.)

# Incorrect Use of Models

The most widespread misuse of manipulative materials occurs when the teacher tells students, "Do as I do." There is a natural temptation to get out the materials and show children exactly how to use them. Children will blindly follow the teacher's directions, and it may even look as if they understand. It is just as possible to get students to move blocks around mindlessly as it is to teach them to "invert and multiply" mindlessly. Neither promotes thinking or aids in the development of concepts (Ball, 1992; Clements & Battista, 1990).

A natural result of overly directing the use of models is that children begin to use them as answer-getting devices rather than as thinker toys. When getting answers rather than solving problems becomes the focus of a lesson, children will gravitate to the easiest method available to get the answers. For example, if you have carefully shown and explained to children how to get an answer with a set of counters, then an imitation of that method is what they will most likely select. By strictly following your directions, little or no reflective thought will go into exploring the concepts involved. When an activity is not reflective, little real growth occurs, and little understanding is constructed.

# TEACHING DEVELOPMENTALLY

Teaching involves decision making. Decisions are made as you plan lessons. *What is the best task to propose tomorrow? Considering what happened today, what will move the children forward?* And decisions are made minute to minute in the classroom. *How should I respond? Should they struggle some more, or should I intervene? Is progress being made? How can I help Suzy move in the correct direction without discouraging her?*

The ideas that have been discussed in this chapter provide a theoretical foundation for making those decisions.

# Foundations of a Developmental Approach

Following is a summary of the major implications of the theory that has been discussed. A teacher who keeps these ideas in mind can be said to be basing his or her instruction on a constructivist view of learning or, in the terminology of this book, a *developmental approach*.

1. *Children construct their own knowledge and understanding; we cannot transmit ideas to passive learners.* Each child comes to us with a unique but rich collection of ideas. These ideas are the tools that will be used to construct new concepts and procedures as students wrestle with ideas, discuss solutions, challenge their own and others' conjectures, explain their methods, and solve engaging problems. Ideas cannot be poured into children as if they were empty vessels.

2. *Knowledge and understanding are unique for each learner.* Each child's network of ideas is different from that of the next child. As new ideas are formed, they will be integrated into that web of ideas in a unique way as well. We should not try to make all children the same.

3. *Reflective thinking is the single most important ingredient for effective learning.* For children to create new ideas and to connect them in a rich web of interrelated ideas, children must be mentally engaged. They must find the relevant ideas they possess and bring them to bear on the development of new ideas and the solutions to new problems. Only by being mentally engaged with the task at hand can relational understanding of new ideas ever develop. "Passive learning" is an oxymoron!

4. *Effective teaching is a child-centered activity.* In a constructivist classroom, the emphasis is on learning rather than teaching. Students are given the task of learning. The role of the teacher is to engage the students by posing good problems and creating a classroom atmosphere of exploration and sense making. The source of mathematical truth is found in the reasoning carried out by the class. The teacher is not the arbiter of what is mathematically correct.

# Strategies for Effective Teaching

How can we structure lessons to promote appropriate reflective thought? Purposeful mental engagement or reflective thought about the ideas we want students to develop is the single most important key to effective teaching. Without actively thinking about the important concepts of the lesson, learning will not happen. How can we make it happen? Here are seven suggestions based on the perspectives of this chapter. Perhaps you will be able to add to the list.

1. Create a mathematical environment.
2. Pose worthwhile mathematical tasks.
3. Use cooperative learning groups.
4. Use models and calculators as thinking tools.
5. Encourage discourse and writing.
6. Require justification of student responses.
7. Listen actively.

## Creating a Mathematical Environment

In a mathematical environment, students feel comfortable trying out ideas, sharing insights, challenging others, seeking advice from other students and the teacher, explaining their thinking, and taking risks. No one is permitted to be a passive observer. An environment with these features is built around expectations, respect, and the belief that *all* children can learn. Learning takes effort, and children need to know that as a class, their task is to work at doing mathematics. The interactions of a mathematical environment require students and teachers alike to respect one another, to listen attentively, and to learn to disagree without offending.

We cannot simply tell children how to think or what habits to acquire. Processes and habits of thought are developed over time within a community where such processes and thinking are the norm. In a community of mathematical discourse, students evaluate their own assumptions and those of others and argue about what is mathematically true (Corwin, 1996; Lampert, 1990). The goal is to let all students believe that they are the authors of mathematical ideas and logical arguments. In this environment, reasoning and mathematical argument—not the teacher—are the sources of an idea's legitimacy. "Doing mathematics is an act of sense-making" (Schoenfeld, 1994, p. 60). The classroom environment should be a place where figuring it out and "sense-making" are common practices, not just for individuals but for the class as a whole.

In an urban school in Montgomery County, Maryland, fourth graders were observed to raise their hands during a discussion and say, "I would like to add to what Marcel just said" or "I disagree with Tawanna." All students would face the speaker and listen attentively. In the same school, second-grade students raised their hands with the index finger pointing up to indicate "a point of interest," a polite way to disagree. In both classrooms, it was clear that teachers had spent time and effort developing this atmosphere of respect. "Creating contexts where students can safely express their own mathematical ideas is a central teaching task and a step toward developing students' mathematical power" (Smith, 1996, p. 397).

## Posing Worthwhile Mathematical Tasks

The single most important principle for reform in mathematics is to allow students to make the subject of mathematics problematic (Hiebert et al., 1996). By problematic, these authors mean "allowing students to wonder why things are, to inquire, to search for solutions, and to resolve incongruities. It means that both curriculum and instruction should begin with problems, dilemmas, and questions for students"

(p. 12). When students are actively looking for relationships, analyzing patterns, finding out which methods work and which don't, justifying results, or evaluating and challenging the thoughts of others, they are necessarily and optimally engaging in reflective thought about the ideas involved.

Tasks or problems must be designed to engage the students in the concepts of the curriculum. Tasks should be based on a knowledge of the mathematical content and an informed guess about the concepts the students in the class bring to the task (Fennema, Carpenter, Franke, & Carey, 1993; Simon, 1995). Time must be given to permit students to wrestle with these tasks individually or in groups and also to discuss solutions and strategies with the class as a whole.

The selection of good tasks requires that you listen each day to the way students are thinking about whatever mathematics is currently being discussed. The selection of the next day's task should be made in such a way as to help students reflect on the new ideas you want them to develop. Look for explorations that embody the big ideas of the chapter. As students wrestle with these problems, the tiny skills and ideas of the traditional curriculum will emerge. In a good task, students will "bump into" the important mathematics you have in mind for them to learn (Lappan & Briars, 1995).

## Using Cooperative Learning Groups

Placing children in groups of three or four to work on a problem is an extremely useful strategy for encouraging the discourse and interaction envisioned in a mathematical community. A classroom arranged in small groups has many times more interaction and discussion going than can be accomplished in a full-class setting. Frequently, a simple pairing of students is all that is necessary. In groups or pairs, children are much more willing and able to speak out, explore ideas, explain things to their group, question and learn from one another, pose arguments, and have their own ideas challenged in a friendly atmosphere of learning. Children will take risks within a small group that they would never dream of taking in front of an entire class. Groups should usually be heterogeneous in ability so that all students are exposed to good thinking and reasoning.

While the groups are at work, the teacher has the opportunity to be an active listener to six or more different discussions. Time should always be allotted for full-class discussions so that group members can share their group's ideas and the teacher can focus attention on important ideas. (See Chapter 22 for a more detailed discussion of cooperative groups.)

## Using Models and Calculators as Thinking Tools

The use of models has already been thoroughly discussed. It is worth repeating that models help children explore ideas and make sense of them. Many good explorations are actually posed in terms of physical materials. For example, "Try to find different ways to make the number 437 using ones, tens, and hundreds pieces. What patterns can you find? What else do you notice about the ways you can make 437?" Here

the model is the focus of the problem rather than a way of exploring a different task.

Manipulatives and calculators should always be readily available for student use as a regular part of your classroom environment. This is just as true for middle school classrooms as for the kindergarten.

## Encouraging Discourse and Writing

To explain an idea orally or in written form forces us to wrestle with that idea until it is really ours and we personally understand it. The more we try to explain something or argue reasonably about something, the more connections we will search for and use in our explanation or in our argument. Talking gets the talker involved.

When children are asked to respond to and critique others, they are similarly forced to attend and to assimilate what is being said into personal mental schemes. Frequently, when we get involved verbally with an idea, we find ourselves changing or modifying the idea in midstream. The reflective thought required to make an explanation or argue a point is a true learning experience in itself (Corwin, 1996; Whitin & Wilde, 1995; Yackel, Cobb, Wood, Wheatley, & Merkel, 1990).

Writing can be a part of nearly every problem posed. Not only does it help children structure their thoughts, but writing also causes each student to commit to an idea and rehearse an explanation or defense in preparation for the class discussion. Of course, writing includes journals, formal essays, and reports. It is also a significant tool in assessment. Countryman (1992) states, "The writer reflects on, returns to, and builds upon what has gone before" (p. 59).

## Requiring Justification of Student Responses

Requiring children to explain or defend their responses has a positive effect on how children view mathematics and their own mathematical abilities. Doing so also promotes confidence and self-worth. Justification of responses forces students to think reflectively. To defend or explain eliminates guessing or responses based on rote learning. Thus having children explain their answers is another excellent mechanism for getting the same benefits as from discourse and writing.

Requiring students to explain why, to tell how, and to detail their ideas communicates that mathematics is not mysterious or unfathomable. There is no need for the teacher to pose as the source of mathematical truth.

## Listening Actively

To promote reflective thinking requires that teaching be child-centered, not teacher-centered. By placing attention on the children's thoughts instead of our own, we encourage children to do more thinking and hence to search for and strengthen more internal connections—in short, to develop understanding. When children respond to questions or make an observation in class, an interested but nonevaluative response is a way to ask for an elaboration: "Tell me more about that, Karen" or "I see. Why do you think that?" Even a simple "Um-hmm" followed by silence is very effective, permitting the child and others to continue their thinking.

Active listening requires that we believe in children's ideas. To wait 45 seconds, a minute, or even longer for a child to find a response or formulate even a simple idea is much easier when we believe that whatever the child says reflects a unique and valuable understanding. When you believe in children, children sense it and respond accordingly.

# REFLECTIONS ON CHAPTER 3

## Writing to Learn

1. Describe in your own words what it means to say *we construct our own knowledge* as opposed to *we absorb knowledge*.

2. Explain why we should assume that each child's knowledge and understanding of an idea is unique for that child.

3. What is reflective thought? Why is it so important to promote reflective thinking in the classroom?

4. Contrast knowing an idea with understanding an idea. What does it mean to say that understanding exists on a continuum from relational to instrumental? Give an example of an idea, and explain how it might be understood at different places along this continuum.

5. Examine the seven benefits of relational understanding. Select the ones that you think are most important. Describe each benefit and why you personally believe it is significant.

6. Describe conceptual knowledge of mathematics and procedural knowledge of mathematics. Provide examples of each.

## For Discussion and Exploration

1. Discuss the meaning and validity of the following statement from Labinowicz (1985): "We see what we understand rather than understand what we see" (p. 7).

2. Consider your most recent classroom experience when mathematics was being taught. Compare and contrast this experience with the suggestions for developmental teaching given in this chapter. Would you say that the teaching reflected a constructivist view of learning? Why or why not?

3. Not every educator believes in constructivism. A common argument goes something like this: There is not enough time to let kids discover everything. Basic facts and ideas are more efficiently taught through careful, well-planned, and meaningful explanations. Students should not have to "reinvent the wheel." How would you respond to someone with this perception of school and learning?

## Recommendations for Further Reading

### Highly Recommended

Ball, D. L. (1997). From the general to the particular: Knowing our own students as learners of mathematics. *Mathematics Teacher, 90,* 732–737.

Don't be fooled because this article is in *The Mathematics Teacher.* Deborah Ball, one of the leading advocates for classroom discourse and listening to children, offers a thought-provoking example of third-grade thinking about fractions while raising our awareness of how difficult it is to see into the minds of children. She makes the point that understanding is not an all-or-nothing idea. Trying to know what students know is not an easy task. Ball provides us with useful food for thought.

Brooks, J. G., & Brooks, M. G. (1993). *In search of understanding: The case for the constructivist classroom.* Alexandria, VA: Association for Supervision and Curriculum Development.

Though not about teaching mathematics, this is a readable and informative book on teaching in a constructivist manner. Examples span all curricular areas and all grades.

Fosnot, C. T. (Ed.). (1996). *Constructivism: Theory, perspectives, and practice.* New York: Teachers College Press.

The first section of this book develops the theory of constructivism in three readable chapters. The next five chapters examine the application of constructivist theory in different disciplines. Deborah Schifter provides the perspective on teaching mathematics. The final section includes four chapters on classroom practice. You will not find this book overly theoretical or hard to read. At the same time, Fosnot's book is not exactly a light read. You will be challenged and rewarded.

Schifter, D. (Ed.). (1996). *What's happening in math class? Envisioning new practices through teacher narratives* (Vol. 1). New York: Teachers College Press.

In each of the five chapters of this book, three or four teachers share their personal struggles at becoming more of a constructivist teacher. Noted mathematics educators then offer their personal perspectives on what the teachers have so candidly shared. This is a book about constructivism in practice. The teacher-authors each work in quite different schools and represent a range of grades. However, the common threads among all of them help us understand why constructivism is such a popular theory in education today.

### Other Suggestions

Ball, D. L. (1996). Teacher learning and the mathematics reforms: What we think we know and what we need to learn. *Phi Delta Kappan, 77,* 500–508.

Brandt, R. (1994). On making sense: A conversation with Magdalene Lampert. *Educational Leadership, 55*(5), 26–30.

Brooks, M. G., & Brooks, G. B. (1999). The courage to be constructivist. *Educational Leadership, 57*(3), 18–24.

Campbell, P. F., & Johnson, M. L. (1995). How primary students think and learn. In I. M. Carl (Ed.), *Seventy-five years of progress: Prospects for school mathematics* (pp. 21–42). Reston, VA: National Council of Teachers of Mathematics.

Clements, D. H. (1997). (Mis?)constructing constructivism. *Teaching Children Mathematics, 4,* 198–200.

Cobb, P., & Bauersfeld, H. (Eds.). (1995). *The emergence of mathematical meaning: Interaction in classroom cultures.* Mahwah, NJ: Erlbaum.

Cobb, P., Wood, T., Yackel, E., & McNeal, E. (1993). Mathematics as procedural instructions and mathematics as meaningful activity: The reality of teaching for understanding. In R. B. Davis & C. A. Maher (Eds.), *School, mathematics, and the world of reality* (pp. 119–133). Needham Heights, MA: Allyn & Bacon.

Fennema, E., Carpenter, T. P., Franke, M. L., & Carey, D. A. (1993). Learning to use children's mathematics thinking: A case study. In R. B. Davis & C. A. Maher (Eds.), *School, mathematics, and the world of reality* (pp. 93–117). Needham Heights, MA: Allyn & Bacon.

Ginsburg, H. P., & Baron, J. (1993). Cognition: Young children's construction of mathematics. In R. J. Jensen (Ed.), *Research ideas for the classroom: Early childhood mathematics* (pp. 3–21). Old Tappan, NJ: Macmillan.

Greenes, C. (1999). Ready to learn: Developing young children's mathematical powers. In J. V. Copley (Ed.), *Mathematics in the early years* (pp. 39–47). Reston, VA: National Council of Teachers of Mathematics.

Hiebert, J. C. (1990). The role of routine procedures in the development of mathematical competence. In T. J. Cooney (Ed.), *Teaching and learning mathematics in the 1990s* (pp. 31–40). Reston, VA: National Council of Teachers of Mathematics.

Labinowicz, E. (1985). *Learning from children: New beginnings for teaching numerical thinking.* Menlo Park, CA: AWL Supplemental.

Noddings, N. (1993). Constructivism and caring. In R. B. Davis & C. A. Maher (Eds.), *School, mathematics, and the world of reality* (pp. 35–50). Needham Heights, MA: Allyn & Bacon.

Perkins, D. (1999). The many faces of constructivism. *Educational Leadership, 57*(3), 6–11.

Russell, S. J., & Corwin, R. B. (1993). Talking mathematics: "Going slow" and "letting go." *Phi Delta Kappan, 74,* 555–558.

Schifter, D. (1996). A constructivist perspective on teaching and learning mathematics. *Phi Delta Kappan, 77,* 492–499.

Smith, J. P., III. (1996). Efficacy and teaching mathematics by telling: A challenge for reform. *Journal for Research in Mathematics Education, 27,* 387–402.

Thompson, P. W. (1994). Concrete materials and teaching for mathematical understanding. *Arithmetic Teacher, 41,* 556–558.

Whitin, D. J. (1993). Number sense and the importance of asking "why?" In S. Brown & M. Walter (Eds.), *Problem posing: Reflections and applications* (pp. 121–129). Mahwah, NJ: Erlbaum.

Wiske, M. S. (1994). How teaching for understanding changes the rules in the classroom. *Educational Leadership, 51*(5), 18–21.

Wood, T. (1995). An emerging practice of teaching. In P. Cobb & H. Bauersfeld (Eds.), *The emergence of mathematical meaning: Interaction in classroom cultures* (pp. 203–227). Mahwah, NJ: Erlbaum.

# Chapter 4

# Teaching Through Problem Solving

*We believe that if we want students to understand mathematics, it is more helpful to think of understanding as something that results from solving problems, rather than something we can teach directly.*

*Hiebert et al. (1997, p. 25)*

*There is no other decision that teachers make that has a greater impact on students' opportunity to learn and on their perceptions about what mathematics is than the selection or creation of the tasks with which the teacher engages the students in studying mathematics.*

*Lappan and Briars (1995, p. 138)*

In 1989, the NCTM *Curriculum and Evaluation Standards* said that problem solving should be "a primary goal of all mathematics instruction and an integral part of all mathematical activity" (p. 23) and that students should "use problem-solving approaches to investigate and understand mathematical content" (p. 75). Over the next 10 years, evidence continued to mount that problem solving was a powerful and effective vehicle for learning. In 2000, NCTM's *Principles and Standards* document makes the case in even stronger language:

> Solving problems is not only a goal of learning mathematics but also a major means of doing so. . . . Problem solving is an integral part of all mathematics learning, and so it should not be an isolated part of the mathematics program. Problem solving in mathematics should involve all the five content areas described in these Standards. . . . Good problems will integrate multiple topics and will involve significant mathematics. (p. 52)

This vision is far from being realized. However, in classrooms where teachers have adopted this approach, teacher and student excitement is high and no one wants to return to traditional instruction.

## PROBLEM SOLVING AS A PRINCIPAL INSTRUCTIONAL STRATEGY

The following statement is a major thesis of this chapter. It is a clear reflection of the *Principles and Standards* document as just noted and represents the current thinking of a wide segment of mathematics education researchers.

> *Most, if not all, important mathematics concepts and procedures can best be taught through problem solving. That is, tasks or problems can and should be posed that engage students in thinking about and developing the important mathematics they need to learn.*

This proposition may strike some as extreme or unrealistic. Rather than accept it blindly or reject it, let's first consider why it may make sense.

### Starting Where the Students Are: A Shift in Thinking About Mathematics Instruction

Traditionally, the teacher taught the mathematics, the students practiced it for a while, and then they were expected to use the new skills or ideas in solving problems. This approach, strongly engrained in our culture, rarely works well. First, it begins where the teacher is rather than where the children are, ignoring what the children may or may not bring to the lesson. It assumes that wonderful explanations, perhaps enhanced by hands-on materials, will produce understanding. Although this approach sometimes succeeds with some children, showing and telling depends on passive absorption of ideas and leaves most students believing that mathematics is mysterious and beyond understanding.

The second difficulty with the teach-then-solve paradigm is that problem solving is separated from the learning process. Children who have come to expect the teacher to tell them the rules are unlikely to solve problems for which solution methods have not been provided. By separating teaching from problem solving, learning mathematics is separated from doing mathematics. This simply does not make sense.

Effective lessons begin where the students are, not where we are. That is, teaching should begin with the ideas that children already have, the ideas they will use to create new ones. To engage students requires tasks or activities that are problematic and require thought. Students learn mathematics as a *result* of solving problems. Mathematical ideas are the *outcomes* of the problem-solving experience, rather than elements that must be taught before problem solving (Hiebert et al., 1996, 1997). Furthermore, the process of solving problems is now completely interwoven with the learning; children are *learning* mathematics by *doing* mathematics!

## An Illustration

Suppose that you are teaching fifth grade and the topic is comparison of fractions—given two fractions, tell which is greater. The teach-by-telling approach provides a rule: Get common denominators, and compare the numerators. You accompany the rule with a conceptual explanation and pictures so that students will see the concept. However, students are aware of the exercises to come and how to do them. The explanation is of little value since the rule is all that is necessary to get through the day. As your students find the common denominators and complete the exercises, they are doing little more than third-grade multiplication. They are not thinking about fraction concepts at all.

In contrast, at the 1999 NCTM annual conference, Marilyn Burns shared these two solutions given by fifth graders who were asked to compare $\frac{6}{8}$ and $\frac{4}{5}$. No rules or procedures had been provided.

*I know that $\frac{4}{5}$ is the same as $\frac{8}{10}$ and $\frac{8}{10}$ is two-tenths away from a whole. I know that $\frac{6}{8}$ is two-eighths away from a whole. And since tenths are smaller than eighths, $\frac{8}{10}$ must be closer to the whole and so $\frac{4}{5}$ is larger.*

*I know that $\frac{6}{8}$ is the same as $\frac{12}{16}$ and $\frac{4}{5}$ is the same as $\frac{12}{15}$. Since fifteenths are bigger than sixteenths, $\frac{4}{5}$ must be larger.*

These students were concentrating on the meaning of fractions and the size of fractional parts. The second student actually used a common *numerator* approach that is never taught in schools but is completely reasonable. These students and the others in their class almost certainly learned more than had they blindly followed rules.

## The Value of Teaching with Problems

There is no doubt that teaching with problems is difficult. Tasks must be designed or selected each day, taking into consideration the current understanding of the students and the needs of the curriculum. It is often difficult to plan more than a few days in advance. If you have a traditional textbook, modifications will need to be made. There are good reasons to go to this effort.

- *Problem solving places the focus of the students' attention on ideas and sense making.* When solving problems, students are necessarily reflecting on the ideas that are inherent in the problems. Developing ideas are more likely to be integrated with existing ones, thereby improving understanding. By contrast, no matter how skillfully a teacher provides explanations and directions, students will be attending to "doing it right" or following the directions the teacher has provided.

- *Problem solving develops "mathematical power."* Students solving problems in class will be engaged in all five of the process standards described by the *Principles and Standards* document: problem solving, reasoning, communication, connections, and representation. These are the processes of doing mathematics and go well beyond the content understanding that is developed.

- *Problem solving develops the belief in students that they are capable of doing mathematics and that mathematics makes sense.* Every time you pose a problematic task and expect a solution, you say to students, "I believe you can do this." Every time the class solves a problem and students develop their understanding, confidence and self-worth are developed.

- *Problem solving provides ongoing assessment data that can be used to make instructional decisions, help students succeed, and inform parents.* Students engaging in problem solving will be discussing ideas, drawing pictures or using manipulatives, defending their solutions and evaluating others', and writing reports or explanations. This activity provides you with a steady stream of valuable information for planning the next lesson, helping individual students, evaluating their progress, and communicating with parents.

- *It is a lot of fun!* Teachers who experience teaching in this manner never return to a teach-by-telling mode. The excitement of students' developing understanding through their own reasoning is worth all the effort. And of course it is fun for the students.

# PROBLEMS AND TASKS FOR LEARNING MATHEMATICS

We have been talking about using problems to teach mathematics without having clearly defined what we mean by a problem. In the context of this discussion, the concept of "problem" is quite broad. The main point is that the problem, task, or activity engage students in making sense of the key ideas you want them to learn.

## A Description of Tasks or Problems

A *problem* is defined here as any task or activity for which the students have no prescribed or memorized rules or methods, nor is there a perception by students that there is a specific "correct" solution method (Hiebert et al., 1997).

A problem for learning mathematics also has these features:

- *It must begin where the students are.* The design or selection of the task must take into consideration the current understanding of the students. They should have the appropriate ideas to engage and solve the problem and yet still find it challenging and interesting. They should see the task as something to make sense of.

- *The problematic or engaging aspect of the problem must be due to the mathematics that the students are to learn.* Although it is acceptable and even desirable to have contexts or external conditions for problems that make them interesting, these aspects should not be the focus of the activity. In solving the problem or doing the activity, students should be concerned primarily with making sense of the mathematics involved and thereby developing their understanding of those ideas.

- *It must require justifications and explanations for answers and methods.* Students should understand that the responsibility for determining if answers are correct and why rests with them. Students should also expect to explain their solution methods.

Problems may be posed for individual students, pairs, or groups. They may involve hands-on materials or drawings. At other times, the work may involve pencil-and-paper tasks or be strictly mental work. Calculators may or may not be used.

It is important to understand that mathematics is to be taught *through* problem solving. That is, problematic tasks or activities are the vehicle by which the desired curriculum is developed. The learning is an outcome of the problem-solving process.

# Examples of Problematic Tasks

In Chapter 3, you saw that mathematical ideas could be categorized as conceptual or procedural. Students can learn both types of mathematics through problematic activities. Here are some examples in each category.

## Conceptual Mathematics

The following problem may be used for different purposes, depending on the students.

---

**Think about the number 6 broken into two different amounts. Draw a picture to show a way that six things can be in two parts. Think up a story to go with your picture.**

---

At the kindergarten or first-grade level, the teacher may want students simply to think about different parts of 6 and to connect these ideas into a context. In first or second grade, the teacher may challenge children to find all of the combinations rather than focus on the story or context. There is a nice relationship and pattern to be constructed. In a class discussion following work on the task, students are likely to develop an orderly process for listing all of the combinations: As one part grows from 0 to 6, the other part begins at 6 and shrinks by ones to 0. There are seven combinations for 6.

The following task might be used in grades 3–6 as part of the development of fraction concepts.

---

**Place an X on the number line about where $\frac{11}{8}$ would be. Explain why you put your X where you did. Perhaps you will want to draw and label other points on the line to help explain your answer.**

---

Note that the task includes a suggestion for how to respond but does not specify exactly what must be done. Students are able to use their own level of reasoning and understanding to justify their answers. In the follow-up discussion, the teacher may well expect to see a variety of justifications from which to help the class refine ideas about fractions that are greater than 1.

---

**I used two identical shapes to make a rectangle. What might they have been?** (Baker & Baker, 1991)

---

This task, appropriate for grades 3–8, is very open-ended. There is a good potential for students to learn about congruent shapes and rotations. (When two congruent shapes form a rectangle, one can be rotated around the center of the rectangle to match the other.) With this problem, everyone will be able to contribute some ideas and will be ready to reflect on the ideas of others.

---

**Use your graphing calculator to find the intersection of the lines for $y = 3x - 6$ and $y = -2x + 4$. What do the coordinates of the point of intersection have to do with the two equations? Explain.**

---

Students in an eighth-grade algebra class can use a variety of methods to find the point of intersection (graphing calculator, tables, graphs sketched on paper). They will find that the coordinates are solutions to both equations. This problem is a good example of a significant relationship that students can best understand by figuring it out on their own, rather than by having it explained to them in the text or by the teacher.

## Procedures and Processes

Critics of the problem-solving approach often point to the need for students to learn basic skills, saying that these must be taught through direct instruction. In reality, students can develop procedures via a problem-solving approach. Imagine a class of second graders who had never been taught to add two-digit numbers in the conventional manner. They are challenged to find the sum of 48 and 25. In one second-grade classroom, at least seven different solution methods were offered by the students. Two children employed two different counting techniques using a hundreds chart for assistance. Here are solutions of some of the others:

4⃞8⃞ + 2⃞5⃞   (Boxed digits help "hold" them.)

40 + 20 = 60

⃞3⃞   (The 3 is left from the 5.)

8 + 2 = 10

60 + 10 = 70

70 + 3 = 73

---

40 + 20 = 60

60 + 8 = 68

68 + 5 = 73

---

48 + 20 = 68

68 + 2 ("from the 5") = 70

"Then I still have that 3 from the 5."

70 + 3 = 73

---

25 + 25 = 50   ⃞23⃞

50 + 23 = 73

Teacher: Where does the 23 come from?

*"It's sort of from the 48."*

How did you split up the 48?

*"20 and 20 and I split the 8 into 5 and 3."*

---

48 − 3 = 45   ⃞3⃞

45 + 25 = 70

70 + 3 = 73

In this class (reported by Russell, 1997), the students show a variety of levels of thinking and many interesting techniques. They had learned from each other the trick of placing numbers in "hold boxes," although not everyone used it. The children who are counting on the chart are showing that they may not yet have developed adequate place-value tools to understand these more sophisticated methods. Or the class discussion may help them activate those ideas or "dots" they simply had not considered. One question is this: Are these invented methods efficient or adequate? Regardless of how you feel about that, these children are at least minimally prepared to consider a variety of methods because they are developing meaningful ideas about the process. One option is to offer students an efficient way of adding two-digit numbers and asking the students to figure out why it works and to decide if it will work every time.

Imagine for yourself what might happen if fifth-grade students were asked to add 3.72 + 1.6 before having been told about lining up decimal points. Many students will do it incorrectly, perhaps aligning the 2 and 6 or the 3 and 1. The decimal may be placed in various places. But students attempting to defend their solutions will need to confront the size of the answer and the meaning of the digits in each position. A class of problem solvers will soon develop a good method for adding decimals.

Gary Tsuruda is a middle school teacher. His classes frequently work in small groups to solve problems. Figure 4.1 (p. 44) shows one example. Notice that the initial questions bring the requisite ideas needed for the task to the students' conscious level. Next they are asked to do some exploration and look for patterns. From these explorations the group must come up with a formula, test it, describe how it was developed, and illustrate its use.

Tsuruda (1994) reports that every group was able to produce a formula. "Not all the formulas looked like the typical textbook formula, but they were all correct, and more important, each formula made sense according to the way the students in that group had constructed the knowledge from the data they themselves had generated" (p. 6).

In all of these examples, the students are very much engaged in the processes of doing mathematics—figuring out procedures, not accepting them blindly. What is abundantly clear is that the more problem solving that students do, the more willing they are to solve problems and the more

## TRAPEZOID AREA

**GOAL:** *Find an easy way to determine the area of any trapezoid.*

Be sure that you understand the answers to each of these questions:

1. What does "area" mean?
2. What is a trapezoid?
3. How do you find the area of other polygons? Show as many different ways as you can.

*Now see if your group can find an easy way to determine the area of any trapezoid.*

**HINTS:**

1. Draw several trapezoids on dot paper and find their areas. Look for patterns.
2. Consider how you find the area of other polygons. Are any of the key ideas similar?
3. You might try cutting out trapezoids and piecing them together.
4. If you find a way to determine the area, make sure it is as easy as you can make it and that it works for *any* trapezoid.

**WRITE-UP:**

1. Explain your answers to the first three questions in detail. Tell how your group reached agreement on the answers.
2. Tell what you did to get your formula for the area of any trapezoid. Did you use any of the hints? How did they help you?
3. Show your formula and give an illustration of how it works.

**Figure 4.1**  **A middle school example in which students are required to construct a formula.**
*Source:* From *Putting It Together: Middle School Math in Transition* (p. 7), by G. Tsuruda, 1994 Portsmouth, NH: Heinemann, a division of Reed Elsevier Inc. Reprinted by permission of Gary Tsuruda .

methods they develop for attacking problems (Campbell, 1996; Lester, 1994; Rowan & Bourne, 1994; Schifter & Fosnot, 1993; Silver, Smith, & Nelson, 1995; Silver & Stein, 1996; Wood, Cobb, Yackel, & Dillon, 1993).

# A THREE-PART LESSON FORMAT

U.S. teachers typically spend a small portion of a lesson explaining or reviewing an idea and then go into "production mode,"

where students wade through a list of exercises. Lessons set up in this explain-then-practice pattern condition students to focus on procedures so that they can get through the exercises. Teachers find themselves going from desk to desk reteaching and explaining to individuals. This is in significant contrast to a lesson built around a single problem, an approach that is quite typical in Asian classrooms (see Figure 4.2). Much more learning occurs and much more assessment information is available when a class works on a single problem and engages in discourse about the validity of the solution.

---

**The emphasis on understanding is evident in the steps typical of Japanese eighth-grade mathematics lessons:**

- Teacher poses a complex thought-provoking problem.
- Students struggle with the problem.
- Various students present ideas or solutions to the class.
- Class discusses the various solution methods.
- The teacher summarizes the class's conclusions.
- Students practice similar problems.

**In contrast, the emphasis on skill acquisition is evident in the steps common to most U.S. and German math lessons:**

- Teacher instructs students in a concept or skill.
- Teacher solves example problems with class.
- Students practice on their own while the teacher assists individual students.

---

**Figure 4.2**  **Comparison of the steps typical of eighth-grade mathematics lessons in Japan, the United States, and Germany.**
*Source:* Unpublished tabulations from the Third International Mathematics and Science Study, Videotape Classroom Study, University of California, Los Angeles, 1996. Used with permission.

## Before, During, and After

Teaching through problem solving does not mean simply providing a problem or task, sitting back, and waiting for magic to happen. The teacher is responsible for making the atmosphere and the lesson work. To this end, think of a lesson as consisting of three main parts: *before, during,* and *after.* Each portion carries specific agendas and requires specific teacher actions that are necessary to make the lesson effective (see Figure 4.3).

- *Before.* The agenda in this part of the lesson is to get students mentally prepared to work on the problem and thinking about the kinds of ideas that will help them the most. You want to be sure they understand the task. You want to be sure they understand their responsibilities. At the end of this portion of the lesson, there should be no questions regarding the task or what is to be done. Students have already begun to think about the relevant ideas and are ready to go to work.

**Getting Ready**
- Get students mentally ready to work on the task.
- Be sure all expectations for products are clear.

**Students Work**
- Let go!
- Listen carefully.
- Provide hints.
- Observe and assess.

**Class Discourse**
- Accept student solutions without evaluation.
- Conduct discussion as students justify and evaluate results and methods.

**Figure 4.3** **Teaching through problem solving suggests a simple three-part structure for lessons.**

- *During.* The first agenda item here is to *let go!* Give students a chance to work without your constant guidance. Give them the opportunity to use *their* ideas and not simply follow directions. Have faith in their abilities. The second point is to *listen.* Find out how different children or groups are thinking, what ideas they are using, and how they are approaching the problem.

- *After.* In this portion of the lesson, you want to engage the class in productive discourse and help students begin to work as a community of learners. *Do not evaluate.* Students must learn to both contribute to and participate in these discussions. They must listen to others and help decide which approaches and solutions make the most sense and why. Thinking must not stop when the problem is solved. Now is the time to encourage reflection on solutions, methods, and extensions.

If you allot time for each before, during, and after segment, it is quite easy to devote a full period to one seemingly simple problem. As long as the problematic feature of the task is the mathematics you want students to learn, a lot of good learning will result from engaging students in only one problem. The same three-part structure can be applied to small tasks, resulting in a 10- to 20-minute minilesson (common in kindergarten). There are also times when the during and after portions extend into the next day or even longer.

## Teacher Actions in the Before Phase

The kinds of things you do in the before phase of a lesson will vary with the task. Some tasks you can begin with

immediately. More likely, however, you will first engage students in some form of activity directly related to the problem in order to get them prepared. Consider the following "before actions."

### Begin with a Simple Version of the Task

Suppose that you are interested in developing some ideas about area and perimeter in the fourth or fifth grade. This is the task you plan to present (Lappan & Even, 1989).

Assume that the edge of a square is 1 unit. Add squares to this shape so that it has a perimeter of 18.

Instead of beginning your lesson with this problem, you might consider one of the following simpler tasks:

- Draw a 3-by-5 rectangle of squares on the board, and let students tell things they know about the shape. (It's a rectangle. It has squares. There are 15 squares. There are three rows of five.) If no one mentions the words *area* and *perimeter,* you could write those two words on the board and ask if those words can be used in talking about this figure.

- Provide students with some square tiles or grid paper. "I want everyone to make a shape that has a perimeter of 12 units. After you make your shape, find out what its area is." After a short time, have several students share their shapes.

Each of these "warm-ups" gets the vocabulary you will need for your exploration out in the open. The second activity suggests the tiles as a possible model that students may choose to use. It has the added benefit of hinting that there are different figures with the same perimeter.

Dad says it is 503 miles to the beach. When we stopped for gas, we had gone 267 miles. How much farther do we have to drive?

This problem is designed to help children develop an add-on method of subtraction. Before presenting this problem, have students supply the missing part of 100 after you supply one part. Try numbers like 80 or 30 at first; then try 47 or 62. After presenting the actual task, you might ask students if the answer to the problem is more or less than 300.

## Brainstorm

If your activity or task will present a new concept or if the problem is relatively complex, a preliminary brainstorming session may help get students on the right track before they get too lost in doing the problem.

A second-grade teacher in an urban school was planning an initial discussion of fractions. She needed to find out just what ideas her students had before she could decide exactly what to do next. On the overhead projector, she drew a simple square with both diagonals (see Figure 4.4) "Today we are going to begin talking about fractions. I want to find out what you know. Look at the figure on the screen, and think of one thing you can say about it." She used a "think-pair-share" strategy, suggesting that after they had thought of an idea, they should talk about their ideas with a partner. This gave all students the opportunity to put their ideas into words before having to share with the full class. When she then began calling on children to share their ideas, most children were ready. All ideas were written on the overhead without comment or judgment: "There is an X." "It is a fraction." "All the triangles are equal." The full list of ideas covered the board. Acceptance of the ideas gave all students a sense of confidence and involvement.

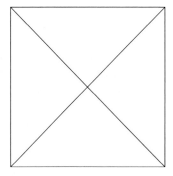

**Figure 4.4**  **This figure was used to initiate a brainstorming session with second graders to find out what they knew about fractions.**

When the brainstorming had fairly well exhausted ideas, the teacher focused on the comment about the triangles all being equal. "In your groups, I want you to talk about this: Does it matter that the pieces are equal fractions?" The resulting discussion helped develop the ideas of fair shares for fractions and also connected with some ideas about symmetry the students had been working on earlier.

Often you can have students suggest solutions or strategies. Their suggestions will not solve the problem for others because students must still work out the solution and an explanation. The following problem for middle grade students is designed to address the ideas of ratio and proportion as well as data analysis. Since this is not a straightforward task, brainstorming will likely produce a variety of approaches, resulting in more profitable solutions by more students.

Enrollment data for the school provide information about the students and their families as shown here:

|  | School | Class |
|---|---|---|
| Siblings |  |  |
| None | 36 | 5 |
| One | 89 | 4 |
| Two | 134 | 17 |
| More than two | 93 | 3 |
| Race |  |  |
| African American | 49 | 11 |
| Asian American | 12 | 0 |
| White | 219 | 15 |
| Travel-to-school method |  |  |
| Walk | 157 | 10 |
| Bus | 182 | 19 |
| Other | 13 | 0 |

If someone asked you how typical your class was of the rest of the school, how would you answer? Write an explanation of your answer. Include one or more charts or graphs that you think would support your conclusion.

## Estimate or Use Mental Computation

When the task is aimed at the development of a computational procedure, a useful before action is to have students actually do the computation mentally or suggest a ballpark answer. Have students independently think of an estimate or compute mentally, and then list these "pre-answers" on the board. You may even have students explain their reasoning. Again, this process will not spoil the problem for the class.

This technique would be useful with the earlier problem concerning how many miles to go to the beach. The following task is another example where preliminary estimates or mental computations would be useful.

How many small squares (ones or units) will fit in a rectangle that is 54 units long and 36 units wide? Use base-ten pieces to help you with your solution.

Make a plan for figuring out the total number of pieces without doing too much counting. Explain how your plan would work on a rectangle that is 27 units by 42 units.

Prior to estimation or mental computation for this problem, several simpler problems will also help. For example, rectangles such as 30 by 8 or 40 by 60 could be explored, or these may have been problems from earlier days.

## Be Sure the Task Is Understood

You must always be sure that students understand the problem before setting them to work. Remember that their perspective is different from yours.

Consider the task of mastering the multiplication facts. The most difficult facts can each be connected or related to an easier fact already learned.

Use a fact you already know to help you solve each of these facts: $4 \times 6$, $6 \times 8$, $7 \times 6$, $3 \times 8$.

For this task, it is essential that students understand the idea of using a helping fact. They have most likely used helping facts in addition. You can build on this by asking, "When you were learning addition facts, how could knowing $6 + 6$ help you figure out $6 + 7$?" You may also need to help students understand what is meant by a fact they know—one they have mastered and know without counting.

When using a word problem, it is useful in the lower grades to ask a series of direct questions that can be answered just by looking at the problem.

The local candy store purchased candy in cartons holding 12 boxes per carton. The price paid for one carton was $42.50. Each box contained 8 candy bars that the store planned to sell individually. What was the candy store's cost for each candy bar?

"What did the candy store do? What is in a carton? What is in a box? What is the price of one carton? What does that mean when it says 'each box'?" The last question here is to identify vocabulary that may be misunderstood. It is also useful to be sure students can explain to you what the problem is asking. Rereading a problem does little good, but having students restate the problem in their own words forces them to think about what the problem is asking.

## Establish Expectations

Students need to be clearly told what is expected of them beyond an answer. It is always a good idea to have students write out an explanation for their solution. There is a significant difference between "Show how you got your answer" and "Explain why you think your answer is correct." With the former direction, students may simply record their steps ("First we did . . . , and then we . . .") or present their work

as self-evident. You can't expect students to explain their mental processes unless you ask for an explanation. In Figure 4.5 (p. 48), the work of two students' illustrates the contrast.

When students are working in groups, only one written explanation should come from the group. All in the group must understand what is written, all should put their names on it, and any one in the group should be ready to make an oral presentation.

It is never too early to begin written explanations, even in kindergarten. There the writing may be in the form of drawings and numbers, but this early form of written communication is just as important. Figure 4.6 (p. 48) shows one student's solution to ways to make 5.

The written explanations may be in a journal or on a separate sheet of paper. Sometimes a group report can be prepared on a large sheet of newsprint. This is useful when students are going to make a presentation.

There may be occasions when you will not require written work. A very simple yet useful technique is to have students share their ideas with a partner and then between the two of them select the best approach to be presented. This causes students to defend their ideas to a peer and prepares them to talk to the class.

Students preparing to explain and defend their answers will spend time reflecting on the validity of their results and will often make revisions even before sharing them. They will have a greater interest in the class discussion because they will want to compare their solution with others'. They will have "rehearsed" for the class discussion and be ready to participate. Even when students fail to solve a problem, they should be expected to show the ideas and the work that they have considered.

# Teacher Actions in the During Phase

Once you are comfortable that students are ready to work on the task, it is time to let go. You must demonstrate confidence and respect for your students' abilities. Set them to work with the expectation that they will solve the problem. You *must* let go!

Students should get in the habit of working in groups so that there is no lost time in moving from the full-class discussion to the small groups. Groups of three or at most four work well, but pairs of students, especially at the K–2 level, are often best. (Chapter 22 includes a detailed discussion of cooperative group work.) Your role now shifts to that of facilitator and active listener. You might sit down with a group, listen for a while, have the students explain what they are doing, or just take notes.

## Provide Hints and Suggestions

How much help to give students is always going to be an issue. Should you let them stumble down the wrong path? How much direction should you provide? Do you correct errors you see?

$\frac{9}{10}$

Math
P.O.T.W.                                    Betsy
                                            Nov. 18, 1992

Karen and Fran have 28 goldfish.
Fran has 4 more goldfish than Karen. How
many goldfish does each girl have?

$28 - 4 = 24$     $24 \div 2 = 12$     $12 + 4 = 16$

$\boxed{16} + \boxed{12} = 28$

          First I subtracted 4 from 28.          Why did
Then I divided by 2. I then added the          you do
4 that was left to that answer. Then I added    this?
those 2 #'s.

          Fran has 16 goldfish, and Karen
has 12 goldfish.

$\frac{10}{10}$  Excellent!

Math
P.O.T.W.                                    Ryan
                                            Nov. 17, 1992

Karen and Fran have 28 goldfish.
Fran has 4 more goldfish than Karen.
How many goldfish does each girl
have?

$$\begin{array}{r} 14 \\ 2\overline{)28} \\ \underline{2} \\ 08 \\ \underline{8} \\ 00 \end{array}$$

          What I did was to
divide the 28 goldfish in half.
when I did this each girl
had 14. Since Fran had 4
more goldfish than Karen I
took 2 of Karen's goldfish and
gave two to Fran. Fran now
had 16 and Karen had 12.
The total is 28 and Fran has
4 more than Karen.

Answers Fran has 16 goldfish and Karen has 12

**Figure 4.5**  **Betsy tells each step in her solution but provides no explanation. In contrast, Ryan's work includes reasons for his steps.**

**Kindergarten**
How many ways can you show what 5 means?

**Figure 4.6**  **A kindergarten student shows her thinking about ways to make 5.**

If a group is searching for a place to begin, a hint may be appropriate. You might suggest that the students try using a particular manipulative or draw a picture if that seems appropriate.

In Fern's Furniture Store, Fern has priced all of her furniture at 20 percent over wholesale. In preparation for a sale, she tells her staff to cut all prices by 10 percent. Will Fern be making 10 percent profit, less than 10 percent profit, or more than 10 percent profit? Explain your answer.

For this problem, consider the following hints:

■ Try drawing a picture or a diagram of something that shows what 10 percent off means.

■ Try drawing a picture or a diagram that shows what 20 percent more means.

■ Maybe you could pick a price of something and see what happens.

■ Let's try a simpler problem. Suppose that you had 8 blocks and got 25 percent more. Then you lost 25 percent of the new collection.

## Encourage Testing of Ideas

Students will look to you for approval of their results or ideas. Avoid being the source of "truth" or of right and wrong. When asked if a result or method is correct ask, "How can you decide?" or "Why do you think that might be right?" or "I see what you have done. How can you check that somehow?" Even if not asked for an opinion, asking, "How can we tell if that makes sense?" reminds students that answers without reasons are not acceptable.

## Suggest Extensions or Generalizations

Lots of good problems are simple on the surface. It is the extensions that are excellent. The area and perimeter task is a case in point. Many students will quickly come up with one or two solutions. "I see you found one way to do this. Are there any other solutions? Are any of the solutions different or more interesting than others? Which of the shapes you found with a perimeter of 18 is the largest and which the smallest? Does the perimeter always change when you add another tile?"

*What can you find out about that?* This general question is at the very heart of mathematics as a science of pattern and order. It asks students to look for something interesting, to generalize. For example, in the area and perimeter problem, squares can be added to a shape in three situations: If a new square touches the old shape on only one side, the perimeter increases by 2. If it touches on two sides, there is no increase. If it fits into a "U" and touches on three sides, the perimeter actually decreases by 2.

Questions that begin "What if you tried . . . ?" or "Would that same idea work for . . . ?" are also ways to suggest different extensions. For example, "Suppose you tried to find all the shapes possible with a perimeter of 18. What could you find out about the areas?"

## Find a Second Method

The value of students' solving a problem in more than one way cannot be overestimated. It shifts the value system in the classroom from answers to processes and thinking. It is a good way for students to make new and different connections.

For example, consider this sixth-grade problem.

**The dress was originally priced at $90. If the sale price is 25 percent off, how much will it cost on sale?**

This is an example of a straightforward problem with a single answer. Many students will solve it by multiplying by 0.25 and subtracting the result from $90. The suggestion to find another way may be all that is necessary. Others may require specific directions: "How would you do it with frac-

tions instead of decimals?" "Draw me a diagram that explains what you did." "How could this be done in just one step?" "Think of a way that you could do this mentally."

Second graders will frequently solve the next problem by counting or using addition.

**Maxine had saved up $9. The next day, she received her allowance. Now she has $12. How much allowance did she get?**

"How would you do that on a calculator?" and "Can you write an equation that tells what you did?" are ways of encouraging children to connect 9 plus ? = 12 with 12 − 9.

Solving a problem in a second way can help students who have made an error find their own mistake. Perhaps a student has used a symbolic method of her own invention and has made an error in reasoning. Suggesting only that she try to do the problem with physical models ("so that I can understand what you did") may be all that is necessary to have her make a self-correction.

# Teacher Actions in the After Phase

Be certain to plan ample time for this portion. Often this is when the best learning will take place. Twenty minutes or more is not at all unreasonable for a good class discussion and sharing of ideas. This is not a time to check answers but for the class to share ideas. Over time, you will develop your class into a community of learners who together are involved in making sense of mathematics. This atmosphere will not develop easily or quickly. You must teach your students about your expectations for this time and how to interact with their peers.

## Engage the Class in Discussion

You may want simply to list answers from all of the groups and put them on the board without comment. Following that, you can return to one or more students to get explanations for their solutions or to explain their processes. At other times, you may choose to call on groups or individuals that you noticed earlier doing something interesting or something of special value. This should not be restricted to correct solutions.

When there are different answers, the full class should be involved in the discourse concerning which answers are correct. Allow those responsible for the answers to defend them, and then open the discussion to the class. "Who has an idea about this? George, I noticed that you got a different answer than Tomeka. What do you think of her explanation?" Resist with every fiber in you the temptation to judge the correctness of an answer. Even when the class fails to come to a conclusion, rather than provide your solution, suggest that perhaps you will need to return to this later. Later will be when students have gained some additional insights to help them.

One of your functions is to make sure that all students participate, that all listen, and that all understand what is being said. Moving along too quickly cheats students who are not quite able to follow the faster explanations of the best children in the room. Encourage students to ask questions. "Pete, did you understand how they did that? Do you want to ask Mary a question?"

## Identify Rules, Hypotheses, and Future Problems

When you are satisfied with the discussion around the answer and the solution, summarize the main points of the discussion, and make sure that all students understand what has been agreed on. When a problem involves creating a procedure, the class may decide on one or more methods of solution, and these may be written on the board. For example, suppose that the task involved finding clever methods of adding when one of the addends is a 9 (e.g., 5 + 9 or 9 + 3). Some students may have devised a method of taking 1 off of the smaller number and putting it with the 9. This might be listed as Maggie's rule: *Shift 1 from the little number to make 10. 5 + 9 becomes 4 + 10.* Other students may have added 10 to the smaller number and subtracted 1. Yolanda's rule might be written: *Add 10 instead of 9 and then take 1 off. 5 + 9 is 5 + 10 − 1.* When students invent procedures for computation or measurement formulas, you may want to help them find a good way to write them, but do not change the students' basic ideas. No student should be required to use the ideas of others, but all students must try to understand them.

Often someone will make a generalization or an observation that he or she strongly believes in but cannot completely justify. These ideas should always be listened to with interest, even if they are incorrect. Untested ideas can be written up on the board as "Andrew's Hypothesis." Explain the meaning of *hypothesis* as an idea that may or may not be true. Testing the hypothesis may become the problem for another day, or the hypothesis may simply be kept on the board until additional evidence comes up that either supports or disproves it. For example, when comparing fractions, suppose that a group makes this generalization and you write it on the board: *When deciding which fraction is larger, the fraction in which the bottom number is closer to the top number is the larger fraction. Example: $\frac{4}{7}$ is not as big as $\frac{7}{8}$ because 7 is only 1 from 8 but 4 is 3 away from 7.* This is not an unusual conclusion, but it is not correct in all instances. A problem for a subsequent day would be to decide if the hypothesis is always right or to find fractions for which it is not right (counterexamples.)

Even when students have not suggested hypotheses, discussions will often turn up interesting questions that can profitably be used for tasks to help clarify an emerging idea.

## Use Praise Cautiously

Be an attentive listener to both good and not so good ideas. Support and praise effort and risk taking, but *expect* students to do good work. Praise offered for correct solutions or excitement over interesting ideas suggests that the students did something unusual or unexpected. This can be negative feedback for those who do not get praise. Comments such as "Good job!" and "Super work!" roll off the tongue easily. We use these statements to help children feel good about themselves. There is evidence to suggest that we should be cautious when using expressions of praise, especially with respect to student products and solutions (Schwartz, 1996). Praise not only supports students' feelings but also evaluates. "Good job!" says, "Yes, you did that correctly." "Nice work" can establish an expectation for others that products must be neat or beautiful in order to have value. This can make students who do excellent mathematical science hide their efforts if they appear sloppy or poorly presented.

In place of praise that is judgmental, Schwartz (1996) suggests comments of interest and extension: "I wonder what would happen if you tried . . ." or "Please tell me how you figured that out." Notice that these phrases express interest and value the child's thinking. They also can and should be used regardless of the validity of the responses.

## Engage *All* Class Members

Teachers are finding a wider range of academic diversity in their classrooms. NCTM in its *Standards* documents is very clear in expressing the belief that all children can learn the mathematics of the regular curriculum. This view is supported by a number of prominent mathematics educators who have worked extensively with at-risk populations (Campbell, 1996; NCTM, 1989, 1991; Silver & Stein, 1996; Trafton & Claus, 1994).

But the needs and abilities of children are different, and it requires skill and practice to conduct a large group discussion that is balanced and includes all children. Rowan and Bourne (1994) offer some excellent suggestions based on their work in an urban, multiracial, multiethnic, low-socioeconomic school district. They emphasize that the most important factor is to be clear about the purpose of group discussion—that is, to share and explore the variety of strategies, ideas, and solutions generated by the class and to learn to communicate these ideas in a rich mathematical discourse. Every class has a handful of students who are always ready to respond. Other children learn to be passive or do not participate. So rule number one is that the discussion is more important than hearing an answer.

A second suggestion is to begin discussions by calling first on the children who tend to be shy or lack the ability to express themselves well. Rowan and Bourne (1994) note that the more obvious ideas are generally given at the outset of a discussion. When asked to participate early and given sufficient time to formulate their thoughts, these reticent children can more easily participate and thus be valued.

Make it a habit to ask for explanations to accompany *all* answers. Soon the request for an explanation will not signal an incorrect response, as children initially believe. Many incorrect answers are the result of small errors in the context of otherwise excellent thinking. Likewise, many correct answers may not represent the insightful thinking you might have assumed. A child who has given an incorrect answer is very likely to see the error and correct it during the explanation. Try to support children's thinking without evaluating responses. "Does someone have a different idea or want to comment on what Daniel just said?" All children should hear the same teacher reactions that only the "smart kids" used to hear.

Many times a student will get stuck in the middle of an explanation. The silence can be difficult, and there is a temptation to call on someone else to "help out" or to suggest that the child get assistance from a classmate. Though well intentioned, the message this sends to the child is that he is not capable on his own. Children must learn that time will be given and that their classmates trust and believe in one another. This attitude conveys support and confidence and is usually all that is necessary to get a quality response.

There will, of course, be times when a response is simply not forthcoming. When this occurs, you might suggest taking some time to get thoughts together or to work out the idea with some materials. Promise to return to the child later, and then be *certain* to return to hear what was figured out.

# DESIGNING AND SELECTING EFFECTIVE TASKS

A task is effective when it helps students learn the ideas you want them to learn. It must be the mathematics in the task that makes it problematic for the students so that it is the mathematical ideas that are their primary concern. Therefore, the first and most important consideration for selecting any task for your class must be the mathematics. That said, where do you look for tasks?

## Your Textbook

Most teachers find their textbook to be the main guide to their day-to-day curriculum. However, when teachers let the text determine the next lesson, they assume that children learned from each page what was intended. Avoid the "myth of coverage": If we covered it, they must have learned it. Good teachers use their text as a resource and as a basic guide to their curriculum. In the face of the current pressures from state-level standards, the state curriculum guide is also an important consideration.

### Using Traditional Textbooks

Traditional textbooks are designed to be teacher-directed, a contrast to the approach you have been reading about. But they should not be discarded. Much thought went into the content and the pedagogical ideas. Your book can still be used

as a prime resource if you think about translating units and lessons to a problem-oriented approach.

Adopt a *unit perspective.* Avoid the idea that every lesson and idea in the unit requires attention. Examine a chapter or unit from beginning to end, and identify the two to four *big ideas,* the essential mathematics in the chapter. (Big ideas are listed at the start of each chapter in Section 2 of this book. These may be helpful as a reference.) Temporarily ignore the smaller subideas that often take up a full lesson.

With the big ideas of the unit in mind, you can now do two things: (1) adapt the best or most important lessons in the chapter to a problem-solving format and (2) create or find tasks in the text's teacher notes and other resources that address the big ideas. The combination will almost certainly provide you with an ample supply of tasks.

### Adapting a Traditional Textbook Lesson

Figure 4.7 (p. 52) shows a page from a first-grade textbook. The lesson addresses an important idea: the connection of addition and subtraction. The approach on this page is fine: a bar of cubes in two colors is used to suggest an addition and a subtraction equation, thus connecting these concepts. However, as is typical of traditional K–2 texts, there are blanks to be filled in with very specific correct answers. Student attention turns almost immediately to how to get the right numbers in the blanks. Imagine for a moment how you might help students complete this page correctly. It is easy to slip into a how-to mode that focuses more on the blanks than on addition and subtraction. Let's convert this lesson to a problem-oriented task. How can children be challenged to wrestle with this idea? You might want to try this before reading on.

One thought is to provide a bar of cubes of one color and have students break the bar into two parts. The students' task is to write addition and subtraction equations that tell what they did with the bar. They should draw a picture to show how they broke the bar.

Another idea is to create a scenario where there are two amounts, such as toy cars, on two different shelves. *In the toy store, there were 11 cars, 4 on the top shelf and 7 on the next shelf.* Have the students create two story problems about the 11 cars, one that is an addition story and another that is a subtraction story.

In the first modification, the page was translated directly to a task. In the second, a similar task was designed that did not look the same but addressed exactly the same mathematics. In each case, the students will do only one or two examples rather than the eight that are on this page and on the other side. But in the during and after portions of either modified lesson, there will be a much greater opportunity for students to develop the connection between addition and subtraction. That concept will be the focus of the discussion, not filling in the blanks.

Figure 4.8 (p. 53) is a geometry lesson from a fifth-grade book. The content involves classification of triangles by relative side lengths and by the size of the angles, but notice

**Figure 4.7  A first-grade lesson from a traditional textbook.**
*Source:* From *Scott Foresman–Addison Wesley Math: Grade 1* (p. 117), by R. I. Charles et al., 1998, Glenview, IL: Scott Foresman–Addison Wesley. Copyright 1998 by Scott Foresman–Addison Wesley. Reprinted with permission.

how much of the lesson is simply providing definitions. The lesson is easily translated to a problematic task. Consider what *you* might do before reading on.

To make this a classification *task,* students need some triangles in all six categories, with two or three triangles per category. You might prepare a set of triangles, reproduce them, and have students cut them out, or geoboards could be used if they are available. (These and other ideas are discussed in Chapter 17.) Given a set of triangles, the task is to find two ways to sort the triangles into three separate piles. You could specify doing this first by sides and then by angles, or let students develop their own classification schemes. In the during portion, you can

provide hints that will help assure that some students create the categories you want. After students have created the categories, you can provide the appropriate vocabulary.

## Using Reform Programs

If your school is using a "reform-oriented" textbook series (see p. 14), then you will likely find that most of the lessons are already geared to a problem-solving mode. Your main difficulty may be assuring yourself that all of the skills and concepts of your local curriculum are appropriately emphasized. Some units may need additional activities or modifications based on the needs of your students, and others you

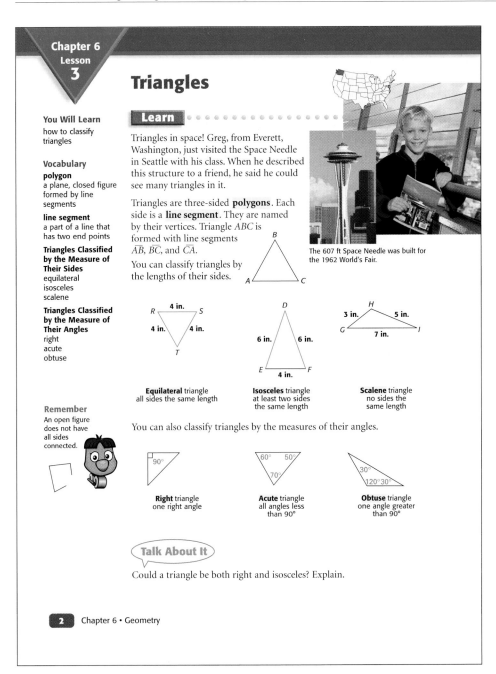

**Figure 4.8** A fifth-grade lesson from a traditional textbook.
*Source:* From *Scott Foresman–Addison Wesley Math: Grade 5* (p. 272), by R. I. Charles et al., 1998, Glenview, IL: Scott Foresman–Addison Wesley. Copyright 1998 by Scott Foresman–Addison Wesley. Reprinted with permission.

may decide to skip. Some teachers use these programs as resource books, selecting only a few units or activities to augment their regular program.

## Children's Literature

The use of children's literature is sufficiently important as a source of problems that it deserves some separate attention. Children's stories can be used in numerous ways to create reflective tasks at all grade levels, and there are many excellent books to help you in this area (Bresser, 1995; Burns,

1992a; Sheffield, 1995; Theissen, Matthias, & Smith, 1998; Welchman-Tischler, 1992; Whitin & Wilde, 1992, 1995).

By way of example, a very popular children's book, *The Doorbell Rang* (Hutchins, 1986), can be used with different agendas at various grade levels. The story is a sequential tale of children sharing 12 cookies. On each page, more children come to the kitchen, and the 12 cookies must be redistributed. This simple yet engaging story can lead to exploring ways to make equal parts of almost any number for children at the K–2 level. It is a springboard for multiplication and division at the 3–4 level. It can also be used to explore fraction concepts at the 4–6 level.

Most of the chapters in Section 2 of this text include a section titled "Literature Connection" that suggests a few ideas for using literature to explore the mathematics of that chapter. Literature ideas are often found in the articles of NCTM's journals. It is an exciting approach to developing lessons.

## Other Resources

You will never compile a perfect set of tasks for your class; every class is different. As already noted, your textbook is a good place to begin, and children's literature should always be considered. Here are some additional options to consider:

- Read the NCTM journals regularly: *Teaching Children Mathematics* (for grades K–6) or *Mathematics Teaching in the Middle School* (for grades 5–8). Copy and file articles to go with each chapter in your text or each section of your curriculum. Don't wait until you need an idea to begin flipping through journals.

- Begin to develop your personal professional library of resource books. Check out NCTM publications. The Addenda Series books are an excellent place to begin, but NCTM's catalog has lots of resources. Don't forget the book in your hands! Many teachers use it as their first resource. A number of commercial publishers and distributors specialize in materials for teaching mathematics, including resource books for teachers and activity books and manipulatives for students.

- Check out the reform curricula at your grade level, even if you don't use them regularly. Buy a single module to get your feet wet. Check out these implementation centers on the Web: for elementary school, Alternatives for Rebuilding Curricula at http://www.comap.com/arc; for middle school, Show-Me Center at http://showmecenter.missouri.edu

- Surf the Web. There are lots of Web sites designed to offer help and teaching ideas for teachers. Many include complete lesson plans. One caution: Just because it's on the Web doesn't mean it's good. The things you will find range widely in quality. Good sites to get you started are noted in Chapter 24.

## A Task Selection Guide

Throughout this book, in every student textbook, and in every article you read or in-service workshop you attend, you will hear and read about suggestions for activities, problems, tasks, or explorations that someone believes are effective in helping children learn some aspect of mathematics. Selecting activities or tasks is, as Lappan and Briars (1995) contend, the most significant decision affecting your students' learning. In the accompanying box is a four-step guide you can use when considering a new activity for your students.

---

### Activity Evaluation and Selection Guide

**STEP 1: How Is the Activity Done?**

Actually do the activity. Try to get "inside" the task or activity to see how it is done and what thinking might go on.

How would *children* do the activity or solve the problem? (They don't know what you do!)
- What materials are needed?
- What is written down or recorded?

**STEP 2: What Is the Purpose of the Activity?**

What *mathematical ideas* will the activity develop?
- Are the ideas concepts or procedural skills?
- Will there be connections to other related ideas?

**STEP 3: Will the Activity Accomplish Its Purpose?**

What is *problematic* about the activity? Is the problematic aspect related to the mathematics you identified in the purpose?

What *must* children reflect on or think about to complete the activity? (Don't rely on wishful thinking.)

Is it possible to complete the activity without much reflective thought? If so, can it be modified so that students will be required to think about the mathematics?

**STEP 4: What Must You Do?**

What will you need to do in the *before* portion of your lesson?
- How will you prepare students for this task?
- What will be the students' responsibilities?

What difficulties might you anticipate seeing in the *during* portion of your lesson?

What will you want to focus on in the *after* portion of your lesson?

---

To evaluate the effectiveness of a task or activity you think may be good, begin by actually doing the activity yourself, trying to think of the ways children in your class might do it. Consider the information and skills *they* will bring to the activity.

The second step has you focus on what ideas and what mathematics the activity is likely to help children develop. Beware! The author's stated objective is not always an accurate indication of the mathematics in the task.

The third step is the most important point in determining if an activity will or will not accomplish its purpose. What is problematic about the activity? What will improve the chances that the children will be mentally active, reflecting on and constructing the ideas you identified in step 2? Try to predict what students will do with the activity. Think about how students might have difficulty with the task. Difficulties are usually the best opportunities for learning, but you would like to anticipate them if possible.

The fourth step in the guide focuses your attention on implementation issues. Consider possible before, during, and after actions of a lesson built on the task that will add to its effectiveness.

Practice using this guide with activities throughout this book. Work toward thinking about tasks or activities from the view of what is likely to happen inside children's minds, not just what they are doing with their hands. Good tasks are minds-on activities, not just hands-on activities.

# TEACHING TIPS AND QUESTIONS

The ideas expressed here have been gathered from elementary and middle school teachers who have been working hard at developing a problem-solving approach in their classrooms and from the research literature on teaching via problem solving.

## Four Suggestions

1. *Predict! Don't hope.* When planning a task, it is not sufficient to think about how it will work if everything goes well. Think about your students—all of them. Predict their likely responses, and be prepared to deal with them. Things rarely go as you hope they will.

2. *Be clear in your own mind about the purpose of the task or activity.* Don't select problems simply because they are interesting. Always ask, "What *mathematics* will students be working with or develop by working on this task?" The purpose of an activity is not the same as what the students are asked to do. For example, students don't use blocks or graphing calculators to learn about blocks or graphing calculators.

3. *Recognize that there is much more to a problem than the answer.* Often the most learning occurs during the class discussion. Children's social interaction is at least as important as their independent reflection. Discussion of various paths to the solution and, most important, deciding why an answer is right or wrong are learning opportunities that should not be passed up. When children discover that they can determine the validity of answers, they learn that mathematics makes sense.

4. *Do not confuse open-ended problem solving with encouraging creativity.* Open-ended solutions are not the same as creative stories, artistic drawings, or students' supplying their own numbers for a problem. These latter approaches often detract from the mathematics of the task as students spend time coloring or writing stories. An "expensive" task is one in which students spend 50 percent or more of the time involved with context, materials, "cut and paste," and similar tasks with no mathematics being addressed.

# How Much to Tell and Not to Tell

When teaching through problem solving, one of the most perplexing dilemmas is how much to tell. On one hand, telling diminishes student reflection. Students who sense that the teacher has a preferred method or approach are extremely reluctant to use their own strategies. Nor will students develop self-confidence and problem-solving abilities by following teacher directions. On the other hand, to tell too little can sometimes leave students floundering and waste precious class time.

Researchers connected with four different constructivist programs, while noting that there will never be a simple solution to this dilemma, offer the following guidance: Teachers should feel free to share relevant information as long as the mathematics in the task remains problematic for the students (Hiebert et al., 1997). That is, "information can and should be shared as long as it does not solve the problem [and] does not take away the need for students to reflect on the situation and develop solution methods they understand" (p. 36).

They go on to suggest three types of information that teachers should provide to their students:

- *Mathematical conventions.* The social conventions of symbolism and terminology that are important in mathematics will never be developed through reflective thought. For example, representing "three and five equals eight" as "$3 + 5 = 8$" is a convention. Definitions and labels are also conventions. What is important is to offer these symbols and words only when students need them or will find them useful. As a rule of thumb, symbolism and terminology should only be introduced *after* concepts have been developed and then specifically as a means of expressing or labeling ideas. They should rarely be presented solely as things to be memorized.

- *Alternative methods.* You can, with care, suggest to students an alternative method or approach for consideration. You may also suggest more efficient recording procedures for student-invented computational methods. A teacher must be cautious in not conveying to students that their ideas are second-best. Nor should students ever be forced to adopt a teacher's suggestion over their own approach. The rule of thumb here is that the value of a procedure should always be a judgment of the students, not a dictate of the teacher. In this spirit, students can learn to appraise a teacher's suggestion without feeling obligated to use it.

- *Clarification of students' methods.* You should help students clarify or interpret their ideas and perhaps point out related ideas. A student may add 38 and 5 by noting that 38 and 2 more is 40 with 3 more making 43. This strategy can be related to the make-ten strategy used to add $8 + 3$. The selection of 40 as a midpoint in this procedure is an important place-value concept. Such clarifications reinforce the students who have the ideas. Discussion or clarification of students' ideas focuses attention on ideas you want the class to learn. Care must be taken that attention to one student's ideas does not diminish those of other students. Nor should teacher attention to one method suggest that it is the preferred approach.

## Frequently Asked Questions

The following are questions teachers have asked about this problem-based approach to teaching mathematics.

1. *How can I teach all the basic skills I have to teach?* Many teachers, especially those feeling the current pressures of state testing programs, resort to rote drill and practice to teach "basic skills." There is a tendency to believe that mastery of the basics is incompatible with a problem-solving approach. However, the evidence strongly suggests otherwise. First, drill-oriented approaches in U.S. classrooms have consistently produced poor results (Battista, 1999; Kamii & Dominick, 1998; O'Brien, 1999). Short-term gains on low-level skills may possibly result from drill, but even state testing programs require more. Both NAEP data (Kenney & Silver, 1997) and the TIMSS results (U.S. Department of Education, 1996, 1997b) suggest that drill is an inadequate answer.

   Second, research data indicate that students in constructivist programs based on a problem-solving approach do as well or nearly as well as students in traditional programs on basic skills as measured by standardized tests (Campbell, 1995; Carpenter, Franke, Jacobs, Fennema, & Empson, 1998; Hiebert & Wearne, 1996; Silver & Stein, 1996). Any deficit in skill development is more than outweighed by strength in concepts and problem solving.

   Finally, traditional skills such as basic fact mastery and computation can be effectively taught in a problem-solving approach (for example, see Campbell, Rowan, & Suarez, 1998; Huinker, 1998).

2. *Why is it OK for students to "tell" or "explain" but not for me?* There are two answers to this question. First, students will question their peers when an explanation does not make sense to them, whereas explanations from the teacher are usually accepted without scrutiny (and hence without understanding). Second, when students are responsible for explaining, the class members develop a sense of pride and confidence that *they* can figure things out and make sense of mathematics. *They* have power and ability.

3. *Where can I find the time to cover everything?* Mathematics is much more connected and integrated than the itemized objectives like those found on many state "stan-dards" lists would suggest. To deal with coverage, the first suggestion is to teach with a goal of developing the "big ideas," the main concepts in a unit or chapter. Most of the skills and ideas on your list of objectives will be addressed as you progress. If you focus separately on each item on the list, big ideas and connections, the essence of understanding, are unlikely to develop. Second, we spend far too much time reteaching because students don't retain ideas. Time spent up front to help students develop meaningful networks of ideas drastically reduces the need for reteaching, thus creating time in the long term.

4. *Is there any place for drill and practice?* Absolutely! The tragic error is to believe that drill is a method of developing ideas. Drill is only appropriate when (a) the desired concepts have been meaningfully developed, (b) flexible and useful procedures have been developed, *and* (c) speed and accuracy are needed. Watch children drilling basic facts who are counting on their fingers or using some other inefficient method. What they may be improving is their ability to count quickly. They are not learning their facts. Too many children are still counting in middle school because drill has not helped them develop efficient strategies. When you accept that drill does not produce understanding, you find there are really not many topics aside from basic fact mastery that should ever require drill.

5. *What do I do when a task bombs?* It will happen, although not as often as you think, that students just do not know what to do with a problem you pose no matter how many hints and suggestions you offer. Do not give in to the temptation to "tell 'em." Set it aside for the moment. Ask yourself why it bombed. Did the students have the ideas they needed? Was the task too advanced? Often we need to regroup and offer students a simpler related task that gets them prepared for the one that proved difficult. When you sense that a task is not going anywhere, regroup! Don't spend days just hoping that something wonderful might happen. If you listen to your students, you will know where to go next.

## TEACHING ABOUT PROBLEM SOLVING

The integration of problem solving and mathematics has obviously been a thrust of this chapter. But the standard on problem solving in *Principles and Standards* also speaks to the need to develop problem-solving *strategies and processes, metacognitive habits* of monitoring and regulating problem-solving activity, and a *positive disposition* toward mathematical problem solving. Each area suggests objectives or goals for the development of good problem solvers.

# Strategies and Processes

*Strategies* for solving problems are identifiable methods of approaching a task that are completely independent of the specific topic or subject matter. Strategy goals play a part in all phases of problem solving: understanding the problem, solving the problem, and reflecting on the answer and solution.

### Strategy and Process Goals

- *Develop problem analysis skills*—to improve students' ability to analyze an unfamiliar problem, identify wanted and needed information, ignore nonessential information, and clearly state the goal of the problem or task

- *Develop and select strategies*—to help students acquire a collection of problem-solving strategies that are useful in a variety of problem-solving settings and to select and use those strategies appropriately

- *Justify solutions*—to improve students' ability to assess the validity of answers

- *Extend or generalize problems*—to help students learn to go beyond the solution to problems; to consider results or processes applied in other situations or used to form rules or general procedures

# Metacognition

*Metacognition* refers to conscious monitoring (being aware of how and why you are doing something) and regulation (choosing to do something or deciding to make changes) of your own thought process. Good problem solvers monitor their thinking regularly and automatically. They recognize when they are stuck or do not fully understand. They make conscious decisions to switch strategies, rethink the problem, search for related content knowledge that may help, or simply start afresh (Schoenfeld, 1992).

There is evidence that metacognitive behavior can be learned (Campione, Brown, & Connell, 1989; Garofalo, 1987; Lester, 1989). Further, students who learn to monitor and regulate their own problem-solving behaviors do show improvement in problem solving.

### Metacognitive Goal

- *Monitor and regulate actions*—to help students develop the habit and ability to monitor and regulate their strategies and progress as they solve problems

# Disposition

*Disposition* refers to the attitudes and beliefs that students possess about mathematics. Students' beliefs concerning their abilities to do mathematics and to understand the nature of

mathematics have a significant effect on how they approach problems and ultimately on how well they succeed.

Students' attitudes (likes, dislikes, and preferences) about mathematics are nearly as important as their beliefs. Children who enjoy solving problems and feel satisfaction or pleasure at conquering a perplexing problem are much more likely to persevere, make second and third attempts, and even search out new problems. Negative attitudes have just the opposite effect.

### Attitudinal Goals

- *Gain confidence and belief in abilities*—to develop students' confidence in their ability to do mathematics and to confront unfamiliar tasks

- *Be willing to try and to persevere*—to improve students' willingness to attempt unfamiliar problems and to develop their perseverance in solving problems without being discouraged by initial setbacks

- *Enjoy doing mathematics*—to help students learn to enjoy and sense personal reward in the process of thinking, searching for patterns, and solving problems

# WORKING TOWARD PROBLEM-SOLVING GOALS WHILE STUDENTS LEARN

All of the goals of problem solving can and will be attained in classrooms that employ a problem-solving approach to the regular curriculum on a daily basis. A separate problem-solving strand is neither desirable nor necessary. It is important that the teacher be clearly aware of the goals of problem solving and focus attention on them regularly.

## Developing Problem-Solving Strategies

Problem-solving strategies and processes are not so much taught as *modeled*. Your task as teacher is to suggest appropriate strategies and to point them out to students in class discussions as important ways of doing mathematics.

### Strategies for Understanding the Problem

Your before actions provide a daily model of problem analysis skills. By entertaining a discussion of what is known, needed, and asked for or expected in the task, children will begin to understand that this is part of what solving problems is about. Soon you can say, "Before we get started, what should we do first?" Let students articulate good understanding strategies such as "Tell what we know" in their own language. Eventually, you can put students in groups and present problems or tasks without having to provide such explicit guidance. Give the responsibility to the students to do the things that you have modeled.

## Plan-and-Carry-Out Strategies

The after phase of your lesson will inevitably include a discussion of methods that were used. When important or especially useful strategies crop up, they should be identified, highlighted, and discussed. Labeling a strategy provides a useful means for students to talk about their methods and for you to provide hints and suggestions. Hints or suggestions about a particular strategy may be appropriate in the before or during phases of your lesson.

In the 1980s and early 1990s, it was popular to select problems for the purpose of teaching a particular strategy or heuristic. The following strategies are just a few of those that became popular during that period. These are strategies most likely to appear in lessons where mathematical content is the main objective.

- *Draw a picture, act it out, use a model.* This is the strategy of using models as "thinker toys" as described in Chapter 3. "Act it out" extends models to a real interpretation of the problem situation.

- *Look for a pattern.* Pattern searching is at the heart of many activities, especially in the algebraic reasoning strand. Patterns in number and in operations play a huge role in helping students learn about and master basic facts and continues to be a major factor into the middle and high school years.

- *Make a table or chart.* Charts of data, function tables, tables for operations, and tables involving ratios or measurements are a major form of analysis and communication within mathematics. The use of a chart is often combined with pattern searching as a means of solving problems or constructing new ideas.

- *Try a simpler form of the problem.* Here the general idea is to modify or simplify the quantities in a problem so that the resulting task is easier to understand and analyze. By solving the easier problem, the hope is to gain insights that can then be used to solve the original, more complex problem.

- *Guess and check.* This might be called "try and see what you can find out." A good way to work on a task that has you stumped is to *do something*. Make an attempt! Reflection even on a failed attempt can lead to a better idea. Another form of this strategy is to make an educated or reasoned guess at the solution and then see how the guess fits the conditions.

- *Make an organized list.* This strategy involves systematically accounting for all possible outcomes in a situation, either to find out how many possibilities there are or to be sure that all possible outcomes have been accounted for. One area where organized lists are very important is in probability.

## Looking-Back Strategies

Looking-back strategies are the things that should always be done after a solution has been found: justify the answer, consider how the problem was solved, and look for possible extensions or generalizations. These are developed as you follow the teacher actions for the after portion of a lesson. Students in the upper grades should begin to accept responsibility for doing these things themselves without your leading every discussion. Help students understand that postproblem reflection is not just something that one does in school but something that should be done whenever a problem is solved.

## Developing Metacognitive Habits

We know that it is important to help students learn to monitor and control their own progress in problem solving. A simple formula that can be employed consists of three questions: *What* are you doing? *Why* are you doing it? *How* does it help you?

Though the exact form of the three questions is not significant, the idea is to be persistent with this reflective questioning as students work through problems or explorations. You can ask the questions as you sit down to listen to any group. By joining the group, you model questioning that you want the students eventually to do on their own. In the upper grades, each group will soon be able to designate a member to be the monitor. The monitor's job is to be the reflective questioner the same way you have modeled when working with the group.

Students can also be helped in developing self-monitoring habits after their problem-solving activity is over. A brief discussion after a problem is over can focus on what types of things were done in solving the problem. "What did you do that helped you understand the problem? Did you find any numbers or information you didn't need? How did you decide what to do? Did you think about your answer after you got it? How did you decide your answer was right?"

Questioning similar to this tells students that all of these things are important. If they know you are going to be asking such questions, students will think about them ahead of time. Oral discussions with the class will be most helpful with younger children.

## Attending to Attitudinal Goals

A classroom environment built on high expectations for all students and respect for each student's thoughts will go a long way toward achieving the attitudinal goals. Here are some additional ideas to help with these goals for all students.

- *Build in success.* In the beginning of the year, plan problems that you are confident your students can solve. Avoid creating a false success that depends on your showing the way at every step and curve.

■ *Praise efforts and risk taking.* Students need to hear frequently that they are "good thinkers" capable of good, productive thought. When students volunteer ideas, listen carefully and actively to each idea, and give credit for the thinking and the risk that children take by venturing to speak out. Be careful to focus praise on the risk or effort and not the products of that effort, regardless of the quality of the ideas. Children whose weak or incorrect ideas are slighted or ignored develop a low sense of self-worth: "I'm no good. I can't think of good ideas." The same negative message comes through when praise is reserved only for the "best" ideas.

■ *Listen to all students.* Avoid ending a discussion with the first correct answer. As you make nonevaluative responses, you will find many children repeating the same idea. Were they just copying a known leader?

Perhaps, but more likely they were busy thinking and did not even hear what had already been said by those who were a bit faster. If ten hands go up, ten children may have been doing good thinking. Don't forget the suggestion made earlier to call on less secure students early in a discussion so that the most obvious ideas are not taken by the more aggressive students.

■ *Provide special successes for special children.* Not all children will develop the same problem-solving abilities, but all have abilities and can contribute. This must be something you truly believe because it is difficult to fake. One way to provide success for students who are slower or not as strong is to involve them in groups with strong and supportive children. In group settings, all children can be made to feel the success of the group work.

# REFLECTIONS ON CHAPTER 4

## Writing to Learn

1. Explain the difference between teaching that begins where the teacher is and teaching that begins where the students are.

2. Discuss each of the benefits of teaching with problems.

3. Describe what is meant by tasks or problems that can be used for teaching mathematics. Be sure to include the three important features that are required to make this method effective.

4. What is the teacher's purpose or agenda in each of the three parts of a lesson—before, during, and after?

5. Describe the kinds of actions or things that a teacher should be doing in each of the three parts of a lesson. (Note that not all of these would be done in every lesson.)

6. Select an activity from any chapter in Section 2 of this text. How can the activity be used as a problem or task for the purpose of instruction as described in this chapter? If you were using this activity in the classroom, what specifically would you do during the "before" section of the lesson?

7. The first of the four suggestions for teaching through problem solving is to predict rather than hope. Explain what this means. How should good predictions affect your lesson planning?

8. Goals for the development of good problem solving were separated under the headings of "Strategies and Processes," "Metacognition," and "Disposition." Describe what is meant by each of these types of goals.

9. For each category of problem-solving goals, describe how a teacher can help students develop these goals in the "before," "during," and "after" phases of a lesson.

## For Discussion and Exploration

1. If you were to begin teaching a class of students who had never experienced learning mathematics in a problem-solving envi-

ronment, they are likely not to know how to work at solving problems, work with a partner, or engage in a classroom discussion. How would you begin to deal with these and similar challenges so that students would develop an understanding of their role in such a classroom?

2. Find a traditional basal textbook for any grade level. Look through a chapter, and find at least one lesson that you could convert to a problem-solving lesson without drastically altering the lesson as it was written. Is there any content in the chapter, other than conventions, that you do not feel you could teach through problem solving?

3. Examine a lesson from one of the reform curricula. (See Chapter 1 for a list.) How does the general structure of the lesson you selected compare to the problem-solving approach to teaching described in this chapter?

## Recommendations for Further Reading

### Highly Recommended

Borasi, R. (1992). *Learning mathematics through inquiry.* Portsmouth, NH: Heinemann.

Borasi describes in great detail a ten-lesson "mini-course" on mathematical definitions conducted with two 16-year-old girls. It includes insights into the girls' thoughts as they change their perceptions of doing and learning mathematics as well as Borasi's unique perspectives on mathematics as a humanistic discipline and learning as meaning-making. The topics are only slightly above the middle grades level, but the discussion as a reflection of the current chapter are worth reading by all teachers of mathematics.

Burns, M. (1996). *50 problem-solving lessons: Grades 1–6.* Sausalito, CA: Math Solutions Publications.

The 50 lessons each reflect the spirit of teaching through problem solving. The content strands include number, geometry, measurement, statistics, probability, patterns and functions, algebra, and logic. Each is described in a few pages with ample examples of children's work, all in the spirit of this master teacher of mathematics. Not just a good resource but a good model.

Corwin, R. B. (1996). *Talking mathematics: Supporting children's voices.* Portsmouth, NH: Heinemann.

It is difficult to find a book that while explaining the value of discourse and the struggles that teachers encounter in developing discourse also provides practical suggestions for making it happen in the classroom. Corwin's little book comes as close as any. It is based on a project that worked with teachers exploring how to create classrooms that valued and supported mathematical talk. It is written in simple terms that inform and inspire. Included are eight related readings from other sources.

Hiebert, J. C., Carpenter, T. P., Fennema, E., Fuson, K. C., Wearne, D., Murray, H. G., Olivier, A. I., & Human, P. G. (1997). *Making sense: Teaching and learning mathematics with understanding.* Portsmouth, NH: Heinemann.

The authors of this highly readable and significant book are connected to four problem-based, long-term research projects. They make one of the best cases currently in print for developing mathematics via problematic tasks. After reviewing features of the general approach and the supporting theory, they present a vignette from each project and discuss it in detail. *Making Sense* and the companion article by the same authors in *The Educational Researcher* (see "Other Suggestions") have guided my revision of Chapter 4 in this text.

Rowan, T. E., & Bourne, B. (1994). *Thinking like mathematicians: Putting the K–4 Standards into practice.* Portsmouth, NH: Heinemann.

A must read for any teacher in the K–5 range. Rowan and Bourne describe in 132 pages the spirit of the *Standards* as carried out by teachers in urban, multiethnic Montgomery County, Maryland, schools. The schools described were part of a project funded by the National Science Foundation to explore the effectiveness of a constructivist approach (see Campbell, 1996). The book contains practical suggestions and inspiring stories from teachers and from the classroom.

## Other Suggestions

Arvold, B., Turner, P., & Cooney, T. J. (1996). Analyzing teaching and learning: The art of listening. *Mathematics Teacher, 89,* 326–329.

Baker, A., & Baker, J. (1991). *Maths in the mind: A process approach to mental strategies.* Portsmouth, NH: Heinemann.

Baker, J., & Baker, A. (1990). *Mathematics in process.* Portsmouth, NH: Heinemann.

Ball, D. L. (1996). Connecting to mathematics as part of learning to teach. In D. Schifter (Ed.), *What's happening in math class? Reconstructing professional identities* (Vol. 2, pp. 36–45). New York: Teachers College Press.

Bickmore-Brand, J. (Ed.). (1990). *Language in mathematics.* Portsmouth, NH: Heinemann.

Brown, S. L., & Walter, M. I. (1990). *The art of problem posing* (2nd ed.). Mahwah, NJ: Erlbaum.

Brownell, W. A., & Chazal, C. B. (1935). The effects of premature drill in third-grade arithmetic. *Journal of Educational Research, 29,* 17–28.

Campbell, P. F. (1996). Empowering children and teachers in the elementary mathematics classrooms of urban schools. *Urban Education, 30,* 449–475.

Chambers, D. L. (1995). Improving instruction by listening to children. *Teaching Children Mathematics, 1,* 378–380.

Dacey, L. S., & Eston, R. (1999). *Growing mathematical ideas in kindergarten.* Sausalito, CA: Math Solutions Publications.

English, L. D., Cudmore, D., & Tilley, D. (1998). Problem posing and critiquing: How it can happen in your classroom. *Mathematics Teaching in the Middle School, 4,* 124–129.

Henningsen, M., & Stein, M. K. (1997). Mathematical tasks and student cognition: Classroom-based factors that support and inhibit high-level mathematical thinking and reasoning. *Journal for Research in Mathematics Education, 28,* 524–549.

Hiebert, J. C., Carpenter, T. P., Fennema, E., Fuson, K. C., Human, P. G., Murray, H. G., Olivier, A. I., & Wearne, D. (1996). Problem solving as a basis for reform in curriculum and instruction: The case of mathematics. *Educational Researcher, 25,* 12–21.

Hiebert, J. C., & Wearne, D. (1993). Instructional tasks, classroom discourse, and students' learning in second-grade arithmetic. *American Educational Research Journal, 30,* 393–425.

Hyde, A. A., & Hyde, P. R. (1991). *Mathwise: Teaching mathematical thinking and problem solving.* Portsmouth, NH: Heinemann.

Lappan, G., & Briars, D. (1995). How should mathematics be taught? In I. M. Carl (Ed.), *Seventy-five years of progress: Prospects for school mathematics* (pp. 115–156). Reston, VA: National Council of Teachers of Mathematics.

Lubienski, S. T. (1999). Problem-centered mathematics teaching. *Mathematics Teaching in the Middle School, 5,* 250–255.

Manouchehri, A., & Enderson, M. C. (1999). Promoting mathematical discourse: Learning from classroom examples. *Mathematics Teaching in the Middle School, 4,* 216–222.

McNeal, B. (1995). Learning not to think in a textbook-based mathematics class. *Journal of Mathematical Behavior, 14,* 205–234.

Mokros, J., Russell, S. J., & Economopoulos, K. (1995). *Beyond arithmetic: Changing mathematics in the elementary classroom.* White Plains, NY: Cuisenaire–Dale Seymour.

Parker, R. E. (1993). *Mathematical power: Lessons from a classroom.* Portsmouth, NH: Heinemann.

Reys, B. J., & Long, V. M. (1995). Teacher as architect of mathematical tasks. *Teaching Children Mathematics, 1,* 296–299.

Ritchhart, R. (1999). Generative topics: Building a curriculum around big ideas. *Teaching Children Mathematics, 5,* 462–468.

Romagnano, L. (1994). *Wrestling with change: The dilemmas of teaching real mathematics.* Portsmouth, NH: Heinemann.

Rowan, T. E., & Robles, J. (1998). Using questions to help children build mathematical power. *Teaching Children Mathematics, 4,* 504–509.

Sawada, D. (1997). Mathematics as reasoning: Episodes from Japan. *Mathematics Teaching in the Middle School, 2,* 416–421.

Sawada, D. (1999). Mathematics as problem solving: A Japanese way. *Teaching Children Mathematics, 6,* 54–58.

Schifter, D., & Fosnot, C. T. (1993). *Reconstructing mathematics education: Stories of teachers meeting the challenge of reform.* New York: Teachers College Press.

Schwartz, S. L. (1996). Hidden messages in teacher talk: Praise and empowerment. *Teaching Children Mathematics, 2,* 396–401.

Schweitzer, K. (1996). The search for the perfect resource. In D. Schifter (Ed.), *What's happening in math class? Reconstructing professional identities* (Vol. 2, pp. 47–65). New York: Teachers College Press.

Silver, E. A., & Smith, M. S. (1996). Building discourse communities in mathematics classrooms: A worthwhile but challenging journey. In P. C. Elliott (Ed.), *Communication in mathematics, K–12 and beyond* (pp. 20–28). Reston, VA: National Council of Teachers of Mathematics.

Smith, J. P., III. (1996). Efficacy and teaching mathematics by telling: A challenge for reform. *Journal for Research in Mathematics Education, 27,* 387–402.

Smith, M. S., & Stein, M. K. (1998). Selecting and creating mathematical tasks: From research to practice. *Mathematics Teaching in the Middle School, 3,* 344–350.

Stein, M. K., & Smith, M. S. (1998). Mathematical tasks as a framework for reflection: From research to practice. *Mathematics Teaching in the Middle School, 3,* 268–275.

Stigler, J. W., & Hiebert, J. C. (1999). *The teaching gap: Best ideas from the world's teachers for improving education in the classroom.* New York: Free Press.

Tsuruda, G. (1994). *Putting it together: Middle school math in transition.* Portsmouth, NH: Heinemann.

Wood, T. (1999). Creating a context for argument in mathematics class. *Journal for Research in Mathematics Education, 30,* 171–191.

Wood, T., & Sellers, P. (1996). Assessment of a problem-centered mathematics program: Third grade. *Journal for Research in Mathematics Education, 27,* 337–353.

Yackel, E. (1995). Children's talk in inquiry mathematics classrooms. In P. Cobb & H. Bauersfeld (Eds.), *The emergence of mathematical meaning: Interaction in classroom cultures* (pp. 131–162). Mahwah, NJ: Erlbaum.

# Chapter 5

# Building Assessment into Instruction

*Assessment should be the servant of teaching and learning. Without information about their students' skills, understanding, and individual approaches to mathematics, teachers have nothing to guide their work.*

Mokros, Russell, and Economopoulos (1995, p. 84)

It is not surprising that one of the six principles of *Principles and Standards for School Mathematics* is assessment. Appropriate assessment practices, integral to the instructional process, will inform teaching so that student learning is improved. As teachers rethink what mathematics instruction means, they must also rethink the process of assessment. Chapter-end tests and reliance on formal testing programs are simply inadequate in a truly student-centered, problem-oriented classroom. The challenge for teachers in this first decade of the 21st century is to develop and rely on quality assessment strategies and not be overwhelmed by the pressures of testing from outside the classroom.1

## THE ASSESSMENT STANDARDS

In 1995, NCTM's *Assessment Standards for School Mathematics* called for a shift away from "assessing only students' knowledge of specific facts and isolated skills" and toward "assessing students' full mathematical power" (p. 83). Traditional testing has focused on what students *do not know* (how many wrong answers). The general spirit of the *Assessment Standards* is to find out what students *do know*. The document contains six standards for assessment and details four purposes that assessment practices should serve.

## What Is Assessment?

The term *assessment* is defined in the *Assessment Standards* as "the process of gathering evidence about a student's knowl-

edge of, ability to use, and disposition toward mathematics and of making inferences from that evidence for a variety of purposes" (p. 3). It is important to note that assessment is not at all the same as testing, measurement, or evaluation of students. These latter terms include the elements of value or worth. Assessment data are certainly used in evaluation of both students and programs. However, assessment focuses on data collection. There are multiple ways to collect and use these data. Only one of the four uses of data described in the *Assessment Standards* is related to assigning evaluative grades.

As illustrated in Figure 5.1, assessment should be seen as an ongoing but very deliberate process. Assessments must be planned and then data gathered in the classroom. The evidence is then interpreted and is used to design instruction and inform students. This leads to planning the next assessment, and the cycle continues.

**Figure 5.1  Assessment involves four stages that usually operate in a cycle.**

*Source:* Reprinted with permission from *Principles and Standards for School Mathematics.* Copyright ©2000 by the National Council of Teachers of Mathematics. All rights reserved.

# Six Assessment Standards

The six assessment standards are statements against which assessment practices can be judged. They are not prescriptions for how to create assessments. The classroom teacher should periodically reflect on his or her assessment methods using the standards as a benchmark.

## 1. The Mathematics Standard

> *Assessment should reflect the mathematics that all students need to know and be able to do. (NCTM, 1995, p. 11)*

*Principles and Standards* provides teachers with a broad perspective of the five content strands in the curriculum. Further, there are the five process standards that reflect students' mathematical power. Assessment practices should reflect these ten standards. In most school districts, state or local standards will provide a finer description of mathematical content. When the pressures of testing accompany these local standards, the danger is to focus on tests and low-level skills rather than the broader view of doing mathematics. This does not, however, exclude appropriate attention to computational skills and traditional basics.

## 2. The Learning Standard

> *Assessment should enhance mathematics learning. (NCTM, 1995, p. 13)*

The Learning standard suggests that the main purpose of assessment is to improve performance, not merely to audit it. Classroom assessment practices should communicate to students *during* the learning process, guiding students to improve their learning and know what is valued.

In like manner, assessment should guide teachers in their design of instruction by providing a constant stream of information by which decisions can be made during a unit rather than when instruction is finished.

For assessment to support and enhance learning, it must be viewed and designed as an integral part of instruction, not as an addendum or an interruption.

## 3. The Equity Standard

> *Assessment should promote equity. (NCTM, 1995, p. 15)*

Equitable assessment respects the unique qualities, experiences, and expertise of each student. Equity in assessment sets high mathematical standards for all students, including those with special needs. This standard is reflected in the equity principle of *Principles and Standards*, which says that we must hold high expectations for all students while recognizing that students need different forms of instructional support. Equity aims directly at finding out what all students *do* know rather than establishing a narrow hurdle that too often screens students from further mathematics or suggests only that they have failed to achieve.

## 4. The Openness Standard

> *Assessment should be an open process. (NCTM, 1995, p. 17)*

Students need to know what is expected of them and how they can demonstrate what they have learned. The criteria for quality performance must also be clear to students. Reasoning, communication, and problem solving must be integrated with content knowledge. Performance should be viewed in a holistic manner, based on much more than correct answers. Students need to be involved in setting the criteria and even using the criteria to assess their own performance. Openness also means that parents and other teachers are aware of the methods and criteria that are valued in the classroom.

## 5. The Inferences Standard

> *Assessment should promote valid inferences about mathematics learning. (NCTM, 1995, p. 19)*

The question that teachers in a developmental approach to instruction must constantly ask is, "What does this performance tell me about this student's understanding or reasoning?" Assessments are based on students' doing mathematics—communicating, reasoning, justifying results, testing hypotheses, looking for patterns. An examination of the number of correct exercises provides only a shallow glimpse into a student's understanding. No objectively scored test can determine the workings of children's thought processes or individual understandings.

This standard requires that teachers reflect seriously and honestly on what students are revealing about what they know. The use of multiple assessment techniques is one way that teachers can improve the validity of their inferences. Lessons developed around problems using the three-part format described in Chapter 4 will provide ample data for valid assessments.

## 6. The Coherence Standard

> *Assessment should be a coherent process. (NCTM, 1995, p. 21)*

This assessment cycle (Figure 5.1) must be in complete accord with the objectives of instruction—what you want students to learn—as well as the methods of instruction. There must be a balance of assessment methods that reflect conceptual and procedural understanding as well as mathematical processes. Traditional paper-and-pencil tests alone will not be sufficient. The Coherence standard also suggests an alignment of assessment methods with the methods of instruction. That is, students should be evaluated using the same methods, materials, and approaches with which they learned.

# Purposes of Assessment

Even a cursory glance at the six assessment standards suggests a complete integration of assessment and instruction. The *Assessment Standards* outlines four specific purposes of

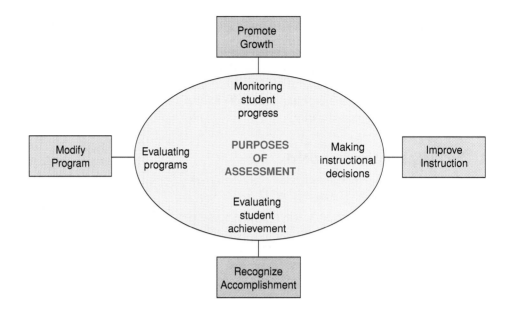

**Figure 5.2** **Four purposes of assessment and their results.**
*Source:* Adapted from NCTM (1995, p. 25). Used with permission.

assessment as depicted in Figure 5.2. With each purpose, the rectangle to the outside indicates a corresponding result.

## Monitoring Student Progress

As a teacher, you establish high goals for students. Assessment should provide both teacher and students with ongoing feedback concerning progress toward those goals. Assessment should inform each individual student and the teacher about growth toward mathematical power and problem-solving ability, not just mastery of procedural skills. Furthermore, the feedback should be received during instruction, not at the end of the unit, when it is perhaps too late to promote student learning.

## Making Instructional Decisions

Teachers planning tasks each day to develop student understanding must have daily information about how students are thinking and what ideas they are using and developing. When teaching with problems and tasks, this information is readily available, especially in the during and after stages of a lesson. Daily problem solving and discussion provide a much richer and more useful array of data than can ever be gathered from a chapter test. It comes at a time when you can formulate plans to help students develop ideas, rather than remediate after the fact. Thus daily assessment data are essential to the effective design of instruction.

## Evaluating Student Achievement

Assessment differs from evaluation. *Assessment* is the collection of data; *evaluation* is "the process of determining the worth of, or assigning a value to, something on the basis of careful examination and judgment" (NCTM, 1995, p. 3). Evaluation involves a teacher's judgment about a student's demonstrated understanding. It may include test data but should take into account a wide variety of sources and types

of information gathered during the course of instruction. Most important, evaluation should reflect performance criteria about what students know and understand; it should not be used to compare one student with another.

Traditional evaluation was nearly synonymous with the end-of-unit test. There was a clear line between instruction and evaluation. The *Assessment Standards* view of appropriate assessment, reiterated in *Principles and Standards,* is to eradicate that line by gathering assessment data continuously in informal ways and frequently in more structured ways and by including these data in evaluation. (A more complete discussion of grading can be found near the end of this chapter.)

## Evaluating Programs

Assessment data should be used as one significant component in answering the question "How well did this program work to achieve my goals?" In this context, *program* refers to any organized unit of study and need not be restricted to school or district decisions such as which textbook should be adopted. For the classroom teacher, program includes such things as self-designed units of instruction, a chapter from a resource book or text, or even a particular strategy for cooperative groups or learning centers. In evaluation of these as well as larger curricular programs, students' knowledge, understanding, processes, and disposition—based on multiple sources of information—should all be taken into account.

# WHAT SHOULD BE ASSESSED?

A quality assessment program will not only include the specific concepts and skills of your current unit but will also attend to the processes of doing mathematics. You can and should develop a general framework within which you can assess information concerning all content and processes.

# Concepts and Procedures

Recall that understanding occurs on a continuum determined by the number and quality of connections that an individual has made. A good assessment strategy will provide opportunity for students to demonstrate how they themselves understand the concepts under discussion. The traditional test generally targets only one way to know an idea, that determined by the test designer. If you collect information from students as they complete an activity, while it is being discussed, as results are justified—in short, while students are doing mathematics—you will gain information that provides insight into the nature of the students' understanding of that idea.

Procedural knowledge, including skill proficiency, should be included, although it should not be considered as more important than conceptual understanding. If your state objectives emphasize skills, be careful to see that the conceptual foundations are there as well. If a student can compute with fractions yet has no idea of why he needs a common denominator for addition but not for multiplication, then the rules that have been "mastered" are poorly connected to meaning. This would indicate only the tenuous presence of a skill. Whereas a routine skill such as mastering addition with regrouping can easily be checked with a traditional test, the desired conceptual connections require assessment of a different nature.

# Mathematical Processes

Guidelines for defining the specifics of mathematical power can be found in the five process standards of *Principles and Standards*. Now, it is not reasonable to try to assess all of these processes, and certainly not every day. For each grade band, *Principles and Standards* describes what the process standards might look like at that level. Use these descriptions to craft statements about doing mathematics that your students can understand. Here are a few examples, but you should write your own or use those provided by your school system.

### Problem Solving

- Works at understanding a problem before beginning work.
- Uses drawings, graphs, and physical models to help solve problems.
- Has and uses appropriate strategies for solving problems.
- Assesses the validity of answers.

### Reasoning

- Justifies solution methods and results.
- Makes conjectures based on reasoning.
- Observes and uses patterns in mathematics.

### Communication

- Explains ideas in writing.
- Communicates ideas clearly in class discussions.

These statements should be discussed with your students to help clarify them and to let students know that these are values to you. Periodically, use the statements to rate students' mathematical processes based on their individual work, group work, and participation in class discussions. If you use portfolios, work developed and collected over time, process assessment should almost certainly be considered. Processes must also be used in your grading or evaluation scheme, or students will not take them seriously.

# Disposition

You will recall that attitudinal goals were a separate component of the objectives of problem solving. It is important to make occasional efforts to collect data on students' confidence and beliefs in their own mathematical abilities as well as their likes and dislikes about mathematics. This information is most easily obtained with self-reported checklists and journal writing. Information on perseverance and willingness to attempt problems is available to you every day in a problem-solving approach. These too are data that you must make an effort to collect, perhaps with anecdotal notes or a checklist attached to an observation scheme.

# COMBINING INSTRUCTION AND ASSESSMENT

Real change in the classroom cannot be achieved without simultaneously changing and integrating both instruction and assessment. If your instruction becomes more problem-based but your assessment methods focus on recall and closed-response items, the instruction is doomed to failure. Students quickly learn that what is valued is getting answers. Older students tune out or even refuse to participate in the tasks provided. "Just show us how to get the answer." Assessment strategies must reflect our values in exactly the same manner as our instruction.

The reverse situation—to engage in "traditional," teacher-directed instruction with open-ended, problem-solving tasks for assessment—asks children to demonstrate mathematical power without ever having experienced it. Students who are accustomed to being told how to do everything in the mathematics classroom, when facing novel, problem-solving tasks, will understandably complain, "You've never told us how to do this!" Teachers who have tried various "alternative assessments" without significantly altering their instruction find these assessments difficult or impossible for their students, and all involved become frustrated.

Quality instruction and appropriate assessment need not be different activities. Assessment and instruction should become nearly indistinguishable. We can assess as we provide opportunities for learning. The search for quality assessment tasks is simultaneously a search for quality learning tasks. They are one and the same!

## Performance Tasks

Recall from Chapter 4 that a problem was any task or activity for which the students have no prescribed or memorized rules or specific correct solution method. The same definition should be used for performance tasks. The assessment literature often refers to "performance assessment tasks" or "alternative assessments," but those expressions imply tasks that are in some way different from those used in instruction. They are not different.

Problems for instruction also have three features that should be revisited in the context of assessment.

First, a problem must *begin where the students are*. Good tasks should permit every student in the class, regardless of mathematical prowess, to demonstrate some knowledge, skill, or understanding. Lower-ability students should be encouraged to use the ideas they do possess to work on a problem even if these are not the same skills or strategies used by others in the room. A forgotten computational procedure should not preclude a student from working on a performance task. At the same time that we consider accessibility, we should strive to select or design tasks that are sufficiently rich to challenge the thinking and reasoning of all students.

Second, the *problematic or engaging aspect of the problem must be due to the mathematics that the students are to learn*. Too often what has been promoted as "alternative assessments" focus on the real-world or authentic contexts of the problems. We must remember that we are most likely assessing students' understanding of mathematics. So although contextual situations are often nice, how a student completes a task and justifies the solution should inform us about his or her understanding. That agenda should not be overshadowed because of difficulties that may arise from context or because students spent more time on the nonmathematical aspects of the task than on the mathematical ideas.

Third, problems must *require justifications and explanations for answers and methods*. The justifications, even those given orally, will almost certainly provide more information than the answers alone. Perhaps no better method exists for getting at student understanding.

The unfortunate separation of learning and assessment tasks is partly due to our lengthy history of equating assessment with summative, evaluative testing. There may be times when you do decide to use a task as a summative evaluation and therefore choose not to interact with students as they are working. In these instances, you will have already provided students with an opportunity to access and develop the content that is essential to the task. The task should not be identical to a previous learning experience; if it were, the students would simply be following an earlier example, not doing mathematics. Using a task as a summative assessment simply changes the purpose and intent of the task. Taken out of this evaluative context, the task should still look exactly like a learning task.

## Selecting Tasks for Assessment

Anne is a third-grade teacher. During an academic year, she was one of a group of teachers learning to use appropriate assessment techniques in mathematics. Anne used the following task with her class arranged in groups of three or four working together.

---

**Find ways to add consecutive numbers in order to reach sums between 1 and 15. For example, $3 + 4 + 5 = 12$, and 3, 4, and 5 are consecutive numbers.**

---

Anne reports:

I wanted to assess if my students were able to both estimate and solve math facts mentally. In addition, I wanted to assess how far my students had come in cooperative learning. I developed a checklist for myself to use when making my observations. Some items on the list included "able to recall basic facts," "able to add mentally," "adding by counting up on fingers," "interacted with peers positively," and "participating with the group." The task was long enough and engaging enough that I was able to spend time with each group listening to the interaction and questioning the members about their thinking.

By thinking of her objective ahead of time, Anne was able to listen actively to her students and know what she was looking for. Anne stated her objectives in very procedural language: "able to recall," "able to add mentally." Alternatively, she might have focused on how children connect facts. For example, do children see that $4 + 5$, $5 + 6$, and $6 + 7$ are odd sums or are each 2 apart? Do those who are still counting use one fact, say, $4 + 5$, to arrive at $3 + 4 + 5$? By focusing on behaviors, Anne forgot to plan a discussion that would allow her to see the ideas students may have constructed. She did use this opportunity to assess some group skills.

When selecting a task for assessment purposes, it is most important to be very clear about what you want to assess. In this example, there were lots of things that Anne could have focused on. The essential content of this task was addition and number relationships. Yet the focus could be on either procedural or conceptual knowledge and may or may not include attention to problem solving or other skills. Anne also had a written report from each group that she could take home and reflect on for communication skills. Had she entertained a class discussion after the task, she would have opened the door for whatever thoughts students may have had. There would be an opportunity to wonder how many sums were possible for different numbers. "Do all numbers have consecutive sums? How do we know? What else do you notice?"

# Examples of Problems for Assessment

Each of the following tasks provides ample opportunity for students to learn. At the same time, it provides data for the teacher to use in assessment. Notice that these are not elaborate tasks and yet along with a discussion, each could engage students for most of a period. As you read each task, think about the following questions to decide what specific information might be assessed:

- What is the essential conceptual content in the task?
- What problem-solving processes might be observed?
- What opportunity might there be to observe communication skills?
- What about reasoning (if-then thinking)?
- Are there opportunities for students to connect the content with other content either in or outside of mathematics?
- Is the task accessible to a range of students in some way?

### SHARES (GRADES K–3)

**Leila has 6 gumdrops, Darlene has 2, and Melissa has 4. They want to share them equally. How will they do it? Draw a picture to help explain your answer.**

At second or third grade, the numbers in Shares would probably be larger. What would happen if the problem were about cookies and the total number of cookies were 14?

### SUBTRACTION (GRADES 1–2)

**If you did not know the answer to 12 − 7, what are some ways you could find the answer?**

### HOW MUCH? (GRADES 1–2)

**Gustavo has saved $15 to buy a game that he wants. The game costs $23. How much money does Gustavo still need?**

These two problems are similar in that they involve subtraction and allow the teacher to see what strategies a student might use. In the second problem, the context increases the chances that students will use an "add-on" approach (15 and how much more to make 23?). Without context, you get a better chance to see what strategies students are using most regularly.

### BROKEN KEYS (GRADES 2–4)

**If the ⑤ key on your calculator were broken, how could you do this problem: 458 + 548 + 354? Is there more than one way? Which way do you like the best? Why?**

Broken Keys is a good example of a task with many solutions. As students are working, you will be able to assess how easily students arrive at different approaches.

### THE WHOLE SET (GRADES 3–5)

**Mary counted 15 cupcakes left from the whole batch that Mother made for the picnic. "We've already eaten two-fifths of these," she noted. How many cupcakes did Mother bake?**

This last problem could easily have been posed without any context. What is the value of context in tasks such as these?

### TOP AND BOTTOM (GRADES 4–6)

**In the fraction $\frac{3}{4}$, how would you explain the meaning of the top number to a third grader? Do the same for the bottom number. Use two different ways to explain each.**

A great source of problems is to have students explain an idea that has been developed in class. The explanations can be addressed to another grade level, as in Top and Bottom, or to a fictional peer who missed yesterday's lesson. Here the task tells you quite directly how effective the previous lesson was.

In the following task, students are asked to judge the performance of other students. Analysis of student performance is another good way to create tasks.

### DECIMALS (GRADES 4–6)

**Alan tried to make a decimal number as close to 50 as he could using the digits 1, 4, 5, and 9. He arranged them in this order: 51.49. Jerry thinks he can arrange the same digits to get a number that is even closer to 50. Do you agree or disagree? Explain.**

### MENTAL MATH (GRADES 4–8)

**Explain two different ways to multiply 4 × 276 in your head. Which way is easier to use? Would you use a different way to multiply 5 × 98? Explain why you would use the same or different methods.**

Mental computation tasks should be done frequently at all grade levels beginning around grade 2. Other students pick up the methods that students share. The explanations also offer a lot of information about students' concepts and the types of strategies that they have already acquired. This information can be recorded with a variety of simple methods over time.

---

### TWO TRIANGLES (GRADES 4–8)

**Tell everything you can about these two triangles.**

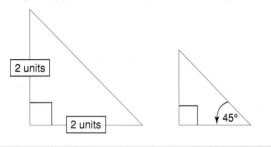

---

This task is a good example of a very open-ended assessment. Consider how much more valuable this task is than asking for the angle measure in the left-hand triangle.

---

### ALGEBRA: GRAPHING (GRADES 7–8)

**Does the graph of $y = x^2$ ever intersect the graph of $y = x^2 + 2$? What are some ways that you could test your idea?**

---

Even with a graphing calculator, you cannot prove that these two graphs will not intersect. The task requires reasoning and an understanding of how graphs are related to equations.

## More Thoughts About Assessment Tasks

In some instances, the real value of the task or what can be learned about students will come only in the discussion that follows. For others, the information will be in the written report. In many of Marilyn Burns's books, you will see the phrase "We think the answer is . . . We think this because . . ." Students must develop the habit of adding and listening to justifications. If explanations are not a regular practice in your room, do not expect students to offer good explanations in assessments, either written or oral.

Much of the assessment literature has placed a significant value on situational problems or realistic problems and open-ended problems. There is no doubt that such problems have an important place in the mathematics classroom. But neither open-endedness nor real-world contexts are necessary for students to be meaningfully engaged in constructing mathematics. Nor are these features necessary for quality assessment. An open-ended, very realistic problem can be interesting and engaging and be mathematically trivial. For example, tasks involving spending money from a fast-food menu or a catalog are rarely more than glorified addition

exercises. *Keep your focus on the mathematics.* The inclusion of real connections and open-ended tasks is possible without sacrificing the mathematics.

Many activities have no written component and no "answer" or result. For example, students may be playing a game where dice or dominoes are being used. A teacher who sits in on the game will see great differences in how children use numbers. Some will count every dot on the card or domino. Others will use a counting-on strategy. Some will recognize certain patterns without counting. Others may be unsure if 13 beats 11. This information significantly differentiates students relative to their understanding of number concepts. Data gathered from listening to a pair of children work on a simple activity or an extended project provide significantly greater insight into students' thinking than almost any written test we could devise. Data from student conversations and observations of student behavior can be recorded and used for the same purposes that written data can, including evaluation and grading. Especially in the case of grading, it is important to keep dated written notes that can be referred to later.

If you have been helping children develop a computational procedure or a formula or some other routine procedure, you may be tempted to restrict assessment to using the procedure to get answers. A conceptual understanding must also be assessed. This can be done by asking for students to explain a particular step (*What does this little "1" stand for up on the top of the tens column?*) or to find and correct an error, with an appropriate explanation, that is made by a fictional student.

# RUBRICS AND PERFORMANCE INDICATORS

A *rubric* is a framework that can be designed or adapted by the teacher for a particular group of students or a particular mathematical task (Kulm, 1994). A rubric consists of a scale of three to six points that is used as a rating of performance rather than a count of how many items are correct or incorrect. The rating is applied by examining total performance on a task as opposed to counting the number of items correct.

Note that a rubric is a scale to judge performance on a single task, not a series of exercises.

## Simple Rubrics

The simplest form of a rubric consists of three or four points and is a good type of scale to use on a regular basis. The following simple four-point rubric was developed by the New Standards Project and is used in the Pittsburgh Public School System:

4   Excellent: Full Accomplishment

3   Proficient: Substantial Accomplishment

2   Marginal: Partial Accomplishment

1   Unsatisfactory: Little Accomplishment

This simple rubric allows a teacher to rate performances using a double-sort technique as illustrated in Figure 5.3. The broad categories of the first sort are relatively easy to discern. The scale then allows you to separate each category into two levels as shown. Some teachers use a 4+ rating to note truly exceptional performance. A rating of 0 is given for no response or effort or for responses that are completely off task.

The advantage of the four-point scale is the relatively easy double sort that can be made. Others prefer a three-point rubric such as the following example:

3    Above and beyond—uses exemplary methods, shows creativity, goes beyond the requirements of the problem

2    On target—completes the task with no more than minor errors, uses expected approaches

1    Not there yet—makes significant errors or omissions, uses inappropriate approaches

These relatively simple scales are *general* rubrics. They label general categories of performance but do not define the specific criteria for a particular task. For any given task or process, it is usually helpful to create performance indicators for each level.

## Performance Indicators

*Performance indicators* are task-specific statements that describe what performance looks like at each level of the rubric and in so doing establish criteria for acceptable performance (Ann Arbor Public Schools, 1993).

A rubric and its performance indicators should focus you and your students on your goals and away from the self-limiting question "How many can you miss and still get an A?" Like athletes who continually strive for better performances rather than "good enough," students should always see the possibility to excel. When you take into account the total performance (processes, answers, justifications, extension, and so on), it is always possible to "go beyond."

Typically rubrics are used for written work where you can consider thoughtfully each student's performance. The rubric is just as valuable a tool for observations and for judgment of oral performance by students and can make your recording schemes more valuable and easier to use.

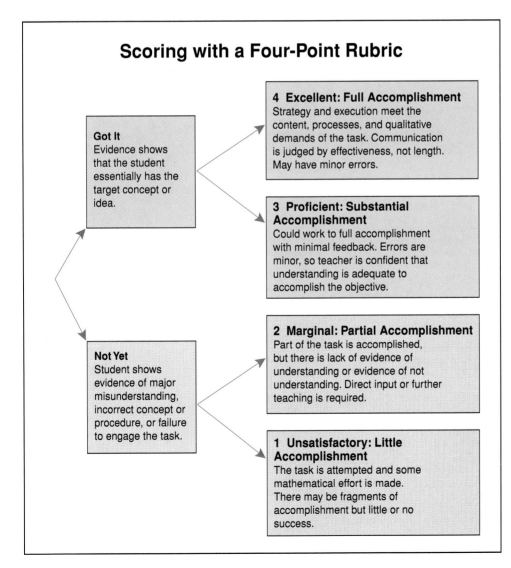

## Scoring with a Four-Point Rubric

**Got It**
Evidence shows that the student essentially has the target concept or idea.

**Not Yet**
Student shows evidence of major misunderstanding, incorrect concept or procedure, or failure to engage the task.

**4  Excellent: Full Accomplishment**
Strategy and execution meet the content, processes, and qualitative demands of the task. Communication is judged by effectiveness, not length. May have minor errors.

**3  Proficient: Substantial Accomplishment**
Could work to full accomplishment with minimal feedback. Errors are minor, so teacher is confident that understanding is adequate to accomplish the objective.

**2  Marginal: Partial Accomplishment**
Part of the task is accomplished, but there is lack of evidence of understanding or evidence of not understanding. Direct input or further teaching is required.

**1  Unsatisfactory: Little Accomplishment**
The task is attempted and some mathematical effort is made. There may be fragments of accomplishment but little or no success.

**Figure 5.3** With a four-point rubric, performances are first sorted into two categories. Each performance is then considered again and assigned to a point on the scale.

## Deciding on Performance Indicators

What performance at different levels of your rubric will or should look like may be difficult to predict. Much depends on your experience with children at that grade level, your past experiences with students working on the same task, and your insights about the task itself and the ideas that it embodies or that children may use as they work on it.

If possible, it is good to write out indicators of "proficient" or "on target" performances before you use the task in class. This is an excellent self-check to be sure that the task is likely to accomplish the purpose you selected it for in the first place. Think about your process goals as well as your content goals. Think about how children are likely to approach the activity. Remember, *predict, don't hope.* Consider different materials that might be used, different ways to describe the results, and how the product can be explained or the answer justified.

Remember that rubrics are applied to performance on a single task, although the task may have multiple components. If you find yourself writing performance indicators in terms of number of correct responses, you are most likely looking at practice exercises and not tasks for which a rubric is appropriate.

If you are clear in your mind what performance looks like that meets your goals, then you will easily recognize performance that goes beyond and performance that is marginal.

Unexpected methods and solutions happen. Don't box students into demonstrating their understanding only as you thought or hoped they would when there is evidence that they are accomplishing your objectives in different ways.

Even if you have not written a performance indicator ahead of time, the double-sorting strategy described earlier (two categories, each then separated into two piles) is a useful approach

## Table 5.1
### Kid-Friendly Math Rubric: Example of a Six-Point Analytic Rubric

| | Understanding | Support for Thinking | Communication |
|---|---|---|---|
| **6**<br>Exceptional, awesome, goes beyond | • Finds *all* important parts of problem<br>• Has *full* understanding of math needed<br>• Uses unusual, creative thinking | • Finds more than one way to solve problem<br>• Uses many ways to show thinking like diagrams, charts, graphs, etc.<br>• Experiments, designs, analyzes<br>• Does *more* than problem asks | • Writes a clear, convincing, thoughtful answer<br>• Writes to an audience<br>• Diagrams very clear |
| **5**<br>Very good, clear, strong | • Finds *most* of the important parts of problem<br>• Has good understanding of math needed | • Finds one or more ways to solve problem<br>• Uses several ways to show thinking like diagrams, charts, graphs, etc.<br>• May experiment, design, analyze<br>• May compare problem to another, predict | • Writes clearly<br>• Makes sense<br>• Writes to an audience<br>• Diagrams clear |
| **4**<br>Pretty good, gets the job done | • Finds *most* of the important parts of problem—some less important are missing<br>• Understands *most* of math needed | • Uses one way to solve problem<br>• Some ways to show thinking may be missing<br>• May experiment, design, or analyze | • Addresses all parts of the problem<br>• Writes to an audience<br>• Writing may be unclear |
| **3**<br>OK, good try, unclear | • Finds a *few* of the important parts of problem<br>• Understands *some* of math needed<br>• Thinking gets mixed up<br>• Might miss the big idea | • May or may not solve the problem<br>• Mathematical thinking is unclear or limited<br>• Chooses wrong ways to solve problem | • Has trouble writing ideas<br>• May or may not write to an audience<br>• Diagrams or charts not clear |
| **2**<br>Incomplete, confusing | • Has little understanding of problem<br>• Finds less important parts of problem<br>• Understands bits and pieces of math needed | • Doesn't explain thinking<br>• Uses ways to solve problem which don't fit the problem | • Writes in a confusing way<br>• May or may not write to an audience |
| **1**<br>May or may not make an effort, no understanding | • Doesn't understand problem | • Answer difficult to understand<br>• Makes little or no attempt to explain results | • Writes in a way that is very hard to understand |

*Source:* From "Kid Friendly Math Rubric," Conejo Valley School District, CA, 1994. Reprinted with permission.

to help you identify on-target performance. There will almost always be differences across your class, although you should make no attempt to have equal piles, and some categories may even have no students in them. Always relate assessments to your mathematical goals for the activity. Avoid comparisons of one student with another, and don't be fooled by creative or elaborate reports that miss the mathematical ideas.

When you have finished your sorting process for a task you plan to use again, write a description of the on-target behavior. You may find it useful to make a copy of performances representative of different points on your rubric. File the descriptions and examples with the activity for future use.

## Student Involvement with Rubrics

When mathematics consisted primarily of arithmetic, students knew that correct computation was the goal—the only goal. Today, not only is the curriculum significantly broader than computation, but the focus is on *doing mathematics* and all that that entails. Students need information about what doing good mathematics looks like, and they need to know what your expectations are for acceptable and exceptional performance. This is part of the Openness standard for assessment.

In the beginning of the year, discuss your general rubric with the class. Post it prominently. Many teachers use the same rubric for all subjects; others prefer to use a special rubric for mathematics. In your discussion, let students know that as they do activities and solve problems in class, you will look at their work and listen to their explanations and provide them with feedback in terms of the rubric, rather than as a letter grade or a percentage.

When students start to understand what the rubric really means, begin to discuss performance on tasks in terms of the general rubric. You might have students rate their own work according to the general rubric and explain their reasons for the rating. Older students can do this in written form, and you can respond in writing. For all students, you can have class discussions about a task that has been done and what might constitute good and exceptional performance.

## More Examples of Rubrics

Simple rubrics with three or four levels may be the easiest to use in most classroom situations. Just as some teachers like the simplicity of these scales, others find that a more detailed rubric with as many as six points suits their needs better. Regardless of the scale you select, let your needs dictate what you use.

The four-point scale in Figure 5.3 (p. 69) is an example of a *holistic scale,* a single scale used to rate a complete task as a whole while possibly covering many subtopics and agendas. One rating on the scale summarizes the full performance. A single grade on a report card is also a holistic rating.

However, suppose that you want to provide feedback to students concerning one or more particular aspects of their work. You may be interested in separating out one or more of the following: procedural skill, conceptual understanding, problem-solving processes, communication skills, or reasoning. It is never reasonable to rate any given task for every one of these features, but you may want to focus on two or three. It is possible to add several dimensions to your scale or rubric. A scale that rates a performance separately on each of two or more traits is known as an *analytic scale.* Table 5.1 is a six-point analytic scale that examines understanding, support for thinking, and communication. A valuable feature of this scale is the language that is intended to communicate to students in words they can understand.

The analytic scale in Figure 5.4 has become popular as a means of focusing on different aspects of students' problem-solving skills. Generally, this scale is used to rate written performance on a problem-solving task. An interesting feature of the scale is the differential weighting used. Using this scale, a score of 3, 3, 6 would mean something quite different from a score of 6, 6, 0, although both scores total 12 points. The point total becomes a holistic rating based on an analytic process.

---

### Analytic Scoring Scale

**Understanding the Problem**
0 – Complete misunderstanding of the problem
3 – Part of the problem misunderstood or misinterpreted
6 – Complete understanding of the problem

**Planning a Solution**
0 – No attempt, or totally inappropriate plan
3 – Partially correct plan based on correct interpretation of part of the problem
6 – Plan could lead to a correct solution if implemented properly

**Getting an Answer**
0 – No answer, or wrong answer based on an inappropriate plan
1 – Copying error, computational error, or partial answer for a problem with multiple answers
2 – Incorrect answer although this answer follows logically from an incorrect plan
3 – Correct answer and correct label for the answer

**Figure 5.4** **An analytic scale for problem solving with differential weightings.**

*Source:* Adapted from *How to Evaluate Progress in Problem Solving,* by R. I. Charles, F. K. Lester Jr., & P. O'Daffer, 1987, Reston, VA: National Council of Teachers of Mathematics, as presented in "Cooperative Problem Solving: But What About Grades?" by D. L. Kroll, J. O. Masingila, & S. T. Mau, 1992, *Arithmetic Teacher, 39*(6), p. 18. Reprinted by permission of the National Council of Teachers of Mathematics.

# USING OBSERVATION IN ASSESSMENT

All teachers learn useful bits of information about their students every day. When the three-part lesson format suggested in Chapter 4 is used, the flow of data increases dramatically, especially in the *during* and *after* portions of lessons. If you have a systematic plan for gathering this information while observing and listening to students, at least two very valuable things occur. First, you will likely gather a lot more information. Information that may have gone unnoticed is suddenly visible and important. Second, observation data gathered systematically can be added to other data and used in planning lessons, providing feedback to students, conducting parent conferences, and determining grades.

Depending on what information you may be trying to gather, a single observation scheme may require several days to two weeks before it has been observed. Long-term goals can be observed over a full marking period. Shorter periods of observation will focus on a particular cluster of concepts or skills. Over longer periods, you can note growth in various aspects of mathematical power, such as particular problem-solving skills or communication skills. To use observation effectively as a means of gathering assessment data from performance tasks, you should take seriously the following maxim: *Do not attempt to observe every student in a single class period.*

No single observation recording format will serve all purposes. Further, formats and methods of gathering observation data are going to be influenced by your individual teaching style and habits. Observation methods also vary with the purposes for which they are used.

## Anecdotal Notes

A simple system for recording observations is to write short notes either during or immediately after a lesson in a brief narrative style. One possibility is to have a card for each student. Some teachers keep the cards on a clipboard with each taped at the top edge (see Figure 5.5). Each card can then be accessed quickly. Another option is to select cards for about five students a day, focusing your observations on those five. On another day, different students are selected. The students selected may be members of one or two cooperative groups. An alternative to cards is the use of large peel-off file labels, possibly preprinted with student names on your computer. The label notes are then moved to a more permanent notebook page for each student.

## An Observation Rubric

Another possibility is to use your three- or four-point general rubric on a reusable form as in Figure 5.6. Include space for content-specific descriptors and another space to jot down names of students. A quick note or comment may be amended to a name when appropriate. This method is especially useful for planning purposes.

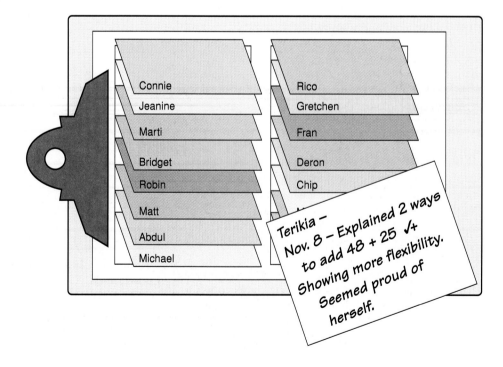

**Figure 5.5** Cards for observation notes can be taped to a clipboard or folder for quick access.

**Figure 5.6** **Record names in a rubric during an activity or for a single topic over several days.**

## Checklists or Forms for Individuals

To cut down on writing and to help focus your attention, a small form with several specific processes or content areas of interest can be devised and duplicated for each student (see Figure 5.7). Some teachers have found methods of printing these on their computer, perhaps on sticky labels. Once a computer format is worked out, it is easy to change the items on the checklist without retyping all the student names. Regardless of the checklist form, a place for comments should be included.

## Checklists for Full Classes

Another format involves listing all students in a class on a single page or not more than three pages (see Figure 5.8 on p. 74). Across the top of the page are specific things to look for. Pluses and minuses, checks, or codes corresponding to your general rubric can be entered in the grid. A space left for comments is useful. A full-class checklist is more likely to be used for long-term objectives. Topics that might be appropriate for this format include problem-solving processes, communication skills, and such skills as basic facts or estimation. Dating entries or noting specific activities observed is also helpful.

# JOURNALS AND WRITING

Having students write in mathematics is a natural and very important way to help them reflect on what they are learning.

**Figure 5.7** **A focused checklist and rubric can be printed for each student with the help of a computer.**

| NAME: _Sharon V._ <br><br>FRACTIONS | NOT YET | OK | SUPER | COMMENTS |
|---|---|---|---|---|
| Understands numerator/denominator | | ✓ | | |
| Area models | | ✓ | | |
| Set models | ✓ | | | |
| Uses fractions in real contexts | ✓ | | | |
| Estimates fraction quantities | | ✓ | | getting better |
| PROBLEM SOLVING | | | | |
| Understands problem before beginning work | | ✓ | | this is good |
| Is willing to take risks | ✓ | | | problem area |
| Justifies results | | | | |
| | | | | |

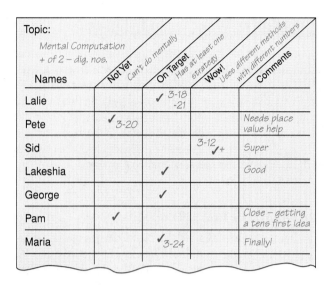

**Figure 5.8**   **A full-class observation checklist can be used for longer-term objectives or for several days to cover a short-term objective.**

Some teachers have students write explanations and justifications for every problem or task. Writing is a form of communication, a major objective for mathematics instruction. Though many children have difficulty writing in mathematics initially, persistence pays off.

Writing has some real advantages over oral communication. It can include pictures, graphs, and symbols that are powerful communication tools not available orally. Written expression is usually preceded with time spent to organize one's thoughts. It can be revised or edited by scratching out and writing over, whereas oral responses are immediate and irretrievable. Finally, written expression can be organized so that it is a private communication between teacher and student. Students can learn to put trust in your respect for what they write. Trust will come through thoughtful, helpful responses and respect for students' privacy.

## Journals

Writing can of course be done on a single sheet of paper and turned in separately, but the use of a journal has real value. A journal may take the form of a composition booklet or, for K–1 children, folded writing paper stapled within a construction-paper cover. Binders and spiral notebooks are other options, but teachers find these bulky, and students are more likely to remove unwanted pages.

Journals are a way to make written communication a regular part of doing mathematics. Journals help you abandon the mistaken, counterproductive myth "If they write it,

I must grade it." Journals are a place for students to write about such things as

- Their conceptual understandings and problem solving, including descriptions of ideas, solutions, and justifications of problems, graphs, charts, and observations

- Their questions concerning the current topic, an idea that they may need help with, or an area they don't quite understand

- Their feelings about aspects of mathematics, their confidence in their understanding, or their fears of being wrong

Even if you have students write in their journals nearly every day, be sure that these journals are special places for writing about mathematics. Drill and practice, for example, should not be done in a journal. Lengthy projects done over several days should be separate from journals and given a special presentation. A performance task you plan to use primarily for evaluation purposes should probably not be in a journal. But the work for many of your performance tasks can and should go in the journal as part of doing mathematics. In this way, you communicate that the work is important and you do want to see it but you are not going to grade it.

Journals are vehicles for communication, not evaluation. To grade journal writing defeats its purpose as a way to learn about students' ideas and to provide them with valuable feedback and direction. Graded journals would communicate that there is a specific "right" response you are seeking. That would not have the same flavor as communication. It is essential, however, that you read and respond to journal writing. One form of response for a performance task would be to use the classroom's general rubric along with a helpful comment. This is another way to distinguish between rubrics and grades and still provide feedback.

On a regular basis, it is manageable to read and respond to about five journals a night. Following an especially interesting lesson, you might want to read the journal entry of every student in the class. Allow students to flag entries for which they want your special attention or response. If you do not read and respond to journals, students will quickly come to regard them as busywork and conclude that you do not value their efforts. Teachers whose students have learned to communicate honestly through their journals find them a key element in their assessment program, prized above all other sources of information to improve learning and instruction.

## Writing Prompts and Ideas

Students should always have a clear, well-defined purpose for writing in their journals. They need to know exactly what to write about and who the audience is (you, an imaginary friend, a student in a lower grade, an adult, a Martian), and they should be given a definite time frame within which to write. Journal writing that is completely open-ended without goal or purpose will be a waste of time. Here are some suggestions for prompts to get you thinking; however, the possibilities are endless.

### Concepts and Problem Solving

- "I think the answer is . . . I think this because . . ." (The journal can be used to solve and explain any problem. Always be sure to include the problem. Some teachers duplicate the problem and have students tape it into the journal to save time and effort.)

- Write an explanation for other students (or for students in a lower grade) of why 4 × 7 is the same as 7 × 4 and why this works for 6 × 49 and 49 × 6.

- Draw four different quadrilaterals that are alike in some way. Tell why they are alike. Draw one that is different. Tell why it is different.

- Explain to a student in grade X (or who was absent today) what you learned about decimals today.

- What about the work we did today was easy? What was hard? What do you still have questions about?

- If you got stuck today in solving a problem, where did you get stuck? Why do you think you had trouble there? If you did not get stuck, what idea helped you solve the problem?

- After you got the answer to today's problem, what did you do so that you were convinced your answer was correct? How sure are you that you got the correct answer?

- How can addition help you do subtraction facts like 12 − 4 and 15 − 6?

- Write a story problem that goes with this picture (this graph, this diagram, this equation).

### Affective Ideas

- "What I like most (or least) about mathematics is . . ."

- Write a mathematics autobiography. Tell about your experiences in mathematics outside of school and how you feel about the subject.

- "Mathematics is like a . . . because . . ."

- Write to an imaginary friend who is the same age as you, telling how you feel about what we did in mathematics this week.

## Journals for Early Learners

If you are interested in working with K–1 children, the writing suggestions presented may have sounded discouraging because it is difficult for prewriters and beginning writers to express ideas like those suggested. There are specific techniques for journals in kindergarten and first grade that have been used successfully.

### The Giant Journal

To begin the development of the writing-in-mathematics process, one kindergarten teacher uses a language experience approach. After an activity, she writes the heading "Giant Journal" and a topic or prompt on a large flipchart. Students respond to the prompt, and she writes their ideas, adding the contributor's name and even drawings when appropriate, as in Figure 5.9.

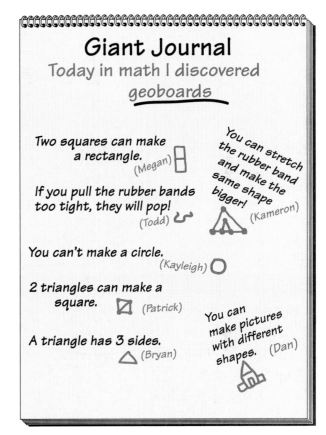

**Figure 5.9** **A journal in kindergarten may be a class product on a flipchart.**

### Drawings and Early Writing

All students can draw pictures of some sort to describe what they have done. Dots can represent counters or blocks. Shapes and special figures can be cut out from duplicated sheets and pasted onto the journal page.

It is important for the "writing" to be a record of something the student has just done and is comfortable with. Figure 5.10 (p. 76) shows problems solved in first and second grade. Do not be concerned about invented spellings to communicate ideas. Have students read their papers to you.

### Brainstorming

Young children have difficulty translating what they say and think into written form. One way to help is to use discussion time to help children think about their journal entries. Record ideas on the board as they are contributed by

Grade 1
Read the problem. Think and use "stuff" to help you solve it.

There were 7 owls.
They found some mice in the woods to eat. Each owl got 5 mice.
How many mice did they find? How do you know?
Use pictures and words to show how you solved the problem.

Grade 2
The farmer saw five cows and four chickens. How many legs and tails in all did he see?

**Figure 5.10**  **Journal entries of early-grades children.**

students. For kindergartners and first graders, use very simple abbreviated versions of what they say. For children in grades 2 and 3, you may limit your recording to key phrases and special words. In this manner, the ideas that have been generated are now recorded for students to assemble into their own writing. When a student says, "I don't know what to write," have him tell you about his task or idea. Then have him write what he just told you.

# Student Self-Assessment

Stenmark (1989) notes that "the capability and willingness to assess their own progress and learning is one of the greatest gifts students can develop. . . . Mathematical power comes

with knowing how much we know and what to do to learn more" (p. 26).

In a self-assessment, students may tell you

- How well they think they understand a piece of content

- What they believe or how they feel about some aspect of mathematics, perhaps what you are covering right now

- How well they perceive they are working in class or in their group

It is important to see that this is not your measure of their learning, disposition, or behavior but rather a record of how *they perceive* these things.

In each of these three possible areas for student self-assessment (content, disposition, and behavior), there is potential for interesting and useful inputs into your instructional program. What are the implications when a student feels she knows content better than (or not as well as) she actually does? How do you react to positive attitudes from a poorly performing student or negative attitudes from a generally strong student? How can you use students' assessment of their group behaviors as a tool for improving group behavior? These and similar questions are aimed at getting you to think about why you might want to use periodic self-assessments in your class. It is important to consider how you want the assessment to help you as a teacher before you begin collecting the data. Tell your students why you are having them do this activity. Encourage them to be honest and candid. Though it may seem like fun to collect class information early in the year on a topic such as "Why I like mathematics," do not assign a self-assessment activity just to make yourself feel good about your students.

You can gather self-assessment data in several ways. A common method is to use some form of a questionnaire to which students respond. These can have open-ended questions, response choices (e.g., *seldom, sometimes, often; disagree, don't care, agree*), mind maps, drawings, and so on. Many such instruments appear in the literature, and many textbook publishers provide examples. Whenever you use a form or questionnaire that someone else has devised, be certain that it serves the purpose you intend. Often these forms are too long or include questions in which you have little interest. Modify them to suit your purposes. The fact that a form was professionally prepared or accompanies your text does not necessarily make it appropriate or useful to you.

An open-ended writing prompt such as was suggested for journals is one method of getting self-assessment data:

- How well do you think you understand the work we have been doing the last few days on fractions? If there is something that is causing you difficulty with fractions, please tell me what it is.

■ Write one thing you liked and one thing you did not like about math class today (or this week).

■ In your group, how well do you think you have followed the rules about helping others? About asking for ideas from others? About keeping the group on task?

These questions indicate how an open-ended writing prompt can be directed at any of the three areas of self-assessment. You may find that a simple prompt can become familiar to students if you use it on a regular basis. For example, midway through a unit is a good time to listen to what students regard as things they know and do not know. As students learn that you will react in some way that is helpful to them, they will be more apt to provide you with candid, useful information.

## Attitude Inventories

Students may find it difficult to write about attitudes and beliefs. An inventory where they can respond "yes," "maybe," or "no" to a series of statements is another approach. Encourage students to add comments under an item if they wish. Here are some items you could use to build such an inventory:

■ I feel sure of myself when I get an answer to a problem.

■ I sometimes just put down anything so I can get it over with.

■ I like to work on really hard math problems.

■ Math class makes me feel nervous.

■ If I get stuck, I usually just quit or go to another problem.

■ I am not as good in math as most of the other students in this class.

■ Mathematics is my favorite subject.

■ I do not like to work at problems that are hard to understand.

■ Memorizing rules is the only way I know to learn mathematics.

■ I will work a long time at a problem until I think I've solved it.

Another technique is to ask students to write a sentence at the end of any work they do in mathematics class saying how that activity made them feel. Young children can draw a face on each page to tell you about their feelings.

## Frequency of Self-Assessments

How often should self-assessment data be gathered? The answer varies with the type of assessment and the purpose.

You should always have a clear purpose for asking students for information, and that purpose should be tied directly to helping students learn. There should never be any grades attached to affective assessments, nor should students be asked to take time and effort if the information is not serving a real purpose.

Finding out about student attitudes or likes and dislikes can help you get to know your students early on in a new year. Periodic follow-up assessments can help you gauge how well you are connecting with your students throughout the year. Once per grading period is probably often enough. Discuss the results with your students, or find other ways to let them know you value their thoughtful responses. Do not collect affective data simply to make yourself feel good.

Information about student confidence concerning content being learned suggests a quite different timetable. Some teachers have students make it a habit to rate every written performance as "easy," "OK," or "difficult." Obviously, this information is of little value after a unit has been covered and you are ready to move on. Lack of confidence suggests a potential problem, or perhaps statements made in class will have to be evaluated accordingly. In most instances, you will want to give students feedback individually. If there is a consensus belief in the class, you might let students know that you are ready to "raise the bar" or, alternatively, continue to work on an area of discomfort.

Self-evaluation of group work should be conducted periodically. As will be discussed in Chapter 22, cooperative group behavior needs to be an ongoing objective. As you focus on various specific group behaviors, a group self-assessment may be in order.

# TESTS

Tests will always be a part of assessment and evaluation no matter how adept we become at blending assessment with instruction. However, a test need not be a collection of low-level skill exercises. Although simple tests of computational skills may have some role in your classroom, the use of such tests should be limited. Like all other forms of assessment, tests should reflect the goals of your instruction. Tests can be designed to find out what concepts students have and how their ideas are connected. Tests of procedural knowledge should go beyond just knowing how to perform an algorithm and should allow and require the student to demonstrate a conceptual basis for the process. The following examples will illustrate these ideas.

1. Write a multiplication problem that has an answer between the answers to these two problems:

$$
\begin{array}{cc}
49 & 45 \\
\times 25 & \times 30
\end{array}
$$

2. a. In this division exercise, what number tells how many tens were shared among the 6 sets?

   b. Instead of writing the remainder as "R 2," Elaine writes "$\frac{1}{3}$" Explain the difference between these two ways of handling the leftover part.

$$\begin{array}{r} 49\,\text{R}2 \\ 6\overline{)296} \end{array} \qquad \begin{array}{r} 49\frac{1}{3} \\ 6\overline{)296} \end{array}$$

3. On the grid, draw two figures with the same area but different perimeters. List the area and perimeter of each.

4. For each subtraction fact, write an addition fact that helps you think of the answer to the subtraction.

$$\begin{array}{r} 12 \\ -3 \\ \hline 9 \end{array} \qquad \begin{array}{r} 9 \\ +3 \\ \hline 12 \end{array} \qquad \begin{array}{r} 9 \\ -4 \\ \hline \end{array} \qquad \begin{array}{r} 14 \\ -7 \\ \hline \end{array}$$

5. Draw pictures of arrows to show why $^-3 + {}^-4$ is the same as $^-3 - {}^+4$.

If a test is well constructed, much more information can be found than simply the number of correct or incorrect answers. Here are some things to think about when constructing a test:

1. *Permit calculators all the time.* Except for tests of computational skills, the calculator allows students to focus on what you really want to test. It also communicates a positive attitude about calculator use to your students.

2. *Use manipulatives and drawings.* Students can use appropriate models to work on test questions when those same models have been used to develop concepts. (Note the use of drawings in Example 5 above.) Simple drawings can be used to represent counters, base-ten pieces, fraction pieces, and the like (see Figure 5.11). Be sure to provide examples in class of how to draw the models before you ask students to draw on a test.

3. *Include opportunities for explanations.*

4. *Assess affective factors on the test.* One idea is to have students rate their personal confidence level on each question as A (high), B (moderate), or C (low). Another idea is to have students draw a face showing how they feel about the question or the test in general. Ask students to complete a sentence that begins "I liked this test because . . ." or "I did not like this test because . . ."

5. *Avoid "preanswered" tests.* These are tests where questions have only one correct answer, whether it is a calculation, a multiple-choice, or a fill-in-the-blank. Tests of this type tend to fragment what children have learned and hide most of what they know. Rather, construct tests that allow students the opportunity to show what they know.

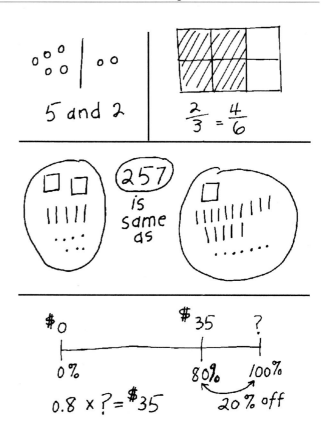

**Figure 5.11** **Students can use drawings to illustrate concepts on tests.**

# DEALING WITH STANDARDIZED TESTING

States and local school districts nearly all employ some form of testing program. These external tests (originating externally to the classroom) are usually referred to as "standardized" tests because the same tests are given to large numbers of students. External tests are a legitimate concern for teachers, who are often evaluated in terms of their students' performance. It is important to be informed about the nature of high-stakes tests and how you can help your students perform well.

## State Standards and State Tests

A large number of states have adopted a set of objectives for mathematics for students by grade level. The word *standard* is used differently in this context than in the NCTM *Standards* documents. Whereas the standards discussed in *Principles and Standards* are broad statements applicable to 3-year grade bands, a state standard is generally a very specific objective or benchmark goal. States wishing to ensure that districts implement or teach these standards almost always implement a corresponding testing program. This not only enforces implementation but also permits reporting of scores for purposes of accountability.

The variability in state standards and in the types of state testing programs is vast. In some states, the tests are entirely in multiple-choice format. In others, they include open-response items (fill in the answer, no choices), and some include items where students must show their work and provide explanations. There are also states that use a portfolio assessment program (see next section of this chapter).

Teachers should be aware of the nature of the testing program for their state. If a norm-referenced test is used, the assumption is that the state standards will be reflected in the results even though not all standards are tested. Since norm-referenced tests are designed to spread performance rather than test all objectives, they are likely to include items not on the state standards list and omit many that are. It is always a serious error for a teacher to "teach to the test," but this is especially true if the test is a norm-referenced exam.

Other states hire testing companies to design criterion-referenced tests, crafted to assess a specific list of objectives. The advantage for teachers is that the tests are supposed to reflect the objectives that they are under contract to teach. That still does not control for the difficulty of the test or the types of items included.

## Teachers and State Standards

The consequences of low scores on state tests are almost certainly going to cause teachers to be anxious and concerned. Regardless of the state, the tests, or the consequences, the best advice is to teach to the big ideas in the mathematics curriculum. Students who have strong, relational understanding of the main ideas in mathematics and who have good mathematics process skills will always do well on standardized tests. When teachers try to teach to the test or gear their teaching specifically to a list of objectives, they tend to leave their students with an array of isolated bits of information. The dots will simply not be well connected. This does not mean to ignore objective lists but rather to identify broad concepts on which the specific objectives can be built. To obsess over objectives and tests and ignore big ideas and conceptual understanding will almost certainly be counterproductive.

## Improving Performance on High-Stakes Tests

There is no doubt that your students can benefit from a bit of test "savvy" and test preparation on your part. Here are some strategies for improving performance:

- *Ensure an opportunity to learn the content.* Plan your year so that the big ideas for most or all of the objectives will be taught before the test is given.

- *Provide ongoing review and practice.* For skills such as computation, mental computation, estimation, use of formulas, and other procedural ideas, short regularly spaced reviews are much more effective than a massive practice effort the week before the test.

- *Provide experience with different question formats.* If you have information about the types of formats the standardized test will employ, be sure to use these question formats regularly (not exclusively) in class.

- *Teach test-taking strategies.* Students are often not very efficient test takers, so helping them learn to take tests can have some benefits. Here are some teachable strategies:

    Read questions carefully. Practice identifying what questions are asking and what information is given to get the answer.

    Estimate the answer before spending time with computation. On multiple-choice tests, estimation and good number sense is often all that is needed to select the correct answer.

    Eliminate choices. Look at the available options. Some will almost certainly be unreasonable. Does a choice make sense? Can looking at the ones digit eliminate answers?

    Work backward from an answer.

*Caution!* Test-taking strategies require good concepts, skills, and number sense. Without good understanding, test strategies will do little good. Invest most of your efforts teaching mathematics rather than test skills.

## PORTFOLIOS IN THE ASSESSMENT PLAN

A *portfolio* is an assemblage of many types of student work selected with both student and teacher input, designed to provide a holistic view of some aspect of mathematics that may not be evident from examination of any single entry. The portfolio should demonstrate and help students reflect on their mathematical power and what that really means. It may be used to focus on progress and growth, understandings, or problem-solving processes. The materials in the portfolio may include assignments, projects, reports, student writing, worksheets from texts or other sources, comments by teachers, observations from interviews, and self-evaluations of group and individual efforts. A portfolio should be more than a folder of student papers. It should tell a story that goes beyond the individual entries. The portfolio is an excellent form of communication between student and teacher, student and parent, and parent and teacher.

## Portfolio Content Suggestions

Your own portfolio program should be carried out to serve the particular goals you have in mind and to communicate achievement of these goals to students and parents. These plans and goals should be discussed with your students from the outset and revisited periodically so that the students are fully involved in the process.

Table 5.2 is from a superb NCTM booklet, *Mathematics Assessment: Myths, Models, Good Questions, and Practical Suggestions* (Stenmark, 1991). It provides ideas for the types of entries that could be included to correspond to different goals. Any given portfolio will include only a sampling of these ideas and may contain only eight to ten entries.

Teachers who have used portfolios have noted that students begin to take more pride in their work and make extra efforts. Portfolios can add a sense of importance to daily work.

## Portfolio Management

At first, the idea of keeping a portfolio for every child is a bit daunting. Included in this section are some ideas found in the Stenmark (1991) booklet.

### A Working Portfolio

Set up folders for each student, and keep them where students can easily get to them. These folders serve as working portfolios and will hold students' potential portfolio entries. Encourage students to revise or correct work on special projects, but always keep the original versions to be able to track progress. The working portfolio is also the place where your observation notes or other items that originate with you can be kept. When groups turn in reports or projects, make copies for each group member's work portfolio.

### Assembling the Portfolio

At the end of the unit or grading period, or whenever it is time to assemble the final portfolio, students select and clip together the items from the working portfolio that they want to be included in their final portfolio. Have a class discussion about how to select items and what the items should show. Encourage children to pick things that tell about themselves in mathematics: their strengths, weaknesses, points of pride, places they need help, and progress made over the period. Students should write a few sentences explaining each selection and why it was included. You should designate two or three items as "must include," usually the same ones for the whole class.

Students then review their portfolios and write a cover letter that discusses the content as a whole and gives their personal perspective on such things as problem-solving skills, confidence, attitudes, and growth in understanding, depending on the goals you and your class have established. This portfolio is now ready for evaluation and subsequent sharing with parents.

### Portfolio Evaluation

You will probably have made comments on most or all of the materials as they were completed. Now you are looking at the portfolio as a whole. It is very important to provide feedback. It is an excellent way to encourage students and to build confidence and communicate perspective about mathematics. Your comments should be made with this in mind. If you plan to include the portfolio in your grading scheme, a rubric will be useful.

# DIAGNOSTIC INTERVIEWS

An interview is simply a one-on-one discussion with a child to help you see how she is thinking about a particular subject, what processes she uses in solving problems, or what attitudes and beliefs she may have. A structured interview may be as short as 5 to 10 minutes. More open-ended or exploratory interviews may last as long as a half hour.

## Reasons to Consider an Interview

There are several reasons why it may occasionally be well worth the time and effort to conduct interviews. The most obvious reason is that you need more information concerning a particular child and how he or she is constructing concepts or using a procedure. Remediation will almost always be more successful if you can pinpoint *why* a student is having difficulty before you try to fix the problem.

A second reason is to get information either to plan your instruction or to assess the effectiveness of your instruction. For example, are you sure that your students have a good understanding of equivalent fractions, or are they just doing the exercises according to rote rules? At the end of Chapter 9, a collection of tasks is suggested to get at students' understanding of place value. Concept tasks such as these might be used in interviews conducted at the beginning of a unit to see what ideas you need to work on. They can be used later in the unit or at the end to assess growth or retention of ideas.

Another reason is to grow as a teacher, to learn more about the way children learn and think. You might decide to conduct at least one interview a week, changing the topic and the children you interview. In addition to growth in your knowledge of children, you will also grow in your ability to conduct good interviews.

## Planning an Interview

There is no magic right way to plan or structure an interview. In fact, flexibility is a key ingredient. You should, however, have some overall game plan before you begin, and be prepared with key questions and materials. Begin an interview with questions that are easy or closest to what the child is

## Table 5.2
### Goals and Suggested Portfolio Contents

| Goal | Evidence, Examples, and Comments |
|---|---|
| **Positive mathematical disposition**<br>Motivation<br>Curiosity<br>Perseverance<br>Risk taking<br>Flexibility<br>Self-responsibility<br>Self-confidence | • Journal entries depicting enthusiasm for mathematics<br>• Photographs of large, colorful mathematics graphics by students<br>• Problem solution with an added paragraph beginning with "On the other hand …" or "What if …"<br>• Log of a week's or month's work showing a single important problem or investigation worked on over a period of time<br>• Homework paper with a description of several approaches to a problem<br>• Student-written planning calendar outlining work to be done<br>• Mathematics autobiography |
| **Growth in mathematical understanding**<br>Concept development<br>Problem-solving skills<br>Communication skills<br>Construction of mathematics<br>Reflection on approaches and<br>   solutions to problems or tasks | • Similar items collected at regular intervals from the beginning of the year<br>• Written explanation of why an algorithm works<br>• Diagram, table, or similar organized representation that clarifies a problem situation<br>• Solution that defines assumptions, includes counterexamples<br>• Photographs of a mathematics project<br>• Journal entries delineating solution justifications and variations in strategies<br>• Student identification of papers that need more work, with reasons<br>• A paper that starts with "Today in math class I learned …"<br>• Inclusion of drafts as well as finished work |
| **Mathematical reasoning in a variety of mathematical topics**<br>Estimation, number sense, number<br>   operations, and computation<br>Measurement, geometry, and<br>   spatial sense<br>Statistics and probability<br>Fractions and decimals<br>Patterns and relationships | • Report on an investigation (e.g., number patterns in sums of sequential numbers)<br>• Student-planned statistical survey, with accompanying graphic designs<br>• Written report of a probability experiment and accompanying theoretical design<br>• Response to an open-ended question regarding measurement of geometric shapes<br>• Student explanation of what $\frac{1}{2}$ minus $\frac{1}{3}$ means<br>• Diagram examples of multiplication using a number line, a rectangular array, and repeated groups of physical objects<br>• Annotated drawing illustrating the Pythagorean theorem<br>• Representation of an area model solution for a statistical problem |
| **Mathematical connections**<br>Connecting a mathematical idea to<br>   other mathematical topics, to other<br>   subject areas, and to real-world<br>   situations | • Papers that show authentic use of mathematics in other curricular areas such as science or social studies<br>• Student reflections on how mathematics is meaningful as it is used in the adult world<br>• Examples from nature of occurrences of Pascal's triangle number patterns<br>• A report on the relationship among arithmetic, algebra, and geometry with demonstrative examples on a coordinate grid<br>• Student-constructed table of equivalent fractions, decimal numbers, and percents, with examples of where each type of number is used<br>• Mathematical art project<br>• Report about a person in history or personally known who contributed to mathematics |
| **Group problem-solving**<br>Development of skills in working<br>   with others<br>Communication | • A task design or plan<br>• Group paper that includes the names of the members of the group and the tasks each did<br>• Group self-assessment sheet<br>• Videotape or audiotape of group working on problems or making oral reports<br>• Group-work report of trying a second or third strategy applied when the first one didn't work |
| **Use of tools**<br>Integration of technology—use of<br>   calculators and computers and so on<br>Use of manipulatives | • Computer-generated statistical analysis of a problem<br>• Frequent mention of use of calculators on open-ended problems<br>• Diagrams representing use of manipulative material |
| **Teacher and parent involvement**<br>Communication between teacher and<br>   parent and between parent and student<br>Parental understanding of educational<br>   objectives and values | • Consistency of program demonstrated by items from every grading period<br>• Anecdotal report<br>• Informal assessment sheet<br>• Interview of student<br>• Teacher- or parent-written comments<br>• Assessment by teacher of student work<br>• Student presentation of portfolio to parent during parent-teacher conference |

*Source:* National Council of Teachers of Mathematics © 1991. In J. K. Stenmark (Ed.), *Mathematics Assessment.* Reprinted by permission.

likely to be able to do, usually some form of procedural exercise. For numeration or computation topics, for example, begin with a pencil-and-paper task such as a computation, writing or comparing numerals, or a simple translation problem. When the opening task has been completed, ask the child to explain what was done. "How would you explain this to a second grader (or your younger sister)?" "What does this (point to something on the paper) stand for?" "Tell me about why you do it that way." At this point, you may try a similar task but with a different feature; for example, after doing

372 − 54, try 403 − 37. The second problem has a zero in the tens place, a possible source of difficulty.

The next phase in the interview involves the use of models or drawings that the child can use to demonstrate understanding of the earlier procedural task. Computations can be done with base-ten materials, blocks or counters can be used, number lines explored, grid paper used for drawing, and so on. Be careful not to interject or teach. The temptation to do so is sometimes overwhelming. Watch and listen. Next, explore connections between what was done with models and what was done with pencil and paper. Many children will do the very same task and get two different answers. Does it matter to the children? How do they explain the discrepancy? Can they connect actions using models to what they wrote or explained earlier?

Alternative beginnings to an interview include making an estimate of the answer to either a computation or a word problem, doing a computation mentally, or trying to predict the solution to a given task. Notice that the interview does not generally proceed the way instruction does. That is, in an interview, the conceptual explanations and discussions in general come after the procedural activity. Your goal is not to use the interview to teach but rather to find out where the child is in terms of concepts and procedures at this time.

## Suggestions for Effective Interviews

The following suggestions have been adapted from excellent discussions of interviewing children by Labinowicz (1985, 1987), Liedtke (1988), and Scheer (1980).

- *Be accepting and neutral as you listen to the child.* Smiles, frowns, or other body language can make the child think that the answer he or she gave is right or wrong. Develop neutral responses such as "Uh-huh," "I see," or even a silent nod of the head.

- *Avoid cuing or leading the child.* "Are you sure about that?" "Now look again closely at what you just did." "Wait. Is that what you mean?" These responses will indicate to children that they have made some mistake and cause them to change their responses. This can mask what they really think and understand. A similar form of leading is a series of easily answered questions that direct the student to a correct response. That is teaching, not interviewing.

- *Wait silently.* Give the student plenty of time before you ask a different question or probe. After the child makes a response, wait again! This second wait time is even more important because it allows and encourages the child to elaborate on the initial thought and provide you with more information. Wait even when the response is correct. Waiting can also give you a bit more time to think about the direction you want the interview to take. Your wait time will almost never be as long as you imagine it is.

- *Do not interrupt.* Let children's thoughts flow freely. Encourage children to use their own words and ways of writing things down. Interjecting questions or correcting language can be distracting to the child's thinking.

- *Use imperatives rather than questions.* Say, "show me," "tell me," "do," or "try," rather than "Can you . . . ?" or "Will you . . . ?" In response to a question, the child can simply say no, leaving you in a vacuum.

- *Avoid confirming a request for validation.* Students frequently follow answers or actions with, "Is that right?" This query can easily be answered with a neutral, "That's fine," or "You're doing OK," regardless of whether the answer is right or wrong. Interviewing is not an easy thing to do well. Many teachers are timid about it and fail to take the time. But not much damage is possible, and the rewards of listening to children, both for you and your students, are so great that you really do not want to pass it up.

## GRADING

*Myth:* A grade is an average of a series of scores on tests and quizzes. The accuracy of the grade is dependent primarily on the accuracy of the computational technique used to calculate the final numeric grade.

*Reality:* A grade is a statistic that is used to communicate to others the achievement level that a student has attained in a particular area of study. The accuracy or validity of the grade is dependent on the information that is used in preparing the grade, the professional judgment of the teacher, and the alignment of the assessments with the true goals and objectives of the course.

## Confronting the Myth

Most experienced teachers will tell you that they know a great deal about their students in terms of what the students know, how they perform in different situations, their attitudes and beliefs, and their various levels of skill attainment. Good teachers have always been engaged in ongoing performance assessment, albeit informal and usually with no recording. However, even good teachers have relied on test scores to determine grades, essentially forcing themselves to ignore a wealth of information that reflected a truer picture of their children.

The myth of grading by statistical number crunching is so firmly ingrained in schooling at all levels that you may find it hard to abandon. If one thing is clear from the discussions in this chapter, it should be that it is quite possible to gather a wide variety of rich information about students' understanding, problem-solving processes, and attitudes and beliefs. To ignore all of this information in favor of a handful of numbers based on tests, tests that usually focus on low-level skills, is unfair to students, to parents, and to you as the teacher.

# Grading Issues

For effective use of the assessment information gathered from problems, tasks, and other appropriate methods to assign grades, some hard decisions are inevitable. Some are philosophical, some require school or district agreements about grades, and all require us to examine what we value and the objectives we communicate to students and parents.

## Values

In contrast to the many myths of grading, one thing is undeniably true: *What gets graded is what gets valued.* Using rubric scales to provide feedback and to encourage a pursuit of excellence must also relate to grades. However, "converting four out of five to 80 percent or three out of four to a grade of C can destroy the entire purpose of alternative assessment and the use of scoring rubrics" (Kulm, 1994, p. 99). Kulm explains that directly translating rubrics to grades focuses attention on grades and away from the purpose of every good problem-solving activity, to strive for an excellent performance. When papers are returned with less than top ratings, the purpose is to help students know what is necessary to achieve at a higher level. Early on, there should be opportunities to improve based on feedback. When a grade of 75 percent or a C– is returned, all the student knows is that he or she did poorly. If, for example, a student's ability to justify her own answers and solutions has improved, should she be penalized in the averaging of numbers by a weaker performance early in the marking period?

What this means is that grading must be based on the performance tasks and other activities for which you assigned rubric ratings; otherwise, students will soon realize that these are not important scores. At the same time, they need not be added or averaged in any numeric manner. The grade at the end of the marking period should reflect a holistic view of where the student is now relative to your goals and your value system. That value system should be clearly reflected in your framework for rating tasks.

## Alignment

The grades you assign should reflect all of your objectives. Procedural skills remain important but should be weighted in proportion to other goals in keeping with your value system. If you are restricted to assigning a single grade for mathematics, different factors probably have different weights or values in making up the grade. Student X may be fantastic at reasoning and truly love mathematics yet be weak in traditional skills. Student Y may be mediocre in problem solving but possess good communication skills. How much weight should you give to cooperation in groups, to written versus oral reports, to computational skills? There are no simple answers to these questions. However, they should be addressed at the beginning of the grading period and not the night you set out to assign grades.

A multidimensional reporting system is a big help. If you can assign several grades for mathematics and not just one, your report to parents is more meaningful. Even if the school's report card does not permit multiple grades, you can devise a supplement indicating several ratings for different objectives. A place for comments is also helpful. This form can be shared with students periodically during a grading period and can easily accompany a report card.

You can always involve students and parents in a discussion of a multidimensional approach to determining a grade based on rubric ratings for different components of your goals. Traditional test averaging has always done this. Not every test covers the same thing, and various scores (quizzes, homework, exams) are often assigned different weights. These are subjective, teacher-made decisions. The same subjective approach can be used with rubric scores without computing numeric averages.

# REFLECTIONS ON CHAPTER 5

## Writing to Learn

1. The six assessment standards concern *mathematics, learning, equity, openness, inferences,* and *coherence.* For each, describe in your own words what the standard says and its importance for you as a teacher.

2. Describe the four purposes of assessment as outlined by the *Assessment Standards.* How do these purposes relate to you as a teacher?

3. What should we look for if we are trying to assess "mathematical power"?

4. In looking at procedural knowledge, what should be assessed in addition to skill proficiency? Why?

5. How can a learning task or problem be an assessment task? Why should these be the same thing?

6. Describe the essential features of a rubric. What are performance indicators? What is the difference between a rubric and a performance indicator? What is the difference between a holistic rubric and an analytic rubric?

7. How can students be involved in understanding and using rubrics to help with their learning?

## For Discussion and Exploration

1. Examine a few chapter-end tests in various textbooks. How well do the tests reflect what is important in the chapter? Concepts and understanding? Mathematical power?

2. Select any good performance task for a grade level you are interested in. Try to answer the six questions on page 67, just above the

examples of problems for assessment. If possible, get some other people to do the same for the same task. Compare your ideas.

3. Pick a topic and a grade level. Try to write three good test questions for that topic.

4. The pressures of state testing are causing teachers in some school systems to give practice tests that are similar to the state-mandated exams. What is your personal reaction to such practice testing? What are the pros and cons of this practice?

# Recommendations for Further Reading

## Highly Recommended

Bright, G. W., & Joyner, J. M. (Eds.). (1998). *Classroom assessment in mathematics: Views from a National Science Foundation working conference.* Lantham, MD: University Press of America.

In 1997, a conference was held in North Carolina on the topic of classroom assessment in mathematics. Experts from around the country shared their personal perspective and expertise on this issue. This book contains 3 position papers and 23 working papers presented at the conference, providing a wonderful resource for anyone looking for information on mathematics assessment practices.

Kuhs, T. M. (1997). *Measure for measure: Using portfolios in K–8 mathematics.* Portsmouth, NH: Heinemann.

If you want to know about portfolios in mathematics, this is a must book. Kuhs is purposely nonprescriptive about how to conduct a portfolio program but writes from an informed perspective. The five chapters cover how-to ideas, grading issues, and practical questions that typically concern teachers.

Kulm, G. (1994). *Mathematics assessment: What works in the classroom.* San Francisco: Jossey-Bass.

Kulm has excellent credentials in the area of both mathematics and science assessment. This book provides perspective, detailed guidance, and models that can be copied for direct use in the classroom. One of the best books on assessment in mathematics available.

Lambdin, D. V., Kehle, P. E., & Preston, R. V. (Eds.). (1996). *Emphasis on assessment: Readings from NCTM's school-based journals.* Reston, VA: National Council of Teachers of Mathematics.

An assembly of 30 articles on assessment taken from NCTM's various journals and organized in four categories: rationale for change, testing and grading, alternative assessment options, and evaluation of teacher effectiveness. At the end of the book are three annotated bibliographies—one for elementary and middle grade teachers, a second for high school teachers, and a third from the *Journal for Research in Mathematics Education*.

Stenmark, J. K. (Ed.). (1991). *Mathematics assessment: Myths, models, good questions, and practical suggestions.* Reston, VA: National Council of Teachers of Mathematics.

If you want a comprehensive look at new directions in assessment with examples, alternatives, ideas, and formats, this book is indispensable. Since its publication, it has been one of NCTM's most popular books. The author is associated with the EQUALS project and has written extensively on assessment. You'll find this an excellent resource.

## Other Suggestions

Ann Arbor Public Schools. (1993). *Alternative assessment: Evaluating student performance in elementary mathematics.* White Plains, NY: Cuisenaire–Dale Seymour.

Billstein, R. (1998). Assessment: The STEM model. *Mathematics Teaching in the Middle School, 3,* 282–286, 294–296.

Brown-Herbst, K. (1999). So math isn't just answers. *Mathematics Teaching in the Middle School, 4,* 448–455.

Burns, M. (1995). *Writing in math class.* Sausalito, CA: Math Solutions Publications.

Cai, J., Lane, S., & Jakabcsin, M. S. (1996). The role of open-ended tasks and holistic scoring rubrics: Assessing students' mathematical reasoning and communication. In P. C. Elliott (Ed.), *Communication in mathematics, K–12 and beyond* (pp. 137–145). Reston, VA: National Council of Teachers of Mathematics.

Cai, J., Magone, M. E., Wang, N., & Lane, S. (1996). Describing student performance qualitatively. *Mathematics Teaching in the Middle School, 1,* 828–835.

Cole, K. A. (1999). Walking around: Getting more from informal assessment. *Mathematics Teaching in the Middle School, 4,* 224–227.

Helton, S. M. (1995). I thik the citanre will hoder lase: Journal keeping in mathematics class. *Teaching Children Mathematics, 1,* 336–340.

Huinker, D. M., & Laughlin, C. (1996). Talk your way into writing. In P. C. Elliott (Ed.), *Communication in mathematics, K–12 and beyond* (pp. 81–88). Reston, VA: National Council of Teachers of Mathematics.

Karp, K. S., & Huinker, D. M. (1997). Portfolios as agents of change. *Teaching Children Mathematics, 3,* 224–228.

Moon, J. (1997). *Developing judgment: Assessing children's work in mathematics.* Portsmouth, NH: Heinemann.

National Council of Teachers of Mathematics. (1995). *Assessment standards for school mathematics.* Reston, VA: Author.

Newman, V. (1994). *Math journals: Tools for authentic assessment.* San Leandro, CA: Watten/Poe Teaching Resource Center.

O'Brien, D. C. (1996). Math journals: First attempts in third grade. In D. Schifter (Ed.), *What's happening in math class? Reconstructing professional identities* (Vol. 2, pp. 146–157). New York: Teachers College Press.

Peressini, D., & Bassett, J. (1996). Mathematical communication in students' responses to a performance-assessment task. In P. C. Elliott (Ed.), *Communication in mathematics, K–12 and beyond* (pp. 146–158). Reston, VA: National Council of Teachers of Mathematics.

Popham, W. J. (1999). Why standardized tests don't measure educational quality. *Educational Leadership, 56*(6), 8–15.

Reys, B. J., & Long, V. M. (1995). Teacher as architect of mathematical tasks. *Teaching Children Mathematics, 1,* 296–299.

South Carolina Educational Television (T. M. Kuhs, Director). (1992). *Mathematics assessment: Alternative approaches* [Video and guidebook]. Reston, VA: National Council of Teachers of Mathematics.

Vincent, M. L., & Wilson, L. (1996). Informal assessment: A story from the classroom. *Mathematics Teacher, 89,* 248–250.

Webb, N. L. (Ed.). (1993). *Assessment in the mathematics classroom.* Reston, VA: National Council of Teachers of Mathematics.

Webb, N. L., & Briars, D. (1990). Assessment in mathematics classrooms, K–8. In T. J. Cooney (Ed.), *Teaching and learning mathematics in the 1990s* (pp. 108–117). Reston, VA: National Council of Teachers of Mathematics.

Webb, N. L., & Welsch, C. (1993). Assessment and evaluation for middle grades. In D. T. Owens (Ed.), *Research ideas for the classroom: Middle grades mathematics* (pp. 299–315). Old Tappan, NJ: Macmillan.

Zawojewski, J. S. (1996). Polishing a data task: Seeking better assessment. *Teaching Children Mathematics, 2,* 372–378.

Zazkis, R., & Hazzan, O. (1999). Interviewing in mathematics education research: Choosing the questions. *Journal of Mathematical Behavior, 17,* 429–439.

# Development of Mathematical Concepts and Procedures

A cross the K–8 grade span, the mathematics curriculum encompasses a large number of concepts and procedures. No teacher is expected to be an expert on every one of these. That is why the foundational ideas of the first five chapters are so important. Each of the 16 chapters in this section provides specific instructional ideas that are built on those foundations. In addition, the chapters serve as a source of ideas for nearly every topic in the K–8 range.

At any grade level, there are overarching mathematical ideas that tie together the endless list of objectives often mandated by state or local school systems. To address these objectives, it is often useful to focus on larger mathematical ideas of a unit or chapter. In this section, each chapter begins with a listing of "big ideas," the mathematical concepts that form an umbrella for the smaller ideas discussed in the chapter. This list can help you focus on the big ideas of a corresponding unit of study in the classroom. Numerous activities, along with ideas for incorporating children's literature, technology, and assessment, are built into every chapter.

# Chapter 6

# Developing Early Number Concepts and Number Sense

**N**umber is a complex and multifaceted concept. A rich understanding of number, a relational understanding, involves many different ideas, relationships, and skills. Experience suggests that these relationships do not develop automatically, and it is our job to provide children with a wide assortment of activities that will help them construct these many ideas of number.

## BIG Ideas

1. Counting tells how many things are in the set.
2. Numbers are related to each other through a wide variety of relationships.
3. Numbers have different values when connected to real objects and measures: 5 elephants is a big amount, but 5 crayons is a small amount though the same number; 12 minutes is not much more than 10 minutes, but it is a lot more than 30 seconds.

## EARLY NUMBER SENSE

*Number sense* was described by Howden (1989) as a "good intuition about numbers and their relationships. It develops gradually as a result of exploring numbers, visualizing them in a variety of contexts, and relating them in ways that are not limited by traditional algorithms" (p. 11). This definition may still be the best more than a decade later. *Principles and Standards* calls for Pre-K–2 students to understand numbers, have ways of representing them, and explore relationships among numbers. Flexible, intuitive thinking with numbers should continue to be developed throughout the school years as larger numbers, fractions, decimals, and percents are added to students' repertoire of number ideas. But number sense

development must begin in kindergarten, as it forms the foundation of number-related ideas to be accumulated throughout the school years.

In this chapter, we will focus on a small yet important piece of number sense, relationships for numbers up to about 20. The focus is on helping children construct a variety of important relationships with these numbers and connections to the real world. These are the relationships on which all further numeric thinking and number sense development will be built.

## NUMBER DEVELOPMENT IN PRE-K AND KINDERGARTEN

Parents help children count their fingers, toys, people at the table, and other small sets of objects. Questions concerning "who has more?" or "are there enough?" are part of the daily life of children as young as 2 or 3 years of age. Considerable evidence indicates that these children have some understanding of the concepts of number and counting (Baroody, 1987; Fuson & Hall, 1983; Gelman & Gallistel, 1978; Gelman & Meck, 1986; Ginsburg, 1977).

In school, conceptual knowledge of numbers is developed alongside the related procedural skills of counting, numeral recognition, and numeral writing. The procedural skills become tools that children use to refine their understanding of number concepts.

## The Relationships of More, Less, and Same

The concepts of "more," "less," and "same" are basic relationships contributing to the overall concept of number.

Children begin to develop these ideas before they begin school. An entering kindergarten child can almost always choose the set that is *more* if presented with two sets that are quite obviously different in number. In fact, Baroody (1987) states, "A child unable to use 'more' in this intuitive manner is at considerable educational risk" (p. 29). Classroom activities should help children build on this basic notion and refine it.

Though the concept of less is logically equivalent to the concept of more (selecting the set with more is the same as *not* selecting the set with less), the word *less* proves to be more difficult for children than *more*. A possible explanation is that children have many opportunities to use the word *more* but have limited exposure to the word *less*. To help children with the concept of less, frequently pair it with the word *more* and make a conscious effort to ask "which is less?" questions as well as "which is more?" questions. For example, suppose that your class has correctly selected the set that has more from two that are given. Immediately follow with the question "Which is less?" In this way, the less familiar term and concept can be connected with the better-known idea.

For all three concepts (more, less, and same), children should construct sets using counters as well as make comparisons or choices between two given sets. The activities described here include both types. These activities should be conducted in a spirit of inquiry followed whenever possible with requests for explanations. "Why do you think this set has less?"

---

**A**CTIVITY

## 6.1 Make Sets of More/Less/Same

At a workstation or table, provide about eight cards with sets of 4 to 12 objects, a set of small counters or blocks, and some word cards labeled "More," "Less," and "Same." Next to each card, have students make three collections of counters: a set that is more, one that is less, and one that is the same. The appropriate labels are placed on the sets (see Figure 6.1).

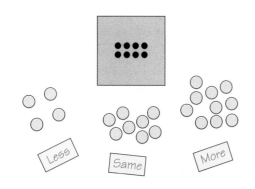

**Figure 6.1** Making sets that are more, less, and the same.

---

In Activity 6.1, students create a set with counters, which gives them the opportunity to reflect on the sets and adjust them as they work. The next activity is done without counters. Although it addresses the same basic ideas, it provides a different problem situation.

**A**CTIVITY

## 6.2 Find the Same Amount

Give children a collection of cards with sets on them. Dot cards are one possibility (see the Blackline Masters at the back of this book). Have the children pick up any card in the collection and then find another card with the same amount to form a pair. Continue to find other pairs.

---

Activity 6.2 can be altered to have children find dot cards that are "less" or "more."

Watch how children do this task. Children whose number ideas are completely tied to counting and nothing more will select cards at random and count each dot. Others will begin by selecting a card that appears to have about the same number of dots. This is a significantly higher level of understanding. Also observe how the dots are counted. Are the counts made accurately? Is each counted only once? Another milestone for children occurs when they begin recognizing small patterned sets without counting.

The same concepts of more, less, and same are developed in the following game of "More and Less War."

**A**CTIVITY

## 6.3 More and Less War

The familiar game of "War" can be played with the dot cards or any cards that have sets on them; it can also be played with dominoes. In this version, children spin a more/less spinner before each turn (see Figure 6.2). If the spinner shows "Less," the player with less wins, and vice versa.

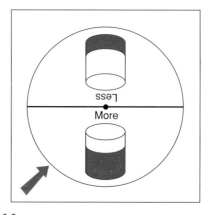

**Figure 6.2** A more/less spinner.

# Early Counting

Meaningful counting activities can begin in preschool. Generally, children at midyear in kindergarten should have a fair understanding of counting, but children must construct this idea. It cannot be forced. Only the counting sequence is a rote procedure. The *meaning* attached to counting is the key conceptual idea on which all other number concepts are developed.

## The Development of Counting Skills

Counting involves at least two separate skills. First, one must be able to produce the standard list of counting words in order: "One, two, three, four, . . ." Second, one must be able to connect this sequence in a one-to-one manner with the items in the set being counted. Each item must get one and only one count.

Experience and guidance are the major factors in the development of these counting skills. Many children come to kindergarten able to count sets of ten or beyond. At the same time, children from impoverished backgrounds may require considerable practice to make up their experience deficit. The size of the set is also a factor related to success in counting. Obviously, longer number strings require more practice to learn. The first 12 counts involve no pattern or repetition, and many children do not recognize a pattern in the teens.

Counting a set of objects that can be moved as they are counted is easier than counting objects that cannot be moved or touched. Counting a set that is ordered in some way, such as in a string of dots or other pattern, is easier than counting a randomly displayed set. There seems to be little advantage in making counting tasks difficult. Therefore, children still learning the skills of counting—that is, matching oral number words with objects—should be given sets of blocks or counters that they can move or pictures of sets that are arranged for easy counting.

## Meaning Attached to Counting

There is a difference between being able to count (as just described) and knowing what counting tells. When we count a set, the last number word used is the name of the "many-ness" of the set or the *cardinality* of the set. Though very young children seem to have some concept of quantity, they do not immediately connect this concept with the act of counting. When children understand that the last count word names the quantity of the set, they are said to have the *cardinality principle*. Most children by age $4\frac{1}{2}$ have made this connection (Fuson & Hall, 1983).

To determine if children have the cardinality rule, they can be given a set of objects and asked, "How many?" If they repeat or emphasize the last count, it can be inferred that they have switched meaning from a count use of the last word to a cardinality use of the last word. For example, "One, two, three, four, five, six. There are six." If this cardinal usage is not clear, the "How many?" question can be repeated. If the child then

announces the total without counting, it is clear that he or she is using the cardinal meaning of the counting word. However, a recount of the entire set would indicate that the question "How many?" was interpreted by the child as a command to count rather than a request for the quantity in the set.

In the classroom, you can help students develop a deeper sense of cardinality through almost any counting activity. The following two suggestions also provide you with some insight into children's current development.

---

**ACTIVITY**

### 6.4  Counting Sets

Have children count several sets where the number of objects is the same but the objects are very different in size. Discuss how they are alike and different. "Were you surprised that they were the same amount? Why or why not?"

---

**ACTIVITY**

### 6.5  Count and Rearrange

Have students count a set. Then rearrange the set and ask, "How many now?" If they see no need to count over, you can infer that they have connected the cardinality to the set regardless of its arrangement. If they choose to count again, discuss why they think the answer is the same.

---

# Numeral Writing and Recognition

Helping children read and write single-digit numerals is similar to teaching them to read and write letters of the alphabet. Traditionally, instruction has involved various forms of repetitious practice. Children trace over pages of numerals, repeatedly write the numbers from 0 to 10, make the numerals from clay, trace them in sand, write them on the chalkboard or in the air, and so on. The principle has been that numeral form is a rote activity that can best be learned through practice.

Baroody (1987) argues convincingly that while some numeral writing practice is clearly necessary, much time can be saved by focusing on the defining characteristics of each numeral and on a motor plan for forming the numerals. The characteristics of the numerals should be articulated and discussed. For example, 1, 4, and 7 are made up of straight lines, whereas 2 and 5 mix straight and curved. Similar numerals should be taught together in order to focus on the properties that are necessary to distinguish them from each other. The numerals 6 and 9, for example, are distinguished from all other numerals by a closed loop on a stick. The loop for the 6 is at the bottom, and the loop for the 9 is at the top. These features distinguish one from the other.

The calculator is a good instructional tool for numeral recognition. In addition to helping children with numerals, early activities can help develop familiarity with the calculator so that more complex activities are possible.

---

**ACTIVITY**

### 6.6 Find and Press

Every child should have a calculator. Always begin by having the children press the clear key. Then you say a number, and the children press that number on the calculator. If you have an overhead calculator, you can then show the children the correct key so that they can confirm their responses, or you can write the number on the board for children to check. Begin with single-digit numbers. Later, progress to two or three numbers called in succession. For example, call, "Three, seven, one" (not "Three hundred seventy-one"). Children press the complete string of numbers as called.

---

Perhaps the most common kindergarten textbook exercises have children match sets with numerals. Children are given pictured sets and asked to write or match the number that tells how many. Alternatively, they may be given a number and told to make or draw a set with that many objects. Many teacher resource books describe cute learning center activities where children put a numeral with the correct-sized set—frogs (with dots) on numbered lily pads, for example. It is important to note that these frequently overworked activities involve only the skills of counting sets and numeral recognition or writing. When children are successful with these activities, little is gained by continuing to do them.

## TECHNOLOGY NOTE

Computer software that allows children to create sets on the screen with the click of a mouse is quite common. *Unifix Software* (Hickey, 1996) is an electronic version of the popular Unifix cubes, plastic cubes that snap together to make bars. The software allows the teacher to add features to counting activities that are not available with the cubes alone. In its most basic form, children can make bars of cubes in any color, break the bars, move them around, add sounds to each cube, and more. The teacher can choose to have a numeral appear on each bar showing the total. From one to four loops can be created, with the loop total another option. Not only can students count to specified numbers and have the numerals appear for reinforcement, but they can informally begin to explore the idea that two quantities can form a larger amount.

Do not let these computer tools become play toys. It is important to keep the task problematic. For example, in early kindergarten, students could make a set of single blocks in one loop that is just as many as (or more or less than) a bar

the teacher has made in the first loop. (Files can be prepared ahead of time.) Later, students can explore different combinations of two bars that would equal a third bar.

Other software titles that can assist with early number development include *Number Meanings and Counting* (Tenth Planet, 1998c) and *MathKeys: Unlocking Whole Numbers, Grades K–2* (MECC, 1996b). ■

## Counting On and Counting Back

Although the forward sequence of numbers is relatively familiar to most young children, counting on and counting back are difficult skills for many. Frequent short practice drills are recommended.

---

**ACTIVITY**

### 6.7 Up and Back Counting

Counting up to and back from a target number in a rhythmic fashion is an important counting exercise. For example, line up five children and five chairs in front of the class. As the whole class counts from 1 to 5, the children sit down one at a time. When the target number, 5, is reached, it is repeated; the child who sat on 5 now stands, and the count goes back to 1. As the count goes back, the children stand up one at a time, and so on, "1, 2, 3, 4, 5, 5, 4, 3, 2, 1, 1, 2, . . ." Kindergarten and first-grade children find exercises such as this both fun and challenging. Any movement (clapping, turning around, doing jumping jacks) can be used as the count goes up and back in a rhythmic manner.

---

A variation of Activity 6.7 is to count up and back between two numbers. For example, start with 4 and count to 11 and back to 4, and so on. Keep a rhythm as in the other exercises. The calculator provides an excellent counting exercise for young children because they see the numerals as they count.

---

**ACTIVITY**

### 6.8 Calculator Up and Back

Have each child press ⊞ 1 ⊟ ⊟ ⊟ ⊟ ⊟. The display will go from 1 to 5 with each ⊟ press. The count should also be made out loud in a rhythm as in the other exercises. To start over, press the clear key and repeat. Counting up and back is also possible, but the end numbers will not be repeated. The following illustrates the key presses and what the children would say in rhythm:

3 ⊞ 1 ⊟⊟⊟⊟ ⊟ 1 ⊟⊟⊟⊟ ⊞ 1 ⊟⊟ . . .

"3 plus 1, 4, 5, 6, 7, minus 1, 6, 5, 4, 3, plus 1, 4, 5, . . ."

---

The last two activities are designed only to help students become fluent with the number words in both forward and reverse order and to begin counts with numbers other than 1. Although not at all easy for young students, these activities do not address counting on or counting back in a meaningful manner. The next two activities are designed for that purpose.

**Figure 6.4** **"There are four under the card. How many are there altogether? Count."**

─ **A**CTIVITY ─

## 6.9 Counting On with Counters

Give each child a collection of 10 or 12 small counters that the children line up left to right on their desks. Tell them to count four counters and push them under their left hands (see Figure 6.3). Then say, "Point to your hand. How many are there?" (Four.) "So let's count like this: f-o-u-r (pointing to their hand), five, six, . . ." Repeat with other numbers under the hand.

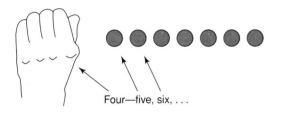

Four—five, six, . . .

**Figure 6.3** **Counting on: "Hide four. Count, starting from the number of counters hidden."**

The following activity addresses the same concept in a bit more problematic manner.

─ **A**CTIVITY ─

## 6.10 Real Counting On

On the overhead, cover some counters with a card before the light is turned on and place additional counters to the side of the card, as in Figure 6.4. Point to the card, and tell students how many are hidden. Ask how many counters there are in all.

How students respond is a good assessment of where they are in the development of this important idea. Do they repeat the count of the first set? Is it necessary for them to see the covered set? Or can they count on meaningfully and confidently? Do not forget to challenge results. "Why do you think there are 12?"

Applying counting-back skills is more difficult for children but can be developed in a manner similar to counting on. To learn about counting back, the children first count out a set as they did in the counting-on activities. These are covered. The covered set is pointed to, saying the number covered. Then, as counters are removed one at a time, the backward count is made. As a problem, count and cover a set. Remove a few counters, and ask how many remain covered.

# RELATIONSHIPS AMONG NUMBERS 1 THROUGH 10

Set-to-numeral matching and other counting activities are vitally important to number development. However, they focus only on the basic meaning of number and on accurate counting skill. Once children have acquired a concept of cardinality and can meaningfully use their counting skills, little more is to be gained from the kinds of counting activities described so far. More relationships must be created for children to develop number sense, a flexible concept of number not completely tied to counting.

## A Collection of Number Relationships

Figure 6.5 (p. 92) illustrates the four different types of relationships that children can and should develop with numbers:

- *Spatial relationships:* Children can learn to recognize sets of objects in patterned arrangements and tell how many without counting. For most numbers, there are several common patterns. Patterns can also be made up of two or more easier patterns for smaller numbers.

- *One and two more, one and two less:* The two-more-than and two-less-than relationships involve more than just the ability to count on two or count back two. Children should know that 7, for example, is 1 more than 6 and also 2 less than 9.

- *Anchors or "benchmarks" of 5 and 10:* Since 10 plays such a large role in our numeration system and because two fives make up 10, it is very useful to develop relationships for the numbers 1 to 10 to the important anchors of 5 and 10.

- *Part-part-whole relationships:* To conceptualize a number as being made up of two or more parts is the most important relationship that can be developed about numbers. For example, 7 can be thought of as a set of 3 and a set of 4 or a set of 2 and a set of 5.

The traditional number curriculum has placed almost no emphasis on these relationships. When children have learned to count and to read and write numerals, the next step has been, unfortunately, to begin addition and subtraction. The development of these relationships requires many months at the kindergarten and first-grade levels. The principal tool that children will use in this development is the one number tool they possess: counting. Initially, then, you will notice a lot of counting, and you may wonder if you are making progress. Have patience! Counting will become less and less necessary as children construct these new relationships and begin to use the more powerful ideas.

# Spatial Relationships: Patterned Set Recognition

Many children learn to recognize the dot arrangements on standard dice due to the many games they have played that use dice. Similar instant recognition can be developed for other patterns as well. The activities suggested here encourage reflective thinking about the patterns so that the relationships will be constructed. The patterns represent more than an abstract symbolism for the number of dots. Since much repetitive counting goes into learning to recognize the patterns, they are intimately connected to knowledge of the particular number concept. Quantities up to 10 can be known and named without the routine of counting. This can then aid in counting on (from a known patterned set) or learning combinations of numbers (seeing a pattern of two known smaller patterns). In general, the idea is to help children access real quantities and yet be free of the tedium of counting.

A good set of materials to use in pattern recognition activities is a set of dot plates. These can be made using small paper plates and the peel-off dots commonly available in stationery stores. A reasonable collection of patterns is shown in Figure 6.6. Note that some patterns are combinations of two smaller patterns or a pattern with one or two additional dots. These should be made in two colors. Keep the patterns compact. If the dots are spread out, the patterns are hard to see.

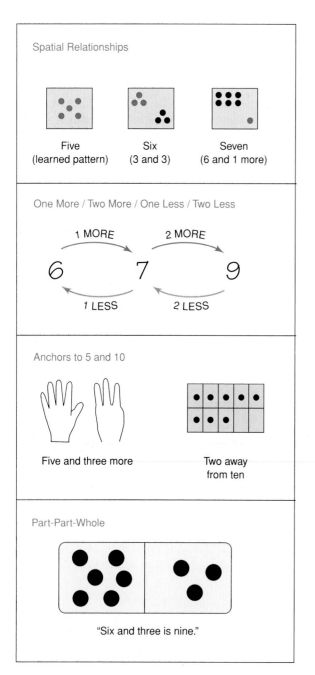

**Figure 6.5    Four relationships to be developed involving small numbers.**

---

**A**CTIVITY

## 6.11  Learning Patterns

To introduce the patterns, provide each student with about 10 counters and a piece of construction paper as a mat. Hold up a dot plate for about 3 seconds. "Make the pattern you saw using the counters on the mat. How many dots did you see? How did you see them?" Spend some time discussing the configuration of the pattern and how many dots. Do this with a few new patterns each day.

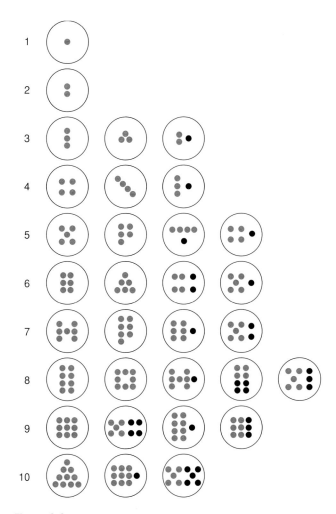

**Figure 6.6** **A useful collection of dot patterns for "dot plates."**

---

## ACTIVITY

### 6.12 Dot Plate Flash

Hold up a dot plate for only 1 to 3 seconds. "How many? How did you see it?" Children like to see how quickly they can recognize and say how many dots. Include lots of easy patterns and a few with more dots as you build their confidence. Students can also flash the dot plates to each other as a workstation activity.

---

## ACTIVITY

### 6.13 Dominoes

Make a set of dominoes out of poster board and put a dot pattern on each end. The dominoes can be about 2 inches by 4 inches. The same patterns can appear on lots of dominoes with different pairs of patterns making up each one. Let the children play dominoes in the regular way, matching up the ends. As a speed

---

activity, spread out all of the dominoes and see how fast the children play all of the dominoes or play until no more can be played. Regular dominoes could also be used, but there are not as many patterns.

The dot plates and patterned sets in general can easily be used in many other activities, as we will see. However, the instant recognition activities with the plates are exciting and can be done in 5 minutes at any time of day or between lessons. There is value in using them at any primary grade level and at any time of year.

## One and Two More, One and Two Less

When children count, they have no reason to reflect on the way one number is related to another. The goal is only to match number words with objects until they reach the end of the count. To learn that 6 and 8 are related by the twin relationships of "two more than" and "two less than" requires reflection on these ideas within tasks that permit counting. Counting on (or back) one or two counts is a useful tool in constructing these ideas.

---

## ACTIVITY

### 6.14 One-Less-Than Dominoes

Use the dot-pattern dominoes or a standard set to play "one-less-than" dominoes. Play in the usual way, but instead of matching ends, a new domino can be added if it has an end that is one less than the end on the board. A similar game can be played for two less, one more, or two more.

---

The following activities can be done for any of the four relationships; each will be described for only one.

---

## ACTIVITY

### 6.15 Make a Two-More-Than Set

Provide students with about six dot cards. Their task is to construct a set of counters that is two more than the set shown on the card. Similarly, spread out eight to ten dot cards, and find another card for each that is two less than the card shown. (Omit the 1 and 2 card for two less than, and so on.)

---

In activities where children find a set or make a set, they can add a numeral card (a small card with a number written on it) to all of the sets involved. They can also be encouraged to take turns reading a number sentence to their partner. If, for example, a set has been made that is two more than a set of four, the child can read this by saying the number sentence, "Two more than four is six."

The following activities involve numerals and sets together or just numerals. These are especially important in late first grade through the third grade.

— **A**CTIVITY —

## 6.16 One-More-Than Response Cards

**Provide each child with six to eight number cards about the size of index cards. (Children can cut up paper and make their own.) On the cards, put the numbers you will need for the day (e.g., 5 through 10). Now flash a dot plate and have students hold up the card that is one more than the plate. Nothing is said out loud, and all students respond. Similarly, you can hold up a numeral card or say a number orally, and they respond with their numeral cards.**

The calculator can be an exciting device to practice the relationships of one more than, two more than, one less than, and two less than.

— **A**CTIVITY —

## 6.17 A Calculator Two-More-Than Machine

**Teach children how to make a two-more-than machine. Press 0 ⊞ 2 ⊜. This makes the calculator a two-more-than machine. Now press any number— for example, 5. Children hold their finger over the ⊜ key and predict the number that is two more than 5. Then they press ⊜ to confirm. If they do not press any of the operation keys (+, −, ×, ÷) the "machine" will continue to perform in this way.**

What is really happening in the two-more-than machine is that the calculator "remembers" or stores the last operation, in this case "+ 2," and adds that to whatever number is in the window when the ⊜ key is pressed. If the child continues to press ⊜, the calculator will count by twos. At any time, a new number can be pressed followed by the equal key. To make a two-less-than machine, press 2 ⊟ 2 ⊜. (The first press of 2 is to avoid a negative number.) In the beginning, students forget and press operation keys, which change what their calculator is doing. Soon, however, they get the hang of using the calculator as a machine.

## Anchoring Numbers to 5 and 10

Here again, we want to help children relate a given number to other numbers, specifically 5 and 10. These relationships are especially useful in thinking about various combinations of numbers. For example, in each of the fol-

lowing, consider how the knowledge of 8 as "5 and 3 more" and as "2 away from 10" can play a role: 5 + 3, 8 + 6, 8 − 2, 8 − 3, 8 − 4, 13 − 8. (It may be worth stopping here to consider the role of 5 and 10 in each of these examples.) Later, similar relationships can be used in the development of mental computation skills on larger numbers such as 68 + 7.

The most common and perhaps most important model for this relationship is the ten-frame. Generally attributed to Robert Wirtz (1974), the ten-frame is simply a 2 × 5 array in which counters or dots are placed to illustrate numbers (see Figure 6.7). Ten-frames can be simply drawn on a full sheet of construction paper (or use the Blackline Master). Nothing fancy is required, and each child can have one. The ten-frame has been incorporated into a variety of activities in this book and is now popular in standard textbooks for children.

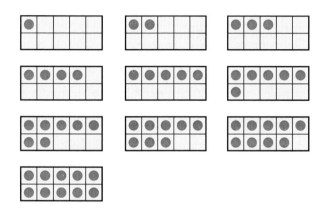

**Figure 6.7** **Ten-frames.**

For children in kindergarten or early first grade who have not yet explored a ten-frame, it is a good idea to begin with a five-frame. This row of five sections is also drawn on a sheet of construction paper (or use the Blackline Master). Provide children with about ten counters that will fit in the five-frame sections, and conduct the following activity.

— **A**CTIVITY —

## 6.18 Five-Frame Tell-About

**Explain that only one counter is permitted in each section of the five-frame. No other counters are allowed on the five-frame mat. Have the children show 3 on their five-frame. "What can you tell us about three from looking at your mat?" After hearing from several children, try other numbers from 0 to 5. Children may place their counters on the five-frame in any manner. What they observe will differ a great deal from child to child. For example, with four counters, a child with two on each end may say, "It has a space in the middle" or "It's two and two." There are no wrong answers. Focus attention on how many more counters are needed to make 5 or how far away from 5 a number is. Next try numbers between 5 and 10. The rule**

of one counter per section still holds, but don't explain how to do this. As shown in Figure 6.8, numbers greater than 5 are shown with a full five-frame and additional counters on the mat but not in the frame. In discussion, focus attention on these larger numbers as 5 and some more: "Eight is five and three more."

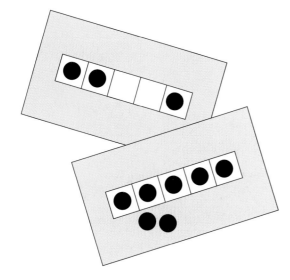

**Figure 6.8** A five-frame focuses on the 5 anchor. Counters are placed one to a section, and students tell how they see their number in the frame.

Notice that the five-frame really focuses on the relationship to 5 as an anchor for numbers but does not anchor numbers to 10. When five-frames have been used for a week or so, introduce ten-frames. You may want to play a ten-frame version of a "Five-Frame Tell-About," but soon introduce the following rule for showing numbers on the ten-frame: *Always fill the top row first, starting on the left, the same way you read. When the top row is full, counters can be placed in the bottom row, also from the left.* This will produce the "standard" way to show numbers on the ten-frame as in Figure 6.7.

For a while, many children will count every counter on their ten-frame. Some will take all counters off and begin each number from a blank frame. Others will soon learn to adjust numbers by adding on or taking off only what is required, often capitalizing on a row of five without counting. Do not pressure students. With continued practice, all students will grow. How they are using the ten-frame provides insight into students' current number concept development.

## ACTIVITY

### 6.19 Crazy Mixed-Up Numbers

This activity is adapted from *Mathematics Their Way* (Baratta-Lorton, 1976). All children make their ten-frame show the same number. The teacher then calls out random numbers between 0 and 10. After each number, the children change their ten-frames to show the new number. Children can play this game inde-

pendently by preparing lists of about 15 "crazy mixed-up numbers." One child plays "teacher," and the rest use the ten-frames. Children like to make up their own number lists.

"Crazy Mixed-Up Numbers" is much more of a problem than it first appears. How do you decide how to change your ten-frame? Some children will wipe off the entire frame and start over with each number. Others will have learned what each number looks like. To add another dimension, have the children tell, *before changing their ten-frames,* how many more counters need to be added ("plus") or removed ("minus"). They then call out plus or minus whatever amount is appropriate. If, for example, the frames showed 6, and the teacher called out "four," the children would respond, "Minus two!" and then change their ten-frames accordingly. A discussion of how they know what to do is valuable.

## ACTIVITY

### 6.20 Ten-Frame Translation

Give students a number in some form other than a ten-frame, and have them show that number on their ten-frames. Show them a dot card, hold up fingers, show some counters on the overhead, hold up a numeral card, or simply say a number out loud. These activities could also be done independently at a workstation by providing the number cards or sets along with the ten-frames and counters. Worksheets could be prepared for independent seatwork, as shown in Figure 6.9. The children would use an actual ten-frame and then record the result on the paper.

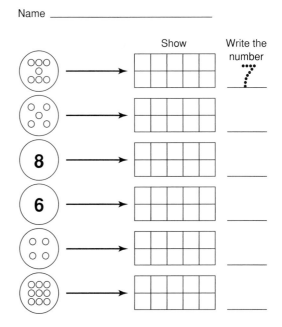

**Figure 6.9** A ten-frame record sheet. Children can use a large ten-frame with counters and then draw dots in the ten-frames on the worksheet.

Ten-frame flash cards are an important variation of ten-frames. Make cards from poster board about the size of a small index card, with a ten-frame on each and dots drawn in the frames. A set of 20 cards consists of a 0 card, a 10 card, and two each of the numbers 1 to 9. The cards allow for simple drill activities to reinforce the 5 and 10 anchors.

---

**ACTIVITY**

## 6.21 Ten-Frame Flash

**Flash ten-frame cards to the class or group, and see how fast the children can tell how many dots are shown. This activity is fast-paced, takes only a few minutes, can be done at any time, and is a lot of fun if you encourage speed.**

---

Important variations of "Ten-Frame Flash" include

- Saying the number of spaces on the card instead of the number of dots
- Saying one more than the number of dots (or two more, and also less than)
- Saying the "ten fact"—for example, "Six and four make ten"

After students have become familiar with the ten-frame, simply having a large blank ten-frame drawn on the board can profitably influence children's thinking about 5 and 10 as they do number activities or discuss numbers at any time. Try looking at a ten-frame while doing the following two activities.

---

**ACTIVITY**

## 6.22 Five-And

**In "Five-And," the teacher calls out numbers between 5 and 10. The children respond "Five and _____" using the appropriate number. For example, if you say, "Eight!" the children respond, "Five and three."**

---

**ACTIVITY**

## 6.23 Make-Ten

**Call out numbers between 0 and 10. The children respond by saying how many more are needed to make 10. This is most effective with numbers between 5 and 10.**

---

Ten-frame tasks are surprisingly problematic for students. Even in the drill activities just described, students must reflect on the two rows of five, the spaces remaining, and how a particular number of dots is so much more or less than 5. The early discussions of how numbers are seen on the five-frames or ten-frames are examples of brief after activities in which students learn from one another.

# Part-Part-Whole Relationships

Consider what you think about when you count a set of seven objects. What is significant is what you do *not* think about. Specifically, counting a set will never cause you to focus on the fact that it could be made up of two parts and what the size of those parts might be. Without activities that focus on quantities in terms of two or more parts, many children simply continue to use counting as their principal means of accessing quantity. A noted researcher in children's number concepts, Lauren Resnick (1983), states:

> Probably the major conceptual achievement of the early school years is the interpretation of numbers in terms of part and whole relationships. With the application of a Part-Whole schema to quantity, it becomes possible for children to think about numbers as compositions of other numbers. This enrichment of number understanding permits forms of mathematical problem solving and interpretation that are not available to younger children. (p. 114)

A study of kindergarten children examined the effects of part-part-whole activities on number concepts (Fischer, 1990). With only 20 days of instruction to develop the part-part-whole structure, children showed significantly higher achievement than the control group on number concepts, word problems, and place-value concepts.

## Basic Ingredients of Part-Part-Whole Activities

Most part-part-whole activities focus on a single number for the entire activity. Thus a child or group of children working together might work on the number 7 throughout the activity. Either children build the designated quantity in two or more parts, using a wide variety of materials and formats, or else they start with the full amount and separate it into two or more parts. A group of two or three children may work on one number in one activity for 5 to 20 minutes. Kindergarten children will usually begin these activities working on the number 4 or 5. As concepts develop, the children can extend their work to numbers 6 to 12. It is not unusual to find children in the second grade who have not developed firm part-part-whole constructs for numbers in the 7-to-12 range.

When children do these activities, have them say or "read" the parts aloud or write them down on some form of recording sheet (or do both). Reading or writing the combinations serves as a means of encouraging reflective thought focused on the part-whole relationship. Writing can be in the form of drawings, numbers written in blanks (_____ and _____), or addition equations if these have been introduced ($3 + 5 = 8$). There is a clear connection between part-part-whole concepts and addition and subtraction ideas.

A special and important variation of part-part-whole activities is referred to as *missing-part* activities. In a missing-part activity, children know the whole amount and use their already developed knowledge of the parts of that whole to try to tell what the covered or hidden part is. If they do not know or are unsure, they simply uncover the unknown part and say the full combination as they would normally. These activities should never be conducted as "problems" or "tests" with right and wrong answers. They are simply learning activities where children try to think of a part they cannot see. Missing-part activities provide maximum reflection on the combinations for a number. They also serve as the forerunner to subtraction concepts. With a whole of 8 but with only 3 showing, the child can later learn to write "8 − 3 = 5."

In most of the part-part-whole activities that involve materials, children will display sets with the designated number of objects in two or more parts each. It is reasonable to have children make at least eight ways to show a number with one set of materials. Each number display can be placed on a small mat or piece of construction paper. Two or three children working together may have quite a large number of displays, all using the same materials and all representing the same quantity in two or more parts. As you come around to observe, ask individuals to "read a number sentence" to go with the designs. Encourage children to read their designs to each other.

## Part-Part-Whole Activities

┌─ **A**CTIVITY ─────────────
### 6.24 Build It in Parts

**The ideas here are illustrated in Figure 6.10.**

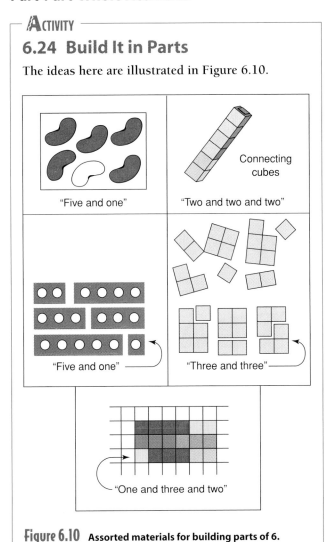

**Figure 6.10** Assorted materials for building parts of 6.

- Make sets with "two-color counters" such as lima beans spray-painted on one side (also available in plastic).
- Make bars of connecting cubes or other plastic cubes that interlock. Make each bar with two colors.
- Color rows of squares on 1-inch grid paper.
- Make combinations with "dot strips," which are simply strips of poster board with dots on them. Make lots of strips with one to four dots and some strips with five to ten dots. The strips are only as long as the row of dots that is on them. (Punch holes in the dots to make a set for the overhead projector.)
- Make combinations with two-column strips. These are cut from tagboard ruled in 1-inch squares. Except for the single square, all pieces are cut from two columns of squares. Odd numbers will have an odd square on one end. (Punch holes in center of the squares to make a set for the overhead projector.)

As a variation of "Build It in Parts," have students make designs with different materials. Each design has the same prescribed number of objects. When talking with the children about their designs, ask how they can see their design in two parts or in three parts.

- Make arrangements of wooden cubes.
- Make designs with pattern blocks. It is a good idea to use only one or two shapes at a time.
- Make designs with flat toothpicks. These can be dipped in white glue and placed on small squares of construction paper to create a permanent record.
- Make designs with touching squares or triangles. Cut a large supply of small squares or triangles out of construction paper. These can also be pasted down.

It is both fun and useful to challenge children to see their designs in different ways, producing different number combinations. In Figure 6.11 (p. 98), decide how children look at the designs to get the combinations listed under each.

┌─ **A**CTIVITY ─────────────
### 6.25 Two out of Three

**Make lists of three numbers, two of which total the whole that children are focusing on. Here is an example list for the number 5:**

2—3—4
5—0—2
1—3—2
3—1—4
2—2—3
4—3—1

With the list on the board or overhead, children can take turns selecting the two numbers that make the whole. As with all problem-solving activities, children should be challenged to justify their answers. The same activity can be used in a worksheet format, but the real value lies in the discussion and justification.

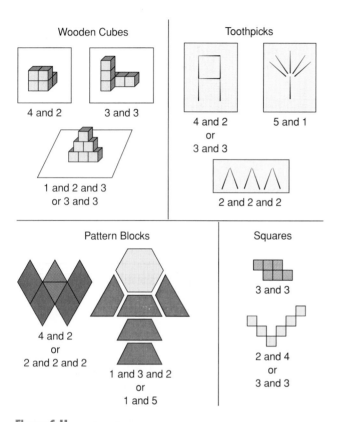

**Figure 6.11**  Designs for 6.

## Missing-Part Activities

Missing-part activities require some way for a part to be hidden or unknown. Usually this is done with two children working together or else in a teacher-directed manner with the class. Again, the focus of the activity remains on a single designated quantity as the whole.

---

### ACTIVITY

### 6.26 Covered Parts

A set of counters equal to the target amount is counted out, and the rest are put aside. One child places the counters under a margarine tub or piece of tagboard. The child then pulls some out into view. (This amount could be none, all, or any amount in between.) For example, if 6 is the whole and 4 are showing, the other child says, "Four and *two* is six." If there is hesitation or if the hidden part is unknown, the hidden part is immediately shown. The focus is on learning and thinking, not on testing and anxiety.

---

### ACTIVITY

### 6.27 Missing-Part Cards

For each number 4 to 10, make missing-part cards on strips of 3-by-9-inch tagboard. Each card has a numeral for the whole and two dot sets with one set covered by a flap. For the number 8, you need nine cards with the visible part ranging from 0 to 8 dots. Students use the cards as in "Covered Parts," saying, "Four and two is six" for a card showing four dots and hiding two (see Figure 6.12).

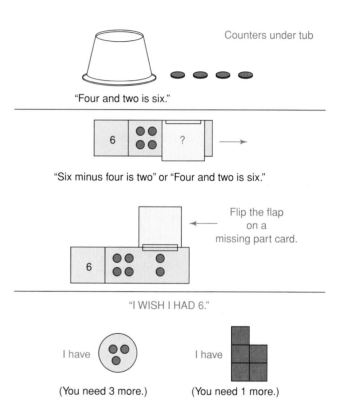

**Figure 6.12**  Missing-part activities.

---

### ACTIVITY

### 6.28 I Wish I Had

Hold out a bar of connecting cubes, a dot strip, a two-column strip, or a dot plate showing 6 or less. Say, "I wish I had six." The children respond with the part that is needed to make 6. Counting on can be used to check. The game can focus on a single whole, or the "I wish I had" number can change each time.

---

The following are also missing-part activities but are completely symbolic.

## ACTIVITY

### 6.29 Calculator Parts of 8 Machine

Make a parts of 8 machine by pressing 8 ⊟ 8 ⊟. Now if any number from 0 to 8 is pressed followed by ⊟, the display shows the other part. (The second part shows as a negative number. Tell students that is how they can tell it is the second part.) Children should try to say the other part before they press ⊟. Though this is basically a drill activity, a discussion with any child concerning his or her reasoning returns it to a problem orientation. Machines can be made for any number in the same way.

## TECHNOLOGY NOTE

There are lots of ways you can use computer software to create part-part-whole activities. All that is needed is a program that permits students to create sets of objects on the screen. *Unifix Software* (Hickey, 1996) is especially nice for this purpose. One approach has students create two-part bars to match a single bar that you specify. Here students could make many bars all for the same number. Alternatively, students could put counters in two set loops formed by the computer. As always, the computer should offer something beyond the simple manipulative. In this instance, the advantage is your ability to control the type of feedback provided. Options include showing the total in a bar, the total in a loop, and the total of all blocks on the screen. For example, a student can make a bar of two and a bar of six with a numeral showing on each. When the bars are snapped together, the new bar total of eight appears.

*Combining and Breaking Apart Numbers* (Tenth Planet, 1998a) is specifically designed for part-part-whole activities. Although the early activities in this package are fairly passive and slow, the "Through" or last section makes the mathematics reasonably problematic. In various animated settings, children attempt to make a number either in two parts or by adding two groups and then removing one or two groups. This is an example of software that requires some teacher guidance to create good problems or else students will not stay engaged. The printed support material includes suggestions for corresponding off-line activities that make this a worthwhile program. ■

## Dot Card Activities

Many good number development activities involve more than one of the relationships discussed so far. As children learn about ten-frames, patterned sets, and other relationships, the dot cards in the Blackline Masters at the back of this book provide a wealth of activities (see Figure 6.13). The cards contain dot patterns, patterns that require counting, combina-

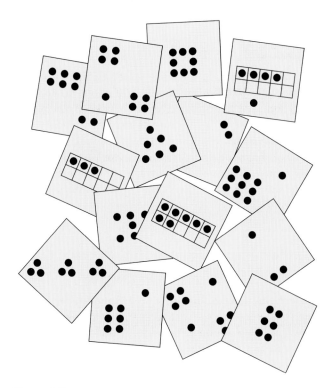

**Figure 6.13**  **Dot cards can be made using the Blackline Masters at the back of this book.**

tions of two and three simple patterns, and ten-frames with "standard" as well as unusual placements of dots. When children use these cards for almost any activity that involves number concepts, the cards make them think about numbers in many different ways. The dot cards add another dimension to many of the activities already described and can be used effectively in the following activities.

## ACTIVITY

### 6.30 Double War

The game of "Double War" (Kamii, 1985) is played like war, but on each play, both players turn up two cards instead of one. The winner is the one with the larger total number. Children playing the game can use many different number relationships to determine the winner without actually finding the total number of dots.

## ACTIVITY

### 6.31 Dot-Card Trains

Make a long row of dot cards from 0 up to 9, then go back again to 1, then up, and so on. Alternatively, begin with 0 or 1 and make a two-more/two-less train.

---

**ACTIVITY**

## 6.32 Difference War

Besides dealing out the cards to the two players as in regular "War," prepare a pile of about 50 counters. On each play, the players turn over their cards as usual. The player with the greater number of dots wins as many counters from the pile as the difference between the two cards. The players keep their cards. The game is over when the counter pile runs out. The player with the most counters wins the game.

---

**ACTIVITY**

## 6.33 Missing-Part Combos

Select a number between 5 and 12, and find combinations of two cards that total that number. When students have found at least ten combinations, one student can then turn one card in each group face down. The next challenge is to name the card that was turned down. ("Before you check, why do you think you are right?")

---

# RELATIONSHIPS FOR NUMBERS 10 TO 20

Even though kindergarten, first-, and second-grade children daily experience numbers up to 20 and beyond, it should not be assumed that they will automatically extend the set of relationships they have developed on smaller numbers to the numbers beyond 10. And yet these numbers play a big part in many simple counting activities, in basic facts, and in much of what we do with mental computation. Relationships with these numbers are just as important as relationships involving the numbers through 10.

## A Pre-Place-Value Relationship with 10

A set of ten should play a major role in children's initial understanding of numbers between 10 and 20. When children see a set of six with a set of ten, they should know without counting that the total is 16. However, the numbers between 10 and 20 are not an appropriate place to discuss place-value concepts. That is, prior to a much more complete development of place-value concepts (appropriate for second grade and beyond), children should not be asked to explain

the 1 in 16 as representing "one ten." (Stop for a moment and say to yourself: "one ten." Think about it! What would this mean to a 5-year-old? Ten is a lot. How can it be one? This is initially a strange idea.) The inappropriateness of discussing "one ten and six ones" (what's a one?) does not mean that a set of ten should not figure prominently in the discussion of the teen numbers. The following activity illustrates this idea.

---

**ACTIVITY**

## 6.34 Ten and Some More

Use a simple two-part mat, and have children count out ten counters onto one side. Next have them put five counters on the other side. Together count all of the counters by ones. Chorus the combination: "Ten and five is fifteen." Turn the mat around: "Five and ten is fifteen." Repeat with other numbers in a random order but without changing the 10 side of the mat.

---

Activity 6.34 is designed to teach new number names and thus requires a certain amount of directed teaching. Following this activity, explore numbers to 20 in a more open-ended manner. Provide each child with two ten-frames drawn one under the other on a construction paper mat. In random order, have children show numbers to 20 on their mats. There is no preferred way to do this as long as there are the correct number of counters. What is interesting is to discuss how the counters can be placed on the mat so that it is easy to see how many are there. Have children share their ideas. Not every child will use a full set of ten, but as this idea becomes more popular, the notion that ten and some more is a teen amount will soon be developed. Do not forget to include numbers less than ten as well. As you listen to your children, you may want to begin challenging them to find ways to show 26 counters or even more.

## Extending More and Less Relationships

The relationships of one more than, two more than, one less than, and two less than are important for all numbers. However, these ideas are built on or connected to the same concepts for numbers less than 10. The fact that 17 is one less than 18 is connected to the idea that 7 is one less than 8. Children may need help in making this connection.

---

**ACTIVITY**

## 6.35 More and Less Extended

On the overhead, show 7 counters, and ask what is two more, or one less, and so on. Now add a filled ten-frame to the display (or 10 in any pattern), and repeat the questions. Pair up questions by covering and uncovering the ten-frame as illustrated in Figure 6.14.

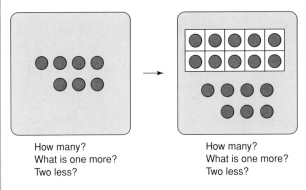

How many?
What is one more?
Two less?

How many?
What is one more?
Two less?

**Figure 6.14** Extending relationships to the teens.

## Double and Near-Double Relationships

The use of doubles (double 6 is 12) and near-doubles (13 is double 6 and 1 more) is generally considered a strategy for memorizing basic addition facts. There is no reason why children should not begin to develop these relationships long before they are concerned with memorizing basic facts. Doubles and near-doubles are simply special cases of the general part-part-whole construct.

Relate the doubles to special images. Thornton (1982) helped first graders connect doubles to these visual ideas:

Double 3 is the bug double: three legs on each side.

Double 4 is the spider double: four legs on each side.

Double 5 is the hand double: two hands.

Double 6 is the egg carton double: two rows of six eggs.

Double 7 is the two-week double: two weeks on the calendar.

Double 8 is the crayon double: two rows of eight crayons in a box.

Double 9 is the 18-wheeler double: two sides, nine wheels on each side.

Children can draw pictures or make posters that illustrate the doubles for each number. There is no reason that the images need be restricted to those listed here. Any images that are strong ideas for your children will be good for them.

Periodically conduct oral exercises in which students double the number you say. Ask children to explain how they knew a particular double. Many will not use the pictures.

**ACTIVITY**

### 6.36 The Double Maker

Make the calculator into a "double maker" by pressing 2 ⊠ ▭. Now a press of any digit followed by ▭ will produce the double of that number. Children can work in pairs or individually to try to beat the calculator.

As a related oral task, say a number, and ask students to tell what double it is. "What is fourteen?" (Double 7!) When students can do this well, use any number up to 20. "What is seventeen?" (Double 8 and 1 more.)

## NUMBER SENSE AND THE REAL WORLD

So far we have discussed the development of number meanings and some very specific relationships involving numbers. These ideas are very much a part of what is meant by number sense. Here we examine ways to broaden the early knowledge of numbers even further. Relationships of numbers to real-world quantities and measures and the use of numbers in simple estimations can help children develop the flexible, intuitive ideas about numbers that are most desired.

### Estimation and Measuring

One of the best ways for children to think of real quantities is to associate numbers with measures of things. In the early grades, measures of length, weight, and time are good places to begin. Just measuring and recording results will not be very effective, however, since there is no reason for children to be interested in or think about the result. To help children think or reflect a bit on what number might tell how long the desk is or how heavy the book is, it would be good if they could first write down or tell you an estimate. To produce an estimate is, however, a very difficult task for young children. They do not understand the concept of "estimate" or "about." For example, suppose that you have cut out of poster board an ample supply of very large footprints, say, about 18 inches long. All are exactly the same size. You would like to ask the class, "About how many footprints will it take to measure across the rug in our reading corner?" The key word here is *about,* and it is one that you will need to spend a lot of time helping children understand. To this end, the request of an estimate can be made in ways that help with the concept of "about" and still permit children to respond.

The following estimation questions can be used with most early estimation activities:

- *More or less than* _____? Will it be more or less than 10 footprints? Will the apple weigh more or less than 20 wooden blocks? Are there more or less than 15 connecting cubes in this long bar?

- *Closer to* _____ *or to* _____? Will it be closer to 5 footprints or closer to 20 footprints? Will the apple weigh closer to 10 blocks or closer to 30 blocks? Does this bar have closer to 10 cubes or closer to 50 cubes?

- *Less than* _____, *between* _____ *and* _____, *or more than* _____? Will it take less than 10, between 10 and 20, or more than 20 footprints? Will the apple weigh less than 5 blocks, between 5 and 15 blocks, or more than 15 blocks? Are there less than 20, between 20 and 50, or more than 50 cubes in this bar?

- *About* _____. Use one of these numbers: 5, 10, 15, 20, 25, 30, 35, 40, . . . About how many footprints? About how many blocks will the apple weigh? About how many cubes are in this bar?

This list of estimation question formats is arranged from the easiest to the most difficult. However, notice that each clearly indicates to the children that they need not come up with an exact amount or number. Asking for estimates using these formats helps children learn what you mean by "about." Every child can make an estimate without having to pull a number out of the air.

For almost all measurement estimation activities at the K–2 level, it is good to use an informal measuring unit instead of standard units such as feet, centimeters, pounds, or kilograms. This avoids the problem of children's lack of familiarity with the unit. If, however, you want them to learn about a unit of measure, say, the meter, then by all means include that unit in these exercises.

Another suggestion is to estimate several things in succession using the same unit. This will help children develop an understanding of relative measures. For example, suppose that you are estimating and measuring "around things" using a string. To measure, the string is wrapped around the object and then measured in some unit such as craft sticks. After measuring the distance around Demetria's head, estimate the distance around the wastebasket or around the globe or around George's wrist. Each successive measure helps children with the new estimates.

An alternative approach is to estimate and measure the same item successively with different-sized units. You will be surprised when young children guess that the measure is smaller when the unit gets smaller. The ideas that smaller

units produce larger measurements and large units small measurements are difficult relationships for children to construct. (See Chapter 16 for a more complete discussion of measurement.)

## More Connections

Here are some additional activities that can help children connect numbers to real situations.

### ACTIVITY

### 6.37  Add a Unit to Your Number

Write a number on the board. Now suggest some units to go with it, and ask the children what they can think of that fits. For example, suppose the number is 9. "What do you think of when I say 9 *dollars? 9 hours? 9 cars? 9 kids? 9 meters? 9 o'clock? 9 hand spans? 9 gallons?*" Spend some time in discussion of each. Let children suggest units as well. Be prepared to explore some of the ideas either immediately or as projects or tasks to share with parents at home.

### ACTIVITY

### 6.38  Is It Reasonable?

Select a number and a unit—for example, 15 feet. Could the teacher be 15 feet tall? Could your living room be 15 feet wide? Can a man jump 15 feet high? Could three children stretch their arms 15 feet? Pick any number, large or small, and a unit with which children are familiar. Then make up a series of these questions.

Once children are familiar with Activity 6.38, have them select the number and the unit or things (10 kids, 20 bananas, . . .), and see what kinds of questions children make up. When a difference of opinion develops, capitalize on the opportunity to explore and find out. Resist the temptation to supply your adult-level knowledge. Rather, say, "Well, how can we find out if it is or is not reasonable? Who has an idea about what we could do?"

### ACTIVITY

### 6.39  Things That Are Seven

Pick any number (7 is used here as an example), and have groups of children find ways to tell about that number. Seven might be the days in a week, the number of people in Mandy's family, or the number of kittens in Inky's litter. Other children might want to show 7 in some measurement way, such as a stack of 7 books, 7 glasses of water in a jug, 7 long giant steps, the length of 7 children lying down head to toe, or how many hops they can hop in 7 seconds. Groups can present their ideas orally, make a written report, contribute a page to put on the bulletin board, or present a demonstration.

These activities are really problems in the truest sense. Not only are there no clear answers, but children can easily begin to pose their own questions and explore number in the part of the environment most interesting to them. Children will not have these real-world connections when you begin, and you may be disappointed in their limited ideas about number. Howden (1989) writes about a first-grade teacher of children from very impoverished backgrounds who told her, "They all have fingers, the school grounds are strewn with lots of pebbles and leaves, and pinto beans are cheap. So we count, sort, compare, and talk about such objects. We've measured and weighed almost everything in this room and almost everything the children can drag in" (p. 6). This teacher's children had produced a wonderfully rich and long list of responses to the question "What comes to your mind when I say twenty-four?" In another school in a professional community where test scores are high, the same question brought almost no response from a class of third graders. It can be a very rewarding effort to help children connect their number ideas to the real world.

# Graphs

Graphing activities are another good way to connect children's worlds with number. Chapter 18 discusses ways to make graphs with children in grades K–2. Graphs can be quickly made of almost any data that can be gathered from the students: favorite ice cream, color, sports team, pet; number of sisters and brothers; kids who ride different buses; types of shoes; number of pets; and so on. Graphs can be connected to content in other areas. A unit on sea life might lead to a graph of favorite sea animals.

Once a simple bar graph is made, it is very important to take a few minutes to ask as many number questions as is appropriate for the graph. In the early stages of number development (grades K–1), the use of graphs for number relationships and for connecting numbers to real quantities in the children's environment is a more important reason for building graphs than the graphs themselves. The graphs focus attention on counts of realistic things. Equally important, bar graphs clearly exhibit comparisons between and among numbers that are rarely made when only one number or quantity is considered at a time. See Figure 6.15

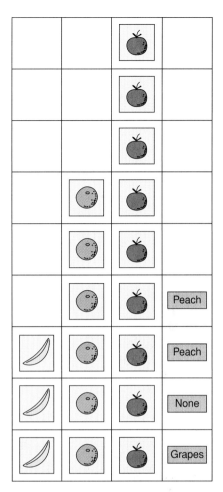

Class graph showing fruit brought for snack. Paper cutouts for bananas, oranges, apples, and cards for "others."

- — Which bar (or refer to what the graph represents) is most, least?
- — Which are more (less) than 7 (or some other number)?
- — Which is one less (more) than this bar?
- — How much more is _____ than _____? (Follow this question immediately by reversing the order and asking how much less.)
- — How much less is _____ than _____? (Reverse this question after receiving an answer.)
- — How much difference is there between _____ and _____ ?
- — Which two bars together are the same as _____ ?

**Figure 6.15** **Relationships and number sense in a bar graph.**

for an example of a graph and questions that can be asked. At first, children will have trouble with the questions involving differences, but repeated exposure to these ideas in a bar graph format will improve their understanding.

These comparison concepts add considerably to children's understanding of number.

 LITERATURE CONNECTIONS

Children's literature abounds with wonderful counting books. Involving children with books in a variety of ways can serve to connect number to reality, make it a personal experience, and provide ample opportunities for problem solving. Be sure to go beyond simply reading a counting book or a number-related book and looking at the pictures. Find a way to extend the book into the children's world. Create problems related to the story. Have children write a similar story. Extend the numbers and see what happens. Create a mural, graphs, or posters. The ideas are as plentiful as the books. Here are a few ideas for making literature connections to number concepts and number sense.

## Anno's Counting House
### (Anno, 1982)

In the beautiful style of Anno, this book shows ten children in various parts of a house. As the pages are turned, the house front covers the children, and a few are visible through cutout windows. A second house is on the opposite page. As you move through the book, the children move one at a time to the second house, creating the potential for a 10–0, 9–1, 8–2, . . . , 0–10 pattern of pairs. But as each page shows part of the children through the window, there is an opportunity to discuss how many in the missing part. Have children use counters to model the story as you "read" it the second or third time.

What if the children moved in pairs instead of one at a time? What if there were three houses? What if there were more children? What else could be in the house to count? How many rooms, pictures, windows? What about your house? What about two classrooms or two buses instead of houses?

## The Very Hungry Caterpillar
### (Carle, 1969)

This is a predictable-progression counting book about a caterpillar who eats first one thing, then two, and so on. Children can create their own eating stories and illustrate them. What if more than one type of thing were eaten at each stop? What combinations for each number are there? Are seven little things more or less than three very large things? What does all of this stuff weigh? How many things are eaten altogether?

## Two Ways to Count to Ten
### (Dee, 1988)

This Liberian folktale is about King Leopard in search of the best animal to marry his daughter. The task devised involves throwing a spear and counting to 10 before the spear lands. Many animals try and fail. Counting by ones proves too lengthy. Finally, the antelope succeeds by counting "2, 4, 6, 8, 10."

The story is a perfect lead-in to skip counting. Can you count to 10 by threes? How else can you count to 10? How many ways can you count to 48? What numbers can you reach if you count by fives? The size of the numbers you investigate is limited only by the children. A hundreds board or counters are useful thinker toys to help with these problems. Be sure to have children write about what they discover in their investigations.

Another fun book to use is *The King's Commissioners* (Friedman, 1994), a hilarious tale that also opens up opportunities to count by different groupings or skip counting.

# EXTENSIONS TO EARLY MENTAL MATHEMATICS

Teachers in the second and third grades can capitalize on some of the early number relationships and extend them to numbers up to 100. A useful set of materials to help with these relationships is the little ten-frames found in the Blackline Masters. Each child should have a set of 10 tens and a set of frames for each number 1 to 9 with an extra 5.

The following three ideas are illustrated with the little ten-frames in Figure 6.16. First are the relationships of one more than and one less than. If you understand that one more than 6 is 7, then in a similar manner, ten more than 60 is 70 (that is, one more ten). The second idea is really a look ahead to fact strategies. If a child has learned to think about adding on to 8 or 9 by first adding up to 10 and then adding the rest, the extension to similar two-digit numbers is quite simple; see Figure 6.16(b). Finally, the most powerful idea for small numbers is thinking of them in parts. It is a very useful idea (though not one found in textbooks) to take apart larger numbers to begin to develop some flexibility in the same way. Children can begin by thinking of ways to take apart a multiple of 10 such as 80. Once they do it with tens, the challenge can be to think of ways to take apart 80 when one part has a 5 in it, such as 25 or 35.

More will be said about early mental computation in Chapter 10. The point to be made here is that early number relationships have a greater impact on what children know than may be apparent at first. Even teachers in the upper grades may profitably consider the use of ten-frames and part-part-whole activities.

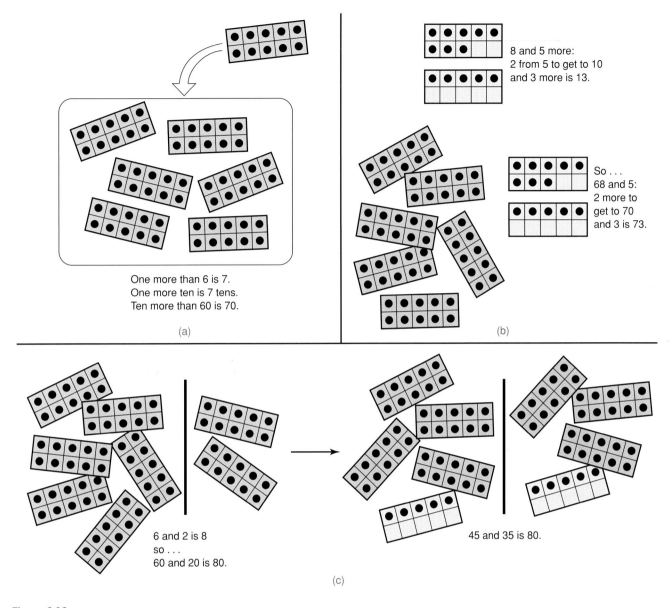

8 and 5 more:
2 from 5 to get to 10
and 3 more is 13.

So . . .
68 and 5:
2 more to
get to 70
and 3 is 73.

One more than 6 is 7.
One more ten is 7 tens.
Ten more than 60 is 70.

(a)

(b)

6 and 2 is 8
so . . .
60 and 20 is 80.

45 and 35 is 80.

(c)

**Figure 6.16** **Extending early number relationships to mental computation activities.**

# REFLECTIONS ON CHAPTER 6

## Writing to Learn

1. How can you tell if children are attaching any meaning to their counting?

2. Describe an activity that is a "set-to-numeral match" activity. What ideas must a child have to do these activities meaningfully and correctly?

3. What are the four types of relationships that have been described for small numbers? Explain briefly what each of these means, and suggest at least one activity for each.

4. Describe a missing-part activity. What should happen if the child trying to give the missing part does not know it?

5. How can a calculator be used to develop early counting ideas connected with number? How can a calculator be used to help

a child practice number relationships such as part-part-whole or one less than?

6. For numbers between 10 and 20, describe how to develop each of these ideas:

   a. The idea of the teens as a set of 10 and some more

   b. Extension of the one-more/one-less concept to the teens

7. Describe briefly your own idea of what number sense is.

8. What are three ways that children can be helped to connect numbers to real-world ideas?

9. Give two examples of how early number relationships can be used to develop some early mental computation skills.

## For Discussion and Exploration

1. Examine a textbook series for grades K–2. Compare the treatment of counting and number concept development with that presented in this chapter. What ideas are stressed? What ideas are missed altogether? If you were teaching in one of these grades, how would you plan your number concept development program? What part would the text play?

2. Many teachers in grades above the second find that their children do not possess the number relationships discussed in this chapter but rely heavily on counting. Given the pressures of other content at these grades, how much effort should be made to remediate these number concept deficiencies?

## Recommendations for Further Reading

### Highly Recommended

Burton, G. (1993). *Number sense and operations: Addenda series, grades K–6.* Reston, VA: National Council of Teachers of Mathematics.
   For developing number concepts, either this book or the *Number Sense and Operations* book in the Addenda Series for your grade level should be a must. The activities are developed in sufficient detail to give you clear guidance and yet allow considerable flexibility.

National Council of Teachers of Mathematics. (1989). Number sense [Focus issue]. *Arithmetic Teacher, 36*(6).
   This remains one of the best focus issues of *The Arithmetic Teacher* (predecessor of *Teaching Children Mathematics*). It contains the Howden article referenced in this chapter and several others worth reading. It is still timely.

Van de Walle, J. A., & Watkins, K. B. (1993). Early development of number sense. In R. J. Jensen (Ed.), *Research ideas for the classroom: Early childhood mathematics* (pp. 127–150). Old Tappan, NJ: Macmillan.
   This chapter includes a discussion of many of the K–2 topics covered in this text as well as a broader discussion of number sense, including mental computation and estimation. It provides a good mix of practical ideas with ample references to the research literature.

### Other Suggestions

Baroody, A. J., & Wilkins, J. L. M. (1999). The development of informal counting, number, and arithmetic skills and concepts. In J. V. Copley (Ed.), *Mathematics in the early years* (pp. 48–65). Reston, VA: National Council of Teachers of Mathematics.

Bresser, R., & Holtzman, C. (1999). *Developing number sense.* Sausalito, CA: Math Solutions Publications.

Clements, D. H. (1999). Subitizing: What is it? Why teach it? *Teaching Children Mathematics, 5,* 400–405.

Fuson, K. C. (1989). *Children's counting and concepts of number.* New York: Springer-Verlag.

Greenes, C., Schulman, L., & Spungin, R. (1993). Developing sense about numbers. *Arithmetic Teacher, 40,* 279–284.

Kouba, V. L., Zawojewski, J. S., & Strutchens, M. E. (1997). What do students know about numbers and operations? In P. A. Kenney & E. A. Silver (Eds.), *Results from the sixth mathematics assessment of the National Assessment of Educational Progress* (pp. 87–140). Reston, VA: National Council of Teachers of Mathematics.

Leutzinger, L. P., & Bertheau, M. (1989). Making sense of numbers. In P. R. Trafton (Ed.), *New directions for elementary school mathematics* (pp. 111–122). Reston, VA: National Council of Teachers of Mathematics.

McClain, K., & Cobb, P. (1999). Supporting students' ways of reasoning about patterns and partitions. In J. V. Copley (Ed.), *Mathematics in the early years* (pp. 112–118). Reston, VA: National Council of Teachers of Mathematics.

McIntosh, A., Reys, B. J., & Reys, R. E. (1997). *Number SENSE: Simple effective number sense experiences* [Grades 1–2]. White Plains, NY: Cuisenaire–Dale Seymour.

National Council of Teachers of Mathematics. (1990). *Number sense now! Reaching the NCTM Standards* [Video and teacher's guide]. Reston, VA: Author.

Payne, J. N., & Huinker, D. M. (1993). Early number and numeration. In R. J. Jensen (Ed.), *Research ideas for the classroom: Early childhood mathematics* (pp. 43–71). Old Tappan, NJ: Macmillan.

Schwartz, S. L. (1995). Enchanting, fascinating, useful number. *Teaching Children Mathematics, 1,* 486–491.

Tenth Planet. (1998). *Combining and breaking apart numbers* [Computer Software]. Pleasantville, NY: Sunburst Communications.

Tenth Planet. (1998). *Number meanings and counting* [Computer Software]. Pleasantville, NY: Sunburst Communications.

Van de Walle, J. A. (1990). Concepts of number. In J. N. Payne (Ed.), *Mathematics for the young child* (pp. 63–87). Reston, VA: National Council of Teachers of Mathematics.

Weinberg, S. (1996). Going beyond ten black dots. *Teaching Children Mathematics, 2,* 432–435.

Whitin, D. J., Mills, H., & O'Keefe, T. (1994). Exploring subject areas with a counting book. *Teaching Children Mathematics, 1,* 170–174.

Whitin, D. J., & Wilde, S. (1995). *It's the story that counts: More children's books for mathematical learning, K–6.* Portsmouth, NH: Heinemann.

Wicket, M. S. (1997). Serving up number sense and problem solving: *Dinner at the panda palace. Teaching Children Mathematics, 3,* 476–480.

# Chapter 7

# Developing Meanings for the Operations

This chapter is about helping children connect different meanings, interpretations, and relationships to the four operations of addition, subtraction, multiplication, and division so that they can effectively use these operations in real-world settings.

The main thrust of this chapter is helping children develop what might be termed *operation sense,* a highly integrated understanding of the four operations and the many different but related meanings these operations take on in real contexts. As children solve simple word problems, they learn about the operations. At the same time, they will be constructing new number relationships and thinking strategies that will help them master basic facts. Thus the ideas in this chapter are significantly related to the relationships discussed in Chapter 6 and to the skills covered in Chapter 8.

## BIG Ideas

1. Addition and subtraction are connected. Addition names the whole in terms of the parts, and subtraction names a missing part.

2. Multiplication involves counting groups of like size and determining how many are in all (multiplicative thinking).

3. Multiplication and division are related. Division names a missing factor in terms of the known factor and the product.

4. Models can be used to solve story problems for all operations and to figure out what operation is involved in a problem regardless of the size of the numbers.

## TWO SOURCES OF OPERATION MEANINGS

For all four operations, word problems and models (usually sets of counters and number lines) are the two basic tools the teacher has to help students develop operation concepts. As you will see, each of the four operations is a little more complex than you may have thought. For example, as many as 14 different types of word problems have been identified for addition and subtraction.

### Operation Meanings from Word Problems

The most important way in which children construct operation meanings is solving word problems. The word problem provides an opportunity for examining a diverse set of meanings for each operation. Word problems can and should be handled in a spirit of inquiry, allowing children to use their own methods and justify their solutions.

We know from research that children as early as kindergarten can and do solve story problems. This is much earlier than is commonly acknowledged in traditional textbooks. Young children who have not yet learned to grab the numbers in a story problem and perform an operation are forced to think very hard about the problem. As long as the numbers are relatively simple, children are usually able to solve these problems by directly modeling the meaning of the problem with counters and counting. In the process, many children also develop new and more efficient counting strategies.

To see the difference between simple models and story problems, consider the action of joining 4 counters with

7 counters to create a set of 11. Although this is a model for 7 + 4 = 11, word problems for this situation may be quite different. Look at the following two problems:

**Molly earned $4 babysitting. She had already earned $7. How much does Molly have now?**

**Jerome was picking apples. He had 7 apples in his bag and then picked some more. When he counted again, he had 11 apples. How many more apples did he pick?**

The action with counters is not completely the same for the two problems. In the apple problem, an unknown number of counters must be added to 7 until the total is 11. In the money problem, the 4 is known; it can be counted out and then joined with the 7. How would you solve the apple problem if it were changed like this?

**You had 34.8 bushels of apples, received a new shipment, and now have a total of 72.5 bushels. How many bushels were shipped?**

To compute the answer or to use a calculator, you will have to perform the operation 72.5 − 34.8, a subtraction. The action was joining, but subtraction names the amount joined. This example highlights the complexity of learning operation meaning and connecting that with computational procedures.

## Basic Meanings Developed with Models

Counter or set models for the operations include movable objects, pictures of sets in various arrangements, arrays (things arranged in rows and columns), and variations of these basic ideas. Number lines are also a good model at the upper grade levels but can be more confusing than helpful at the primary level.

An activity with only models lacks a problem to solve. The teacher must be more directive in explaining what is to be done. Children do something with the model (arrange, separate, join, draw arrows on the number line, count rows and lengths of rows, and so on) and then write number sentences (equations) that mean the same thing as the model. The purpose is to associate or connect a new symbolic language (the equation and operation sign) with the concept of the operation as seen in the model.

Models serve both as a thinker toy to analyze what the structure of the story problem may be and also as a connection between the meaning in the story problem and the symbolic equation. Your knowledge of different ways that models can represent operations can assist children in this process.

Often a suggestion from you can help children clarify their own thought processes. Models and drawings used in the after portion of a lesson can also help communicate to other children ideas that may be difficult to explain otherwise. There is evidence that models often help make the underlying structure of a story problem more apparent to the students.

As much as possible, the modeling should flow from the students and not be imposed artificially. Your suggestions should be kept as close to the children's thought processes as possible. Never impose a "correct" model, forcing students to "do as you show them." Models should not become the objective of a lesson. There is no reason to have students "learn a model" (Gutstein & Romberg, 1995).

# TEACHING SYMBOLISM FOR THE OPERATIONS

The symbols we use for the operations and the equal sign are all conventions; you have to show students how to use this symbolism to express their ideas. This is best done in the after portion of a lesson, once students have solved a word problem. You can show students how to write an appropriate equation for the problem just solved.

As you will soon see, each of the operations has many different meanings. Care must be made to help students see that multiple meanings are given to the same symbol. For example, the minus sign (−) is often read as "take away." This is an unfortunately narrow definition.

Return to the problem of 7 apples, picking some more, and ending up with 11 apples. The action is "put together," yet it is solved as a subtraction problem. One child may write 7 + 4 = 11 and another 11 − 7 = 4. A discussion will serve to help children see that both make sense and that they are actually equivalent equations. Forcing children to write exactly the equation we have in mind or to solve a problem as we would solve it may be a waste of precious classroom time. The time may better be spent allowing children to solve problems and write equations in ways that make the most sense to them and discussing these solutions to share and develop a rich array of ideas (Gutstein & Romberg, 1995).

## Using Models to Learn About Symbolism

With the understanding that symbolism for the operations is an arbitrary convention that children must learn from us, the use of more directed activities is appropriate, even in a problem-oriented classroom. In a models-only activity, children write complete equations. The activities begin with models, and what is written is a full equation that tells about the model. The model tells something about 12 − 8 = 4 and how this equation relates the quantities 12, 8, and 4. As children use similar models to solve word problems, they can be expected to select an appropriate equation based on how they understood the problem and also how they modeled the problem. The model becomes an intermediate linkage between operation meanings and the symbolism. One model can be used to represent various meanings for an operation. Therefore, models make it possible for students to see how one operation symbol can represent all the different meanings.

## Connecting Operations

You have often heard that subtraction is the "inverse of addition" or that division is the "inverse of multiplication." Although technically correct, saying that to children is not very helpful to them. The concept of "inverse operation" is fairly sophisticated. However, it is very important to connect addition and subtraction and to connect multiplication and division. As you will see, models form that connection much better than words. The models for subtraction are precisely the same as those for addition. Similarly, the models for multiplication and division are alike. It is only a matter of which numbers are unknown in the problem.

When students have a model for one operation and have written an equation to go with it, it is often useful to ask what other equation can be written for the same model. This will not only help students see how the inverse operations are connected but also help with the connection between multiplication and division.

## Translations: Models, Words, and Symbols

It is useful to think of models, word problems, and symbolic equations as three separate languages. Each language can be used to express the relationships involved in one of the operations. Given these three languages, a powerful approach to helping children develop operation meaning is to have them make translations from one language to another. Once children develop a familiarity with an assortment of models and drawings and they gain exposure to a variety of meanings through word problems, they can begin to make translations from any one language to the other two, as shown in Figure 7.1. Note that Figure 7.1 is actually a simplification of the five representations discussed in Chapter 3 (see Figure 3.9, p. 34).

In a translation exercise, students are provided with an expression in one of the three languages: a model (usually in the form of a drawing), a word problem, or an equation. They are then asked to come up with expressions in each of the other two languages that represent the same relationships. For example, students could be asked to make up a story problem to go with the equation $4 \times 7 = 28$ and to illustrate the meaning with a drawing. Since different cooperative groups or individuals will devise different ideas, the results provide a wonderful source of discussion.

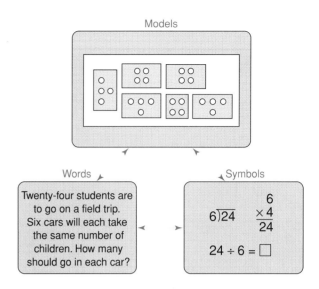

**Figure 7.1** **Translations from any one language to the others helps develop students' concepts of the operators.**

# WORD PROBLEMS FOR ADDITION AND SUBTRACTION

Researchers have separated addition and subtraction problems into categories based on the kind of relationships involved. These include *join* problems, *separate* problems, *part-part-whole* problems, and *compare* problems (Carpenter & Moser, 1983; Gutstein & Romberg, 1995; Fennema, Carpenter, Levi, Franke, & Empson, 1997). The basic structure for each of these four types of problems is illustrated in Figure 7.2 (p. 110). A different problem results depending on which of the three quantities in the structure is unknown.

## Examples of Problems for Each Structure

The number family 4, 8, 12 is used in each of the story problems that follow. For each problem, refer to the structure in Figure 7.2, and determine which of the three elements is the unknown. Note that the drawings are not intended for children but to help you as a teacher consider the different structures. Also note that the problems are described in terms of their structure and not as addition or subtraction problems. Joining action does not always mean addition, nor does separate always mean subtraction.

### Join Problems

For the action of joining, there are three quantities involved: an initial amount, a change amount (the part being added or joined), and the resulting amount (the amount after the action is over).

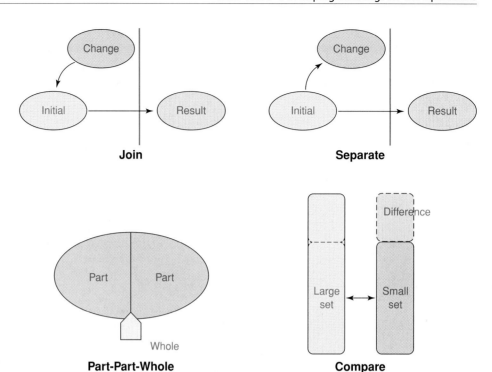

**Figure 7.2**  **Four basic structures for addition and subtraction story problems. Each structure has three numbers. Any one of the three numbers can be the unknown in a story problem.**

**Join**

**Separate**

**Part-Part-Whole**

**Compare**

### JOIN: RESULT UNKNOWN

Sandra had 8 pennies. George gave her 4 more. How many pennies does Sandra have altogether?

### JOIN: CHANGE UNKNOWN

Sandra had 8 pennies. George gave her some more. Now Sandra has 12 pennies. How many did George give her?

### JOIN: INITIAL UNKNOWN

Sandra had some pennies. George gave her 4 more. Now Sandra has 12 pennies. How many pennies did Sandra have to begin with?

## Separate Problems

Notice that in the separate problems, the initial amount is the whole or the largest amount, whereas in the join problems, the result was the whole. Again, refer to Figure 7.2 as you consider these problems. Be sure you can identify what quantities are the initial, change, and result amounts.

### SEPARATE: RESULT UNKNOWN

Sandra had 12 pennies. She gave 4 pennies to George. How many pennies does Sandra have now?

### SEPARATE: CHANGE UNKNOWN

Sandra had 12 pennies. She gave some to George. Now she has 8 pennies. How many did she give to George?

### SEPARATE: INITIAL UNKNOWN

Sandra had some pennies. She gave 4 to George. Now Sandra has 8 pennies left. How many pennies did Sandra have to begin with?

## Part-Part-Whole Problems

Part-part-whole problems involve two parts that are combined into one whole. The combining may be a physical action, or it may be a mental combination where the parts are not physically combined.

There are only two part-part-whole problems instead of three as with the other structures. There is no meaningful distinction between the two parts in a part-part-whole situation, so there is no need to have a different problem for each part as the unknown. For each possibility (whole unknown and part unknown), two problems are given here. The first is a mental combination where there is no action. The second problem involves a physical action.

### PART-PART-WHOLE: WHOLE UNKNOWN

George has 4 pennies and 8 nickels. How many coins does he have?

George has 4 pennies and Sandra has 8 pennies. They put their pennies into a piggy bank. How many pennies did they put into the bank?

### PART-PART-WHOLE: PART UNKNOWN

George has 12 coins. Eight of his coins are pennies, and the rest are nickels. How many nickels does George have?

George and Sandra put 12 pennies into the piggy bank. George put in 4 pennies. How many pennies did Sandra put in?

## Compare Problems

Compare problems involve the comparison of two quantities. The third amount is not actually present but is the difference between the two amounts. There are three types of compare problems, corresponding to which quantity is unknown (smaller, larger, or difference). For each of these, two examples are given: one problem where the difference is stated in terms of more and another in terms of less.

### COMPARE: DIFFERENCE UNKNOWN

George has 12 pennies and Sandra has 8 pennies. How many more pennies does George have than Sandra?

George has 12 pennies. Sandra has 8 pennies. How many fewer pennies does Sandra have than George?

### COMPARE: LARGER UNKNOWN

George has 4 more pennies than Sandra. Sandra has 8 pennies. How many pennies does George have?

Sandra has 4 fewer pennies than George. Sandra has 8 pennies. How many pennies does George have?

### COMPARE: SMALLER UNKNOWN

George has 4 more pennies than Sandra. George has 12 pennies. How many pennies does Sandra have?

Sandra has 4 fewer pennies than George. George has 12 pennies. How many pennies does Sandra have?

# Reflections on the Four Problem Types

An exercise to help you, the teacher, grasp these problem structures is to match the numbers in each problem with the parts in the corresponding structure. A second thing to do would be to write an equation to go with each problem. Other good ideas are to change the context entirely, to use two-digit numbers or decimals, and to make up new problems for each structure.

## Computational and Semantic Forms of Equations

If you write an equation for each of the problems as just suggested, you may write some equations where the unknown quantity is not isolated on one side of the equal sign. For example, a likely equation for the join problem with initial part unknown is $\boxed{8} + 4 = 12$. This is referred to as the *semantic* equation for the problem since the numbers are

listed in the order that follows the meaning of the problem. When the semantic form does not isolate the unknown, an equivalent equation can be written for the same problem. In this case, the equation $12 - 4 = \boxed{8}$ is referred to as the *computational* form of the equation; it isolates the unknown. For some of the problems, the computational form and the semantic form are the same. When they are not the same, children must eventually come to see the equivalence of these equations. With larger numbers that cannot be handled mentally or with counters, the computational form must be used to get an answer with a calculator or with pencil and paper.

## Problem Difficulty

The various types of problems are not at all equal in difficulty for children (Thompson & Hendrickson, 1986). The change problems where the initial part is unknown are among the most difficult, probably because children modeling the problems directly do not know how many counters to put down to begin with. Problems where the change amounts are unknown are also difficult.

Compare problems are significantly different because they do not exactly match up with the part-part-whole model. When a child models a problem with the difference unknown, there is a good chance that the two quantities will be represented. The tendency is to see the two amounts and put them together. This is even more likely to happen when children try to solve compare problems without using a model.

Many children will solve these compare problems as part-part-whole problems without making separate sets of counters for the two amounts. The whole is used as the large amount, one part for the small amount and the second part for the difference. There is absolutely no reason this should be discouraged as long as children are clear about what they are doing. Again, the best value of these problems is in the discussion of how they are approached by different children.

## Inadvertent Definitions

In traditional textbook programs, there is an almost exclusive emphasis on join and change problems with result unknown. These become the de facto definitions of addition and subtraction: Addition is "put together," and subtraction is "take away." The reasons for this are teachers' reluctance to let children wrestle with a difficult problem and the fact that they have themselves learned that the result-unknown problems "define" addition and subtraction. The other problems receive very little attention in books and are generally seen as "nonstandard" problems. This emphasis on the two easiest forms of problems is a serious curricular error that causes difficulties as children face all of these problem structures and as they encounter larger numbers in the upper grades.

# Using Addition and Subtraction Word Problems in the Classroom

No one is suggesting that children should be taught the four structures of word problems as illustrated in Figure 7.2.

These are presented for your understanding so that you can create and discuss story problems with children. When making up your own problems, a good idea is first to think of a context (Martians, shopping, a magic tree that grows doughnuts and a child who comes to eat them, a car going down the road and how many miles it has gone). With a context to provide a story line, put some numbers into the various structures to create problems. The examples presented here have been very sterile to allow you to focus on the meaning. It is much better to embellish your problems when you work with children. Put them in contexts that relate to the children's own lives; use students' names, add unnecessary information, or leave out a number. Use problems related to literature that you are reading. Let children make up problems, but supply a context to inspire them. Unless children are exposed to all of these types of problems, the problems they make up will most likely be result-unknown.

The important goal here is to analyze relationships and discuss approaches. Children should have access to a variety of familiar materials to work with as they think about a problem. Present a problem orally as well as in written form. If children work in pairs or small groups, they can discuss their ideas and come to some common agreement. It is almost always a good idea to request a written explanation of how the problem was solved, including a picture if that is helpful. A full-sentence answer should always be required: "Now George has 12 cents."

The task for an entire class period can be one or two problems. Remember to leave time for discussion. Have children explain how they solved the problem. If children are ready—if they have been exposed to the necessary symbolism—have them include an equation that "goes with the solution." Some teachers have children circle the number in the equation that was the answer to the problem. Trial equations can be "written" with numeral and symbol cards so that changes can be made easily. The tendency in the United States is to have students solve a lot of problems or do a lot of exercises in a single class period. In Japan, however, a complete lesson will often revolve around one or two problems and the related discussion (Reys & Reys, 1995).

Even though your text will likely not include this wide variety of problem types, all of these problems should be proposed to children, even at the K–l level. By second grade, begin to put numbers like 56 and 39 in the problems or even numbers in the hundreds. These problems, even when presented before children learn to compute, will challenge children to invent ways to work with the larger numbers as well as move students to the computational form of the equations. Calculators should of course always be available for use.

## TECHNOLOGY NOTE

The *Fizz & Martina* series (Tom Snyder Productions, 1998) embed problems in "real-life" adventures of Fizz and Martina.

Available in videotape, videodisk, and CD formats, the stories require students to pay attention and take notes. A story is stopped when the problem is posed, and students work in groups without the video or computer. Printed support material is included. This model fits nicely with the before, during, and after format of a problem-solving lesson.

At present, few programs offer addition and subtraction word problems with the variety of problem types we have just explored. However, there are two other ways that you can take advantage of your classroom computers using almost any basic tool software you happen to have. First, you can provide problems yourself using your word processor or any program that allows shapes to be easily drawn and words to be typed. An example of the latter type is *Kid Pix* (Brøderbund, 1996a). Open a new file, and write a word problem in an appropriate space. Students open the file and use the drawing capabilities to record their solution. They may use counters before using the computer. The advantage here is the increased recording capability of the computer. The students' work is either not saved or renamed so that your file remains as an activity. Children can also write on the page before printing their solutions.

These same programs can be used to reverse the process. Bridget Phipps, a first-grade teacher, notes that her children were much better at writing story problems on the computer than they were by hand, and she often had students write problems for pictures she created. Make a file with a drawing involving counters in two parts or with a whole specified and one part showing. Students write and solve a story problem on the computer to go with the drawing. A program such as *MathKeys: Unlocking Whole Numbers* (MECC, 1995b, 1996b) has a large variety of stamps to create counters and a readily available writing space beneath the pictures. ■

# MODELS FOR ADDITION AND SUBTRACTION

As noted earlier, some more directed activities with models are useful to help children learn the conventions of the symbols +, −, and = and to serve as linkages between these equations and the richer meanings of addition and subtraction word problems.

## Part-Part-Whole Models

The part-part-whole concept as discussed in Chapter 6 is a way of understanding that a quantity or whole can be composed of two or more separate quantities or parts. All materials that can be used to model a part-part-whole meaning of addition or subtraction are simply variations of the ideas in Chapter 6. To some extent, addition and subtraction can be thought of as adding symbolism onto number concepts through similar activities. With the exception of action (join or separate), the part-part-whole models for addition and subtraction are the same.

## Addition

When the parts of a set are known, addition is used to name the whole in terms of the parts. This simple, albeit sterile, definition of addition serves both action situations (join and separate) and static or no-action situations.

As noted earlier, an activity without a word problem involves having children *do* something with the manipulatives and then *write* a designated equation that tells what they did. There really is no problem to solve. At the same time, this is one of the things that children simply need to be told—it is a convention that we write equations with plus signs and equal signs to stand for these meanings. There is an opportunity for reflection and discussion as children use different models for the same equation and begin to see the same idea in different contexts.

Each of the part-part-whole models shown in Figure 7.3 is a model for 5 + 3 = 8. Some of these are the result of a definite put-together or joining action, and some are not. Notice that in every example, both of the parts are distinct, even after the parts are joined. If counters are used, the two parts should be kept in separate piles or in separate sections of a mat or should be two distinct colors. For children to see a relationship between the two parts and the whole, the image of the 5 and 3 must be kept as two separate sets. This helps children reflect on the action after it has taken place. "These red chips are the ones 1 started with. Then I added these five blue ones, and now 1 have eight altogether."

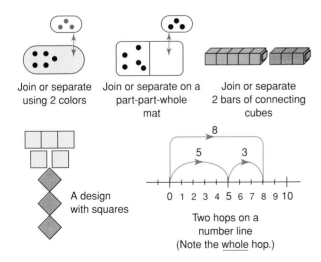

**Figure 7.3** Part-part-whole models for 5 + 3 = 8 and 8 − 3 = 5.

A number line presents some real conceptual difficulties for first and second graders. Its use as a model at that level is generally not recommended. A number line measures distances from zero the same way a ruler does. In the early

grades, children focus on the dots or numerals on a number line instead of the spaces. They think of numbers in terms of sets and objects, not lengths. However, if arrows (hops) are drawn for each number in an exercise, the length concept is more clearly illustrated. To model the part-part-whole concept of 5 + 3, start by drawing an arrow from 0 to 5, indicating, "This much is five." Do not point to the dot for 5, saying "This is five."

### ACTIVITY

## 7.1 Equations with Number Patterns

Recall Activity 6.24 (p. 97) and its variations, in which children made designs or built sets for a specific number. When children seem ready to deal with written symbolism, simply show them how to write a plus or addition number sentence (equation) for each design. In those initial activities, children said a combination, such as "Four and five is nine." Now they have a new symbolic way to match what they say.

Two children can work together, do something with a model, say the combination, and together write the equation. The children can vary the total amounts they construct each time—within appropriate limits, of course.

## Subtraction

In a part-part-whole model, when the whole and one of the parts are known, subtraction names the other part. This definition is in agreement with the drastically overused language of "take away." If you start with a whole set of 8 and remove a set of 3, the two sets that you know are the sets of 8 and 3. The expression 8 − 3, read "eight minus three," names the five remaining. Therefore, eight minus three is five. Notice that the models in Figure 7.3 are models for subtraction as well as addition (except for the action). Helping children see that they are using the same models or pictures aids in connecting the two operations.

Directed activities for part-part-whole subtraction concepts are similar to those for addition, with two important differences:

1. The amount left (for action situations) or the unknown part (for nonaction situations) should initially be covered. The child is encouraged to "think addition": "What goes with this part to make the whole amount?"

2. Two equations should almost always be written for the model. That is, if the whole amount is 9, and 3 are showing, the child first writes "9 − 3 = 6." Then the unknown part is uncovered, and the corresponding addition equation is written as well. The single model for both equations serves as a means of helping the child construct the relationship between addition and subtraction.

---

## Activity

## 7.2 Missing-Part Subtraction

A fixed number of counters is placed on a mat. One child separates the counters into two parts while the other child hides his or her eyes. The first child covers one of the two parts with a sheet of tagboard, revealing only the other part (see Figure 7.4). The second child says the subtraction sentence. For example, "Nine minus four [the visible part] is five [the covered part]." The covered part can be revealed if necessary for the child to say how many are there. Both the subtraction equation and the addition equation can then be written.

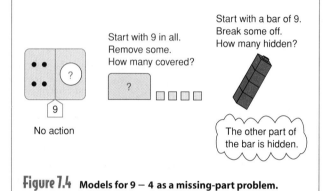

**Figure 7.4** **Models for 9 − 4 as a missing-part problem.**

"Missing-Part Subtraction" can be played with any materials where one part of the whole is hidden.

### Subtraction as Think-Addition

Note that in Activity 7.2, the situation ends with two parts clearly distinct, even when there is a remove action. The removed part remains in the activity or on the mat as a model for an addition equation to be written after writing the subtraction equation. A discussion of how these two equations can be written for the same model situation is an important opportunity to connect addition and subtraction. This is significantly better than the traditional worksheet activity of "fact families" in which children are given a family of numbers such as 3, 5, and 8 and are told to write two plus equations and two minus equations. Very quickly this becomes a matter of dropping the numbers in the various slots.

This modeled activity for subtraction has another value that is extremely significant for later learning to master subtraction facts. Because the counters for the remaining or unknown part are left hidden under the cover, when children do these activities, they are encouraged to think about the hidden part: "What goes with the part I see to make the whole?" For example, if the total or whole number of counters is 9, and 6 are removed from under the cover, the child is likely to think in terms of "6 and what makes 9?" or "What goes with 6 to make 9?" The mental activity is "think-addition" instead of a "count what's left" approach. Later, when working on subtrac-

tion facts, a subtraction fact such as 9 − 6 = ☐ should trigger the same thought pattern: "6 and what makes 9?" This relationship between addition and subtraction must be constructed by the children. However, a more traditional approach to subtraction facts has no hope of getting children thinking about addition and thus connecting a known addition fact to subtraction. The traditional approach with counters for 9 − 6 = ☐ is first count out 9, next count and take away 6, and then count what is left. The 6 removed are just that—removed. They do not form the other part in the part-part-whole model.

## Comparison Models

The comparison relationship involves two distinct sets or quantities and the difference between them. Several ways of modeling the difference relationship are shown in Figure 7.5. The same kind of model can be used whether the difference or one of the two quantities is unknown.

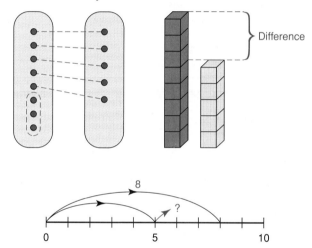

**Figure 7.5** **Models for the difference between 8 and 5.**

Children modeling comparison word problems will frequently use a model like those in the figure to solve the problem. Note, however, that it is not immediately clear how you would associate either the addition or subtraction operations with a comparison situation. That is another reason this is a difficult type of problem. From an adult vantage point, you can see that if you match part of the larger amount with the smaller amount, the large set is now a part-part-whole model that can solve the problem. In fact, many children do model compare problems in just this manner. But that is a very difficult idea to show children if they do not construct the idea themselves.

To approach the model and comparison idea as a problem situation, have children make two amounts, perhaps with two bars of connecting cubes. Discuss the difference between the two bars to generate the third number. For example, if the children make a bar of 10 and a bar of 6, the difference is 4. "What equations can we make with these three numbers?" Have children make up story problems that involve two amounts of 10 and 6. Discuss which equations go with the problems that are created.

## The Order Property and the Zero Property

Put simply, the *order* property (or *commutative* property) for addition says that it makes no difference in which order two numbers are added. Most children find little difficulty with this idea. Since it is quite useful in problem solving, mastering basic facts, and mental mathematics, there is value in spending some time helping children construct the relationship. The name of the property is not important, but the idea is.

Show a set on a two-part mat on the overhead projector. Ask the children to say the addition name for how much is shown—for example, "Eight plus four." Now draw careful attention to the mat as you turn it completely around. Again request the addition name, "Four plus eight." Discuss which is more, 8 plus 4 or 4 plus 8. "Will this work for other numbers? What if we had really big numbers like 432 on one side and 189 on the other?" A discussion similar to this will very likely generate the order property. Notice that the rule is not arbitrary but comes from the students and the model.

Many children have difficulty with addition and subtraction when zero is involved. Zero as a number is probably not understood as early as other numbers. Also, there is an intuitive idea that addition "makes numbers bigger" and subtraction "makes numbers smaller." Avoid providing arbitrary-sounding "rules" about zero. Rather, use and model story problems involving addition and subtraction with zero and make a special effort to discuss ways to make sense of these with your students. What you do not want to do is make a

statement such as "Whenever you add zero, you get the same number back." That may make sense to you, but it sounds like an arbitrary rule to a child. It is always better to have a good discussion through a story problem and models. Have faith. Children can figure these things out.

## WORD PROBLEMS FOR MULTIPLICATION AND DIVISION

Most researchers identify four different classes of multiplicative structures (Greer, 1992). Of these, the two described in Figure 7.6, *equal groups* (*repeated addition, rates*) and *multiplicative comparison*, are by far the most prevalent in the elementary school. Problems matching these structures can be modeled with sets of counters, number lines, or arrays. They represent a large percentage of the multiplicative problems in the real world. (The term *multiplicative* is used here to describe all problems that involve multiplication and division structure.)

The two other types of problems, *combinations* (*Cartesian products*) and *product-of-measures* problems (e.g., length times width equals area), are also important but receive much less attention in school. These problems will be described in terms of real-world contexts instead of a general structure.

The diagrams of the two basic structures are presented here for you as a teacher to organize your thoughts. The structures are not consciously recognized by children, nor should any attempt be made to teach the abstract structures of these problems to children.

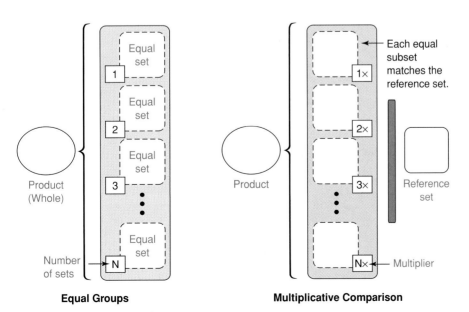

**Figure 7.6** Two of the four basic structures for multiplication and division story problems. Each structure has three numbers. Any one of the three numbers can be the unknown in a story problem.

**Equal Groups**                              **Multiplicative Comparison**

# Examples of Problems for Each Structure

Multiplicative problems differ from additive problems in that the numbers involved represent different kinds of things. One number or *factor* counts how many sets, groups, or parts of equal size are involved. The other factor tells the size of each set or part. These two factors have traditionally been referred to as the *multiplier* (number of parts) and the *multiplicand* (size of each part). These terms are not particularly useful to children and will not be used here unless needed for clarity. The third number in each of these two structures is the *whole* or *product* and is the total of all of the parts. The parts and wholes terminology is useful in making the connection to addition.

## Equal-Group Problems

When the number and size of groups are known, the problem is a multiplication situation. When either the number or the size of sets is unknown, division results. But note that these latter two situations are not alike. Problems where the size of the sets is unknown are called *fair-sharing* or *partition* problems. The whole is shared or distributed among a known number of sets to determine the size of each. If the number of sets is unknown but the size of the equal sets is known, the problems are called *measurement* or sometimes *repeated-subtraction* problems. The whole is "measured off" in sets of the given size. These terms are used with the examples to follow. Keep in mind the structure in Figure 7.6 to see which numbers are given and which is unknown.

There is also a subtle difference between problems that might be termed *repeated-addition* problems (If 3 children have 4 apples each, how many apples are there?) and those that might be termed *rate* problems (If there are 4 apples per child, how many apples would 3 children have?). For each category, two examples of rate problems are provided.

### EQUAL GROUPS: WHOLE UNKNOWN (MULTIPLICATION)

Mark has 4 bags of apples. There are 6 apples in each bag. How many apples does Mark have altogether?

If apples cost 7 cents each, how much did Jill have to pay for 5 apples? (*rate*)

Peter walked for 3 hours at 4 miles per hour. How far did he walk? (*rate*)

### EQUAL GROUPS: SIZE OF GROUPS UNKNOWN (PARTITION DIVISION)

Mark has 24 apples. He wants to share them equally among his 4 friends. How many apples will each friend receive?

Jill paid 35 cents for 5 apples. What was the cost of 1 apple? (*rate*)

Peter walked 12 miles in 3 hours. How many miles per hour (how fast) did he walk? (*rate*)

### EQUAL GROUPS: NUMBER OF GROUPS UNKNOWN (MEASUREMENT DIVISION)

Mark has 24 apples. He put them into bags containing 6 apples each. How many bags did Mark use?

Jill bought apples at 7 cents apiece. The total cost of her apples was 35 cents. How many apples did Jill buy? (*rate*)

Peter walked 12 miles at a rate of 4 miles per hour. How many hours did it take Peter to walk the 12 miles? (*rate*)

## Multiplicative Comparison Problems

In multiplicative comparison problems, there are really two different sets, as there were with comparison situations for addition and subtraction. One set consists of multiple copies of the other. Two examples of each possibility are provided here. It may be useful for you to consider the distinction between additive comparisons and multiplicative comparisons. In the former, the comparison is an amount or quantity difference. In multiplicative situations, the comparison is based on one set's being a particular multiple of the other.

### COMPARISON: PRODUCT UNKNOWN (MULTIPLICATION)

Jill picked 6 apples. Mark picked 4 times as many apples as Jill. How many apples did Mark pick?

This month Mark saved 5 times as much money as last month. Last month he saved $7. How much money did Mark save this month?

### COMPARISON: SET SIZE UNKNOWN (PARTITION DIVISION)

Mark picked 24 apples. He picked 4 times as many apples as Jill. How many apples did Jill pick?

This month Mark saved 5 times as much money as he did last month. If he saved $35 this month, how much did he save last month?

### COMPARISON: MULTIPLIER UNKNOWN (MEASUREMENT DIVISION)

Mark picked 24 apples, and Jill picked only 6. How many times as many apples did Mark pick as Jill did?

This month Mark saved $35. Last month he saved $7. How many times as much money did he save this month as last?

## Combinations Problems

Combinations problems involve counting the number of possible pairings that can be made between two sets. The product consists of *pairs* of things, one member of each pair taken from each of the two given sets. The two factors in these problems each represent the size of a set, so there is no reason to distinguish between two division situations.

### COMBINATIONS: PRODUCT UNKNOWN

Sam bought 4 pairs of pants and 3 jackets, and they all can be worn together. How many different outfits consisting of a pair of pants and a jacket does Sam have?

You want to make a set of attribute pieces that have 3 colors and 6 different shapes. If you want your set to have exactly one piece for every possible combination of shapes and colors, how many pieces will you need to make?

An experiment involves tossing a coin and rolling a die. How many different possible results or outcomes can this experiment have?

### COMBINATIONS: SIZE OF A SET UNKNOWN

Sam bought some new pants and jackets. He has a total of 12 different outfits. If he bought 4 pairs of pants, how many jackets did Sam buy?

Your set of attribute materials consists of 18 different pieces. There are 3 colors, and each color comes in different shapes. How many different shapes are in the set?

In the experiment of tossing a coin and rolling a die, there are 12 possible outcomes. Of course, the coin has two sides. How many sides does the die have?

Note in the last "outfits" example that if the unknown were the number of pairs of pants instead of the number of jackets, the problem would be structurally the same. A similar observation could be made of the other two problems in that category.

There are different ways to model these problems: indicate pairings using lines, model all pairs directly, or use an array. Figure 7.7 gives examples of all of these possibilities.

Combinations problems can have more than two quantities. For example, Sam may also have six different ties

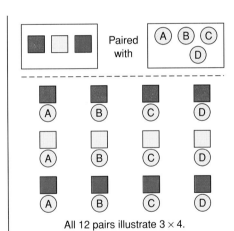

**Figure 7.7** Models for combinations situations.

2 × 5 pairs

Each line indicates a possible pair.

All 12 pairs illustrate 3 × 4.

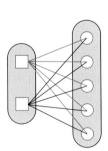

5 × 3 possible ice cream cones

Each section is one combination of a flavor and a type of cone.

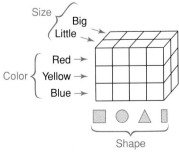

How many different pieces with these attributes?

(3 × 4) × 2 different pieces (concept extended to 3 factors)

($4 \times 3 \times 6$), the attribute pieces could include two sizes and have one, two, or three holes in each piece ($3 \times 6 \times 2 \times 3$), and the experiment may include two coins instead of one ($2 \times 2 \times 6$). Modeling combinations from three or more sets is possible but quickly becomes tedious. The lower-right example in Figure 7.7 shows a three-dimensional array, although a line drawing or pairings could also have been used. In the upper grades, it is worthwhile exploring such combinations with small numbers to see that this concept of multiplication can be extended to any number of sets. As probability and finite mathematics become more and more common in the curriculum, experiences with combinations problems become more important.

### Product-of-Measures Problems

What distinguishes product-of-measures problems from the others is that the product is literally a different type of thing from the other two factors. In a rectangle, the product of two lengths (length × width) is an area, usually square units. Figure 7.8 illustrates how different the square units are from each of the two factors of length: 4 feet times 7 feet is not 28 feet but 28 *square* feet. The factors are each one-dimensional entities, but the product consists of *two*-dimensional things. If the area of the rectangle and the length of one side were given, division would be used to determine the length of the unknown side.

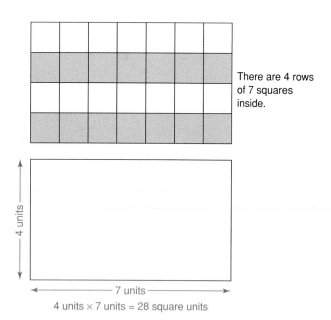

There are 4 rows of 7 squares inside.

4 units × 7 units = 28 square units

**Figure 7.8** Length times length equals area.

Two other fairly common examples in this category are number of workers × hours worked = worker-hours and kilowatts × hours = kilowatt-hours.

## Reflections on Multiplicative Problems

The remainder of this chapter will focus on equal-group and multiplicative comparison problems. These are the most common multiplication and division problems found in the elementary and middle grades.

Extensive research on children's multiplicative thinking suggests that children are slow to think of sets of objects as singular items to be counted (Clark & Kamii, 1996; Kouba, 1989; Steffe, 1988). However, there is also evidence that kindergarten and first-grade children are quite successful at solving multiplication and division problems, even division involving remainders (Carpenter, Ansell, Franke, Fennema, & Weisbeck, 1993; Carpenter, Carey, & Kouba, 1990; Fennema et al., 1997). Mulligan and Mitchelmore (1997), based on their own research and that of others, make a strong argument that students should be exposed to all four operations from the first year of school and that multiplication and division should be much more closely linked in the curriculum. (Traditionally, multiplication is taught prior to and separate from division.) In the early years, the strategies students use may not reflect multiplicative thinking, but the exposure will improve understanding of all four operations and lead to an earlier development of multiplicative strategies.

## Notation and Language

In most books, the convention is that the first factor in a product indicates the number of sets and the second the size of the sets. Thus $4 \times 8$ refers to four sets of eight, not eight sets of four. There is no reason to be rigid about this convention, but it will be useful for communication and for reading textbooks to establish it in your classroom. Introduction of this convention and the operation symbols × and ÷ is best done as students are solving multiplicative problems. In the after portion of a lesson, you can simply explain that these are symbols used to represent the ideas in the problems.

Unfortunately, there are two commonly used symbols for division: $24 \div 6$ and $6\overline{)24}$. The second form is the computational form. It would probably not exist if there were no pencil-and-paper computational procedure that made use of it. (For the other three operations, the vertical format is the computational form.)

These two forms cause some troubles worth noting. First, the order of the numbers is reversed. To read them both as "twenty-four divided by six," one must be read from left to right and the other from right to left. Compounding this difficulty is the meaningless but traditional phrase, "six goes into twenty-four," which probably originated in conjunction with the question, "How many sixes are in twenty-four?" The "goes into" terminology is so ingrained in our society that most adults continue to use it as if it carried some clear meaning.

The phrase has not been in student textbooks for many years. Perhaps it would help if we realize that "goes into" is language connected to our tradition and our understanding but not to children's. If "goes into" is in your vernacular, and it probably is, try not to use it in the classroom.

# Remainders

More often than not, division does not result in a simple whole number. For example, problems with 6 as a divisor will "come out even" only one time out of six. In the absence of a word-problem context, a remainder can be dealt with in only two ways: It can either remain a quantity left over or be partitioned into fractions. In Figure 7.9, the problem $11 \div 4$ is modeled to show fractions.

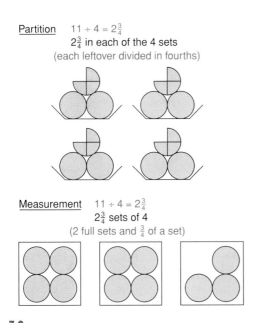

**Figure 7.9** **Remainders expressed as fractions.**

In real contexts, remainders sometimes have three additional effects on answers:

The remainder is discarded, leaving a smaller whole-number answer.

The remainder can "force" the answer to the next highest whole number.

The answer is rounded to the nearest whole number for an approximate result.

The following problems illustrate all five possibilities.

**You have 30 pieces of candy to share fairly with 7 children. How many pieces of candy will each child receive?**
*Answer:* 4 pieces of candy and 2 left over. (*left over*)

**Each jar holds 8 ounces of liquid. If there are 46 ounces in the pitcher, how many jars will that be?**
*Answer:* 5 and $\frac{6}{8}$ jars. (*partitioned as a fraction*)

**The rope is 25 feet long. How many 7-foot jump ropes can be made?**
*Answer:* 3 jump ropes. (*discarded*)

**The ferry can hold 8 cars. How many trips will it have to make to carry 25 cars across the river?**
*Answer:* 4 trips. (*forced to next whole number*)

**Six children are planning to share a bag of 50 pieces of bubble gum. About how many pieces will each child get?**
*Answer:* About 8 pieces for each child. (*rounded, approximate result*)

Students should not just think of remainders as "R 3" or "left over." Remainders should be put in context and dealt with accordingly. It is useful for you to make up problems in different contexts. Include continuous quantities such as length, time, and volume. See if you can come up with problems in each division category for equal-group and comparison problems that would have remainders dealt with as fractions or as rounded-up or rounded-down results.

# Using Multiplication and Division Word Problems in the Classroom

Multiplication and division word problems are excellent examples of tasks that should be used to structure a lesson using the before, during, and after format described in Chapter 4. If you are teaching in grades K–2, you may need to make up your own problems. By third grade, most textbooks have good problems to select from. However, the traditional textbook lesson will likely have a short illustration of some multiplication idea with a series of problems to be solved at the end. The need to complete many problems encourages children to ignore the problems, pull out the numbers, and perform an operation. If instead you structure a lesson around one to three problems and include a full discussion of strategies, models, and reasoning, students have a much greater opportunity to develop multiplicative thinking. Division and multiplication problems presented in pairs give you an opportunity to focus on the relationships between these operations.

The numbers in multiplicative problems are generally larger than in additive problems. Fairly early in third grade, you will want to move to problems involving $14 \times 8$ or even larger numbers. Large numbers are tedious to model with counters or drawings. Children encouraged to wrestle with large numbers can and will invent a variety of methods for doing the computation in these problems. Another alternative is to encourage the use of the calculator. Children should, however, be able to defend anything they do on the calculator. For example, if they do not know what 14 × 8 means or why they are using the multiplication key instead of ⊞ or ⊟, they have not solved the problem.

As has been noted, with division problems, the numbers involved frequently do not produce answers that "come out even." Textbooks are especially notorious about shielding children from remainders in division. The result is that many children believe their answers must be wrong when the division doesn't work out evenly. In the real world, division situations rarely result in whole-number answers. The emphasis in your word problems at all grade levels should therefore be on realistic numbers. There is a lot of value in discussing with children how to interpret these results.

## TECHNOLOGY NOTE

The *Fizz & Martina* series (Tom Snyder Productions, 1998) was mentioned earlier as a vehicle for embedding story problems into real contexts. For the upper grades, the problems are both one- and two-step and involve a wider range of mathematical concepts than have been discussed here. Many teachers like the idea of a video format for its ease of use.

A few other programs have been found that use word problems. *Word Problem Square Off* (Gamco, 1994) and *Math for the Real World* (Davidson), are two examples. Both are designed for grade 3 and higher, with *Square Off* available in three grade levels. Unless you find a value in the extrinsic motivation provided by the computer or by game formats that have nothing to do with the mathematics, the programs are little more than problem banks. There are no models to solve the problems or to explain solutions. No help is provided. Until something better is developed, you are almost certainly better off using problems in your textbook and making up your own. ■

## MODELS FOR MULTIPLICATION AND DIVISION

In the beginning, children will be able to use the same models—sets and number lines—for all four operations. A model not generally used for addition but extremely important and widely used for multiplication and division is the array. An *array* is any arrangement of things in rows and columns, such as a rectangle of square tiles or blocks.

To make clear the connection to addition, early multiplication activities should also include writing an addition sentence for the same model. A variety of models is shown in Figure 7.10. Notice that the products are not included, only addition and multiplication "names" are written. This is another way to avoid the tedious counting of large sets. A similar approach is to write one sentence that expresses both

concepts at once, for example, $9 + 9 + 9 + 9 = 4 \times 9$. Note again that the first factor tells the number of sets and the second factor the size of the sets.

## Multiplication and Division Activities

Along with story problems, children can also benefit from a few activities with models and no context. The purpose of such activities is to focus on the meaning of the operation and the associated symbolism. Activity 7.3 has a good problem-solving spirit. The language you use depends on what you have used with your children in the past.

---

**ℕACTIVITY**

### 7.3  Finding Factors

**Start by assigning a number that has several factors— for example, 12, 18, 24, 30, or 36. Have students find multiplication expressions for their assigned number. With counters, students attempt to find a way to separate the counters into equal subsets. With arrays (perhaps made from square tiles or cubes or drawn on grid paper), students try to build rectangles that have the given number of squares. For each such arrangement of sets or appropriate rectangles, both an addition and a multiplication equation should be written.**

---

Consider for a moment how you would go about doing each of the following tasks: First, take 18 counters and find out how many sets of 6 counters you can make. Draw a picture of the result. Write a simple story problem that fits with what you just did. Second, take 18 counters and separate them into 6 equal sets. Draw another picture, and write a story problem that fits with what you did. Now look at your pictures. What is interesting is that each is a picture of a different multiplication situation.

For the first task, you should have made 3 sets of 6. That is a model for $\boxed{3} \times 6 = 18$. The second time you created 6 sets of 3 each. That is a model for $6 \times \boxed{3} = 18$. Division involves finding a missing factor. It is related to multiplication in the same way that subtraction is related to addition.

Your first word problem should have been a measurement problem involving measuring out *groups of 6*. The second word problem should be a partition problem. You partitioned or shared the 18 among *6 sets*. It is important as a teacher that you be able to create problems that fit the measurement and partition concepts.

Activity 7.3 can also include division concepts. When children have learned that 3 and 6 are factors of 18, they can write the equations $18 \div 3 = 6$ and $18 \div 6 = 3$ along with

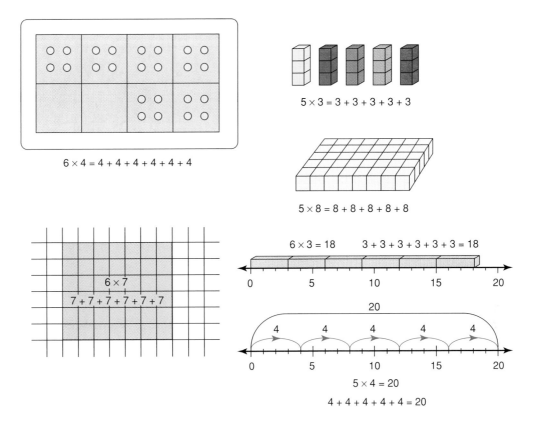

**Figure 7.10** Models for equal-group multiplication.

$3 \times 6 = 18$ and $6 + 6 + 6 = 18$ (assuming that three sets of six were modeled). The following variation of the same activity focuses on division. Having children create word problems is another excellent elaboration of this activity. Require children to explain how their story problems fit with what they did with the counters.

─ **A**CTIVITY ─

## 7.4 Learning About Division

Provide children with an ample supply of counters and some way to place them into small groups. Small paper cups work well. Have children count out a number of counters to be the whole or total set. They record this number: "Start with thirty-one." Next specify either the number of equal sets to be made or the size of the sets to be made: "Separate your counters into four equal-sized sets," or "Make as many sets of four as is possible." Next have the children write the corresponding multiplication equation for what their materials show; under that, have them write the division equation.

Be sure to include both types of exercises: number of equal sets and size of sets. Discuss with the class how these two are different, yet each is related to multiplication and

each is written as a division equation. You can show both ways to write division equations at this time. Do Activity 7.4 several times. Start with whole quantities that are multiples of the divisor (no remainders), but soon include situations with remainders. (Note that it is technically incorrect to write $31 \div 4 = 7$ R 3. However, in the beginning, that form may be the most appropriate to use.)

The activity can be varied by changing the model. Have children build arrays using square tiles or blocks or by having them draw arrays on centimeter grid paper. Present the exercises by specifying how many squares are to be in the array. You can then specify the number of rows that should be made (partition) or the length of each row (measurement). How could children model fractional answers using drawings of arrays on grid paper?

─ **A**CTIVITY ─

## 7.5 The Broken Multiplication Key

The calculator is a good way to relate multiplication to addition. Students can be told to find various products on the calculator without using the ⊠ key. For example, $6 \times 4$ can be found by pressing ⊞ 4 ⊟ ⊟ ⊟ ⊟ ⊟ ⊟. (Successive presses of ⊟ add 4 to the display each time. You began with zero and added 4 six times.) Students can be challenged to demonstrate their result with sets of counters. But note that this same technique can be used to determine products such as 23 × 459 ($\boxed{+}$ 459 and then 23 presses of $\boxed{=}$). Students will want to compare to the same product using the $\boxed{\times}$ key.

"The Broken Multiplication Key" can profitably be followed by "The Broken Division Key."

---

**/A**CTIVITY

## 7.6  The Broken Division Key

Have children work in groups to find methods of using the calculator to solve division exercises without using the divide key. The problems can be posed without a story context. "Find at least two ways to figure out 61 ÷ 14 without pressing the divide key." If the problem is put in a story context, one method may actually match the problem better than another. Good discussions may follow different solutions with the same answers. Are they both correct? Why or why not?

---

There is no reason ever to show children how to do Activity 7.6. However, it would be a good idea for *you* to see if you can find *three* ways to solve 61 ÷ 14 on a calculator without using the divide key. For a hint, see the footnote.*

# Useful Multiplication and Division Properties

As with addition and subtraction, there are some multiplicative properties that are useful and thus worthy of attention. The emphasis should be on the ideas and not terminology or definitions.

## The Order Property in Multiplication

Because the two factors in a multiplication expression carry different meanings, it is not intuitively obvious that 3 × 8 is the same as 8 × 3 or that, in general, the order of the numbers makes no difference (the *order* or *commutative* property). A picture of 3 sets of 8 objects cannot immediately be seen as 8 piles of 3 objects. Eight hops of 3 land at 24, but it is not clear that 3 hops of 8 will land at the same point.

The array, by contrast, is quite powerful in illustrating the order property, as is shown in Figure 7.11. Children should draw or build arrays and use them to demonstrate

---

*There are two measurement approaches or two ways to find out how many 14s are in 61. A third way is essentially related to partitioning or finding 14 times what number is close to 61.

---

why each array represents two different multiplications with the same product.

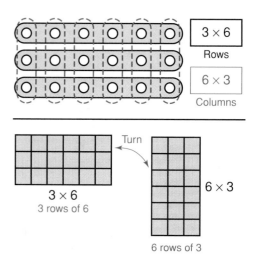

**Figure 7.11**  **Two ways an array can be used to illustrate the order (commutative) property for multiplication.**

## The Role of Zero and One in Multiplication

Zero and, to a lesser extent, 1 as a factor often cause difficulty for children. In one recent third-grade text (Charles et al., 1998), a lesson on factors of 0 and 1 has children use a calculator to examine a wide range of products involving 0 or 1 (423 × 0, 0 × 28, 1536 × 1, etc.) and look for patterns. The pattern suggests the rules for factors of 0 and 1 but not a reason. In the same lesson, a word problem asks how many grams of fat there are in 7 servings of celery with 0 grams of fat in each serving. This approach is far preferable to an arbitrary rule, since it asks students to reason. Make up interesting word problems involving 0 or 1, and discuss the results. Problems with 0 as a first factor are really strange. Note that on a number line, 5 hops of 0 land at 0 (5 × 0). What would 0 hops of 5 be? Another fun activity is to try to model 6 × 0 or 0 × 8 with an array. (Try it!) Arrays for factors of 1 are also worth investigating.

## The Distributive Property

It may not be essential for young children to know the *distributive* property in the form $a \times (b + c) = (a \times b) + (a \times c)$. But the concept involved is very useful in relating one basic fact to another, and it is also involved in the development of two-digit computation. Figure 7.12 illustrates how the array model can be used to illustrate that a product can be broken up into two parts. Children could be asked to draw specific rectangles, slice them into two parts, and write the corresponding equation.

## Why Not Division by Zero?

Some children are simply told "Division by zero is not allowed." Though this fact is quite important, it is not always understood by children. To avoid an arbitrary rule, pose

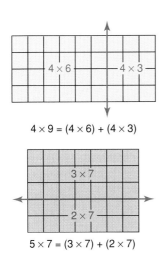

$$4 \times 9 = (4 \times 6) + (4 \times 3)$$

$$5 \times 7 = (3 \times 7) + (2 \times 7)$$

**Figure 7.12** **Models for the distributive property.**

problems to be modeled that involve zero: "Take thirty counters. How many sets of zero can be made?" or "Put twelve blocks in zero equal groups. How many in each group?" Even if children think they have a result that makes sense, suggest that they write the corresponding multiplication equations as they have done for other exercises.

# STORY PROBLEMS IN THE UPPER GRADES

So far in this chapter, we have discussed the meanings of the operations and simple one-step problems that amplify the meanings of those operations. The word problems have been relatively simple, and the numbers involved have been relatively small. The value of these problems is that they allow children to use simple models to analyze the problems. By fourth grade and beyond, most children have developed meanings for the operations. The problems that are encountered at that point include large numbers with decimals and fractions, the data are frequently embedded in charts or tables, problems involve more data than necessary, and many problems have two or sometimes even three steps. Here we will discuss how the methods that have been used in this chapter can be applied to help children analyze these more complex situations.

## Dealing with Large Numbers in Problems

Consider the following problem:

**In building the road through the subdivision, a low section in the land was filled in with dirt that was hauled**

**in by trucks. The complete fill required 638 truckloads of dirt. The average truck carried $6\frac{1}{4}$ cubic yards of dirt, which weighed 17.3 tons. How many tons of dirt were used in the fill?**

Typically, in a sixth- to eighth-grade book, problems of this type are found as part of a series of problems revolving around a single context or theme. Data may be found in a graph or chart or perhaps a short news item or story. Most likely the problems will include all four of the operations. Students have difficulty deciding on the correct operation and even finding the appropriate data for the problem. Many students will find two numbers in the problem and guess at the correct operation. These children simply do not have any tools for analyzing problems. At least two strategies can be taught that are very helpful: Think about the answer before solving the problem, or solve a simpler problem that is just like this one.

## Think About the Answer Before Solving the Problem

Poor problem solvers fail to spend adequate time thinking about the problem and what it is about. They rush in and begin doing calculations, believing that "number crunching" is what solves problems. That is simply not the case. Rather, students should spend time talking about (later, thinking about) what the answer might look like. For our sample problem, it might go as follows:

*What is happening in this problem?* Some trucks were bringing dirt in to fill up a hole.

*What will the answer tell us?* How many tons of dirt were needed in the fill.

*Will that be a small number of tons or a large number of tons?* Well, there were 17.3 tons on a truck, but there were a lot of trucks, not just one. It's probably going to be a whole lot of tons.

*About how many do you think it will be?* It's going to be really big. If there were just 100 trucks, it would be 1,730 tons. It might be close to 10,000 tons. That's a lot of tons!

In this type of discussion, two things are happening. First, the students are asked to focus on the problem and the meaning of the answer instead of on numbers. The numbers are not important in thinking about the structure of the problem. Second, the thinking leads to a rough estimate of the answer. Sometimes, for everyday things, this can simply be based on common sense. In any event, thinking about what the answer tells and about how large it might be is a useful first step. When an answer is finally arrived at, it should be given in a full sentence and compared with the early ballpark estimate.

## Work a Simpler Problem

The reason that models are rarely used with problems such as the dirt problem is that the numbers are impossible to model easily. Dollars and cents, distances in thousands of miles, and time in minutes and seconds are all examples of data likely to be found in the upper grades, and all are difficult to model. The general problem-solving strategy of "try a simpler problem" can almost always be applied to problems with unwieldy numbers.

A simple strategy has the following steps:

1. Substitute small whole numbers for all relevant numbers in the problem.
2. Model the problem using the new numbers (counters, drawing, number line, array).
3. Write an equation that solves the small-number version of the problem.
4. Write the corresponding equation with the original numbers used where the small-number substitutes were.
5. Use a calculator to do the computation.
6. Write the answer in a complete sentence, and decide if it makes sense.

A good rule of thumb is to substitute numbers between 3 and 25. Avoid the use of 1 and 2, as relationships might be obscured. Figure 7.13 shows what might be done for the dirt problem. It also shows an alternative in which only one of the numbers is made smaller and the other number is illustrated symbolically. Both methods are effective. The use of symbols in a conceptual drawing is a powerful strategy in itself.

The idea is to provide a tool students can use to analyze a problem and not just guess at what computation to do. It is much more useful to have students do a few problems where they must use a model of a drawing to justify their solution than to give them a lot of problems where they guess at a solution but don't know if their guess is correct.

# Two-Step Problems

Students often have difficulty with multistep problems. If your students are going to work with multistep problems, be sure they can analyze one-step problems in the way that we have discussed. The following ideas, adapted from suggestions by DeAnn Huinker (1994), are designed to help children see how two problems can be chained together.

1. Give students a one-step problem, and have them solve it. Before discussing the answer, have each student or group make up a second problem that uses the answer to the first problem. The rest of the class can then be asked to use the answer to the first problem to solve the second problem. Here is an example:

*Given problem:* **It took $3\frac{1}{3}$ hours for the Joneses to drive the 195 miles to Washington. What was their average speed?**

*Second problem:* **The Jones children remember crossing the river at about 10:30, or 2 hours after they left home. About how far from home is the river?**

2. Make a "hidden question." Repeat the first exercise by beginning with a one-step problem. You might give different problems to different groups. This time, have students write out both problems as before. Then write a single related problem that leaves out the question from the first problem. That question from the first problem is the "hidden question." Here is a simple example:

*Given problem:* **Tony bought three dozen eggs for 89 cents a dozen. How much was the bill?**

**Figure 7.13** **Working a simpler problem: two possibilities.**

Change all numbers:

$\overset{7}{\cancel{638}}$ trucks of dirt          don't need this

$\boxed{6\frac{1}{4} \text{ yards of dirt in a truck}}$

weighs $\cancel{17.3}$ tons
$\phantom{weighs }4$

$\boxed{\text{11,037 tons of dirt were used.}}$

$7 \times 4 = 28$

$638 \times 17.3 = 11{,}037$

Leave one number alone:

| 17.3 tons | 17.3 tons | 17.3 tons | 17.3 tons |

$4 \times 17.3$

$638 \times 17.3 = 11{,}037$

*Second problem:* **How much change did Tony get back from $5?**

*Hidden-question problem:* **Tony bought three dozen eggs for 89 cents a dozen. How much change did Tony get back from $5?**

Have other students identify the hidden question. Since all students are working on a similar task but with different problems (be sure to mix the operations), they will be more likely to understand what is meant by a hidden question.

3. Pose standard two-step problems, and have the students identify and answer the hidden question. Consider the following problem:

**Willard Sales decides to add widgets to its line of sale items. To beginF with, Willard bought 275 widgets wholesale for $3.69 each. In the first month, the company sold 205 widgets at $4.99 each. How much did Willard make or lose on the widgets? Do you think Willard Sales should continue to sell widgets?**

Begin by considering the questions that were suggested earlier: "What's happening in this problem?" (Something is being bought and sold at two different prices.) "What will the answer tell us?" (How much profit or loss there was.) These questions will get you started. If students are stuck, you can ask, "Is there a hidden question in this problem?"

## ASSESSMENT NOTES

Simple one- and two-step word problems are excellent assessment tasks. Because similar tasks can be provided on different days, observation data can easily be gathered over time. The problems lend themselves to both group work and independent work. All children, even the youngest, can produce a written report of their work so that there is evidence to keep and also evidence of written communication skills.

Not only does using story problems make data gathering easy, but the problems also provide a wonderful opportunity to assess a wide range of information about your students. The obvious data is about conceptual understanding of the operations involved, connections between related operations, connections with operation symbolism (equations), and connections to real-world information.

Another area of conceptual knowledge and understanding is number sense. After students have decided what computation to do in a problem, it is useful to see how they go about doing it. Several programs, most notably *Cognitively Guided Instruction* (CGI) (Fennema et al., 1997; Hankes, 1996), rely almost entirely on solutions to word problems for the development of basic fact mastery and the invention of computational procedures. Regardless of how computational

methods are developed in your class, children will exhibit their most spontaneous and personal approaches to computation when solving realistic story problems.

Finally, all aspects of problem solving, including the metacognitive and affective goals, can be observed as children work on simple story problems.

The message is that using a few story problems each week at all grade levels (including kindergarten and the middle grades) is an excellent way to help children construct meanings of the operations and provide you with a wealth of ongoing feedback that is crucial to your overall assessment strategies.

## LITERATURE CONNECTIONS

Finding an exciting and fun way to use literature to develop or expand understanding of the operations is extremely easy. There are lots of books with stories or pictures concerning sets of things, buying things, measures, and so on, that can be used to pose problems or, better, to stimulate children to invent their own problems. Perhaps the most widely mentioned book in this context is *The Doorbell Rang,* by Pat Hutchins (1986). You can check that one out yourself. Here are three additional suggestions.

### *How Many Snails?*
### (Giganti, 1988)

Appropriate for the K–2 set, this book includes a variety of pictures where the objects belonging to one collection have various subcollections (parts and wholes). For example, a sky full of clouds has various types of clouds. The text asks, "How many clouds are there? How many clouds are big and fluffy? How many clouds are big and fluffy and gray?" These pages lead directly to addition and subtraction situations matching the part-part-whole concepts. Of special note is the opportunity to have missing-part thinking for subtraction. Children can think of collections that they would like to draw so that subcollections have a variety of attributes. They can then pose their own questions about the drawing and add appropriate number sentences. In discussion, children could explain why they selected the particular equation and how it fits the picture.

### *More than One*
### (Hoban, 1981)

The wonderful black-and-white photos of Tana Hoban are designed to introduce group words such as a *crowd* of people, a *herd* of elephants, or a *bundle* of wood. A discussion of group words (animal groups fit nicely with science—*flock, pride, covey,* etc.) beyond those that are in the book can be interesting in and of itself. Do different groups typically contain different numbers of things? Is it likely that there would be two elephants in a herd? Could there be 50? What is typical? These grouping words provide a real opportunity for children to develop *group* as a single entity but with separate things inside. Now suppose that there are many groups (herds, flocks, crowds). If we know the size of one, and we know how many herds, do we know how many elephants in all? Imagine a situation where that was always the case—all groups with group names have the same number of things. If there are 87 pieces of wood in 3 bundles, how many in a bundle? Clever one- and two-step multiplication and division stories can be generated.

## Each Orange Had 8 Slices
### (Giganti, 1992)

Each two-page spread shows objects grouped in three ways. For example, one spread has four trees, three bird's nests in each tree, and two eggs in each nest. The author asks three questions: "How many trees? How many nests? How many eggs?" The three questions with each picture extend multiplication to a three-factor product. In the case of the trees, nests, and eggs, the product is $4 \times 3 \times 2$. After children get a handle on the predictable arrangement of the book's pictures, they can not only write multiplication stories that go with the pictures but also make up situations of their own. What similar situations can be found in the classroom? Perhaps desks, books, and pages or bookshelves, shelves, and books. There is no need to restrict the discussion to three nestings of objects. The same idea is present in measurements: yards, feet, inches or gallons, quarts, pints, cups, ounces. New problems can be posed that require division. What if there were some boxes with 6 cartons in each? Each carton has 4 widgets. If there are 72 widgets, how many boxes are there?

# REFLECTIONS ON CHAPTER 7

## Writing to Learn

1. Make up a context for some story problems, and make up six different join and separate problems: three with a join action and three with a separate action. For all six problems, use the same number family: 9, 4, 13.

2. Make up a comparison word problem. Next change the problem to provide an example of all six different possibilities for comparison problems.

3. Make up multiplication word problems to illustrate the difference between equal groups and multiplicative comparison. Can you create problems involving rates or continuous quantities?

4. Make up two different word problems for $36 \div 9$. For one, the modeling should result in four sets of nine, and for the other, the modeling should result in nine sets of four. Which is which? Which of your problems is a measurement problem, and which is a partition problem?

5. Make up realistic measurement and partition division problems where the remainder is dealt with in each of these three ways: (a) it is discarded (but not left over); (b) it is made into a fraction; (c) it forces the answer to the next whole number.

6. Use three different models to illustrate what $3 \times 7$ means in terms of repeated addition. What is the meaning of each factor? What is the meaning of $3 \times 7$ in the combination concept? Make a drawing to illustrate what you mean.

7. Explain how to help students analyze problems when the numbers are not small whole numbers but rather are large or are fractions or decimals that do not lend themselves to using counters.

8. What roles can story problems play in your assessment scheme? What will you have to do in the classroom to make the most of story problems as assessment opportunities?

## For Discussion and Exploration

1. *Cognitively Guided Instruction* is not a curriculum program but a professional development program in which teachers learn to use students' thinking to guide instruction. The predominant thrust of CGI is the use of story problems, not only for learning the operations but also for number and fact development and even for computation development with larger numbers. Select either basic fact mastery or computation development, and describe how you think these goals might be achieved primarily through story problems. If possible, view some of the CGI videotapes and the accompanying teacher's guide (Fennema et al., 1997) to compare your thoughts with theirs.

2. Examine a basal textbook at one or more grade levels. Identify how, and in what chapters, the meanings for the operations are developed. Discuss the relative focus on meanings of the operations with one-step story problems, use of models, and mastery of basic facts.

3. See how many different types of story problems you can find in a basal textbook. In the primary grades, look for join, remove, part-part-whole, and compare problems. For grades 4 and up, look for the four multiplicative types. (Look in the multiplication and division chapters and also at special problem-solving lessons.) Are the various types of problems well represented?

## Recommendations for Further Reading
### Highly Recommended

Fennema, E., Carpenter, T. P., Levi, L., Franke, M. L., & Empson, S. (1997). *Cognitively guided instruction: Professional development in primary mathematics.* Madison: Wisconsin Center for Education Research.

Although this book is designed for leaders of in-service or pre-service workshops, it is a valuable and affordable reference for any teacher wanting to understand the CGI approach to instruction. In particular, the classifications of word problems for all operations, as discussed in this chapter, are explained in detail, along with methods for using these problems. With the book come six videotapes that detail children's strategies for solving problems and provide a look at several CGI classrooms.

Gutstein, E., & Romberg, T. A. (1995). Teaching children to add and subtract. *Journal of Mathematical Behavior, 14,* 283–324.

A bit more research-oriented than Carpenter et al. (1990) and yet very worthwhile reading for a teacher who wants to have a clear understanding of how children develop addition and subtraction concepts. The article explores several research programs that have investigated different strategies for teaching addition and subtraction. It extends beyond operation meaning to the development of computational strategies.

Kouba, V. L., & Franklin, K. (1993). Multiplication and division: Sense making and meaning. In R. J. Jensen (Ed.), *Research ideas for the classroom: Early childhood mathematics* (pp. 103–126). Old Tappan, NJ: Macmillan.

This chapter, which seeks to help teachers understand the intricacies of multiplicative concepts, is complete and readable, providing teachers at the 3–4 level with a good perspective without being too technical.

Schifter, D., Bastable, V., & Russell, S. J. (1999). *Developing mathematical ideas: Numbers and operations, Part 2: Making meaning for operations* (Casebook). White Plains, NY: Cuisenaire–Dale Seymour.

In this casebook, teachers in grades K–7 share their stories of working with children as they develop meanings for the four operations. The teachers discuss the kinds of actions and situations that students use as they come to understand the operations. This is a companion book to an extended in-service guide. There is also a video available to augment the series. However, the casebook is worthwhile by itself.

## Other Suggestions

Baroody, A. J., & Standifer, J. D. (1993). Addition and subtraction in the primary grades. In R. J. Jensen (Ed.), *Research ideas for the classroom: Early childhood mathematics* (pp. 72–102). Old Tappan, NJ: Macmillan.

Bell, A., Greer, B., Grimison, L., & Mangan, C. (1989). Children's performance on multiplicative word problems: Elements of a descriptive theory. *Journal for Research in Mathematics Education, 20,* 434–449.

Burns, M. (1989). Teaching for understanding: A focus on multiplication. In P. R. Trafton (Ed.), *New directions for elementary school mathematics* (pp. 123–133). Reston, VA: National Council of Teachers of Mathematics.

Burns, M. (1992). *About teaching mathematics: A K–8 resource.* Sausalito, CA: Math Solutions Publications.

Burns, M. (1995). *Math by all means: Multiplication, grade 3.* Sausalito, CA: Math Solutions Publications.

Carey, D. A. (1991). Number sentences: Linking addition and subtraction word problems and symbols. *Journal for Research in Mathematics Education, 22,* 266–280.

Carpenter, T. P., Carey, D. A., & Kouba, V. L. (1990). A problem-solving approach to the operations. In J. N. Payne (Ed.), *Mathematics for the young child* (pp. 111–131). Reston, VA: National Council of Teachers of Mathematics.

Clark, F. B., & Kamii, C. K. (1996). Identification of multiplicative thinking in children in grades 1–5. *Journal for Research in Mathematics Education, 27,* 41–51.

Hankes, J. E. (1996). An alternative to basic-skills remediation. *Teaching Children Mathematics, 2,* 452–457.

Kamii, C. K. (1994). *Young children continue to reinvent arithmetic: 3rd grade.* New York: Teachers College Press.

Kouba, V. L., Zawojewski, J. S., & Strutchens, M. E. (1997). What do students know about numbers and operations? In P. A. Kenney & E. A. Silver (Eds.), *Results from the sixth mathematics assessment of the National Assessment of Educational Progress* (pp. 87–140). Reston, VA: National Council of Teachers of Mathematics.

Ohanian, S., & Burns, M. (1995). *Math by all means: Division, grades 3–4.* Sausalito, CA: Math Solutions Publications.

Rathmell, E. C., & Huinker, D. M. (1989). Using "part-whole" language to help children represent and solve word problems. In P. R. Trafton (Ed.), *New directions for elementary school mathematics* (pp. 99–110). Reston, VA: National Council of Teachers of Mathematics.

Schwartz, S. L., & Curcio, F. R. (1995). Learning mathematics in meaningful contexts: An action-based approach in the primary grades. In P. A. House (Ed.), *Connecting mathematics across the curriculum* (pp. 116–123). Reston, VA: National Council of Teachers of Mathematics.

# Chapter 8

# Helping Children Master the Basic Facts

*Basic facts* for addition and multiplication refer to combinations where both addends or both factors are less than 10. Subtraction and division facts correspond to addition and multiplication facts. Thus $15 - 8 = 7$ is a subtraction fact because both parts are less than 10.

*Mastery of a basic fact* means that a child can give a quick response (in less than 3 seconds) without resorting to noneffient means, such as counting. Work toward mastery of addition and subtraction facts typically begins in the first grade. Most books include all addition and subtraction facts for mastery in the second grade, although much additional drill is usually required in grade 3 and even after. Multiplication and division facts are generally a target for mastery in the third grade, with more practice required in grades 4 and 5. Unfortunately, many children in grade 8 and above do not have a complete command of the basic facts.

The use of calculators in no way diminishes the importance of basic fact mastery; quite the contrary. With the shift in emphasis from pencil-and-paper computation to mental computation and estimation skills, command of the basic facts is more important than ever. Further, it is true that *all* children are able to master the basic facts—including children with learning disabilities and slow learners. Children simply need to construct efficient mental tools that will help them. This chapter is about helping children develop those tools.

## BIG Ideas

1. Number relationships can be used to help remember basic facts.
2. For subtraction facts, the concept "think addition" is the most important idea.

3. There are patterns and relationships in basic facts. You can figure out new or unknown facts from the ones you already know.
4. All the facts can be learned with the help of efficient strategies.

## A THREE-STEP APPROACH TO FACT MASTERY

Every teacher of grades 4 to 10 knows children who are still counting on their fingers, making marks in the margins to count on, or simply guessing at answers. These children have certainly been given more than adequate opportunity to practice their facts over their years in school. They have not mastered their facts because they have not developed efficient methods of producing a fact answer. Drill of inefficient methods does not produce mastery!

Fortunately, we know quite a bit about helping children develop fact mastery, and it has little to do with quantity of drill or drill techniques. Three components or steps to this end can be identified:

1. Help children develop a strong understanding of the operations and of number relationships.
2. Develop efficient strategies for fact retrieval.
3. Then provide practice in the use and selection of those strategies.

### The Role of Number and Operation Concepts

Number relationships play a significant role in fact mastery. For example, an efficient mental strategy for $8 + 5$ is to think "8 and 2 more is 10. That leaves 3. 10 and 3 is 13." This requires the relationship between 8 and 10 (8 is 2 away from 10), the part-part-whole knowledge of 5 (2 and 3 more makes 5), and the fact that 10 and 3 is 13. For 6 × 7, it is efficient to think "5 times 7 and 7 more." For many children, the efficiency of this approach is lost because they need to count on 7 to get from 35 to 42. With an extension of the number relationships just noted, it is possible to think "35 and 5 more is 40, and 2 more is 42." Every relationship discussed in Chapter 6 can contribute to fact mastery.

The meanings of the operations also play a role in the construction of efficient strategies. The ability to relate 6 × 7 to "5 times 7 and 7 more" is based on an understanding of the meanings of the first and second factors. To relate 13 − 7 to "7 and what makes 13" requires an understanding of how addition and subtraction are related. The commutative or "turnaround" properties for addition and multiplication reduce the number of addition and multiplication facts from 100 each to 55 each. These are just a few examples of the role that operation sense plays in the mastery of basic facts.

Teachers in the upper grades with students who have not mastered basic facts will do well to investigate what command of number relationships and operations the students have. Without these relationships and concepts, the strategies discussed throughout this chapter will necessarily be learned in an instrumental manner. The results will not be nearly as effective as they would had these basic ideas been established first.

# Development of Efficient Strategies

An efficient strategy is one that can be done mentally and quickly. The emphasis is on *efficient*. Counting is not efficient. If drill is undertaken when counting is the only strategy available, all you provide is practice in counting.

The use of strategies is not at all a new idea. Brownell and Chazal (1935) recognized that children use different thought processes with different facts. Since the mid-1970s, there has been a strong interest among mathematics educators in the idea of directly teaching strategies to children (e.g., Baroody, 1985; Bley & Thornton, 1995; Fuson, 1984, 1992; Rathmell, 1978; Steinberg, 1985; Thornton & Noxon, 1977; Thornton & Toohey, 1984). Many of the ideas that appear in this chapter have been adapted from the work of these researchers.

We have already seen some efficient strategies: the use of building up through 10 in adding 8 + 5 and the use of the related fact 5 × 7 to help with 6 × 7. Consider for a moment how you think about 6 + 6. What about 9 + 5? You may think that you just "know" these. What is more likely is that you used some ideas similar to double six (for 6 + 6) and 10 and 4 more (for 9 + 5). Your response may be so automatic by now that you are not reflecting on the

use of these relationships or ideas. That is one of the features of efficient mental processes—they become automatic with use.

Many children have learned basic facts without being taught efficient strategies. They develop or learn many of these methods in spite of the drill they may have endured. With an understanding of numbers and operations, many children invent their own strategies, usually without conscious thought. The challenge for teachers is to devise lessons in which all children will develop strategies that are useful. A strategy is most useful to students when it is theirs, built on and connected to concepts and relationships they already own.

For your students to develop effective strategies, you yourself need to have a command of as many good strategies as possible, even if you have never used them. This will help you recognize your students' invented strategies and capitalize on those ideas.

Next you need to plan lessons in which specific strategies are likely to be developed. There are two basic types of lessons suggested for this purpose. The first is to use simple story problems designed in such a manner that students are most likely to develop a strategy as they solve it. In the discussion of these solution methods, you can focus attention on the methods that are most useful. You can have all students try the methods others have developed. Often a suggestion of an idea is all that is necessary. A second type of lesson has students focus on a collection of facts and try to develop strategies for working with this group of facts. The problematic feature of these lessons is the development of a strategy.

There is a huge temptation simply to tell students about a strategy and then have them practice it. Though this can be effective for some students, many others will not personally relate to your ideas or may not be ready for them. Continue to discuss strategies invented in your class and plan lessons that encourage strategies, but do not force strategies on your students.

# Drill of Efficient Methods and Strategy Selection

Drill plays a significant role in fact mastery, and the use of old-fashioned methods such as flash cards and fact games can be effective if used wisely.

## Avoid Premature Drill

Many activities suggested in this chapter involve drill using simple flash cards. It is critical, however, that you do not introduce or suggest such drill too soon. Suppose that a child does not know the 9 + 5 fact and has no way to deal with it other than to count fingers or use counters. These are inefficient methods. Premature drill introduces no new information and encourages no new connections. It is both a waste of time and a frustration to the child.

The strategies for some facts may not seem completely efficient at first glance. However, if practice is delayed until a strategy has been rather firmly developed, the practice will be *of that strategy* and will not be aimed at rote memory. The repetitious use of the strategy makes its use much quicker. Once again, it is not necessary that the strategies be your strategies, only that they be efficient and meaningful and useful to the child. Fact responses learned via strategies do become quick and automatic with practice.

## Practice Strategy Selection or Strategy Retrieval

*Strategy selection* or *strategy retrieval* is the process of deciding what strategy is appropriate for a particular fact. If you don't think to use a strategy, you probably won't. Many teachers who have tried teaching fact strategies report that the method works well while the children are focused on whatever strategy they are working on. They acknowledge that children can learn and use strategies. But, they continue, when the facts are all mixed up or the child is not in "fact practice" mode, old counting habits return. Students need to know not only how to use the strategy but also how to select the appropriate strategy when it is needed. This selection of a strategy or retrieval of the strategy from a personal repertoire is as important a part of fact strategy instruction as the strategies themselves.

For example, suppose that your children have been practicing the near-doubles facts for addition: Use the better-known double, 7 + 7, to derive the unknown 8 + 7. Children become quite skilled at doubling the smaller addend and adding 1. All of the facts they are practicing are selected to fit this model. On other days, they have learned and practiced other strategies. Later, on a worksheet or in a mental math exercise, the children are presented with a mixture of facts. In a single exercise, a child might see

$$\begin{array}{cccc} 7 & 4 & 2 & 8 \\ +\,6 & +\,9 & +\,6 & +\,5 \end{array}$$

There is no mind-set or reminder to use different processes for each. Especially if the children have previously been habituated to counting to get answers, they will very likely revert to counting and ignore the efficient methods they recently practiced. When they were practicing the strategy, there was no need to decide what strategy might be useful. All of the facts during the near-doubles practice were near-doubles, and the strategy worked. Later, however, there is no one to suggest the strategy.

A simple activity that is useful is to prepare a list of facts selected from two or more strategies and then, one fact at a time, ask children to name a strategy that would work for that fact. Once again, the strategies a particular child uses may not be the same as those you emphasized in class. Regardless, children still need to develop the habit of using

the relationships they have constructed and not fall back on inefficient methods. They should explain why they picked the strategy and demonstrate its use. This type of activity turns the attention to the features of a fact that lend it to this or that strategy.

## Overview of the Approach

For each particular strategy, from development to eventual drill when the strategy is well understood, the general approach for instruction is very similar.

### Make Strategies Explicit in the Classroom

As has been discussed, your students will develop strategies as they solve word problems or as they investigate a category of facts you present. When a student suggests a new strategy, be certain that everyone else in the room understands how it is used. Suppose that Maggie explains how she figured out 3 × 7 by starting with double 7 (14) and then adding 7 more. She knew that 6 more onto 14 is 20 and one more is 21. You can ask another student to explain what Maggie just shared. This requires students to attend to ideas that come from their classmates. Now explore with the class to see what other facts would work with Maggie's strategy. This discussion may go in a variety of directions. Some may notice that all of the facts with a 3 in them will work. Others may say that you can always add one more set on if you know the smaller fact. For example, for 6 × 8 you can start with 5 × 8 and add 8.

Don't expect to have a strategy introduced and understood with just one word problem or one exposure such as this. Try on several successive days problems in which the same type of strategy might be used. Children need lots of opportunities to make a strategy their own. Many children will simply not be ready to use an idea the first few days, and then all of a sudden something will click and a useful idea will be theirs.

It is a good idea to write new strategies on the board or make a poster of strategies students develop. Give the strategies names that make sense. (*Double and add one more set. Maggie's idea. Use with 3s.*)

Your agenda is to get students to think about different strategies and to try them out. No student should be forced to adopt someone else's strategy, but every student should be required to understand strategies that are brought to the discussion.

### Practice the Strategy

When you are comfortable that children are able to use a strategy without recourse to physical models and that they are beginning to use it mentally, it is time to practice it. It is a good idea to have as many as ten different activities for each strategy or group of facts. File folder or boxed activities can be used by children individually, in pairs, or even in small groups. With a large number of activities, children can work on strategies they understand and on the facts that they need the most.

Flash cards are among the most useful approaches to fact strategy practice. For each strategy, make several sets of flash cards using all of the facts that fit that strategy. On the cards, label the strategy or use drawings or cues to remind the children of the strategy. Examples appear throughout the chapter.

Other activities involve the use of special dice made from wooden cubes, teacher-made spinners, matching activities where a helping fact or a relationship is matched with the new fact being learned, and games of all sorts. Almost any existing game involving fact drill can be modified to drill only one strategy or one collection of facts. A child or group of children may even want to make their own flash cards or drill games to match their own newly invented ideas.

### Individualize

If you have been successful in creating a mathematical community in which problem-solving discourse takes place regularly, it is not unlikely that children will band together in groups to help each other with fact mastery. Either with or without student input, create small study groups of two to four students where each child has similar needs or is working on similar facts. Let the members of each group discuss and practice the strategies for a specific cluster of facts together. Beyond the middle of the second grade, it is extremely unlikely that all students in your class will have the same needs or will approach facts the same way. Plan small periods of time for children to work together. These periods should be interspersed with your ongoing curriculum. Do not make fact mastery a burden that prevents you from moving forward.

### Practice Strategy Selection

After children have worked on two or three strategies, strategy selection drills are very important. These can be conducted quickly with the full class or a group, or independent games and activities can be prepared. Examples are described toward the end of the chapter.

# STRATEGIES FOR ADDITION FACTS

The strategies for addition facts are directly related to one or more number relationships. In Chapter 6, numerous activities were suggested to develop these relationships. When the class is working on addition facts, the number relationship activities can and should be included with those described here. The teaching task is to help children connect these number relationships to the basic facts.

# One-More-Than and Two-More-Than Facts

Each of the 36 facts highlighted in the chart has at least one addend of 1 or 2. These facts are a direct application of the one-more-than and two-more-than relationships.

| + | 0 | 1 | 2 | 3 | 4 | 5 | 6 | 7 | 8 | 9 |
|---|---|---|---|---|---|---|---|---|---|---|
| 0 |   | 1 | 2 |   |   |   |   |   |   |   |
| 1 | 1 | 2 | 3 | 4 | 5 | 6 | 7 | 8 | 9 | 10 |
| 2 | 2 | 3 | 4 | 5 | 6 | 7 | 8 | 9 | 10 | 11 |
| 3 |   | 4 | 5 |   |   |   |   |   |   |   |
| 4 |   | 5 | 6 |   |   |   |   |   |   |   |
| 5 |   | 6 | 7 |   |   |   |   |   |   |   |
| 6 |   | 7 | 8 |   |   |   |   |   |   |   |
| 7 |   | 8 | 9 |   |   |   |   |   |   |   |
| 8 |   | 9 | 10 |   |   |   |   |   |   |   |
| 9 |   | 10 | 11 |   |   |   |   |   |   |   |

Join or part-part-whole problems in which one of the addends is a 1 or a 2 are easy to make up. For example, *When Tommy was at the circus, he saw 8 clowns come out in a little car. Then 2 more clowns came out on bicycles. How many clowns did Tommy see in all?* Ask different students to explain how they got the answer of 10. Some will count on from 8. Some may still need to count 8 and 2 and then count all. Others will say they knew that 2 more than 8 is 10. The last response gives you an opportunity to talk about facts where you can use the two-more-than idea.

The different responses will provide you with a lot of information about students' number sense. As students are ready to use the two-more-than idea without counting all, they can begin to practice with activities such as the following.

┌─ **A**CTIVITY ─────────────
### 8.1 One-/Two-More-Than Dice
Make a die labeled +1, +2, +1, +2, "one more," and "two more." Use with another die labeled 4, 5, 6, 7, 8, and 9. After each roll of the dice, children should say the complete fact: "Four and two is six."
└──────────────────────────

┌─ **A**CTIVITY ─────────────
### 8.2 One-/Two-More-Than Match
In a matching activity, children can begin with a number, match that with the one that is two more, and then connect that with the corresponding basic fact.
└──────────────────────────

— **A**CTIVITY —
## 8.3 Lotto for +1/+2

A lotto-type board can be made on a file folder. Small fact cards can be matched to the numbers on the board. The back of each fact card can have a small answer number to use as a check.

Figure 8.1 illustrates some of these activities and shows several possibilities for flash cards. Notice that activities such as the dice or spinner games and the lotto-type activity can be modified for almost all of the strategies in the chapter. These are not repeated for each strategy.

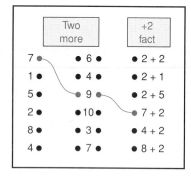

**Figure 8.1** **One-more and two-more facts.**

## Facts with Zero

Nineteen facts have zero as one of the addends. Though such problems are generally easy, some children overgeneralize the idea that answers to addition are bigger. Word problems

involving zero will be especially helpful. In the discussion, use drawings that show two parts with one part empty.

| + | 0 | 1 | 2 | 3 | 4 | 5 | 6 | 7 | 8 | 9 |
|---|---|---|---|---|---|---|---|---|---|---|
| 0 | 0 | 1 | 2 | 3 | 4 | 5 | 6 | 7 | 8 | 9 |
| 1 | 1 | | | | | | | | | |
| 2 | 2 | | | | | | | | | |
| 3 | 3 | | | | | | | | | |
| 4 | 4 | | | | | | | | | |
| 5 | 5 | | | | | | | | | |
| 6 | 6 | | | | | | | | | |
| 7 | 7 | | | | | | | | | |
| 8 | 8 | | | | | | | | | |
| 9 | 9 | | | | | | | | | |

— **A**CTIVITY —
## 8.4 What's Alike? Zero Facts

Write about ten zero facts on the board, some with the zero first and some with the zero second. Discuss how all of these facts are alike. Have children use counters and a part-part-whole mat to model the facts at their seats.

Figure 8.2 suggests some practice ideas.

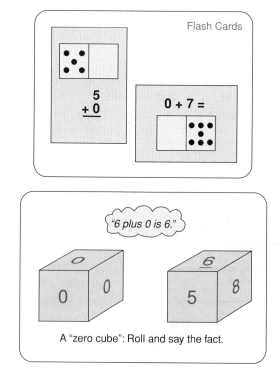

**Figure 8.2** **Facts with zero.**

## Doubles

There are only ten doubles facts from 0 + 0 to 9 + 9, as shown here. These ten facts are relatively easy to learn and become a powerful way to learn the near-doubles (addends one apart). Some children use them as anchors for other facts as well.

| + | 0 | 1 | 2 | 3 | 4 | 5 | 6 | 7 | 8 | 9 |
|---|---|---|---|---|---|---|---|---|---|---|
| 0 | 0 |   |   |   |   |   |   |   |   |   |
| 1 |   | 2 |   |   |   |   |   |   |   |   |
| 2 |   |   | 4 |   |   |   |   |   |   |   |
| 3 |   |   |   | 6 |   |   |   |   |   |   |
| 4 |   |   |   |   | 8 |   |   |   |   |   |
| 5 |   |   |   |   |   | 10 |   |   |   |   |
| 6 |   |   |   |   |   |   | 12 |   |   |   |
| 7 |   |   |   |   |   |   |   | 14 |   |   |
| 8 |   |   |   |   |   |   |   |   | 16 |   |
| 9 |   |   |   |   |   |   |   |   |   | 18 |

**A**CTIVITY

## 8.5 Double Images

Have students make picture cards for each of the doubles, and include the basic fact on the card as shown in Figure 8.3.

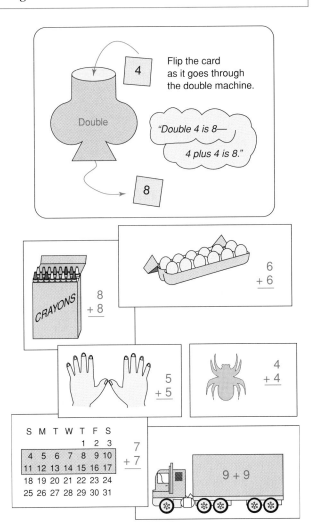

**Figure 8.3** Doubles facts.

Word problems can focus on pairs of like addends. *Alex and Zack each found 7 seashells at the beach. How many did they find together?*

**A**CTIVITY

## 8.6 Calculator Doubles

Use the calculator and enter the "double maker" (2 ⊠ ▭ ). Let one child say, for example, "Seven plus seven." The child with the calculator should press 7, try to give the double (14), and then press ▭ to see the correct double on the display. (Note that the calculator is also a good way to practice +1 and +2 facts.)

# Near-Doubles

Near-doubles are also called the "doubles plus one" facts and include all combinations where one addend is one more than the other. The strategy is to double the smaller number and add 1. Be sure students know the doubles before you focus on this strategy.

| + | 0 | 1 | 2 | 3 | 4 | 5 | 6 | 7 | 8 | 9 |
|---|---|---|---|---|---|---|---|---|---|---|
| 0 |   | 1 |   |   |   |   |   |   |   |   |
| 1 | 1 |   | 3 |   |   |   |   |   |   |   |
| 2 |   | 3 |   | 5 |   |   |   |   |   |   |
| 3 |   |   | 5 |   | 7 |   |   |   |   |   |
| 4 |   |   |   | 7 |   | 9 |   |   |   |   |
| 5 |   |   |   |   | 9 |   | 11 |   |   |   |
| 6 |   |   |   |   |   | 11 |   | 13 |   |   |
| 7 |   |   |   |   |   |   | 13 |   | 15 |   |
| 8 |   |   |   |   |   |   |   | 15 |   | 17 |
| 9 |   |   |   |   |   |   |   |   | 17 |   |

After discussing the strategy with the class, write 10 or 15 near-doubles facts on the board. Use vertical and horizontal formats, and vary which addend is the smaller. Quickly go through the facts. First have students only identify which number to double. The next time through, have students name the double that will be used. The third time, have students say the double and then the near-double.

Before using the following activity or the two shown in Figure 8.4 (p. 134), be sure to try word problems involving near-doubles. The discussion will give you a good idea of who is ready to practice this strategy.

**A**CTIVITY

## 8.7 Double Dice plus One

Roll a single die with numerals or dot sets, and say the complete double-plus-one fact. That is, for 7, students should say, "Seven plus eight is fifteen."

**Figure 8.4** **Near-doubles facts.**

# Make-Ten Facts

These facts all have at least one addend of 8 or 9. One strategy for these facts is to build onto the 8 or 9 up to 10 and then add on the rest. For 6 + 8, start with 8, then 2 more makes 10, and that leaves 4 more for 14.

| + | 0 | 1 | 2 | 3 | 4 | 5 | 6 | 7 | 8 | 9 |
|---|---|---|---|---|---|---|---|---|---|---|
| 0 | | | | | | | | | | |
| 1 | | | | | | | | | | 10 |
| 2 | | | | | | | | | 10 | 11 |
| 3 | | | | | | | | | 11 | 12 |
| 4 | | | | | | | | | 12 | 13 |
| 5 | | | | | | | | | 13 | 14 |
| 6 | | | | | | | | | 14 | 15 |
| 7 | | | | | | | | | 15 | 16 |
| 8 | | | 10 | 11 | 12 | 13 | 14 | 15 | 16 | 17 |
| 9 | | 10 | 11 | 12 | 13 | 14 | 15 | 16 | 17 | 18 |

Before using this strategy, be sure that children have learned to think of the numbers 11 to 18 as 10 and some more. Many second- and third-grade children have not constructed this relationship. (Refer to "Relationships for Numbers 10 to 20" in Chapter 6, pp. 100–101.)

---

**Ⓐctivity**

## 8.8 Make 10 on the Ten-Frame

Give students a mat with two ten-frames (see Figure 8.5). Flash cards are placed next to the ten-frames, or a fact can be given orally. The students should first model each number in the two ten-frames and then decide on the easiest way to show (without counting) what the total is. The obvious

---

(but not the only) choice is to move counters into the frame showing either 8 or 9. Get students to explain what they did. Focus especially on the idea that 1 (or 2) can be taken from the other number and put with the 9 (or 8) to make 10. Then you have 10 and whatever is left.

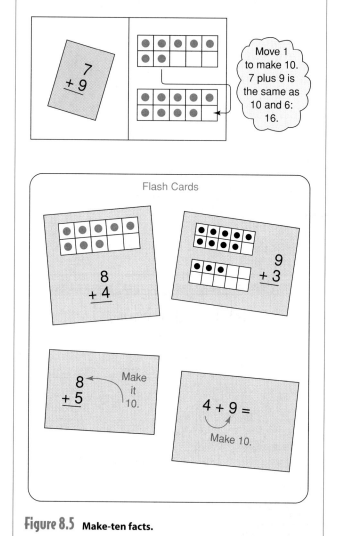

**Figure 8.5** **Make-ten facts.**

Provide a lot of time with the make-ten activity. Encourage discussion and exploration of "easy ways" to think about adding two numbers when one of them is 8 or 9. Perhaps discuss why this is not a useful idea for a fact such as 6 + 5 where neither number is near 10. Note that children will have many other ways of using 10 to add with 8 or 9. For example, with the fact 9 + 5, some will add 10 + 5 and subtract 1. This is a perfectly good strategy, and it uses 10. You may want to give efficient strategies unique names determined by the children and discuss which ones seem especially useful.

When children seem to have the make-ten idea, try the same activity without counters. Use the little ten-frame cards found in the Blackline Masters. Make a transparency set for the overhead. Show an 8 (or 9) card on the overhead. Place other cards beneath it one at a time. Suggest *mentally* "moving" two dots into the 8 ten-frame. Have students say orally what they are doing. For 8 + 4, they might say, "Take 2 from the 4 and put it with 8 to make 10. Then 10 and 2 left over is 12." The activity can be done independently with the little ten-frame cards.

Make flash cards with either one or two ten-frames, with reminders to "make ten" out of the 8 or the 9.

# Other Strategies and the Last Six Facts

To appreciate the power of strategies for fact learning, consider the following. We have discussed only five ideas or strategies (one or two more than, zeros, doubles, near-doubles, and make-ten), yet these ideas have covered 88 of the 100 addition facts! Further, these ideas are not really new but rather the application of important relationships. The 12 remaining facts are really only six facts, and their respective turnarounds as shown on the chart.

|+|0|1|2|3|4|5|6|7|8|9|
|---|---|---|---|---|---|---|---|---|---|---|
|0| | | | | | | | | | |
|1| | | | | | | | | | |
|2| | | | | | | | | | |
|3| | | | | | |8|9|10| | |
|4| | | | | | | |10|11| | |
|5| | | |8| | | | |12| | |
|6| | | |9|10| | | | | | |
|7| | | |10|11|12| | | | | |
|8| | | | | | | | | | |
|9| | | | | | | | | | |

Before trying to develop any particular strategies for these facts, spend several days with word problems where these facts are the addends. Listen carefully to the ideas that students use in figuring out the answers. If no strategies seem to emerge, try the following activity with any one of these facts.

---

**𝔸CTIVITY**

## 8.9 If You Didn't Know

Pose the following task to the class: **If you did not know the answer to 7 + 5** (or any fact that you want to work on), **what are some clever ways you can think of to get the answer?**

---

The value of this activity is the same as the word problem but focuses attention on the development of a strategy. In the event that no one comes up with a practical strategy, you can offer one that a fictional friend shared with you—perhaps a student you heard about in another school. Then provide one of the strategies discussed here, and ask students what they think of it.

## Doubles plus Two, or Two-Apart Facts

Of the six remaining facts, three have addends that differ by 2: 3 + 5, 4 + 6, and 5 + 7. There are two possible relation-

ships that might be useful here, each depending on knowledge of doubles. Some children find it easy to extend the idea of the near-doubles to double plus 2. For example, 4 + 6 is double 4 and 2 more. A different idea is to take 1 from the larger addend and give it to the smaller. Using this idea, the 5 + 3 fact is transformed into the double 4 fact—*double the number in between*.

## Make-Ten Extended

Three of the six facts have 7 as one of the addends. The make-ten strategy is frequently extended to these facts as well. For 7 + 4, the idea is *7 and 3 more makes 10 and 1 left is 11*. You may decide to suggest this idea at the same time that you initially introduce the make-ten strategy. It is interesting to note that Japan, mainland China, Korea, and Taiwan all teach an addition strategy of building through 10 and do so in the first grade. Many U.S. second graders do not know what 10 plus any number is (Fuson, 1992).

## Counting On

Counting on is the most widely promoted strategy. It is generally taught as a strategy for all facts that have 1, 2, or 3 as one of the addends and thus includes the one- and two-more-than facts. For the fact 3 + 8, the child starts with 8 and counts three counts: *9, 10, 11*. There are several reasons this approach is downplayed in this text. First, it is frequently applied to facts where it is not efficient, such as 8 + 5. It is difficult to explain to young children that they should count for some facts but not others. Second, it is much more procedural than conceptual. Finally, if other strategies are used, it is not necessary.

## Ten-Frame Facts

If you have been keeping track, all of the remaining six facts have been covered by the discussion so far, with a few being touched by two different thought patterns. The ten-frame model is so valuable in seeing certain number relationships that these ideas cannot be passed by in thinking about facts. The ten-frame helps children learn the combinations that make 10. Ten-frames immediately model all of the facts from 5 + 1 to 5 + 5 and the respective turnarounds. Even 5 + 6, 5 + 7, and 5 + 8 are quickly seen as two fives and some more when depicted with these powerful models (see Figure 8.6, p. 136).

A good idea might be to group the facts shown in the chart here and practice them using one or two ten-frames as a cue to the thought process.

|+|0|1|2|3|4|5|6|7|8|9|
|---|---|---|---|---|---|---|---|---|---|---|
|0| | | | | |5| | | | |
|1| | | | | |6| | | |10|
|2| | | | | |7| | |10| |
|3| | | | | |8| |10| | |
|4| | | | | |9|10| | | |
|5|5|6|7|8|9|10|11|12|13|14|
|6| | | | | |10|11| | | |
|7| | | |10| |12| | | | |
|8| | |10| | |13| | | | |
|9| |10| | | |14| | | | |

Flash Cards

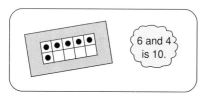

**Figure 8.6** **Ten-frame facts.**

The next two activities are suggestive of the type of relationships that can be developed.

**ACTIVITY**

### 8.10  A Plus-Five Machine

Use the calculator to practice adding five. Enter ⊞ 5 ▭. Next enter any number, and say the sum of that number plus 5 before pressing ▭. Continue with other numbers. (The ⊞ 5 ▭ need not be repeated.) If a ten-frame is present, the potential for strengthening the 5 and 10 relationships is heightened.

Obviously, the calculator can be made into a machine for adding any number and is a powerful drill device.

**ACTIVITY**

### 8.11  Say the Ten Fact

Hold up a ten-frame card, and have children say the "ten fact." For a card with 7 dots, the response is "seven and three is ten." Later, with a blank ten-frame drawn on the board, say a number less than 10. Children start with that number and complete the "ten fact." If you say, "four," they say, "four plus six is ten." Use the same activities in independent or small group modes.

# STRATEGIES FOR SUBTRACTION FACTS

Subtraction facts prove to be more difficult than addition. This is especially true when children have been taught subtraction through a "count-count-count" approach; for 13 − 5, *count* 13, *count off* 5, *count* what's left. There is little evidence that anyone who has mastered subtraction facts has found this approach helpful. Unfortunately, many sixth, seventh, and eighth graders are still counting.

## Subtraction as Think-Addition

In Figure 8.7, subtraction is modeled in such a way that students are encouraged to think, "What goes with this part to make the total?" When done in this *think-addition* manner, the child uses known addition facts to produce the unknown quantity or part. (You might want to revisit missing-part activities in Chapter 6 and part-part-whole subtraction concepts in Chapter 7.) If this important relationship between parts and wholes—between addition and subtraction—can be made, subtraction facts can be much easier. When children see 9 − 4, you want them to think spontaneously, "Four and *what* makes nine?" By contrast, observe a third-grade child who struggles with this fact. The idea of thinking addition never occurs. Instead, the child will begin to count either back from 9 or up from 4. The value of think-addition cannot be overstated.

Connecting Subtraction to Addition Knowledge

1. Count out 13 and cover.

2. Count and remove 5. Keep these in view.

3. Think: "Five and what makes thirteen?" 8! 8 left. 13 minus 5 is 8.

4. Uncover.

8 and 5 is 13.

**Figure 8.7** **Using a think-addition model for subtraction.**

Word problems that promote think-addition are those that sound like addition but have a missing addend: *join, initial part unknown; join, change unknown;* and *part-part-whole, part unknown* (see Chapter 7). Consider this problem: *Janice had 5 fish in her aquarium. Grandma gave her some more fish. Then she had 12 fish. How many fish did Grandma give Janice?* Notice that the action is join and thus suggests addition. There is a high probability that students will think *5 and how many more makes 12.* In the discussion in which you use problems such as this, your task is to connect this thought process with the subtraction fact, 12 − 5.

## Subtraction Facts with Sums to 10

Think-addition is most immediately applicable to subtraction facts with sums of 10 or less. These are generally introduced with a goal of mastery in the first grade. Sixty-four of the 100 subtraction facts fall into this category.

If think-addition is to be used effectively, it is essential that addition facts be mastered first. Evidence suggests that children learn very few, if any, subtraction facts without first mastering the corresponding addition facts. In other words, mastery of 3 + 5 can be thought of as prerequisite knowledge for learning the facts 8 − 3 and 8 − 5.

Even though there are 64 subtraction facts that are easily learned with a think-addition strategy, it is useful to consider breaking these down into groups that match the corresponding addition facts. For example, children are more likely to use a think-addition strategy for 8 − 4 and 6 − 3 because these are "doubles." Actually, it is the corresponding addition fact that is the double. With this idea on the floor, you can ask, "How could we use an idea like that with these facts: 9 − 4 or 7 − 3?" Here the related think-addition fact is a near-double. All of the facts with a sum of 10 (10 − 3, 10 − 4, etc.) are also nicely clustered for think-addition with a ten-frame. A group of these facts could be written on the board. The task might be to find an easy way to use the ten-frame to get the answers. Similarly, facts involving minus 5 (8 − 5, 9 − 5, etc.) are also related to the ten-frame in a think-addition manner.

Facts involving 0, 1, and 2 may be solved by different children in many different ways including think-addition. These facts are closely related to important basic number relationships. If children experience difficulties with facts such as 8 − 0 or 7 − 2, it would be a good idea to investigate their number concepts. A child who says that 7 − 0 is 6 may have overgeneralized that subtraction makes the number smaller.

## The 36 "Hard" Subtraction Facts: Sums Greater than 10

Before reading further, look at the three subtraction facts shown here, and try to reflect on what thought process you use to get the answers. Even if you "just know them," think about what a likely process might be.

$$\begin{array}{ccc} 14 & 12 & 15 \\ -\ 9 & -\ 6 & -\ 6 \end{array}$$

Many people will use a different strategy for each of these facts. For 14 − 9, it is easy to start with 9 and work up through 10: *9 and 1 more is 10, and 4 more makes 5.* For the 12 − 6 fact, it is quite common to hear "double 6," a think-addition approach. For the last fact, 15 − 6, 10 is used again but probably by working backward from 15—a take-away process: *Take away 5 to get 10, and 1 more leaves 9.* We could call these three approaches, respectively, build up through 10, think-addition, and back down through 10. Each of the remaining 36 facts with sums of 11 or more can be learned using one or more of these strategies. Figure 8.8 shows how these facts, in three overlapping groups, correspond to these three strategies. Keep in mind that these are not required strategies. Some children may use a think-addition method for all. Others may have a completely different strategy for some or all of these. The three approaches suggested here are based on ideas already developed: the relationship between addition and subtraction and the power of 10 as a reference point.

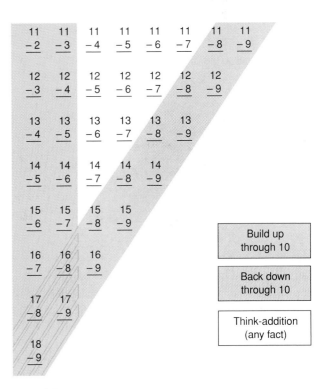

**Figure 8.8** The 36 "hard" subtraction facts.

## Build Up Through 10

This group includes all facts where the part or subtracted number is either 8 or 9. Examples are 13 − 9 and 15 − 8.

**ACTIVITY**

### 8.12 Build Up Through the Ten-Frame

On the board or overhead, draw a ten-frame with 9 dots. Discuss how you can build numbers between

11 and 18, starting with 9 in the ten-frame. Stress the idea of *one more to get to 10* and then the rest of the number. Repeat for a ten-frame showing 8. Next, with either the 8 or 9 ten-frame in view, call out numbers from 11 to 18, and have students explain how they can figure out the difference between that number and the one on the ten-frame. Later, use the same approach, but show fact cards to connect this idea with the symbolic subtraction fact (see Figure 8.9).

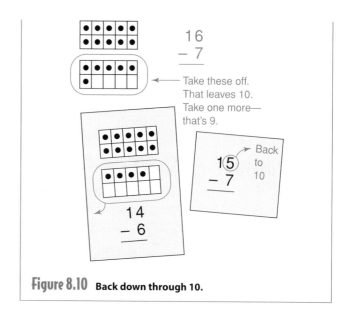

**Figure 8.10**    **Back down through 10.**

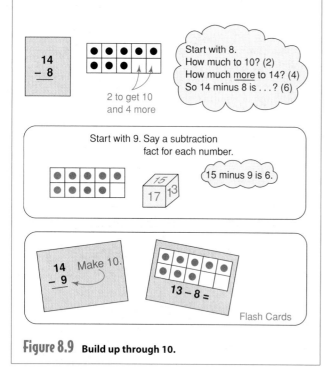

**Figure 8.9**    **Build up through 10.**

## Back Down Through 10

Here is one strategy that is really take-away and not think-addition. It is useful for all facts that have a difference of 8 or 9, such as 15 − 6 or 13 − 5. For example, with 15 − 6, you start with the total of 15 and take off 5. That gets you down to 10. Then take off 1 more to get 9. For 14 − 6, just take off 4 and then take off 2 more to get 8. Here we are working backward with 10 as a "bridge."

— **A**CTIVITY —

## 8.13 Back Down Through the Ten-Frame

Start with two ten-frames on the overhead, one filled completely and the other partially filled as in Figure 8.10. For 13, for example, discuss what is the easiest way to think about taking off 4 counters or 5 counters. Repeat with other numbers between 11 and 18. Have students write or say the corresponding fact.

## Extend Think-Addition

Think-addition remains one of the most powerful ways to think about subtraction facts. When the think-addition concept of subtraction is well developed, many children will use that approach for all subtraction facts. (Notice that virtually everyone uses a think-multiplication approach for division. Why?)

What may be most important is to listen to children's thinking as they attempt to answer subtraction facts that they have not yet mastered. If they are not using one of the three ideas suggested here, it is a good bet that they are counting—an inefficient method. Work hard at the think-addition concept. Return to missing-part activities as found in Chapter 6. Use wholes greater than 10, and have the students write both an addition and subtraction fact for each. Perhaps most important, continue lessons built around word problems—*join, initial or change unknown,* and *part-part-whole, part unknown.* The following activities are also effective.

The activities that follow are all of the think-addition variety. There is of course no reason why these activities could not be used for all of the subtraction facts. They need not be limited to the "hard facts."

— **A**CTIVITY —

## 8.14 Missing-Number Cards

Show children, without explanation, families of numbers with the sum circled as in Figure 8.11(a). Ask why they think the numbers go together and why one number is circled. When this number family idea is fairly well understood, show some families with one number replaced by a question mark, as in Figure 8.11(b), and ask what number is missing. When students understand this activity, explain that you have made some missing-number cards based on this idea. Each card has two of three numbers that go together in the same way. Sometimes the circled number is missing (the sum), and sometimes one of the other numbers is missing (a part). The cards can be made both vertically and horizontally with the sum appearing in different positions. The object is to name the missing number.

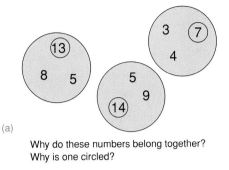

(a)

Why do these numbers belong together?
Why is one circled?

(b)

Which number is missing?
How can you tell what it is?

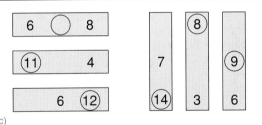

(c)

These missing-number cards are just like the number families. Say the missing number.

**Figure 8.11** **Introducing missing-number cards.**

─ **A**CTIVITY ─────────────

### 8.15 Missing-Number Worksheets

Make copies of the blank form found in the Blackline Masters to make a wide variety of drill exercises. In a row of 13 "cards," put all of the combinations from two families with different numbers missing, some parts and some wholes. Put blanks in different positions. An example is shown in Figure 8.12. After filling in numbers, run the sheet off, and have students fill in the missing numbers. Another idea is to group facts from one strategy or number relation or perhaps mix facts from two strategies on one page. Have students write an addition fact and a subtraction fact to go with each missing-number card. This is an important step because many children are able to give the missing part in a family but do not connect this knowledge with subtraction.

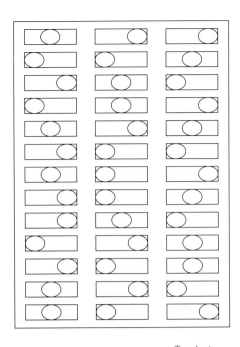

**Figure 8.12** **Missing-part worksheets. The blank version can be used to fill in any sets of facts you wish to emphasize (see Blackline Masters).**

─ **A**CTIVITY ─────────────

### 8.16 Find a Plus Fact to Help

Select a group of subtraction facts that you wish to practice. Divide a sheet of paper into small cards, about 10 or 12 to a sheet. For each subtraction fact, write the corresponding addition fact on one of the cards. Two subtraction facts can be related to each addition fact. Duplicate the sheet, and have students cut the cards apart. Now write one of the subtraction facts on the board. Rather than call out answers, students find the addition fact that helps with the subtraction fact. On your signal, each student holds up the appropriate fact. For 12 − 4 or 12 − 8, the students would select 4 + 8. The same activity can be made into a matching card game.

# STRATEGIES FOR MULTIPLICATION FACTS

Multiplication facts can also be mastered by relating new facts to existing knowledge. For example, the fact 4 × 7 can be found from double 7 and then double again. Rote memory is not required.

Since the first and second factors in multiplication stand for different things (7 × 3 is 7 threes and 3 × 7 is 3 sevens), it is imperative that students completely understand the commutative property (go back and review Figure 7.11, p. 122). For example, 2 × 8 is related to the addition fact double 8. But the same relationship also applies to 8 × 2. Most of the fact strategies are more obvious with the factors in one order than in the other, but turn-around facts should always be learned together.

Of the five groups or strategies discussed next, the first four strategies are generally easier and cover 75 of the 100 multiplication facts. You are continually reminded that these strategies are suggestions, not rules, and that the most general approach with children is to have them discuss ways that *they* can use to think of facts easily.

## Doubles

Facts that have 2 as a factor are equivalent to the addition doubles and should already be known by students who know their addition facts. The major problem is to realize that not only is 2 × 7 double 7, but so is 7 × 2. Try word problems where 2 is the number of sets. Later use problems where 2 is the size of the sets.

**Activity**

## 8.17 Calculator 2× Facts

Review the concept of doubles from addition. Play "Say the Double." You say a number, and the children say the double of that number. Use the calculator to practice doubles (press 2 × =).

Make and use flash cards with the related addition fact or word *double* as a cue (see Figure 8.13).

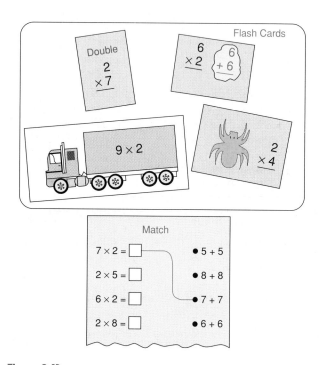

**Figure 8.13**  **Multiplication doubles.**

## Fives Facts

This group consists of all facts with 5 as the first or second factor, as shown here.

Practice counting by fives to at least 45. Connect counting by fives with rows of 5 dots. Point out that six rows is a model for 6 × 5, eight rows is 8 × 5, and so on.

## 8.18 Clock Facts

Focus on the minute hand of the clock. When it points to a number, how many minutes after the hour is it? Draw a large clock, and point to numbers 1 to 9 in random order. Students respond with the minutes after. Now connect this idea to the multiplication facts with 5. Hold up a flash card, and then point to the number on the clock corresponding to the other factor. In this way, the fives facts become the "clock facts."

Include the clock idea on flash cards or to make matching activities (see Figure 8.14).

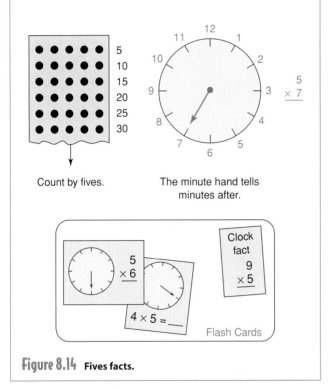

**Figure 8.14** **Fives facts.**

## Zeros and Ones

Thirty-six facts have at least one factor that is either 0 or 1. These facts, though apparently easy, tend to get confused with "rules" that some children learned for addition. The fact $6 + 0$ stays the same, but $6 \times 0$ is always zero. The $1 + 4$ fact is a one-more idea, but $1 \times 4$ stays the same. Make flash cards and games that reflect a conceptual approach to these facts. The concepts behind these facts can be developed through discussion and story problems. Above all else, avoid rules that sound arbitrary and without reason such as "Any number multiplied by zero is zero." Though true, it is an idea that should come from the chil-

dren and should never be generalized unless they can explain why it is so.

| × | 0 | 1 | 2 | 3 | 4 | 5 | 6 | 7 | 8 | 9 |
|---|---|---|---|---|---|---|---|---|---|---|
| 0 | 0 | 0 | 0 | 0 | 0 | 0 | 0 | 0 | 0 | 0 |
| 1 | 0 | 1 | 2 | 3 | 4 | 5 | 6 | 7 | 8 | 9 |
| 2 | 0 | 2 | | | | | | | | |
| 3 | 0 | 3 | | | | | | | | |
| 4 | 0 | 4 | | | | | | | | |
| 5 | 0 | 5 | | | | | | | | |
| 6 | 0 | 6 | | | | | | | | |
| 7 | 0 | 7 | | | | | | | | |
| 8 | 0 | 8 | | | | | | | | |
| 9 | 0 | 9 | | | | | | | | |

## Nifty Nines

Facts with a factor of 9 include the largest products but can be among the easiest to learn. The table of nines facts includes some nice patterns that are fun to discover. Two of these patterns are useful for mastering the nines: (1) The tens digit of the product is always one less than the "other" factor (the one other than 9), and (2) the sum of the two digits in the product is always 9. So these two ideas can be used together to get any nine fact quickly. For $7 \times 9$, *1 less than 7 is 6, 6 and 3 make 9, so the answer is 63.*

| × | 0 | 1 | 2 | 3 | 4 | 5 | 6 | 7 | 8 | 9 |
|---|---|---|---|---|---|---|---|---|---|---|
| 0 | | | | | | | | | | 0 |
| 1 | | | | | | | | | | 9 |
| 2 | | | | | | | | | | 18 |
| 3 | | | | | | | | | | 27 |
| 4 | | | | | | | | | | 36 |
| 5 | | | | | | | | | | 45 |
| 6 | | | | | | | | | | 54 |
| 7 | | | | | | | | | | 63 |
| 8 | | | | | | | | | | 72 |
| 9 | 0 | 9 | 18 | 27 | 36 | 45 | 54 | 63 | 72 | 81 |

Children are not likely to invent this strategy simply by solving word problems involving a factor of 9. Therefore, consider building a lesson around the following task.

## 8.19 Patterns in the Nines Facts

In column form, write the nines table on the board ($9 \times 1 = 9, 9 \times 2 = 18, \ldots, 9 \times 9 = 81$). The task is to find as many patterns as possible in the table. As you listen to the students work on this task, be sure that somewhere in the class the two patterns necessary for the strategy have been found. After discussing all the patterns, a follow-up task is to use the patterns to think of a clever way to figure out a nine fact if you didn't know it. (Note that even for students who know their nines facts, this remains a valid task.)

Once children have invented a strategy for the nines, practice activities such as those shown in Figure 8.15 are appropriate. Also consider word problems with a factor of 9 and check to see if the strategy is in use.

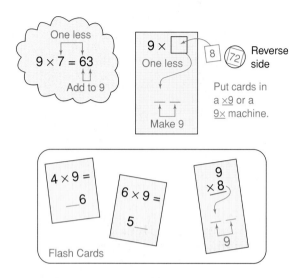

**Figure 8.15** *"Nifty nines" rule.*

*Warning:* Although the nines strategy can be quite successful, it also can cause confusion. Because two separate rules are involved and a conceptual basis is not apparent, children may confuse the two rules or attempt to apply the idea to other facts. It is not, however, a "rule without reason." It is an idea based on a very interesting pattern that exists in the base-ten numeration system. One of the values of patterns in mathematics is that they help us do seemingly difficult things quite easily. The nifty-nine pattern illustrates clearly one of the values of pattern and regularity in mathematics.

An alternative strategy for the nines is almost as easy to use. Notice that $7 \times 9$ is the same as $7 \times 10$ less one set of 7, or $70 - 7$. This can easily be modeled by displaying rows of 10 cubes, with the last one a different color, as in Figure 8.16. For students who can easily subtract 4 from 40, 5 from 50, and so on, this strategy may be preferable.

$4 \times 10 = 40$

$4 \times 9$ is 4 less,

36

**Figure 8.16** **Another way to think of the nines.**

## Helping Facts

The chart shows the remaining 25 multiplication facts. It is worth pointing out to children that there are actually only 15

facts remaining to master because 20 of them consist of 10 pairs of turnarounds.

| × | 0 | 1 | 2 | 3 | 4 | 5 | 6 | 7 | 8 | 9 |
|---|---|---|---|---|---|---|---|---|---|---|
| 0 | | | | | | | | | | |
| 1 | | | | | | | | | | |
| 2 | | | | | | | | | | |
| 3 | | | | 9 | 12 | | 18 | 21 | 24 | |
| 4 | | | | 12 | 16 | | 24 | 28 | 32 | |
| 5 | | | | | | | | | | |
| 6 | | | | 18 | 24 | | 36 | 42 | 48 | |
| 7 | | | | 21 | 28 | | 42 | 49 | 56 | |
| 8 | | | | 24 | 32 | | 48 | 56 | 64 | |
| 9 | | | | | | | | | | |

These 25 facts can be learned by relating each to an already known fact or *helping* fact. For example, $3 \times 8$ is connected to $2 \times 8$ (double 8 and 8 more). The $6 \times 7$ fact can be related to either $5 \times 7$ (5 sevens and 7 more) or to $3 \times 7$ (double $3 \times 7$). The helping fact must be known, and the ability to do the mental addition must also be there. For example, to go from $5 \times 7$ is 35 and then add 7 for $6 \times 7$, a student must be able to add 35 and 7. If you see finger counting at that stage, the idea of make-ten can be extended: 35 and 5 more is 40 and 2 left makes 42.

How to find a helping fact that is useful varies with different facts and sometimes depends on which factor you focus on. Figure 8.17 illustrates models for four overlapping groups of facts and the thought process associated with each.

The *double and double again* approach is applicable to all facts with 4 as one of the factors. Remind children that the idea works when 4 is the second factor as well as when it is the first. For $4 \times 8$, double 16 is also a difficult fact. Help children with this by noting, for example, that $15 + 15$ is 30, $16 + 16$ is two more, or 32. Adding $16 + 16$ on paper defeats the purpose.

*Double and one more set* is a way to think of facts with one factor of 3. With an array or a set picture, the double part can be circled, and it is clear that there is one more set. Two facts in this group involve difficult mental additions.

If either factor is even, a *half then double* approach can be used. Select the even factor, and cut it in half. If the smaller fact is known, that product is doubled to get the new fact. For $6 \times 7$, half of 6 is 3. 3 times 7 is 21. Double 21 is 42. For $8 \times 7$, the double of 28 may be hard, but it remains an effective approach to that traditionally hard fact. (Double 25 is $50 + 2$ times 3 is 56.)

Many children prefer to go to a fact that is "close" and then *add one more set* to this known fact. For example, think of $6 \times 7$ as 6 sevens. Five sevens is close: That's 35. Six sevens is one more seven, or 42. When using $5 \times 8$ to help with $6 \times 8$, the set language "6 eights" is very helpful in remembering to add 8 more and not 6 more. Admittedly difficult, this approach is used by many children, and it becomes the best way to think of one or two particularly difficult facts. "What is seven times eight? Oh, that's 49 and 7 more—56." The process can become almost automatic.

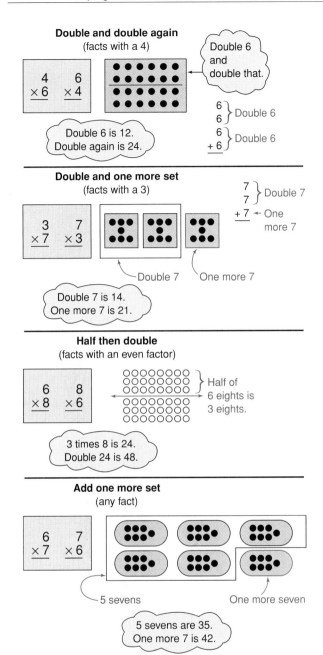

**Figure 8.17** Finding a helping fact.

The relationships among easy and hard facts are fertile ground for good problematic tasks. Rather than tell students what helping facts to use and how to use them, select a fact from one of the strategies. Use the same formulation as in Activity 8.9, "If You Didn't Know" (p. 135). For example, "If you didn't know what 6 × 8 is, how could you figure it out by using something that you do know?" Students should be challenged to find as many as possible interesting and useful ways to answer a hard multiplication fact.

Since arrays are a powerful thinking tool for these strategies, provide students with copies of the ten-by-ten dot array (Figure 8.18, also in Blackline Masters). A tagboard *L* is used

to outline specific product arrays. The lines in the array make counting the dots easier and often suggest the use of the easier fives facts as helpers. For example, 7 × 7 is 5 × 7 plus double 7 ⟶ 35 + 14.

**Figure 8.18** An array is a useful model for developing strategies for the hard multiplication facts. (A Blackline Master is in the back of the text.)

Don't forget to use word problems as a vehicle for developing these harder facts. Consider this problem: *Connie bundled up all of her old crayons into bags of 7 crayons each. She was able to make 8 bags with 3 crayons left over. How many crayons did she have?* As students work to get an answer, many of the strategies just discussed are possible. Plus there is the added benefit of the assessment value gained by listening to the methods different children bring to a situation that does not look like a fact drill.

Word problems can also be structured to prompt a strategy. *Carlos and Jose kept their baseball cards in albums with 6 cards on each page. Carlos had 4 pages filled, and Jose had 8 pages filled. How many cards did each boy have?*

As with other strategies, drill activities can be devised that reflect the strategies that students invent (see Figure 8.19, p. 144).

# DIVISION FACTS AND "NEAR FACTS"

Children are likely to use the corresponding multiplication fact to think of a division fact. If we are trying to think of 36 ÷ 9, we tend to think, "Nine times what is thirty-six?" For most, 42 ÷ 6 is not a separate fact but is closely tied to 6 × 7. (Would it not be wonderful if subtraction were so closely related to addition? It can be!)

An interesting question to ask is, "When children are working on a page of division facts, are they practicing division or

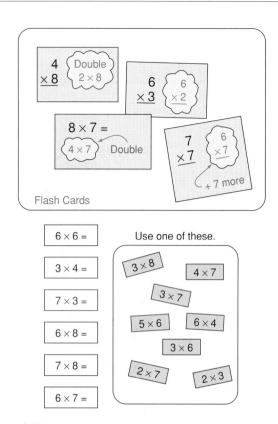

**Figure 8.19** **Practice thinking of a helping fact.**

Find the largest factor without going over the target number.

4 × ☐ ⟶ 23, ☐ left over
7 × ☐ ⟶ 52, ☐ left over
6 × ☐ ⟶ 27, ☐ left over
9 × ☐ ⟶ 60, ☐ left over

multiplication?" There is undoubtedly some value in limited practice of division facts. However, mastery of multiplication facts and connections between multiplication and division are the key elements of division fact mastery. Word problems continue to be a key vehicle to create this connection.

Exercises such as 50 ÷ 6 might be called "near facts." Divisions that do not come out evenly are much more prevalent in computations and in real situations than division facts or division without remainders. To determine the answer to 50 ÷ 6, most people run through a short sequence of the multiplication facts, comparing each product to 50: "6 times 7 (low), 6 times 8 (close), 6 times 9 (high). Must be 8. That's 48 and 2 left over." This process can and should be practiced. That is, children should be able to do problems with one-digit divisors and one-digit answers plus remainders mentally and with reasonable speed.

**ACTIVITY**

## 8.20 How Close Can You Get?

To practice "near facts," try this exercise. As illustrated, the idea is to find the one-digit factor that makes the product as close as possible to the target without going over. Help children develop the process of going through the multiplication facts that was just described. This can be a drill with the full class by preparing a list for the overhead, or it can be a worksheet activity.

# EFFECTIVE DRILL AND PRACTICE

There is little doubt that strategy development and general number sense (number relationships and operation meanings) are the best contributors to fact mastery. Drill in the absence of these factors has repeatedly been demonstrated as ineffective. However, the positive value of practice should not be completely ignored. Practice of nearly any mental activity strengthens memory and retrieval capabilities (Ashcraft & Christy, 1995).

## When and How to Practice

The proliferation of drill-and-practice software and endless worksheet activities is evidence that teachers and parents hold tenaciously to their belief in drill. Certainly, there are some positive gains. However, far too much time is devoted to inefficient drill of basic facts, often with a negative impact on students' attitudes toward mathematics and beliefs in their abilities.

### Avoid Inefficient Practice

Adopt this simple rule and stick with it: *Do not subject any student to fact drills unless the student has developed efficient strategies for the facts being practiced.* Practice will strengthen strategies and make them increasingly automatic. Therefore, practicing strategies such as those discussed in this chapter will allow students to use them with increased efficiency, even to the point of recalling the fact without even being conscious of the strategy use. Counting on fingers and making marks on paper can never become automatic regardless of the amount of practice. Strictly rote drill offers no assistance when the fact is unknown. Short-term gains are almost certain to be lost over time. Practice prior to development of efficient methods is simply a waste of precious instructional time.

### Individualize Practice

It is unreasonable to expect every student in your class to develop and be comfortable with the same strategies. As you have seen, there are multiple paths to most facts. Different students will bring different number tools to the task and will develop strategies at different rates. This means that there are few drills that are likely to be efficient for a full class at any given time. That is why so many of the suggested activities are designed as flash cards, games, or simple repeatable worksheets. By creating a large number of drill activities promoting different strategies and addressing different collections of facts, it is not at all unreasonable to direct students to activities that are most useful for them.

By third grade, students can help you with this individualization process by keeping their own chart of facts mastered and facts yet to be mastered. If games and drill activities are well labeled, students can even select the activities they are ready to work on.

It is also important to listen carefully to the strategies different students are using. For example, if a student tends to solve multiplication facts with a 9 by multiplying by 10 and subtracting, it is not profitable to suggest the "nifty nine" strategy. A student who has not mastered addition facts is not ready for subtraction practice.

### Practice Strategy Retrieval

When students are involved in a drill exercise that is designed to practice a particular strategy, it is likely that they will use that strategy. However, when facts are practiced without a reminder of a strategy, students need to practice by selecting from their memory the mental method that works best for them. Drills can be devised that help students look at a fact and recall a strategy that works. The next two activities suggest how this might be done.

---

**ACTIVITY**

### 8.21 Circle the Strategy

On a worksheet, have students circle the facts that belong to a strategy they have been working on and answer only those facts. The same approach can be used with two or three strategies on one sheet.

---

**ACTIVITY**

### 8.22 Sort Them as You Do Them

Mix ordinary flash cards from two or more strategies into a single packet. Prepare simple pictures or labels for the strategies in the packet. Students first match a card with a strategy and then use the strategy to answer that fact.

---

Both of these activities can be tailored to match the strategies that an individual student is using and working on. Talk with the students, and have them help you put the activity together.

 **TECHNOLOGY NOTE**

There are literally hundreds of software programs that offer drill and practice of basic facts. Nearly all fact programs offer games or exercises at various difficulty levels. Unfortunately, there do not seem to be any programs that organize facts the

way they are organized in this chapter. It should be clear that computerized fact practice should be used only after students have developed some strategies.

A few representative programs are described here.

In *Math Munchers Deluxe* (MECC, 1995d), students move their muncher in a 3-D grid format. By answering questions, they can avoid six Troggles that chase the muncher and try to eat it. Like many programs, *Math Munchers* encourages speed and is highly motivating. It is aimed at grades 3 to 6 and could profitably provide practice up through grade 8.

*Mega Math Blaster* (Davidson) promotes speed through an arcade format. There are children who are attracted to this approach and many who are not. For some, the formats in fancy, high-paced programs is a distraction to the mathematical thinking you want to promote. Like most programs, *Mega Math Blaster* includes drills for more than just facts. It is not uncommon to see drill with multidigit computation, decimals, fractions, percents, estimation, and other topics, all in the same format.

One aspect of a program you should be aware of is how a student inputs answers. For fact practice, numbers are usually typed left to right. But in the same program, multidigit computation may be entered beginning with the ones place or right to left. In *Gold Medal Mathematics* (EdVenture Software, 1997), responses are always in multiple-choice format. This is not uncommon, especially for programs designed for younger children.

*Teasers by Tobs* (O'Brien) uses a 3 × 3 operation grid for either addition or multiplication. Addends or factors appear on two sides of the grid, sums or products on the inside. Interestingly, blank spaces are sometimes inside the grid (sums or products) and sometimes on the sides. In this way, subtraction and division are implicitly linked to addition and multiplication. (This is similar to the missing number worksheets in Figure 8.12, p. 139).

Many (not all) programs automatically keep performance records of individual students. Others offer teachers the option of customizing the difficulty level in some way. *Performance Mathematics* (Jazz Interactive) drills only basic facts. However, the program presents facts in small increments of increasing difficulty and keeps track of which facts are "mastered" (determined by correct responses within a fixed time). New sets of facts are tailored to the progress of the individual student, including a number of mastered facts and a few new facts. ■

## What About Timed Tests?

Teachers who use timed tests believe that the tests help children learn basic facts. This perspective makes no instructional sense. Children who perform well under time pressure display their skills. Children who have difficulty with skills or who work more slowly run the risk of reinforcing wrong practices under pressure. Also, they can become fearful about, and negative toward, their mathematics learning. (Burns, 1995a, p. 408)

Think about this quotation whenever you are tempted to give a timed test. Reasoning and pattern searching are never facilitated by restricting time. Some children simply cannot work well under pressure or in situations that provoke stress.

Speed tests have been most popular for tests of basic facts. Although speed may encourage children to memorize facts, it is effective only for students who are goal-oriented and who can perform in pressure situations. Speed in a testing situation is debilitating for many and provides no positive benefits. Very short speed drills (say, one row of eight facts), if presented in a lighthearted manner, may be useful. Drills of this nature should not, however, be used as assessments and *never* for grading purposes. A short, five-fact drill with a soft emphasis on quickness can encourage efficient strategies and provide feedback. But the results should be for the individual child, not your grade book.

In every instance, timed tests reward few and punish many. They can have a lasting negative impact on student attitudes. They should be avoided whenever possible.

# FACT REMEDIATION WITH UPPER-GRADE STUDENTS

Children who have not mastered their basic facts by the sixth or seventh grade are in need of something other than more practice. They have certainly seen and practiced facts countless times over the past several school years. There is no reason to believe that the drills *you* provide will somehow be more effective than last year's. These students need something better. The following key ideas can guide your efforts to help these older students.

1. *Recognize that more drill will not work.* Students' fact difficulties are due to a failure to develop or to connect concepts and relationships such as those that have been discussed in this chapter, not a lack of practice. At best, more practice will provide temporary results. At worst, it will cause negative attitudes about mathematics.

2. *Inventory the known and unknown facts for each student in need.* Find out from each student what facts are known quickly and comfortably and which are not. Middle grade students can do this diagnosis for you. Provide sheets of all facts for one operation in random order, and have the students circle the facts they are hesitant about and answer all others. Suggest that finger counting or making marks in the margin is not permitted.

3. *Diagnose strengths and weaknesses.* Find out what students do when they encounter one of their unknown facts. Do they count on their fingers? Add up numbers in the margins? Guess? Try to use a related fact? Write down times tables? Are they able to use any of the relationships that might be helpful as suggested in this chapter? Some of this you may be able to accomplish by having students write reflective papers about two or three specific facts. More efficiently, you should conduct a 15-minute diagnostic interview with each student in need. Simply pose unknown facts and ask how the student approaches them. Try an idea from this chapter, and see what connections are already there. Don't try to teach; just find out.

4. *Provide hope.* Children who have experienced difficulty with fact mastery often believe that they cannot learn facts or that they are doomed to finger counting forever. Let these children know that you will help them and that you will provide some new ideas that will help them as well. Take that burden on yourself, and spare them the prospect of more defeat.

5. *Build in success.* As you begin a well-designed fact program for a child who has experienced failure, be sure that successes come quickly and easily. Begin with easy strategies, and introduce only a few new facts at a time. Even with pure rote drill, repetitive practice with five facts in three days will provide more success than introducing 15 facts in a week. Success builds success! With strategies as an added assist, success comes even more quickly. Point out to children how one idea, one strategy, is all that is required to learn many facts. Use fact charts to show what set of facts you are working on. It is surprising how the chart quickly fills up with mastered facts. Keep reviewing newly learned facts and those that were already known. This is success. It feels good, and failures are not as apparent. Short practice exercises can be designed as homework. Explain strategies and build them into the exercises. At the end of the exercises, have students write about which ideas are helpful and which are not. Use this information to design the next exercise.

Your extra effort beyond class time can be a motivation to a student to make some personal effort on his or her own time. During class, these students should continue to work with all students on the regular curriculum. You must believe and communicate to these students that the reason they have not mastered basic facts is not a reflection of their ability. With efficient strategies and individual effort, success will come. Believe!

# FACTS: NO BARRIER TO GOOD MATHEMATICS

Students who have total command of basic facts do not necessarily *reason better* than those who, for whatever reason, have not yet mastered facts. Today, mathematics is not about computation, especially pencil-and-paper computation. Mathematics is about reasoning and patterns and making sense of things. Mathematics is problem solving. There is no reason that a child who has not yet mastered all basic facts should be excluded from real mathematical experiences.

The most obvious alternative is the calculator. It should be on the desk every day for all students. There is absolutely no evidence that the presence of a calculator will impede basic fact mastery. On the contrary, the more students use the calculator, the more proficient they will be with it. This will make many of the calculator fact drills more effective and provide students with ready access to electronic flash cards. In a classroom climate where most students do know their facts and where students help one another and share thinking strategies as has been suggested, very few students will rely on the calculator for any prolonged period.

Students who are relegated to drill of facts when the rest of the class is engaged in meaningful experiences will soon feel stupid and incapable of doing "real" mathematics. By contrast, when students who have not mastered facts are engaged in exciting and meaningful experiences, they have real motivation to learn facts and real opportunities to develop relationships that can aid in that endeavor. Do not allow students who are behind in fact mastery to fall behind in mathematics.

# REFLECTIONS ON CHAPTER 8

## Writing to Learn

1. Explain briefly each part of the three-step approach to fact mastery.

2. Explain how a teacher can use word problems as a means of helping students construct strategies for the basic facts. What type of word problem would you use for subtraction fact strategies? Explain.

3. For each addition fact strategy:
   a. List at least three facts for which the strategy can be used.
   b. Explain the thinking process or concepts that are involved in using the strategy. Use a specific fact as an illustration.

4. What is meant by subtraction as "think-addition"? How can you help children develop a think-addition thought pattern for subtraction?

5. For subtraction facts with sums greater than 10, it is reasonable that as many as three different thought patterns or strategies might be used. Describe each of those suggested in the text.

6. Why is the turnaround property (commutative property) more important in multiplication fact mastery than in addition?

7. For each multiplication strategy except "use a helping fact," answer the questions in item 3.

8. The "last 25" multiplication facts involve using a fact that has already been learned and working from that fact to the new or harder fact. Four different ways to make this connection with a helping fact were described. Some are applicable only to certain facts. Describe each of these approaches, and list the facts for which the approach is applicable.

9. Describe when it is appropriate to use drill and how it can help. What is "premature" drill?

10. Why not use speed drills to learn facts?

11. How do you help children who have been drilling their basic facts for years and still have not mastered them?

## For Discussion and Exploration

1. Explore a computer software program that drills basic facts. What features does your program have that are good? Not so good? Explain. In general, do you think these programs are effective? How would you use such software in a classroom with only one or two available computers?

2. One view of thinking strategies is that they are little more than a collection of tricks for kids to memorize. Discuss the question, "Is teaching children thinking strategies for basic fact mastery in keeping with a constructivist view of teaching mathematics?" Carole Thornton (1990), a leading researcher in the area of basic-fact strategies, suggests a fairly direct approach to teaching strategies.

3. Examine a recently published second-, third-, or fourth-grade textbook to determine how thinking strategies for the basic facts have been developed. Compare what you find with the groupings of facts in this chapter. How would you use the text effectively in your program?

## Recommendations for Further Reading

### Highly Recommended

Fennema, E., Carpenter, T. P., Levi, L., Franke, M. L., & Empson, S. (1997). *Cognitively guided instruction: Professional development in primary mathematics.* Madison: Wisconsin Center for Education Research.
   The CGI program believes that students develop their own strategies for mastering the basic facts. They are helped in this process by solving well-selected story problems. Teachers listen carefully to students' emerging processes and encourage increasingly efficient methods. This book provides detailed explanations. (See also the annotation for this book in Chapter 7, pp. 126–127.)

Hope, J. A., Leutzinger, L. P., Reys, B. J., & Reys, R. E. (1988). *Mental math in the primary grades.* White Plains, NY: Cuisenaire–Dale Seymour.
   This first book in a series of three on mental mathematics devotes roughly the first half of its pages to the development of basic facts using strategies similar to those found in this chapter. The lessons include transparency masters as well as activity sheets for children and encourage appropriate use of manipulatives such as ten-frames.

Thornton, C. A. (1990). Strategies for the basic facts. In J. N. Payne (Ed.), *Mathematics for the young child* (pp. 133–151). Reston, VA: National Council of Teachers of Mathematics.
   Carole Thornton was one of the first researchers to test the effectiveness of basic-fact strategies. She has coauthored two series of Blackline Masters for fact development and has done research in both the United States and Australia. This chapter is a good supplement to what you have read in this chapter.

## Other Suggestions

Baroody, A. J. (1985). Mastery of the basic number combinations: Internalization of relationships or facts? *Journal for Research in Mathematics Education, 16,* 83–98.

Baroody, A. J., & Standifer, D. J. (1993). Addition and subtraction in the primary grades. In R. J. Jensen (Ed.), *Research ideas for the classroom: Early childhood mathematics* (pp. 72–102). Old Tappan, NJ: Macmillan.

Brownell, W. A., & Chazal, C. B. (1935). The effects of premature drill in third-grade arithmetic. *Journal of Educational Research, 29,* 17–28.

Burns, M. (1995). Timed tests. *Teaching Children Mathematics, 1,* 408–409.

Carpenter, T. P., Carey, D. A., & Kouba, V. L. (1990). A problem-solving approach to the operations. In J. N. Payne (Ed.), *Mathematics for the young child* (pp. 111–131). Reston, VA: National Council of Teachers of Mathematics.

Kamii, C. K., Lewis, B. A., & Booker, B. M. (1998). Instead of teaching missing addends. *Teaching Children Mathematics, 4,* 458–461.

Labinowicz, E. (1985). *Learning from children: New beginnings for teaching numerical thinking.* Menlo Park, CA: AWL Supplemental.

Leutzinger, L. P. (1999). Developing thinking strategies for addition facts. *Teaching Children Mathematics, 6,* 14–18.

Leutzinger, L. P. (1999). *Facts that last: A balanced approach to memorization* [one volume for each operation]. Chicago: Creative Publications.

Rathmell, E. C. (1978). Using thinking strategies to teach the basic facts. In M. N. Suydam (Ed.), *Developing computational skills* (pp. 13–38). Reston, VA: National Council of Teachers of Mathematics.

Rightsel, P. S., & Thornton, C. A. (1985). 72 addition facts can be mastered by mid–grade 1. *Arithmetic Teacher, 33*(3), 8–10.

Steinberg, R. M. (1985). Instruction on derived facts strategies in addition and subtraction. *Journal for Research in Mathematics Education, 16,* 337–355.

Thornton, C. A., & Jones, G. A. (1994). Computation sense. In C. A. Thornton & N. S. Bley (Eds.), *Windows of opportunity: Mathematics for students with special needs* (pp. 205–227). Reston, VA: National Council of Teachers of Mathematics.

Thornton, C. A., & Smith, P. (1988). Action research: Strategies for learning subtraction facts. *Arithmetic Teacher, 35*(8), 8–12.

Thornton, C. A., & Toohey, M. A. (1984). *A matter of facts: Addition, subtraction, multiplication, division.* Mountain View, CA: Creative Publications.

# Chapter 9

# Whole-Number Place-Value Development

A full understanding of place value includes a complex array of ideas and relationships that develop over the K–6 grade span. In kindergarten, children begin learning to count to 100. By second grade, they are talking about tens and ones and are using these ideas in many ways. By fourth grade, students are working with numbers involving four or more digits. Numbers are experienced in computations, on calculators, in mental computations and estimations, and in connection with real-world quantities and measures. In fourth and fifth grades, the ideas of whole-number place value are extended to decimals.

In addition to number meanings, students should begin in the early grades to develop some number sense for large numbers. Number sense must continue to be developed throughout the elementary years. Number sense for the whole numbers refers to the following concepts:

- A sense of the relative size of numbers (185 is large compared to 15, small compared to 1219, and about the same as 179)

- A connection to real-world concepts (estimation of quantities, knowing what would be reasonable numbers for the capacity of a football stadium or school cafeteria, the dollars required to purchase a sweatshirt or a TV or a car, or the weight of an adult)

- A flexible use of numbers in estimation (using 250 instead of 243 in a computation because "four 250s" is easy to work with; thinking about 1296 as "about thirteen hundred")

- A knowledge of the effect of operating with large numbers (adding 1000 increases 3472 by less than a third; 1000 times 3472 will be over 3 million; division by 1000 will produce a very small result)

The *Principles and Standards* document uses the term *computational fluency* to refer to the possession of efficient and accurate methods of computing. NCTM has made it clear that computation is as important as ever. The emphasis, however, is on multiple methods of computation, including mental computation and estimation strategies, and paper methods that may or may not be the traditional procedures of the past. All computational methods are intimately connected with place-value understanding. Neither number sense nor computational understanding can possibly be developed without a firm understanding of place value.

## BIG Ideas

1. Sets of ten (and tens of tens) must be perceived as single entities. These sets can then be used to describe how many. This is the main principle of base-ten numeration.

2. The positions of digits in numbers determine what they represent—which size group they count. This is the main principle of place-value numeration.

3. There are patterns to the way numbers are formed.

4. The groupings of ones, tens, and hundreds can be taken apart in different ways. For example, 256 can be 1 hundred, 14 tens, and 16 ones.

5. "Really big" numbers are best understood in terms of familiar real-world referents.

## EARLY DEVELOPMENT OF PLACE-VALUE IDEAS

It is important for teachers to understand the ideas about numbers that children are likely to have before they develop place-value concepts and to reflect on how these new and complex concepts are built on the early ideas.

# Number Ideas Before Place Value

It is tempting to think that children know a lot about numbers with two digits (10 to 99) even as early as kindergarten. After all, most kindergartners can and should learn to count to 100 and even to count out sets of things that may have 20 or 30 objects in them. They do daily calendar activities, count children in the room, turn to specified page numbers in their books, and so on. However, their understanding is quite different from yours. It is based on a one-more-than or count-by-ones approach to quantity.

## Children's Pre-Base-Ten View of Number

Ask first- or second-grade children to count out 53 tiles, and most will be able to do so or will make only careless errors. It is a tedious but not formidable task. If you watch closely, you will note that the children count out the tiles one at a time and put them into the pile with no use of any type of grouping. Have the children write the number that tells how many tiles they just counted. Most children will be able to write it. Some may write "35" instead of "53," a simple reversal.

So far, so good. Now ask the children to write the number that is 10 more than the number they just wrote. Most will begin to count, either starting from 1 or starting from 53. Those counting on from 53 will also find it necessary to keep track of the counts, probably on their fingers. Many, if not most, children in the first and early second grade will not be successful at this task, and almost none will know immediately that 10 more is 63. Asking for the number that is 10 less is even more problematic.

Finally, show a large collection of cards, each with a ten-frame drawn on it. Explain that the cards each have ten spaces and that each will hold ten tiles. Demonstrate putting tiles on the cards by filling up one of the ten-frames with tiles. Now ask, "How many cards like this do you think it will take if we want to put all of these tiles [the 53 counted out] on the cards?" A not unusual response is "53." Other children will say they do not know, and a few will try to put the tiles on the cards to figure it out.

## Pre-Base-Ten Quantity Tied to Counts by Ones

The children just described know that there are 53 tiles "because I counted them." Writing the number and saying the number are usually done correctly, but this procedural knowledge is connected to the count by ones. With minimal instruction, children can tell you that the 5 is in the tens place or that there are "3 ones." It is likely that this is simply a naming of the positions with little understanding. If children have been exposed to base-ten materials, they may name a rod of ten as a "ten" and a small cube as a "one." These same chil-

dren, however, may not be readily able to tell how many ones are required to make a ten. It is easy to attach words to both materials and groups without realizing what the materials or symbols represent.

Children do know that 53 is "a lot" and that it's more than 47 (because you count past 47 to get to 53). They think of the "53" that they write as a single numeral. They do not know that the 5 represents five groups of ten things and the 3 three single things (Fuson et al., 1997; Ross, 1989). Fuson and her colleagues refer to children's pre-base-ten understanding of number as "unitary." That is, there are no groupings of ten, even though a two-digit number is associated with the quantity. They rely on unitary counts to understand quantities.

# Basic Ideas of Place Value

Place-value understanding requires an integration of new and difficult-to-construct concepts of grouping by tens (the base-ten concept) with procedural knowledge of how groups are recorded in our place-value scheme, how numbers are written, and how they are spoken.

## Integration of Base-Ten Groupings with Counts by Ones

Recognizing that children can count out a set of 53, we want to help them see that making groupings of tens and leftovers is a way of counting that same quantity. Each of the groups in Figure 9.1 has 53 tiles. We want children to construct the idea that all of these are the same and that the sameness is clearly evident by virtue of the groupings of tens.

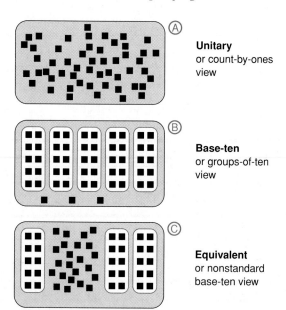

**Unitary** or count-by-ones view

**Base-ten** or groups-of-ten view

**Equivalent** or nonstandard base-ten view

**Figure 9.1** Three equivalent groupings of 53 objects. Group A is 53 because "I counted them (by ones)." Group B has 5 tens and 3 more. Group C is the same as B, but now some groups are broken into singles.

There is a subtle yet profound difference between two groups of children: those who know that group B is 53 because they understand the idea that 5 groups of 10 and 3 more is the same amount as 53 counted by ones and those who simply say, "It's 53," because they have been told that when things are grouped this way, it's called 53. The latter children may not be sure how many they will get if they count the tiles in set B by ones or if the groups were "ungrouped" how many there would then be. The children who understand will see no need to count set B by ones. They understand the "fifty-threeness" of sets A and B to be the same.

*The ideas in the preceding paragraph are important for you to understand so that the activities discussed later will make sense. Spend some time with these ideas before reading further.*

Recognition of the equivalence of groups B and C is another step in children's conceptual development. Groupings with fewer than the maximum number of tens can be referred to as *equivalent groupings* or *equivalent representations*. Understanding the equivalence of B and C indicates that grouping by tens is not just a rule that is followed but that any grouping by tens, including all or some of the singles, can help tell how many.

## The Role of Counting in Constructing Base-Ten Ideas

Just as counting is the vehicle with which children construct ideas about small numbers up to 10, counting plays a key role in constructing base-ten ideas about quantity and connecting these concepts to symbols and oral names for numbers.

Children can count sets such as those in Figure 9.1 in three different ways. Each way helps children think about the quantities in a different way (Thompson, 1990).

1. *Counting by ones.* This is the method children have to begin with. Initially, a count by ones is the only way they are able to name a quantity or "tell how many." All three of the sets in Figure 9.1 can be counted by ones. Before base-ten ideas develop, this is the only way children can be convinced that all three sets are the same.

2. *Counting by groups and singles.* In group B in Figure 9.1, counting by groups and singles would go like this: "One, two, three, four, five bunches of 10, and one, two, three singles." Consider how novel this method would be for a child who had never thought about counting a group of things as a single item. Also notice how this counting does not tell directly how many items there are. This counting must be coordinated with a count by ones before it can be a means of telling "how many."

3. *Counting by tens and ones.* This is the way adults would probably count group B and perhaps group C: "Ten, twenty, thirty, forty, fifty, fifty-one, fifty-two, fifty-three." While this count ends by saying the number that is there, it is not as explicit as the second method in counting the

number of groups. Nor will it convey a personal understanding of "how many" unless it is coordinated with the more meaningful count by ones.

Regardless of the specific activity that you may be doing with children, helping them integrate the grouping-by-tens concept with what they know about number from counting by ones should be your foremost objective. Children should frequently have the opportunity to count sets of objects in several ways. If first counted by ones, the question might be, "What will happen if we count these by groups and singles (or by tens and ones)?" If a set has been grouped into tens and singles and counted accordingly, "How can we be really certain that there are 53 things here?" or "What do you think we will get if we count by ones?" It is inadequate to *tell* children that these counts will all be the same. That is a relationship they must construct themselves through reflective thought, not because the teacher says it works that way.

## Integration of Groupings with Words

The way we say a number such as "fifty-three" must also be connected with the grouping-by-tens concept. The counting methods provide a connecting mechanism. The count by tens and ones results in saying the number of groups and singles separately: "five tens and three." This is an acceptable, albeit nonstandard, way of naming this quantity. Saying the number of tens and singles separately in this fashion can be called *base-ten language* for a number. Children can associate the base-ten language with the usual language: "five tens and three—fifty-three."

Notice that there are several variations of the base-ten language for 53—5 tens and 3; 5 tens and 3 ones; 5 groups of 10 and 3 leftovers; 5 tens and 3 singles; and so on. Each may be used interchangeably with the standard name, "fifty-three." For three-digit numbers, the same flexibility is available: 230 can be 23 tens or 2 hundreds and 3 tens. For a number with singles, there are more options.

It can easily be argued that base-ten language should be used throughout the second grade, even in preference to standard oral names.

## Integration of Groupings with Place-Value Notation

In like manner, the symbolic scheme that we use for writing numbers (ones on the right, tens to the left of ones, and so on) must be coordinated with the grouping scheme. Activities can be designed so that children physically associate a tens and ones grouping with the correct recording of the individual digits, as Figure 9.2 (p. 152) indicates.

Language again plays a key role in making these connections. The explicit count by groups and singles matches the individual digits as the number is written in the usual left-to-right manner.

A similar coordination is necessary for hundreds.

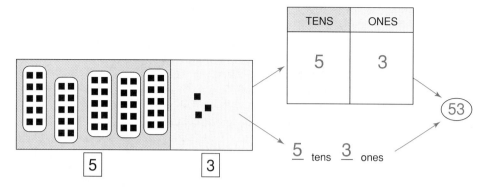

**Figure 9.2** Groupings by 10 are matched with numerals, placed in labeled places, and eventually written in standard form.

## Relational Understanding

Figure 9.3 summarizes the ideas that have been discussed so far.

- The conceptual knowledge of place value consists of the base-ten grouping ideas.

  A collection of objects can be grouped in sets of 10 and some leftover singles.

  There can be equivalent representations with fewer than the maximum groupings.

- The base-ten grouping ideas must be integrated with oral and written names for numbers.

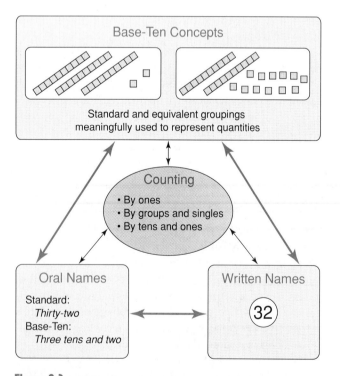

**Figure 9.3** Relational understanding of place value integrates three components, shown as the corners of the triangle: base-ten concepts, oral names for numbers, and written names for numbers. Counting is a key activity by which children can construct and integrate these three ideas and connect them to the pre-place-value concepts of number that they have to begin with.

- In addition to counting by ones, children use two other ways of counting: by groups and singles separately and by tens and ones. All three methods of counting are coordinated as the principal method of integrating the concepts, the written names, and the oral names.

Remember that these ideas are built on a count-by-ones understanding of number. The notion of sets of 10 as single entities must be constructed as a completely new way of thinking about number. Simply showing children groups of 10 and telling them that "10 ones is the same as 1 ten" will not construct that idea for them.

The base-ten or grouping ideas are the conceptual knowledge of place value, whereas counting, oral names, and written names fall under the category of procedural knowledge. A relational understanding of place value integrates all of these ideas.

# MODELS FOR PLACE VALUE

Physical models for base-ten concepts can play a key role in helping children develop the idea of "a ten" as both a single entity and as a set of 10 units. Remember, though, that the models do not "show" the concept to the children. The children must construct the concept and impose it on the model.

## Base-Ten Models and the Ten-Makes-One Relationship

A good base-ten model for ones, tens, and hundreds is *proportional*. That is, a ten model is physically ten times larger than the model for a one, and a hundred model is ten times larger than the ten model. Base-ten models can be categorized as *groupable* and *pregrouped*.

### Groupable Models

Models that most clearly reflect the relationships of ones, tens, and hundreds are those for which the ten can actually be made or grouped from the singles. When you bundle 10 Popsicle sticks, the bundle of 10 literally *is the same as* the 10 ones from which it was made. Examples of these groupable models are shown in Figure 9.4(a). These could also be called "put-together-take-apart" models.

Of the groupable models, beans or counters in cups are the cheapest and easiest for children to use. (Plastic portion cups can be purchased from restaurant supply houses.) Plastic connecting cubes are attractive and provide a good transition to pregrouped tens sticks. Plastic chain links in ten-link chains are another popular model. Bundles of Popsicle sticks are perhaps the best-known base-ten model, but small hands have trouble with rubber bands and actually making the bundles. With most groupable materials, hundreds are possible but are generally not practical for most activities in the classroom.

As children become more and more familiar with these models, collections of tens can be made up in advance by the children and kept as ready-made tens. Lids can be purchased for the plastic portion cups, and the connecting cubes or the links can be left prebundled. This is a good transition into the pregrouped models described next.

## Pregrouped or Trading Models

At some point, you will need to represent hundreds. Models that are pregrouped must be introduced. As with all base-ten models, the ten piece is physically equivalent to 10 ones and a hundred piece equivalent to 10 tens, as in Figure 9.4(b). However, children cannot actually take them apart or put them together. When 10 single pieces are accumulated, they must be exchanged or *traded* for a ten, and likewise, tens must be traded for hundreds.

The chief advantage of these models is their ease of use and the efficient way they model large numbers. Since they do not come apart, there are always readily available tens and hundreds. The disadvantage is the potential for children to use them without reflecting on the ten-to-one relationships. For example, if children are told to trade 10 ones for a ten, it is quite possible for them to make this exchange without attending to the "tenness" of the piece they call a ten. Similarly, children can learn to make the number 42 with 4 tens and 2 ones pieces without understanding that if the pieces all came apart there would be 42 ones pieces that could be counted by ones.

Though no model including a groupable model, will guarantee that children are reflecting on the ten-to-one relationships in the materials, with pregrouped models we need to make an extra effort to see that children understand that a ten piece really is the same as 10 ones.

(See the Blackline Masters and Materials Construction Tips for making base-ten strips and squares and the bean sticks.)

## Nonproportional Materials

In this text, colored counters, abacuses, and money are not considered to model base-ten ideas because the materials play no part in developing those relationships. With an abacus like the ones shown in Figure 9.5 (p. 154), ten beads in one column are exchanged for one bead in the next column

**(a) Groupable Base-Ten Models**

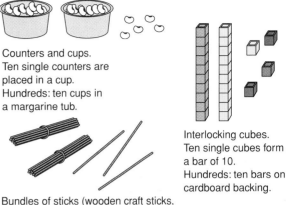

Counters and cups. Ten single counters are placed in a cup. Hundreds: ten cups in a margarine tub.

Interlocking cubes. Ten single cubes form a bar of 10. Hundreds: ten bars on cardboard backing.

Bundles of sticks (wooden craft sticks, coffee stirrers). (If bundles are left intact, these are a pregrouped model.) Hundreds: ten bundles in a big bundle.

**(b) Pregrouped Base-Ten Models**

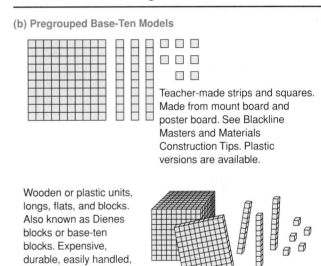

Teacher-made strips and squares. Made from mount board and poster board. See Blackline Masters and Materials Construction Tips. Plastic versions are available.

Wooden or plastic units, longs, flats, and blocks. Also known as Dienes blocks or base-ten blocks. Expensive, durable, easily handled, the only model with 1000.

Bean sticks. Beans glued to craft sticks. Ten sticks in a raft is also made from cardboard.

"Raft"

See directions and alternatives in Blackline Masters and Materials Construction Tips.

**Figure 9.4** **Groupable and pregrouped base-ten models.**

to the left. Although this is no more or less arbitrary than the convention of using base-ten instead of base-six or base-eight, for example, there is nothing in the representation that illustrates the relationship between ten beads and the single bead to its left. A stack of numeral cards from 0 to 9 in each position could easily replace the abacus with no decrease in representational value. By first grade, students do not need beads to understand numbers to 9. Nonproportional materials can keep track of numbers, but they do not illuminate an understanding of them in the same manner as proportional materials.

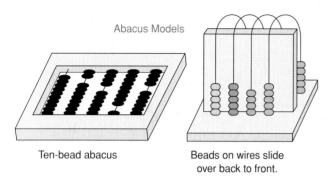

Abacus Models

Ten-bead abacus

Beads on wires slide over back to front.

**Figure 9.5** **Abacus models are nonproportional.**

Teachers and textbooks frequently use pennies, dimes, and dollars as a place-value model. If the relationship that a dime is worth 10 pennies and that a dollar is worth 10 dimes is part of the children's existing understanding, money will model base-ten place value. But if the teacher must explain or impose this relationship, the trade rate between pennies and dimes is simply a "rule of the game" from the children's view. They can learn to obey the rule, but the model is not helping them see why 10 ones is the same as 1 ten. The relationship should be in the model.

The pivotal question may be, "Why not just use proportional models?"

# DEVELOPING PLACE-VALUE CONCEPTS AND PROCEDURES

Now that you have some idea of what we want to accomplish, we can look at some activities designed to help. This is one area of mathematics where the conceptual and procedural knowledge are developed in an integrated or coordinated manner. While a particular activity may focus on grouping or on oral or written names, all activities involve models and add to the complete coordination of concepts, oral names, and written symbols as depicted in Figure 9.3 (p. 152).

## Grouping Activities

Because children come to their development of base-ten concepts with a count-by-ones idea of number, you must begin there. You cannot arbitrarily impose grouping by 10 on children. At the same time, why groups of 10 and not groups of some other number? The decision to use 10 as the base of our numeration system is certainly arbitrary. It most likely stems

from the fact that humans have ten fingers. And so we want children to experiment with showing amounts in groups of like size and perhaps to come to an agreement that 10 is a very useful size to use. The following activity could be done in late first grade or second grade and is designed as an example of a first effort at developing grouping concepts.

---
**A**CTIVITY

### 9.1 Counting in Groups

Find a collection of things that children might be interested in counting—perhaps the number of eyes in the classroom or the number of shoes, a mystery jar of buttons or cubes, a long chain of plastic links, or the number of crayons in the crayon box. The quantity should be countable, somewhere between 25 and 100. Pose the question, "How could we count our shoes in some way that would be easier than counting by ones?" Whatever suggestions you get, try to implement them. After trying several methods, you can have a discussion of what worked well and what did not. If no one suggests counting by tens, you might casually suggest that as possibly another idea.

---

One teacher had her second-grade students find a good way to count all the connecting cubes being held by the children after each had been given a cube for each of their pockets. The first suggestion was to count by sevens. That was tried but did not work very well because none of the second graders could count by sevens. In search of a faster way, the next suggestion was to count by twos. This did not seem to be much better than counting by ones. Finally, they settled on counting by tens and realized that this was a pretty good method, although counting by fives worked pretty well also.

This and similar activities provide you with the opportunity to suggest that materials actually be arranged into groups of tens before the "fast" way of counting is begun. Remember that children may count "ten, twenty, thirty, thirty-one, thirty-two" but not fully realize the "thirty-two-ness" of the quantity. To connect the count-by-tens method with their understood method of counting by ones, the children need to count both ways and discuss why they get the same result.

The idea in the next activity is for children to make groupings of 10 and record or say the amounts. Number words are used so that children will not mechanically match tens and ones with individual digits. It is important that children confront the actual quantity in a manner meaningful to them.

---
**A**CTIVITY

### 9.2 Groups of 10

Prepare bags of counters of different types. Bags may have toothpicks, buttons, beans, plastic chips, connecting cubes, craft sticks, or other items. Children have a record sheet similar to the top example in

**Name** _____

| Bag of | Number word | | |
|---|---|---|---|
| Toothpicks | | Tens | ☐ |
| | | Singles | ☐ |
| Beans | | Tens | ☐ |
| | | Singles | ☐ |
| Washers | | Tens | ☐ |
| | | Singles | ☐ |

**Get this many.**

**Write the number word.**

_____

Tens _____ Ones _____

**Fill the tens.**

Get forty-seven beans.

Fill up ten-frames. Draw dots.

Tens _____ Extras _____

**Loop this many.**

Loop [sixty-two] in groups of ten.

Tens _____ Ones _____

**Figure 9.6** **Number words and making groups of 10.**

Figure 9.6. The bags can be placed at stations around the room, or each pair of children can be given one. Children dump out and count the contents. The amount is recorded as a number word. Then the counters are grouped in as many tens as possible. The groupings are recorded on the form. Bags are traded, or children move to another station after returning all counters to the bag.

| Number Words | | |
|---|---|---|
| eleven | ten | one |
| twelve | twenty | two |
| thirteen | thirty | three |
| fourteen | forty | four |
| fifteen | fifty | five |
| sixteen | sixty | six |
| seventeen | seventy | seven |
| eighteen | eighty | eight |
| nineteen | ninety | nine |

**Figure 9.7** **A chart to help children write number words.**

If children have difficulty writing the number words, a chart can be displayed for students to copy from (see Figure 9.7).

Variations of the "Groups of 10" activity are suggested by the other record sheets in Figure 9.6. In "Get This Many," the children count the dots and then count out the corresponding number of counters. Small cups in which to put the groups of 10 should be provided. Notice that the activity requires students to address quantities in a way they understand, record the amount in words, and then make the groupings.

The activity starts where the students are and develops the idea of groups. Make various countable designs with the dots. "Fill the Tens" and "Loop This Many" each begin with a verbal name (number word), and students must count the indicated amount and then make groups. As you watch children doing these activities, you will be able to learn a lot about their base-ten concept development. For example, how do children count out the objects? Do they make groupings of 10 as they go? Do they count to 10 and then start again at 1? Children who do that are already using the base-ten structure. But what you will more likely see early on is children counting a full set without any stopping at tens and without any effort to group the materials in piles. A second-grade teacher had her students count a jar of small beans. After they had recorded the number, they were to ask for plastic cups in which to make cups of 10. Several children, when asked how many cups they thought they might need, had no idea or made random guesses.

The following activity is another variant but includes an estimation component that adds interest, makes the activity more problematic, and contributes to number sense. It is helpful to add estimation to these early counting and grouping activities. Estimates encourage children to think about total quantities. Listening to students' estimates is also a useful assessment opportunity that tells you a lot about children's concepts of numbers in the range of your current activities.

---

**ACTIVITY**

### 9.3 Estimating Groups of Tens and Ones

Show students a length that they are going to measure—for example, the length of a student lying down or the distance around a sheet of newspaper. At one end of the length, line up 10 units (e.g., 10 cubes in a bar, 10 toothpicks, rods, or blocks). On a recording sheet (see Figure 9.8), students write down a guess of how many groups of 10 and leftovers they think will fit into the length. Next they find the actual measure, placing units along the full length. These are counted by ones and also grouped in tens. Both results are recorded.

---

Notice that all place-value components are included in Activity 9.3. Children can work in pairs to measure several lengths around the room. A similar estimation approach could be added to "Groups of 10" (Activity 9.2), where students first estimate the quantity in the bags. Estimation requires reflective thought concerning quantities expressed in groups.

## TECHNOLOGY NOTE

*Unifix Software* (Hickey, 1996) allows you to create useful grouping activities on the computer. As many as 100 individual cubes can be "stamped" onto the screen. The cubes are easily snapped into rods. With the "bar total" option on, the size of each rod is printed on the rod. A single cube shows "1." You could prepare a file with, say, 78 cubes and have students estimate how many tens. This could be done with or without displaying the total cubes on the screen. With both displays (rod and screen totals), students will note that the total does not change when cubes are made into bars of 10 or when bars are broken into singles. Another alternative is to have students show a specific number of bars (all totals turned off). Will students use bars of 10 to keep track of counts?

*Grouping and Place Value* (Tenth Planet, 1997) offers three animated grouping tasks: Balls are packed by a machine in groups of tens and then 10 tens form a hundred; a "space money" scenario has children match hundreds, tens, and ones "coins" to specified amounts; and children try to find which of four collections of objects matches a given number. Children have little control over the ball packing, but the animation is catchy. The money task involves more interaction but is symbolic. The last is perhaps the best. Children select a gadget that groups objects by twos, fives, or tens, thereby providing three grouping possibilities. After grouping, the counting is not done for the students as it is in the warm-up exercises. As with other Tenth Planet products, the print material offers excellent suggestions for using the software as well as related off-computer tasks. ■

## The Strangeness of Ones, Tens, and Hundreds

As students begin to make groupings of 10, the language of these groupings must also be introduced. At the start, language such as "groups of 10 and leftovers" or "bunches of tens and singles" is most meaningful. For tens, use whatever terminology fits: bars of 10, cups of 10, bundles of 10. Eventually you can abbreviate this simply to "ten." There is no hurry to use the word "ones" for the leftovers. Language such as "four tens and seven" works very well.

---

**Figure 9.8** Record sheet for estimating groups of tens and ones.

Reflect for a moment on how strange it must sound to say "seven ones." Certainly children have never said they were "seven ones" years old. The use of the word *ten* as a singular group name is even more mysterious. Consider the phrase "Ten ones makes one ten." The first *ten* carries the usual meaning of 10 things, the amount that is 1 more than 9 things. But the other *ten* is a singular noun, a thing. How can something the child has known for years as the name for a lot of things suddenly become one thing? Bunches, bundles, cups, and groups of 10 make more sense in the beginning than "a ten."

The word *hundred* is equally strange and yet usually gets less attention. It must be understood in three ways: as 100 single objects, as 10 tens, and as a singular thing. These word names are not as simple as they seem!

### Equivalent Representations

An important variation of the grouping activities is aimed at the equivalent representations of numbers. (See Figure 9.3, p. 152.) For example, with children who have just completed the "Groups of 10" activity for a bag of counters, ask, "What is another way you can show your 42 besides 4 groups and 2 singles? Let's see how many ways you can find." Interestingly, most children will go next to 42 singles. The following activities are also directed to the idea of equivalent representations.

┌─ **A**CTIVITY ─────────────────────────
### 9.4 Odd Groupings

Show a collection of materials that are only partly grouped in sets of 10. For example, you may have 5 chains of 10 links and 17 additional links. Be sure the children understand that the groups each have 10 items. Count the number of groups, and also count the singles. Ask, "How many in all?" Record all responses, and discuss before you count. Let the children use whatever way they wish to count. Next change the groupings (make a ten from the singles, or break apart one of the tens) and repeat the questions and discussion. Do not change the total number from one time to the next. Once students begin to understand that the total does not change, ask in what other ways the items could be grouped if you use tens and singles.
└────────────────────────────────────

The next activity is similar but is done using pregrouped materials.

┌─ **A**CTIVITY ─────────────────────────
### 9.5 Three Other Ways

Students work in groups or pairs. First they show "four hundred sixty-three" on their desks with strips and squares in the standard representation. Next they find and record at least three other ways of showing this number.
└────────────────────────────────────

A variation of "Three Other Ways" is to challenge students to find a way to show an amount with a specific number of pieces. "Can you show 463 with 31 pieces?" (There is more than one way to do this.) Students in grades 4 or 5 can get quite involved with finding all the ways to show a three-digit number.

After children have had sufficient experiences with pregrouped materials, a "dot, stick, and square" notation can be used for recording ones, tens, and hundreds. By third grade, children can use small squares for hundreds, as shown in Figure 9.9. Use the drawings as a means of telling the children what pieces to get out of their own place-value kits and as a way for children to record results.

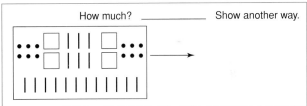

**Figure 9.9** Equivalent representation exercises using square-stick-dot pictures.

The next activity begins to incorporate oral language with equivalent representation ideas.

┌─ **A**CTIVITY ─────────────────────────
### 9.6 Base-Ten Riddles

Base-ten riddles can be presented orally or in written form. In either case, children should use base-ten materials to help solve them. The examples here illustrate a variety of possibilities with different levels of difficulty.

I have 23 ones and 4 tens. Who am I?

I have 4 hundreds, 12 tens, and 6 ones. Who am I?

I have 30 ones and 3 hundreds. Who am I?

I am 45. I have 25 ones. How many tens do I have?

I am 341. I have 22 tens. How many hundreds do I have?

I have 13 tens, 2 hundreds, and 21 ones. Who am I?

If you put 3 more tens with me, I would be 115. Who am I?

I have 17 ones. I am between 40 and 50. Who am I?

I have 17 ones. I am between 40 and 50. How many tens do I have?

# Oral Names for Numbers

The standard name of the collection in Figure 9.10 is "forty-seven." A more explicit terminology in *base-ten language* is "four tens and seven ones." Base-ten language is rarely misunderstood by children working with base-ten materials and encourages thinking in terms of groups instead of a large pile of singles.

"Four tens and seven ones—forty-seven"

**Figure 9.10   Mixed model of 47.**

## Two-Digit Number Names

In first and second grade, children need to connect the base-ten concepts with the oral number names they have used many times. They know the words but have not thought of them in terms of tens and ones. The following sequence is suggested:

1. Start with the names *twenty, thirty, forty,* through *ninety.*

2. Next do all names *twenty* through *ninety-nine.*

3. Emphasize the teens as exceptions. Acknowledge that they are formed "backward" and do not fit the patterns.

Almost always use base-ten models while teaching oral names. Use base-ten language paired with standard language.

— **A**CTIVITY —————————————

## 9.7  Counting Rows of 10

Use a 10 × 10 array of dots on the overhead projector. Cover up all but two rows, as shown in Figure 9.11(a). "How many tens? (2.) Two tens is called *twenty.*" Have the class repeat. "Sounds a little like *twin.*" Show another row. "Three tens is called *thirty.* Four tens is *forty.* Five tens should have been *fivety* rather than *fifty.*" The names *sixty, seventy, eighty,* and *ninety* all fit the pattern. Slide the cover up and down the array, asking how many tens and the name for that many.

Use the same 10 × 10 array to work on names for tens and ones. Show, for example, four full lines, "forty." Next expose one dot in the fifth row. "Four tens and one. Forty-one." Add more dots one at a time. "Four tens and two. Forty-two." "Four tens and three. Forty-three." This is shown in Figure 9.11(b). When that pattern is established, repeat with other decades from twenty through ninety.

(a)          "Two tens—twenty"

(b)

"Four tens—forty"

"Four tens and three—forty-three"

**Figure 9.11   10 × 10 dot arrays are used to model sets of 10 and singles.**

Repeat this basic approach with other base-ten models. The next activity shows how this might be done.

— **A**CTIVITY —————————————

## 9.8  Counting with Base-Ten Models

Show some tens pieces on the overhead. Ask how many tens. Ask for the usual name. Add a ten or remove a ten, and repeat the questions. Next add some ones. Always have children give the base-ten name and the standard name. Continue to make changes in the materials displayed by adding or removing 1 or 2 tens and by adding and removing ones. For this activity, show the tens and ones pieces in different arrangements rather than the standard left-to-right order for tens and ones. The idea is to connect the names to the materials, not the order they are in.

Reverse the activity by having children use base-ten pieces at their desks. For example, you say, "Make 63." The children make the number with the models and then give the base-ten name.

Note that Activities 9.7 and 9.8 will be much enhanced by discussion. Have children explain their thinking. If you don't require children to reflect on these responses, they soon learn how to give the response you want, matching number words to models, without actually thinking about the total quantities.

---

**ACTIVITY**

## 9.9 Tens, Ones, and Fingers

Ask your class, "How can you show 37 fingers?" (It is fun to precede this question by asking for different ways to show 6 fingers, 8 fingers, and other amounts less than 10.) Soon children will figure out that four children are required. Line up four children, and have three hold up 10 fingers and the last child 7 fingers. Have the class count the fingers by tens and ones. Ask for other children to show different numbers. Emphasize the number of sets of 10 fingers and the single fingers (base-ten language) and pair this with the standard language.

---

In the last three activities, it is important occasionally to count an entire representation by ones. Remember that the count by ones is the young child's principal linkage with the concept of quantity. For example, suppose you have just had children use connecting cubes to make 42. Try asking, "Do you think there really are 42 blocks there?" Many children are not convinced, and the count by ones is very significant.

The language pattern for two-digit numbers is best developed and connected with models using numbers 20 and higher. That is where the emphasis should be. Teens can and should appear in the activities but should be noted as exceptions to the verbal rules you are developing.

One approach to the teen numbers is to "back into them." Show, for example, 6 tens and 5 ones. Get the standard and base-ten names from the children as before. Remove tens one at a time, each time asking for both names. The switch from 2 tens and 5 ("twenty-five") to 1 ten and 5 ("fifteen") is a dramatic demonstration of the "backward" names for the teens. Take that opportunity to point them out as exceptions. Count them by ones. Say them in both languages.

Add tens to get to numbers that follow the rules. Return to a teen number. Continue to contrast the teens with the numbers 20 and above.

### Three-Digit Number Names

The approach to three-digit number names is essentially the same as for two-digit names. Show mixed arrangements of base-ten materials. Have children give the base-ten name and the standard name. Vary the arrangement from one example to the next by changing only one type of piece. That is, add or remove only ones or only tens or only hundreds.

Similarly, have children at their desks model numbers that you give to them orally using the standard names. By the time that children are ready for three-digit numbers, the two-digit number names, including the difficulties with the teens, have usually been mastered. The major difficulty is with numbers involving no tens, such as 702. As noted earlier, the use of base-ten language is quite helpful here. The zero-tens difficulty is more pronounced when writing numerals. Children frequently write 7002 for "seven hundred two." The emphasis on the meaning in the oral base-ten language form will be a significant help.

## Written Symbols

The discussion so far has stressed the ideas of groups of 10 and the connection of these base-ten concepts to oral number names. No one would expect that written numbers are completely absent during this development. At the same time, it is correct to focus on the ideas of base-ten concepts before emphasizing the written numbers.

### Place-Value Mats

Place-value mats are simple mats divided into two or three sections to hold ones and tens or ones, tens, and hundreds pieces as shown in Figure 9.12 (p. 160). You can suggest to your students that the mats are a good way to organize their materials when working with base-ten pieces. Explain that the standard way to use a place-value mat is with the space for the ones on the right and tens and hundreds places to the left.

Though there is no requirement to have anything printed on the mats, it is strongly recommended that two ten-frames be drawn in the ones place as shown. (See Blackline Masters and Materials Construction Tips for directions for making the mats.) That way, the amount of ones on the ten-frames is always clearly evident, eliminating the need for frequent and tedious counting (Thompson & Van de Walle, 1984). The ten-frame also makes it very clear how many additional counters would be needed to make the next set of 10. If children are modeling two numbers at the same time, one ten-frame can be used for each number. Most illustrations of place-value mats in this book will show two ten-frames, even though that feature is not commonly seen in standard texts.

Strips and squares show
237 on three-place mat.

With two ten-frames,
cups and beans show 53.

**Figure 9.12** **Place-value mats with two ten-frames in the ones place to organize the counters and promote the concept of groups of 10.**

As children use their place-value mats, they can be shown how the left-to-right order of the pieces is also the way that numbers are written. The place-value mat becomes a link between the base-ten models and the written form of the numbers. Once again, be aware of how easy it would be for a child to show a number on a mat using tens and ones pieces and learn to write the number without any understanding of what the number represents. First- and second-grade textbooks often show a model and have children record numbers in this manner:

    <u> 7 </u> tens and <u> 3 </u> ones is <u> 73 </u> in all.

It is all too easy to copy down the number of sticks and single blocks and rewrite these digits in a single number 73 and not confront what these symbols stand for.

## The 0–99 Chart

A 0–99 chart is a 10 × 10 grid with the numbers written in order from 0 to 99 (see Figure 9.13). It is a good idea to have a large chart like this somewhere prominent in your room. A large blank 10 × 10 grid is even more important for class discussions and activities. An overhead transparency can be made of the grid in the Blackline Masters, or a transparency master can be purchased. Some teachers prefer to buy a commercial chart that has pockets into which numeral cards can be inserted. Both the 0–99 chart and the blank chart lend themselves to useful activities that involve the written form

of numbers. (A hundreds chart goes from 1 to 100. It can be used just as well. There are some minor pros and cons to each version.) A Blackline Master of four small charts is also in the back of the text.

> **ACTIVITY**
>
> ## 9.10 Patterns on the 0–99 chart
>
> Display a 0–99 chart prominently, or give the children their own charts on paper. Have children work in pairs to find patterns on the chart. First- and second-grade children will have difficulty describing these patterns in writing. Solicit ideas orally from the class. Have children explain patterns found by others to be sure that all understand the ideas that are being suggested.

There are many different patterns on the 0–99 chart. In a discussion, different children will describe the same pattern in several ways. Accept all ideas. Here are some of the patterns they may point out:

- The numbers in a column all end with the same number (the same ones digit, which is the same as the number at the top). A child may point this out for the number 7 and then other children note the same idea for 3, then 5, and so on.

- In a row, one number counts (the ones digit goes 0, 1, 2, 3, . . . , 9; the "second" number goes up by ones, but the first number (tens digit) stays the same.

| 0 | 1 | 2 | 3 | 4 | 5 | 6 | 7 | 8 | 9 |
|---|---|---|---|---|---|---|---|---|---|
| 10 | 11 | 12 | 13 | 14 | 15 | 16 | 17 | 18 | 19 |
| 20 | 21 | 22 | 23 | 24 | 25 | 26 | 27 | 28 | 29 |
| 30 | 31 | 32 | 33 | 34 | 35 | 36 | 37 | 38 | 39 |
| 40 | 41 | 42 | 43 | 44 | 45 | 46 | 47 | 48 | 49 |
| 50 | 51 | 52 | 53 | 54 | 55 | 56 | 57 | 58 | 59 |
| 60 | 61 | 62 | 63 | 64 | 65 | 66 | 67 | 68 | 69 |
| 70 | 71 | 72 | 73 | 74 | 75 | 76 | 77 | 78 | 79 |
| 80 | 81 | 82 | 83 | 84 | 85 | 86 | 87 | 88 | 89 |
| 90 | 91 | 92 | 93 | 94 | 95 | 96 | 97 | 98 | 99 |

**Figure 9.13** **A 0–99 chart.**

- In a column, the first number (tens digit) counts or goes up by ones.
- You can count by tens going down the left-hand column.
- The numbers under the 2 are all even numbers. (Every other number is even.)
- If you count by fives, you get two columns, the first column and the 5 column.

These are just a few ideas that are easy to see. If you have students start to mark or color numbers that fit a rule, many more patterns emerge. Examine numbers that have a 7 in them or those where the two digits add up to 4. Skip-count by twos, threes, fives, and so on, and have the students color the numbers as they go. This will produce nice patterns that will spark a search for others.

The 0–99 chart patterns will help focus on the way numbers are written. Consider the following interactions between the chart and children making numbers with base-ten models:

- Have children make a number with their base-ten models and find the number on the chart.
- Try the reverse. Point to a number, and have children make the number.
- If you make all the numbers in a row, how would they be alike? How would they be different?
- What about the numbers in a column?
- What would you have to change to go from one number to the next in a row? In a column?
- What if you went diagonally from one number to the next? How would the materials change?

## TECHNOLOGY NOTE

Several software packages include hundreds charts. In *Math-Keys: Unlocking Whole Numbers* (MECC, 1995b, 1996b), the number chart offers very little in the way of problematic tasks. Students select a pattern from a menu (multiples, primes, odds, etc.), and the computer fills in all the corresponding numbers. Patterns can be combined so that even multiples of 3 would be colored in.

*Math and More 3: Patterns on Lattices* (EduQuest, 1994) allows the chart to scroll to 1000. Both programs focus on finding and describing patterns on the chart. Here is a situation where the computer does not seem to improve on the overhead projector. ∎

### More Connections with Numbers

The next three activities are designed to help children make connections among all three representations: models, oral language, and written forms. They can be done with two- or three-digit numbers in grades 1–4.

---

### ACTIVITY

### 9.11 Say It/Press It

Display some ones and tens (and hundreds) so that the class can see. (Use the overhead projector or magnetized pieces on the board, or simply draw using the square-stick-dot method.) Arrange the materials in a mixed design, not in the standard left-to-right format. Students say the amount shown in base-ten language ("four hundreds, one ten, and five") and then in standard language ("four hundred fifteen"), and finally they enter it on their calculators. Have someone share his or her display and defend it. Make a change in the materials and repeat.

"Say It/Press It" is especially good for helping with teens (note the example in the activity description) and for three-digit numbers with zero tens. If you show 7 hundreds and 4 ones, the class says "seven hundreds, zero tens, and four—seven hundred (*slight pause*) four." The pause and the base-ten language suggest the correct three-digit number to press or write. Many students have trouble with this example and write "7004," writing exactly what they hear in the standard name. Similarly, first- and second-grade children often write "504" for fifty-four. This activity will help. The next two activities simply change the representation that is presented first to the students.

---

### ACTIVITY

### 9.12 Show It/Press It

Say the standard name for a number (with either two or three digits). At their desks, students use their own base-ten models to show that number and press it on their calculators (or write it). Again, pay special attention to the teens and the case of zero tens.

---

### ACTIVITY

### 9.13 Write It/Say It

In this variant, you silently write a number (or press it on your overhead calculator), and the students show it at their desk with their models. On your cue, all say the amount in unison.

---

In Activities 9.12 and 9.13, you could have students record each example on paper using the square-stick-dot notation. Students having difficulties should put materials on a place-value mat. Worksheet activities can combine all three forms for numbers. Figure 9.14 (p. 162) shows two variations. A third variation would give the numeral and have children supply the number and draw the model.

Name _____

Supply the missing parts: number word, drawing, number

Number word

_____

Four hundred three

: ‖=‖ :
: ☐ ☐ :     Number                    Number

**Figure 9.14** **Connecting language, models, and numerals.**

# NUMBER SENSE DEVELOPMENT

The discussion so far has addressed the three main components of place-value understanding: the integration of base-ten groupings, oral names, and written names. But students need to expand these ideas beyond basic numeration concepts and reading and writing numerals in order to develop number sense. Even though this section highlights number sense activities, number sense is not a new or separate curriculum topic. These activities should be an ongoing feature of your instruction.

## Relative Magnitude

Relative magnitude refers to the size relationship one number has with another—is it much larger, much smaller, close, or about the same? There are several quick activities that can be done with a number line sketched on the board. The number line can help children see how one number is related to another.

### ACTIVITY

#### 9.14 Who Am I?

Sketch a line labeled 0 and 100 at opposite ends. Mark a point that corresponds to your secret number. (Estimate the position the best you can.) Students try to guess your secret number. For each guess, place and label a mark on the line.

Continue marking each guess until your secret number is discovered. As a variation, the endpoints can be other than 0 and 100. For example, try 0 and 1000, 200 and 300, or 500 and 800.

### ACTIVITY

#### 9.15 Squeeze

Label only the endpoints of the number line, but subdivide the line into ten equal segments. Have one student stand at each end with a marker card. As students guess your secret number, announce that the guess is either too high or too low. If the guess is too high, the student on the high end moves in to mark the guess by holding the marker card at the appropriate place. When the guess is too low, the left-end student moves in and marks that number in a similar manner. Guessing continues as the ends squeeze in on the secret number.

### ACTIVITY

#### 9.16 Who Could They Be?

Label two points on a number line (not necessarily the ends).

Ask students what numbers they think different points labeled with letters might be and why they think that. In the example shown here, B and C are less than 100 but probably more than 60. E could be about 180. You can also ask where 75 might be or where 400 is. About how far apart are A and D? Why do you think D is more than 100?

In the next activity, some of the same ideas are discussed without benefit of a number line.

### ACTIVITY

#### 9.17 Close, Far, and in Between

Put any three numbers on the board. If appropriate, use two-digit numbers.

With these three numbers as referents, ask questions such as the following, and encourage discussion of all responses:

**Which two are closest? Why?**

Which is closest to 300? To 250?

Name a number between 457 and 364.

Name a multiple of 25 between 219 and 364.

Name a number that is more than all of these.

About how far apart are 219 and 500? 219 and 5000?

If these are "big numbers," what are some small numbers? Numbers about the same? Numbers that make these seem small?

## Connections to Real-World Ideas

We should not permit children to study place-value concepts without encouraging them to see number in the world about them. You do not need a prescribed activity to bring real numbers into the classroom.

Children in the second grade should be thinking about numbers under 100 first and, soon after, numbers up to 1000. Quantities larger than that are difficult to think about. Where are numbers like this? Around your school: the number of children in each class, the numbers on the school buses, the number of minutes devoted to mathematics each day and then each week, the number of cartons of chocolate and plain milk served in the cafeteria each day, the numbers on the calendar (days in a week, month, year), the number of days since school has started. And then there are measurements, numbers at home, numbers on a field trip, and so on.

What do you do with these numbers? Turn them into interesting graphs, write stories using them, make up problems, devise contests.

As children get a bit older, the interest in numbers can expand beyond the school and classroom. All sorts of things can and should be measured to create graphs, draw inferences, and make comparisons. For example, what numbers are associated with the "average" fifth grader? Height, weight, arm span, age in months, number of siblings, number of grandparents, distance from home to school, length of standing broad jump, number of pets, hours spent watching TV in a week. How can you find the average for these or other numbers that may be of interest to the students in your room? Is anyone really average?

The particular way you bring number and the real world together in your class is up to you. But do not underestimate the value of connecting the real world to the classroom.

## Approximate Numbers and Rounding

In our number system, some numbers are "nice." They are easy to think about and work with. What makes a nice number is sort of fuzzy. However, numbers such as 100, 500, and 750 are easier to use than 94, 517, and 762. Multiples of 100 are very nice, and multiples of 10 are not bad either. Multiples of 25 (50, 75, 425, 675, etc.) are nice because they combine into 100s and 50s rather easily, and we can mentally place those between multiples of 100s. Multiples of 5 are a little easier to work with than other numbers.

Flexible thought with numbers and many estimation skills are related to the ability to substitute a nice number for one that is not so nice. The substitution may be to make a mental computation easier, to compare it to a familiar reference, or simply to store the number in memory more easily.

The choice of a nice number to substitute for a less manageable one is never completely clear-cut. There is no "correct" or "best" substitute for $327.99 or 57 pounds. The choices depend on the need for clarity and accuracy and how the substitute will be used. Nice substitutes for $327.99 might be $300, $325, $328, $330, or even $350. In a given situation, there may be more than one good choice of substitutes. For example, $325 might be used in combinations with other prices "rounded" to the nearest $5. An amount like $325 lends itself easily to multiplication. For instance, for 7 times $325, we might think 7 × 300 is $2100 plus 7 × $25 is $175 (four 25s is 100, and three more is 75). Note that $350 is also not a nearest ten or hundred but the nearest 50. That makes a nice round number that allows a little extra in an estimation situation. "Our vacation expenses were approximately $350."

In the past, students were taught rules for rounding numbers to the nearest 10 or nearest 100. Unfortunately, the emphasis was placed on applying the rule correctly. (If the next digit is 5 or more, round up; otherwise, leave the number alone.) A context to suggest why they may want to round numbers was usually a lesser consideration.

The activities here are designed to help students recognize what nice numbers are and to identify a nice-number substitute. (*Note:* The term *nice number* is not found in standard textbooks. It is an invention of mine. There is no commonly accepted definition.)

---

**A**CTIVITY

### 9.18 Nice-Number Skip Counts

Count by 5s, 10s, 25s, and 50s with your students. The 5s and 10s are fairly easy, but the skill is certainly worth practicing. Counts by 25s or 50s may be hesitant at first. Students can use a calculator to assist with their counting and connect the counts with numerals (press ⊞ 25 ⊟ ⊟ ⊟ . . .). At first, start all counts at zero. Later, start at some multiple of your skip amount. For example, begin at 275 and count by 25s. Counts by 10s should also begin at numbers ending in 5 as well as multiples of 10. Also count backward by these same amounts (press 650 ⊟ 50 ⊟ ⊟ ⊟ . . .).

For children in grades 1 and 2, a 0–99 chart can be used in connection with skip-counting 5s and 10s. Older children should count to at least 1000 and should discuss the patterns that they see in these counts.

## Counting Money

Too often children are expected to count coins without any preparation or background. It is not that money is hard for children but rather that skip-counting by different amounts is difficult. The next activity extends "Nice-Number Skip Counts" in preparation for counting money by shifting from one skip count to another.

---

### ᴀ̸ᴄᴛɪᴠɪᴛʏ

### 9.19 Money Counts

Explain to the students that they will start counting by one number and at your signal they will shift to a count by a different number. Begin with only two different amounts, say, 25 and 10. Write these numbers on the board. Point to the larger number (25), and have students begin to count. After three or more counts, raise your hand to indicate a pause in the counting. Then lower your hand and point to the smaller number (10). Children continue the count from where they left off but now count by 10s. Use any two of these numbers: 100, 50, 25, 10, 5, 1. Always start with the larger. Later, try three numbers, still in descending order.

---

Note that the counts in "Money Counts" are the same as are used when counting coins or money. These skills can be applied to bills and coins. Plastic money is available for use on the overhead and is an effective substitute.

## Rounding

To round a number simply means to substitute a nice number that is close so that some computation can be done more easily. The close number can be any nice number and need not be a multiple of 10 or 100, as has been traditional. It should be whatever makes the computation or estimation easier or simplifies numbers sufficiently in a story, chart, or conversation. You might say, "Last night it took me 57 minutes to do my homework" or "Last night it took me about one hour to do my homework." The first expression is more precise; the second substitutes a rounded number for better communication.

---

### ᴀ̸ᴄᴛɪᴠɪᴛʏ

### 9.20 Near and Nice

The idea is to say or write a number and have students select a close nice-number substitute. Begin by requesting a close multiple of 50. Explain that

these are the numbers that you get when you count by 50s. It is a good idea to include a real-world measurement as well. For example, "Instead of 243 feet, let's use _____ feet." Pause at the blank, and students fill in an appropriate number, here 250 feet. Finding the nearest 25 is sometimes difficult. For example, is 463 miles closer to 450 or 475 miles? Actually, either is quite a good substitute. In fact, place your emphasis on selecting a close nice number rather than the closest or best nice number.

---

A number line with nice numbers highlighted can be useful in helping children select near nice numbers. An unlabeled number line like the one shown in Figure 9.15 can be made using three strips of poster board taped end to end. Labels are written above the line on the chalkboard. The ends can be labeled 0 and 100, 100 and 200, . . . , 900 and 1000. The other markings then show multiples of 25, 10, and 5. Indicate a number above the line that you want to round. Discuss the marks (nice numbers) that are close.

**Figure 9.15**   **A blank number line can be labeled in different ways to help students with near and nice numbers.**

# NUMBERS BEYOND 1000

For children to have good concepts of numbers beyond 1000, the conceptual ideas that have been carefully developed must be extended. This is sometimes difficult to do because physical models for thousands are not commonly available. At the same time, number sense ideas must also be developed. In many ways, it is these informal ideas about very large numbers that are the most important.

## Extending the Place-Value System

Two important ideas developed for three-digit numbers should be carefully extended to larger numbers. First, the grouping idea should be generalized. That is, 10 in any position makes a single thing (group) in the next position, and vice versa. Second, the oral and written patterns for numbers in three digits are duplicated in a clever way for every three digits to the left. These two related ideas are not as easy for children to understand as adults seem to believe. Because models for large numbers are so difficult to have or picture, textbooks must deal with these ideas in a predominantly symbolic manner. That is not sufficient!

---

## 9.21 What Comes Next?

Have a "What Comes Next?" discussion with the use of base-ten strips and squares. The unit or ones piece is a 1 centimeter (cm) square. The tens piece is a 10 × 1 strip. The hundreds piece is a square, 10 cm × 10 cm. What is next? Ten hundreds is called a thousand. What shape? It could be a strip made of 10 hundreds squares. Tape 10 hundreds together. What is next? (Reinforce the idea of "ten makes one" that has progressed to this point.) Ten one-thousand strips would make a square measuring 1 meter (m) on a side. Once the class has figured out the shape of the thousand piece, the problematic task is "What comes next?" Let small groups work on the dimensions of a ten-thousand piece.

---

If your students become interested in seeing the big pieces from "What Comes Next?" engage them in measuring them out on paper. Ten ten-thousand squares (100,000) go together to make a huge strip. Draw this strip on a long sheet of butcher paper, and mark off the 10 squares that make it up. You will have to go out in the hall.

How far you want to extend this square, strip, square, strip sequence depends on your class. The idea that 10 in one place makes 1 in the next can be brought home dramatically. It is quite possible with older children to make the next 10 m × 10 m square using masking tape on the cafeteria floor or chalk lines on the playground. The next strip is 100 m × 10 m. This can be measured out on a large playground with kids marking the corners. By this point, the payoff includes an appreciation of the increase in size of each successive amount as well as the ten-makes-one progression. The 100 m × 10 m strip is the model for 10 million, and the 10 m × 10 m square models 1 million. The difference between 1 million and 10 million is dramatic. Even the concept of 1 million tiny centimeter squares is dramatic.

The three-dimensional wooden or plastic base-ten materials are all available with a model for thousands, which is a 10-cm cube. These models are expensive, but having at least one large cube to show and talk about is a good idea.

Try the "What Comes Next?" discussion in the context of these three-dimensional models. The first three shapes are distinct: a *cube*, a *long*, and a *flat*. What comes next? Stack 10 flats and they make a cube, same shape as the first one only 1000 times larger. What comes next? (See Figure 9.16.) Ten *cubes* make another *long*. What comes next? Ten big *longs* make a big *flat*. The first three shapes have now repeated! Ten big flats will make an even bigger cube, and the triplet of shapes begins again.

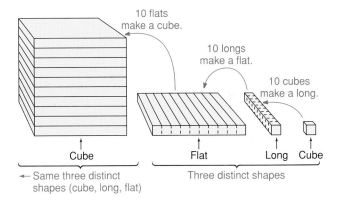

**Figure 9.16**  **With every three places, the shapes repeat. Each cube represents a 1, each long represents a 10, and each flat represents a 100.**

Each cube has a name. The first one is the *usnit* cube, the next is a *thousand*, the next a *million*, then a *billion*, and so on. Each long is 10 cubes: 10 units, 10 thousands, 10 millions. Similarly, each flat shape is 100 cubes.

To read a number, first mark it off in triples from the right. The triples are then read, stopping at the end of each to name the unit (or cube shape) for that triple (see Figure 9.17). Leading zeros are ignored. If students can learn to read

**Figure 9.17**  **The triples system for naming large numbers.**

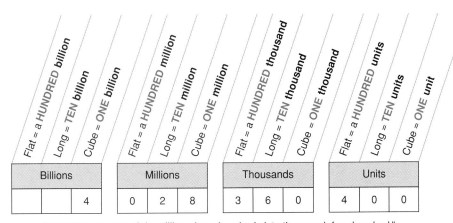

"Four billion, twenty-eight million, three hundred sixty thousand, four hundred."

numbers like 059 (fifty-nine) or 009 (nine), they should be able to read any number. To write a number, use the same scheme. If first mastered orally, the system is quite easy.

It is important for children to realize that the system does have a logical structure, is not totally arbitrary, and can be understood.

# Conceptualizing Large Numbers

The ideas just discussed are only partially helpful in thinking about the actual quantities involved in very large numbers. For example, in extending the square, strip, square, strip sequence, some appreciation for the quantities of 1000 or of 100,000 is included. But it is hard for anyone to translate quantities of small squares into quantities of other items, distances, or time.

## Creating References for Special Big Numbers

In these activities, numbers like 1000, 10,000, or even 1 million are translated literally or imaginatively into something that is easy or fun to think about. Interesting quantities become lasting reference points or benchmarks for large numbers and thereby add meaning to numbers encountered in real life.

### ACTIVITY
### 9.22 Collecting 10,000

*Collections.* As a class or grade-level project, collect some type of object with the objective of reaching some specific quantity—for example, 1000 or 10,000 buttons, walnuts, old pencils, jar lids, or pieces of junk mail. If you begin aiming for 100,000 or I million, be sure to think it through. One teacher spent nearly 10 years with her classes before amassing a million bottle caps. It takes a small dump truck to hold that many!

### ACTIVITY
### 9.23 Showing 10,000

*Illustrations.* Sometimes it is easier to create large amounts. For example, start a project where students draw 100 or 200 or even 500 dots on a sheet of paper. Each week, different students contribute a specified number. Another idea is to cut up newspaper into pieces the same size as dollar bills to see what a large quantity would look like. Paper chain links can be constructed over time and hung down the hallways with special numbers marked. Let the school be aware of the ultimate goal.

### ACTIVITY
### 9.24 How Long?/How Far?

*Real and imagined distances.* How long is a million baby steps? Other ideas that address length: toothpicks, dollar bills, or candy bars end to end; children holding hands in a line; blocks or bricks stacked up; children lying down head to toe. Real measures can also be used: feet, centimeters, meters.

### ACTIVITY
### 9.25 A Long Time

*Time.* How long is 1000 seconds? How long is a million seconds? A billion? How long would it take to count to 10,000 or 1 million? (To make the counts all the same, use your calculator to do the counting. Just press the ☰.) How long would it take to do some task like buttoning a button 1000 times?

## Estimating Large Quantities

Activities 9.22 through 9.25 focus on a specific number. The reverse idea is to select a large quantity and find some way to measure, count, or estimate how many.

### ACTIVITY
### 9.26 Really Large Quantities

Ask how many

Candy bars would cover the floor of your room

Steps an ant would take to walk around the school building

Grains of rice would fill a cup or a gallon jug

Quarters could be stacked in one stack floor to ceiling

Pennies can be laid side by side down an entire block

Pieces of notebook paper would cover the gym floor

Seconds you have lived

Big-number projects need not take up large amounts of class time. They can be explored over several weeks as take-home projects or group projects or, perhaps best of all, be translated into great schoolwide estimation contests. One of the best ways to motivate projects around large numbers is with the many children's books that examine these ideas in inventive ways. A few suggestions follow.

# LITERATURE CONNECTIONS

Books that emphasize groups of things, even simple counting books, are a good beginning to the notion of 10 things in a single group. Many books have wonderful explorations of large quantities and how they can be combined and separated.

## Moira's Birthday
### (Munsch, 1987)

As Moira plans her birthday party, she invites more and more children until she has invited all the children in the kindergarten, first, second, third, fourth, fifth, and sixth grades. Then she needs to order food. She orders 200 cakes and 200 pizzas. Wonderful bedlam ensues as the food and the children all arrive at the party. A second-grade teacher, Diane Oppedal (1995), used this story as a background for the question "How can you show 200 things in different ways?" As children work on this or similar projects, they can be encouraged to use some form of groups to keep track of their collections.

The same book can also be used to motivate a variety of computation situations that could be used prior to structured computation instruction. "How many children are in three classrooms?" "What if everyone at the party got two pieces of pizza?" "If Moira gave 37 of her 94 presents back to the children who helped her clean up, how many presents did she have left?"

## How to Count like a Martian
### (St. John, 1975)

This book explores number systems from different ancient cultures (Chinese, Roman, Egyptian, etc.) and so has a culture connection as well as a mathematics connection. The contrast of the different systems, most of which are not place-value systems, can be a good way for children in the fourth and fifth grades to appreciate and discuss the base-ten place-value system. Most other numeration systems do not have a zero, for example. Several numeration systems use the same symbol repeatedly to express multiples of a certain quantity. Children could write numbers in different systems, try to compute in another system, or discuss how they might make up a system of their own. Why is it that most of the world has adopted the system we use?

## The King's Commissioners
### (Friedman, 1994)

The king has so many commissioners, he can't keep track of how many there are. In a hilarious tale, the commissioners are marched into the throne room to be counted. One per-son tries to count them by twos and another by fives. The princess convinces the king that there are many other excellent ways to count. The story is a natural background for place-value concepts, including grouping and different counting methods, large numbers, and informal early computation challenges. Stephanie Sheffield (1995) offers specific suggestions for using this story with children at about the second-grade level.

## A Million Fish . . . More or Less
### (McKissack, 1992)

This story, which takes place in lower Louisiana, is a tall tale of a boy who catches three fish . . . and then a million more. The story is full of exaggerations such as a turkey that weighs 500 pounds and a jump-rope contest (using a snake) where the story's hero wins with 5553 jumps. "Could these things really be? How long would it take to jump 5553 times? Could Hugh put a million fish in his wagon? How do you write half of a million?" Rusty Bresser (1995) suggests a number of excellent ways this tale can be used to investigate large numbers and how they are written. The connections to real things and real ideas is just the ticket to add number sense to an upper-grade unit on place value.

Many other excellent books investigate very large numbers in interesting contexts. *How Much Is a Million?* (1985) and *If You Made a Million* (1989), both by David Schwartz, have become very popular. Wanda Gag's *Millions of Cats* (1928) is a classic that is still worth the time to investigate. Just one more of many possibilities is *Six Dogs, Twenty-Three Cats, Forty-Five Mice, and One Hundred Sixteen Spiders* (Chalmers, 1986). The imagination that these books inspire can lead children into fascinating investigations of large numbers, and with a bit of guidance, good place-value concepts can be visited along the way.

# ASSESSMENT NOTES
## Ongoing Assessment

Most of the activities suggested in this chapter serve as opportunities to find out what children know and understand about place value. They are performance tasks. A lot of the assessment information you will need can come from watching and listening as children do these tasks.

- How do children count or estimate quantities? Do they spontaneously use sets of tens?

- When materials are already arranged in groups of 10 (counters in cups, dots in ten-frames) or in groups of 100, do the children use these structures to tell how many?

■ How flexible are children with their thinking about numbers? Can they take them apart and combine them in ways that reflect an understanding of ones, tens, and hundreds?

■ How well are they able to relate numbers appropriate for their age to real quantities, measures, and events?

The following activity is frequently used in interviews with individual students but could easily be a task posed to the whole class or a small group for discussion. As you listen to how children solve these problems, you will realize that there is a lot more information to be found out about their thinking beyond simply getting the answer correct.

---

**ACTIVITY**

## 9.27 Mystery Mats

First, show a mat or board with some base-ten pieces covered and some showing. Tell the child how many pieces are hidden under the cover, and ask him or her to figure out how much is on the board altogether, as in Figure 9.18(a).

After that, show a board partially covered as before. Tell the child how many pieces are on the board altogether, and ask how many are hidden, as in Figure 9.18(b).

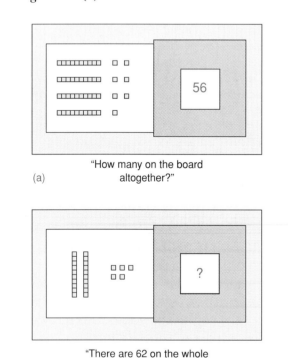

(a)    "How many on the board altogether?"

(b)    "There are 62 on the whole board. How many covered?"

**Figure 9.18** Two useful assessment activities.

---

Activity 9.27 could also involve hundreds. The amounts that you tell the child could be given in written form instead of orally.

# Diagnosis of Place-Value Concepts

Much information can be had from observation and discussion. However, you may still be curious to know exactly what level of understanding a few particular children may have about place-value concepts. Children are often able to disguise their lack of understanding in this area by following directions, using the tens and ones pieces in prescribed ways, and using the language of place value.

Another reason for a short diagnostic interview with a few students may be to confirm that the assessments you have made through observation are in fact valid.

The diagnostic tasks presented here are designed to help you look more closely at children's understanding of place value. They are not suggested as definitive tests but as means of obtaining information for the thoughtful teacher. These tasks have been used by several researchers and are adapted primarily from Labinowicz (1985) and Ross (1986). The tasks are designed for one-on-one settings. They should not be used as instructional activities.

## Counting Skills

A variety of oral counting tasks provide insight into the counting sequence.

■ Count forward for me, starting at 77.

■ Count backward, starting at 55.

■ Count by tens.

■ Count by tens, starting at 34.

■ Count backward by tens, starting at 130.

In the tasks that follow, the manner in which the child responds is as important as the answers. For example, counting individual squares on tens pieces that are known to the child as "tens" will produce correct answers but indicates that the structure of tens is not being used.

## One More and Ten More, One Less and Ten Less

Write the number 342. Have the child read the number. Then have the child write the number that is 1 more than the number. Next ask for the number that is 10 more than the number. You may wish to explore further with models. One less and 10 less can be checked the same way.

## Digit Correspondence

Dump out 36 blocks. Ask the child to count the blocks, and then have the child write the number that tells how many there are. Circle the 6 in 36 and ask, "Does this part of your 36 have anything to do with how many blocks there are?" Then circle the 3 and repeat the question exactly. Do not give clues. Based on responses to the task, Ross (1989) has identified five distinct levels of understanding of place value:

1. *Single numeral.* The child writes 36 but views it as a single numeral. The individual digits 3 and 6 have no meaning by themselves.

2. *Position names.* The child identifies correctly the tens and ones positions but still makes no connections between the individual digits and the blocks.

3. *Face value.* The child matches 6 blocks with the 6 and 3 blocks with the 3.

4. *Transition to place value.* The 6 is matched with 6 blocks and the 3 with the remaining 30 blocks but not as 3 groups of 10.

5. *Full understanding.* The 3 is correlated with 3 groups of 10 blocks and the 6 with 6 single blocks.

## Using Tens

Dump out 47 counters, and have the child count them. Next show the child at least ten cards, each with a ten-frame drawn on it. Ask, "If we wanted to put these counters in the spaces on these cards, how many cards could we fill up?" (If the ten-frame has been used in class to model sets of 10, use a different frame such as a 10-pin arrangement of circles. Be sure the child knows there are 10 spaces on each card.)

## Using Groups of 10

Prepare cards with beans or other counters glued to the cards in an obvious arrangement of 10. Supply at least ten cards and a large supply of the beans. After you are sure that the child has counted several cards of beans and knows there are 10 on each, say, "Show me 34 beans." (Does the child count individual beans or use the cards of 10?) The activity can also be done with hundreds.

# REFLECTIONS ON CHAPTER 9

## Writing to Learn

1. Explain how a child who has not yet developed base-ten concepts understands quantities as large as, say, 85. Contrast this with a child who understands these same quantities in terms of base-ten groupings.

2. What is meant by *equivalent representations?*

3. Explain the three ways one can count a set of objects and how these methods of counting can be used to coordinate concepts and oral and written names for numbers.

4. Describe the two types of physical models for base-ten concepts. What is the significance of the difference between these two types of models? Why is an abacus not considered a model for place value?

5. Describe an activity for developing base-ten grouping concepts, and reflect on how the activity encourages children to construct base-ten concepts.

6. How do children learn to write two- and three-digit numbers in a way that is connected to the base-ten meanings of ones and tens or ones, tens, and hundreds?

7. How would you describe good place-value number sense? There are a variety of aspects to number sense with large numbers. Describe activities that are designed to help develop these different features of good number sense with larger numbers.

8. What are two different ideas that you would want children to know about very large numbers (beyond 1000)? Describe one or two activities for each.

## For Discussion and Exploration

1. Based on the suggestions toward the end of this chapter and on the content of a standard basal textbook, design a diagnostic interview for a child at a particular grade level, and conduct the interview. It is a good idea to take a friend to act as an observer or to use a tape recorder or video recorder to keep track of how the interview went.

2. A popular collection of activities, sometimes referred to as "trading activities," are done with base-ten models. In all of these activities, children have a place-value mat on which they accumulate materials or from which they remove materials. The activities generally take a game format. Perhaps a die is rolled and the die tells the child how many ones are to be placed on the mat or how many may be removed. Whenever 10 pieces in one section are accumulated, a trade is made for a single piece in the next place: 10 ones for a ten, 10 tens for a hundred. Similarly, in the process of removing pieces, trades are made in the reverse manner: 1 ten for 10 ones.

Do these trading activities contribute any new connections or ideas to place-value understanding? If so, what are they? Are trading activities problematic? Are there any activities in this chapter that get at the same ideas?

## Recommendations for Further Reading

### Highly Recommended

Burns, M. (1994). *Math by all means: Place value, grade 2.* Sausalito, CA: Math Solutions Publications.

Burns provides 25 days of very detailed lessons in place value for second-grade children. In her usual style, she provides numerous examples of children's written work and descriptions of interactions that took place in the classroom. It is possible to take issue with the claims Burns makes for the complete development resulting from these lessons, but that does not detract from the value of most of the activities. Perhaps most important is the way that Burns brings you into the classroom to get a feel for how these activities will work with children.

Hiebert, J. C., & Wearne, D. (1992). Links between teaching and learning place value with understanding in first grade. *Journal for Research in Mathematics Education, 23,* 98–122.

This study compares four first-grade classrooms where a highly conceptual approach to place value was used with two classrooms where the teachers essentially followed the traditional textbook. The article provides an excellent, objective description of a constructivist approach to this complex topic in the first grade and stark contrast with the traditional text-based methods. For example, one major difference that was found was between materials used to "work through an idea" and materials used to "show."

Richardson, K. (1990). *A look at children's thinking: Video II and study guide.* Norman, OK: Educational Enrichment.

This tape showing diagnostic interviews is must viewing for anyone interested in how children develop number concepts and place value in particular. Richardson uses the same series of questions with several children at different stages of development. Her commentary clearly describes why the questions are asked, what she is looking for, and an analysis of the students' responses. You cannot watch this tape and not fully appreciate the complexity of place-value concepts and the difficulty children have developing them.

Schifter, D., Bastable, V., & Russell, S. J. (1999). *Developing mathematical ideas: Numbers and operations, Part 1: Building a system of tens* (Casebook). White Plains, NY: Cuisenaire–Dale Seymour.

Schifter and her colleagues at TERC have compiled in this book a wonderful collection of cases, each written by a classroom teacher, in which the complexities of place-value development truly come to light. Although this is a companion book to an in-service program, the cases by themselves are worth reading. They will provide useful insights into children's thinking and useful points of discussion. The book contains 29 different cases from grades 1 to 6 and covers situations involving invented computations and decimals as well as whole-number meanings.

## Other Suggestions

Bove, S. P. (1995). Place value: A vertical perspective. *Teaching Children Mathematics, 1,* 542–546.

Fuson, K. C., Wearne, D., Hiebert, J. C., Murray, H. G., Human, P. G., Olivier, A. I., Carpenter, T. P., & Fennema, E. (1997). Children's conceptual structures for multidigit numbers and methods of multidigit addition and subtraction. *Journal for Research in Mathematics Education, 28,* 130–162.

Kamii, C. K. (1986). Place value: An explanation of its difficulty and educational implications for the primary grades. *Journal of Research in Childhood Education, 1,* 75–86.

Labinowicz, E. (1985). *Learning from children: New beginnings for teaching numerical thinking.* Menlo Park, CA: AWL Supplemental.

Larsen, N. (1996). Making cents. *Teaching Children Mathematics, 2,* 520–522.

Little, C. (1999). Counting grass. *Mathematics Teaching in the Middle School, 5,* 7–10.

Nagel, N. G., & Swingen C. C. (1998). Students' explanations of place value in addition and subtraction. *Teaching Children Mathematics, 5,* 164–170.

O'Connell, S. R. (1995). Newspapers: Connecting the mathematics classroom to the world. *Teaching Children Mathematics, 1,* 268–274.

Oppedal, D. C. (1995). Mathematics is something good. *Teaching Children Mathematics, 2,* 36–40.

Payne, J. N., & Huinker, D. M. (1993). Early number and numeration. In R. J. Jensen (Ed.), *Research ideas for the classroom: Early childhood mathematics* (pp. 43–71). Old Tappan, NJ: Macmillan.

Reys, B. J. (1991). *Developing number sense in the middle grades: Addenda series, grades 5–8.* Reston, VA: National Council of Teachers of Mathematics.

Ross, S. H. (1989). Parts, wholes, and place value: A developmental perspective. *Arithmetic Teacher, 36*(6), 47–51.

Schwartz, S. L., & Curcio, F. R. (1995). Learning mathematics in meaningful contexts: An action-based approach in the primary grades. In P. A. House (Ed.), *Connecting mathematics across the curriculum* (pp. 116–123). Reston, VA: National Council of Teachers of Mathematics.

Thompson, C. S. (1990). Place value and larger numbers. In J. N. Payne (Ed.), *Mathematics for the young child* (pp. 89–108). Reston, VA: National Council of Teachers of Mathematics.

Whitin, D. J. (1995). Connecting literature and mathematics. In P. A. House (Ed.), *Connecting mathematics across the curriculum* (pp. 134–141). Reston, VA: National Council of Teachers of Mathematics.

# Chapter 10

# Strategies for Whole-Number Computation

In the context of reform mathematics, the new NCTM *Principles and Standards* document, and the public push for accountability and testable standards, computation is a major issue. In the past, only one method of computing was developed for each operation. Prior to calculators, it was important to have an efficient method of computing, applicable to all situations regardless of the size of the numbers. Today, technology appropriately handles large, tedious computations that demand an exact result. At the same time, we now know that there are numerous methods of computing that can be handled either mentally or with pencil and paper. In most everyday instances, these alternative strategies for computing are easier and faster, can often be done mentally, and contribute to our overall number sense. The traditional algorithms (procedures for computation) do not have these benefits.

In the 1980s, a large number of second- and third-grade students were asked to compute $300 - 1$. Almost all resorted to the traditional algorithm of borrowing, and many students made errors (UCSMP, 1999). The example may seem extreme or unusual. However, every day, students and adults resort to error-prone pencil-and-paper strategies when other, more meaningful methods would be faster and less susceptible to error. Flexibility with a variety of computational strategies is a significant component of number sense and an important tool for successful daily living. It is time to broaden our perspective of what it means to compute.

## BIG Ideas

1. Flexible methods of computation involve taking apart and combining numbers in a wide variety of ways, most depending on place value.

2. Invented strategies, mental computation, estimation, and the traditional algorithms are all based on place-value concepts and an understanding of the different meanings of the operations and how they are related.

3. Each of the traditional algorithms is simply a clever way to record an operation for a single place value with transitions (trades, "borrows," or "carries") to an adjacent position. As such, traditional algorithms have a digit orientation.

## INVENTED STRATEGIES

In the past decade, a number of research projects have focused attention on how children handle computational situations when they have not been taught a specific algorithm.* In addition to these research efforts, the elementary reform curricula each base the development of computational methods on student-invented strategies. "There is mounting evidence that children both in and out of school can construct methods for adding and subtracting multi-digit numbers without explicit instruction" (Carpenter, Franke, Jacobs, Fennema, & Empson, 1998, p. 4). Data supporting students' construction of useful methods for multiplication and division have also been gathered (Baek, 1998; Kamii & Dominick, 1997; Schifter, Bastable, & Russell, 1999b).

---

*The Cognitively Guided Instruction project (CGI), directed by Carpenter, Fennema, and Franke at the University of Wisconsin; the Conceptually Based Instruction project (CBI), directed by Hiebert and Wearne at the University of Delaware; the Problem Centered Mathematics Project (PCMP), directed by Human, Murray, and Olivier at the University of Stellenbosch, South Africa; the Supporting Ten-Structured Thinking project (STST), directed by Fuson at Northwestern University; and ongoing research by Kamii at the University of Alabama are all examples of efforts that have informed thinking about invented strategies for computation.

Try solving the following problem using some other method than the usual algorithm you were taught in school. Can you do it mentally?

Mary had 114 spaces in her photo album. So far she has 89 photos in the album. How many more photos can she put in before the album is full?

Here are just four of many methods that have been used by students in the primary grades:

89 + 11 is 100. 11 + 14 is 25.

90 + 10 is 100 and 14 more is 24 plus 1 is 25.

Take away 14 and then take away 11 more. 25 in all.

89, 99, 109 (that's 20), 110, 111, 112, 113, 114 ⟶ 25 (keep track on fingers).

Carpenter et al. (1998) refer to any strategy other than the traditional algorithm that does not involve using physical materials such as base-ten blocks or drawings as an *invented strategy*. The developmental step that usually precedes invented strategies is called *direct modeling*: the use of manipulatives or drawings to represent directly the meaning of the operation or story problem (see Figure 10.1). Invented strategies are often but not always done mentally. For example, 75 + 19 can be done mentally (75 and 20 is 95, less 1 is 94). For 847 + 256, some students may write down intermediate steps to help with memory. In the classroom, some written support is often used as strategies develop, and then for some students the same methods will become entirely mental.

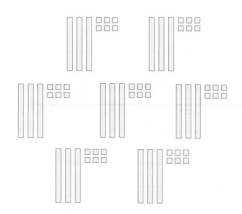

**Figure 10.1**  **A possible direct modeling of 36 × 7 using base-ten models.**

Not all students invent their own strategies. Strategies invented by class members are shared, explored, and tried out by others. However, no student should be permitted to use any strategy without understanding it (Campbell, Rowan, & Suarez, 1998).

# Contrasts with Traditional Algorithms

There are significant differences between invented strategies and the traditional algorithms.

1. *Invented strategies are number-oriented rather than digit-oriented.* For example, an invented strategy for 68 × 7 begins 7 × 60 is 420 and 56 more is 476. The first product is 7 times *sixty*, not the digit 6, as would be the case in the traditional algorithm. Using the traditional algorithm for 45 + 32, children never think of 40 and 30 but rather 4 + 3. Kamii, long a crusader against standard algorithms, claims that they "unteach" place value (Kamii & Dominick, 1998).

2. *Invented strategies are left-handed rather than right-handed.* Invented strategies begin with the largest parts of numbers, those represented by the leftmost digits. For 26 × 47, invented strategies will begin with 20 × 40 is 800, providing some sense of the size of the eventual answer in just one step. The traditional algorithm begins with 7 × 6 is 42. By beginning on the right with a digit orientation, traditional methods hide the result until the end. Long division is an exception.

3. *Invented strategies are flexible rather than rigid.* Invented strategies tend to change with the numbers involved in order to make the computation easier. Try each of these mentally: 465 + 230 and 526 + 98. Did you use the same method? The traditional algorithm suggests using the same tool on all problems. The traditional algorithm for 7000 − 25 typically leads to student errors, yet a mental strategy is relatively simple (Carroll & Porter, 1997).

# Benefits of Invented Strategies

The development of invented strategies delivers more than computational facility. Both the development of these strategies and their regular use have positive benefits that are difficult to ignore.

- *Base-ten concepts are enhanced.* There is a definite interaction between the development of base-ten concepts and the process of inventing computational strategies (Carpenter et al., 1998). "Invented strategies demonstrate a hallmark characteristic of understanding" (p. 16). The development of invented strategies should be integrated with the development of base-ten concepts, even as early as first grade.

- *Invented strategies are built on student understanding.* Because invented strategies are so dependent on base-ten concepts and are developed in a problem-solving atmosphere, students rarely use an invented strategy they do not understand. In contrast, students are frequently seen to use traditional algorithms without being able to explain why they work (Carroll & Porter, 1997).

■ *Students make fewer errors with invented strategies.* Data collected by Kamii and Dominick (1997) provide some hard evidence for this claim. With traditional algorithms, students tend to develop systematic errors or "buggy algorithms" that they use again and again. Careless errors often result from confusion with carried digits or column alignment. Systematic errors are not typical of invented strategies.

■ *Use of invented strategies promotes mathematical thinking.* Invented strategies grow out of students' thinking, guided by the teacher. Sense making is a hallmark of their development. Students use invented strategies in meaningful ways. Thus the development and use of these strategies is an example of *doing mathematics.* In contrast, the traditional algorithms are often accepted on faith because the teacher says, "This is how you are to do it."

■ *Invented strategies serve students at least as well on standard tests.* Evidence from the reform programs suggests that students not taught traditional algorithms fare about as well in computation on standardized tests as students in traditional programs (Campbell, 1996; Carroll, 1996, 1997; Chambers, 1996). As an added bonus, students tend to do quite well with word problems, since they are the principal vehicle for developing invented strategies. The pressures of external testing do not dictate a focus on the traditional algorithms.

# DEVELOPMENT OF INVENTED STRATEGIES

Students do not spontaneously invent wonderful computational methods while the teacher sits back and watches. Among different experimental programs, students tended to develop or gravitate toward different strategies suggesting that teachers and the programs do have an effect on what methods students develop (Fuson et al., 1997). This section discusses general pedagogical methods for helping children develop invented strategies.

## Use Story Problems Frequently

When computational tasks are embedded in simple contexts, students seem to be more engaged than they are with bare computations. Furthermore, the choice of story problems influences the strategies students use to solve them. Consider these problems:

**Max had already saved 68 cents when Mom gave him some money for running an errand. Now Max has 93 cents. How much did Max earn for his errand?**

**George took 93 cents to the store. He spent 68 cents. How much does he have left?**

The computation 93 − 68 solves both problems, but the first is more likely than the second to be solved by an add-on method. In a similar manner, fair-share division problems are more likely to encourage a share strategy than a measurement or repeated subtraction problem.

Problems need not be elaborate but should involve themes and topics of interest to the students. Use the students themselves in the problems. Build problems around sets of data collected in the class or literature that you've been reading. Use the measurements from your measurement unit to create problems.

Not every task need be a story problem. Especially when students are engaged in figuring out a new strategy, bare arithmetic problems are quite adequate.

## Use the Three-Part Lesson Format

The three-part lesson format described in Chapter 4 is a good structure for an invented-strategy lesson. The task is simply a story problem or even a bare computation but always with the expectation that the method of solution will be discussed. Sometimes you can provide variations with different numbers to different groups to adjust for difficulty.

In the before section, some teachers solicit estimates or solutions done mentally and record these on the board. This gets everyone thinking before setting students free to work in pairs or independently (Lester, 1996). Familiar materials such as base-ten models and counters should be readily available but never required for a solution. It is often useful to have students write or use pictures to explain their methods (Whitin & Whitin, 1998).

Allow plenty of time to solve a problem. Listen to the different strategies students are using, but do not interject your own. Challenge able students to find a second method, solve a problem without models, or improve on a written explanation. Encourage slower children using even the simplest counting methods. Students who finish quickly may share their methods with others before sharing with the class.

The most important portion of the lesson comes when students explain their solution methods. Avoid focusing on the same students each time. Help students write their explanations on the board or overhead. Encourage students to ask questions of their classmates. Occasionally have the class try a particular method with different numbers to see how it works. When students find a particular idea worthwhile, record it on a "strategies chart." Remember, not every student will invent strategies. However, students can and will try strategies that they have seen and that make sense to them. Make a firm rule that *no one may use a strategy that he or she does not understand.*

# Allow for a Range of Methods

Virtually all methods can be separated into three categories: *direct modeling, invented strategies,* and *traditional algorithms* (see Figure 10.2). Many teachers who hope to develop invented strategies are disappointed when students rely on very primitive and tedious counting methods. Another frustration is the use of a traditional algorithm, even if it has never been introduced by the teacher. It is important to view all methods that students use from the perspective of what students know and understand.

**Figure 10.2** **The typical progress of computational strategies.**

## Direct Modeling

Direct modeling methods generally fall into one of two categories: those that involve a counting-by-ones method with no evidence of base-ten concepts being used and those in which students use their knowledge of tens and hundreds to model more efficiently.

Students who consistently count by ones most likely have not developed base-ten grouping concepts. That does not mean that they should not continue to solve problems involving two-digit numbers. As you work with these children, suggest (don't force) that they group counters by tens as they count. Perhaps instead of making large piles, they might make bars of ten from connecting cubes or organize counters in cups of ten. Some students will use the ten-stick as a counting device to keep track of counts of ten, even though they are counting each segment of the stick by ones.

If you feel students are capable of more sophisticated strategies, perhaps the counters should mysteriously "dis-

appear" for a few days, or you might challenge students to find a more clever way to solve a problem.

When children have plenty of experience with base-ten concepts and models, they begin to use these ideas in the direct modeling of the problems. Remember the power of drawing squares, sticks, and dots for hundreds, tens, and ones. Some students will find such drawings more useful than the actual blocks. Even when students use base-ten materials, they will find many different ways to solve problems.

### Progression to Invented Strategies

Direct modeling involving tens and ones can and will lead eventually to invented strategies, methods that rely solely on mental processes or are supported by pencil and paper. However, students do tend to stick with comfortable strategies. Students may need to be encouraged to move away from the direct modeling process. Here are some ideas:

- Record students' verbal explanations on the board in ways that they and others can model. Have the class follow the recorded method using different numbers.
- Ask students who have just solved a problem with models to see if they can do it in their heads.
- Pose a problem to the class, and ask students to solve it mentally if they are able.
- Ask children to make a written numeric record of what they did when they solved the problem with models. Explain that they are then going to try to use the same method on a new problem.

### Unsolicited Introduction of Traditional Algorithms

You probably cannot keep the traditional algorithms out of your classroom. Children pick up the traditional algorithms from older siblings, last year's teacher, well-meaning parents ("My dad showed me an easy way"). Traditional algorithms are in no way evil, and so to forbid their use is somewhat arbitrary. However, students who latch on to a traditional method often resist the invention of more flexible strategies. What do you do then?

First and foremost, apply the same rule to traditional algorithms as to all strategies: *If you use it, you must understand why it works and be able to explain it.* In an atmosphere that says, "Let's figure out why this works," students can profit from making sense of these algorithms just like any other. But the responsibility should be theirs, not yours.

Accept a traditional algorithm (once it is understood) as one more strategy to put in the class "tool box" of methods. But reinforce the idea that like the other strategies, it may be more useful in some instances than in others. Pose problems where a mental strategy is much more useful, such as 504 − 498 or 75 × 4. Discuss which method seemed best. Point out that for a problem such as 4568 + 12,813, the traditional algorithm has some advantages. But in the real world, most people do those computations on a calculator.

# INVENTED STRATEGIES FOR ADDITION AND SUBTRACTION

Research has demonstrated that children will invent a lot of different strategies for addition and subtraction. Your goal might be that each of your children has at least one or two methods that are reasonably efficient, mathematically correct, and useful with lots of different numbers. Expect different children to settle on different strategies.

Many of the techniques for addition and subtraction are easily done mentally without recording. It is not at all unreasonable for students to be able to add and subtract two-digit numbers mentally by third grade. However, daily recording of strategies on the board not only helps communicate ideas but also helps children who need the short-term memory assistance of recording intermediate steps.

## Adding and Subtracting Single Digits

Children can easily extend addition and subtraction facts to higher decades.

**Tommy was on page 47 of his book. Then he read 8 more pages. How many pages did Tommy read in all?**

If students are simply counting on by ones, an activity in which students solve a series of problems may be useful. Suggest that students use the little ten-frames to help, as shown in Figure 10.3. It is especially powerful to extend the make-ten idea to other decades. For example, "How can we add 38 + 5 without counting on?" (38 and 2 gets to 40 and 3 more is 43.)

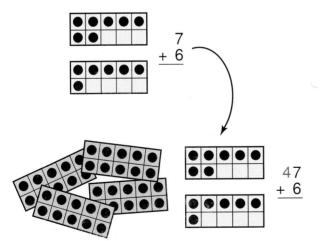

**Figure 10.3** Little ten-frame cards can help children extend the make-ten idea to larger numbers.

Subtracting a single digit by backing down through a decade number is just as valuable a skill. For 53 − 7, take off 3 to 50, then 4 more is 46.

## Adding and Subtracting Tens and Hundreds

Have children solve a problem such as the following:

**Tilly got a new bag of marbles to add to her collection. The new bag had 200 marbles. Tilly already had 438 marbles. How many marbles does Tilly have now?**

Sums and differences involving multiples of 10 or 100 are easily computed mentally. Write a problem such as the following on the board:

$$300 + 500 + 20$$

Challenge children to solve it mentally. Ask students to share how they did it. Look for use of place-value words: "3 *hundred* and 5 *hundred* is 8 *hundred,* and 20 is 820."

Use base-ten models to help children begin to think in terms of tens and hundreds. Early examples should not include any trades. The exercise 420 + 300 involves no trades, whereas 70 + 80 may be more difficult

## Adding Two-Digit Numbers

For the examples that follow, a possible recording method is offered. These are intended to be suggestions, not prescriptions. Children have difficulty inventing recording techniques. If you record their ideas on the board as they explain their ideas, you are helping them develop written techniques. You may even discuss recording methods with individuals or with the class to decide on a form that seems to work well. Horizontal formats encourage students to think in terms of numbers instead of digits. A horizontal format is also less likely to encourage use of the traditional algorithms.

Students will often use a counting-by-tens-and-ones technique for some of these methods. That is, instead of "46 + 30 is 76," they may count "46 $\longrightarrow$ 56, 66, 76." These counts can be written down as they are said to help students keep track. Eventually, students should move toward a more efficient approach.

Figure 10.4 (p. 176) illustrates four different strategies for addition of two two-digit numbers. The following story problem is a suggestion.

**The two scout troops went on a field trip. There were 46 girl scouts and 38 boy scouts. How many scouts went on the trip?**

---

### Invented Strategies for Addition with Two-Digit Numbers

**Add Tens, Add Ones, then Combine**

46 + 38

40 and 30 is 70.
6 and 8 is 14.
70 and 14 is 84.

$$\begin{array}{r} 46 \\ +38 \\ \hline 70 \\ 14 \\ \hline 84 \end{array}$$

**Add On Tens, then Add Ones**

46 + 38

46 and 30 more is 76.
Then I added on the other 8.
76 and 4 is 80 and 4 is 84.

$$46 + 38 \rightarrow$$
$$76 + 8 \rightarrow 80, 84$$

**Move Some to Make Tens**

46 + 38

Take 2 from the 46 and put
it with the 38 to make 40.
Now you have 44 and 40
more is 84.

$$\overset{2}{46} + 3\!\!\!/8$$
$$44 + 40$$
$$84$$

**Use a Nice Number and Compensate**

46 + 38

46 and 40 is 86.
That's 2 extra, so it's 84.

$$46 + 38$$
$$46 + 40 \rightarrow$$
$$86 - 2 \rightarrow 84$$

**Figure 10.4** Four different invented strategies for adding two two-digit numbers.

---

The *move to make ten* and *compensation* strategies are useful when one of the numbers ends in 8 or 9. To promote that strategy, present problems with addends like 39 or 58. Note that it is only necessary to adjust one of the two numbers.

## Subtracting by Counting Up

This is an amazingly powerful way to subtract. Most of us have never thought of using it since in the traditional curriculum, subtraction as take-away predominates. Students working on the *think-addition* strategy for their basic facts can also be solving problems with larger numbers. The concept is the same. It is important to use *join with change unknown* problems or *missing-part* problems to encourage the counting-up strategy. Here is an example of each.

Sam had 46 baseball cards. He went to a card show and got some more cards for his collection. Now he has 73 cards. How many cards did Sam buy at the card show?

Juanita counted all of her crayons. Some were broken and some not. She had 73 crayons in all. 46 crayons were not broken. How many were broken?

The numbers in these problems are used in the strategies illustrated in Figure 10.5.

## Take-Away Subtraction

Using take-away is considerably more difficult to do mentally. However, take-away strategies are common, probably because traditional textbooks emphasize take-away as the meaning of subtraction. Four different strategies are shown in Figure 10.6.

There were 73 children on the playground. The 46 second-grade students came in first. How many children were still outside?

**Figure 10.5** Subtraction by counting up is a powerful method.

---

### Invented Strategies for Subtraction by Counting Up

**Add Tens to Get Close, then Ones**

73 − 46

46 and 20 is 66.
  (30 more is too much.)
Then 4 more is 70 and 3 is 73.
That's 20 and 7 or 27.

$$\begin{array}{r} 46 \searrow 20 \\ 66 \searrow 4 \\ 70 \searrow 3 \\ 73 \phantom{\searrow} \\ \hline 27 \end{array}$$

**Add Tens to Overshoot, then Come Back**

73 − 46

46 and 30 is 76.
That's 3 too much,
so it's 27.

$$73 - 46$$
$$46 + 30 \rightarrow 76 - 3 \rightarrow 73$$
$$30 - 3 = 27$$

**Add Ones to Make a Ten, then Tens and Ones**

73 − 46

46 and 4 is 50.
50 and 20 is 70 and 3
more is 73. The 4 and 3
is 7 and 20 is 27.

$$73 - 46$$
$$46 + 4 \rightarrow 50$$
$$+20 \rightarrow 70$$
$$+3 \rightarrow 73$$
$$\hline 27$$

Similarly,

46 and 4 is 50.
50 and 23 is 73.
23 and 4 is 27.

$$46 + 4 \rightarrow 50$$
$$50 + 23 \rightarrow 73$$
$$23 + 4 = 27$$

---

### Invented Strategies for Take-Away Subtraction

**Take Tens from the Tens, then Subtract Ones**

73 − 46
70 minus 40 is 30.
Take away 6 more is 24.
Now add in the 3 ones → 27.

$73 - 46$
$70 - 40 \rightarrow 30 - 6 \rightarrow$
$24 + 3 \rightarrow 27$

Or

70 minus 40 is 30.
I can take those 3 away, but I need 3 more from the 30 to make 27.

$$
\begin{array}{r}
7\not{3} \\
-\ 46 \\
\hline
30 \\
-\ 3 \\
\hline
27
\end{array}
$$

**Take Away Tens, then Ones**

73 − 46
73 minus 40 is 33.
Then take away 6:
3 makes 30 and
3 more is 27.

$73 - 40 \rightarrow 33 - 3$
$30 - 3 \rightarrow 27$

**Take Extra Tens, then Add Back**

73 − 46
73 take away 50 is 23.
That's 4 too many.
23 and 4 is 27.

$73 - 50 \rightarrow 23 + 4$
$27$

**Add to the Whole if Necessary**

73 − 46
Give 3 to 73 to make 76.
76 take away 46 is 30.
Now give 3 back → 27.

$+3$
$73 - 46$
$76 - 46 \rightarrow 30$
$-3 \rightarrow 27$

**Figure 10.6** Take-away strategies work reasonably well for two-digit problems. They are a bit more difficult with three digits.

---

The two methods that begin by taking tens from tens are reflective of what most students do with base-ten pieces (Madell, 1985). The other two methods leave one of the numbers intact and subtract from it. Try 83 − 29 in your head by first taking away 30 and adding 1 back. This is a good mental method when subtracting a number that is close to a multiple of ten.

Sometimes we need to be reminded of what comes naturally to children. Campbell (1997) tested over 2000 students in Baltimore who had not been taught the traditional algorithm for subtraction. Not one student began with the ones place!

## Extensions and Challenges

Each of the examples in the preceding sections involved sums less than 100 and all involved *bridging a ten;* that is, if done with a traditional algorithm, they require carrying or borrowing. Bridging, the size of the numbers, and the potential for doing problems mentally are all issues to consider.

### Bridging

For most of the strategies, it is easier to add or subtract when bridging is not required. Try each strategy with 34 + 52 or 68 − 24 to see how it works. Easier problems instill confidence. They also permit you to challenge your students with a "harder one." There is also the issue of bridging 100 or 1000. Try 58 + 67 with different strategies. Bridging across 100 is also an issue for subtraction. Problems such as 128 − 50 or 128 − 45 are more difficult than ones that do not bridge 100.

### Larger Numbers

Most curricula will expect third graders to add and subtract three-digit numbers. Your state standards may even require

work with four-digit numbers. Try seeing how *you* would do these without using the traditional algorithms: 487 + 235 and 623 − 247. For subtraction, a counting-up strategy is usually the easiest. Occasionally, other strategies appear with larger numbers. For example, "chunking off" multiples of 50 or 25 is often a useful method. For 462 + 257, pull out 450 and 250 to make 700. That leaves 12 and 7 more ⟶ 719.

### Pencil or Mental Strategies

You may want to be sure that by third grade every student has a pencil-and-paper method that is adequate for most purposes. This need not be the traditional algorithm. Many invented strategies will work quite adequately for large numbers and later for decimals. A single invented strategy will generally not be adequate for dealing with all problems. Often the heart of the matter is in devising a recording strategy that will work for larger numbers.

As students develop invented strategies, they (and you) will find that doing mental addition and subtraction is actually fairly easy, even with three-digit numbers. Try it! Every once in a while, have a "no paper day" when all computations are to be done mentally.

# TRADITIONAL ALGORITHMS FOR ADDITION AND SUBTRACTION

It can easily be argued that students no longer need the traditional algorithms for addition and subtraction. However, for various reasons, you may feel that your students need to learn them. The traditional algorithms require an understanding of *regrouping*, exchanging 10 in one place-value position for 1 in the position to the left—or the reverse, exchanging 1 for 10 in the position to the right. The corresponding terms *carrying* and *borrowing* are obsolete and conceptually misleading. The word *regroup* also has little meaning for young children. A preferable term is *trade*. Ten ones are *traded* for a ten. A hundred is *traded* for 10 tens. It is a serious error to work for mastery of nonregrouping problems before tackling regrouping. To keep these problems separate has been the documented source of many error patterns. Teaching nonregrouping problems first causes bad habits that children must later unlearn.

If you develop traditional algorithms in a problem-solving manner, there is no reason why your students should not be expected to understand them!

## The Addition Algorithm

Explain to the students that they are going to learn a method of adding that most "big people" learned when they were in school. It is not the only way or even the best way; it is just a method you want them to learn.

### Begin with Models Only

In the beginning, avoid any written work except for the possible recording of an answer. Provide children with place-value mats and base-ten models. The mat with two ten-frames in the ones place (Blackline Masters) is suggested.

Have students make one number at the top of the mat and a second beneath it as shown in the top portion of Figure 10.7. If children are still developing their base-ten concepts, a groupable model such as counters in cups is most helpful.

Explain this one rule: *You begin in the ones column.* "This is a way people came up with a long time ago, and it worked for them." Let students solve the problem on their own. Provide plenty of time, and then have students explain what they did and why. Let students use overhead models or magnetic pieces to help with their explanations.

One or two problems in a lesson with lots of discussion is much more productive than a lot of problems based on rules children don't understand.

### Develop the Written Record

Reproduce pages with simple place-value charts similar to those shown in Figure 10.8. The charts will help young children record numerals in columns. The general idea is to have children record on these pages each step of the procedure they do with the base-ten models *as it is done*. The first few times you do this, guide each step carefully, as illustrated in Figure 10.9. A similar approach would be used for three-digit problems.

A suggestion is to have children work in pairs. One child is responsible for the models and the other for recording the steps. Children reverse roles with each problem.

Figure 10.10 shows a variation of the traditional recording scheme that is quite reasonable, at least for up to three dig-

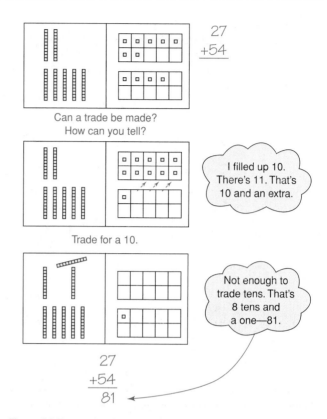

**Figure 10.7**  **Working from right to left in addition.**

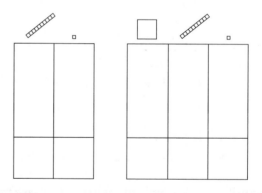

**Figure 10.8**  **Blank recording charts are helpful (see Blackline Masters).**

its. It avoids the little "carried ones" and focuses attention on the value of the digits. If students were permitted to start adding on the left as they are inclined to do, this recording procedure is the same as that shown for the invented strategy "Add tens, add ones, then combine" (Figure 10.4, p. 176). Why not let students start on the left and use this method of recording?

## The Subtraction Algorithm

The general approach to developing the subtraction algorithm is the same as for addition. When the procedure is completely understood with models, a do-and-write approach connects it with a written form.

How much is in the ones column? (14)

Will you need to make a trade? (yes)

How many tens will you make? (1) How many ones will be left? (4)

Good! Make the trade now.

Let's stop now and record exactly what we have done. You had 14 ones, and you made 1 ten and 4. Write a small "1" at the top of the tens column to show the ten you put there and a "4" in the answer space of the ones column for the 4 ones left.

Look at the tens column on your mat. You have 1 ten on top, 3 from the 36, and 4 more from the 48. See how your paper shows the same thing?

Now add all the tens together. Write how many tens that is in the answer space for the tens column.

**Figure 10.9** **Help students record on paper each step they do on their mats as they do it.**

**Figure 10.10** **An alternative recording scheme for addition. Notice that this can be used from left to right as well as from right to left.**

## Begin with Models Only

Start by having children model the top number in a subtraction problem on the top half of their place-value mats. For the amount to be subtracted, have children write each digit on a small piece of paper and place these pieces near the bottom of their mats in the respective columns, as in Figure 10.11 (p. 180). To avoid inadvertent errors, suggest making all trades first. That way, the full amount on the paper slip can be taken off at once. Also explain to children that they are to begin working with the ones column first, as they did with addition.

## Anticipate Difficulties with Zeros

Exercises in which zeros are involved anywhere in the problem tend to cause special difficulties. Give extra attention to these cases while still using models. A zero in the ones or tens place of the bottom number means there is nothing to take away and leaves some children wondering what they are supposed to do. Zeros in the top number mean there are no materials in that column, which presents an unusual situation.

The very common error of "borrowing across zero" is best addressed at the modeling stage. For example, in 403 − 138, children must make a double trade, exchanging a hundreds piece for 10 tens and then one of the tens for 10 ones.

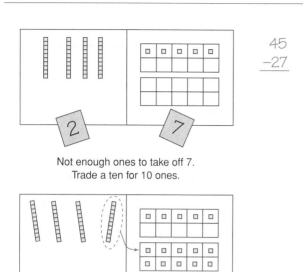

45
−27

Not enough ones to take off 7.
Trade a ten for 10 ones.

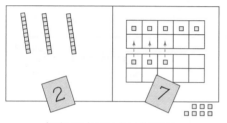

Now there are 15 ones.
I can take 7 off easily.

It does not matter which ones come off. Put the leftovers together.

And now I can take off 2 tens.

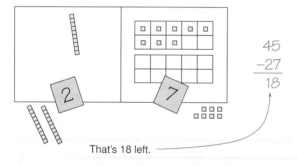

45
−27
18

That's 18 left.

**Figure 10.11** Two-place subtraction with models.

## Develop the Written Record

The process of recording each step as it is done is the same as was suggested for addition. The same recording sheets (Figure 10.8, p. 178) are also recommended.

When a problem has been solved and recorded, children should be able to explain the meanings of all of the markings at the top of the problem in terms of base-ten materials. This ability to explain symbolism is a signal for moving children on to a completely symbolic level. Again, be attentive to problems with zeros.

If students are permitted to follow their natural instincts and begin with the big pieces (from the left instead of the right), recording schemes similar to that shown in Figure 10.12 are possible. The trades are made from the pieces remaining *after* the subtraction in the column to the left has been done. A "borrow across zero" difficulty will still occur, but in problems like this: 462 − 168. Try it.

```
   13 14
  7̸3̸4̸
 −275
 ─────
  5̸0̸0
  4̸6̸0
   59
 ─────
  459
```

**Figure 10.12** A left-hand recording scheme for subtraction. Other methods can also be devised.

# INVENTED STRATEGIES FOR MULTIPLICATION

Computation strategies for multiplication are considerably more complex than for addition and subtraction. Often, but by no means always, the strategies that students invent are very similar to the traditional algorithm. The big difference is that students think about numbers, not digits. They always begin with the large or left-hand numbers.

For multiplication, the ability to break numbers apart in flexible ways is even more important than in addition or subtraction. The distributive property is another concept that is important in multiplication computation. For example, to multiply 43 × 5, one might think about breaking 43 into 40 and 3, multiplying each by 5, and then adding the results. Children require ample opportunities to develop these concepts by making sense of their own ideas and those of their classmates.

## Useful Representations

The problem 34 × 6 may be represented in a number of ways, as illustrated in Figure 10.13. Often the choice of a model is influenced by a story problem. To determine how many Easter eggs 34 children need if each colors 6 eggs, children may model 6 sets of 34 (or possibly 34 sets of 6). If the problem is about the area of a rectangle that is 34 cm by 6 cm, then some form of an array is likely. But each representation is appropriate for thinking about 34 × 6 regardless of the context, and students should get to a point where they select ways to think about multiplication that are meaningful to them.

**Figure 10.13** **Different ways to model 34 × 6 may support different computational strategies.**

How children represent a product interacts with their methods for determining answers. The groups of 34 might suggest repeated additions—perhaps taking the sets two at a time. Double 34 is 68 and there are three of those, so 68 + 68 + 68. From there a variety of methods are possible.

The 6 sets of base-ten pieces might suggest breaking the numbers into tens and ones: 6 times 3 tens or 6 × 30 and 6 × 4. Some children use the tens individually: 6 tens make 60. So that's 60 and 60 and 60 (180). Then add on the 24 to make 204.

It is not uncommon to arrange the base-ten pieces in a nice array, even if the story problem does not suggest it. The area model is very much like an arrangement of the base-ten pieces.

All of these ideas should be part of students' repertoire of models for multidigit multiplication. Introduce different representations (one at a time) as ways to explore multiplication until you are comfortable that the class has a collection of useful ideas. At the same time, do not force students who reason very well without drawings to use models when they are not needed.

# Multiplication by a Single-Digit Multiplier

As with addition and subtraction, it is helpful to place multiplication tasks in contextual story problems. Let students model the problems in ways that make sense to them. Do not be concerned about mixing of factors (6 sets of 34 or 34 sets of 6). Nor should you be timid about the numbers you use. The problem 3 × 24 may be easier than 7 × 65, but the latter provides challenge. The types of strategies that students use for multiplication are much more varied than for addition and subtraction. However, the following three categories can be identified from the research to date.

## Complete-Number Strategies

Children who are not yet comfortable breaking numbers into parts using tens and ones will approach the numbers in the sets as single groups. For students who think this way, Figure 10.14 illustrates two methods they may use. These children will benefit from listening to children who use base-ten models. They may also need more work with base-ten grouping activities where they take numbers apart in different ways.

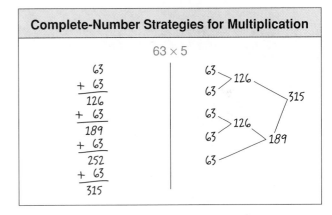

**Figure 10.14** **Children who use a complete-number strategy do not break numbers apart into decades or tens and ones.**

## Partitioning Strategies

Children break numbers up in a variety of ways that reflect an understanding of base-ten concepts, at least four of which are illustrated in Figure 10.15 (p. 182). The "By Decades" approach is the same as the standard algorithm except that students always begin with the large values. It extends easily to three digits and is very powerful as a mental math strategy. Another valuable strategy for mental methods is found in the "Other Partitions" example. It is easy to compute mentally with multiples of 25 and 50 and then add or subtract a small adjustment. All partition strategies rely on the distributive property.

## Compensation Strategies

Children look for ways to manipulate numbers so that the calculations are easy. In Figure 10.16 (p. 182), the problem

**Figure 10.15** Numbers can be broken apart in different ways to make easier partial products, which are then combined. Partitioning by decades is useful for mental computation and is very close to the standard algorithm.

$27 \times 4$ is changed to an easier one, and then an adjustment or compensation is made. In the second example, one factor is cut in half and the other doubled. This is often used when a 5 or a 50 is involved. Because these strategies are so dependent on the numbers involved, they can't be used for all computations. However, they are powerful strategies, especially for mental math and estimation.

---

**Compensation Strategies for Multiplication**

| | |
|---|---|
| $27 \times 4$ <br> $27 + 3 \longrightarrow 30 \times 4 \to 120$ <br> $3 \times 4 = 12 \longrightarrow -12$ <br> $\overline{108}$ | $250 \times 5$ <br> I can split 250 in half and multiply by 10. <br> $125 \times 10 = 1250$ |

$17 \times 70 \qquad 3 \times 70$
$20 \times 70 \to 1400 - 210 \to 1190$

**Figure 10.16** Compensation methods use a product related to the original. A compensation is made in the answer, or one factor is changed to compensate for a change in the other factor.

## Using Multiples of 10 and 100

There is a value in exposing students early to products involving multiples of 10 and 100.

The scout troop wanted to package up 400 fire starter kits as a fund-raising project. If each pack will have 12 fire starters, how many fire starters are the scouts going to need?

Children will use $4 \times 12 = 48$ to figure out that $400 \times 12$ is 4800. There will be discussion around how to say and write

"forty-eight hundred." Be aware of students who simply tack on zeros without understanding why. Try problems such as $30 \times 60$ or $210 \times 40$ where tens are multiplied by tens.

Some teachers suggest "cluster problems," a list of simpler but related products that can be used to solve the larger task. For $210 \times 40$, a cluster of simple products might be

$4 \times 2 \quad 4 \times 21 \quad 4 \times 10 \quad 4 \times 20 \quad 40 \times 20 \quad 40 \times 200 \quad 40 \times 21$

Students discuss which problems in the cluster could be used to help solve the larger problem. Initially the teacher suggests the cluster problems, but later students can create their own (Schifter et al., 1999b).

## Two-Digit Multipliers

A problem such as this one can be solved in many different ways:

**The parade had 23 clowns. Each clown carried 18 balloons. How many balloons were there altogether?**

Some children look for smaller products such as $6 \times 23$ and then add that result three times. Another method is to do $20 \times 23$ and then subtract $2 \times 23$. Others will calculate four separate partial products: $10 \times 20 = 200$, $8 \times 20 = 160$, $10 \times 3 = 30$, and $8 \times 3 = 24$. And still others may add up a string of 23s. Two-digit multiplication is both complex and challenging. But children can solve these problems in a variety of interesting ways, many of which will contribute to the development of the traditional algorithm or one that is just as efficient. Time devoted to working on these tasks in the fourth through sixth grades is well spent.

A valuable exploration is to prepare large rectangles for each group of two or three students. The rectangles should be measured carefully, with dimensions between 25 cm and 60 cm, and drawn accurately with square corners. (Use the corner of a piece of poster board for a guide.) The students' task is to determine how many small ones pieces (base-ten materials) will fit inside. Wooden or plastic base-ten pieces are best, but cardboard strips and squares are adequate. Alternatively, rectangles can be drawn on base-ten grid paper (see Blackline Masters), or students can simply be given the task verbally: *What is the area of a rectangle that is 47 cm by 36 cm?*

Most children will fill the rectangle first with as many hundreds pieces as possible. One obvious approach is to put the 12 hundreds in one corner. This will leave narrow regions on two sides that can be filled with tens pieces and a final small rectangle that will hold ones. Especially if students have had earlier experiences with finding products in arrays, figuring out the size of each subrectangle is not terribly difficult. The sketch in Figure 10.17 shows the four regions. If you did not already know the algorithm, how would you determine the size of the rectangle? Use your method on a rectangle that measures 68 cm by 24 cm. Make a sketch to explain your work.

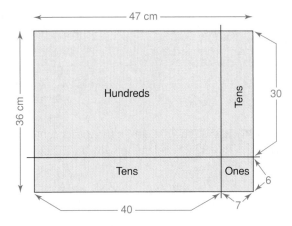

**Figure 10.17** **Ones, tens, and hundreds pieces fit exactly into the four sections of this 47 × 36 rectangle. Figure the size of each section to determine the size of the whole rectangle.**

# THE TRADITIONAL ALGORITHM FOR MULTIPLICATION

The traditional multiplication algorithm is probably the most difficult of the four algorithms if students have not had plenty of opportunities to explore their own strategies. Without

understanding, children put numbers in wrong columns, add in carried digits before they multiply, and make a host of other errors. When children are recording methods that make sense to them, these errors are much less likely.

The multiplication algorithm can be meaningfully developed using either a repeated addition model or an area model. For single-digit multipliers, the difference is minimal. When you move to two-digit multipliers, the area model has some advantages. For that reason, the discussion here will use the area model.

## One-Digit Multipliers

As with the other algorithms, as much time as possible should be devoted to the conceptual development of the algorithm with the recording or written part coming later.

### Begin with Models

Give students a drawing of a rectangle 47 cm by 6 cm. *How many small square centimeter pieces will fit in the rectangle?* (What is the area of the rectangle in square centimeters?) Let students solve the problem in groups before discussing it as a class.

As shown in Figure 10.18, the rectangle can be "sliced" or separated into two parts so that one part will be 6 ones by 7 ones, or 42 ones, and the other will be 6 ones by 4 tens, or 24 tens. Notice that the base-ten language "6 ones times 4 tens is 24 tens" tells how many *pieces* (sticks of ten) are in the big section. To say "6 times 40 is 240" is also correct and tells how many units or square centimeters are in the section. Each section is referred to as a *partial product*. By adding the two partial products, you get the total product or area of the rectangle.

To avoid the tedium of drawing large rectangles and arranging base-ten pieces, use the base-ten grid paper found in the Blackline Masters. On the grid paper, students can easily draw accurate rectangles showing all of the pieces. Check to be sure students understand that for a product such as 74 × 8, there are two partial products, 70 × 8 = 560 and 4 × 8 = 32, and the sum of these is the product. Do not force any recording technique on students until they understand how to use the two dimensions of a rectangle to get a product.

**Figure 10.18** **A rectangle filled with base-ten pieces is a useful model for two-digit-by-one-digit multiplication.**

## Develop the Written Record

To help with a recording scheme, provide sheets with base-ten columns on which students can record problems. When the two partial products are written separately as in Figure 10.19(a), there is little new to learn. Students simply record the products and add them together. As illustrated, it is possible to teach students how to write the first product with a carried digit so that the combined product is written on one line. This traditional recording scheme is known to be problematic. The little carried digit is often the source of difficulty—it gets added in before the second multiplication or is forgotten.

(a)                                             (b)

**Figure 10.19** (a) In the standard form, the product of ones is recorded first. The tens digit of this first product can be written as a "carried" digit above the tens column. (b) It is quite reasonable to abandon the carried digit and permit the partial products to be recorded in any order.

There is absolutely no practical reason why students can't be allowed to record both partial products and avoid the errors related to the carried digit. When you accept that, it makes no difference in which order the products are written. Why not simply permit students to do written multiplication as shown in Figure 10.19(b)? When the factors are in a word problem, chart, or other format, all that is really necessary is to write down all the partial products and add. Furthermore, that is precisely how this is done mentally. It is time to make this change!

Most standard curricula progress from two digits to three digits with a single-digit multiplier. Students can make this progression easily. They still should be permitted to write all three partial products separately and not have to bother with carrying.

## Two-Digit Multipliers

With the area model, the progression to a two-digit multiplier is relatively straightforward. Rectangles can be drawn on base-ten grid paper, or full-sized rectangles can be filled in with base-ten pieces. There will be four partial products, corresponding to four different sections of the rectangle.

Several variations in language might be used. Consider the product 47 × 36 as illustrated in Figure 10.20. In the partial product 40 × 30, if base-ten language is used—*4 tens times 3 tens is 12 hundreds*—the result tells how many hundreds pieces are in that section. Verbally, the product "forty times thirty" is formidable. Try to avoid "four times three," which promotes thinking about digits rather than numbers. It is well worth stressing the idea that in all cases, a product of *tens times tens is hundreds*.

Figure 10.20 also shows the recording of four partial products in the traditional order and how these can be collapsed to two lines if carried digits are used. Here the second "carry" technically belongs in the hundreds column but it rarely is written there. Often it gets confused with the first and is thus an additional source of errors. The lower left of the figure shows the same computation with all four products written in a different order. This is quite an acceptable algorithm. In the rare instance when someone multiplies numbers such as 538 × 29 with pencil and paper, there would be six partial products. But far fewer errors would occur, requiring less instructional time and much less remediation.

# INVENTED STRATEGIES FOR DIVISION

Even though many adults think division is the most onerous of the computational operations, it can be considerably easier than multiplication. Conceptual methods are easily developed through the use of simple story problems. It is appropriate to begin thinking about division computation in the third and fourth grades, but even second graders can solve story problems with two-digit dividends and single-digit divisors via direct modeling.

Recall that there are two concepts of division. First there is the partition or fair-sharing idea, illustrated by this story problem:

**The bag has 783 jelly beans, and Maggie and her four friends want to share them equally. How many jelly beans will Maggie and each of her friends get?**

Then there is the measurement or repeated subtraction concept:

**Jumbo the elephant loves peanuts. His trainer has 625 peanuts. If he gives Jumbo 20 peanuts each day, how many days will the peanuts last?**

Students should be challenged to solve both types of problems. However, the fair-share problems are often easier

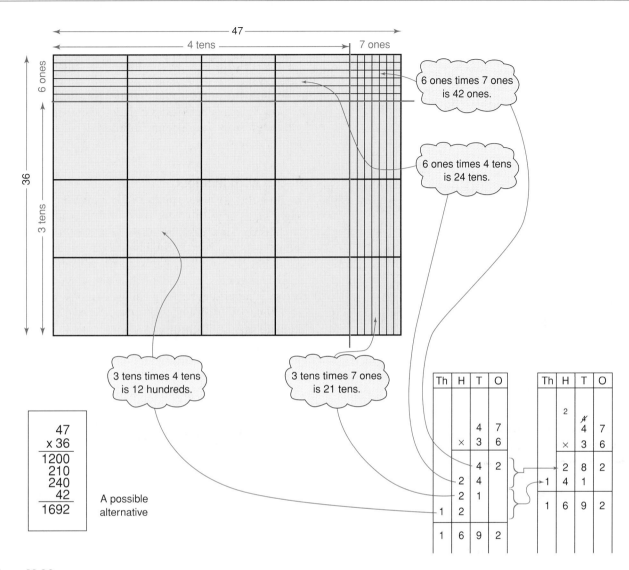

**Figure 10.20** A 47 × 36 rectangle filled with base-ten pieces. Base-ten language connects the four partial products to the traditional written format. Note the possibility of recording the products in some other order.

to solve with base-ten pieces. Furthermore, the traditional algorithm is built on this idea. Eventually, students will develop strategies that they will apply to both types of problem, even when the process does not match the action of the story.

Figure 10.21 (p. 186) shows some strategies that fourth-grade children have used to solve division problems. The first example illustrates 92 ÷ 4 using base-ten pieces and a sharing process. A ten is traded when no more tens can be passed out. Then the 12 ones are distributed, resulting in 23 in each set. This direct modeling approach with base-ten pieces is quite easy even for third-grade students to understand and use.

In the second example, the student sets out the base-ten pieces and draws a "bar graph" with six columns. After not-

ing that there are not enough hundreds for each kid, he splits the 3 hundreds in half, putting 50 in each column. That leaves him with 1 hundred, 5 tens, and 3 ones. After trading the hundred for tens (now 15 tens), he gives 20 to each, recording 2 tens in each bar. Now he is left with 3 tens and 3 ones, or 33. He knows that 5 × 6 is 30, so he gives each kid 5, leaving him with 3. These he splits in half and writes $\frac{1}{2}$ in each column.

The child in the third example is solving a sharing problem but tries to do it as a measurement process. She wants to find out how many 8s are in 143. Initially she guesses. By multiplying 8 first by 10, then by 20, and then by 14, she knows the answer is more than 14 and less than 20. After some more work (not shown), she rethinks the problem as how many 8s in 100 and how many in 40.

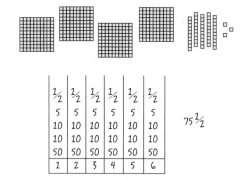

**(b)  453 ÷ 6**
**(share with 6 kids)**

| ½ | ½ | ½ | ½ | ½ | ½ |
|---|---|---|---|---|---|
| 5 | 5 | 5 | 5 | 5 | 5 |
| 10 | 10 | 10 | 10 | 10 | 10 |
| 10 | 10 | 10 | 10 | 10 | 10 |
| 50 | 50 | 50 | 50 | 50 | 50 |
| 1 | 2 | 3 | 4 | 5 | 6 |

75½

**(c)  143 jelly beans shared with 8 kids**

Try 14 × 8 → 112
12 groups of 8 is 96.
12 groups in 100 leaves 4.
 5 groups of 8 in 40.
And 3 more left over.
12 + 5 is 17 with 7 left.

**Figure 10.21** **Students use both models and symbols to solve division tasks.**

*Source:* Adapted from *Developing Mathematical Ideas: Numbers and Operations, Part I: Building a System of Tens Casebook,* by D. Schifter, V. Bastable, & S. J. Russell. Copyright ©1999 by the Educational Development Center, Inc. Published by Dale Seymour Publications, an imprint of Pearson Learning. Used by permission.

# THE TRADITIONAL ALGORITHM FOR DIVISION

Long division is the one traditional algorithm that starts with the left-hand or big pieces. The conceptual basis for the algorithm most often taught in textbooks is the partition or fair-share method.

## One-Digit Divisors

Typically, the division algorithm with one-digit divisors is introduced in the third grade. If done well, it should not have to be retaught, and it should provide the basis for two-digit divisors. Students in the upper grades who are having difficulty with the division algorithm can also benefit from a conceptual development.

### Begin with Models

Traditionally, if we were to do a problem such as 4)583, we might say "4 goes into 5 one time." This is quite mysterious to children. How can you just ignore the "83" and keep changing the problem? Preferably, you want students to think of the 583 as 5 hundreds, 8 tens, and 3 ones, not as the independent digits 5, 8 and 3. One idea is to use a context such as candy bundled in boxes of ten with 10 boxes to a carton. Then the problem becomes *We have 5 boxes, 8 cartons, and 3 pieces of candy to share between 4 schools evenly.* In this context, it is reasonable to share the cartons first until no more can be shared. Those remaining are "unpacked," and the boxes shared, and so on. Money ($100, $10, and $1) can be used in a similar manner. Figure 10.22 shows the process in detail. Make up a three-digit problem, and try this yourself using base-ten pieces.

### Develop the Written Record

The recording scheme for the long-division algorithm is not completely intuitive. You will need to be quite directive in helping children learn to record the fair sharing with models. There are essentially four steps:

1. *Share* and record the number of pieces put in each group.
2. *Record* the number of pieces shared in all. Multiply to find this number.
3. *Record* the number of pieces remaining. Subtract to find this number.
4. *Trade* (if necessary) for smaller pieces, and combine with any that are there already. Record the new total number in the next column.

When students model problems with a one-digit divisor, steps 2 and 3 seem unnecessary. Explain that these steps really help when you don't have the pieces there to count.

### Record Explicit Trades

Figure 10.23 (p. 188) details each step of the recording process just described. On the left, you see the traditional algorithm. To the right is a suggestion that matches the actual action with the models by explicitly recording the trades. Instead of the somewhat mysterious "bring-down" procedure, the traded pieces are crossed out, as is the number of existing pieces in the next column. The combined number of pieces is written in this column using a two-digit number. In

The task is to share these 5 hundreds, 8 tens, and 3 ones among these four sets so that each set gets the same amount.

I'll begin with the hundreds pieces. There are enough so that each set can get 1 hundred. That leaves 1 hundred left that cannot be shared.

I can trade the hundred for 10 tens. That gives me a total of 18 tens. With 18 I can put 4 tens in each of the four sets and have 2 tens left. Two is not enough to go around to all four sets.

Trade for 10 tens

I can trade the 2 tens for 10 ones each or a total of 20 ones. With the 3 ones I already had, that gives me 23 ones. I can put 5 ones in each of the four sets. That leaves me with only 3 ones left over as a remainder.

Trade for 20 ones

Each set got 145. I record that on the top of the problem in the right place-value columns. The answer tells how much went to each set.

If I added up how much they got altogether, that would be 4 × 145 or 580. The remainder of 3 makes the 583 I started with.

**Figure 10.22**   **Sharing pieces within each place value and trading leftovers for the next smaller place is the entire conceptual basis for the long-division algorithm.**

the example, 2 hundreds are traded for 20 tens, combined with the 6 that were there for a total of 26 tens. The 26 is therefore written in the tens column.

Students who are required to make sense of the long-division procedure find the explicit-trade method easier to follow. Blank division charts with wide place-value columns are highly recommended. These can be found in the Blackline Masters. Without the charts, it is important to spread out the digits in the dividend when writing down the problem. (The explicit-trade method is an invention of mine. It has been used successfully in grades 3 to 8. You will not find it in textbooks.)

Both the explicit-trade method and the use of place-value columns will help with the problem of leaving out a middle zero in a problem (see Figure 10.24, p. 189).

## Two-Digit Divisors

There is almost no justification for having children master division with two-digit divisors. A large chunk of the fourth, fifth, and sometimes sixth grade is frequently spent on this outdated skill. The cost in terms of time and students' attitudes toward mathematics is enormous. Only a few times in any adult's life will an exact result to such a computation be required and a calculator not be available. If you can possibly influence the removal of this outdated skill from your school's curriculum, you are encouraged to speak up.

With a two-digit divisor, it is hard to come up with the right amount to share at each step. A guess too high or too low means you have to erase and start all over.

**Figure 10.23** The traditional and explicit-trade methods are connected to each step of the division process. Every step can and should make sense.

## An Intuitive Idea

Suppose that you were sharing a large pile of candies with 36 friends. Instead of passing them out one at a time, you conservatively estimate that each person could get at least 6 pieces. So you give 6 to each of your friends. Now you find there are more than 36 pieces left. Do you have everyone give

back the 6 pieces so you can then give them 7 or 8? That would be silly! You simply pass out more.

The candy example gives us two good ideas for sharing in long division. First, always underestimate how much can be shared. You can always pass out some more. Second, if there is enough left to share some more, just do it! To avoid

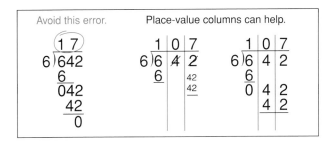

**Figure 10.24** **Using lines to mark place-value columns can help avoid forgetting to record zeros.**

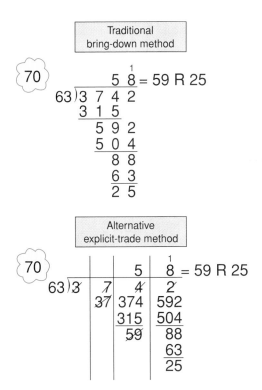

**Figure 10.25** **Round the divisor up to 70 to think with, but multiply what you share by 63. In the ones column, share 8 with each set. Oops! 88 left over. Just give 1 more to each set.**

ever overestimating, always pretend there are more sets among which to share than there really are. For example, if you are dividing 312 by 43 (sharing among 43 sets or "friends"), pretend you have 50 sets instead. Round *up* to the next multiple of 10. You can easily determine that 6 pieces can be shared among 50 sets because 6 × 50 is an easy product. Therefore, since there are really only 43 sets, clearly you can give *at least* 6 to each. Always consider a larger divisor; *always round up.* If your underestimate leaves you with more to share, simply pass out some more.

### Using the Idea Symbolically

These ideas are used in Figure 10.25. Both the traditional method and the explicit-trade method of recording are illustrated. The rounded-up divisor, 70, is written in a little "think bubble" above the real divisor. Rounding up has another advantage: it is easy to run through the multiples of 70 and compare them to 374. Think about sharing base-ten pieces (thousands, hundreds, tens, and ones). Work through the problem one step at a time, saying exactly what each recorded step stands for.

This approach has proved successful with children in the fourth grade learning division for the first time and with children in the sixth to eighth grades in need of remediation. It reduces the mental strain of making choices and essentially eliminates the need to erase. If an estimate is too low, that's OK. And if you always round up, the estimate will never be too high. Nor is there any reason ever to change to the more familiar approach. It is just as good for adults as for children. The same is true of the explicit-trade notation. It is certainly an idea to consider.

 **TECHNOLOGY NOTE**

Most software programs that provide drill of any sort will also provide drill in multidigit computation. Most simply provide problems at different levels and evaluate answers. These programs have limited advantages for the teacher. In *Gold Medal Mathematics* (EdVenture Software, 1997), for example, students are first "warmed up" with fact practice. Then, in a practice setting, students continue to solve problems until they complete ten in a row correctly. The challenge round

encourages speed. Somewhat unusual is the fact that all answers are in multiple-choice format. This permits students to use any strategy, encourages mental computation, and may be good practice for standardized tests. The program includes two-digit addition and subtraction as well as multiplication and division.

Some programs provide base-ten blocks on the screen that students can manipulate to help solve problems. Before purchasing these programs, see how much freedom is provided, and ask what the computer program does that could not be accomplished at least as well with physical materials. *MathKeys* (MECC, 1995a, 1996b), for example, includes very attractive screen graphics that permit modeling numbers into the thousands. However, the computer forces trading and always updates totals. Perhaps this can provide a form of explanation, but there is no problem-solving spirit to this program. ■

 **LITERATURE CONNECTIONS**

Children's literature can play a very useful role in helping you develop problems for your invented strategies and mental computation lessons. Your simple story problems every day may be great, but children deserve a change. Turn to children's books. There are a great many fascinating books that involve large numbers and opportunities to compute. Some are about real data, and others are fictional.

## Cookies
### (Jaspersohn, 1993)

This is the true story of Wally Amos and his Famous Amos Chocolate Chip Cookies. (Are you interested already?) The text includes a large number of color and black-and-white photos that show the production and distribution of Famous Amos cookies. Because it is filled with facts about the cookies—numbers sold, number the average person eats in a year, and so on—you can easily pose questions that require computation and that children will find interesting. Although actual computations can be done on a calculator, this context clearly suggests that estimates and round numbers make more sense. As you discuss ideas generated by the book, some computations can be done mentally to determine exact answers. Other computations will be estimates. Students can extend the story to a project to research cookie consumption in their home, data from grocery stores about other cookies, or the number of trucks or miles required to get cookies to market. The possibilities are endless. During these projects, suggest that students pay attention to where an estimate makes more sense than an exact computation. Find out if there are places as they are working on their project where they made a quick mental estimate or did a mental computation.

## Is a Blue Whale the Biggest Thing There Is?
### (Wells, 1993)

This is one of the most intriguing books you will find about large things and large distances. Blue whales look small next to Mount Everest, which in turn looks small next to the earth. The data in the book allow children to make other comparisons, such as the number of fourth graders that would have the same weight or volume as a blue whale or

would fill the gymnasium. As with the Famous Amos data, these comparisons are the perfect place for estimations and discussions about how much accuracy is necessary to make a meaningful comparison. Bresser (1995) provides excellent insights into the use of this story with fourth-, fifth-, and sixth-grade students.

 ## ASSESSMENT NOTES

Parents are perhaps more interested in their children's computational skills than in any other area. It is quite easy to give a test of computation like those provided in traditional textbooks. When students do well on these tests, parents are pleased. But what do you know when students do not do well? At best you can make inferences based on the papers turned in. You can look for basic-fact errors and carelessness or perhaps find a systematic error in an algorithm. What you do not know is how children are solving these problems and what ideas and strategies they have developed that are useful or need further development.

## Ongoing Assessment

When computational strategies and algorithms are developed in the manner suggested in this chapter, every day you are presented with a wealth of assessment data. The important thing is to gather, record, and use these data for individual children the same as you would for tests and quizzes. A simple chart something like the one in Figure 10.26 may be all you need. Note that the third column includes a minirubric or a three-point scale. Students' names can be arranged in groups, by how they sit in the room, or alphabetically—any way that makes them easy to find.

As you walk around in the during portion of your lessons, and also in the after portion when children explain their computation strategies and reasoning, you can make

**Figure 10.26** A checklist with space for comments or notes lets you record daily observations of students' direct modeling and invented strategies.

| Topic: Mental addition and subtraction / Student | Adds 2-digit + 1-digit numbers | Adds 2-digit + 2-digit numbers; note methods | Flexibility in choosing a method: 1, 2, 3 | Comments |
|---|---|---|---|---|
| Lalie | | | | |
| Pete | | | | |
| Sid | | | | |
| Lakeshia | | | | |

notes on the chart. Make a new chart each week, but keep the old ones to provide evidence of growth over time. These charts can be useful for grading and for parent conferences. There is no harm in giving an occasional quiz or test of computational skills. But avoid giving more value to tests simply because they are objective. Compare the results with the information you have gathered through observation. Did you get any new information? Were the results consistent? If not, why not?

## Occasional Interviews

It is not always easy to tell what concepts or thought processes individual students are using. For example, some students may get overly attached to a particular approach and not be flexible enough to switch to a more efficient method when the numbers call for it. Some children do not provide as much information in class as you need because they are shy or not very verbal. You may need to find out more about underlying conceptual understanding of base-ten concepts.

For these and many other reasons, it is often useful to stop and listen more carefully to a single child. A little interview may take 5 to 10 minutes. Perhaps you can do it while others are working on a problem you have posed, or maybe you will find a time outside of the lesson.

The interview format is similar to the lessons that have been described. Pose a word problem or computation, and ask the student to "think out loud" while she works. Explain that you want to find out how she is thinking. Avoid any teaching at this time. Do not make evaluative comments. Show your interest in the student's thinking. Ask questions to clarify thinking that may not be clear. If a child is making errors with symbolic techniques, ask if he can show you how to do the same task with counters or base-ten models. Similarly, a student who seems to rely heavily on physical models can be challenged in an interview to try a problem without models.

Some children will give you a much clearer picture of their abilities and understanding in an interview than when they feel pressured by talking in a full-class setting.

# REFLECTIONS ON CHAPTER 10

## Writing to Learn

1. What is the difference between solving a problem with direct modeling and solving a problem with an invented strategy? What is a traditional algorithm?

2. How are traditional algorithms different from invented strategies? Explain the benefits of invented strategies over traditional algorithms.

3. When a problem has been solved, how do you manage all of the different methods that students may propose, and what should you do about students who propose no ideas of their own?

4. What do you do when someone brings a traditional algorithm into the classroom before you have introduced it? What if you never plan to teach the traditional algorithm but students want to use it anyway?

5. Explain how strategies for problems such as 58 + 6 or 72 − 5 are similar to the make-ten strategies for basic facts. How can you help children extend their basic fact strategies to these larger numbers?

6. Illustrate three different strategies for adding 46 + 39. Which ones are easy to do mentally? Is there a strategy that is easier because 39 is close to 40? What strategies work well for sums such as 538 + 243? For each strategy you work with, think about how you could record it on the board so that other students will be able to follow what is being done.

7. Use two different adding-up strategies for 93 − 27 and for 545 − 267. Make up a story problem that would encourage an adding-up strategy.

8. Describe how you would go about developing the traditional algorithms for addition and subtraction. How would you deal with the issue of beginning on the right with the ones place when students' natural tendency is to begin on the left? Use 385 + 128 to illustrate a reasonable written algorithm that begins on the left instead of the right. Do the same for 453 − 278.

9. Draw pictures showing how 57 × 4 could be modeled: with counters, with base-ten pieces, with rectangles or arrays on base-ten grids.

10. How might you help a student who is using a complete-number strategy for multiplication?

11. Try to develop some skill using an invented strategy for multiplying by single-digit numbers. Can you do 327 × 6 mentally? How would you record the steps on the chalkboard if a student gave them to you the way you did it?

12. Use a compensation strategy for these: 68 × 20, 5 × 46, 25 × 480.

13. Draw a rectangle for 28 × 57, and explain how it could be used to compute the product.

14. Which division concept, measurement or partition, is easier for direct modeling and is also the one used to develop the usual long-division algorithm? Make up an appropriate word story with that concept to go with 735 ÷ 6.

15. Use the traditional algorithm for 735 ÷ 6, and then repeat the process using the text's suggestion of recording trades explicitly. With the two algorithms side by side, explain every recorded number in terms of what it stands for when sharing base-ten pieces.

16. To avoid erasures in long division, a rounded-up divisor can be used to make estimates of the quotient in each place value. Show how this method works and avoids erasures using the problem 4589 ÷ 62.

# For Discussion and Exploration

1. Examine any or all of these three books on mental computation (or similar resource books on the same topic):

   *Mental Math in the Primary Grades* (Hope, Leutzinger, Reys, & Reys, 1988)

   *Mental Math in the Middle Grades* (Hope, Reys, & Reys, 1987)

   *Mental Math in the Junior High School* (Hope, Reys, & Reys, 1988)

   Although the ideas suggested in these books are excellent, you will notice that the instructional strategy is considerably more guided than that described in this chapter. Would you use these books or their equivalent in your computational program? Would you use this approach instead of the one suggested here, or should methods such as these be integrated into a problem-solving approach?

2. Select any grade between 2 and 6, and discuss what you feel is an appropriate skill level for whole-number computation at that grade. Should these skills be taught at that grade or earlier? How do your views compare with the treatment given whole-number computation in a traditional textbook for that grade level? How does the textbook treatment compare with the general position offered in this chapter?

3. Examine one of the three reform curricula (see Chapter 1, p. 14) for the elementary grades. How is whole-number computation developed?

# Recommendations for Further Reading

## Highly Recommended

Campbell, P. F., & Johnson, M. L. (1995). How primary students think and learn. In I. M. Carl (Ed.), *Prospects for school mathematics* (pp. 21–42). Reston, VA: National Council of Teachers of Mathematics.

Campbell and Johnson describe a project in an urban school system that is completely based in a constructivist paradigm. Their purpose is to describe how children are able to construct their own ideas. Interestingly, most of the examples provided involve computation and student-invented methods. Absolutely worth reading.

Creative Publications. (1996). *Smart arithmetic* [Video]. Chicago: Author.

This inexpensive video shows real classrooms in which children share their completely mental strategies for computation at all grade levels. The teachers accept all methods and expect students to understand the ideas of others. Between episodes, the teachers discuss the implementation of their mental math programs and provide practical tips. (Note that the *Smart Arithmetic* books, Irvine & Walker, 1996a, 1996b, are not closely connected to the video.)

Morrow, L. (Ed.). (1998). *The teaching and learning of algorithms in school mathematics*. Reston, VA: National Council of Teachers of Mathematics.

Mastery of algorithms is and always has been a topic that anti-reformers choose to attack, usually because they believe that reform means to stop teaching computation. This NCTM yearbook offers well-articulated perspectives on the issue. More important, it contains numerous articles with practical teaching suggestions at the elementary, middle, and secondary levels.

Schifter, D., Bastable, V., & Russell, S. J. (1999). *Developing mathematical ideas: Numbers and operations, Part 1: Building a system of tens* (Casebook). White Plains, NY: Cuisenaire–Dale Seymour.

The cases in this book clearly demonstrate the interaction between children's place-value understanding and their invented strategies for computation. It is from this book and its companion in-service guide that much of the information in this chapter regarding invented strategies was derived. For any teacher seriously interested in the development of student-invented methods of computation, this book provides practical insights.

## Other Suggestions

Baek, J. (1998). Children's invented algorithms for multidigit multiplication problems. In L. J. Morrow (Ed.), *The teaching and learning of algorithms in school mathematics* (pp. 151–160). Reston, VA: National Council of Teachers of Mathematics.

Bresser, R., & Holtzman, C. (1999). *Developing number sense: Grades 3–6*. Sausalito, CA: Math Solutions Publications.

Burns, M. (1992). *About teaching mathematics: A K–8 Resource*. Sausalito, CA: Math Solutions Publications.

Campbell, P. F., Rowan, T. E., & Suarez, A. R. (1998). What criteria for student-invented algorithms? In L. J. Morrow (Ed.), *The teaching and learning of algorithms in school mathematics* (pp. 49–55). Reston, VA: National Council of Teachers of Mathematics.

Carpenter, T. P., Franke, M. L., Jacobs, V. R., Fennema, E., & Empson, S. B. (1998). A longitudinal study of invention and understanding in children's multidigit addition and subtraction. *Journal for Research in Mathematics Education, 29,* 3–20.

Carroll, W. M. (1996). Use of invented algorithms by second graders in a reform mathematics curriculum. *Journal of Mathematical Behavior, 15,* 137–150.

Carroll, W. M., & Porter, D. (1997). Invented strategies can develop meaningful mathematical procedures. *Teaching Children Mathematics, 3,* 370–374.

Chambers, D. (1996). Direct modeling and invented procedures: Building on students' informal strategies. *Teaching Children Mathematics, 3,* 92–95.

Cobb, P., & Merkel, G. (1989). Thinking strategies: Teaching arithmetic through problem solving. In P. R. Trafton (Ed.), *New directions for elementary school mathematics* (pp. 70–81). Reston, VA: National Council of Teachers of Mathematics.

Coburn, T. G. (1989). The role of computation in the changing mathematics curriculum. In P. R. Trafton (Ed.), *New directions for elementary school mathematics* (pp. 43–56). Reston, VA: National Council of Teachers of Mathematics.

Hiebert, J. C., & Wearne, D. (1996). Instruction, understanding, and skill in multidigit addition and subtraction. *Cognition and Instruction, 14,* 251–283.

Hope, J. A., Leutzinger, L. P., Reys, B. J., & Reys, R. E. (1988). *Mental math in the primary grades*. White Plains, NY: Cuisenaire–Dale Seymour.

Hope, J. A., Reys, B. J., & Reys, R. E. (1987). *Mental math in the middle grades*. White Plains, NY: Cuisenaire–Dale Seymour.

Hope, J. A., Reys, B. J., & Reys, R. E. (1988). *Mental math in the junior high school*. White Plains, NY: Cuisenaire–Dale Seymour.

Hope, J. A., & Sherrill, J. M. (1987). Characteristics of unskilled and skilled mental calculators. *Journal for Research in Mathematics Education, 18,* 98–111.

Irvine, R., & Walker, K. (1996). *Smart arithmetic: A thinking approach to computation, grades 1–3.* Mountain View, CA: Creative Publications.

Irvine, R., & Walker, K. (1996). *Smart arithmetic: A thinking approach to computation, grades 4–6.* Mountain View, CA: Creative Publications.

Kamii, C. K. (1989). *Double-column addition: A teacher uses Piaget's theory* [Videotape]. New York: Teachers College Press.

Kamii, C. K. (1994). *Young children continue to reinvent arithmetic: 3rd grade.* New York: Teachers College Press.

Kamii, C. K., & Dominick, A. (1997). To teach or not to teach algorithms. *Journal of Mathematical Behavior, 16,* 51–61.

Kamii, C. K., & Lewis, B. A. (1993). The harmful effects of algorithms in primary arithmetic. *Teaching K–8, 23*(5), 36–38.

Reys, B. J., & Reys, R. E. (1999). Computation in the elementary curriculum: Shifting the emphasis. *Teaching Children Mathematics, 5,* 236–241.

Reys, R. E., & Nohda, N. (Eds). (1994). *Computational alternatives for the twenty-first century: Cross-cultural perspectives from Japan and the United States.* Reston, VA: National Council of Teachers of Mathematics.

Reys, R. E., Reys, B. J., Nohda, N., & Emori, H. (1995). Mental computation performance and strategy use of Japanese students in grades 2, 4, 6, and 8. *Journal for Research in Mathematics Education, 26,* 304–326.

Silver, E. A., Shapiro, L. J., & Deutsch, A. (1993). Sense making and the solution of division problems involving remainders: An examination of middle school students' solution processes and their interpretations of solutions. *Journal for Research in Mathematics Education, 24,* 117–135.

Skinner, P. (1999). *It all adds up! Engaging 8-to-12-year-olds in math investigations.* Sausalito, CA: Math Solutions Publications.

Thornton, C. A., & Jones, G. A. (1994). Computation sense. In C. A. Thornton & N. S. Bley (Eds.), *Windows of opportunity: Mathematics for students with special needs* (pp. 205–227). Reston, VA: National Council of Teachers of Mathematics.

Trafton, P. R., & Hartman, C. L. (1997). Developing number sense and computational strategies in problem-centered classrooms. *Teaching Children Mathematics, 4,* 230–233.

# Chapter 11

# Number Sense and Estimation with Whole Numbers

All of the topics related to whole numbers are intimately related. Number meanings and relationships (Chapter 6) are connected to the way students understand the operations (Chapter 7), and both of these collections of ideas contribute to basic fact mastery (Chapter 8). As children solve story problems, the numbers that are used begin to get larger, and they use the ideas of place value (Chapter 9) to invent a variety of computational strategies (Chapter 10).

The ideas discussed in this chapter are part of the full development of flexible and fluent thinking with whole numbers. The number sense activities will help children build relationships specifically related to computation. The skills of estimation can begin as early as third grade and later extend already developed mental strategies to deal with real-world situations that do not demand exact answers.

## BIG Ideas

1. Multidigit numbers can be taken apart in a wide variety of ways, including by decades (36 is 30 and 6), with place-value concepts (36 is 2 tens and 16 ones), and with other multiples (480 is 500 less 20 or 475 and 5). Numbers can easily be recombined when these parts are recognized.

2. Nearly all computational estimations involve replacing or substituting difficult-to-handle numbers with close "nice" numbers so that the resulting computation can be done mentally.

## NUMBER SENSE FOR WHOLE-NUMBER COMPUTATION

Number sense has been a part of every topic discussed so far in this text. It refers to flexible thinking and intuitive ideas about number. Here we examine only a small slice of number sense, the ability to take numbers apart and combine them in flexible ways. This flexibility with multidigit numbers is extremely important for students to develop if they are to improve their use of invented strategies and algorithms for whole numbers.

## Working with Tens and Hundreds

Most invented strategies for whole-number computation grow out of children's work with direct modeling. Initially, students require support for their thinking by writing the steps they use on paper. Because they are in the process of creating the strategies they are using, it is not reasonable to expect them to operate completely mentally. However, many invented strategies can become automatic, and when that happens, students can begin to use them without resorting to pencil and paper. This is somewhat analogous to mastering the basic facts. Efficient strategies for the facts are developed using assorted models, and children appear to be very slow and deliberate about something as simple as adding 6 + 8. But soon these strategies become so ingrained that students can quickly respond to basic facts. The activities here will help students become more efficient with their invented computational strategies by providing them with greater flexibility with numbers.

### ACTIVITY

#### 11.1 Arrow Math

With a 0–99 chart in view, write a number on the chart followed by one or more arrows. The arrow can point up, down, left, right, or diagonally. Each arrow represents a move of one square on the board.

63 ↓ ↓ →
Read: "63, 73, 83, 84"

45 ↑ ↑ ↖ ← ←
Read: "45, 35, 25, 14, 13, 12"

After students become adept at "Arrow Math," talk about what each arrow means. The left and right arrows are one-less and one-more arrows. The up and down arrows are the same as 10 less and 10 more. What do each of the four possible diagonal arrows represent? (adapted from Hope, Leutzinger, Reys, & Reys, 1988).

The possibility of a 0–999 chart can be discussed with your class, and you may even want to make one. Show a 0–99 chart, and draw a second 10 × 10 grid below it. "What number would go in these squares?" (100 to 199) "And if we had some more charts below this one, what numbers would be in each of them?" Each new grid is the next 100 numbers: 200 to 299, 300 to 399, and so on.

With an extended chart idea, the "Arrow Math" activity can be extended to include "super arrows."

426 ⇓ ⇓ ↓ → →
Read: "426, 526, 626, 636, 637, 638"

In the next example, note how three super up arrows and a regular down arrow are actually a good way to subtract 290.

674 ⇑ ⇑ ⇑ ↓
"674 minus 300 is 374, plus 10 is 384"

"Arrow Math" is only mildly problematic, and there is some evidence that the activity does not directly contribute to computation strategies (Cobb, 1995). However, the following activity connects arrows on the chart more directly to computation.

┌─ **A**CTIVITY ───────────────────
**11.2 More Arrow Math**

Begin with an arrow math task as before. For example:

56 ↓ ↓ →

After getting a result, ask, "How much did we add?" (21) "Now write an equation to go with this arrow problem." (56 + 21 = 77)

This works well in a similar manner for up and then left arrows for subtraction:

81 ↑ ↑ ↑ ↑ ← ←
81 − 43 = 38
└──────────────────────────────

That is, one way to subtract 43 from 81 is first to subtract 40 and then to subtract 3 more. The next two examples offer another twist.

64 ↓ ↓ ← and 72 ↑ ↑ ↑ →

In the first example, you add 20 and then subtract 1, a nice way of adding 19. In the second example, 30 is subtracted and then 1 added—a good way to subtract 29.

"More Arrow Math" certainly requires more than four examples. After the more straightforward tasks like the first two, begin with the equations, and have students write and complete the arrow problem: For 27 + 34, you first go down 3 (add 30) and then right 4 (add 4). How would you do 457 − 238? When adding or subtracting a number ending in 8 or 9, a good strategy, as indicated in "More Arrow Math," is to add or subtract a close multiple of 10 and then compensate.

 # TECHNOLOGY NOTE

*Math and More 3: Patterns on Lattices* (EduQuest, 1994) allows students to create a wide variety of arrow paths on a number chart that scrolls as high as 999. The software is a tool only, providing the number chart and arrows. Unfortunately, the start and end numbers are always visible. However, the software is well designed to explore this idea, and the teacher support material provides good explanations. It is important to ask, however, does using the computer add something of value to the task of doing and engaging in mathematics that you wouldn't have without it? ■

┌─ **A**CTIVITY ───────────────────
**11.3 Calculator Tens and Hundreds**

Two students work together with one calculator. They press ⊞ 10 ⊟ to make a "+10 machine." One child enters any number. The other student says or writes the number that is 10 more. The ⊟ is pressed for confirmation. The roles are then reversed. The same activity can be done with plus any multiple of 10 or multiple of 100. On their turn to challenge, students can select what kind of machine to use. For example, they may first press 0 ⊞ 300 ⊟ and then press 572. The other student would say or write 872 and then press ⊟ for confirmation. This game can also be played using ⊟ instead of ⊞ to practice mentally subtracting tens or hundreds.
└──────────────────────────────

As described, "Calculator Tens and Hundreds" is very similar to "Arrow Math" without the 0–99 chart. Students doing these activities will soon discover that it is fairly easy to add and subtract hundreds and tens mentally. In "Calculator Tens and Hundreds," students could easily begin to add or subtract numbers such as 240 or 73. Every student who has not been taught to add and subtract in the traditional pencil-and-paper manner will begin these tasks mentally starting with the largest amounts, just as in "Arrow Math."

Many of the skills and concepts developed so far also appear in the next activity, which combines symbolism with base-ten representations. In all of these activities, class discussion should have children explain how they did the exercises or tell how they thought about them.

---

**ACTIVITY**

## 11.4 Numbers, Squares, Sticks, and Dots

As illustrated in Figure 11.1, prepare a worksheet or overhead transparency on which a numeral and some base-ten pieces are shown. Use small squares, sticks, and dots for base-ten pieces to keep drawing simple. Students write the totals that they compute mentally.

Figure 11.2 is a take-away version of the same activity. As shown, the amount removed can be either the numeral or the squares and sticks. Try it both ways.

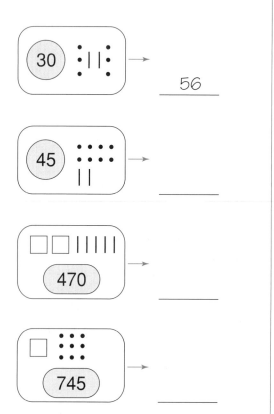

**Figure 11.1**  **Flexible counting on or addition using both models and numerals.**

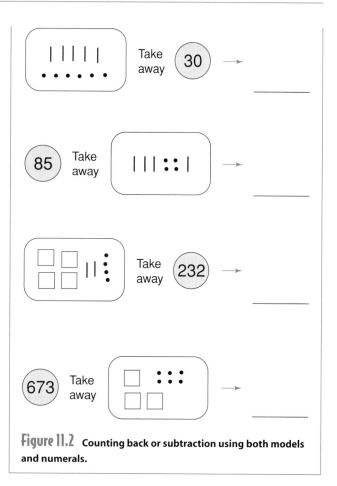

**Figure 11.2**  **Counting back or subtraction using both models and numerals.**

Notice how many ideas related to invented strategies and counting money are included in Activity 11.4. The next two activities push for the same thinking done mentally.

---

**ACTIVITY**

## 11.5 Moving Models Mentally

Display some tens and hundreds base-ten models on the overhead. Students say the number shown. Next tell how much will be added or subtracted, as in "minus 300," and have students say the result. Build another number and repeat. Finally, move to examples with trades. Show 820. "Minus 50." (Think: "Minus 20 is 800, and 30 more is 770.")

---

**ACTIVITY**

## 11.6 The Chain Game

Each student has one or more cards with a number written on it. After naming a start number, the teacher calls out, for example, "Plus 300" or "Minus 70." The student holding the result card calls out the result. Then the teacher reads the next change, and the chain continues. If the cards are prepared so that some numbers occur more than once, all students must remain alert even after their numbers have been called. Figure 11.3 illustrates the ideas with only seven cards.

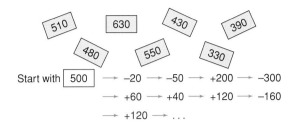

Start with [ 500 ] → –20 → –50 → +200 → –300 → +60 → +40 → +120 → –160 → +120 → . . .

**Figure 11.3** **A chain game for adding and subtracting tens and hundreds.**

# Thinking About Parts of Numbers

The activities in the previous section had children counting on or counting back in various ways. The next few activities focus on taking numbers apart.

─ **A**CTIVITY ─────────────────

## 11.7 Break It in Two Parts

Pick any two-digit or three-digit number. The task is to find ways to make the number in two parts. For example, 375 can be 300 and 75 or 215 and 160. Children should be permitted to use base-ten pieces or other models if they wish.

Several potential problems may arise from the last activity. Treat them as opportunities for learning. Children who do not have good place-value concepts may write 3 and 75 for 375. This may be inadvertent, or it may be a signal of a larger problem. Suggest modeling the number with base-ten pieces, and see how the child connects the pieces and the digits.

Some children may see an easy pattern: 374 and 1, 373 and 2, 372 and 3, and so on. Compliment the nice pattern. Then ask, "What would the other part be if one part is 120? Would you have to continue your pattern all the way to 120?"

The next activity is similar but focuses on parts of important nice numbers such as 50, 100, or 300.

─ **A**CTIVITY ─────────────────

## 11.8 The Other Part of 100

Give students a number, say, 28, and have them determine "the other part of 100" (72). Discuss strategies. If students are having difficulty with this, try using the little ten-frame cards (Blackline Masters). Show the given part of 100 with the little ten-frame cards as in Figure 11.4. When students are more adept, they can practice by themselves or

with a partner using their calculator. They make the calculator into a Parts of 100 Machine by pressing 100 [–] 100 [=]. Now when they press any number less than 100 followed by [=], the calculator will give the other part of 100 (with a minus sign).

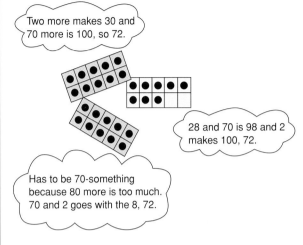

Two more makes 30 and 70 more is 100, so 72.

28 and 70 is 98 and 2 makes 100, 72.

Has to be 70-something because 80 more is too much. 70 and 2 goes with the 8, 72.

**Figure 11.4** **Using little ten-frames to help think about the "other part of 100."**

Students can play "The Other Part" of 50 or 200 or 450 or any round number; 50 is probably the best number to begin with. In the following activity, the nice number is seen as a part of another number. Often in computations, it is useful to recognize a nice part of a number, operate on that part, and then deal with the rest.

─ **A**CTIVITY ─────────────────

## 11.9 50 and Some More

Say a number between 50 and 100. Students respond with "50 and ___." For 63, the response is "50 and 13." Use other numbers that end in 50, such as "450 and Some More."

Compatible numbers for addition and subtraction are numbers that go together easily to make nice numbers. Numbers that make tens or hundreds are the most common examples. Compatible sums also include numbers that end in 5, 25, 50, or 75, since these numbers are easy to work with as well. The teaching task is to get students accustomed to looking for combinations that work together and then looking for these combinations in computational situations.

─ **A**CTIVITY ─────────────────

## 11.10 Compatible Pairs

Searching for compatible pairs can be done as a worksheet activity or with the full class using the overhead projector. Prepare a transparency, or duplicate a page with a search task. Five possibilities of different difficulty levels are shown in Figure 11.5. Students call out or connect the compatible pairs as they see them.

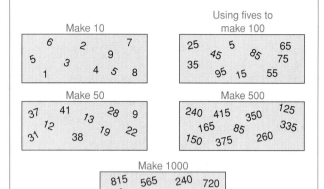

**Figure 11.5**  **Compatible-pair searches.**

---

## 11.11  Compatible Calculations

Present strings of numbers that use compatibles:

$$30 + 80 + 40 + 50 + 10$$
$$25 + 125 + 75 + 250 + 50$$
$$95 + 15 + 35 + 5 + 65$$

Strings such as these can be approached in two ways, and each should be practiced. One way is to search out compatible combinations such as 5 and 95 in the third example. The other way is simply to add one addend at a time, saying the result as you go. For the first example, that would be "30, 110, 150, 200, 210."

Change some of the operations to subtraction for a good variation.

## Flexible Thinking

Students may approach the following activities in a variety of ways. While they are good for workstation activities, it is often useful to have a class discussion of the strategies students are using.

## 11.12  Calculator Challenge Counting

Students press any number on the calculator (e.g., 17), then ⊞ 8. They say the sum before they press

⊟. Then they continue to add 8 mentally, challenging themselves to say the number before they press ⊟. They should see how far they can go before making a mistake.

The constant addend in "Challenge Counting" can be any number, even a two- or three-digit number. Try 20 or 25. Try 40 and then 48. As an added challenge, after a student has progressed eight or ten counts, have the student reverse the process by pressing ⊟ followed by the same number and then ⊟, ⊟, . . . Discuss patterns that appear.

## 11.13  Little Ten-Frame Addition and Subtraction

Provide a set of little ten-frame cards for each of two students. Each student makes a number with his or her cards. When both have their number ready, they place it out so both can see. Then they try to be the first to tell the total. For the subtraction version, one student makes a number greater than 50 and the other writes a number on paper that is less than 50. The written number is to be subtracted from the modeled number. Students should be encouraged to share strategies to see how fast they can get.

##  ASSESSMENT NOTES

The activities presented so far in this chapter not only develop appropriate number sense skills but also provide clues when students are having difficulty going beyond counting by ones when solving multidigit story problems. Students who exhibit difficulty with any of these activities will also have difficulty with almost any type of invented computation and certainly with the estimation activities to come. For example, how do students go about the exercises in Activity 11.4, "Numbers, Squares, Sticks, and Dots" (p. 196)? This activity demands that children have sufficient understanding of base-ten concepts that they can use them in meaningful counts. If students are counting by ones, perhaps on their fingers, then more practice with these activities may be misplaced. Consider additional counting and grouping activities (Chapter 9) where students have the opportunity to see the value of groups of ten. In Activity 11.7, "Break It in Two Parts" (p. 197), look for the types of numbers children use. Can they be encouraged to use parts that are nice or round numbers? When they select one part, how do they go about finding the other part? Perhaps the task should be modified to use numbers such as 20 or 30 so that you can see what number concepts are being employed.

These are just two examples of using the activities in this section in a diagnostic manner. Consider thinking about other activities in this way. Build them into a brief interview with students you need more information about.

# INTRODUCING COMPUTATIONAL ESTIMATION

The long-term goal of computational estimation is to be able quickly to produce an approximate result for a computation that will be adequate for the situation. In everyday life, estimation skills are valuable time savers. Many situations do not require an exact answer, so reaching for a calculator or a pencil is not necessary if one has good estimation skills.

Good estimators tend to employ a variety of computational strategies they have developed over time. Teaching these strategies to children has become a regular part of the curriculum. Beginning about grade 3, we can help children develop an understanding of what it means to estimate a computation and start to develop some early strategies that may be useful. From then on through middle school, children should continue to develop and add to their estimation strategies and skills.

## Understanding the Concept of an Estimate

Estimation of measures and quantities is a significant part of the measurement strand. Students estimate lengths, weights, and other measures as both a practical skill and a means to develop unit familiarity. Students also estimate quantities: How many jelly beans in the jar?

Computational estimation is a significantly different skill. There are no physical materials; it is not a visual task. Consider that computation has always meant "get the exact correct answer." Computational estimation involves some computation; it is not a guess at all. Since it is based on computation, how can there be different answers to estimates? The answer, of course, is that any particular estimate depends on the strategy used and the kinds of adjustments in the numbers that might be made. Estimates also tend to vary with the need for the estimate. Estimating your gas mileage is quite different from trying to decide if your last $5 will cover the three items you need at the Fast Mart. These are new and difficult ideas for young students.

## Suggestions for Estimation Instruction

Here are some general principles that are worth keeping in mind as you help your students develop estimation skills.

## Find Real Examples of Estimation

Discuss situations where computational estimations are used in real life. Some simple examples include figuring gas mileage, dealing with grocery store situations (doing comparative shopping, determining if there is enough to pay the bill), adding up distances in planning a trip, determining approximate yearly or monthly totals of all sorts of things (school supplies, haircuts, lawn-mowing income, time watching TV), and figuring the cost of going to a sporting event or show including transportation, tickets, and snacks. Help children see how each of these involves a computation (in contrast to measurement estimates). You could sit down with a calculator or pencil and paper and compute an exact answer. Discuss why exact answers are not necessary in some instances and why they are necessary in others. Look in a newspaper or magazine to find where numbers are the result of estimation and where they are the result of exact computations.

## Use the Language of Estimation

Words and phrases such as *about, close, just about, a little more* (or *less*) *than,* and *between* are part of the language of estimation. Students should understand that they are trying to get as close as possible using quick and easy methods, but there is no correct estimate. Language can help convey that idea.

## Build on Related Skills and Concepts

Estimation skills are related to mental computation skills and number sense. Most estimation strategies are based on the idea of using nice numbers that are close to the numbers in the computation. The nice-number substitutes lend themselves to a mental computation that was not possible with the actual numbers.

A real-world number sense also plays a role. Is $2.10, $21, or $210 most reasonable for thirty 69-cent soft drinks? It is much easier to focus on $7 \times 3$ and use a result that makes sense than to compute $0.69 \times 30$ and try to place the decimal correctly. Similar assists come from knowing if the cost of a car would likely be $950 or $9500. Could attendance at the school play be 30 or 300 or 3000? A simple computation can provide the important digits, with number sense providing the rest.

## Accept a Range of Estimates

What estimate would you give for $27 \times 325$? If you use $20 \times 300$, you might say 6000. Or you might use 25 for the 27, noting that four 25s make 100. Since $325 \div 4$ is about 81, that would make 8100. If you use $30 \times 300$, your estimate is 9000, and $30 \times 320$ gives an estimate of 9600. Is one of these "right"?

By listing the estimates of many students and letting students discuss how and why different estimates resulted, they can begin to see that estimates generally fall in a range around the exact answer. Different approaches provide different results. And don't forget the context. Some situations call for more careful estimates than others.

## Beginning Formats for Estimation

Consider the threat a third-grade student perceives when you ask for an estimate of the sum $349.29 + $85.99 + $175.25. The requirement is to come up with *a number*. Even textbooks, in an attempt to teach a particular estimation strategy, will lead students through a series of rounding and adding and come up with a singular answer. This is contrary to the idea of what an estimate really is: producing answers that are "good enough" for the purposes. The purposes often determine what we need to know. For the three prices, the question "About how much?" is quite different from "Is it more than $600?" How would you answer each of those questions?

Each activity that follows suggests a format for estimation where a specific numeric response is not required.

─ **A**CTIVITY ─────────────

## 11.14  Over or Under?

Prepare several estimation exercises on a transparency. With each, provide an "over or under number." In Figure 11.6, each is either over or under $1.50, but the number need not be the same for each task.

**Figure 11.6** *"Over or Under?"* is a good beginning estimation activity.

─ **A**CTIVITY ─────────────

## 11.15  Which One's Closest?

Make a transparency of a page of drill-and-practice computations (see Figure 11.7). Have students focus on a single row or other collection of five to eight problems. Ask them to find the one with an answer that is closest to some round number that you provide. One transparency could provide a week's worth of 5-minute drills.

Which of these is closest to 600? To 1000? To 100?

**Figure 11.7**  **A textbook drill page can be a good source of estimation exercises.**

─ **A**CTIVITY ─────────────

## 11.16  Best Choice

For any single estimation task, offer three or four possible estimates.

How close the choices are will determine the difficulty of the task. Sometimes it is a good idea to use multiples of ten, such as $21, $210, and $2100.

Even with these multiple-choice tasks, the three-part lesson format remains useful. Present the exercise, have students quickly write their choice on paper (this commits them to an answer), and then discuss why the choice was made. All three parts may take only 5 or 10 minutes. In the discussion, a wide variety of estimates and estimation methods will be shared. This will help students see that estimates fall in a range and that there is no single correct estimate or method.

# COMPUTATIONAL ESTIMATION STRATEGIES

Estimation strategies are specific algorithms that produce approximate results rather than exact results. The strategies discussed in this section are the ones good estimators use.

It is always a good idea simply to present an estimation task and see what strategies and ideas students will use, in much the same spirit as developing invented strategies. However, it is most likely that you will need to be more directive in suggesting at least some of these strategies. After introducing a strategy, you can have students practice it so that it is clearly understood.

When students have seen a variety of strategies, stop specifying which strategy to use. Rather, provide a task, and let students come up with an estimate using whatever strategy makes sense to them. Even in groups of three or four, students can each make an estimate and then compare both estimates and strategies. This helps in the selection of a strategy as well as in allowing for a range of answers.

# Front-End Methods

Front-end methods focus on the leading or leftmost digits in numbers, ignoring the rest. After an estimate is made on the basis of only these front-end digits, an adjustment can be made by noticing how much has been ignored.

## Front-End Addition and Subtraction

Front end is a good beginning strategy for addition or subtraction. This approach is reasonable when all or most of the numbers have the same number of digits. Figure 11.8 illustrates the idea. Notice that when a number has fewer digits than the rest, that number is ignored completely.

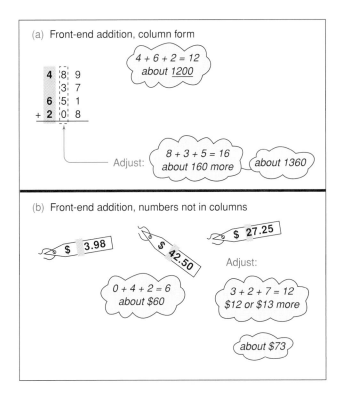

**Figure 11.8** **Front-end estimation in addition.**

After adding or subtracting the front digits, an adjustment is made to correct for the digits or numbers that were ignored. Making an adjustment is actually a separate skill. For young children, practice first just using the front digits. Pay special attention to numbers of uneven length when not in a column format.

When teaching this strategy, present additions or subtractions in column form, and cover all but the leading digits. Discuss the sum or difference estimate using these digits. Is it more or less than the actual amount? Is the estimate off by a little or a lot? Later, show numbers in horizontal form or on price tags that are not lined up. What numbers should be added?

The leading-digit strategy is easy to use and easy to teach because it does not require rounding or changing numbers. The numbers used are there and visible, so children can see what they are working with. It is a good first strategy for children as early as the third grade.

## Front-End Multiplication and Division

For multiplication and division, the front-end method uses the first digit in each factor. The computation is then done using zeros in the other positions. For example, a front-end estimation of $48 \times 7$ is 40 times 7, or 280. When both numbers have more than one digit, the front ends of both are used. For $452 \times 23$, consider $400 \times 20$, or 8000.

Division with pencil and paper is almost a front-end strategy already. First determine in which column the first digit of the quotient belongs. For $7\overline{)3482}$, the first digit is a 4 and belongs in the hundreds column, over the 4. Therefore, the front-end estimate is 400. This method always produces a low estimate, as students will quickly figure out. In this particular example, the answer is clearly much closer to 500, so 480 or 490 is a good adjustment.

# Rounding Methods

Rounding is the most familiar form of estimation. Estimation based on rounding is a way of changing the problem to one that is easier to work with mentally. Good estimators follow their mental computation with an adjustment to compensate for the rounding. To be useful in estimation, rounding should be flexible and well understood conceptually.

## Rounding in Addition and Subtraction

When a lot of numbers are to be added, it is usually a good idea to round them to the same place value. Keep a running sum as you round each number. In Figure 11.9 (p. 202), the same total is estimated two ways using rounding. A combination of the two is also possible.

In subtraction situations, there are only two numbers to deal with. For subtraction and for additions involving only two addends, it is generally necessary to round only one of the two numbers. For subtraction, round only the subtracted number. In $6724 - 1863$, round 1863 to 2000. Then it is easy: $6724 - 2000$ is 4724. Now adjust. You took away a

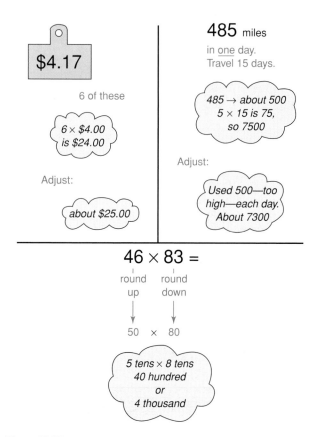

**Figure 11.9**  **Rounding in addition.**

bigger number, so the result must be too small. Adjust to about 4800. For 627 + 385, you might round 627 to 625 because multiples of 25 are almost as easy to work with as multiples of 10 or 100. After substituting 625 for 627, you may or may not want to round 385 to 375 or 400. The point is that there are no rigid rules. Choices depend on the relationships held by the estimator, on how quickly the estimate is needed, and on how accurate an estimate is required. The more adjusting and "playing around" with the numbers, the more accurate you are likely to be. After a while, however, you should reach for the calculator.

### Rounding in Multiplication and Division

The rounding strategy for multiplication is no different from that for other operations. However, the error involved can be significant, especially when both factors are rounded. In Figure 11.10, several multiplication situations are illustrated, and rounding is used to estimate each.

If one number can be rounded to 10, 100, or 1000, the resulting product is easy to determine without adjusting the other factor.

When one factor is a single digit, examine the other factor. Consider the product 7 × 836. If 836 is rounded to 800, the estimate is relatively easy and is low by 7 × 36. If a more accurate result is required, round 836 to 840, and add two partial products. Then the estimate is 5600 plus 280, or 5880 (7 × 800 and 7 × 40).

If possible, round only one factor—select the larger one if it is significantly larger. (Why?) For example, in 47 × 7821, 47 × 8000 is 376,000, but 50 × 8000 is 400,000.

Another good rule of thumb with multiplication is to round one factor up and the other down (even if that is not the closest round number). When estimating 86 × 28, 86 is between 80 and 90, but 28 is very close to 30. Try rounding 86 down to 80 and 28 up to 30. The actual product is 2408, only 8 off from the 80 × 30 estimate. If both numbers were

**Figure 11.10**  **Rounding in multiplication.**

rounded to the nearest 10, the estimate would be based on 90 × 30, with an error of nearly 300.

With one-digit divisors, it is almost always best to search for a compatible dividend rather than to round off. For example, $7\overline{)4325}$ is best estimated by using the close compatible number, 4200, to yield an estimate of 600. Rounding would suggest a dividend of 4000 or 4300, neither of which is very helpful.

When the divisor is a two-digit or three-digit number, rounding it to tens or hundreds makes looking for a missing factor much easier. For example, for $425\overline{)3890}$, round the divisor to 400. Then think, 400 times *what* is close to 3890?

## Using Compatible Numbers

When adding a long list of numbers, it is sometimes useful to look for two or three numbers that can be grouped to make 10 or 100. If numbers in the list can be adjusted slightly to produce these groups, that will make finding an estimate easier. This approach is illustrated in Figure 11.11.

In subtraction, it is often possible to adjust only one number to produce an easily observed difference, as illustrated in Figure 11.12.

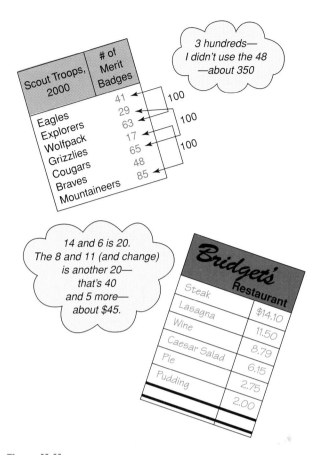

**Figure 11.11** **Compatibles used in addition.**

**Figure 11.12** **Compatibles can mean an adjustment that produces an easy difference.**

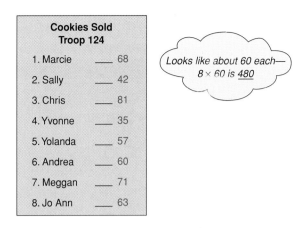

**Figure 11.13** **Estimating sums using averaging.**

**Figure 11.14** **Adjusting to simplify division.**

*Source:* From *GUESS (Guide to Using Estimation Skills and Strategies)* (box II, cards 2 and 3), by B. J. Reys and R. E. Reys, 1983, White Plains, NY: Dale Seymour Publications. Copyright 1983 by Dale Seymour Publications. Reprinted by permission of Dale Seymour Publications.

Frequently in the real world, an estimate is needed for a large list of addends that are relatively close. This might happen with a series of prices of similar items, attendance at a series of events in the same arena, cars passing a point on successive days, or other similar data. In these cases, as illustrated in Figure 11.13, a nice number can be selected as representative of each, and multiplication can be used to determine the total. This is more of an *averaging technique* than a compatible-numbers strategy.

One of the best uses of the compatible-numbers strategy is in division. The two exercises shown in Figure 11.14 illustrate adjusting the divisor or dividend (or both) to create a

division that comes out even and is therefore easy to do mentally. Many percent, fraction, and rate situations involve division, and the compatible-numbers strategy is quite useful, as shown in Figure 11.15 (p. 204).

73% of our 132 eighth graders watch more than 2 hours of TV per day.

> 73% → about 75% or $\frac{3}{4}$.
>
> If I use 120, one-fourth is 30 and three-fourths is 90. (That's probably a little low. I used a bigger percentage but fewer students.) About 90 to 95.

The chances of getting a winning lottery ticket are about 1 in 8. Zeke bought 60 tickets. About how many "winners" is reasonable?

> $\frac{1}{8}$ of 60 → $\frac{1}{8}$ of 64 is 8.
>
> About 7 or 8 winners.

A box of 36 thank-you cards is $6.95. How much is that per card?

> 36 × 2 is 72 → or 36 × 20 is 720.
>
> $6.95 is close to $7.20. So these cards cost a little less than 20¢ each.

**Figure 11.15** **Using compatible numbers in division.**

# ESTIMATION EXERCISES

The ideas presented so far illustrate some of the types of estimation and thought patterns you want to suggest to your students. But making up examples and putting them into a realistic context is not easy and is very time-consuming. Fortunately, good estimation material is now being included in virtually all textbooks. This exposure, however, will probably not be sufficient to provide an ongoing, intensive program for developing estimation skills. Try adding to the text using one or more of the many good teacher resource materials that are available commercially. Some of these are listed at the end of the chapter.

The examples presented here are not designed to teach estimation strategies but offer useful formats to provide your students with practice using skills as they are being developed. These will be a good addition to any estimation program.

## Calculator Activities

The calculator is not only a good source of estimation activities but also one of the reasons estimation is so important. In the

real world, we frequently hit a wrong key, leave off a zero or a decimal, or simply enter numbers incorrectly. An estimate of the expected result alerts us to these errors. The calculator as an estimation-teaching tool lets students work independently or in pairs in a challenging, fun way without fear of embarrassment. With a calculator for the overhead projector, some of the activities described here work very well with a full class.

┌─ **A**CTIVITY ─────────────────────────

### 11.17 The Range Game

This is an estimation game for any of the four operations. First pick a start number and an operation. The start number and operation are stored in the calculator. Students then take turns entering a number and pressing $\boxed{=}$ to try to make the result land in the target range. The following example for multiplication illustrates the activity: Suppose that a start number of 17 and a range of 800 to 830 are chosen. Press 17 $\boxed{\times}$ $\boxed{=}$ to store 17 as a factor. Press a number and then $\boxed{=}$. Perhaps you try 25. (Press 25 $\boxed{=}$.) The result is 425. That is about half the target. Try 50. The result is 850—maybe 2 or 3 too high. Try 48. The result is 816—in the target range! Figure 11.16 gives examples for all four operations. Prepare a list of start numbers and target ranges. Let students play in pairs to see who can hit the most targets on the list (Wheatley & Hersberger, 1986).

After entering the setup with the start # as shown, players take turns pressing a number, then $\boxed{=}$ to try to get a result in the target range.

Addition:

Press: 0 $\boxed{+}$ (start #) $\boxed{=}$

| START | | TARGET |
|---|---|---|
| 153 | ⟶ | 790 → 800 |
| 216 | ⟶ | 400 → 410 |
| 53 | ⟶ | 215 → 220 |

Subtraction:

Press: 0 $\boxed{-}$ (start #) $\boxed{=}$

| START | | TARGET |
|---|---|---|
| 18 | ⟶ | 25 → 30 |
| 41 | ⟶ | 630 → 635 |
| 129 | ⟶ | 475 → 485 |

Multiplication:

Press: (start #) $\boxed{\times}$ 0 $\boxed{=}$

| START | | TARGET |
|---|---|---|
| 67 | ⟶ | 1100 → 1200 |
| 143 | ⟶ | 3500 → 3600 |
| 39 | ⟶ | 1600 → 1700 |

Division:

Press: 0 $\boxed{\div}$ (start #) $\boxed{=}$

| START | | TARGET |
|---|---|---|
| 20 | ⟶ | 25 → 30 |
| 39 | ⟶ | 50 → 60 |
| 123 | ⟶ | 15 → 20 |

**Figure 11.16** **"The Range Game"—a calculator game.**

"The Range Game" can be played with an overhead calculator with the whole class, by an individual, or by two or three children with calculators who can race one another. The speed element is important. The width of the range and the type of numbers used can all be adjusted to suit the level of the class.

─ **A**CTIVITY ───────

### 11.18 Secret Sum

This calculator activity uses the memory feature. A target number is selected—for example, 100. Students take turns entering a number and pressing the ⊞ M+ ⊟ key. Each of the numbers is accumulated in the memory, but the sum is never displayed on the screen. If one player thinks that the other player has made the sum go beyond the target, he or she announces "over," and the ⊟ MRC ⊟ (memory return) key is pressed to check. If a player is able to hit the target exactly, bonus points can be awarded. Interesting strategies quickly develop.

"Secret Sum" can also be played with the ⊟ M− ⊟ key. First enter a total amount in the memory. Each player's number is followed by a press of ⊟ M− ⊟ and is subtracted from the memory. Here the first to announce correctly that the other player has made the memory go negative is the winner.

─ **A**CTIVITY ───────

### 11.19 The Range Game: Sequential Versions

Select a target range as before. Next enter the starting number in the calculator, and hand it to the first player. For addition and subtraction, the first player then presses either ⊞ or ⊟, followed by a number, and then ⊟. The next player begins his or her turn by entering ⊞ or ⊟ and an appropriate number, operating on the previous result. If the target is 423 to 425, a sequence of turns might go like this:

Start with 119.

  ⊞ 350 ⊟ ⟶ 469 (too high)
  ⊟ 42 ⊟ ⟶ 427 (a little over)
  ⊟ 3 ⊟ ⟶ 424 (success)

For multiplication or division, only one operation is used through the whole game. After the first or second turn, decimal factors are usually required. This variation provides excellent understanding of multiplication or division by decimals. A sequence for a target of 262 to 265 might be like this:

Start with 63.

  ⊠ 5 ⊟ ⟶ 315 (too high)
  ⊠ 0.7 ⊟ ⟶ 220.5 (too low)
  ⊠ 1.3 ⊟ ⟶ 286.65 (too high)
  ⊠ 0.9 ⊟ ⟶ 257.985 (too low)
  ⊠ 1.03 ⊟ ⟶ 265.72455 (very close!)

(**What would you press next?**)

Try a target of 76 to 80, begin with 495, and use only division.

## TECHNOLOGY NOTE

Estimation skills are often embedded in software drill-and-practice packages, although very few are designed for estimation skills alone. *Mega Math Blaster* (Davidson), *Power Rangers ZEO: Power Active Math* (MacWarehouse, 1996), and *CornerStone Mathematics, Grades 3–8* (SkillsBank, 1996) are three examples. *Power Rangers* has six levels for each of its skills, including one called "estimation," which proves to be exercises in rounding. The estimation activities in *Mega Math Blaster* are in an arcade format. This adds the useful element of speed but may be a turn-off for students who do not care for the format. *CornerStone Math* has test materials both in the software and in paper form that are useful for evaluation and practice in test taking.

The *Blue Falls Elementary* title in *Fizz & Martina's Math Adventures* (Tom Snyder Productions, 1998) includes three estimation problems in each of the four episodes. (The *Fizz & Martina* programs are each built around adventure stories with group problem solving in a realistic context.) Students are encouraged to estimate and then explain the strategy they have used. At least one strategy is provided. ■

## Activities for the Overhead Projector

The overhead projector offers several advantages. You can prepare the computational exercises ahead of time. You can control how long a particular computation is viewed by the students. There is no need to prepare handouts. Commercial materials such as GUESS cards (Figure 11.14, p. 203) can be copied onto transparencies for instructional purposes.

─ **A**CTIVITY ───────

### 11.20 What Was Your Method?

Select any single computational estimation problem, and put it on the board or overhead. Allow 10 seconds for each class member to get an estimate. Discuss briefly the various estimation techniques that were used. As a variation, prepare a problem with an estimation illustrated. For example, 139 × 43 might be estimated as 6000. Ask questions concerning this estimate: "How do you think that estimate was arrived at? Was that a good approach? How should it be adjusted? Why might someone select 150 instead of 140 as a substitute for 139?" Almost every estimate can involve different choices and methods. Alternatives make good discussions, helping students see different methods and learn that there is no single correct estimate.

---

### ▶ ᴀᴄᴛɪᴠɪᴛʏ

## 11.21  In the Ballpark

Using a page of problems from a workbook, write in answers to six or seven problems. On one or two problems, make a significant error that can be caught by estimation. For example, write 5408 ÷ 26 = 28 (instead of 208) or 36 × 17 = 342 (instead of 612). Other answers should be correct. Encourage the class to estimate each problem to find errors "not even in the ballpark."

---

# ESTIMATING WITH FRACTIONS, DECIMALS, AND PERCENTS

Fractions, decimals, and percents are three different notations for rational numbers. Many real-world situations that call for computational estimation involve the part-to-whole relationships of rational numbers. A few examples are suggested here:

> SALE! $51.99. Marked one-fourth off. What was the original price?
>
> About 62 percent of the 834 students bought their lunch last Wednesday. How many bought lunch?
>
> Tickets sold for $1.25. If attendance was 3124, about how much was the total gate?
>
> I drove 337 miles on 12.35 gallons of gas. How many miles per gallon did my car get?

The examples in this chapter have not used fractions, decimals, or percents. To estimate with such numbers first involves an ability to estimate with whole numbers. Beyond this, it involves an understanding of fractions and decimals and what these two types of numbers mean. Calculations with percents are always done as fractions or as decimals. The key is to be able to use an appropriate fraction or decimal equivalent.

In the first of the examples just presented, one approach is based on the realization that if $51.99 (or $52) is the result of one-fourth off, that means $52 is three-fourths of the total. So one-fourth is a third of $52, or a little less than $18. Thus about $52 + $18 = $70, or about $69, seems a fair estimate of the original cost. Notice that the conceptualization of the problem involves an understanding of fractions, but the estimation skill

involves only whole numbers. This is also the case for almost all problems involving fractions, decimals, or percents.

From a developmental perspective, it is important to see that the skills of estimation are separate from the conceptual knowledge of rational numbers. It would be a mistake to work on the difficult processes of estimation using fractions or percents if concepts of those numbers are poorly developed. In later chapters, where rational number numeration is discussed, it is shown that an ability to estimate can contribute to increased flexibility or number sense with fractions, decimals, and percents.

##  LITERATURE CONNECTIONS

Interesting literature often provides a diversionary context in which the mathematics may be a bit more fun and possibly more realistic. Even if realism in these two books is a bit stretched, the context makes a welcome change of pace.

### *The Twelve Circus Rings*
(Chwast, 1993)

Based on the same pattern as "The Twelve Days of Christmas," the 12 circus rings each contain more animals or more acts: "six acrobats, five dogs a-barking, four aerialists zooming, three monkeys playing, two elephants, and a daredevil on high wire." The colorful illustrations add to the excitement of the circus and the growing number of performers. After 12 days, how many aerialists are zooming? Remember that there are four aerialists not only in ring 4 but also in rings 5 through 12. The story lends itself to some early estimation but can easily be extended to create some fun questions. "About how much do the bows cost for all the dogs a-barking if each bow costs $1.29?" Both you and your students can make up estimation questions that challenge the skills you've been developing. In addition to the potential for both estimation and mental computation, the author also considers patterns as another extension.

### *The 329th Friend*
(Sharmat, 1979)

This book not only offers the opportunity to examine mental math strategies and practice in the context of the story but is also about friendship and the need to be liked. The story is about Emery Raccoon, who has no friends. Because he is lonely, Emery invites 328 strangers to lunch to make new friends. There are considerations about the number of dishes, knives, forks, and spoons that suggest multiplying 329 by small numbers and different ways of doing this. The story is easily expanded into other similar number questions. At the end, Emery discovers that although his guests ignored him, there was one friend that was there all along—himself.

## ASSESSMENT NOTES

Since estimation involves a certain element of speed, teachers often wonder how they can test it so that students are not computing on paper and then rounding the answer to look like an estimate. One method is to prepare a short list of about three estimation exercises on a transparency. The cards in the GUESS boxes (Reys & Reys, 1983) are a ready source for these, or you can simply write bare computations. Students have their paper ready as you very briefly show one exercise at a time on the overhead, perhaps for 20 seconds, depending on the task. Students write their estimate immediately and indicate if they think their estimate is "low" or "high"—that is, lower or higher than the exact computation.

They are not to do any written computation. Continue until you are finished. Then show all the exercises, and have students write down how they did each estimate. They should also indicate if they think the estimate was a good estimate or not so good and why. By only doing a few estimates but having the students reflect on them in this way, you actually receive more information than you would with just the answers to a longer list.

A theme of these assessment notes is that your students give you a lot of information each day, and all you have to do is record it. Information can be gathered from your daily estimation activities in much the same way as for invented strategy computations, by using a recording sheet for your observations (see Chapter 10).

# REFLECTIONS ON CHAPTER 11

## Writing to Learn

1. Describe specific examples where number sense plays a direct role in the development of invented computational strategies, mental computation, and estimation.

2. Why might the idea of an estimate for a computation be a difficult concept?

3. Describe each of the general strategies that were offered for conducting estimation activities.

4. Young children often find it difficult to come up with an estimate. What are the suggested techniques where students are required to estimate but not to actually produce an estimate?

5. Describe each of these estimation strategies. Be able to make up a good example and use it in your explanation.

   a. Front-end addition and subtraction.

   b. Front-end multiplication.

   c. Rounding in addition.

   d. Rounding in subtraction.

   e. Rounding in multiplication.

   f. Compatible numbers in addition and subtraction.

   g. Compatible numbers in division.

6. How can the calculator be used to practice estimation strategies?

## For Discussion and Exploration

1. In the past, the computation curriculum focused only on the traditional algorithms. There was only one way to compute. In the K–8 curriculum today, how much emphasis should be given to each of the forms of computation that have been discussed (invented strategies both with pencil and paper and mental, traditional algorithms and variations, and finally estimation)? Try to support your argument on the basis of real-world use.

2. Do the curriculum standards for your state require computational estimation? Mental computation? For "straightforward computation," is there any requirement that a particular algorithm or method of computation be used? How does your state's computational guidelines influence what computation methods are taught in school? Do you agree with what is required?

## Recommendations for Further Reading

### Highly Recommended

Bresser, R., & Holtzman, C. (1999). *Developing number sense: Grades 3–6.* Sausalito, CA: Math Solutions Publications.
Bresser and Holtzman are classroom teachers who have compiled 13 worthwhile number sense activities covering a range of topics including mental computation, number meanings, and estimation. With each activity, the authors provide pages of extensions, practical suggestions, and answers to questions concerning using the activity in the classroom. Most activities include examples of students' work.

Reys, R. E., & Nohda, N. (Eds.). (1994). *Computational alternatives for the twenty-first century: Cross-cultural perspectives from Japan and the United States.* Reston, VA: National Council of Teachers of Mathematics.
This book addresses similarities and differences in computation in the United States and Japan. Divided into three sections, the articles discuss mental computation, estimation, and the use of calculators in the two countries. Respected researchers from both countries have contributed to this work. Although not designed as a resource book, the thoughtful teacher will find practical ideas as well as interesting perspectives.

Reys, R. E., & Reys, B. J. (1983). *Guide to using estimation skills and strategies (GUESS)* (Boxes I and II). White Plains, NY: Cuisenaire–Dale Seymour.
Still among the best materials for teaching computational estimation strategies, these two hefty boxes of cards provide the

teacher of grades 4–8 with a complete program. Two of the cards are shown in Figure 11.14. Use them as transparencies, in small groups, or as independent work.

## Other Suggestions

Auriemma, S. H. (1999). How huge is a hundred? *Teaching Children Mathematics, 6,* 154–159.

Hunting, R. P. (1999). Rational-number learning in the early years: What is possible? In J. V. Copley (Ed.), *Mathematics in the early years* (pp. 80–87). Reston, VA: National Council of Teachers of Mathematics.

Leutzinger, L. P., Rathmell, E. C., & Urbatsch, T. D. (1986). Developing estimation skills in the primary grades. In H. L. Schoen (Ed.), *Estimation and mental computation* (pp. 82–92). Reston, VA: National Council of Teachers of Mathematics.

McIntosh, A., Reys, B. J., & Reys, R. E. (1997). *Number SENSE: Simple effective number sense experiences, grades 3–4.* White Plains, NY: Cuisenaire–Dale Seymour.

McIntosh, A., Reys, B. J., & Reys, R. E. (1997). *Number SENSE: Simple effective number sense experiences, grades 4–6.* White Plains, NY: Cuisenaire–Dale Seymour.

McIntosh, A., Reys, B. J., & Reys, R. E. (1997). *Number SENSE: Simple effective number sense experiences, grades 6–8.* White Plains, NY: Cuisenaire–Dale Seymour.

Reys, B. J. (1986). Teaching computational estimation: Concepts and strategies. In H. L. Schoen (Ed.), *Estimation and mental computation* (pp. 31–44). Reston, VA: National Council of Teachers of Mathematics.

Reys, R. E. (1998). Computation versus number sense. *Mathematics Teaching in the Middle School, 4,* 110–112.

Reys, R. E., Trafton, P. R., Reys, B. J., & Zawojewski, J. S. (1987). *Computational estimation (grades 6, 7, 8).* White Plains, NY: Cuisenaire–Dale Seymour.

Reys, R. E., & Yang, D. (1998). Relationship between computational performance and number sense among sixth- and eighth-grade students in Taiwan. *Journal for Research in Mathematics Education, 29,* 225–237.

Sowder, J. T., & Kelin, J. (1993). Number sense and related topics. In D. T. Owens (Ed.), *Research ideas for the classroom: Middle grades mathematics* (pp. 41–57). Old Tappan, NJ: Macmillan.

Sowder, J. T., & Wheeler, M. M. (1989). The development of concepts and strategies used in computational estimation. *Journal for Research in Mathematics Education, 20,* 130–146.

Thornton, C. A., Jones, G. A., & Neal, J. L. (1995). The 100s chart: A stepping stone to mental mathematics. *Teaching Children Mathematics, 1,* 480–483.

Trafton, P. R. (1986). Teaching computational estimation: Establishing an estimation mind-set. In H. L. Schoen (Ed.), *Estimation and mental computation* (pp. 16–30). Reston, VA: National Council of Teachers of Mathematics.

Van de Walle, J. A., & Watkins, K. B. (1993). Early development of number sense. In R. J. Jensen (Ed.), *Research ideas for the classroom: Early childhood mathematics* (pp. 127–150). Old Tappan, NJ: Macmillan.

# Chapter 12

# Developing Fraction Concepts

Fractions are not trivial concepts, even for middle school children. However, most programs teach some fraction ideas in grade 1 or 2 and have a full development of fraction concepts in grades 3 and 4.

A fraction is an expression of a relationship between a part and a whole. Helping children construct that relationship and connect it meaningfully to symbolism is the topic of this chapter.*

## BIG Ideas

1. Fractional parts are equal shares or equal-sized portions of a whole thing or a whole set.

2. Fractional parts have special names that tell how many parts of that size are needed to make a whole. For example, *thirds* require three parts to make a whole.

3. The more parts required to make a whole, the smaller the parts.

4. The numerator of a fraction tells how many parts are being considered. The denominator indicates the kind or size of parts the numerator counts.

5. Two equivalent fractions are two ways of describing the same amount using different-sized fractional parts.

---

*Technically, the relationship between a part and a whole is a *rational number,* and a fraction is one type of symbolism used to represent a rational number. This distinction between number and symbol is ignored in this book, however, primarily because it is not meaningful to children before approximately grade 8. The context will generally make the intent clear.

## THREE CATEGORIES OF FRACTION MODELS

Models must be used at all grade levels to develop fraction concepts adequately, and children should have experiences with a wide assortment of models. Three categories of models are presented here: region, length, and set. Most of the activities in the chapter can be done with all three model types. A change in the model usually marks a significant change in the activity from the viewpoint of the children. As you examine the ideas in the chapter, consider how the same activity could be done with different models and different types of models.

### Region or Area Models

In region models, a surface or area is subdivided into smaller parts. Each part can be compared with the whole. Figure 12.1 (p. 210) shows a variety of models in this category.

Circular regions and rectangle models can be duplicated on tagboard or construction paper, laminated, and cut into fraction kits kept in plastic bags. (Masters for circular models are included in the Blackline Masters and Materials Construction Tips.) Rectangles permit almost any piece to be designated as the whole so that other pieces change in fractional values accordingly. Pattern blocks, geoboards, and grid paper provide the same flexibility. With grid paper or dot paper, children can easily draw pictures to explore fraction ideas. Paper folding is a model available to everyone. Plastic area models are commercially available in several shapes.

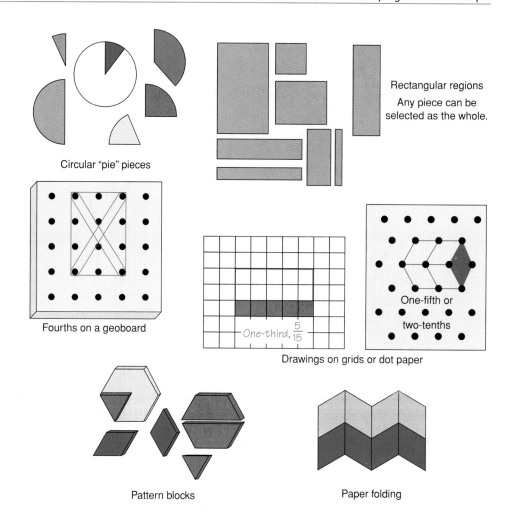

Circular "pie" pieces

Rectangular regions
Any piece can be
selected as the whole.

Fourths on a geoboard

One-third, $\frac{5}{15}$

One-fifth or
two-tenths

Drawings on grids or dot paper

**Figure 12.1** **Area or region models
for fractions.**

Pattern blocks

Paper folding

# Length or Measurement Models

With measurement models, lengths are compared instead of
areas. Either lines are drawn and subdivided, or physical
materials are compared on the basis of length, as shown in
Figure 12.2. Manipulative versions provide more opportunity for trial and error and for exploration.

Fraction strips are a teacher-made version of Cuisenaire
rods. Both the strips and the rods have pieces that are in
lengths of 1 to 10 measured in terms of the smallest strip or
rod. Each length is a different color for ease of identification.
As an alternative, strips of construction paper or adding-
machine tape can be folded to produce equal-sized subparts.
Older children can simply draw line segments on paper and
subdivide them visually.

The rod or strip model provides the most flexibility
while still having separate pieces for comparisons. To make
fraction strips, cut 11 different colors of poster board into
strips 2 cm wide. Cut the smallest strips into 2-cm squares.
Other strips are then 4, 6, 8, . . . , 20 cm, producing lengths
1 to 10 in terms of the smallest strip. Cut the last color into
strips 24 cm long to produce a 12 strip. If you are using
Cuisenaire rods, tape a red 2 rod to an orange 10 rod to
make a 12 rod. In this chapter's illustrations, the colors of

the strips will be the same as the corresponding lengths of
the Cuisenaire rods:

| 1 | White | 7 | Black |
|---|---|---|---|
| 2 | Red | 8 | Brown |
| 3 | Light green | 9 | Blue |
| 4 | Purple | 10 | Orange |
| 5 | Yellow | 12 | Pink or red-orange |
| 6 | Dark green | | |

The number line is a significantly more sophisticated
measurement model (Bright, Behr, Post, & Wachsmuth,
1988). From a child's vantage point, there is a real difference
between putting a number on a number line and comparing
one length to another. Each number on a line denotes the distance of the labeled point from zero. Place the numbers $\frac{2}{3}$ and
$\frac{3}{4}$ on a number line, and consider how a child would think
about these numbers in the context of that model.

# Set Models

In set models, the whole is understood to be a set of objects,
and subsets of the whole make up fractional parts. For exam-

Fraction strips or Cuisenaire rods

Number lines

Line segment drawings

Folded paper strips

**Figure 12.2** **Length or measurement models for fractions.**

ple, 3 objects are one-fourth of a set of 12 objects. The set of 12, in this example, represents the whole or 1. It is the idea of referring to a collection of counters as a single entity that makes set models difficult for primary school children. However, the set model helps establish important connections with many real-world uses of fractions and with ratio concepts. Figure 12.3 illustrates several set models for fractions.

Sets of 6

Two-color counters in arrays. Rows and columns help show parts. Each array makes a whole. Here $\frac{3}{5} = \frac{9}{15}$.

Two-color counters in loops drawn on paper.

Shows $1\frac{2}{6}$.

Drawings using Xs and Os.

Shows $\frac{2}{3} = \frac{10}{15}$.

**Figure 12.3** **Set models for fractions.**

Any type of counter can be used to model fractional parts of sets, including drawing Xs and Os. However, if the counters are colored in two colors on opposite sides, they can easily be flipped to change their color to model various fractional parts of a whole set. Two-sided counters can be purchased, or colored picture-mount board can be cut into 2-cm squares.

# DEVELOPING THE CONCEPT OF FRACTIONAL PARTS

Fractions are the first place in children's experiences where a number represents something other than a count. The notion of a fractional part is completely relative to the whole and, in terms of models, may consist of one piece in some instances and many pieces in others. Helping children develop a firm understanding of fractional parts and of all the related nuances is critical if children are to have any number sense with fractions.

## Constructing Fractional Parts

A first goal in the development of fractions is to help children construct the idea of *fractional parts of the whole*—the parts that result when the whole has been partitioned into *equal-sized portions* or *fair shares*.

The one idea that young children do bring to the concept of fractions is the notion of partitioning or sharing. Children seem to understand the idea of separating a quantity into two or more parts to be shared among friends. This understood concept of sharing is therefore a good place to begin the discussion of fractional parts.

### Two Requirements for Fractional Parts

In Figure 12.4 (p. 212), some of the regions are divided into fourths, and some are not. Examine those that are not fourths. Are they cut into *equal* or *fair shares?* If they are, why are they not fourths? (To have fourths, you need four parts making up the whole.) But other wholes are cut into four parts. Why are these not fourths? (The parts are not fair shares or equal parts.)

For any particular fractional part, children need to reflect on two aspects or components:

1. The whole must be made up of the *correct number* of parts or shares.
2. Each of the parts must be *equal* or *fair shares;* they must be the same size.

The *names* of fractional parts are determined by the number of fair shares making up the whole: *halves,* two fair shares; *thirds,* three fair shares; *fourths,* four fair shares; and so on.

Note that the equal parts need not be the same shape. Congruence is not necessary to have fractional parts. Nor should the concept of "part" be considered a singular entity. The term *share* may be more appropriate. For example, a

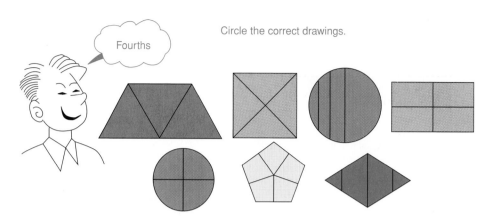

**Figure 12.4 Find correct examples of fourths. Why are the nonexamples wrong?**

pizza cut into 12 equal slices can be partitioned into four equal shares or parts. Each share would consist of three pieces. The fact that the individual slices are also fractional parts (twelfths) in no way negates the fact that three of them make up one-fourth of the pie.

We are in the habit of saying "four equal parts" when talking about fourths. The phrase comes out so quickly that the emphasis on the two requirements of four parts and fair shares may be lost.

Children can generalize the notion of fractional parts right from the beginning. A mistake that is frequently made is to assume that halves, thirds, and fourths are somehow easier than sixths, eighths, or twelfths. By introducing the general notion of fractional parts, children have more to explore and discuss. Once this generalization is made, all fractional parts are available. The traditional artificial restriction to one-half, one-third, and one-fourth in the early grades defeats learning more general relationships.

## Activities with Fractional Parts and Fraction Words

Fractional parts should be explored using all available models. The terminology of *the whole* or *one whole* or simply *one* should also be introduced informally at the same time. In all activities, the *fraction words—halves, thirds, fourths, fifths,* and so on—are used orally and written out. These fractional parts or equal shares are the nouns or things or objects of fractions. They are the building blocks of virtually all fraction concepts. The early emphasis is on *thirds* or *sixths,* not on one-third or one-sixth.

### ⓐCTIVITY
### 12.1 Correct Shares

As in Figure 12.4, show examples and nonexamples of specified fractional parts. Have students identify the wholes that are correctly divided into requested fractional parts and those that are not. For each response, have students explain their reasoning. The activity should be done with a variety of models, including length and set models.

In the "Correct Shares" activity, the most important part is the discussion of the nonexamples. The wholes are already partitioned either correctly or incorrectly, and the children were not involved in the partitioning. It is also useful for children to create designated equal shares given a whole, as they are asked to do in the next activity.

### ⓐCTIVITY
### 12.2 Finding Fair Shares

Give students models, and have them find fifths or eighths or other fractional parts using the models. (The models should never have fractions written on them.) The activity is especially interesting when different wholes can be designated in the same model. That way, a given fractional part does not get identified with a special shape or color but with the relationship of the part to the designated whole. Some ideas are suggested in Figure 12.5.

Folding paper is another good way to involve children in construction of fractional parts, as in Activity 12.2. Folds into halves, fourths, and eighths are the easiest because they are successive halves. With some help, children can fold strips into three parts and from these thirds fold sixths.

Having children draw slices to subdivide a circle or even a rectangle is very difficult and is not recommended. On a rectangle, children will frequently draw four lines for fourths and then realize they have made five parts. Others will make three nice equal parts and then realize that the last one is far too large for fourths. These and other difficulties with eye-hand coordination get in the way of concept development. Try to keep the focus on the number and fairness of the shares and less on the ability to draw them.

Notice when partitioning sets that children frequently confuse the number of counters in a share with the name of the share. In the example in Figure 12.5, the 12 counters are partitioned into four sets—*fourths.* Each share or part has 3 counters, but it is the number of shares that makes the partition show *fourths.*

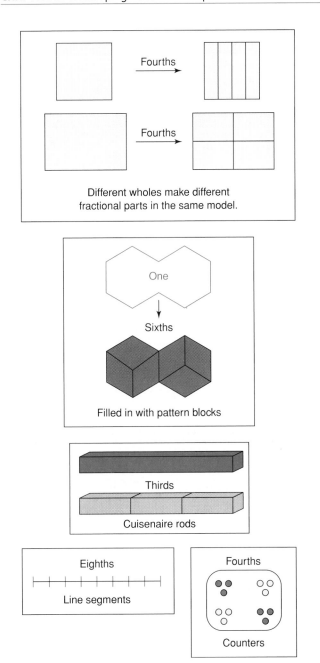

**Figure 12.5** Given a whole, find fractional parts.

## 12.3 Counting Fractional Parts

Once students have identified fourths, for example, count fourths. Show five or six fourths on the overhead. "How many fourths? Let's count: *one*-fourth, *two*-fourths, *three*-fourths, *four*-fourths, *five*-fourths, *six*-fourths." Count other collections of fourths. Ask if a collection that has been counted is more or less than a whole or more or less than two wholes. As shown in Figure 12.6, make informal comparisons among different counts. "Why did we get almost two wholes with seven-fourths, and yet we don't even have one whole with seven-twelfths? What is another way we could say seven-thirds?" (Two wholes and one-third or one whole and four-thirds.)

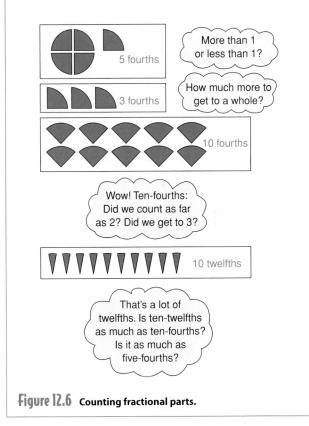

**Figure 12.6** Counting fractional parts.

## Counting Fractional Parts

The importance of fractional parts will become increasingly obvious as you read this chapter. Once fractional parts or equal shares are developed as ideas, they can then be called fourths or thirds or whatever and counted in the same way one counts apples or other objects. Fractions greater than one whole can similarly be understood this way. Seven-thirds is just seven things called thirds. By counting fractional parts, we can help children develop a completely generalized system for naming fractions before they learn about fraction symbolism. The oral names then can be connected easily to the fraction notation.

Counting fractional parts can lay the groundwork for several important ideas. The idea that eighths are smaller than thirds, for example, is an elusive idea. Counting different-sized parts and discussing how many parts it takes to make one whole is an opportunity to begin reflection on this idea. "Count three-fourths and then count three-twelfths. Which is more? Why?"

Counts should frequently include sets such as 5 thirds or 11 fourths or other sets greater than one whole. When the count gets to one whole (3 thirds or 4 fourths), stop and discuss other names for that amount. Such counts will dispel the notion that a fraction is something less than 1. With older children, counts can also be stopped at places where equivalent fractions are evident such as 6 twelfths (1 half) or 9 sixths (1 whole and 1 half). These discussions will provide nice forerunners for equivalent fractions and mixed fractions.

# Connecting Concepts with Symbolism

Fraction symbolism should be delayed as long as possible. The first three activities can all be done orally and with the use of written fraction words such as 7 *fourths* or 3 *eighths*. Eventually, the standard symbolic form must be used.

Always write fractions with a horizontal bar, not a slanted one. Write $\frac{3}{4}$, *not* 3/4.

## Meaning of the Top and Bottom Numbers

Consider a grocer who has developed a special way to take orders for his produce. If the order is for "seven apples and three bananas," he simply writes:

$$\frac{7}{A} \qquad \frac{3}{B}$$

The number on the top tells him *how many* items he needs. The letter on the bottom tells him *what* he needs. The grocer's idea can be used to explain fraction symbolism: The top counts, and the bottom tells what is counted.

Display several collections of fractional parts, and have children count each set and write the count using fraction words such as "3 fourths." Explain that you are going to show how these fraction words can be written more easily. For each collection, write the standard fraction next to the word. Display some other collections, and ask students if they can tell you how to write the fraction. Rather than an explanation, use the already developed oral language both with models and when writing the fraction symbols.

Next have children count by fourths as you write the fractions on the board. Repeat for other parts.

$$\frac{1}{4}, \frac{2}{4}, \frac{3}{4}, \frac{4}{4}, \frac{5}{4}, \frac{6}{4}, \frac{7}{4}, \frac{8}{4}, \frac{9}{4}$$

$$\frac{1}{6}, \frac{2}{6}, \frac{3}{6}, \frac{4}{6}, \frac{5}{6}, \frac{6}{6}, \frac{7}{6}, \frac{8}{6}, \frac{9}{6}$$

$$\frac{1}{8}, \frac{2}{8}, \frac{3}{8}, \frac{4}{8}, \frac{5}{8}, \frac{6}{8}, \frac{7}{8}, \frac{8}{8}, \frac{9}{8}$$

Discuss each row. How are the fractions alike? How are they different? What part of each row is like counting? Why does the bottom number stay the same as you count fourths or sixths or eighths? Finally, ask:

What does the top number in a fraction tell you?

What does the bottom number in a fraction tell you?

*Answer those two questions yourself.* Think in terms of fractional parts and what has been covered to this point. Write

your explanations for the meanings of top and bottom numbers using children's language. Explore several ways of saying each. Your meaning should not be tied to a particular model.

Here are some reasonable explanations for the top and bottom numbers.

- *Top number:* This is the counting number. It tells how many shares or parts we have. It tells how many have been counted. It tells how many parts we are talking about. It counts the parts or shares.
- *Bottom number:* This tells what is being counted. It tells what fractional part is being counted. If it is a 4, it means we are counting *fourths;* if it is a 6, we are counting *sixths;* and so on.

This formulation of the meanings of the top and bottom numbers may seem unusual to you. It is often said that the top number tells "how many" (this phrase seems unfinished) and the bottom tells "how many parts it takes to make a whole." This may be correct but can be misleading. For example, a $\frac{1}{6}$ piece is often cut from a cake without making any slices in the remaining $\frac{5}{6}$ of the cake. That the cake is only in two pieces does not change the fact that the piece taken is $\frac{1}{6}$. Or if a pizza is cut in 12 pieces, 2 pieces still make $\frac{1}{6}$ of the pizza. In neither of these instances does the bottom number tell how many pieces make a whole.

There is growing evidence that an iterative notion of fractions, one that views a fraction such as $\frac{3}{4}$ as a count of three things called *fourths,* is an important idea for children to develop (Post, Wachsmuth, Lesh, & Behr, 1985; Tzur, 1999). The iterative concept is most clear when focusing on these two ideas about fraction symbols:

- The top number *counts.*
- The bottom number tells *what is being counted.*

The *what* of fractions are the fractional parts. They can be counted. Fraction symbols are just a shorthand for saying *how many* and *what.*

## *Numerator* and *Denominator*

To count a set is to *enumerate* it. *Enumeration* is the process of counting. The common name for the top number in a fraction is the *numerator.*

A $1 bill, a $5 bill, and a $10 bill are said to be bills of different denominations. Similarly, the word *denomination* is used to differentiate among branches of religions (such as Baptists, Presbyterians, Episcopalians, and Catholics). A denomination is the name of a class or type of thing. The common name for the bottom number in a fraction is the *denominator.*

Up to this point, the terms *numerator* and *denominator* have not been used, as will be the case in most of the rest of the chapter. Why? No child in the third grade would mistake the designations *top number* and *bottom number.* The words *numerator* and *denominator* have no common reference for children. Whether these words are used or not, the words themselves will not help young children understand the meanings.

## Mixed Numbers and Improper Fractions

In the fourth National Assessment of Educational Progress, about 80 percent of seventh graders could change a mixed number to an improper fraction, but fewer than half knew that $5\frac{1}{4}$ was the same as $5 + \frac{1}{4}$ (Kouba et al., 1988a). The result indicates that many children are using a mindless rule that is in fact relatively easy to construct.

If you have been counting fractional parts beyond a whole, your students already know how to write $\frac{13}{6}$ or $\frac{11}{3}$. Ask, "What is another way that you could say 13 *sixths*?" Students may suggest "two wholes and one-sixth more," or "two plus one-sixth." Explain that these are correct and that $2 + \frac{1}{6}$ is usually written as $2\frac{1}{6}$ and is called a *mixed number.* Note that this is a symbolism convention and must be explained to children. What is not at all necessary is to teach a rule for converting mixed numbers to common fractions and the reverse. Rather, consider the following task.

┌─ **A**CTIVITY ─────────────────────

### 12.4 Mixed-Number Names

Give students a mixed number such as $3\frac{2}{5}$. Their task is to find a single fraction that names the same amount. They may use any familiar materials or make drawings, but they must be able to give an explanation for their result. Similarly, have students start with a fraction greater than 1, such as $\frac{17}{4}$, and have them determine the mixed number and provide a justification for their result.

└──────────────────────────────────

Repeat the "Mixed-Number Names" task several times with different fractions. After a while, challenge students to figure out the new fraction name without the use of models. A good explanation for $3\frac{1}{4}$ might be that there are 4 fourths in one whole, so there are 8 fourths in two wholes and 12 fourths in three wholes. The extra fourth makes 13 fourths in all, or $\frac{13}{4}$. (Note the iteration concept playing a role.)

There is absolutely no reason ever to provide a rule about multiplying the whole number by the bottom number and adding the top number. Nor should students need a rule about dividing the bottom number into the top to convert fractions to mixed numbers. These rules will readily be developed by the students but in their own words and with complete understanding.

┌─ **A**CTIVITY ─────────────────────

### 12.5 Calculator Fraction Counting

Calculators that permit fraction entries and displays are now quite common in schools. The TI-Math Explorer Plus and the Casio FX-55 are two examples. If these are available, they can be quite effective in helping children understand fraction symbolism. Counting by fourths, for example, can be done by pressing ⊞ 1 ⧄ 4 ⊟. The display will show 1/4.

Students should have models for fourths to manipulate as they count. When they add successive fourths to the pile, they press ⊟ for each piece. At four-fourths, the calculator shows 4/4. Continued presses simply add on to the numerator. To see the corresponding mixed number, press the ⎡a,b/c⎤ key. The mixed number for $\frac{6}{4}$ is shown as 1_2/4. Since the calculator will not reduce the fraction automatically, the count agrees with the physical models.

Fraction calculators provide an exciting and powerful way to help children develop fractional symbolism. A variation on Activity 12.5 is to show children a mixed number such as $3\frac{1}{8}$ and ask how many counts of $\frac{1}{8}$ on the calculator it will take to count that high. The students should try to stop at the correct number ($\frac{25}{8}$) before pressing the ⎡a,b/c⎤ key.

## Exercises with Parts and Wholes

The exercises presented here can help children develop their understanding of fractional parts as well as the meanings of the top and bottom numbers in a fraction. Models are used to represent wholes and parts of wholes. Written or oral fraction names represent the relationship between the parts and wholes. Given any two of these—whole, part, and fraction—the students can use their models to determine the third.

Any type of model can be used as long as different sizes can represent the whole. For region and area models, it is also necessary that single regions or lengths be used to represent nonunit fractions. Traditional pie pieces do not work because the whole is always the circle, and all the pieces are *unit fractions.* (A *unit fraction* is a single fractional part. The fractions $\frac{1}{3}$ and $\frac{1}{8}$ are unit fractions.)

Examples of each type of exercise are provided in Figure 12.7, Figure 12.8, and Figure 12.9 (p. 216). Each figure includes examples with a region model (freely drawn rectangles), a length model (Cuisenaire rods or fraction strips), and set models. It would be a good idea to work through these exercises before reading on. For the rectangle models, simply sketch a similar rectangle on paper. For the rod or strip models, use Cuisenaire rods or make fraction strips. The colors used correspond to the actual rod colors. Lengths are not given in the figures so that you will not be tempted to use an adult-type numeric approach. If you do not have access to rods or strips, just draw lines on paper. The process you use with lines will correspond to what is done with rods.

The questions that ask for the fraction when given the whole and part require a lot of trial and error and can frustrate young students. Be sure that appropriate fractional parts are available for the region and length versions of these questions.

Two or three challenging parts-and-whole questions can make an excellent lesson. The tasks should be presented to the class in just the same form as in Figures 12.7, 12.8, and 12.9. Physical models are often the best way to present the tasks so that students can use a trial-and-error

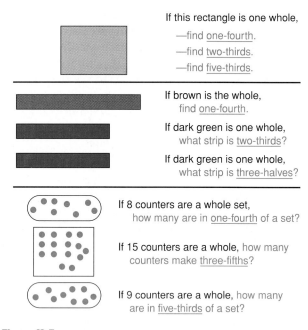

If this rectangle is one whole,
—find <u>one-fourth</u>.
—find <u>two-thirds</u>.
—find <u>five-thirds</u>.

If brown is the whole,
find <u>one-fourth</u>.

If dark green is one whole,
what strip is <u>two-thirds</u>?

If dark green is one whole,
what strip is <u>three-halves</u>?

If 8 counters are a whole set,
how many are in <u>one-fourth</u> of a set?

If 15 counters are a whole, how many
counters make <u>three-fifths</u>?

If 9 counters are a whole, how many
are in <u>five-thirds</u> of a set?

**Figure 12.7**   **Given the whole and the fraction, find the part.**

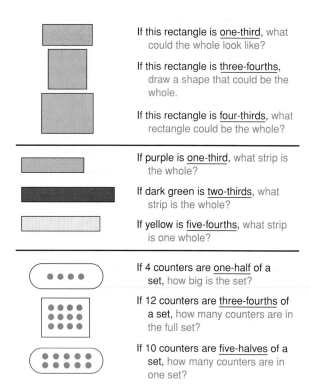

If this rectangle is <u>one-third</u>, what
could the whole look like?

If this rectangle is <u>three-fourths</u>,
draw a shape that could be the
whole.

If this rectangle is <u>four-thirds</u>, what
rectangle could be the whole?

If purple is <u>one-third</u>, what strip is
the whole?

If dark green is <u>two-thirds</u>, what
strip is the whole?

If yellow is <u>five-fourths</u>, what strip
is one whole?

If 4 counters are <u>one-half</u> of a
set, how big is the set?

If 12 counters are <u>three-fourths</u> of
a set, how many counters are in
the full set?

If 10 counters are <u>five-halves</u> of a
set, how many counters are in
one set?

**Figure 12.8**   **Given the part and the fraction, find the whole.**

approach to determine their results. As with all tasks, it
should be clear that an explanation is required to justify
each answer. For each task, let several students supply
answers and explanations.

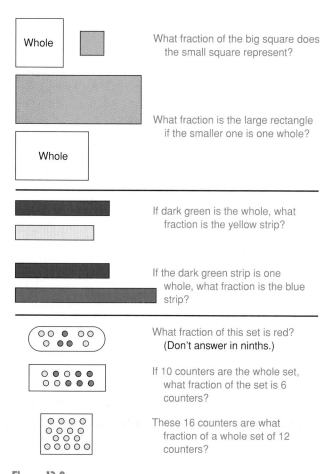

What fraction of the big square does
the small square represent?

What fraction is the large rectangle
if the smaller one is one whole?

If dark green is the whole, what
fraction is the yellow strip?

If the dark green strip is one
whole, what fraction is the blue
strip?

What fraction of this set is red?
(Don't answer in ninths.)

If 10 counters are the whole set,
what fraction of the set is 6
counters?

These 16 counters are what
fraction of a whole set of 12
counters?

**Figure 12.9**   **Given the whole and the part, find the fraction.**

Sometimes it is a good idea to create simple story problems that ask the same questions.

Mr. Samuels has finished $\frac{3}{4}$ of his patio. It looks like this:

Draw a picture that might be the shape of the finished
patio.

The problems can also involve numbers instead of
models:

If the swim team sold 400 raffle tickets, it would have
enough money to pay for new team shirts. So far the
swimmers have $\frac{5}{8}$ of the necessary raffle tickets sold.
How many more tickets do they need to sell?

In the second problem, the number 400 is easily divis-
ible by 8. If the total or whole had been given as 500, for

example, you could ask for "about" how many more tickets are necessary. The first problem asks for the whole, given the part and fraction. The second problem asks for the part, given the whole and fraction. Make up a story problem where the whole and part are given and the fraction is asked for.

With some models, it is necessary to be certain that the answer exists within the model. For example, if you were using fraction strips, you could ask, "If the blue strip (9) is the whole, what strip is two-thirds?" The answer is the 6 strip, or dark green. You could not ask students to find "three-fourths of the blue strip" because each fourth of 9 would be $2\frac{1}{4}$ units, and no strip has that length. Similar caution must be taken with rectangular pieces.

Questions involving unit fractions are generally the easiest. The hardest questions usually involve fractions greater than 1. For example, "If 15 chips are five-thirds of one whole set, how many chips are in a whole?" If asked in terms of a mixed number (15 chips are the same as $1\frac{2}{3}$), the question is even more difficult because it must first be translated to an improper fraction. However, in every question, the unit fraction plays a significant role. If you have $\frac{5}{3}$ and want the whole, you first need to find $\frac{1}{3}$.

Avoid being the answer book for your students. Make students responsible for determining the validity of their own answers. In these exercises, the results can always be confirmed in terms of what is given. Students will learn that they can understand these ideas. There are no obscure rules. Everything makes sense!

# FRACTION NUMBER SENSE

The focus on fractional parts is an important beginning because it helps students reflect on the meanings of the part-to-whole relationship and the corresponding meanings of the top and bottom numbers. But number sense with fractions demands more—it requires that students have some intuitive feel for fractions. They should know "about" how big a particular fraction is and be able to tell easily which of two fractions is larger. These ideas require building further on the relationships already discussed.

## Flexibility with Fractional Parts

Children have a tremendously strong mind-set about numbers that causes them difficulties with the relative size of fractions. In their experience, larger numbers mean "more." The tendency is to transfer this whole-number concept to fractions: Seven is more than four, so sevenths should be bigger than fourths (Mack, 1995). The inverse relationship between number of parts and size of parts cannot be told but must be a creation of each student's own thought process.

> **ACTIVITY**
> ## 12.6 Ordering Unit Fractions
> List a set of unit fractions such as $\frac{1}{3}$, $\frac{1}{8}$, $\frac{1}{5}$, and $\frac{1}{10}$. Ask children to put the fractions in order from least to most. Challenge children to defend the way they ordered the fractions. The first few times you do this activity, have them explain their ideas by using models. Encourage the language of sharing—the more shares in one whole, the smaller each share will be.

This idea is so basic to the understanding of fractions that arbitrary rules ("Larger bottom numbers mean smaller fractions") are not only inappropriate but dangerous. Come back to this basic idea periodically. Children will seem to understand one day and revert to their more comfortable ideas about big numbers a day or two later.

Another way to help children think about fractional parts in a flexible manner is similar to the way we help younger children think about small whole numbers: Take them apart.

> **ACTIVITY**
> ## 12.7 Taking Fractions Apart
> Assign a fraction to work with. For example, consider $1\frac{1}{4}$. The task is to find ways to write the fraction in terms of two parts. $1\frac{1}{4}$ is clearly 1 and $\frac{1}{4}$. But what are some other ways to think about this fraction in two parts? Have children make lists and see what they can find out. You will probably want to let them use a physical model, perhaps one of their own choosing. Or you may suggest that they do the activity without a model as a means of stretching themselves.

How children will approach Activity 12.7 will vary a lot with the age and experience of the children. The activity could be done at any grade from 3 to 8. Consider just a few possibilities for $1\frac{1}{4}$:

All ways to use fourths: $\frac{1}{4}$ and $\frac{4}{4}$, $\frac{2}{4}$ and $\frac{3}{4}$

All ways with some other denominator: $\frac{1}{8}$ and $\frac{9}{8}$, $\frac{2}{8}$ and $\frac{8}{8}$, $\frac{3}{8}$ and $\frac{7}{8}$, . . .

Using two or more different fractions: $\frac{1}{2}$ and $\frac{3}{4}$, $\frac{1}{3}$ and $\frac{2}{3}$ and $\frac{1}{4}$, or $\frac{1}{3}$ and $\frac{11}{12}$

Thinking in terms of money or decimals: 75 cents and 50 cents, 0.8 and 0.45

There is ample opportunity to develop patterns and relationships among fractions. As a variation, you could supply one part and ask children for one or more ways to determine what the other part is. Children will not think about this as subtraction but will use their own concepts to come up with solutions. This activity is a good assessment of how children are thinking about fractions.

# Benchmarks of Zero, One-Half, and One

The most important reference points or benchmarks for fractions are 0, $\frac{1}{2}$, and 1. For fractions less than 1, simply comparing them to these three numbers gives quite a lot of information. For example, $\frac{3}{20}$ is small, close to 0, whereas $\frac{3}{4}$ is between $\frac{1}{2}$ and 1. The fraction $\frac{9}{10}$ is quite close to 1. Since any fraction greater than 1 is a whole number plus an amount less than 1, the same reference points are just as helpful: $3\frac{3}{7}$ is almost $3\frac{1}{2}$.

---

**A**CTIVITY

## 12.8  Zero, One-Half, or One

On the board or overhead, write a collection of 10 to 15 fractions. A few should be greater than 1 ($\frac{9}{8}$ or $\frac{11}{10}$), with the others ranging from 0 to 1. Let students sort the fractions into three groups: those close to 0, close to $\frac{1}{2}$, and close to 1. For those close to $\frac{1}{2}$, have them decide if the fraction is more or less than $\frac{1}{2}$. The difficulty of this task is largely dependent on the fractions. The first time you try this, use fractions such as $\frac{1}{20}$, $\frac{53}{100}$, or $\frac{9}{10}$ that are very close to the three benchmarks. On subsequent days, use fractions with most of the denominators less than 20. You might include one or two fractions such as $\frac{2}{8}$ or $\frac{3}{4}$ that are exactly in between the benchmarks. As usual, require explanations for each fraction.

---

The next activity is also aimed at developing the same three reference points for fractions. In "Close Fractions," however, the students must come up with the fractions rather than sort them.

---

**A**CTIVITY

## 12.9  Close Fractions

Have your students name a fraction that is close to 1 but not more than 1. Next have them name another fraction that is even closer to 1 than that. For the second response, they have to explain why they believe the fraction is closer to 1 than the previous fraction. Continue for several fractions in the same manner, each one being closer to 1 than the previous fraction. Similarly, try close to 0 or close to $\frac{1}{2}$ (either under or over). The first several times you try this activity, let the students use models to help with their thinking. Later, see how well their explanations work when they cannot use models or drawings. Focus discussions on the relative size of fractional parts.

---

Understanding why a fraction is close to 0, $\frac{1}{2}$, or 1 is a good beginning for fraction number sense. It begins to focus on the size of fractions in an important yet simple manner. The next activity also helps students reflect on fraction size.

---

**A**CTIVITY

## 12.10  About How Much?

Draw a picture like one of those in Figure 12.10 (or prepare some ahead of time for the overhead). Have each student write down a fraction that he or she thinks is a good estimate of the amount shown (or the indicated mark on the number line). Listen without judgment to the ideas of several students, and discuss with them why any particular estimate might be a good one. There is no single correct answer, but estimates should be "in the ballpark." If children have difficulty coming up with an estimate, ask if they think the amount is closer to 0, $\frac{1}{2}$, or 1.

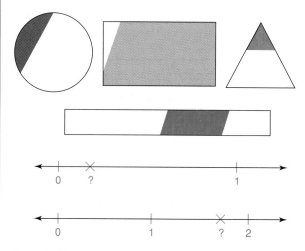

**Figure 12.10**   **About how much? Name a fraction for each drawing, and explain why you chose that fraction.**

---

# Thinking About Which Is More

The ability to tell which of two fractions is greater is another aspect of number sense with fractions. That ability is built around concepts of fractions, not on an algorithmic skill or symbolic tricks.

## Concepts, Not Rules

You have probably learned rules or algorithms for comparing two fractions. The usual approaches are finding common denominators and using cross-multiplication. These rules can be effective in getting correct answers but require no thought about the size of the fractions. This is especially true of the cross-multiplication procedure. If children are taught these rules before they have had the opportunity to think about the relative size of various fractions, there is little chance that they will develop any familiarity with or number sense about fraction size. Comparison activities (which fraction is more?) can play a significant role in helping children develop concepts of relative fraction sizes. But keep in mind that reflective thought is the goal, not an algorithmic method of choosing the correct answer.

Before reading further, try the following exercise. Assume for a moment that you know nothing about equivalent fractions or common denominators or cross-multiplication. Assume that you are a fourth- or fifth-grade student who was never taught these procedures. Now examine the pairs of fractions in Figure 12.11 and select the larger of each pair. Write down or explain one or more reasons for your choice in each case.

Which fraction in each pair is greater?
Give one or more reasons. Try not to use drawings or models.
<u>Do</u> not <u>use</u> common denominators or cross-multiplication.
Rely on concepts.

A. $\frac{4}{5}$ or $\frac{4}{9}$  G. $\frac{7}{12}$ or $\frac{5}{12}$

B. $\frac{4}{7}$ or $\frac{5}{7}$  H. $\frac{3}{5}$ or $\frac{3}{7}$

C. $\frac{3}{8}$ or $\frac{4}{10}$  I. $\frac{5}{8}$ or $\frac{6}{10}$

D. $\frac{5}{3}$ or $\frac{5}{8}$  J. $\frac{9}{8}$ or $\frac{4}{3}$

E. $\frac{3}{4}$ or $\frac{9}{10}$  K. $\frac{4}{6}$ or $\frac{7}{12}$

F. $\frac{3}{8}$ or $\frac{4}{7}$  L. $\frac{8}{9}$ or $\frac{7}{8}$

**Figure 12.11** **Comparing fractions using concepts.**

## Conceptual Thought Patterns for Comparison

The first two comparison schemes listed here rely on the meanings of the top and bottom numbers in fractions and on the relative sizes of unit fractional parts. The third and fourth ideas use the additional ideas of 0, $\frac{1}{2}$, and 1 as convenient anchors or benchmarks for thinking about the size of fractions.

1. *More of the same-size parts.* To compare $\frac{3}{8}$ and $\frac{5}{8}$, it is easy to think about having 3 of something and also 5 of the same thing. When the fractions are given orally, this is almost trivial. When given in written form, it is possible for children to choose $\frac{5}{8}$ as larger simply because 5 is more than 3 and the other numbers are the same. Right choice, wrong reason. Comparing $\frac{3}{8}$ and $\frac{5}{8}$ should be like comparing 3 apples and 5 apples.

2. *Same number of parts but parts of different sizes.* Consider the case of $\frac{3}{4}$ and $\frac{3}{7}$. If a whole is divided into 7 parts, the parts will certainly be smaller than if divided into only 4 parts. Many children will select $\frac{3}{7}$ as larger because 7 is more than 4 and the top numbers are the same. That approach yields correct choices when the parts are the same size, but it causes problems in this case. This is like

comparing 3 apples with 3 melons. You have the same number of things, but melons are larger.

3. *More and less than one-half or one whole.* The fraction pairs $\frac{3}{7}$ versus $\frac{5}{8}$ and $\frac{5}{4}$ versus $\frac{7}{8}$ do not lend themselves to either of the previous thought processes. In the first pair, $\frac{3}{7}$ is less than half of the number of sevenths needed to make a whole, and so $\frac{3}{7}$ is less than a half. Similarly, $\frac{5}{8}$ is more than a half. Therefore, $\frac{5}{8}$ is the larger fraction. The second pair is determined by noting that one fraction is less than 1 and the other is greater than 1. The benchmark numbers of $\frac{1}{2}$ and 1 are useful for making size judgments with fractions.

4. *Distance from one-half or one whole.* Why is $\frac{9}{10}$ greater than $\frac{3}{4}$? Not because the 9 and 10 are big numbers, although you will find that to be a common student response. Each is one fractional part away from one whole, and tenths are smaller than fourths. Similarly, notice that $\frac{5}{8}$ is smaller than $\frac{4}{6}$ because it is only one-eighth more than a half, while $\frac{4}{6}$ is a sixth more than a half. Can you use this basic idea to compare $\frac{3}{5}$ and $\frac{5}{9}$? (*Hint:* Each is half of a fractional part more than $\frac{1}{2}$.)

How did your reasons for choosing fractions in Figure 12.11 compare to these ideas?

Classroom activities should help children develop informal ideas like those just explained for comparing fractions. However, the ideas should come from student experiences and discussions. To teach "the four ways to compare fractions" would be nearly as defeating as teaching cross-multiplication.

### ACTIVITY
### 12.11 Compare and Test

Provide students with a familiar fraction model. Present a pair of fractions for comparison. (They should be fractions that can be illustrated with the model.) Have the students think about which is more (compare), write down their choice, and then test their selection with the models. Be sure they make a commitment first, before they use the models.

When students begin to do well with the "Compare and Test" activity, see if they can give reasons without the use of models. Be sure you include fraction pairs that cover all of the possibilities discussed earlier.

### ACTIVITY
### 12.12 Why Is It More?

Give students a pair of fractions to compare. The task is to find as many good explanations for their choice as possible. Explanations should be written down and then discussed as a full class. The same exercise is a very good homework assignment and is also a good assessment activity.

ACTIVITY

### 12.13 Line 'Em Up

Have students put four or five fractions in order from least to most. In this way, a variety of methods for making comparisons can be included in the same exercise. As with all conceptual fraction activities, limit the denominators to reasonable numbers. It is rarely necessary to consider fractions with denominators greater than 12.

A word of caution is implicit in the following situation. Mark is offered the choice of a third of a pizza or a half of a pizza. Since he is hungry and likes pizza, he chooses the half. His friend Jane gets a third of a pizza but ends up with more than Mark. How can that be? Figure 12.12 illustrates how Mark got misdirected in his choice. The point of the "pizza fallacy" is that whenever two or more fractions are discussed in the same context, the correct assumption (the one Mark made in choosing a half of the pizza) is that the fractions are all parts of the same whole.

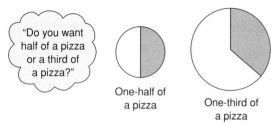

What assumption is made when answering this question?

**Figure 12.12**   The "pizza fallacy."

Comparisons with any model can be made only if both fractions are parts of the same whole. For example, $\frac{2}{3}$ of a light green strip cannot be compared to $\frac{2}{5}$ of an orange strip.

## Other Methods of Comparison

Not all fractions can be compared by reliance on the conceptual approaches that have been discussed. Most adults would be hard-pressed to compare $\frac{2}{3}$ and $\frac{3}{5}$ without some other methods.

When simple methods fail, a more sophisticated and usually more complex method is required. The most common approach is to convert the fraction to some other form. When equivalent fractions are well developed, one or both of the fractions can be rewritten so that both fractions have the same denominator. Although common denominator is the most often taught method, why not use a common numerator? Another idea is to translate the fraction to a different notation—decimals or percents. Many decimal and percent equivalents can and should become second nature and require no computation.

With good fraction concept development, you can easily argue that there is never a need to teach an algorithm for comparing two fractions. The repeated application of rules permits students to stop thinking about fraction size. When students have a good understanding of equivalent fractions and the equivalent representation of fractions as decimals and percents, they will have plenty of meaningful tools to compare fractions. Marilyn Burns (1999) told of fifth graders comparing $\frac{6}{8}$ to $\frac{4}{5}$. One child changed the $\frac{4}{5}$ to $\frac{8}{10}$ so that both fractions would be two parts away from a whole. Since tenths are smaller than eighths, he concluded that $\frac{4}{5}$ was larger. Another child used common numerators. When percents are connected to fractions, these two fractions might quickly be seen as 75 percent and 80 percent and compared that way.

Remember, restrict comparison exercises to fractions with denominators of 12 or less.

## TECHNOLOGY NOTE

*Representing Fractions* (Tenth Planet, 1998d) is software that offers a range of challenges for fraction development. In two of the four activities, students build given fractions using models of unit fractions. Though not open-ended, these activities may reinforce the iterative concept of fractions. The computer orally counts to the fraction target when a solution is offered: "One-fourth, two-fourths, three-fourths." Another task area requires students to build a whole based on a given fractional part. This activity is similar to building a whole with fraction strips, given the fraction and the part as described earlier in this chapter.

"Open-Ended Build and Play" is a component of *Representing Fractions* in which the user can slice up squares, circles, or triangles by connecting equally spaced dots on the edges. Parts can then be cut into even smaller pieces. The individual pieces can be painted different colors and dragged to any part of the screen. This open-ended model provides teachers or students with a tool that is more flexible than any physical model. Note that this is a pure model or tool. No fraction symbols are provided, nor are any problems posed. The computer does no evaluation. The teacher can pose tasks and let students use the program to work on solutions. Alternatively, students can devise their own challenges for each other using the drawing tool. As with all Tenth Planet activities, a journal permits students to copy a picture of their work, write about it, and even record a short message.

*Fizz & Martina's Math Adventures: Lights, Camera, Fractions* (Tom Snyder Productions, 1998) is software supposedly designed for grades 5 and 6. However, the concepts and presentation are closer to grade 4. Fraction problems are embedded in an elaborate cartoon video involving Fizz and Martina. The software is designed to be shown to a full class and stopped at appropriate times to let students work in groups to solve the problem and write on the journal sheets provided. Multiple-solution strategies are encouraged. The problems are good, but the story line is a bit corny and very time-intensive. Most tasks involve finding fractional parts of amounts ($\frac{1}{4}$ of 120 words, $\frac{2}{3}$ of $180). The ideas and the support material are good, and the program is designed in the same spirit as the three-part lesson format described in this text. Since each episode involves only a few problems, the program is somewhat limited in its use. ■

## Estimation

A frequently quoted result from the Second National Assessment (Post, 1981) concerns the following item:

**Estimate the answer to $\frac{12}{13} + \frac{7}{8}$. You will not have time to solve the problem using paper and pencil.**

Here is how 13-year-olds answered:

| Response | Percent of 13-Year-Olds |
|----------|-------------------------|
| 1 | 7 |
| 2 | 24 |
| 19 | 28 |
| 21 | 27 |
| Don't know | 14 |

This result vividly demonstrates that a good concept of fractions is more significant for estimation purposes than mastery of the pencil-and-paper procedures. Knowing if a fraction is closer to 0, $\frac{1}{2}$, or 1 proves quite useful. Numbers can be rounded to the nearest whole or nearest half and then added easily. For example, $2\frac{1}{8} + \frac{4}{9}$ is about the same as $2 + \frac{1}{2}$. A front-end approach is also possible: Deal with the whole numbers, and then look at the fractions using estimates to the nearest half to make an adjustment. The following activities are useful for developing these ideas.

┌─ **A**CTIVITY ─────────────────────

### 12.14  Pick the Best

**Flash sums or differences of proper fractions. Response options can vary with the age and experience of the students. More than 1 or less than 1 is one alternative. Closer to 0, 1, or 2 is also an easy option. A more sophisticated option is to give the result to the nearest half: 0, $\frac{1}{2}$, 1, $1\frac{1}{2}$, or 2.**

┌─ **A**CTIVITY ─────────────────────

### 12.15  Speed Estimates

**Provide short speed drills for estimating sums and differences with mixed numbers, as illustrated in Figure 12.13.**

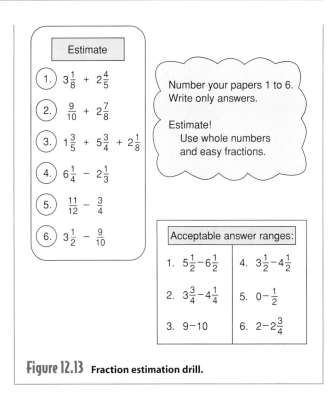

Estimate

1.) $3\frac{1}{8} + 2\frac{4}{5}$

2.) $\frac{9}{10} + 2\frac{7}{8}$

3.) $1\frac{3}{5} + 5\frac{3}{4} + 2\frac{1}{8}$

4.) $6\frac{1}{4} - 2\frac{1}{3}$

5.) $\frac{11}{12} - \frac{3}{4}$

6.) $3\frac{1}{2} - \frac{9}{10}$

Number your papers 1 to 6. Write only answers.

Estimate!
Use whole numbers
and easy fractions.

| Acceptable answer ranges: | |
|---------------------------|---|
| 1. $5\frac{1}{2} - 6\frac{1}{2}$ | 4. $3\frac{1}{2} - 4\frac{1}{2}$ |
| 2. $3\frac{3}{4} - 4\frac{1}{4}$ | 5. $0 - \frac{1}{2}$ |
| 3. $9 - 10$ | 6. $2 - 2\frac{3}{4}$ |

**Figure 12.13** **Fraction estimation drill.**

When more than two addends are involved, an acceptable range may be a bit wider. Encourage students to give whole-number estimates at first, and later practice refining estimates to the nearest half. Discuss both front-end and rounding techniques.

# EQUIVALENT-FRACTION CONCEPTS

How do you know that $\frac{4}{6} = \frac{2}{3}$? Before reading further, think of at least two different explanations.

## Concepts Versus Rules

Here are some possible answers to the question just posed:

1. They are the same because you can reduce $\frac{4}{6}$ and get $\frac{2}{3}$.

2. If you have a set of 6 things and you take 4 of them, that would be $\frac{4}{6}$. But you can make the 6 into groups of 2. So then there would be 3 groups, and the 4 would be 2 groups out of the 3 groups. That means it's $\frac{2}{3}$.

3. If you start with $\frac{2}{3}$, you can multiply the top and the bottom numbers by 2, and that will give you $\frac{4}{6}$, so they are equal.

4. If you had a square cut into 3 parts and you shaded 2, that would be $\frac{2}{3}$ shaded. If you cut all 3 of these parts in half, that would be 4 parts shaded and 6 parts in all. That's $\frac{4}{6}$, and it would be the same amount.

These answers, all correct, exemplify the distinction between conceptual and procedural knowledge. Responses 2 and 4 are very conceptual, although not efficient. The procedural responses, 1 and 3, are quite efficient but indicate no conceptual knowledge. All students should eventually know how to write an equivalent fraction for a given fraction. At the same time, the rules should never be taught or used until the students understand what the result means.

> *Concept:* Two fractions are equivalent if they are representations for the same amount or quantity—if they are the same number.
>
> *Rule:* To get an equivalent fraction, multiply (or divide) the top and bottom numbers by the same nonzero number.

The rule or algorithm for equivalent fractions has no intuitive connection with the concept. As a result, students can easily learn and use the rule in exercises such as "List the first four equivalent fractions for $\frac{3}{5}$" without any idea of how the fractions in the list are related. It becomes an exercise in

multiplication. A developmental approach suggests that students should be led to see that the algorithm is a meaningful and efficient way to find equivalent fractions.

# Finding Different Names for Fractions

The general approach to a conceptual understanding of equivalent fractions is to have students use models to generate different names for models of fractions.

## Area or Region Models

Examples of equivalent fraction representations using area models are illustrated in Figure 12.14.

---

**A**CTIVITY

### 12.16 Different Fillers

Using the models that students have, draw the outline of several fractions on paper, and duplicate them. For example, if the model is rectangles, you might draw an outline (no subdivisions) of a rectangle for $\frac{2}{3}$, $\frac{1}{2}$, and perhaps $\frac{5}{4}$. Have children try to fill the outlines with various unit fraction pieces to determine as many simple fraction names for the regions as possible. In class discussion, see if students can go beyond the actual models they have. For example, if the model has no tenths, it would be interesting to ask what other names could be generated if tenths were available. An easier question involves pieces that can be derived

---

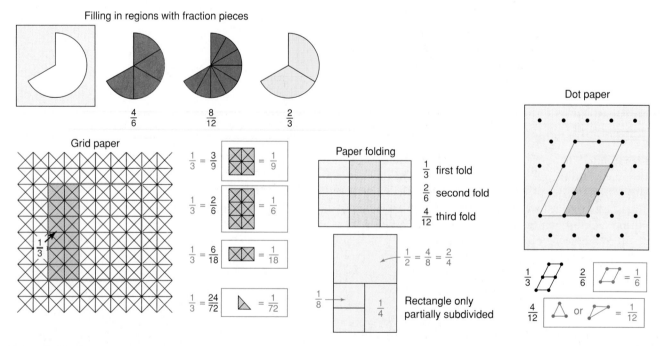

**Figure 12.14**   **Area models for equivalent fractions.**

from existing pieces. "You found out that $\frac{5}{4}$ and $\frac{10}{8}$ and $\frac{15}{12}$ are all the same. What if we had some sixteenths pieces? Could we cover this same region with those? How many? How can you decide?"

---

**ACTIVITY**

## 12.17 Folding and Refolding

Paper folding effectively models the equivalent fraction concept. Have students fold a sheet of paper into halves or thirds. Unfold and color a fraction of the paper. Write the fraction. Now refold and add one more fold. It is fun to discuss, before opening, how many sections will be in the whole sheet and how many will be colored. Open and discuss what fraction names can now be given to the shaded region. Is it still the same? Why? Repeat until the paper cannot be folded any more.

---

**ACTIVITY**

## 12.18 Dot Paper Equivalencies

Use grid paper or dot paper so that regions can easily be subdivided into many smaller parts. Have students draw a model for a whole and shade in some fraction that can be determined using the lines or dots on the paper. Now see how many different names for the shaded part they can find with the aid of the smaller regions in the drawing (see Figure 12.14). Make a transparency of a grid or dot pattern, and do this exercise with the full class. Teams or individuals can take turns explaining different names for the shaded part.

---

Although subdivided regions illustrate why there are multiple names for one fractional part, students should learn that the existence of the subdivisions is not required. Half of a rectangle is still $\frac{2}{4}$, even if no subdivisions are present and even if the other half is divided into three parts. Work toward this understanding by drawing models for fractions and then erasing the subdivision lines. "Is this $\frac{2}{3}$ still $\frac{4}{6}$?"

## Length Models
Equivalent fractions are modeled with length models in much the same way as area models. One fraction is modeled, and then different lengths are used to determine other fraction names. Some examples are shown in Figure 12.15.

## Set Models
The general concept of equivalent fractions is the same with set models as with length and area models, although there are more limitations to how a particular set can be partitioned.

**Figure 12.15** **Length models for equivalent fractions.**

For example, if $\frac{2}{3}$ is modeled with 8 out of 12 counters, that particular representation can also be seen as $\frac{4}{6}$ and $\frac{8}{12}$ but not as $\frac{6}{9}$ or $\frac{10}{15}$. As shown in Figure 12.16 (p. 224), a given number of counters in two colors can be arranged in different subgroups to illustrate equivalent fractions.

---

**ACTIVITY**

## 12.19 Arrange the Counters, Find the Names

Have students set out a specific number of counters in two colors—for example, 32 counters, 24 of them red and the rest yellow. This set will be the whole. Then have them find as many names as they can for each color by arranging the counters into different subgroups. Drawings can be made using Xs and Os to produce a written record of the activity.

---

## A Transitional Activity
Each of the following four equations is typical of equivalent fraction exercises found in textbooks. Notice the differences among the examples.

$$\frac{5}{3} = \frac{\square}{6} \qquad \frac{2}{3} = \frac{6}{\square} \qquad \frac{8}{12} = \frac{\square}{3} \qquad \frac{12}{8} = \frac{3}{\square}$$

An excellent task is to have students complete an equation of this type by using a model to determine the missing number. Some care must be taken to select exercises that can be solved with the model being used. For example, most pie-piece sets do not have ninths. Counters are a model that can always be used. Make students responsible for justifying their results with the use of models or drawings. Explanations

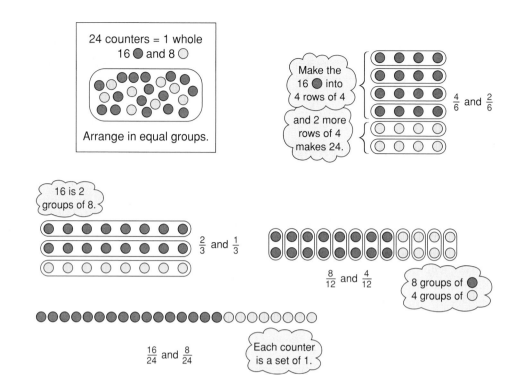

**Figure 12.16** **Set models for equivalent fractions.**

$\frac{16}{24}$ and $\frac{8}{24}$

should be shared with the class. Kamii and Clark (1995) argue that undue reliance on physical models does not help children construct equivalence schemes. When children understand that fractions can have different names, they should be challenged to develop a method for finding equivalent names.

# Developing an Equivalent-Fraction Algorithm

## An Area Model Approach

Though there are many possible ways to model the procedure of multiplying top and bottom numbers by the same number, the most commonly used approach is to slice a square in two directions.

── **A**CTIVITY ────────────

### 12.20 Slicing Squares

Give students paper with rows of squares about 3 cm on each side. Have them shade the same fraction in several squares using vertical subdividing lines. Next slice each rectangle horizontally into different fractional parts, as shown in Figure 12.17. Help students focus on the products involved by having them write the top and bottom numbers in the fraction as a product. Notice that for each model, the top and bottom numbers will always have a common factor. (Paper folding provides a similar result.)

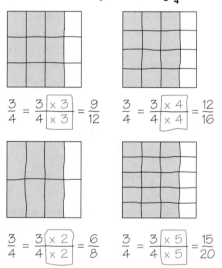

Start with each square showing $\frac{3}{4}$.

$\frac{3}{4} = \frac{3 \times 3}{4 \times 3} = \frac{9}{12}$       $\frac{3}{4} = \frac{3 \times 4}{4 \times 4} = \frac{12}{16}$

$\frac{3}{4} = \frac{3 \times 2}{4 \times 2} = \frac{6}{8}$       $\frac{3}{4} = \frac{3 \times 5}{4 \times 5} = \frac{15}{20}$

What <u>product</u> tells how many parts are shaded?
What <u>product</u> tells how many parts in the whole?
Notice that the same factor is used for both part and whole.

**Figure 12.17** **A model for the equivalent-fraction algorithm.**

Examine examples of equivalent fractions that have been generated with other models, and see if the rule of multiplying top and bottom numbers by the same number holds there also. If the rule is correct, how can $\frac{6}{8}$ and $\frac{9}{12}$ be equivalent?

What about fractions like $2\frac{1}{4}$? How could it be demonstrated that $\frac{9}{4}$ is the same as $\frac{27}{12}$?

## Writing Fractions in Simplest Terms

The multiplication rule for equivalent fractions produces fractions with larger denominators. To write a fraction in *simplest terms* means to write it so that numerator and denominator have no common whole number factors. (Some texts use the name *lowest terms* instead of *simplest terms*.) One meaningful approach to this task of finding simplest terms is to reverse the earlier process, as illustrated in Figure 12.18. Try to devise a problematic task that will help students develop this reverse idea.

Lower terms →

$$\frac{8}{12} = \frac{2\ \times\ 4}{3\ \times\ 4} = \frac{2}{3}$$

← Higher terms

**Figure 12.18** Using the equivalent-fraction algorithm to write fractions in simplest terms.

Of course, finding and eliminating a common factor is the same as dividing both top and bottom by the same number. The search for a common factor keeps the process of writing an equivalent fraction to one rule: Top and bottom numbers of a fraction can be multiplied by the same nonzero number. There is no need for a different rule for rewriting fractions in lowest terms.

Two additional notes:

1. Notice that the phrase "reducing fractions" was not used. This unfortunate terminology implies making a fraction smaller and is rarely used anymore in textbooks.

2. Many teachers seem to believe that fraction answers are incorrect if not in simplest or lowest terms. This is also unfortunate. When students add $\frac{1}{6} + \frac{1}{2}$ and get $\frac{4}{6}$, they have added correctly and have found the answer. Rewriting $\frac{4}{6}$ as $\frac{2}{3}$ is a separate issue.

## Multiplying by One

Many junior high textbooks use a strictly symbolic approach to equivalent fractions. It is based on the multiplication identity property of rational numbers that says that any number multiplied by 1 remains unchanged. Any fraction of the form $\frac{n}{n}$ can be used as the identity element. Therefore, $\frac{3}{4} = \frac{3}{4} \times 1 = \frac{3}{4} \times \frac{2}{2} = \frac{6}{8}$. Furthermore, the numerator and denominator of the identity element can also be fractions. In this way, $\frac{6}{12} = \frac{6}{12} \times \left(\frac{1/6}{1/6}\right) = \frac{1}{2}$.

This explanation relies on an understanding of the multiplicative identity property, which most students in grades 4 to 6 do not fully appreciate. It also relies on the procedure for multiplying two fractions. Finally, the argument uses solely

deductive reasoning based on an axiom of the rational number system. It does not lend itself to intuitive modeling. A reasonable conclusion is to delay this important explanation until at least seventh or eighth grade in an appropriate pre-algebra context and not as a method or a rationale for producing equivalent fractions.

# TECHNOLOGY NOTE

A lot of computer software seems to be better at providing a high-tech model to illustrate equivalent fractions than it does at creating a problem-solving mode where students can think through an equivalent fraction task. *MathKeys: Unlocking Fractions and Decimals, Grades 3–5* (MECC, 1996a) provides a counter model, a bar model, and a circle model for fractions. In circles, two fractions can be modeled side by side, subdivided, and shaded in up to 16 sections. However, the symbolic fractions are never in lowest terms, and the symbols for each model are always present with the relation symbol ($<$, $>$, $=$) placed between them. The graphics are easy to manipulate and are quite good. However, this software is an example of students being able to use a model without reflective thought to solve a problem. The symbolic form is always correct with no student input. Programs such as this may be best used as a class demonstration tool.

*CampOS Math* (Pierian Spring Software, 1996) is a multiconcept package with at least two fraction components. Both use circular pie models to help students learn concepts. Although presented much more intriguingly than in *Math-Keys*, the models in *CampOS Math* provide so much help that students may not connect the model with the fraction symbolism. The "Fractionator" component permits changing numerator and denominator to create circular region models including fractions greater than 1. When the computer "locks" either the numerator or the denominator, the student is challenged to create a given fraction in an equivalent form. A nonmodel drill of equivalent fractions is provided. ■

# LITERATURE CONNECTIONS

Fractions in textbooks and even in the activities in this chapter lack context. Context takes children away from rules and encourages them to explore ideas in a more open and informal manner. The way that children approach fraction concepts in these contexts may surprise you.

## *The Doorbell Rang*
### (Hutchins, 1986)

Often used to investigate whole-number operations of multiplication and division, this book is also an excellent early introduction to fractions. The story is a simple tale of two children preparing to share a plate of 12 cookies. Just as they have figured out how to share the cookies, the doorbell rings and more children arrive. This continues to happen until there are more children than cookies. Grandma saves the day. By changing the number of children to create an uneven division, children have to figure out how to divide the remaining cookies fairly. If given drawings of circles for cookies, investigations of situations such as four cookies for six children provide a variety of ways to solve fraction problems and discuss the need for fractional parts consisting of equal shares.

## Gator Pie
(Mathews, 1979)

Appropriate even for grades 5 and 6, this delightful book has Alvin, Alice, and other alligators sharing a pie they find in the woods. As more and more gators arrive, the need for cutting the pie into more and more pieces is evident, finally ending in hundredths, making a nice connection between decimals and fractions. An interesting exploration involves cutting a pie (or a rectangle) into halves or thirds and then deciding how to share it among a larger number once already cut. To go from halves to sixths is reasonably easy

but may surprise you. What if the pie is cut in thirds and then we want to share it in tenths?

## The Man Who Counted: A Collection of Mathematical Adventures
(Tahan, 1993)

This book contains a story, "Beasts of Burden," about a wise mathematician, Beremiz, and the narrator, who are traveling together on one camel. They are asked by three brothers to solve an argument. Their father has left them 35 camels to divide among them: half to one brother, one-third to another, and one-ninth to the third. The story provides an excellent context for discussing fractional parts of sets and how fractional parts change as the whole changes. However, if the whole is changed from 35 to, say, 36 or 34, the problem of the indicated shares remains unresolved. The sum of $\frac{1}{2}$, $\frac{1}{3}$, and $\frac{1}{9}$ will never be one whole, no matter how many camels are involved. Bresser (1995) describes three full days of wonderful discussions with his fifth graders, who proposed a wide range of solutions. Bresser's suggestions are worth considering.

# REFLECTIONS ON CHAPTER 12

## Writing to Learn

1. Give examples of three categories of fraction models. What real models have you used that correspond to each of these?

2. Why are set models more difficult for younger children?

3. Describe fractional parts. What are the two distinct requirements of fractional parts? Explain how children's concepts of partitioning need to be refined to produce a concept of fractional parts.

4. What are children learning in activities in which you count fractional parts? How can this type of activity help children learn to write fractions meaningfully?

5. Give a fourth-grade explanation of the meaning of the top number and the bottom number in a fraction.

6. Using a length model, make up part-and-whole questions for each of the following cases:

   a. Given a part and a nonunit fraction less than 1, find the whole.

   b. Given a part and a nonunit fraction greater than 1, find the whole.

   c. Given a whole and a nonunit fraction less than 1, find the part.

   d. Given a whole and a nonunit fraction greater than 1, find the part.

   Try your questions with a friend. Then change each question so that it is in terms of sets. With sets, be sure that a unit fraction

is never a single counter. That is, if the question is about fourths, use whole sets of size 8 or 12 or more.

7. Describe several types of ideas for number sense with fractions and an activity for each.

8. Make up pairs of fractions that can be compared ("select the larger") without using an algorithm. See if you can make up examples that use the four different ideas that were suggested for comparing fractions.

9. Explain the difference between understanding the concept of equivalent fractions and knowing the algorithm for writing an equivalent fraction.

10. Describe some activities that will help children develop the equivalent-fraction concept.

11. How can you help children develop the algorithm for equivalent fractions?

## For Discussion and Exploration

1. A common error that children make is to write $\frac{3}{5}$ for the fraction represented here:

Why do you think that they do this? In this chapter, the notation of fractional parts and counting by unit fractions were introduced before any symbols. How could this help avoid the type of thinking that is involved in this common error?

2. Experiment with rods made of connecting cubes as a model for fractions. For example, if a bar of 12 cubes is a whole, then bars of 3 cubes would be fourths. Since the bars can be taken apart and put together and since the individual cubes can be counted, there are some significant differences between this model and those suggested in the text. Is this a length model or a set model?

3. In an editorial in *Mathematics Teaching in the Middle School,* Patrick Groff (1996) questions the importance of teaching fractions in the upper-elementary and middle grades. His arguments are based in part on the difficulty of learning fraction ideas at this level, the decreased use of fractions in everyday life, and the press for space in the curriculum from other topics that have recently been introduced. His opinion is rebutted in the "Readers Write" section of the September-October 1996 issue by a former physicist and by a current teacher. The discussion has merit. Which side of this argument makes more sense? Why?

# Recommendations for Further Reading

## Highly Recommended

Payne, J. N., Towsley, A. E., & Huinker, D. M. (1990). Fractions and decimals. In J. N. Payne (Ed.), *Mathematics for the young child* (pp. 175–200). Reston, VA: National Council of Teachers of Mathematics.

These authors explore many of the ideas covered in this chapter, provide additional activities or variations on those found here, and show how the early development of fractions can be connected to decimal concepts. Do not be put off by the date; this resource will be timely for many years to come.

Reys, B. J., Kim, O., & Bay, J. M. (1999). Establishing fraction benchmarks. *Mathematics Teaching in the Middle School, 4,* 530–532.

This short article describes a simple three-question interview administered to 20 fifth-grade students. The results are both sad and surprising. A significant conclusion is that the teaching of benchmarks for fractions, specifically 0, $\frac{1}{2}$, and 1, is generally neglected in the standard curriculum. The questions used in the interview can profitably be used with children in grades 4–7.

Tzur, R. (1999). An integrated study of children's construction of improper fractions and the teacher's role in promoting learning. *Journal for Research in Mathematics Education, 30,* 390–416.

Tzur's teaching experiment is described in detail, providing the reader with a real understanding of the construction of fraction concepts at the fourth-grade level.

Watanabe, T. (1996). Ben's understanding of one-half. *Teaching Children Mathematics, 2,* 460–464.

This provocative article examines three very interesting tasks that were presented to a second-grade child. Even if you are interested in the upper grades, this is a worthwhile article. Not only are the tasks or variations of them quite interesting for all children, but the implications are also worth considering. Listening carefully to children informs us best.

## Other Suggestions

Armstrong, B. E., & Larson, C. N. (1995). Students' use of part-whole and direct comparison strategies for comparing partitioned rectangles. *Journal for Research in Mathematics Education, 26,* 2–19.

Behr, M. J., Post, T. R., & Wachsmuth, I. (1986). Estimation and children's concept of rational number size. In H. L. Schoen (Ed.), *Estimation and mental computation* (pp. 103–111). Reston, VA: National Council of Teachers of Mathematics.

Behr, M. J., Wachsmuth, I., & Post, T. R. (1985). Construct a sum: A measure of children's understanding of fraction size. *Journal for Research in Mathematics Education, 16,* 120–131.

Bezuk, N. S., & Bieck, M. (1993). Current research on rational numbers and common fractions: Summary and implications for teachers. In D. T. Owens (Ed.), *Research ideas for the classroom: Middle grades mathematics* (pp. 118–136). Old Tappan, NJ: Macmillan.

Dorgan, K. (1994). What textbooks offer for instruction in fraction concepts. *Teaching Children Mathematics, 1,* 150–155.

Groff, P. (1996). It is time to question fraction teaching. *Mathematics Teaching in the Middle School, 1,* 604–607.

Kieren, T., Davis, B., & Mason, R. (1996). Fraction flags: Learning from children to help children learn. *Mathematics Teaching in the Middle School, 2,* 14–19.

Langford, K., & Sarullo, A. (1993). Introductory common and decimal fraction concepts. In R. J. Jensen (Ed.), *Research ideas for the classroom: Early childhood mathematics* (pp. 223–247). Old Tappan, NJ: Macmillan.

Mack, N. K. (1995). Confounding whole-number and fraction concepts when building on informal knowledge. *Journal for Research in Mathematics Education, 26,* 422–441.

Middleton, J. A., van den Heuvel-Panhuizen, M., & Shew, J. A. (1997). Using bar representations as a model for connecting concepts of rational number. *Mathematics Teaching in the Middle School, 3,* 302–312.

Moss, J., & Case, R. (1999). Developing children's understanding of the rational numbers: A new model and an experimental curriculum. *Journal for Research in Mathematics Education, 30.* 122–147.

Pothier, Y., & Sawada, D. (1983). Partitioning: The emergence of rational number ideas in young children. *Journal for Research in Mathematics Education, 14,* 307–317.

Reys, B. J. (1991). *Developing number sense in the middle grades: Addenda series, grades 5–8.* Reston, VA: National Council of Teachers of Mathematics.

Saenz-Ludlow, A. (1994). Michael's fraction schemes. *Journal for Research in Mathematics Education, 25,* 50–85.

Schifter, D., Bastable, V., & Russell, S. J. (1999). *Developing mathematical ideas: Numbers and operations, Part 2: Making meaning for operations* (Casebook). White Plains, NY: Cuisenaire– Dale Seymour.

# Chapter 13

# Computation with Fractions

The authors of *Principles and Standards for School Mathematics* are much more explicit about what fraction computational skills should be taught than the authors of the 1989 *Standards* were. *Principles and Standards* calls for estimation with fraction sums and differences in grades 3–5, with an emphasis on benchmarks such as $\frac{1}{2}$. Students are to develop strategies for addition and subtraction using a variety of methods. In grades 6–8, *Principles and Standards* calls for students to extend their understanding of the operations to include fractions and decimals. All methods of fraction computation (mental, estimation, paper-and-pencil, and calculator) are recommended (NCTM, 2000).

## BIG Ideas

1. For fraction computation, use the same ideas developed for whole-number computation. Apply these ideas to fractional parts instead of whole numbers.

2. Estimation of computation with fractions helps all fraction computation make sense. Many fraction computations can be done mentally without relying on formal algorithms.

## NUMBER SENSE AND FRACTION ALGORITHMS

In contrast to the new *Principles and Standards* document, many state-level standards call for fraction computation skills before the sixth grade. Too often the rush to computation limits the all-important conceptual development time for the fundamental ideas discussed in Chapter 12. Traditional text-

books will typically explore addition and subtraction of fractions in grade 4 and develop all four operations in grade 5. The result is usually a collection of procedures that students do not fully understand.

## The Danger of Rules

In the short term, the rules for fraction computation can be relatively simple to teach. Students can become proficient at finding common denominators during a chapter on adding and subtracting simple fractions. Multiplying fractions is such an easy procedure that some suggest that it should be taught first. Division, following the invert-and-multiply rule, is nearly as easy. Fraction rules can easily become the focus of rote instruction.

Focusing attention on fraction rules and answer getting has two significant dangers. First, none of the rules help students think in any way about the meanings of the operations or why they work. Second, the mastery observed in the short term is quickly lost. The group of rules governing fraction computation become similar and confusing. "Do I need a common denominator, or can you just add the bottoms?" "Do you invert the second number or the first?"

## A Problem-Solving, Number Sense Approach

Without a firm understanding of fraction concepts, the development of computational algorithms for fractions can quickly become superficial, rule-oriented, and confusing. That is why this chapter was written separately from the preceding chapter—to place more emphasis on fraction concepts themselves.

The following guidelines should be kept in mind when developing computational strategies for fractions:

1. *Begin with simple contextual tasks.* Huinker (1998) makes an excellent case for the use of contextual problems and for letting students develop their own methods of computation with fractions. Problems or contexts need not be elaborate or themselves problematic. What you want is a context for both the meaning of the operation and the fractions involved.

2. *Connect the meaning of fraction computation with whole-number computation.* To consider what $2\frac{1}{2} \times \frac{3}{4}$ might mean, we should ask, "What does $2 \times 3$ mean?" The concepts of each operation are the same, and benefits can be had by connecting these ideas.

3. *Let estimation and informal methods play a big role in the development of strategies.* "Should $2\frac{1}{2} \times \frac{3}{4}$ be more or less than 1? More or less than 3?" Estimation keeps the focus on the meanings of the numbers and the operations, encourages reflective thinking, and helps build informal number sense with fractions. For many computations, there is no need for a standard algorithm, and children can, if they are asked to try, find interesting ways to get answers. Here is a simple example: $\frac{7}{8} + \frac{1}{2}$ is $1\frac{1}{2}$ less $\frac{1}{8}$, so it is $1\frac{3}{8}$.

4. *Explore each of the operations using models.* Use a variety of models. Have students defend their solutions using the models. You will find that sometimes it is possible to get answers with models that do not seem to help with pencil-and-paper approaches. That's fine! The ideas will help children learn to think about the fractions and the operations, contribute to mental methods, and provide a useful background when you eventually do get to the standard algorithms.

In the discussions that follow, informal exploration is encouraged for each operation. There is also a guided development of each traditional algorithm.

# ADDITION AND SUBTRACTION

The idea of developing invented strategies for fractions beginning with contextual problems is similar to the approach described in Chapter 10 for whole-number computation. As with whole numbers, expect that students will use a variety of methods and that the methods will vary widely with the fractions encountered in the problems.

No attempt is made in this chapter to describe all of the solution strategies that students might develop. Students will continue to find ways to solve problems with fractions, and their informal approaches will contribute to the development of more standard methods (Huinker, 1998; Lappan & Mouck, 1998; Schifter, Bastable, & Russell, 1999c).

## Informal Exploration

Consider the following simple context:

**Paul and his brother were each eating the same kind of candy bar. Paul had $\frac{3}{4}$ of his candy bar. His brother still had $\frac{7}{8}$ of a candy bar. How much candy did the two boys have together?**

This is an example of the type of task you can pose to students from the very beginning of their exploration with fraction computation. Most of your problems should involve simple fractions with denominators of 12 or smaller. Avoid a focus on traditional categories such as like and unlike denominators or mixed and common fractions. Rather, include a mix of problem types so that artificial rules do not develop that later must be unlearned.

Encourage students to use drawings or models of their choice. However, there should be a clear connection between the context of the problem, the models, and the symbolism used. When using flexible models like strips or counters, students will first need to decide on a representation of the whole so that both fractions can be modeled correctly. (Recall the pizza fallacy from Figure 12.12, p. 220). For example, in the candy bar problem, students might incorrectly draw two different-sized rectangles or use a set of 4 for fourths and a set of 8 for eighths. When such errors occur, let students work through the resulting difficulties in your class discussions.

Figure 13.1 (p. 230) illustrates how three different models might be used to solve simple addition tasks. Many other strategies are possible. For example, can you find at least two ways to solve the candy bar problem?

Subtraction of two fractions with models is a similar process, as shown in Figure 13.2 (p. 230). Notice that it is sometimes possible to find the sum or difference of two fractions without subdividing either one. Instead, attention is focused on the size of a leftover part. When area models are used for addition and subtraction, common denominators are frequently not involved at all. Selecting a set size or length that permits modeling of two fractions is mathematically the same as finding a common denominator. (Why?)

When making up addition and subtraction exercises to be done with models, do not be afraid of difficult problems. Include exercises with unlike denominators, fractions greater than 1, and mixed numbers. For subtraction, explore problems such as $3\frac{1}{8} - 1\frac{1}{4}$, where a trade of wholes for eighths might occur. At this stage, avoid directing students with a completely formulated method. The problem-solving approach, combined with the use of models, will help students develop relationships.

## The Myth of Common Denominators

Teachers commonly tell students, "In order to add or subtract fractions, you must first get common denominators."

Find a strip for a whole that allows both fractions to be modeled.

Whole

$\frac{5}{6}$

$\frac{1}{2}$

$\frac{5}{6} + \frac{1}{2}$

The sum is 1 whole and a red rod more than a whole. A red is $\frac{1}{3}$ of a dark green.

So $\frac{5}{6} + \frac{1}{2} = 1\frac{1}{3}$.

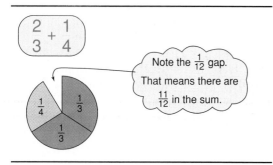

Note the $\frac{1}{12}$ gap. That means there are $\frac{11}{12}$ in the sum.

What set size can be used for the whole? The smallest is a set of 15.

$\frac{2}{5}$        $\frac{4}{3}$

Combine (add) the fractions.
$\frac{2}{5}$ is 6 counters, and $\frac{4}{3}$ is 20 counters.
In sets of 15, that is $\frac{26}{15}$, or $1\frac{11}{15}$.

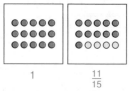

1       $\frac{11}{15}$

**Figure 13.1**   **Using models to add fractions.**

The explanation usually goes something like, "After all, you can't add apples and oranges." This well-intentioned statement is essentially false. A correct statement might be, "In

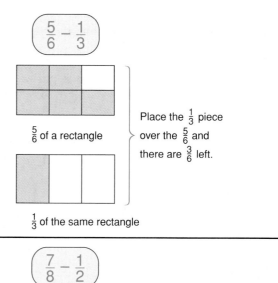

$\frac{5}{6}$ of a rectangle

$\frac{1}{3}$ of the same rectangle

Place the $\frac{1}{3}$ piece over the $\frac{5}{6}$ and there are $\frac{3}{6}$ left.

Find a rod that can be broken into eighths and halves: brown.

$\frac{1}{2}$

$\frac{7}{8}$

Whole

$\frac{7}{8} - \frac{1}{2}$ is the difference between a purple and a black rod. That is three whites, or $\frac{3}{8}$. So $\frac{7}{8} - \frac{1}{2} = \frac{3}{8}$.

Get a set that can be divided into both halves and thirds. Use sets of 6.

8 counters minus 3 counters is 5 counters, or $\frac{5}{6}$.

$1\frac{1}{3}$       $\frac{1}{2}$

**Figure 13.2**   **Using models to subtract fractions.**

order *to use the standard algorithm* to add or subtract fractions, you must first get common denominators." And the explanation is then, "The algorithm is designed to work only with common denominators."

If students have spent adequate time solving contextual and noncontextual addition and subtraction problems using their own invented strategies, you will find that many correct solutions are found without ever getting a common denominator, especially when a physical model is used. Consider these sums and differences:

$$\frac{3}{4} + \frac{1}{8} \quad \frac{1}{2} - \frac{1}{8} \quad \frac{2}{3} + \frac{1}{2} \quad 1\frac{1}{2} - \frac{3}{4} \quad 1\frac{2}{3} + \frac{3}{4}$$

Working with the ways different fractional parts are related one to another often provides solutions without common denominators. For example, how are halves, fourths, and eighths related? Also, picture three thirds making up a whole, either in a circle or on a line segment. Have you ever noticed that one-half of the whole is one-and-a-half thirds? That is, the difference between a half and a third is half of a third, or one-sixth. Similarly, the difference between a third and a fourth is a twelfth. With relationships such as these, many fraction computations can be solved without first getting common denominators.

## Developing the Algorithm

The foregoing notwithstanding, it is important to develop an algorithm for addition and subtraction, and children will likely need some guidance in doing so. At the same time, they can easily build on their informal explorations and see that the common-denominator approach is meaningful.

### Like Denominators

Most lists of objectives first specify addition and subtraction with like denominators. This is both unfortunate and unnecessary! If students have a good foundation with fraction concepts, they should be able to add or subtract like fractions immediately. Students who are not confident solving problems such as $\frac{3}{4} + \frac{2}{4}$ or $3\frac{7}{8} - 1\frac{3}{8}$ almost certainly do not have good fraction concepts and will be lost in any further development. The idea that the top number counts and the bottom number tells what is counted makes addition and subtraction of like fractions the same as adding and subtracting whole numbers.

### Unlike Denominators

To get students to move to common denominators, consider a task such as $\frac{5}{8} + \frac{2}{4}$. Let students use pie pieces to get the result of $1\frac{1}{8}$ using any approach. Many will note that the models for the two fractions make one whole and there is $\frac{1}{8}$ extra. The key question to ask at this point is, "How can we change this problem into one that is just like the easy ones where the parts are the same?" For this example, it is relatively easy to see that fourths could be changed into eighths. Have students use models to show the original problem and also the converted problem. The main idea is to see that $\frac{5}{8} + \frac{2}{4}$ is exactly the same problem as $\frac{5}{8} + \frac{4}{8}$.

Next try some examples where both fractions need to be changed—for example, $\frac{2}{3} + \frac{1}{4}$. Again, focus attention on *rewriting the problem* in a form that is like "adding apples and apples," where the parts of both fractions are the same. As students discuss solutions, be sure they understand clearly that the new form of the problem is the same problem. This can and should be demonstrated with models. However, if your students express any doubt about the equivalence of the two problems ("Is $\frac{11}{12}$ really the answer to $\frac{2}{3} + \frac{1}{4}$?"), that should be a clue that the concept of equivalent fractions is not well understood.

As a result of modeling and rewriting fractions to make the problems easy, students should come to understand that

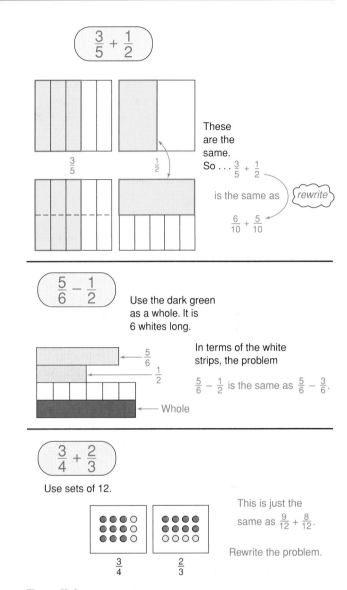

**Figure 13.3** Rewriting addition and subtraction problems involving fractions.

the process of getting a common denominator is really one of looking for a way to change the *statement* of the problem without changing the problem itself. These ideas are illustrated in Figure 13.3.

Subtraction of two simple fractions follows exactly the same approach.

### Common Multiples

Many students have trouble with finding common denominators because they are not able to come up with common multiples of the denominators quickly. That is a skill that can be practiced. It also depends on having a good command of the basic facts for multiplication. Here are two activities aimed at the skill of finding least common multiples or common denominators.

**Figure 13.4**    Least common multiple (LCM) flash cards.

### Mixed Numbers

A separate algorithm for mixed numbers in addition and subtraction is not necessary even though mixed numbers are often treated as separate topics in traditional textbooks and in some lists of objectives. Avoid layering fractions with yet another rule. Include mixed numbers in all of your activities with addition and subtraction, and let students solve these problems in ways that make sense to them. Furthermore, it is almost certain that students will add the whole numbers first and then deal with the fractions using the algorithm or whatever method makes sense.

For subtraction, dealing with the whole numbers first still makes sense. Consider this problem: $5\frac{1}{8} - 3\frac{5}{8}$. After subtracting 3 from 5, students will need to deal with the $\frac{5}{8}$. Some will take $\frac{5}{8}$ from the whole part, 2, leaving $1\frac{3}{8}$, and then $\frac{1}{8}$ more is $1\frac{4}{8}$. Others may take away the $\frac{1}{8}$ that is there and then $\frac{4}{8}$ from the remaining 2. A third but unlikely method is to trade one of the wholes for $\frac{8}{8}$, add it to the $\frac{1}{8}$,

and then take $\frac{5}{8}$ from the resulting $\frac{9}{8}$. This last method is the same as the traditional algorithm.

## Estimation and Simple Methods

Almost all computation with fractions, even on standardized tests, will involve small denominators. Occasionally, the need for a common denominator might require sixteenths or twentieths, but even that is rare. With denominators of 16 or less, estimation using "nice" fractions like halves and fourths is usually possible and should be encouraged. Estimation also leads to informal methods that are often easier than traditional algorithms for getting exact answers.

Consider $7\frac{1}{8} - 2\frac{3}{4}$. A first estimate might be 5, ignoring the fractions. Will it be more or less than 5? Others may begin by thinking $7\frac{1}{8}$ is close to 7 and $2\frac{3}{4}$ is close to 3 $\longrightarrow$ about 4, maybe a little more. Once students begin to think in these terms, a meaningful method for an exact answer is often possible without using an algorithm.

Examine the fraction exercises for addition and subtraction in a middle grades textbook. See how many of them you can do without pencil and paper. Challenge students to do the same.

# MULTIPLICATION

When working with whole numbers, we would say that $3 \times 5$ means "3 sets of 5." The first factor tells how much of the second factor you have or want. *Billy bought 3 packages of 5 balloons.* Here Billy bought whole sets of things that were also whole numbers. This is a good place to begin. Simple story problems are a significant help in this development.

## Informal Exploration

The story problems that you use to pose multiplication tasks to children need not be elaborate, but it is important to think about the numbers that you use in the problems. A possible progression of problem difficulty is developed in the sections that follow.

### Beginning Concepts

Consider these two problems as good starting tasks:

> There are 15 cars in Michael's toy car collection. Two-thirds of the cars are red. How many red cars does Michael have?

> Suzanne has 11 cookies. She wants to share them with her three friends. How many cookies will Suzanne and each of her friends get?

In both of these problems, the task is to find a fractional part of a whole number. Notice that in the first problem, the 15 cars can be easily divided into thirds. Students will first need to find thirds and then take two of those. In the second problem, a type of unit that can be subdivided (cookies) is used because 11 cannot be broken into fourths. Students will solve this problem in different ways, as illustrated in Figure 13.5.

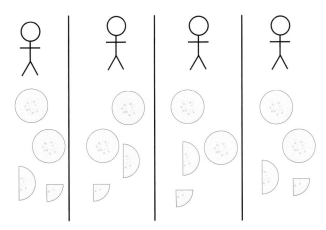

Pass out whole cookies. Cut 2 cookies in half.

Cut last cookie in fourths. $2\frac{3}{4}$ for each.

Cut all 11 cookies in fourths. Give a fourth of each cookie to each girl. Each will get $\frac{11}{4}$, or $2\frac{3}{4}$ cookies.

**Figure 13.5** **Two ways to solve the problem of sharing 11 cookies among four children.**

Problems in which the first factor is a whole number are also important.

Wayne filled 5 glasses with $\frac{2}{3}$ liter of soda in each glass. How much soda did Wayne use?

This problem may be solved in different ways. Some children will put the thirds together, making wholes as they go. Others will count all of the thirds and then find out how many whole liters are in 10 thirds.

In this last problem, replace $\frac{2}{3}$ liter with $\frac{2}{7}$ liter. Initial attention is on the number of parts in each (2), so there are 10 unit parts, just as in the original problem. Then the focus changes to the size of the parts to determine the number of wholes.

## Unit Parts Without Subdivisions

To expand on the ideas just presented, consider these three problems:

You have $\frac{3}{4}$ of a pizza left. If you give $\frac{1}{3}$ of the leftover pizza to your brother, how much of a whole pizza will your brother get?

Someone ate $\frac{1}{10}$ of the cake, leaving only $\frac{9}{10}$. If you eat $\frac{2}{3}$ of the cake that is left, how much of a whole cake will you have eaten?

Gloria used $2\frac{1}{2}$ tubes of blue paint to paint the sky in her picture. Each tube holds $\frac{4}{5}$ ounce of paint. How many ounces of blue paint did Gloria use?

Notice that the units or fractional parts in these problems do not need to be subdivided further. The first problem is $\frac{1}{3}$ of three things, the second is $\frac{2}{3}$ of nine things, and the last is $2\frac{1}{2}$ of four things. The focus remains on the number of unit parts in all, and then the size of the parts determines the number of wholes. Figure 13.6 (p. 234) shows how problems of this type might be modeled. However, it is very important to let students model and solve these problems in their own way, using whatever models or drawings they choose. Require only that they be able to explain their reasoning.

## Subdividing the Unit Parts

When the pieces must be subdivided into smaller unit parts, the problems become more challenging.

Zack had $\frac{2}{3}$ of the lawn left to cut. After lunch, he cut $\frac{3}{4}$ of the grass he had left. How much of the whole lawn did Zack cut after lunch?

The zookeeper had a huge bottle of the animals' favorite liquid treat, Zoo Cola. The monkey drank $\frac{1}{5}$ of the bottle. The zebra drank $\frac{2}{3}$ of what was left. How much of the bottle of Zoo Cola did the zebra drink?

Stop for a moment and figure out how you would solve each of these problems. Draw pictures to help you, but do not use a computational algorithm.

In Zack's lawn problem, it is necessary to find fourths of two things, the 2 *thirds* of the grass left to cut. In the Zoo Cola problem, you need thirds of four things, the 4 *fifths* of the cola that remain. Again, the concepts of the top number counting and the bottom number naming what is counted play an important role. Figure 13.7 (p. 234) shows two possible

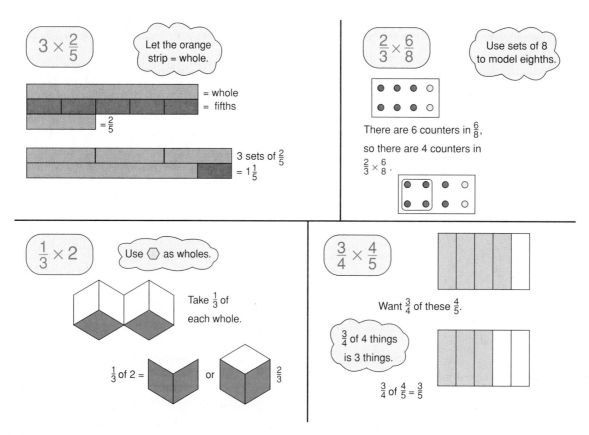

**Figure 13.6**  Modeling multiplication problems in which the unit pieces do not require further subdivision.

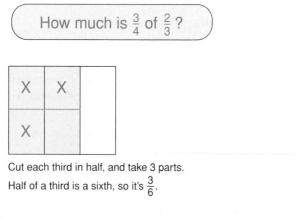

How much is $\frac{3}{4}$ of $\frac{2}{3}$ ?

Cut each third in half, and take 3 parts.
Half of a third is a sixth, so it's $\frac{3}{6}$.

Cut all 3 thirds into 4 parts. Each part is $\frac{1}{12}$.
Three-fourths of the 8 twelfths of the grass
left to cut is $\frac{6}{12}$.

**Figure 13.7**  Solutions to fraction products when the unit parts must be subdivided.

solutions for Zack's lawn problem. Similar approaches can be used for the Zoo Cola problem. You may have used different drawings, but the ideas should be the same.

If students use counters to model problems where the units require subdivision, an added difficulty arises. Figure 13.8 illustrates what might happen solving the problem $\frac{3}{5} \times \frac{2}{3}$. (*Three-fifths of $\frac{2}{3}$ of a whole is how much of a whole?*) The typical way to show $\frac{2}{3}$ is with two out of three counters. But the thirds need to be divided into five parts in order to get 3 fifths of them. Here the representation of a whole must be changed so that the thirds can be subdivided. Do not discourage students from using counters, but be prepared to help them find ways to show thirds using larger sets.

The problem in Figure 13.8 offers another possible twist worth mentioning. Since there is no context to the problem, why not use the commutative property—turn the factors around and consider $\frac{2}{3}$ of $\frac{3}{5}$. Wow! Do you see that the answer is $\frac{2}{5}$ almost immediately?

## Developing the Algorithm

If you have spent adequate time exploring multiplication of fractions as just described, the traditional multiplication algorithm is relatively simple to develop. A square or other rectangle to represent the whole is the most commonly used model for developing the algorithm.

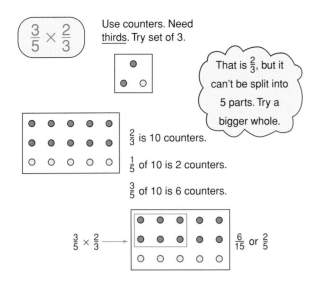

**Figure 13.8** **Modeling multiplication of fractions with counters.**

## A Beginning Task

To make the development problematic for students, provide them with a drawing of $\frac{3}{4}$ of a square as shown in Figure 13.9. The task is to use the drawing to determine the product $\frac{3}{5} \times \frac{3}{4}$ (three-fifths of three-fourths of a whole) and explain the result.

Drawn as shown, the easiest way to get $\frac{3}{4}$ of the shaded region is to divide it into fourths using lines in the opposite direction. Then the problem is to determine what types of unit pieces these are. Although students may not think of it, an easy method of doing this is to extend the lines, subdividing the entire whole into fourths. Then the product of the denominators tells how many pieces are in the whole

(the kind of unit), and the product of the numerators tells the number of pieces in the product.

Begin with problems where the units must be subdivided, as in this example. If you were to use $\frac{3}{4} \times \frac{4}{5}$, there would be no reason to subdivide the unit pieces and thus no reason to multiply the numerators and denominators.

Avoid pushing students to formalize the rule or algorithm of multiplying tops and bottoms. Many students will simply count each small part in the drawings and not notice that the numbers of rows and columns are actually the two numerators and the two denominators, respectively. You might steer students in this direction by posing a problem with the initial sketch but asking them to determine the product without additional drawing. Try this with $\frac{7}{8} \times \frac{4}{5}$, where the numbers make it almost mandatory that you multiply.

A cautionary note: Many texts make this sliced-square approach so mechanical that it actually becomes a meaningless algorithm in itself. Students are told to shade a square one way for the first factor and the opposite way for the second factor. Without rationale, they are told that the product is the region that is double-shaded. You might as well give students the rule and forget about explanations.

## Factors Greater than One

Once students have explored products with both factors less than 1, it may be challenging to have them see if they can use a similar type of drawing to explain products with either or both factors greater than 1. Figure 13.10 (p. 236) shows how this might look when both factors are mixed numbers. Keep the task problematic. This can be a significant and worthwhile challenge. There is no need to explain how to do this.

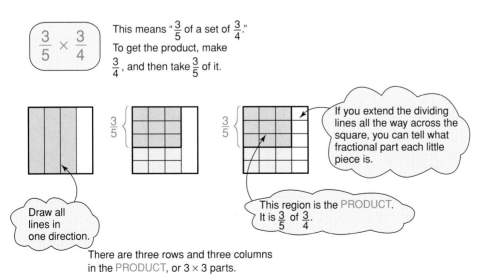

**Figure 13.9** **Development of the algorithm for multiplication of fractions.**

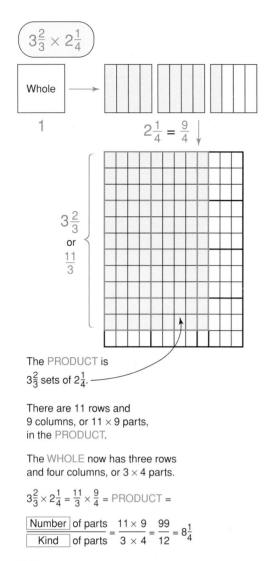

The PRODUCT is
$3\frac{2}{3}$ sets of $2\frac{1}{4}$.

There are 11 rows and
9 columns, or $11 \times 9$ parts,
in the PRODUCT.

The WHOLE now has three rows
and four columns, or $3 \times 4$ parts.

$$3\frac{2}{3} \times 2\frac{1}{4} = \frac{11}{3} \times \frac{9}{4} = \text{PRODUCT} =$$

$$\frac{\boxed{\text{Number}} \text{ of parts}}{\boxed{\text{Kind}} \text{ of parts}} = \frac{11 \times 9}{3 \times 4} = \frac{99}{12} = 8\frac{1}{4}$$

**Figure 13.10**   **The same approach used to develop the algorithm for fractions less than 1 can be expanded to mixed numbers.**

It is useful to have students explore products with fractions greater than 1 as area problems. For example, using the same numbers as in Figure 13.10, the task might be: *Find the area of a rectangle that is $2\frac{1}{4}$ yards by $3\frac{2}{3}$ yards* (see Figure 13.11). In this context, students may approach the task in a manner very similar to two-digit multiplication of whole numbers. There are four different sections to the rectangle, just as with whole numbers. The size of each can be determined by figuring out a partial product. The largest part is the product of the two whole numbers, $2 \times 3$. The smallest part is the product of the two fractions, $\frac{1}{4} \times \frac{2}{3}$. The other two parts are products of whole numbers times fractions.

This area context has a significant advantage in connecting mathematical ideas. Not only is it the same approach used for a product such as $36 \times 48$, but it can also be used for decimals ($3.4 \times 2.6$). The same concept is used again in algebra for products such as $(2x + 3)(x + 4)$. You may have learned this as the "FOIL" method: *First, Outer, Inner,* and

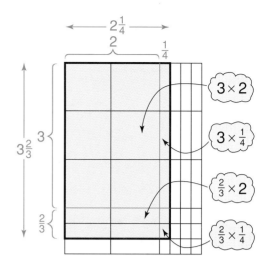

**Figure 13.11**   **The product of two mixed numbers as four partial products.**

*Last* are the same as the four partial products found in all of these examples.

## A Disadvantage of the Algorithm

Interestingly, the multiplication algorithm *always* subdivides the parts, even when it is not necessary. For example, $\frac{3}{4} \times \frac{8}{5}$ results in $\frac{12}{20}$ using the algorithm. However, a student with a good understanding might say, "Three fourths of 8 is 6, so it's 6 fifths, or $1\frac{1}{5}$." As is true with most algorithms, they sometimes steer us away from simple solutions that can be handled mentally. The simpler, nonalgorithmic solutions always involve smaller denominators and are often more useful.

## More Mental Techniques

In the real world, there are many instances when the product of a whole number times a fraction occurs, and a mental estimate or even an exact answer is quite useful. For example, sale items are frequently listed as "$\frac{1}{4}$ off," or we read of a "$\frac{1}{3}$ increase" in the number of registered voters. Fractions are excellent substitutes for percents, as you will see in the next chapter. To get an estimate of 60 percent of $36.69, it is useful to think of 60 percent as $\frac{3}{5}$ or as a little less than $\frac{2}{3}$.

These products of fractions with large whole numbers can be calculated mentally by thinking of the meanings of the top and bottom numbers. For example, $\frac{3}{5}$ is 3 one-fifths. So if you want $\frac{3}{5}$ of 350, for example, first think about *one*-fifth of 350, or 70. If *one*-fifth is 70, then *three*-fifths is $3 \times 70$, or 210. Although this example has very accommodating numbers, it illustrates a process for mentally multiplying a large number by a fraction: First determine the unit fractional part, and then multiply by the number of parts you want. Once again, you can see the importance of the fractional-part concept and the meanings of the top and bottom numbers.

When numbers are not so nice, encourage students to use compatible numbers. To estimate $\frac{3}{5}$ of $36.69, a useful compatible is $35. One-fifth of 35 is 7, so three-fifths is

3 × 7, or 21. Now adjust a bit—perhaps add an additional 50 cents, for an estimate of $21.50.

Students should practice estimating fractions times whole numbers in lots of real contexts: $3\frac{1}{4}$ gallons of paint at $14.95 per gallon or $\frac{7}{8}$ of the 476 students who attended Friday's football game. When working with decimals and percents, these skills will be revisited, and once again mathematics will seem more connected than disconnected.

# DIVISION

Invert the divisor and multiply is probably one of the most mysterious rules in elementary mathematics. We want to avoid this mystery at all costs. However, first it makes sense to examine division with fractions from a more familiar perspective.

As with the other operations, go back to the meaning of division with whole numbers. Recall that there are two meanings of division: partition and measurement. We will review each briefly and look at some story problems that involve fractions. (Can you make up a word problem right now that would go with the computation $2\frac{1}{2} \div \frac{1}{4}$?)

You should have students explore both measurement and partition problems. Here we will discuss each type of problem separately for the purpose of clarity. In the classroom, the types of problems should probably be mixed. As with multiplication, how the numbers relate to each other in the problems tends to affect the difficulty.

## Informal Exploration: Partition Concept

In the partition concept for 13 ÷ 3, the task is to share 13 things among 3 sets and determine the amount in 1 set. Since

partition problems involving fractional divisors are often about rates, put this whole-number situation in a rate context: *If 3 widgets cost $13, how much does one widget cost? That is, what is the price per widget?*

## Whole-Number Divisors

Almost any fair-share problem can involve sharing a fractional amount.

**Cassie has $5\frac{1}{4}$ yards of ribbon to make three bows for birthday packages. How much ribbon should she use for each bow if she wants to use the same length of ribbon for each?**

In this problem, the idea of sharing equally is clear. When the $5\frac{1}{4}$ is thought of as fractional parts, there are 21 fourths to share, or 7 fourths for each ribbon. Alternatively, one might think of 1 yard per bow, leaving $2\frac{1}{4}$ yards, or 9 fourths. These 9 fourths are then shared, 3 fourths per bow, for a total of $1\frac{3}{4}$ yards for each bow. Regardless of the particular process, the unit parts required no further subdivision in order to do the division. In the following problem, the parts must be split into smaller parts.

**Darlene has $1\frac{1}{4}$ hours to finish her three household chores. If she divides her time evenly, how many hours can she give to each?**

The 5 fourths of an hour that Darlene has do not split neatly into three parts. So some or all of the parts must be subdivided. Figure 13.12 shows three different models for figuring this out. In each case, all of the fourths are subdivided into three equal parts, producing twelfths. There are a total of 15

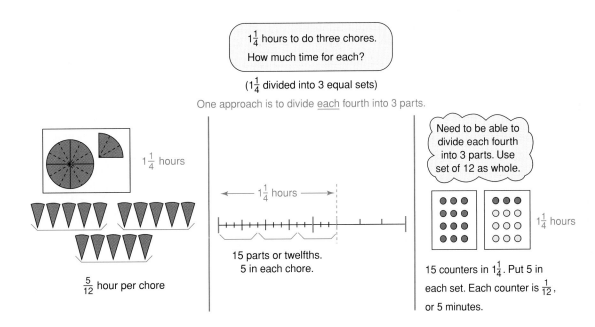

**Figure 13.12** Three models of partition division with a whole-number divisor.

twelfths, or $\frac{5}{12}$ hour for each chore. (Test this answer against the solution in minutes: $1\frac{1}{4}$ hours is 75 minutes, which divided among 3 chores is 25 minutes per chore.)

## Fractional Divisors

It seems counterintuitive to think about sharing an amount across fractional sets. It doesn't make sense to share cupcakes with $3\frac{1}{2}$ friends. However, rate problems with fractional divisors are quite common. Here is an example:

**Elizabeth bought $3\frac{1}{3}$ pounds of tomatoes for $2.50. How much did she pay per pound?**

It may be hard to think about sharing the $2.50 among the $3\frac{1}{3}$ pounds. But how would you figure the price per $\frac{1}{3}$ pound? There are 10 thirds. Therefore, one-tenth of the money was used to buy each $\frac{1}{3}$ pound; that's 25 cents for each third, or three times that much, 75 cents, for each pound.

Now you try these two problems:

**Dan paid $2.40 for a $\frac{3}{4}$-pound box of candy. How much is that per pound?**

**Maggie found out that if she walks really fast during her morning exercise, she can cover $2\frac{1}{2}$ miles in $\frac{3}{4}$ of an hour. She wonders how fast she is walking in miles per hour.**

With the candy, think in terms of sharing the money among 3 *fourths,* and then figure the amount per pound.

With Maggie, the task is the same: Distribute the miles over each of the 3 equal *fourths* of an hour, and then determine the number of miles in 1 hour. What makes this problem a bit different is that the $2\frac{1}{2}$ miles, or 5 half-miles, must first be broken into smaller units so that they can be distributed across the 3 fourths. Try dividing each half into three parts. Draw pictures or use models to finish the solution.

## Thoughts About Partition Problems

You will have to look long and hard in textbooks to find partition problems with fractional divisors. Students will undoubtedly find these problems challenging. However, understanding of both fractions and rate problems is certainly enhanced by these explorations. For children in grades 4 and 5, it makes sense to stick with whole-number divisors.

Why do these problems seem so difficult? Obviously, problems involving finding a unit rate do occur in the real world. However, most of these are likely to be done using decimals rather than fractions.

If you explore partition situations with fractions a bit more, it is possible to come up with the invert-and-multiply algorithm. Suppose the divisor is $\frac{3}{4}$. You first divide the given quantity into three parts (the amount per fourth) and then multiply by 4 to find the amount in one whole. That is, you

divide the dividend by the numerator and multiply by the denominator. That's what is done when you multiply by the reciprocal fraction, $\frac{4}{3}$.

# Informal Exploration: Measurement Concept

Almost all division explorations with fractions found in the elementary and middle school curriculum involve the measurement concept. To review, $13 \div 3$ with this concept means "How many sets of 3 are in 13?" Here is a contextual setting: *If you have 13 quarts of lemonade, how many canteens holding 3 quarts each can you fill?* A key idea to get from this example involves how to deal with that last quart after filling the first four canteens. If you continue to fill a fifth canteen, it will get only one quart. It will be only one-third full. So one answer is $4\frac{1}{3}$ *canteens.*

Since this is the concept of division that is almost always seen in textbooks and will be used to develop an algorithm for dividing fractions, it is important for students to explore this idea in contextual situations.

## Whole-Number Results

Students readily understand problems such as the following:

**You are going to a birthday party. From Ben and Jerry's ice cream factory, you order 6 pints of ice cream. If you serve $\frac{3}{4}$ of a pint of ice cream to each guest, how many guests can be served? (Schifter, Bastable, & Russell, 1999b, p. 120)**

Students typically draw pictures of six things divided into fourths and count out how many sets of $\frac{3}{4}$ can be found. The difficulty is in seeing this as $6 \div \frac{3}{4}$, and that part will require some direct guidance on your part. One idea is to compare the problem to one involving whole numbers (6 pints, 2 per guest) and make a comparison.

Here is a slightly more complex problem:

**Farmer Brown found that he had $2\frac{1}{4}$ gallons of liquid fertilizer concentrate. It takes $\frac{3}{4}$ gallon to make a tank of mixed fertilizer. How many tankfuls can he mix?**

Try solving this problem yourself. Use any model or drawing you wish to help explain what you are doing. Notice that you are trying to find out *How many sets of 3 fourths are in a set of 9 fourths?* Your answer should be 3 tankfuls (not 3 fourths). Here is another problem to try:

**Linda has $4\frac{2}{3}$ yards of material. She is making baby clothes for the bazaar. Each dress pattern requires $1\frac{1}{6}$ yards of material. How many dresses will she be able to make from the material she has?**

What makes this problem a bit different is that the given quantity is in thirds and the divisor is in sixths. Since you want to measure off "sets" of $1\frac{1}{6}$, someplace in the solution, sixths will need to be used. Two ideas are shown in Figure 13.13.

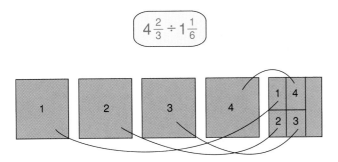

I broke the 2 thirds into 4 sixths. Then I used 1 whole and 1 sixth for each piece. There were four pieces.

I broke it all up into sixths. That made 24 (from the 4) and 4 more from the $\frac{2}{3}$. That's 28 in all. Then $1\frac{1}{6}$ is $\frac{7}{6}$, so I divided the 28 by 7 and got 4.

**Figure 13.13** Two solutions to the problem *How many lengths of $1\frac{1}{6}$ yards can be cut from $4\frac{2}{3}$ yards of cloth?*

## Answers That Are Not Whole Numbers

If Linda had 5 yards of material, she could still make only four dresses because a part of a dress does not make sense. But suppose that Farmer Brown began with 4 gallons of concentrate. After making five tanks of mix, he would have used $\frac{15}{4}$, or $3\frac{3}{4}$ gallons, of the concentrate. With the $\frac{1}{4}$ gallon remaining he could make a *partial* tank of mix. He could make $\frac{1}{3}$ of a tank of mix, since it takes 3 fourths to make a whole, and he has 1 fourth of a gallon.

Here is another problem to try:

John is building a patio. Each section requires $\frac{2}{3}$ of a cubic yard of concrete. The concrete truck holds $2\frac{1}{4}$ cubic yards of concrete. If there is not enough for a full section at the end, John can put in a divider and make a partial section. How many sections can John make with the concrete in the truck?

You should first try to solve this problem in some way that makes sense to *you*. (Stop and do this now.)

After you have solved it your way, try this method. Change all of the numbers to the same unit (twelfths). Then the problem becomes *How many sets of 8 twelfths are in a set of 27 twelfths?* Figure 13.14 shows two noncontextual problems solved in this same way, each with a different model. That is, both the dividend or given quantity and the divisor are expressed in the same type of fractional parts. This results in a whole-number division problem. (In the concrete problem, the answer is the same as $27 \div 8$.) In the classroom, after students have solved problems such as this using their own methods, suggest this common-unit approach.

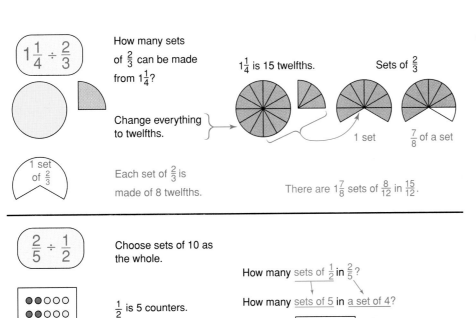

**Figure 13.14** Models for the measurement concept of fraction division.

# Developing the Algorithms

There are two different algorithms for division of fractions. Methods of teaching both algorithms are discussed here.

## The Common-Denominator Algorithm

The common-denominator algorithm relies on the measurement or repeated subtraction concept of division. Consider the problem $\frac{5}{3} \div \frac{1}{2}$. As shown in Figure 13.15, once each number is expressed in terms of the same fractional part, the answer is exactly the same as the whole-number problem $10 \div 3$. The name of the fractional part (the denominator) is no longer important, and the problem is one of dividing the numerators. The resulting rule or algorithm, therefore, is as follows: *To divide fractions, first get common denominators, and then divide numerators.* For example, $\frac{5}{3} \div \frac{1}{4} = \frac{20}{12} \div \frac{3}{12} = 20 \div 3 = \frac{20}{3} = 6\frac{2}{3}$.

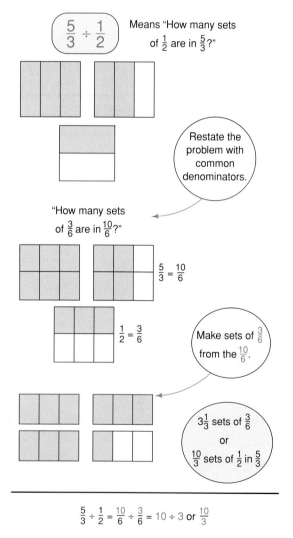

$$\frac{5}{3} \div \frac{1}{2} = \frac{10}{6} \div \frac{3}{6} = 10 \div 3 \text{ or } \frac{10}{3}$$

**Figure 13.15** **Models for the common-denominator method for fraction division.**

Try using pie pieces, fraction strips, and then sets of counters to model $1\frac{2}{3} \div \frac{3}{4}$ and $\frac{5}{8} \div \frac{1}{2}$.

## The Invert-and-Multiply Algorithm

The more traditional algorithm for division by a fraction is to invert the divisor and multiply. As noted earlier, it is possible to develop this algorithm by exploring the partition concept of division. There is very little research to support such an approach. The usual development of the invert-and-multiply approach relies on a symbolic rationale as is outlined in Figure 13.16.

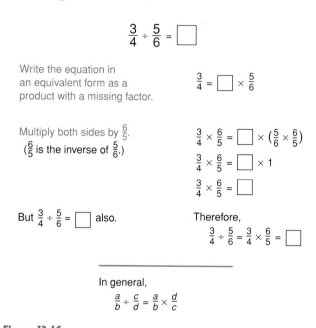

**Figure 13.16** **To divide, invert the divisor and multiply.**

## Curricular Decisions

Which of these two division algorithms for fractions is "preferred"? Each has value. The common-denominator approach can be explained quite well with models and story problems. From a developmental point of view, this is a compelling argument. Very few children below the eighth grade will be able to appreciate the explanation for the invert-and-multiply approach. The result may be that they simply learn the rule: Turn the second one upside down and multiply. The idea of "turning a fraction upside down" is antithetical to any meaningful approach to mathematics.

For students who are able to understand the symbolic explanation of the invert-and-multiply approach, it is certainly much more quickly explained with no ambiguities or special cases to consider. For some students in the eighth grade, this may be a very appropriate approach.

Invert and multiply is generally the algorithm taught in algebra, although the common-denominator algorithm works in algebra almost as well.

# TECHNOLOGY NOTE

Very few software programs adequately address the four operations with fractions. Tenth Planet's *Fraction Operations* (1998b) is one of the better programs in this arena. All Tenth Planet packages have three sections called "Into," "Through," and "Beyond." In *Fraction Operations,* the "Through" section focuses entirely on finding common denominators. Students will see that common denominators are the same as common subdivisions. The software cleverly helps find them in a visual manner. However, as is true with this entire program, there is nothing in the presentation that will help students develop an independent or symbolic method of finding common denominators. The program finds a common subdivision but does not relate this to a common multiple of the denominators.

The "Beyond" section has four components, one for each of the four operations. In each, a contextual setting remains fixed, with different problems randomly generated for that context. For addition, two bars shown end to end (segments of a carpeted path into the castle) must be "added" so that a single red carpet can replace them, permitting the royal family to enter the castle. A measuring tool makes it easy to find a common subdivision for each bar and thus a common denominator to complete the addition. The subtraction component is similar. A fractional amount designates the length of a gap in a railway bridge. One fraction bar is in place. The task is to find the length of the missing bar to complete the bridge. The measuring tool is used in the same way as with addition.

For multiplication, a square model, the floor plan of a house, is used. Part of the floor is shaded in vertical segments. The student is told what fraction of the shaded portion is to be his or her bedroom. The task is to find what fraction of the whole house the bedroom will be. The graph-

ics are wonderful and are identical to the approach described in Figure 13.9 (p. 235). Interestingly it is possible but not required to extend the horizontal lines subdividing the shaded region across the entire square.

The division model starts with an amount of liquid shown in a vertical cylinder. The laboratory setting requires that the liquid be transferred into a number of smaller beakers. The size of the smaller beakers represents the divisor. Both the dividend and the divisor are always amounts less than 1. A problem might be to transfer $\frac{2}{3}$ of a liter of liquid to beakers that hold $\frac{1}{5}$ of a liter each. A measuring device helps determine the fractional amount in the final beaker. Only the final beaker can be subdivided so that the common-denominator method is not likely to evolve.

With each of these four components, the concept is very nicely and correctly illustrated. The development of the harder concepts of multiplication and division (measurement concept) are especially well designed. The downside is that there is nothing in the program to promote reflective thinking or problem solving. The clever graphics and audio information provide all the directions. The measurement tools even make finding the common denominators and fractional parts nearly mechanical.

How can these programs be used profitably? One idea is to use them to pose problems to the class. Even with numbers randomly generated, it is easy to flip through problems until you find one you would like students to solve. The essential parts of the graphics are easy to sketch on paper. Students can solve the problems themselves, pose solutions, and discuss as usual. Student solutions and methods can then be compared with the computer solutions.

Students who need special help with the concept can work with the program on their own. Remember, it is not likely that students will develop an independent strategy by working with this program. ■

# REFLECTIONS ON CHAPTER 13

## Writing to Learn

1. Make up an example, and use pie pieces (or draw pictures) to show how two fractions with unlike denominators can be added without first getting a common denominator. In your example, did you get your answer by either looking at the part that was more than a whole or at the missing part that was just less than a whole? Explain both of these ideas.

2. Suppose that you got pie pieces out to show $\frac{2}{3} + \frac{1}{2}$ and by some informal means your students are now convinced that the sum is $1\frac{1}{6}$. Now suppose that you substitute $\frac{16}{24}$ for the $\frac{2}{3}$ and $\frac{7}{14}$ for the $\frac{1}{2}$. "What is this sum ($\frac{16}{24} + \frac{7}{14}$)?" Explain why you would want

students to say *immediately* that the sum was $1\frac{1}{6}$. Why is this idea important to the use of common denominators in addition and subtraction?

3. Explain why it is obvious that $\frac{3}{4} \times \frac{8}{5} = \frac{6}{5}$ without using the algorithm and without first getting $\frac{24}{20}$.

4. Draw pictures of squares for the whole to illustrate these products and explain each:
$$3 \times \frac{2}{5} \qquad \frac{3}{4} \times \frac{2}{3} \qquad 2\frac{1}{2} \times \frac{2}{3}$$

5. Explain at least one mental method (estimation or mental computation) for each of these:
$$\frac{3}{4} \times 5\frac{1}{2} \qquad 1\frac{1}{8} \text{ of } 679$$

6. Make up a word problem with a fraction as a divisor. Is your problem a measurement problem or a partition problem? Make up a second word problem with fractions of the other type (measurement or partition).

7. Draw pictures to explain each of these divisions using a measurement approach:

$$\frac{2}{4} \div \frac{1}{4} \qquad 2\frac{1}{3} \div \frac{2}{3} \qquad \frac{3}{4} \div \frac{1}{8} \qquad 2\frac{3}{4} \div \frac{2}{3}$$

In the second and fourth examples, the answer is not a whole number. To help you explain the fractional part of the answer, use a set of counters to explain why $13 \div 5 = 2\frac{3}{5}$ also using a measurement approach. (That is, how many sets of 5 are in a set of 13?)

8. Use the same problems you modeled in item 7 to explain a common-denominator algorithm for division. Use the same rationale to explain why $\frac{13}{79} \div \frac{5}{79} = 13 \div 5 = \frac{13}{5}$.

9. What is one strong reason for not teaching "invert and multiply"?

## For Discussion and Exploration

1. Give two reasons why the following argument is flawed:

$$\frac{1}{2} \qquad\qquad \frac{1}{3}$$

●○          ●○○

add

●●○○○

Therefore, $\frac{1}{2} + \frac{1}{3} = \frac{2}{5}$.

Add tops and bottoms.

2. Examine a textbook series, and see where each fraction algorithm is first introduced. Does the preparation for the algorithm seem appropriate? How guided is the development? Will students develop an understanding of the rule or simply apply it to the exercises?

3. Several calculators are now available that do computations in fractional form as well as in decimal form. Some of these automatically give results in simplest terms. If you have access to such a calculator, discuss how it might be used in teaching fractions and especially fraction computation. If such calculators become commonplace, should we continue to teach fraction computation?

## Recommendations for Further Reading

### Highly Recommended

Huinker, D. M. (1998). Letting fraction algorithms emerge through problem solving. In L. J. Morrow (Ed.), *The teaching and learning of algorithms in school mathematics* (pp. 170–182). Reston, VA: National Council of Teachers of Mathematics.

Huinker takes the idea of students inventing algorithms as described for whole numbers in Chapter 10 and applies it to problems involving fractions. With examples of children's work, this article makes a good case for avoiding rules and letting students work with ideas that make sense. As always, Huinker is worth reading.

Kamii, C. K., & Warrington, M. A. (1999). Teaching fractions: Fostering children's own reasoning. In L. V. Stiff (Ed.), *Developing mathematical reasoning in grades K–12* (pp. 82–92). Reston, VA: National Council of Teachers of Mathematics.

Kamii begins with a quick review of Piagetian constructivism but quickly moves to apply this theory to the development of fraction operations. As always, Kamii avoids the use of models and relies on carefully selected word problems. All four operations are discussed.

Kieren, T., Davis, B., & Mason, R. (1996). Fraction flags: Learning from children to help children learn. *Mathematics Teaching in the Middle School, 2,* 14–19.

The authors began with a simple area model involving rectangular pieces cut from a standard sheet of paper. When smaller pieces were placed on larger pieces with spaces in between, the results looked like flags and presented interesting problematic tasks for the students. These researchers have a long history of work with fractions, and this article offers useful insights as well as a suggestion for an easily made model.

### Other Suggestions

Behr, M. J., Wachsmuth, I., & Post, T. R. (1985). Construct a sum: A measure of children's understanding of fraction size. *Journal for Research in Mathematics education, 16,* 120–131.

Bezuk, N. S., & Bieck, M. (1993). Current research on rational numbers and common fractions: Summary and implications for teachers. In D. T. Owens (Ed.), *Research ideas for the classroom: Middle grades mathematics* (pp. 118–136). Old Tappan, NJ: Macmillan.

Graeber, A. O., & Tanenhaus, E. (1993). Multiplication and division: From whole numbers to rational numbers. In D. T. Owens (Ed.), *Research ideas for the classroom: Middle grades mathematics* (pp. 99–117). Old Tappan, NJ: Macmillan.

Groff, P. (1996). It is time to question fraction teaching. *Mathematics Teaching in the Middle School, 1,* 604–607.

Mack, N. K. (1998). Building a foundation for understanding the multiplication of fractions. *Teaching Children Mathematics, 5,* 34–38.

Nowlin, D. (1996). Division with fractions. *Mathematics Teaching in the Middle School, 2,* 116–119.

Post, T. R., Wachsmuth, I., Lesh, R. A., & Behr, M. J. (1985). Order and equivalence of rational numbers: A cognitive analysis. *Journal for Research in Mathematics Education, 16,* 18–36.

Warrington, M. A., & Kamii, C. K. (1998). Multiplication with fractions: A Piagetian, constructivist approach. *Mathematics Teaching in the Middle School, 3,* 339–343.

# Chapter 14

# Decimal and Percent Concepts and Decimal Computation

In most U.S. programs, fractions receive earlier attention than decimals. However, decimal concepts are typically introduced as early as grade 3. What is clear is that the ideas of fractions and decimals must be closely connected. Most of this chapter focuses on that connection.

## BIG Ideas

1. Decimal numbers are simply another way of writing fractions. Connections between fraction and decimal symbolism can help in understanding both.

2. The base-ten place-value system extends infinitely in two directions: to very tiny values as well as to large values.

3. The decimal point indicates the units position.

4. Percents are simply hundredths and as such are a third way of writing fractions and decimals.

## CONNECTING TWO DIFFERENT REPRESENTATIONAL SYSTEMS

The symbols 3.75 and $3\frac{3}{4}$ represent the same quantity, yet on the surface the two appear quite different. For children especially, the world of fractions and the world of decimals are very distinct. Even adults tend to think of fractions as sets or regions (three-fourths *of* something), whereas we think of decimals as being more like numbers. The reality is that fractions and decimals are two different ways that have been developed to represent the same ideas. When we tell children that 0.75 is the same as $\frac{3}{4}$, this can be especially confusing. Even though different ways of writing the numbers have been invented, the numbers themselves are not different. A significant goal of instruction in decimal and fraction numeration should be to help students see that both systems represent the same concepts.

For example, in many contexts, it is easier to think about $\frac{3}{4}$ than 75 hundredths or 0.75. Conversely, the decimal system makes it easy to use numbers that are close to $\frac{3}{4}$, such as 0.73 or 0.78. An obvious use of the decimal system is in digital equipment such as calculators, computers, and electronic meters.

To help students see the connection between fractions and decimals, we can do three things. First, we can use familiar fraction concepts and models to explore rational numbers that are easily represented by decimals: tenths, hundredths, and thousandths. Second, we can extend the base-ten decimal system to include numbers less than 1 as well as large numbers. Third, we can help children use models to make meaningful translations between fractions and decimals. These three components are discussed in turn.

## Base-Ten Fractions

Fractions that have denominators of 10, 100, 1000, and so on will be referred to in this chapter as *base-ten fractions*. This is simply a convenient label and is not one commonly found in the literature. Fractions such as $\frac{7}{10}$ or $\frac{63}{100}$ are examples of base-ten fractions.

### Base-Ten Fraction Models

Most of the common models for fractions are somewhat limited for the purpose of depicting base-ten fractions. Generally, the familiar fraction models cannot show hundredths or thousandths. It is important to provide models for these fractions using the same conceptual approaches that were used for fractions such as thirds and fourths.

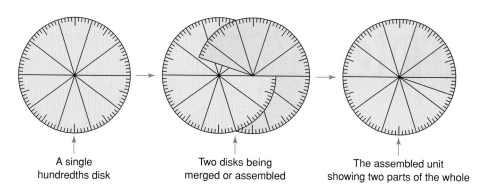

**Figure 14.1**   **A hundredths disk for modeling base-ten fractions.**

A single hundredths disk     Two disks being merged or assembled     The assembled unit showing two parts of the whole

Two very important region models can be used to model base-ten fractions. First, to model tenths and hundredths, circular disks such as the one shown in Figure 14.1 can be printed on tagboard (see Blackline Masters). Each disk is marked with 100 equal intervals around the edge and is cut along one radius. Two disks of different colors, slipped together as shown, can be used to model any fraction less than 1. Fractions modeled on this hundredths disk can be read as base-ten fractions by noting the spaces around the edge but are still reminiscent of the traditional pie model.

The most common model for base-ten fractions is a 10 × 10 square. These squares can be run off on paper for students to shade in various fractions (see Figure 14.2 and Blackline Masters). Another important variation is to use base-ten place-value strips and squares. As a fraction model, the 10-cm square that was used as the hundreds model for whole numbers is taken as the whole or 1. Each strip is then 1 tenth, and each small square is 1 hundredth. The *Decimal Squares* materials (Bennett, 1982) include squares in which each hundredth is again partitioned into ten smaller sections. This permits modeling of thousandths by shading in portions of the square. Even one more step is provided by the large square in the Blackline Masters that is subdivided into 10,000 tiny squares. When shown on an overhead projector, individual squares or ten-thousandths can easily be identified and shaded in with a pen on the transparency.

One of the best length models is a meter stick. Each decimeter is one-tenth of the whole stick, each centimeter is one-hundredth, and each millimeter is one-thousandth. Any number-line model broken into 100 subparts is likewise a useful model for hundredths.

Many teachers use money as a model for decimals, and to some extent this is helpful. However, for children, money is almost exclusively a two-place system: Numbers like 3.2 or 12.1389 do not relate to money. Children's initial contact with decimals should be more flexible, and so money is not recommended as a decimal model. Money is certainly an important *application* of decimal numeration.

## Multiple Names and Formats

Early work with base-ten fractions is designed primarily to acquaint students with the models, to help them begin to think of quantities in terms of tenths and hundredths, and to learn to read and write base-ten fractions in different ways.

10 × 10 squares on paper. Each square is one whole. Students shade fractional parts.

Base-ten strips and squares can be used to model base-ten fractions. Instead of shading in the large square, strips and small squares are placed on it to show a fractional part.

**Figure 14.2**   **10 × 10 squares model base-ten fractions.**

Have students show a base-ten fraction using any base-ten fraction model. Once a fraction, say, $\frac{65}{100}$, is modeled, the following things can be explored:

- Is this fraction more or less than $\frac{1}{2}$? Than $\frac{2}{3}$? Than $\frac{3}{4}$? Some familiarity with these fractions can be developed by comparison with fractions that are easy to think about.

- What are some different ways to say this fraction using tenths and hundredths? ("6 tenths and 5 hundredths," "65 hundredths") Include thousandths when appropriate.

- Show two ways to write this fraction ($\frac{65}{100}$ or $\frac{6}{10} + \frac{5}{100}$).

The last two questions are very important. When base-ten fractions are later written as decimals, they are usually read as a single fraction. That is, 0.65 is read "sixty-five hundredths." But to understand them in terms of place value, the same number must be thought of as 6 tenths and 5 hundredths. A mixed number such as $5\frac{13}{100}$ is usually read the same way as a decimal: 5.13 is "five and thirteen-hundredths." For purposes of place value, it should also be understood as $5 + \frac{1}{10} + \frac{3}{100}$. Special attention should also be given to numbers such as the following:

$$\frac{30}{1000} = \frac{0}{10} + \frac{3}{100} + \frac{0}{1000}$$

$$\frac{70}{100} = \frac{7}{10} + \frac{0}{100}$$

The expanded forms will be helpful in translating these fractions to decimals. In oral form, fractions or decimals with trailing zeros are sometimes used to indicate a higher level of precision. Seven-tenths is numerically equal to 70 hundredths, but the latter conveys precision to the nearest hundredth.

Exercises at this introductory level should include all possible connections between models, various oral forms, and various written forms. Given a model or a written or oral fraction, students should be able to give the other two forms of the fraction, including equivalent forms where appropriate.

## Extending the Place-Value System

Before considering decimal numerals with students, it is advisable to review some ideas of whole-number place value. One of the most basic of these ideas is the 10-to-1 relationship between the value of any two adjacent positions. In terms of a base-ten model such as strips and squares, 10 of any one piece will make 1 of the next larger, and vice versa.

### A Two-Way Relationship

The 10-makes-1 rule continues indefinitely to larger and larger pieces or positional values. This concept is fun to explore in terms of how large the strips and squares will actually be if you move six or eight places out.

If you are using the strip-and-square model, for example, the strip and square shapes alternate in an infinite progression as they get larger and larger. Having established the progression to larger pieces, focus on the idea that each piece to the right in this string gets smaller by one-tenth. The critical question becomes "Is there ever a smallest piece?" In the students' experience, the smallest piece is the centimeter square or unit piece. But couldn't even that piece be divided into 10 small strips? And couldn't these small strips be divided into 10 very small squares, and so on? In the mind's eye, there is no smallest strip or smallest square.

The goal of this discussion is to help students see that a 10-to-1 relationship can extend *infinitely in two directions*. There is no smallest piece and no largest piece. The relationship between adjacent pieces is the same regardless of which two adjacent pieces are being considered. Figure 14.3 illustrates this idea.

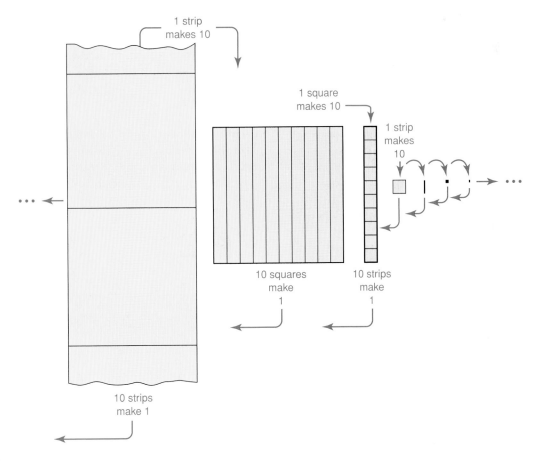

**Figure 14.3** Theoretically, the strips and squares extend infinitely in both directions.

## The Role of the Decimal Point

An important idea to be realized in this discussion is that there is no built-in reason why any one position should naturally be chosen to be the unit or ones position. In terms of strips and squares, for example, which piece is the ones piece? The small centimeter square? Why? Why not a larger or a smaller square? Why not a strip? *Any piece could effectively be chosen as the ones piece.*

When a number such as 1624 is written, the assumption is that the 4 is in the units or ones position. But if a position to the left of the 4 is selected as the ones position, some method of designating that position must be devised. Enter the decimal point. As shown in Figure 14.4, the same amount can be written in different ways, depending on the choice of the unit. The decimal point is placed between two positions with the convention that the position to the left of the decimal is the units or ones position. Thus the role of the decimal point is *to designate the units position,* and it does so by sitting just to the right of that position.

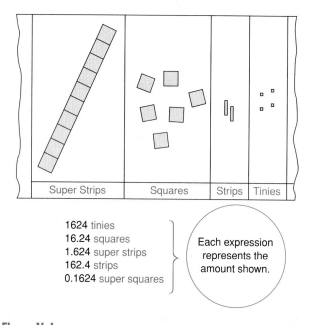

**Figure 14.4**  **The decimal point indicates which position is the units.**

A fitting caricature of the decimal is shown in Figure 14.5. The "eyes" of the decimal always focus up toward the name of the units or ones. A tagboard disk of this decimal-point face can be used between adjacent base-ten models or on a place-value chart (found with the hundredths disk in the Blackline Masters). If such a decimal point were placed between the squares and strips in Figure 14.4, the squares would then be designated as the units, and 16.24 would be the correct written form for the model.

### ACTIVITY
## 14.1 The Decimal Names the Unit

Have students display a certain amount of base-ten pieces on their desks. For example, put out 3 squares,

7 strips, and 4 tinies. Refer to the pieces as "squares," "strips," and "tinies," and reach an agreement on names for the theoretical pieces both smaller and larger. To the right of tinies can be "tiny strips" and "tiny squares." To the left of squares can be "super strips" and "super squares." Each student should also have a tagboard smiley decimal point. Now ask students to write and say how many squares they have, how many super strips, and so on, as in Figure 14.4. The students position their decimal point accordingly and both write and say the amounts.

Activity 14.1 illustrates vividly that the decimal indicates the named unit and that the unit can change without changing the quantity. A related discussion could involve multiplication or division of the quantity by powers of 10. If the display shows, for example, 3.74 squares, what would 10 times this amount be? Here the decimal remains looking at the squares position since 10 times 3.74 squares will still be squares. However, while the decimal remains in the same place-value position, each piece in the display would be enlarged 10 times, and hence each digit will shift to a position one place to the left. The result would be 37.4 squares, with the 3 squares becoming 3 super strips, the 7 strips becoming 7 squares, and the 4 tinies becoming 4 strips.

## The Decimal with Measurement and Monetary Units

The notion that the decimal "looks at the units place" is useful in a variety of contexts. For example, in the metric system, seven place values have names. As shown in Figure 14.6, the decimal can be used to designate any of these places as the unit without changing the actual measure. Our monetary system is also a decimal system. In the amount $172.95, the decimal point designates the dollars position as the unit. There are 1 hundred (of dollars), 7 tens, 2 singles, 9 dimes, and 5 pennies or cents in this amount of money regardless of how it is written. If pennies were the designated unit, the

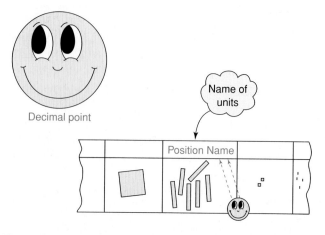

**Figure 14.5**  **The decimal point always "looks up at" the name of the units position.**

| kilometer | hectometer | dekameter | meter | decimeter | centimeter | millimeter | |
|---|---|---|---|---|---|---|---|
| | | 4 | 3 | 8 | 5 | | |

4 dekameters, 3 meters, 8 decimeters, and 5 centimeters =

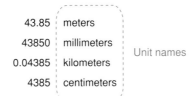

| 43.85 | meters |
| 43850 | millimeters |
| 0.04385 | kilometers |
| 4385 | centimeters |

Unit names

**Figure 14.6** **In the metric system, each place-value position has a name. The decimal point can be placed to designate which length is the unit length.**

same amount would be written as 17,295 cents or 17,295.0 cents. It could just as correctly be 0.17295 thousands of dollars or 1729.5 dimes.

In the case of actual measures such as metric lengths or weights or the U.S. monetary system, the name of the unit is written after the number. You may be 1.62 meters tall, but it does not make sense to say you are "1.62 tall." In the paper, we may read about Congress spending $7.3 billion. Here the units are billions of dollars, not dollars. A city may have a population of 2.4 million people. That is the same as 2,400,000 individuals.

## Other Decimal Models

Technically, any base-ten place-value model can be used as a model for decimals. With the strip-and-square model, students can each have a set of materials at their desks. If the kit includes a tagboard smiley decimal point, no place-value mat is required. Students can arrange their base-ten pieces in order and put the decimal point to the right of the designated unit piece. Usually, the 10-cm square is selected. This allows students to model decimal fractions to hundredths. Some teachers even cut wooden toothpicks into 1-cm lengths to represent the next smaller strip or thousandths. These show up very nicely on an overhead projector.

The three-dimensional wooden or plastic base-ten blocks have four different pieces. If the 10-cm cube or "block" is designated as 1, then the flats, sticks, and small cubes can be used to model decimals to three places.

Any base-ten fraction model is also a decimal model since decimals and fractions are simply two different ways to represent the same amounts. Three-fourths is shown on the hundredths disk as 7 tenths and 5 hundredths. If these pieces could be cut up and put on a place-value chart, they would be shown as 0.75 with the decimal looking up at the circles place, as in Figure 14.7.

## Making the Fraction-Decimal Connection

To connect the two numeration systems, fractions and decimals, students should make concept-oriented translations.

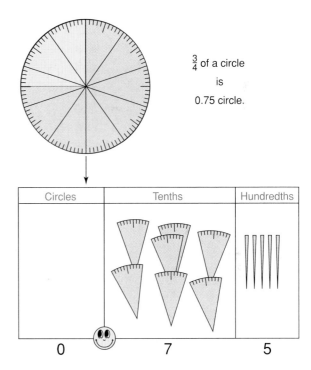

$\frac{3}{4}$ of a circle

is

0.75 circle.

| Circles | Tenths | Hundredths |
|---|---|---|
| 0 | 7 | 5 |

**Figure 14.7** **Fraction models could be decimal models.**

The purpose of such activities has less to do with the skill of converting a fraction to a decimal than with construction of the concept that both systems express the same ideas.

**ACTIVITY**

## 14.2 Fractions to Decimals

Start with a base-ten fraction, such as $\frac{35}{100}$ or $\frac{28}{10}$. Have students use at least two different base-ten fraction models to show these amounts. Discuss how each model shows the same relationship. Include as one of the models a set of strips and squares with the $10 \times 10$ square designated as the unit. The strip-and-square model can then be rearranged in standard place-value format, indicating how the fraction can be expressed as a decimal (see Figure 14.8, p. 248).

Once a fraction is modeled and written as both a fraction and a decimal, both symbolisms should be read. The oral language for both fraction and decimal will be the same.

$\frac{35}{100}$ = 0.35 = "thirty-five hundredths"

**Figure 14.8** **Translation of a base-ten fraction to a decimal.**

Activity 14.2 starts with a fraction and ends with a decimal. The reverse activity is equally important: Begin with a decimal number, and have students use several models to represent it and then read and write it as a fraction. As long as the fractions are restricted to base-ten fractions, the conversions are straightforward.

The calculator can also play a significant role in decimal concept development.

─ **A**CTIVITY ─────────

## 14.3 Calculator Decimal Counting

Recall how to make the calculator "count" by pressing ⊞ 1 🟰 🟰 . . . Now have students press ⊞ 0.1 🟰 🟰 . . . When the display shows 0.9, stop and discuss what this means and what the display will look like with the next press. Many students will predict 0.10 (thinking that 10 comes after 9). This prediction is even more interesting if, with each press, the students have been accumulating base-ten strips as models for tenths. One more press would mean one more strip, or 10 strips. Why should the calculator not show 0.10? When the tenth press produces a display of 1 (calculators never display trailing zeros to the right of the decimal), the discussion should revolve around trading 10 strips for a square. Continue to count to 4 or 5 by tenths. How many presses to get from one whole num-

ber to the next? Try counting by 0.01 or by 0.001. These counts illustrate dramatically how small one-hundredth and one-thousandth really are. It requires 10 counts by 0.001 to get to 0.01 and 1000 counts to reach 1.

Activity 14.3 provides an excellent opportunity for class discussion. Never cite the calculator as the reason for any result or as a source of truth. The fact that the calculator counts 0.8, 0.9, 1., 1.1 instead of 0.8, 0.9, 0.10, 0.11 should give rise to the question "Does this make sense? If so, why?" After all, experts made the calculator this way. Did they do it right? Why did they make it this way?

─ **A**CTIVITY ─────────

## 14.4 Double Calculator Counting

A fascinating variation of Activity 14.3 is to use two calculators side by side, the second calculator being one that displays fractions. On the fraction calculator, enter ⊞ 1 ⧸ 10 🟰, and on the standard calculator, ⊞ 0.1 🟰. Repeatedly press 🟰 on the two calculators simultaneously. At 10 presses, the standard calculator shows 1, as discussed earlier, but the fraction calculator shows $\frac{10}{10}$ and will continue to increment the numerator to $\frac{11}{10}$ and so on. If the ⓐ,b/c key is pressed, the mixed number is displayed. The display can be made to toggle back and forth among the mixed number, the improper fraction, and the decimal equivalent. If models are also coordinated with the counting, the activity helps relate two symbol systems and a conceptual model in a powerful illustration.

The Texas Instruments TI-15 Explorer and TI-73 graphing calculators have the most flexible fraction and decimal displays available. They can be set to automatically simplify fractions to lowest terms or to permit "manual" simplification, letting the user select a common factor. In the manual simplify mode, the ⟨F↔D⟩ key converts 0.25 to ↓25/100. The down arrow indicates that lower terms are possible. In the simplify mode, 0.25 is converted to $\frac{1}{4}$. Results will be either mixed or improper fractions, depending on another mode choice. Activities such as "Calculator Decimal Counting" and "Double Calculator Counting" are enhanced with these calculators because of these mode choices, because both the calculation and results are displayed for successive counts, and because fractions are nicely displayed with a horizontal fraction bar.

# DEVELOPING DECIMAL NUMBER SENSE

So far, the discussion has revolved around the connection of decimals with base-ten fractions. Number sense implies more. It means having intuition about or a friendly understanding of numbers. To this end, it is useful to connect decimals to the fractions with which children are familiar, to be able to compare and order decimals readily, and to approximate decimals with useful familiar numbers.

# Familiar Fractions Connected to Decimals

Chapter 12 showed how to help students develop a conceptual familiarity with simple fractions, especially halves, thirds, fourths, fifths, and eighths. We should extend this familiarity to the same concepts expressed as decimals. One way to do this is to have students translate familiar fractions to decimals by means of a base-ten model.

---

## ACTIVITY

### 14.5 Friendly Decimal Fractions

Have students shade in familiar fractions on a $10 \times 10$ grid. Because the grid effectively translates any fraction to a base-ten fraction, the fractions can then easily be written as decimals. Under each shaded figure, write the fraction in familiar form, then as a base-ten fraction, and finally as a decimal, as shown in Figure 14.9.

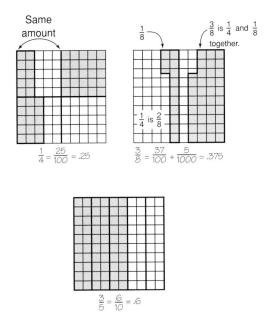

$$\frac{1}{4} = \frac{25}{100} = .25$$

$$\frac{3}{8} = \frac{37}{100} + \frac{5}{1000} = .375$$

$$\frac{3}{5} = \frac{6}{10} = .6$$

**Figure 14.9** **Familiar fractions converted to decimals using a $10 \times 10$ square.**

Begin with halves and fifths, since these can be shown with strips of 10 squares. Next explore fourths. Many students will shade $\frac{1}{4}$ by shading in a $5 \times 5$ square of the grid. See if they can then shade the same amount using strips and fewer than 10 small squares. Repeat for other fourths, such as $\frac{3}{4}$ or $\frac{7}{4}$. Eighths present an interesting challenge. One way

---

to find $\frac{1}{8}$ of a $10 \times 10$ square is to take half of $\frac{1}{4}$. Since $\frac{1}{4}$ is $\frac{2}{10}$ and $\frac{5}{100}$, then $\frac{1}{8}$ is $\frac{1}{10} + \frac{2}{100} + \frac{5}{1000}$. The $\frac{5}{1000}$ part is the same as half of $\frac{1}{100}$. Rather than "explain" all this to students, use the potential difficulty of figuring out $\frac{1}{8}$ as an opportunity for valuable discussion. The result should come from the students.

The exploration of modeling $\frac{1}{3}$ as a decimal is a good introduction to the concept of an infinitely repeating decimal. Try to partition the whole square into 3 parts using strips and squares. Each part receives 3 strips with 1 left over. To divide the leftover strip, each part gets 3 small squares with 1 left over. To divide the small square, each part gets 3 tiny strips with 1 left over. (Recall that with base-ten pieces, each smaller piece must be $\frac{1}{10}$ of the preceding size piece.) Each of the 3 parts will get 3 tiny strips with 1 left over. It becomes obvious that this process is never-ending. As a result, $\frac{1}{3}$ is the same as 0.333333 . . . or 0.$\overline{3}$. For practical purposes, $\frac{1}{3}$ is about 0.333. Similarly, $\frac{2}{3}$ is a repeating string of sixes, or about 0.667. Later, students will discover that many fractions cannot be represented by a finite decimal.

---

## ACTIVITY

### 14.6 Dual Counts with Friendly Fractions

Repeat Activity 14.4, "Double Calculator Counting," but this time begin with a familiar or friendly fraction such as $\frac{1}{5}$ or $\frac{1}{4}$ on the fraction calculator and the corresponding decimal on the other calculator. Again explore counts beyond 1 or 2 wholes, and also switch between mixed and improper fractions. Notice also that while the [F←D] key changes a fraction to a decimal, when going from a decimal to a fraction it uses a base-ten fraction. Thus 2.6 is changed to $2\frac{6}{10}$. The [Simp] key can then be used to find the fraction $2\frac{3}{5}$ that you are working with.

---

Results of National Assessment of Educational Progress (NAEP) examinations consistently reveal that students have difficulties with fraction-decimal equivalences. Kouba et al. (1988a) note that students could express proper fractions as decimals but only 40 percent of seventh graders could give a decimal equivalent for a mixed number. In the sixth NAEP, students had difficulty placing decimals on a number line where the subdivisions were fractions (Kouba, Zawojewski, & Strutchens, 1997). These results indicate that students may be memorizing equivalences without thinking about the conceptual relationships. Having students explain a decimal equivalent for a mixed number such as $4\frac{2}{3}$ or a fraction equivalent for $25\frac{3}{4}$ is much more important than mastering a rule for conversion. Division of the numerator by the denominator may be a means of converting fractions to decimals, but it contributes nothing to understanding the resulting equivalence. Note that this method has not been and will not be suggested in this chapter.

# Approximation with a Nice Fraction

In the real world, decimal numbers are rarely those with exact equivalents to nice fractions. What fraction would you say approximates the decimal 0.52? In the sixth NAEP exam, only 51 percent of eighth graders selected $\frac{1}{2}$. The other choices were $\frac{1}{50}$ (29 percent), $\frac{1}{5}$ (11 percent), $\frac{1}{4}$ (6 percent), and $\frac{1}{3}$ (4 percent) (Kouba et al., 1997). Again, the most plausible explanation for this performance is a reliance on rules. Students need to wrestle with the size of decimal numbers and begin to develop a sense of familiarity with them. And this must extend to all decimal numbers, not just those such as 0.75 that have exact equivalents.

As with fractions, the first benchmarks that should be developed are 0, $\frac{1}{2}$, and 1. For example, is 7.3962 closer to 7 or 8? Why? (Would you accept this response: "Closer to 7 because 3 is less than 5"?) Is it closer to 7 or $7\frac{1}{2}$? Often the 0, $\frac{1}{2}$, or 1 benchmarks are good enough to make sense of a situation. If a closer approximation is required, students should be encouraged to consider the other friendly fractions (thirds, fourths, fifths, and eighths). In this example, 7.3962 is close to 7.4, which is $7\frac{2}{5}$. A good number sense with decimals would imply the ability to think quickly of a meaningful fraction that is a close substitute for almost any number.

To develop this type of familiarity with decimals, children do not need new concepts or skills. They do need the opportunity to apply and discuss the related concepts of fractions, place value, and decimals in activities such as the following.

---
**A**CTIVITY

## 14.7 Close to a Friendly Fraction

Make a list of decimal numbers that do not have nice fractional equivalents. Have students suggest a nearby decimal number that does have a nice equivalent. Try this yourself with this list:

  24.8025     6.59     0.9003     124.356

Different students may select different fractions for these numbers. The rationale for their choice presents an excellent opportunity for discussion.

---
**A**CTIVITY

## 14.8 Best Match

On the board, list a scattered arrangement of five familiar fractions and at least five decimals that are close to the fractions but not exact. Students are to pair each fraction with the decimal that best matches it. Figure 14.10 is an example. The difficulty is determined by how close the various fractions are one to another.

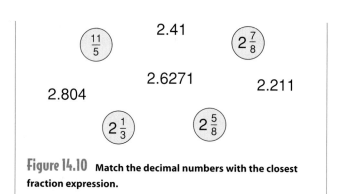

**Figure 14.10** **Match the decimal numbers with the closest fraction expression.**

In Activities 14.7 and 14.8, students will have a variety of reasons for their answers. Sharing their thinking with the class provides a valuable opportunity for all to learn. Do not focus on the answers but on the rationales.

# Ordering Decimal Numbers

Putting a list of decimal numbers in order from least to most is a skill closely related to the one just discussed. In the fourth NAEP (Kouba et al., 1988a), only about 50 percent of seventh graders could identify the largest number in the following list: 0.36, 0.058, 0.375, and 0.4. The most common error is to select the number with more digits, which is an incorrect application of whole-number ideas. Some students later pick up the idea that digits far to the right represent very small numbers. They then incorrectly identify numbers with more digits as smaller. Both errors reflect a lack of conceptual understanding of how decimal numbers are constructed. The following activities can help promote discussion about the relative size of decimal numbers.

---
**A**CTIVITY

## 14.9 The Larger Decimal Number

Present two decimal numbers, and have students use models to explain which is larger. A meter stick or a $10 \times 10$ square is useful for this purpose.

---
**A**CTIVITY

## 14.10 Close "Nice" Numbers

Write a four-digit decimal on the board—3.0917, for example. Start with the whole numbers: "Is it closer to 3 or 4?" Then go to the tenths: "Is it closer to 3.0 or 3.1?" Repeat with hundredths and thousandths. At each answer, challenge students to defend their choices with the use of a model or other conceptual explanation. A large number line without numerals, shown in Figure 14.11, is useful.

Cut four strips of poster board measuring 6 × 28 inches. Tape end to end. Place on chalk tray.
Write on board above. Endpoints can be any interval of 1, $\frac{1}{10}$, $\frac{1}{100}$.

**Figure 14.11**  **A decimal number line.**

Too often, the process of rounding numbers is taught as an algorithm without any reflection on why the algorithm makes sense. Children come to believe that to "round" a number means to do something to it or change it in some way. In reality, to *round* a number means that you *substitute* a "nice" number as an approximation for the cumbersome original number. In this sense, we can also round decimal numbers to "nice fractions" and not just to tenths and hundredths. For example, instead of rounding 6.73 to the nearest tenth, a number sense perspective might suggest rounding it to the nearest quarter (6.75 or $6\frac{3}{4}$) or to the nearest third (6.67 or $6\frac{2}{3}$).

---

**ACTIVITY**

## 14.11  Line 'Em Up

**Prepare a list of four or five decimal numbers that students might have difficulty putting in order. They should all be between the same two consecutive whole numbers. Have students first predict the order of the numbers, from least to most. Next have them place each number on a number line with 100 subdivisions, as in Figure 14.11. As an alternative, have students shade in the fractional part of each number on a separate 10 × 10 grid using estimates for the thousandths and ten-thousandths. In either case, it quickly becomes obvious which digits contribute the most to the size of a decimal.**

---

 **TECHNOLOGY NOTE**

The key ingredient for making the connection between fractions and decimals is the discussions involving comparisons and equivalent expressions as in the activities already described. Although not designed exactly for this purpose, *MathKeys: Unlocking Fractions and Decimals* (MECC, 1996a) has one decimal component that you may find useful in these discussions. The software permits easy "stamping" of squares for wholes, strips for tenths, and small squares for hundredths. When the addition mode is selected, two numbers can be made side by side, one in red and the other in yellow. The decimal numerals are shown in an addition equation. The two numbers can then be visually compared quite nicely.

Clicking on the ⊟ button unfortunately combines the two models automatically and displays the sum in both horizontal and vertical format with no student input.

The drill program *Math Munchers Deluxe* (MECC, 1995d) provides useful practice of decimal-fraction equivalence in a format students seem to like. An array of 25 fractions, decimals, fraction region models, percents, and ratios is presented. The student is to find all instances that are equivalent to a given decimal number. The game can also be played with less than or greater than rather than equivalent. The 17 levels of difficulty provide ample challenge. This is a good example of worthwhile drill. However, it must come after conceptual ideas are well developed. The program offers no feedback or conceptual assistance. ■

## Other Fraction-Decimal Equivalents

The only fraction-decimal equivalents discussed so far are those for the nice fractions: halves, thirds, fourths, fifths, and eighths. Also, any base-ten fraction is immediately converted to a decimal. These fractions and decimal equivalents provide a significant degree of number sense with decimal numbers. The major component of decimal instruction should be a conceptual focus on these ideas.

At times, however, other fractions must be expressed as a decimal. For example, how do you enter $\frac{5}{6}$ or $\frac{3}{7}$ on a calculator that does not accept fraction notation? The answer is based on the fact that $\frac{3}{7}$ is also an expression for 3 ÷ 7. If this division is carried out on paper, an infinite but repeating decimal will result. The ninths have very interesting decimal equivalents, and looking for a pattern is a worthwhile activity (try 1 ÷ 9, 2 ÷ 9, . . . , on your calculator). The division process should also be checked out for familiar fraction equivalents. If students have constructed a good understanding of familiar fractions and decimal equivalents, the concept will confirm the division result. If the division 4 ÷ 5 is the only explanation students have for why $\frac{4}{5}$ = 0.8, a significant lack of a conceptual linkage between fractions and decimals is likely.

In the seventh or eighth grade, students are frequently taught to convert a repeating decimal to a fraction. These conversions demonstrate that every repeating decimal can also be represented as a fraction and therefore as a rational number. This important theoretical result is useful primarily for distinguishing between rational and irrational numbers. The contribution such tedious activities have for number sense is minimal.

# INTRODUCING PERCENTS

Textbooks have traditionally treated percents as a separate topic from fractions and decimals or stuck them in a chapter on ratios. The connection of percents to fraction and decimal concepts is so strong that it makes better sense to discuss percents as students begin to have a good grasp of the fraction-decimal relationships.

## A Third Operator System

One of the big ideas of the chapter has been that decimal numerals and fractions are simply two different symbol systems for the same part-to-whole relationships. In this sense, both fractions and decimals are interpreted as real numbers. But when we say "three-fifths of a cake" or "three-fifths of the students," the number meaning comes from the cake or the set of students. In fact, it is precisely this operator notion that makes it difficult for children to think of fractions as numbers. They initially learn about them as parts of things.

When children have made a strong connection between the concepts of fractions and decimals, the topic of percents can be introduced. Rather than approach percents as a new idea, children should see that percents are simply a different way to record ideas they have already developed about fractions and decimals. Rather than a third *numeration* system, percents are essentially a third *symbolism for operators*.

### Another Name for Hundredths

The term *percent* is simply another name for *hundredths*. If students can express common fractions and simple decimals as hundredths, the term *percent* can be substituted for the term *hundredth*. Consider the fraction $\frac{3}{4}$. As a fraction expressed in hundredths, it is $\frac{75}{100}$. When $\frac{3}{4}$ is written in decimal form, it is 0.75. Both 0.75 and $\frac{75}{100}$ are read in exactly the same way, "seventy-five hundredths." When used as operators, $\frac{3}{4}$ of something is the same as 0.75 or 75 percent of that same thing. Thus percent is merely a new notation and terminology, not a new concept.

Models provide the main link among fractions, decimals, and percents, as shown in Figure 14.12. Base-ten fraction models are suitable for fractions, decimals, and percents, since they all represent the same idea.

Another helpful approach to the terminology of percent is through the role of the decimal point. Recall that the decimal identifies the units. When the unit is ones, a number such as 0.659 means a little more than 6 tenths of 1. The word *ones* is understood (6 tenths of 1 *one*). But 0.659 is also

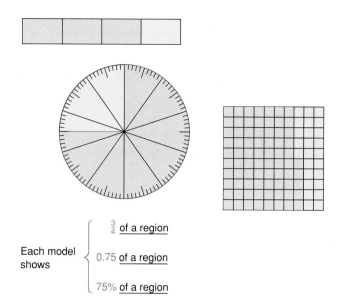

Each model shows
$\frac{3}{4}$ of a region
0.75 of a region
75% of a region

**Figure 14.12**    **Models connect three different notations.**

6.59 tenths and 65.9 hundredths and 659 thousandths. In each case, the name of the unit must be explicitly identified, or else the unit ones would be assumed. In 6.59 tenths, the interpretation is 6 and 59 hundredths *of the things called tenths*. Since *percent* is another name for *hundredths*, when the decimal identifies the hundredths position as the units, the word *percent* can be specified as a synonym for *hundredths*. Thus 0.659 (of some whole or 1) is 65.9 hundredths or 65.9 percent of that same whole. As illustrated in Figure 14.13, the notion of placing the decimal point *to identify the percent position* is conceptually more meaningful than the apparently arbitrary rule: "To change a decimal to a percent, move the decimal two places to the right." A better idea is to equate hundredths with percent both orally and in notation.

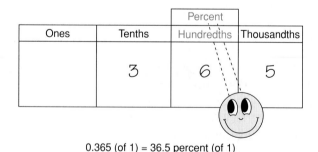

0.365 (of 1) = 36.5 percent (of 1)

**Figure 14.13**    **Hundredths are also known as percents.**

## Using Percent with Familiar Fractions

Students should use base-ten models for percents in much the same way as for decimals. The disk with 100 markings around the edge is now a model for percents as well as a fraction model for hundredths. The same is true of a 10 × 10 square. Each tiny square inside is 1 percent of the square.

Each row or strip of 10 squares is not only a tenth but also 10 percent of the square.

Similarly, the familiar fractions (halves, thirds, fourths, fifths, and eighths) should become familiar in terms of percents as well as decimals. Three-fifths, for example, is 60 percent as well as 0.6. One-third of an amount is frequently expressed as $33\frac{1}{3}$ percent instead of 33.3333 . . . percent. Likewise, $\frac{1}{8}$ of a quantity is $12\frac{1}{2}$ percent or 12.5 percent of the quantity. These ideas should be explored with base-ten models and not as rules about moving decimal points.

## Realistic Percent Problems

### The Three Percent Problems

Junior high school teachers talk about "the three percent problems." The sentence "_____ is _____ percent of _____" has three spaces for numbers; for example, "20 is 25 percent of 80." The classic three percent problems come from this sterile expression; two of the numbers are given, and the students are asked to produce the third. Students learn very quickly that you either multiply or divide the two given numbers, and sometimes you have to move a decimal point. But they have no way of determining when to do what, which numbers to divide, or which way to shift the decimal. As a result, performance on percentage problems is very poor. Furthermore, commonly encountered expressions using percent terminology, such as sales figures, taxes, census data, political information, and trends in economics, are almost never in the "_____ is _____ percent of _____" format. So when asked to solve a realistic percent problem, students are frequently at a loss.

Chapter 12 explored three types of exercises with fractions, in which one element—part, whole, or fraction—was unknown. Students used models and simple fraction relationships in those exercises. Those three types of exercises are precisely the same as the three percent problems. Developmentally, then, it makes sense to help students make the connection between the exercises done with fractions and those done with percents. How? Use the same types of models and the same terminology of parts, wholes, and fractions. The only thing that is different is that the word *percent* is used instead of *fraction*. In Figure 14.14, three exercises from Chapter 12 have been changed to the corresponding percent terminology. A good idea for early work with percents would be to review (or explore for the first time) all three types of exercises in terms of percents. The same three types of models can be used (refer to Figures 12.7, 12.8, and 12.9 on p. 216).

### Realistic Percent Problems and Nice Numbers

Though students must have some experience with the non-contextual situations in Figure 14.14, it is important to have them explore these relationships in real contexts. Find or make up percent problems, and present them in the same way that they appear in newspapers, on television, and in

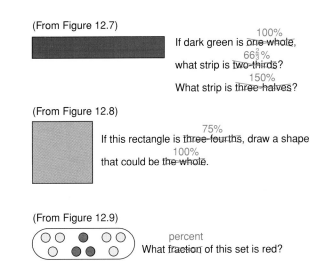

**Figure 14.14** Part-whole-fraction exercises can be translated into percent exercises.

other real contexts. In addition to realistic problems and formats, follow these maxims for your unit on percents:

- Limit the percents to familiar fractions (halves, thirds, fourths, fifths, and eighths) or easy percents ($\frac{1}{10}$, $\frac{1}{100}$), and use numbers compatible with these fractions. The focus of these exercises is the relationships involved, not complex computational skills.

- Do not suggest any rules or procedures for different types of problems. Do not categorize or label problem types.

- Use the terms *part, whole,* and *percent* (or *fraction*). *Fraction* and *percent* are interchangeable. Help students see these percent exercises as the same types of exercises they did with simple fractions.

- Require students to use models or drawings to explain their solutions. It is better to assign three problems requiring a drawing and an explanation than to give 15 problems requiring only computation and answers. Remember that the purpose is the exploration of relationships, not computational skill.

- Encourage mental computation.

The following sample problems meet these criteria for easy fractions and numbers. Try working each problem, identifying each number as a part, a whole, or a fraction. Draw length or area models to explain or work through your thought process. Examples of this informal reasoning are illustrated with additional problems in Figure 14.15 (p. 254).

1. **The PTA reported that 75 percent of the total number of families were represented at the meeting last night. If children from 320 families go to the school, how many were represented at the meeting?**

2. The baseball team won 80 percent of the 25 games it played this year. How many games were lost?

3. In Mrs. Carter's class, 20 students, or $66\frac{2}{3}$ percent, were on the honor roll. How many students are in her class?

4. George bought his new computer at a $12\frac{1}{2}$ percent discount. He paid $700. How many dollars did he save by buying it at a discount?

5. If Joyce has read 60 of the 180 pages in her library book, what percent of the book has she read so far?

6. The hardware store bought widgets at 80 cents each and sold them for $1 each. What percent did the store mark up the price of each widget?

## Estimation in Percent Problems

Of course, not all real percent problems have nice numbers. Frequently in real life, an approximation or estimate in percent situations is all that is required or is enough to help one think through the situation. Even if a calculator will be used to get an exact answer, an estimate based on an understanding of the relationship can confirm that a correct operation was performed or that the decimal was positioned correctly.

To help students with estimation in percent situations, two ideas that have already been discussed can be applied. First, when the percent is not a "nice" one, substitute a close percent that is easy to work with. Second, select numbers that are compatible with the percent involved, to make the calculation easy to do mentally. In essence, convert the not-nice percent problem into one that is nice. Here are some examples. Try your hand at estimating each.

1. The 83,000-seat stadium was 73 percent full. How many people were at the game?

2. The treasurer reported that 68.3 percent of the dues had been collected, for a total of $385. How much more money could the club expect to collect if all dues are paid?

3. Max McStrike had 217 hits in 842 at-bats. What was his batting average?

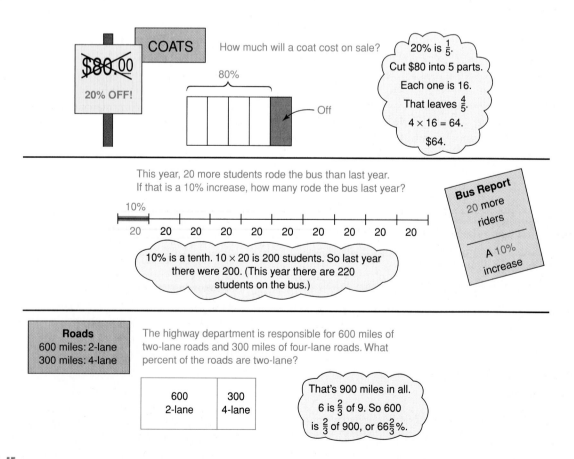

**Figure 14.15** Real percent problems with nice numbers. Simple drawings help with reasoning.

**Possible Estimates**

1. (Use $\frac{3}{4}$ and 80,000) $\longrightarrow$ about 60,000

2. (Use $\frac{2}{3}$ and $380; will collect $\frac{1}{3}$ more) $\longrightarrow$ about $190

3. ($4 \times 217 > 842$; $\frac{1}{4}$ is 25 percent, or 0.250) $\longrightarrow$ a bit more than 0.250

The following activities are also useful in helping students with estimation in percent situations.

---

**A**CTIVITY

## 14.12 Percents as Nice Fractions

Choose the closest nice fraction. For example, which fraction is closest to 78 percent: $\frac{1}{2}$, $\frac{2}{3}$, or $\frac{4}{5}$? Multiple-choice exercises such as this one can be done with a full class or can be made into worksheet exercises. Later, students can give a nice fraction that is close to the percent without a multiple choice. Have students justify their answers.

---

**A**CTIVITY

## 14.13 Easy Percents

Work with "easy percents," especially 1 percent and 10 percent. Begin with exercises where students give 1 percent and 10 percent of numbers. Then show them how to use these easy percents to get other percentages, either exact or approximate. For example, to get 15 percent of $349, think that 10 percent is about $35.00 and 5 percent is half of that, or $17.50. So 15 percent is $35.00 + $17.50, or $52.50. Similar reasoning can be used to adjust an estimate by 1 percent or 2 percent. To find 82 percent of $400, it is easy to think of $\frac{4}{5}$ (80 percent) as $4 \times \frac{1}{5}$ of 400, or $4 \times $80, which is $320. Since each 1 percent is $4, add on $8.

---

Sometimes an exact result, and therefore some calculation, is required. The emphasis on conceptual thinking, nice fractions, and estimation of results will all pave the way for easy work when an exact result is desired. The use of an estimate will determine if the result is in the correct ballpark or if it makes sense. Frequently, the same estimation process will dictate what computation to do so that the problem can be entered on a calculator.

# COMPUTATION WITH DECIMALS

In 1989, the NCTM *Standards* said, "It is no longer necessary or useful to devote large portions of instructional time to performing routine computations by hand. Other mathematical experiences for middle school students deserve far more

emphasis" (p. 94). NCTM's call for less emphasis on computation has been misinterpreted and often criticized by those who believe that the *Standards* were "watering down" mathematics. The issue is especially significant in the area of decimal computation. Many state-level curricula have students learning traditional computational algorithms for decimals in fifth grade with reteaching almost inevitable in the middle grades. This requires a significant consumption of scarce instructional time and tends to place the focus on rules that are often learned without a firm rationale.

The *Principles and Standards* document calls only for *estimation* of computations with decimal numbers in grades 3–5. The 6–8 band says that students should "understand the meaning and effects of arithmetic operations with fractions, decimals, and integers" (NCTM, 2000, p. 214). According to *Principles and Standards,* students in grades 6–8 should develop "the ability to compute efficiently and accurately" with these numbers by the time they leave middle school (p. 220). These statements stop short of specifying levels of computational proficiency with decimals. For example, it is reasonable for students to compute $2.7 \times 25$, and they should be able to estimate this product as a bit less than 75. However, one should question time devoted to tedious exercises such as $3.78 \times 24.62$ or $16.51 \div 2.54$. Anyone needing an exact answer to such computations should use a calculator.

Due to their prescribed curriculum, some teachers will undoubtedly feel compelled to teach more decimal computation or teach it earlier than is suggested by NCTM. Even so, the operations on decimal numbers can be developed as extensions of students' understanding of whole-number computation. Students can develop algorithms that they understand. Estimation can and should play a significant role in this development. There is no reason to revert to mindless rules of "lining up decimal points" or "counting decimal places."

## The Role of Estimation

Students should learn to estimate decimal computations before they learn to compute with pencil and paper. For many decimal computations, rough estimates can be made easily by rounding the numbers to nice whole numbers or simple base-ten fractions. In almost all cases, a minimum goal for your students should be to have the estimate contain the correct number of digits to the left of the decimal—the whole-number part. Select problems for which estimates are not terribly difficult. Before going on, try making easy whole-number estimates of the following computations. Do not spend time with fine adjustments in your estimates.

1. $4.907 + 123.01 + 56.1234$
2. $459.8 - 12.345$
3. $24.67 \times 1.84$
4. $514.67 \div 3.59$

Your estimates might be similar to the following:

1. Between 175 and 200

2. More than 400, or about 425 to 450

3. More than 25, closer to 50 (1.84 is more than 1 and close to 2)

4. More than 125, less than 200 (500 ÷ 4 = 125 and 600 ÷ 3 = 200)

In these examples, an understanding of decimal numeration and some simple whole-number estimation skills can produce rough estimates. When estimating, thinking focuses on the meaning of the numbers and the operations and not on counting decimal places. However, students who are taught to focus primarily on the pencil-and-paper algorithms for decimals may find even simple estimations difficult.

Therefore, a good *place* to begin decimal computation is with estimation. Not only is it a highly practical skill, but it also helps children look at answers in ballpark terms, can form a check on pencil-and-paper computation, and is one way of placing the decimal in multiplication and division.

A good *time* to begin computation with decimals is as soon as a conceptual background in decimal numeration has been developed. Learning the pencil-and-paper algorithms for decimals will do little or nothing to help students understand decimal numeration.

# Addition and Subtraction

Consider this problem:

---

**Max and Moe each timed his own quarter-mile run with a stopwatch. Max says that he ran the quarter in 74.5 seconds. Moe was more accurate. He reported his run as 81.34 seconds. How many seconds faster did Max run than Moe?**

---

Students who understand decimal numeration should first of all be able to tell approximately what the difference is—close to 7 seconds. With an estimate as a beginning, students should then be challenged to figure out the exact difference. The estimate will help them avoid the typical error of lining up the 5 under the 4. A variety of student strategies are possible. For example, students might note that 74.5 and 7 is 81.5 and then figure out how much extra that is. Others may count on from 74.5 by adding 0.5 and then 6 more seconds to get to 81 seconds and then add on the remaining 0.34 second. These and other strategies will eventually confront the difference between the one-place decimal (.5) and the two-place decimal (.34). Students will resolve this issue by returning to their understanding of place value. Similar story problems for addition and subtraction, some involving

different numbers of decimal places, will help develop students' understanding of these two operations. Always request an estimate prior to computation.

If you want to work toward a more typical algorithm, you might suggest writing the numbers on a place-value chart. This simple suggestion focuses attention on the idea of adding or subtracting like place values (see Figure 14.16). It also indicates a separation of the whole-number and decimal parts of the problem. Students may work from the left, computing first the whole-number portion and then the decimal part.

**Figure 14.16** **Using a place-value chart to develop rules for adding and subtracting decimals.**

# Multiplication

Estimation should play a significant role in developing an algorithm for multiplication. As a beginning point, consider this problem:

---

**The farmer fills each jug with 3.7 liters of cider. If you buy 4 jugs, how many liters of cider is that?**

---

Begin with an estimate. It is more than 12 liters. What is the most it could be? Could it be 16 liters? Once an estimate of the result is decided on, let students use their own methods for determining an exact answer. Many will use repeated addition: 3.7 + 3.7 + 3.7 + 3.7. Others may begin by multiplying 3 × 4 and then adding up 0.7 four times. Eventually, students will agree on the exact result of 14.8 liters. Explore other problems involving whole-number multipliers. Multipliers such as 3.5 or 8.25 that involve nice fractional parts—here, one-half and one-fourth—are also reasonable.

As a next step, have students compare a decimal product with one involving the same digits but no decimal. For example, how are 23.4 × 6.5 and 234 × 65 alike? Interestingly, both products have exactly the same digits: 15210. (The zero may be missing from the decimal product.) Using a calculator, have students explore other products that are alike except for the decimals involved. The digits in the answer are always alike. Try multiplying each of these numbers by 2.6: 347 and 3.47. The first product is 902.2 and the second is 9.022. This result leads to the following task:

**If the numbers turn out the same except for the decimal point, how can we use this idea to figure out 83.48 × 0.35?**

The result is actually a very good algorithm for multiplication: *Ignore the decimal points, and do the computation as if all numbers were whole numbers. When finished, place the decimal by estimation.* See Figure 14.17 for an example.

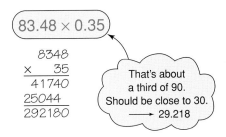

**Figure 14.17** Using estimation to place decimals.

## Division

Division can be extended in a similar manner.

**In 8 days, Max ran a total of 23.5 miles. What was his average miles per day?**

This is a partition problem that calls for sharing the 23.5 miles evenly across 8 days. The same algorithm developed for whole numbers extends very nicely, as shown in Figure 14.18. The 7 extra in the ones column are traded 1 for 10 to the next column, just as with whole numbers. The explicit-trade method (see Chapter 10) makes this quite clear.

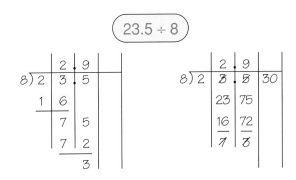

Trade 2 tens for 20 ones, making 23 ones.
Put 2 ones in each group, or 16 in all.
That leaves 7 ones.

Trade 7 ones for 70 tenths, making 75 tenths.
Put 9 tenths in each group, or 72 in all.

Trade the 3 tenths for 30 hundredths.

(Continue trading for smaller pieces as long as you wish.)

**Figure 14.18** Extension of the division algorithm.

As with multiplication, compare two divisions of numbers with and without decimal points—for example, 14.6 ÷ 8 = 1.825 and 146 ÷ 8 = 18.25. Both have the same digits. Have students try this with other quotients using a calculator. The only difference is the placement of the decimal point! Therefore, the algorithm for multiplication can also be used for division: *Ignore the decimal points, and do the computation as if all numbers were whole numbers. When finished, place the decimal by estimation.*

Outside the classroom it is unusual for ordinary people to perform divisions with decimal divisors using pencil and paper. This is not to say that such computation cannot be taught meaningfully. It simply means that such computation is not a productive use of school time.

## 📖 LITERATURE CONNECTIONS

Few interesting stories inspire exploration of decimals and percents for children in the fifth grade and higher. One notable exception is *The Phantom Tollbooth*, a story that should not be missed regardless of its mathematical significance.

In the daily paper and weekly magazines, you will find decimal and percent situations with endless real-world connections. One issue with percents in news stories is the frequent omission of the base amount or the whole on which the percent is determined. "March sales of widgets were reported to be up 3.6 percent." Does that mean an increase over February or over March of the previous year? Increase and decrease by percents are interesting to project over several years. If the consumer price index rises 3 percent a year, how much will a $50 basket of groceries cost by the time your students are 21 years old?

## The Phantom Tollbooth
### (Juster, 1961)

References to mathematical ideas abound throughout this book. Milo enters a world of crazy places and imaginative creatures after driving his toy car through a model of a turnpike tollbooth. Several chapters involve adventures in Digitopolis, where everything is number-oriented. In Digitopolis, Milo meets a boy who is only half of a boy, appearing in the drawing to be the left half of a boy cut top to bottom. As it turns out, the boy is actually 0.58 since he is a member of the average family: a mother, father, and 2.58 children. The boy is the 0.58. One advantage, he explains, is that he is the only one who can drive the $\frac{3}{10}$ of a car, the average family owning 1.3 cars. This section of the tale involves a great discussion of averages that come out in decimal numbers.

An obvious extension of the story is to explore averages of things that are interesting to the students (average number of siblings, average arm span, etc.) and see where these odd decimal parts come from. In the case of measures of length, for example, an average length can be a real length even if no one has it. But an average number of something like cars or sisters can be very humorous as discussed in the story. Where else are fractions and decimals used in this way?

 ## ASSESSMENT NOTES

The real danger in teaching the topics discussed in this chapter is in emphasizing skills instead of the concepts and big ideas. Traditional tests will focus on children's ability to round numbers, order decimals, compute with pencil and paper,

and solve sterile percent problems. These assessments are far too skill-oriented.

The activities described in this chapter will involve discussions and explanations. For example, Activity 14.7, "Close to a Friendly Fraction" (p. 250), will very likely produce an array of answers as your students select a "nice" decimal and fractional equivalent. How did they make that choice? Which seems "best"? Is there always a best answer? When students use a 10 × 10 square to find a decimal equivalent for $\frac{3}{8}$ or $\frac{2}{3}$, there will be lots of discussion if you are not overly directive. From these discussions, you can gather data about your students' understanding of concepts.

So as not to rely totally on listening to discussions, you can and should have students write out explanations and draw pictures to support their answers to many of the activities. Here are two questions that could serve as assessments or as instructional tasks:

1. Consider these two computations: $3\frac{1}{2} \times 2\frac{1}{4}$ and $2.276 \times 3.18$. Without doing the calculations, which do you think is larger? Provide a reason for your answer that can be understood by someone else in this class.

2. How much larger is $0.76 \times 5$ than $0.75 \times 5$? How can you tell without doing the computation? (Kulm, 1994)

Realistic percent problems are still the best way to assess a student's understanding of percent. Assign one or two, and have students explain why they think their answer makes sense. You might take a realistic percent problem and substitute fractions for percents (e.g., use $\frac{1}{8}$ instead of 12.5 percent) to see how students handle these problems with fractions compared to decimal numbers.

If your focus is on reasons and justifications rather than number of problems correct, you will be able to collect all the information you need.

# REFLECTIONS ON CHAPTER 14
## Writing to Learn

1. Describe three different base-ten models for fractions and decimals, and use each to illustrate how base-ten fractions can easily be represented.

2. Explain why the place-value system extends infinitely in two directions. How can this idea be developed with students in the fifth or sixth grade?

3. Use an example involving base-ten pieces to explain the role of the decimal point in identifying the units position. Relate this idea to changing units of measurement as in money or metric measures.

4. What are the suggested "familiar fractions"? How can these fractions be connected to their decimal equivalents in a conceptual manner?

5. What should be emphasized if you want children to have good number sense with decimals?

6. Describe one or two ways in which a calculator can be used to develop number ideas with decimals.

7. What does rounding mean? What type of rounding can we do that is different from rounding to the nearest tenth or hundredth? Explain how a number line can be used in rounding.

8. Make up three realistic percent problems in which the percents are actually nice fractions and the numbers involved are com-

patible with the fractions. One problem should ask for the part, given the whole and the percent. One should ask for the percent, given the whole and the part. The third should ask for the whole, given the part and the percent. Model each, and show how each can be solved using fraction ideas.

9. Why should we not spend a lot of time with pencil-and-paper computation with decimals?

10. For addition and subtraction, the line-up-the-decimals rule can be reasonably taught without much trouble. Explain.

11. Give an example explaining how, in most problems, multiplication and division with decimals can be replaced with estimation and whole-number methods.

## For Discussion and Exploration

1. For each of the four operations, discuss what computational skill with decimals is necessary for children to have. For example, if you believe that division with decimal numbers is important, what is the most tedious problem you would consider having students master? What alternatives to traditional pencil-and-paper computation do you think should be included in the curriculum?

2. One way to order a series of decimal numbers is to annex zeros to each number so that all numbers have the same number of decimal places. For example, rewrite

|  |  |  |
|---|---|---|
| 0.34 |  | 0.3400 |
| 0.3004 | as | 0.3004 |
| 0.059 |  | 0.0590 |

Now ignore the decimal points and any leading zeros, and order the resulting whole numbers. Discuss the merits of teaching this approach to children.

3. Talk individually with some seventh- or eighth-grade students. First find out if they can do simple fraction exercises that ask for the part, the whole, or the fraction given the other two (as in Chapter 12). Encourage them to make drawings and give explanations. Next ask them to solve simple percent word problems that require the same type of reasoning using simple fractions and compatible numbers. Compare students' abilities with these mathematically identical problems.

## Recommendations for Further Reading

### Highly Recommended

Bennett, A. B., Jr., & Nelson, L. T. (1994). A conceptual model for solving percent problems. *Mathematics Teaching in the Middle School, 1,* 20–25.
This article introduces a useful twist on using the 10 × 10 grid to understand percents. The authors provide a series of increasingly difficult tasks that can easily be used in a constructivist environment to challenge a range of students. Realistic percent problems are used throughout.

McIntosh, A., Reys, B. J., & Reys, R. E. (1997). *Number SENSE: Simple effective number sense experiences* (3 vols.: grades 3–4; 4–6, with J. Hope; and 6–8). White Plains, NY: Cuisenaire–Dale Seymour.
These three activity resource books provide Blackline Masters that are designed to help students develop a wide range of useful number relationships. Of special note are activities that use benchmarks

of 0, $\frac{1}{2}$, and 1 for fractions and for decimals. There are also good activities for connecting fractions and decimals. The pages can be used individually or with a full class as overhead transparencies.

Moss, J., & Case, R. (1999). Developing children's understanding of the rational numbers: A new model and an experimental curriculum. *Journal for Research in Mathematics Education, 30,* 122–147.
These authors devised and taught a fourth-grade sequence that began with percents, moved on to decimals, and covered fractions last—the exact opposite of the sequence suggested in this text. A linear model was the main representation used. Although quite nontraditional, much can be learned from this study by two thoughtful researchers who have done considerable work in the area of fraction and decimal conceptual development.

Owens, D. T., & Super, D. B. (1993). Teaching and learning decimal fractions. In D. T. Owens (Ed.), *Research ideas for the classroom: Middle grades mathematics* (pp. 137–158). Old Tappan, NJ: Macmillan.
Owens and Super offer insights from research on how children develop decimal concepts and the difficulties involved. The chapter also provides a variety of useful activities for decimal concept development. The authors have also included results of NAEP testing that give some perspective on "typical" student development.

### Other Suggestions

Allinger, G. D., & Payne, J. N. (1986). Estimation and mental arithmetic with percent. In H. L. Schoen (Ed.), *Estimation and mental computation* (pp. 141–155). Reston, VA: National Council of Teachers of Mathematics.

Chappell, M. F., & Thompson, D. R. (1999). Modifying our questions to assess students' thinking. *Mathematics Teaching in the Middle School, 4,* 470–474.

Hiebert, J. C., Wearne, D., & Taber, S. (1991). Fourth graders' gradual construction of decimal fractions during instruction using different physical representations. *Elementary School Journal, 91,* 321–341.

Huinker, D. M. (1992). Decimals and calculators make sense! In J. T. Fey (Ed.), *Calculators in mathematics education* (pp. 56–64). Reston, VA: National Council of Teachers of Mathematics.

Langford, K., & Sarullo, A. (1993). Introductory common and decimal fraction concepts. In R. J. Jensen (Ed.), *Research ideas for the classroom: Early childhood mathematics* (pp. 223–247). Old Tappan, NJ: Macmillan.

Lembke, L. O., & Reys, B. J. (1994). The development of, and interaction between, intuitive and school-taught ideas about percent. *Journal for Research in School Mathematics, 25,* 237–259.

Oppenheimer, L., & Hunting, R. P. (1999). Relating fractions and decimals: Listening to students talk. *Mathematics Teaching in the Middle School, 4,* 318–321.

Reys, B. J. (1991). *Developing number sense in the middle grades: Addenda series, grades 5–8.* Reston, VA: National Council of Teachers of Mathematics.

Thompson, C. S., & Walker, V. (1996). Connecting decimals and other mathematical content. *Teaching Children Mathematics, 2,* 496–502.

Wearne, D., Hiebert, J. C., & Taber, S. (1991). Fourth graders' gradual construction of decimal fractions during instruction using different physical representations. *Elementary School Journal, 91,* 321–341.

Williams, S. E., & Copley, J. V. (1994). Promoting classroom dialogue: Using calculators to discover patterns in dividing decimals. *Mathematics Teaching in the Middle School, 1,* 72–75.

# Chapter 15

# Developing Concepts of Ratio and Proportion

The topics of ratio and proportion have long been a difficult area of the middle grades curriculum. Even so, the importance of developing an understanding of proportional reasoning cannot be diminished. Proportional reasoning has been referred to as the capstone of the elementary curriculum and the cornerstone of algebra and beyond (Lesh, Post, & Behr, 1987). The ability to reason proportionally was a hallmark of Piaget's distinction between concrete levels of thought and formal operational thought. It represents the ability to begin to understand multiplicative relationships where most arithmetic concepts are additive in nature. In 1989, the *Curriculum Standards* noted that proportional reasoning was "of such great importance that it merits whatever time and effort must be expended to assure its careful development" (NCTM, 1989, p. 82). *Principles and Standards* suggests that the topic should be addressed in grades 6–8 with "a strong intuitive basis" (NCTM, 2000, p. 221). In an era of increasingly strict state standards, there is pressure to develop rules for solving routine problems. Where proportional reasoning is concerned, however, the rush to rules is a serious error. Time must be allowed for development of intuitive ideas, as the *Standards* suggests.

## BIG Ideas

1. Ratio is a multiplicative comparison of two numbers or measures or quantities.
2. Proportional situations are based on multiplicative relationships. Equal ratios result from multiplication or division, not from addition or subtraction.

## PROPORTIONAL REASONING

So that the reading of this chapter is based on common ground, several exercises are provided for your exploration.

Each typifies the relationships that make up the concepts of ratio and proportion. It does not matter what your personal mathematical acquaintance with ratio actually is. Try each of the following problems. You may wish to discuss and explore the exercises in a group or with a friend.

### SHORT AND TALL

**Mr. Green sells trophies on the basis of height. A short trophy measures 6 paper clips tall, as shown in Figure 15.1. According to his price chart, this short trophy sells for $4.00. Mr. Green has a taller trophy that is worth $6.00 according to the same scale. How many paper clips tall is the $6.00 trophy?**

**Figure 15.1**   The "Short and Tall" trophy problem.

### LAPS

Yesterday, Mary counted the number of laps she ran and recorded the amount of time it took. Today she ran fewer laps in more time than yesterday. Did she run faster, slower, or at about the same speed today—or can't you tell? What if she had run more laps in more time?

### SIMILAR SHAPES

Place a piece of paper over the dot grid in Figure 15.2. Using the dots as a guide, draw a shape that is *like* the one shown but larger. How many different shapes that are like the given shape can you draw and still stay within the grid provided?

**Figure 15.2**  **Draw some shapes just like this, only larger.**

### COLLECTION

Deron bought a new collection of baseball cards. It has 8 Hall of Fame players and 12 other players who are only rookies. Mom says Deron has to share part of the collection with Derik, his younger brother, and she notes that Deron should include a fair number of valuable cards. If he gives Derik 2 of the Hall of Famers, how many of the other players' cards should he give Derik if the mix of valuable and ordinary cards is to be the same as in the original set Deron bought?

## Examples of Ratios in Different Contexts

A *ratio* is an ordered pair of numbers or measurements that express a comparison between the numbers or measures. This definition covers a wide range of situations. To students, ratios in different settings or contexts may present very different ideas and different difficulties.

## All Fractions Are Ratios

Fractions are a means of comparing parts to the whole. The fraction $\frac{3}{4}$ is a comparison of 3 parts to the 4 parts that make up the whole. Both the whole and the part are measured in fourths. Such a comparison of parts to wholes is also a ratio. So all fractions are ratios. The fraction $\frac{9}{12}$ is an expression of the same ratio as $\frac{3}{4}$.

## Ratios Can Compare Two Parts of the Same Whole

Some ratios are comparisons of one part of a whole to another part. In the "Collection" exercise, there were 8 of one kind of card and 12 of the other. The ratio of valuable cards to the whole set is 8 to 20. But you can also compare the two kinds of cards to each other instead of one part of the set to the total. A comparison of valuable to regular cards is not a fraction but a ratio of a part to a part. The valuable and less valuable cards are in the ratio of 8 to 12, or 2 to 3. Other examples of part-to-part ratios are Democrats to Republicans, boys to girls, and sailboats to speedboats.

## Ratios Can Be Expressions of Rates

Both part-to-whole and part-to-part ratios compare two measures of the same type of thing. A ratio can also be a *rate*. A rate is a comparison of the measures of two different things or quantities; the measuring unit is different for each value.

In the "Short and Tall" exercise, the comparison between paper clips and money is a ratio that is a rate—in this case, dollars per paper clip. If you figured out the ratio of $2.00 for every 3 clips, you could determine that the tall trophy should be 9 clips tall. All prices are rates and are also ratios: 69 cents each, 3 for a dollar, 12 ounces for $1.39. A price is a ratio of money to a measure of quantity.

The "Laps" exercise involved comparisons of time to distance, another example of rate. There are no numbers involved in that exercise, so the reasoning is qualitative rather than quantitative, but the ratio concept is basically the same. All rates of speed are comparisons of time and distance: for example, driving at 55 miles per hour (time to distance) or jogging at 9 minutes per mile (distance to time).

Other rates that we may not think of as ratios are miles per gallon, square yards of coverage per gallon of paint, inches of tape per roll, passengers per busload, and roses per bouquet. Changes between two units of measure are also rates or ratios. Examples include inches per foot, milliliters per liter, and centimeters per inch. The distance scale on a map is another example of a ratio as a rate.

## Other Examples of Ratio

In geometry, the ratio of the circumference of a circle to the diameter is designated by the Greek letter $\pi$ (pi). The ratios of corresponding parts of similar geometric figures are always the same, as in the "Similar Shapes" exercise. The diagonal of a square is always $\sqrt{2}$ times a side. The trigonometric functions can be developed from ratios of sides of right triangles. The slope of a line or of a roof is a ratio of rise for each unit of horizontal distance or run.

The chances of rolling a sum of 7 with two dice are 6 in 36, or 1 in 6. Probabilities are part-to-whole ratios: the number of favorable outcomes compared to the total number of possible outcomes.

In music, you find a set number of beats to a measure, 8 whole notes or 12 tones to an octave. Pleasant-sounding chords involve tones with wavelengths in specific ratios.

In nature, the ratio known as the *golden ratio* is found in many spirals, from nautilus shells to the swirls of a pinecone or a pineapple. Artists and architects have used the same ratio in creating shapes that are naturally pleasing to the eye.

# Proportions

As students begin to reflect on a variety of examples of ratios, they will also begin to see comparisons that are in the *same ratio*. In the "Similar Shapes" exercise, the ratio of any two sides of a small shape is the same as the ratio of the corresponding sides of a larger but similar shape. In the "Collection" exercise, the ratios of good to ordinary cards in Deron's set of 15 cards, in Derik's set of 5 cards, and in the original set of 20 cards can be seen to be the same even though there are different numbers in each situation.

A *proportion* is a statement of equality between two ratios. Different notations for proportions can be used, for example:

$$3 : 9 = 4 : 12 \quad \text{or} \quad \frac{3}{9} = \frac{4}{12}$$

These might be read "3 is to 9 as 4 is to 12" or "3 and 9 are in the same ratio as 4 and 12."

A ratio that is a rate usually includes the units of measure when written, for example:

$$\frac{\$12.50}{1 \text{ gallon}} = \frac{\$37.50}{3 \text{ gallons}}$$

Similarly, 12 inches per foot is the same as 36 inches per 3 feet.

There is a distinction between a proportion and the idea of equivalent fractions. Equivalent fractions are different symbols for the same quantity or amount; they represent the same rational number in different forms. If one bag has 3 red and 9 white balls and another has 4 red and 12 white, the number of red balls in each bag is different. But the ratios of red to white and red to total—the comparisons of these quantities—is the same for both bags.

Finding one number in a proportion when given the other three is called *solving* a proportion.

# Proportional Reasoning and Children

*Proportional reasoning* includes an understanding of ratios but is also much more. It involves the ability to compare ratios and to predict or produce equivalent ratios. It requires the ability to make comparisons, not just of the quantities involved but of the relationships between quantities as well. As the exercises have shown, proportional reasoning involves quantitative as well as qualitative thinking yet is not dependent on a skill with a mechanical or algorithmic procedure.

## A Developmental Perspective

Considerable research has been conducted to determine how children reason in various proportionality tasks and to determine if developmental or instructional factors are related to proportional reasoning (for example, see Karplus, Pulos, & Stage, 1983; Lamon, 1993; Lo & Watanabe, 1997; Noelting, 1980; and Post, Behr, & Lesh, 1988). These research efforts clearly indicate that proportional reasoning is not an automatic result of natural growth and development. Many adults have not acquired the skills of proportional thinking, and the performance of junior high school students on proportional tasks has been disappointing.

The research provides direction for how to help children develop proportional thought processes. Some of these ideas are outlined here.

1. Provide ratio and proportion tasks in a wide range of contexts. These might include situations involving measurements, prices, geometric and other visual contexts, and rates of all sorts.

2. Encourage discussion and experimentation in predicting and comparing ratios. Help children distinguish between proportional and nonproportional comparisons by providing examples of each and discussing the differences.

3. Help children relate proportional reasoning to existing processes. The concept of unit fractions is very similar to unit rates. Research indicates that the use of a unit rate for comparing ratios and solving proportions is the most common approach among junior high students even when cross-product methods have been taught. (This approach is explained later.)

4. Recognize that symbolic or mechanical methods, such as the cross-product algorithm, for solving proportions do not develop proportional reasoning and should not be introduced until students have had many experiences with intuitive and conceptual methods.

## Contrast with a Mechanical Approach

Suppose that you have been given a procedure for solving proportions of the following form:

1. Set up a proportion: $\dfrac{a}{b} = \dfrac{c}{x}$

2. Cross-multiply: $a \times x = b \times c$

3. Solve for the unknown: $x = \dfrac{b \times c}{a}$

After exercises involving this procedure, you are given problems like "Short and Tall" and guided to set up the proportion:

$$\frac{4 \text{ dollars}}{6 \text{ clips}} = \frac{6 \text{ dollars}}{n \text{ clips}}$$

Ignoring the fact that it does not make a lot of sense to multiply clips times dollars, you cross-multiply ($4 \times n = 6 \times 6$) and solve for $n$ by division. Would this activity help you conceptualize ratio in any general way or even help you solve additional exercises?

Sixth-, seventh-, and eighth-grade curricula have traditionally focused on the procedural knowledge associated with ratio and proportion. That includes deciding if two ratios given symbolically are equal or unequal (check the cross-products) and solving proportions as in the preceding example. This emphasis has been due partly to standardized testing, which has required such skills, and partly to the difficulty of specifying thought processes, such as proportional reasoning, in lists of objectives.

It takes considerable class time to provide students with experiences that permit intuitive thought and reflection. Situations that are very different on the surface must be explored before commonalities show through. Contextual and numeric differences in problems play a significant role in how children approach proportion tasks and how difficult they are to solve (Lamon, 1993; Thompson & Thompson, 1994). A focus on procedures does not help students think about relationships in any global manner.

Time can be found for these exciting activities over the sixth- to eighth-grade years, and procedural knowledge can easily be connected to the resulting concepts.

## Exploration of Intuitive Methods for Solving Proportions

To illustrate some intuitive approaches for solving proportions, consider the following tasks:

**Tammy bought 3 widgets for $2.40. At the same price, how much would 10 widgets cost?**

**Tammy bought 4 widgets for $3.75. How much would a dozen widgets cost?**

Before reading further, solve these two problems using an approach for each that seems most reasonable to you.

In the first situation, it is perhaps easiest to determine the cost of one widget—the unit rate or unit price. This can be found by dividing the price of three widgets by 3. Multiplying this unit rate of $0.80 per widget by 10 will produce the answer. This approach is referred to as a *unit-rate* method of solving proportions.

In the second problem, a unit-rate approach could be used, but the division does not appear to be easy. Since 12 is a multiple of 4, it is easier to notice that the cost of a dozen is 3 times the cost of 4. This is called a *factor-of-change* method. It could have been used on the first problem but would have been awkward. The factor of change between 3 and 10 is $3\frac{1}{3}$. Multiplying $2.40 by $3\frac{1}{3}$ will produce the correct answer. Although the factor-of-change method is a useful way to think about proportions, it is most frequently used when the numbers are compatible. Students should be given problems in which the numbers lend themselves to both approaches so that they will explore both methods. When the numbers involved do not favor either the unit-rate or factor-of-change method, students should use and justify whichever method makes sense to them.

Notice that the unit-rate method is exactly the same as that used in solving many fraction problems. Consider the following fraction exercise: "If a given rectangle is $\frac{3}{10}$ of the whole, how big is the whole?" Dividing the rectangle into three parts forms a unit fractional part, which can then be "multiplied" to produce any related part, including the whole.

As illustrated in Figure 15.3, graphs provide another way of thinking about proportions, and they connect proportional thought to algebraic interpretations. All graphs of equivalent ratios fall along straight lines through the origin. If the equation of one of these graphs is written in the form $y = mx$, the slope $m$ is always one of the equivalent ratios.

**Figure 15.3**  **Graph of price-to-item ratios.**

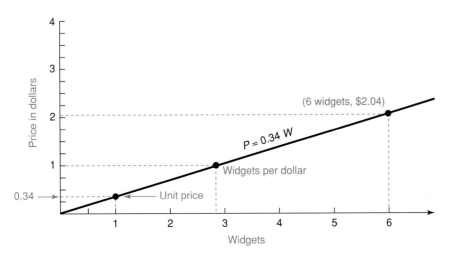

No one method for solving a proportion should be favored over another, and none should be taught in a rote manner. Rather, activities and guided discussions should help students learn to think proportionally in a variety of ways and contexts.

# INFORMAL ACTIVITIES TO DEVELOP PROPORTIONAL REASONING

Three categories of activities are suggested here: selection of equivalent ratios, scaling or table activities, and construction and measurement activities. Each provides a different opportunity for the development of proportional reasoning. The activities are not in any definitive sequence, nor are they designed to teach specific methods for solving proportions. Some activities can be modified or repeated using different numbers or contexts to produce more or less difficult situations or to suggest different thought processes.

## Equivalent Ratio Selections

In selection activities, a ratio is presented, and students select an equivalent ratio from others presented. The focus should be on an intuitive rationale for why the pairs selected are in the same ratio. Sometimes numeric values will play a part to help students develop numeric methods to explain their reasoning. In later activities, students will be asked to construct an equivalent ratio without choices being provided.

It is extremely useful in these activities to include pairs of ratios that are not proportional but have a common difference. For example, $\frac{5}{8}$ and $\frac{9}{12}$ are not equivalent ratios, but the corresponding differences are the same: $8 - 5 = 12 - 9$. Students who focus on this additive relationship are not seeing the multiplicative relationship of proportionality.

### ACTIVITY

#### 15.1 Look-Alike Rectangles

Draw a collection of 13 rectangles on one sheet of paper. Use a sheet of centimeter grid paper, and trace the rectangles using whole-number measures for at least one dimension of each rectangle. Make four rectangles with sides in the ratio of 1 to 4, four in the ratio 2 to 5, four in the ratio 5 to 8, and one square about midsize to the other 12 rectangles. Label the rectangles A to M in a mixed order.

The students' task is to group the rectangles into three sets of four that "look alike" with one "oddball." Do not tell them that the oddball is the square. When they have decided on their groupings, stop and discuss reasons they classified the rectangles as they did. Be prepared for some students to try to match

sides or look for rectangles that have the same amount of difference between them. Do not evaluate any rationale offered. Next have them measure and record the sides of each rectangle to the nearest half-centimeter and calculate the ratios of the short to long sides for each. You may want to prepare a little worksheet as shown in Figure 15.4. Discuss these results, and ask students to offer explanations. If the groups are formed of proportional (similar) rectangles, the ratios within each group will all be the same.

If you laminate the rectangles before cutting them out, they can be used from year to year.

**Figure 15.4** A recording sheet for "Look-Alike Rectangles."

The "Look-Alike Rectangles" are actually groups of similar figures. The same activity can be done with triangles or any sets of shapes designed as groups of similar figures. The focus in this activity is on observing like ratios. From a geometric standpoint, this is an activity about similarity. The two concepts—proportionality and similarity—are closely connected.

Another feature of proportional rectangles can be observed by stacking like rectangles aligned at one corner, as in Figure 15.5. Place a straightedge across the diagonals, and you will see that opposite corners also line up. If the rectan-

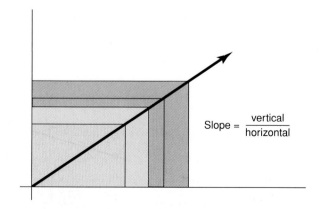

**Figure 15.5** The slope of a line through a stack of proportional rectangles is equal to the ratio of the two sides.

gles are placed on a coordinate axis with the common corner at the origin, the slope of the line joining the corners is the ratio of the sides. Here is a connection between proportional reasoning and algebra.

---

**ACTIVITY**

## 15.2 Different Objects, Same Ratios

Prepare cards with distinctly different objects, as shown in Figure 15.6. Given one card, students are to select a card on which the ratio of the two types of objects is the same. This task moves students to a numeric approach rather than a visual one and introduces the notion of ratios as rates. A unit rate is depicted on a card that shows exactly one of either of the two types of objects. For example, the card with three boxes and one truck provides one unit rate. A unit rate for the other ratio is not shown. What would it be? Objects paired with coins or bills is a way to introduce price as a ratio.

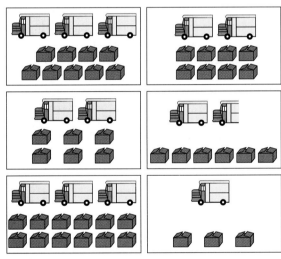

On which cards is the ratio of trucks to boxes the same? Also, compare trucks to trucks and boxes to boxes.

**Figure 15.6** **Rate cards: Match cards with the same rate of boxes per truck.**

---

# Within and Between Ratios

When comparing ratios, it is sometimes useful to think of them as being either *within* ratios or *between* ratios. A ratio between two measures in the same setting is a *within* ratio. If a 12-ounce box of cereal costs $1.39, the ratio of price to weight is a within ratio. If I have a larger box of the same cereal, the price-to-weight ratio will be the same if the cereal is priced the same. Suppose that the larger box holds 32 ounces and is priced at $2.59. The within ratio, 2.59/32 is about $0.08 per ounce. The

same ratio for the smaller box, 1.39/12, is about $0.12 per ounce. These prices are not proportional.

A *between* ratio is a ratio of two corresponding measures in different situations. In the cereal example, the two between ratios are cost to cost and price to price. The between ratio for cost is 32 ounces to 12 ounces, or 2.67. The between ratio for price, $2.59 to $1.39, is 1.86. You get 2.67 times as much cereal for only 1.86 times as much money.

In the "Look-Alike Rectangles" activity, students calculate within ratios. The ratio of two sides within one rectangle is equal to the like ratio within a look-alike rectangle. When doing that activity, challenge your students to find examples of between ratios that are alike (long side to long side and short side to short side). The between ratios will be alike for any *two* rectangles in the same group but not for all pairs of rectangles in the group. Why?

The simple drawing in Figure 15.7 is a nice generic way of looking at two ratios and determining if a ratio is between or within. A drawing similar to this is often very helpful for organizing ratios in proportional contexts.

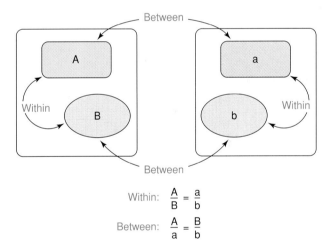

Within: $\dfrac{A}{B} = \dfrac{a}{b}$

Between: $\dfrac{A}{a} = \dfrac{B}{b}$

**Figure 15.7** **Given a proportional situation, the two between ratios and the two within ratios will be the same.**

In each of the following pairs, the two ratios are equivalent, but the proportionality is more easily seen when there are integral multiples in either the within or the between ratios. The type of ratio indicated to the right is the one most easily compared. Put the numbers in the drawing in Figure 15.7 to help make this clear. Notice that the order of the numbers in one ratio is not important as long as the corresponding order is used in the other ratio.

| | | | |
|---|---|---|---|
| 3 to 12 | and | 5 to 20 | (within) |
| 2 to 6 | and | 6 to 18 | (between and within) |
| 3 to 7 | and | 6 to 14 | (between) |
| 4 to 6 | and | 10 to 15 | (neither) |

When there is an even multiple within, the ratio can easily be converted to a unit ratio. For example, 3 to 12 is the same as 1 to 4. Pairs that involve between but not within multiples lend themselves to the factor-of-change approach: 6 to 14 is an even multiple of the 3-to-7 ratio.

# Scaling Activities

Scaling activities involve filling in charts where paired entries are related in some way. The format of a chart is not important, and different formats can be used. Scaling up is a matter of providing entries with larger numbers, and scaling down is entering smaller numbers. The following are examples of scaling up:

| | | | | |
|---|---|---|---|---|
| 1 foot | → | 12 inches | 1 can | → | $0.55 |
| 2 feet | → | 24 inches | 2 cans | → | $1.10 |
| 3 feet | → | ? inches | 3 cans | → | $ ? |

The items in the charts can be related measures such as time (minutes to hours), money (nickels to quarters), weight (pounds to ounces or kilograms), or common pairings such as crayons to boxes, hands to fingers, or wheels to tricycles. They can also be arbitrary ratios, such as a man who eats three bagels for every two bananas.

In a scaling-down activity, one or two larger entries in the list or table are given, and students are asked to provide smaller entries:

| | | | | | |
|---|---|---|---|---|---|
| 28 days | → | 4 weeks | 12 cups | → | 24 sugar cubes |
| 21 days | → | 3 weeks | 11 cups | → | 22 sugar cubes |
| ? days | → | 2 weeks | 10 cups | → | ? sugar cubes |

Be careful not to make these exercises too long or tedious. Allow students to use repeated addition or subtraction as well as multiplication and division. Also be sure to permit the use of calculators to make computation easy.

Notice that in the examples so far, the unit ratio is easy to determine without the use of fractions. These easier scaling activities can be done at an early grade. Later, fractions and decimals can be used. Students can scale down with one division to get a unit ratio and multiply to get a particular requested entry, as in the following example:

3 boxes for $2.25 → 5 boxes for ?
 1 box is $0.75 (unit ratio), so 5 boxes is
5 × $0.75 = $3.75.

Scaling can also be done up or down without using a unit ratio:

| Minutes: | 5 | ? | 15 | 20 | 25 | 30 | 35 |
|---|---|---|---|---|---|---|---|
| Widgets made: | ? | 14 | 21 | ? | ? | ? | ? |

The next two activities are related to scaling but are less structured.

## ACTIVITY

### 15.3 What's in the Bag?

This activity involves informal probability concepts as well as ratio. Put colored cubes or other counters of two colors in a bag. For example, use 4 red and 8 blue. Explain that there are cubes of different colors in the bag, but do not tell students the number of cubes or number of colors. Shake the bag, and have students draw out a cube, record the color, and return the cube to the bag. After 10 or 15 trials, ask students how many of each color they think might be in the bag, and record the guesses. After some more trials, you could ask what is the fewest possible number of cubes that they think could be in the bag.

Then you can give them one of the following clues: the total counters that are in the bag or the number of cubes of one color. See if with this information they can predict how many of each color are in the bag. "What if there were more cubes? What are other numbers of each color that might be in the bag?" The discussion is useful even if the students do not guess the correct ratio of colors. You can continue pulling out blocks to see that the ratio stays approximately, but not exactly, the same. Besides changing the ratio of colors on different days, you can add a third color. After seeing the actual contents of the bag, discuss what other numbers of each color would produce the same result. Groups might explore drawing cubes from bags with equal ratios of colors but different numbers and compare the results.

## ACTIVITY

### 15.4 Graphs Showing Ratios

Have students make a graph of the data from a collection of equal ratios that they have scaled or discussed. The graph in Figure 15.8 is of the ratios of two sides of similar rectangles. If only a few ratios have actually been computed, the graph can be drawn carefully and then used to determine other equivalent ratios. This is especially interesting when there is a physical model to coincide with the ratio. In the rectangle example, students can draw rectangles with sides determined by the graphs and compare them to the original rectangles. A unit ratio can be found by locating the point on the line that is directly above or to the right of the number 1 on the graph. (There are actually two unit ratios for every ratio. Why?) Students can then use the unit ratio to scale up to other values and check to see that they are on the graph as well. Note that the slope of any line through the origin is a ratio.

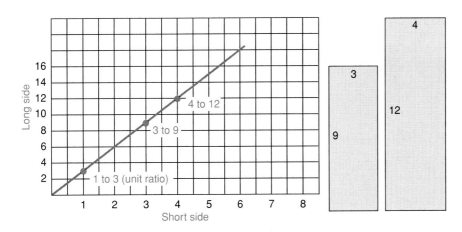

**Figure 15.8** **Graphs show ratios of sides in similar rectangles.**

A spreadsheet can be a real asset for investigating proportions in table form. How much direction you provide depends on students' familiarity with spreadsheets. Even if only a few ratios in a table are provided, students can enter these in two columns and use the spreadsheet to divide the values in one column by the other. The division produces one of the two unit ratios. Assuming that the ratios are proportional, each unit ratio computed in each row will be the same. The spreadsheet can then be used to extend the table, either scaling up or scaling down using the unit ratio. Formulas are easily entered in one row and then extended down the column. In fact, this activity may be a good place to introduce students to formulas on the spreadsheet and how to extend them.

## Construction and Measurement Activities

In these activities, measurements are made to construct physical or visual models of equivalent ratios in order to provide a tangible example of a proportion as well as look at numeric relationships.

### ACTIVITY

### 15.5 Different Units, Equal Ratios

**Cut strips of adding machine tape all the same length, and give one strip to each group in your class. Each group is to measure the strip using a different unit. Possible units include different Cuisenaire rods, a piece of chalk, a pencil, the edge of a book or index card, or standard units such as inches or centimeters. When every group has measured the strip, ask for the measure of one of the groups, and display the unit of measure. Next, hold up the unit of measure used by another group, and have the class compare it with the first unit. See if the class can estimate the measurement that the second group found. The ratio of the measuring units should be the inverse of the mea-**surements made with those units. For example, if two units are in a ratio of 2 to 3, the respective units will be in a ratio of 3 to 2. Examine measurements made with other units. Finally, present a unit that no group has used, and see if the class can predict the measurement when made with that unit.

Activity 15.5 can be profitably extended by providing each group with an identical set of four strips of quite different lengths. Good lengths might be 20, 50, 80, and 120 cm. As before, each group measures the strips using a different length.

This time, have each group enter data into a common spreadsheet. (Alternatively, share group data so that all groups can enter data on their own spreadsheets.) Figure 15.9 (p. 268) shows what a spreadsheet might look like for three groups. A template can be prepared ahead of time, or students can create their own spreadsheets. Almost all spreadsheets will offer a variety of graphing options. In this activity, bar graphs show the actual measurements for each group and circle graphs show each measure in ratio to the sum of the measures (i.e., a percentage of total measures.)

Once the graphs are completed, there are numerous opportunities to observe and explore proportions. The bar graphs, though different, all look "alike." Since the circle graphs illustrate the ratios rather than the actual measurements, they will be identical or nearly so. Within and between ratios are easily calculated with the spreadsheet.

Continue the exploration by introducing a new strip. If you know its measure with any one of the units, what will its measure be with the other units? Similarly, if a new unit of measure is introduced, how can the measures of the strips be determined? Can this be done by comparing the new unit with an old one? If a known strip is measured with the new unit, can all other measures and ratios be determined?

Bar graphs and circle plots are also easily made with a TI-73 graphing calculator. If technology is not available, this same activity can be done by hand. To make circle graphs, use the hundredths disk in the Blackline Masters.

| | A | B | C | D | E | F | G | H | I |
|---|---|---|---|---|---|---|---|---|---|
| **2** | | | Four strips measured with three different units. | | | | | | |
| **3** | | | | | | | | | |
| **4** | | Unit A | Unit B | Unit C | | | | | |
| **5** | Strip 1 | 19.2 | 32 | 12.8 | | | | | |
| **6** | Strip 2 | 28.8 | 48 | 19.2 | | | | | |
| **7** | Strip 3 | 4.8 | 8 | 3.2 | | | | | |
| **8** | Strip 4 | 12.0 | 20 | 8.0 | | | | | |
| **9** | | | | | | | | | |
| **10** | | | Within Ratios | | | | | | |
| **11** | 1 to 2 | 0.7 | 0.7 | 0.7 | | | | | |
| **12** | 1 to 3 | 4.0 | 4.0 | 4.0 | | | | | |
| **13** | 1 to 4 | 1.6 | 1.6 | 1.6 | | | | | |
| **14** | 2 to 3 | 6.0 | 6.0 | 6.0 | | | | | |
| **15** | 2 to 4 | 2.4 | 2.4 | 2.4 | | | | | |
| **16** | 3 to 4 | 0.4 | 0.4 | 0.4 | | | | | |
| **17** | | | | | | | | | |
| **18** | | | | | | | | | |
| **19** | | | Between Ratios | | | | | | |
| **20** | | A to B | A to C | B to C | | | | | |
| **21** | Strip 1 | 0.6 | 1.5 | 2.5 | | | | | |
| **22** | Strip 2 | 0.6 | 1.5 | 2.5 | | | | | |
| **23** | Strip 3 | 0.6 | 1.5 | 2.5 | | | | | |
| **24** | Strip 4 | 0.6 | 1.5 | 2.5 | | | | | |
| **25** | | | | | | | | | |
| **26** | | | | | | | | | |

**Figure 15.9** **A spreadsheet can be used to record data, create tables of interesting ratios, and produce bar and circle graphs.**
*Source:* Screen reprinted with permission from Apple Computer, Inc.

## ACTIVITY

### 15.6 Density Ratios

This activity involves weight and density ratios. Provide each group with four small containers of different sizes. The four containers must be the same for each group. Have each group fill its containers with a different filler. Select fillers that vary greatly in density—for example, dry oatmeal, rice, sand, and small metal washers. Each group weighs the contents of its containers (not including the containers) to the nearest gram. The results will be similar to the length experiment. Instead of different units of measure, the different densities of the fillers will produce different weights. Use a spreadsheet to produce the graphs and compute the ratios of interest.

## ACTIVITY

### 15.7 Scale Drawings

On grid or dot paper (see the Blackline Masters), have students draw a simple shape using straight lines with vertices on the dots. After one shape is complete, have them draw a larger or smaller shape that is the same as or similar to the first. This can be done on a grid of the same size or a different size, as shown in Figure 15.10. After completing two or three pictures of different sizes, the ratios of the lengths of different sides can be compared.

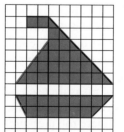

Use a metric ruler
- Choose two lengths on one boat and form a ratio (use a calculator). Compare to the ratio of the same parts of the other boats.
- Choose two boats. Measure the same part of each boat, and form a ratio. Compare with the ratios of another part.
- Compare the areas of the big sails with the lengths of the bottom sides.

**Figure 15.10** **Comparing similar figures drawn on grids.**

Corresponding sides from one figure to the next should all be in the same ratio. The ratio of two sides within one figure should be the same as the ratio of the corresponding two sides in another figure. This activity connects the geometric idea of similarity with the numeric concept of ratio.

## ✏ACTIVITY

# 15.8 Length, Surface, and Volume Ratios

A three-dimensional version of Activity 15.7 can be done with blocks, as shown in Figure 15.11. Using 1-inch or 2-cm wooden cubes, make a simple "building." Then make a similar but larger building, and com-

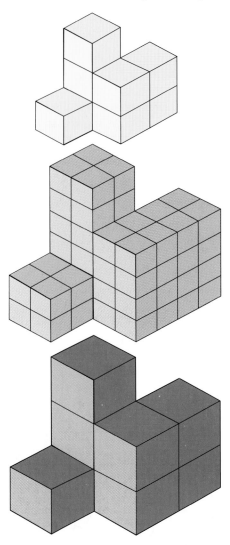

Similar "buildings" can be made by changing the number of blocks in each dimension (factor of change) or by using different-sized blocks.

**Figure 15.11** **Similar constructions.**

pare measures. A different size can also be made using different-sized blocks. To measure buildings made with different blocks, use a common unit such as centimeters. (Notice that volumes and surface areas do not vary proportionally with the edges of solids. However, these are relationships that are interesting to observe.)

Activities 15.7 and 15.8 involve area and volume as well as length. Comparisons of corresponding lengths, areas, and volumes in proportional figures lead to some interesting ratios. If two figures are proportional (similar), any two linear dimensions you measure will be in the same ratio on each, say, 1 to $k$. Corresponding areas, however, will be in the ratio of 1 to $k^2$, and corresponding volumes in the ratio of 1 to $k^3$. Try this with some constructions of your own.

As a means of contrasting proportional situations with additive ones, try starting with a figure on a grid or a building made with blocks and adding two units to every dimension in the figure. The result will be larger but will not look at all the same. Try this with a simple rectangle that is 1 cm by 15 cm. The new rectangle is twice as "thick" (2 cm) but only a bit longer. It will not appear to be the same shape as the original.

Dynamic geometry software such as *The Geometer's Sketchpad* (Key Curriculum Press, 1995) offers a very effective method of exploring the idea of ratio. In Figure 15.12, two lengths are drawn on a grid using the "snap-to-grid" option. The lengths are measured, and two ratios are computed. As the length of either line is changed, the measures and ratios are updated instantly. A screen similar to this could be used to discuss ratios of lengths as well as inverse ratios with your full class. In this example, notice that the second pair of lines has the same difference but that the ratios are not the same. A similar drawing could be prepared for the overhead on a transparency of a centimeter dot grid if software was not available.

**Figure 15.12** **Dynamic geometry software or just a centimeter grid can be used to discuss ratios of two lengths.**

*Source:* From *The Geometer's Sketchpad.* Key Curriculum Press, 1150 65th Street, Emeryville, CA 94608; (800)995-MATH. Used by permission.

Activity 15.9 is a useful follow-up to the discussion of equal ratios of line segments. Measures and ratios can be turned on or off, so that the information the student receives can change the activity considerably.

---

**ACTIVITY**

## 15.9 Match the Ratios

Create a sketch like the one shown in Figure 15.13 using *The Geometer's Sketchpad*. The lengths of each of the four segments can be adjusted by dragging the right endpoints along the dotted-line rays. If the top pair of segments (AB and CD) is set, the students' task is to adjust segments EF and GH so that they are in the same ratio as AB:CD. Segment EF can be preset, or students can be free to change it as well. In the figure, all measures and ratios are shown. The Hide and Show buttons turn the indicated information on or off. The ratio EF:GH should be hidden for use as a check when students feel they have the two pairs of lines in the same ratio. If measures and ratios are hidden, the task is purely visual. If the ratio of AB:CD or the measures of segments are shown, the task changes considerably. All modes should be explored.

---

Similar tasks can be created using *Cabri Geometry* (Texas Instruments, 1994) or *Geometry Inventor* (LOGAL, 1994a). The computer screen can be projected for use as a class discussion or used by pairs or individuals at separate computers. A low-tech version of this activity can be conducted with the chalkboard and a meter stick. Draw segments AB, CD, and EF on the board. The student task is to draw GH as in Activity 15.9. As with the computer version, measures of the segments can be given to the students or not. Ratios can be computed with a calculator.

Other activities can also be transformed into estimation activities. For example, prepare a figure on plain paper using graph paper placed underneath as a guide. The figure can be as simple as a right triangle or more complicated, such as a drawing of a truck or a house. Make a transparency of the drawing. Students will see a very large figure with no measurements or grid. On paper with a very small grid, perhaps 0.5 cm, students attempt to draw a figure similar to the one on the overhead. Producing a perfectly similar figure may be difficult, but many may be close or even exact.

## SOLVING PROPORTIONS

The activities to this point have been designed to lead students to an intuitive concept of ratio and proportion, to help in the development of proportional reasoning.

**Compare the ratio of AB and CD to the ratio of EF and GH.**

Drag the right-hand endpoints to change the lengths of the segments. Set AB and CD first. Then adjust EF and GH so that those two segments are in the same ratio.

**Figure 15.13**  **This activity was created with *The Geometer's Sketchpad*. The task is to adjust segments EF and GH to be in the same ratio as AB and CD. To change the difficulty, the measures and ratios can be hidden by clicking on the Hide and Show buttons.**

*Source:* From *The Geometer's Sketchpad*. Key Curriculum Press, 1150 65th Street, Emeryville, CA 94608; (800)995-MATH. Used by permission.

One practical value of proportional reasoning is to use observed proportions to find unknown values. Knowledge of one ratio can often be used to find a value in the other. Comparison pricing, using scales on maps, and solving percentage problems are just a few everyday instances where solving proportions is required. Students need to learn to set up proportions symbolically and to solve them.

# An Informal Approach

Traditional textbooks show students how to set up an equation of two ratios involving an unknown, "cross-multiply," and solve for the unknown. This can be a very mechanical approach and will almost certainly lead to confusion and error. Although you may wish eventually to cover the cross-product algorithm, it is well worth the time for students to find ways to solve proportions using their own ideas first. If you have been exploring proportions in various activities, students will have a good foundation on which to build their own approaches.

For each of the following two problems, place the numbers in a little drawing of two ratios similar to Figure 15.7 (p. 265). Solve each problem. Think about within or between ratios matching up. Do not use cross-multiplication.

---

At the Office Super Store, you can buy plain #2 pencils, four for 59 cents. The store also sells the same pencils in a large box of 5 dozen pencils for $7.79. How much do you save by buying the large box?

---

The price of a box of 2 dozen candy bars is $4.80. Bridget wants to buy 5 candy bars. What will she have to pay?

---

To solve the pencil problem, you might notice that the between ratio of pencils to pencils is 4 to 60, or 1 to 15. If you multiply the 59 cents by 15, the factor of change, you will get the price of the box of 60 if the pencils were sold at the same price. In the candy problem, the within ratio of 24 to $4.80 is easy to use to get the unit rate of 20 cents per candy bar. But what do you do if the numbers don't "come out nicely" like they do in these problems?

Try solving the same problems with new numbers that do not work out so easily. If you are having difficulty with the new problems, discuss them with a friend.

Finally, try the following problem. Make a little sketch as before, and use a technique you have figured out yourself. (Do this now before reading on.)

---

Brian can run 5 km in 18.4 minutes. If he keeps on running at the same speed, how far can he run in 23 minutes?

---

The first situation for your sketch is Brian's 5-km run (5 km and 18.4 minutes). The second situation is the unknown distance and 23 minutes. There are at least two things you might consider, and one is no easier than the other. You could look at the between ratios of minutes to minutes in order to find a factor of change. That is, what do you multiply 18.4 by to get 23? On the calculator, compute 23 ÷ 18.4 to get 1.25, the factor of change. Now 5 km × 1.25 is 6.25 km.

The second possibility is to get a unit rate for the 5 km and multiply by 23. That would mean divide both the 5 and the 18.4 by 18.4 (like simplifying a fraction to a denominator of 1). The calculator yields 0.2717391, or about 0.27 km per minute. Multiply this unit rate by 23 minutes and you get 6.2499993 km. In both cases, the longer distance is 6.25 km.

What is important here is to see how to use multiplication to solve the proportional situation. Further, notice that the calculations are based on ideas already developed. The sketch of the two ratios helps keep things straight and avoids any ambiguous cross-multiplying.

# The Cross-Product Algorithm

The methods just described come close to being well-defined algorithms, though they are a bit more flexible than cross-product methods. The reality is that the computations involved are exactly the same as in cross-multiplication. Yet some teachers may still want to teach cross-multiplication.

## Draw a Simple Model

Given a ratio word problem, the greatest difficulty students have is setting up a correct proportion or equation of two ratios, one of which includes the missing value. "Which fractions do I make? Where does the $x$ go?"

Rather than drill and drill in the hope that they will somehow eventually get it, show students how to sketch a simple picture that will help them determine what parts are related. In Figure 15.14, a simple model is drawn for a typical rate or price problem. The two equations in the figure come from setting up within and between ratios.

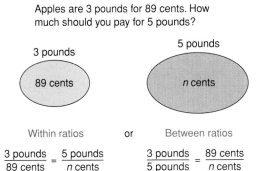

$$\frac{3 \text{ pounds}}{89 \text{ cents}} = \frac{5 \text{ pounds}}{n \text{ cents}} \qquad \frac{3 \text{ pounds}}{5 \text{ pounds}} = \frac{89 \text{ cents}}{n \text{ cents}}$$

**Figure 15.14** A simple drawing helps in a price-to-ratio problem.

## Solve the Proportion

Examine the left (within) ratios in the same way as for Brian's 5-km race: Find out what to multiply the left fraction by to get the right. To do this, we would divide 5 by 3 and then multiply that result by 89:

$$\frac{5}{3} \times 89$$

Looking at the same left equation in Figure 15.14, we could also determine the unit price or the price for 1 pound by dividing the 89 cents by 3 and then multiplying this result by 5 to determine the price of 5 pounds:

$$\frac{89}{3} \times 5$$

Now look what happens if we cross-multiply in the original equation:

$$3n = 5 \times 89$$

$$n = \frac{5 \times 89}{3}$$

This equation can be solved by dividing the 5 by 3 and multiplying by 89 or dividing 89 by 3 and multiplying by 5. These are exactly the two devices we employed in our more intuitive approach. If you cross-multiply the between ratios, you get exactly the same result. Furthermore, you get the same result if you had written the two ratios inverted, that is, with the reciprocals of each fraction. Try it!

So if you want to develop a cross-product algorithm, it is not unreasonable to do problems like these while encouraging students to use their own methods. If you write out the computations involved, a very small amount of direct teaching can develop the cross-product approach. But why hurry?

In Figure 15.15, a problem involving rates of speed is modeled with simple lines representing the two distances. The distance and the time for each run is modeled with the same line. You cannot see time, but it fits into the distance covered. All equal-rates-of-speed problems can be modeled this way. There really is no significant difference from the

drawing used for the apples. Again, it is just as acceptable to write between ratios as within ratios, and students need not worry about which one goes on top as long as the ratios are written in the same order. The model helps with this difficulty.

# Activities Involving Proportions

In the preceding discussion, simple rate problems were used to help students develop a technique for solving proportions. The next two activities illustrate other common uses of proportional reasoning.

---

**A**CTIVITY

### 15.10  Scale Drawings

Provide students with a drawing of a simple geometric figure, including its dimensions. The task is to create a new drawing that is either larger or smaller than the given one. One dimension of the new drawing is specified (see Figure 15.16 for an example). Students can set up between or within ratios and determine the other dimensions by solving the proportion.

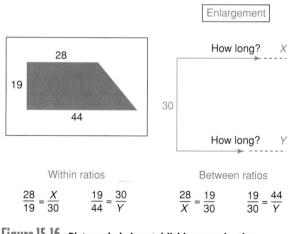

**Figure 15.16** Pictures help in establishing equal ratios.

---

This activity is somewhat simplistic, but it provides students with the essential ideas for solving proportions in more realistic situations such as these:

- If you wanted to make a scale model of the solar system and use a Ping-Pong ball for the earth, how far away should the sun be? How large a ball would you need?

- What scale should be used to draw a scale map of your city (or some interesting region) so that it will nicely fit onto a standard piece of poster board?

- Use the scale on a map to estimate the distance and travel time between two points of interest.

- Roll a toy car down a ramp, timing the trip with a stopwatch. How fast was the car traveling in miles per hour? If the speed is proportional to the size of the car, how fast would this have been for a real car?

**Figure 15.15**  **Line segments can be used to model both time and distance.**

■ Your little sister wants a table and chair for her doll. Her doll is 14 inches tall. How big should you make the table?

■ Determine the various distances that a ten-speed bike travels in one turn of the pedals. You will need to count the sprocket teeth on the front and back gears.

Have you ever wondered how scientists estimate the number of bass in a lake or the number of monarch butterflies that migrate each year to Mexico? One method often used is a capture-recapture technique modeled in the next activity.

---

**ACTIVITY**

### 15.11 Capture-Recapture

Prepare a shoebox full of some uniform small object such as centicubes or plastic chips. You could also use a larger box filled with Styrofoam packing "peanuts." If the box is your lake and the objects are the fish you want to count, how can you estimate the number without actually counting them? Remember, if they were fish, you couldn't even see them! Have a student reach into the box and "capture" a representative sample of the "fish." For a large box, you may want to capture more than a handful. "Tag" each fish by marking it in some way—marking pen or sticky dot. Count and record the number tagged, and then return them to the box. The assumption of the scientist is that tagged animals will mix uniformly with the larger population, so mix them thoroughly. Next, have five to ten students make a recapture of fish from the box. Each counts the total captured and the number in the capture that are tagged. Accumulate these data.

Now the task is to use all of the information to estimate the number of fish in the lake. The recapture data provide an estimated ratio of tagged to untagged fish. The number tagged to the total population should be in the same ratio. After solving the proportion, have students count the actual items in the box to see how close their estimate is.

---

For a more detailed description of the "Capture-Recapture" activity, see the NCTM Addenda Series book *Understanding Rational Numbers and Proportions* (Curcio & Bezuk, 1994).

## Percent Problems as Proportions

Percent has traditionally been included as a topic with ratio and proportion because percent is one form of ratio, a part-to-whole ratio. In Chapter 14, it was shown that percent problems can be connected to fraction concepts. Here the same part-to-whole fraction concept of percent will be extended to ratio and proportion concepts. Ideally, all of these ideas (fractions, decimals, ratio, proportion, and percent) should be conceptually integrated. The better that students

connect these ideas, the more flexible and useful their reasoning and problem-solving skills will be.

## Equivalent Fractions as Proportions

First consider how equivalent fractions can be interpreted as a proportion using the same simple models already used. In Figure 15.17, a line segment is partitioned in two different ways: in fourths on one side and in twelfths on the other. In the previous examples, proportions were established based on two amounts of apples, two different distances or runs, and two different sizes of drawings. Here only one thing is measured—the part of a whole—but it is measured or partitioned two ways: in fourths and in twelfths.

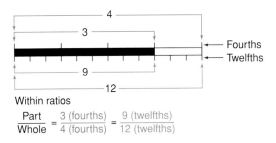

$$\frac{\text{Part}}{\text{Whole}} = \frac{3 \text{ (fourths)}}{4 \text{ (fourths)}} = \frac{9 \text{ (twelfths)}}{12 \text{ (twelfths)}}$$

**Figure 15.17** **Equivalent fractions as proportions.**

The within ratios are ratios of part to whole within each measurement. Within ratios result in the usual equivalent fraction equation, $\frac{3}{4} = \frac{9}{12}$ (3 fourths are to 4 fourths as 9 twelfths are to 12 twelfths). The between proportion equates a part-to-part ratio with a whole-to-whole ratio, or $\frac{3}{9} = \frac{4}{12}$ (3 fourths are to 9 twelfths as 4 fourths are to 12 twelfths).

A simple line segment drawing similar to the one in Figure 15.17 could be drawn to set up a proportion to solve any equivalent-fraction problem, even ones that do not result in whole-number numerators or denominators. Two examples are shown in Figure 15.18 (p. 274).

## Percent Problems

All percent problems are exactly the same as the equivalent-fraction examples. They involve a part and a whole measured in some unit and the same part and whole measured in hundredths—that is, in percents. A simple line segment drawing can be used for each of the three types of percent problems. Using this model as a guide, a proportion can be written and solved by the cross-product algorithm. Examples of each type of problem are shown in Figure 15.19 (p. 274).

It is tempting to teach all percent problems in this one way. Developmentally, such an approach is not recommended. Even though the approach is conceptual, it does not translate easily to intuitive ideas, mental arithmetic, or estimation as discussed in Chapter 14. The modeling and proportion approach of Figure 15.19 is suggested only as a way to help students analyze problems that may verbally present some difficulty. The approach of Chapter 14, which relates percent to part-whole fraction concepts, should probably receive more emphasis.

$$\frac{3}{5} = \frac{\square}{8}$$

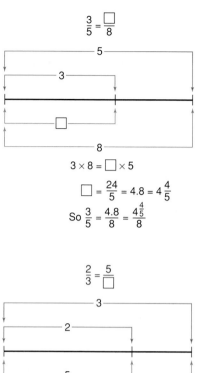

$$3 \times 8 = \square \times 5$$

$$\square = \frac{24}{5} = 4.8 = 4\frac{4}{5}$$

$$\text{So } \frac{3}{5} = \frac{4.8}{8} = \frac{4\frac{4}{5}}{8}$$

$$\frac{2}{3} = \frac{5}{\square}$$

$$2 \times \square = 3 \times 5$$

$$\square = \frac{15}{2} = 7\frac{1}{2} = 7.5$$

$$\frac{2}{3} = \frac{5}{7\frac{1}{2}} = \frac{5}{7.5}$$

Can you interpret these fractions?

**Figure 15.18**   **Solving equivalent-fraction problems as equivalent ratios using cross-products.**

## TECHNOLOGY NOTE

You have already seen how spreadsheets can be used to create tables and compute ratios. Dynamic geometry programs allow figures to be scaled to larger or smaller sizes by using either a specified ratio or the dilation feature. This provides an excellent connection between the concepts of similarity and proportion.

Very few computer programs specifically address the issue of proportionality. *CampOS Math* (Pierian Spring Software, 1996) has an activity called the Color Mixer in which the concept of ratio is applied to the mixing of red, green, and blue light to create new colors. By way of example, the student may be asked to set the color mixer so that the blue light is at 30 percent intensity and R:G (the ratio of red to green) = 5:9. There is some potential confusion between types of ratios. The program provides a somewhat realistic use of ratio and some minimal problem solving. ■

In 1960, U.S. railroads carried 327 million passengers. Over the next 20 years, there was a 14 percent decrease in passengers. How many passengers rode the railroads in 1980?

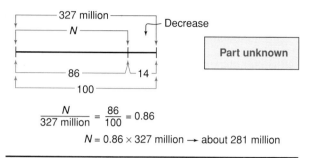

$$\frac{N}{327 \text{ million}} = \frac{86}{100} = 0.86$$

$$N = 0.86 \times 327 \text{ million} \rightarrow \text{about 281 million}$$

Sylvia's new boat cost $8950. She made a down payment of $2000. What percent of the sales price was Sylvia's down payment?

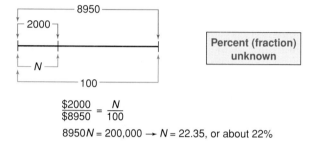

$$\frac{\$2000}{\$8950} = \frac{N}{100}$$

$$8950N = 200,000 \rightarrow N = 22.35, \text{ or about 22\%}$$

The average dressed weight of a beef steer is 62.5 percent of its weight before being slaughtered. If a dressed steer weighs 592 pounds, how much did it weigh "on the hoof"?

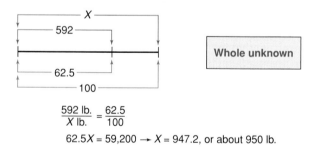

$$\frac{592 \text{ lb.}}{X \text{ lb.}} = \frac{62.5}{100}$$

$$62.5X = 59,200 \rightarrow X = 947.2, \text{ or about 950 lb.}$$

**Figure 15.19**   **The three percentage problems solved by setting up a proportion using a simple line segment model.**

## LITERATURE CONNECTIONS

Literature brings an exciting dimension to the exploration of proportional reasoning. Many books and stories discuss comparative sizes; concepts of scale as in maps; giants and miniature people who are proportional to regular people; comparative rates, especially rates of speed; and so on. A book may not appear to explore proportions, and the author may not have had that in mind at all, but comparisons are the stuff of many excellent stories and are at the heart of proportional ideas. The suggestions here are intended to give you an idea of what you might look for.

## *If You Hopped like a Frog*
### (Schwartz, 1999)

David Schwartz, the author of *How Much Is a Million?* and *If You Made a Million,* has found some wonderful mathematics in nature with this new book. Here Schwartz uses proportional reasoning to determine what it would be like if we had the powers or dimensions of familiar animals. "If you hopped like a frog, you could jump from home plate to first base in one mighty leap." This short picture book contains 12 of these fascinating proportions: if you were as strong as an ant . . . , if you flicked your tongue like a chameleon . . . , and so on. At the end of the book, Schwartz provides some factual data on which the proportions are based. The book could be read at least twice at the start of a lesson, and students could find their own comparisons to calculate. This is a wonderful connection to science. There is no reason the comparisons need be between animals and humans as in this book. The toy-car to real-car ratio is an example of comparisons students could be encouraged to explore using this delightful book as a springboard.

## *Counting on Frank*
### (Clement, 1991)

We will refer to this wonderful book again when we discuss measurement in Chapter 16. It is hard to imagine that more mathematics could spring from 24 pages mostly covered with pictures. But the ideas appeal to all ages, and the potential for good investigations is clearly there for older children. The narrator and his pet dog, Frank, estimate, figure, and ponder interesting facts, usually about large numbers in odd settings (enough green peas to be level with the kitchen tabletop). But three spreads of the book are wonderful fantasies of proportions that could easily inspire an entire unit of proportional reasoning projects.

> "If I had grown at the same speed as the tree—6 feet per year—I'd now be almost 50 feet tall!" How fast do we grow? What if we kept growing at the same rate? How old is the narrator? How old would he be when he is 75 feet tall?
>
> If the mosquito that bothers him were 4 million times bigger . . . What would any common object be like if it were a million times bigger?
>
> If the toaster that shoots toast 3 feet in the air were as big as the house . . .

## *The Borrowers*
### (Norton, 1953)

This is the classic tale of little folk living in the walls of a house. The furnishings and implements are created from odds and ends from the full-size human world. The potential to make scale comparisons is endless.

A similar tale unfolds in Shel Silverstein's poem "One Inch Tall" (1974), in which you are invited to imagine being 1 inch tall.

At the other extreme are stories about giants and dinosaurs, but the concepts of scale are similar. Suppose that a giant were 18 feet tall, or three times the height of a tall man. All linear dimensions (arm span, foot length, etc.) would also be three times that of the man. But the surface area would be $3^2$ or 9 times as large, and the giant's volume and hence his weight would be $3^3$ or 27 times as much as the man's. That would make the giant weigh about 5400 pounds. With a cross-sectional area of the bones only 9 times more, the bones would not be able to hold the weight. This is one reason there are no real giants.

 **ASSESSMENT NOTES**

Proportional reasoning is a way of thinking that includes the ability to understand and compare ratios. It is one of the hallmarks of Piaget's formal operational stage of development, acquired around adolescence. But this form of reasoning may not develop in persons who have not had ample opportunities to reflect on proportional situations.

As you work with your students in solving proportional reasoning tasks, it will be useful for you to think about the type of reasoning that students are using.

- Do they distinguish between proportional situations and additive or nonproportional ones?

- Are they flexible in the way that they attempt to solve proportions? A nonflexible or algorithmic approach, even if correct, may signal that a student is simply following rules.

- Are there differences in thinking about different types of proportional situations? For example, discrete (countable) items in a proportion are sometimes easier to deal with than continuous quantities such as time, distance, or volume.

- Do students seem to understand rates (miles per hour, inches per yard, dollars per pound) as ratios? How students deal with these ideas reflects the development of their proportional thinking.

Keep in mind that proportional reasoning develops slowly over the middle school years. A first unit of two or three weeks' duration in the sixth grade may not be enough for many children to develop true proportional thought. It will be useful to collect anecdotal evidence related to the questions just listed. If most of your students seem to be at the beginning levels of proportional thought, activities involving selection of equal ratios, constructions, and scaling will be more useful than harder proportion problems. Using numbers that lend themselves to easy relationships will also make it easier for students to describe different methods for solving proportion tasks.

# REFLECTIONS ON CHAPTER 15

## Writing to Learn

1. Describe the idea of a ratio in your own words. Explain how your idea fits with each of the following statements:

    a. A fraction is a ratio.

    b. Ratios can compare things that are not at all alike.

    c. Ratios can compare two parts of the same whole.

    d. Rates such as prices or speeds are ratios.

2. What is a proportion? For each of the statements in item 1, give an example of a proportion. Also give an example of a comparison that is additive rather than proportional.

3. Make up a realistic proportional situation that can be solved by a factor-of-change approach and another that can be solved by a unit-rate approach. Explain each.

4. Much of this chapter is about activities that help students observe ratios and develop proportional reasoning abilities. These activities were placed in three groups:

    a. Selection of equivalent ratios

    b. Scaling activities

    c. Construction and measurement activities

    For each group, pick one activity presented in the text that you did not do as part of class experiences. Do the activity, and describe briefly how you think the activity would contribute to students' proportional reasoning.

5. Consider this problem: If 50 gallons of fuel oil cost $56.95, how much can be purchased for $100? Draw a sketch to illustrate the proportion, and set up the equation in two different ways. One equation should equate within ratios and the other between ratios.

6. Make up a realistic percentage problem, and set up a proportion. Draw a model to help explain why the proportion makes sense. Illustrate how this method could be used for any of the three types of percentage problems.

## For Discussion and Exploration

1. Examine a teacher's edition of a basal textbook for the sixth, seventh, or eighth grade. How is the topic of ratio developed? What is the emphasis? Select one lesson, and write a lesson plan that extends the ideas found on the student pages and actively involves the students.

2. In Chapter 14, the three percent problems were developed around the theme of which element was missing—the part, the whole, or the fraction that related the two. In this chapter, percent is related to proportions, an equality of two ratios with one of these ratios a comparison to 100. How are these two approaches alike? Do you prefer one or the other?

## Recommendations for Further Reading

### Highly Recommended

Lo, J., & Watanabe, T. (1997). Developing ratio and proportion schemes: A story of a fifth grader. *Journal for Research in Mathematics Education, 28,* 216–236.

The two authors tell of their work with a fifth-grade student in 15 sessions over a 6-month period in which they presented a wide variety of proportion problems of varying difficulty. They conclude that much of students' difficulties with proportional reasoning stems from difficulties with multiplication, division, fraction, and decimal concepts. At the same time, they suggest that there is an advantage in beginning proportional tasks early. The tasks and the discussion both provide useful information for any teacher concerned with the development of proportional reasoning.

Middleton, J. A., & van den Heuvel–Panhuizen, M. (1995). The ratio table. *Mathematics Teaching in the Middle School, 1,* 283–287.

These authors provide the most elaborate and helpful discussion of tables or scaling activities that can be found. There are interesting discussions of real children's work with contrasts made to help the reader see different levels of proportional thought. This is an excellent article and should be considered must reading for anyone teaching proportions in the middle grades.

Miller, J. L., & Fey, J. T. (2000). Proportional reasoning. *Mathematics Teaching in the Middle School, 5,* 310–313.

This short article, one of a very few recently published on this topic, describes three proportionality tasks with a total of seven questions that were posed to middle grade students. The results compared students in a reform curriculum with those in a traditional curriculum. The interesting tasks are quite reproducible. The discussion is also valuable.

## Other Suggestions

Ben-Chaim, D., Fey, J. T., Fitzgerald, W. M., Benedetto, C., & Miller, J. L. (1998). Proportional reasoning among 7th grade students with different curricular experiences. *Educational Studies in Mathematics, 36,* 247–273.

Cramer, K., Bezuk, N. S., & Behr, M. J. (1989). Proportional relationships and unity rates. *Mathematics Teacher, 82,* 537–544.

Cramer, K., & Post, T. R. (1993). Making connections: A case for proportionality. *Arithmetic Teacher, 40,* 342–346.

Cramer, K., Post, T. R., & Currier, S. (1993). Learning and teaching ratio and proportion: Research implications. In D. T. Owens (Ed.), *Research ideas for the classroom: Middle grades mathematics* (pp. 159–178). Old Tappan, NJ: Macmillan.

Haubner, M. A. (1992). Percents: Developing meaning through models. *Arithmetic Teacher, 40,* 232–234.

Hoffer, A. R., & Hoffer, S. A. K. (1992). Ratios and proportional thinking. In T. R. Post (Ed.), *Teaching mathematics in grades K–8: Research-based methods* (2nd ed., pp. 303–330). Needham Heights, MA: Allyn & Bacon.

Lamon, S. J. (1993). Ratio and proportion: Connecting content and children's thinking. *Journal for Research in Mathematics Education, 24,* 41–61.

Lappan, G., Fitzgerald, W. M., Winter, M. J., & Phillips, E. (1986). *Middle grades mathematics project: Similarity and equivalent fractions.* Menlo Park, CA: AWL Supplemental.

Post, T. R., Behr, M. J., & Lesh, R. A. (1988). Proportionality and the development of prealgebra understandings. In A. F. Coxford (Ed.), *The ideas of algebra, K–12* (pp. 78–90). Reston, VA: National Council of Teachers of Mathematics.

Strickland, J. F., & Denitto, J. F. (1989). The power of proportions in problem solving. *Mathematics Teacher, 82,* 11–13.

# Chapter 16

# Developing Measurement Concepts

In its new *Principles and Standards* document, NCTM chose to organize the content around only five standards, each spanning K–12. It is significant to note that one of these content standards is Measurement. This suggests an emphasis that the measurement strand has not received in most traditional curricula. The authors of *Principles and Standards* note that measurement is pervasive in our lives and provides opportunities for learning and applying other mathematics. Measurement can enhance or contribute to the study of number, geometry, statistics, and functions.

That measurement was given its own standard in *Principles and Standards* also points to the complexity of the subject. Between kindergarten and eighth grade, students must learn the attributes that they will be measuring (length, weight, capacity, and so on); what it means to measure, including an understanding of units of measure and how unit size affects measures; the selection and use of measurement instruments; systems of measurement (metric and customary); and formulas that can be used for determining measurements. Measurement is far more complex than we often realize.

## BIG Ideas

1. Measurement involves a comparison of an item that is being measured with a unit that has the same attribute (length, volume, weight, etc.). To measure anything meaningfully, the attribute to be measured must be understood.

2. Meaningful measurement and estimation of measurements depend on a personal familiarity with the unit of measure being used.

3. Measurement instruments are devices that replace the need for actual measurement units in making comparisons.

4. Area and volume formulas are ways of using length measures to count the area or volume units in an object without using area or volume units.

## THE MEANING AND PROCESS OF MEASURING

Suppose that you were asked to measure an empty bucket. The first thing you would need to know is *what* about the bucket is to be measured. Various lengths could be measured: height or depth, diameter (distance across), circumference (distance around). The surface area of the side could be determined. A bucket also has volume and weight. Each of these *aspects that can be measured* is an *attribute* of the bucket.

Once you determine the attribute to be measured, you can choose a unit of measure. The unit must have the attribute that is being measured. Length is measured with units that have length, volume with units that have volume, and so on.

Technically, a *measurement* is a number that indicates a comparison between the attribute of the object being measured and the same attribute of a given unit of measure. We commonly use small units of measure to determine in some way a numeric relationship (the measurement) between what is measured and the unit. For example, to measure a length, the comparison can be done by lining up copies of the unit directly against the length being measured. Notice that this is what you do when you use a ruler or tape measure. To measure weight, which is a pull of gravity or a force, the weight of the object might first be applied to a spring. Then the comparison is made by finding out how many units of weight produce the same effect on the spring. In either case, the number of units is the measure of the object.

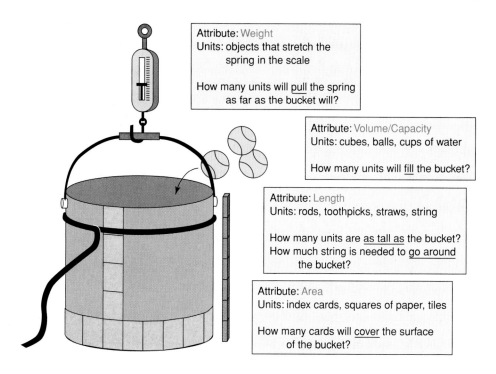

Attribute: Weight
Units: objects that stretch the
spring in the scale

How many units will <u>pull</u> the spring
as far as the bucket will?

Attribute: Volume/Capacity
Units: cubes, balls, cups of water

How many units will <u>fill</u> the bucket?

Attribute: Length
Units: rods, toothpicks, straws, string

How many units are <u>as tall as</u> the bucket?
How much string is needed to <u>go around</u>
the bucket?

Attribute: Area
Units: index cards, squares of paper, tiles

How many cards will <u>cover</u> the surface
of the bucket?

**Figure 16.1** **Measuring different attributes of a bucket.**

For most of the attributes that are measured in schools, we can say that *to measure* means that the attribute being measured is "filled" or "covered" or "matched" with a unit of measure with the same attribute (as illustrated in Figure 16.1). This concept of measurement will adequately serve the purposes of this chapter and is a good way to discuss with children what a measurement is. It is appropriate with this understanding, then, to say that the measure of an attribute is a count of how many units are needed to fill, cover, or match the attribute of the object being measured.

In summary, to measure something, one must perform three steps:

1. Decide on the attribute to be measured.

2. Select a unit that has that attribute.

3. Compare the units, by filling, covering, matching, or some other method, with the attribute of the object being measured.

Measuring instruments such as rulers, scales, protractors, and clocks are devices that make the filling, covering, or matching process easier. A ruler lines up the units of length and numbers them. A protractor lines up the unit angles and numbers them. A clock lines up units of time and marks them off.

# DEVELOPING MEASUREMENT CONCEPTS AND SKILLS

A typical group of first graders measures the length of their classroom by laying strips 1 meter long end to end. But the strips sometimes overlap, and the line weaves in a snakelike fashion around the desks. Do they understand the concept of length as an attribute of the classroom? Do they understand that each strip of 1 meter has this attribute of length? Do they understand that their task is to fill smaller units of length into the longer one? What they most likely understand is that they are supposed to be making a line of strips stretching from wall to wall (and from their vantage point, they are doing quite well). They are performing a procedure instrumentally, without a conceptual basis.

## A General Plan of Instruction

A basic understanding of measurement suggests how to help children develop a conceptual knowledge of measuring.

| Conceptual Knowledge to Develop | Type of Activity to Use |
|---|---|
| 1. Understand the attribute being measured. | 1. Make comparisons based on the attribute. |
| 2. Understand how filling, covering, matching, or making other comparisons of an attribute with units produces what is called a measure. | 2. Use physical models of measuring units to fill, cover, match, or make the desired comparison of the attribute with the unit. |
| 3. Understand the way measuring instruments work. | 3. Make measuring instruments and use them along with actual unit models to compare how each works. |

Let's briefly discuss each of these instructional activities.

## Making Comparisons

When students compare objects on the basis of some measurable attribute, that attribute becomes the focus of the activity. For example, is the capacity of one box more than, less than, or about the same as the capacity of another? No measurement is required, but some manner of comparing one volume to the other must be devised. The attribute of "capacity" (how much a container can hold) is inescapable.

Many attributes can be compared directly, such as placing one length directly in line with another. In the case of volume or capacity, some indirect method is probably required, such as filling one box with beans and then pouring the beans into the other box. Using a string to compare the height of a wastebasket to the distance around is another example of an indirect comparison. The string is the intermediary. It is impossible to compare these two lengths directly.

Constructing or making something that is the same in terms of a measurable attribute is another type of comparison activity—for example, "Cut the straw to be just as long as this piece of chalk" or "Draw a rectangle that is about the same size (has the same area) as this triangle."

## Using Models of Units

For most attributes that are measured in elementary schools, it is possible to have physical models of the units of measure. Time and temperature are exceptions. (Many other attributes not commonly measured in school also do not have physical units of measure. Light intensity, speed, loudness, viscosity, and radioactivity are just a few examples.) Unit models can be found for both informal units and standard units. For length, for example, drinking straws (informal) or tagboard strips 1 foot long (standard) might be used as units.

The most easily understood use of unit models is actually to use as many copies of the unit as are needed to fill or match the attribute measured. To measure the area of the desktop with an index card unit, you can literally cover the entire desk with index cards. Somewhat more difficult, especially for younger children, is to use a single copy of the unit with an iteration process. The same desktop area can be measured with a single index card by moving it from position to position and keeping track of which areas the card has covered.

It is useful to measure the same object with different-sized units. Results should be predicted in advance and discussed afterward. This will help students understand that the unit used is as important as the attribute being measured. The fact that smaller units produce larger numeric measures, and vice versa, is hard for young children to understand. This inverse relationship can only be constructed by reflecting on measurements with varying-sized units. Predictions and discussions of results add to the reflective nature of the activities.

## Making and Using Measuring Instruments

In the sixth National Assessment of Educational Progress (Kenney & Kouba, 1997), only 24 percent of fourth-grade students and 62 percent of eighth-grade students could give the correct measure of an object not aligned with the end of a ruler, as in Figure 16.2. These results point to the difference between using a measuring device and understanding how it works. Students also experienced difficulty when the increments on a measuring device were other than one unit.

**Figure 16.2** **"How long is this segment?"**

If students actually make simple measuring instruments using unit models with which they are familiar, it is more likely that they will understand how an instrument measures. A ruler is a good example. If students line up physical units along a strip of tagboard and mark them off, they can see that it is the *spaces* on rulers and not the marks or numbers that are important. It is essential that the measurement with actual unit models be compared with the measurement using an instrument. Without this comparison, students may not understand that these two methods are really two means to the same end. Always have students explain how the ruler, scale, or other device compares to using actual units.

A discussion of student-made measuring instruments for each attribute is provided in the text that follows. Of course, children should also use standard, ready-made instruments such as rulers and scales and should compare the use of these devices with the use of the corresponding unit models.

# Informal Units and Standard Units: Reasons for Using Each

It is common in primary grades to use nonstandard or informal units to measure length and sometimes area. Unfortunately, measurement activities in the upper grades, where other attributes are measured, often do not begin with informal units. The use of informal units for beginning measurement activities is beneficial at all grade levels.

- Informal units make it easier to focus directly on the attribute being measured. For example, instead of using square inches to measure area, an assortment of different units, some of which are not square, can be used to help understand the essential features of area and units of area.

- By selecting units carefully, the size of the numbers in early measurements can be kept reasonable. The measures of length for first-grade students can be kept less than 20 even when measuring long distances. An angle unit much larger than a degree can be significantly easier for a sixth grader to use because a degree is so small.

- The use of informal units can avoid conflicting objectives in the same beginning lesson. Is your lesson about what it means to measure area or about understanding square centimeters? Learning to measure is different from learning about the standard units used to measure.

- Informal units provide a good rationale for standard units. A discussion of the need for a standard unit can have more meaning after groups in your class have measured the same objects with their own units.

- Informal units can be fun.

The use of standard units is also important in your measurement program at any grade level.

- Knowledge of standard units is a valid objective of a measurement program and must be addressed. Students must not only develop a familiarity with standard units but must also learn appropriate relationships between them.

- Once a measuring concept is fairly well developed, it is frequently just as easy to use standard units. If there is no good instructional reason for using informal units, why not use standard units and provide the exposure?

There is no simple rule for when to use standard or informal units. Children's initial measurement of any attribute should probably begin with informal units and progress over time to the use of standard units and standard measuring tools. The amount of time that should be spent using informal unit models varies with the age of the children and the attributes being measured. First-grade children need a lot of experience with a variety of informal units of length, weight, and capacity. Informal units might be used at this level all year. Conversely, the benefits of nonstandard measuring units may last only two or three days for measurements of mass or capacity at the middle school level.

# The Role of Estimation in Learning Measurement

It is very important to have students estimate a measurement before they make it. This is true with both informal and standard units. There are three reasons for including estimation in measurement activities:

- Estimation helps students focus on the attribute being measured and the measuring process. Think how you would estimate the area of the front of this book with standard playing cards as the unit. To do so, you have to think about what area is and how the units might be fitted into the book cover.

- Estimation provides intrinsic motivation to measurement activities. It is fun to see how close you can come in your estimate or if your team can make a better estimate than the other teams in the room.

- When standard units are used, estimation helps develop familiarity with the unit. If you estimate the height of the door in meters before measuring, you have to devise some way to think about the size of a meter.

# Helping Children with Measurement Estimates

Having said that estimating measures should be included in almost all measurement activities, there remains the problem of how to go about doing so. Later we will discuss teaching children specific estimating strategies that can be used throughout life. However, until these strategies are developed, children will have difficulty making estimates. Here are three ways to ask for estimates that avoid asking children to come up with an actual number or measure estimate.

1. Ask for a comparison estimate rather than a measure. For example, is the teacher taller, shorter, or about the same as 2 meters? Does the book weigh more, less, or about the same as 1 pound? The same can be done with informal units: Is the area of the desktop more, less, or about the same as 20 index cards?

2. Ask which of two or more suggested measures the actual measure is closer to. For example, is the angle measure closer to 15, 60, or 90 degrees? Is the capacity of the box closer to 1 liter or 3 liters?

3. Provide an actual unit or set of units as a comparison. The children can make an initial estimate privately on paper. Then show the unit or set of 10 or 100 units, and let them adjust their first estimate accordingly. The use of the provided set of units allows them mentally to mark off or compare in some way. Making the first estimate adds a bit of interest. For example, after seeing a bar of 10 cubes placed at one end of the chalkboard, the children can count by tens as they visually mark off these bars along the board. The use of 10 or 100 is suggested for place-value reasons. For large units such as a meter or a kilogram, one copy of the unit can be placed directly alongside the object being estimated. Of course, with an attribute such as weight, the children should be able to handle the unit as well as the object.

Notice that there is a progression to these three ideas in terms of how specific an estimate is requested. Use this progression as you develop estimation skills with children.

# The Approximate Nature of Measurement

In all measuring activities, emphasize the use of approximate language. The desk is *about* 15 orange rods long. The chair is *a little less than* 4 straws high. The use of approximate language is very useful for younger children because many measurements do not come out even. Older children will begin to search for smaller units or will use fractional units to try to measure exactly. Here is an opportunity to develop the idea that all measurements include some error. Each smaller unit or subdivision does produce a greater degree of precision. For example, a length measure can never be more than one-half unit in error. And yet, since there is mathematically no "smallest unit," there is always some error involved.

The notion of precision related to the size of the unit is an important idea in all measuring tasks. Sometimes precision is not required, and a larger unit is much easier to deal with. At other times, precision is significant, and smaller units become important. For example, measuring a pane of glass for a window requires a different precision than measuring a wall to decide how many 4-by-8-foot panels are needed to cover it. An awareness of precision due to unit size and the need for precision in different situations is an important aspect of measurement, especially at the upper grades.

## Suggested Measurement Sequence

For each attribute to be measured, we can identify the three types of activities that have been discussed. Comparison activities should generally precede the use of units, and measuring instruments should come last. Within each of these categories, there is also a rough guideline of progression that can be considered:

Almost all activities should include an estimation component. Familiarity with standard units is a separate but important objective. In the discussions that follow, the focus is on activities for comparison, use of units, and use of instruments for each attribute. Separate discussions of standard units and estimation are also provided.

## MEASURING LENGTH

Length is usually the first attribute students learn to measure. Be aware, however, that length measurement is not immediately understood by young children.

## Comparison Activities

At the kindergarten level, children should begin with direct comparisons of two or more lengths.

---

**ACTIVITY**

### 16.1 Longer, Shorter, Same

Make a sorting-by-length station at which students sort objects as longer, shorter, or about the same as a specified object. It is easy to have several such stations in your room. The reference object can be changed occasionally to produce different sorts. A similar task is to put objects in order from shortest to longest.

---

**ACTIVITY**

### 16.2 Length Hunt

Give pairs of students a strip of tagboard, a stick, a length of rope, or some other object with an obvious length dimension. The task on one day might be to find five things in the room that are shorter than or longer than or about the same as their object. They can draw pictures or write the names of the things they find.

---

It is important to compare lengths that are not in straight lines. One way to do this is with string or rope. Students can wrap string around objects in a search for things that are, for example, as long around as the distance from the floor to their belly button or as long as the distance around one's head or waist. Body measures are always fun.

Indirect comparisons are a next step in length comparisons.

---

**ACTIVITY**

### 16.3 Crooked Paths

Make some crooked or curvy paths on the floor with masking tape. The task is to determine which path is longest, next longest, and so on. The students should find a way to make straight paths that are just as long as the crooked paths so that they can be compared easily. (You may or may not wish to offer this suggestion.) Provide pairs of students with a long piece of rope. The task is easier if the rope is longer than the crooked paths. The students can draw their straight paths on the board, mark them with tape on the floor, or use some other method that you devise. Have students explain how they solved the problem. (This is a good outdoor activity also.)

---

The "Crooked Paths" activity can also be done with the small distances at students' desks. A simple worksheet like the one in Figure 16.3 (p. 282) might be prepared. Instead of crooked paths, students can make straight paths that are as long as the distance around simple shapes (their perimeters).

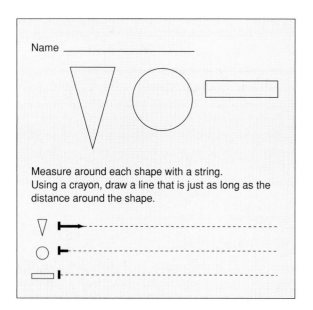

**Figure 16.3**  **Making a straight path just as long as a crooked path.**

# Using Units of Length

Students can use a variety of informal units to begin measuring length, for example:

*Giant footprints:* Make about 20 copies of a large footprint about $1\frac{1}{2}$ to 2 feet long cut out of poster board.

*Measuring strips:* Cut strips of poster board about 5 cm wide. Several sets can be made to provide different units. Some can be the long dimension of the poster board, some the short, and a third set about 1 foot long. Make each set of a different color.

*Measuring ropes:* Cut cotton clothesline into lengths of 1 m. These are useful for measuring curved lines and the circumference of large objects such as the teacher's desk.

*Plastic straws:* Drinking straws are inexpensive and provide large quantities of a useful unit. Straws are easily cut into smaller units. You can link straw units together with a long string. The string of straws is an excellent bridge to a ruler or measuring tape.

*Short units:* Toothpicks, connecting cubes, wooden cubes, and paper clips are all useful units for measuring shorter lengths. Cuisenaire rods are one of the nicest sets of units because they come in ten different lengths, are easily placed end to end, and can be related to each other. Paper clips can readily be made into chains.

For young children, initial measurements should be along lines or edges. If different teams of students measure the same distances and get different results, discuss the differences. The discussion can help focus on why units need to be lined up end to end and in a straight line and why units such as ropes must be stretched to their full length.

## 16.4 Guess and Measure

Make lists of things in the room to measure (see Figure 16.4). For younger children, run a piece of masking tape along the dimension of each object to be measured. On the list, designate the units to be used. Do not forget to include curves or other distances that are not straight lines. Include estimates before the measures. Young children will not be very good at estimating distances at first.

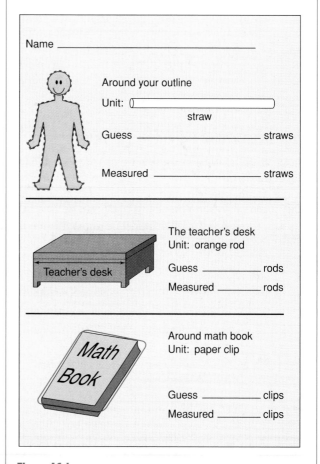

**Figure 16.4**  **Record sheet for measuring with informal length units.**

## 16.5 Changing Units

Have students measure a distance with one unit; then provide them with a different unit and see if they can predict the measure with the new unit. Students should write down their predictions and explanations of how they were made. Then have them make the actual measurement. In the class discussions that follow, the predictions and explanations will be the most educational part of the activity. The first few times you do this activity, the larger unit should be a simple multiple of the smaller unit. If the two units are not related by a whole-number multiple, the task becomes numerically difficult.

## Two Units and Fractional Parts of Units

As children develop a need for more precision, two units can be used at the same time. The second unit should be a sub-unit of the first. For example, with connecting cubes, the first unit can be bars of 10 cubes, and the second can be individual cubes. With measuring strips, make subunits that are one-fourth or one-tenth as long as the longer strip. Cut plastic straws so that an even number of paper clips is equal to one straw. Cuisenaire rods allow for more variety. For example, 4 reds make a brown, or 10 whites make an orange. Have children measure with the larger unit until no more of that unit will fit, and then add on sufficient smaller units to fill up the distance (see Figure 16.5). Report measures in two parts: "8 straws and 3 clips long." For older students, smaller units can simply be fractional parts of longer units.

Width = 5 orange and 4 red

**Figure 16.5** **Using two units to measure length.**

After a measurement with two related units has been made and recorded, have students figure out how to report the same measurement in terms of either unit—for example, $5\frac{2}{3}$ blue rods or 17 light green rods (3 light green = 1 blue). This provides a readiness exercise for standard units. For example, a measurement of 4 feet 3 inches is sometimes reported as 51 inches or as $4\frac{1}{4}$ feet. The use of two units is also good readiness for subdivision marks on a ruler.

## Making and Using Rulers

Rulers or tape measures can be made for almost any unit of measure. It is important that students have used the actual unit models before making the rulers.

Ruler construction should be directly related to a measuring experience with a unit that is small but not less than 5 cm. Rulers can be made on long strips of tagboard about

5 cm wide. If you precut narrow strips of construction paper, students can cut these into shorter pieces using their unit model as a guide. Discuss how the paper strips could be used for measuring just as well as the actual units. Next, students can paste the paper units along the edge of the tagboard. Use two contrasting colors, and alternate them as shown in Figure 16.6.

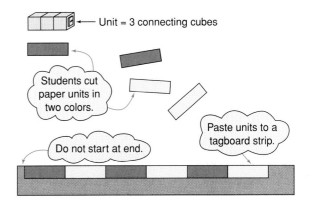

**Figure 16.6** **Making a simple ruler.**

Pasting down copies of the units on a ruler maximizes the connection between the spaces on a ruler and the actual units. Older children can make rulers by using a real unit to make marks along a tagboard strip and then coloring in the spaces. Children should not be encouraged to use the end of a ruler as a starting point; many real rulers are not made that way. If the first unit on a ruler does not coincide with the end of the ruler, the student is forced to attend to aligning the units on the ruler with the object measured.

Students should eventually put numbers on their homemade rulers, as shown in Figure 16.7. For young children, numbers can be written in the center of each unit to make it clear that the numbers are a way of precounting the units.

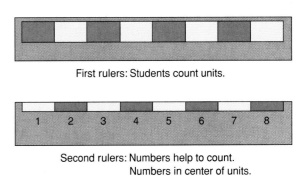

First rulers: Students count units.

Second rulers: Numbers help to count.
Numbers in center of units.

Standard rulers: Numbers are at ends of units. Notice where 0 is.

**Figure 16.7** **Give meaning to numbers on rulers.**

When numbers are written in the standard way, at the ends of the units, the ruler becomes a number line. This format is more sophisticated and should be carefully discussed with children. (Number lines are generally a poor number model for children below the third grade.)

## Assessment Note

Although Figure 16.7 illustrates a developmental progression, children should be encouraged to make and number their rulers in ways that make sense to them. By having students make their own rulers in their own way and by having them explain the measures obtained by using their rulers, you receive an enormous amount of assessment data about how well students understand the measurement process. By contrast, if you carefully direct how children should construct and use their rulers, they may very well use the rulers mechanically, without understanding what they are doing.

Putting measurement tasks into problem-solving exercises increases your information flow. For example, how could you explain in a letter to a class in another state just how large your classroom is or the size of the model of a blue whale you have been building? Let different groups decide how to do this and make the measurements. Then compare results and see if each solution actually conveys the meaning.

## Using Rulers and Tape Measures

It is important to use the rulers students have made. In addition to the estimate-and-measure activities mentioned earlier, have teams measure items once with a ruler and a second time with actual unit models. Although the results should be the same, inaccuracies or incorrect use of the ruler may produce differences that are important to discuss. Also, use the ruler to measure lengths that are longer than the ruler.

### ⒶCTIVITY

### 16.6 More than One Way

Challenge students to find different ways to measure the same length with one ruler. (Start from either end; start at a point not at the end; measure different parts of the object and add the results.)

Tape measures, especially for measuring around objects, can be made in a variety of ways using the same approach as rulers. With long units such as meters, a clothesline can be marked with a piece of masking tape or a marking pen at the end of each meter. Grosgrain ribbon is easily marked with a ballpoint pen. Even adding-machine tape can be used to make temporary tape measures.

After working with simple rulers and tapes, have students make rulers with subunits or fractional units. This should follow the use of two units for measuring, as described earlier.

Much of the value of student-made rulers can be lost if you do not transfer this knowledge to standard rulers. Give children a standard ruler, and discuss how it is like and how it differs from the ones they have made. What are the units? Could you make a ruler with paper units the same as this? Could you make some cardboard units and measure the same way as with the ruler? What do the numbers mean? What are the other marks for? Where do the units begin?

# MEASURING AREA

Data from the sixth National Assessment of Educational Progress suggests that fourth- and eighth-grade students have an incomplete understanding of area (Kenney & Kouba, 1997).

## Comparison Activities

When comparing two areas, the added consideration of shape causes difficulties not present in length measures. One of the purposes of early comparison activities with areas is to help students distinguish between size (or area) and shape, length, and other dimensions. A long, skinny rectangle may have less area than a triangle with shorter sides. This is an especially difficult concept for young children to understand. Piagetian experiments indicate that many 8- or 9-year-olds do not understand that rearranging areas into different shapes does not affect the amount of area.

Direct comparison of two areas is nearly always impossible except when the shapes involved have some common dimension or property. For example, two rectangles with the same width can be compared directly, as can any two circles. Comparison of these special shapes, however, fails to deal with the attribute of area. Instead, activities in which one area is rearranged are suggested. Cutting a shape into two parts and reassembling it in a different shape can show that the before and after shapes have the same area, even though they are different shapes. This idea is not at all obvious to children in the K–2 grade range.

### ⒶCTIVITY

### 16.7 Two-Piece Shapes

Give children a rectangle of construction paper, and have them fold and cut it on the diagonal, making two identical triangles. Next, have them rearrange the triangles into different shapes, including the original rectangle. The rule is that only sides of the same length can be matched up and must be matched exactly. Have each group find all the shapes that can be made this way, pasting the triangles on paper as a record of each shape (see Figure 16.8). Discuss the size and shape of the different results. Is one shape bigger than the rest? How is it bigger? Did one take more paper to make, or do they all have the same amount of paper? Help children conclude that although each figure is a different shape, all the figures have the same *area*. (*Size* in this context is a useful substitute for *area* with very young children, although it does not mean exactly the same thing.)

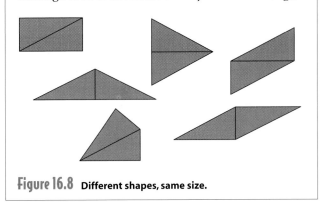

**Figure 16.8** **Different shapes, same size.**

Tangrams, a very old and popular set of puzzle shapes, can be used in a similar way. The standard set of seven tangram pieces is cut from a square, as shown in Figure 16.9. The two small triangles can be used to make the parallelogram, the square, and the medium triangle. Four small triangles will make the large triangle. This permits a similar discussion about the pieces having the same size (area) but different shapes (Seymour, 1971). (Tangram pieces can be found in the Blackline Masters.)

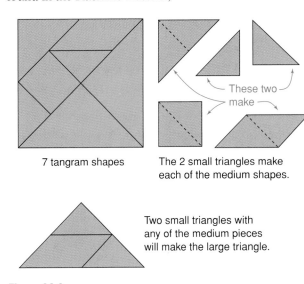

7 tangram shapes

The 2 small triangles make each of the medium shapes.

These two make

Two small triangles with any of the medium pieces will make the large triangle.

**Figure 16.9** **Tangrams provide a nice opportunity to investigate size and shape concepts.**

The following activities suggest methods for comparing areas without measuring.

━ **A**CTIVITY ━

## 16.8 Tangram Areas

**Draw the outline of several shapes made with tangram pieces, as in Figure 16.10. Let students use tangrams to decide which shapes are the same size, which are larger, and which are smaller. Shapes can**

be duplicated on paper, and children can work in groups. Let students explain how they came to their conclusions. There are several different approaches to this task, and it is best if students determine their own solutions rather than blindly follow your directions. You might stop here, get a set of tangrams, and make the area comparisons suggested in Figure 16.10.

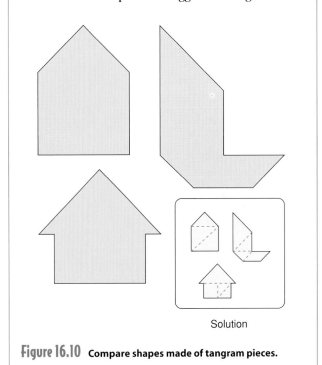

Solution

**Figure 16.10** **Compare shapes made of tangram pieces.**

━ **A**CTIVITY ━

## 16.9 Fill and Compare

**Draw two or three shapes on a piece of paper and duplicate them. The shapes can be irregular blobs or more familiar shapes such as triangles, circles, or rectangles. In pairs or small groups, have students decide simply by observation which of the shapes is largest and which smallest. Then have them find a way to determine if their original estimates are correct. You can suggest methods of comparison, or you can leave the methods completely to the students' invention.**

Activity 16.9 allows you to observe what kinds of ideas your children bring to the concept of area. In a completely open approach, you might suggest a wide variety of "tools" from which they may choose, or they can decide on their own methods of determining which shape is largest. For example, you could provide scissors, 1-inch plastic squares (such as Color Tiles), lima beans, string, centimeter grid paper, tangrams, or any other type of counter or tile. By not prescribing the method of comparison, you will be able to see children's current understanding of the area concept.

Methods of comparison include filling one shape with counters and then moving these same counters to a second shape to see if it takes more or fewer counters to fill its interior. Another possibility is to cut out the shapes and place one on top of the other. Some children may think of cutting a shape into two or more pieces so that it can be rearranged to compare with another. Shapes may be traced onto grid paper to count the squares that are inside. String is not really useful for comparing areas. However, if someone does use string to compare the boundaries of the shapes, for example, the discussion of what was actually compared can be very helpful.

## Using Units of Area

Although squares are very nice units of area (and the most commonly used), any tile that conveniently fills up a plane region can be used. Even filling a region with uniform circles or lima beans provides a useful idea of what it means to measure areas. Here are some suggestions for area units that are easy to gather or make in the large quantities you will need.

Cut squares or triangles (diagonals of squares) from cardboard. (Use a paper cutter.) Large squares or triangles (about 20 cm on a side) work well for large areas. Smaller units should be about 5 to 10 cm on a side.

Sheets of newspaper make excellent units for very large areas.

Poster board can easily be cut into large quantities of congruent tiles for smaller units. Include 2 × 1 rectangles, equilateral triangles, and right triangles as well as squares. These tiles can be from 2 to 5 cm on a side.

Pattern blocks provide six different units. The hexagon, trapezoid, large diamond, and triangle can be related to each other in a manner similar to the tangrams.

Playing cards, index cards, or old business cards make good medium-sized units.

Round plastic chips, pennies, or lima beans can be used. It is not necessary at a beginning stage that the area units fit with no gaps.

Children can use units to measure surfaces in the room such as desktops, bulletin boards, or books. Large regions can be outlined with masking tape on the floor. Use the gym or hallway for very large areas. Small regions can be duplicated on paper so that students can work at their desks. Odd shapes and curved surfaces provide more challenge and interest. The surfaces of a watermelon or of the side of the wastebasket provide useful challenges.

When measuring length, it is only the last unit that may not completely fit. In area measurements, there may be lots of units that only partially fit. You may wish to begin with shapes in which the units fit. Build a shape with units, and draw the outline. By third or fourth grade, students should begin to wrestle with partial units and mentally put together two or more partial units to count as one (see Figure 16.11).

Your objective in the beginning is to develop the idea that area is a *measure of covering*. Do not introduce formulas. Simply have the students fill the shapes and count the units. Be sure to include estimation before measuring (this is significantly more difficult than for length), use approximate language, and relate precision to the size of the units in the same manner as with length. Groups are very likely to come up with different measures for the same region. Discuss these differences with the children, and point to the difficulties involved in making estimates around the edges. Avoid the idea that there is a "right" answer.

The following activity is similar to Activity 16.9, "Fill and Compare." What is different is that you are now asking students not only to make comparisons but also to use a measurement of some sort to order the shapes by size.

**Figure 16.11**  **Measuring the area of a large shape drawn with tape on the floor. Units are pieces of tagboard all cut to the same shape.**

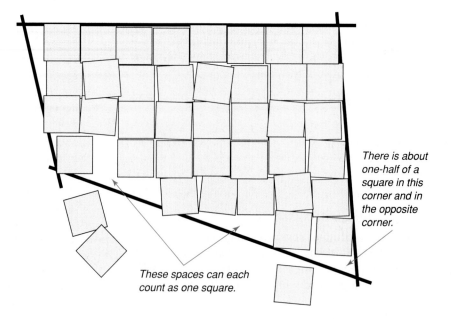

There is about one-half of a square in this corner and in the opposite corner.

These spaces can each count as one square.

## 16.10 Smaller to Larger

Present a series of quite different shapes with only slightly different areas. Students first predict the order of the shapes from the smallest to largest and record their prediction. The task is then to determine the correct order using any methods and units they wish. The determination of the "correct" order is left to the students. This can lead to a profitable class discussion about different methods.

The next activity requires an application of ideas developed about area so far.

## 16.11 Same-Size Rectangle

Have students make a rectangle that has the same size as another shape that you have given them. The given shape may be a blob or some other irregular shape, or it may be a triangle or even a rectangle. The activity can be done with small shapes that can be drawn on paper or very large shapes on the floor with tape or chalk. This activity works best when children work in groups. All groups in the class should be given the same shape to work with but no directions as to how to design their same-size rectangle. Each group will almost certainly come up with a rectangle of different dimensions, even if all have very good solutions. Groups must explain why they believe their rectangle has the same area as the given shape. They should be allowed to use whatever materials they wish. This activity can be done before the area formula has been introduced.

# Using Grids

With the exception of computer drafting equipment, there really are no instruments designed for measuring area. However, grids of various types can be thought of as a kind of "area ruler." A grid of squares does exactly what a ruler does: It lays out the units for you. Square grids are available in the Blackline Masters. Note that triangular grids can also be used. Make transparencies of any grid paper. Have students place the grid over a region to be measured and count the units inside. An alternative method is to trace around a region on a paper grid.

## 16.12 Floor Grids

For larger regions on the floor, make two lines with tape in an L, as shown in Figure 16.12. On the tape, mark off appropriate units of length. Explain that the

two lines are the edges of a grid and can be used to help visualize imaginary squares without drawing them. To demonstrate, large shapes cut from butcher paper or other flat items can be positioned in the corners of the L.

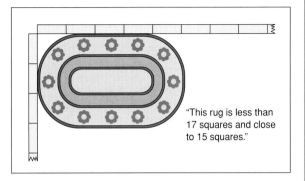

"This rug is less than 17 squares and close to 15 squares."

**Figure 16.12** **Two masking-tape rulers on the floor make an imaginary grid for measuring the area of large shapes.**

Of course, the most useful grid is one of squares, since most standard units of area are squares derived from standard units of length (square inches, square centimeters, etc.). As children use square grids to determine areas of rectangular shapes, many will begin to see that the product of the number of rows times the number of columns is an easy way to count the squares. The L approach (which can also be used for small shapes on paper) provides a hint at using the lengths of sides to determine areas.

# MEASURING VOLUME AND CAPACITY

*Volume* and *capacity* are both terms for measures of the "size" of three-dimensional regions. Standard units of volume are expressed in terms of length units, such as cubic inches or cubic centimeters. Capacity units are generally applied to liquids or the containers that hold liquids. Standard capacity units include quarts and gallons, liters and milliliters.

## Comparison Activities

Most solid shapes and containers must be compared indirectly. By far the easiest comparisons are made between containers that can be filled with something that is then poured into another container.

Young children should have lots of experiences directly comparing the capacities of different containers. Collect a large assortment of cans, small boxes, and plastic containers. Gather as many different shapes as possible. Also gather some plastic scoops. Cut a plastic 2-liter bottle in half, and use the top portion as a funnel. Rice or dried beans are good fillers to use. Sand and water are both considerably messier.

## 16.13 Capacity Sort

Provide a collection of labeled containers, with one marked as the "target." The students' task is to sort the collection into those that hold more than, less than, or about the same amount as the target container. Provide a recording sheet on which each container is listed and a place to circle "holds more," "holds less," and "holds about the same." List the choices twice for each container. The first choice is to record a guess made by observation. The second is to record "what was found." Provide a filler (such as beans or rice), scoops, and funnels. Avoid explicit directions, but later discuss students' ideas for solving the task.

## 16.14 Capacity Lineup

Given a series of five or six labeled containers of different sizes and shapes, the task is to order them from least volume to most. This can be quite challenging. Do not provide answers. Let students work in groups to come up with a solution and also explain how they arrived at it.

Solids such as a rock, a ball, a block, an apple, or an eggplant can also be compared in terms of volume, but it is a bit more difficult. Some method of displacement must be used. One approach is to use a container that will hold each of the items. Place an object in the container and fill with rice to a level that will be above all of the objects. Mark this level on the container. Then remove the object and mark the new level. Each new object should be put in the container and buried with rice to the same initial level. The problem-solving nature of the activity is enhanced if students are challenged to devise their own methods.

## Using Units of Volume

Two types of units can be used to measure volume and capacity: solid units and containers. Solid units are things like wooden cubes or old tennis balls that can be used to fill the container being measured. The other type of unit model is a small container that is filled and poured repeatedly into the container being measured. The following are a few examples of units that you might want to collect.

Thimbles, plastic caps, and liquid medicine cups are all good for very small units.

Plastic jars and containers of almost any size can serve as a unit.

Wooden cubic blocks or blocks of any shape can be units as long as you have a lot of the same size.

Styrofoam packing peanuts, walnuts, or even marbles can be used. Even though they do not pack perfectly, they still produce conceptual measures of volume.

Measuring activities for volume and capacity are similar to those for length and area. Estimation of volumes is a lot more fun as a class activity because it is much more difficult. Finding ways to measure containers such as a large cardboard carton in terms of a relatively small container-type unit can be an excellent challenge for groups of fourth or fifth graders. This can be done long before volume formulas are developed.

When measuring with solid units such as cubes or balls, it is difficult to use only one and iterate it, as can be done with length or area. However, a worthwhile challenge is to determine the volumes of containers given only enough units to cover the bottom. Do not forget very large volumes such as your room. How many cubic meters will the room hold? Be sure to make these projects where groups devise their methods and provide written explanations and drawings.

## Making and Using Measuring Cups

Instruments for measuring capacity are generally used for small amounts of liquids or pourable materials such as rice or water. These tools are commonly found in kitchens and laboratories. As with other instruments, if children make their own, they are likely to develop a better understanding of the units and the approach to the measuring process.

A measuring cup can be made by using a small container as a unit. Select a large, transparent container for the cup and a small container for a unit. Fill the unit with beans or rice, empty it into the large container, and make a mark indicating the level. Repeat until the cup is nearly full. If the unit is small, marks may only be necessary after every 5 units. Numbers need not be written on the container for every marking. Students frequently have difficulty reading scales in which not every mark is labeled or where each mark represents more than one unit. This is an opportunity to help them understand how to interpret lines on a real measuring cup.

Students should use their measuring cups and compare the measures with those made by directly filling the container from the unit. The cup is likely to produce errors due to inaccurate markings. This is an opportunity to point out that measuring instruments themselves can be a source of error in measurement. The more accurately made the instrument, and the finer the calibration, the less the error from that source.

# MEASURING WEIGHT AND MASS

*Weight* is a measure of the pull or force of gravity on an object. *Mass* is the amount of matter in an object and a measure of the force needed to accelerate it. On the moon, where gravity is much less than on earth, an object has a smaller weight but the identical mass as on earth. For practical purposes, on the earth, the measures of mass and weight will be about the same. In this discussion, the terms *weight* and *mass* will be used interchangeably.

## Making Comparisons

The most conceptual way to compare the weights of two objects is to hold one in each hand, extend your arms, and experience the relative downward pull on each—effectively communicating to a young child what "heavier" or "weighs more" means. This personal experience can then be transferred to one of two basic types of scales—balances and spring scales. Figure 16.13 shows a homemade version of each. Simple scales of each type are available through school-supply catalogs.

Children should first use their hands to estimate which of two objects is heavier. When they then place the objects in the two pans of a balance, the pan that goes down can be

Two-pan balance

Rubber-band (spring) scales
Marks show where different objects
pulled the scale.

**Figure 16.13** **Two simple scales.**

understood to hold the heavier object. Even a relatively simple balance will detect small differences. If two objects are placed one at a time in a spring scale, the heavier object pulls the pan down farther. Both balances and spring scales have real value in the classroom. (Technically, spring scales measure weight and balance scales measure mass. Why?)

With either scale, sorting and ordering tasks are possible with very young children. For older children, comparison activities for weight are not necessary. (Why?)

## Using Units of Weight or Mass

Any collection of uniform objects with the same mass can serve as weight units. For very light objects, wooden or plastic cubes work well. Large metal washers found in hardware stores are effective for weighing slightly heavier objects. You will need to rely on standard weights to weigh things as heavy as a kilogram or more.

In a balance scale, place an object in one pan and weights in the other until the two pans balance. In a spring scale, first place the object in and mark the position of the pan on a piece of paper taped behind the pan. Remove the object and place just enough weights in the pan to pull it down to the same level. Discuss how equal weights will pull the spring or rubber band with the same force.

While the concept of heavier and lighter is learned rather early, the notion of units of weight or mass is a bit more mysterious. At any grade level, even a brief experience with informal unit weights is good preparation for standard units and scales.

## Making and Using a Scale

Most scales that we use in our daily lives produce a number when an object is placed on or in it. There are no visible unit weights. How does the scale produce the right number? By making a scale that gives a numeric result without recourse to units, children can see how scales work.

Students can use informal weight units and calibrate a simple rubber-band scale like the one in Figure 16.13. Mount the scale with a piece of paper behind it, and place weights in the pan. After every five weights, make a mark on the paper. The resulting marks correspond to the markings around the dial of a standard scale. The pan serves as the pointer. In the dial scale, the downward movement of the pan mechanically causes the dial to turn. The value of this activity is seeing how scales are made. Even digital readout scales are based on the same principle.

## MEASURING ANGLES

Angle measurement causes difficulty for two reasons: The attribute of angle size is often misunderstood, and protractors are introduced and used without understanding how they work.

## Comparing Angles

The attribute of angle size might be called the "spread of the angle's rays." Angles are composed of two rays that are infinite in length. The only difference in their size is how widely or narrowly the two rays are spread apart.

Some authors have students think of how much one ray has rotated away from the other. Two rulers held together near the ends can be used to demonstrate this idea. As one ruler is rotated, the size of the angle is seen to get larger. However, when we see angles, the rays have already been spread—there is no rotation. Do you think of the angles in a triangle as one side being rotated away from the other?

To help children conceptualize the attribute of the spread of the rays, two angles can be directly compared by tracing one and placing it over the other, as in Figure 16.14. Be sure to have students compare angles with sides of different lengths. A wide angle with short sides may seem smaller than a narrow angle with long sides. This is a common misconception among students. As soon as students can tell the difference between a large angle and a small one, regardless of the length of the sides, you can move on to measuring angles.

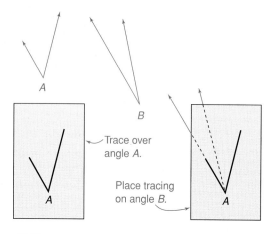

**Figure 16.14   Which angle is larger? Use tracings to compare.**

## Using Units of Angular Measure

A unit for measuring an angle must be an angle. Nothing else has the same attribute of spread that we want to measure. (Contrary to popular opinion, you do not need to use degrees to measure angles.)

— **A**CTIVITY —

### 16.15  A Unit Angle

Give each student an index card or a small piece of tagboard. Have students draw a narrow angle on the tagboard using a straightedge and then cut it out. The resulting wedge can then be used as a unit of angular measure by counting the number that will fit in a given angle. Pass out a worksheet with assorted

angles on it, and have students use their unit to measure them. Because students made their own unit angles, the results will differ and can be discussed in terms of unit size.

Activity 16.15 illustrates that measuring an angle is the same as measuring length or area. Unit angles are used to fill or cover the spread of an angle just as unit lengths fill or cover a length. Once this concept is well understood, you can move on to the use of measuring instruments.

## Making a Protractor

The protractor is one of the most poorly understood measuring instruments found in schools. Part of the difficulty arises because the units (degrees) are so very small. It would be physically impossible to cut out a single degree and use it in, say, Activity 16.15. Another problem is that there are no visible angles showing; there are only little marks around the outside edge of the protractor. Finally, the numbering that appears on most protractors runs both clockwise and counterclockwise along the marked edges. "Which numbers do I use?" By making a protractor with a large unit angle, all of these mysterious features can be understood. A careful comparison with a standard protractor will then permit that instrument to be used with understanding.

Tear off about a foot of ordinary waxed paper for each student. Have the students fold the paper in half and crease the fold tightly. Fold in half again so that the folded edges match. Repeat this two more times, each time bringing the folded edges together and creasing tightly. Cut or tear off the resulting wedge shape about 4 or 5 inches from the vertex and unfold. If done correctly, there will be 16 angles surrounding the center, as in Figure 16.15. This serves as an excellent protractor with a unit angle that is one-eighth of a straight angle. It is sufficiently transparent that it can be placed over an angle on paper, on the blackboard, or on the

Fold a piece of waxed paper, tear off the uneven ends, and unfold to a 16-"wedge" protractor.

**Figure 16.15   Making a waxed-paper protractor.**

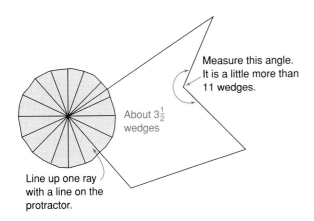

**Figure 16.16** **Measuring angles in a polygon using a waxed-paper protractor.**

overhead projector to measure angles, as shown in Figure 16.16. Reasonable estimates of angle measures can be made with a waxed-paper protractor as small as the one in Figure 16.16. In that figure, one angle of a free-form polygon is measured for you. Use a waxed-paper protractor to measure the other four angles in this polygon as carefully as possible. Use fractional estimates. Your sum for all five interior angles should be very close to 24 wedges. There are two possible ways to get the measure of the angle indicated with the arrow. How would you measure that angle if your protractor was only a half circle instead of a full circle?

The waxed-paper protractor makes it quite clear how a protractor fits unit angles into an angle for measurement. When measuring angles, students can easily estimate halves, thirds, or fourths of a "wedge," a possible name for this informal unit angle. This is sufficiently accurate to measure, for example, the interior angles of a polygon and discover the usual relationship between number of sides and sum of the

interior angles. For a triangle, the sum is 8 wedges, recorded as $8^w$. For a quadrilateral, the sum is $16^w$. And in general, the sum for an $n$-sided polygon is $(n - 2) \times 8^w$. The superscript $w$ is a forerunner of the degree symbol ($°$).

Figure 16.17 illustrates how a tagboard semicircle can be made into a protractor to measure angles in wedges. This tagboard version is a bit closer to a standard protractor, since the rays do not extend down to the vertex and the markings are numbered in two directions. The only difference between this protractor and a standard one is the size of the unit angle. The standard unit angle is the *degree,* which is simply a very small angle. A standard protractor is not very helpful in teaching the meaning of a degree. But an analogy between wedges and degrees and between these two protractors is a very effective approach.

# INTRODUCING STANDARD UNITS

As pointed out earlier, there are a number of reasons for teaching measurement using nonstandard units. However, measurement sense demands that children be familiar with the common measurement units and that they be able to make estimates in terms of these units and meaningfully interpret measures depicted with standard units.

Perhaps the biggest error in measurement instruction is the failure to recognize and separate two types of objectives: first, understanding the meaning and technique of measuring a particular attribute and, second, learning about the standard units commonly used to measure that attribute. These two objectives can be developed separately; when both objectives are attempted together, confusion is likely. Reread the list of reasons

**Figure 16.17** **Comparisons of protractors and unit angles.**

The marks on the tagboard wedge protractor are the rays on the waxed-paper version.
The marks on a plastic protractor are the rays of <u>degrees</u>. A degree is just a very small angle.

for using nonstandard units (p. 279), and be very clear about why you would use them. It is only when students are comfortable with measurement of an attribute that they can focus on things like cups and quarts or the number of inches in a foot or feet in a yard or have a feel for grams and kilograms. Though both domains of knowledge are important, it may be useful to keep the objectives separate when planning your lessons.

# Instructional Goals

Three broad goals relative to standard units of measure can be identified:

1. *Familiarity with the unit.* Familiarity means that students should have a basic idea of the size of commonly used units and what they measure. Without this familiarity, measurement sense is impossible. It is more important to know about how much 1 liter of water is or to be able to estimate a shelf as 5 feet long than to have the ability to measure either of these accurately.

2. *Ability to select an appropriate unit.* Related to unit familiarity is knowing what is a reasonable unit of measure in a given situation. The choice of an appropriate unit is also a matter of required precision. (Would you measure your lawn to purchase grass seed with the same precision as you would use in measuring a window to buy a pane of glass?) Students need practice in using common sense in the selection of appropriate standard units.

3. *Knowledge of a few important relationships between units.* The emphasis should be kept to those relationships that are commonly used, such as inches, feet, and yards or milliliters and liters. Tedious conversion exercises do little to enhance measurement sense. The goal of unit relationships is the least important of all measurement objectives.

## Developing Unit Familiarity

The importance of familiarity with standard units of measure is highlighted by the reluctance (even fear) on the part of a majority of U.S. citizens to adopt the metric system. The average adult develops a "feel" for units used throughout life: inch, foot, mile, pound, cup, gallon. These *customary* units are not easier to use than metric units, but they are familiar, whereas *metric* units are not. Helping students develop familiarity with the most frequently used units of measure in both systems is thus an important goal of instruction.

Two types of activities can help develop familiarity with standard units: (1) comparisons that focus on a single unit and (2) activities that develop personal referents or benchmarks for single units or easy multiples of units.

### ⒶCTIVITY

### 16.16  About One Unit

Give students a model of a standard unit, and have them search for things that measure about the same as that one unit. For example, to develop familiarity with the meter, give students a piece of rope 1 meter long. Have them make lists of things that are about 1 meter. Keep separate lists for things that are a little less (or more) or twice as long (or half as long). Encourage students to find familiar items in their daily lives. In the case of lengths, be sure to include circular lengths. Later, students can try to predict if a given object is more than, less than, or close to 1 meter.

The same activity can be done with other unit lengths. Parents can be enlisted to help students find familiar distances that are about 1 mile or about 1 kilometer. Suggest in a letter that they check the distances around the neighborhood, to the school or shopping center, or along other frequently traveled paths.

For capacity units such as cup, quart, and liter, students need a container that holds or has a marking for a single unit. They should then find other containers at home and at school that hold about as much, more, and less. Remember that the shapes of containers can be very deceptive when estimating their capacity.

For the standard weights of gram, kilogram, ounce, and pound, students can compare objects on a two-pan balance with single copies of these units. It may be more effective to work with 10 grams or 5 ounces. Students can be encouraged to bring in familiar objects from home to compare on the classroom scale.

Standard area units are in terms of lengths such as square inches or square feet, so familiarity with lengths is important. Familiarity with a single degree is not as important as some idea of 30, 45, 60, and 90 degrees. The turtle graphics of Logo provide an excellent avenue for degree familiarity. (Logo is a very accessible computer language with a simple graphics capability that even first-grade children can control. This language is discussed more fully in Chapter 17.)

The second approach to unit familiarity is to begin with very familiar items and use their measures as references or benchmarks. A doorway is a bit more than 2 meters. A bag of flour is a good reference for 5 pounds. Your bedroom may be about 10 feet long. A paper clip weighs about a gram and is about 1 centimeter wide. A gallon of milk weighs a little less than 4 kilograms.

### ⒶCTIVITY

### 16.17  Familiar References

For each unit of measure you wish to focus on, have students make a list of at least five familiar things and measure those things using that unit. For lengths, encourage them to include long and short things; for weight, to find both light and heavy things; and so on. The measures should be rounded off to nice whole numbers. Discuss lists in class so that different ideas are shared.

**293**

Of special interest for length are benchmarks found on our bodies. These become quite familiar over time and can be used as approximate rulers in many situations. Even though young children grow quite rapidly, it is useful for them to know the approximate lengths that they carry around with them.

### 16.18 Personal Benchmarks

**Measure your body. About how long is your foot, your stride, your hand span (stretched and with fingers together), the width of your finger, your arm span (finger to finger and finger to nose), the distance around your wrist and around your waist, and your height to waist, to shoulder, and to head? Perhaps you cannot remember all of these, but some may prove to be useful benchmarks, and some may be excellent models for single units. (The average child's fingernail width is about 1 cm, and most people can find a 10-cm length somewhere on their hands.)**

To help remember these references, they must be used in activities where lengths, volumes, and so on are compared to the benchmarks to estimate measurements.

### Choosing Appropriate Units

Should the room be measured in feet or inches? Should the concrete blocks be weighed in grams or kilograms? The answers to questions such as these involve more than simply knowing how big the units are, although that is certainly required. Another consideration involves the need for precision. If you were measuring your wall in order to cut a piece of molding or woodwork to fit, you would need to measure it very precisely. The smallest unit would be an inch or a centimeter, and you would also use small fractional parts. But if you were determining how many 8-foot molding strips to buy, the nearest foot would probably be sufficient.

### 16.19 Guess the Unit

**Find examples of measurements of all types in newspapers, on signs, or in other everyday situations. Present the context and measures but without units. The task is to predict what units of measure were used. Have students discuss their choices.**

### Developing Relationships Between Units

The number of inches in a foot or a yard or the number of cups in a quart is the type of information that must eventually be committed to memory. Practice with conversions is something that lends itself well to pencil-and-paper work. This procedural aspect of unit familiarity has been over-

worked in the curriculum largely due to the ease of testing rather than the need to know.

Many students may know that there are 16 ounces in 1 pound, but when they try to determine how many pounds are in 90 ounces, they get confused over which operation to use. This is partly a matter of understanding the meanings of operations. However, simple common sense can help. In this example, since pounds are heavier than ounces, it is reasonable to end up with fewer pounds than ounces.

The customary system involves an unfortunate variety of conversion factors, and as long as the United States continues to use it, teachers will have to deal with helping children commit the most commonly used factors to memory.

Exact conversions between the metric and the customary system should never be done. From the standpoint of familiarity with these systems, "soft" or "friendly" conversions are useful as long as we live in a country that seems bent on having two systems of measurement. For example, a liter is "a gulp more" than a quart, and a meter is "a bit longer" than a yard. The same is true for benchmarks. One hundred meters is about one football field plus one end zone, or about 110 yards.

## Important Standard Units

Both the customary and metric systems include many units that are not used in everyday living. Table 16.1 lists the units that are most common.

### Table 16.1
**Commonly Encountered Units of Measure**

| | Metric System | Customary System |
|---|---|---|
| **Length** | millimeter | inch |
| | centimeter | foot |
| | meter | yard |
| | kilometer | mile |
| **Area** | square centimeter | square inch |
| | square meter | square foot |
| | | square yard |
| **Volume** | cubic centimeter | cubic inch |
| | cubic meter | cubic foot |
| | | cubic yard |
| **Capacity** | millimeter | ounce* |
| | liter | cup |
| | | quart |
| | | gallon |
| **Weight** | gram | ounce* |
| | kilogram | pound |
| | metric ton | ton |

*In the U.S. customary system, the term *ounce* refers to a weight or *avoirdupois* unit, 16 of which make a pound, and also a volume or capacity unit, 8 of which make a cup. Though the two units have the same name, they are not related.

### The Metric System

Unit familiarity with the popularly used units should be the principal focus of almost all instruction with standard units.

Before students have developed a full understanding of decimal notation, there is little advantage in teaching the very nice relationships in the metric system. Whereas the customary system frequently mixes units (3 pounds 6 ounces, or 6 feet 2 inches), the metric system uses a single unit for each measure. To adhere to this "rule" would mean that primary-grade children, who do not understand decimal numbers, should report a measure in the smallest unit used. For example, a length would be recorded as "235 cm" instead of "2.35 m" or "2 m and 35 cm." How important this rule is for the second grade may be open to debate.

Perhaps one of the worst errors in the metric measurement curriculum is having students "move decimal points" to convert from one metric unit to another prior to a complete development of decimal notation. Confused, children memorize rules about moving decimals so many places this way or that, and the focus becomes rules and right answers.

As children begin to appreciate the structure of decimal notation, the metric system can and should be developed with all seven places: three prefixes for smaller units (*deci-, centi-, milli-*) and three for larger units (*deka-, hecto-, kilo-*). With decimal knowledge and familiarity with the basic and popularly used units, the complete metric system is easy to learn.

Making conversions within the metric system can be approached in two related ways. As we saw in Figure 14.6 in Chapter 14 (p. 247), a place-value chart gives a metric name to each of seven consecutive places. If it is understood that the decimal point always identifies the units position, then given any metric measurement, each digit is in a position with a metric name. The decimal point can be repositioned if the name of the unit is changed. In the measure 17.238 kg, the decimal indicates that the 7 is in the units position. The label "kg" indicates that the name of the position is kilograms. Therefore, the 2 is in the hectogram position, the 3 in the dekagram position, and the 8 in the gram position. Repositioning the decimal to indicate grams as the units makes the same measure read 17,238 g or 17,238.0 g.

An alternate rationale is to think of decimal point shifting as multiplying or dividing by powers of 10. In our example, since there are 1000 grams in a kilogram, change to grams by multiplying by 1000, or shift the decimal three places to the right.

It should be emphasized once again that unit conversion is perhaps the least important part of learning the metric system or any standard system. It is a skill that is not used frequently in daily life.

## The Customary System

The "familiar" system of units is technically known as the U.S. customary system. After an attempt in the 1970s to go completely metric, most schools and textbooks have resigned themselves to teaching both metric and customary systems.

Conversion of units within the customary system is difficult for children for two reasons: There are more conversion ratios to memorize, and they are not conveniently related to the decimal system. For example, many children will add

3 feet 8 inches to 5 feet 6 inches and get 9 feet 4 inches instead of 9 feet 2 inches. (Why?) Similar difficulties occur with all conversions in the customary system. Once again, while it is important to know how many inches in a foot and a few other common relationships, overemphasis on conversions in the customary system is unwarranted.

# ESTIMATING MEASURES

Measurement estimation is the process of using mental and visual information to measure or make comparisons without the use of measuring instruments. It is a practical skill. Almost every day, we make estimates of measures. Do I have enough sugar to make the cookies? Will the car fit in that space? Can you throw the ball 50 feet? Is this suitcase over the weight limit? About how long is the fence? Will this paper cover the box? Each of these involves estimation.

Besides its value outside the classroom, estimation in measurement activities helps students focus on the attribute being measured, adds intrinsic motivation, and helps develop familiarity with standard units. Therefore, measurement estimation both improves measurement instruction and develops a valuable life skill.

## Techniques of Measurement Estimation

Just as for computational estimation, specific strategies exist for estimating measures. Four strategies can be taught specifically:

1. *Develop and use benchmarks or referents for important units.* (This strategy was also mentioned as a way to develop familiarity with units.) Students should have a good referent for single units and also useful multiples of standard units. Referents or benchmarks for 1, 5, 10, and perhaps 100 pounds might be useful. A referent for 500 milliliters is very useful. These benchmarks can then be compared mentally to objects being estimated: "That tree is about as tall as four doorways, or between 8 and 9 meters tall."

2. *Use "chunking" when appropriate.* Figure 16.18 is an example. It may be easier to estimate the shorter chunks along the wall than to estimate the whole length as one. The weight of a stack of books is easier if some estimate is given to an "average" book.

3. *Use subdivisions.* This is a similar strategy to chunking, with the chunks imposed on the object by the estimator. For example, if the wall length to be estimated has no useful chunks, it can be mentally divided in half and then in fourths or even eighths by repeated halving until a more manageable length is arrived at. Length, volume, and area measurements all lend themselves to this technique.

4. *Iterate a unit mentally or physically.* For length, area, and volume, it is sometimes easy to mark off single units visually. You might use your hands or make marks or folds to keep

Estimate the room length.
Use: windows, bulletin board, and spaces between as "chunks."
Use: cabinet length—looks like about three cabinets will fit into
the room—plus a little bit.

**Figure 16.18**  **Estimating measures by chunking.**

track as you go. For length, it is especially useful to use a body measure as a unit and iterate with that. If you know, for example, that your stride is about $\frac{3}{4}$ meter, you can walk off a length and then multiply to get an estimate. Hand and finger widths are useful for shorter measures.

## Tips for Teaching Estimation

Each of the four strategies just listed should be taught directly and discussed with students. But the best approach to improving estimation skills is to have students do a lot of estimating. Keep the following tips in mind:

1. Help students learn strategies by having them use a specified approach. Later activities should permit students to choose whatever techniques they wish.

2. Periodically discuss how different students made their estimates. This will help students understand that there is no single right way to estimate and also remind them of different approaches that are useful.

3. Accept a range of estimates. Think in relative terms about what is a good estimate. Within 10 percent for length is quite good. Even 30 percent off may be reasonable for weights or volumes.

4. Sometimes have students give a range of measures that they believe includes the actual measure. This not only is a practical approach in real life but also helps focus on the approximate nature of estimation.

5. Let students measure to check estimates. However, it is only necessary that one or two students or one team do the measurement if the focus is on estimation. If all students are required to follow their estimates with a measure, they may correctly wonder why they bothered estimating.

6. Make measurement estimation an ongoing activity. A daily measurement to estimate can be posted on the bulletin board. Students can turn in their estimates on paper and discuss them in a 5-minute period. Older students

can even be given the task of making up the things to estimate, with a team assigned this task each week.

7. Make an effort to include estimations of all attributes. It is easy to get carried away with length and forget about area, volume, weight, and angles.

## Measurement Estimation Activities

Estimation activities need not be elaborate. Any measurement activity can have an "estimate first" component. For more emphasis on the process of estimation itself, simply think of things that can be estimated, and have students estimate. Here are a few suggestion.

---
**A**CTIVITY

### 16.20 Estimation Quickie

Select a single object such as a box, a watermelon, a jar, or even the principal. Each day, select a different attribute or dimension to estimate. For a watermelon, for example, students can estimate its length, girth, weight, volume, and surface area.

---

---
**A**CTIVITY

### 16.21 Estimation Scavenger Hunt

Conduct measurement scavenger hunts. Give teams a list of measurements, and have them find things that are close to having those measurements. Permit no measuring instruments. A list might include the following items:

A length of 3.5 m

Something that weighs more than 1 kg but less than 2 kg

A container that holds about 200 ml

Let students suggest how to judge results in terms of accuracy.

---

### 16.22 E-M-E Sequences

Use estimate-measure-estimate sequences (Lindquist, 1987a). Select pairs of objects to estimate that are somehow related or close in measure but not the same. Have students estimate the measure of the first and check by measuring. Then have them estimate the second. Here are some examples of pairs:

Width of a window, width of a wall

Volume of a coffee mug, volume of a pitcher

Distance between the eyes, width of the head

Weight of a handful of marbles, weight of a bag of marbles

Activity 16.22 can help students understand how benchmarks are used in estimation.

# DEVELOPING FORMULAS

Frequently, measurement and geometry are presented together in textbooks. The relationship between these two areas of mathematics is most evident in the development of formulas for measures of geometric figures. Formulas help us use easily made measures to determine indirectly some other measure that is not so easily found. For example, it is easy to measure the three dimensions of a box with a ruler, but it is not easy to actually measure the volume of the same box. By using a formula, the volume can be determined from the length measures.

Children should never use formulas without participating in the development of those formulas. Formulas for area and volume should all be developed by children. Developing the formulas and seeing how they are connected and interrelated is significantly more important than blindly plugging numbers into formulas, which is primarily computational tedium.

## Common Difficulties

Many children become so encumbered with the use of formulas and rules that an understanding of what these formulas are all about is completely lost.

### Overemphasizing Formulas

In the sixth National Assessment of Educational Progress, students were asked to draw on a square grid a rectangle with an area of 12 square units. Correct responses were given by 42 percent of fourth-grade and 66 percent of eighth-grade students. When asked for the area of a carpet 9 feet long and

6 feet wide, correct responses for these grades were given 19 percent and 65 percent of the time, respectively. Most fourth-grade students selected the sum of the dimensions (15) as their answer. The eighth-grade performance is consistent with that of drawing the 12-square-unit rectangle but is not a strong performance (Kenney & Kouba, 1997).

Many such items from this assessment and earlier NAEP studies indicate that children often have difficulty applying area measurement formulas and that formulas for area and perimeter are often confused. The most likely explanation is a premature emphasis on formulas with little effort to develop an understanding of why the formulas work.

The tasks in Figure 16.19 cannot be solved with simple formulas; they require an understanding of concepts and how formulas work. "Length times width" is not a definition of area.

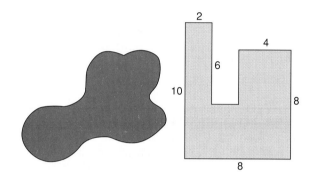

"How would you determine the areas of these shapes?"

Note: Many children believe that such shapes do not have areas or that the areas are impossible to determine because there are no formulas.

**Figure 16.19** **Understanding the attribute of area.**

### Height or Side

Another common error when students use formulas comes from failure to conceptualize the meaning of height in geometric figures, both two- and three-dimensional. The shapes in Figure 16.20 each have a slanted side and a height given. Students tend to confuse these two. Any side or flat surface of a figure can be called a *base* of the figure. For each base that a figure has, there is a corresponding height. If the figure were to slide into a room on its base, the *height* would be the height of the shortest door it could pass through without bending over—that is, the perpendicular distance to the base. Children have a lot of early experiences with the length-times-width formula for rectangles, in which the height is exactly the same as the length of a side. Perhaps this is the source of the confusion.

Before formulas involving heights are discussed, children should be able to identify where a height could be measured for any base that a figure has.

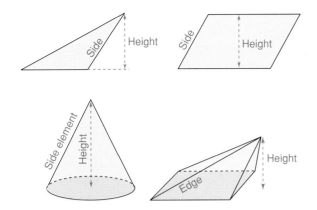

**Figure 16.20** **Heights of figures are not always measured along an edge or a surface.**

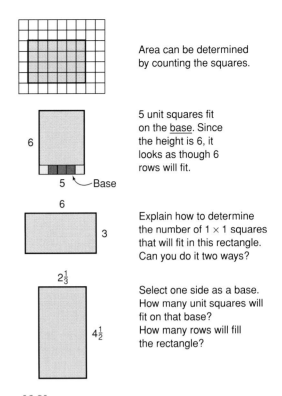

Area can be determined by counting the squares.

5 unit squares fit on the <u>base</u>. Since the height is 6, it looks as though 6 rows will fit.

Explain how to determine the number of 1 × 1 squares that will fit in this rectangle. Can you do it two ways?

Select one side as a base. How many unit squares will fit on that base? How many rows will fill the rectangle?

**Figure 16.21** **Determining the area of a rectangle.**

# The Area of Rectangles Parallelograms, Triangles, and Trapezoids

The development of area formulas is a fantastic opportunity to follow the spirit of the NCTM *Principles and Standards*. First, a problem-solving approach can meaningfully involve students and help them see that mathematics is a sense-making endeavor. Second, the connectedness of mathematics is evident. Here you will see that all of the standard area formulas are intimately related and can be developed and learned as an integrated whole rather than as a collection of isolated facts.

## Rectangles

The formula for the area of a rectangle is one of the first that is developed and is usually given as $A = L \times W$, "area equals length times width." Looking forward to other area formulas, an equivalent but more unifying idea might be $A = b \times h$, "area equals *base* times *height*." The base-times-height formulation can be generalized to all parallelograms and is useful in developing the area formulas for triangles and trapezoids. Furthermore, the same approach can be extended to three dimensions, where volumes of cylinders are given in terms of the *area of the base* times the height. Base times height, then, helps connect a large family of formulas that otherwise must be mastered independently.

The following sequence of exercises to develop the area formula for a rectangle is illustrated in Figure 16.21. Approach each step of this sequence with a problem-solving spirit: How can we figure this out?

1. Have students determine the areas of rectangles drawn on square grids or geoboards. Or have students draw rectangles that have specified areas (but do not give the dimensions). Some may count every square; others may multiply to find the total number of squares.

2. Examine rectangles not on a grid but with whole-number dimensions. Designate one side as the base, and line unit squares along this side. How many such rows can fit into the rectangle? On the same rectangle, repeat this approach using the other side as the base.

3. Give students rectangles with only the dimensions provided, and have them determine the area. Require them to justify their results. Encourage approaches similar to those in step 2.

4. Examine rectangles with dimensions that are not whole numbers. If the base is $4\frac{1}{2}$ units, then $4\frac{1}{2}$ unit squares will fit along the base. If the height is $2\frac{1}{3}$ units, then there are $2\frac{1}{3}$ rows with $4\frac{1}{2}$ squares in each, or $2\frac{1}{3}$ sets of $4\frac{1}{2}$.

## From Rectangles to Parallelograms

Once students understand the base-times-height formula for rectangles, the next challenge is to determine the areas of parallelograms. Do not provide a formula or other explanation. Rather, give students a rectangle drawn on a grid or on a plain sheet of paper. Their task is to develop a method for finding the area of the parallelogram that they can use with any parallelogram, not just the one they are working with. If students are stuck, ask them to examine ways that the parallelogram is like a rectangle or how it can be changed into a rectangle. As shown in Figure 16.22 (p. 298), a parallelogram can always be transformed into a rectangle with the same base, the same height, and the same area. Thus the formula for the area of a parallelogram is exactly the same as for a rectangle: base times height.

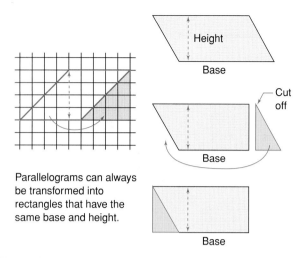

Parallelograms can always be transformed into rectangles that have the same base and height.

**Figure 16.22** **Area of a parallelogram.**

## From Parallelograms to Triangles

It is very important for students to understand the parallelogram formula before exploring triangle area. With that background, the area of a triangle is relatively simple.

As with parallelograms, students should be challenged to figure the area of a triangle in such a manner that the method applies to all triangles. They can explore the areas of triangles drawn on grids or geoboards, just as with parallelograms. As a hint toward a formula, have students fold a piece of paper in half, draw a triangle on the folded paper, and cut it out, making two identical copies. Suggest that they try using the two triangles to construct a figure for which they have an area formula.

As shown in Figure 16.23, two congruent triangles can always be arranged to form a parallelogram with the same base and the same height as the triangle. The area of the triangle will therefore be one-half as much as the parallelogram. Have students further explore all three possible parallelograms, one for each triangle side serving as base. Will the computed areas always be the same?

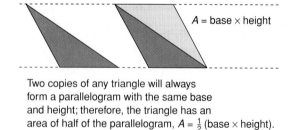

$A = \text{base} \times \text{height}$

Two copies of any triangle will always form a parallelogram with the same base and height; therefore, the triangle has an area of half of the parallelogram, $A = \frac{1}{2} (\text{base} \times \text{height})$.

**Figure 16.23** **Two triangles always make a parallelogram.**

## From Parallelograms to Trapezoids

After developing formulas for parallelograms and triangles, your students may be interested in tackling trapezoids without any further assistance. (See Figure 4.1, p. 44, for an example of a completely open challenge.) There are several methods of arriving at a formula for trapezoids, each related to the area of par-

allelograms or rectangles. One of the nicest methods uses the same general approach that was used for triangles. Suggest that students try working with two trapezoids that are identical, just as they did with triangles. Figure 16.24 shows how this method results in the formula. Now, not only are all of these formulas connected, but similar methods were used to develop them.

(Do you think that a special formula for the area of squares should be taught? What about formulas for perimeters?)

base = base 1 + base 2
$A = \text{height} \times (\text{base 1} + \text{base 2})$

Two trapezoids always make a parallelogram with the same height and a base equal to the sum of the bases in the trapezoid. Therefore,

$$A = \frac{1}{2} \times \text{height} \times (\text{base 1} + \text{base 2})$$

**Figure 16.24** **Two trapezoids always form a parallelogram.**

 # TECHNOLOGY NOTE

The relationship among the areas of rectangles, parallelograms, and triangles can be dramatically illustrated using a dynamic geometry program such as *The Geometer's Sketchpad* (Key Curriculum Press, 1995) or *Geometry Inventor* (LOGAL, 1994a). Draw two congruent segments on two parallel lines, as shown in Figure 16.25. Then connect the endpoints of the segments to form a parallelogram and two triangles. A segment between the parallel lines and perpendicular to each indicates the height. Either of the two line segments can be dragged left or right to "sheer" the parallelogram and triangle but without changing the base or height. All area measures remain fixed! ■

Explore the area of parallelograms and triangles.

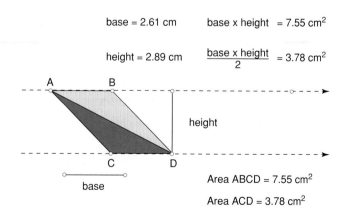

base = 2.61 cm     base x height   = 7.55 cm²

height = 2.89 cm     $\dfrac{\text{base x height}}{2}$ = 3.78 cm²

Area ABCD = 7.55 cm²
Area ACD = 3.78 cm²

Drag A or C to sheer the parallelogram left or right.
Drag D to change the height.

**Figure 16.25** **Dynamic geometry software shows that figures with the same base and height maintain the same area.**

# Circle Formulas

The relationship between the *circumference* of a circle (the distance around) and the length of the *diameter* (a line through the center joining two points on the circle) is one of the most interesting that children can discover. The circumference of every circle is about 3.14 times as long as the diameter. That exact ratio is an irrational number close to 3.14 and is represented by the Greek letter $\pi$. So $\pi = C/D$, the circumference divided by the diameter. In a slightly different form, $C = \pi D$. Half the diameter is the radius ($r$), so the same equation can be written $C = 2\pi r$. (Chapter 17 will discuss in detail the concept of $\pi$ and how students can discover this important ratio.)

Figure 16.26 presents an argument for the area formula $A = \pi r^2$. This development is one commonly found in textbooks. Another informal proof is based on the notion that the area of a polygon inscribed in a circle gets closer and closer to the area of the circle as the number of sides increases. (The relationship between regular polygons and the circle is well known to those who have drawn circles with Logo. For them, this approach to the area of a circle may be especially appealing.)

Regardless of the approach you use to develop the area formula, students should be challenged to figure it out on their own. Perhaps you show students how to arrange 8 or 12 sectors of a circle into an approximate parallelogram. Their task should be to use this as a hint toward development of an area formula for the circle. You may need to help them notice that the arrangement of sectors is an approximate par-allelogram and that the smaller the sectors, the closer the arrangement gets to a rectangle. But the complete argument for the formula should come from your students.

# Volumes of Common Solid Shapes

The relationships between the formulas for volume are completely analogous to those for area. As you read, notice the similarities between rectangles and prisms, between parallelograms and "sheered" (oblique) prisms, and between triangles and pyramids. Not only are the formulas related, but the process for development of the formulas is similar.

## Volumes of Cylinders

A *cylinder* is a solid with two congruent parallel bases and sides with parallel elements. There are several special classes of cylinders, including *prisms* (with polygons for bases), *right prisms, rectangular prisms,* and *cubes* (see Chapter 17). Interestingly, all of these solids have the same volume formula, and that one formula is analogous to the area formula for parallelograms.

Provide students with some wooden cubes and square grid paper that matches the face of the cubes. Have students draw a 3 × 5 rectangle on the paper, and place 15 cubes on the rectangle. This makes a box with a height of 1 unit. The volume of this box is 1 times the area of the base. Now place a second layer of cubes on the first. What is the height? The volume? Continue to add layers up to 5 or 6 (see Figure 16.27, p. 300). For each new layer, notice that the total number is

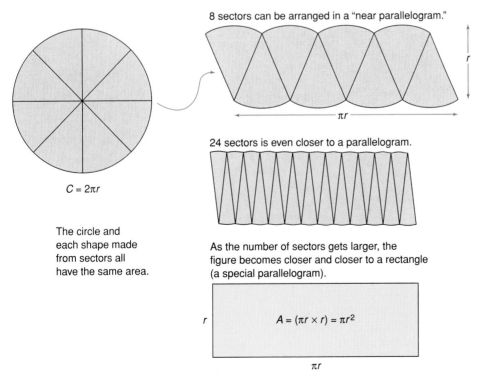

**Figure 16.26** Development of the circle area formula.

8 sectors can be arranged in a "near parallelogram."

$\pi r$

$r$

24 sectors is even closer to a parallelogram.

$C = 2\pi r$

The circle and each shape made from sectors all have the same area.

As the number of sectors gets larger, the figure becomes closer and closer to a rectangle (a special parallelogram).

$A = (\pi r \times r) = \pi r^2$

$r$

$\pi r$

Students can cut a circle into eight sectors or perhaps even more and rearrange them to form a near rectangle with dimensions of half the circumference by the radius.

the number of cubes on the bottom layer times the number of layers. The number on the bottom layer (or any layer) is the area of the base. The number of layers is the height. Therefore, the volume of the solid is $V = A \times h$, *the area of the base times the height.*

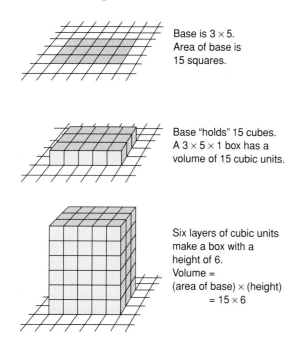

Base is $3 \times 5$.
Area of base is
15 squares.

Base "holds" 15 cubes.
A $3 \times 5 \times 1$ box has a
volume of 15 cubic units.

Six layers of cubic units
make a box with a
height of 6.
Volume =
(area of base) × (height)
= $15 \times 6$

**Figure 16.27**   **Volume of a prism.**

Recall how the area formula for rectangles was developed (see Figure 16.21, p. 297), and notice how that development is like the one for volume. Instead of *length* of the base × height (for *area* of rectangles), in three dimensions, the *volume* formula for the corresponding figure is *area* of the base × height.

Recall that a parallelogram can be thought of as a "sheered" rectangle, as was illustrated with the dynamic geometry software (Figure 16.25, p. 298). Show students a stack of three or four decks of playing cards (or a stack of books or paper). When stacked straight, they form a rectangular solid. The volume, as just discussed, is $V = A \times h$, with *A* equal to the area of one card. Now if the stack is sheered or slanted to one side as shown in Figure 16.28, what will the volume of this new figure be? Students should be able to argue that this figure has the same volume (and same volume formula) as the original stack.

What if the cards in this activity were some other shape? If they were circular, the volume would still be the area of the base times the height; if they were triangular, still the same. The conclusion is that the volume of *any* cylinder is equal to the *area of the base* times the *height.*

## Volumes of Cones and Pyramids

Just as there is a nice relationship between the areas of parallelograms and triangles, there is a similar relationship between the volumes of cylinders and cones.

Height

**Figure 16.28**   **Two cylinders with the same base and height have the same volume.**

Help students make a poster board prism and a pyramid with the same height and base. (Plastic models of these related shapes can be purchased.) Leave the base of each open. Score fold lines for accurate folds. Dimensions for a square pyramid and prism are given in Figure 16.29. Have students estimate the number of times the pyramid will fit into the prism. Then have them test their prediction by filling the pyramid with beans or rice and emptying it into the prism. They will discover that exactly 3 pyramids will fill a prism with the same base and height. (An alternative method is carefully to make models from clay and compare the weights.)

The 3-to-1 ratio of volumes is true of all cylinders and cones with the same base and height regardless of the shape of the base or the position of the vertex. That is, for any cone or pyramid, $V = \frac{1}{3}(A \times h)$. Recall that for parallelograms and triangles that have the same base and height, the areas are in a 2-to-1 ratio. *Area* is to *two*-dimensional figures what *volume* is to *three*-dimensional figures. Further, triangles are to parallelograms as pyramids are to prisms.

# MEASURING TIME

Time is measured in the same way that other attributes are measured: A unit of time is selected and used to "fill" the time to be measured. *Time* can be thought of as the duration of an event from its beginning to its end. An informal unit of time might be the duration of a pendulum swing, the steady drip of a water faucet, or the movement of the sun's shadow between two fixed points (as on a sundial). To measure time, the units of time are started at the same time as the activity being measured ("timed") and counted until the activity is finished. Thus the pendulum swings, for example, are "fitted into" the duration of time that it takes the child to print his or her name. Young children enjoy timing events with informal units. Older children can appreciate the measurement of time as a process similar to the measurement of other attributes and thus see commonality in all measuring.

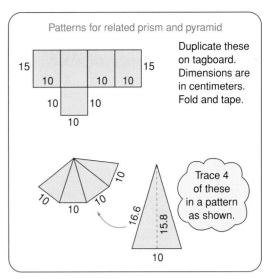

Patterns for related prism and pyramid

Duplicate these on tagboard. Dimensions are in centimeters. Fold and tape.

Trace 4 of these in a pattern as shown.

Same base

Same base

The volume of a pyramid or cone is one-third the volume of a prism or cylinder with the same base and same height.

**Figure 16.29** **Comparing volumes of prisms to pyramids and cones to cylinders.**

# Clock Reading

Telling time has little to do conceptually with the measurement of time. The skills of clock reading are related to the skills of reading any meter that uses pointers on a numbered scale. Clock reading is a difficult skill to teach in the early grades, yet nearly everyone learns to tell time by middle school.

## Some Difficulties

Young children's problems with clock reading may be due to the curriculum. Children are usually taught first to read clocks to the hour, then the half and quarter hours, and finally to 5- and 1-minute intervals. In the early stages of this sequence, children are shown clocks set exactly to the hour or half hour. Many children who can read a clock at 7:00 or 2:30 have no idea what time it is at 6:58 or 2:33.

Digital clocks permit students to read times easily but do not relate times very well. To know that a digital reading of 7:58 is nearly 8 o'clock, the child must know that there are 60 minutes in an hour, that 58 is close to 60, and that 2 minutes is not a very long time. These concepts have not been developed by most first-grade and many second-grade children. The analog clock (with hands) shows "close to" times without the need for understanding big numbers or even how many minutes in an hour.

Further, the standard approach to clock reading ignores the distinctly different actions and functions of the two hands. The little hand indicates broad, approximate time (nearest hour), and the big hand indicates time (minutes) before or beyond an hour. When we look at the hour hand, we focus on where it is pointing. With the minute hand, the focus is on the distance that it has gone around the clock or the distance yet to go for the hand to get back to the top.

## Suggested Approach

The following suggestions can help students understand and read analog clocks.

1. Begin with a one-handed clock. A clock with only an hour hand can be read with reasonable accuracy. Use lots of approximate language: "It's about 7 o'clock." "It's a little past 9 o'clock." "It's halfway between 2 o'clock and 3 o'clock" (see Figure 16.30).

"About 7 o'clock"

"Halfway between 2 o'clock and 3 o'clock"

"A little bit past 9 o'clock"

**Figure 16.30** **Approximate time with one-handed clocks.**

2. Discuss what happens to the big hand as the little hand goes from one hour to the next. When the big hand is at 12, the hour hand is pointing exactly to a number. If the hour hand is about halfway between numbers, about where would the minute hand be? If the hour hand is a little past or before an hour (10 to 15 minutes), about where would the minute hand be?

3. Use two real clocks, one with only an hour hand and one with two hands. (Break off the minute hand from an old clock.) Cover the two-handed clock. Periodically during the day, direct attention to the one-handed clock. Discuss the time in approximate language. Have students predict where the minute hand should be. Uncover the other clock and check.

4. Teach time after the hour in 5-minute intervals. After step 3 has begun, count by fives going around the clock. Instead of predicting that the minute hand is pointing at the 4, encourage students to say it is about 20 minutes after the hour. As skills develop, suggest that students always look first at the little or hour hand to learn approximately what time it is and then focus on the minute hand for precision.

5. Predict the reading on a digital clock when shown an analog clock, and vice versa; set an analog clock when shown a digital clock. This can be done with both one-handed and two-handed clocks.

## A Teaching Clock

A simple clock for use on the overhead projector can be made easily with three sheets of acetate. On one, draw a simple clock face but leave off the hands. Cut a small hole in the center, and insert a brass fastener from the back side. Leave the fastener sticking straight up; do not spread the prongs. Cut two circles from the other sheets. The radius of the circles should be the same as the minute and hour hands of the clock. Cut small holes in the center of these circles, and draw a clock hand on each that extends from the center to the edge of the circle. If you slip just the smaller hour hand over the brass fastener, you have a very nice one-handed clock. For a clock with two hands, place the larger circle on first.

Use your overhead clock to practice one-handed clock reading, emphasizing approximate language. Set the little hand at various places on the clock, and have children suggest how to read it. Let students set the hour hand at times like half-past 5 or a little before 8 o'clock.

## Related Concepts

Students also need to learn about seconds, minutes, and hours and to develop some concept of how long these units are. You can help by making a conscious effort to note the duration of short and long events during the day. Timing small events of $\frac{1}{2}$ minute to 2 minutes is fun and

useful. TV shows and commercials are a good standard. Have students time familiar events in their daily lives: brushing teeth, eating dinner, riding to school, spending time in the reading group.

As students learn more about two-digit numbers, the time after the hours can also be related to the time left before the hour. This is helpful not only for telling time but for number sense as well. Note that in the sequence suggested, time after the hour is stressed almost exclusively. Time before or till the hour can come later.

Problem-solving exercises such as "If it was 7:30 when Bill left home and the trip took 8 hours, what time did he arrive?" are important. Even middle school students have difficulty with these ideas. Adding and subtracting time involves understanding the relationships between minutes and hours and also the two cycles of 12 hours in the day.

## ASSESSMENT NOTES

Gathering useful assessment data in the area of measurement requires open-ended activities that permit students to show how they understand measurement concepts. Traditional textbook tests tend to focus on prescriptive, procedural skills such as conversion of units from feet to inches or the use of a formula. Examine these test items, and ask yourself if they really tell you what you want to know about your students and measurement.

## Focus on Ideas

As you progress through your measurement unit, think about what students really need to know to develop an understanding of measurement of any given attribute.

How well do students understand the attribute being measured? Observing how students do comparison activities ("Which of these regions is the largest? How can you tell?") will tell you what you need to know. Be wary of overly directing students; make sure that the ideas you observe are theirs, not yours. Rather than direct a student to measure something the way you prescribe, have students select their own methods and explain what they did and why they made the choices they made. If reasonable, ask them to find more than one way to measure the same object.

Do students use measuring tools meaningfully? Rulers, protractors, and clocks are often poorly understood. Ask students to find two different ways to measure with a ruler, or have them react to the technique used by another student. ("Monique measured the width of her locker. She lined up the 10 cm mark on one side. The other side of the locker was lined up between the 42 and 43 cm marks. Monique was confused. Without measuring the locker again, how would you help Monique?") Another technique is to have students explain how a ruler or protractor works to make a measurement. To help with their explanations, have them compare a student-made device, such as the waxed-paper protractor, with the standard device.

## Standard Units

Again, the danger is the traditional focus on conversions of units rather than familiarity with the units. Consider these two tasks:

1. 427 centimeters = _____ meters
2. Estimate the length of this rope in centimeters and in meters. What ideas did you use to help make your estimate?

Both tasks relate centimeters to meters. The second task requires a student to have unit familiarity as well. Does the child use a meter-centimeter relationship or make two independent estimates? How are the estimates made? Are familiar benchmarks for the unit being used? Feedback related to these questions is available as children do the second task but not the first. As with all assessment, the information can be used to guide your instruction or for evaluation purposes.

## Formulas

Plugging numbers into formulas, even requiring students to memorize the formulas, does very little to develop measurement understanding. Spend time in conceptual development of formulas and less time on practice with their use.

 **LITERATURE CONNECTIONS**

Various fantasy books about giants, or strange lands, and unusual occurrences prompt comparisons of measures with our everyday world. There are also a large number of "concept books" for measurement, books that are designed to help children explore interesting aspects of measurement. The selections here are offered as examples.

## How Big Is a Foot?
### (Myller, 1990)

The story in this concept book is very attractive to younger children. The king measures his queen (crown included) using his feet and orders a bed made that is 6 feet long and 3 feet wide. The chief carpenter's apprentice, who is very small, makes the bed according to his own feet. The problems give rise to the need for standard units. But children are also motivated to use their own measuring methods for different purposes. Lubinski and Thiessen (1996) show how students create a "ruler" with footprints linked together and share activities conducted in a first-grade class.

## Jim and the Beanstalk
### (Briggs, 1970)

A variation on the classic tale of *Jack and the Beanstalk*, Jim helps the giant, who is growing quite old. Jim makes him a giant-sized pair of glasses and eventually measures the giant for false teeth and a wig. As with the books for ratio concepts discussed in Chapter 15, children are intrigued with the notion of how big these giant things would be and with discussing other large things that would fit in the story.

A similar story is Jonathan Swift's classic, *Gulliver's Travels*. A fourth-grade unit titled *My Travels with Gulliver* (Education Development Center, 1991) guides students to create drawings and use measurements to explore the lands in Gulliver's journey. The land of the Brobdingnag is a place where objects are about ten times normal size.

## Counting on Frank
### (Clement, 1991)

The dog, Frank, and his young master, the narrator of the story, engage in a series of estimations of everyday things: the length of a line that can be drawn by the average ballpoint pen, the number of Franks that would fit in the bedroom, or the time it would take to fill the entire bathroom with water if the tap were left on. These fanciful ideas and hilarious drawings easily motivate students to make their own estimates. Younger children may not be able to go further than a guess of one of their own ideas. By third grade, students can investigate how well their estimate agrees with reality. This book can lead children to investigate length, weight, volume, area, and time and connect each to their personal world. "If I filled my room with stuffed duffel bags, I estimate it would take 3000 bags. Altogether these bags would weigh over 15,000 pounds. If the duffel bags were each as big as my dad's car, they would take a space as big as the football stadium." Ideas such as this are fun to imagine but can also be tested against reality through measurement and calculations. One idea is to have class members contribute to their very own Frank book and provide an appendix that explains their estimates.

## 8,000 Stones
### (Wolkstein, 1972)

This is an interesting folktale concerning the Supreme Governor of China, who wishes to find a method of weighing an elephant that has been received as a gift. The emperor's son solves the problem by putting the elephant in a boat and noticing the water level on the side. The amount of weight to produce the same effect is that of the elephant. This is a wonderful introduction to indirect methods of measurement for middle grade students. Not only can the same weighing method be explored, but students can research other measurements and find out how they are made. For example, how do we measure temperature with a mercury thermometer, and how is it done with a bimetal thermometer, the kind that causes a dial to rotate?

# REFLECTIONS ON CHAPTER 16

## Writing to Learn

1. Explain what it means to measure something. Does your explanation work equally well for length, area, weight, volume, and time?

2. A general instructional plan for measurement has three parts. Explain how the type of activity to use with each part accomplishes the instructional goal.

3. Five reasons were offered for using informal units instead of standard units in instructional activities. Which of these seem most important to you, and why?

4. For each of the following attributes, describe a comparison activity, one or two possible informal units, and a group activity that includes an estimation component:

   a. Length    d. Weight

   b. Area      e. Capacity

   c. Volume

5. With a straightedge, draw a triangle, a quadrilateral, and a five-sided figure. Make each about as large as a sheet of notebook paper. Make a waxed-paper protractor, and measure each interior angle. Did the sum of the angles for each figure come close to what is predicted?

6. What is a degree? How would you help children learn what a degree is?

7. What do students need to know about standard units? Of these, which is the most and least important?

8. Develop in a connected way the area formulas for rectangles, parallelograms, triangles, and trapezoids. Draw pictures and provide explanations.

9. Explain how the volume formula for a right rectangular prism can be developed in an analogous manner to the area formula for a rectangle.

10. Explain how the area of a circle can be determined using the basic formula for the area of a parallelogram. (If you have a set of fraction "pie pieces," these can be used as sectors of a circle.)

11. Describe the differences between the typical approach for teaching clock reading and the one-handed approach discussed in this chapter.

## For Discussion and Exploration

1. Make your own measuring instrument for an informal unit of measure. Use your instrument to measure, and then make the same measurement directly with a unit model. What are the values and limitations of each method? Can you see the importance of having children do this both ways?

2. Frequently, a textbook chapter on measurement will cover length, area, volume, and capacity with both metric and customary units. This means a very light treatment of each. An alternative for the publisher is to focus on one area of measurement in each grade and risk not matching the curriculum guides for many states and districts. Get a teacher's edition of a basal textbook for any grade level, and look at the chapters on measurement. How well does the book cover measurement ideas? How would you modify or expand on the lessons found there?

3. Read Chapter 10, "Foot Activities," in *A Collection of Math Lessons from Grades 3 Through 6* (Burns, 1987). Identify two good ideas in the sequence of lessons. Modify the activities to suit your own needs, and try them out with a class of children.

## Recommendations for Further Reading

### Highly Recommended

Nitabach, E., & Lehrer, R. (1996). Developing spatial sense through area measurement. *Teaching Children Mathematics, 2*, 473–476.

This is a superb article. The authors describe six principles of measurement, giving special attention to area measurement. They then proceed to describe some nice activities with first and second graders and the children's responses. Too often we take simple measurement ideas for granted. This article provides a research-based view of reality.

Rubenstein, R. N., Lappan, G., Phillips, E., & Fitzgerald, W. M. (1993). Angle sense: A valuable connector. *Arithmetic Teacher, 40*, 352–358.

This is an important article for the middle grade teacher. The authors describe a series of investigations of angles in various polygons using pattern blocks and an angle-measuring device called a *goniometer*. Among other interesting ideas is a discussion of the question "Why are there 360 degrees in a circle?" and a graphical exposition of the interior angles of polygons that goes beyond the usual.

Wilson, P. S., & Rowland, R. E. (1993). Teaching measurement. In R. J. Jensen (Ed.), *Research ideas for the classroom: Early childhood mathematics* (pp. 171–194). Old Tappan, NJ: Macmillan.

There is an interesting research-based idea for every teacher in this well-written review of measurement in the classroom. All areas of measurement are discussed, with clear descriptions of some of the difficulties children experience. The chapter contains great activities as well.

### Other Suggestions

Battista, M. T. (1999). Fifth graders' enumeration of cubes in 3D arrays: Conceptual progress in an inquiry-based classroom. *Journal for Research in Mathematics Education, 30*, 417–448.

Clopton, E. L. (1991). Area and perimeter are independent. *Mathematics Teacher, 84*, 33–35.

Coburn, T. G., & Shulte, A. P. (1986). Estimation in measurement. In H. L. Schoen (Ed.), *Estimation and mental computation* (pp. 195–203). Reston, VA: National Council of Teachers of Mathematics.

Corwin, R. B., & Russell, S. J. (1990). *Measuring: From paces to feet* (Unit of study for grades 3–5 from *Used numbers: Real data in the classroom*). White Plains, NY: Cuisenaire–Dale Seymour.

Friederwitzer, F. J., & Berman, B. (1999). The language of time. *Teaching Children Mathematics, 6*, 254–259.

Gerver, R. (1990). Discovering pi: Two approaches. *Arithmetic Teacher, 37*(8), 18–22.

Kenney, P. A., & Kouba, V. L. (1997). What do students know about measurement? In P. A. Kenney & E. A. Silver (Eds.), *Results from the sixth mathematics assessment of the National Assessment of Educational Progress* (pp. 141–163). Reston, VA: National Council of Teachers of Mathematics.

Liedtke, W. W. (1990). Measurement. In J. N. Payne (Ed.), *Mathematics for the young child* (pp. 229–249). Reston, VA: National Council of Teachers of Mathematics.

McClain, K., Cobb, P., Gravemeijer, K., & Estes, B. (1999). Developing mathematical reasoning within the context of measurement. In L. V. Stiff (Ed.), *Developing mathematical reasoning in grades K–12* (pp. 93–106). Reston, VA: National Council of Teachers of Mathematics.

Rectanus, C. (1998). *Math by all means: Area and perimeter, grades 5–6.* Sausalito, CA: Math Solutions Publications.

Reynolds, A., & Wheatley, G. H. (1997). Third-grade students engage in a playground measuring activity. *Teaching Children Mathematics, 4,* 166–170.

Rhone, L. (1995). Measurement in a primary-grade integrated curriculum. In P. A. House (Ed.), *Connecting mathematics across the curriculum* (pp. 124–133). Reston, VA: National Council of Teachers of Mathematics.

Richardson, K. (1997). Too easy for kindergarten and just right for first grade. *Teaching Children Mathematics, 3,* 432–437.

Shaw, J. M., & Cliatt, M. J. P. (1989). Developing measurement sense. In P. R. Trafton (Ed.), *New directions for elementary school mathematics* (pp. 149–155). Reston, VA: National Council of Teachers of Mathematics.

Szetela, W., & Owens, D. T. (1986). Finding the area of a circle: Use a cake pan and leave out the pi. *Arithmetic Teacher, 33*(9), 12–18.

Whitin, D. J. (1994). Exploring estimation through children's literature. *Arithmetic Teacher, 41,* 436–441.

Wilson, P. S. (1990). Understanding angles: Wedges to degrees. *Mathematics Teacher, 83,* 294–300.

Wilson, P. S., & Adams, V. M. (1992). A dynamic way to teach angle and angle measure. *Arithmetic Teacher, 39*(5), 6–13.

Zweng, M. J. (1986). Introducing angle measurement through estimation. In H. L. Schoen (Ed.), *Estimation and mental computation* (pp. 212–219). Reston, VA: National Council of Teachers of Mathematics.

# Chapter 17

# Geometric Thinking and Geometric Concepts

The geometry curriculum in grades K–8 should provide an opportunity to experience shapes in as many different forms as possible. These should include shapes built with blocks, sticks, or tiles; shapes drawn on paper or with a computer; and shapes observed in art, nature, and architecture. Hands-on, reflective, and interactive experiences are at the heart of good geometry activities at the elementary and middle school levels. The geometry curriculum should aim at the development of geometric reasoning and spatial sense. The three Big Ideas parallel three levels of thinking that characterize development over the K–8 school years.

## BIG Ideas

1. Shapes, both two- and three-dimensional, exist in great variety. There are many different ways to see and describe similarities and differences among shapes. The more ways that one can classify and discriminate shapes, the better one understands them.

2. Shapes have properties that can be used when describing and analyzing them. Awareness of these properties helps us appreciate shapes in our world. Properties can be explored and analyzed in a variety of ways.

3. An analysis of geometric properties leads to deductive reasoning in a geometric environment.

## THREE EXPLORATORY ACTIVITIES

To provide some common view of the nature of elementary and middle school geometry and how young children approach geometric concepts, three simple activities are offered here for you to do. The activities will provide some idea of the spirit of informal geometry as well as background for a discussion of children's geometric thinking. All you will need is a pencil, several pieces of paper, scissors, and 15 to 20 minutes.

### DIFFERENT TRIANGLES

Draw a series of at least five triangles. After the first triangle, each new one should be different in some way from those already drawn. Write down why you think each is different.

### SHAPES WITH TRIANGLES

Make a few copies of the 2-cm isometric grid found in the Blackline Masters, or simply place a sheet of paper over the grid. Draw three or four different figures by following the grid lines. Make each figure so that it has an area of 10 triangles. Count to find the distance around each figure (the perimeter), and record this next to each drawing. Examine your results for any ideas you may observe. Explore any ideas you have by drawing additional figures.

### A TILING PATTERN

First make at least eight copies of any shape in Figure 17.1. An easy way to do this is to fold a piece of paper so that there are eight thicknesses. Trace the shape on an outside section, and cut through all eight thicknesses at once.

Think of the shapes you cut out as tiles. The task is to use the tiles to make a regular tiling pattern. A tiling pattern made with one shape has two basic properties. First, there are no holes or gaps. The tiles must fit together without overlapping and without leaving any spaces. Second, the tiles must be arranged in a repeating pattern that could be extended indefinitely. That is, if you were to tile an endless floor with your pattern, the design in one section of the floor would be the same as that in any other section. Several different tiling patterns are possible for each of the three tiles. Experiment to decide on a pattern that you like.

Notice that each of the tile shapes is made up of triangles and can be drawn on a triangle grid such as the 2-cm isometric grid or on the isometric dot grid, both found in the Blackline Masters. When you have decided on a tiling pattern, place a piece of paper over one of these two grids, and draw your tiling pattern using the grid as a guide. Cover most of the grid with your pattern.

Finally, suppose that your tiles come in two colors. With a pen or pencil, shade in some of the tiles to make a regular pattern in two colors.

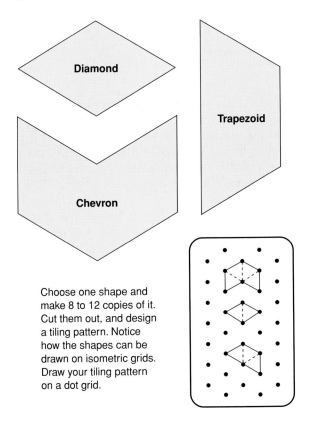

Choose one shape and make 8 to 12 copies of it. Cut them out, and design a tiling pattern. Notice how the shapes can be drawn on isometric grids. Draw your tiling pattern on a dot grid.

**Figure 17.1** **Three tile patterns.**

## Reflections on the Activities

The following observations apply to all geometry activities in school as well as the activities you have just completed.

## Different People Think About Geometric Ideas in Different Ways

Compare your response to the three exploration activities with those of your peers. Are there qualitative differences as well as objective differences? How would primary-age children's approaches to these activities compare to an eighth grader's? Figure 17.2 (p. 308) shows how two students, one in the fifth grade and one in the eighth grade, responded to the triangle task. Research indicates that age is not the major criterion for how students think geometrically. The kinds of experiences a child has may be a more significant factor.

## Explorations Can Help Develop Relationships

The more you play around with and think about the ideas in these activities, the more there is to think about. You might be able to extend each of these activities to develop the ideas beyond the obvious. For example:

### FOR "DIFFERENT TRIANGLES"

How many different ways can two triangles be different? Could you draw five or more *quadrilaterals* that were each different?

### FOR "SHAPES WITH TRIANGLES"

What did you notice about the shapes that had smaller perimeters as opposed to those with the larger perimeters? If you tried the same activity with rectangles on a square grid, what would the shapes with the largest and smallest perimeters look like? What about three-dimensional boxes? If you were to build different boxes with the same number of cubes, what could you say about the surface areas?

### FOR "A TILING PATTERN"

How many different tiling patterns are there for this shape? Can any shape be used to tile with? Can you see any larger shapes within your pattern?

Notice that it takes more than just doing an activity to learn or create a new idea. The greatest learning occurs when you stop and reflect on what you did and begin to ask questions or make observations. Like all mathematics, geometry is best developed in a spirit of problem solving.

## Geometry Activities and Hands-On Materials

Even the simple paper tiles used in "A Tiling Pattern" gave you the opportunity to explore spatial relationships and search for

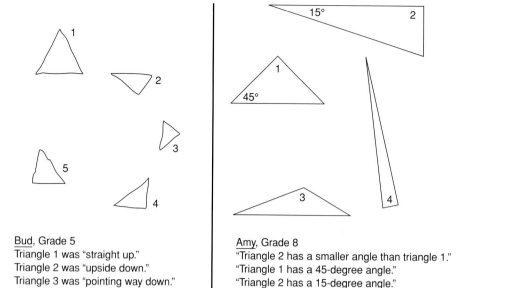

Bud, Grade 5
Triangle 1 was "straight up."
Triangle 2 was "upside down."
Triangle 3 was "pointing way down."
Triangle 4 was "pointing way to the left."
Triangle 5 "has crooked lines."

Amy, Grade 8
"Triangle 2 has a smaller angle than triangle 1."
"Triangle 1 has a 45-degree angle."
"Triangle 2 has a 15-degree angle."
"Triangle 3 has a wider angle than triangles 1 and 2."
"Triangle 4 has a 90-degree angle and a really small angle."

**Figure 17.2** **Two children show markedly different responses to the task of drawing a series of different triangles.**

*Source:* From "Characterization of the van Hiele Levels of Development in Geometry," by W. F. Burger and J. M. Shaughnessy, 1986, *Journal for Research in Mathematics Education, 17*(1), pp. 38–39. Reprinted by permission of the National Council of Teachers of Mathematics.

patterns much more easily than without them. Activities on paper such as the dot grid in "Shapes with Triangles" are a second-best alternative to real physical objects. The same area and perimeter activity is much more effective with a collection of cardboard triangles that can be rearranged to form different shapes. The first activity is the least enticing of the three, but at least you could freely draw pictures. Virtually *every activity* that is appropriate for K–8 geometry should involve some form of hands-on materials, models, or at least paper (graph paper or dot paper) that lends itself to easy spatial explorations.

# INFORMAL GEOMETRY AND SPATIAL SENSE

In *Principles and Standards for School Mathematics,* the authors chose only five broad content standards, one of which is Geometry. The prominence of this strand, appropriately kept separate from measurement, speaks to the importance that should be placed on the development of geometric ideas at all grade levels. Prior to the 1989 *Standards* document, geometry received only limited attention in the traditional curriculum. State standards now place a heavier emphasis on geometry than in the past. There is still a serious concern that in international comparisons, U.S. students fall short in this area.

## Informal Geometry

The term *informal geometry* has been used for many years to refer to geometric activities appropriate for students in ele-

mentary and middle school. Informal geometry activities provide children with the opportunity to explore, to feel and see, to build and take apart, to make observations about shape in the world around them as well as in the world they create with drawings, models, and computers. Activities involve constructing, visualizing, comparing, transforming, and classifying geometric figures. The experiences and explorations can take place at different levels of sophistication: from shapes and their appearances to properties of shapes to relationships among properties. The spirit of informal geometry is one of exploration, almost always in a hands-on, engaging activity.

## Spatial Sense

Just as a good definition of number sense is an intuition about numbers and their relationships, *spatial sense* can be defined as an intuition about shapes and the relationships among shapes. Individuals with spatial sense have a feel for the geometric aspects of their surroundings and the shapes formed by objects in the environment.

Many people say they aren't very good with shape or that they have poor spatial sense. The typical belief is that you are either born with spatial sense or not. This simply is not true! We now know that rich experiences with shape and spatial relationships, when provided consistently over time, can and do develop spatial sense. Without geometric experiences, most people do not grow in their spatial sense or spatial reasoning. Between 1990 and 1992, NAEP data indicated a significant improvement in students' geometric reasoning at all three grades tested, 4, 8, and 12 (Strutchens & Blume, 1997). Students did not just get smarter. What is more likely is that there has been an increasing emphasis on geometry at all grades. Still, much more needs to be done if U.S. children are to rise to the same level as their European and Asian counterparts.

## The Importance of Geometry

In the past, most elementary and middle grades teachers spent very little time on geometry. Possibly they felt uncomfortable with the topic themselves or did not regard the topic as important. Traditional norm-referenced tests did not give a lot of weight to geometric thinking. Thanks to the increased NCTM emphasis on geometry and its inclusion in state testing programs, more geometry is being taught. Still, it is fair to ask, "Why study geometry?" Here are a few reasons that come to mind.

1. Geometry can provide a more complete appreciation of the world. Geometry can be found in the structure of the solar system, in geological formations, in rocks and crystals, in plants and flowers, even in animals. It is also a major part of our synthetic universe: Art, architecture, cars, machines, and virtually everything that humans create have elements of geometric form.

2. Geometric explorations can develop problem-solving skills. Spatial reasoning is an important form of problem solving, and problem solving is one of the major reasons for studying mathematics.

3. Geometry plays a key role in the study of other areas of mathematics. For example, fraction concepts are related to geometric part-to-whole constructs. Ratio and proportion are directly related to the geometric concept of similarity. Measurement and geometry are clearly related.

4. Geometry is used daily by many people. Scientists of all sorts, architects and artists, engineers, and land developers are just a few of the professions that use geometry regularly. At home, geometry helps build a fence, design a dog house, plan a garden, arrange a living room.

5. Geometry is enjoyable. If geometry increases students' fondness for mathematics more in general, that makes the effort worthwhile.

## THE DEVELOPMENT OF GEOMETRIC THINKING

Until recently, the geometry curriculum in the United States has been poorly defined. Teachers and curriculum developers have had little guidance on what is important. However, the work of two Dutch educators, Pierre van Hiele and Dina van Hiele-Geldof, is beginning to have an impact on the design of geometry instruction and curriculum.

## The van Hiele Levels of Geometric Thought

The van Hieles' work began in 1959 and immediately attracted a lot of attention in the Soviet Union but for nearly two decades got little notice in this country (Hoffer, 1983; Hoffer & Hoffer, 1992). But today, the van Hiele theory has become the most influential factor in the American geometry curriculum.

The most prominent feature of the model is a five-level hierarchy of ways of understanding spatial ideas. Each of the five levels describes the thinking processes used in geometric contexts. The levels describe how one thinks and what types of geometric ideas one thinks about, rather than how much knowledge one has. As one progresses from one level to the next, the object of one's geometric thinking changes.

### Level 0: Visualization

*The objects of thought at level 0 are shapes and what they "look like."*

Students recognize and name figures based on the global, visual characteristics of the figure—a gestaltlike approach to shape. Students operating at this level are able to make measurements and even talk about properties of shapes, but these properties are not thought about explicitly. It is the appearance of the shape that defines it for the student. A square is a square "because it looks like a square." Because appearance is dominant at this level, appearances can overpower properties of a shape. For example, a square that has been rotated so that all sides are at a 45° angle to the vertical may not appear to be a square for a level 0 thinker. Students at this level will sort and classify shapes based on their appearances—"I put these together because they all look sort of alike."

*The products of thought at level 0 are classes or groupings of shapes that seem to be "alike."*

### Level 1: Analysis

*The objects of thought at level 1 are classes of shapes rather than individual shapes.*

Students at the analysis level are able to consider all shapes within a class rather than a single shape. Instead of talking about *this* rectangle, it is possible to talk about *all* rectangles. By focusing on a class of shapes, students are able to think about what makes a rectangle a rectangle (four sides, opposite sides parallel, opposite sides same length, four right angles, congruent diagonals, etc.). The irrelevant features (e.g., size or orientation) fade into the background. At this level, students begin to appreciate that a collection of shapes goes together because of properties. Ideas about an individual shape can now be generalized to all shapes that fit that class. If a shape belongs to a particular class such as cubes, it has the corresponding properties of that class. "All cubes have six congruent faces, and each of those faces is a square." These properties were only implicit at level 0. Students operating at level 1 may be able to list all the properties of squares, rectangles, and parallelograms but not see that these are subclasses of one another, that all squares are rectangles and all rectangles are parallelograms. In defining a shape, level 1 thinkers are likely to list as many properties of a shape as they know.

*The products of thought at level 1 are the properties of shapes.*

### Level 2: Informal Deduction

*The objects of thought at level 2 are the properties of shapes.*

As students begin to be able to think about properties of geometric objects without the constraints of a particular object, they are able to develop relationships between and among these properties. "If all four angles are right angles, the shape must be a rectangle. If it is a square, all angles are right angles. If it is a square, it must be a rectangle." With greater ability to engage in "if-then" reasoning, shapes can be classified using only minimum characteristics. For example, four congruent sides and at least one right angle can be sufficient to define a square. Rectangles are parallelograms with a right angle. Observations go beyond properties themselves and begin to focus on logical arguments *about* the properties. Students at level 2 will be able to follow and appreciate an informal deductive argument about shapes and their properties. "Proofs" may be more intuitive than rigorously deductive. However, there is an appreciation that a logical argument is compelling. An appreciation of the axiomatic structure of a formal deductive system, however, remains under the surface.

*The products of thought at level 2 are relationships among properties of geometric objects.*

### Level 3: Deduction

*The objects of thought at level 3 are relationships among properties of geometric objects.*

At level 3, students are able to examine more than just the properties of shapes. Their earlier thinking has produced conjectures concerning relationships among properties. Are these conjectures correct? Are they "true"? As this analysis of the informal arguments takes place, the structure of a system complete with axioms, definitions, theorems, corollaries, and postulates begins to develop and can be appreciated as the necessary means of establishing geometric truth. At this level, students begin to appreciate the need for a system of logic that rests on a minimum set of assumptions and from which other truths can be derived. The student at this level is able to work with abstract statements about geometric properties and make conclusions based more on logic than intuition. This is the level of the traditional high school geometry course. A student operating at level 3 can clearly observe that the diagonals of a rectangle bisect each other, just as a student at a lower level of thought can. However, at level 3, there is an appreciation of the need to prove this from a series of deductive arguments.

The level 2 thinker, by contrast, follows the argument but fails to appreciate the need.

*The products of thought at level 3 are deductive axiomatic systems for geometry.*

### Level 4: Rigor

*The objects of thought at level 4 are deductive axiomatic systems for geometry.*

At the highest level of the van Hiele hierarchy, the object of attention is axiomatic systems themselves, not just the deductions within a system. There is an appreciation of the distinctions and relationships between different axiomatic systems. This is generally the level of a college mathematics major who is studying geometry as a branch of mathematical science.

*The products of thought at level 4 are comparisons and contrasts among different axiomatic systems of geometry.*

# Characteristics of the van Hiele Levels

You no doubt noticed that the products of thought at each level are the same as the objects of thought at the next. This object-product relationship between levels of the van Hiele theory is illustrated in Figure 17.3. The objects (ideas) must be created at one level so that relationships among these objects can become the focus of the next level. In addition to this key concept of the theory, four related characteristics of the levels of thought merit special attention.

1. The levels are sequential. To arrive at any level above level 0, students must move through all prior levels. To move through a level means that one has experienced geometric thinking appropriate for that level and has created in one's own mind the types of objects or relationships that are the focus of thought at the next level. Skipping a level rarely occurs.

2. The levels are not age-dependent in the sense of the developmental stages of Piaget. A third grader or a high school student could be at level 0. Indeed, some students and adults remain forever at level 0, and a significant number of adults never reach level 2. But age is certainly related to the amount and types of geometric experiences that we have. Therefore, it is reasonable for all children in the K–2 range to be at level 0, as well as the majority of children in grades 3 and 4.

3. Geometric experience is the greatest single factor influencing advancement through the levels. Activities that permit children to explore, talk about, and interact with content at the next level, while increasing their experiences at their current level, have the best chance of advancing the level of thought for those children.

4. When instruction or language is at a level higher than that of the student, there will be a lack of communication. Students required to wrestle with objects of thought

**The van Hiele Theory of Geometric Thought**

**Figure 17.3** **At each level of geometric thought, the ideas created become the focus or object of thought at the next level.**

that have not been constructed at the earlier level may be forced into rote learning and achieve only temporary and superficial success. A student can, for example, memorize that all squares are rectangles without having constructed that relationship. A student may memorize a geometric proof but fail to create the steps or understand the rationale involved (Fuys, Geddes, & Tischler, 1988; Geddes & Fortunato, 1993).

# Implications for Instruction

The van Hiele theory provides the thoughtful teacher with a framework within which to conduct geometric activities. The theory does not specify content or curriculum but can be applied to most activities. Most activities can be designed to begin with the assumption of a particular level and then be raised or lowered by means of the types of questioning and guidance provided by the teacher.

## Instructional Goals: Content and Levels of Thought

The Geometry standard in *Principles and Standards* focuses on process as well as content. Verbs such as *describe, compare, relate, represent, investigate, sort, reason, analyze, predict, test* (conjectures), and *critique* (arguments) are all used in the description of the standard (see Appendix A). The goals are much broader than a collection of facts and bits of knowledge about geometric ideas. The term *spatial sense* best sums up the Geometry standard.

The van Hiele theory fits very nicely with a *Principles and Standards* view of geometry. It focuses our attention on how students think in geometric contexts and the object of their thinking: shapes ⟶ properties ⟶ informal logic ⟶ deductive principles. If the van Hiele theory is correct—and there is much evidence to support it—then a major goal of the K–8 curriculum must be to advance students' level of geometric thought. If students are to be adequately prepared for

the deductive geometry curriculum of high school, their thinking should have advanced to at least level 2.

This is not to say that content knowledge is not important. Spatial sense is clearly enhanced by an understanding of shapes, what they look like, and even what they are named. The concepts of symmetry, congruence, and similarity contribute to understanding our geometric world. And the interaction with measurement that allows us to analyze angle measures and relationships between geometric entities is also valuable. But these must all be developed not in the context of "things to master" but rather as ways of knowing and understanding the geometric world.

## Teaching at the Student's Level of Thought

A developmental approach to instruction demands that we listen to children and begin where we find them. The van Hiele theory highlights the necessity of teaching at the child's level. However, almost any activity can be modified to span two levels of thinking, even within the same classroom. We can respect the responses and observations made by children that suggest a lower level of thought while encouraging and challenging children to operate at the next level. Remember that it is the type of thinking that children are required to do that makes a difference in learning, not the specific content.

The following are some suggested features of instruction appropriate for the first three van Hiele levels.

### Features of Level 0 Activities

Involve lots of sorting, identifying, and describing of various shapes.

Use lots of physical models that can be manipulated by the students.

Include many different and varied examples of shapes so that irrelevant features do not become important. (Many students, for example, believe that only equilateral triangles are really triangles or that squares turned 45° are no longer squares.)

Provide opportunities to build, make, draw, put together, and take apart shapes.

### Features of Level 1 Activities

Begin to focus more on properties of figures than on simple identification. Define, measure, observe, and change properties with the use of models.

Use problem-solving contexts in which properties of shapes are important components.

Continue to use models, as with level 0, but include models that permit the exploration of various properties of figures.

Classify figures based on properties of shapes as well as by names of shapes. For example, find different properties of triangles that make some alike and others different.

### Features of Level 2 Activities

Continue to use models, with a focus on defining properties. Make property lists, and discuss which properties are necessary and which are sufficient conditions for a specific shape or concept.

Include language of an informal deductive nature: *all, some, none, if-then, what if,* and the like.

Investigate the converse of certain relationships for validity. For example, the converse of "If it is a square, it must have four right angles" is "If it has four right angles, it must be a square."

Use models and drawings as tools to think with, and begin to look for generalizations and counterexamples.

Encourage the making and testing of hypotheses.

Most of the content of the K–8 curriculum can be adapted to any of the three levels. An exception may be an inappropriate attention to abstract concepts such as point, line, ray, and plane as basic elements of geometric forms. These abstract ideas are not appropriate even at level 2.

Listen to your students during a geometry activity. Compare their comments and observations with the descriptions of the first two van Hiele levels. Be sure that the activities you plan do not require that students reason above their level of thought.

The activities suggested in the remainder of this chapter are grouped according to the first three van Hiele levels. These are just suggestions for getting started. Most activities have the potential of being addressed at slightly lower or higher levels.

The intent here is to illustrate the wide variety of things that can be done. Find ideas that you like, and develop them fully. Search out additional resource books to help you.

# INFORMAL GEOMETRY ACTIVITIES: LEVEL 0

The emphasis at level 0 is on shape and form experiences. Though properties of figures are included, they are explored only informally. Remember that a level 0 activity does not necessarily mean a primary-grade activity. Some students in the upper grades have had insufficient opportunity to develop their thinking beyond a beginning level.

Any categorization of informal geometry activities according to van Hiele levels is likely to be a bit fuzzy. You may think some of the following activities represent level 1 better, and many can be extended easily to include that level.

## Exploring Shapes and Properties

The activities here all begin with shapes already made or drawn, and students work with them in various ways. The shapes may be two- or three-dimensional. Some activities can be done either with a set of flat two-dimensional shapes or equally well with a set of solid shapes.

### Sorting and Classifying Shapes

At level 0, perhaps the most important type of activity you can do is to have students work with a wide varieties of shapes and find similarities and differences. Many students will focus on nonstandard features such as "pointed" or "curvy" or "looks like a house." Others will notice things that really are not part of the shape at all: "points up" or "is close to the edge of the desk."

---

**A**CTIVITY

#### 17.1  Shape Sort

**Make collections of a wide variety of shapes by running them off on card stock, laminating them, and cutting them out. Figure 17.4 provides some ideas, but you will want many more shapes than those shown. Have students select a shape at random and then find other shapes that are like it in some way. All shapes should be alike in the same way. By finding only one set at a time, you avoid the problem of trying to put every shape into a category. Students should describe what makes their set of shapes alike either orally or in writing. Challenge them to draw a new shape that fits the category and explain why it belongs.**

---

If your set of shapes has five or six examples of a commonly named shape (for example, rectangle or rhombus), it is likely that some students will sort these out. Or you can ask them to find other shapes that are "like" the special shape that you select. In this way, the concept of that particular class of shapes is being formed without any definition from you. You can then label the concept or provide the proper name for the shape. Names of shapes should always come after the concept of the shape has been developed. Figure 17.5 indicates some concepts that can be explored this way.

Shape sorts can be done with three-dimensional shapes. Wooden or plastic collections are available as one option. Another is to make some solids from tagboard or modeling clay. Real objects such as cans, boxes, balls, or Styrofoam

**Figure 17.4** An assortment of shapes for sorting.

Shapes with curved edges

Opposite sides "go the same way"—parallelograms

Three sides—triangles

Shapes with a "square corner"—right angle

These all "dent in"—concave

**Figure 17.5** By sorting shapes, students begin to recognize properties.

shapes are another source of three-dimensional models. Figure 17.6 (p. 314) illustrates some classifications of solids.

## Matching Shapes

### ⲀⲤⲦⲒⲂⲒⲦⲨ
### 17.2 Feel-It Match

Prepare two identical collections of shapes. One set is placed in view. Out of children's sight, place a shape from the other set in a box or bag. Children reach into the box, feel a shape without looking, and attempt to find the matching shape from those that are displayed. The activity can be done with either two-dimensional tagboard shapes or solids. The shapes in the collection determine what ideas might develop and how difficult the activity is. For example, all shapes may have different numbers of sides or faces, or all shapes may be different but belong to one category, such as quadrilaterals, triangles, pyramids, prisms, curved surfaces, curved edges.

The following matching activity is similar but can be done with the entire class and provides more opportunity for informal discussion of shapes and properties.

### ⲀⲤⲦⲒⲂⲒⲦⲨ
### 17.3 What's like This?

Display a collection of shapes (either two- or three-dimensional) for all to see. Show the class a "target" shape that has something in common with one or more of the shapes in the collection. Students are to select a shape that is like the target shape in some way and explain their choice. There may be excellent choices and reasons that you did not even think about. Figure 17.7 (p. 314) illustrates only a few of the many possibilities for this activity.

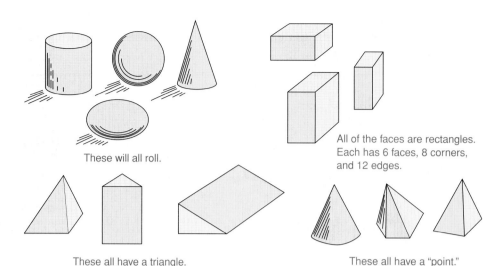

These will all roll.

All of the faces are rectangles. Each has 6 faces, 8 corners, and 12 edges.

These all have a triangle.

These all have a "point."

**Figure 17.6** **Early classifications of three-dimensional shapes.**

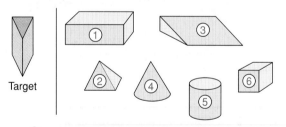

Target

Like ④ – Both are squares.
Like ⑤ – All four sides same, squeezed in a little.
Like ⑥ – Has the same kind of corner.
        – Looks like half of it.
Like ② – Same except it's longer.

Target

Like ③ – Both are wedges.
        – Both have two triangles.
Like ①, ③, and ⑥ – All have a rectangle face.
Like ①, ⑤, and ⑥ – All have a "flat top"
                (i.e., two parallel faces—so does ③).
Like ② and ③ – Have triangles.

**Figure 17.7** **Playing "What's like This?" involves finding a shape that's like the target. There are usually many good solutions.**

Matching activities can also match solid shapes with copies of the faces. "Face cards" can be made by tracing around the different faces of a solid shape, as in Figure 17.8.

---

**A**CTIVITY

## 17.4  Face Match

Two different matching activities can be done with face cards: Given a face card, find the solid, or given a solid, find the face card. If cards are made with only one face per card, students can select from a larger collection those faces that belong with a particular shape. Another variation is to show only one face at a time as clues.

Going on a "shape hunt" is a well-worn but still worthwhile activity. The activity can be modified to accommodate level 0 and level 1 thought within the same classroom by altering what is being searched for. Discussions of objects in the environment contribute to the geometric experiences of all students.

**A**CTIVITY

## 17.5  Shape Hunt

Have students search not just for triangles, circles, squares, and rectangles but also for properties of shapes. A shape hunt will be much more successful if you let students look for either one thing or a specific list. Different groups can hunt for different things, for example:

Parallel lines (lines "going in the same direction")

Right angles ("square corners")

Curved surfaces or curved lines

Two or more shapes that make another shape

Circles inside each other (concentric)

Shapes with "dents" (concave) or without dents (convex)

Shapes used over and over in a pattern (brick wall, chain link fence)

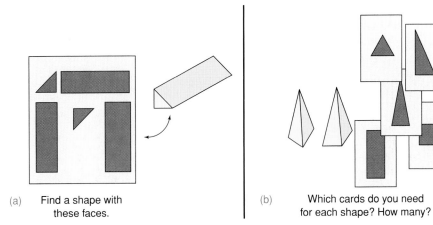

(a)  Find a shape with these faces.

(b)  Which cards do you need for each shape? How many?

**Figure 17.8  Matching face cards with solid shapes.**

> Solids that are somehow like a box, a cylinder (tube), a pyramid, a cone
>
> Five shapes that are alike somehow (specify solid or flat)
>
> Shapes that are symmetrical

# Constructing Shapes

These activities have children building, drawing, or constructing shapes in some way. It is good to begin by letting students freely make whatever shapes or designs they wish. This permits children to experience the new materials. Prepared activities can then go beyond this free-play level and challenge children to build shapes that have a particular feature. These challenges promote reflective thinking about the properties involved and are a good way to encourage level 1 thinking without pushing children too hard.

Several commercial materials permit fairly creative building of geometric solids (for example, 3D Geoshapes, Polydron, and the Zome System). Pattern blocks, Color Tiles, and tangrams are among the most popular sets of "tiles." In addition to commercial products, all sorts of other materials can be used. Modeling clay is an obvious choice for solids. Plastic straws can be fastened together in different ways to make skeletal models. Special tiles such as a collection of right triangles made by cutting on the diagonal of a rectangle can be constructed from poster board. Geoboards and various grid papers provide excellent methods for children to make drawings of shapes.

## Using Tiles to Make Shapes

A good way to explore shapes at level 0 is to use smaller shapes or tiles to create larger shapes. Among the best materials for this purpose are pattern blocks, but many teacher-made materials can be used too. A variety of shapes are suggested in Figure 17.9. Class sets can be cut from poster board and placed in plastic bags for individual or group use.

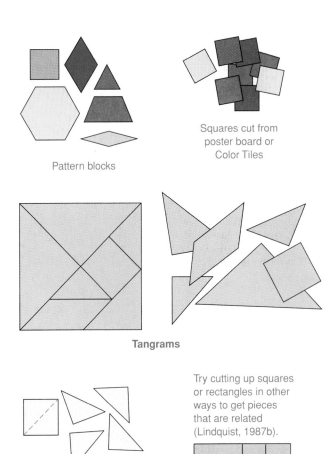

Pattern blocks

Squares cut from poster board or Color Tiles

Tangrams

Triangles cut from squares

Try cutting up squares or rectangles in other ways to get pieces that are related (Lindquist, 1987b).

**Figure 17.9  Activities with tiles can involve an assortment of shapes or can be designed with just one shape.**

Some of the activities that follow can be repeated using a different set of tiles to provide not only variety but also a different perspective.

## Geoboard Explorations

The geoboard is one of the best devices for drawing two-dimensional shapes. Here are just a few of many activities for using geoboards at a beginning level.

---

**A**CTIVITY

### 17.6 Geoboard Copy

Copy shapes, designs, and patterns from prepared cards as in Figure 17.10. Begin with designs shown with dots as on a geoboard, and later have students copy designs drawn without dots.

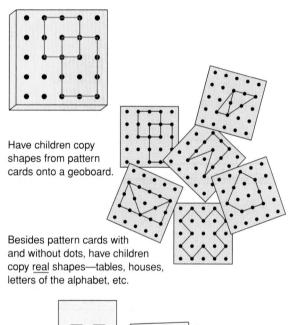

Have children copy shapes from pattern cards onto a geoboard.

Besides pattern cards with and without dots, have children copy <u>real</u> shapes—tables, houses, letters of the alphabet, etc.

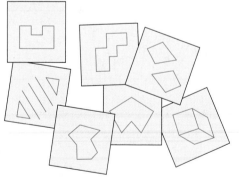

**Figure 17.10**   **Shapes on geoboards.**

---

**A**CTIVITY

### 17.7 Geoboard Tiles

Challenge the students to make shapes on the geoboard using combinations of only one smaller shape as if the smaller shape were a tile (Figure 17.11). Cards with the smaller shapes can be prepared to direct the activity.

---

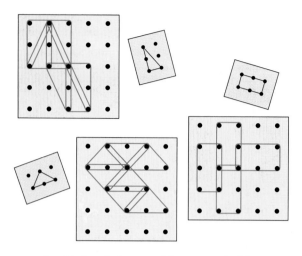

Provide "small shape cards" to suggest building blocks to students.

**Figure 17.11**   **Bigger shapes from smaller shapes.**

---

**A**CTIVITY

### 17.8 Congruent Parts

Copy a shape from a card, and have students subdivide or cut it into smaller shapes. Specify the number of smaller shapes. Also specify whether they are all to be congruent or simply of the same type as shown in Figure 17.12. Depending on the shapes involved, this activity can be made quite easy or relatively challenging.

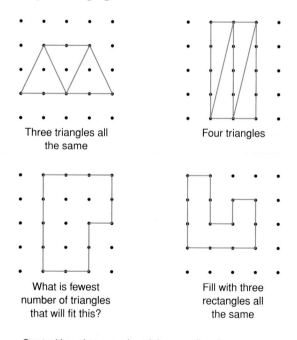

Start with a shape, and cut it into smaller shapes. Add special conditions to make the activity challenging.

**Figure 17.12**   **Subdividing shapes.**

Aᴄᴛɪᴠɪᴛʏ

## 17.9 Geoboard Challenges

Challenge students to see how many different shapes they can make of a specific type or with a particular property. (Very young children will feel more comfortable searching for three shapes or four shapes rather than "many" shapes.) Here are some appropriate ideas for level 0:

Make shapes with five sides (or some other number of sides).

Make shapes with all square corners. Can you make one with three sides? Four sides? Six, seven, eight sides?

Make some trapezoids that are all different (or suggest any other shape that students can identify).

Make a shape that has a line of symmetry. Check it with a mirror.

Two practical comments should be made about the use of geoboards. First, have lots of them available in the classroom. It is better for two or three children to have 10 or 12 boards at a station than for each to have only one. That way, a variety of shapes can be made and compared before they are changed.

This leads to the second point. Teach students from the very beginning to copy their geoboard designs onto paper. Paper copies permit students to create complete sets of drawings that fulfill a particular task. Drawings can be placed on the bulletin board for classification and discussion, made into booklets illustrating a new idea that is being discussed, and sent home to show parents what is happening in geometry.

Younger students can use paper with a single large geoboard on each sheet. Later, a paper board about 10 cm square is adequate. Older children can use centimeter dot paper or a page of small boards, each about 5 cm square. (See the Blackline Masters.)

In the very early grades, children will have some difficulty copying geoboard designs onto paper, especially designs with slanted lines. To help, suggest that they first mark the dots for the corners of their shape ("Second row, end peg"). With the corners identified, it is much easier for them to draw lines to make the shape.

## Dot and Grid Paper Explorations

Geoboards are excellent due to the ease with which drawings can be made and changed, but they have limitations in terms of size, arrangement, and number of pegs. Assorted dot and grid papers provide an alternative. Virtually all of the activities suggested for tiles and geoboards can also be done on dot or grid paper. Changing the type of paper changes the activity and provides new opportunity for insight and discovery. Figure 17.13

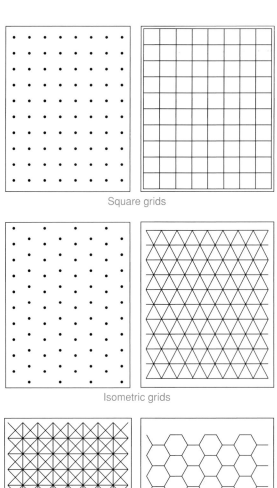

Square grids

Isometric grids

Square and diagonal grid        Hex grid

**Figure 17.13** **Dot and grid paper of various types and sizes can be used for many geometric explorations.**

shows several possibilities for dot and grid papers, all found in the Blackline Masters.

Here are some additional ideas that lend themselves particularly well to dot and grid paper.

Aᴄᴛɪᴠɪᴛʏ

## 17.10 Three-Dimensional Drawings

Isometric dot paper is an effective way to draw solid shapes built with cubes. Square dot paper can be used to draw side and top views, as shown in Figure 17.14 (p. 318). Building a simple shape with cubes and then drawing plan and perspective views is an excellent activity for middle grade students to help with perspective. (See Winter, Lappan, Phillips, & Fitzgerald, 1986, for a series of excellent activities.)

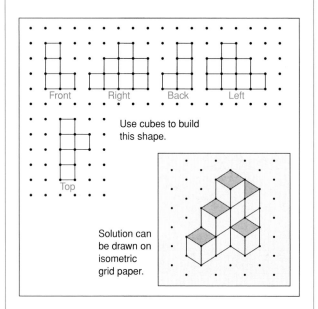

A slightly different idea is to reverse Activity 17.10. Provide students with a perspective drawing that you have made, and have them build the structure with blocks. Drawings can be prepared on worksheets, or you can develop a collection of cards for use at workstations. A top view with the number of cubes indicated in each square can be used as an answer key. However, it is best to let students work together to decide if they have made an accurate construction.

## ▲CTIVITY

## 17.11 Slides, Flips, and Turns

Slides, flips, and turns can be investigated on any grid. Start with a simple shape. Draw the same shape flipped over, turned, or placed in a different orientation. Trace the original shape, and cut it out. This copy can be flipped or reoriented to test the drawings that are made (see Figure 17.15).

## Building Solids

Building three-dimensional shapes presents a little more difficulty than two-dimensional shapes but is perhaps even more important. Building a model of a three-dimensional shape is an informal way to get to understand the shape intuitively in terms of its component parts.

As noted earlier, commercial plastic building sets can be used to build a wide variety of solids. The pieces are all equi-

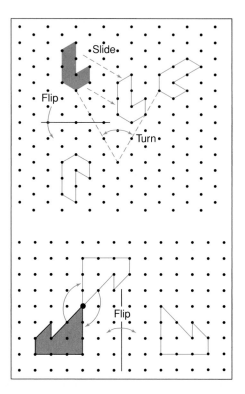

Figure 17.15 **Slides, flips, and turns can be explored on almost any type of grid.**

lateral polygons (triangles, squares, pentagons, and hexagons) with all edges the same length. The resulting shapes are quite rigid.

Skeleton models are three-dimensional "solids" built using sticks of some sort. In addition to commercial materials such as the Zome System, the following two ideas are highly recommended.

■ *Plastic drinking straws with flexible joints.* Cut the straws lengthwise with scissors from the top down to the flexible joint. These slit ends can then be inserted into the uncut bottom ends of other straws, making a strong but flexible joint. Three or more straws are joined in this fashion to form two-dimensional polygons. To make skeletal solids, use tape or wire twist ties to join polygons side to side.

■ *Rolled newspaper rods.* Fantastic superlarge skeletons can be built using newspaper and masking tape. Roll three large sheets of newspaper on the diagonal to form a rod approximately 1 meter long. The more tightly the paper is rolled, the less likely the rod is to bend. Secure the roll at the center with a bit of tape. The ends of the rods are thin and flexible for about 6 inches where there is less paper. Connect rods by bunching this thin part together and fastening with tape. Use tape freely, wrapping it several times around each joint. Additional rods can be joined after two or three are already taped (see Figure 17.16).

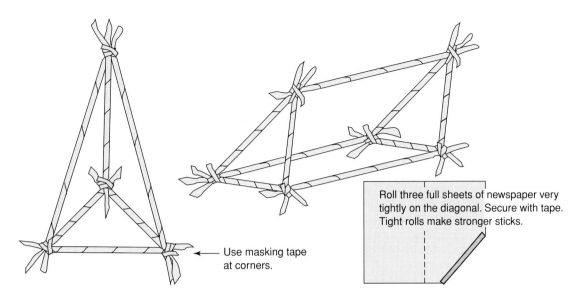

**Figure 17.16** **Large skeletal structures and special shapes can be built with tightly rolled newspaper. Young children can build free-form sculptures. Older children can be challenged to build shapes with specific properties. Overlap the ends about 6 inches to ensure strength.**

Regardless of the method used, students should compare the rigidity of a triangle with the lack of rigidity of polygons with more than three sides. Point out that the rigidity of the triangle is used in many bridges, in the long booms of construction cranes, in gates, and in the structural parts of buildings. As children build large skeleton structures, they will find that they need to add diagonal members to form triangles. The more triangles, the less likely their structure will collapse.

The newspaper rod method is exciting because the structures quickly become large. Let students work in groups of four or five. They will soon discover what makes a structure rigid and ideas of balance and form. Primary-grade students can benefit from creating free-form structures. Older students can be challenged to make more well-defined shapes.

---

**ACTIVITY**

## 17.12 Unfolded Solids

Have students design nets for various solids. (A *net* for a solid is a flat shape that will fold up to make a solid.) On a square centimeter grid, parallel lines and angles can be drawn without tedious measuring (see Figure 17.17, p. 320). Paper nets can be traced or pasted onto tagboard for a sturdier solid. Circular cones are easily made by cutting a sector from a circle. Experiment with different circle sizes and different sectors. Much of the value in folding up a solid is planning what shape the faces will be and where the faces can be connected. Encourage groups to solve these problems themselves; provide only as much help as necessary.

Plastic building sets like Polydron provide a great way to explore nets since every possible solid made with these sets can be unfolded into a flat net. A potential net is made by linking the desired faces together in a flat array on the desk. If the construction is actually a net, the shape will fold to the desired shape. There is spatial visualization value in predicting if a given potential net will in fact create the specified shape. In a reverse manner, a shape can be unfolded to its net. The potential challenges here are to predict in advance the shape of the net or to try to find how many different nets for a shape there are. For example, how many distinct nets are there for a simple cube? Is every arrangement of six squares a net of a cube? Polydron and 3D Geoshapes consist only of regular polygons (all sides and angles congruent). Use two shapes for one face to add more variety to nets and solids.

Solids can also be built from blocks such as wooden cubes (1 inch or 2 cm). Plastic connecting cubes can be linked on any side and then turned in other orientations. The following tasks can make such activities challenging.

---

**ACTIVITY**

## 17.13 Block Boxes

In groups, have students see how many different rectangular solids can be made using just 12 cubes each. (A rectangular solid has six faces, and each face is a rectangle.) Try other numbers of cubes. When are two rectangular solids congruent (exactly the same)? How would you have to turn one solid to get it in the same orientation as another that is the same shape?

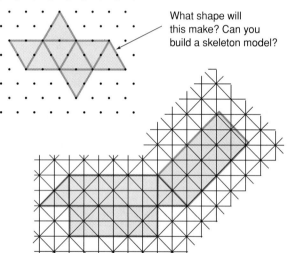

What shape will this make? Can you build a skeleton model?

**Figure 17.17** Nets are easily drawn on grid paper. After making one net for a solid, try to find others that will fold up to make the same solid.

- ACTIVITY

## 17.14 Building Plans

From a simple building that you have built, make a task card with five views of the building, as in Figure 17.18. Students use trial and error to try to build the same building from the five views. Slightly harder is to omit the top view but give the total number of cubes. This is a good exercise in spatial perception.

# Geometric Challenges for Level 0

In many activities, the traditional content may be minimal but the problem-solving value is significant. These geometric problem-solving activities provide opportunity for growth in geometric thinking and spatial sense.

At level 0, geometric problems involve manipulating, drawing, and creating shapes of all types. The tasks revolve around global features of shapes, rather than any analysis of properties or relationships between classes or figures. Many activities already suggested have a problem-solving orientation. The following are additional suggestions.

- ACTIVITY

## 17.15 Tangram Puzzles

Tangrams have been popular geometric puzzles for years. Figure 17.19 shows tangram puzzles of different difficulties. Easy ones are appropriate even for preschool children. The 1999 Dale Seymour catalog listed 11 different tangram books and sets of activities, including the classic *Tangramath* (Seymour, 1971).

**Figure 17.18** Views of a simple building.

Top — Left — Front — Right — Back

(Lines indicate different faces.)

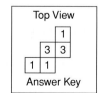

Given the five cards at the top, use wooden cubes to build the building. An answer key can be made by putting the numbers of cubes in each vertical stack on the top view. To make your own task cards, start by building a building, and then make the cards.

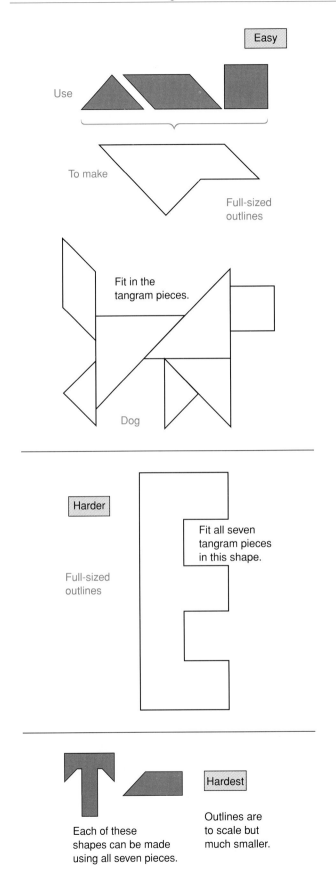

Easy

Use

To make

Full-sized outlines

Fit in the tangram pieces.

Dog

Harder

Full-sized outlines

Fit all seven tangram pieces in this shape.

Hardest

Each of these shapes can be made using all seven pieces.

Outlines are to scale but much smaller.

**Figure 17.19** **Four types of tangram puzzles illustrate a range of difficulty levels.**

**ACTIVITY**

## 17.16 Pentominoes

A pentomino is a shape formed by joining five squares as if cut from a square grid. Each square must have at least one side in common with another. Provide students with five square tiles and a sheet of square grid paper for recording. Challenge them to see how many different pentomino shapes they can find. Shapes that are flips or turns of other shapes are not considered different. Do not tell students how many pentomino shapes there are. Good discussions will come from deciding if some shapes are really different and if all shapes have been found.

Once students have decided that there are just 12 pentominoes (see Figure 17.20), the 12 pieces can then be used in a variety of activities. Paste the grids with the children's pentominoes onto tagboard, and let them cut out the 12 shapes. These can be used in the next two activities.

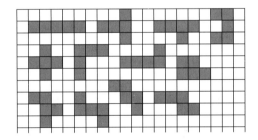

There are 12 pentominoes.

Finding all possible shapes made with five squares—or six squares (called "hexominoes") or six equilateral triangles and so on—is a good exercise in spatial problem solving.

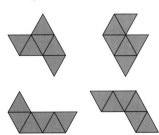

Four of the different shapes that six equilateral triangles will make.

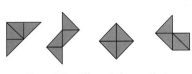

Four of the different shapes that four "half-square" triangles will make.

**Figure 17.20** **Pentominoes and related shape challenges.**

## Activity

### 17.17 Pentomino Puzzles

A variety of puzzles can be made from the pentominoes. Students can make puzzles to challenge their classmates by selecting four or more pieces and putting them together into a single shape. The outline of this shape is then drawn on grid paper. The challenge is to find a way to create the shape without knowing which pieces were used. The more pieces there are, the more difficult the puzzle will be. Many puzzles will have more than one solution. Much harder is to use all 12 pieces to construct a rectangle. It is possible to make a $6 \times 10$, $5 \times 12$, and $4 \times 15$ rectangle using the 12 pieces.

## Activity

### 17.18 Pentomino Squeeze

Play "Pentomino Squeeze" on an $8 \times 8$ grid of squares. Pieces are dealt out randomly to two players. The player with the cross places it on the board. In turn, players place pieces on the board without overlapping any piece that is already placed. The last player to be able to play is the winner. Smaller boards can be used to make the game more difficult.

An extended challenge is to find out how many *hexominoes* there are (shapes made from six squares). It is also fun to explore the number of shapes that can be made from six equilateral triangles or from four 45-degree right triangles (halves of squares). With the right triangles, sides that touch must be the same length. How many of each of these "ominoes" do you think there are?

## Tessellations

A *tessellation* is a tiling of the plane using one or more shapes in a repeated pattern with no holes or gaps. The "Tiling Pattern" activity at the beginning of the chapter was a tessellation activity. Making tessellations is an artistic way for level 0 students from first grade to eighth grade to engage in geometric problem solving. One-shape or two-shape tessellation activities can vary considerably in relative difficulty and still remain level 0 activities.

Some shapes are easier to tessellate than others (see Figure 17.21). When the shapes can be put together in more than one pattern, both the problem-solving level and the creativity increase. Literally hundreds of shapes can be used as tiles for tessellations. Every one of the 12 pentominoes will tessellate. It is fun to create shapes on various grid papers and then test them to see if they can be used to tessellate.

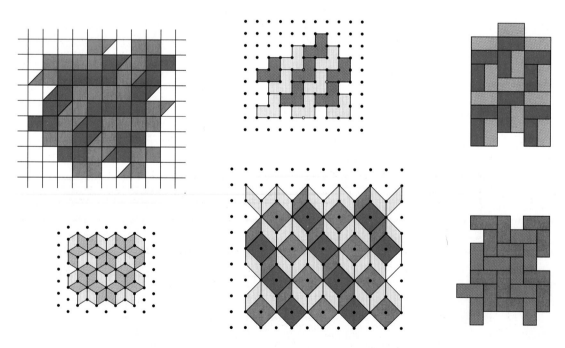

Tessellations can be drawn on grids or made of construction paper tiles. They are challenging and provide an opportunity for both artistic creativity and spatial reasoning.

**Figure 17.21**  **Tessellations.**

Most children will benefit from using actual tiles to create patterns. Simple construction paper tiles can be cut quickly on a paper cutter. Other tiles can be traced onto construction paper and several thicknesses cut at once with scissors. Older children may be able to use dot or line grids and plan their tessellations with pencil and paper. Spend one period with tiles or grids, letting children experiment with tiling patterns. To plan a tessellation, use only one color so that the focus is on the spatial relationships. To complete an artistic-looking tessellation, add a color design. Use only two colors with younger children and never more than four. Color designs are also repeated regularly all over the tessellation.

Tessellations can be made by gluing paper tiles to large sheets of paper, by drawing them on dot or line grids, or by tracing around a poster board tile. Do not worry about the edges of tessellations. Work from the center out, leaving ragged edges to indicate that the pattern goes on and on.

 # TECHNOLOGY NOTE: LEVEL 0

Geometry is one area of the curriculum for which a variety of fascinating computer programs exist. Many programs allow students to "stamp" geometric shapes onto the screen and then manipulate them with the mouse. Other programs mimic geoboards. These allow much more flexibility and ease of use than a physical geoboard. The Logo programming language challenges children to draw shapes by entering directions and offers a unique approach to geometric reasoning. All of these have real value for level 0 thinkers. You can find software that is appropriate for all grade levels.

## Shape and Geoboard Software

*Shape Up* (Sunburst, 1995) and *Shapes* (Clements & Sarama, 1995) are two good examples of computer versions of physical tiles. Both programs include a pattern block and tangram format in which students can stamp pieces onto a blank screen. Pieces are easily moved around, rotated, or flipped through either a vertical or horizontal line. In *Shapes,* two or more pieces can be "glued together" to create new shapes. The pattern blocks include a quarter circle that adds to the variability. Both programs allow shapes to be enlarged or reduced in size. Some puzzles are included with the packages, and new puzzles similar to those in Figure 17.19 are easily created. *Shape Up* has a third mode in which six regular shapes can be manipulated and each can be cut into many smaller shapes and rearranged in endless ways.

The critical question to ask is, "What do these programs provide that cannot be accomplished with real blocks?" Both modes are enticing to children, but the computer versions require more deliberate actions. For example, the rotate button must be clicked, and a piece must be rotated in incremental amounts. The ability to enlarge or shrink pieces is at least interesting and may help with the understanding of similarity. It is not clear that any greater geometric benefit is gained, but the environment and the experience are sufficiently different to warrant the use of this type of program along with physical models. Students who have difficulty with fine motor control are often unable to produce drawings or cut-and-paste recordings of their geometry activities. Since the computer permits students to print colorful copies of their work and include written journal entries, these students take real pride in the products they produce.

*James Discovers Math* (Brøderbund, 1995a) and *Millie's Math House* (Edmark, 1993) also have components in which shapes can be stamped and arranged. Designed for the 3- to 6-year-old set, these programs are much more limited. *James Discovers Math* also has a feature in which any one of several tessellations can be colored in to make wonderful shape patterns. Although students only color in the shapes, the activity has plenty of spatial value for young children.

*GeoComputer* (Edmark, 1996) is an example of an electronic geoboard. This program shows a dot grid (geoboard) on which students can draw lines between points. Lines can be stretched over other pegs just like rubber bands on a geoboard. *GeoComputer* allows students to manipulate shapes by dragging edges of shapes without changing the lengths. Regions can be colored with a palette of colors. Any shape can be flipped over or rotated 90 degrees, moves that are not simple to accomplish on a physical board. This program will also measure areas and perimeters of regions. *MathKeys: Geometry, Vol. 1* (MECC, 1995a) includes a similar geoboard but without the measuring and reflection capabilities. A larger array of pegs, ease of shape manipulation, and the ability to save and print work are the major advantages of electronic geoboards. As with shape programs, they should be used in tandem with the hands-on versions.

## Logo

Logo is a highly accessible yet powerful computer language. Although Logo is technically a computer programming language, versions developed in recent years such as *Turtle Math* (Clements & Meredith, 1994) make programming easy enough for third graders. Briefly, in Logo's graphics mode, a "turtle" (a small triangle or a picture of a turtle) is controlled with simple keyboard commands. It can be made to go forward or backward any distance and to turn left or right any number of degrees. The turtle draws a line in its path. The string of commands **fd 50 rt 90 fd 30 rt 90** will cause the turtle to draw a long and a short segment at right angles to each other. If this set of commands were repeated again, a rectangle would be formed. Any collection of commands can be given a name and then used as a single command. For

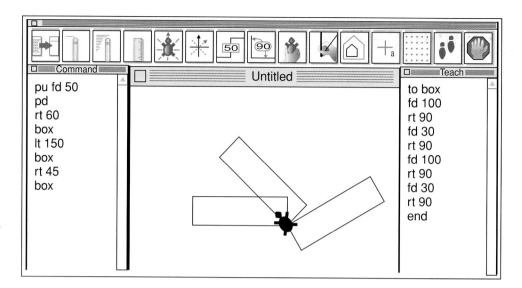

**Figure 17.22** **The** *Turtle Math* **window. The buttons at the top provide powerful assists to Logo programming. Notice how the box command can be executed in various positions.**

example, **repeat 2[fd 60 rt 90 fd 30 rt 90]** will create a 60 by 30 rectangle. If you name this set of commands with a single word of your choosing—for example, **box**—simply entering the command **box** will have the same effect. In this way, an entire collection of "procedures" can be defined and used repeatedly.

This may sound tedious, and in the original versions of Logo, the necessary typing and editing did create obstacles. In *Turtle Math*, a toolbar takes away nearly all of the tedium. For example, it is possible to move and turn the turtle with the mouse and have corresponding commands created automatically. Rulers help determine distances, and other buttons provide help with turning the turtle. If a shape is drawn and then changed with the mouse, the commands that produced the shape are also changed. For those willing to work with the language, in this form it is very accessible to children by grade 3 if not earlier. Figure 17.22 shows the *Turtle Math* screen. Commands are entered in the left portion, and procedures are defined in the right-hand window.

Logo brings a completely different perspective on geometric shapes and thus on geometric explorations and spatial development. Because students are required to draw shapes by issuing precise commands, Logo requires that a drawing be conceptualized in terms of its component parts—dimensions of sides, angle sizes, turn directions, and orientation in the plane. Consider a child trying to draw a house (a rectangle with a triangle on top). The child has a visual image of the house and can probably draw one on paper. But to teach the turtle to draw the house, each part must be drawn separately and the relationship between the parts (angles, orientations, lengths of lines) must all be taken into account and articulated.

A more profound difference between visualizing shapes and defining procedures can be observed when children try to make the turtle draw a circle. The turtle moves only in straight lines, not curves. A common suggestion is to "play

turtle." That is, if you were a turtle, how would you "walk" the shape you want to make? Children soon realize that they can walk a circle by repeatedly going forward a tiny bit and turning a tiny bit. A common "first circle" is produced by this command: **repeat 360[fd 1 rt 1]**. This is actually a 360-sided regular polygon, but on the screen it looks exactly like a circle. How would you make a larger circle? What if you repeated only 36 times? What should the turn amount be? How would you make a hexagon? What about a triangle or square? How are all of these polygons like the "circle"? How are they different?

A typical Logo challenge is to draw a rectangle that is tilted on the screen like the one in Figure 17.22. To accomplish this, students must learn that the right-angle turns that make rectangles are the same turns when the rectangle is tilted. Most know that before they begin the rectangle, the turtle must be turned a bit. When they get to the first turn, however, it is no longer obvious that a turn of 90 is necessary.

*Turtle Math* is a component of *Investigations in Number Data and Space* (Cuisenaire–Dale Seymour Publications, 1995), one of the reform curricula for the elementary grades. ■

# INFORMAL GEOMETRY ACTIVITIES: LEVEL 1

The activities at level 1 begin to focus more on the properties of shapes and include some analysis of those properties. For example, at level 0, triangles might have been sorted by "big" and "little," "pointy" and "not as pointy," or even "with square corners" and "without square corners." At level 1, the same set of triangles can be sorted by the relative sizes of the angles or the relative lengths of the sides. Combinations of these categories give rise to even more relationships.

# Transitions to Level 1

Most of the materials in the suggested activities are the same as those used at level 0, and many level 0 activities are easily extended to level 1. For example, consider Activity 17.6, "Geoboard Copy" (p. 316). If students who seem to be ready for more challenging work have successfully copied a parallelogram, talk briefly about what makes that shape special. Can other shapes be made that also have sides that are parallel? Make at least five different parallelograms, and copy them onto dot paper. What is alike about all five? Now this activity has begun to focus the attention on the *class* of *all* parallelograms and the properties of that class.

It is quite reasonable to have several similar but related investigations proceeding in the same classroom, with different groups pursuing tasks at different van Hiele levels.

# Classifying Shapes by Properties

Sorting activities are grouped here in a manner similar to that used for level 0 activities. To promote the kind of thinking that is appropriate for level 1, shapes are presented so that specific properties and categorizations are clearly evident. For example, the shapes used might be quadrilaterals or even a collection of two or three types of quadrilaterals. In other words, the children are looking at a class of shapes and producing the ideas that make the class special—properties of the class and all potential members.

You may have to be more direct in pointing out particular properties or categories that students do not notice. When a classification of shapes has been made and discussed and is well understood, the appropriate name for the classification can be supplied.

## Special Categories of Two-Dimensional Shapes

Table 17.1 lists some important categories of two-dimensional shapes. Examples of these shapes can be found in Figure 17.23 (p. 326).

In the classification of quadrilaterals and parallelograms, the subsets are not all disjoint. For example, a square is a rectangle and a rhombus. All parallelograms are trapezoids, but not all trapezoids are parallelograms.* Children at level 1 have difficulty seeing this type of subrelationship. They may quite correctly list all the properties of a square, a rhombus, and a rectangle and still identify a square as a "nonrhombus" or a "nonrectangle." Is it wrong for students to refer to subgroups as disjoint sets? By fourth or fifth grade, it is only wrong to encourage such thinking. Burger (1985) points out

---

*Some definitions of trapezoid specify *only one* pair of parallel sides, in which case parallelograms would not be trapezoids. The University of Chicago School Mathematics Project (UCSMP) uses the "at least one pair" definition meaning that parallelograms and rectangles are trapezoids.

## Table 17.1
**Categories of Two-Dimensional Shapes**

| Shape | Description |
| --- | --- |
| **Simple Closed Curves** | |
| Concave, convex | An intuitive definition of *concave* might be "having a dent in it." If a simple closed curve is not concave, it is *convex*. A more precise definition of *concave* may be interesting to explore with older students. |
| Symmetrical, nonsymmetrical | Shapes may have one or more lines of symmetry and may or may not have rotational symmetry. These concepts will require more detailed investigation. |
| Polygons   Concave, convex   Symmetrical, nonsymmetrical | Simple closed curves with all straight sides. |
| Regular | All sides and all angles are congruent. |
| **Triangles** | |
| Triangles | Polygons with exactly three sides. |
| *Classified by sides* | |
|   Equilateral | All sides are congruent. |
|   Isosceles | At least two sides are congruent. |
|   Scalene | No two sides are congruent. |
| *Classified by angles* | |
|   Right | Has a right angle. |
|   Acute | All angles are smaller than a right angle. |
|   Obtuse | One angle is larger than a right angle. |
| **Convex Quadrilaterals** | |
| Convex quadrilaterals | Convex polygons with exactly four sides. |
| Kite | Two opposing pairs of congruent adjacent sides. |
| Trapezoid   Isosceles trapezoid | At least one pair of parallel sides. A pair of opposite sides is congruent. |
| Parallelogram   Rectangle   Rhombus   Square | Two pairs of parallel sides. Parallelogram with a right angle. Parallelogram with all sides congruent. Parallelogram with a right angle and all sides congruent. |

that upper elementary students correctly use such classification schemes in other contexts. For example, individual students in a class can belong to more than one club. A square is an example of a quadrilateral that belongs to two other clubs.

Several types of sorting activities can help students grow in their understanding of how shapes are related.

---

**ACTIVITY**

## 17.19 Shape Sort II

Sort shapes by naming properties and not by names of the shapes. When two or more properties are combined, sort by one property at a time. "Find all of the shapes that have opposite sides parallel." (Find these.) "Now find those that also have a right angle." (This group should include squares as well as nonsquare rectangles.) After sorting, discuss what the name of the shapes is. Also try sorting by the same combinations of properties but in a different order.

Use loops of string to keep track of shapes as you sort them. Lay two loops out on a flat surface. Have students put all of the shapes with four congruent sides in one loop and those with a right angle in the other. Where do squares go? Let them wrestle with this dilemma until they realize that the two loops must be overlapped, with the squares placed in the overlapping region.

**Figure 17.23** **Classification of two-dimensional shapes.**

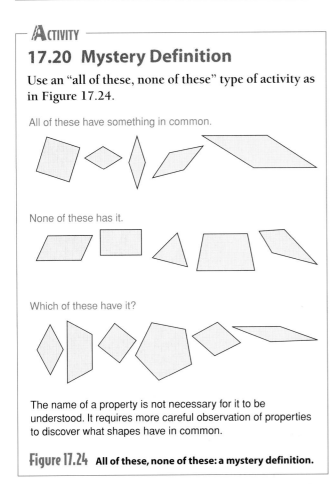

**ACTIVITY**

## 17.20 Mystery Definition

Use an "all of these, none of these" type of activity as in Figure 17.24.

All of these have something in common.

None of these has it.

Which of these have it?

The name of a property is not necessary for it to be understood. It requires more careful observation of properties to discover what shapes have in common.

**Figure 17.24** **All of these, none of these: a mystery definition.**

## Special Categories of Three-Dimensional Shapes

Important and interesting shapes and relationships also exist in three dimensions. Some classifications of solids are given here. Three-dimensional figures can be sorted in a variety of ways without resorting to classes with special names (see Table 17.2). Figures 17.25 and 17.26 (p. 328) show examples and nonexamples of cylinders and cones. It is useful to see that prisms are to cylinders what pyramids are to cones: special cases in which the bases are polygons.

## Constructing and Measuring Shapes

Constructing shapes in two and three dimensions is one of the most profitable activities that can be done in geometry. As children begin to demonstrate level 1 thinking, construction activities can be posed as tasks. Students are given the properties of shapes rather than their appearance.

In addition, measurements of shapes can help students recognize even more relationships. Area, perimeter, surface area, volume, angle, radius, and circumference can be measured on various shapes. For example, students who measure interior angles of various polygons can discover that when the number of sides of two polygons is the same, so is the

**Table 17.2**
**Categories of Three-Dimensional Shapes**

| Shape | Description |
|---|---|
| **Sorted by Edges and Vertices** | |
| Spheres and "egglike" shapes | Shapes with no *edges* and no *vertices* (corners). |
| | Shapes with *edges* but no *vertices* (e.g., a flying saucer). |
| | Shapes with *vertices* but no *edges* (e.g., a football). |
| **Sorted by Faces and Surfaces** | |
| Polyhedron | Shapes made of all faces (a *face* is a flat surface of a solid). If all surfaces are faces, all the edges will be straight lines. |
| | Some combination of faces and rounded surfaces (cylinders are examples, but this is not a definition of a cylinder). |
| | Shapes with all curved surfaces. |
| | Shapes with and without edges and with and without vertices. |
| | Faces can be parallel. Parallel faces lie in planes that never intersect. |
| **Cylinders** | |
| Cylinder | Two congruent, parallel faces called *bases*. Lines joining corresponding points on the two bases are always parallel. These parallel lines are called *elements* of the cylinder. |
| Right cylinder | A cylinder with elements perpendicular to the bases. A cylinder that is not a right cylinder is an *oblique cylinder*. |
| Prism | A cylinder with polygons for bases. All prisms are special cases of cylinders. |
| Rectangular prism | A cylinder with rectangles for bases. |
| Cube | A square prism with square sides. |
| **Cones** | |
| Cone | A solid with exactly one face and a vertex that is not on the face. Straight lines (elements) can be drawn from any point on the edge of the base to the vertex. The base may be any shape at all. The vertex need not be directly over the base. |
| Circular cone | Cone with a circular base. |
| Pyramid | Cone with a polygon for a base. All faces joining the vertex are triangles. Pyramids are named by the shape of the base: *triangular* pyramid, *square* pyramid, *octagonal* pyramid, and so on. All pyramids are special cases of cones. |

sum of the measures of the interior angles. Direct comparisons, informal units, and simple student-made measuring devices are sufficient for exploring almost all interesting relationships involving measures.

## Two-Dimensional Constructions

Tiles, geoboards, and dot and grid paper are among the best construction materials for two-dimensional shapes. On the

**Figure 17.25** **Cylinders and prisms.**

Cylinders have two parallel faces, and parallel lines join corresponding points on these faces. If the parallel faces are polygons, the cylinder can be called a prism.

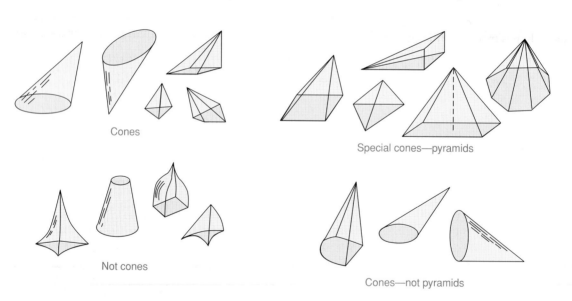

Cones and cones with a polygon base (pyramids) all have straight-line elements joining every point of the base with the vertex. (Yes, a pyramid is just a special type of cone.)

**Figure 17.26** **Cones and pyramids.**

computer, dynamic geometry programs such as *The Geometer's Sketchpad* (Key Curriculum Press, 1995), *Geometry Inventor* (LOGAL, 1994a), and *Cabri Geometry II* (Texas Instruments, 1994) are fantastic for students beginning about grade 4 or 5.

The first activity here (adapted from the 5–8 section of NCTM's 1989 *Standards*) uses ordinary flat toothpicks to draw lines.

**ACTIVITY**

## 17.21 Toothpick Triangles

Provide children with a supply of toothpicks. They are to arrange the toothpicks in straight lines to make triangles. Begin with three picks, then move to four, then five, and so on. For each number of picks, the children first decide if any triangle is possible. If so, they sketch it (showing each pick) and then see if there are other possible triangles that can be made with the same number of picks. For example, only one triangle is possible with three picks, none are possible with four picks, and two different triangles can be made with seven picks.

"Toothpick Triangles" is an example of an opportunity to extend reasoning to level 2. If students are asked to explain why certain triangles are impossible ("Why is only one triangle possible with eight picks?"), they may go beyond just looking at properties of triangles and begin to do some informal reasoning. The sum of any two sides of a triangle must be greater than the third side. (Why?)

## ACTIVITY

### 17.22 Property Challenges

This activity can be done with almost any materials that allow students to draw or construct shapes easily. List properties or relationships, and have students construct as many shapes as possible that have those properties or exhibit those relationships. Compare shapes made by different groups. Here are some examples:

Make a four-sided shape with two opposite sides the same length but not parallel.

Make some six-sided shapes. Make some with one, two, and then three pairs of parallel sides and some with no parallel sides.

Make shapes with all square corners. Can you make one with three sides? Four sides? Five sides? Six, seven, or eight sides?

Make some six-sided shapes with square corners. Count how many squares are inside each. What is the distance around each?

Make five different triangles. How are they different? (This is also good for four-, five-, or six-sided shapes.)

Make some triangles with two equal (congruent) sides.

Make some four-sided shapes with three congruent sides.

Try five-sided shapes with four congruent sides.

Make some quadrilaterals with all sides equal (or with two pairs of equal sides).

Make a shape with one or more lines of symmetry or with rotational symmetry. (A longer discussion of symmetry is provided later in the chapter.)

It is easy (and fun) to make up property challenges. Explore some of these, and make up others that suit your

needs. One idea is to use combinations of previously explored concepts. Can you make a triangle with two right angles? Can you make a rhombus that has a right angle? A parallelogram with only two equal sides?

Make a chart like the one shown here: Challenge children to draw or construct triangles that fit into each of the nine cells. Of the nine, two are impossible. (Can you tell which ones?)

|  | Equilateral | Isosceles | Scalene |
|---|---|---|---|
| Right |  |  |  |
| Acute |  |  |  |
| Obtuse |  |  |  |

Combination challenges can also include the notions of perpendicular, angle measurement, area, perimeter, similarity, concave and convex, regularity, and symmetry, to name just a few. Also encourage your students to come up with some of their own. Notice that some of the challenges in Activity 17.22 are not possible. Discovering that some combination of relationships is not possible—and why—is just as valuable as learning the relationships themselves.

## ACTIVITY

### 17.23 Measure Investigation

Ask students to make shapes according to special measurement requirements.

Make at least five different shapes with an area of _____ (approximate number for your materials). What is the perimeter of each?

Make shapes with a fixed perimeter, and examine the area of each.

Try to make the shape with the largest area for a given perimeter or the smallest perimeter for a given area. (For polygons, the largest area for a fixed perimeter is always regular. Try it.)

Angle and side specifications provide lots of opportunities to examine properties. Angles can usually be kept to multiples of 30 and 45, or informal units can be used.

Make several different triangles that all have one angle the same. Next make some different triangles with two angles the same (for example, 30 and 45 degrees). What do you notice?

Can you make a parallelogram with a 60-degree angle? Make several. Are they all alike? How? How are they different?

Make some parallelograms with a side of 5 and a side of 10. Are they all the same?

Draw some polygons with 4, 5, 6, 7, and 8 sides. Divide them all up into triangles, but do not let any lines cross or triangles overlap. What do you discover? Measure the angles inside each polygon.

Draw an assortment of rectangles, and draw the diagonals in each. Measure the angles that the diagonals make with each other. Measure each part of each diagonal. What do you observe? Try this exercise with squares, rhombuses, other parallelograms, and kites (quadrilaterals with two pairs of adjacent sides congruent).

## Three-Dimensional Constructions

The only way to experience some of the truly interesting relationships in three dimensions is with models.

## ACTIVITY

### 17.24 Clay Shapes and Slices

You can make almost any shape with modeling clay and then slice it to investigate the resulting faces on the slices. Use an oil-based craft clay that will not dry out. An inexpensive tool called a *piano wire*, a wire with two handles, is used to cut the clay. This works much better than a knife and can be purchased at an art supply store. Have students make cubes, cones, prisms, cylinders, a torus (doughnut shape), and

other shapes. Precision is not important as long as the essential features are there.

Given a solid, ask students to find a way to slice the shape to produce a slice face with a particular shape. For example, how could you slice a cube so that the slice face is a trapezoid? Will it be isosceles? Always? Figure 17.27 suggests a few ways that different solids can be cut (Carroll, 1988).

If clay slicing seems too problematic, plastic three-dimensional shapes can serve the same purpose. (For example, *Power Solids* from Cuisenaire are reasonably priced and include 12 shapes.) Pour a small amount of water into the hollow shape. The surface of the water is the same shape as a slice. By tilting the solid in different ways, different "slices" are formed. Students may have to add or remove a little water to get the slice in the right place.

Note that predicting ahead of time where to make the slice or how it might be possible to get the desired slice shape is the key to making this last activity profitable. With the water and plastic shapes, it is all too easy to experiment without a lot of reflective thought.

Shape slicing helps students see how a plane intersects with a solid shape. Another connection between two and three dimensions involves "generating" solids from a two-dimensional shape. Sliding (translating) or revolving a plane surface, as shown in Figure 17.28, can generate imaginary solids. Spinning a shape about an edge can make unusual as well as standard shapes.

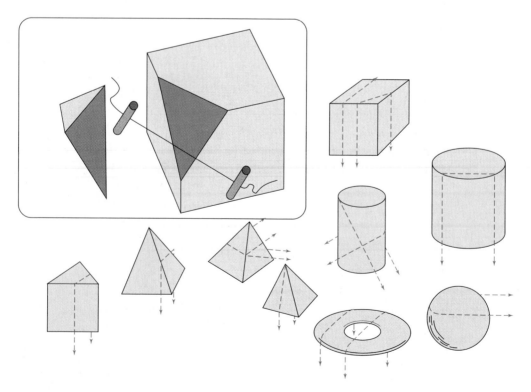

**Figure 17.27** **Predict the slice face before you cut a clay model with a piano wire.**

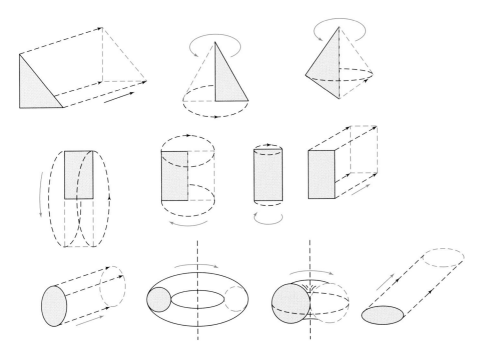

Use a poster board model of a flat shape to generate solids in the air. Slide or rotate the shape. Try to make your generated solid from clay.

**Figure 17.28** **Generating imaginary solids.**

---

┌─ **A**CTIVITY ─────────────────────

## 17.25 Solid Generation Challenges

There are two similar types of challenges:

1. Start with a generator. Provide students with a shape cut from tagboard. The task is to describe, draw, or make from clay all solids that can be generated from this one shape. The shape may be spun or translated in any way. Can some shapes be generated in more than one way?

2. Start with a solid. Give students a model of a solid, or describe one orally. Students are to draw and cut out one or more shapes that will generate the solid and describe how the generation is to be done.

**What solids cannot be generated in this way? What can you say about any solid generated by sliding? How else can cylinders be generated? What about prisms? What types of cones can be generated and how?**

└───────────────────────────────────

Using cubes to build shapes was a suggestion for level 0. At level 1, it is interesting to examine rectangular prisms (box shapes) using cubes because surface area and volume are easily determined in this format. These tasks are analogous to those in two dimensions involving area and perimeter.

┌─ **A**CTIVITY ─────────────────────

## 17.26 Surface and Volume Inquiry

Working with 36 cubes, have students figure out how many boxes (rectangular prisms) they can make that use all 36 cubes. For each, they should list the dimensions and the total surface area. What can you say about boxes with larger surface areas? Smaller surface areas? Try 60 cubes and then 64 cubes. (Good numbers to use will have several factorizations into three factors.) Later, reverse the problem. Have students construct boxes that have a given surface area. Can boxes with the same surface area have different volumes? Try surface areas of 24, 54, or 96 squares.

└───────────────────────────────────

One general conclusion from the "Surface and Volume Inquiry" activity is that boxes that are the closest to cubical will have the smallest surface areas. (Recall that the rectangles with the smallest perimeters were squares.) If the experiment could be carried out for boxes with more and more sides, you would see that shapes with the most volume and least surface area tend to get closer and closer to the shape of a sphere. (A cube is sort of a six-sided "sphere.") This explains why soap bubbles are spherical. The volume of air is fixed (trapped inside), and the soap film tends to contract. When the surface is minimal for the amount of air, the bubble is a sphere.

# Exploring Special Properties and Relationships

Some geometric properties of shape merit special attention. Here you will recognize some of the traditional content of geometry. The activities are generally adaptable to several levels. Since the activities are designed to investigate properties, they are suitable for level 1 thinking. Students still at level 0 will be able to work at the activities but may not apply the properties to whole classes of shapes. Those ready for level 2 thinking can be challenged to see how properties are related or what conditions give rise to particular properties.

## Line Symmetry

*Line symmetry* (bilateral or mirror symmetry) is fun and challenging to explore using a variety of materials.

---

**⚡ ACTIVITY**

## 17.27 Symmetry on a Grid

On a geoboard or on dot or grid paper, draw a line to be a mirror line. Next, draw a shape on one side that touches the line, as in Figure 17.29. Try to draw the mirror or symmetric image of the shape on the other side of the line. Try starting with two intersecting lines of symmetry. Draw the beginning shape between two of the rays formed by these lines. Reflect the shape across each line, a step at a time, until further reflections produce no new lines on your drawing. Mirrors can be used to test the results.

---

**⚡ ACTIVITY**

## 17.28 Line Symmetry Analysis

On a piece of dot paper, use the technique of Activity 17.27 to create a symmetric drawing. Fold the paper on the mirror line, and notice how corresponding points on each side of the line match up. Open the paper, and connect several corresponding points with a straight line. Notice that the mirror line is a perpendicular bisector of the lines joining the points. Use this property to create a symmetric drawing on plain paper. Draw the line and half of the figure as before. From several critical points, draw perpendicular lines to the mirror line and extend them an equal distance beyond (see Figure 17.30).

---

A *flip* or *reflection* of a shape through a line is related to the concept of symmetry. If you plan to investigate *transformations* (slides, flips, and turns), Activities 17.27 and 17.28 are good beginnings.

A useful device for studying symmetry and transformations is the Mira, a piece of red Plexiglas (see Figure 17.31)

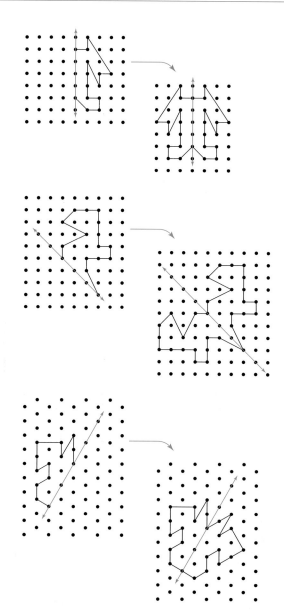

**Figure 17.29** **Exploring symmetry on dot grids.**

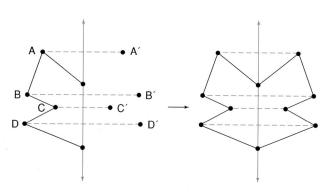

**Figure 17.30** **From points on one side, draw perpendicular lines to the mirror line, and extend them an equal distance beyond.**

**Figure 17.31** The Mira is a "see-through mirror" that allows you to draw the image that you see in the glass.

that stands perpendicular to the table surface. The Mira is essentially a see-through mirror. You can reach behind the Mira and draw the image that you see in the mirror. Since you can see the image behind the Mira as well as the reflected image, it is possible to match images with reflections and draw the mirror line at the base of the Mira. This feature of the Mira allows one to draw perpendicular bisectors and angle bisectors, reflect images, and make a variety of constructions more easily than with a compass and straightedge and in a very conceptual manner.

The following activity offers a slightly different view of symmetry and provides a good preparation for rotational symmetry.

---

┌─ **A**CTIVITY ─────────────────────────────┐

## 17.29 Flip into the Box

Cut out a small rectangle from paper or cardboard. Color one side, and label the corners A, B, C, and D so that they have the same label on both sides. Place

└──────────────────────────────────────────┘

the rectangle on a sheet of paper, and trace around it. Refer to the traced rectangle as a "box" for the cutout rectangle. The question is, "How many different ways can you flip the rectangle over so that it fits in the box?" Before each flip, place the rectangle in the box in the initial orientation. As shown in Figure 17.32, each flip into the box is a flip through a line, and these lines are also lines of symmetry. Students can discover that for a plane shape, there are as many lines of symmetry as there are ways to flip a figure over and still have it fit into its box. Try with other figures: square, nonsquare rhombus, kite, parallelogram with unequal sides and angles, triangles, regular pentagons, and others.

## Rotational Symmetry

One of the easiest introductions to rotational symmetry is to create a box for a shape by tracing around it, as in Activity 17.29. If a shape will fit into its box in more than one way without flipping it over, it has *rotational symmetry*. The *order of rotational symmetry* is the number of different ways it can fit into the box. Thus a square has rotational symmetry of order 4, as well as four flip lines or lines of symmetry. A parallelogram with unequal sides and angles has rotational symmetry of order 2 but no lines of symmetry (see Figure 17.33, p. 334).

---

┌─ **A**CTIVITY ─────────────────────────────┐

## 17.30 Building "Rotatable" Shapes

Use tiles, geoboards, or dot or grid paper to draw a shape that has rotational symmetry of a given order. Except for regular polygons, this can be quite challenging. To test a result, trace around it, and cut out a copy of the shape. Try to rotate it on the drawing.

└──────────────────────────────────────────┘

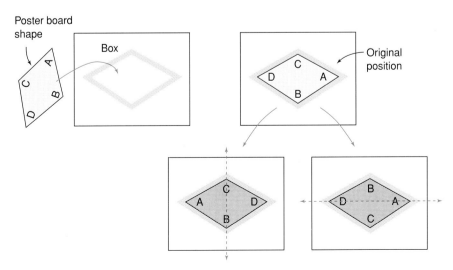

**Figure 17.32** There are at least two ways to flip this diamond into its box. Are there more? Cut one out and try it!

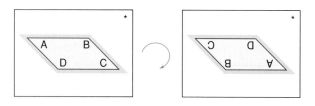

**Figure 17.33**  **This parallelogram fits in its box two ways without flipping it over. Therefore, it has rotational symmetry of order 2.**

## Symmetries in Three-Dimensional Figures

A plane of symmetry in three dimensions is analogous to a line of symmetry in two dimensions. Each point in a symmetric solid corresponds to a point on the other side. The plane of symmetry is the perpendicular bisector of the line segments joining each pair of points. Figure 17.34 illustrates a shape built with cubes that has a plane of symmetry.

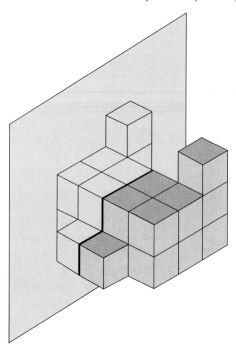

**Figure 17.34**  **A block building with one plane of symmetry.**

## ACTIVITY

### 17.31  Plane Symmetry Buildings

With cubes, build a building that has a plane of symmetry. If the plane of symmetry goes between cubes, slice the shape by separating the building into two symmetrical parts. Try making buildings with two or more planes of symmetry. Build various prisms. Do not forget that a plane can slice diagonally through the blocks. Try using clay to build solids with planes of symmetry, and slice through these planes with a piano wire.

Rotational symmetry in the plane has an analogous counterpart in three dimensions. Whereas a figure in a plane is rotated about a point, a three-dimensional figure is rotated about a line. Such a line is called an *axis of symmetry*. As a solid with rotational symmetry revolves around an axis of symmetry, it will occupy the same position in space (its box), but in different orientations. Whereas plane figures have only one center of rotation, a solid can have more than one axis of rotation. For each axis of symmetry, there is a corresponding order of rotational symmetry. A regular square pyramid has only one axis of symmetry that runs through the vertex and the center of the square. A cube, by contrast, has a total of 13 axes of symmetry: three (through opposite faces) of order 4, four (through diagonally opposite vertices) of order 3, and six (through midpoints of diagonally opposite edges) of order 2.

## ACTIVITY

### 17.32  Find the Spin Lines

Give students a solid shape that has one or more axes of rotational symmetry. Color or label each face of the solid to help keep track. The students' task is to find all axes of rotational symmetry (spin lines) and determine the order of rotational symmetry for each. Suggest that students use one finger of each hand to hold the solid at the two points where the axis of symmetry emerges. A partner can then slowly turn the solid, and both can decide when the solid is again "in its box"—that is, in the same space it was in originally (see Figure 17.35).

## Diagonals of Quadrilaterals

The usual approach to quadrilaterals is in terms of the sides (parallel or not, congruent or not) and angles. Another way to analyze quadrilaterals is in terms of the *diagonals*. Consider the following relationships for diagonals of quadrilaterals:

*Length:* Either equal in length or not (two possibilities)

*Angle of intersection:* Either right angle or not (two possibilities)

*Ratio of parts* (from the corners to the intersection): One diagonal bisected, both bisected, neither bisected but parts proportional, or none of these (four possibilities)

## ACTIVITY

### 17.33  Diagonal Investigation

Have students select a particular type of quadrilateral (say, parallelogram) and draw several different examples of it. Use dot or grid paper to make drawing parallel lines and congruent angles easy. For each example, students should draw the diagonals and make whatever measurements and calculations they desire. The goal is to discover what properties the

With A on top, the cube fits in its "box" four ways. Through this axis, the order of rotational symmetry is order 4.

These two axes also have rotational symmetry of order 4.

Edge-to-edge axes each have symmetry of order 2. How many are there?

If the axis is corner to opposite corner, what is the order of symmetry? How many of these axes are there?

**Figure 17.35** **Rotations of a cube.**

diagonals of that particular type of quadrilateral might have. Different groups of students can investigate different quadrilaterals, and information can be shared and discussed.

In Activity 17.33, the students begin with a quadrilateral and examine properties of the diagonals. A similar activity begins with the diagonals.

— **A**CTIVITY —
## 17.34 Diagonal Strips

For this activity, students need three strips of tagboard about 2 cm wide. Two should be the same

length (about 30 cm) and the third somewhat shorter (about 20 cm). Punch nine holes equally spaced along the strip. (Punch a hole near each end. Divide the distance between the holes by 8. This will be the distance between the remaining holes.) Use a brass fastener to join two strips. A quadrilateral is formed by joining the four end holes as shown in Figure 17.36. Provide students with the list of possible relationships for angles, lengths, and ratios of parts. Their task is to use the strips to determine the properties of diagonals that will produce different quadrilaterals. The strips are there to help in the exploration. Students may want to make additional drawings on dot grids to test the various hypotheses.

**Figure 17.36** **Diagonals of quadrilaterals.**

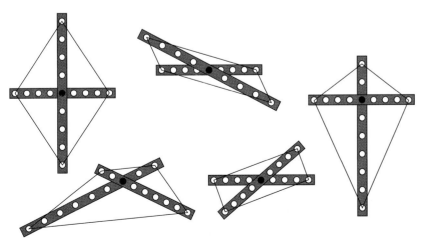

Quadrilaterals can be determined by their diagonals. Consider the length of each, where they cross, and the angles between them. What conditions will produce parallelograms? Rectangles? Rhombuses? Challenge: What properties will produce a nonisosceles trapezoid?

Every type of quadrilateral can be uniquely described in terms of its diagonals using only the conditions of length, angle of intersection, and ratio of parts. Some students will work with the diagonal relationships to see what shapes can be made. Others will begin with examples of the shapes and observe the diagonal relationships. A dynamic geometry program such as *The Geometer's Sketchpad* is an excellent vehicle for this investigation.

## Angles, Lines, and Planes

The relationships between angles within a figure can be explored quite well by tracing angles for comparisons, by comparing angles to a square corner, and by using informal units. With only such simple techniques, students can begin to look at relationships such as the following:

- The angles made by intersecting lines or by lines crossing two parallel lines: Which angles are equal? Which add up to a straight angle?

- The sum of the interior angles of polygons of different types: Is there a relationship in the number of sides and the sum of the angles? What if the shape is concave?

- The exterior angles of polygons: Extend each side in the same direction (for example, clockwise), and observe the sum of these angles. How is the exterior angle related to the interior angle?

In three dimensions, students can begin to observe the angles formed by intersecting planes and between lines and planes. How can two lines not intersect but not be parallel? Can a line and a plane be parallel? How could you describe a line that is perpendicular to a plane? Where would you find examples of these relationships in the real world?

## Similar Figures

In both two and three dimensions, two figures can be the same shape but be different sizes. At level 0, students can sort out shapes that look alike. At that level, the concept of "similar" is strictly visual and not likely to be precise. At level 1, students can begin to measure angles, lengths of sides, areas, and volumes (for solids) of shapes that are similar. By investigation, relationships between similar shapes can be observed. For example, students will find that all corresponding angles must be congruent, but other measures vary proportionately. If one side of a larger yet similar figure is triple that of the smaller figure, so will all linear dimensions be triple those of the smaller figure. If the ratio of corresponding lengths is 1 to $n$, the ratio of areas will be 1 to $n^2$, and the ratio of volumes will be 1 to $n^3$.

All similar figures have proportional measures. It only makes sense to combine this geometric area with the study of proportional reasoning. In Chapter 15, similar rectangles were used to help students observe equal ratios. Recognition of similar figures and proportional reasoning are very much connected and are a good place to make connections in the mathematics curriculum.

A good first definition of *similar figures* is that they are figures that "look alike" but are different in size. To help with this, draw three rectangles on the board. Make two of them similar, say, with sides in the ratio of 1 to 2. The third rectangle should be very different, perhaps long and skinny with sides closer to a 1-to-10 ratio. "Which rectangles look most alike?" As in Chapter 15, this initial concept should be developed intuitively. Later a more precise definition of similarity can be provided: Two shapes are *similar* if all corresponding angles are congruent and all corresponding lengths are proportional. The following activity could be done before students have been given this definition.

---

### ⒶCTIVITY

### 17.35 Build a Similar Figure

**The initial task is to draw or construct at least three shapes similar to a shape you provide. (In two dimensions, good shapes are rectangles, triangles, or circles, but any polygon will work. In three dimensions, rectangular prisms or circular cylinders are good choices.) After making the shapes, students should measure at least three lengths on each shape. Also have them compute the areas of each shape. In the case of three-dimensional shapes, they should compute areas of corresponding surfaces. For three-dimensional shapes, they should also measure or compute the volume of each shape. All measures should be entered into a table so that comparisons can be made. The follow-up task is to look for special relationships in the table of measures. If necessary, suggest that students examine various ratios.**

---

Figure 17.37 shows some measures for similar rectangles and cylinders illustrating length, area, and volume ratios. Note how these three are related. Of course, the measures your students make will not likely have nice whole numbers like these, so calculators or spreadsheets are indispensable. Once students determine that similar figures have proportional measures, the more formal definition can be provided.

## Circles

The circle is a simple shape encountered frequently in our world. Many interesting relationships can be observed between measures of different parts of the circle. Among the most astounding and important is the ratio between measures of the circumference and the diameter.

Similar rectangles

Compare the ratios of lengths
of sides and ratios of areas.

Example: Small to Large

| | | | |
|---|---|---|---|
| Length | 2 to | 6 | (1 to 3) |
| Area | 12 to | 108 | (1 to 9) |

Similar shapes have corresponding dimensions
in predictable ratios. What measures stay
the same? How do lengths, areas, and volumes
change? Is that true of all shapes?

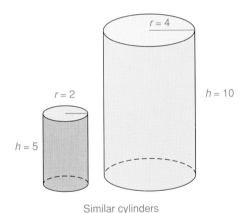

Similar cylinders

Height, radius, and circumference
are all in ratio 1 to 2.

Surface Areas:

| | | | | |
|---|---|---|---|---|
| Sides | 20π | to | 80π | } 1 to 4 |
| Tops | 4π | to | 16π | |
| Volumes: | 20π | to | 160π or 1 to 8 | |

**Figure 17.37** **Similar solids.**

### 17.36 Discovering Pi

Have groups of students carefully measure the circumference and diameter of many different circles.
Groups should each measure different circles.

Measure both the circumference and diameter of
circular items such as jar lids, tubes, cans, and waste-

baskets. To measure circumference, carefully wrap
string once around the object and then measure that
length of string.

Draw larger circles using a string, as shown in Figure 17.38. String can be used to measure the circumference. Also measure large circles marked on
gym floors and playgrounds. Use a trundle wheel or
rope to measure the circumference.

Measures of circumference and diameter should
be collected from all groups and entered in a table.
Ratios of the circumference to the diameter should
also be computed for each circle. A scatter plot of the
data should be made with the horizontal axis representing diameters and the vertical axis circumfer-
ences. If the data are entered on a spreadsheet or in
a graphing calculator, the scatter plot can be generated easily and all ratios computed at once.

Most ratios should be in the neighborhood of 3.1
or 3.2. The scatter plot should approximate a straight
line through the origin. The slope of the line should
also be close to 3.1. (Recall from Chapter 15 that
graphs of equivalent ratios are always straight lines
through the origin.) The exact ratio is an irrational
number, about 3.14159, represented by the Greek
letter $\pi$ (pi).

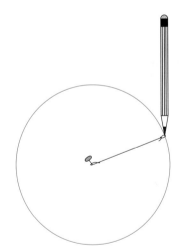

A string with two loops can be used to draw
very large circles that are larger than those drawn
with a compass. Two students working together
will have better success than just one.

**Figure 17.38** **Drawing a circle.**

What is most important in Activity 17.36 is that students
develop a clear understanding of $\pi$ as the ratio of circumference to diameter in any circle. The quantity $\pi$ is not some

strange number that appears in math formulas; it is a naturally occurring and universal ratio.

There are many other explorations that can be done with circles. For example, drawing circles with compasses and then drawing arcs with the same radius through the center has delighted students for ages. Making three folds of a circular disk into the center forms a very nice equilateral triangle, complete with flaps on each edge. These can then be glued together to make three of the five Platonic solids (to be discussed in connection with level 2). It is interesting to notice that all triangles drawn with two vertices on opposite ends of a diameter and the third at some other point on the circle have something in common.

## Assorted Problem-Solving Activities

Problem solving continues to be an important feature of geometry activities at level 1. A few additional explorations are suggested here.

┌─ **A**CTIVITY ────────────────────────────┐

### 17.37 Triangle Communication

Draw any triangle. Choose exactly three measurements of either angles or lengths of sides, and use only these to tell a partner how to draw a triangle that is congruent to yours. What combinations of angles and sides will work?

└──────────────────────────────────────────┘

┌─ **A**CTIVITY ────────────────────────────┐

### 17.38 Area Problems

Determine the areas of odd shapes and surfaces such as those in Figure 17.39 for which there are no formulas or for which dimensions are not provided.

└──────────────────────────────────────────┘

┌─ **A**CTIVITY ────────────────────────────┐

### 17.39 A Geometric Probability Problem

If a dart has an equal chance of landing at any point on a circular target, is it more likely to land closer to the center or closer to the edge?

└──────────────────────────────────────────┘

## Tessellations Revisited

Students at level 1 can begin to create more complex tessellations with attention being given to certain geometric properties.

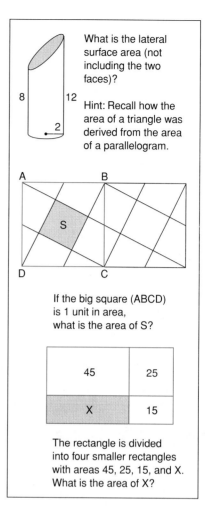

**Figure 17.39** **Examples of area problems that require some analysis.**
*Source:* Adapted from Milauskas (1987).

The Dutch artist M. C. Escher is well known for his tessellations, where the tiles are very intricate and usually take the shape of things like birds, horses, angels, or lizards. What Escher did was take a simple shape such as a triangle, parallelogram, or hexagon and perform transformations on the sides. For example, a curve drawn along one side might be translated (slid) to the opposite side. Another idea was to draw a curve from the midpoint of a side to the adjoining vertex. This curve was then rotated about the midpoint to form a totally new side of the tile. These two ideas are illustrated in part (a) of Figure 17.40. Dot paper is used to help draw the lines. *Escher-type tessellations,* as these have come to be called, are quite popular projects for students in the sixth to eighth grades. Once the tile has been designed, it can be cut from two different colors of construction paper instead of drawing the tessellation on a dot grid.

A *regular tessellation* is made of a single tile that is a regular polygon (all sides and angles congruent). Each vertex of a regular tessellation has the same number of tiles meeting

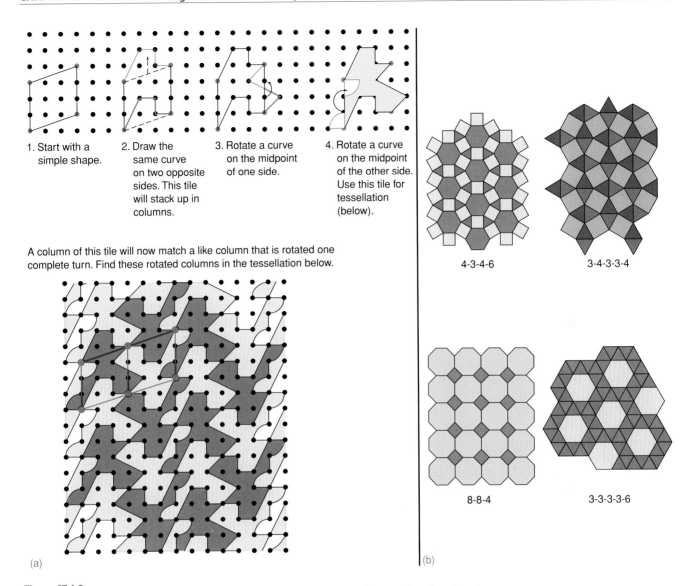

1. Start with a simple shape.

2. Draw the same curve on two opposite sides. This tile will stack up in columns.

3. Rotate a curve on the midpoint of one side.

4. Rotate a curve on the midpoint of the other side. Use this tile for tessellation (below).

A column of this tile will now match a like column that is rotated one complete turn. Find these rotated columns in the tessellation below.

4-3-4-6

3-4-3-3-4

8-8-4

3-3-3-3-6

(a)

(b)

**Figure 17.40** **(a) One of many ways to create an Escher-type tessellation. (b) Examples of semiregular tessellations.**

at that point. A checkerboard is a simple example of a regular tessellation. A *semiregular tessellation* is made of two or more tiles, each of which is a regular polygon. At each vertex of a semiregular tessellation, the same collection of regular polygons come together in the same order. A vertex (and therefore the complete semiregular tessellation) can be described by the series of shapes meeting at a vertex. Under each example of these tessellations in part (b) of Figure 17.40, the vertex numbers are given. Students can figure out what polygons are possible at a vertex and design their own semiregular tessellations.

Tessellations are very popular with teachers in grades 3 through 10. A number of excellent resource books can be found in catalogs such as Cuisenaire.

An alternative method of tiling the plane is to use *rep-tiles*. A rep-tile is a geometric figure for which congruent copies can be made and assembled to produce a larger similar figure. All squares, rectangles, parallelograms, and triangles are rep-tiles. Take any one of these shapes, cut out four copies of it, and you can rearrange them so that the larger figure has the same shape as the smaller one.

Begin with a small triangle. Put four together to make a larger one. Make three copies of the new larger triangle and with the first four small triangles make an even larger triangle—the third generation. Make three copies of this and assemble with the third-generation triangle to make the fourth-generation triangle, and so on. This process will theoretically tile the entire plane but is not a tessellation. After the first four triangles, there are never more than three tiles of any one size. See Fosnaugh and Harrell (1996) for further discussion of this unique idea.

# TECHNOLOGY NOTE: LEVEL I

As students begin to do more than build with geometric "blocks" (tangrams, pattern blocks, grid drawing, etc.), the computer begins to offer powerful tools for explorations.

## Dynamic Geometry Software

In a dynamic geometry program, points, lines, and geometric figures are drawn on the screen using only the computer mouse. Once drawn, the geometric objects can be moved about and manipulated in endless variety. Distances, lengths, areas, angles, slopes, and perimeters can be measured. When the figures are changed, the measurements update instantly.

Most significant, geometric objects can be created with special relationships to other objects. For example, lines can be drawn perpendicular or parallel to other lines or segments. Angles and segments can be drawn congruent to other angles and segments. A point can be placed at the midpoint of a segment. A figure can be produced that is a reflection, rotation, or dilation of another figure. The amazing thing is that when a geometric object is created with a particular relationship to another, that relationship is maintained no matter how either object is moved or changed.

Three of the best known dynamic geometry programs are *The Geometer's Sketchpad* (Key Curriculum Press, 1995), *Geometry Inventor* (LOGAL, 1994a), and *Cabri Geometry II* (Texas Instruments, 1994). Although each operates somewhat differently, they are sufficiently alike that separate descriptions are not required here. *Cabri* and *Sketchpad* were originally designed for high school students, whereas *Geometry Inventor* was designed for use in the middle school. *Inventor* and *Sketchpad* can be used profitably starting about grade 4.

## Dynamic Geometry Examples

To appreciate the potential (and the fun) of dynamic geometry software, you really need to experience it on a computer. In the meantime, two examples are offered here in an attempt to illustrate how these programs work.

Follow these steps in Figure 17.41 (the example uses *Sketchpad*):

1. Points A, B, and C were placed freely, and a segment was drawn between A and B.
2. A line was drawn through C parallel to AB.
3. A point D was placed on the line through C, and segments AD and DB were drawn.

(At this time, the line through C can be moved, but it will remain parallel to AB. If A or B is moved, C remains fixed, but the line through C will rotate so that it remains parallel to AB. Through all of this, the point D will remain on the line, and triangle ABD will adjust accordingly.)

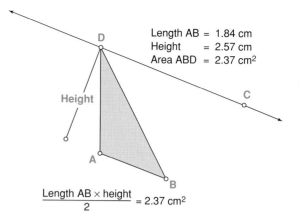

Length AB = 1.84 cm
Height = 2.57 cm
Area ABD = 2.37 cm²

$$\frac{\text{Length AB} \times \text{height}}{2} = 2.37 \text{ cm}^2$$

**Figure 17.41** A *Sketchpad* construction. When D is moved along the line DC, all measures are updated.

4. A segment is constructed (some steps are omitted here) so that it runs from D to a hidden line through AB and is always perpendicular to AB. This line is clearly the height of triangle ABD. *Sketchpad* permits labeling any way you wish.
5. Measures are made of AB, the height, and the area of ABD. The formula AB × height/2 is also calculated.

Now D can be dragged along line DC, and the height of ABD will remain constant, as will the length of AB. The area of the triangle remains fixed as long as the base and height remain fixed.

In Figure 17.42, the midpoints of a freely drawn quadrilateral ABCD have been joined. The diagonals of the resulting quadrilateral (EFGH) are also drawn and measured. No matter how the points A, B, C, and D are dragged around the screen, even inverting the quadrilateral, the other lines will maintain the same relationships (joining midpoints and diagonals), and the measurements will be instantly updated on the screen.

Remember that at level 1, the objects of thought are *classes* of shapes. In a dynamic geometry program, if a quadrilateral is drawn, only one shape is observed, as would be the case on paper or on a geoboard. But now that quadrilateral can be stretched and altered in endless ways. Students actually explore not one shape but an enormous number of examples from that class of shapes. If a property does not change when the figure changes, the property is attributable to the *class* of shapes rather than any particular shape.

As another example, suppose you draw a triangle with a segment joining the midpoints of two sides (called a *mid-segment*). Measures of various lengths, angles, and areas are placed on the screen. Now you drag vertices and sides to change the specific shape of the triangle. Each time you stop, the measures of the current triangle are added to a chart. Regardless of the angles in the triangle, certain pairs of angles always seem to be the same. The length of the midsegment is exactly half of the third side. It seems always to be parallel to it as well. You are experiencing a property of midsegments of *all* triangles, not just a few.

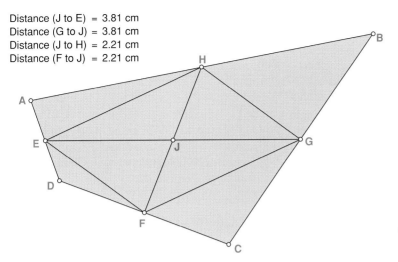

Distance (J to E)  =  3.81 cm
Distance (G to J)  =  3.81 cm
Distance (J to H)  =  2.21 cm
Distance (F to J)  =  2.21 cm

**Figure 17.42** A *Sketchpad* **construction illustrating an interesting property of quadrilaterals.**

"Property Challenges" (Activity 17.22, p. 329), "Measure Investigation" (Activity 17.23, p. 329), all of the symmetry investigations (both line symmetry and rotational symmetry), "Diagonal Investigation" (Activity 17.33, p. 334), investigations of similarity, and "Discovering Pi" (Activity 17.36, p. 337) can all be explored profitably with dynamic geometry programs. The publishers of these programs provide excellent activities that are appropriate for level 1 investigations. Many activities are included with the software, and others are found in supplementary publications.

## Tessellations on the Computer

*TesselMania!* (MECC, 1994) is a popular software program that makes it very easy to produce intricate tessellations that are similar in spirit to those of Escher. Using the mouse to alter one or more sides of a simple tile such as a parallelogram, square, diamond, or triangle produces the tessellations. By selecting the type of pattern in advance, the program automatically performs the necessary translations or rotations to the other sides of the tile. With a single click, the screen is filled with the resulting tessellation (see Figure 17.43). Color and other drawing objects can be added to the tiles to create results that are quite striking. This program must be used with care. It is so easy to create intricate results with no understanding of what has been done geometrically that it can easily become an art tool rather than an opportunity to learn about transformations. But if a desired tessellation is carefully designed and planned away from the computer, the software can be used to do the tedious work of creating the finished product. Tessellations created with the program can also be analyzed to determine exactly what transformations were involved.

## Logo in Level 1 Explorations

Two features of Logo make it ideal for level 1 explorations. First, as noted in an earlier section, *procedures* or small programs can be written and used repeatedly. For example, sup-

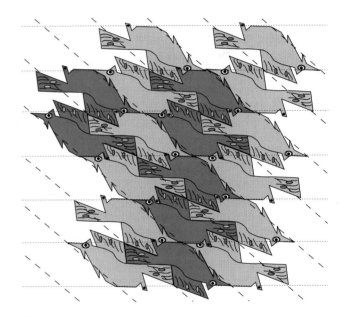

**Figure 17.43** **An example of a tessellation produced with TesselMania! Deluxe. Only complete tiles are shown. Notice the grid. The tile was created using the same types of transformations as illustrated in Figure 17.40 (p. 339).**

pose that you have drawn a rectangle with these commands: **fd 60 rt 90 fd 30 rt 90 fd 60 rt 90**. These commands can be labeled with the command **to box** or **to rect** or **to [anyword]**. The **to** tells Logo that the word following it is going to be defined. Once defined, all that is necessary is to type the word. If these commands had been used to label **box,** then typing **box** will cause the turtle to execute them immediately. There is no limit on the number of words that can be defined. An already defined word can be used to define a new word.

Suppose that the word **tri** (short for *triangle*) were defined as follows:

> **to tri**
>
> > **repeat 3 [fd 30 rt 120]**

Now you can define **house**:

> to house
>> box
>> fd 60
>> rt 30
>> tri

Stop for a moment and sketch what you think the procedure **house** will draw. Why are the two commands between **box** and **tri** required? How would you make the turtle draw the house lying on its side or upside down?

Variables are another powerful feature of Logo. For example, the following procedure will draw rectangles of any dimension:

> to rect :l :w
>> repeat 2 [fd :l rt 90 fd :w]

Now if you type **rect 100 70**, Logo draws a rectangle that is 100 units on the first side and 70 units on its second side. **Rect 70 100** draws the same rectangle but with the short side first. **Rect 50 50** draws a square. If variables are used in the **box** and **tri** procedures, then the **house** procedure can be written with two variables, allowing the house shape to be drawn any size at all.

Procedures and variables allow students to explore geometric properties by trying to create procedures that might produce certain effects. For example, how can you draw two similar rectangles? Are all rectangles drawn with the **rect :l :w** procedure the same shape? Given the procedure for any particular shape, how can the procedure for its mirror image be drawn? Why are the turns in the **tri** procedure (p. 341) 120 instead of 60 or some other angle? How would you define a procedure that draws a parallelogram? These are only a few simple examples to illustrate how students working in a Logo environment can begin to explore properties of shapes. Tasks such as these can be explored by level 1 thinkers. However, as students begin to ask "Why does that work?" the thinking begins to take on a deductive quality that pushes the thought process to the next level. ■

# INFORMAL GEOMETRY ACTIVITIES: LEVEL 2

At van Hiele level 2 of geometric thinking, students begin to use informal deductive reasoning. That is, they can follow and use logical arguments, although they may have a difficult time constructing a proof of their own. Physical models and drawings are still important, but for different reasons. At level 1, students' explorations lead to inductive conclusions about shapes. Students at level 1 are satisfied that this is true because it seems to happen that way when they try it. At level 2, students can use a drawing to help them follow a

deductive argument supplied by the teacher. They may also use models to test conjectures or to find counterexamples. Models become more a tool for thinking and verification than one for exploration.

Many topics in the seventh- and eighth-grade curriculum lend themselves to projects that promote level 2 thinking. It is important to challenge students to reason through these topics and not just memorize formulas and procedures. Eighth-grade geometry may be one of the last opportunities for good activities that prepare students for the level 3 thinking required in a high school geometry course.

## Definitions and Properties

Activities at level 2 can begin to focus on the definitions of shapes and how different classes of shapes are related.

---
**ACTIVITY**

### 17.40 Minimal Property Lists

Give each group of students a particular type of shape, for example, rectangles. The first task is to list all possible properties of that shape that they can think of. It is useful to share the property lists for different shapes with the class. Others may have new properties to add or may wish to challenge a property as not holding for all possible shapes of that type. A possible list for rectangles is offered here.

The next challenge is to find *minimal property lists*, subsets of the property lists that if true would guarantee a shape of that type *and* no extra properties. If a property is removed from a minimal list, the list should no longer guarantee the shape. For most shapes, there are several different minimal property lists.

<u>Rectangle Properties</u>

**Four sides**

**Four right angles**

**Opposite sides parallel**

**Diagonals bisect each other**

**Adjacent sides perpendicular**

**Opposite sides equal in length**

**Diagonals congruent**

**Lines of symmetry through opposite sides**

**Rotational symmetry of *at least* order 2**

---

Creation of property lists is an important exercise for beginning level 2 thinkers. Using rectangles as an example, some students will note that the diagonals are not perpendicular. This is true only of nonsquare rectangles. Similarly, it would be incorrect to say that rectangles had rotational symmetry of order 2 since squares, a subset of rectangles, have rotational symmetry of order 4.

Finding *minimal* lists is a clear example of level 2 reasoning. Here students must reason "*If* a shape has these properties, *then* it must necessarily have all of the rest of these properties." Notice that every minimal list is a potential definition of that shape. The diagonals are especially interesting for quadrilaterals, since each type of quadrilateral can be uniquely defined by describing only the properties of its diagonals.

Minimal lists are also a good way to examine relationships between shapes. Students will find, for example, that every property of a rectangle is also a property of a square but not the reverse. Property lists and minimal property lists can be used in the logical arguments required in the next activity.

---

**ACTIVITY**

## 17.41 If-Then, True or False

Explore statements in these forms:

If it is a _____, then it is also a _____.

All _____ are _____.

**Fill the blanks with names of shapes or statements of properties and relationships. Let students use drawings or models to decide if the statements are true or to find counterexamples. A few examples are suggested here.**

If it is a cylinder, then it is a prism.

If it is a prism, then it is a cylinder.

If it is a square, then it is a rhombus.

All parallelograms have congruent diagonals.

All quadrilaterals with congruent diagonals are parallelograms.

If two rectangles have the same area, then they are congruent.

All prisms have a plane of symmetry.

All right prisms have a plane of symmetry.

If a prism has a plane of symmetry, then it is a right prism.

**Obviously, not all of these statements are true. For those that you think may be false, find a counterexample. You and your students can make up similar puzzles to stump the class.**

---

# Informal Proofs

Perhaps the notion of geometric proof in the seventh or eighth grade seems a bit difficult. That may be a result of your personal experience with proof in your tenth-grade course. The typical high school geometry proof is based on axioms, definitions, and theorems that have already been established. Each tiny statement must be defended.

What is quite possible at the middle grade level is to require students to build informal arguments that involve everyday logic. These arguments can easily be made by middle grade students if they are given the opportunity to explore an idea and get a good feel for what is involved. Here are some simple examples.

---

**ACTIVITY**

## 17.42 Two Congruent Parts

**"I have a rectangle that has been divided into two congruent parts. What could the parts be?" There is no single answer to this question, and some answers depend on the specific rectangle in question. How students respond will depend somewhat on what materials you provide. If you suggest that students use a rectangular dot grid, you will likely get different answers than if you simply have them make sketches on plain paper.**

---

The interesting part of "Two Congruent Parts" is the discussion that can surround any given answer. Many answers can be generalized to apply to any original rectangle or to a specific rectangle. A generalized answer is now a conjecture that can potentially be proved. You may want to explore this activity on your own for a while before reading further. Here are a few possible conjectures that are probable results of such an investigation:

1. The two shapes could be right triangles.

2. The two shapes could be squares.

3. The two shapes could be rectangles with one side the same as the given rectangle and the other half the length of the given rectangle.

4. The line dividing the rectangle will always go through the center of the rectangle (the intersection of the diagonals).

Each of these statements is open to some scrutiny, even though most seem to be true on the surface. Consider statement 1. Here is a possible argument: If you draw a line from one corner to the opposite corner, there will be two triangles. Because the shape is a rectangle, the remaining two corners are right angles and are angles in the two triangles. Therefore, they are right triangles. The two shapes are congruent because all of the sides are congruent: One side is the same—the diagonal; the two legs of one triangle are adjacent sides of the rectangle. These sides match the opposite sides of the rectangle and are the legs of the second triangle.

Statement 2 is true only for a special class of rectangles but can be proved just as easily. Statement 4 is the toughest to prove but is certainly worthy of a class struggle.

Another opportunity for proof is found in the next activity.

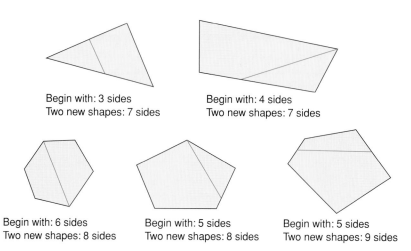

**Figure 17.44** **Start with a polygon, and draw a segment to divide it into two polygons. How many sides will the two new polygons have?**

Begin with: 3 sides
Two new shapes: 7 sides

Begin with: 4 sides
Two new shapes: 7 sides

Begin with: 6 sides
Two new shapes: 8 sides

Begin with: 5 sides
Two new shapes: 8 sides

Begin with: 5 sides
Two new shapes: 9 sides

---

**ACTIVITY**

### 17.43  Two Polygons from One

Begin with a convex polygon with a given number of sides. Connect two points with a segment. How many sides do the two resulting polygons have altogether (see Figure 17.44)? (Sconyers, 1995)

The answer to the question of course depends on how many sides the original polygon has. It also depends on how the segment is drawn. However, with some exploration, it is reasonable to discover that for any polygon with more than three sides, there are three cases to consider for the segment and for each case a clear answer to how many sides will result. (The proof is left to you.) As students work together, perhaps with some hints or suggestions from you, they will be able to construct a good argument for a generalized answer to the question posed.

What is significant about these informal proof activities is that the generalizations come from students' explorations. If you write a theorem on the board and ask students to prove it, you have already told them the statement is true. The proof becomes an uninteresting exercise. If, by contrast, a student makes a statement about a geometric situation the class is exploring, it can be written on the board with a question mark—it is a *conjecture*, a statement whose truth has not yet been determined. "Is it true? Always? What do you think? Can we prove it? Can you find a counterexample?" Out of discussions such as this, good deductive arguments can be developed by the class.

As students begin to construct and analyze arguments such as these fairly simple ones, they will begin to develop an appreciation for what deductive argument is about. What happens is in keeping with level 2 of the van Hiele theory: Students look at properties of shapes (objects of thought) and construct logical arguments (products of thought).

## Other Topics for Level 2 Investigation

The middle grades geometry curriculum often includes content that is new and therefore treated in a show-and-tell manner. When possible, these topics should be explored or extended in a way that challenges students to reason in a deductive manner. Here are some examples.

### The Pythagorean Theorem

An area interpretation of the *Pythagorean theorem* states that if a square is made on each side of a right triangle, the areas of the two smaller squares will together be equal to the area of the square on the longest side or hypotenuse. Figure 17.45 illustrates two proofs that students can follow.

As a variation on the Pythagorean theorem, have students explore what happens if the squares formed on each side of a right triangle are replaced by triangles or semicircles. Will the same relationship between the three areas hold? What about other shapes (pentagons, hexagons, etc.)?

### Area and Volume Formulas

Chapter 16 contains suggestions for helping students develop formulas for areas and volumes of common shapes. Formula development is a major connection between measurement and geometry and is also a good bridge between level 1 and level 2 of geometric thinking.

### The Platonic Solids

The *Platonic solids* are *completely regular polyhedrons*. "Completely regular" means that each face is a regular polygon and every vertex has exactly the same number of faces joining at that point. Level 2 students can work through an informal argument that demonstrates there can be only five completely regular polyhedrons and allows the excitement of constructing them.

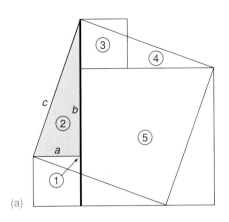

$c^2$ = regions ① + ② + ③ + ④ + ⑤

$a^2$ = regions ① + ③

$b^2$ = regions ② + ④ + ⑤

Therefore, $c^2 = a^2 + b^2$

(The second and third equations require some thought. Do you see why they are correct?)

(a)

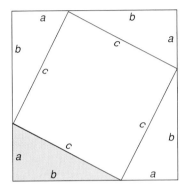

(b)

The area of the large square is $(a + b)^2 = a^2 + 2ab + b^2$

The same area is also $c^2$ plus 4 times the area of one triangle.

$c^2 + 4(\frac{1}{2}ab) = c^2 + 2ab$

So $c^2 + 2ab = a^2 + 2ab + b^2$

$c^2 = a^2 + b^2$

**Figure 17.45** **Two proofs of the Pythagorean theorem.**

---

**ACTIVITY**

## 17.44 Search for the Platonic Solids

Provide students with a supply of congruent equilateral triangles, squares, regular pentagons, and a few regular hexagons. These can be cut from tagboard, but plastic construction kits such as Polydron or Geoshapes are excellent for the purpose. (If you use tagboard shapes, an ample supply of tape will also be necessary.) Explain what completely regular polyhedrons are, focusing on the idea that these will have the same number of faces meeting at every vertex and every face will be a congruent regular polygon. Students should work in small groups to find as many completely regular solids as possible. As a class, decide if each construction is in fact completely regular and entertain arguments for why students think they have found them all.

Since finding and building the Platonic solids is such a powerful exploration, one possible approach to finding them, coupled with an argument that there are only five such solids, is outlined here for your benefit. Resist the urge to guide your students through this development; level 2 thinking will be better served by letting students work through this argument on their own.

Since the polyhedrons must have regular faces, begin with the simplest possible face, an equilateral triangle, and see what polyhedrons can be constructed.

1. Put three triangles together at a point. Join the edges to form a pyramid. This will leave a space for one more triangle to be inserted as a base forming a *tetrahedron* (*tetra* = four). Observe that this is a completely regular polyhedron. (Why is a six-sided polyhedron made of two tetrahedrons placed face to face not completely regular?)

2. Start over, this time with four triangles coming together at a point. Joining these will form a square pyramid. Attach another triangle to each edge of the square and bring these four to a point. This will result in a completely regular eight-sided polyhedron or *octahedron* (*octa* = eight).

3. Begin again with triangles. Join five at a point to form a pentagonal pyramid. Continue to add triangles on open edges until there are five at each vertex. It is very exciting to see and feel this form into a ball-like structure of 20 triangles, an *icosahedron* (*icosa* = twenty).

4. When you try six triangles at a point, they make a flat surface, not a solid. No more than six will work either. Therefore, there are no more

completely regular polyhedrons possible with triangular faces.

5. The next regular polygon after a three-sided one is a four-sided polygon, a square. Put three together at a point, and attach the sides. Add an additional square at the three open vertices, and you have formed a cube. Now, however, you know to call it a *hexahedron* (*hex* = six). As with the triangles, no other polyhedrons can be made with squares.

6. The next polygon is a regular pentagon. Three can be put together at one vertex, and you can continue to add pentagons on open edges with three coming together at every point until 12 pentagons form a complete polyhedron, a *dodecahedron* (*dodeca* = twelve).

7. Finally, conclude by experimentation that no other polyhedrons are possible with pentagons or with hexagons. After seeing that three hexagons lay flat, it is fairly clear that three septagons would not fit around a point. Thus there are no other possible regular polyhedrons, and you have found all five of the Platonic solids.

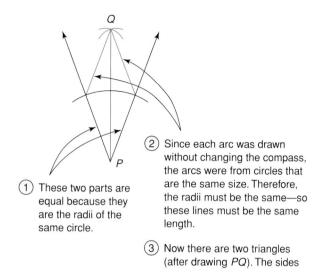

① These two parts are equal because they are the radii of the same circle.

② Since each arc was drawn without changing the compass, the arcs were from circles that are the same size. Therefore, the radii must be the same—so these lines must be the same length.

③ Now there are two triangles (after drawing *PQ*). The sides all match up, so they are the same (congruent). If that is so, then the two angles at *P* must be the same.

**Figure 17.46**   **A possible informal explanation for bisecting an angle with compass and straightedge.**

A fantastic skeletal icosahedron can be built out of the newspaper rods described earlier in the chapter. Start with five at a point, and join the other ends with five rods to form a pentagonal pyramid. Add two more rods at each vertex of the base, and continue from there. Keep in mind that you want five rods at each vertex and that all faces make triangles. The icosahedron will be about 4 feet in diameter and will be amazingly rigid.

Another way to make all of the Platonic solids in skeletal form is to use the bendable drinking straws described earlier. There is enough rigidity that even the cube and dodecahedron will turn out all right.

## Constructions

Too frequently, students are taught to perform constructions with a straightedge and compass but have no idea why the constructions work. In most instances, the constructions represent simple theorems that students can follow and provide reasons for the steps. An example of bisecting an angle is illustrated in Figure 17.46.

## TECHNOLOGY NOTE: LEVEL 2

Dynamic geometry software (*The Geometer's Sketchpad, Geometry Inventor,* and *Cabri*) was discussed in the context of level 1 thinking. These programs allow students to explore an entire class of figures and observe properties or relationships that are attributable to that class. At level 2, however, the

focus is on reasoning or deductive thinking. Can these computer programs help students develop deductive arguments to support the relationships they come to believe through inductive reasoning?

## Finding Relationships Versus Explaining Relationships

Suppose that you have students use a dynamic geometry program to draw a triangle, measure all of the angles, and add them up. As the triangle vertices are dragged around, the sum of the angles would remain steadfast at 180 degrees. Students can conjecture that the sum of the interior angles of a triangle is always 180 degrees, and they would be completely convinced of the truth of this conjecture based on their inductive experiences. (The same exploration is easily done with paper drawings and measurement with a protractor.)

However, no matter how convincing the experience, it fails to explain *why it is so.* As Michael de Villiers notes in his excellent book *Rethinking Proof with the Geometer's Sketchpad* (1999), "The observation that the sun rises every morning does not explain why this is true" (p. 24). De Villiers points out that the experience leading to the conjecture or truth should also help students develop a rationale for the result. In the case of interior angles of a triangle, the experience just described does not help students understand why it is so. Consider the following activity, which can be done easily with paper and scissors or quite dramatically with a dynamic geometry program.

---

**A**CTIVITY

## 17.45  Angle Sum in a Triangle

Have all students cut out three congruent triangles. (Stack three sheets of paper, and cut three shapes at one time.) Place one triangle on a line and the second directly next to it in the same orientation. Place the third triangle in the space between the triangles as shown in Figure 17.47(a). Based on this experience, what conjecture can you make about the sum of the angles in a triangle?

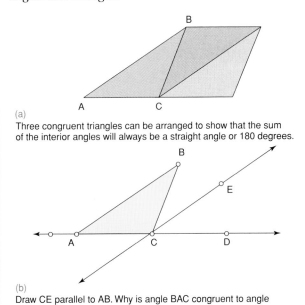

(a)
Three congruent triangles can be arranged to show that the sum of the interior angles will always be a straight angle or 180 degrees.

(b)
Draw CE parallel to AB. Why is angle BAC congruent to angle ECD? Why is angle ABC congruent to angle BCE?

**Figure 17.47**  **Deductive, logical reasoning is necessary to *prove* relationships that appear true from observations.**

In a dynamic geometry program, the three triangles in Figure 17.47(a) can be drawn by starting with one triangle, translating it to the right the length of AC, and then rotating the same triangle about the midpoint of side BC. When vertices of the original triangle are dragged, the other triangles will change accordingly and remain congruent. We still do not know why the angle sum is always a straight angle, but this exploration allows students to see why it might be so. In the figure, there are lines parallel to each side of the original triangle. By using properties of angles formed by cutting two lines with a transverse line, it is easy to argue that the sum of the angles will always be a straight line [see Figure 17.47(b); the proof is left to you]. By setting up the three triangles and focusing on parallel lines, students can develop the deductive argument or can follow an argument developed by the class.

Dynamic geometry software can be enormously powerful for helping students observe geometric relationships and make conjectures. The truth of the conjectures will often be obvious. At level 2, however, we must begin to ask why. The following activity further illustrates the point.

**A**CTIVITY

## 17.46  Triangle Midsegments

Using a dynamic geometry program, draw a triangle, and label the vertices A, B, and C. Draw the segment joining the midpoints of AB and AC, and label this segment DE, as in Figure 17.48. Measure the length of DE and BC. Also measure angles ADE and ABC. Drag points A, B, and C. What conjectures can you make about the relationships between segment DE, the *midsegment* of ABC, and BC, the base of ABC?

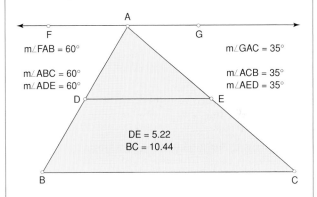

**Figure 17.48**  **The midsegment of a triangle is always parallel to the base and half as long.**

It is very clear that the midsegment is half the length of the base and parallel to it, but why is this so? Students will need a bit more guidance, but you should not necessarily have to provide the argument for them. Suggest that they draw a line through A parallel to BC. List all pairs of angles that they know are congruent. Why are they congruent? Note that triangle ABC is similar to triangle ADE. Why is it similar? With hints such as these, many middle grade students can begin to make logical arguments for why the things they observe to be true are in fact true.

## Defining Shapes

Some dynamic geometry programs come with built-in shapes. For example, in *Geometry Inventor,* selecting the correct icon and dragging the mouse will draw a square. The resulting shape will remain a square no matter how the vertices are dragged about the screen. Suppose that you did not have this capability.

**A**CTIVITY

## 17.47  Squares That Remain Square

Challenge students to find a way to use their dynamic geometry program to create a square (without using a built-in capability) that will remain a square even when its sides or vertices are dragged about the screen.

There are numerous ways of solving the "Squares That Remain Square" task. Note that lines, circles, or points that may be necessary in the construction but are not part of the square can be hidden in the final drawing so that only the square remains. Different groups will come up with different methods. To solve the problem, reasoning must proceed from the properties to the square: If my shape maintains these relationships (properties), it must therefore remain a square. Students can be challenged to find efficient methods for creating a square. Solutions from different groups can be displayed and discussed. If a particularly interesting approach has not been used, challenge students to use that method. For example, can you make a square by using what you know about the diagonals?

Activity 17.47 can easily be changed from a square to an equilateral triangle, an isosceles triangle, a rhombus, a kite, a trapezoid, a parallelogram, and other shapes. As students become more familiar with the workings of their dynamic geometry program, the possibilities for these constructions increases. For example, reflections and rotations are often useful. Even finding ways to draw a segment congruent to another segment involves valuable reasoning.

## Shape Makers

If you begin with a collection of shapes that retain their properties, these can then be used to explore the relationships among classes of shapes. As a simple example, suppose you have a shape that remains a parallelogram and one that remains a rectangle. Is there a shape that can be made with the rectangle maker that cannot be made with the parallelogram maker? What about the reverse: Can the parallelogram maker make any rectangle shapes? What conjecture can you make based on these explorations?

*Shape Makers: Developing Geometric Reasoning with the Geometer's Sketchpad* (Battista, 1998) is a book of explorations based on this type of reasoning. The activities are appropriate for students in grades 5–8. The book includes a disk of files with all the shape makers already developed. The research-based explorations are designed to move students into level 2 thinking. With or without Battista's book, the idea of using shape makers to explore the relationships between shapes is very powerful. ■

## ASSESSMENT NOTES

Typical assessments in geometry require only limited recall information from students. To properly assess and evaluate activities like those suggested in this chapter, you need a clear understanding of your goals and objectives.

## What to Assess

An understandable conflict arises when we examine the breadth of engaging activities that are available in the area of geometry. On the one hand, intuition suggests that these are good experiences for children as they explore the geometric world around them. On the other hand, we ask ourselves, "Exactly what did they learn?" Many good geometric experiences, especially those suitable for level 0 and level 1 students, are explorations in which children can develop their spatial sense.

If students are filling in outlines with tangram pieces or finding all of the 12 pentominoes, we are not concerned that they "master" these skills. It is not a curricular objective to find the 12 shapes that can be made with five squares on a grid. Perhaps it is precisely because these activities do not show up on lists of objectives that schools and textbooks in the United States have traditionally not allocated much time to geometry in the elementary and middle grades.

Many teachers find themselves trying to apply a grade to geometry activities that have no right or wrong answers and for which there is no clear objective. Even when the activity is aimed at a particular geometric concept, such as line symmetry or similarity, the answer to "Do they know it?" may be fuzzy. In level 2, many activities invite class or group discussions of informal proofs and conjecture making. Again, the objective is often unclear.

## Clarifying Your Geometry Objectives

The greatest mistake that can be made is to take the fuzziness of geometry goals to mean that geometry is not important. You must clearly articulate the goals of your geometry program and find ways to assess them. You will then know when you are being successful, know how to defend or explain what you are doing in your geometry program, and be able to make well-documented evaluations of your students.

The most important geometric agenda of the K–8 teacher is to provide experiences that move students from level 0 thinking to level 2 thinking by the end of the eighth grade. Not every teacher will be able to move children to the next level. However, all teachers should be aware that the experiences they provide are the single most important factor in moving children up this developmental ladder. Every teacher should be able to see some growth in geometric thinking over the course of the year.

A useful idea is to separate your objectives into those that deal with content and those that deal with general geometric growth. By attending to geometric growth in a general way, you can avoid the trap of teaching to content objectives so specifically that students are parroting back what you tell them without really developing their spatial sense.

### Spatial Sense and van Hiele Objectives

In the early grades, when you can expect your students to be level 0 thinkers, you want to be sure that their thinking is increasing in its sophistication and is moving toward level 1. Here are suggestions for things to look for:

- Child attends to a variety of characteristics of shapes in sorting and building activities.
- Child uses language that is descriptive of geometric shapes.

- Child shows evidence of geometric reasoning in solving puzzles, exploring shapes, creating designs, and analyzing shapes.
- Child recognizes shapes in the environment.
- Child solves spatial problems.

Each of these statements can be assessed as indicative of either a level 0 thinker or a level 1 thinker. For example, at level 0, the types of characteristics that students are likely to pay attention to are not properties of general classes of shapes ("pointy," "fat," "has five sides," "goes up," etc.). Properties such as "parallel" or "symmetrical" may be used by level 0 thinkers as well as those at level 1. The distinction is found in what the properties are attributed to. At level 0, students are restricted in thought to the shapes they are currently working with, while at level 1, students attribute properties to classes of shapes (*all* rectangles or *all* cylinders). Language, reasoning, shape recognition, and spatial problem solving can all be assessed as being appropriate for level 0 or level 1. By thinking in this manner, teachers can begin to get a sense of the geometric growth of their students beyond the specific content knowledge that may have been developed.

At the upper elementary and middle grades, teachers can begin to think in terms of students being at level 1 or level 2 in their geometric thought. Before grade 6 or 7, very few students will have achieved level 2 thinking, but teachers need to be aware of progress in that direction. The following general indicators are more indicative of level 2 thinkers rather than level 1:

- Child shows improvement in spatial visualization skills.
- Child has an inclination to make and test conjectures in geometric situations.
- Child makes use of logical explanations in geometric problem solving.
- Child justifies conclusions in geometric contexts.
- Child assesses the validity of logical arguments in geometric situations.

Most of these indicators or objectives include elements of reasoning and logical sophistication that are not generally present in a level 1 thinker. As noted in the discussions of dynamic geometry software, a level 1 thinker is using inductive reasoning to discover relationships in shapes, whereas a level 2 thinker is, with guidance, beginning to develop arguments that explain why a particular relationship exists.

## Geometric Concept Objectives

Helping students grow in geometric thought includes the development of specific concepts and ideas. As with concepts in other strands of mathematics, understanding of most ideas will vary considerably from one student to the next, and you will want to be aware of different levels of understanding.

Children should begin at level 0 and continue in level 1 to attach appropriate names to classifications of shapes that they readily recognize. It will be useful to see if the ideas are present even if the actual names are not. Shape recognition, however, should not be a major focus of your program and should not dominate your assessment agenda.

Rather than focus on mastery of definitions, be more aware of the appropriate use of terms in student activities. A student who can give you a memorized definition of a ray and an angle but shows little understanding when using these terms in an activity has not learned much of value. Similar statements can be made about a host of other geometric terms and relationships (*parallel, perpendicular, diameter, radius, tangent, skew, congruence, supplemental angles,* etc.).

For some larger concepts, understanding grows over the years as new connections and sophistication with the concepts develop. These include *line symmetry, rotational symmetry, similarity,* and *transformations (slides, flips, turns).* The concept of line symmetry, for example, may be introduced as early as the second grade and continue to be developed in sophistication through the eighth grade. It is not reasonable to say that Johnny "knows symmetry." It may be appropriate to note that Johnny can recognize line symmetry in simple geometric designs and can produce a symmetric image if given a simple design and a line of symmetry. Johnny may not, for example, use or even recognize the relationship of corresponding elements in a symmetrical pattern to the line of symmetry or know how symmetry and the reflection transformation are related. For the purpose of assessment, you need to make descriptive statements that indicate what a student does know about the concepts. Your objectives should also be articulated in descriptive form.

*Principles and Standards* is extremely helpful for articulating growth in geometry across the grades (refer to Appendix A to see how the general standards for geometry are articulated for each grade band). These statements can help you decide on the level of sophistication that is appropriate for the particular topics you are teaching in your classroom.

## Putting It All Together

In deciding what to assess and how, it is best to take a long-term view of geometry rather than a more traditional mastery-oriented approach. Two large perspectives have been suggested:

- Growth in spatial sense and geometric thought
- Understanding of geometric concepts and the corresponding terminology and notation

As a teacher, you should establish and articulate goals for your geometry program in each area. Share them with others at your grade level. Create checklists, observation schemes, and rubrics that reflect long-range objectives. In this way, you can gather data that will inform and support your geometry program. By thinking in terms of long-range objectives, you will be able to articulate the value of a pentomino activity or other geometric challenge. Furthermore, you will learn what things to look for and listen for during a geometry exploration. What a child "knows" in geometry is not just a list of mastered terms but a way of thinking in geometric contexts.

# REFLECTIONS ON CHAPTER 17

## Writing to Learn

*Note:* There are so many activities in this chapter that you may feel overwhelmed. The best way to get excited about and comfortable with informal geometry is to start doing the same activities that are designed for students. Do not worry about being "right." What is right is to *do something,* to think about what you are doing, and to have fun. As you get interested, you will begin to search for ideas and relationships, and you may even decide you want to do further reading. Good geometry resource books for teachers are plentiful, and articles in the journals *Teaching Children Mathematics* and *Mathematics Teaching in the Middle School* are often excellent. You could not go wrong by simply exploring activities from this chapter.

1. Describe what is meant by informal geometry. How is it different from the geometry usually taught in high school? How is it different from what you remember from school? What is spatial sense?

2. What do you think are the two best reasons for studying geometry? Explain.

3. Describe in your own words the first three van Hiele levels of geometric thought (levels 0, 1, and 2). Note in your description the object of thought and the product of thought. How do these ideas create a progression from one level to the next?

4. Describe the four characteristics of the van Hiele levels of thought. For each, reflect on why each characteristic might be important for teachers.

5. How would activities aimed at levels 0, 1, and 2 differ?

6. Select an activity from each of the levels, and do it (perhaps with a friend). Describe your experiences. If you were a child operating at the corresponding level, how would you describe your approach to the activity?

7. What can you do when the students in your classroom are at different van Hiele levels of thought?

8. The use of computers was discussed at each of the three van Hiele levels. Describe at least one computer activity appropriate for each level, and explain why each is targeted at that level rather than a higher or lower level. If possible, try some geometric software that you can access, and consider its usefulness in terms of the van Hiele levels of thought.

9. How can a teacher assess students in terms of general geometric growth or spatial sense? Assuming that the van Hiele theory is correct, why is it important to understand where your students are in terms of that theory?

## For Discussion and Exploration

1. How important should geometry be in the primary grades, the intermediate grades, and the middle school grades? Consider, at each of these levels, the competing demands of other areas of the mathematics curriculum, and suggest how many of the roughly 36 weeks of the year should be spent on geometry. What justification can you give for your position?

2. Examine the teacher's edition of a basal textbook at any grade level. Select any lesson on geometry. Remember that the authors of the pupil's book are restricted to the printed page by the very nature of books. Teachers are not so restricted. How would you teach this lesson so that it was a *good* informal geometry lesson? Your lesson should include a hands-on activity and have a problem-solving spirit.

3. At the elementary and middle school levels, computer software should be an important component of your instructional tools. If you are not familiar with the types of software discussed in this chapter, find out what you have access to, and play around to learn what each program can do. Consult the manual for teaching suggestions.

   If you are interested in grades K–4, you will want to see a program where students stamp shapes and manipulate them on the screen. A computer version of a geoboard is also important. If your interests are in the upper grades or middle school, become familiar with a dynamic geometry program. Such programs are the most significant tools available for upper-grades geometry.

   Seek out the software described in this chapter, or consult your school media specialist to find out what is available.

## Recommendations for Further Reading

### Highly Recommended

Bertheau, M. (1994). The most important thing is . . . *Teaching Children Mathematics, 1,* 112–115.

This short article reminds us that children's literature is a wonderful springboard for mathematics even if the book is not about mathematics. In addition to a nice idea for a good geometry lesson, the suggested discussion about shapes and what is important about them makes a good activity to begin moving children from level 0 to level 1 thinking. It is also a good assessment activity in the spirit of finding out what children know.

Del Grande, J. (1993). *Geometry and spatial sense: Addenda series, grades K–6.* Reston, VA: National Council of Teachers of Mathematics.

Geddes, D. (1992). *Geometry in the middle grades: Addenda series, grades 5–8.* Reston, VA: National Council of Teachers of Mathematics.

These two *Addenda* books are outstanding. Each provides useful perspective on geometry for the grade span and exciting activities. As with all the *Addenda Series* books, the activities are accompanied by discussions of how to "get into" the activity and develop the ideas with children. Blackline Masters are provided when appropriate. The K–6 activities are also found in each of the elementary grade-level *Addenda* books from NCTM.

National Council of Teachers of Mathematics. (1999). Geometry and geometric thinking [Focus Issue]. *Teaching Children Mathematics, 5*(6).

One of the best focus issues in recent years, this issue of *TCM* is full of practical ideas and useful perspectives on geometry for the early grades. Of special note is a wonderful article by Pierre van Hiele in which he describes a series of activities with a unique collection of shapes (the mosaic puzzle). This focus issue is a valuable resource for any teacher.

Wyat, K. W., Lawrence, A., & Foletta, G. M. (1998). *Geometry activities for middle school students with the Geometer's Sketchpad.* Emeryville, CA: Key Curriculum Press.

As noted in this chapter, dynamic geometry software belongs in the upper elementary and middle grades. This book of explorations for the *Geometer's Sketchpad* can be used to introduce students (and you) to the software even if you have never used *Sketchpad* before. The activities explore triangles, quadrilaterals, symmetry, transformations, and constructions. This book will convince you of the value of dynamic geometry in grades 4–8. (Also see Battista, 1998.)

## Other Suggestions

Battista, M. T. (1998). *Shape makers: Developing geometric reasoning with the Geometer's Sketchpad.* Emeryville, CA: Key Curriculum Press.

Bennett, D. (1999). *Exploring geometry with the Geometer's Sketchpad* (2nd ed.). Emeryville, CA: Key Curriculum Press.

Brahier, D. J., & Speer, W. R. (1997). Worthwhile tasks: Exploring mathematical connections through geometric solids. *Mathematics Teaching in the Middle School, 3,* 20–28.

Bruni, J. V., & Seidenstein, R. B. (1990). Geometric concepts and spatial sense. In J. N. Payne (Ed.), *Mathematics for the young child* (pp. 203–207). Reston, VA: National Council of Teachers of Mathematics.

Carroll, W. M. (1998). Middle school students' reasoning about geometric situations. *Mathematics Teaching in the Middle School, 3,* 398–403.

Clements, D. H. (1999). Geometric and spatial thinking in young children. In J. V. Copley (Ed.), *Mathematics in the early years* (pp. 66–79). Reston, VA: National Council of Teachers of Mathematics.

Confer, C. (1994). *Math by all means: Geometry, grade 2.* Sausalito, CA: Math Solutions Publications.

Crowley, M. L. (1987). The van Hiele model of the development of geometric thought. In M. M. Lindquist (Ed.), *Learning and teaching geometry, K–12* (pp. 1–16). Reston, VA: National Council of Teachers of Mathematics.

Dana, M. E. (1987). Geometry: A square deal for elementary teachers. In M. M. Lindquist (Ed.), *Learning and teaching geometry, K–12* (pp. 113–125). Reston, VA: National Council of Teachers of Mathematics.

de Villiers, M. D. (1999). *Rethinking proof with the Geometer's Sketchpad.* Emeryville, CA: Key Curriculum Press.

Enderson, M. C., & Manouchehri, A. (1998). Technology-based geometric explorations for the middle grades. In L. P. Leutzinger (Ed.), *Mathematics in the middle* (pp. 193–200). Reston, VA: National Council of Teachers of Mathematics.

Ernie, K. T. (1995). Mathematics and quilting. In P. A. House (Ed.), *Connecting mathematics across the curriculum* (pp. 170–176). Reston, VA: National Council of Teachers of Mathematics.

Flores, A. (1993). Pythagoras meets van Hiele. *School Science and Mathematics, 93,* 152–157.

Fosnaugh, L. S., & Harrell, M. E. (1996). Covering the plane with rep-tiles. *Mathematics Teaching in the Middle School, 1,* 666–670.

Fuys, D. J., & Liebov, A. K. (1993). Geometry and spatial sense. In R. J. Jensen (Ed.), *Research ideas for the classroom: Early childhood mathematics* (pp. 195–222). Old Tappan, NJ: Macmillan.

Geddes, D., & Fortunato, I. (1993). Geometry: Research and classroom activities. In D. T. Owens (Ed.), *Research ideas for the classroom: Middle grades mathematics* (pp. 199–222). Old Tappan, NJ: Macmillan.

Giganti, P., Jr., & Cittadino, M. J. (1990). The art of tessellation. *Arithmetic Teacher, 37*(7), 6–16.

Kleiman, G. M. (1995). Seeing and thinking mathematically in the middle school. In P. A. House (Ed.), *Connecting mathematics across the curriculum* (pp. 153–158). Reston, VA: National Council of Teachers of Mathematics.

Lehrer, R., & Curtis, C. L. (2000). Why are some solids perfect? Conjectures and experiments by third graders. *Teaching Children Mathematics, 6,* 324–329.

Malloy, C. (1999). Perimeter and area through the van Hiele model. *Mathematics Teaching in the Middle School, 5,* 87–90.

Manouchehri, A., Enderson, M. C., & Pugnucco, L. A. (1998). Exploring geometry with technology. *Mathematics Teaching in the Middle School, 3,* 436–442.

Mercer, S., & Henningsen, M. A. (1998). The pentomino project: Moving students from manipulatives to reasoning and thinking about mathematical ideas. In L. P. Leutzinger (Ed.), *Mathematics in the middle* (pp. 184–192). Reston, VA: National Council of Teachers of Mathematics.

Rectanus, C. (1994). *Math by all means: Geometry, grade 3.* Sausalito, CA: Math Solutions Publications.

Rubenstein, R. N., & Thompson, D. R. (1995). Making connections with transformations in grades K–8. In P. A. House (Ed.), *Connecting mathematics across the curriculum* (pp. 65–78). Reston, VA: National Council of Teachers of Mathematics.

Sandberg, S. E. (1998). A plethora of polyhedra. *Mathematics Teaching in the Middle School, 3,* 388–391.

Sconyers, J. M. (1995). Proof and the middle school mathematics student. *Mathematics Teaching in the Middle School, 1,* 516–518.

Senk, S. L., & Hirschhorn, D. B. (1990). Multiple approaches to geometry: Teaching similarity. *Mathematics Teacher, 83,* 274–280.

Serra, M. (1993). *Discovering geometry: An inductive approach.* Emeryville, CA: Key Curriculum Press.

Seymour, D., & Britton, J. (1989). *Introduction to tessellations.* White Plains, NY: Cuisenaire–Dale Seymour.

Shroyer, J., & Fitzgerald, W. (1986). *Mouse and elephant: Measuring growth.* Menlo Park, CA: AWL Supplemental.

Strutchens, M. E., & Blume, G. W. (1997). What do students know about geometry? In P. A. Kenney & E. A. Silver (Eds.), *Results from the sixth mathematics assessment of the National Assessment of Educational Progress* (pp. 165–193). Reston, VA: National Council of Teachers of Mathematics.

Teppo, A. R. (1991). Van Hiele levels of geometric thought revisited. *Mathematics Teacher, 84,* 210–221.

Walter, M. J. (1970). *Boxes, squares, and other things.* Reston, VA: National Council of Teachers of Mathematics.

Winter, M. J., Lappan, G., Phillips, E., & Fitzgerald, W. (1986). *Middle grades mathematics project: Spatial visualization.* Menlo Park, CA: AWL Supplemental.

# Chapter 18

# Exploring Concepts of Probability and Data Analysis

The related topics of probability and data analysis represent two of the most prominent uses of mathematics in our everyday lives. We hear about the possibility of contracting a particular disease, having twins, winning the lottery, or living to be 100. Simulations of complex situations are frequently based on simple probabilities used in the design of highways, storm sewers, medical treatments, sales promotions, and spacecraft. Graphs and statistics bombard the public in advertising, opinion polls, reliability estimates, population trends, health risks, and the progress of students in schools and schools in school systems, to name only a few areas.

To deal with this information, students should have ample opportunity throughout their school years to have informal yet meaningful experiences with the basic concepts involved. The emphasis from the primary level into high school should be placed on activities leading to intuitive understanding and conceptual knowledge rather than computations and formulas.

## BIG Ideas

1. The possible occurrence of a future event, compared to the chance of its nonoccurrence, can be characterized as impossible, less likely, equally likely, more likely, or certain. To determine the likelihood of an event along this continuum is to determine the probability of its happening.

2. Data sets can be analyzed in various ways to provide a sense of the shape of the data, including how spread out they are (range, variance) and how they are centered (mean, median, mode).

3. The same set of objects can be considered in different ways, leading to the creation of different classifications. A single object can belong to more than one class.

4. Data are organized so as to help with the making of decisions or inferences or the development of new ideas about situations or the populations from which the data are drawn.

## PROBABILITY AND DATA ANALYSIS IN SCHOOLS

A number of factors have led to an increase in the quantity and quality of probability and data analysis instruction in elementary and middle schools in recent years:

Increased awareness of the importance of probability and data analysis concepts and methods

An emphasis on experimental or simulation approaches to probability (instead of rules and formulas)

The use of simplified yet powerful technology to describe data visually without complicated procedures

The use of calculators and computers, especially graphing calculators, to conduct thousands of random trials of experiments, from flipping coins to simulating baseball batting performances; to do the tedious work of constructing graphs; and to perform computations on large sets of numbers almost instantly

NCTM focused attention on the topics of probability and statistics in 1989 when it included standards for all grades addressing these topics specifically. With *Principles and Standards for School Mathematics*, NCTM expands the emphasis on these topics by making Data Analysis and Probability one of the five content standards for all grades. The term *data analysis* is actually broader than *statistics*. Data analysis refers to the collection and organization of data so that the information can be used to answer questions about the data or supply information about the population from which the data were taken. Statistics are numbers that describe data, such as *mean* and *range*. So even kindergarten children can be involved in gathering data and making graphs to describe data—doing data analysis. As children move through school, the methods of data analysis become more sophisticated with new graphing techniques and the use of statistics.

Similarly, concepts of chance can be developed long before sophisticated ideas of probability are introduced. *Principles and Standards* recognizes that children need to begin these experiences in the earliest grades so that an intuitive understanding of probability is developed on which more traditional methods can be built.

# INTRODUCTION TO PROBABILITY

Let's first experiment with some basic ideas of probability before considering how to help children develop these ideas.

## Two Experiments

Consider answering the following two questions by actually performing the experiments enough times to make a reasonable guess at the results.

### TOSSING A CUP

Toss a small "portion" cup or other small cup once or twice, letting it land on the floor. Notice that there are three possible ways for the cup to land: upside down, right side up, or on its side. If the cup were tossed this way 100 times, about how many times do you think it would land in each position?

### FLIPPING TWO COINS

If you were to flip one coin 100 times, you would expect that it would come up heads about as many times as tails. If two coins were tossed 100 times, about how many times do you think that they would both come up heads?

A quick way to conduct these experiments is to work in groups. If ten people each do ten trials and pool their data, the time needed for 100 trials is not long. Twenty cups can be placed on a tray and tossed at one time. Even if you do not actually do the experiments, jot down your predictions now before reading on.

## Theoretical Versus Experimental Probability

In the cup toss, there is no practical way to determine the results before you start. However, once you had results for 100 flips, you would undoubtedly feel more confident in predicting the results of the next 100 flips. If you gathered data on that same cup for 1000 trials, you would feel even more confident. Say that your cup lands on its side 78 times out of 100. You might choose a round figure of 75 or 80 for the 100 tosses. If, after 200 flips, there were 163 sideways landings, you would feel even more confident of the 4-out-of-5 ratio and predict about 800 sideways landings for 1000 tosses. The more flips that are made, the more confident you become. You have determined an *experimental probability* of $\frac{4}{5}$ or 80 percent for the cup to land on its side. It is experimental because it is based on the results of an experiment rather than a theoretical analysis of the cup.

In a one-coin toss, the prediction of about 50 percent heads could confidently be made before you flipped the coin, based on your understanding of a fair coin. Your prediction for two heads in the two-coin version may be more difficult. It is quite common for people to observe that there are three types of outcomes: both heads, both tails, and one of each; so they predict that two heads will come up about one-third of the time. (What did you predict?) The prediction is based on their analysis of the experiment, not on experimental results. After conducting the experiment, however, they are surprised to find that two heads come up only about one-fourth of the time. This experience might cause them to return to their original analysis and look for an error in their thinking.

There is only one way for two heads to occur and one way for two tails to occur, but there are *two* ways that a head and a tail could result: Either the first coin is heads and the second tails, or vice versa. As shown in Figure 18.1, that makes a total of four possible outcomes, not three. The assumption that each outcome is equally likely was correct. Therefore, the correct probability of two heads is 1 out of 4, or $\frac{1}{4}$, not $\frac{1}{3}$. This *theoretical probability* is based on a logical analysis of the experiment, not on experimental results.

| First Coin | Second Coin |
|---|---|
| Head | Head |
| Head | Tail |
| Tail | Head |
| Tail | Tail |

**Figure 18.1** **Four possible outcomes of flipping two coins.**

When we talk about probabilities, we are assigning some measure of chance to an experiment. An *experiment* is any activity that has two or more clearly discernible results or *outcomes*. Both tossing the cup and tossing the two coins were experiments. Observing tomorrow's weather and shooting ten free throws on the basketball court are also experiments. The collection of all outcomes is generally referred to as the *sample space*. As you have already seen, the toss of two coins has four outcomes in the sample space. Tomorrow's weather can be described in many ways: precipitation or no precipitation, or dry, rain, sleet, or snow. An *event* is any subset of the outcomes or any subset of the sample space. For the two-coin experiment, the event we were concerned with was getting two heads. For the free-throw shoot, we might be interested in the event of getting five or more baskets out of the ten tosses.

When all possible outcomes of a simple experiment are equally likely, the *theoretical probability* of an event is

$$\frac{\text{Number of outcomes in the event}}{\text{Number of possible outcomes}}$$

In real-world situations, outcomes are often not equally likely, as they are for coin flips or dice rolls. The cup-tossing experiment, though not a practical situation, is "muddy" and real. The outcomes are difficult to predict, and they are not equally likely. In situations like these, we can determine the observed relative frequency of the event by performing the experiment a lot of times. The *relative frequency* of an event is

$$\frac{\text{Number of observed occurrences of the event}}{\text{Total number of trials}}$$

It should be clear that the relative frequency is not a good predictor of the chance of the event's happening unless the number of trials is very large. The *experimental probability* of an event is the ratio that the relative frequency approaches as the number of trials gets infinitely large. Because it is impossible to perform an infinite number of trials, we must be satisfied with some large number of trials. The more trials, the more confident we might be that the experimental probability is close to the actual probability.

## Implications for Instruction

There are many reasons why an experimental approach to probability, actually conducting experiments and examining outcomes, is important in the classroom.

- It is significantly more intuitive. Results begin to make sense and do not result from some abstract rule.
- It eliminates guessing at probabilities and wondering, "Did I get it right?" Counting or trying to determine the number of elements in a sample space can be very difficult without some intuitive background information.
- It provides an experiential background for examining the theoretical model. When you begin to sense that the probability of two heads is $\frac{1}{4}$ instead of $\frac{1}{3}$, the analysis in Figure 18.1 seems more reasonable.

- It helps students see how the ratio of a particular outcome to the total number of trials begins to converge to (get closer and closer to) a fixed number. For an infinite number of trials, the relative frequency and theoretical probability would be the same.
- It develops an appreciation for a simulation approach to solving problems. Many real-world problems are actually solved by conducting experiments or simulations.
- It is a lot more fun and interesting! Even searching for a correct explanation in the theoretical model is more interesting.

Whenever possible, then, try to use an experimental approach in the classroom. If a theoretical analysis (such as with the two-coin experiment) is possible, it should also be examined, and the results should be compared. Rather than correcting a student error in an initial analysis, we can let experimental results guide and correct student thinking.

# DEVELOPING PROBABILITY CONCEPTS

Informal ideas about chance and probability, when developed early, provide necessary background for concepts to be constructed at the middle and secondary levels.

## Early Concepts of Chance

Children in kindergarten and the primary grades need to develop an intuitive concept of chance: the idea that some events, when compared with others, have a better or worse likelihood or an approximately equal likelihood of happening.

Many young children believe that an event will happen "because it's my favorite color" or "because it's lucky" or "because it did it that way last time." Many games such as CandyLand or Chutes and Ladders are very exciting for young children who do not comprehend that the outcomes are entirely random. When they finally learn that they have no control over the outcome, children begin to look for other games where there is some element of player determination.

---

**ACTIVITY**

### 18.1 Is It Likely?

**Ask students to judge various events as *certain*, *impossible*, or *possible* ("might happen"). Consider these examples:**

It will rain tomorrow.

Drop a rock in water, and it will sink.

Trees will talk to us in the afternoon.

The sun will rise tomorrow morning.

Three students will be absent tomorrow.

George will go to bed before 8:30 tonight.

You will have two birthdays this year.

Children describe or make up events that are certain, impossible, or possible. For each event, they should justify their estimate of likelihood.

## ACTIVITY

### 18.2 Who Will Win?

Play simple games where the chance of one side's winning can be controlled. Before playing the games, have students predict who will win and why. Afterward, discuss why they think things turned out as they did. For example, the hockey game in Figure 18.2 starts with a counter in the center. Two players take turns spinning a spinner. The counter moves one space toward the goal that comes up on the spinner. Play the game with different spinners. As a variation, let students choose a spinner on each turn. Ask them to explain their choices.

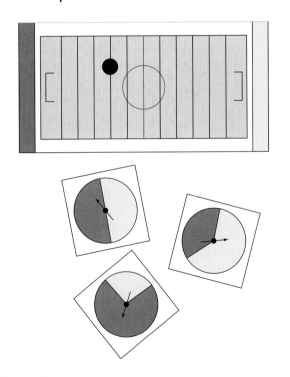

**Figure 18.2** **A simple game of chance played with different spinners helps young children with basic concepts of chance.**

## ACTIVITY

### 18.3 Predictions

Have students make predictions about the outcomes of simple experiments using the terms *more, less, all,* and *none.* For example, show children how many

each of red and yellow cubes you have in a bag. You will let children draw cubes one at a time and put them back each time. "If we do this ten times, will there be more reds, less reds, all reds, or no reds?" Change the number of each color cube, and repeat. The same activity can be done by spinning spinners, rolling dice, drawing cards, or using any random device that you can adjust. Include situations that are certain, such as placing all yellow cubes in the bag.

## Determining Probabilities for Simple Events

From a basic understanding that one event can be more or less likely than another, students can begin to predict specific ratios of outcomes of simple events. Before students have worked with part-to-whole ratios, use language such as "65 out of 100" instead of using fractions. A discussion of reasons for students' predictions is always important. The experiment should then be conducted and the results compared with expected outcomes.

Figure 18.3 (p. 356) illustrates a number of simple random devices that can be used for experiments. To get large numbers, let groups of students conduct the same experiment and combine results. Ask students to notice that the results for smaller numbers of trials are all different and that they are frequently quite different from what might be expected.

Occasionally, have students list the outcomes of their experiments in a row, to show the order of the outcomes. Interestingly, truly random events do not alternate. They frequently appear in clusters or runs. If eight odd numbers in a row come up on a die roll, the chance remains exactly $\frac{1}{2}$ (1 out of 2) that the next roll will be odd. The die has no memory. The previous roll of a die cannot affect the next roll. It is very unlikely that even numbers will come up seven times in a row (1 chance in 128). However, if that does happen, the chance for an even number on the next roll is still $\frac{1}{2}$.

## Experiments with Two or More Independent Events

Flipping two coins and observing the result of each is an example of an experiment with two independent events. The flip of one coin has no effect on the other. The events are *independent*. Another example is that of drawing a card and spinning a spinner. Many interesting experiments involve two or more separate, independent events.

Determining the experimental probability of compound events is no different than for simple events. The experiment is performed numerous times, and the number of favorable results is compared to the total trials as before. The challenge comes in trying to reconcile experimental results with theoretical ones.

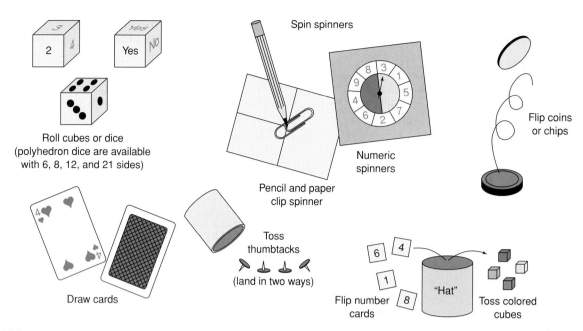

**Figure 18.3**   **There are many simple ways to produce random outcomes.**

**Sum of Two Dice**

| 2 | ~~HH~~ I |
| 3 | ~~HH~~ ~~HH~~ |
| 4 | ~~HH~~ ~~HH~~ ~~HH~~ IIII |
| 5 | ~~HH~~ ~~HH~~ ~~HH~~ IIII |
| 6 | ~~HH~~ ~~HH~~ ~~HH~~ ~~HH~~ ~~HH~~ IIII |
| 7 | ~~HH~~ ~~HH~~ ~~HH~~ ~~HH~~ ~~HH~~ ~~HH~~ ~~HH~~ IIII |
| 8 | ~~HH~~ ~~HH~~ ~~HH~~ ~~HH~~ ~~HH~~ ~~HH~~ IIII |
| 9 | ~~HH~~ ~~HH~~ ~~HH~~ ~~HH~~ ~~HH~~ |
| 10 | ~~HH~~ ~~HH~~ ~~HH~~ I |
| 11 | ~~HH~~ II |
| 12 | ~~HH~~ ~~HH~~ |

(a)

**Red Die**

|  | 1 | 2 | 3 | 4 | 5 | 6 |
|---|---|---|---|---|---|---|
| **1** | ~~HH~~ | ~~HH~~ I | ~~HH~~ III | ~~HH~~ II | ~~HH~~ III | ~~HH~~ II |
| **2** | ~~HH~~ IIII | ~~HH~~ III | ~~HH~~ I | ~~HH~~ ~~HH~~ | ~~HH~~ II | ~~HH~~ II |
| **3** | ~~HH~~ ~~HH~~ | ~~HH~~ | ~~HH~~ II | ~~HH~~ II | ~~HH~~ ~~HH~~ II | ~~HH~~ IIII |
| **4** | ~~HH~~ II | ~~HH~~ ~~HH~~ II | ~~HH~~ III | ~~HH~~ ~~HH~~ | ~~HH~~ ~~HH~~ II | ~~HH~~ III |
| **5** | ~~HH~~ IIII | ~~HH~~ ~~HH~~ II | ~~HH~~ ~~HH~~ | ~~HH~~ III | ~~HH~~ | ~~HH~~ IIII |
| **6** | ~~HH~~ III | ~~HH~~ IIII | ~~HH~~ III | ~~HH~~ II | ~~HH~~ III | ~~HH~~ III |

(Green Die — vertical label on left)

There are six ways to get 7.

(b)

**Figure 18.4**   **Tallies can account only for the total (a) or keep track of the individual dice (b).**

Suppose that a class is conducting an experiment to determine the probability of rolling a 7 with two dice. They might tally their results in a chart showing each sum from 2 to 12 as a single event, as in part (a) of Figure 18.4.

The results of their experiment will show clearly that these events are not equally likely and that in fact the sum of 7 has the best chance of occurring. To explain this, they might look for the combinations that make 7: 1 and 6, 2 and 5, and 3 and 4. But there are also three combinations for 8. It seems as though 8 should be just as likely as 7, and yet it is not.

Now suppose that the experiment is repeated. This time, for the sake of clarity, suggest that students roll two different-colored dice and that they keep the tallies in a chart like the one in part (b) of Figure 18.4.

The results of a large number of dice rolls indicate what one would expect, namely, that all 36 cells of this chart are equally likely. But there are more cells with a sum of 7 than any other number. Therefore, students were really looking for the event that consists of any of the six ways, not three ways, that two dice can add to 7. There are six outcomes in the desired event out of a total of 36, for a probability of $\frac{6}{36}$, or $\frac{1}{6}$.

When investigating the theoretical probability of a compound event, it is helpful to use a chart or diagram that keeps the two independent events separate and illustrates the combinations. The matrix in Figure 18.4(b) is one good suggestion when there are only two events. A tree diagram (Figure 18.5) is another method that can be used with any number of events.

┌─ **A**CTIVITY ─

## 18.4 Compound Outcomes

The following are examples of compound events composed of independent events.

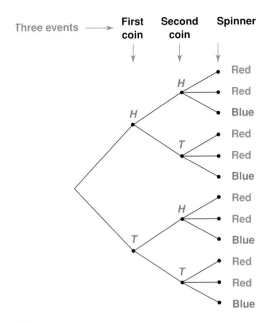

**Figure 18.5** **A tree diagram showing all possible outcomes for two coins and a spinner that is $\frac{2}{3}$ red.**

Rolling an even sum with two dice

Spinning blue and flipping a cup on end

Getting two blues out of three spins (depends on spinner)

Having a tack or a cup land up if each is tossed once

Getting *at least* two heads from a toss of four coins

Have students first make and defend a prediction of the probability of the event. Then they should conduct an experiment with a large number of trials, comparing their results to their predicted probabilities. Finally, they should reconcile differences. Where appropriate, students can try to determine the theoretical probability as part of their final analysis of the experiment.

Words and phrases such as *and, or, at least,* and *no more than* can also cause children some trouble. Of special note is the word *or,* since its everyday usage is generally not the same as its strict logical use in mathematics. In mathematics, *or* includes the case of *both.* So in the tack-and-cup example, the event includes tack up, cup up, and *both* tack *and* cup up.

# Theoretical Probabilities with an Area Model

One way to determine the theoretical probability of a compound event is to list all possible outcomes and count those that are favorable, that is, those that make up the event. This is useful and intuitive as a first approach. However, it has some limitations. First, what if the events are not all equally

likely? For example, the spinner may be only $\frac{1}{4}$ blue. Second, it is difficult to move from that approach to even slightly more sophisticated methods. An area model approach has been used successfully with fifth-grade students and is quite helpful for some reasonably difficult problems.

Suppose that after many experiences, you have decided that your cup lands on its side 82 percent of the time. The experiment is to toss the cup and then draw a card from a deck. What is the probability that the cup will land on its side *and* you will draw a spade? Draw a square to represent one whole. First partition the square to represent the cup toss, 82 percent and 18 percent, as in Figure 18.6(a). Now partition the square in the other direction to represent the four equal card suits. As shown in Figure 18.6(b), one region is the proportion of time that both events, sideways and spades, happen. The area of this region is $\frac{1}{4}$ of 82 percent, or 20.5 percent.

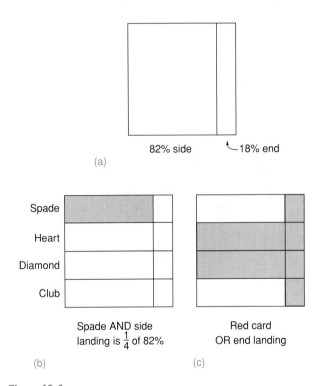

**Figure 18.6** **An area model for determining probabilities.**

You can use the same drawing to determine the probability of other events in the same experiment. For example, what is the probability of the cup landing on either end *or* drawing a red card? As shown in Figure 18.6(c), half of the area of the square corresponds to drawing a red card. This section includes the case of drawing a red card *and* an end landing. The other half of the 18 percent end landings happen when a red card is not drawn. Half of 18 percent is 9 percent of the area. The total area for a red card *or* an end landing is 59 percent.

The area approach is easy for students to use and understand for experiments involving two independent events when the probability of each is known. For more than two independent events, further subdivision of each region is required but is still quite reasonable. The use of *and* and *or* connectives is easily dealt with. It is quite clear to students, without memorization of formulas, how probabilities should be combined.

# Exploring Dependent Events

The next level of difficulty occurs when the probability of one event depends on the result of the first. For example, suppose that there are two identical boxes. In one box is a dollar bill and two counterfeit bills. In the other box is one of each. You may choose one box and from that box select one bill without looking. What are your chances of getting a genuine dollar? Here there are two events: selecting a box and selecting a bill. The probability of getting a dollar in the second event depends on which box is chosen in the first event. These events are *dependent,* not independent.

As another example, suppose that you are a prisoner in a faraway land. The king has pity on you and gives you a chance to leave. He shows you the maze in Figure 18.7. At the start and at each fork in the path, you must spin the spinner and follow the path that it points to. You may request that the key to freedom be placed in one of the two rooms. In which room should you place the key to have the best chance of freedom? Notice that the probability of ending the maze in any one room is dependent on the result of the first spin.

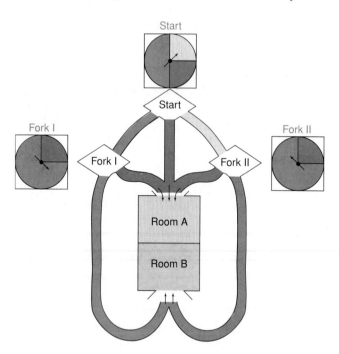

**Figure 18.7**   **Should you place your key to freedom in Room A or Room B? At each fork, the spinner determines your path.**

Either of these two problems could be solved with an experimental approach, a simulation. A second approach to both problems is to use the area model to determine the theoretical probabilities. An area model solution to the prisoner problem is shown in Figure 18.8. How would the area model for the prisoner problem be different if the spinner at Fork II were a $\frac{1}{3}$ versus $\frac{2}{3}$ spinner?

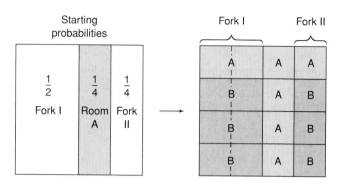

At Fork I, $\frac{3}{4}$ of the time you will go to Room B. (Note: Not $\frac{3}{4}$ of the square but $\frac{3}{4}$ of the times you go to Fork I.)

At Fork II, $\frac{3}{4}$ of these times (or $\frac{3}{16}$ of total time) you will go to Room B.

Therefore, you will end up in Room A $\frac{7}{16}$ of the time and Room B $\frac{9}{16}$ of the time.

**Figure 18.8**   **Using the area model to solve the maze problem.**

It would be good to stop at this point and try the area approach for the problem of the counterfeit bills. (The chance of getting a dollar is $\frac{5}{12}$.)

The area model will not solve all probability problems. However, it fits very well into a developmental approach to the subject because it is conceptual, it is based on existing knowledge of fractions, and more symbolic approaches can be derived from it. Figure 18.9 shows a tree diagram for the same problem, with the probability of each path of the tree written in. After some experience with probability situations, the tree diagram model is probably easier to use and adapts to a wider range of situations. You should be able to match up each branch of the tree diagram in Figure 18.9 with a section of the square in Figure 18.8. Use the area model to explain why the probability for each complete branch of the tree is determined by multiplying the probabilities along the branch.

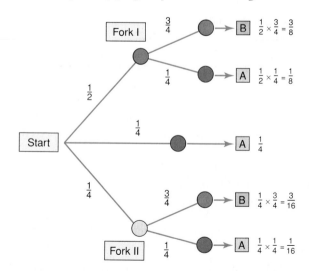

**Figure 18.9**   **A tree diagram is another way to model the outcomes of two or more dependent events.**

# SIMULATIONS

*Simulation* is a technique used for answering real-world questions or making decisions in complex situations where an element of chance is involved. To see what is likely to happen in the real event, a model must be designed that has the same probabilities as the real situation. For example, in designing a rocket, a large number of related systems all have some chance of failure. Various combinations of failures might cause serious problems with the rocket. Knowing the probability of serious failures will help determine if redesign or backup systems are required. It is not reasonable to make repeated tests of the actual rocket. Instead, a model that simulates all of the chance situations is designed and run repeatedly, most likely with the help of a computer. The computer model can simulate hundreds or even thousands of flights, and an estimate of the chance of failure can be made.

Many real-world situations lend themselves to simulation analysis. In a business venture, the probability of selling a product might depend on a variety of chance factors, some of which can be controlled or changed and others not. Will advertising help? How likely is it that a competitor will enter the market? Should high-cost materials be used? What location provides the best chance of sales? If a reasonable model can be set up that simulates these factors, an experiment can be run before actually entering into the venture to determine the best choices.

The following problem and model are adapted from the excellent materials developed by the Quantitative Literacy Project (Gnanadesikan, Schaeffer, & Swift, 1987). In Figure 18.10, a diagram shows water pipes for a pumping system connecting A to B. The five pumps are aging, and it is estimated that at any given time, the probability of pump failure is $\frac{1}{2}$. If a pump fails, water cannot pass that station. For example, if pumps 1, 2, and 5 fail, water can flow only through 4 and 3. Consider the following questions that might well be asked about such a system:

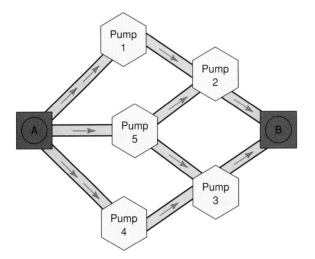

**Figure 18.10**   **Each of these five pumps has a 50 percent chance of failure. What is the probability that some path from A to B is working?**

What is the probability that water will flow at any time?

On the average, about how many stations need repair at any time?

What is the probability that the 1–2 path is working at any time?

For any simulation, a series of steps or a model can serve as a useful guide.

1. *Identify key components and assumptions of the problem.* The key component in the water problem is the condition of a pump. Each pump is either working or not. The assumption is that the probability that a pump is working is $\frac{1}{2}$.

2. *Select a random device for the key components.* Any random device can be selected that has outcomes with the same probability as the key component—in this case, the pumps. Here a simple choice might be tossing a coin, with heads representing a working pump.

3. *Define a trial.* A *trial* consists of simulating a series of key components until the situation has been completely modeled one time. In this problem, a trial could consist of tossing a coin five times, each toss representing a different pump.

4. *Conduct a large number of trials, and record the information.* For this problem, it would be good to keep the record of heads and tails in groups of five because each set of five is one trial and represents all of the pumps.

5. *Use the data to draw conclusions.* There are four possible paths for the water, each flowing through two of the five pumps. As they are numbered in the drawing, if any one of the pairs 1–2, 5–2, 5–3, and 4–3 is open, it makes no difference whether the other pumps are working. By counting the trials in which at least one of these four pairs of coins both came up heads, we can estimate the probability of water flowing. To answer the second question, the number of tails per trial can be averaged. How would you answer the third question concerning the 1–2 path's being open?

Steps 4 and 5 are the same as solving a probability problem by experimental means. The interesting problem-solving aspects of simulation activities are in the first three steps, where the real-world situation is translated into a model. Translation of real-world information into models is the essence of applied mathematics.

Here are a few more examples of problems that can be solved by simulation and are easy enough to be tackled by middle school students.

---

In a true-or-false test, what is the probability of getting 7 out of 10 questions correct by guessing alone? (*Key component:* answering a question. *Assumption:* Chance of getting it correct is $\frac{1}{2}$.) What if the test were multiple-choice with 4 choices?

In a group of five people, what is the chance that two were born in the same month? (*Key component:* month of birth. *Assumption:* All 12 months are equally likely.)

Casey's batting average is .350. What is the chance he will go hitless in a complete nine-inning game? (*Key component:* getting a hit. *Assumptions:* Probability of a hit for each at-bat is .35. Casey will get to bat four times in the average game.)

Krunch-a-Munch cereal packs one of five games in each box. About how many boxes should you expect to buy before you get a complete set? (*Key component:* getting one game. *Assumption:* Each game has a $\frac{1}{5}$ chance. *Trial:* Use a $\frac{1}{5}$ random device repeatedly until all five outcomes appear; the average length of a trial answers the question.) What is the chance of getting a set in eight or fewer boxes?

 **TECHNOLOGY NOTE**

Truly random events often occur in unexpected groups; a fair coin may turn up heads five times in a row. A 100-year flood may hit a town twice in ten years. Hands-on random devices such as spinners, dice, or cubes drawn from a bag give students an intuitive feel for the imperfect distribution of randomness. Students believe in the unbiased outcomes of these devices. The downside is that the use of spinners and bags of cubes requires a lot of time to produce a large number of trials and keep track of the results. This is where technology can help enormously.

Electronic devices, including some relatively simple calculators and graphing calculators, are designed to produce random outcomes at the press of a button. Computer software is available that flips coins, spins spinners, or draws numbers from a hat. Calculators produce random numbers that can then be interpreted in terms of the desired device. As long as students accept the results generated by the technology as truly random or equivalent to the hands-on device, they offer significant advantages for performing experiments.

## Probability Software

Software for exploring probability concepts can generally be described as computer-animated random devices. Graphics show students the coins being flipped or the spinner being spun. Most allow different speeds. In a slow version, students may watch each spin of a spinner or coin flip. Faster

speeds show the recording of each trial but omit the graphics. An even quicker mode simply shows the cumulative results. The number of trials can be set by the user. Volume 1 of *MathKeys: Unlocking Probability* (MECC, 1995c) includes options for a single coin, a single die, a choice of six different two-color spinners, or two colors of marbles drawn from a bag. In Volume 2, compound experiments using multiple spinners, dice, or marble bags can be designed and run. As is typical of these programs, results are not only tallied but also shown on a bar graph for a visual display of outcome ratios. Both volumes include some interesting games that are problematic and permit students to apply their understanding of probability.

*The Probability Constructor* (LOGAL, 1994b), designed for students at the middle grades, is more sophisticated and offers many more options. Within each of six devices, the probability of the outcomes is adjustable. An area model allows for the exploration of compound events, and outcomes can be displayed in a variety of ways. The support materials include a complete series of lessons and teacher notes that are quite well done.

Even with only one computer in the room, a good probability program is a worthwhile investment.

## Probability with Calculators

Many relatively simple calculators include a key that will produce a random number. Examples are the Casio FX-55, the TI-32 Explorer Plus, and of course any graphing calculator. Usually, the random numbers generated are between 0 and 1. Students who are going to use these random number generators will need some direction in using them to their advantage. Each number generated will likely have 8 or more decimal places. A list of five numbers might look like this:

    0.8904433368
    0.0232028877
    0.1669322714
    0.1841957303
    0.5523714952

How could a list of decimals like this replace flipping a coin or spinning a spinner? Suppose each was multiplied by 2. The results would be between 0 and 2. If you ignore the decimal part, you would have a series of zeros and ones that could stand for heads and tails, boys and girls, true and false, or any other pair of equally likely outcomes. For three outcomes, the same as a $\frac{1}{4}$-$\frac{1}{4}$-$\frac{1}{2}$ spinner, you might decide to look at the first two digits of the number and assign values from 0 to 24 and 25 to 49 to the two quarter portions and values 50 to 99 for the one-half portion. Alternatively, each number could be multiplied by 4, the decimal part ignored, resulting in random numbers 0, 1, 2, and 3. These could then be assigned to the desired outcomes. In effect, random numbers can simulate any simple random device.

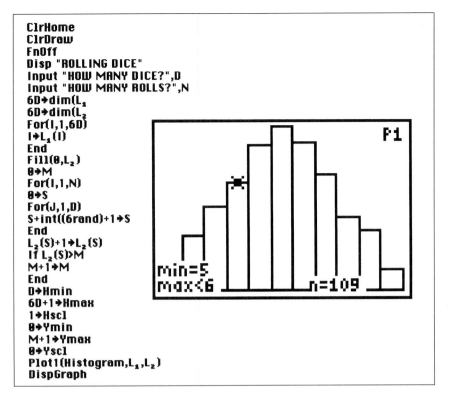

```
ClrHome
ClrDraw
FnOff
Disp "ROLLING DICE"
Input "HOW MANY DICE?",D
Input "HOW MANY ROLLS?",N
6D→dim(L₁
6D→dim(L₂
For(I,1,6D)
I→L₁(I)
End
Fill(0,L₂)
0→M
For(I,1,N)
0→S
For(J,1,D)
S+int((6rand)+1→S
End
L₂(S)+1→L₂(S)
If L₂(S)>M
M+1→M
End
D→Hmin
6D+1→Hmax
1→Hscl
0→Ymin
M+1→Ymax
0→Yscl
Plot1(Histogram,L₁,L₂)
DispGraph
```

**Figure 18.11**   **This TI-82 program can be used to simulate thousands of dice rolls and accumulate the results.**

With graphing calculators, the random number generator can be used inside of a simple program that produces the numbers and stores them in a list. The list can then be displayed graphically. The program in Figure 18.11 is for a TI-82 or TI-83 calculator. It will "roll" as many dice as you request. At the end of the program, a histogram displays the totals for each sum. With the TRACE feature, the value for each bar in the graph is displayed. The figure shows the result of rolling two dice 1000 times. It took about $2\frac{1}{2}$ minutes to run the program and produce the graph. (Computer programs produce the result almost instantly.) The TI-73 calculator designed for middle school has a built-in coin and dice function.

Although computer programs are much faster, allow for more variation, and include attractive graphics, the advantage of calculator approaches is availability. Every student can design and run an experiment individually. When computers are at a premium, this is a significant advantage. ■

# GATHERING DATA TO ANSWER QUESTIONS

The first bullet in the Data Analysis and Probability standard of *Principles and Standards* says that students should "formulate

questions that can be addressed with data and collect, organize, and display relevant data to answer them" (NCTM, 2000, p. 48). The significant feature of this statement that has been missing in the past is that data collection should be for a purpose, to answer a question, just as in the real world. At all grades, the analysis of data should have the agenda of adding information about some aspect of our world. This is what political pollsters, advertising agencies, market researchers, census takers, wildlife managers, and hosts of others do: gather data to answer questions. This means that the process of data analysis should begin with questions. Preferably, these questions should be about things of interest to the students.

When students formulate the questions they want to ask, the data they gather become more and more meaningful. How they organize the data and the techniques for analyzing them have a purpose. For example, one class of students gathered data concerning which cafeteria foods were most often thrown in the garbage. As a result of these efforts, certain items were removed from the regular menu. The activity illustrated to students the power of organized data, and it helped them get food that they liked better.

## Ideas for Questions and Data

Often the need to gather data will come from the class naturally in the course of discussion or from questions arising in other content areas. Science, of course, is full of measurements and thus abounds in data requiring analysis. Social studies is also full of opportunities to pose questions requiring data analysis. The next few sections suggest some additional ideas.

## Classroom Questions

Young children can learn about themselves, their families and pets, the animals in their neighborhood, measures such as arm span or time to get to school, their likes and dislikes, and so on. At the K–2 level, the easiest questions to deal with are those that can be answered by each class member's contributing one piece of data. When there are lots of possibilities, suggest that students restrict the number of choices. Here are a few ideas:

> *Favorites:* TV shows, fruit, season of the year, color, football team, pet, ice cream flavor
>
> *Numbers:* Number of pets, sisters, or brothers; hours watching TV or hours of sleep; birthdays (month or day of month); bedtime
>
> *Measures:* Height, arm span, area of foot, long-jump distance, letters in name, time to button a sweater, daily temperature, weather, shadow length, rainfall

## Beyond the Classroom

As children get older, they can begin to think about various populations and differences between them. For example, how are fifth graders similar or different from middle school students? Students might examine questions concerning boys versus girls, adults or teachers versus students, or categories of workers or college graduates. These situations involve issues of sampling and making generalizations and comparisons.

The news media frequently report what the latest survey reveals about the "typical" family, business, teenager, drug addict, or member of some other population or group. How did they survey everyone, and what does "typical" mean? Do the students in your classroom believe they are typical? Are they like those in the next classroom or the next grade level? To describe a group usually involves asking a variety of questions, and deciding on which questions to ask is not nearly as easy as it may sound. How many questions should be asked? Should they be multiple-choice? If not, how will the answers be handled? To describe a large group (say, the school), how many people should be surveyed? How should they be selected? Students should be involved in making these decisions as they formulate their questions and design surveys.

## Other Sources of Information

Do not restrict students from asking questions that can be answered by gathering the data themselves. Gathering data can mean using data that have been collected by others. For example, newspapers, almanacs, sports record books, maps, and various government publications are sources of data that may be used to answer student questions. Students may be interested in facts about another country as a result of a social studies unit. Olympic records in various events over the years or data related to space flight are other examples of topics around which student questions may be formulated. For these and hundreds of other questions, data can be found on the World Wide Web. (See Chapter 24.)

## The Shape of Data

A big conceptual idea in data analysis can be referred to as the *shape of data:* a sense of how data are spread or grouped, what characteristics they have, and what they tell us in a global way about the population from which they are taken.

Each of the graphical techniques we will discuss gives a visual picture of the shape of data. Students should learn that different graphs provide different snapshots of the data. For the particular question being answered, the choice of graphs is made around the notion of the shape of the data.

Statistical techniques provide a numeric picture of the shape of the data. The numbers can be thought of as measures of the shape. For example, the median tells us where the center is. The range tells about the spread of the data.

The better we can answer the question "What is the shape of the data?" the better we can answer the question that caused the data to be gathered in the first place.

# CLASSIFICATION AND DATA ANALYSIS

Classification involves making decisions about how to categorize things. This basic activity is fundamental to data analysis. In order to formulate questions and decide how to represent data that have been gathered, decisions must be made about how things might be categorized. Farm animals, for example, might be grouped by number of legs; by type of product they provide; by those that work, provide food, or are pets; by size or color; by the type of food they eat; and so on. Each of these groupings is based on a different attribute of the animals.

Young children need experiences with categorizing things in different ways in order to learn to make sense of real-world data. Attribute activities are explicitly designed to develop this flexible reasoning about the characteristics of data.

## Attribute Materials

*Attribute materials* are sets of objects that lend themselves to being sorted and classified in different ways. *Unstructured* attribute materials include such things as seashells, leaves, the children themselves, or the set of the children's shoes. The *attributes* are the ways that the materials can be sorted. For example, hair color, height, and gender are attributes of children. Each attribute has a number of different *values:* for example, blond, brown, or red (for the attribute of hair color); tall or short (for height); male or female (for gender).

A *structured* set of attribute pieces has exactly one piece for every possible combination of values for each attribute. For example, several commercial sets of plastic attribute materials have four attributes: color (red, yellow, blue), shape (circle, triangle, rectangle, square, hexagon), size (big, little), and thickness (thick, thin). In the set just described, there is exactly one large, thin, red triangle, just as there is one each of all other combinations. The specific values, number of values, or number of attributes that a set may have is not important. Three teacher-made sets of structured attribute pieces are illustrated in Figure 18.12.

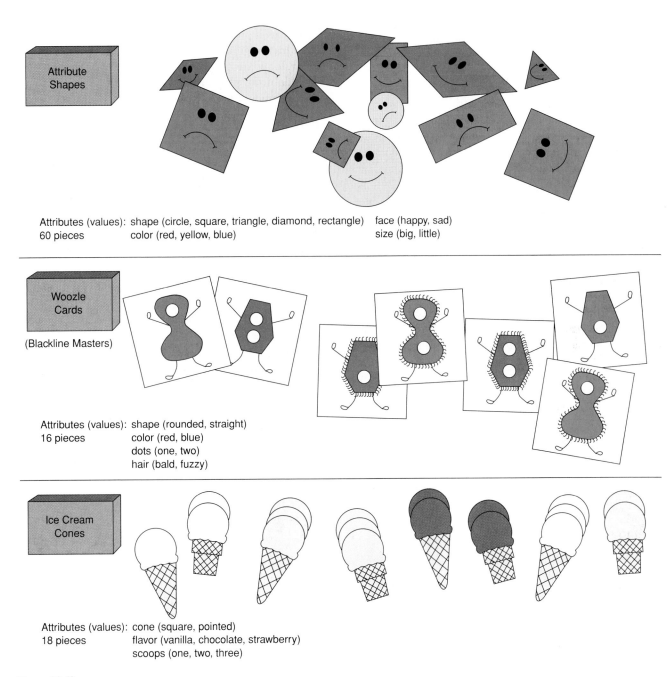

Attributes (values): shape (circle, square, triangle, diamond, rectangle)   face (happy, sad)
60 pieces            color (red, yellow, blue)                               size (big, little)

Attributes (values): shape (rounded, straight)
16 pieces            color (red, blue)
                     dots (one, two)
                     hair (bald, fuzzy)

Attributes (values): cone (square, pointed)
18 pieces            flavor (vanilla, chocolate, strawberry)
                     scoops (one, two, three)

**Figure 18.12** **Three teacher-made attribute sets. Attribute shapes are made in large sizes from poster board and laminated. Woozle Cards can be duplicated on card stock, quickly colored in two colors, laminated, and cut into cards (see Blackline Masters). The ice cream cones are made from construction paper and laminated. They could also be duplicated, colored, and cut out by students.**

The value of using structured attribute materials is that the attributes and values are clearly identified and easily described by students. There is no confusion about what values a particular piece possesses, so you can focus your attention on the reasoning skills that the activities are meant to serve.

# Activities with Attribute Materials

Most attribute activities are best done with young children sitting on the floor in a large circle where all can see and have access to the materials. Older children can work in groups of four to six students, each group with its own set of materials. In that format, problems can be addressed to the full class, and groups can explore them independently. All activities should be conducted in an easygoing manner that encourages risk taking, clear thinking, attentiveness, and discussion of ideas.

Most of the activities here will be described using the geometric shapes in Figure 18.12. However, each could be done with any structured set, and some could be done with nonstructured materials.

## Learning Classification Schemes

Several attribute activities involve using overlapping loops, each containing a designated class of materials such as pieces that are "red" or "not square." Loops can be made of yarn or drawn on large sheets of paper. When two loops overlap, the area that is inside both loops is for the pieces that have both properties. Children as young as kindergarten can have fun with simple loop activities. With the use of words such as *and, or,* and *not,* the loop activities become quite challenging.

Loops or *Venn diagrams* should be thought of as a method of representing data. Loops are much easier for young children to use than bar graphs and yet permit them to show data in a powerful way.

Before children can use loops in a problem-solving activity, the scheme itself must be understood. A good way to accomplish this is to do a few activities that involve the loops. Children find these interesting and fun. After several days of working with these initial activities, you can move on to problem-solving activities involving the same formats.

┌─ **A**CTIVITY ─────────────────

## 18.5 The First Loops

Give children two large loops of yarn or string. Direct them to put all the red pieces inside one string and all triangles inside the other. Let the children try to resolve the difficulty of what to do with the red triangles. When the notion of overlapping the strings to create an area common to both loops is clear, more challenging activities can be explored.

└──────────────────────────────

Later, "strings" or loops can be drawn on poster board or on large sheets of paper. If you happen to have a magnetic

blackboard, try using small magnets on the backs of the pieces, and conduct full-class activities with the pieces on the board. Students can come to the board to place or arrange pieces inside loops drawn on the board with colored chalk.

┌─ **A**CTIVITY ─────────────────

## 18.6 Labeled Loops

**Label overlapping loops with cards indicating values of different attributes. Children take turns randomly selecting a piece from the pile. The task is to decide in which region it belongs. Pieces belonging in neither loop are placed outside. Let other students decide if the placement is correct, and occasionally have someone else explain. Do this even when the choice of regions is correct.**

└──────────────────────────────

A significant variation of Activity 18.6 is to introduce negative attributes such as "not red" or "not small." Also important is the use of the *and* and *or* connectives, as in "red and square" or "big or happy." The use of *and, or,* and *not* significantly widens children's classification schemes. It also makes these activities quite difficult for very young children. In Figure 18.13, three loops are used in a string game illustrating some of these ideas.

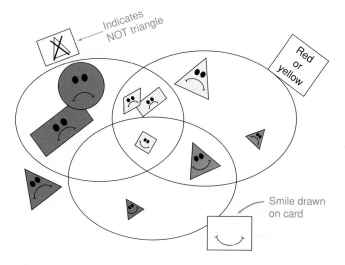

**Figure 18.13** A three-loop activity with attribute pieces.

## Solving Logic Problems

The activities described so far have students attempting to classify materials according to *our* schemes—the teacher creates a classification, and the children fit pieces into it. All that is required in these activities is an understanding of the loop method of classification and the ability to discriminate the attributes. When the words *and, or,* and *not* are used, children gain experience with those logical connectives. However, very limited logical reasoning is involved. A more significant activity is to infer how things have been classified when the scheme is not clearly articulated. The following activities require students to make and test conjectures about how things are being classified. These activities more directly prepare students to analyze their world, formulate questions, and do data analysis.

## ACTIVITY

### 18.7 Guess My Rule

For this activity, try using students instead of shapes as attribute "pieces." Decide on an attribute of your students such as "blue jeans" or "stripes on clothing," but do not tell your rule to the class. Silently look at one child at a time and move the child to the left or right according to this attribute rule. After a number of students have been sorted, have the next child come up and ask students to predict which group he or she belongs in. Before the rule is articulated, continue the activity for a while so that others in the class will have an opportunity to determine the rule. This same activity can be done with virtually any materials that can be sorted. When unstructured materials such as students, students' shoes, shells, or buttons are used, the classifications may be quite obscure, providing an interesting challenge.

## ACTIVITY

### 18.8 Hidden Labels

The same inference approach can be applied to "Labeled Loops" (Activity 18.6). Select label cards for the loops of string, and place the cards face down. Begin to sort pieces according to the turned-down labels. As you sort, have students try to determine what the labels are for each of the loops. Let students who think they have guessed the labels try to place a piece in the proper loop, but avoid having them guess the labels aloud. Students who think they know the labels can be asked to "play teacher" and respond to the guesses of the others. Point out that one way to test an idea about the labels is to select pieces that you think might go in a particular section. Do not turn the cards up until most students have figured out the rule. Notice that some rules or labels are equivalent: "Not large" is the same as "small." With simple, one-value labels and only two loops, this activity can easily be played in kindergarten. With the use of three loops and logical connectives, it can become challenging even for middle school students.

## ACTIVITY

### 18.9 Which One Doesn't Belong?

Select four pieces so that three of the pieces have some feature in common that is not a feature of the fourth. The students try to decide which piece is different. In Figure 18.14, there are two pieces that are each different from the other three. Frequently, there can be three or even four possible choices, each for a different reason. The students should explain their reasons, and classmates should decide if the reason is good. Be sure to emphasize good reasoning and not right answers.

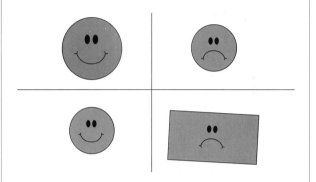

**Figure 18.14** **"One of these things is not like the others."**

## ACTIVITY

### 18.10 Sets of Four

Choose one value for each of two attributes, such as "happy triangles" or "large red pieces." Select any four pieces that share both values, and arrange them in a 2 × 2 array. The challenge is to make more arrays similar to or like the original one. To make new arrays, you must first decide how the pieces in the original array are alike and then use those same attributes but with different values to make the other arrays. Look at the example in Figure 18.15 (p. 366). The original array was all happy triangles: attributes of face and shape. The values of color and size are mixed. Within each new array, face and shape values are the same. Corresponding pieces each match the original array in color and size. If this activity is done with the Woozle Cards, where each of the attributes has exactly two values, four arrays will use up all of the pieces.

Be prepared to adjust the difficulty of these and similar activities according to the skills and interests of your children. Remember that children like to be challenged, but an activity that is either too easy or too difficult is likely to result in restlessness and discipline problems.

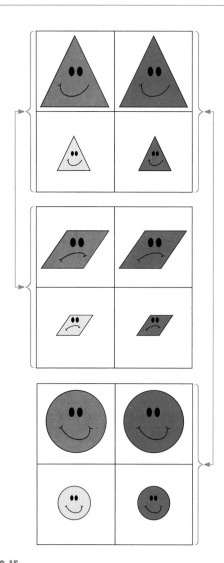

**Figure 18.15**  **Making sets of four.**

## Difference Games

As an introduction to these activities, let each child select an attribute piece. Then you hold up one piece for all to see and ask questions such as these:

Who has one that is like mine? How is it like mine?

Who has one that is different? Explain how it is different.

Look at your neighbor's piece. Tell how yours is like that one. Let your partner explain how your neighbor's is different from your piece.

These same questions used with real objects (leaves, farm animals, students) help students think of categories for sorting. They will also help with the formulation of questions for data analysis.

Students will soon find that sometimes a piece differs in three or four ways and other pieces will differ in perhaps one or two ways. To focus attention on this, ask, "Who has a piece that is different in *just exactly one way* from mine? Who has a piece that is different in *exactly two ways*?" Notice

that for a set with four attributes, a piece differing in three ways is alike in one way.

**ACTIVITY**

### 18.11 Difference Trains and Tracks

Place an attribute piece in the center of the group. The first student finds a piece that is different from this piece in exactly one way. Let students take turns finding a piece that differs from the *preceding* piece in just one way, creating a "one-difference train." The train can be made as long as the students wish or until no more pieces will fit the one-difference rule.

As a variation, draw a circular track on a piece of paper or poster board with six to ten sections on it. Place the first piece in one of the sections. Subsequent pieces can be placed to the right or the left around the track but must differ in one way from the adjacent piece. Placing the last piece may be difficult or even impossible; it must differ in exactly one way from the piece on either side. A sample is shown in Figure 18.16.

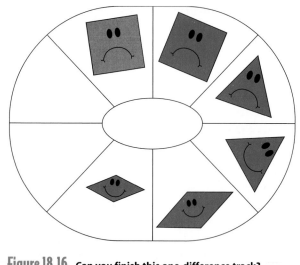

**Figure 18.16**  **Can you finish this one-difference track?**

Difference games can be two-difference games as well as one-difference games. These are not significantly more difficult but add variety.

## TECHNOLOGY NOTE

Few computer programs address issues of classification. Attribute activities are actually quite effective without a computer. One of the most challenging and most interesting programs in this area is *Logical Journey of the Zoombinis* (Brøderbund, 1996b). Zoombinis are little creatures with variations in hair, eyes, nose, and feet. The program has 12 problems of increasing difficulty to solve, each in an adventure context involving the Zoombini creatures.

A bit closer to the issue of creating classification schemes and using loop diagrams is *Tabletop, Jr.* (Brøderbund, 1995b). This program can be used by individuals or the full class. The program provides a wide variety of objects that can each be constructed with varying attributes. Various sorting choices are available, including the loop diagrams and the difference patterns seen in this chapter. Objects can also be sorted according to a hidden rule specified by a user, a computer version of "Guess My Rule" with a lot of variation. Picture graphs can be constructed with the objects providing a direct link to data graphing. ■

# GRAPHICAL REPRESENTATIONS

Once data have been gathered, what are you going to do with them? Students should be involved in the decisions that go into answering this question. To whom do you want to communicate the information? What ideas in the data are most important, and what are some good ways to show these off?

Children with little experience with the various ways of picturing data will not even be aware of the many options that are available to them. Sometimes you can suggest a new way of displaying data and have children learn to construct that type of graph or chart. Once they have made the display, they can discuss its value. Did this graph (or chart or picture) tell about our data in a clear way? Compared to other ways of displaying data, how is this better?

The emphasis or goal of our instruction should be to help children see that graphs and charts tell about information, that different types of representations tell different things about the same data. The value of having students actually construct their own graphs is not so much that they learn the techniques but that they are personally invested in the data and that they learn how a graph conveys information. Once a graph is constructed, the most important activity is discussing what it tells the people who see it, especially those who were not involved in making the graph. Discussions about graphs of real data that the children have themselves been involved in gathering will help them interpret other graphs and charts that they see in newspapers and on TV.

What we should *not* do is get overly anxious about the tedious details of graph construction. The issues of analysis and communication are *your* agendas and are much more important than the technique! In the real world, technology will take care of details.

There are two equally good possibilities you may consider when planning to have your students construct graphs or charts. First, you can simply encourage students to do their best and make charts and graphs that make sense to them and that they feel communicate the information they wish to con-

vey. This is not to say that children do not need guidance. They should have seen and been involved in group constructions of various types of graphs and charts. This provides them with some ideas from which to choose for their own graphs. This informal approach may be best with younger students because they will be more personally invested in their work and not distracted by the techniques of the technology. Care should be taken not to worry about fancy labeling or nice, neat pictures. The intent is to get the students involved in communicating a message about their data.

The second option is to use technology. The computer and graphing calculators have provided us with many tools for constructing simple yet powerful representations. With the help of technology, it is possible to construct several different pictures of the same data with very little effort. The discussion can then focus on the message or information that each format provides. Students can make their own selections of various graphs and can justify their choice based on their own intended purposes. As just one example, Figure 18.17 (p. 368) shows four graphs produced by *The Graph Club* (Tom Snyder, 1993). When two or more graphs are being created from the same data, it is possible to see all graphs change accordingly. How does a pie graph show information differently than a picture graph?

## Bar Graphs

Bar graphs and tally charts are among the first ways to group and present data and are especially useful in grades K–3. At this early level, bar graphs should be made so that each bar consists of countable parts such as squares, objects, tallies, or pictures of objects. No numeric scale is necessary. Graphs should be simple and quickly constructed. Figure 18.18 (p. 369) illustrates a few techniques that can be used to make a graph quickly with the whole class.

A "real graph" uses the actual objects being graphed. Examples include types of shoes, seashells, and books. Each item can be placed in a square so that comparisons and counts are easily made.

Picture graphs use a drawing of some sort that represents what is being graphed. Students can make their own drawings, or you can duplicate drawings to be colored or cut out to suit particular needs.

Symbolic graphs use something like squares, blocks, tallies, or Xs to represent the things being counted in the graph. An easy idea is to use sticky notes as elements of a graph. These can be stuck directly to the chalkboard or other chart and rearranged if needed.

To make a quick graph of class data, follow these steps:

1. Decide on what groups of data will make up the different bars. It is good to have two to six different bars in a graph.

2. Have each participant prepare a contribution to the graph before you begin. For real or picture graphs, the object or picture should be ready to be placed on the

Fruits We Like Best

**Figure 18.17**   **Four graphs produced with *Graph Club* software.**

graph. For symbolic graphs, students should write down or mark their choice.

3. Have students, in small groups, quickly place or mark their entry on the graph. A graph mat can be placed on the floor, or a chart can be prepared on the wall or chalkboard. If tape or pins are to be used, have these items ready.

A class of 25 to 30 students can make a graph in less than 10 minutes, leaving ample time to use it for questions and observations.

Once a graph has been constructed, engage the class in a discussion of what information the graph tells or conveys. "What can you tell about our class by looking at this shoe graph?" Graphs convey factual information (more people wear sneakers than any other kind of shoe) and also provide

opportunities to make inferences that are not directly observable in the graph (kids in this class do not like to wear leather shoes). The difference between actual facts and inferences is an important idea in graph construction and is also an important idea in science. Older students can examine graphs found in newspapers or magazines and discuss the *facts* in the graphs and the *message* that may have been intended by the person who made the graph.

As children begin to see different types of graphs, they can begin to make their own graphs of information gathered independently or by a group. A simple way to move graphing from the entire class to a small group is to assign different data collection tasks to different groups of children. The task is to gather the data and decide on and make a graph that displays as clearly as possible the information found.

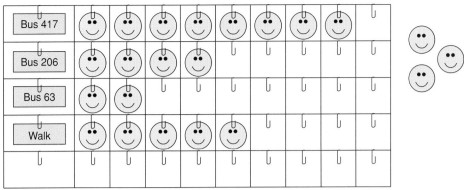

Clip paper pictures or symbols on a chart that
has a paper clip prepared in each square.

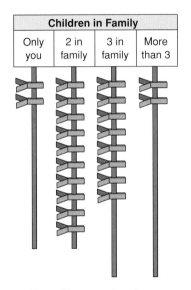

Hang ribbons, and students
clip on pinch-style clothespins

A graph mat can be
made on a sheet of
plastic about 8 to 10
feet long and used
on the floor. Make
5 or 6 columns with
12 to 15 squares in
each column. Students
place real objects in
the columns to show
the number of each.

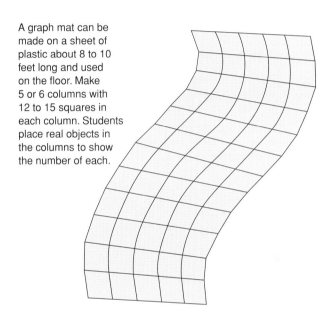

**Figure 18.18** Some ideas for quick graphs that can be used again and again.

## Stem-and-Leaf Plots

*Stem-and-leaf plots* are a popular form of bar graph where numeric data is plotted by using the actual numerals in the data to form the graph. By way of example, suppose that the American League baseball teams had posted the following record of wins over the past season:

| Baltimore | 45 | Milwaukee | 91 |
| Boston | 94 | Minnesota | 98 |
| California | 85 | New York | 100 |
| Chicago | 72 | Oakland | 101 |
| Cleveland | 91 | Seattle | 48 |
| Detroit | 102 | Toronto | 64 |
| Kansas City | 96 | Texas | 65 |

If the data are to be grouped by tens, list the tens digits in order and draw a line to the right, as in Figure 18.19(a) on page 370. These form the "stem" of the graph. Next, go through the list of scores, and write the ones digits next to the appropriate tens digit, as in Figure 18.19(b). These are the "leaves." The process of making the graph groups the data for you. Furthermore, every piece of data can be retrieved from the graph. (Notice that stem-and-leaf plots are best made on graph paper so that each digit takes up the same amount of space.)

To provide more information, the graph can be quickly rewritten, ordering each leaf from least to most, as in Figure 18.19(c). In this form, it may be useful to identify the number that belongs to a particular team, indicating its relative place within the grouped listing.

Stem-and-leaf graphs are not limited to two-digit data. For example, if the data ranged from 600 to 1300, the stem

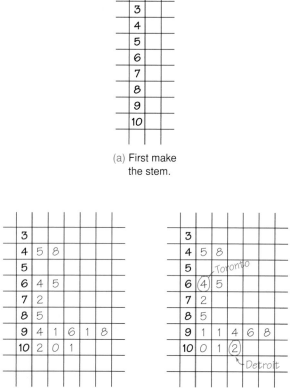

(a) First make the stem.

(b) Write in the leaves directly from the data.

(c) It is easy to rewrite each leaf in numeric order. This puts all of the data in order.

**Figure 18.19**  Making a stem-and-leaf plot.

**Gallons of Water**

| | |
|---|---|
| 6 | 29, 17, 83, 40, 82 |
| 7 | 68, 08, 95, 47, 12, 03, 18, 50, 54 |
| 8 | 44, 13, 29 |
| 9 | 14, 83, 91, 27, 56, 30 |
| 10 | 39, 00, 80, 73, 46, 10, 06 |
| 11 | 93, 11, 09, 25, 36, 66, 68, 57, 32 |
| 12 | 17, 20, 31, 26 |
| 13 | |

**Tens of Gallons of Water**

| | |
|---|---|
| 6 | 3, 2, 8, 4, 8 |
| 7 | 7, 1, 5, 1, 0, 2, 5, 5 |
| 8 | 0, 4, 1, 3 |
| 9 | 1, 8, 9, 3, 6, 3 |
| 10 | 4, 0, 8, 7, 5, 1, 1 |
| 11 | 9, 1, 1, 3, 4, 7, 7, 6, 3 |
| 12 | 2, 2, 3, 3 |
| 13 | |

**Figure 18.20**  In the plot shown in (b), the data from (a) are rounded to the nearest 10.

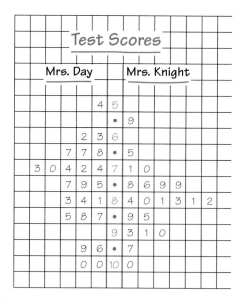

**Figure 18.21**  Stem-and-leaf plots can be used to compare two sets of data.

could be the numerals from 6 to 13 and the leaves made of two-digit numbers separated by commas. If the ones digit is not important, round the data to the nearest 10, and use only the tens digit in the leaves. Figure 18.20 shows the same data in two different stem-and-leaf plots.

Figure 18.21 illustrates two additional variations. When two sets of data are to be compared, the leaves can extend in opposite directions from the same stem. In the same example, notice that the data are grouped by fives instead of tens. When plotting 62, the 2 is written next to the 6; for 67, the 7 is written next to the dot below the 6.

Stem-and-leaf plots are significantly easier for students to make than bar graphs, all of the data are maintained, they provide an efficient method of ordering data, and individual elements of data can be identified.

## Continuous Data Graphs

Bar graphs or picture graphs are useful for illustrating categories of data that have no numeric ordering—for example,

colors or TV shows. When data are grouped along a continuous scale, it makes sense to represent the data in that order and perhaps to show progressions from one point in the scale to the next. Examples of such information include temperatures that occur over time, height or weight over age, and percentages of test takers scoring in different intervals along the scale of possible scores.

## Line Plots

*Line plots* are useful *counts* of things along a numeric scale. To make a line plot, a number line is drawn and an X is made above the corresponding value on the line for every corresponding data element. One advantage of a line plot is that every piece of data is shown on the graph. It is also a very easy type of graph for students to make. It is essentially a bar graph with a potential bar for every possible value. A simple example is shown in Figure 18.22. (A stem-and-leaf plot is a lot like a line plot except that the data are grouped.)

**Line Plot**

Test scores, Period 6

**Histogram** (TI-83)

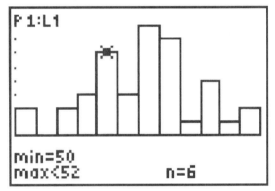

Age of U.S. presidents at inauguration

**Line Graph**

Temperature change over 24 hours

**Figure 18.22** **Three approaches to graphing data over continuous intervals. Notice that the horizontal scale must show some progression and is not just a grouping, as in a bar graph.**

## Histograms

A *histogram* is a form of bar graph in which the categories are consecutive equal intervals along a numeric scale. The height or length of each bar is determined by the number of data elements falling into that particular interval. Histograms are not difficult in concept but can cause problems for the students constructing them. What is the appropriate interval to use for the bar width? What is a good scale to use for the length of the bars? That all of the data must be grouped and counted within each interval causes further difficulty. Technology helps us with all of these decisions, allowing children to focus on the graph and its message. Graphing calculators, for example, produce histograms without much difficulty. They allow for the size of the interval to be specified and easily changed. By connecting the calculator to a computer, the graphs can be printed out or pasted into a word processor for inclusion in a student report. Figure 18.22 shows an example of a histogram produced on a TI-83.

## Line Graphs

A *line graph* is used when there is a numeric value associated with equally spaced points along a continuous number scale. Points are plotted to represent two related pieces of data, and a line is drawn to connect the points. For example, a line graph might be used to show how the length of a flagpole shadow changed from one hour to the next during the day. The horizontal scale would be time, and the vertical scale would be the length of the shadow. Discrete points can be plotted and straight lines drawn connecting them. In the example of the shadow, a shadow did exist at all times, but its length did not jump or drop from one plotted value to the other. It changed continuously as suggested by the graph. See the example in Figure 18.22.

## Circle Graphs

A circle or pie graph is used when data have been partitioned into parts and interest is in the ratio of each part to the whole. In Figure 18.23 (p. 372), each of two graphs shows the percentages of students with different numbers of siblings. One graph is based on classroom data and the other on schoolwide data. Because pie graphs display ratios rather than quantities, the small set of class data can be compared to the large set of school data. That could not be done with bar graphs.

### Easily Made Circle Graphs

You have already seen (in Figure 18.17, p. 368) a computer-generated circle graph (or pie graph) that can be used by children as early as the second grade. Nearly every spreadsheet program has circle graph capabilities.

Even without technology, there are a variety of ways that circle graphs can be made easily. Circle graphs of the students in your room can be made quickly and quite dramatically.

**Number of Siblings in Family**

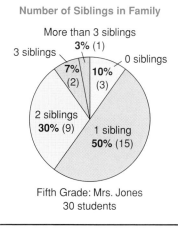

Fifth Grade: Mrs. Jones
30 students

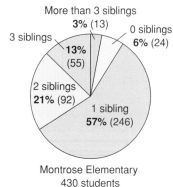

Montrose Elementary
430 students

**Figure 18.23** Circle graphs show ratios of part to whole and can be used to compare ratios.

Suppose, for example, that each student picked his or her favorite basketball team in the NCAA tournament's "Final Four." Line up all of the students in the room so that students favoring the same team are together. Now form the entire group into a circle of students. Tape the ends of four long strings to the floor in the center of the circle, and extend them to the circle at each point where the teams change. Voilà! A very nice pie graph with no measuring and no percentages. If you copy and cut out a hundredths disk (one is in the Blackline Masters) and place it on the center of the circle, the strings will show approximate percentages for each part of your graph (see Figure 18.24).

Another easy approach to circle graphs is similar to the human pie graph. Begin by having students make a bar graph of the data. Once complete, cut out the bars themselves, and tape them together end to end. Next, tape the two ends together to form a circle. Estimate where the center of the circle is, draw lines to the points where different bars meet, and trace around the full loop. The result is, again, a very meaningful circle graph. You can estimate percentages using the hundredths disk as before.

### From Percentages to Pie Graphs

If students have experienced either of the two methods just described, using their own calculations to make pie graphs will make more sense. The numbers in each category are added to form the total or whole. (That's the same as taping all of the

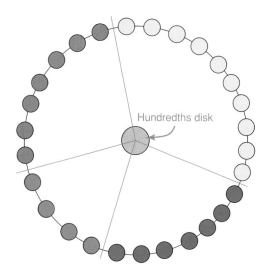

**Figure 18.24**   **A human pie graph: Students are arranged in a circle, with string stretched between them to show the divisions.**

strips together or lining up the students.) By dividing each of the parts by the whole with a calculator, numbers between 0 and 1 result—fractional parts of the whole. If rounded to hundredths, these numbers are now percentages of the whole. (Check that the total is 1 whole, or 100 percent. Rounding may cause some error.) With a copy of the hundredths disk, students can easily make a pie chart and never have to mess with degrees and protractors. Trace around the disk to make the outline of the pie. Mark the center through a small hole in the disk, and draw a line to the circle. Start from that point, and use the disk to measure hundredths around the outside.

# DESCRIPTIVE STATISTICS

Although graphs provide visual images of data, measures of the data are a different and important way to think about the shape of data. Numbers that describe data are *statistics,* measures of the data that quantify some attribute of them. The things that are most often described numerically about a set of data are the distance between the highest and lowest data values (the *range*), some measure of where the center of the data is (an *average*), and how dispersed the data are within the range (the *variance* or *dispersion*). Students can get an idea of the importance of these statistics by exploring the ideas informally.

## Averages

The term *average* is heard quite frequently in everyday usage. Sometimes it refers to an exact arithmetic average, as in "the average daily rainfall." Sometimes it is used quite loosely, as in "She is about average height." In either situation, an average is a single number or measure that is descriptive of a larger collection of numbers. If your test average is 92, it is assumed that somehow all of your test scores are reflected by this number.

The *mean, median,* and *mode* are specific types of averages or *measures of central tendency.* The *mode* is the value that occurs most frequently in the data set. Of these three statistics, the mode is the least useful and could perhaps be ignored completely. Consider the following set of numbers:

1, 1, 3, 5, 6, 7, 8, 9

The mode of this set is 1. The mode is not a very good description of this set, and such is often the case. If the 8 in this string of numbers were a 9, there would be two modes. If one of the ones were changed to a 2, there would be no mode at all. In short, the mode is a statistic that does not always exist, does not necessarily reflect the center of the data, and can be highly unstable, changeable with very small changes in the data.

The *mean* is computed by adding all of the numbers in the set and dividing the sum by the number of elements added. This is the statistic that is sometimes referred to as the *average,* although the terms are not synonymous. The mean of our sample set is 5 (40 ÷ 8). The mean is discussed in more detail later in the chapter.

The *median* is the middle value in an ordered set of data. Half of all values lie at or above the median and half below. For the eight numbers in our sample set, the median is between 5 and 6, or 5.5. The Quantitative Literacy Project (Landwehr & Watkins, 1987) places a heavy emphasis on the median in preference to the mean or the mode. The median is easier to understand and to compute and is not affected, as the mean is, by one or two extremely large or extremely small values outside the range of the rest of the data.

# Box-and-Whisker Plots

*Box-and-whisker plots* (or just *box plots*) are an easy method for visually displaying not only the median statistic but also information about the range and distribution or variance of data. In Figure 18.25, the ages in months for 27 sixth-grade students are given, along with stem-and-leaf plots for the full class and the boys and girls separately. Box-and-whisker plots are shown in Figure 18.26 (p. 374).

Each box-and-whisker plot has these three features:

1. A box that contains the "middle half" of the data, one-fourth to the left and right of the median. The ends of the box are at the *lower quartile,* the median of the lower half of the data, and the *upper quartile,* the median of the upper half of the data.

2. A line inside the box at the median of the data.

3. A line extending from the end of each box to the *lower extreme* and *upper extreme* of the data. Each line therefore covers the upper and lower fourths of the data.

Look at the information these box plots provide at a glance! The box and the lengths of the lines provide a quick indication of how the data are spread out or bunched together. Since the median is shown, this spreading or bunching can be determined for each quarter of the data. The entire class in this example is much more spread out in the upper half than the lower half. The girls are much more closely grouped in age than either the boys or the class as a whole. It is immediately obvious that at least three-fourths of the girls are younger than the median age of the boys. The *range* of the data (difference between upper and lower extremes) is represented by the length of the plot, and the extreme values can be read directly. It is easy to mark and label entries of particular interest. For example, Joe B. and Whitney might be the class officers.

Making box-and-whisker plots is quite simple. First, put the data in order. An easy and valuable method is to make a stem-and-leaf plot and order the leaves, providing another

The following numbers represent the ages in months of a class of sixth-grade students.

| Boys | | Girls | |
|---|---|---|---|
| 132 | 122 | 140 | 131 |
| 140 | 130 | 129 | 128 |
| 133 | 134 | 141 | 131 |
| 142 | 125 | 134 | 132 |
| 134 Joe B. | 147 | 124 | 130 |
| (137) | 131 | 129 Whitney | 127 |
| 139 | 129 | (125) | |

All students

| 12 | 2, 4 |
| • | 5, 5, 7, 8, (9,) 9, 9, |
| 13 | 0, 0, 1, 1, (1,) 2, 2, 3, 4, 4, 4 |
| • | (7,) 9 |
| 14 | 0, 0, 1, 2 |
| • | 7 |

Boys

| 12 | 2 |
| • | 5, 9 |
| 13 | (0,) 1, 2, 3, |4, 4 |
| • | 7, (9) |
| 14 | 0, 2 |
| • | 7 |

Girls

| 12 | 4 |
| • | 5, 7,|8, 9, 9 |
| 13 | (0,) 1, 1, 2, |4 |
| • | |
| 14 | 0, 1 |
| • | |

**Figure 18.25** **Ordered stem-and-leaf plots grouped by fives. Medians and upper and lower quartiles are found on the stem-and-leaf plots. Medians and quartiles are circled or are represented by a bar (I) if they fall between two elements.**

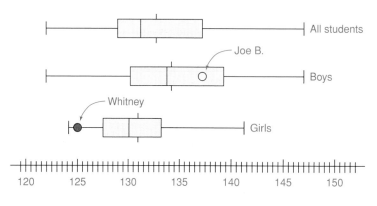

Age (months) of 27 sixth-grade students

**Figure 18.26** Box-and-whisker plots show a lot of information.

visual image as well. Next, find the median. Simply count the number of values and determine the middle one. This can be done directly on the stem-and-leaf plots as was done in Figure 18.25. To find the two quartiles, ignore the median itself, and find the medians of the upper and lower halves of the data. Mark the two extremes, the two quartiles, and the median above an appropriate number line. Draw the box and the lines. Box plots can also be drawn vertically.

Note that the means for the data in our example are each just slightly higher than the medians (class = 132.4; boys = 133.9; girls = 130.8). For this example, the means themselves do not provide nearly as much information as the box plots. In Figure 18.26, the means are shown with small marks extending above and below each box.

Graphing calculators and several computer programs draw box-and-whisker plots, making this relatively simple process even more accessible. The TI-73 and TI-83 calculators can draw box plots for up to three sets of data on the same axis. In Figure 18.27, the data for the top box plot is based on 23 items. The second plot has 122 items. The third plot has 48 items of data. When you compare both large and small sets of data in this manner, the spread or lack of spread of the data becomes much more obvious.

Box-and-whisker plots are pictures of statistics more than pictures of data. They show the range and the median and pictorially indicate a sense of the spread. The more traditional measures of spread, the *variance* and the *standard deviation*, are not necessary to consider at the middle school level. However, once a concept of spread or dispersion of data is developed informally with box-and-whisker plots, the standard deviation may have more meaning. This statistic is rather tedious to compute but is available on scientific and graphing calculators at the press of a button.

## Understanding the Mean

Due to ease of computation and stability, the median when compared to the mean has some advantages as a practical average. However, the mean will continue to be used in pop-

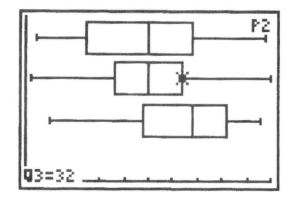

**Figure 18.27** Three box plots of data falling between the values of 0 and 50. Twenty-three items are represented by the top plot, 122 by the middle plot, and 48 by the bottom plot. The cursor on the middle plot shows that the third quartile is 32. What other information can be determined from this plot?

ular media and in books. For smaller sets of data such as your test scores, the mean is perhaps a more meaningful statistic. Finally, the mean is used in the computation of other statistics such as the standard deviation. Therefore, it remains important that students have a good concept of what the mean tells them about a set of numbers.

How do you describe the mean other than how to compute it? There are actually two different ways to think about the mean. First, it is a number that represents what all of the data items would be if they were leveled out. In this sense, the mean represents all of the data items. Statisticians prefer to think of the mean as a central balance point. This concept of the mean is more in keeping with the notion of a measure of the "center" of the data or a measure of central tendency. Both concepts are discussed in the following sections.

### A Leveling Concept of the Mean

When you say that the average score on your class math test was 92, one way to interpret that is as follows: If every student had received the same score, that score would be

92. Higher scores balance out lower scores. This concept of the mean is easy to understand and explain and has the added benefit that it leads directly to the algorithm for computing the mean.

---

**ACTIVITY**

## 18.12 Leveling the Bars

Have students make a bar graph of some data using plastic connecting cubes such as Unifix. Choose a situation with 5 or 6 bars with no more than 10 or 12 cubes in each. For example, the graph in Figure 18.28 shows prices for six toys. The task for students is to use the graph itself to determine what the price would be if all of the toys were the same price, assuming that the total for all the toys remained the same. Students will use various techniques to rearrange the cubes in the graph but will eventually create six equal bars, possibly with some leftovers that could mentally be distributed in fractional amounts. (In the example, the total number of cubes is a multiple of 6.) Do not tell students they are finding the average or mean, only that they are to find equal-length bars.

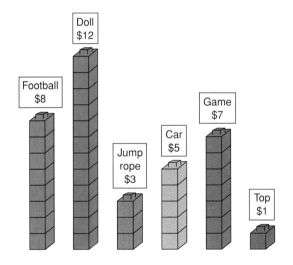

Bar graph made with plastic snap cubes

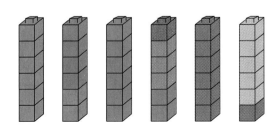

The same cubes rearranged into equal stacks. Their height is the <u>mean</u> value of the bars above.

**Figure 18.28** **Understanding the mean as a leveling of the data.**

Focus attention on methods in which students stacked the bars and then divided the stack into six parts. If no one has done that, create a new bar graph with connecting cubes, show it to the class, and then stack all of the bars into one long bar. Pose this task: "What is a clever way we could use this long bar to determine what size the bars would be if they were all the same?" It is relatively easy to see that you determine the length of the long bar (the total of all of the bars) and divide by the number of bars you began with.

The same leveling activity can begin with any bar graph that students have made on paper. Once the graph is made, have students cut the bars out and tape them together end to end. Ask them to use this long strip to determine the size of the bars if they were all the same. To do this, the students can fold the strip into as many equal parts as there are bars in the graph.

---

**ACTIVITY**

## 18.13 Numeric Leveling

Provide a set of about 15 numbers. They might be student heights in centimeters or any other meaningful data. Ask, "What would these numbers be if the total was the same and yet the numbers were all alike?"

---

The last task more explicitly develops the add-up-and-divide algorithm. Once students see how to use this technique to determine a level number for a data set, then it is time to tell them that this number they are finding is called the *mean.*

The next activity is a good follow-up to early discussions of the mean.

---

**ACTIVITY**

## 18.14 Over and Under the Mean

Duplicate a simple bar graph on graph paper for each student. The task is to estimate the mean and draw a horizontal line across the graph at that point. No computation is to be done! Make a transparency of the graph to use for discussion. Draw a line on a second piece of acetate that can be placed as the estimated mean line. Have students share where they drew their lines and why (see Figure 18.29, p. 376). What is likely to emerge from the discussion is that the total of the parts of the bars above the line must match the total space between the line and the bars below the line. That is, you should be able to cut off the bars above the mean line and fit the pieces in the spaces below the line. After discussion, use a calculator to compute the mean numerically and compare with the estimates.

---

## A Balance Point Concept of the Mean

Statisticians think about the mean as a point on a number line where the data on either side of the point are balanced. To help think about the mean in this way, it is useful to think about the data placed on a line plot rather than as bar graphs.

*A, B,* and *D* are <u>above</u> the line a <u>total</u> of 23 + 45 +1 = 69. *C* and *E* are <u>below</u> the line a total of 22 + 8 = 30. There is more ABOVE than BELOW. This estimate is <u>too low</u>. (Actual mean = 57.8)

Percentage of voters who voted in five precincts

**Figure 18.29** **Estimating the mean on a bar graph.**

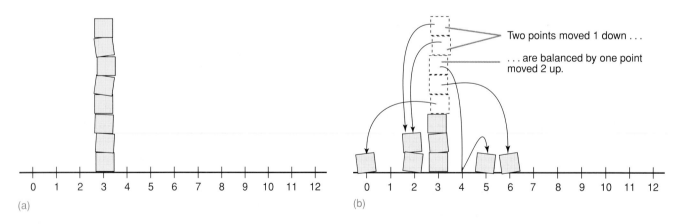

Two points moved 1 down . . .

. . . are balanced by one point moved 2 up.

(a)                    (b)

**Figure 18.30** **(a) If all data points are the same, the mean is that value. (b) By moving data points away from the mean in a balanced manner, different distributions can be found that have the same mean.**

What is important is not how many pieces of data are on either side of the mean or balance point but the distances of data from the mean that must balance.

To illustrate, draw a number line on the board, and arrange eight sticky notes above the number 3 as shown in Figure 18.30(a). Each sticky note represents one family. The notes are positioned on the line to indicate how many pets are owned by the family. Stacked up like this would indicate that all families have the same number of pets. The mean is three pets. But different families are likely to have different numbers of pets. So we could think of eight families with a range of numbers of pets. Some may have zero pets, and some may have as many as ten or even more. How could you change the number of pets for these eight families so that the mean remains at 3? Students will suggest moving the sticky notes in opposite directions, probably in pairs. This will result in a symmetrical arrangement. But what if one of the families has eight pets, a move of five spaces from the 3? This might be balanced by moving two families to the left, one three spaces to the 0 and one two spaces to the 1. Figure 18.30(b) shows one way the families could be rearranged to maintain a mean of 3. You should stop here and find at least two other distributions of the families, each having a mean of 3.

Use the next activity to find the mean or balance point given the data.

─── **A**CTIVITY ───

## 18.15 Finding the Balance Point

Have students draw a number line from 0 to 12 with about an inch between the numbers. Use six small sticky notes to represent the prices of six toys as shown in Figure 18.31. Have them place a light pencil mark on the line where they think the mean might be. For the moment, avoid the add-up-and-divide computation. The task is to determine the actual mean by moving the sticky notes in toward the "center." That is, the students are finding out what price or point on the number line balances out the six prices on the line. For each move of a sticky one space to the left (a toy with a lower price), a different sticky must be moved one space to the right (a toy with a higher price). Eventually, all stickies should be stacked above the same number, the balance point or mean.

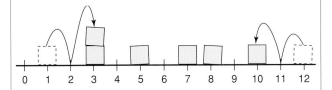

**Figure 18.31** Move data points in toward the center or balance point without changing the balance around that point. When you have all points at the same value, that is the balance or the mean.

Stop now and try this exercise yourself. Notice that after any pair of moves that keep the distribution balanced, you actually have a new distribution of prices with the same mean. The same was true when you moved the stickies out from the mean when they were all stacked on the same point.

The balance concept does not lead to the add-up-and-divide algorithm for computing the mean. However, you can show that the computation will always produce the same value as determined by the balance.

Notice that the mean only defines the center of a set of data and so by itself is not a very useful description of the shape of the data. The balance approach to the mean clearly illustrates that many different distributions can have the same mean.*

## Changes in the Mean

Especially for small sets of data, the mean is significantly affected by extreme values. For example, suppose that another toy with a price of $20 is added to the six we have been using in the examples. How will the mean change? If the $1 toy were removed, how would the mean be affected? Suppose that one new toy is added that increases the mean from $6 to $7. How much does the new toy cost? Students should be challenged with questions such as these using small sets of data and either the balance or the leveling concept.

 Technology provides an efficient method of exploring the mean as well as other statistics. Graphing calculators and spreadsheets will all compute the range, mean, and median for any set of data at the press of a button. On a spreadsheet, these statistics update immediately when a number is changed or added to the data. This is a dynamic, albeit not very conceptual, way to explore how these measures of the data center are affected by changes in the data.

# SCATTER PLOTS AND RELATIONSHIPS

Data are often analyzed to search for or demonstrate relationships between two sets of data or phenomena. For example, what are the relationships, if any, between time spent watching television and overall grade point average? Does the size of a college have anything to do with the cost of attending?

All sorts of real situations exist where we are interested in relationships between two variables or two numeric phenomena. The world of science abounds with experimental data. How far does a toy car roll down an inclined plane as compared to the angle of the plane? How tall do beans grow over a 21-day period from the day they sprout? Such data are generally gathered from some sort of experiment that is set up and observed, with measurements taken. The experiment defines the various variables to look at.

Data that may be related are gathered in pairs. For example, if you were going to examine the possible relationship

---

*The balance concept of the mean is the one developed in the Connected Math Project, one of the three reform programs for the middle grades. It is also developed in the *Used Numbers* book *Statistics: Middles, Means, and In-Betweens* (Friel, Mokros, & Russell, 1992).

between hours of TV watched and grades, each person in the survey or sample would produce a pair of numbers, one for TV time and one for grade point average.

## Scatter Plots

Regardless of the source of the data, a good first attempt at examining them for possible relationships is to create a *scatter plot* of the two variables involved, a graph of points on a coordinate grid with each axis representing one of the two variables. Each pair of numbers from the two sets of data, when plotted, produces a visual image of the data as well as a hint concerning any possible relationships. Suppose that the following information was gathered from 25 eighth-grade boys: height in inches, weight in pounds, and number of letters in their last name. The two graphs in Figure 18.32 show two possibilities. Graph (a) is a scatter plot of height to weight, and graph (b) is a plot of name length to weight. Both were made with a graphing calculator.

As you would expect, the boys' weights seem to increase as their heights increase. However, the relationship is far from perfect. We all know there are short chubby people and tall

lanky people and many variations in between. However, the dots in the graph illustrate a general trend. Similarly, there is no reason to expect any relationship between name length and weight, and indeed the dots appear to be almost randomly distributed.

## Best-Fit Lines

If your scatter plot indicates a relationship, it can be simply described in words. "As boys get taller, they tend to get heavier." This is correct but not particularly useful. What exactly is the relationship? If I knew the height of a boy, could I predict what his weight might be based on this information? Like much of statistical analysis, the value of a statistic is to predict what has not yet been observed. We poll a small sample of voters before an election to predict how the full population will vote. Here, can a sample of 30 students predict the weights of other students?

The relationship in these cases is not a number like a mean or a standard deviation but rather a line or curve. Is there a line that can be drawn through the scatter plot that represents the "best" approximation of all of the dots and reflects the observed trend? If the scatter plot seems to indicate a steadily increasing or steadily decreasing relationship (as in the height-weight graph), you would probably try to find a straight line that approximates the dots. Sometimes the plot will indicate a curved relationship, in which case you might try to draw a smooth curve like a parabola to approximate the dots.

### What Determines Best Fit?

From a strictly visual standpoint, the line you select defines the observed relationship and could be used to predict other values not in the data set. The more closely the dots in the scatter plot hug the line you select, the greater the confidence you would have in the prediction value of the line. Certainly you could draw a straight line somewhere in the name length–weight graph, but you would not have much faith in its predictive capability because the dots would be quite dispersed from any line you might draw.

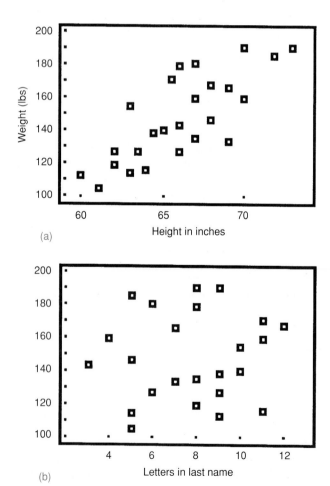

(a)

(b)

**Figure 18.32** **Scatter plots show potential relationships or lack of relationships.**

> **ACTIVITY**
>
> ### 18.16 Best-Fit Line
>
> Once students have collected related data and prepared a scatter plot, duplicate an accurate version of the plot for each group of students. Provide the groups with a piece of spaghetti to use as a line. The task is to tape the line on the plot so that it is the "best" line to represent the relationship in the dots. Further, the students are to develop a rationale for why they positioned the line as they did.
>
> Using an overhead transparency of the plot, compare the lines chosen by various groups and their rationales.

Before reading further, return to the height-weight plot in Figure 18.32, graph (a), and draw a straight line that you think would make a good line of best fit. You may want to make a photo enlargement of that figure to use with your class. What reason would you offer for why you drew the line where you did?

Many of the reasons students will give for their best-fit line will be rather subjective: "It just looks right" or "There are just as many points above as below." Others will see how many points they can make the line touch. Most intuitive ideas fail to consider all of the points. Two different people using the same criteria might well come up with very different lines. There is a need for a better definition of a best-fit line.

Encourage students to use a more "mathematical" reason for why a line might be best. Since a good line is one around which most dots cluster, a good-fitting line is one where the distances from all of the dots to the line is minimal. This general notion of least distance to the line for all points can lead to an algorithm that will always produce a unique line for a given set of points. Two such algorithms are well known and used in statistics. The more complicated approach is called the *least squares regression* line. It is an algebraic procedure that is not accessible to middle grade students and is also rather tedious to compute. The second algorithm produces what is called the *median-median* line and is quite easy to determine.

## Median-Median Line

The median-median line can be determined directly from the graph or from the data. It is based on the simple median statistic. The method for determining the median-median line essentially consists of these steps:

1. Separate the data into three "equal" sets of points along the horizontal axis. (In the example of Figure 18.33, since there are 25 points, put the extra point into the middle third.)

2. Find the *median point* in each third of the points. (This is described in the text that follows.)

3. Connect the median points in the first and third sets of data. This line takes into consideration all points in these two sections but ignores the points in the middle third.

4. Draw a parallel line one-third of the distance between this first line and the center median point. This gives the center collection of points a proportional influence on the position of the line.

A *median point* in a scattered collection of points is the point with its first coordinate equal to the median of all the first coordinates and its second coordinate equal to the median of all the second coordinates. Another way of saying this is that the median point is one that is midway vertically and midway horizontally. Using this second formulation, the median point can be found by counting points from the bottom up until you have half the points below and half above.

With an odd number of points, draw a horizontal line through the middle point. With an even number of points, draw the line halfway between the two middle points. The median point will fall on this horizontal line. Repeat the process, moving from left to right. The vertical line you find this way will intersect the horizontal line at the median point. Note that it is not necessary for the median point to be a data point.

In Figure 18.33, the median point in the left-hand third of the data (the first eight points counting left to right) is shown as a single pixel. Find the other two median points on your own, and complete steps 3 and 4.

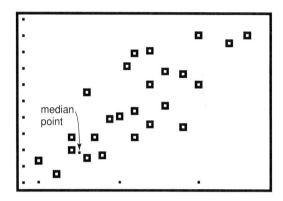

**Figure 18.33** A height-versus-weight scatter plot. Use the graph to find the median-median line. The single pixel in the lower left is the median point for the left third of the points.

## Median-Median Lines with a Calculator

The TI-73 and TI-83 calculators will compute the median-median line for you. Data are entered in two lists, one for the first coordinates of each point and one for the corresponding second coordinates. Figure 18.34 shows the calculator plot of the median-median line for the same height-versus-weight data.

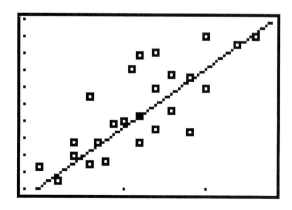

**Figure 18.34** The median-median line for the points plotted in Figure 18.33.

# Thinking About Functional Relationships

It is worth noting that the median-median line is a graphical representation of a function relating the variable on the horizontal axis to the variable on the vertical axis. Using the height-weight example, it is appropriate to say that *the weight of a boy is a function of his height*. The best-fit line is a mathematical method of determining what the function might be. Different methods of finding the best-fit line will likely develop slightly different lines.

Note that if the function (line) that we found accurately predicted the weight of a boy based on his height, all of the data points would fall along a perfectly straight line. That they do not is a vivid picture of the difference between data found in the world (the points on the graph) and a mathematical model of the real world (the line).

Scatter plots and best-fit lines will be discussed again in Chapter 20 on functions. The connection among the real world, statistics, and algebraic ideas is a valuable one to make.

 TECHNOLOGY NOTE

Throughout this discussion of data analysis, there have been numerous references to graphing calculators, spreadsheets, and graphing software. This is an area of the curriculum where technology really changes the way we teach. In the past, the emphasis was on how to create the graph and how to compute the statistic. Students had to labor over graph paper, drawing scales, labeling axes, coloring the graphs, and so on. Today, every graphical technique and every statistic mentioned in this chapter is readily available in a variety of technologies. An exception may be stem-and-leaf plots. With the help of technology, the focus of instruction in data analysis can and should shift to the big ideas of using graphs and statistics: to describe data, to get a sense of the shape of data, to answer questions with data, and to communicate this information to others.

At the primary level, it is useful to have a software program into which children can enter data and select from a variety of graphical representations. *The Graph Club* (Tom Snyder, 1993), though not new, is an excellent example of software in this category (see Figure 18.11, p. 361). By fourth grade, students are able to use a spreadsheet. *Cruncher* (SRA/McGraw-Hill, 1996) is a slightly simplified spreadsheet designed for grades 3 and up. Every popular spreadsheet will compute any statistic for columns or rows of data. If the data are changed, the statistics change instantly. Spreadsheets also make very nice bar graphs, line graphs, and circle graphs. Since spreadsheets are often bundled with the software that comes with computers, this software is nearly as available as the computers. Teachers should also check to see if the publisher of their textbook offers graphing software.

The graphing calculator puts data analysis technology in the hands of every student. The TI-73 calculator is designed for middle grade students. It will produce eight different kinds of plots or graphs, including pie charts, bar graphs, and picture graphs that are not available on the TI-83. All graphing calculators will compute and graph best-fit lines using either the median-median method or the regression method.

An argument can be made for having students do some graphing and computing of statistics without technology. Appropriate methods have been suggested in this chapter. However, the intent of by-hand methods should always be to help understand the graphs or the statistics. Given today's readily available technology, there is no reason for repetitious exercises with tedious by-hand methods. Keep the emphasis on data interpretation by taking advantage of technology. ■

 ASSESSMENT NOTES

Care should be taken in assessment of probability and statistical ideas to distinguish between the use of related algorithms and techniques and the quite different kind of knowledge that involves judgment and interpretation.

## Probability

The skills that are easy to assess involve the computation of probabilities. Even young children should be able to tell if an event is possible or impossible or is very likely or not very likely. Older children should be able to determine probabilities in well-designed experiments such as those discussed in this chapter.

You also want to be aware of students' understanding of chance and probability. What does it mean that an event has a probability of 89 percent or $\frac{2}{3}$? How many times should a simulation or an experiment be conducted before you can have confidence in the results? What does "confidence in the results" mean? Can knowing the probability of an event ever predict what will happen on the next trial? How are probability ideas used in the real world?

These more subtle ideas can be determined by having class discussions and listening for the reasoning of students and making efforts to check students' understanding of the key ideas you are looking for. You might use a four-point rubric to rate students quickly on their understanding. Middle school students can write short reports about a situation that includes your main ideas, and you can have them specifically address the issues you want to assess.

## Statistics

In the area of statistics and data analysis, the same distinction is important. Of course, you want your students to know how to make a stem-and-leaf plot and a box plot or find the mean and the median. But many students can learn to do these things without interpreting them. Choice and interpretation of graphs and statistics are more important than the ability to construct and compute.

## Choice

Computers and calculators will make graphs even when they are inappropriate to your needs. Students must be able to select appropriate graphs and statistics to suit their purposes. It is important to pose situations that include a real context and have students decide what statistics and what graphs would best serve the purposes. Is a bar graph or a line graph more appropriate? Why? Which statistic is better in this situation, the mean or the median?

## Interpretation

In a similar manner, making the graph or computing the best-fit line does not help me understand what it tells me about the data. There are a number of ways to get at interpretation. For example, several graphs and statistics for the same situation and data can be presented. "Suppose you were a newspaper editor. Which of these statistics and graphs should you use in your story? Explain your selection. Are any of these statistics of no value to the message?" In this type of interpretation, several options are provided, and the choice is based on the intended audience and purpose. There is no need actually to compute the statistics or create the graphs.

Another idea is to provide graphs and statistics for two related situations: your class and the rest of the school, your state and the rest of the country, hamburgers at McDonald's and hamburgers at Burger King. What can be determined for sure from these data? What inferences can be made? What would help you make a decision about _____ that you cannot determine from the information gathered? How could you use this information to argue in favor of _____? How could you use the same information to argue on the reverse side of the issue?

 ## LITERATURE CONNECTIONS

It may be difficult to find books that specifically address the concept of probability or data analysis. The books suggested here will provide springboards for discussions of chance, classification, and comparisons.

## Do You Wanna Bet? Your Chance to Find Out About Probability
### (Cushman, 1991)

The two characters in this book, Danny and Brian, become involved in everyday situations both in and out of school.

Each situation has an element of probability involved. For example, two invitations to birthday parties are for the same day. What is the chance that two friends would have the same birthday? In another situation, Brian wonders if he should do his homework because the weather forecaster predicts a 60 percent chance that there will be enough snow to close schools. When it doesn't snow at all, the question is, was the forecaster wrong? Secret notes passed in class lead to the discussion of letter frequencies in our language. These and other situations woven into an interesting story can each lead to a probability experiment or discussion. Students might create simulations to examine some of the same ideas, or the story may provoke similar questions for exploration.

## Frog and Toad Are Friends
### (Lobal, 1970)

When Frog and Toad go walking, Frog loses a button. As they search to find the button, they find many buttons. Whenever one of Frog's friends asks, "Is this your button?" Frog responds (with a touch of anger), "No, that is not my button! That button is _____, but my button was _____." The phrase is repeated with each newly found button. It turns out that Frog did not lose the button on the walk but in his own home before they left. This provides another value to the story as Frog must find a way to make up for being so angry with his friends.

The approach to finding the button is very much like the game "One of These Things Is Not like the Others." It is also a perfect lead-in to secret sorting activities as described in this chapter. Young students can model the story directly with sets of buttons, shells, attribute blocks, Woozle Cards, or other objects with a variety of attributes. With a highly varied set of geometric shapes, the children could play the game and explore their geometric language and perceptions of geometric attributes.

## Incredible Comparisons
### (Ash, 1996)

Not a story but an amazing collection of facts and comparisons, Ash's book includes 23 topics for comparison, each graphically displayed. For example, different-sized squares are used to compare the size of the continents. Maps of major countries are layered on top of each other to indicate relative areas. Data about area and distances are also provided in different units of measure. The amount of time needed to travel the widths of countries is demonstrated as well. Data and drawings such as these can prompt students to find clever but acceptable ways to display the information or to research similar information in other resources. Other topics include big buildings, animal speeds, growth and age, and population.

# REFLECTIONS ON CHAPTER 18

## Writing to Learn

1. Describe the difference between theoretical probability, relative frequency, and experimental probability.

2. Why is it a good idea to have students conduct experiments before trying to figure out probabilities?

3. What are the first ideas that young students should develop about the concept of chance? How can this be done?

4. Describe how you could use a random-number generator on a computer or calculator to produce a simulation of a three-part spinner with all parts equal.

5. What is the purpose of a simulation? Set up a simulation for at least one of the examples on pages 359–360. Conduct a few trials.

6. Use an area model and a tree diagram to determine the theoretical probability for the following experiment:

   > Dad puts a $5 bill and three $1 bills in the first box. In a second box, he puts another $5 bill but just one $1 bill. Junior, for washing the car, gets to take one bill from the first box without looking and put it in the second box. After these have been well mixed, he then gets to take one from the second box without looking. What is the probability that he will get $5?

   Design a simulation for the problem, and try it out. Does it agree with your theoretical probability?

7. Explain why attribute activities are important in the development of data analysis skills. Why would you use structured attribute materials for these activities instead of informal or unstructured materials such as buttons?

8. In initial loop activities, the teacher tells the students how to sort the attribute pieces. What is the purpose of these not-so-problematic activities? What are students learning in activities where the loop labels are not shown or the sorting rule is a secret?

9. How is a two-difference game played on an oval track? Draw a picture showing a two-difference solution for a track with seven spaces. Use attribute blocks or Woozle Cards.

10. Draw a picture of a line plot, a histogram, and a line graph. How are all of these alike?

11. Put at least 30 numbers in a stem-and-leaf plot, and use it to determine the median, the upper and lower quartiles, and the range and to draw a box-and-whisker plot.

12. What are three ways to make a circle graph? What does a circle graph tell you that a bar graph does not? What does it not tell?

13. What are three different forms of averages? Which is the most stable? Explain.

14. Describe two different concepts of the mean. How can each be developed? Which idea leads to the method of computing the mean?

15. Describe what is meant by a best-fit line. When would you want to find such a line?

16. On a grid, make a scatter plot of about 30 points that appear to have a negative linear relationship or correlation. Use these points to draw the median-median line. Suppose that your points represented number of yearly visits to the mall as related to miles between home and mall. How could your best-fit line be used to predict the number of visits to the mall for a person who was not included in your data set? How much potential error would you assign to your prediction based solely on the scatter plot that you drew?

## For Discussion and Exploration

1. Examine one of six books from the Used Numbers Project or the two *Teach-Stat Activities* books (see Recommendations for Further Reading). These books have some of the best statistics activities for elementary students. You might share an activity or idea in the book that excited you, react to a lesson described in the book, or share an idea in the book with a teacher and get his or her reaction.

2. How important is it, in your opinion, to teach probability concepts in the early grades (K–4)? What about in the middle grades? Does your answer change if you substitute statistics for probability? Explain your position. Some experts have argued that the ability to understand probability and statistical ideas is so much more important than the related skills that being able to compute probabilities and statistics or to make graphs are skills that we could skip in favor of increased reasoning in this area. What position would you take on this issue?

## Recommendations for Further Reading

### Highly Recommended

National Council of Teachers of Mathematics. (1999). Data and chance in the middle school curriculum [Focus issue]. *Mathematics Teaching in the Middle School, 4*(6).
   In keeping with the overall quality of this journal, this focus issue is a valuable resource for the twin topics of data and probability. The first article describes a fascinating activity involving killer bees with a solid connection to biology. Other articles are equally useful.

University of North Carolina Mathematics and Science Education Network. (1997). *Teach-stat activities: Statistics investigations for grades 1–3.* White Plains, NY: Cuisenaire–Dale Seymour.

University of North Carolina Mathematics and Science Education Network. (1997). *Teach-stat activities: Statistics investigations for grades 3–6.* White Plains, NY: Cuisenaire–Dale Seymour.
   These two books contain a wealth of superb data activities developed through a National Science Foundation grant under the direction of some of North Carolina's top mathematics educators. The activities are each designed to follow a four-stage model: pose the question, collect the data, analyze the data, interpret the results. In other words, data are collected for the purpose of answering a question. The activities are each described in detail with all necessary Blackline Masters included. A companion professional development manual is also available.

*Used numbers: Real data in the classroom.* White Plains, NY: Cuisenaire–Dale Seymour.
   This set of six books, each covering two or three grades between kindergarten and sixth, is a result of an NSF-supported project at Technical Education Research Centers (TERC) and Lesley Col-

lege. The books are an excellent resource for elementary statistics activities. Each book is a unit of study, most with subtopics that can be used independently. The authors (authorship varies with each book) include ample detail to help you get a feel for what might happen in the classroom. The spirit of these activities is excellent! The suggestions are realistic and can all be implemented as suggested. Blackline Masters are included when needed. (All six titles are included under "Other Suggestions.")

Zawojewski, J. S. (1991). *Dealing with data and chance: Addenda series, grades 5–8.* Reston, VA: National Council of Teachers of Mathematics.

Middle school teachers interested in teaching probability and statistics must have this book. It is not timid in its suggestions for demanding activity, yet all activities are appropriate for middle grade students. The book is organized around the four theme standards of the *Curriculum Standards.*

## Other Suggestions

Bright, G. W., & Hoeffner, K. (1993). Measurement probability, statistics, and graphing. In D. T. Owens (Ed.), *Research ideas for the classroom: Middle grades mathematics* (pp. 78–98). Old Tappan, NJ: Macmillan.

Burns, M. (1995). *Math by all means: Probability, grades 3–4.* Sausalito, CA: Math Solutions Publications.

Corwin, R. B., & Friel, S. N. (1990). *Statistics: Prediction and sampling* (Unit of study for grades 5–6 from *Used numbers: Real data in the classroom*). White Plains, NY: Cuisenaire–Dale Seymour.

Corwin, R. B., & Russell, S. J. (1990). *Measuring: From paces to feet* (Unit of study for grades 3–5 from *Used numbers: Real data in the classroom*). White Plains, NY: Cuisenaire–Dale Seymour.

Creative Publications. (1986). *Hands-on attribute blocks.* Chicago: Author.

Curcio, F. R., & Artzt, A. F. (1996). Assessing students' ability to analyze data: Reaching beyond computation. *Mathematics Teacher, 89,* 668–673.

Curcio, F. R., Nimerofsky, B., Perez, R., & Yaloz-Femia, S. (1998). Developing concepts in probability: Designing and analyzing games. In L. P. Leutzinger (Ed.), *Mathematics in the middle* (pp. 206–211). Reston, VA: National Council of Teachers of Mathematics.

Dessart, D. J. (1995). Randomness: A connection to reality. In P. A. House (Ed.), *Connecting mathematics across the curriculum* (pp. 177–181). Reston, VA: National Council of Teachers of Mathematics.

Elementary Quantitative Literacy Project. (1998). *Exploring statistics in the elementary grades: Book 1 (K–6).* White Plains, NY: Cuisenaire–Dale Seymour.

Friel, S. N., Mokros, J. R., & Russell, S. J. (1992). *Middles, means, and in-betweens* (Unit of study for grades 5–6 from *Used numbers: Real data in the classroom*). White Plains, NY: Cuisenaire–Dale Seymour.

Gnanadesikan, M., Schaeffer, R. L., & Swift, J. (1987). *The art and techniques of simulation: Quantitative literacy series.* White Plains, NY: Cuisenaire–Dale Seymour.

Haruta, M. E., Flaherty, M., McGivney, J., & McGivney, R. J. (1996). Coin tossing. *Mathematics Teacher, 89,* 642–645.

Jones, G. A., Thornton, C. A., Langrall, C. W., & Tarr, J. E. (1999). Understanding students' probabilistic reasoning. In L. V. Stiff (Ed.), *Developing mathematical reasoning in grades K–12* (pp. 146–155). Reston, VA: National Council of Teachers of Mathematics.

Karp, K. S. (1994). Telling tales: Creating graphs using multicultural literature. *Teaching Children Mathematics, 1,* 87–91.

Landwehr, J. M., Swift, J., & Watkins, A. E. (1987). *Exploring surveys and information from samples: Quantitative literacy series.* White Plains, NY: Cuisenaire–Dale Seymour.

Landwehr, J. M., & Watkins, A. E. (1987). *Exploring data: Quantitative literacy series.* White Plains, NY: Cuisenaire–Dale Seymour.

Leutzinger, L. P. (1990). Graphical representation and probability. In J. N. Payne (Ed.), *Mathematics for the young child* (pp. 251–263). Reston, VA: National Council of Teachers of Mathematics.

Lindquist, M. M. (1992). *Making sense of data: Addenda series, grades K–6.* Reston, VA: National Council of Teachers of Mathematics.

Martin, H. M., & Zawojewski, J. S. (1993). Dealing with data and chance: An illustration from the middle school addendum to the standards. *Arithmetic Teacher, 41,* 220–223.

Newman, C. M., Obremski, T. E., & Schaeffer, R. L. (1987). *Exploring probability: Quantitative literacy series.* White Plains, NY: Cuisenaire–Dale Seymour.

Phillips, E., Lappan, G., Winter, M. J., & Fitzgerald, W. M. (1986). *Middle grades mathematics project: Probability.* Menlo Park, CA: AWL Supplemental.

Russell, S. J., & Corwin, R. B. (1989). *Statistics: The shape of the data* (Unit of study for grades 4–6 from *Used numbers: Real data in the classroom*). White Plains, NY: Cuisenaire–Dale Seymour.

Russell, S. J., & Corwin, R. B. (1990). *Sorting: Groups and graphs* (Unit of study for grades 2–3 from *Used numbers: Real data in the classroom*). White Plains, NY: Cuisenaire–Dale Seymour.

Russell, S. J., & Friel, S. N. (1989). Collecting and analyzing real data in the elementary classroom. In P. R. Trafton (Ed.), *New directions for elementary school mathematics* (pp. 134–148). Reston, VA: National Council of Teachers of Mathematics.

Russell, S. J., & Stone, A. (1990). *Counting: Ourselves and our families* (Unit of study for grades K–1 from *Used numbers: Real data in the classroom*). White Plains, NY: Cuisenaire–Dale Seymour.

Shaughnessy, J. M., & Dick, T. (1991). Monty's dilemma: Should you stick or switch? *Mathematics Teacher, 84,* 252–256.

Uccellini, J. C. (1996). Teaching the mean meaningfully. *Mathematics Teaching in the Middle School, 2,* 112–115.

Wallace, E. C. (1993). Exploring regression with a graphing calculator. *Mathematics Teacher, 86,* 741–743.

Zawojewski, J. S., & Heckman, D. S. (1997). What do students know about data analysis, statistics, and probability? In P. A. Kenney & E. A. Silver (Eds.), *Results from the sixth mathematics assessment of the National Assessment of Educational Progress* (pp. 195–224). Reston, VA: National Council of Teachers of Mathematics.

# Chapter 19

# Algebraic Reasoning

It is significant that the authors of *Principles and Standards for School Mathematics* chose Algebra as one of the five content standards to span all grades, pre-K–12. Clearly, they are not talking about algebra in the eighth grade or high school or even that every child should take an algebra "course." Rather, the *Principles and Standards* Algebra standard is about the development of algebraic thinking and algebraic concepts to be developed throughout the K–12 curriculum. The focus is on patterns, functions, and the ability to analyze situations with the help of symbols.

*Algebraic reasoning* involves representing, generalizing, and formalizing patterns and regularity in all aspects of mathematics. As Kaput (1998) notes, it is difficult to find an area of mathematics that does not involve generalizing and formalizing in some central way. In fact, this type of reasoning is at the heart of mathematics as a science of pattern and order.

In this chapter, we will look specifically at activities that focus on this thinking and reasoning throughout the grades. As algebraic reasoning develops, so must the language and symbolism that have been developed to support and communicate that thinking, specifically equations, variables, and functions. Function and functional notation are such important ideas in mathematics that a separate chapter has been devoted to them.

## BIG Ideas

1. Logical patterns exist and are a regular occurrence in mathematics. They can be recognized, extended, or generalized. The same pattern can be found in many different forms. Patterns are found in physical and geometric situations as well as in numbers.

2. Symbolism, especially that involving equations and variables, is used to express generalizations of patterns and relationships.

3. Variables are symbols that take the place of numbers or ranges of numbers. They have different meanings depending on whether they are being used as representations of quantities that vary or change, representations of specific unknown values, or placeholders in a generalized expression or formula.

4. Equations and inequalities are used to express relationships between two quantities.

## REPEATING PATTERNS

Identifying and extending patterns is an important process in algebraic thinking. Simple repetitive patterns can be explored as early as kindergarten. Young children love to work with patterns such as those made with colored blocks, connecting cubes, and buttons.

## Using Materials in Patterning

When possible, patterning activities should involve some form of physical materials. This is especially true of repeating patterns in grades K–4. When patterns are built with materials, children are able to test the extension of a pattern and make changes without fear of being wrong.

Many kindergarten and first-grade textbooks have pages where students are given a pattern such as a string of colored beads. The task may be to color the last bead or two in the string. There are two differences between this and the same activity done with actual materials. First, by coloring on the page, the activity takes on an aura of right versus wrong. If a mistake is made, correction on the page is difficult and can cause feelings of inadequacy. Materials allow a trial-and-error approach to be used. Second, pattern activities on worksheets prevent children from extending patterns beyond the few spaces provided by the page. Most children enjoy using materials such as colored blocks, buttons, and connecting cubes to extend their patterns well beyond the printed page. Children are frequently observed continuing a pattern with materials halfway across the classroom floor. In doing so, children receive a great deal of satisfaction and positive feedback from the activity itself. "Hey, I understand this! I can do it really well. I feel good about how I solved my pattern problem."

# Repeating-Pattern Activities

The concept of a repeating pattern and how a pattern is extended or continued can be introduced to the full class in several ways. One possibility is to draw simple shape patterns on the board and extend them in a class discussion. Oral patterns can be joined in by all children. For example, "do, mi, mi, do, mi, mi, ..." is a simple singing pattern. Up, down, and sideways arm positions provide three elements with which to make patterns: up, side, side, down, up, side, side, down, ... Boy-girl patterns or stand-sit-squat patterns are also fun. From these ideas, the youngest children learn quickly the concept of patterns. Students can begin to work more profitably in small groups or even independently once a general notion of patterns is developed.

┌─ **A**CTIVITY ────────────────────

## 19.1 Pattern Strips

Students can work independently or in groups of two or three to extend patterns made from simple materials: buttons, colored blocks, connecting cubes, toothpicks, geometric shapes—items you can gather easily. For each set of materials, draw two or three complete repetitions of a pattern on strips of tagboard about 5 cm by 30 cm. The students' task is to use actual materials, copy the pattern shown, and extend it as far as they wish. Discussions with students will help them describe their patterns and uncover errors. Figure 19.1 illustrates possible patterns for a variety of materials. It is not necessary to have class-sized sets of materials. Make 10 to 15 different pattern strips for each set of materials. With six to eight sets, your entire class can work at the same time, in small groups working with different patterns and different materials.

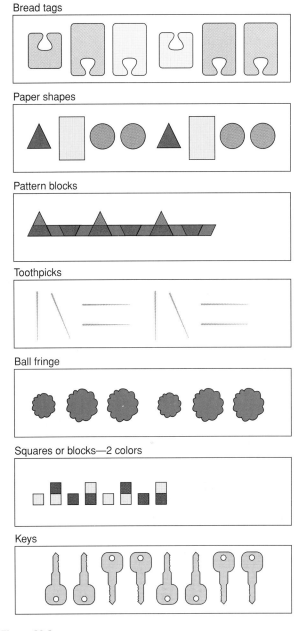

**Figure 19.1** Examples of pattern cards drawn on tagboard. Each pattern repeats completely and does not split in the middle of a core.

The *core* of a repeating pattern is the shortest string of elements that repeats. Notice in Figure 19.1 that the core is always fully repeated and never only partially shown. If the core of a pattern is –oo, a card might have –oo–oo (two repetitions of the core), but it would be ambiguous if the card showed –oo–oo– or –oo–.

A significant step forward mathematically is to see that two patterns constructed with different materials are actually the same pattern. For example, the first pattern in Figure 19.1 and the first pattern in Figure 19.2 (p. 386) can both be

**Figure 19.2  More examples of repeating patterns.**

"read" A-B-B-A-B-B-, and the pattern below those in both figures is A-B-C-C-A-B-C-C-. Challenging students to translate a pattern from one medium to another or to find two patterns that are alike, even though made with different materials, helps students focus on the relationships that are the essence of repeated patterns.

┌─ **A**CTIVITY ────────────────────────────────

## 19.2  Pattern Match

Using the chalkboard or overhead projector, show six or seven patterns with different materials or pictures. Teach students to use an A, B, C method of reading a pattern. Half of the class can close their eyes while the other half uses the A, B, C scheme to read a pattern that you point to. After hearing the pattern, the students who had their eyes closed examine the patterns and try to decide which pattern was read. If two of the patterns in the list have the same structure, the discussion can be very interesting.

└──────────────────────────────────────────────

The following independent activity involves translation of a pattern from one medium to another, which is another way of helping students separate the relationship in a pattern from the materials used to build it.

┌─ **A**CTIVITY ────────────────────────────────

## 19.3  Same Pattern, Different Stuff

Have students make a pattern with one set of materials given a pattern strip showing a different set. This activity can easily be set up by simply switching the pattern strips from one set of materials to another. A similar idea is to mix up the pattern strips for four or five different sets of materials and have students find strips that have the same pattern. To test if two patterns are the same, children can translate each of the strips into a third set of materials or can write down the A, B, C pattern for each.

└──────────────────────────────────────────────

The challenge in the next activity is a forerunner to looking at the function aspect of patterns.

## ACTIVITY

### 19.4 Predict Down the Line

For most repeating patterns, the elements of the pattern can be numbered 1, 2, 3, and so on. Provide students with a pattern to extend. Before students begin to extend the pattern, have them predict exactly what element will be in, say, the fifteenth position. Students should be required to provide a reason for their prediction, preferably in writing. Students should then extend the pattern as before and check their prediction. If their prediction is incorrect, have them examine their reasoning and try to figure out why the prediction was off.

The prediction activity may be quite challenging before the second grade. Eventually, students will figure out that the length of the core of the pattern plays a significant role. If you ask for a prediction of the hundredth element or even the three-hundredth element, students will not be able to check the prediction by extending the pattern. Verification focuses on the rationale for the prediction. Students may need to use a calculator to skip-count or multiply. But it is always the reasoning that is most important.

## GROWING PATTERNS

Beginning at about the fourth or fifth grade and extending through the junior high years, students can explore patterns that involve a progression from step to step. In technical terms, these are called *sequences;* we will simply call them *growing patterns*. With these patterns, students not only extend patterns but also look for a generalization or an algebraic relationship that will tell them what the pattern will be at any point along the way. Growing patterns also demonstrate the concept of function and can be used as an entry point to this very important mathematical idea.

Figure 19.3 illustrates some growing patterns that are built with various materials or drawings. The patterns consist of a series of separate elements or *frames,* each new frame related to the previous one according to the pattern.

The first thing to do with patterns in the upper and middle grades is to get students comfortable with building patterns and talking about how they can be extended in a logical manner. Building the patterns with physical materials such as tiles, counters, or flat toothpicks allows students to make changes if necessary and to build on to one frame to make a new frame. It is also more fun!

## ACTIVITY

### 19.5 Extend and Explain

As an introduction to growing patterns, show students the first three elements or frames of a pattern. Provide them with appropriate materials or grid paper, and have them extend the patterns and explain why their extension indeed follows the pattern. For some patterns, there may be more than one way to extend the first two or three frames. If, for example, you were to suggest only the first two elements of the block pattern at the top of Figure 19.3, students might well develop four or five patterns that are different from the stairsteps shown in the figure. The purpose would simply be to explore the idea of a progression from one frame or part of a growing pattern to the next.

When discussing a pattern, students should try to determine how each frame in the pattern differs from the preceding

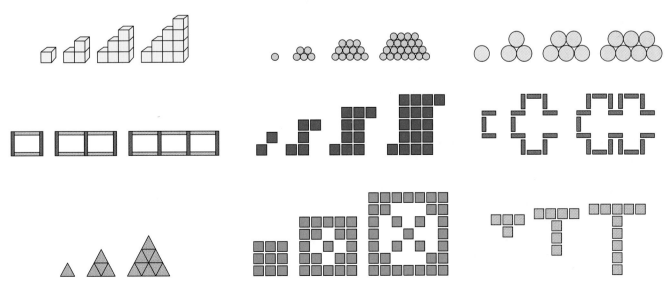

**Figure 19.3** **Growing patterns with materials or drawings.**

frame. If each new frame can be built by adding on to or changing the previous frame, the discussion should include how this can be done. For example, each stairstep in Figure 19.3 can be made by adding a column of blocks to the preceding stairsteps. In contrast, the pattern of red tiles involves a form of expansion rather than adding on.

Growing patterns also have a numeric component, the number of objects in each frame. As shown in Figure 19.4, a table can be made for any growing pattern. One row of the table or chart is always the frame number, and the other is for recording how many objects are in that frame. Frequently, a pattern grows so quickly and requires so many blocks or spaces to draw it that it is only reasonable to build or draw the first five or six frames. This leads to the following activity.

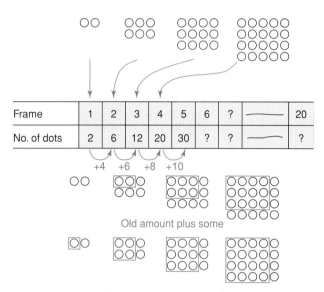

**Figure 19.4** Two different relationships in a visual pattern.

## ACTIVITY

### 19.6 Predict How Many

Have students begin to extend a growing pattern you provide. They should also make a table showing how many items are needed to make each frame of the pattern. The task is to predict the number of items in the twentieth frame of the pattern. The challenge is to see if there is a way to do this without filling in the first 19 entries of the table. Predictions should also be accompanied by an explanation.

Activity 19.6 is a natural progression from the earlier prediction activity with repeating patterns. Finding a way to determine the twentieth or even the hundredth entry in the table gets at the heart of finding a relationship that later students will understand is an example of a function. We next look at how to help students find these relationships.

# Searching for Relationships

Once a table or chart is developed, students have two representations of the pattern: the one created with the drawing or materials and the numeric version that is in the table. When looking for relationships, some students will focus on the table and others will focus on the physical pattern. It is important for students to see that whatever relationships they discover, they exist in both forms. So if a relationship is found in a table, challenge students to see how that plays out in the physical version.

## Patterns from Frame to Frame: Recursive Relationships

For most students, it is easier to see the patterns from one frame to the next. When you have a chart constructed, the differences from one frame to the next can be written next to or below it, as in Figure 19.4. In that example, the number in each frame can be determined from the previous frame by adding successive even numbers. The description that tells how a pattern changes from any given frame to the next frame is known as a *recursive relationship*.

Whenever there is a pattern in the table, see if students can find that same pattern in the physical version. In Figure 19.4, notice that in each frame, the previous frame has been outlined. That lets you examine the amount added and see how it creates the pattern of adding on even numbers. The picture or physical pattern and the table should be as closely connected as possible.

## Patterns from Frame Number to Frame: Functional Relationships

The recursive frame-to-frame pattern is almost certainly the first that your students will observe. However, to find the table entry for the hundredth frame, the only way a recursive pattern can help is to find all of the prior 99 entries in the table. If a rule or relationship can be discovered that connects the number of objects in a frame to the frame number, any table entry can be determined without building or calculating all of the intermediate entries. A rule that determines the number of elements in a frame from the frame number is an example of a *functional relationship*.

There is no single best method for finding this relationship between frame number and frame. Some students may get insight by simply "playing around" with the numbers and asking, "How can I operate on the frame number to get the corresponding number in the table?" Most will benefit from examining the physical pattern for regularities. At the bottom of Figure 19.4, a square array is outlined for each frame. Each successive square is one larger on a side. What relationship might exist between this subset of the pattern and the frame numbers? In this example, the side of each square is the same as the frame number. The row to the right of each square is also the frame number. With that information, how would you describe the twentieth frame? Can you determine how many elements will be in it without drawing the picture? At this point, a significant activity is to write a numeric expression for each frame number using the same pattern. For example, the first four frames in Figure 19.4 are $1^2 + 1$, $2^2 + 2$, $3^2 + 3$, and $4^2 + 4$.

It may take much searching and experimenting for students in groups or as a class to come up with an expression that is similar for each frame. Do not be upset if students have difficulty. Encourage the search for relationships to continue, even if it takes more than one day. The search for relationships is the most significant portion of these activities.

## Moving from Patterns to Function and Variable

When students have discovered numeric expressions for each frame using frame numbers, write them with brackets around the frame numbers as shown in Figure 19.5. If this results in a pattern, the bracketed numbers will change from one frame to the next while the other numbers in the expressions remain the same. Now the bracketed numbers can be replaced by a letter or variable, resulting in a general formula. The formula defines the functional relationship between frame numbers and frame values.

Before reading on, explore each of the patterns in Figure 19.3 (p. 387) to see if you can find formulas (functional relationships) for each. You should be able to "plug in" the frame numbers in your formulas and get the value for that frame. Some are much harder than others.

The discussion to this point is summarized in the following activity, an elaboration of "Predict How Many." It is best to do this in groups so that ideas can be generated more freely.

### ACTIVITY

## 19.7 Find the Function in the Pattern

Give students the beginning of a pattern, usually at least three frames. Their tasks are as follows:

1. Extend the pattern several more frames until they are sure they understand the pattern. They should always look backward to the beginning of the pattern to see that their idea works for all frames. Record this in a drawing.

2. Make a table that shows frame numbers and elements in each frame for every frame they have constructed.

3. Find and describe in writing as many patterns as possible in the table and in the physical pattern. For each pattern found in the table, they should see how that idea can be found in the physical pattern. The most important pattern to look for is the one from frame number to frame, the functional relationship.

4. Write the frame number–to–frame relationship as a formula in terms of the frame number. Show how the formula works for each part of the table already constructed. Use the formula to predict the next entry in the table, and check this with an actual construction of the pattern, if possible. Use the formula to predict the twentieth entry in the table.

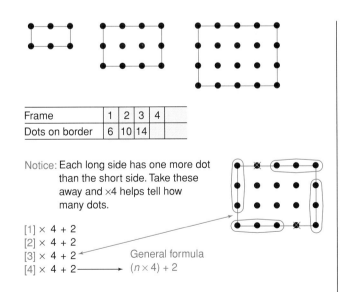

| Frame | 1 | 2 | 3 | 4 |
|---|---|---|---|---|
| Dots on border | 6 | 10 | 14 | |

Notice: Each long side has one more dot than the short side. Take these away and ×4 helps tell how many dots.

[1] × 4 + 2
[2] × 4 + 2
[3] × 4 + 2
[4] × 4 + 2     General formula
               $(n \times 4) + 2$

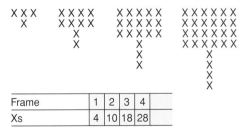

| Frame | 1 | 2 | 3 | 4 |
|---|---|---|---|---|
| Xs | 4 | 10 | 18 | 28 |

Notice: If the tail part is added to the side of the top part, there is always a square and three more columns.

[1] × [1] + (3 × [1])
[2] × [2] + (3 × [2])
[3] × [3] + (3 × [3])
    ⋮    General formula
$n \times n + 3n = n^2 + 3n$

**Figure 19.5** Finding functional relationships in patterns.

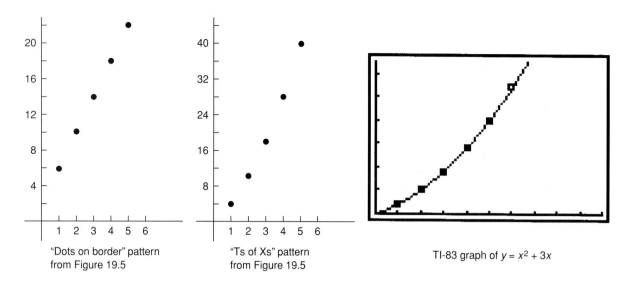

**Figure 19.6** **Graphs of growing patterns.**

## Graphing the Patterns

So far, growing patterns are represented by the physical materials or drawings, by a chart, and by a symbolic rule. A graph adds a fourth representation. The individual points in a pattern can be plotted even if the physical pattern has not been discovered. Figure 19.6 shows the graph for each of the two patterns in Figure 19.5. Notice that the first is a straight-line (linear) relationship and the other is a curved line that would make half of a parabola if the points were joined.

 Do not forget how easy it is both to plot points and to draw curves on the graphing calculator. The second graph in Figure 19.6 is also shown on a graphing calculator with the function $y = x^2 + 3x$ (same as $n^2 + 3n$) drawn through it. Spreadsheets can be used in exactly the same way.

## OTHER PATTERNS TO EXPLORE

It would be an error to leave the impression that repeated patterns and growing patterns as discussed so far are all that students need to know about patterns. Mathematicians continue to search for and discover new patterns and relationships. Applications of mathematical patterns have led to solutions of real-world problems that were once thought to be unsolvable. Patterns are powerful ideas.

## Patterns on the Hundreds Chart

The hundreds chart is a rich field for exploring number relationships and should not be thought of solely as a device for teaching numeration.

### 19.8 Skip-Count Patterns on a Hundreds Chart

Duplicate lots of small copies of a hundreds chart (or a 0-to-99 chart as in the Blackline Masters). Let children pick a number from 2 to 10. Their task is to begin with zero and skip-count by that number. For each count, they should color in the corresponding number on their chart and look for patterns. When they have finished skip-counting and coloring all the way to 100, they should write a description of their pattern. The written report can then accompany the colored pattern on the hundreds chart. See Figure 19.7 for two examples of patterns.

| 1 | 2 | 3 | 4 | 5 | 6 | 7 | 8 | 9 | 10 |
|---|---|---|---|---|---|---|---|---|---|
| 11 | 12 | 13 | 14 | 15 | 16 | 17 | 18 | 19 | 20 |
| 21 | 22 | 23 | 24 | 25 | 26 | 27 | 28 | 29 | 30 |
| 31 | 32 | 33 | 34 | 35 | 36 | 37 | 38 | 39 | 40 |
| 41 | 42 | 43 | 44 | 45 | 46 | 47 | 48 | 49 | 50 |
| 51 | 52 | 53 | 54 | 55 | 56 | 57 | 58 | 59 | 60 |
| 61 | 62 | 63 | 64 | 65 | 66 | 67 | 68 | 69 | 70 |
| 71 | 72 | 73 | 74 | 75 | 76 | 77 | 78 | 79 | 80 |
| 81 | 82 | 83 | 84 | 85 | 86 | 87 | 88 | 89 | 90 |
| 91 | 92 | 93 | 94 | 95 | 96 | 97 | 98 | 99 | 100 |

**Figure 19.7** **Skip counts by sixes (colored blue) and threes (circled with red).**

Here are some possible follow-up problems to accompany Activity 19.8:

Which numbers make diagonal patterns? Which make column patterns?

Can you find two skip-count patterns with one "on top of" the other? That is, all of the squares for one pattern are on the pattern for the other. How are these two skip-count numbers related? Are there other patterns that are on top of each other?

What patterns only have a few squares in common? On what numbers do the patterns cross? Can you tell without looking at the charts?

What happens to the patterns if you use the same skip-count number but start with 1 or some other number instead of starting with 0?

Fours on a 5-wide chart

Threes and fives
on a 4-wide chart

**Figure 19.8** **Patterns on hundreds charts of different widths.**

---

Have students look for relationships involving the skip-count number, the width of the chart, and whether the pattern is diagonal or makes columns.

Students will find that the same patterns are on top of each other as with the usual chart. However, patterns go in columns only when skip-counting by a factor or a multiple of the chart width. For example, on a chart of width 9, the threes make columns but the twos make diagonals. What will a 6 do on a 9-wide chart? What if the width of the chart is a prime number? You can also explore charts that are wider than 10.

## Number Patterns

Many worthwhile patterns can be observed with numbers alone. These can be simple repeating patterns such as 1, 2, 1, 2, . . . Even very young children can use numbers in patterns like these. Generally, however, numeric patterns involve some form of progression. The pattern 1, 2, 1, 3, 1, 4, 1, 5, . . . is a simple example that even young students can discover. Here are some more numeric patterns:

| | |
|---|---|
| 2, 4, 6, 8, 10, . . . | (even numbers; add 2 each time) |
| 1, 4, 7, 10, 13, . . . | (start with 1; add 3 each time) |
| 1, 4, 9, 16, . . . | (squares: $1^2$, $2^2$, $3^2$, etc.) |
| 0, 1, 5, 14, 30, . . . | (add the next square number) |
| 2, 5, 11, 23, . . . | (double the number and add 1) |
| 2, 6, 12, 20, 30, . . . | (multiply successive pairs) |
| 3, 3, 6, 9, 15, 24, . . . | (add the two preceding numbers— an example of a Fibonacci sequence) |

The challenge in these patterns or sequences of numbers is not only to find and extend the pattern but also to try to determine a general rule to produce the *n*th number in the sequence. Informal or exploratory approaches are similar to those described for growing patterns.

---

**ACTIVITY**

### 19.10 Pairs of Patterns: Alike and Different

Give students two patterns that are related in some way. To indicate that they understand the patterns, they should first extend each one by at least five more numbers. Next, they should write an explanation of how the two patterns are *alike* and how the two patterns are *different*. Here are some pairs to use:

2, 4, 6, 8, 10, . . . and 3, 5, 7, 9, 11, . . .

2, 4, 6, 8, 10, . . . and 2, 4, 8, 16, 32, . . .

3, 4, 3, 4, 3, 4, . . . and 7, 9, 7, 9, 7, 9, . . .

5, 10, 15, 20, 25, . . . and 2, 7, 12, 17, 22, . . .

10, 20, 30, 40, 50, . . . and 50, 100, 150, 200, 250, . . .

---

**ACTIVITY**

## 19.9 Change the Charts, Change the Patterns

Have students make number charts with fewer than ten numbers in a row. Use centimeter grid paper. Repeat the skip-count tasks from Activity 19.8. The challenge is to discover which skip counts will form diagonal patterns and which will form column patterns. The answer will vary, depending on the width of the chart. (See Figure 19.8 for two examples.)

After solving several pairs of related number patterns, students can make up their own pairs of patterns and challenge other students to discover how they are alike and different.

The calculator provides a powerful approach to patterns. A few examples are presented here, but there are many more.

### Ⱥ CTIVITY

## 19.11 Skip-Count Patterns

Choose a start number between 0 and 9, and add a constant (skip number) repeatedly to that number. Remember to use the automatic constant feature. For example, to start with 7 and add 4 repeatedly, you press 7 ⊞ 4 ⊟ ⊟ ⊟ . . . What digits appear in the ones place? (1, 5, 9, 3, 7, 1, 5, 9, 3, 7, . . .) How long is the pattern before it repeats? Are all patterns the same length? Are there shorter ones? Can you find one that is length 6? Why not? How does this change when the start number changes? How does it change when the skip number changes?

An extended discussion of this last activity can be found in Chapter 2, "Start and Jump Numbers" (p. 17).

### Ⱥ CTIVITY

## 19.12 Secret Function I

This game can be introduced using an overhead calculator with the full class, and then pairs of children can play independently. Without the class looking, store a one-step operation (secret function) in the calculator. Here is an example for each operation:

Addition:        Secret = +8     Press 0 ⊞ 8 ⊟ ± ⊟

Subtraction:     Secret = −24    Press 0 ⊟ 4 ⊟ ± ⊟

Multiplication:  Secret = ×36    Press 6 ⊠ 0 ⊟

Division:        Secret = ÷3     Press 0 ⊞ 3 ⊟

The display will show 0 after the function has been stored. After a secret function has been entered, students try to guess the secret rule or function. They can get up to three clues. To get the first clue, they enter any number and press ⊟ to see what the secret function does to the entered number. They can get a second clue to the secret by pressing ⊟ again and the third clue by pressing ⊟ a third time. After each clue, they should try to guess the secret function and predict the display after the next ⊟ press.

"Secret Function I" can be played at any grade level with addition and subtraction. Be prepared to talk about numbers less than zero. When division is used, decimals will appear. At the upper grade levels, the multiplication and division functions may be decimals or fractions. Consider the discus-

sion when the rule is ×0.5 and a student guesses ÷2. As a variation, instead of pressing ⊟ successively, a different number can be entered each time before pressing ⊟. If any of the operation keys are pressed, the function will no longer be stored. (Your calculator must have a sign-change key ± to enter addition or subtraction functions. Some calculators store the second rather than the first factor for multiplication. In that case, reverse the order in the hidden function.)

### Ⱥ CTIVITY

## 19.13 Secret Function II

A graphing calculator allows for a different version of "Secret Function I." Compound functions such as $(2x + 1)/2$ or $x^2 − 4x$ can be stored. Students attempt to guess the rule by entering different numbers and seeing the output. The goal is to try to guess the function using as few input trials as possible. On the TI-73 or TI-83, the following simple program will take an entry, display the output, and continue to accept inputs until you press ⸢Quit⸥.

```
Prgm 1: GUESS
:Lbl 1
:Disp "ENTER X"
:Input X
:2X+5⇒A  (This line stores the secret function.)
:Disp A
:Goto 1
```

Students using the program will see only

```
Prgm 1: GUESS
"ENTER X"
?3
                    11
ENTER X
?5
                    15
```

The function line of the program is easily changed.

### Ⱥ CTIVITY

## 19.14 Amazing Digits

Enter 9 ⊠ $n$, where $n$ is any number from 1 to 9. Press ⊟. Now press other numbers followed by ⊟. Even if students know their nines facts, this step will serve to clarify the process and illustrate that each new press of ⊟ multiplies the display by 9. Now enter 99 ⊠ $n$ ⊟. Try other values of $n$ followed by ⊟. What is the pattern? Try 999 ⊠ $n$ and even 9999 or 99999 ⊠ $n$. Students should play with and explore this idea as long as they wish. Next try using repeating digits for $n$ (3333 or 66). Instead of using nines for the multiplier, try using 0.009 or 99.9. Also experiment with other repeat-digit multipliers. If students are interested, the patterns with nines might be analyzed by looking at 999 as 1000 − 1 or as 9 × 111.

─ **A**CTIVITY ─

## 19.15  More Amazing Digits

Especially if students have shown interest in "Amazing Digits," try division by 9. Begin by just dividing single-digit numbers by 9. (The calculator remembers the last divisor, so after the first division, just enter the new number and press ⊟.) After this, there are all sorts of variations to try:

> a. Divide by 99, 999, . . .
>
> b. Divide by 0.9, 0.09, 0.009, . . .
>
> c. Divide by 9, but use two-digit dividends. Can you predict the results?
>
> d. Try three-digit dividends and a divisor of 9.
>
> e. Combine (a) or (b) with (c) or (d).

The patterns in "More Amazing Digits" are spectacular and interesting by themselves, but you may want to also try using a digit other than 9 in that exercise.

─ **A**CTIVITY ─

## 19.16  Consecutive Odd Numbers

Before doing this activity, you will need to explain what consecutive odd numbers are and how to add them on the calculator. Consecutive odd numbers are odd numbers that come together in the counting order. Thus 1, 3, 5, 7 are consecutive odd numbers, as are 27, 29, 31. To add a string of these numbers, some students may benefit by writing the numbers down before they begin to add them on the calculator. Young students are confused when adding more than two numbers in a row. When they press ⊞ after the second addend, the display shows the sum as if ⊟ had been pressed.

### Part 1
Have students use their calculators to make a chart that lists the sums of the first *n* consecutive odd numbers.

| | |
|---|---|
| 1 | 1 |
| 1 + 3 | 4 |
| 1 + 3 + 5 | 9 |
| 1 + 3 + 5 + 7 | 16 |

and so on.

The sums should look familiar. If students (around grades 5 to 8) do not recognize these as squares, suggest that they press the √ key after they get the sum.

It would be a good idea for them to express the sums as squares ($1^2, 2^2, 3^2, 4^2, \ldots$). Can they predict the sum of the first 20 or first 50 consecutive odd numbers?

### Part 2
If the consecutive odd numbers are written in a triangular list as shown here, and the sum of each horizontal row is recorded, there is an interesting result:

1

3   5

7   9   11

13   15   17   19

and so on.

As follow-up to the odd sum activity, students may want to examine consecutive even numbers or simply consecutive numbers. For example, what can you tell about the sum of any four consecutive numbers? Any five? Pick a number less than 100. Can you find a string of consecutive numbers that add up to your number? Can you find two different consecutive strings of numbers that have the same sum? (3 + 4 + 5 + 6 = 5 + 6 + 7). What numbers have only one sum?

## The Fibonacci Sequence

For a growing pattern that is just a little bit different, see Figure 19.9. It begins with a little square. Each successive frame is formed by building a new and larger square onto the previous design. (Can you see how to continue drawing this pattern?) If the side of the first two little squares is 1 each, then the sides of each new square are the numbers of most interest in this pattern. For those squares shown in the figure, the

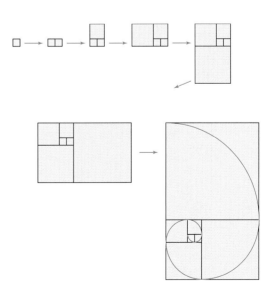

**Figure 19.9**  **A growing pattern of squares: Each new rectangle is a little closer to a "golden rectangle."**

sides are 1, 1, 2, 3, 5, 8, and 13. What would the side of the next square be? This series of numbers, known as the *Fibonacci sequence,* is named for the Italian mathematician Leonardo Fibonacci (c. 1180–1250). The sequence occurs in a variety of living things. For example, if you count the sets of spirals that go in opposite directions on a pineapple or the seeds of a sunflower, the two numbers will be adjacent numbers in the Fibonacci sequence, usually 8 and 13 for a pineapple and 55 and 89 for sunflowers.

Another interesting fact about the Fibonacci sequence is that the ratio of adjacent numbers in the sequence gets closer and closer to a single fixed number known as the *golden ratio,* a number very close to 1.618. Each larger rectangle in Figure 19.9 has sides in ratio a little closer to the golden ratio. A rectangle in that ratio is called a *golden rectangle,* examples of which can be found in most of the prominent examples of ancient Greek architecture as well as in much art and architecture through the ages. The spiral that is drawn in the last rectangle shown (made from quarter circles drawn in each square) is the same spiral found in the shell of the chambered nautilus.

The usual Fibonacci sequence begins with 1, 1. After these first two terms, the next term is found by adding the two preceding terms: $1 + 1 = 2$, $1 + 2 = 3$, $2 + 3 = 5$, $3 + 5 = 8$, and so on. What happens if you use the same rule for generating each new number but you begin with numbers other than 1 and 1? This is an interesting exploration. Among other things you may discover is that the ratio of successive pairs of terms also gets closer and closer to the same golden ratio, 1.618 . . . , as in the regular Fibonacci sequence. On a graphing calculator, the following simple program will produce successive numbers in the sequence and the current ratio of the last two terms with every press of the Enter key.

```
ClrHome
ClrList L₂,L₁
1→N
Disp "ENTER 1ST"
Disp "SEED"
Input H
1→L₁(N)
Disp "ENTER 2ND"
Disp "SEED"
Input Y
H/Y→L₂(1)
ClrHome
Disp "FIRST 2 NOS.",H,Y
Disp "RATIO",H/Y
Pause
ClrHome
Lbl 1
N+1→N
H+Y→A
Y→Z
H→Y
A→H
Disp "LAST 3 NOS.",Z,Y,H
Disp "RATIO OF LAST 2",H/Y
N→L₁(N)
H/Y→L₂(N)
Pause
ClrHome
Goto 1
```

The Fibonacci sequence and the golden ratio are fascinating phenomena of mathematics. For those who would like to learn more about the connections of this sequence with nature, art, and mathematics, books by Runion (1990) and by Garland (1987) are highly recommended.

# VARIABLES AND EQUATIONS

One of the most powerful ways we have of expressing the regularities found in mathematics is with variables. Variables enable us to use mathematical symbolism as a tool to think and help better understand mathematical ideas in the same way physical objects and drawings are used. But if variables are to be included with these other "thinker toys," it is important to help students develop an understanding of the various ways they are used.

## Variables

A *variable* is a symbol that can stand for any one of a set of numbers or other objects. Although correct, this simple-sounding definition has a variety of interpretations, depending on how the variables are used. A less than clear understanding can lead to a host of misinterpretations.

### Misunderstandings About Variables

Even though students are exposed throughout the elementary years to boxes and letters in arithmetic expressions, studies indicate that most children have a very narrow understanding of the concept of "variable" (Booth, 1988; Chalouh & Herscovics; Lodholz, 1990).

Some students believe that $7w + 22 = 109$ and $7n + 22 = 109$ will have different solutions. Students readily accept L for length but have difficulty accepting another letter for the same quantity. Letters are sometimes taken to represent objects rather than numeric values. Converting the expression "John has three times as many apples as Mary" to symbols, we might use $3a$ for John's apples. Here the $a$ stands not for *apples* but for the *number of apples.*

Conventions of notation also compound the difficulty. For example, we use $ab$ to mean $a \times b$, but $3 \times 5 \neq 35$. Similarly, $ab = ba$, but $35 \neq 53$; and $4 + 0.75 = 4.75$, but $2x + y \neq 2xy$.

### Different Uses of Variables

Meanings of variables change with the way they are used. Usiskin (1988) identified three uses of variables that are commonly encountered in school mathematics:

1. *As a specific unknown.* In the early grades, this is the use found in equations such as $8 + \square = 12$. Later, we see exercises such as this: If $3x + 2 = 4x - 1$, solve for $x$.

2. *As a pattern generalizer.* Variables are used in statements that are true for all numbers. For example, $a \times b = b \times a$

for all real numbers. Formulas such as $A = L \times W$ also show a pattern.

3. *As quantities that vary in joint variation.* Joint variation occurs when change in one variable determines a change in another. In $y = 3x + 5$, as $x$ changes or varies, so does $y$. Formulas are also an example of joint variation. In $C = 2\pi r$, as $r$, the radius, changes, so does $C$, the circumference.

## Variables as Unknowns

The following activity is a reasonable way for students to experience the meaning of a variable as a placeholder.

┌─ **A**CTIVITY ──────────────────────────────

### 19.17 Story Translations

Read a simple story problem to students, but omit the question. Their task is to write an equation that means the same thing. For example: *There are 3 full boxes of pencils and 5 extra pencils. There are 41 pencils in all.* ($3 \times \square + 5 = 41$) Be sure to include all meanings of all four operations as described in Chapter 7. The activity can be reversed by providing an equation with an unknown and letting students make up a story to go with it. Once equations are agreed on, students should use whatever means they wish to find values that make the sentences true. Trial and error is a reasonable first strategy.

└──────────────────────────────────────────────

Sometimes students will write what may look like different equations. For example, *If Yolanda has 12 cards and Karl has 5, write the equation that tells how many more cards Yolanda has.* Both of these equations might be written: $12 - 5 = \square$ and $5 + \square = 12$. Students should decide how these equations are alike and how they are different.

┌─ **A**CTIVITY ──────────────────────────────

### 19.18 Number Tricks

Have students do the following sequence of operations:

*Write down any number.*
*Add to it the number that comes after it.*
*Add 9.*
*Divide by 2.*
*Subtract the number you began with.*

Now you can "magically" read their minds. Everyone ended up with 5!

The challenge is to see if students can discover the secret to the trick. If students need a hint, suggest that instead of using an actual number, they use a box or a letter to begin with. Start with $N$. Add the next number: $N + (N + 1) = 2N + 1$. Adding 9 gives $2N + 10$. Dividing by 2 leaves $N + 5$. Now subtract the number you began with, leaving 5.

└──────────────────────────────────────────────

There are endless trick sequences like the one in this activity. Here are two more:

Pick a number between 1 and 9, multiply by 5, add 3, multiply by 2, add another number between 1 and 9, subtract 6. What do you see?

Pick a number, multiply by 6, add 12, take half of the result, subtract 6, divide by 3. What happens?

These tricks can also be explored with models by using a small box or a cube for the unknown. Figure 19.10 shows how the first of the two tricks above might be modeled. Notice the place-value component required to understand the result.

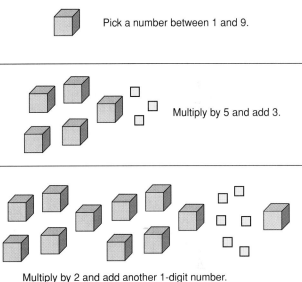

Pick a number between 1 and 9.

Multiply by 5 and add 3.

Multiply by 2 and add another 1-digit number.

Subtract 6, and then . . .

$$10 \times \boxed{\phantom{}} + \boxed{\phantom{}} = \boxed{\phantom{}}\boxed{\phantom{}}$$
(a 2-digit number)

**Figure 19.10** Number tricks can be modeled using a block or a box for the unknown. Additional numbers are shown with counters or base-ten pieces.

## Variables as Pattern Generators

Variables are often used to illustrate rules or regularities that exist in our number system. We often write down these rules using variables without giving much thought to the fact that students may not understand the variables involved.

┌─ **A**CTIVITY ──────────────────────────────

### 19.19 What's True for All Numbers?

Ask students how they know that $465 + 137 = 137 + 465$ without doing the computation. Students' explanations should show evidence of understanding the commutative property for addition, although the name of the property is not important. How can this be written to show that it's a rule that is true for every number, even fractions and decimals? If students do not suggest it, offer the idea that letters or shapes could be used like this:

$$\Delta + \square = \square + \Delta \quad \text{or} \quad n + m = m + n$$

Be sure students understand that the choice of letter or shape is totally arbitrary as long as it is understood that each stands for any number and that when the same letter or shape appears in the same equation, it must represent the same value.

With this introduction, challenge students to find other statements that are true for all numbers.

Students may need some prodding to think about things that are always true, but it is best that they come up with the ideas themselves. One way to provide hints is to explore some specific examples. For example, draw a divided rectangle as shown in Figure 19.11. What are two ways to calculate the area? This can lead to the generalized version of the distributive property: $a(b + c) = (a \times b) + (a \times c)$. In addition to properties of the number system, also think about definitions of exponents or rules for negative numbers, all of which can be expressed in a general form using variables.

**Figure 19.11** **The distributive property is just one of many ideas that can be generalized using variables.**

---

**ACTIVITY**

## 19.20 Special Quantities

What numeric expression would tell the number of chair legs on 376 chairs? ($376 \times 4$) What about 195 chairs? ($195 \times 4$) How would you write the number of legs on any number of chairs? ($N \times 4$) Using this as an example, challenge students to write expressions for other types of quantities: fingers on students, eggs in cartons, crayons in boxes, wheels on tractor trailers, hours in days, inches in feet, quarts in gallons, and so on. Similarly, use variables to express these special numbers: any odd number, any even number, any multiple of 7, a multiple of 3 plus a different multiple of 5, any two-digit number, any power of 2. Once students get the idea, have them make up their own special quantities and see if others can describe them verbally.

---

 The way that variables are used in the "Special Quantities" activity is essentially the way variables are used in spreadsheets. In Figure 19.12, odd and even numbers are generated from the numbers in column A. These values are then used in the sums and products columns.

Formulas that relate two or more quantities also express generalizations. For example, the formula $A = B \times h$ shows the relationship between the area of a rectangle and the product of its base and height. $F = (9/5)C + 32$ illustrates the relationship between Fahrenheit and Celsius temperatures. What equation would you use to indicate the relationship between feet and yards? A common error is to write $3F = Y$. However, substituting 6 for $F$ in this formula results in 18 yards instead of 2 yards. The difficulty is found in the syntax. Contrast "There are 3 feet in 1 yard" with "The number of feet is 3 times the number of yards." The variables stand for the *number* of feet and the *number* of yards, not feet and yards. Therefore, the correct relationship is $F = 3Y$.

### Variables as Quantities That Vary

"Joint variation is at the heart of understanding patterns and functions. As students grow in their ability to derive meaning for variables in contexts, they encounter variables that are changing in relation to each other" (Lappan, 1998, p. 57). Whenever students develop charts that list the corresponding values of two related quantities, they are exploring the idea of *joint variation*; the value in one row varies according to the value in the other row. Young children make charts showing the number of eyes for different numbers of kids. In the study of ratio and proportion, students make charts relating cost to the number of units purchased or relating miles driven to gallons of gasoline used. In measurement, charts are made that relate circumference to diameter or volume to the area of the base of a cylinder. In data analysis, best-fit lines produce generalizations of the way two variables are approximately related, for example, height and arm span. In this chapter, we have seen that the study of growing patterns results in formulas that connect the frame number to the number of elements in that frame of the pattern.

All of these are examples of joint variation—one value changing in relation to another. They are also examples of functions, the rule that determines the way that the two variables are related. Chapter 20 is devoted to helping children understand and analyze functions. There we will examine ways to help students explore joint variation of variables expressed in contextual situations, in equations, in charts, in graphs, and in words.

## Equations and Inequalities

In the expression $3B + 7 = B - C$, the equal sign means that the quantity on the left *is the same as* the quantity on the right. To understand expressions in this way, students must interpret simple arithmetic expressions such as $3 + 5$ or $4 \times 87$ as *single quantities*.

| | A | B | C | D | E | F | G | H | I |
|---|---|---|---|---|---|---|---|---|---|
| 1 | **Exploring Odd and Even Numbers** | | | | | | | | |
| 2 | | | | | | | | | |
| 3 | **N** | **Even** | **Odd** | **E + E** | **E + O** | **O + O** | **E × E** | **E × O** | **O × O** |
| 4 | 1 | 2 | 3 | 4 | 5 | 6 | 4 | 6 | 9 |
| 5 | 2 | 4 | 5 | 8 | 9 | 10 | 16 | 20 | 25 |
| 6 | 7 | 14 | 15 | 28 | 29 | 30 | 196 | 210 | 225 |
| 7 | 10 | 20 | 21 | 40 | 41 | 42 | 400 | 420 | 441 |
| 8 | 15 | 30 | 31 | 60 | 61 | 62 | 900 | 930 | 961 |

| | A | B | C | D | E | F | G | H | I |
|---|---|---|---|---|---|---|---|---|---|
| 1 | **Exploring Odd and Even Numbers** | | | | | | | | |
| 2 | | | | | | | | | |
| 3 | **N** | **Even** | **Odd** | **E × E** | **E + O** | **O + O** | **E × E** | **E × O** | **O × O** |
| 4 | 1 | =2*A4 | =2*A4+1 | =B4+B4 | =B4+C4 | =C4+C4 | =B4*B4 | =B4*C4 | =C4*C4 |
| 5 | 2 | =2*A5 | =2*A5+1 | =B5+B5 | =B5+C5 | =C5+C5 | =B5*B5 | =B5*C5 | =C5*C5 |
| 6 | 7 | =2*A6 | =2*A6+1 | =B6+B6 | =B6+C6 | =C6+C6 | =B6*B6 | =B6*C6 | =C6*C6 |
| 7 | 10 | =2*A7 | =2*A7+1 | =B7+B7 | =B7+C7 | =C7+C7 | =B7*B7 | =B7*C7 | =C7*C7 |
| 8 | 15 | =2*A8 | =2*A8+1 | =B8+B8 | =B8+C8 | =C8+C8 | =B8*B8 | =B8*C8 | =C8*C8 |

**Figure 19.12** A spreadsheet formula uses variables to represent values in other cells. The expression in a cell is a pattern generalizer for that cell. The same spreadsheet is shown twice here, once with the formula in each cell and once with the cell values calculated. Note that any change column A will produce changes in the entire row.

Unfortunately, students tend to look on expressions such as 3 + 5 and 4 × 87 as commands or things to do. The = tells you to add, and students think of *add* as a verb or an operator button, like pressing ⊟ on a calculator. As students read left to right in an equation, the = tells them, "Now give the answer." Because of this "get an answer" view of operations and equal signs, students fail to think of 5 + 2 as another way to write 7.

## A Balance Pan Approach to Equality

The following activities are ways to help students with the basic concepts needed to understand equations.

### ⫴CTIVITY

### 19.21 Names for Numbers

Challenge students to find different ways to express a particular number, say, 10. Give a few simple examples, such as 5 + 5 or 12 − 2. Encourage the use of two or more different operations. "How many names for 8 can you find using only numbers less than 10 and at least three operations?" In your discussion, emphasize that each expression is a way of representing or writing a number. Notice that there are no equal signs in this activity.

The next activity develops the concept of the equal sign. It begins with numbers only but is quickly extended to include variables.

### ⫴CTIVITY

### 19.22 Tilt or Balance

On the board, draw a simple two-pan balance. In each pan, write a numeric expression, and ask which pan will go down or whether the two will balance (see Figure 19.13, p. 398). Challenge students to write expressions for each side of the scale to make it balance. For each, write a corresponding equation to illustrate the meaning of =. Note that when the scale "tilts," either a "greater than" or "less than" symbol (> or <) is used.

After a short time, add variables to the two-pan balance activity.

For middle grade students, the graphing calculator may be a more "sophisticated" approach to the two-pan balance concept. On graphing calculators, expressions involving relationship symbols such as =, ≠, >, or ≤ are evaluated by the calculator as either true or false. If you enter 3 + 2 = 6 and press ⌷Enter⌷, the calculator

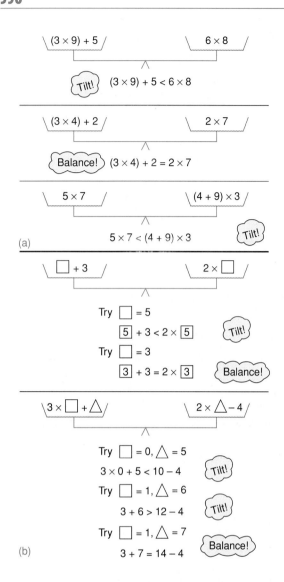

**Figure 19.13** Using expressions and variables in equations and inequalities. The two-pan balance helps develop the meaning of =, <, and >.

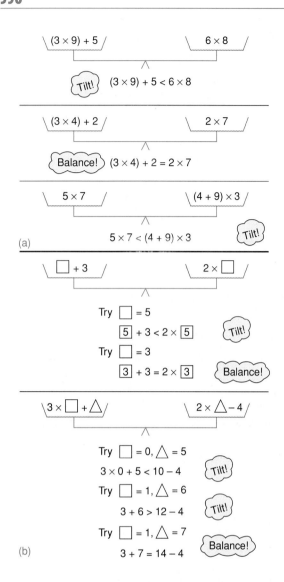

**Figure 19.14** Testing expressions with variables on a graphing calculator.

responds with a 0, meaning "false." For true expressions, the calculator responds with a 1. Any letter can be a variable and assigned a value with the STO or Store key. Once an expression is entered, the values of the variables can be changed, and the expression can be recalled and tested. An example is shown in Figure 19.14.

## Solving Equations

Variables and equations lead to the task of *solving equations* or finding values of the variables that make the equations true (balance). Activities that use the two-pan balance idea help develop concepts of both equality and variable.

---

**A**CTIVITY

### 19.23  Variables in the Balance

Provide a drawing of a two-pan balance with three different shapes, some in each pan. For example, show two boxes, and a triangle balancing a triangle, and a hexagon. Students are challenged to find values for each of the shapes that keep the scale balanced. Explain that like shapes must represent the same number. This is true of variables in any equation. Students will generally use trial and error, but you may see students begin to try other problem-solving approaches. For an equation with three variables, there will be many solutions.

---

**A**CTIVITY

### 19.24  Scales and More Scales

Provide pictures of balances or scales involving variables represented as either shapes or letters. The task is to find values for the variables that make all of the scales balance. Identical shapes or variables must have the same value on all scales. Examples are shown in Figure 19.15. Notice that some scales are two-pan balances and others are spring scales with a value showing. The latter are like equations in which all the variables are on one side set equal to a number. What students will quickly determine is that they can use relationships on one scale to replace variables on another scale, thus arriving at a solution. Often there are multiple paths to the same result.

---

Encourage students to find methods other than trial and error to solve problems such as those in Figure 19.15. For example, can you tell how much more one shape weighs than another? What if you combine the amounts on two or more scales either by adding or subtracting? Be sure to have students share their solution strategies so that all will hear different methods. Scale problems are easily designed by working backward from a solution. Assign values to the

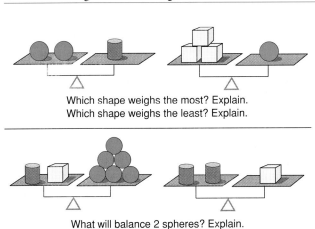

Which shape weighs the most? Explain.
Which shape weighs the least? Explain.

What will balance 2 spheres? Explain.

| 8 | 12 |

How much does each shape weigh? Explain.

| 13 | 21 | 14 |

How much does each shape weigh? Explain.

| 7 | 6 | 9 |

How much does each shape weigh? Explain.

**Figure 19.15** **Examples of problems with multiple scales (equations).**

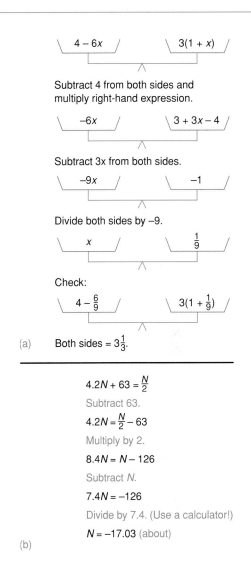

$4 - 6x$     $3(1 + x)$

Subtract 4 from both sides and multiply right-hand expression.

$-6x$     $3 + 3x - 4$

Subtract 3x from both sides.

$-9x$     $-1$

Divide both sides by $-9$.

$x$     $\frac{1}{9}$

Check:

$4 - \frac{6}{9}$     $3(1 + \frac{1}{9})$

(a)     Both sides $= 3\frac{1}{3}$.

$4.2N + 63 = \frac{N}{2}$

Subtract 63.

$4.2N = \frac{N}{2} - 63$

Multiply by 2.

$8.4N = N - 126$

Subtract $N$.

$7.4N = -126$

Divide by 7.4. (Use a calculator!)

$N = -17.03$ (about)

(b)

**Figure 19.16** **Using a balance scale to think about solving equations.**

variables, and arrange them in the scales. For three variables, be sure to provide three scales.

Eventually, students will need more general techniques for solving simple equations in one variable. The following task challenges students to begin to develop these methods.

— **A**CTIVITY —

## 19.25 Adjust the Balance

Show a balance with variable expressions in each side. Use only one variable. Make the tasks such that a solution by trial and error is not reasonable. For example, the solution to $3x + 2 = 11 - x$ is not a whole number. Suggest that adjustments can be made to the quantities in each pan as long as the balance is maintained. If you begin with simple equations such as $x - 17 = 31 - x$, students should be able to

develop skills and explain their rationale. Students should also be challenged to devise a method of proving that their solutions are correct. (Solutions can be tested by substitution in the original equation.)

Figure 19.16 shows solutions for two equations, one in a balance and the other without. Even after you have stopped using the balance, it is a good idea to refer to the scale or balance pan concept of equality and the idea of keeping the scales balanced.

## LITERATURE CONNECTIONS

Many teachers find pattern explorations sufficiently interesting that they may not think of using literature to provide a springboard for student explorations. However, here are three examples of books that are excellent beginnings for patterns and chart building.

## Pattern
### (Pluckrose, 1988)

This book brings pattern from the real world to the classroom in the form of brilliantly colored photographs. Pattern is seen in the soles of tennis shoes, dishes, butterflies, leaves, and flowers. The book provides a jumping-off point for an exploration of pattern in the world around us. A photo collage could be made of patterns found by the children. Drawings of patterns with explanations of the source and descriptions of the patterns can be assembled into a book. A display of patterns from your class activities and those found in nature, in the home, and in the neighborhood would make an excellent show for parents.

## Anno's Mysterious Multiplying Jar
### (Anno & Anno, 1983)

Like all of the books illustrated by Mitsumasa Anno, this one is beautiful. It tells an imaginative story of a mysterious jar that contains a sea. On the sea is one island. The island has two mountains. Each mountain has three countries. Within each country are four walled kingdoms. . . . Finally, each of nine boxes contains ten jars. The illustrations help develop the quickly expanding numbers of factorials. After the story, the authors help conceptualize the size of each factorial with arrays of tiny stars and suggest other ways to explore this fascinating number pattern.

Children of almost any age are likely to be interested in exploring the factorial concept due to the large numbers. A simple idea is to create a multiplying story and illustrate it or collect objects to show how many items are involved. Another idea is to examine nested situations in the real world even if they are not factorials. For example, talk to a grocery store about how small items such as chewing gum are shipped to the store. There will likely be cartons in which there are smaller boxes. In each box there may possibly be packages. Each package might contain several packs of gum and then finally single sticks. How many in all is determined by the same multiplication process.

## Anno's Magic Seeds
### (Anno, 1994)

Another wonderful book by Mitsumasa Anno, *Magic Seeds* develops a pattern that changes throughout, becoming a bit more elaborate with each change. A wise man gives Jack two magic seeds. He is told to eat one and plant the other. The seed he eats will keep him from hunger for a whole year, and the planted seed will produce two new seeds by the following year. Several years later, Jack decides to plant both seeds rather than eating one. This new pattern continues until he marries, has a child, and starts to sell seeds.

At each stage of the story, there is an opportunity to develop a chart and extend the current pattern into the future. Austin and Thompson (1997) outline in considerable detail how they used the story to develop patterns and charts with sixth- and seventh-grade students. Their article is worth looking up. However, you will have no problem developing good pattern lessons from this book without any assistance.

 ## ASSESSMENT NOTES

The main content of this chapter is found in the ideas related to patterns (repeating, number, and growing) and the related ideas of variables and equations. At any particular grade level, your particular curriculum will likely specify particular skills in these areas. To assess this particular knowledge is straightforward. Can your students recognize and extend patterns of the appropriate type for their grade level? Do they use variables in ways that suggest an understanding of the various uses and meanings of *variable*—again, commensurate with their grade level? And do they solve equations appropriate for their grade level? Answers to these questions should be found in the way students respond to the activities you conduct in class or in end-of-unit tests that assess these ideas directly.

More pervasive than these specific ideas, however, is the general notion of algebraic reasoning. It is appropriate to gather data that indicate the degree to which students make generalizations based on their mathematical experiences and use appropriate language and symbolism to represent these generalizations. Since pattern and regularity can be found in nearly all areas of mathematics, algebraic reasoning should be developed and assessed throughout the curriculum. Students who ask questions like "Will that work for any numbers?" or who observe similarities from one area of mathematics to another are using algebraic reasoning. Students who have difficulty seeing and expressing relationships such as the way two patterns are alike or who have difficulty expressing rules and formulas are not as strong in their algebraic reasoning.

Make a conscious effort to observe and keep anecdotal records of behaviors that are indicative of algebraic reasoning. It is quite likely that such records over time will give you useful insights into the mathematical talents of your students.

# REFLECTIONS ON CHAPTER 19

## Writing to Learn

1. Describe in your own words what algebraic reasoning means. At what grade level should algebraic reasoning begin?

2. Make up three pattern strips showing repeating patterns for some common objects that might be found in the classroom. Label each using an A, B, C scheme. No two schemes should be alike, but all should use the same materials. What is the core of each pattern? What will be the twenty-fifth element of each?

3. What is a recursive relationship? Where in a growing pattern would you look for a recursive relationship? In terms of growing patterns, what is a functional relationship?

4. The following growing pattern consists of square borders. The elements of each frame are the number of squares or tiles that make up the border. Draw the fifth border and the tenth border in the sequence. Make a chart showing the number of tiles in each of the first ten borders. Find a recursive relationship that permits you to get from one frame to the next. With attention to the drawings of this growing pattern, try to find one or more ways to express the general functional relationship that the pattern defines.

5. How can a hundreds chart (or a 0-to-99 chart) be used to develop pattern ideas?

6. Using a simple calculator, show how it is used to play "Secret Function I" (p. 392) for all four operations.

7. Give an example of each of the three different uses of variables. For each use, describe at least one activity that addresses students' understanding of variables used in that manner.

8. Make up a scales problem involving three different variables. After you have made it up, show at least one way that it can be solved other than by trial and error.

9. What misconceptions do children have about expressions such as 4 + 8 and the equal sign that can cause difficulty working with equations?

10. Explain how to solve the equation $4x + 3 = x + 12$ using a pan balance.

## For Discussion and Exploration

1. The Reasoning standard in *Principles and Standards for School Mathematics* is meant to permeate all content areas. However, it has special significance for the types of activities found in this chapter. Read the Reasoning standard, either the overview found in Chapter 3 of *Principles and Standards* or the corresponding elaboration found in the grade band of most interest to you. Discuss how the inclusion of algebraic reasoning throughout the elementary and middle school grades emphasizes the use of reasoning for all students.

2. Explorations of patterns such as the number and calculator patterns or the Fibonacci sequence are not presented in typical textbooks except as enrichment or extras, especially in the upper grades. (Repeat patterns are quite popular in grades K and 1.) Is it reasonable to spend time in the fourth through eighth grades on explorations of this sort? Take a position and defend it.

3. The Disney film *Donald in Mathmagic Land* is a classic from the 1940s that is now available on videotape and occasionally aired on the Disney Channel. The film explores pattern and several related beauties of mathematics in a timeless manner. Your mathematics education is not quite complete if you haven't seen it. It will intrigue children from third grade to high school, and a creative teacher can find many ways to follow up with explorations. View it if you can, and share an idea for using the film with children.

## Recommendations for Further Reading

### Highly Recommended

Coburn, T. G. (1993). *Patterns: Addenda series, grades K–6.* Reston, VA: National Council of Teachers of Mathematics.

This is one of the best resource books on patterns for the K–6 grades. Examples of virtually every type of pattern activity are included. As with other elementary *Addenda Series* books, the same activities are found in each of the grade-level books. What you get in this book are not only good activities but also a view of how pattern can easily progress from kindergarten to grade 6.

Moses, B. (Ed.). (1999). *Algebraic thinking, grades K–12: Readings from NCTM's school-based journals and other publications.* Reston, VA: National Council of Teachers of Mathematics.

In this collection, NCTM has assembled nearly 60 articles addressing the broad topic of algebraic thinking. After looking at definitions and issues surrounding the teaching of algebra at various levels, the book provides classroom activities from patterns to functions. Technology gets a special section, as does assessment. This is an excellent single source for a lot of information.

National Council of Teachers of Mathematics. (1997). Algebraic thinking [Focus Issue]. *Teaching Children Mathematics, 3*(6).

National Council of Teachers of Mathematics. (1997). Algebraic thinking: Opening the gates [Focus issue]. *Mathematics Teaching in the Middle School, 2*(4).

National Council of Teachers of Mathematics. (1997). Algebraic thinking [Focus issue]. *Mathematics Teacher, 90*(2).

In 1997, NCTM responded to the growing interest in algebraic reasoning by publishing focus issues on the topic in all three of its school-based journals. Together, these journals provide not just algebraic activities at all levels but also a long-range perspective on the growth of algebraic reasoning across the grades. These are especially valuable publications.

## Other Suggestions

Baratta-Lorton, M. (1976). *Mathematics their way*. Menlo Park, CA: AWL Supplemental.

Burk, D., Snider, A., & Symonds, P. (1988). *Box it or bag it mathematics: Teachers resource guide (K–2)*. Salem, OR: Math Learning Center.

Burns, M. (1992). *About teaching mathematics: A K–8 resource*. Sausalito, CA: Math Solutions Publications.

Driscoll, M. J. (1999). *Fostering algebraic thinking: A guide for teachers, grades 6–10*. Portsmouth, NH: Heinemann.

English, L. D., & Warren, E. A. (1998). Introducing the variable through pattern exploration. *Mathematics Teacher, 91*, 166–172.

Esty, W. W., & Teppo, A. R. (1996). Algebraic thinking, language, and word problems. In P. C. Elliott (Ed.), *Communication in mathematics, K–12 and beyond* (pp. 45–53). Reston, VA: National Council of Teachers of Mathematics.

Falkner, K. P., Levi, L., & Carpenter, T. P. (1999). Children's understanding of equality: A foundation for algebra. *Teaching Children Mathematics, 6*, 232–236.

Feinberg-McBrian, C. (1996). The case of trapezoidal numbers. *Mathematics Teacher, 89*, 16–24.

Greenes, C., & Findell, C. (1999). Developing students' algebraic reasoning abilities. In L. V. Stiff (Ed.), *Developing mathematical reasoning in grades K–12* (pp. 127–137). Reston, VA: National Council of Teachers of Mathematics.

Greenes, C., & Findell, C. (1999). *Groundworks: Algebraic thinking* (3 vols.: grades 1, 2, and 3). Chicago: Creative Publications.

Greenes, C., & Findell, C. (1999). *Groundworks: Algebra puzzles and problems* (4 vols.: grades 4, 5, 6, and 7). Chicago: Creative Publications.

MacGregor, M., & Stacey, K. (1999). A flying start to algebra. *Teaching Children Mathematics, 6*, 78–85.

National Council of Teachers of Mathematics & Mathematical Sciences Education Board. (1998). *The nature and role of algebra in the K–14 curriculum: Proceedings of a national symposium, May 27 and 28, 1997*. Washington, DC: National Academy Press.

Phillips, E., Gardella, T., Kelly, C., & Stewart, J. (1991). *Patterns and functions: Addenda series, grades 5–8*. Reston, VA: National Council of Teachers of Mathematics.

Quinn, A. L., Koca, R. M., Jr., & Weening, F. (1999). Developing mathematical reasoning using attribute games. *Mathematics Teacher, 92*, 768–775.

Schifter, D. (1999). Reasoning about operations: Early algebraic thinking in grades K–6. In L. V. Stiff (Ed.), *Developing mathematical reasoning in grades K–12* (pp. 62–81). Reston, VA: National Council of Teachers of Mathematics.

Speer, W. R., & Brahier, D. J. (1996). What comes nex _? *Teaching Children Mathematics, 1*, 100–108.

Swafford, J. O., & Langrall, C. W. (2000). Grade 6 students' pre-instructional use of equations to describe and represent problem situations. *Journal for Research in Mathematics Education, 13*, 89–112.

Vance, J. H. (1998). Number operations from an algebraic perspective. *Teaching Children Mathematics, 4*, 282–285.

Williams, S. E., & Copley, J. V. (1994). Promoting classroom dialogue: Using calculators to discover patterns in dividing decimals. *Mathematics Teaching in the Middle School, 1*, 72–75.

# Chapter 20

# Exploring Functions

The concept of function is one of the big ideas in all of mathematics. In the past, a study of functions was relegated to the course called Algebra I. Algebra I is typically offered in grade 8 or 9, and not all students take it. In today's world, it is important that all students develop algebraic reasoning, especially with regard to functions. *Principles and Standards for School Mathematics* suggests that function concepts should be integrated throughout the middle school program rather than relegated to a special algebra course. Furthermore, the study of functions should focus on relationships in meaningful contexts and multiple methods of representing and examining these relationships. This is in stark contrast to the traditional focus on notation, vertical-line tests, range and domain, and methods of graphing equations, all without much purpose.

In this chapter, you will see how an investigation of meaningful contexts can result in the development and articulation of function concepts in ways that make sense to students. An emphasis is on connecting representations of functions so that each can provide a different picture of the relationship. Technology, most significantly the graphing calculator, is a powerful tool that aids in this development.

## BIG Ideas

1. Functions are relationships or rules that uniquely associate members of one set with members of another set.

2. Functional relationships can be expressed in real contexts, graphs, algebraic equations, tables, and words. All representations for a given function are simply different ways of expressing the same idea, yet each representation provides a different view of the function.

## FUNCTION CONCEPTS AND REPRESENTATIONS

A study of functions is a study of the way change in one variable affects change in another; it is a study of *joint variation* of variables. A function is the rule that defines how the first variable affects the second. Technically, a *function* is a rule of correspondence between two sets that uniquely associates elements of the first set with elements of the second. The variable representing elements from the first set is called the *independent* variable. Since the value of the second variable in the function depends on the value of the first, it is called the *dependent* variable. Though correct, these definitions are not very good starting points for students. The best way to develop functional relationships is to consider real-world contexts that are examples of functions.

There are at least five different ways to interpret or represent a function. Each is a different way of communicating the same rule of correspondence or relationship. It is important to see that each representation expresses the same idea yet provides a different way of looking at or thinking about the relationship. We will use the hot-dog vendor situation to illustrate all five representations.

Brian is trying to make money to help pay for college by selling hot dogs from a hot-dog cart at the coliseum during major performances and ball games. He pays the cart owner $35 per night for the use of the cart. He sells hot dogs for $1.25 each. His costs for the hot dogs, condiments, napkins, and other paper products are about 60 cents per hot dog on average. The profit from a single hot dog is therefore 65 cents.

# Contextual Representations of Functions

This function begins with a context: selling hot dogs and the resulting profit. We are interested in Brian's profit in terms of the number of hot dogs sold: The more hot dogs Brian sells, the more profit he will make. Brian does not begin to make a profit immediately because he must pay the $35 rent on the vending cart. Nonetheless, Brian's profit is dependent on—is *a function of*—the number of hot dogs he sells.

Not every function has a real-world context, but at the middle school level, it is useful to place functions in contexts that make sense to students. Here are some other contexts in which functional relationships are to be found:

- Suppose that the value of a new car depreciates at the rate of 20 percent each year. There is a definite relationship between the age of the car and its current value.

- If you measure the height and arm span of a lot of different people, from very short to very tall, you will likely find that there is a predictable relationship between these two measures. Arm span is related to height.

- A ride on a roller coaster has several possible relationships. As time passes from the beginning of the ride to the end of the ride, the height of the cars above the ground changes. It increases slowly at first, then most likely has a fast decrease followed by a series of lesser increases and decreases. The speed of the cars on the roller coaster is also a function of time. The speed of the cars has an effect on how loud the passengers scream, and so it is reasonable to say that speed and screams are related, although perhaps not as precisely as the height is related to the time.

- If you build rectangles so that all have the same fixed perimeter, the length of the rectangles will decrease as the widths increase. If you begin with a very small width and a longer length, the area of the rectangles first increases as the width increases from zero and then decreases.

These are all contexts in which there is a functional relationship. Some, such as the hot-dog vendor's profit and the declining value of a new car, exist in the real world. The rectangle example has no real-world aspect to it. That context comes up in an investigation of areas and perimeters of rectangles. Regarding height versus arm span and the loudness of roller coaster passengers, the relationship is not easy to determine precisely. Riders will not always scream at exactly the same decibel level, nor will everyone's height-to-arm span ratio be the same. However, all of these situations illustrate functions in meaningful contexts. Each has at least two values that vary jointly, with one being dependent on or related to the other.

# Table Representations of Functions

Brian the hot-dog vendor might well sit down and calculate some possible income figures based on hypothetical sales. This will give him some idea of how many franks he must sell to break even and what his profit might be for an evening. For example, if he sells no hot dogs, he will be $35 in the hole, or his profit will be negative $35. Selling 70 hot dogs would yield a profit of $70 \times 0.65 - 35 = 45.50 - 35$, or $10.50. A table of similar values might look like this:

| Hot Dogs | Profit |
|---|---|
| 0 | − 35.00 |
| 70 | 10.50 |
| 100 | 30.00 |
| 150 | 62.50 |

The number of hot dogs shown in the table is purely a matter of choice. One could calculate the profit for 10,000 hot dogs ($10,000 \times 0.65 - 35$), even though it is not reasonable to expect Brian to sell that many. One of the values of contexts in thinking about functions is to see how mathematical representations can ignore reality. The person who interprets the table must take the context into consideration.

To make a table for the car depreciation example, all we need to know is the sale price of the car. If the car was purchased for $15,000, how would you determine the value of the car after 1 year, 2 years, 5 years? The area of the rectangle can similarly be determined in terms of either the length or the width if we know what the fixed perimeter is. In the case of the roller coaster, some information about the physics of roller coasters would be necessary, or else we would actually have to measure what happens as the roller coaster travels its course.

In the height–arm span situation, a table could be created from actual measurements of a lot of people. However, this table only approximates the "general" relationship. One person who is 5 feet 10 inches tall may have an arm span of 69 inches, while another of the exact same height might have an arm span of 72 inches. Later we will see how a function can be determined that is a good predictor of the height–arm span relationship.

# Language Expressions for Functions

Functional relationships are dependent relationships or rules of correspondence. In the hot-dog vendor situation, Brian's profit depends on the number of hot dogs that are sold. In functional language, we can say, "Profit *is a function of* the number of hot dogs sold." The phrase "is a function of" expresses the dependent relationship. The profit *depends on*—is a function of—the hot-dog sales.

Looking at the other examples, we would say that the current value of a car is a function of its age or its value depends on its age. The speed of the roller coaster is a function of the time since the ride started. If someone were to ask what speed the roller coaster is going, you might respond, "It depends on the time since the ride began," or, in functional terms, "That depends. The speed is a function of the time since the ride began." See if you can express the relationships in the other examples in functional terms.

Language can also help us think about the reverse relationships in a situation. Brian's hot-dog profit is a function of sales. Are his sales a function of profits? Yes, in this sense: If you know how much profit he made in one evening, you can determine precisely how many hot dogs he sold. However, reverse relationships are not always functions. Consider the speed of the roller coaster. Though speed is a function of time, it is not true that time is a function of speed. Why? Suppose you had a table of the roller coaster speed for every 5 seconds from the beginning of the 2-minute ride to the end. If you were asked, "At what time did the roller coaster go 35 mph?" it may be that that speed was reached at eight or ten different times during the ride, as the car accelerated down a hill or slowed going up a hill. Here time cannot be determined by the speed, but the speed can be uniquely determined by the time. Try reversing the functional relationships for all of the examples. Which reverse relationships are functions?

## Graphical Representations of Functions

The old saying goes that a picture is worth a thousand words. This is certainly true of functions. An important representation of a function is with a graph. In Figure 20.1, six different values of hot-dog sales are plotted on a graph. The horizontal axis represents the number of hot dogs sold, and the vertical axis, the profit. As we have already established, the profit goes up as the sales go up. There is, in this situation, a very clear pattern to the six values.

The graph shows that the relationship between sales and profits is *linear*—a straight line—and is increasing. It also allows us easily to answer questions about Brian's profits. How many hot dogs must be sold to break even? The graph shows zero profit (the break-even point) where the line crosses the horizontal axis. (Why?) It looks to be near 53 or 54. What is Brian's profit for 130 hot dogs? How many hot dogs must be sold to make a profit of $100? The context gives meaning to the graph, and the graph adds understanding to the context.

The graph is another mathematical model that, in terms of the context, does not make sense for all portions of the picture. If the line is extended indefinitely, there would be values where Brian's sales were negative (to the left of the vertical axis). This clearly does not make sense. Nor is it reasonable to talk about sales of millions of hot dogs even though the graph can extend as far as is wished.

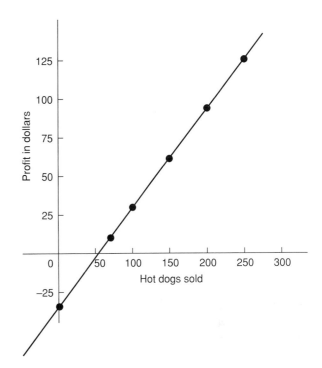

**Figure 20.1** A graph showing profit as a function of hot-dog sales.

Not all graphs of functions are straight lines. Consider the rectangle situation. If you start with a rectangle that has a fixed perimeter of 24 inches and increase the length beginning at 1 inch, both the width and the area will vary accordingly (see Figure 20.2, p. 406). The width graph is linear. It decreases at a constant rate. By contrast, the area graph rises in a curve, reaches a maximum value, and then goes back down.

Figure 20.3 (p. 406) shows a simple roller coaster. Suppose that it takes just 120 seconds to ride. Try to sketch a graph that shows the *height* of the roller coaster throughout the ride. Why will your graph not be exactly the same as the path of the roller coaster? Now make another graph that shows the *speed* of the car over the 120 seconds of the ride. Share your sketches with a friend. How are these two graphs related to each other?

## Equations to Represent Functions

Suppose that we pick a letter, say, $H$, to represent the number of hot dogs Brian sells. For each hot dog sold, his income is $1.25 \times H$ dollars. But to determine his profit, we have to subtract from his income the rental cost of the cart and 60 cents cost per hot dog. Therefore, Brian's profit is represented by $(1.25 \times H) - (0.60 \times H) - 35$, or $(0.65 \times H) - 35$. To make an equation, we can assign another letter to stand for profit: $P = (0.65 \times H) - 35$. This equation defines a mathematical relationship between two values or two variables, profit and hot dogs. Taken out of context, it is simply a relationship between $P$ and $H$. It is the same as the relationship between $x$ and $y$ in the equation $y = 0.65x - 35$.

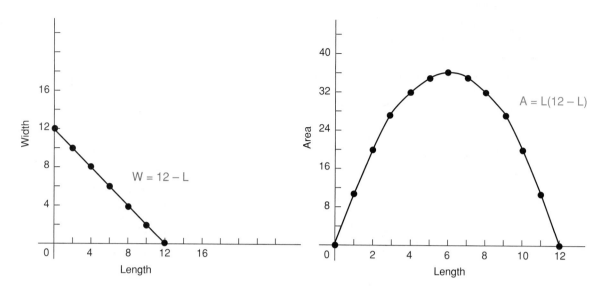

**Figure 20.2** **The width and area graphs as functions of the length of a rectangle with a fixed perimeter of 24 units.**

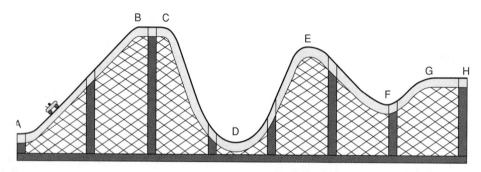

**Figure 20.3** **If it takes 120 seconds to ride this roller coaster, sketch a graph of the height of the car as a function of time. How should the points A through H be spaced along the time line? Sketch a second graph of the speed as a function of time. The time axis with points A to H should be the same. What would a graph of "scream decibels" look like?**

By expressing a function as an equation, it can be examined in its most abstract form. Equations can be categorized in terms of the properties of the entire class of equations. When the properties of a class of equations are understood, they can be applied to the context as well. In our hot-dog example, the equation has the general form of a linear equation, $Y = mX + b$. In this form, the value of $m$ tells us how quickly or steeply the line goes up or down moving from left to right. The value of $b$ tells where the graph will cross the vertical axis.

In the rectangle context, the following two equations represent the width and area, respectively, as functions of the length (assuming that the perimeter is fixed at 24 units):

$$W(L) = \frac{(24 - 2L)}{2} = 12 - L$$

$$A(L) = L(12 - L)$$

Expressing functions in an equation can make it easier to see what is happening. In this example, the function notations $W(L)$ and $A(L)$ were used instead of a single letter for each. $W(L)$ stands for the width. Within this efficient notation is an indication that the width is a function of the length $L$. "The width when the length is 3" can now be represented symbolically as $W(3)$. The symbolic name for the function itself—the relationship between the length and width—is represented by the letter $W$. Similarly for the area function $A$: $A(L)$ is the area for any given value of $L$; $A(4)$ is the area when the length is 4. The area is a function of the length.

Equations also make it easier to calculate values of the function. The equation can be entered into a graphing calculator, and the calculator can do the calculations to produce a table or draw a graph. Without the equation representation of the function, the graphing calculator is much less useful. Figure 20.4 shows the screen of a TI-83 calculator with both the width and the area graphs drawn. The table to the right computes the area for every length in steps of one-half. It requires very little expertise to do this on the calculator and allows the middle school child the chance to see and explore graphs without the tedium of having to plot points.

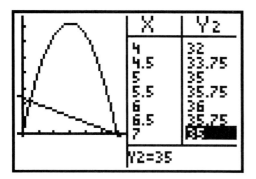

**Figure 20.4** **This graphing calculator shows graphs of both the width and the area of a rectangle of fixed perimeter as functions of the length. The table can show all possible length and area values.**

Sometimes equations come from selecting a curve (and its corresponding equation) that seems to "fit" the data available. That is how an equation for the height–arm span relationship would be determined. A "best-fit curve" would be determined to fit the data. You may recall finding a median-median line for height and weight data in Chapter 18.

# DEVELOPING FUNCTION CONCEPTS IN THE CLASSROOM

If the discussion so far had focused only on Brian the hot-dog vendor, the development would be similar to the approach in a middle school classroom. Begin with a context, explore the relationships, and develop different representations to show what has been found.

## Begin with Meaningful Contexts

Today, algebra is dominated by the study of functions and should begin with meaningful situations in which functions can be found. Numerous contexts contain functional relationships that are completely accessible to students, even as early as sixth grade. By exploring a context and making sense of it, the function relationship is already developed.

In the context of Brian's sales, a discussion can involve finding the number of hot dogs that need to be sold to make a given amount of money and how much profit is made by selling a particular number of hot dogs. By examining and explaining these questions, students are working with the joint variation between hot dogs sold and profit made. They are actually using a function before they have been asked to worry about symbols and definitions.

The search for functional relationships is part of the science of pattern and order—the doing of mathematics. Some contexts can be tied to other strands of the curriculum, providing important connections within mathematics.

- Statistics explorations lead to collecting data and making scatter plots. A function (curve) is found to approximate the data.
- Patterns that grow (*sequences*) combine the direct search for pattern with the idea of functional relationships (see Chapter 19).
- Proportional situations can be graphed and tables made. This produces a special class of linear functions with all graphs passing through the origin (see Chapter 15).
- Geometry and measurement come together in an assortment of formulas that take on new meaning when expressed as functions. You have already seen how area and length can be related in a rectangle with a fixed perimeter.

Just as important as these mathematical connections are the connections to the real world. Our lives abound with situations that involve functional relationships. Making money and the ideas related to profit and loss are both realistic and interesting. Social studies provides many relationships. For example, populations of various regions may be related to health, income, production levels, education levels, death rates, and so on. Science offers another area of investigations. Pendulums can be swung to investigate period as a function of length. The distance a toy car will roll down a ramp can be compared to the angle of the ramp. Plant growth can be related to quantities of fertilizer or to the number of days since germination. These are just a few real contexts that can make the study of functions meaningful.

## Connect Different Representations

Figure 20.5 (p. 408) illustrates the five representations of functions that we explored earlier. The most important idea is to see that for a given function, each of these representations illustrates the same relationship. The *context* provides an embodiment of the relationship outside the world of mathematics. *Language* helps express the relationship in a meaningful and useful manner. *Tables* explicitly match up selected elements that are paired by the function. The joint variation is implicit in the pairings of numbers. The *graph* translates the number pairs into a picture. Any point on the graph of a function has two coordinates. The function is the rule that relates the first coordinate to the second. The *equation* expresses the same functional relationship with the economy and power of mathematical symbolism.

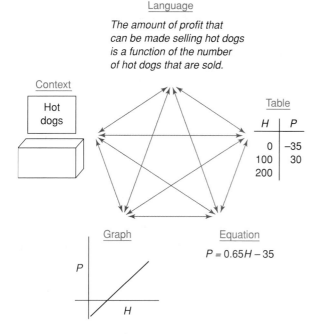

Language

*The amount of profit that can be made selling hot dogs is a function of the number of hot dogs that are sold.*

Context

Hot dogs

Table

| H | P |
|---|---|
| 0 | −35 |
| 100 | 30 |
| 200 | |

Graph

Equation

$P = 0.65H - 35$

**Figure 20.5** **Five different representations of a function. For any given function, students should see that all these representations are connected and illustrate the same relationship. Each representation provides a different perspective on the function.**

 Use Technology

In the past, when students had to plot points and do by hand all the computations that were involved, functions were limited to very simple examples. Eighth-grade students would probably never see a function with an equation much more complicated than $y = 3x + 2$. The tedium of computing and plotting function values meant that examples had to use numbers that were small and relatively easy to work with, making the link to real contexts almost impossible. Thanks to technology, we can now explore realistic contexts involving not-so-nice numbers. Students can investigate all sorts of functions as long as a relationship can be identified.

Consider the examples in the first part of this chapter. The profit example is the easiest to work with and could probably be examined without technology. The car depreciation is an exponential function. The area for a fixed perimeter is a parabolic function. If students can come up with an equation to go with a function rule, technology can be used to make a graph and do the necessary number crunching to make a table. The technology is not "thinking" for the students; on the contrary, student effort is focused on the thinking and not on the mechanics of computation and plotting points.

Students who have talked about exponents and about percents—both middle grades topics—are equipped to develop an equation for the car depreciation situation. That exploration might go like this: If the car loses 20 percent of

its value in 1 year, then it must be worth 80 percent of its value after a year. So after 1 year, the $15,000 car is worth $15,000 × 0.8. In the second year, it loses 20 percent of that value, so it will be worth only 80 percent of its value at the end of year one: ($15,000 × 0.8) × 0.8 = $15,000 × $0.8^2$. At the end of the third year, the value will be $15,000 × $0.8^3$, and so on. In general, at the end of $n$ years, the value of the car can be expressed in this equation: $V = \$15,000 \times 0.8^n$. Figure 20.6 shows the graph and the table of values on a graphing calculator. This equation is no more difficult to enter into a graphing calculator or a computer graphing utility than $y = 3x + 2$. An early study of functions is not a detailed functional analysis. The idea is to see that there are functional relationships and that these can be expressed in different ways.

**Figure 20.6** **The graph and table for $V = 15,000 \times 0.8^n$. The graph shows $n$ for values 0 to 15. The vertical axis runs from 0 to 15,000.**

Real data from measurements, experiments, and surveys can be entered into a graphing calculator or any number of computer programs, and a scatter plot can be easily produced. The same technology can then be used to find a curve that approximates the data. At the middle school level, it is not necessary to know how the calculator determines the quadratic or exponential curve that fits best. But at the same time, there is no reason to hide the idea that a curve can be created, along with an equation, to approximate data that makes sense to students.

## Use Function Machines

Another representation of a function has come into common use: the *function machine*. It can be thought of as a "black box" with input and output slots, as shown in Figure 20.7. Inside the box is the function rule—the rule of correspondence between the input numbers and the output numbers. This representation helps illustrate what makes a function a function. It highlights that a function is a rule of correspondence (the rule inside the box), that for any input there is a unique output value, that the elements the machine will accept are the elements for which the function is defined (also known

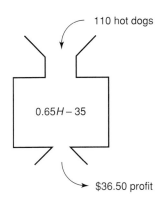

**Figure 20.7** A function machine illustrates the idea that a single input value from the domain of the function produces a unique value in the range of the function. Each in-out pair corresponds to an entry in the function table and a point on the graph of the function.

as the *domain* of the function), and that the set of all possible outputs is the set known as the *range* of the function.

These ideas tend to focus on generic aspects of function and do little to illustrate the specific function that is "in the box." The function machine is most like the table representation of a function. In fact, a table is often generated by recording the inputs and outputs of a function machine.

Function machines are also valuable in a guess-the-rule context. Activity 19.13 (p. 392) shows a simple program to make a graphing calculator into a function machine. Students try different inputs, and the program provides the outputs. If the secret function is also graphed, students guessing the function can use the graph as another clue for guessing the function. This will help make the connection for students between the graphical and symbolic representations of a function. Notice that in a function machine, the input value is the independent variable and the output value is the dependent variable.

# FUNCTIONS FROM PATTERNS

Growing patterns are often used to introduce the idea of function rules connected to a context. Growing patterns or sequences developed from physical or pictorial drawings were discussed at length in Chapter 19. Now that we have a more complete view of the function concept and the various representations of functions, let's explore one more example of a growing pattern and see how all of these ideas fit together in that context.

┌─ **A**CTIVITY ─────────────

## 20.1 Perimeter Patterns

**In this activity, students explore the perimeters of strings of regular polygons. Each string is made up of tiles of the same shape. Adjoining tiles share one side, as shown in Figure 20.8. For a given shape, the task**

is to develop a rule or formula for the perimeter of strings of any number of tiles. For example, if the tiles are square, the perimeter for one square is 4, for two squares is 6, for three squares is 8, and so on. What is a formula for the perimeter of a string of $N$ squares? Figure 20.8 shows strings for three different shapes. Pattern blocks are an excellent manipulative for this task because all edges are 1 inch long except for the trapezoid, which has a long side of 2 inches.

**Figure 20.8** What is the perimeter of a string of $N$ pattern blocks?

Students working at "Perimeter Patterns" should first develop a table by adding tiles to their string one at a time and recording the perimeters in a table as they go. A recursive relationship is easy to determine. For hexagons, it is "add 4 to the preceding perimeter." A table for hexagons looks like this:

| 1 | 2 | 3 | 4 | 5 | 6 | 7 | 8 | ... | $N$ |
|---|---|---|---|---|---|---|---|-----|-----|
| 6 | 10 | 14 | 18 | 22 | 26 | 32 | 36 | ... | ? |

So now we have a table and a contextual situation. The next challenge is the most interesting: Find a rule or equation that tells the perimeter for $N$ hexagons. What students come up with depends on whether they focus on the table of numbers or the string of tiles. In either case, they are likely to have a variety of ideas. Before reading further, see if you can come up with at least two different formulas.

Here are five different-looking formulas:

$$4N + 2$$
$$2(2N + 1)$$
$$6 + (N - 1)4$$
$$(N - 2)4 + (2 \times 5)$$
$$2N + 2N + 2$$

Are your formulas in this list? Perhaps you found a different one. When students share different formulas for the same pattern, others might be challenged to see how they arrived at the patterns. The following three ideas generate three of the five formulas given:

- *The first tile has a perimeter of 6. Each new tile adds 4 more. (This idea can be found in the table as well as the block pattern.)*
- *Each tile has two edges on the top. Include the one extra edge on the left along with the top edges. The bottom edges plus the right edge are the same as this.*
- *Each tile has two edges on the top and two on the bottom plus the two end edges.*

Match these three ways of thinking of the perimeter with three of the formulas. Then try to figure how one may have been thinking to generate the other two. Of course, all of these "different" formulas are equivalent, with the simplest form being $4N + 2$.

To add language to our representations, we can say, "The perimeter of a string of hexagons is a function of the number of hexagons in the string."

Next, a graph of the perimeter relationship provides the fifth representation. The points on the graph will lie along a straight line and go up 4 units for every added tile. The graphs for each of the other tile shapes will go up at different rates or with different *slopes* (see Figure 20.9).

**Figure 20.9** **Graphs of the perimeters of three different pattern-block strings.**

The perimeter problem has an interesting extension. If different groups of students have been working on strings of shapes using different polygons, the resulting formulas will be similar. See if students can find an even more general formula with two variables: *N* representing the number of tiles and *S* representing the number of sides per tile. (This challenge is left to you.)

# FUNCTIONS FROM THE REAL WORLD

Patterns are but one way to get students into an investigation of functions. Here are some other ideas that develop the same concepts.

## Relationships Found in the Real World

Real-world situations, such as the example of Brian selling hot dogs, can be explored with children by having them make tables of data using the information given. By computing several entries in the table, students will begin to see a pattern develop. Consider the following activity.

**A**CTIVITY

### 20.2 How Many Gallons Left?

**Present this situation to students: A car gets 23 miles per gallon of gas. It has a gas tank that holds 20 gallons. Suppose that you were on a trip and had filled the tank at the outset. Make a table showing the number of gallons remaining in the tank for at least three different points in a trip of 350 miles. Plot the data on a graph. Show how you calculated each entry in your table, and be prepared to discuss with the class what you did.**

Notice that very little direction is given in this activity. However, the situation presented to the students is fairly clear. Some teachers may prefer to use numbers that would be easier to compute, but that takes much of the realism out of the situation. If a student decides to make a table entry for 50 miles, he or she will first have to figure out what to do. On a calculator, $50 \div 23 = 2.173913$. This amount should be subtracted from 20 to find out how many gallons remain in the tank. Should you subtract 2 or 2.17 or 2.173913? This is a good example to use to discuss numbers in real contexts. Avoid being prescriptive so that students will do their own thinking and not rely on your directions. Students are bound to make errors in reasoning as well as in computation. Class discussion will sort things out.

As part of the discussion, help students develop functional language to represent the situation. Here the number of gallons in the tank is dependent on how far the car has been driven. Thus the number of gallons remaining *is a function of* the miles driven. In addition to the language, work toward student development of an equation that represents the relationship in the situation. In this case, one possible equation is $g = 20 - \frac{m}{23}$. Or, using functional notation, you might say $G(m) = 20 - \frac{m}{23}$.

Students can draw a line through their plotted points, or with a computer or graphing calculator they can enter the equation and have technology do the graphing. In either case, use the graph to answer questions about the situation: "How can you tell from the graph how much gas will be left after driving 300 miles?" "How many miles can you drive before the gas tank has only 3 gallons left?" "What will happen to the graph if the driver stops to fill the tank after driving 350 miles?" The *trace* feature on a graphing calculator is a great help for getting values from a graph.

Here are a few suggestions for similar explorations.

Mr. Calloway wants to build a fenced pen against one side of his shed. The shed is 15 feet long, and he wants to use the full side of the shed. The pen is to be in the shape of a rectangle with two sides 15 feet long. How much fence will he have to buy if he knows how long the other two sides of the pen will be (side versus fence length)? Add in a gate that is 3 feet long and costs $32. If fencing is $4.25 per foot, rethink the problem in terms of side versus cost. You can also discuss area and side length.

Yolanda's mother agrees to loan her the price of a lawn mower so that Yolanda can earn money over the summer cutting grass. The lawn mower costs $285. Yolanda has determined that she can average $24 per lawn after paying for gasoline. She thinks she will be able to cut about five lawns per week. Examine Yolanda's profit in terms of number of lawns mowed and then in terms of weeks that she works. Suppose that the family takes a vacation during the fourth and fifth weeks of summer. What will the graph of Yolanda's profit in terms of weeks worked look like during this time? Use the graph to figure out when Yolanda will break even and how much profit she will make during the summer.

Mark is an avid cyclist. He can average 17 miles per hour for about 4 hours. He leaves home and travels for $2\frac{1}{2}$ hours at this rate, stops for lunch for $\frac{1}{2}$ hour, and then starts home. What is his distance from home at any given time? Suppose he goes faster for 1 hour and slower for 2 more hours and then returns home. Suppose he has a flat tire and has to stop for 15 minutes to repair it. How fast will he have to go in order to return home at the same time as scheduled, including the same lunch break? Does it make any difference where the breakdown occurs?

Pleasant's Hardware buys widgets for $4.17 each, marks them up 35 percent over wholesale, and sells them at that price. Relate widgets sold to total income. Consider profit instead of income. Incorporate a sale using a reduced price.

## Proportional Situations

In the same spirit, many relationships involving rates or proportions offer a valuable opportunity for examining functions. The following is a typical proportion problem.

**Two out of every three students who eat in the cafeteria drink a pint of white milk. If 450 students eat in the cafeteria, how many gallons of milk are consumed?**

As the problem is stated, there is a fixed number of students (450) and a single answer to the problem. Students would be expected to set up a proportion and solve for the unknown. But if only the first sentence of the problem is provided, students can be asked to create a table showing the number of pints (or gallons) of milk consumed for four or five different numbers of students, plot the data on a graph, and create an equation that shows the relationship between students in the cafeteria and milk consumed. Functional language can be discussed: The number of pints of milk consumed in the cafeteria *is a function of* the number of students who eat there. The graph can be used to answer the question about milk for 450 students. Students can be challenged to find an equation that gives the amount of milk in terms of the number of students.

Each of the following problems has been converted to a function investigation by asking for an answer in terms of an unknown instead of a specific number.

**Mr. Schultz pays $4.00 for a box of 12 candy bars, which he then sells in his store for 45 cents each. How much profit will he make on *n* boxes of candy bars?**

**If each lemonade recipe will serve 20 people, how many recipes are needed to serve *n* people? If it takes three cans of concentrate to make one recipe, how many cans should be purchased to serve *n* people?**

The second example has two questions. One equation can be written to relate the number of recipes as a function of the number of people [$R = f(p)$], and a second equation to give the number of cans of concentrate as a function of the number of recipes [$C = g(R)$]. How can the recipe equation be used in the can equation to produce an equation that gives cans of concentrate as a function of the number of people? This is an example of a *compound function*. For example, the slope of the line relating students to pints of milk is $\frac{2}{3}$. What would the slope be for the line relating students to gallons of milk?

Notice that the graphs of all proportional situations are straight lines that pass through the origin. Students will find that the slope of these lines is also the rate between the two variables.

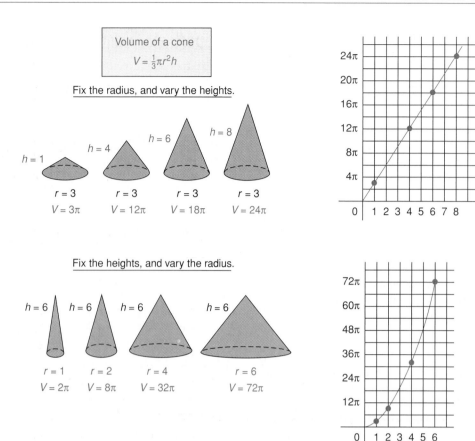

Volume of a cone
$$V = \tfrac{1}{3}\pi r^2 h$$

Fix the radius, and vary the heights.

$h = 1$  $h = 4$  $h = 6$  $h = 8$

$r = 3$  $r = 3$  $r = 3$  $r = 3$
$V = 3\pi$  $V = 12\pi$  $V = 18\pi$  $V = 24\pi$

Fix the heights, and vary the radius.

$h = 6$  $h = 6$  $h = 6$  $h = 6$

$r = 1$  $r = 2$  $r = 4$  $r = 6$
$V = 2\pi$  $V = 8\pi$  $V = 32\pi$  $V = 72\pi$

**Figure 20.10**  **Volume as a function of height or radius. If the radius is fixed, changes in height produce a straight-line graph, but if the height is fixed, changes in the radius produce a curved line.**

# Functions from Formulas

Geometric formulas relate various dimensions, areas, and volumes of shapes. Each of these formulas involves at least one functional relationship.

Consider any familiar formula for measuring a geometric shape. For example, $V = \tfrac{1}{3}\pi r^2 h$ is the formula for the volume of a circular cone. Here the volume is related to both the height of the cone and the radius. If the radius is held constant, the volume is a function of the height. Similarly, for a fixed height, the volume is a function of the radius. Figure 20.10 shows how both of these ideas might be illustrated and the graph that would be associated with each.

The following activity is an example of using functions in a practical way.

─ **A**CTIVITY ────────────

## 20.3  Designing the Largest Box

Begin with a rectangular sheet of cardboard, and from each corner, cut a square. Fold up the four resulting flaps, and tape them together to form an open box. The volume of the box will vary, depending on the size of the squares. (The sheet in Figure 20.11 measures 9 by 12 inches.) Write a formula that

gives the volume of the box as a function of the size of the cutout squares. Use the function to determine what size the squares should be to create the box with the largest volume.

← 12" →

9"

**Figure 20.11**  **If squares are cut from a 9-by-12-inch piece of cardboard so that the four flaps can be folded up, what size squares should be cut so that the volume of the box is the largest possible?**

In "Designing the Largest Box," the resulting equation is a cubic or third-power polynomial. However, any seventh-grade student who knows that the volume of a box is the product of the three dimensions could develop this formula. A table of values and a graph are easily produced on a graphing calculator.

An interesting feature of this problem is that the function is defined for values that do not make sense in the context. The largest square that could be cut out is 4.5 inches on a side, in which case the squares from adjacent corners would touch and there would be no flap to turn up. But the function will produce "negative volumes" for values between 4.5 and 6 and positive volumes for values of the variable greater than 6. The equation representation of the function makes sense in this context *only* for values between 0 and 4.5. This is a useful discussion for students to help them realize that a mathematical model cannot be completely divorced from the context. Figure 20.12 shows the graph on a calculator. The tracer is near the point at which a maximum volume will occur.

**Figure 20.12**  **A graphing calculator plot of the volume function for the problem in Figure 20.11.**

## Functions from Scatter Plot Data

In the contexts discussed so far, patterns and real-world situations, the context gave rise to a specific equation that represented the functional relationship. Often in the real world, phenomena are observed that seem to suggest a functional relationship but not necessarily as clean or as well defined as the situations we have observed so far. In these cases, the data are generally plotted on a graph to produce a scatter plot of points. A visual inspection of the graphed data may suggest what kind of relationship, if any, exists. When a functional relationship seems to be suggested, an equation can be sought that defines a function approximating the data.

A situation like this was explored in Chapter 18. Data representing the heights and weights of people in a sample were plotted on a graph as a set of points, one for each person in the sample. The plot suggested a straight-line relationship between the heights and weights. A median-median line was found. In that case, the median-median line was the function (in graphical form) that approximated the data and was used to define the observed relationship between height and weight. In functional language, we could say that weight appeared to be a function of height.

Students in the middle grades might easily gather data found in an interesting context and perform this same type of analysis—that is, plot the data, look for a possible relationship, and find a best-fit line. When a line is drawn on the scatter plot, all representations of the function are present except the equation—the context produced the data. The graph of the best-fit line is a graphical representation of the function, and functional language can easily be used. A table can be made from points on the best-fit line. (Why would the table be made from the line and not from the actual data?) All that remains is to devise an equation.

The position in this chapter is that functional relationships can be explored as early as the sixth grade. However, in cases where a simple equation is not readily accessible, either that symbolic representation can be overlooked, or technology can be used to produce the equation. There seems little reason to stop students from using graphing calculators or curve-fitting software to see that methods do exist for finding best-fit curves. The calculator permits students to see what these best-fit curves and equations may look like, even though the techniques of finding the equations without technology will have to wait.

┌─────────────────────────────────────────────┐
**A**CTIVITY

### 20.4  Pendulum Swings

Give pairs of students string and a small weight that can be tied to the string (a large washer or a tennis ball, for example). Assign each pair a different length for their pendulum, from about 30 cm to 3 m (if the room is tall enough). The pendulum should be measured from the suspension point to the bottom of the weight. Have students carefully time the swing of the pendulum through ten full (back-and-forth) swings. If time permits, they can perform the experiment several times and take an average of their times to report to the class.
└─────────────────────────────────────────────┘

In the pendulum experiment, the data will form a surprisingly accurate curve without much variation. Students can use their hand-drawn curve to predict the times for other pendulum lengths. The curve is the top half of a parabola that opens to the right. It can be found on the graphing calculator by experimenting with the equation $y = a\sqrt{x}$ for different values of $a$ until a curve is found that fits nicely. What is most important at this level is not the equation but seeing how a physical law can be expressed as a function and represented in table and graphical form.

 **Electronic Data Gathering**

Technology now offers students a way to gather physical data that has exciting implications for connecting function concepts to the real world. The Calculator-Based Laboratory (CBL) is a device that interfaces between the graphing calculator and data sensors to gather and record real data directly into the calculator. Experiments that measure things such as temperature of a liquid, motion of a rolling car or a bouncing ball, light intensity, pH, and force can be conducted, with no pencil-and-paper record keeping. Theories of science that before could only be described can now be observed with real data gathered and analyzed.

Figure 20.13 shows a simple experiment using two different sensors connected through the CBL to a graphing calculator. The motion detector senses the motion back and forth as the hand stretches the rubber bands. The force sensor is connected to the rubber bands and measures the force applied and transmitted through them. A program available with Texas Instruments' manual (Brueningsen, Bower, Antinone, & Brueningsen, 1994) is loaded into the calculator. The program directs the CBL to collect data at regular intervals and store them in the calculator. Like any other data, these can then be plotted and a best-fit line determined. Figure 20.14 shows a scatter plot of data from running this experiment. It is fairly clear that there is a linear relationship and that a best-fit line would likely go through the origin. It is appropriate to say that the force applied to the rubber band is directly proportional to the distance the rubber band is stretched. In functional language, the force *is a function of* the amount the rubber band is stretched.

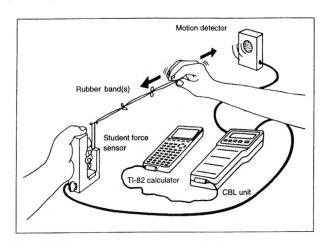

**Figure 20.13**  Two data probes are used to deliver force and motion data directly to a graphing calculator.
*Source:* "Real-World Math with the CBL™ System." Copyright Texas Instruments Inc., Dallas, TX. Reprinted by permission of Texas Instruments, Inc.

**Figure 20.14**  A graphing calculator scatter plot of data gathered in a rubber-band-stretching experiment as depicted in Figure 20.13.

## Other Scatter Plot Ideas

Consider gathering information that may be of personal interest to students. For example, do grades earned in social studies predict grades earned in mathematics? What about science and mathematics? What would the functional relationships be here? Even if a scatter plot of some information that was gathered showed no particular trend, functional language could still be employed—for example, "The grades on last week's mathematics test do *not* appear to be a function of the number of hours' sleep students got the night before the test."

Data can also be obtained from sports records, census reports, the business section of the newspaper, and many other sources. The U.S. Department of Commerce publishes a wide variety of data for each state and often over a series of years. For example, is there a functional relationship over the years between the gross domestic product and the U.S. population?

## Fun Experiments

There are all sorts of experiments that students can invent to see what functional relationships, if any, exist between two variables.

┌ **A**CTIVITY ─

### 20.5 Functional Experiments

The task is to try to develop a functional relationship between two variables by conducting an experiment. Data should be entered in a table and plotted on a graph. The goal is to determine an equation (function) that can be used to make predictions. A graphing calculator or computer will be a useful tool for curve fitting, although for some experiments that may not be necessary. Students should explain which is the independent variable and which the dependent. Here are some ideas for experiments:*

- How long would it take for 100 students standing in a row to complete a wave like the ones done at football games? Experiment with different numbers of students from 5 to 25. Can the relationship predict how many students it would take for a given wave time? (Variation: Have students sequentially stand and do a jumping jack.)

- How far will a Matchbox car roll off of a ramp, based on the height the ramp is raised?

- How is the flight time of a paper airplane affected by the number of paper clips attached to the nose of the plane?

- What is the relationship between the number of dominoes in a row and the time required for them to fall over? (Use multiples of 100 dominoes.)

*Most of these experiments were inspired by the article "Algebra: Real-Life Investigations in a Lab Setting" (McCoy, 1997), which contains additional ideas and useful suggestions.

- Make wadded newspaper balls using different numbers of sheets of newspaper. Rubber bands help hold the paper in a ball. What is the relationship between the number of sheets and the distance the ball can be thrown?

- If colored water is dropped on a paper towel, what is the relationship between the number of drops and the diameter of the spot? Is the relationship different for different brands of towels?

- How much weight can a toothpick bridge hold? Lay toothpicks in a bunch to span a 2-inch gap between two boards. From the toothpicks, hang a bag or other container into which weights can be added until the toothpicks break. Begin with only one toothpick.

Experiments like these are fun. They also provide an opportunity for students to engage in experimental design. Students need practice in identifying independent and dependent variables, controlling experiments for other variables, measuring and recording results, and analyzing data. This is a perfect blend of mathematics and science.

## Graphs Without Equations

A study of functions in the middle school should not get bogged down in techniques of graphing and analysis of equations. That is one reason that the graphing calculator is such an effective tool for early explorations.

The graph is one of the most powerful representations of a function. It is both fun and profitable to interpret and construct graphs related to real situations but without using any specific data, equations, or numbers. The advantage of activities such as these is the focus on how a graph can express the relationships involved.

---

### ACTIVITY

### 20.6 Sketch a Graph

Sketch a graph for each of these situations. No numbers or formulas are to be used.

a. The temperature of a frozen dinner from 30 minutes before it is removed from the freezer until it is removed from the microwave and placed on the table. (Consider time 0 to be the moment the dinner is removed from the freezer.)

b. The value of a 1970 Volkswagen Beetle from the time it was purchased to the present. (It was kept by a loving owner and is in top condition.)

c. The level of water in the bathtub from the time you begin to fill it to the time it is completely empty after your bath.

d. Profit in terms of number of items sold.

e. The height of a baseball in terms of time from when it is thrown straight up to the time it hits the ground.

f. The speed of the baseball in the situation in (e).

Stop here and try to sketch graphs for each of the situations in the activity. In a classroom, it is fun to have students sketch their graphs on transparencies without identifying which situation is being graphed (no labels on the graphs). Let students examine the graphs to see if they can determine which situation goes with each graph that is presented. Examine the graphs for one situation drawn by several students to decide which graph represents a situation best and why. Figure 20.15 contains six graphs that match the six situations described in the "Sketch a Graph" activity. Can you match these graphs with the six situations? How do these graphs compare to the graphs that you sketched?

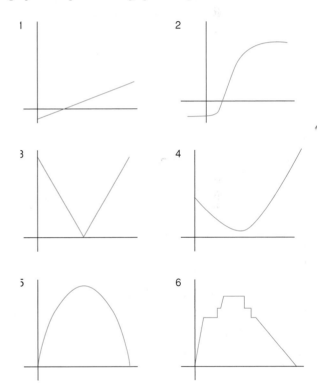

**Figure 20.15** Match each graph with the situations described in Activity 20.6. Talk about what is happening in each case.

A similar example of rates is found in situations involving time and distance. Consider the following:

A car is traveling along a road at about 45 mph and comes to a stop sign. It stops for the sign and then accelerates to the same 45-mph speed.

Sketch a graph of the *distance* the car has traveled from the beginning of the story to the end. The horizontal axis should be *time*. In other words, the graph should show distance as a function of time. How would a graph of the *speed* of the car look over the same interval?

The following activity could be done after children have sketched graphs for a variety of time and distance situations.

---

**A**CTIVITY

### 20.7 Create a Journey Story

Suppose that a student has created the time-distance graphs shown in Figure 20.16. Each is supposed to represent the journey of a single vehicle or person. Some of them are impossible and could not represent any journey. First identify the impossible graphs. Then make up a plausible journey story for each of the remaining graphs.

---

The next activity is similar but begins to develop the idea of rate of change—how rapidly or slowly something changes.

---

**A**CTIVITY

### 20.8 Bottles and Volume Graphs

Figure 20.17 shows six bottles and six graphs. Assume that the bottles are filled at a constant rate. Because of their shapes, the height of the liquid in the bottles will increase either more slowly or more quickly as the bottle gets wider or narrower. Match the graphs with the bottles.

---

Find some bottles or glasses that have different shapes. One place to look is in the science lab. Using a small container such as a medicine cup, pour water into each bottle. Measure the height after each small containerful is poured. Make a graph of the heights as a function of the volume. If students do an actual experiment, the discus-

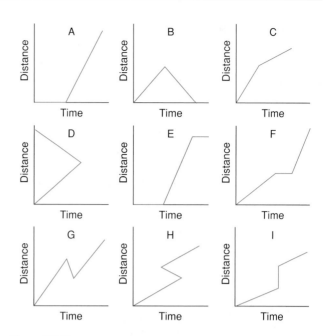

**Figure 20.16** **Which graphs could not possibly describe a journey? Why? Invent a journey story for each of the possible graphs.**

sion of which graph fits which bottle and why will be much more meaningful.

Students could share their stories without telling which graph each story was supposed to match. The class could then discuss which graph best fits each tale.

### ASSESSMENT NOTES

The main thrust of the ideas in this chapter is that students should begin to see functional relationships in a variety of situations—relationships where the change in one quantity has a predictable effect on the change in another.

**Figure 20.17** **If the bottles are filled at a constant rate, match the graphs with the bottles.**

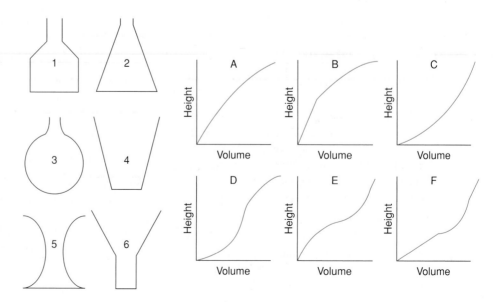

An equally important idea is communication of these functional relationships. Functions can be expressed in terms of context, language, tables, graphs, and equations. What is most important is that students see these representations as different but related methods of telling about a function.

If you keep these big ideas in mind, your assessment plans should be focused accordingly.

■ What kinds of strategies do students use to search for patterns and generalizations? (Do they use the differences from one frame to the next, look for regularities in the physical patterns, coordinate frame numbers with different aspects of the physical pattern, exhibit flexible thinking in the search for patterns?)

■ Do students distinguish between a recursive relationship in a pattern and a functional rule that will produce the frame value for any frame?

■ Do students effectively translate real situations into functional language, graphs, symbols, tables?

■ Are students able to demonstrate the way these various representations of a function are connected?

■ When gathered data only approximate a function rule (scatter plots), do students indicate an understanding of the difference between the real data and the best-fit line or the constructed function rule?

# REFLECTIONS ON CHAPTER 20

## Writing to Learn

1. Describe in your own words the five different representations of a function and how they are related or actually represent the same thing. Use an example of your own (not one from the book) to explain.

2. Describe in general terms how you might develop function concepts through the use of growing patterns, a real-world situation, and an experiment. Indicate how the five representations are used in each method.

3. Make up a real-world situation that defines a functional relationship. Use your example to do the following:
   a. Sketch a graph illustrating the relationship.
   b. State the relationship using the language of functions.
   c. Build a chart with numbers that might go with your relationship.
   d. Explain the graph and the chart as ways of presenting the same information in different forms.
   e. Explain how your example meets the formal definition of a function.

4. The table of values used to create a scatter plot, as in the height versus–arm span example, is not a function table. Explain why not. How do you get a function out of a scatter plot?

5. Regarding graphs without equations, one activity in the text has students sketch graphs for situations, another has students match graphs to a collection of situations, and a third has them make up stories to go with graph sketches. What is the value of these exercises? Are there any differences in what students learn or think about in these different exercises?

## For Discussion and Exploration

1. Some people feel that graphing calculators are too expensive for use in the middle grades. Others argue that students need to know the "basics" before they should be allowed to use these devices. What is your position? Can you defend it?

2. As a part of the Third International Mathematics and Science Study (TIMSS), a video study was done at grade 8. Tapes are available that show algebra lessons from an eighth-grade class in the United States, Japan, and Germany. The lessons show marked differences in the focus and methods of instruction. If at all possible, view the tapes and discuss your reactions.

## Recommendations for Further Reading

### Highly Recommended

Arcidiacono, M. J., & Maier, E. (1993). *Picturing algebra* (Unit 9 in *Math in the mind's eye*). Salem, OR: Math Learning Center.
This is one of the best examples of activities in which patterns lead to equations and functions. Like all *Math in the Mind's Eye* units, this series of lessons actively involves students and provides extensive teacher direction and Blackline Masters for materials and record sheets. Unique to these materials are tiles of unspecified length or dimension that are used to develop a general formula or function.

Edwards, E. L. (Ed.). (1990). *Algebra for everyone*. Reston, VA: National Council of Teachers of Mathematics.
This little book is worth reading by anyone contemplating teaching concepts discussed in this chapter. Short chapters address such issues as change in focus, the transition from arithmetic to algebra, and the use of technology. The annotated list of resources is another plus.

Fey, J. T., & Heid, M. K. (1995). *Concepts in algebra: A technological approach*. Dedham, MA: Janson.
This is a full-year text for beginning algebra that was originally developed under a National Science Foundation grant to illustrate how technology could be used to teach algebra. The authors strongly believe that algebra should be tightly connected to real-world examples, not simply as applications at the ends of a unit but as the springboard of every idea. The emphasis is on functions and graphs. Symbol manipulation is minimal. Factoring is not included as a skill anywhere in the book. Many of the ideas in this book are embedded in the current chapter. This is a highly recommended resource for teachers, as well as a text for a middle grade algebra course.

Phillips, E., Gardella, T., Kelly, C., & Stewart, J. (1991). *Patterns and functions: Addenda series, grades 5–8.* Reston, VA: National Council of Teachers of Mathematics.

It is hard to improve on this book for ideas related to function development. The first section involves students with a wide variety of functions in real contexts, including exponential decay, linear, quadratic, and cubic functions. Throughout the book, the concept of function grows out of pattern development in a variety of creative and interesting activities that connect many middle school mathematics topics to a development of functions. This is an important contribution to the development of function concepts prior to algebra.

## Other Suggestions

Barrett, G., & Goebel, J. (1992). The impact of graphing calculators on the teaching and learning of mathematics. In T. J. Cooney (Ed.), *Teaching and learning mathematics in the 1990s* (pp. 205–211). Reston, VA: National Council of Teachers of Mathematics.

Bell, A. (1995). Purpose in school algebra. *Journal of Mathematical Behavior, 14,* 41–73.

Blume, G. W., & Heckman, D. S. (1997). What do students know about algebra and functions? In P. A. Kenney & E. A. Silver (Eds.), *Results from the sixth mathematics assessment of the National Assessment of Educational Progress* (pp. 225–278). Reston, VA: National Council of Teachers of Mathematics.

Brueningsen, C., Bower, B., Antinone, L., & Brueningsen, E. (1994). *Real-world math with the CBL system: 25 activities using the CBL and TI-82.* Dallas: Texas Instruments.

Coxford, A. F. (Ed.). (1988). *The ideas of algebra, K–12.* Reston, VA: National Council of Teachers of Mathematics.

Day, R. P. (1995). Using functions to make mathematical connections. In P. A. House (Ed.), *Connecting mathematics across the curriculum* (pp. 54–64). Reston, VA: National Council of Teachers of Mathematics.

Day, R. P., & Jones, G. A. (1997). Building bridges to algebraic thinking. *Mathematics Teaching in the Middle School, 2,* 209–212.

Fey, J. T. (1989). School algebra for the year 2000. In S. Wagner & C. Kieran (Eds.), *Research issues in the learning and teaching of algebra* (pp. 199–213). Mahwah, NJ: Erlbaum.

Graphing Technology in Mathematics Project. (1995). *Graphing power: Middle school activities for the TI-81 and TI-82.* White Plains, NY: Cuisenaire–Dale Seymour.

Harvey, J. G., Waits, B. K., & Demana, F. D. (1995). The influence of technology on the teaching and learning of algebra. *Journal of Mathematical Behavior, 14,* 75–109.

Heid, M. K. (1995). *Algebra in a technological world: Addenda series, grades 9–12.* Reston, VA: National Council of Teachers of Mathematics.

McCoy, L. P. (1997). Algebra: Real-life investigations in a lab setting. *Mathematics Teaching in the Middle School, 2,* 220–224.

McCoy, L. P., Baker, T. H., & Little, L. S. (1996). Using multiple representations to communicate: An algebra challenge. In P. C. Elliott (Ed.), *Communication in mathematics, K–12 and beyond* (pp. 40–44). Reston, VA: National Council of Teachers of Mathematics.

Patterson, A. C. (1999). Grasping graphing. *Mathematics Teacher, 92,* 758–762.

Quinn, A. L., & Larson, K. R. (1996). When does a dog become older than its owner? *Mathematics Teacher, 89,* 734–737.

Rubenstein, R. (1996). The function game. *Mathematics Teaching in the Middle School, 2,* 74–78.

Shell Centre for Mathematical Education, University of Nottingham. (1985). *The language of functions and graphs.* Nottingham, England: Author.

Specht, J. (2000). *More than graphs: Mathematics explorations for TI-73, TI-82, TI-83, and TI-83 Plus graphing calculators.* Emeryville, CA: Key Curriculum Press.

Talbert, M. K., & Stallings-Roberts, V. (1994). Introducing pre-algebra skills in an egg-citing way. *Mathematics Teaching in the Middle School, 1,* 198–202.

Taylor, L. J. C., & Nichols, J. A. (1994). Graphing calculators aren't just for high school students. *Mathematics Teaching in the Middle School, 1,* 190–197.

Van Dyke, F. (1998). Visualizing cost, revenue, and profit. *Mathematics Teacher, 91,* 488–493, 500–503.

Wilson, M. R., & Shealy, B. E. (1995). Experiencing function relationships with a viewing tube. In P. A. House (Ed.), *Connecting mathematics across the curriculum* (pp. 219–224). Reston, VA: National Council of Teachers of Mathematics.

Zawojewski, J. S. (1992). *Dealing with data and chance: Addenda series, grades 5–8.* Reston, VA: National Council of Teachers of Mathematics.

# Chapter 21

# Developing Concepts of Exponents, Integers, and Real Numbers

Much of the middle grades curriculum has been discussed in other chapters, including decimals, ratio and proportion, percent, measurement, geometry, probability, statistics, and algebraic reasoning. Each of those topics has its initial development in earlier grades but continues in the middle school. Specifically, students in the middle grades need to develop a more complete understanding of the number system, extend whole numbers to integers, start to think of fractions as rational numbers (both positive and negative), and begin to appreciate the completeness of the real number system.

## BIG Ideas

1. Exponential notation is a powerful way to express repeated products of the same number. Specifically, powers of 10 express very large and very small numbers in an economical manner.

2. Integers add to number the idea of opposite, so that every number has both size and a positive or negative relationship to other numbers. A negative number is the opposite of the positive number of the same size.

3. Every fraction, both positive and negative, is a rational number. Furthermore, every rational number can be expressed as a fraction.

4. Many numbers are not rational and can be expressed only symbolically or approximately using a close rational number.

## LARGE NUMBERS, SMALL NUMBERS, AND EXPONENTS

As numbers in our technological world get very small or very large, expressing them in standard form is cumbersome. Exponential notation is much more efficient for conveying numeric or quantitative information.

### Exponents

In algebra classes, students get confused trying to remember the rules of exponents. For example, when you raise numbers to powers, do you add or multiply the exponents? Here is an example of procedural knowledge that is often learned without supporting conceptual knowledge. Before algebra, students should have ample opportunity to explore working with exponents on whole numbers rather than with letters or variables. By doing so, they are able to deal directly with the concept and actually generate the rules themselves.

A *whole-number exponent* is simply shorthand for repeated multiplication of a number times itself; for example, $3^4 = 3 \times 3 \times 3 \times 3$. That is the only conceptual knowledge required.

Conventions of symbolism must also be learned. These are arbitrary rules with no conceptual basis. The first is that *an exponent applies to its immediate base.* For example, in the expression $2 + 5^3$, the exponent 3 applies only to the 5, so the expression is equal to $2 + (5 \times 5 \times 5)$. However, in the expression $(2 + 5)^3$, the 3 is an exponent of the quantity $2 + 5$ and is evaluated as $(2 + 5) \times (2 + 5) \times (2 + 5)$, or $7 \times 7 \times 7$.

The other convention involves the *order of operations*: Multiplication and division are always done before addition and subtraction. Since exponentiation is repeated multiplication, it also is done before addition and subtraction. In the expression $5 + 4 \times 2 - 6 \div 3$, $4 \times 2$ and $6 \div 3$ are done first. Therefore, the expression is evaluated as $5 + 8 - 2 = 13 - 2 = 11$. If done in left-to-right order, the result would be 4. Parentheses are used to group operations that are to be done first. Therefore, in $(5 + 4) \times 2 - 6 \div 3$, the addition can be done inside the parentheses first, or the distributive property can be used, and the final result is 16. The phrase "*P*lease *e*xcuse *m*y *d*ear *A*unt *S*ally" is sometimes used to help students recall that operations inside *p*arentheses are done first, then *e*xponentiation, and then *m*ultiplication and *d*ivision before *a*ddition and *s*ubtraction.

 ## Calculators and Notation

Most scientific calculators employ "algebraic logic" that will evaluate expressions correctly and also allow grouping with parentheses. However, with the exception of the TI-Math-Mate, the simple four-function calculators generally used in elementary schools do not use algebraic logic. Operations are processed as they are entered. On calculators without algebraic logic, the following two keying sequences produce the same results:

Key: → 3 [+] 2 [×] 7 [=]
Display → 3  2  5 7 35

Key: → 3 [+] 2 [=] [×] 7 [=]
Display → 3  2 5  7 35

Whenever an operation sign is pressed, the effect is the same as pressing [=] and then the operation. Of course, neither result is correct for the expressions $3 + 2 \times 7$, which should be evaluated as $3 + 14$, or 17. Calculators designed for middle grades do use algebraic logic and include parenthesis keys so that both $3 + 2 \times 7$ and $(3 + 2) \times 7$ can be keyed in the order that the symbols appear. Now all of the major manufacturers offer calculators that show an entire expression in the window, including parentheses, as do graphing calculators. Results are shown only after pressing the [Enter] key. With the Explorer Plus and most scientific calculators, the display shows only one number at a time, as illustrated here:

Key: → 3 [+] 2 [×] 7 [=]
Display → 3  2  7 17

Notice that the display does not change when [×] is pressed: A right parenthesis is never displayed. Instead, the expres-

sion that the right parenthesis encloses is calculated and that result displayed.

Key: → [(] 3 [+] 2 [)] [×] 7 [=]
Display → [ 3  2 5  7 35

The graphing calculator offers the best solution to these problems and at the same time provides other significant advantages, as noted in several earlier chapters. When the expression $3 + 2 \times (6^2 - 4)$ is keyed in, the display shows the full expression. Nothing is evaluated until you press [Enter] or [EXE]. Then the result appears on the next line to the right of the screen:

$$3 + 2 * (6^2 - 4)$$
$$67$$

Moreover, the last expression entered can be recalled and edited so that students can see how different expressions are evaluated. Only minimum key presses are required.

| | |
|---|---|
| $3 + 2 * (6^2 - 4)$ | 67 |
| $(3 + 2) * (6^2 - 4)$ | 160 |
| $(3 + 2) * 6^2 - 4$ | 176 |
| $3 + 2 * 6^2 - 4$ | 71 |

Nevertheless, the simple four-function calculator remains a powerful tool regardless of its limitations. For example, to evaluate $3^8$, press 3 [×] [=] [=] [=] [=] [=] [=] [=]. (The first press of [×] will result in 9, or $3 \times 3$.) Students will be fascinated by how quickly numbers grow. Enter any number, press [×], and then repeatedly press [=]. Try two-digit numbers. Try 0.2.

Give students ample opportunity to explore expressions involving mixed operations and exponents with only the conventions and the meaning of exponents to guide them. No rules for exponents should be promoted. When experience has provided a firm background, the rules of exponents will make sense and should not require rote memorization.

---

**A**CTIVITY

### 21.1 **What's in an Expression?**

**Provide students with numeric expressions to evaluate with simple four-function calculators. Here are some examples of the types of expressions that can be valuable:**

| | | | |
|---|---|---|---|
| $3 + 4 \times 8$ $4 \times 8 + 3$ | $3^6 + 2^6$ $(3 + 2)^6$ | $3^4 \times 7 - 5^2$ $(3 \times 7)^4 - 5 \times 2$ | $3^4 \times 5^2$ $(3 \times 5)^6$ |

| | | | |
|---|---|---|---|
| $\dfrac{5^3 \times 5^2}{5^6}$ | $4 \times 3 - 2^3 \times 5 + 23 \times 9$ | $\dfrac{4 \times 3^5}{2}$ | $4 + \dfrac{3^5}{2}$ |

When experiencing difficulty, students should write equivalent expressions without exponents or include parentheses and brackets to indicate explicit groupings. For example:

$$(7 \times 2^3 - 5)^3 = (7 \times (2 \times 2 \times 2) - 5) \times$$
$$(7 \times (2 \times 2 \times 2) - 5) \times$$
$$(7 \times (2 \times 2 \times 2) - 5)$$
$$= ((7 \times 8) - 5) \times$$
$$((7 \times 8) - 5) \times$$
$$((7 \times 8) - 5)$$
$$= (56 - 5) \times (56 - 5) \times (56 - 5)$$
$$= 51 \times 51 \times 51$$

When discussing results, place all of the emphasis on the procedures rather than the answer. The fact that two groups got the same result does not help a group that got a different result. For many expressions, there is more than one way to proceed, and one may be easier to do or to understand than another.

Of course, calculators with algebraic logic will automatically produce correct results. Yet it remains important for students to know the correct order of operations. The calculator should not replace an understanding of the rules. The order-of-operation rules apply to symbolic manipulation in algebra and must also be understood if a calculator without algebraic logic is used.

The following activity involves exponents and estimation and is also a good problem-solving task.

---

**ACTIVITY**

### 21.2 Mystery Number

Before class, write down any simple expression involving exponents, and evaluate it. Give the expression to the class with at least two of the numbers in the expression replaced by stars. Give students the value of the expression, and see which group, using calculators, can find correct values for the stars first. For example:

$$(\star + 7\star)^3 = 41,063,625$$

The size of the result and the fact that it ends in 25 are clues that may help. There is more than one solution to this, so do not be too quick to tell students their answers are not correct.

---

# Very Large Numbers

The real world is full of very large quantities and measures. We see references to huge numbers in the media all the time. Unfortunately, most of us have not developed an appreciation for extremely large numbers. Here are a few examples:

- The annual federal budget is approaching $2 trillion.
- The defense budget alone is about $275 million. Based on 265 million people in the United States, that comes out to about $1040 per person, or about $4160 per family of four—*every year!*
- A state lottery with 41 numbers from which to pick 6 has over 7 million possible combinations of 6 numbers. There are $44 \times 43 \times 42 \times 41 \times 40 \times 39$ possible ways that the balls could come out of the hopper (5,082,517,440). But generally the order in which they are picked is not important. Since there are $6 \times 5 \times 4 \times 3 \times 2 \times 1 = 720$ different arrangements of 6 numbers, each collection appears 720 times. Therefore, there are *only* 5,082,517,440 ÷ 720 possible lottery numbers, or in other words, 1 out of 7,059,052 chances to win.
- An estimate of the size of the universe is 40 billion light-years. One light-year is the number of miles light travels in *one year*. The speed of light is 186,281.7 miles per *second*, or 16,094,738,880 miles in a single day.
- The human body has about 100 billion cells.
- The distance to the sun is about 150 million kilometers.
- The population of the world has surpassed 6 billion.

In class, large numbers should be discussed in real contexts. The opportunity to explore such numbers can very likely be coordinated with teachers in social studies or science. Talk to teachers in the other disciplines, and design a joint exploration for your students to investigate large numbers related to their studies. Individuals or groups can select different facts to look up and discuss.

# Representation of Large Numbers: Scientific Notation

The more common it becomes to find very large numbers in our daily lives, the more important it is to have convenient ways to represent them. One option is to say and write numbers in their common form. However, this practice can at times be cumbersome. Another option is to use exponential notation and our base-ten place-value system.

Students in grade school learn how to multiply by 10, by 100, and by 1000 by simply adding the appropriate number of zeros. Help students expand this idea by examining powers of 10 on a calculator that handles exponents. A graphing calculator is best but not the only option.

---

**ACTIVITY**

### 21.3 Exploring Powers of 10

Have students use any calculator that permits entering exponents to explore some of the following:

a. Explore $10^N$ for various values of N. What patterns do you notice. What does 1E15 mean? (1E15 is the typical calculator form of $1 \times 10^{15}$.)

b. Find out the easiest expressions for one thousand, one million, one billion, one trillion. What patterns are there in these numbers?

c. Enter 45 followed by a string of zeros. How many will your calculator permit? What happens when you press Enter? What does 4.5E10 mean?

d. What does 5.689E6 mean? Can you enter this another way?

e. Try sums like $(4.5 \times 10^N) + (27 \times 10^K)$ for different values of N and K. What can you find out?

f. What happens with products of numbers like those in item (e)?

It is useful to become comfortable with the power-of-10 expressions in Activity 20.3. Students should eventually discover that when scientific or graphing calculators display numbers with more digits than the display will hold, they can use *scientific notation*—a decimal number between 1 and 10 times a power of 10. For example, on a TI-73, the product of $45,000,000 \times 8,000,000$ is displayed as 3.6E14, meaning $3.6 \times 10^{14}$, or 360,000,000,000,000 (360 trillion).

Ask students why there are only 13 zeros. What happens when the numbers in the computation do not involve a lot of zeros? What if each factor in the product had been expressed in scientific notation: $(4.5 \times 10^7) \times (8 \times 10^6)$, or 4.5E7 $\times$ 8.0E6? Discuss the advantages of this latter notation, especially for multiplication and division. Here the significant digits can be multiplied mentally ($4.5 \times 8 = 36$) and the exponents added to produce almost instantly $36 \times 10^{13}$ or $3.6 \times 10^{14}$.

Different notations have different purposes and values. Consider this fact: In 1990, the population of the world was more than 5,050,700,000 persons, about 1 billion fewer than in the year 2000. This can be expressed in various ways:

5 billion 50 million 700 thousand

5,050,700,000

5,0507 $\times 10^9$

Less than 5.1 billion

A little more than 5 billion

Each way of stating the number has value and purpose in different contexts. Rather than spend time with exercises converting numbers from standard form to scientific notation, consider large numbers found in newspapers, magazines, and atlases. How are they written? How are they said aloud? When are they rounded? When not and why? What forms of the numbers seem best for the purposes?

# Negative Exponents

When students begin to explore exponents and have also experienced negative integers, it is interesting to consider what it might mean to raise a number to a negative power. For example, what does $2^{-4}$ mean, if anything? Two related options for exploring the possibilities of negative numbers seem reasonable. First, in the spirit of patterns in mathematics, examine a pattern of numbers, and see how it might best be expanded. As with large numbers, the powers of 10 seem the most profitable to explore because they are directly related to place value. Have students consider $10^N$ as follows:

$10^4 = 10,000$

$10^3 = 1000$

$10^2 = 100$

$10^1 = 10$

$10^0 = ?$

$10^{-1} = ?$

In this sequence, the most obvious entry for $10^0$ is 1, and that is the *definition* of $10^0$. That is, it is a convention that 10 or any other nonzero number raised to the power 0 is 1. So what is $10^{-1}$? If the pattern is to continue, the 1 should move to the right of the decimal:

$10^0 = 1$

$10^{-1} = 0.1$

$10^{-2} = 0.01$

$10^{-3} = 0.001$

and so on. Notice how each of these numbers is written as a fraction:

$$10^{-3} = 0.001 = \frac{1}{1000} = \frac{1}{10^3}$$

Students should be encouraged to explore these numbers on a calculator. That leads to the second way to explore negative exponents: Use a calculator to see if you can figure out what things like $4^{-3}$ or $2^{-5}$ mean. The calculator should of course never be seen as the *reason* for anything in mathematics, but here you are searching for a notation convention. Assuming that one exists, it is reasonable to believe that the calculator will have the correct convention incorporated. If the calculator has decimal-to-fraction conversion, suggest that students use that feature to help develop the meaning of negative exponents. Figure 21.1 gives an example of how this might look on a graphing calculator.

# Very Small Numbers

As with large numbers, it is extremely important to use real examples of very small numbers. Without real contexts, you may be tempted to resort to drill exercises that have little

**Figure 21.1** Graphing calculators routinely evaluate expressions as decimals. However, they also provide a way to convert decimals to fractions. This figure shows the screen of a TI-73 calculator. The `F◂▸D` key converts fractions to decimals and also decimals to fractions as shown here.

meaning for students. Here are a few examples of real-world values to explore:

- The length of a DNA strand in a cell is about $10^{-7}$ m. This is also measured as 1000 *angstroms*. (Based on this information, how long is an angstrom?) How large is a cell?

- Human hair grows at the rate of $10^{-8}$ miles per hour.

- The chances of winning the Virginia lottery, based on selecting six numbers from 1 to 44, is 1 in 7.059 million. That is a probability of less than $1.4 \times 10^{-10}$.

- The mass of one atom of hydrogen is 0.000 000 000 000 000 000 000 001 675 g.

- It takes sound 0.28 second ($2.8 \times 10^{-1}$) to travel the length of a football field. In contrast, a TV signal travels a full mile in about 0.000005368 second, or $5.3 \times 10^{-6}$ second. A TV viewer at home hears the football being kicked before the receiver on the field does.

# INTEGER CONCEPTS

Students almost daily have some interaction with negative numbers or experience phenomena that negative numbers can model. Some examples:

A loss of money is a negative cash flow.

Slowing down the car is negative acceleration, and driving in reverse is negative velocity.

A countdown to blastoff is negative time.

Below-zero temperature and below-ground level are negatives relative to a scale.

In fact, almost any concept that is quantified and has direction probably has both a positive and a negative value.

Generally, negative values are introduced with *integers*—the whole numbers and their negatives or opposites—instead of with fractions or decimals.

# Intuitive Models of Signed Quantities

As with any new types of numbers that students encounter, real models or examples are useful. Negative numbers or situations that model them do exist. It is a good idea to discuss some of these with your class before jumping directly into computation with signed numbers.

### Debits and Credits

Suppose that you are the bookkeeper for a small business. At any time, your records show how many dollars the company has in its account. There are always so many dollars in cash (credits or receipts) and so many dollars in accounts payable (debits). The difference between the debit and credit totals tells the value of the account. If there are more credits than debits, the account is positive, or "in the black." If there are more debits than credits, the account is in debt, shows a negative cash value, or is "in the red." Suppose further that all transactions are handled by mail. The mail carrier can bring mail, a positive action, or take mail away, a negative action. With this scenario, it is easy to discuss addition and subtraction of signed quantities. An example is illustrated in Figure 21.2.

**Figure 21.2** A ledger sheet model for integers.

### Integer Football

The standard football field has a 50-yard line in the center extending to 0 at each goal. A mathematical football field might have the center as the 0-yard line with one goal the +50 goal and the other the −50 goal. Any position on the field is determined by a signed number between +50 and −50. Gains or losses are like positive and negative quantities. A positive team moves toward the positive goal, and a negative team toward the negative goal. If the negative team starts on the −15-yard line and has a loss of 20 yards, it will be on the +5-yard line. (You should sketch a picture of this example and convince yourself that it is numerically the same as the one in Figure 21.2 using the debit-credit model.

Contrived situations such as mailing debits and credits and the football field are suggested as introductory discussion models. They can help students think intuitively about what happens to quantities when an action causes them to be less than 0. They also provide examples of a joining or positive action and a removal or negative action of both positive and negative quantities. With these models we can pose two specific types of questions for students:

1. Give students a beginning and an end value, and have them describe different ways that the change might have occurred. For example, how could the ball get from the +40-yard line to the −10-yard line if the negative team has the ball?

2. Give students either a beginning or an ending value and one or more actions, and have them determine the value not given. For example, if the company received $20 in credits and $35 in debits, resulting in a balance of negative $5, what did the company have to begin with?

The calculator is another model that might be explored early in the discussion of signed numbers. It gives correct and immediate results that students seem to believe. The major drawback is that no rationale for the result is provided.

Have students enter a small number such as 10 in the calculator and press ⊖ 1 ⊜ ⊜ ⊜ . . . until the display shows 0. Discuss what will happen on the next press of ⊜. After pressing the equal button several more times, discuss what they think the result means. (Be aware that the negative sign appears in different places on different calculators.) Similarly, have students explore subtraction problems such as 5 − 8 = ?, and discuss the results.

A negative number is entered on a standard four-function calculator by first pressing the number and then pressing the change-of-sign key (usually ±). Thus to add −3 and −8, press 3 ± + 8 ± ⊜. Students can benefit by using the calculator along with the intuitive models and questions mentioned earlier. For example, how can you get from −5 to −17 by addition? 13 minus *what* is 15?

## Mathematical Definition of Negative Numbers

The mathematician defines a negative number in terms of whole numbers. Therefore, the definition of negative 3 is the solution to the equation 3 + ? = 0. In general, the *opposite of n* is the solution to n + ? = 0. If n is a positive number, the *opposite of n* is a negative number. The set of integers there-

fore consists of the positive whole numbers, the opposites of the whole numbers, or negative numbers, and 0, which is neither positive nor negative. This is the definition found in student textbooks. Like many things in mathematics, abstract or symbolic definitions are best when there is some intuitive or conceptual framework with which to link the idea.

# OPERATIONS WITH INTEGERS

Until students encounter integers, the plus and minus signs are used only for the operations of addition and subtraction. Notation for signed numbers represents a real problem for many students. For example, the sum of 3 and negative 7 can be written as 3 + (−7) or as 3 + −7. The latter form might be clear in a printed book but may be obscure in handwritten form. The use of parentheses is awkward, especially in expressions already involving parentheses. On graphing calculators, the distinction is forced on the user: One key is used for subtraction and another for negatives. They do not work interchangeably.

## Two Models for Integer Operations

Two models are popular for helping students understand how the four operations (+, −, ×, and ÷) work with the integers. One model consists of counters in two different colors, one for positive counts and one for negative counts. Two counters, one of each type, cancel each other out. Thus if yellows are positive and reds are negative, 5 yellows and 7 reds is the same as 2 reds, each representing −2 (see Figure 21.3). It is important with this model that students understand that it is always possible to add to or remove from a pile any number of pairs consisting of one positive and one negative counter without changing the value of the pile. (Intuitively, this is like

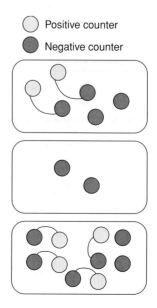

**Figure 21.3** Each collection is a model of negative 2.

adding equal quantities of debits and credits.) The actions of addition and subtraction are the same as for whole numbers; addition is joining or adding counters, and subtraction is removing or taking away counters.

The other commonly used model is the number line. It is a bit more traditional and mathematical, yet many students find it confusing. The football field model provides an intuitive background. Positive and negative numbers are measured distances to the right and left of 0. It is important to remember that signed values are *directed distances* and not points on a line. The points on the number line are not models of integers; the directed distances are. To emphasize this for students, represent all integers with arrows, and avoid referring to the number line coordinates as "numbers." Poster board arrows of different whole-number lengths can be made in two colors, yellow pointing to the right for positive quantities and red to the left for negative quantities (see Figure 21.4). The arrows help students think of integer quantities as directed distances. A positive arrow never points left, and a negative arrow never points right. Furthermore, each arrow is a quantity with both length (magnitude or absolute value) and direction (sign). These properties remain for each arrow regardless of its position on the number line. Small versions of the arrows can easily be cut from poster board for individual students to work with.

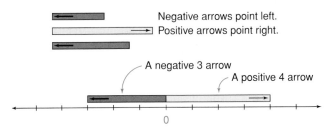

**Figure 21.4** **Number-line model for integers.**

Note that the rules (procedural knowledge) for integer operations are generally easier simply to give to students than explanations with a model are. The conceptual explanations do not make the rules easier to use, and it is never intended that students continue to think in terms of these models as they practice integer arithmetic. Rather, it is important that students not view the procedural rules for manipulating integers as arbitrary and mysterious. Here is a case where we must make students responsible for the conceptual knowledge. If we emphasize only the procedural rules, there is little reason for students to attend to the conceptual justifications. Do not be content with right answers; always demand explanations.

## Which Model to Use

Although the two models appear quite different, they are alike mathematically. Integers involve two concepts—*quantity* and *opposite*. Quantity is modeled by the number of counters or the length of the arrows. Opposite is represented as different colors or different directions.

Many teachers who have tried both models with their students report that students find one model easy and the other hard. (The counter model seems to be the favorite.) As a result, they decide to use only the model that students like or understand better. This is a mistake! Remember that the dual concepts of integers are not in the models but rather must be constructed by the students and imposed on the models. It may be that students find the operations easier when they use counters. This is not the same thing as understanding integer operations. Students should experience both models and, perhaps even more important, discuss how the two are alike. A parallel development using both models at the same time may be the most conceptual approach.

# A PROBLEM-SOLVING APPROACH FOR INTEGERS

The following discussion is more a quick explanation of how counters and arrows can be used to model operations with integers than a suggested pedagogical approach. Once your students understand how integers are represented by each of the models, you can present the operations for the integers in the form of problems. In other words, rather than explaining how addition of integers works and showing students how to solve exercises with the models, you pose an integer computation and let students use their models to find a solution. It may be useful to assign half of the class the arrow model and the other half the counters. When solutions have been reached, the groups can compare and justify their results. Many incorrect ideas will surface, but the learning that will come from the discussion and clarification will be far superior to an expository approach.

## Addition and Subtraction

Adding or subtracting integers with the models is straightforward and analogous to the corresponding debit-credit model or the football model. Since middle school or junior high students will not have used counters or number lines for some time, it would be good to begin work with either of these models using positive whole numbers. After a few examples to help students become familiar with the model for addition or subtraction with whole numbers, have them work through an example with integers using exactly the same reasoning. Remember, the emphasis should be on the rationale and not on how quickly students can get correct answers.

Several examples of addition are modeled in Figure 21.5 (p. 426), each in two ways: with positive and negative counters and with the number-line-and-arrow model. First examine the counter model. After the two quantities are joined, any pairs of positive and negative counters cancel each other out, and students can remove these, making it easier to see the result.

To add using the arrow model, note that each added arrow begins at the point end of the previous arrow. Help students

**Figure 21.5** Relate integer addition to whole-number addition.

with the analogy between these arrows and the football situation: Players always face their own goal. They may go forward or backward, but they never face the opponents' goal. Addition is the advance of a team from the previous position. In the $^+3 + {}^-5$ example, the positive arrow (+ team) starts at 0 and ends at positive 3. From that point, the negative arrow begins (the negative team takes over and *advances* in the negative direction). The result, then, is an arrow beginning at 0 and ending where the second arrow ended. The same change of direction (change of ball possession) takes place in the $^-6 + {}^+2$ example. If a negative were added to a negative, the arrows would each go toward the left or negative (no change of possession), just as there was no change of direction for the 3 + 5 example.

Subtraction is represented as "remove" in terms of the counter model and "back up" in terms of the arrow model. In

Figure 21.6, for $^-5 - {}^+2$, both models begin with a representation of $^-5$. To remove two positive counters from a set that has none, a different representation of $^-5$ must first be made. Since any number of neutral pairs (one positive, one negative) can be added without changing the value of the set, two pairs are added so that two positive counters can be removed. The net effect is to have more negative counters. This is like removing credits from your ledger if you are already in debt. The result is to leave you further in debt. A similar change in the representation of the beginning amount is always necessary when you need to subtract a quantity of a different sign.

With the number-line-and-arrow model, subtraction means to back up or to move in the opposite direction. Using the football field analogy, teams move backward when penalized or they lose yardage. In the example of $^-5 - {}^+2$, the first

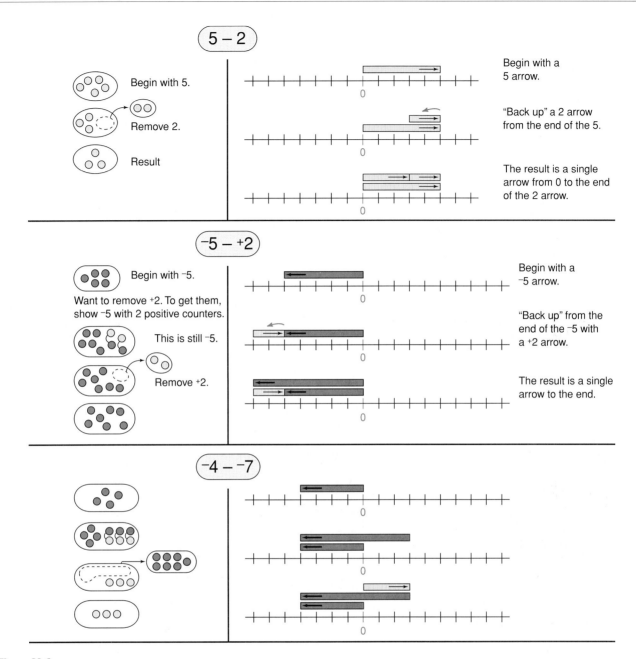

**Figure 21.6**  **Integer subtraction is also related to whole numbers.**

arrow ends at ⁻5. Since a positive quantity is subtracted, use a positive arrow. To subtract it, move it in its opposite direction (left). The forward movement ends at ⁻8. The result of the operation is an arrow from 0 to the back end of the ⁺2 arrow. In the football analogy, the ball is first at the ⁻5-yard line, changes hands to the positive team, which proceeds to lose 2 yards, leaving the ball at the ⁻7-yard line. In the second example, ⁻4 − ⁻7, the ball does not change hands, but the negative team loses yardage.

Have your students draw pictures to accompany integer computations. Set pictures are easy enough; they may consist of Xs and Os, for example. For the arrow model, there is no need for anything elaborate either. Figure 21.7 (p. 428) illustrates how a student might draw arrows for simple addition

and subtraction exercises without even sketching the number line. Directions are shown by the arrows, and magnitudes are written on the arrows. For your initial modeling, however, the poster board arrows in two colors will help students see that negative arrows always point left and that addition is a forward movement and subtraction is a backward movement for either type of arrow.

It is important for students to see that ⁺3 + ⁻5 is the same as ⁺3 − ⁺5 and that ⁺2 − ⁻6 is the same as ⁺2 + ⁺6. With the method of modeling addition and subtraction described here, these expressions are quite discernible and yet have the same result as they should have.

On graphing calculators, these expressions are entered using the "negative" key and the "subtraction" key. The

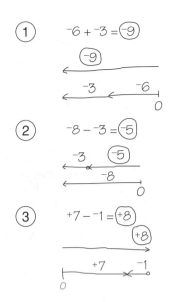

(1)   $^-6 + {}^-3 = \boxed{^-9}$

(2)   $^-8 - {}^-3 = \boxed{^-5}$

(3)   $^+7 - {}^-1 = \boxed{^+8}$

**Figure 21.7**   **Students do not need elaborate drawings to think through the number-line model.**

difference is also evident in the display. The redundant superscript plus signs are not shown. Students can see that $3 + {}^-5$ and $3 - 5$ each results in $^-2$ and that $3 - {}^-5$ and $3 + 5$ are also alike.

## Multiplication and Division

Multiplication of integers should be a direct extension of multiplication for whole numbers, just as addition and subtraction were connected to whole-number concepts. We frequently refer to whole-number multiplication as repeated addition. The first factor tells how many sets there are or how many are added in all, beginning with 0. This translates to integer multiplication quite readily when the first factor is positive, regardless of the sign of the second factor. The first example in Figure 21.8 illustrates a positive first factor and a negative second factor.

What could the meaning be when the first factor is negative, as in $^-2 \times {}^-3$? If a positive first factor means repeated addition (how many times added to 0), a negative first factor

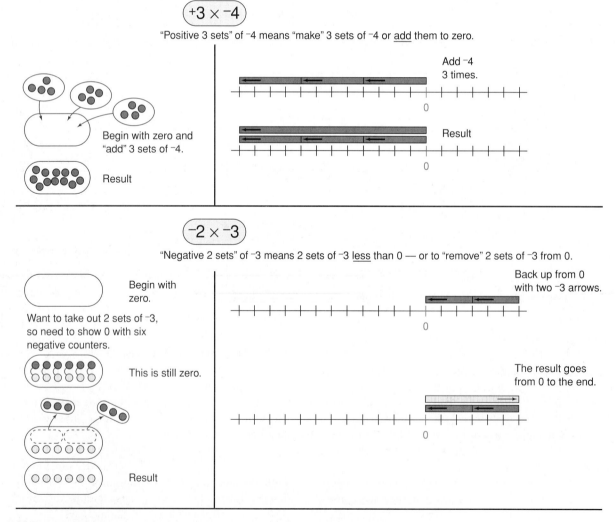

**Figure 21.8**   **Multiplication by a positive first factor is repeated addition. Multiplication by a negative first factor is repeated subtraction.**

should mean repeated subtraction (how many times subtracted from 0). The second example in Figure 21.8 illustrates how multiplication with the first factor negative can be modeled. Understanding integer multiplication depends on how well students understood integer addition and subtraction. There really are no new ideas, only an application of addition and subtraction to multiplication.

The deceptively simple rules of "like signs yield positive products" and "unlike signs yield negative products" are quickly established. However, once more, it is not as important that your students be able to produce answers correctly and skillfully as that they be able to supply a rationale.

With division of integers, again explore the whole-number case first. Recall that $8 \div 4$ with whole numbers has two possible meanings corresponding to two missing-factor expressions: $4 \times ? = 8$ asks, "Four sets of *what* make eight?" whereas $? \times 4 = 8$ asks, "How many fours make eight?" Generally, the measurement approach ($? \times 4$) is the one used with integers, although both concepts can be exhibited with either model. It is helpful to think of building the dividend with the divisor from 0 in the same way that we fill units into an amount when we measure it.

The first example in Figure 21.9 illustrates how the two models work for whole numbers. Following that is an example

**Figure 21.9**  **Division of integers following a measurement approach.**

where the divisor is positive but the dividend is negative. How many sets of $^+2$ will make $^-8$, or ? $\times$ $^+2$ = $^-8$? With the set model, if we try to add positive counters, the result will be positive, not negative. The only way to use sets of $^+2$ to make $^-8$ is to remove them from 0. This means that we must first change the representation of 0 as illustrated. For the arrow model, consider how $^+2$ arrows can be placed end to end to result in a distance 8 to the left of 0. Starting at 0, the arrows must be backed up. In both models, the arrows are being repeatedly subtracted, or added a negative number of times. Try now to model $^+9 \div {}^-3$ using both models. The approach is very similar to this example. Then try a negative divided by a negative. That case is much easier to understand. However, the entire understanding of integer division rests on a good concept of a negative first factor for multiplication and a knowledge of the relationship between multiplication and division.

There is no need to rush your students on to some mastery of use of the models. It is much better that they first think about how to model the whole-number situation and then figure out, with some guidance from you, how to deal with integers.

# RATIONAL NUMBERS

Several number ideas that students have been exposed to in earlier grades, coupled with the ideas of the integers, need to come together in the middle grades. A complete understanding of the rational numbers as positive and negative decimals and equivalently as positive and negative fractions is an important development.

## Fractions as Indicated Division

If four people were to share 12 candies, the number that each would get can be expressed by 12 ÷ 4. If four people were to share three pizzas, the amount that each would get can be expressed similarly by 3 ÷ 4; that is, three things divided four ways. In the pizza example, each person would receive three-fourths of a pizza. So $\frac{3}{4}$ and 3 ÷ 4 are both expressions for the same idea: 3 things divided by 4. Similarly, in the candy example, $\frac{12}{4}$ expresses the number each will receive just as well as 12 ÷ 4. Put simply, a fraction $\frac{a}{b}$ is another way of writing $a \div b$.

Students find this meaning of fractions unusual. First, the indicated division is different from the meaning that has been carefully developed. Second, fractions are commonly thought of as amounts of parts of wholes, not as operations. Similarly, expressions such as 7 ÷ 3 are thought of as operations (things to be done), not numbers. In fact, however, 4, 2 + 2, 12 ÷ 3, and $\frac{8}{2}$ are all symbolic expressions for the same number: 12 ÷ 3 is not the question and 4 the answer; both are expressions for 4. Likewise, 2 ÷ 3 and $\frac{2}{3}$ are both expressions for the quantity two-thirds. Do you find this a little hard to swallow? So do children. For the first time in seven

or eight years of schooling, you are telling students that a symbol can represent two different things. This is a relatively sophisticated idea.

Here are some possible ways to help students develop the idea that a fraction is another way of expressing division.

**ACTIVITY**

### 21.4 How Do You Write It?

**Present students with a simple word problem similar to the following:** *Zach has 18 meters of rope. He cuts off one-fifth of the rope to make a leash for his dog, Sam. How much rope did he use for the leash?* **Three students have solved this problem.**

Student A: Zach cut off 3.6 meters because 18 ÷ 5 = 3.6.

Student B: I did $\frac{1}{5} \times 18$ like this: $\frac{1}{5} \times \frac{18}{1} = \frac{18}{5} = 3\frac{3}{5}$. So the answer is 3 and $\frac{3}{5}$ meters.

Student C: I did the same thing, but I just said the answer was $\frac{18}{5}$ meters.

**Which student is correct? Which has the "best" answer?**

In the discussion of a problem situation like the one in Activity 21.4, you can lead students to see that 18 ÷ 5 and $\frac{18}{5}$ mean exactly the same thing.

Similarly, discuss the difference between these three expressions:

$$\frac{1}{4} \text{ of } 24 \qquad \frac{24}{4} \qquad 24 \div 4$$

In the spirit of looking for patterns, here is a further idea.

**ACTIVITY**

### 21.5 Division Patterns

**Have students do a series of divisions as follows: Begin with 18 and divide by 4. Record the result with a fraction remainder and as an improper fraction. Repeat with 17, then 16, and so on. What can you find out about this?**

In "Division Patterns," students are thinking about division but are recording fractions. In the improper form, each fraction is written as equal to the corresponding division. This becomes more obvious when the dividend (resulting numerator) is less than 4 (3 ÷ 4 = $\frac{3}{4}$, 2 ÷ 4 = $\frac{2}{4}$, 1 ÷ 4 = $\frac{1}{4}$). Some children will explore 0 ÷ 4 = $\frac{0}{4}$ = 0 and continue to negative numbers: $^-1 \div 4 = \frac{-1}{4}$. This gives rise to even further possibilities: What happens if you divide numbers by negative integers instead of positive numbers? Is $\frac{-1}{4}$ the same as $\frac{1}{-4}$? What about the fraction $\frac{-2}{-3}$?

Any or all of these discussions can lead to a general development of the idea that a fraction can be thought of as division of the numerator by the denominator or that $\frac{a}{b}$ is the same as $a \div b$.

# Fractions as Rational Numbers

In the early grades, children develop the idea that fractions are "things" such as parts of circular regions or shaded sections of rectangles. Even when fractions are seen as parts of sets, they remain, in the minds of children, more physical object than number. This is one reason that children have such a difficult time placing fractions on a number line. A significant leap toward thinking about fractions as numbers is made when students begin to understand that a decimal is a representation of a fraction. In Chapter 14, we explored the idea of the "friendly" fractions (halves, thirds, fourths, fifths, eighths) in terms of their decimal equivalents.

In the middle grades, it is time to combine all of these ideas:

- $4\frac{3}{5}$ is 4.6 because $\frac{3}{5}$ is six-tenths of a whole, so 4 wholes and six-tenths is 4.6.

- $4\frac{3}{5}$ is $\frac{23}{5}$, and that is the same as $23 \div 5$, or 4.6 if I use decimals.

- 4.6 is read "four and six-tenths," so I can write that as $4\frac{6}{10} = 4\frac{3}{5}$.

What becomes clear in a discussion building on students' existing ideas is that any number, positive or negative, that can be written as a fraction can also be written as a decimal number. You can also reverse this idea and convert decimal numbers to fractions. Keep in mind that the purpose is to see that there are different symbolic notations for the same quantities—not to become skilled at conversions.

The result of this discussion is a reasonable definition of rational numbers: A *rational number* is any number that can be expressed as a fraction. Equivalently, a *rational number* is any number that can be written as either a terminating or repeating decimal number.

---
## ΛCTIVITY
### 21.6 How Close Is Close?

**Have students select any two fractions or any two decimals that they think are "really close." It makes no difference what numbers students pick or even how close together they really are. Now challenge them to find at least ten more numbers (fractions or decimals) that are between these two numbers. Do not be tempted to show students any clever methods for finding the numbers.**
---

"How Close Is Close?" is an opportunity to find out how your students understand fractions and decimals. (The activity should be done in both forms eventually.) If students haven't been told a method, they must rely on their own ideas to come up with a solution. The activity offers a great opportunity for discussion, assessment of individual students' fraction and decimal concepts, and the introduction of perhaps the most interesting feature of the rational number system:

density. The rational numbers are said to be *dense* because between any two rational numbers there exists an *infinite* number of other rational numbers. In other words, if you tried to plot all of the rationals between 0 and 1, you would have no gaps at all.

A true understanding of the density of the rationals makes the irrationals even more amazing.

# REAL NUMBERS

As just noted, there are *irrational* numbers, numbers that are not rational. The irrationals together with the rational numbers make up the *real* numbers. The real numbers fill in all the holes on the number line even though the holes are infinitesimally small. Students' first experience with irrational numbers typically occurs when exploring roots of whole numbers.

## Introducing the Concept of Roots

The following activity provides a good introduction to square roots and cube roots. From this beginning, the notion of roots of any degree is easily developed.

---
## ΛCTIVITY
### 21.7 Edges of Squares and Cubes

**Show students pictures of three squares (or three cubes) as in Figure 21.10. The edges of the first and last figure are consecutive whole numbers. The areas (volumes) of all three figures are provided. The students' task is to use a calculator to find the edge of the figure in the center. Use of the square root key is not permitted. Solutions will satisfy these equations:**

$$\square \times \square = 45, \text{ or } \square^2 = 45$$

**and**

$$\square \times \square \times \square = 30, \text{ or } \square^3 = 30$$

**Figure 21.10** A geometric interpretation of square roots and cube roots.
---

In "Edges of Squares and Cubes," the calculator permits students to test a possible edge length to see if it is too long or too short. For example, to solve the cube problem, students might start with 3.5 and find that $3.5^3$ is 42.875, much too large. Quickly, they will find that the solution is between 3.1 and 3.2. But where? Again, halfway is a good try: $3.15^3$ is a bit more than 31.255. The next try should be lower. By continued trial and error, a simple calculator can get the result correct to six decimal places and a graphing calculator to as many as nine places.

From this simple introduction, students can be challenged to find solutions to equations such as $\square^6 = 8$. These students are now prepared to understand the general definition of the *nth root* of a number $N$ as the number that when raised to the $n$th power equals $N$. The *square* and *cube roots* are simply other names for the second and third roots. The notational convention of the radical sign comes last. It should then be clear that $\sqrt{6}$ is a number and not an exercise to be done. The cube root of eight is the same as $\sqrt[3]{8}$, which is just another way of writing 2.

## Discussing Real Numbers

Eighth-grade students probably do not need a very sophisticated knowledge of the real number system. A few powerful ideas, however, deserve to be explored informally.

### Irrational Numbers

One characterization of a rational number is that it can be written as a decimal where the decimal part is either finite or repeats infinitely. Thus both 3.45 and 87.19363636 . . . are rational numbers and can each be converted to fractional form. But what about a decimal number that just goes on and on, with no repetition? Or what about the number 3.101001000100001000001 . . . ? These never repeat and are not finite and therefore are not rational. A real number that is not rational is called *irrational*.

The numbers $\pi$ and $\sqrt{2}$ are both irrational numbers. The number $\pi$ is a ratio of two measures in a circle, the circumference and the diameter. Although it is not possible to prove the irrationality of $\pi$ at this level, the fact that it is irrational implies that it is impossible to have a circle with the lengths of both the circumference and the diameter rational. (Why?) A proof that $\sqrt{2}$ is irrational is generally explored at the junior high level. The usual argument assumes that $\sqrt{2}$ *is* rational, which then leads to a contradiction.

### Density of the Real Numbers

If the density of the rationals is impressive, even more astounding is that the irrationals are also dense. And the irrationals and the rationals are all mixed up together. The density of the irrationals is not as easy to demonstrate and is not within the scope of the middle school.

### Rational Roots

One reason it is difficult to comprehend irrational numbers is that we have very little firsthand experience with them. The

ones we are most familiar with are roots of numbers. For example, we just noted that students are frequently shown a proof for the irrationality of $\sqrt{2}$. An intuitive notion of that fact is difficult to come by. Most calculators will show only eight to ten digits, requiring a leap of faith to accept that the decimal representation is infinitely long and nonrepeating.

Unfortunately, what can happen is that whenever students see the radical sign, they think the number is irrational. A possible approach is to consider roots from the opposite direction. Rather than ask what is the square root of 64 or the cube root of 27, we might suggest that *every* number is the square root, the cube root, the fourth root, and so on, of some number (3 is the second root of 9, the third root of 27, etc.). From this vantage point, students can see that "square root" is just a way of indicating a relationship between two numbers. That the cube root of 27 is 3 indicates a special relationship between 3 and 27.

 **LITERATURE CONNECTIONS**

Some topics in this chapter present opportunities for "playing around" with ideas and numbers. Although most teachers in the middle grades do not think of using literature as a springboard for mathematics, here are a few ideas that offer a change of pace in the upper grades.

## The Phantom Tollbooth
### (Juster, 1961)

Milo's remarkable journey through the lands beyond the magic tollbooth are so full of wonderful words and ideas that the story is a must to read and discuss with adolescents regardless of the potential mathematical content. But the first page of Chapter 14, with its road sign indicating three directions to Digitopolis, is worthy of time in your mathematics class. The sign reads:

| DIGITOPOLIS | |
|---:|:---|
| 5 | Miles |
| 1,600 | Rods |
| 8,800 | Yards |
| 26,400 | Feet |
| 316,800 | Inches |
| 633,600 | Half inches |
| AND THEN SOME | |

The discussion about which road is shorter or quicker is just great. Three pages later, Milo is told, "Why, did you know that if a beaver two feet long with a tail a foot and a half long can build a dam twelve feet high and six feet wide in two days, all you would need to build Boulder Dam is a beaver sixty-eight feet long with a fifty-one foot tail?" (p. 175). In the next chapter is an equally humorous discussion of infinity. That is followed by the chapter in which Milo meets the 0.58 boy.

Not only are these fanciful ideas in a story filled with excellent language, but there are also opportunities to wonder what if or to create similar fantasies based on numbers. For example, students could write a new chapter for the book in which Milo journeys to a world in outer space where the distances are enormous and everyone uses scientific notation.

## In One Day
### (Parker, 1984)

This is not literature but an amazing book of 365 facts concerning things that occur in one day in the United States. For example, in one day, Americans "fill in, or at least try to, 50 acres of crossword puzzles" and "buy at least 5 million things that are shaped like Mickey Mouse, or have a picture of Mickey Mouse on them." (That has probably increased since the book was published in 1984.)

It is difficult not to wonder at the amazing numbers in the book. Students may want to test the facts in some way or perhaps do a bit of research to add new facts that interest them. For example, how many footballs are thrown on an average fall day? If there is any interest in finding real-world numbers through some simple research, sharing this book with the class is probably worth the time.

## Math Curse
### (Scieszka & Smith, 1995)

This book was an instant hit probably because there are so many people out there who have math phobias. The first page sets the tone: "On Monday in math class Mrs. Fibonacci says, 'You know, you can think of almost everything as a math prob-

lem.' On Tuesday I start to have problems." Some may argue that this book is so antimathematics that it has no place in the middle grades. But it does provide an opportunity to show your human side as you discuss a wide range of mathematical ideas.

 ## ASSESSMENT NOTES

Middle school teachers frequently get bogged down in the minutiae of their curriculum. Many books emphasize rules and exercises at the expense of opportunities for explorations. The content of this chapter focuses on your students' mathematical power rather than their acquisition of skills.

For example, the discussion of exponents provides good opportunities to see how students reason, communicate ideas, go beyond the answer to generate their own ideas, and generally do mathematics. Once students have learned the relatively simple definition of what an exponent is, the search for easy tricks for multiplying and dividing should be left to students' discovery and their own reasoning. The discussions that ensue will be better than drilling rules about adding exponents when you multiply numbers with like bases. These are good opportunities to assess mathematical power.

With respect to integers, you have already been warned not to focus on the rules for operations. Certainly, the rules are important. However, if the rules for operating on the integers are developed by the students themselves, not only will students have a deeper understanding, but you will have an opportunity to observe and assess their mathematical power.

Similar comments can be made about fractions and decimal relationships and rational numbers. The development of reasoning ability and students' belief that they can do mathematics is far more important than drilling rules.

# REFLECTIONS ON CHAPTER 21

## Writing to Learn

1. Explain the value of the graphing calculator's ability to display a complete arithmetic expression (with or without a variable) on a single line and to evaluate it on another line.

2. How can a calculator be used to explore the order-of-operations convention? Why is this rule something you must simply tell students?

3. Explain how powers of 10 are used to write very small and very large numbers. What is the particular form of the power-of-10 symbolism used in scientific notation and on calculators? What is the value of this notation?

4. Why is it probably better to use two different models for the integers even if one of the two seems to cause students some confusion?

5. Use both the arrow model and the counter model to demonstrate the following:

$$^-10 + {}^+13 = {}^+3 \qquad ^-4 - {}^-9 = {}^+5 \qquad {}^+6 - {}^-7 = {}^+13$$
$$^-4 \times {}^-3 = {}^+12 \qquad {}^+15 \div {}^-5 = {}^-3 \qquad ^-12 \div {}^-3 = {}^+4$$

6. How can you help students understand that a fraction such as $\frac{7}{8}$ means the same thing as $7 \div 8$?

7. How would you explain the difference between a rational and an irrational number to a middle school student?

8. What does $\sqrt{6}$ mean? How is $\sqrt{6}$ different from $\sqrt{4}$? How are they the same?

9. What does it mean to say that the rational numbers are dense?

## For Discussion and Exploration

1. In *Principles and Standards for School Mathematics*, the authors of the 6–8 grade band apparently see the content of this chapter integrated with algebraic reasoning and functions, the content of the two preceding chapters. A traditional self-contained Algebra I course also groups this content with an additional focus on factoring polynomials and other symbolic manipulations. Does your local school system have an Algebra I course in grade 8? Do you think it should? What are some of the pros and cons of a special course?

2. Examine the table of contents in sixth-, seventh-, and eighth-grade books from two or three different publishers or books

specifically intended for middle school mathematics. Using these books as a guide, how would you define "prealgebra"? How much of the curriculum of these three grade levels seems repetitious? Is this the same for all publishers?

3. Use a calculator for the following exercises:

   a. Estimate the cube root of 10 to five decimal places.

   b. What do you think will happen if you enter 1000 in your calculator and then press ⊞ 2 ⊟ ⊟ . . . ? Try it.

   c. What do you think will happen if you enter 1000 in your calculator and then repeatedly press the √ key? Before you try it, try to explain why you think it will happen.

# Recommendations for Further Reading

## Highly Recommended

Fitzgerald, W. M., Winter, M. J., Lappan, G., & Phillips, E. (1986). *Middle grades mathematics project: Factors and multiples.* Menlo Park, CA: AWL Supplemental.

This book is one in a series of five that has stood the test of time. The related topics of prime, factor, composite, prime factorization, divisor, multiple, common multiple, common factor, and relatively prime number are all developed in a succession of interesting games and activities for the middle grades. The focus is on pattern development and logical connections. This is an excellent way to involve students in good mathematics without overwhelming them with tedious algebraic ideas.

Graeber, A. O., & Baker, K. M. (1992). Little into big is the way it always is. *Arithmetic Teacher, 39*(8), 18–21.

This is one of the few articles to discuss fractions as indicated division. The authors look at practices in the elementary school that suggest why the difficulty exists and make practical suggestions for working with middle school students.

Phillips, E., Gardella, T., Kelly, C., & Stewart, J. (1991). *Patterns and functions: Addenda series, grades 5–8.* Reston, VA: National Council of Teachers of Mathematics.

Again, the *Addenda Series* is the place to go for excellent activities. In this volume, you will find sections on exponents and growth patterns, number theory and counting patterns, and rational number patterns. Other topics in the book are related more to the concepts of function and variable.

## Other Suggestions

Battista, M. T. (1983). A complete model for operations on integers. *Arithmetic Teacher, 30*(9), 26–31.

Bennett, A., Jr., Maier, E., & Nelson, L. T. (1989). *Modeling integers* (Unit 6 in *Math in the mind's eye*). Salem, OR: Math Learning Center.

Borlaug, V. (1997). Building equations using M&M's. *Mathematics Teaching in the Middle School, 2,* 290–292.

Chalouh, L., & Herscovics, N. (1988). Teaching algebraic expression in a meaningful way. In A. F. Coxford (Ed.), *The ideas of algebra, K–12* (pp. 33–42). Reston, VA: National Council of Teachers of Mathematics.

Eisen, A. P. (1999). Exploring factor sets with a graphing calculator. *Mathematics Teaching in the Middle School, 5,* 78–82.

Herscovics, N., & Kieran, C. (1980). Constructing meaning for the concept of equation. *Mathematics Teacher, 73,* 572–580.

Kieran, C., & Chalouh, L. (1993). Prealgebra: The transition from arithmetic to algebra. In D. T. Owens (Ed.), *Research ideas for the classroom: Middle grades mathematics* (pp. 179–198). Old Tappan, NJ: Macmillan.

Martinez, J. G. R. (1988). Helping students understand factors and terms. *Mathematics Teacher, 81,* 747–751.

Patterson, A. C. (1997). Building algebraic expressions: A physical model. *Mathematics Teaching in the Middle School, 2,* 238–242.

Paulos, J. A. (1988). *Innumeracy: Mathematical illiteracy and its consequences.* New York: Hill & Wang.

Rubenstein, R. N. (1996). The function game. *Mathematics Teaching in the Middle School, 2,* 74–78.

Shilgalis, T. W. (1994). Are most fractions reduced? *Mathematics Teacher, 87,* 236–238.

Sobel, M. A., & Maletsky, E. M. (1995). *Teaching mathematics: A sourcebook of aids, activities, and strategies* (3rd ed.). Upper Saddle River, NJ: Prentice Hall.

Stacey, K., & MacGregor, M. (1997). Building foundations for algebra. *Mathematics Teaching in the Middle School, 2,* 253–260.

Steinberg, R. M., Sleeman, D. H., & Ktorza, D. (1990). Algebra students' knowledge of equivalence of equations. *Journal for Research in Mathematics Education, 22,* 112–121.

# Issues and Perspectives

The three chapters in this section provide practical suggestions for teaching and, even more important, will help you develop a perspective on some major issues that pervade mathematics education.

Chapter 22 can be thought of as a companion to Chapter 4, where the basic structure for a problem-solving lesson was developed. Here you will find variations on implementing that structure, details of working with cooperative groups, tips for incorporating writing in mathematics, suggestions for homework, and perspectives on using your textbook.

Chapter 23 offers suggestions and perspective on reaching all children. Separate discussions deal with children with special learning problems, multicultural and gender issues, and the mathematically talented.

Although activities and suggestions for using calculators and computers are found throughout the book, Chapter 24 looks at these two forms of technology in a general way. It examines the often contentious issue of calculators and offers perspective on different ways to use and select software for your mathematics classroom.

# Chapter 22

# Planning for Effective Instruction

*Natural learning . . . doesn't happen on a time schedule and often requires more time than schools are organized to provide. Problem-solving experiences take time. It's essential that teachers provide the time that's needed for children to work through activities on their own and that teachers not slip into teaching-by-telling for the sake of efficiency.*

*Burns (1992, p. 30)*

The three-part lesson format described in Chapter 4 provides a basic structure for effective lessons. Even when a lesson does not seem to fit this design exactly, the basic idea of presenting a task *(before),* letting students work on the task *(during),* and discussing results and methods *(after)* provides useful guidance in thinking about how lessons should be conducted.

This chapter describes some adaptations of the basic three-part format as well as some other instructional strategies: cooperative groups, writing in mathematics, homework, and the use of textbooks.

## ADAPTING THE THREE-PART LESSON

The three-part lesson structure is built on the principle that mathematics can and should be taught through problem solving—that is, the mathematics that students are working on should be problematic. It should require them to be mentally active, to reason, to solve problems, to make sense of things, to conjecture, and to evaluate. Lessons that promote this mental engagement with concepts and ideas may not always appear to fit the before-during-after structure described in Chapter 4.

## Discourse

The value of classroom discussion of ideas cannot be overemphasized. As students describe and evaluate solutions to tasks, share approaches, and make conjectures as members of a community of learners, learning will occur in ways that are impossible otherwise. Students begin to take ownership of ideas and develop a sense of power in making sense of mathematics.

Students should understand when given a task that one of their responsibilities is to prepare for discussion that will occur after they have had an opportunity to work on the problem. One fourth-grade teacher discovered that she was too involved in her class discussions. The students tended to wait for her questions rather than tell about their solutions. To help her students be more personally responsible, she devised three posters, inscribed as follows:

*How did you solve the problem?*

*Why did you solve it this way?*

*Why do you think your solution is correct and makes sense?*

In the beginning, students referred to the posters as they made presentations to the class, but soon that was not required. They continued to refer to the posters as they wrote up the solutions to problems in the during portion of lessons. Students began to prompt presenters: "You didn't answer the second question on the poster." One of the best results of these posters was that they helped remove the teacher from the content of the discussions. She was no longer in a position of asking questions that made it seem to students that she had a single "best" answer in mind.

Regardless of the exact structure or time frame for a lesson, an opportunity for discourse should always be built in. After students have played a game, worked in a learning center, completed a challenging worksheet, or engaged in a mental math activity with a full class, they can still discuss their activity: *What strategies worked well in the game? What did you find out in the learning center? What are different ways to do this exercise?*

## Written Work

The three-part format does not preclude students' completing a worksheet or writing explanations in the during portion of a lesson. In fact, a well-planned worksheet can be helpful in focusing attention. Tables, charts, graphs, drawings, and computations can all be part of the work students do, either in groups or independently. Written work in a fill-in-the-blanks format can place undue attention on getting answers. In contrast, a worksheet with questions and plenty of space to show work, answers, and rationale will promote student activity.

Some teachers give each group a transparency with which to share solutions. Not only does the writing help students prepare their thoughts, but it also adds to the importance of written work and saves time in getting ideas before the class during discussions. Younger children may prepare reports on large sheets of newsprint.

## Minilessons

Many tasks do not require the full period. The three-part format can be compressed to as little as 10 minutes. You might plan two or three cycles in a single lesson. For example, consider these tasks:

Grades K–1:  Make up two questions that we can answer using the information in our graph.

Grade 2:  Suppose you did not know the answer to problem 14. How could you start to figure it out?

Grades 4–5:  On your geoboard, make a figure that has line symmetry but not rotational symmetry. Make a second figure that has rotational symmetry but not line symmetry.

Grades 6–7:  Margie has this drawing of the first floor of her house. (Pass out drawing.) She wants to reduce it on the photocopy machine so that it will have a scale of 1 cm to the foot. By what percentage should she reduce it?

These are worthwhile tasks but probably would not require a full period to do and discuss.

A profitable strategy for short tasks is *think-pair-share*. Students are first directed to spend a minute developing their own thoughts and ideas on how to approach the task or even what they think may be a good solution. Then they pair with a classmate and discuss each other's ideas. This provides an opportunity to test out ideas and to practice articulating them. The last step is to share the idea with the rest of the class. The pair may actually have two ideas or can be told to

come to a single decision. The entire process, including some discussion, may take less than 15 minutes.

## Worksheets with Manipulatives

Good activities can be built around a worksheet that requires the use of physical models. Such worksheets guide the specifics of a manipulative activity. Students can draw simple pictures to show what they have done or record numeric results of a manipulative activity.

Figure 22.1 is a worksheet for number combinations that might be used in first grade. Counters are placed in the area at the top of the page and separated into two parts, and dots are drawn in the small versions at the bottom. Many textbooks incorporate physical models into first- and second-grade lessons in this way.

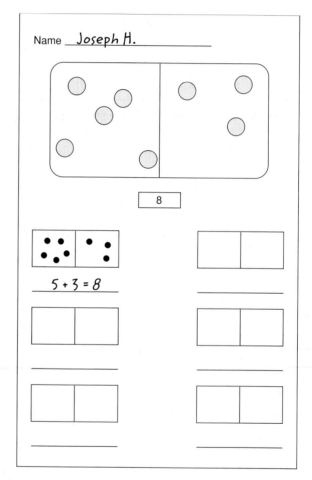

**Figure 22.1**  **A worksheet with counters.**

The worksheet in Figure 22.2 is designed to follow a full-class discussion of trading with base-ten models. Students draw small dots, sticks, and squares to represent the base-ten materials that they worked with to do the exercise.

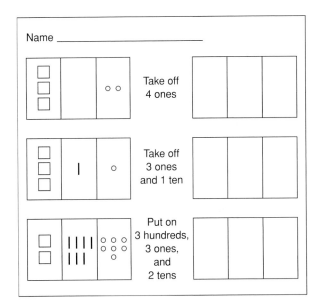

**Figure 22.2** **A worksheet with base-ten materials.**

The seventh-grade example in Figure 22.3 involves percentages approximated by familiar fractions. The students could use pie pieces and the hundredths disk (see Figure 14.1, p. 244) to determine the approximate equivalences without doing any computation.

**Figure 22.3** **A worksheet for decimal-to-fraction estimation.**

Worksheets such as these are appropriate when they are still problematic activities, not routine exercises. They should be followed by discussion, as with any task.

## Workstations

A workstation approach is another alternative for tasks. It can be adapted to any level. For a given topic, you might prepare as many as eight or ten related activities to be placed in workstations. Materials that go with a particular activity are placed in separate tubs or boxes. These materials might include special manipulatives or worksheets to help guide the activity and, if required, such things as scissors, paper, or paste. Some activities may be games to be played by two or three children. Activities may be duplicated at more than one station, perhaps with slightly different levels of difficulty.

For children at the K–2 level, the activities must be taught and practiced in groups or with the full class before being placed in a tub. Older children can be quickly told about an activity, or written directions can guide the activity at the station.

The workstation approach is useful even in middle school. The idea is simply to get all students involved independently or in small groups. For example, during a unit on percentage in the seventh grade, a number of different models and conceptual activities may be introduced during the first week. In the second week, the during portion of each period can involve activities using these models.

If you use workstations regularly, design an organizational scheme that makes the use of stations quick and easy. Use the same containers for activities throughout the year. In K–3 classrooms, label the containers, and assign each to an area of the room: a space on a carpet, a table, or a collection of desks shoved together. A sign or label at each area indicates which tub belongs there. Helpers can set out the tubs at the appropriate places in the room and return them at the end of the period. This procedure can be used all year, with the activities in the tubs changing as they are taught to the class.

Some form of recording or writing should be included when possible. This may involve drawing pictures, pasting down paper counters, or recording symbolically what was done manipulatively. The recording represents accountability and suggests responsibility. The records provide a lasting opportunity for assessment. They can be displayed on bulletin boards, sent home for parents, or placed in students' portfolios.

## PLANNING FOR DIVERSITY

Classrooms are increasingly heterogeneous. While the benefits of broadly inclusive classrooms far outweigh the problems they cause, there are problems. Not all students are ready to tackle the same problem at the same level of sophistication at the same time. Brighter students are more verbal and can dominate class discussions. There are a number of possibilities for dealing with a wide range of student levels.

# Involve Students in Collaborative Activities

Avoid ability grouping! Plan pairs and groups so that students with different abilities work together. Too often teachers feel that lower-skilled students are not able to do the regular work of the classroom. Students who have not mastered computational skills can nevertheless participate in projects that involve reasoning or creative ideas. In fact, the perspective of lower-skilled students can often be a positive factor in a mixed group of students. Help skill-deficient students become proficient with calculators. Expect students to have calculators available at all times.

A mixed-grouping approach is also useful for accommodating students who are performing above grade level. Although certain students at the extreme upper end of the spectrum should be assigned projects and activities for the gifted (see Chapter 23), it is generally inadvisable to separate the more capable children from the rest of the class. Highly skilled students are not necessarily the most creative or even those with the best conceptual backgrounds. Interaction with a mixed group is good for all.

# Plan Differentiated Tasks

Many tasks can be modified up or down in ability level by making small adjustments in the numbers or the requirements involved. A general task can be discussed at the beginning of a lesson. This can be followed by passing out paper with the task written out. Numbers or other variations can be prepared ahead of time for two or three different levels.

For example, in one second-grade class, the teacher regularly has students work on word problems that she prepares ahead of time. Two or three problems are on the page, with space for students to show their reasoning and their work. A problem may look like this:

Eduardo had _____ marbles. He gave Erica _____ marbles. How many marbles does Eduardo now have?

Before class, numbers are written in the blanks so that the same problem serves three different levels. For this example, Eduardo may have 121 marbles, 60 marbles, or 12 marbles and correspondingly give Erica 46, 15, or 5. Thus the same word problem involves $121 - 46$, $60 - 15$, and $12 - 5$, all at the same time.

A similar approach is to put three sets of numbers or three variations of the same task on the board or on the paper itself. Rather than assign students a particular task variation, students select the numbers or variation with which they are comfortable. This student-choice approach puts some control in the hands of the students. It tells students at the lower levels that it is OK to work on easier problems but that they are free to challenge or stretch themselves. It is a form of student self-assessment in the sense that students are telling you what they feel comfortable with. You can compare a student's choice with your sense of his or her abilities. And finally, the

idea that there are several alternatives provides a ready task for those who finish quickly.

# Use Workstations

Another way to modify the level of a task is to create variants of the task at different stations around the room. For example, if a fourth-grade task involved equivalent fractions, a variety of related tasks could be selected and presented at the same time and then placed in different stations. Several stations could be created with different materials (pie pieces, paper for folding, counters, Cuisenaire rods) to find common names for $\frac{2}{3}$. Of these, the pie piece approach is probably least challenging and counters the most challenging and open-ended. Another station might involve slicing squares to develop a procedure for finding equivalent fractions. Yet another station could have students trying to find different ways to compare two fractions, an activity that frequently has equivalent fractions embedded in it. (These activities are all discussed in Chapter 12.)

Students can be assigned to a station that best suits their needs. Students with different abilities can work together at a station that is challenging to the slower learners but not demeaning to the more able. Each can write a separate report.

# Avoid Skill-Oriented Tasks

Tasks that simply practice textbook skills need never be assigned uniformly to the entire class. Though skills are important, they should be practiced at a level appropriate for the individual student. For students who are beyond the need for practice in a particular skill, an assigned practice is boring busywork. For students not ready for the practice level of a skill, the assigned practice reinforces their sense of inadequacy. If a task involves a lot of computation, be certain that all students have calculators. Avoid tasks in which computational proficiency is the objective.

# COOPERATIVE LEARNING GROUPS

As noted, having students work in groups is an extremely effective technique for getting students actively involved in doing mathematics. Group work can be a regular feature of both student-centered and teacher-directed models of instruction. Here you will find some suggestions for establishing and using effective groups.

## Size and Composition

There is no magic number for the size of a group. Johnson, Johnson, and Holubec (1993) point out that the more members in a group, the more possible interactions need to be accommodated. In a group of three, there are three possible student-student interactions. With four students, that number jumps to six. With five students, there are ten different pairs that must be able to interact, and the result is generally disappointing. It may be good to begin with groups of two. In pairs, students can attend more easily to this new idea of working with someone. Later, you will probably want to shift to groups of three or at most four.

For groups to be most effective, students must develop interpersonal skills of cooperation, sharing, listening, and responsibility. The group must view itself as a unit, not as individuals sitting at the same table. These skills are best developed by having groups remain intact for at least several weeks. If you use a fixed-group approach, spend considerable time composing groups. Work on more than balance in abilities. Try also to mix boys and girls, to spread out both the leaders and the followers, to blend troublemakers with those who are cooperative. Avoid putting your problem children all in one group.

# Developing Productive Group Behavior

Working cooperatively and productively in groups is not something that children do automatically or easily. You cannot simply form groups and expect to see the benefits of group work magically happen. Students must be explicitly taught how to work cooperatively with their fellow students.

## Specific Group Skills and Responsibilities

All students should understand what behaviors make a group function effectively. The following are among the most important group behaviors for students to understand.

1. *Share ideas and opinions.* Groups must learn to operate as a group, not as a collection of individuals. Therefore, it is imperative that the members all share their ideas and contribute their best thoughts to the task. Sharing is a two-way street. Each student is responsible for getting his or her ideas to the group and for listening to and accepting the ideas of other members. Sharing is not dominating.

2. *Ask and answer questions.* Each group member is responsible for his or her understanding of the ideas the group generates. If a student lacks some information or does not understand an idea being discussed, he or she has an obligation to ask other group members to explain the idea or task. All group members must be willing to help those who ask. Groups should come to realize that when they work together to share ideas and answer questions, they operate more effectively.

3. *Keep the group on task.* It is easy for students working without teacher direction to stray from the task at hand and begin to play, argue, or discuss things not related to the task. Group members need to learn to help each other attend to the job at hand. This can be done by

reminding the group that there is only so much time, restating the purpose of the activity, or suggesting a direction for the task.

4. *Encourage participation.* Despite rules 1 and 2, there will be students who are reluctant to speak up in a group and who will sit and watch. Students in the group must not permit any member to be passive. When they notice a group member not participating, they need to bring him or her into the process: "What do you think, Nancy?" "Mark, do you think this is a good idea? What do you think we should try?"

These four specific group skills were taken from a much longer list suggested by Johnson, Johnson, and Holubec (1993). However, these four will go a long way to getting your groups to work productively. If you decide to assign roles or have groups select roles for their members, the most important roles should reflect these group skills or rules. For example, an "encourager" can be sure that all participate. A "director" can be assigned to keep the group on task. A "monitor" can be sure that all understand and are sharing ideas.

## Teaching Group Skills

The first thing that must be done to establish effective groups is for students to understand and appreciate the values and benefits of working in a group:

- Everyone has two or three helpers.
- Everyone gets to talk and have his or her ideas heard.
- A collection of ideas is always better than just one idea.
- It is more fun to work with a partner than to work alone.

However, to reap these benefits, the group must learn how to work together.

Don't try to introduce all the group skills at once. Select one or two ideas at a time, and discuss them with the class. Make a poster for the skill being discussed, with space to record students' ideas about what the skill looks and sounds like. Simply telling students to "share ideas" or to "encourage others" is generally a waste of time. Arrange students in temporary groups and have them model one skill such as asking questions. Talk about how the skill sounded and discuss possible ways to ask for information politely. Practice how to use materials and talk about sharing.

## Maintaining Group Skills

Each time you set students to work in groups, there should be two types of objectives that all groups understand. The first objective is the academic task or problem that is the goal of your lesson. The second objective is one or more group skills or general group behavior. In the beginning, have students focus on one particular skill at a time. After assigning the group task for the day, you might say, "Today I want you to work especially hard at helping each other in the group." You might write "Helping each other" on the board or quickly discuss the poster you made that describes that group skill. At the end of the period, have each group assess its performance on the designated group skill. Each student can be asked to respond to a statement such as "Today I offered help in my group: (a) not at all, (b) sometimes, (c) a lot." Also ask the group to respond to a similar statement: "Today our group's members helped each other: (a) really well, (b) sometimes, (c) not as well as we could have." Have the students add one or two sentences that describe their behavior and what they will do to improve.

Continue to have groups work on their group skills throughout the year. Like other skills, these can be improved with practice and periodic evaluation. Group skills can also deteriorate if students forget to work on them.

## Group Recording and Reporting

Students should understand that when they report their group's work, they are sharing the ideas and the work of the group and not their own individual ideas. Groups should always be prepared to share ideas orally or in written form. Preparation for reporting can help groups work together more effectively.

Make it very clear that you may call on any member of the group to share or explain what the group did. In this way, students can be taught to be sure that every group member understands the ideas developed in the group. You may find it useful to stop students just before your class discussion and suggest that the groups make sure that each member understands what was done and is prepared to report if asked to do so.

If you use a record sheet or worksheet, it is a good idea to have only one sheet per group. All group members should put their names at the top of the paper to emphasize that it is group work and that what is written on the page represents the ideas of the group. The person responsible for the writing or recording must be designated at the start of the activity. If you give all students a worksheet, group cooperation tends to break down as students become absorbed in completing their own papers.

## Assessment of Group Work

The main reason for having students work in groups is to promote interaction and therefore learning. In that sense, cooperative groups are an instructional device. Many teachers are concerned that they don't know how to evaluate the work done in groups. With the proper perspective, groups actually make assessment easier and more effective.

As noted in Chapter 5, much assessment data can and should be gathered from observations. Group work makes gathering information much easier and can ensure that data are gathered from all students, not just the vocal minority. If observation schemes are structured around groups, you will be able to focus your attention on the two or three groups you select for that day. Over a few days, all groups and thus all students will have been observed.

Group work provides much more information in any given period than you could possibly gather without groups. When six or eight groups are working at the same time, you have six to eight times as much student activity and talk to observe and listen to than in a full-class environment. It is easy to stand near as many as four groups at once and listen in on all four conversations or watch how all four groups are working.

Having each group submit a single written report substantially reduces the amount of paper you must review for assessment. The smaller amount of written data makes it considerably easier to make instructional decisions and provide feedback than having to face a stack of papers submitted by all students individually.

# WRITING IN THE MATHEMATICS CLASSROOM

Writing in the mathematics classroom is an important instructional technique. It is entirely possible that you were never asked to write during your own mathematics learning and wonder why you should have children write and how to go about it. Here are some ideas to get you started.

## The Value of Writing in Mathematics

When you write, you express your own ideas and use your own words and language. It is personal. In contrast, oral communication in the classroom is very public. Ideas "pop out" without editing or revision. Meaning is negotiated or elaborated on by the class as a whole. The individual reflective quality of writing as compared to classroom discourse is an important factor in considering the value of writing in mathematics.

### Writing as a Learning Tool

> The process of writing requires gathering, organizing, and clarifying thoughts. It demands finding out what you know and don't know. It calls for thinking clearly. Similarly, doing mathematics depends on gathering, organizing, and clarifying thoughts, finding out what you know and don't know, and thinking clearly. Although the final representation of a mathematical pursuit looks very different from the final product of a writing effort, the mental journey is, at its base, the same—making sense of an idea and presenting it effectively. (Burns, 1995b, p. 3)

When students write, they are able to stop first and think. They can incorporate drawings and symbolism to help convey their ideas. They can research an idea or look back on related work to help put ideas together. All of this is very powerful and deliberate reflective thinking. No doubt you have heard or even said, "I never really understood such-and-such until I taught it." Writing is much like teaching in the sense of collecting ideas and having to explain them using only the tools you presently have. In that sense, writing is very much like constructing ideas. Writing is a way to learn.

Because writing is so powerful as a learning device, opportunities for writing should be built into your lesson plans whenever possible. Writing about a solution to a task, how it was done, and why it is correct should be one of the task responsibilities that you explain to students in the before portion of the lesson. Be sure to provide time for the writing to occur. It is useful to provide a signal to the students indicating that they should begin their written report if they haven't already. Writing prior to discussion is excellent rehearsal for students as they prepare to share their ideas. If particular students or groups do not get the opportunity to present their ideas, the written report remains for your evaluation and feedback. This ensures that all voices are heard, even if not during the class period.

Writing time can also come after the class discussion. Here the writing might be about summarizing what was learned during the lesson or unit, or it may give students an opportunity to tell you about ideas they do not yet completely understand.

## Writing as an Assessment Tool

Writing provides a unique window to students' thoughts and the way a student is thinking about an idea. Even a kindergarten child can express ideas in drawings or other markings on paper and begin to explain what he or she is thinking.

Oral communication, valuable as it may be, is gone at the end of the day. No notes you might take can account for all that is said in your class. When you are able to sit down with students' writing, you can reflect on each person individually as well as on the class as a whole. You can use writing to target feedback and design special work for individual students. Written work helps you assess the progress you are making with the current unit. Finally, student writing is an excellent form of communication with parents during conferences. Writing shows students' thinking to their parents, telling them much more than any grade or test score.

For writing to be effective, students need to feel free to tell you what they know and show you how they know it. Do not grade writing as you would a test—that will prevent the writing from being a learning opportunity for the students and a true assessment opportunity for you. Do, however, provide feedback to students—point out serious errors that need attention, comment on interesting ideas, and ask for further clarification. Not responding tells students you do not value what they have written. Help students see that their writing is important to you. Writing should never be busywork for students.

A particular writing task may on occasion be used for evaluation. You can have students do the same kind of writing on a test that they do in their journals or other writings. Because you have had them write outside of these evaluations, they will have learned how to put their ideas on paper, and the evaluation will be much more effective.

## Types of Writing Activities

Regardless of the specific form or label given to writing activities, the act of putting thoughts on paper can be a highly reflective activity that helps students clarify and organize their thoughts.

## Journal Writing

Journal writing has become the most popular form of writing in the mathematics classroom and also the most loosely defined. Two teachers can have their students write in journals, and yet the kind of writing produced may be entirely different. Journals can be thought of as private, to be read only by you unless permission is granted to show a parent or to share with the class.

The journal can be used to have students explain a concept or an idea you have been working on (*What does percent mean?*), to reflect on the day's lesson (*What did you learn today? What was easy to understand today? What was hard?*), or to show how a problem is solved. In fact, practically any writing activity can be done in a journal. It is the private communication format of a journal that makes it unique. (The physical format of journals and suggestions for writing prompts are discussed in Chapter 5.)

## Problem Solving

When a problem is solved, students should learn to write much more than answers. Written explanations of the reasoning and processes students used should convey to others why the solutions are correct. This means that students need to convince themselves that they are correct as well, an important part of doing mathematics. Encourage students to include drawings or any form of explanation that helps the reader understand the solution.

## Explaining an Idea

Somewhat different from solving a problem is the process of explaining an idea. This is prompted by straightforward requests such as, "Explain to me what three-fourths means" or "Show me what you know about the number 10" or "Why does the area formula 'one-half base times height' give the area of a triangle?" Usually, these writing tasks would closely follow the development of the idea in class.

## Reflective Writing

Sometimes it is useful to get a general feel for students' perspective on a unit, how well they think they understand something, or what they like or dislike about mathematics or a topic in mathematics. You may want this type of writing to go in journals, where the element of privacy is useful. But if you make the writing task something a bit more special, you are more likely to get true reflective thinking from your students. Here are a few suggestions for this type of writing assignment:

If mathematics were an animal, it would be . . .

The thing I like best about mathematics is . . .

The hardest part of this chapter on subtraction is . . .

I need help with _____ because . . .

To me, geometry means . . .

## Practical Suggestions

Writing in mathematics is not easy for most students. Many will complain that they don't know what to write. Here are some tips that might help.

### Help Students Get Started

Before offering a writing prompt, have a class discussion concerning the same topic as the prompt. As students suggest ideas, write them on the board in shortened phrases. Make lists of key words that are used in the students' discussion. Do not impose your language; record ideas using the terminology of your students. To help writing about a particular concept in mathematics, you might have students brainstorm and draw a mind map on the board showing how one idea is connected to another. These notes on the board can now be used by students if they wish.

Nearly all of Marilyn Burns's books include examples of children's writing. She recommends the following formulation:

I (we) think the answer is _____.

I (we) think this because . . .

This simple formula can also be used in oral presentations. It is not necessary that children follow the exact wording, but these two lines are a nice way to suggest connecting an answer with its justification.

Many children will tell you they are stuck or don't know what to write. Have them tell you about the problem or the question in the prompt. "Why do you think that is the answer? What did you do to get this? Tell me something you know about this shape you made (this measurement you did, this graph you made, the estimate you made)." Get the student thinking about several ideas before returning to the writing task. Then have the child repeat some of those ideas. "What did you just tell me about how you got that answer?" Now he or she is ready to write. "What you just said to me are the same things you can write. Just pretend you are talking to me, and let those ideas go right through your hand and onto the paper."

Huinker and Laughlin (1996) suggest changing the think-pair-share idea to think-talk-write. The thinking part is the same—a short time for students to get their thoughts together. The talk part is done with a partner or a small group. For the writing part, students are told to use the same ideas and words they just talked about and heard in their conversation. They can add drawings or pictures to help. Think-talk-write can be a regular approach to writing in your classroom.

### Write Often

One thing is certain: If your students write regularly—at least three times every week—they will get better at it. Try sharing some of the writing that has been done by students in your class or another class so that students will have some models. Soon they will be their own good models as writing becomes less of a chore and more of a learning experience.

For young students, the physical act of writing is difficult. If you have computers in your room, take advantage of the word processors. Suggest leaving a blank space for a drawing where necessary. The big advantage of the computer is ease of revision.

### Provide Purpose and Audience

All writers need to have a sense of their audience and the purpose of the writing. For every writing prompt or assignment, make these two points clear. Often you will be the audience. Tell that to the students. "You are writing to me. Give me your best understanding about subtraction so that what I read will let me know what you know."

Other useful audiences include class members (real or fictitious) who may have missed a class. The purpose is to explain the ideas of the day's lesson. Or students can write to explain an idea for a student in a lower grade. This has the advantage of putting them in a position of confidence. Writing a letter to another class, to the principal, to parents, or to a public figure such as the mayor is useful when the purpose is to exhibit the results of a project.

### Help the Prewriter and Early Writer

Children who do not yet have writing skills need to begin the process of recording and communicating their ideas. When we look at pictures and drawings made by young children, we should understand that they are most concerned with communicating to themselves. They do not really have a sense of audience. Burns (1995b) suggests telling young children that what they put on their paper should remind them of what they were thinking. Suggest that they should think about using words, numbers, and pictures to show their ideas. The result will not always make sense at first glance. Be sure to talk to the students about their writing and have them explain what they have written. At this early level, personal expression of ideas is most important.

When time permits, you can have students dictate what they want to write so that their words are on the paper. Be sensitive when using this technique; some children do not like having the teacher write for them.

In Chapter 5, there is an illustration of a large flipchart used by one kindergarten teacher as a "big journal." She writes ideas taken from the class during discussion. This is good modeling, but it does not replace the students' own private writing and formulation of ideas in written form.

# DRILL AND PRACTICE

In the past, drill and practice were the mainstays of the mathematics classroom. Today, the amount of drill should be drastically diminished because our needs are different. Drill does have its place, however. The key is for the practice to be effective and not the predominant feature of the instructional program. No new ideas are ever developed by drilling them.

# What Should Be Practiced

There are many procedural skills in mathematics that are worth practicing. Practice is how the skill becomes automatic after it is learned. A few examples may clarify this point.

Mastery of basic facts is as important today as ever, perhaps even more so. But mindless drill will do little to help students to this end. What needs to become automatic is the use of an effective strategy. As a good way of thinking about a fact is used over and over, it soon becomes an unconscious process. Practice without an efficient strategy relies on rote memory and simply does not work very well.

Children who learn computational procedures without any understanding tend to practice what they think they should be doing. This inevitably leads to *errors* that get practiced and strengthened. When students practice their own invented strategies, they are forced to focus on the ideas of what they are doing rather than follow a collection of rules. Doing many computations with attention to the supporting ideas frees students to invent shortcuts and mental strategies.

Practicing flexible and conceptual approaches to proportion and percent problems is similar to the argument just made for computation. Proportion problems can be solved using a variety of algorithms. Efficient strategies tend to vary from one problem to the next, depending on the numbers involved. Sometimes a simple mental multiplication is all that is necessary. Often a little sketch of the situation helps clarify what the two ratios are and the necessary operation to use. In a similar manner, percent problems can frequently be solved in many ways. What is most important is to be able to think about situations meaningfully and not get totally absorbed by a prescribed procedural maneuver.

Practice should help students become comfortable and flexible with an idea. Lengthy drills of algorithmic skills tend to diminish flexibility and reflective thought. Often teachers want to drill skills in preparation for a standardized test. The result is that when students confront a computation on the test, they respond as they have been drilled to do: They begin immediately to perform the indicated algorithm. Often a mental computation, an estimation, or a nonstandard approach would be twice as fast, especially when the format is multiple-choice. The distracter choices on standardized tests are designed to match the typical errors that students make in mindless application of the algorithms. Students who have practiced thinking are much less likely to make these errors and will actually be able to complete these tests more quickly.

# Suggestions for Practice

The main suggestion for practice has already been made implicitly: Practice the use of flexible conceptual approaches, not isolated and meaningless procedures learned by rote. Here are some additional suggestions:

- Keep practice short. Fifteen minutes three or four times per week is much better than any full class period of practice.

- Individualize practice so that students are actually practicing the things they need to practice. Nothing is more pointless than repetitive drill of a mastered skill.

- Provide conceptual help. Students who are experiencing difficulty in a practice setting are not going to be aided by more practice. A conceptual deficit is nearly always the root cause of a skill deficiency.

- Help students understand that the purpose of practice is to become quick yet flexible. Practice of meaningful skills allows them to be used with greater ease. With this in mind, try to avoid practice of things students will not need to use, such as long division with three-digit divisors.

# HOMEWORK

Homework can be a useful instructional tool. It must be coordinated with your instructional objectives and reflect what happens in your classroom.

## Conceptual Tasks for Homework

Homework has traditionally been a means of providing extra drill and practice on the procedures taught that day. Drill-oriented homework is an obvious extension of lessons that end with a procedural "how to" recipe. In a developmental approach, most lessons require reflection and students justifying their results through the use of models or other methods. Drill-oriented homework is not an appropriate follow-up.

Does it follow that no homework can be assigned? Certainly not! Homework can serve the same purpose as working on a task or a new idea in class. A homework assignment may involve a task similar to one done in class that day. This will provide an opportunity for students to apply again the ideas that were discussed in class. Completely new tasks can also be assigned as homework. Here the *before* portion of a lesson occurs at the end of a class, homework supplies the *during* portion, and the next day begins with the *after* discussion.

Homework is also an effective way to communicate the importance of conceptual understanding and problem solving to both students and parents. When students take work home that involves problem solving, models, writing, or data gathering, parents can see that their children are doing more than drill. Homework is a parent's window to your classroom. Students may discuss homework with their parents, and most parents will see that it is done. If developmental lessons are not followed by similar homework assignments, parents will not see a problem-solving approach to your instruction.

Homework also builds self-reliance as students are forced to grapple with ideas apart from the teacher's guidance.

In this sense, homework is a way of communicating to students, "I know you are able to do this on your own."

## Homework Used for Drill

As already noted, practice does have a place. When you have activities that require practice, from basic-fact drill to solving verbal percent problems, homework can provide appropriate practice. Be sure to follow the suggestions in the preceding paragraphs. Keep drills short, and when possible, individualize them. Avoid drill-oriented homework just because you feel compelled to give a homework assignment.

One idea is to provide an answer key along with the drill. As part of the assignment, have students check their own drills against the key or have them use a calculator to check answers. Encourage them to mark the ones they get wrong and redo these. Then they should write you a note about why they think they got these wrong the first time. Was the error carelessness, or is there something they need help with? If you let students see that the purpose of a drill is to improve their skill, they can help you assess this. With the offer of help when needed, the drill homework becomes an opportunity rather than an irksome chore.

Drill homework should never be graded, especially when students check their own work with an answer key. You can check that it was done, and you must respond to the self-assessments that are written. But do not penalize a student for wrong answers if he or she is aware of them and knows why they are wrong or is asking for help.

## Using Homework in the Classroom

How you attend or do not attend to what was done for homework sends a clear value message to your students. However, checking homework in class can easily become a major time-consuming burden. It is important to find ways of dealing with homework that are quick yet effective.

First, be sure that assigned homework was done, and acknowledge the effort. This does not mean that you need to grade or evaluate it. Checking that homework was completed can be accomplished simply by asking students to place it on their desks for you to see. Make it obvious that you do keep a daily record of homework done and not done.

Checking answers on homework is probably a waste of time. For drill and practice, the self-assessment approach is more effective and requires no class time. When homework is a task or problem, discussing the homework should be just the same as the discussion or after portion of a lesson. Homework with drawings and written explanations should be out on desks during the discussion. Instead of having all students share their work, ask students to compare what they did with what was shown first. "Martha, I see a different drawing on your paper. Can you tell us about that part?" "Pete, it looks like you may have done about the same thing. Is that right, or did you do something differently?" In this approach, homework is a continuation of the learning process. The responsibility to do the homework is the same as the responsibility to work in class.

# THE ROLE OF THE TEXTBOOK

The basal textbook has been the most significant factor influencing instruction in the elementary and middle school classroom. To make decisions about the use of the textbook, it is good to have an objective view of textbooks and the role they can serve in instruction. When you realize that textbooks are not necessarily the best guide to instruction, you can make wiser choices in using them.

## How Are Textbooks Developed?

It is worthwhile to remember that publishing textbooks is a business. If the very best ideas from mathematics educators were incorporated into a textbook that did not sell, those excellent books sitting in warehouses would be of no value to students and would cost the publisher millions of dollars.

Most publishers enlist as authors mathematics educators and teachers who are quite knowledgeable about teaching mathematics. They also do extensive market research to determine what will sell and what teachers think they want in a book. There is frequently a significant gap between what the authors think would be good and what the publisher thinks will sell. Compromise between author and market becomes the rule. Rather than be forward with new ideas for content or pedagogy, publishers make a serious attempt to offend no one. As a consequence, there is frequently a significant time lapse between state-of-the-art mathematics education and what appears in textbooks.

The textbook is a printed medium. Pictures can be put on pages, but manipulative models cannot. To illustrate movement and relationships, such as grouping 10 ones to make a single ten, requires a lot of page space. Young children have a great deal of difficulty following time-lapse-sequence drawings that show materials in several stages of an activity. To use more pages simply creates a book that is too expensive and too heavy. The result is frequently a simple illustration followed by symbolic exercises that require less space.

With exceptions found in occasional lessons, most traditional textbooks remain very close to a "teach by telling" model. It is simply not possible for the text to pose problems or tasks in the student books and not provide the solutions or explanations. Most teachers have not yet adapted the teaching-through-problem-solving approach described in this book. For most of the market, the textbook is expected to teach, not simply pose tasks. The mainstream textbook is designed for a teacher who believes that the best teaching is done by following the text and who values a high proportion of drill and practice.

The reform curricula described in Chapter 1 are very different from traditional texts. The development was funded primarily by the National Science Foundation so that publishers did not have that expense. Authors were not bound by the market concerns. To use these texts, teachers must invest a significant amount of time reading the teacher material provided for them. Often there are no student materials at all. Lessons are problem-oriented and often involve extended explorations by students. Extensive drill is not a feature. The market for these programs is growing slowly; it is currently only around 15 percent at the K–5 level and less than that at the middle and high school levels. Traditional textbooks maintain a dominant presence in most classrooms.

## Teacher's Editions

The teacher's editions give authors considerably more freedom. Many publishers now provide two extra teacher pages for each lesson as well as additional pages with ideas, explanations, and hints in the front and back of each chapter. The teacher's editions nearly always suggest alternative or additional activities completely separate from those presented on the student pages. Teachers should take advantage of this information. Too many teachers interpret the textbook curriculum as "getting students through the student pages" when in fact the real objectives require the much broader scope presented in the teacher's editions. Pupil pages are just one tool for instruction. Pupil pages are not the objective, nor are they the curriculum.

## Two-Page Lesson Format

The typical textbook lesson in the pupil book is presented on two pages. An observable pattern to these lessons can be seen in almost all popular textbook series. A portion of the first page consists of pictures and illustrations that depict the concepts for that lesson. The teacher is to use this section of the page to discuss the concepts with the students. Next are well-explained examples for the students to follow or an exercise guided by the text. Finally, the lesson has a series of exercises or practice activities. Thus many lessons move almost immediately from conceptual development to symbolic or procedural activities.

This three-part characterization of a textbook lesson is unfairly oversimplified. At the K–2 level, where the children write directly in consumable workbooks, what the student writes for all or most of the two pages may be closely tied to meaningful pictures or even simple hands-on models. The clear adherence to the two-page lesson is not always evident in seventh- and eighth-grade texts. There is a definite movement in the textbook industry to develop pupil pages that require some form of hands-on models.

The two-page format sends a clear message to students that the pictures, concepts, and discussion part of a lesson can be ignored. They begin to tune out until the teacher begins to explain how to do the exercises. Following page by page and assigning procedural exercises from every lesson can easily negate all other efforts to communicate the importance of reasoning, of making and testing conjectures, of justifying results—in short, of doing mathematics.

## Suggestions for Textbook Use

Our task as teachers is to help children construct relationships and ideas, not to get them to "do pages." We should look on the textbook as simply one of a variety of teaching resources available in the classroom. The textbook is not the object of instruction.

If one considers the limitations of the print medium and understands that the authors and publishers had to make compromises, the textbook can be a source of ideas for designing lessons rather than prescriptions for what each lesson will be. Here are some suggestions:

- Teach to the big ideas, not the pages. Consider chapter objectives rather than lesson activities. The chapter or unit viewpoint will help focus on the big ideas rather than the activity required to complete a page.
- Consider the conceptual portions of lessons as ideas or inspirations for planning more problematic activities. The students do not actually have to do the page. (Chapter 4 provides two examples.)
- Let the pace of your lessons through a unit be determined by student performance and understanding rather than the artificial norm of two pages per day.
- Use the ideas in the teacher's edition.
- Remember that there is no law saying every page must be done or every exercise completed. Select activities that suit your instructional goals rather than designing instruction to suit the text. Feel free to omit pages and activities you believe to be inappropriate for the needs of your students and your instructional goals.
- If the general approach in the text for a particular unit is not the same as the approach you prefer, omit its use for that unit altogether, or select only exercises that provide appropriate practice after you have developed the concepts with your method.
- When drill and practice at the symbolic level are desired, look to the textbook as one source of such activity. Why write a drill if an acceptable one is there in the book?

The text is usually a good general guide for scope and sequence. There is no reason that you as a teacher should be required to be a curriculum designer. If tasks and activities are adapted from pages covering the objective you are teaching, you can be reasonably sure that they have been designed to work well for that objective. It is not easy to make up good tasks for every lesson. Take advantage of the text.

Textbooks and other supplementary materials (ancillaries) supplied by publishers usually include evaluation instruments that may be of use for diagnosis, for guiding the pace of your instruction, or for evaluation. At present, such tests are more likely to assess computational skills than conceptual understanding, problem solving, or other process objectives. However, there is a definite effort on the part of publishers to develop better assessments for these higher-order skills.

# REFLECTIONS ON CHAPTER 22

## Writing to Learn

1. Discussion or discourse is one of the most important components of a lesson. How can a teacher be a facilitator of a discussion in the after portion of a lesson without asking students specific task-oriented questions? What is the value of removing yourself from this leading role?

2. Describe at least three ways that the three-part lesson format can be modified or adapted.

3. How can differences in student abilities be dealt with in the classroom?

4. With respect to cooperative groups:
   a. Why are larger groups not likely to work as well as groups of two or three?
   b. What are some of the most important group skills needed for cooperative groups to work effectively? How can students be helped to learn them?

5. Describe several ways to include writing in mathematics.

6. Practice is not how the skill is learned but rather how the skill becomes more automatic. What does this mean? Provide an example to explain your answer.

7. How can a task or problem be used as homework within the three-part lesson format? What are some of the advantages to assigning a task for homework?

8. Explain how to use a self-check method of practice for drill-oriented homework.

9. What is the major difference between the instructional method described in this book and the predominant approach found in most mainstream textbooks? Describe briefly what is meant by the "two-page lesson format" that is often adhered to in traditional basal textbooks. What is a serious drawback to lessons of this form?

## For Discussion and Exploration

1. Examine a textbook for any grade level. Look at a topic for a whole chapter, and determine the two or three main objectives or big ideas covered in the chapter. Restrict yourself to no more than three, and be sure that nearly all topics in the chapter can be built into these big ideas. Now look at the individual lessons. Are the lessons really aimed at the big ideas you have identified? Will the lessons effectively develop the big ideas for this chapter? Try to find two or three tasks or explorations related to the big ideas you have described. If students work on these explorations, how many of the individual lesson objectives will be met?

2. Select a lesson or a short series of lessons from a traditional textbook. Using the ideas on the student pages, design a problematic task for students that addresses the same ideas. Will your task and follow-up discussion make an entire lesson? Are any ideas in the textbook lessons likely to be overlooked by using your task instead of the text lesson? Now look at the teacher notes for these same lessons. What ideas can you find there to develop a problematic lesson?

3. What homework would you assign for the lessons you described in question 2? What is the purpose of the homework? What would you do with this homework on the following day when it was due?

## Recommendations for Further Reading

### Highly Recommended

Dacey, L. S., & Eston, R. (1999). *Growing mathematical ideas in kindergarten.* Sausalito, CA: Math Solutions Publications.
Kindergarten teachers often find it difficult to put the practices discussed in a mathematics methods class in the kindergarten context. Dacey and Eston make the kindergarten classroom come alive in practical ways that encompass many of the general themes you have read about here: choosing tasks, learning to talk and listen, gathering assessment data, and much more. This is a must-have book for every kindergarten teacher.

Johnson, D. W., Johnson, R. T., & Holubec, E. J. (1993). *Circles of learning: Cooperation in the classroom* (4th ed.). Alexandria, VA: Association for Supervision and Curriculum Development.
This remains the best available guide for making cooperative learning work in your classroom.

Litton, N. (1998). *Getting your math message out to parents: A K–6 resource.* Sausalito, CA: Math Solutions Publications.
Well-meaning parents who remember mathematics as dominated by memorization and worksheets often challenge a constructivist, student-oriented approach to teaching. Litton is a classroom teacher who has practical suggestions for communicating with parents. The book includes chapters on parent conferences, newsletters, homework, and family math night.

Schroeder, M. L. (1996). Lesson design and reflection. *Mathematics Teaching in the Middle School, 1,* 649–652.
This article makes the suggestion that to become a better teacher, it is important to reflect on what you actually do as a teacher. It is recommended as a guide for looking at your own teaching, whether you are a novice or an experienced teacher.

Thiessen, D., Matthias, M., & Smith, J. (1998). *The wonderful world of mathematics: A critically annotated list of children's books in mathematics* (2nd ed.). Reston, VA: National Council of Teachers of Mathematics.

In this second edition, Thiessen, Matthias, and Smith have compiled over 300 pages of children's books, each with annotation, rating, and suggested grade span. The book is structured by content area. A valuable resource.

## Other Suggestions

Artzt, A. F. (1996). Developing problem-solving behaviors by assessing communication in cooperative learning groups. In P. C. Elliott (Ed.), *Communication in mathematics, K–12 and beyond* (pp. 116–125). Reston, VA: National Council of Teachers of Mathematics.

Artzt, A. F., & Newman, C. M. (1997). *How to use cooperative learning in the mathematics class* (2nd ed.). Reston, VA: National Council of Teachers of Mathematics.

Bickmore-Brand, J. (Ed.). (1990). *Language in mathematics.* Portsmouth, NH: Heinemann.

Borasi, R., Sheedy, J. R., & Siegel, M. (1990). The power of stories in learning mathematics. *Language Arts, 67,* 174–189.

Corwin, R. B., Storeygard, J., & Price, S. L. (1996). *Talking mathematics: Supporting children's voices.* Portsmouth, NH: Heinemann.

Davidson, N. (1990). Small-group cooperative learning in mathematics. In T. J. Cooney (Ed.), *Teaching and learning mathematics in the 1990s* (pp. 52–61). Reston, VA: National Council of Teachers of Mathematics.

Fitzgerald, W. M., & Bouck, M. K. (1993). Models of instruction. In D. T. Owens (Ed.), *Research ideas for the classroom: Middle grades mathematics* (pp. 244–258). Old Tappan NJ: Macmillan.

Griffiths, R., & Clyne, M. (1994). *Language in the mathematics classroom: Talking, representing, recording.* Portsmouth, NH: Heinemann.

Helton, S. M. (1995). I thik the citanre will hoder lase: Journal keeping in mathematics class. *Teaching Children Mathematics, 1,* 336–340.

Hill, S., & Hill, T. (1990). *The collaborative classroom: A guide to cooperative learning.* Portsmouth, NH: Heinemann.

Huinker, D. M., & Laughlin, C. (1996). Talk your way into writing. In P. C. Elliott (Ed.), *Communication in mathematics, K–12 and beyond* (pp. 81–88). Reston, VA: National Council of Teachers of Mathematics.

Johnson, D. W., & Johnson, R. T. (1989). Cooperative learning in mathematics education. In P. R. Trafton (Ed.), *New directions for elementary school mathematics* (pp. 234–245). Reston, VA: National Council of Teachers of Mathematics.

Johnson, D. W., Johnson, R. T., & Holubec, E. J. (1994). *Cooperative learning in the classroom.* Alexandria, VA: Association for Supervision and Curriculum Development.

Leinhardt, G. (1989). Math lessons: A contrast of novice and expert competence. *Journal for Research in Mathematics Education, 20,* 52–75.

Linchevski, L., & Kutscher, B. (1998). Tell me with whom you're learning, and I'll tell you how much you've learned: Mixed-ability versus same-ability grouping in mathematics. *Journal for Research in Mathematics Education, 29,* 533–554.

Madsen, A. L., & Baker, K. (1993). Planning and organizing the middle grades mathematics curriculum. In D. T. Owens (Ed.), *Research ideas for the classroom: Middle grades mathematics* (pp. 285–302). Old Tappan, NJ: Macmillan.

McGrath, K. L. (1998). What is the score on scored discussions? *Mathematics Teaching in the Middle School, 4,* 50–58.

McIntosh, M. E. (1997). 500+ writing formats. *Mathematics Teaching in the Middle School, 2,* 354–358.

Mills, H., O'Keefe, T., & Whitin, D. (1996). *Mathematics in the making: Authoring ideas in primary classrooms.* Portsmouth, NH: Heinemann.

Mousley, J., & Sullivan, P. (Eds.). (1996). *Learning about teaching: An interactive tutorial program to facilitate the study of teaching.* The Australian Association of Mathematics Teachers. (Distributed by the National Council of Teachers of Mathematics.)

Newman, V. (1994). *Math journals: Tools for authentic assessment.* San Leandro, CA: Teaching Resource Center.

Norwood, K. S., & Carter, G. (1994). Journal writing: An insight into students' understanding. *Teaching Children Mathematics, 1,* 146–148.

Rowan, T. E., & Cetorelli, N. D. (1990). An eclectic model for teaching elementary school mathematics. In T. J. Cooney (Ed.), *Teaching and learning mathematics in the 1990s* (pp. xxx–xxx). Reston, VA: National Council of Teachers of Mathematics.

Scheibelhut, C. (1994). I do and I understand, I reflect and I improve. *Teaching Children Mathematics, 1,* 242–246.

Thornton, C. A., & Wilson, S. J. (1993). Classroom organization and models of instruction. In R. J. Jensen (Ed.), *Research ideas for the classroom: Early childhood mathematics* (pp. 269–293). Old Tappan, NJ: Macmillan.

Whitin, D. J., & Whitin, P. E. (1996). Fostering metaphorical thinking through children's literature. In P. C. Elliott (Ed.), *Communication in mathematics, K–12 and beyond* (pp. 60–65). Reston, VA: National Council of Teachers of Mathematics.

Whitin, D. J., & Wilde, S. (1992). *Read any good math lately? Children's books for mathematical learning, K–6.* Portsmouth, NH: Heinemann.

Whitin, D. J., & Wilde, S. (1995). *It's the story that counts: More children's books for mathematical learning, K–6.* Portsmouth, NH: Heinemann.

# Chapter 23

# Teaching All Children Mathematics

*A society can claim success in eradicating the malady of mathematics illiteracy if and only if all its progeny are able to develop to their fullest potential. If its offspring can become employable workers, wisely choosing consumers, and autonomously thinking citizens who can be contributors in the super symbolic quantitative world they will inherit, then society can say, "Victory is ours!"*
*Elliott and Garnett (1994, p. 15)*

All of the NCTM *Standards* documents, beginning with the *Curriculum and Evaluation Standards for School Mathematics* in 1989 and including *Principles and Standards for School Mathematics* in 2000, have provided a vision that *all* children can learn mathematics, not just the mathematically adept. For example, the 1989 *Standards* speaks of its goals for all students, the 1991 *Professional Standards* asserts that "all students can learn to think mathematically (p. 21), and *Principles and Standards for School Mathematics* highlights mathematics learning by all students in its equity principle, one of the six principles on which mathematics instructional programs should be based.

To clarify what is meant by "all students," the NCTM Board of Directors in 1998 adopted its "Every Child" statement, which states:

> By "every child," we mean every child—no exception.
>     We are particularly concerned about students who have been denied access to education opportunities for any reason, such as language, ethnicity, physical impairment, gender, socioeconomic status, and so on. We emphasize that "every child" includes:
>
> - learners of English as a second language and speakers of English as a first language
> - members of underrepresented ethnic groups and members of well-represented groups
> - students who are physically challenged and those who are not

- females and males
- students who live in poverty and those who do not
- students who have not been successful and those who have been successful in school and in mathematics (p. 11)

## MATHEMATICS FOR ALL CHILDREN

Stop and think for a minute. Do you personally believe the quoted statement? Children with disabilities, children from impoverished homes, minority children—can all of these children learn to think mathematically? They certainly can. It is the responsibility of the classroom teacher to make that vision a reality.

### Diversity in Today's Classroom

It is no longer reasonable to talk about "regular education." It is even difficult to talk about the "average child." In recent years, the range of abilities, disabilities, and socioeconomic circumstances in the regular classroom has posed a significant challenge to teachers. Addressing the needs of *all* children means providing opportunity for any or all of the following:

- *Students with learning problems.* These may be students who are identified as having a specific learning disability, such as a problem with visual or auditory perception. The range and types of specific learning problems are quite varied. Other children have difficulties learning because they are slow learners or mildly handicapped.
- *Students from different cultural backgrounds.* The United States and Canada are becoming increasingly multi-

cultural societies. Education policymakers have reached no consensus concerning what to do about multiethnic classrooms. Education remains mostly "mainstream," oriented toward the white middle class, and is not necessarily congruent with other cultures. Yet those are the cultures of the children in our classrooms, the very ones we want to teach.

- *Students who are female.* Girls present the caring teacher with another concern. Traditionally, after about the seventh grade, girls begin to fall behind boys in mathematics, although the difference has decreased in recent years. More troubling is that girls exhibit more hesitancy about mathematics and have poorer self-concepts concerning mathematics than boys do.

- *Students who are mathematically promising.* Nearly every class has at least one child who finds the standard mathematics fairly trivial. These talented children are either bored or constantly providing the answers before others can think. A continued diet of traditional mathematics instruction is not serving this group of students well.

## Challenging Traditional Beliefs

Meeting the needs of all children requires that we challenge and perhaps change many of our long-held assumptions about the mathematics curriculum and about how children learn mathematics.

### Change Beliefs About the Mathematics Curriculum

Our concept of mathematics as a rule-driven, computation-dominated curriculum actually creates much of the difficulty we have in coping with the range of children's talents and abilities. When every child is required to master each algorithm and memorize every basic fact before being permitted to move on to the next procedure or rule, the more able children in the room are quickly bored. Children at the other extreme begin to doubt that they have any mathematical ability.

Computation can be accomplished through invented procedures or with the aid of technology. Geometry, measurement, probability, statistics, and algebra can all be accessed with minimal computational proficiency. There is neither evidence nor any logical argument for the demands of computational proficiency as a prerequisite for meaningful mathematics. Furthermore, the computational curriculum of the past is no longer necessary for the daily lives of citizens once they leave school. What is critically important, however, is the ability to reason and solve problems.

### Change Beliefs About How Children Learn Mathematics

Traditionally, mathematics instruction has broken content into small, bite-sized increments. Each bit is explained, demonstrated, and then practiced until mastery is achieved

and then the next bit is introduced. The belief is that somehow essentially passive children will put the bits together into some sort of cohesive whole. In classrooms for learning-disabled or low-average students, this approach has been even more pronounced and resistant to change. Unfortunately, much of the instruction for children experiencing mathematical difficulties is replete with worksheets and rote drill focused on "basic skills." What we know about how children learn would suggest a quite different approach.

There is no reason to believe that children with special needs, regardless of the nature of those needs, should learn any differently than other children (Baroody & Hume, 1991; Carey, Fennema, Carpenter, & Franke, 1995; Poplin, 1988a, 1988b; Trafton & Claus, 1994).

When skills rather than problem solving and concepts dominate, teachers find it useful to form ability groups. The results of creating ability groups are usually not as good as teachers believe. The degree of skill variability within each of two or three subgroups is not likely to be significantly less than that for the whole class. Furthermore, children in the lower groups are typically denied opportunities for interacting with their peers in situations involving higher-order thinking or reasoning. The mathematics in the bottom group is generally relegated to skill remediation and isolated practice. There is little or no evidence to support the homogeneous grouping of children within classrooms or the creation of special homogeneous classes (Davidson & Hammerman, 1993; Oakes, 1990; Usiskin, 1993).

## CHILDREN WITH LEARNING PROBLEMS

Federal law guarantees access to appropriate education for all children. The Individuals with Disabilities Education Act (IDEA) gives preference to the term *disabled* instead of *handicapped.* The general thrust of the law is to meet the educational needs of children with special needs in the "least restrictive environment."

## Categories of Disabilities

Children bring to the classroom an enormous array of difficulties and differences based on both environmental and psychological factors. Each child is unique in his or her own way and should be regarded as such. IDEA provides legal definitions for a wide range of disabilities, including autism, mental disability (mental retardation, or MR), specific learning disabilities (LD), and various physical disabilities such as hearing or vision impairment and orthopedic handicaps. In 1991, the law was clarified to include children with attention deficit disorder (ADD) and attention deficit–hyperactivity disorder (ADHD). The IDEA definitions of disabilities are used to determine which children are eligible for special services.

Regular classroom teachers need not be expert in all of the potential disabilities they may confront. However, any given class is likely to have a variety of children with special learning problems.

## Inclusion or Referral?

Although IDEA provides special services for eligible students, the "least restrictive environment" is increasingly the regular classroom. Moreover, many children with special learning needs are not eligible under the law, and they will also require the special attention of the regular classroom teacher (Downs, Matthew, & McKinney, 1994).

As the practice of placement in special classes or resource pull-out programs is seen as less and less desirable, the regular classroom teacher faces increasing problems. This is not to say that help is not available. Every classroom teacher should become familiar with the special resources provided. Referral to the school's instructional support or consultation team should always be considered. The objective should be to secure assistance and, most important, information about the child. The more a teacher knows about the nature of a child's learning difficulties, the better prepared that teacher will be to help.

As more and more children with special needs are included in regular classrooms, "the distinction between special and regular education will soon become obsolete" (Greenes, Garfunkel, & De Bussey, 1994, p. 133). The loud and clear message should be, "Get help." Find out about how the special children in your classroom learn.

Rather than be defeated by the reality of a diverse class of children, consider the real benefits of an inclusion model (Borasi, 1994).

- Regular students serve as learning models for special students.
- Special students frequently offer unique alternative solutions to challenging problems encountered by the full class or in small cooperative groups.
- All students develop an awareness of and respect for individual differences.
- All students, not just the "regular" students, are exposed to good mathematics and challenging experiences.

# SPECIFIC LEARNING DISABILITIES

The predominant instructional model for learning-disabled students has historically viewed the learner as passive, with the mastery of skills taking precedence over understanding (Poplin, 1988a). It is this thinking that led to pull-out and self-contained classroom approaches. As noted, these skills-oriented models have produced very limited results.

Poplin's conclusion is that constructivist theory provides the best directions for teachers of special students. That same suggestion is made either implicitly or explicitly by nearly every author in NCTM's excellent book *Windows of Opportunity: Mathematics for Students with Special Needs* (Thornton & Bley, 1994). Put simply, there is no need to change the content of the curriculum for students with learning disabilities. What must be done is what all good constructivist teachers do, and that is pay careful attention to the child and how he or she learns and design instruction (not content) that maximizes the strengths of the child while minimizing the impact of weaknesses.

## A Perspective on Learning Disabilities

Students with learning disabilities have very specific problems with perceptual or cognitive processing. These problems may affect memory or the ability to speak or express ideas in writing, perceive auditory or written information, or integrate abstract ideas. It is insufficient simply to label a child "LD." The following insights offered by Borasi (1994) are an important point of departure for teachers who have learning-disabled children in their classes:

- Learning-disabled students are mentally capable; they are not slow or retarded.
- The classification of LD is not useful to the classroom teacher without a clear understanding of the child's specific learning problem.
- Learning disabilities are not easily remediated and perhaps cannot be remediated.
- Learning disabilities should be compensated for by helping students use their strengths.
- Instructional modifications will be needed to accommodate the specific needs of children with specific learning disabilities.

Borasi suggests that teachers accept the fact that learning disabilities are real in the same sense that being blind or deaf is a real disability. You would not ask a blind person to "look more closely" or a deaf person to "listen more carefully." Hence we should never ask a learning-disabled child to do things that depend heavily on his or her area of deficit.

## Adaptations for Specific Learning Difficulties

Table 23.1 identifies specific disabilities and gives a few examples of the mathematical problems that each might cause. Note that deficits or disabilities may be present as auditory problems, visual problems, or sometimes both. It is important that the teacher have as much detailed information as possible about children who have specific learning difficulties. If the child has already been evaluated by the school psychologist, test information will be available to help pinpoint specific weaknesses and also strengths. Working with the psychologist, you can find ways to adapt instructional strategies to avoid weaknesses and capitalize on strengths *without major modification of the curriculum.*

## Adaptations for Perceptual Deficits

There are many variations of perceptual problems; some are visual and others auditory. All involve confusion of input in one way or another. Children with *figure-ground* difficulties have trouble sorting out or recognizing component parts of what they see or hear. *Discrimination* difficulties refer to the inability to discern differences in things seen or heard. Children with *reversal* problems have difficulty with left-right perceptions and tend to see things in mirror images of what they

## Table 23.1
**Examples of Specific Learning Disabilities and Their Possible Effects on Performance in Mathematics**

| Disability | Visual Deficit | Auditory Deficit |
|---|---|---|
| **Perceptual** | | |
| Figure-ground | • May not finish page or loses place<br>• Has difficulty reading multidigit number | • Has trouble hearing patterns in counting<br>• Has difficulty attending to classroom discourse |
| Discrimination | • Has difficulty differentiating coins<br>• Has difficulty with numerical identification such as 2 for 5 or 3 for 8<br>• Mixes operation symbols | • Has trouble distinguishing between similar-sounding words, such as *thirty* and *thirteen* |
| Reversal | • Reverses digits in numbers<br>• Has difficulty in regrouping | |
| Spatial | • Has trouble writing on lined paper<br>• Fails to notice size differences in shapes (fractions or geometry)<br>• Has difficulty writing numbers, especially fractions and decimals | |
| **Memory** | | |
| Short-term | • Has difficulty retaining newly presented material<br>• Has difficulty copying problems from the board<br>• Has difficulty remembering facts in a word problem | • Has difficulty with oral drills<br>• Has trouble with dictated assignments |
| Long-term | • Has difficulty retaining basic facts or procedures over long period<br>• Has difficulty solving multioperational computation (written or mental) | |
| Sequential | • Has difficulty following through a long or multistep procedure such as computational algorithms<br>• Has difficulty solving multistep word problems | • Cannot retain story problems that are dictated |
| **Integrative** | | |
| Closure | • Has difficulty visualizing groups<br>• Has difficulty with missing addends and missing factors<br>• Is unable to draw conclusions and so has trouble noticing and continuing patterns<br>• Has difficulty with word problems<br>• Has trouble continuing counting patterns from within a sequence | • Has difficulty counting on from within a sequence |
| Expressive language | • Finds rapid oral skills difficult | • Has difficulty counting on<br>• Has difficulty with explanations |
| Receptive language | • Has difficulty relating words to meaning<br>• Has difficulty with words having multiple meanings | • Has difficulty relating words to meanings<br>• Has difficulty writing numbers from dictation |
| Abstract reasoning | • Is unable to solve word problems<br>• Is unable to compare numbers in symbolic form<br>• Cannot understand word problems | |

*Source:* Adapted from *Teaching Mathematics to Students with Learning Disabilities* (3rd ed., pp. 8–9), by N. S. Bley & C. A. Thornton, 1995, Austin, TX: Pro-Ed. Copyright 1995. Reprinted by permission of Pro-Ed.

really are. *Spatial* organization deficits affect children's ability to interpret or implement the positions and arrangements of things. Spatially challenged children have difficulty not only with geometric models and drawings but also with organizing their own writing on paper.

The entire area of perceptual problems is perhaps the clearest area where the maxim "avoid weaknesses and capitalize on strengths" is best observed. The following are simply a few specific suggestions:

- Seat the child near you and the chalkboard.
- Keep the child's desk or workspace free of clutter.
- Maintain a moderate voice. Repeat main ideas.
- Structure text or worksheet pages for the child. Provide templates to block out all but one problem or exercise at a time. (Cut a rectangle in the center of a half-sheet of tagboard. Make several templates with different-sized holes, and have the child keep them in his or her textbook.)
- Help design methods of organizing written work. Have computations done on centimeter grid paper writing one number per square. Provide paper with columns or drawn templates such as those found in the Blackline Masters for traditional algorithms.
- Use a tape recorder (headphones) with instructions explaining what may be difficult to discern from the available visual materials.
- Provide real geometric models whenever possible instead of relying on pictures in the text. Use geoboards and tiles such as pattern blocks for constructions so that drawing will be kept to a minimum.
- Assign a buddy to help read, explain, or repeat directions.

## Adaptations for Memory Deficits

Memory deficits can also be specifically visual or auditory. Some children may have more difficulty recalling things seen than things heard, or vice versa. Children with *short-term memory* deficits can have trouble recalling things for even a few seconds, as when copying from the board or recalling information in a word problem. Lengthy directions are also a problem. *Long-term memory* deficits are quite different. Children with this disability may show no difficulty with material when presented but appear to have not learned at all a day or a week later. Mastery of basic facts is a hallmark problem for children with this disability. *Sequential memory* problems refer to the inability to retain an order to a sequence of events or a series of steps in directions or procedures. These children are likely to ask, "What do I do next?" when working on a computation or extending a pattern. It is important to distinguish this inability to retain order from a lack of understanding.

You can diminish the load on short-term memory by breaking tasks and directions into small steps and providing a buddy to help with recall. Long-term memory problems require overlearning, frequent practice, and as many associations with other ideas as possible. The following more specific suggestions may be useful:

- Rather than a series of instructions, provide only one at a time. With good planning, sequenced instructions can be written out ahead of time.
- When teaching a specific procedure such as an algorithm, work with the student to create a model exercise showing each step. When possible, use the student's own invented strategies.
- For basic facts, use strategies and number relationships (see Chapter 8). Provide fact charts as shown in Figure 23.1, crossing out facts that are mastered.
- Allow use of a calculator at all times.

**Figure 23.1** **Permit the use of fact charts, but encourage memorization.**

Memory deficits tend to be exhibited in procedural work. Remember that no routine procedural knowledge, including mastery of basic facts, should prevent a student from progress in mathematical ideas. Exploration of new concepts is never dependent on mastery of skills.

## Adaptations for Integrative Deficits

Children with integrative problems seem to have difficulty with abstract ideas and conceptualization. These children are not slow or retarded, but they have difficulty making the cognitive connections that others may find easy. Children with an integrative disorder may do quite well at rote procedures such as computational algorithms, but these are no longer the focus of the mathematics curriculum. A general principle for helping these children integrate concepts and develop understanding is similar to a whole-language approach and is not unlike the methods espoused for a good constructivist classroom. In short, help students use experiences and ideas most familiar to them: their own invented procedures for solving problems, familiar models or personal drawings that make sense to them, and their own words in either written or oral form to express their ideas. Of course, these are good approaches for all children. The following more specific approaches may be helpful for children with integrative difficulties:

- Use familiar physical models for longer than the usual period of time.

- Have students verbalize what they do as often as possible. Use both written and oral expression.

- Frequently require explanations and justifications. This self-monitoring can heighten the children's awareness of new ideas, and the verbalization can aid in making connections.

- Allow for repetition or practice of new conceptual ideas.

### Adaptations for Attention Deficits

Many (not all) students with learning disabilities also are identified as having attention deficit disorder or attention deficit–hyperactivity disorder. These children have chronic difficulties with attention span, impulse control, and sometimes hyperactivity. Be careful to distinguish these true disorders from the behavior of children who are discipline problems for other reasons. The following strategies have proved useful:

- Establish clear routines, and discuss them with the child. Make expectations and consequences clear.

- Design learning activities that are active and involving rather than tedious or requiring lengthy periods of silent seatwork.

- Plan for the child to do independent work in an environment free of visual and auditory distractions (a seat near a blank wall, away from classmates, for example).

- Use highlighters to attract attention to important key ideas in textual material.

- Keep assignments short. Shorten exercise lists. Plan smaller subtasks within larger explorations or projects.

- Assign a buddy, and impress on both that the agenda is to stay on task.

- Instead of placing the child in a cooperative group of three or four, use a buddy to form a separate group of two. Larger groups have more distractions and require more patience while others talk.

# MENTAL DISABILITIES

All of us possess different mental capacities in addition to our individual strengths and weaknesses or learning styles. Children with mental disabilities (generally with IQ scores between 50 and 70) will be limited in the kind and degree of mathematical reasoning they can perform. Other children not as severely limited are sometimes labeled *slow learners*. Although severely disabled children are generally best served in a special classroom, a wide range of mental disabilities are likely to be present in the regular classroom.

## Modifications in Instruction

Limited cognitive abilities do not in any way alter the way that children learn. However, those with mental disabilities will learn much more slowly than children with normal intelligence and will much more quickly reach a plateau with respect to the mathematical ideas they can work with (Bley, 1994; Callahan & MacMillan, 1981). These children are likely to have limited memory, attention, and language abilities to assist them in the development of new ideas.

Though a fast-paced, highly interactive classroom may be somewhat overwhelming for slower children, they can benefit from many of the same experiences as the rest of the class. They can and should participate in projects and hands-on activities with their peer group. They can participate in cooperative groups by taking on less demanding roles, such as materials organizer or encourager. They can learn to perform calculations on a calculator and can serve as the person in a group who performs this activity. Many disabled children are good at drawing or making graphs. These helping roles are consistent with the kinds of jobs they are likely to have in the adult world.

Making expectations clear, simple, and appropriate for the child is another important consideration. Within any activity planned for the class, find subtasks or related activities appropriate for the disabled child. Clearly explain these expectations using simple directions. Have the child repeat the expectations in his or her own words.

Partner the disabled child with different students periodically, and have the partner help the child with the same task or idea. In this way, there is opportunity for needed repeated exposure or "overlearning," and other students also will gain from serving as the explainer. It is important for all children in the room to involve slower-learning children in activities and projects. The slow child gains from the richer ideas and interactions and will frequently contribute alternative solutions or ideas. All children gain an appreciation for and acceptance of human differences.

## Modifications in Curriculum

Since mentally disabled children learn much more slowly than other children, it follows that less content can be learned during the years they are in school. It makes sense to focus the available instructional time on those areas that are going to be of the most value to these students as adults. Computational skill is the most obvious area where changes in curricular expectations should be made. There is no reason to be obsessive about fact mastery. Traditional computational algorithms should be eliminated from their curriculum altogether.

Students should be taught to have a calculator handy for all mathematics work. The disabled child should be given careful instruction and lots of practice in using the calculator. A calculator with a printer is useful because it creates a printed record of work done. These students can do the same exercises that others are doing but do them with a calculator.

An area that should be stressed is the relationship of number to the real world. Whereas calculations can be mastered via the calculator, the meanings of numbers in the real world cannot. Do not confuse number meaning with place-value concepts. What is important here is to realize that a bag of flour weighs 5 pounds, that $100 buys a pair of fancy sneakers, or that it takes about 20 minutes to walk a mile. Numbers in the abstract will be of little use.

# MULTICULTURAL AND SOCIAL EQUITY

Traditionally, we have assumed that of all the subjects in the curriculum, mathematics was the most likely to be culturally neutral. After all, 2 + 2 = 4 is a logical fact having little to do with ethnicity or poverty. At the same time, there is clear evidence that African American, Hispanic, and Native American children and children from homes with low socioeconomic status (SES) do poorly in mathematics (Hilliard, 1995; Oakes, 1990, 1995). Do children in these groups not have the same mathematical or even general academic ability as their white, middle-class suburban counterparts? There is no evidence to support such a view, yet discrepancies in achievement levels in mathematics remain a fact.

## A Question of Access

Students in at-risk populations (non-Asian ethnicities and low SES) are simply not getting the same access to quality teachers, to adequate resources and technology, or to quality curriculum as their middle- and upper-class suburban counterparts.

### Access to Quality Teachers

According to Oakes (1990, 1995), low-income and minority students are not being taught mathematics or science by high-quality teachers. It is more difficult to convince quality teachers to accept jobs in predominantly minority schools, and turnover is greater because these schools are experienced as less desirable places in which to teach. Tracking (to be discussed shortly) is also a source of teacher quality discrepancies. Nearly all schools tend to place their least qualified teachers in low-ability classes. In fact, Oakes (1990) reports that "low-track students in the most advantaged schools are likely to have better-qualified teachers than high-track students in the least-advantaged schools" (p. 67).

Teachers can help traditionally at-risk students achieve at the highest levels without any special "minority training," without special technology, and without special texts or materials.

> For some teachers, the surprising reality is that the low achievers change not because of the invention of some culturally specific exotic new method, but because many of them are exposed to regular high-quality instruction, to which many of the traditionally low performers had not been previously exposed. (Hilliard, 1995, p. 109)

### Access to Resources

The disparity in school spending between schools located in areas with low- versus high-income families is increasing. Most low-income and minority children attend schools where fewer dollars have been spent (Oakes, 1995). The result is felt in terms of inadequate facilities, larger class size, inadequate equipment such as computers, and fewer materials. There are examples where huge sums of money have been lavished on disadvantaged schools with little success. These counterexamples notwithstanding, the lack of resources has to have some effect on instruction, if only in terms of teacher and student attitudes toward school. Computers and the Internet are now such important assets in everyday life that access to these technologies is becoming a must rather than a desirable option.

### Access to Curriculum

Evidence suggests that teachers in minority schools tend to place less emphasis on curricular goals such as inquiry and problem solving. Differences occur in both pace or coverage of content as well as emphasis on lower-level skills instead of higher-order thinking and engaging, meaningful explorations. Beginning in the junior high school, the curriculum access issue can be told in terms of available courses. Fewer algebra courses, for example, are taught in low-SES and predominantly minority schools, making access to higher-level mathematics courses in the secondary schools more difficult. In elementary schools, the differences are caused primarily by choices of emphasis that teachers make within the standard curricular materials and by the outside resources available to enrich the curriculum.

## Expectations

It remains true that students will rise or fall to the level of our expectations. Two related factors seem to be working against minority and low-SES students: teachers' beliefs in their abilities and the effects of tracking or homogeneous grouping.

### Teacher Expectations

Among teachers of at-risk children, there is a striking difference between those who believe in the abilities of their students and those who expect very little. The latter group of teachers have found it easy to blame the performance of their students on the myriad factors that exist outside the classroom. *It's the neighborhood. They don't have two parents making them work. The parents are not educated. These kids come from an environment infested with drugs.* Teachers who voice such laments are using real facts as excuses for not making a difference (Ladson-Billings, 1995). If the excuses were valid, no teachers would believe in their students, yet many do and achieve outstanding results.

Experts believe that one of the most important factors for success with disadvantaged or minority students is to develop in them a strong sense of self-esteem, helping children believe in themselves. This is an incredibly difficult task for the teacher whose expectations are low to begin with.

## Negative Effects of Tracking and Homogeneous Grouping

Teachers' assessments of students' abilities play a key role in deciding what types of educational experiences a student may receive. Tracking, curricular access, and belief systems are interrelated. Once students are placed in a lower-level track or in a "slow" class, expectations decline accordingly. Students in low tracks are frequently denied access to challenging material and high-quality mathematics (Silver, Smith, & Nelson, 1995). The mathematics for the lower tracks or classes is almost totally oriented toward day after day of remedial drill with minimal success and no excitement. Teachers become reinforced in their low expectations because students are not encouraged to think, nor are they engaged in activities and interactions that would encourage thinking.

To highlight the negative effects of tracking, Usiskin (1993) described a process of placing students in "special" classes beginning in the early grades of his own child's elementary school. Placements in the "high" class were made on the basis of tests of traditional skills given at the end of the previous year. During the year, the high class spent less time reviewing old material and more time on problem-solving experiences. With more time, they covered more material. At the end of each year, testing was repeated for all students and new placements made. To the surprise of no one, the students in the high class were predominantly the ones who placed into the high class each subsequent year. Usiskin argues that the experiences in the high class were not exceptional and were appropriate for all of the students. Expectations based on the grouping process simply provided greater access to good mathematics. That very first simple skill test, not at all based on higher-order thinking or mathematics, preempted the majority of students from quality experiences from which all could benefit. The reverse phenomenon occurs when students are placed in low or remedial groups. Lower expectations restrict access to quality mathematics and lead to instruction actually targeted at lower achievement.

In addition to the effect on expectations, tracking severely diminishes the potential for valuable interactions in the classroom. Based on their experiences in a small but very diverse school, Davidson and Hammerman (1993) argue that heterogeneity enriches experiences for all students. In their school,

class discussions tend to focus a bit above the middle of the group, keeping work challenging for top and midrange children. Students at the lower end get to see and experience what higher-level interactions are like. Many times, expectations are turned upside down as children perceived as less able come to understand and work meaningfully with concepts to which they would never be exposed in a low-track homogeneous class. Furthermore, exposing all students to higher-level thinking and quality mathematics avoids accentuating differences from year to year caused by low-track expectations.

# Examples of What Works

What we have learned over the years from massive federal programs that have failed is that narrow, skill-focused, highly prescriptive approaches do not work. We have also seen that programs that target disadvantaged kids by grouping them in special classrooms do not work. We *can* point to some recent examples of programs and the efforts of individual teachers that have worked exceptionally well with urban, minority, low-SES children. The common factors in these programs are not money, materials, technology, or tracking. What makes them succeed is a constructivist approach to instruction and a positive belief in the children.

The three examples described here are just that—examples. Many more success stories could be told, but most exhibit the same instructional characteristics as these examples.

## Project IMPACT: CGI in an Urban Setting

Cognitively Guided Instruction (CGI) is a program developed at the University of Wisconsin in the mid-1980s. It is based on the belief that if "teachers had research-based knowledge about children's thinking in general, they would be more able to focus on individual children" (Carey et al., 1995, p. 101). The program is not a curriculum. It focuses on helping teachers listen to how children think and determine what they know and understand. Based on this knowledge of individual children, teachers try to build mathematics ideas on the considerable mathematical understanding that all children naturally bring to school.

Beginning in 1990, the CGI philosophy and approach were brought to three predominantly minority urban public schools outside of Washington, D.C. The schools were diverse in their ethnic makeup and included students speaking a variety of languages. Project IMPACT (Increasing the Mathematical Power of All Children and Teachers) began in grades K–3 and later extended to grade 5. The teachers were trained in CGI techniques during the summer and were supported by a specialist in the schools during the year. Teachers in the project came to recognize that every child, regardless of background or SES, has mathematical knowledge.

The CGI method is essentially a constructivist approach based on the theory that ideas grow as children solve problems using their existing knowledge. IMPACT teachers would frequently propose a task, problem, or investigation; provide an opportunity to work on or consider the task; and then ask questions: *What do you see? Tell us something else about this problem. What do you know? What else do you know? Tell us your thinking. What could we try? Does anyone have a different idea or notice something else about this problem?* All responses were valued by being listened to without judgment or evaluation. All children were expected to be active listeners, and all were called on to participate. When a child was reluctant, students and teacher would be patient until a response was made. IMPACT schools used no tracking, and there was no grouping in the classrooms (Campbell, 1993).

Students in IMPACT were not taught traditional algorithms, nor was there any stress on basic facts and skills. On standardized tests, children excelled at problem solving and concepts and were about average in skill development. A striking effect is the confidence in being able to do mathematics that the children displayed. Teachers also became true believers that all children could do mathematics and could think mathematically (Campbell, 1996).

## The QUASAR Project

QUASAR (Quantitative Understanding: Amplifying Student Achievement and Reasoning), begun in 1989, was a large reform project for middle schools. It focused on schools in economically disadvantaged communities and attempted to improve the participation and performance in mathematics of females, ethnic minorities, and the poor. The belief was that these groups have traditionally failed due primarily to a lack of "access to meaningful, high-quality experiences with mathematics learning" (Silver et al., 1995, p. 10). QUASAR believed that virtually all students can learn middle school mathematics and move on to a challenging program at the secondary level.

The instruction in QUASAR schools was aimed at improving thinking, reasoning, and problem solving. Tasks were designed with multiple entry points and multiple paths to solutions, allowing for heterogeneous classrooms to participate fully in developing solutions. There was an emphasis on communication and discourse in the creation of classroom communities where thinking and reasoning are valued and risk takers are made to feel safe.

At each of its sites, QUASAR nearly eliminated the entrenched practice of academic tracking. A teacher at one site noted that "a lot of the kids that are classified as lost, or turned off, or unintelligent, or whatever, really have some powerful ideas and some powerful ways of thinking, and exposing the other kids to that and them to the ways the other kids think is just too powerful to overlook" (Silver et al., 1995, p. 28). To aid in handling the diversity of the classroom, many teachers used heterogeneous cooperative groups. In one classroom, test scores on a standardized test ranged from the 15th to the 98th percentile. Posters in the room suggested phrases that all students were to use: *Good answer. You can do it! You're on the right track. Give it a try. We'll help you*

*through it.* Trust and mutual respect were key features of the program. Fear of giving wrong answers eventually disappears in this kind of atmosphere as students learn that there is no such thing as a "dumb question" or a "bad answer."

Teachers began to call the QUASAR project the "revolution of the possible."

## Impact of a Single Teacher

For an individual teacher, there is comfort and value in being part of a project that promotes the kind of teaching described in the preceding projects. But for the majority of teachers, the only project will be the one they initiate in their own rooms.

Ms. Rossi is a veteran sixth-grade teacher in a low-SES, predominantly African American school. She is one of eight teachers studied by Ladson-Billings (1995) who are effective working with African American students. In one lesson, Rossi made a point of involving all students individually, assuring them that they were capable of mastering the problems. Students cheered one another and celebrated explanations. Students were pushed to explain "How do you know?" The textbook was generally not used. Rossi would help students see that what they had been doing was the same as what was in the text. The point was always that mathematics was not threatening and that the students were capable of good mathematics and quality thinking.

Based on her study of effective teachers, Ladson-Billings listed five guidelines or principles for the successful teaching of students who are traditionally at risk of failing:

1. *Have high expectations for all students, letting them know that you believe in them.* If you treat students as competent, they are likely to demonstrate competence.

2. *Use "instructional scaffolding."* Instead of worrying about what students do not know, work from what they do know toward what they do not know.

3. *Make instruction the focus of each class.* Avoid busywork. Confront restlessness with an adjustment in instruction rather than a focus on misbehavior.

4. *Extend students' thinking and abilities beyond what they already know.* Provide challenging mathematics for all students, rather than attempting to maintain low levels of performance.

5. *Work at gaining in-depth knowledge of your students as well as knowledge of the subject matter.* Develop a positive identification with all students. Learn to see students of different ethnicities as being like you rather than trying to make minority children "fit in."

Again you notice principles of developmental or constructivist teaching, belief in students, and challenging curriculum. The fifth principle applies to multicultural student populations. It dictates respect for culture, without which the other suggestions may well fail.

# FROM GENDER BIAS TO GENDER EQUITY

Most elementary and middle school teachers are aware of few, if any, differences between boys and girls. Yet when careful comparisons were made over the years, real differences between boys and girls emerged. Elementary school girls have traditionally outperformed boys on standardized tests, although their lead disappears around the seventh grade. By the time of entry to college, many more boys than girls are entering fields of study that include heavy emphases on mathematics and science. Furthermore, there persists a common belief in our society that boys are better than girls at mathematics—what Damarin (1995) refers to as the "maleness of mathematics." In an age in which the ability to reason and solve problems, a knowledge of technology, and competence with general mathematical ideas are all demanded in the workplace, it is more vital than ever that teachers address the issues surrounding gender inequity in mathematics.

## Defining the Problem of Gender Inequity

Three areas of inequity can be examined: differences in achievement, differences in beliefs and attitudes, and differences in representation in mathematics, science, and related careers.

### Achievement

Twenty-five years ago, concern over differences in mathematics achievement between males and females led some observers to suggest that girls were perhaps not as "capable" of doing mathematics as boys. However, research indicated that girls tended to outperform boys until the junior high years, equaled them in early algebra, and began to lag well behind in geometry and beyond. When the range of performance was examined (instead of the average), the top and bottom levels were about the same for males and females. Thus it was not true that girls were outperformed but rather that more boys than girls did well (Burton, 1995).

Further study has indicated that a large part of the differences could be attributed to fewer girls taking mathematics courses in high school. When courses taken is factored into the data, differences diminish. In recent years, gender differences in mathematics achievement have almost disappeared.

Despite that development, two facts remain. First, differences among girls are significantly greater than differences among boys. Many girls for one reason or another are still not achieving well. Second, the perception that boys are better at mathematics remains a seemingly intractable trait of our society. Yet there is no convincing evidence of a biological or genetic basis for gender differences in mathematics achievement.

### Beliefs and Attitudes

The educational system does seem to have an effect on how girls view mathematics. As girls move into the upper grades, they report they like mathematics less and have more self-doubts concerning their personal abilities than boys do. Self-doubts and poor self-concepts concerning mathematics lead to further problems. For example, girls are less likely to persist on challenging tasks than boys are. Weak self-concepts are likely to diminish participation in classroom interactions and group problem solving (Leder, 1995).

Societal norms of the past have another lingering negative effect. In a 1988 study of 9-year-olds, girls were just as likely as boys to say that they were good at mathematics. However, the girls were much less likely to say that mathematics would be useful in their future careers. In general, girls are much more ambivalent concerning the value of mathematics as an occupational prerequisite (Burton, 1995; Leder, 1995). If, as early as age 9, you regard the study of mathematics as irrelevant to your future, this will undoubtedly have an effect on your cognitive efforts and the courses you select at the secondary and college levels.

### Underrepresentation

Choices that students make in terms of coursework and career decisions continue to reflect real differences between the sexes. While it is true girls are taking more mathematics courses than they have in the past, male enrollments continue to be higher in upper-level, more intensive mathematics courses, related applied fields, and occupations requiring mathematical sophistication (Leder, 1995). By opting out of advanced courses in high school, females are effectively excluded from a wide range of college options. Even when the actual mathematics knowledge is not the real issue, mathematics is often used as a filter for entrance into certain demanding career paths. "Equating intelligence with [mathematics] achievement keeps women out of well-paid, high status fields which they would find interesting and exciting and for which they have the talent" (Tyrrell et al., 1994, p. 332). The result has been a substantially unequal distribution of the sexes across careers.

The serious gender gap in upper-level mathematics courses and in career patterns is perhaps the most serious issue in the entire gender equity discussion. With evidence ruling out a genetic difference or the existence of a "math gene," women are still not embarking on career paths that are among the most valuable in today's economy.

## Possible Causes of Gender Inequity

If the problem is not genetic, we should look to the educational system for the causes of gender inequity.

### Teacher Interactions and Gender

Observations of teachers' gender-specific interactions in the classroom indicate that boys get more attention and different kinds of attention than girls do. Boys receive more criticism as well as more praise for correct answers. Boys also tend to be more involved in discipline-related attention and have their work monitored more carefully (Campbell, 1995; Leder, 1995). The increased attention, both positive and negative, that teachers unconsciously provide males contributes to the impression of mathematics as a male domain. Attention is interpreted as value, with a predictable effect on both sexes.

Research has found that teachers wait longer for responses from boys than from girls (Leder, 1995). In one study, females received more wait time on low-level questions concerning facts and procedures, whereas males received longer wait times on more difficult, more challenging, and higher-cognitive questions. Over time, these subtle but real differences suggest to girls that they are not perceived as capable of quality thinking, and they eventually adopt this belief themselves.

## Belief Systems Related to Gender

The belief that mathematics is a male domain persists in our society and is held by both sexes. The "maleness of mathematics" as viewed by males can have negative effects in school. In adolescent years, when girls are significantly interested in and influenced by boys, many girls are afraid to act "too smart" for fear of alienating boys. Campbell (1995) points out that "unless boys as well as girls are convinced that 'real women do math,' efforts toward gender equity in mathematics will encounter obstacles based on stereotyped social roles" (p. 229).

There is evidence that teachers' and parents' erroneous belief that girls can't do math has a transfer effect on girls. It is easy for a mother to reinforce this belief in her daughter and to suggest that it is not important to excel at mathematics "because you're a girl." Teachers and counselors make similar subtle and sometimes not-so-subtle comments that cumulatively convince girls that they are not good at mathematics or that mathematics and science are male domains.

# Working Toward Gender Equity: What Can Be Done?

Campbell (1995) makes a compelling argument that we have tended to address gender inequity as a "girl problem." This places the focus of our solution efforts on girls—to make them somehow like mathematics more or take more courses in mathematics. This approach, she says, makes it seem that there really is something wrong with girls. "If you change a girl so that she 'loves math,' but then you put her back into the same environment and situations that caused her to hate mathematics in the first place, she will revert to hating mathematics" (p. 226). As already noted, the causes of girls' perceptions of themselves vis-à-vis mathematics are largely a function of the educational environment. That is where we should look for solutions.

## Become Aware

Few teachers purposely take gender-specific actions that would have a negative effect on girls, yet many teachers report that even as early as the first grade, if a boy is good at mathematics, it is taken as a reflection of mathematical ability, whereas if a girl excels, it is seen as the result of personal efforts. This differential belief system can be transmitted in the manner that praise is given: "Wow, Mark! You really are showing how smart you are" versus "Margie, I am glad to see how hard you worked on this problem" (Fennema, Peterson, Carpenter, & Lubinski, 1990).

As a teacher, you need to be aware whether you treat boys and girls differently. Work at ensuring equal treatment. Balance the number of questions and overall interactions between boys and girls. A simple approach is to keep a mental tally of girls and boys asked questions. If discipline problems tend to draw more attention to boys, work at being less preoccupied with the boys' disturbances. Instead of reacting to the boys causing trouble, increase your attention to the girls.

Being aware of your gender-specific actions is more difficult than it may sound. To receive feedback, try tape-recording a class or two on a periodic basis. Tally the number of questions asked of boys and girls. Also note which students ask questions and what kind of questions are being asked. At first, you will be surprised at how gender-biased your interaction is. Awareness takes effort.

## Focus on Higher-Level Questioning

Shift from telling to asking. Focus your student interactions on higher-level questioning and problem-solving activities. Take equal interest in the ideas of all students. Especially at the upper grades, it requires extra time to increase questioning and deemphasize telling. When teachers feel this pressure of time and the need to "cover the material," girls are more likely to sense this pressure and avoid asking questions.

Help all children understand, not just those (mostly males) who seek clarification. Instead of asking, "Are there any questions?" address individuals, especially girls: "Sally, do you have any questions?" The latter approach shows interest in the individual and emphasizes your value of understanding over coverage.

## Involve All Students

Find ways to involve all students in your class, not just those who seem eager. Girls tend to shy away from involvement and are not as quick to seek help. The use of physical materials can be a way for all students to be active at the same time and for you to observe the thinking of each student. Cooperative learning groups are another way to encourage involvement. Use mixed-gender groups to avoid gender-oriented competition between groups and to increase boy-girl interactions. Neither suggestion is an automatic solution, however. With physical materials, all students must be required to be active. Similarly, cooperative groups must be continually monitored and evaluated to ensure that all students are participating.

# MATHEMATICS FOR THE GIFTED AND TALENTED

Children who are typically known as "gifted" no doubt deserve consideration in the educational decisions required to provide *all* children the best possible education. Considerable research is available on the education of the gifted but offers little consensus. Alternative views have typically focused on two major questions: What does it mean to be gifted, and should the program for gifted children focus on acceleration or enrichment? In addition, there are practical considerations, not the least of which is how to deliver an appropriate program. Alternatives include pull-out designs, after-school models, and in-class programs. There are also questions of time, teachers, and materials.

## Identification of Mathematically Promising Students

In 1995, NCTM convened the Task Force on the Mathematically Promising to prepare recommendations and draft a policy statement concerning the mathematically talented. The task force preferred to use the term *promising* rather than *gifted* or *talented* because under common definitions of the gifted and talented, many mathematically adept students have been overlooked or excluded. The task force explained that mathematical promise was a function of *ability, motivation, belief,* and *experience or opportunity.* Usiskin (1999) suggests that the vast majority of the population has mathematical promise at birth. He argues that mathematical ability and talent can be nurtured in a large number of students if begun at an early age in school. Students require good teachers, quality curriculum, high expectations, and a supportive environment. With these factors in place, students who *work hard* have a high probability of developing special talents in mathematics. Of course, natural ability is a factor, but the argument is that substantially more people have the ability than make the effort to develop it. With the exception of hard work, the other factors relating to mathematical promise are controlled by schools.

The point that both the task force and Usiskin make is that we must come to understand that mathematical promise or talent is not a matter of heredity. Many Americans tend to believe that children either "have it or they don't," that mathematical ability is a result of the roll of the genetic dice. In contrast, Asians generally believe that success in mathematics, as in any subject, is largely a function of individual effort.

The literature on mathematically promising students suggests that they may not be especially talented in other areas. Nor can mathematical promise be equated with general school achievement or facility with computational algorithms. Promising students generally have good verbal skills, curiosity, imagination, analytic thinking skills, and the ability to concentrate and work independently (House, 1999).

What all of this means for the identification of promising students is that simple criteria built on test scores, IQ, or high grades may exclude those who have a high probability of developing into exceptional mathematical students.

## Acceleration, Enrichment, and Depth

For years, one of the primary debates related to the talented mathematics student was over the relative merits of enrichment versus acceleration. *Acceleration* occurs when students are either placed in a grade ahead of their normal age group or when the pace at which they progress through the regular curriculum is speeded up. *Enrichment* refers to the expansion of the regular curriculum to include additional topics.

### Acceleration and Enrichment

Both merits and cautions are associated with acceleration and enrichment. Capable and promising students should be challenged to move at an appropriate pace through the curriculum and should be exposed to as much quality mathematics as time permits. The NCTM task force chose not to endorse either approach. Acceleration can have the effect of developing a large array of meaningless skills as students are pushed to learn more without exploring the ideas in a full conceptual manner. Even students in the Johns Hopkins University Talent Search for Mathematically Precocious Youth are often moved through textbooks at a fast pace without the chance to explore, extend, and enjoy the mathematics they are learning. Without adequate time, the guidance of a skilled teacher, and the benefit of directed discourse and exploration, students in acceleration programs tend to focus on mechanical skills. This will often be the case as well when students are left to study independently.

Too often enrichment programs result in little more than "fun math time" with topics such as geometric puzzles, computer games, or the "problem of the day." Although good mathematics activities should be fun, they should accomplish much more. They should broaden students' mathematical horizons, require students to think deeply, make connections to earlier ideas and to real contexts, and challenge them to ask questions, make conjectures, and reason about important ideas.

### The Addition of Depth

Recognizing the strengths and pitfalls of enrichment and acceleration, Sheffield (1999) argues for a three-dimensional approach: breadth (enrichment), rate (acceleration), and depth or complexity. That is, the benefits of both acceleration and enrichment should be coupled with the opportunity for studying the complexities of new mathematical ideas, both those in the regular curriculum and those that go beyond it. Sheffield writes that promising students should be introduced to the "joys and frustrations of thinking deeply about a wide range of original, open-ended, or complex problems that encourage them to respond creatively in ways that are original, fluent, flexible, and elegant" (p. 46).

In the regular classroom, teachers often "reward" highly capable students for finishing routine tasks quickly by having them do more exercises or more tedious exercises than those required of the rest of the class. For example, if the full class is working on the multiplication algorithm for multidigit numbers, there is no redeeming value in having promising students who complete their work quickly do more exercises or exercises with more digits. However, they may be asked what would produce the largest or smallest products given four distinct digits to make two factors. Is there a general rule? Why does the rule work? What if there were five digits?

Even more interesting than the max/min task is that for some products, interchanging the digits in each two-digit factor produces the same result:

$$
\begin{array}{cc}
24 & 42 \\
\times\,63 & \times\,36 \\
\hline
1512 & 1512
\end{array}
$$

However, this is obviously not always the case, as a little experimentation will quickly show. When will this interchanging of the digits produce equal products and why? Students working on tasks such as these are engaged in a deeper exploration of the multiplication algorithm than simply understanding how it works and being able to use it.

## The Open-Ended Approach

There is no simple formula for adding depth to mathematical explorations, but some valuable insights may be learned from the Japanese. According to Hashimoto and Becker (1999), the Japanese approach to mathematical problem solving involves making the problem open in one of three ways: the process is open (multiple paths to a solution are explored), the end product is open (there are multiple correct answers to be discovered), or the formulation of new problems is open (students explore new problems related to the one solved). Here is an example of each form of open problem:

### OPEN PROCESS

**Figure 23.2 shows a box of chocolates with some removed. How many chocolates are in the box?**

Of course, the chocolates can be counted one by one. Another method is to note that there are three rows of six and two rows of three ($3 \times 6 + 2 \times 3$). Can you find three or four additional ways to count the chocolates?

### OPEN END PRODUCT

**Given a collection of quite varied geometric shapes, select one. Describe a rule by which some of the other shapes are like the one you selected.**

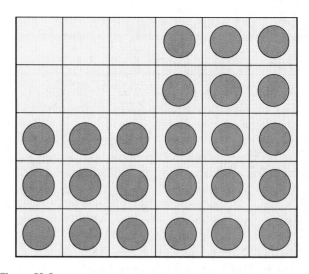

**Figure 23.2**   **This box of chocolates has some removed. How many chocolates remain in the box? How many ways can you find to get the answer?**

For example, if the figure selected were a trapezoid with two right angles, other shapes might be selected that had a pair of parallel sides. Another rule might be that the shape must have exactly two (or at least two) right angles. What other rules can you imagine for this shape?

### OPEN QUESTION

**There are four butterflies on the flower. If three more join them, how many butterflies are there altogether?**

For this primary grade problem, Hashimoto and Becker suggest these possible ways to alter the question:

- Change the number of butterflies.
- Change the objects to something other than butterflies.
- Make the problem into a subtraction problem.

These three approaches to open-ended problem solving are explored in depth in *The Open-Ended Approach: A New Proposal for Teaching Mathematics* (Becker & Shimada, 1997). The authors are not at all suggesting that these are methods to be used only with promising students. On the contrary, these are good ways to challenge *all* students. In fact, many of the tasks found throughout this book are either already open in one of these ways or can be enriched in at least one of the ways suggested here. However, application of the open-ended methods is an excellent way to add depth to both acceleration and enrichment for special students.

# REFLECTIONS ON CHAPTER 23

## Writing to Learn

1. What traditional ideas about curriculum and teaching children must be changed so that the NCTM vision of all children learning mathematics can be realized?

2. How would you argue for the values of a diverse class that includes children with learning problems? That is, what are some of the benefits of including these students in the regular classroom?

3. Briefly describe each of the following specific learning disabilities, and give some indication of how the disability may affect mathematics learning or ability. For each disability, also list at least two ideas that can be used by the classroom teacher to help the child.

   a. Perceptual deficits (figure-ground, discrimination, reversal, spatial)

   b. Memory deficits (short-term and long-term)

   c. Integrative deficits

   d. Attention deficits

4. For children with mental deficits (low-ability students, slow learners), how should content and instruction each be modified?

5. Explain how teacher expectations and tracking have detrimental effects on minorities and low-SES children.

6. Describe in general terms one or more of the most significant ideas that should guide the teacher who is working with students from a cultural minority.

7. What are some factors that contribute to gender inequity, and what are the long-term effects of that inequity?

8. How can teachers in the elementary or middle school work to erase gender inequity?

9. Describe what is meant by enrichment and by acceleration. What are the dangers of each for mathematically promising students?

10. In the context of providing for the mathematically promising, what is meant by depth? How can the Japanese open-ended approaches help provide depth?

## For Discussion and Exploration

1. Two common threads in this chapter are the beliefs that all children will benefit from a developmental or constructivist approach to teaching and that there is real value in teaching children in diverse, heterogeneous classrooms. Some teachers may argue with this position, contending that it is best for the majority of children if "special needs" students are isolated. And besides, the argument continues, their special needs are best met by special teachers in classes with fewer students. Pick a position in this argument, and articulate it in writing or in a classroom discussion.

2. In the discussion of multicultural equity, there was no mention of two ideas that are sometimes discussed in the literature. One

is that students should be exposed to mathematics topics that reflect and honor the cultural heritage of ethnic students. This is a matter of *cultural infusion*. For example, examine the African strategy game of Kalah or the geometry of Native American art. The other idea is that instruction for African Americans should be modified to reflect their particular cognitive learning styles, usually described as "field-dependent" and "global." The learning style argument is also applied to gender differences. How do you feel about either or both of these positions? (You may wish to consult Carey et al., 1995; Downs et al., 1994; or Marolda & Davidson, 1994, for some perspective on these issues.)

3. Based on your personal experiences, do you believe there is a gender problem in mathematics education? Cite some experiences that support your position. What do you think the situation is like today?

4. What would you do if you found yourself teaching a class with one exceptionally talented child who had no equal in the room? Assume that acceleration to the next grade has been ruled out due to social adjustment factors.

## Recommendations for Further Reading

### Highly Recommended

Malloy, C. E., & Brader-Araje, L. (Eds.). (1998). *Challenges of the mathematics education of African American children: Proceedings of the Benjamin Banneker Association leadership conference.* Reston, VA: National Council of Teachers of Mathematics.

The Benjamin Banneker Association is an organization concerned with the mathematics education of African American children. These proceedings of a 1997 conference include six presentations by leaders in the field plus a number of other short papers. They constitute a useful collection of informed perspectives on a subject of great concern for all.

Secada, W. G., Fennema, E., & Adajian, L. B. (Eds.). (1995). *New directions for equity in mathematics education.* New York: Cambridge University Press.

The editors, long known for their research in this field, have assembled one of the best collections of essays to date on the issues of equity. An extremely readable book.

Sheffield, L. J. (Ed.). (1999). *Developing mathematically promising students.* Reston, VA: National Council of Teachers of Mathematics.

This book is the result of a recommendation to NCTM from the Task Force on Mathematically Promising Students. The book is a wealth of ideas and perspectives for working with our most talented students. Rather than the more simplistic approach of NCTM's earlier booklet on teaching the gifted, this book adds depth to any discussion of mathematics for the talented.

Thornton, C. A., & Bley, N. S. (Eds.). (1994). *Windows of opportunity: Mathematics for students with special needs.* Reston, VA: National Council of Teachers of Mathematics.

There are very few books that even attempt to address the issues of special-needs children and mathematics. (NCTM is working on a new book that should be out soon.). Thornton and Bley have put together an excellent book that could be a methods text or a resource for the classroom teacher, consisting of seven chapters on issues, eight that address content through perspective and vignettes, and six that look at promising practices. This book will remain a valuable resource even after the next special-needs book is published.

Trentacosta, J. (Ed.). (1997). *Multicultural and gender equity in the mathematics classroom: The gift of diversity.* Reston, VA: National Council of Teachers of Mathematics.

One of NCTM's finest yearbooks. Numerous articles address virtually every aspect of diversity, including African Americans and other ethnicities, gender, and ethnomathematics.

## Other Suggestions

Bley, N. S., & Thornton, C. A. (1995). *Teaching mathematics to students with learning disabilities* (3rd ed.). Austin, TX: Pro-Ed.

Campbell, P. F. (1996). Empowering children and teachers in the elementary mathematics classrooms of urban schools. *Urban Education, 30,* 449–475.

Cuevas, G., & Driscol, M. (Eds.). (1993). *Reaching all students with mathematics.* Reston, VA: National Council of Teachers of Mathematics.

Education Development Center. (1995). *Equity in education series: Gender-fair math.* Newton, MA: Author.

Edwards, C. A. (1999). *Changing the faces of mathematics: Perspectives on Asian Americans and Pacific islanders.* Reston, VA: National Council of Teachers of Mathematics.

Garrison, L. (1997). Making the NCTM's standards work for emergent English speakers. *Teaching Children Mathematics, 4,* 132–138.

Griffiths, R., & Clyne, M. (1994). *Language in the mathematics classroom: Talking, representing, recording.* Portsmouth, NH: Heinemann.

Hilliard, A. G., III. (1995). Mathematics excellence for cultural "minority" students: What is the problem? In I. M. Carl (Ed.), *Seventy-five years of progress: Prospects for school mathematics* (pp. 99–114). Reston, VA: National Council of Teachers of Mathematics.

Karp, K., Allen, C., Allen, L. G., & Brown, E. T. (1998). Feisty females: Using children's literature with strong female characters. *Teaching Children Mathematics, 5,* 88–94.

Karp, K., Brown, E. T., Allen, L. G., & Allen, C. (1998). *Feisty females: Inspiring girls to think mathematically.* Portsmouth, NH: Heinemann.

Ladson-Billings, G. (1997). It doesn't add up: African-American students' mathematics achievement. *Journal for Research in Mathematics Education, 28,* 697–708.

Litton, N. (1998). *Getting your math message out to parents: A K–6 resource.* Sausalito, CA: Math Solutions Publications.

Mills, H., O'Keefe, T., & Whitin, D. J. (1996). *Mathematics in the making: Authoring ideas in primary classrooms.* Portsmouth, NH: Heinemann.

Oakes, J. (1995). Opportunity to learn: Can standards-based reform be equity-based reform? In I. M. Carl (Ed.), *Seventy-five years of progress: Prospects for school mathematics* (pp. 78–98). Reston, VA: National Council of Teachers of Mathematics.

Ortiz-Franco, L., Hernandez, N. G., & De la Cruz, Y. (Eds.). (1999). *Changing the faces of mathematics: Perspectives on Latinos.* Reston, VA: National Council of Teachers of Mathematics.

Rowser, J. F., & Koontz, T. Y. (1995). Inclusion of African-American students in mathematics classrooms: Issues of style, curriculum, and expectations. *Mathematics Teacher, 88,* 448–453.

Silver, E. A., & Stein, M. K. (1996). The QUASAR project: The "revolution of the possible" in mathematics instructional reform in urban middle schools. *Urban Education, 30,* 476–521.

Tate, W. F. (1997). Race-ethnicity, SES, gender, and language proficiency trends in mathematics achievement: An update. *Journal for Research in Mathematics Education, 28,* 652–679.

Tobias, R. (1992). *Nurturing at-risk youth in math and science: Curriculum and teaching considerations.* Bloomington, IN: National Education Service.

Toney, N. L. (1996). Facing racism in mathematics education. In D. Schifter (Ed.), *What's happening in math class? Reconstructing professional identities* (Vol. 2, pp. 26–36). New York: Teachers College Press.

# Chapter 24

# Technology and School Mathematics

*Rapid developments in technology are changing (and ought to be changing) the way we teach mathematics both because they modify our goals for the mathematics education of people and because they provide new tools with which we can better achieve our goals.*

Willoughby (1990, p. 60)

The term *technology* in the context of school mathematics can refer to everything from simple four-function calculators to video, computers, and the Internet. Technology is so pervasive in our society that it is assumed that children will learn to use technology in schools and that technology will be available to help them learn better. But we should not let the attractiveness of technology blind us to the fact that the fundamental mathematics that students will need in tomorrow's society must be our foremost consideration. Technology must enhance the mathematics students learn. Technology should never be a replacement for good mathematics, nor should it become an end in itself.

To highlight its importance, the authors of *Principles and Standards for School Mathematics* made Technology one of its six principles (see Chapter 1). In 1998, NCTM issued a position statement on technology that begins: "The appropriate use of instructional technology tools is integral to the learning and teaching of mathematics and to the assessment of mathematics learning at all levels" (p. 17).

Calculators and computer software are highlighted throughout Section 2 of this text, with references to specific activities and programs where they are appropriate. The purpose of this chapter is to examine technology and the teaching of mathematics in a more general way that you will be able to make informed judgments about the use of technology in your classroom.

## TECHNOLOGY'S THREEFOLD IMPACT ON MATHEMATICS EDUCATION

Calculators and computers have a profound impact on what mathematics we teach to students as well as the manner in which it is taught. First, some mathematics we used to teach has been made essentially obsolete because of technology. Second, much of the mathematics we teach we can teach better with technology. And third, many topics that we were unable to teach before can now be made accessible to students in meaningful ways.

## Less Important or Obsolete Mathematics

Much of the mathematics that we used to teach has been supplanted by technology. The most obvious example is pencil-and-paper computation, the importance of which has been diminished considerably by the wide availability of calculators. Even most critics of the reform movement would agree that there is no longer any need for drill involving tedious computations. Computational skills remain important, but they should be flexible and helpful to the situation at hand.

Another area where less time need be spent is the techniques of constructing graphs for data analysis. Thanks to computer graphing software and spreadsheets, the tedious by-hand techniques for making charts and graphs have become extraneous, even in the lower grades. This means

465

that emphasis in the classroom can be shifted to the question of which type of graph will best answer and communicate questions about the data. Multiple representations are quickly made, adjusted, and compared with little or no class time wasted in deciding on scales or color schemes.

In the upper grades, graphing calculators and other function graphers make learning to plot points and draw function graphs much less important than in the past. Once students understand how graphs of functions come to be, technology is the best way to create those graphs.

Despite the obsolescence of the *mechanics* of mathematics, it is essential to recognize that mastery of basic facts and flexible methods of computation are just as important as ever, perhaps even more so. Computational fluency is a significant tool for making sense of the world and for mathematical problem solving. Tedious computational drills do not make anyone a better mathematical thinker. Long division with a three-digit divisor should be left to the calculator.

## Better-Taught Mathematics

Whenever technology is used, it should add something to the way students interact with the mathematics involved. There is almost no defense for using technology to do something in mathematics just to say you used technology. But many things we do with technology dramatically improve students' understanding of underlying concepts.

One of the most striking examples of mathematics taught better at the elementary level is the ability to examine real problems with real numbers. This takes problem solving into the real world without the use of artificial constructs. There is no need for answers to "come out even" or to use unrealistic numbers just to ensure that students can compute. Problem solving is further enhanced by removing the distractions of tedious computations, which in the past were so laborious that students often lost sight of the essential features of problems or why they were computing in the first place.

Calculators help very young children learn to count, to skip-count, to practice mental math, and to search for patterns. Connections between decimals and common fractions are clearly enhanced by calculators that permit conversions between these forms.

Geometry is an area where technology has had a dramatic impact. Students with poor motor skills can now assemble beautiful patterns with colorful tiles. Rotation and reflection transformations are easily made, modified, and explored. Dynamic geometry programs such as *The Geometer's Sketchpad* or *Geometry Inventor,* once tools for high school, are now finding increasing use in grades 4–8. These and other geometric tools allow students to explore geometric ideas rather than rely on static drawings and memorize definitions.

Computer versions of some manipulative materials such as base-ten blocks, fractional pie pieces, or fraction strips have the potential for adding to what these same materials can do in their physical modes. Care must be used to ensure that the slick presentations on the computer screen are really enhancing the opportunity to learn. With many programs, the computer does an excellent job of "showing" conceptual ideas. However, these programs often offer little that is problematic for students. As a teaching technique, show and tell is no more effective when done by a computer than when done by a teacher.

## More Accessible Mathematics

Perhaps the most dramatic examples of technology opening mathematical doors for students are found at the high school level. There technology has the potential of radically altering the curriculum to include many topics that were simply not available to students without technology. For example, with only a graphing calculator, polynomials and rational functions of any degree can be explored as easily as a simple quadratic. Computer algebra systems—now found on the TI-92—perform complex symbolic manipulations instantly, making concepts once difficult to work with at the college level now accessible in high school.

At the K–5 level, the enhancement of some topics has been dramatic. We have already discussed the improvement in data analysis, permitting students to explore how a graph helps makes sense of data rather than simply learning how to make the graph. Probability experiments can now be done with thousands of trials, making it possible for students to understand how chance occurrences approach theoretical values in the long run.

The graphing calculator makes it possible for middle school students to explore a wide variety of functions and their corresponding graphical representations. It is as easy to graph $y = 345.39x^2 - 72.3$ as it is to graph $y = 3x + 2$. Calculators and computers can be used to find equations of functions that approximate scatter plots of real data. The wealth of geometric relationships that students can explore with dynamic geometry software is amazing.

# CALCULATORS IN THE MATHEMATICS CLASSROOM

Mathematics educators have long understood the value of calculators in the study of mathematics. In 1976, NCTM published a special issue of *The Arithmetic Teacher* devoted to the use of calculators. Since then, there have been other focus issues, a series of position statements, the 1989 *Curriculum and Evaluation Standards,* an NCTM yearbook (Fey, 1992), and now *Principles and Standards for School Mathematics,* all advocating the regular use of calculators in the teaching of mathematics at all grade levels.

The everyday use of calculators in society, coupled with professional support of calculators in schools, has had a muted impact on the mathematics classroom, especially at the elementary level. Resistance to the use of calculators has diminished but not disappeared. The vocal minority of detractors to the reform movement often assail the use of calculators as "dumbing down" the curriculum or as a "crutch." Their inflammatory rhetoric often resonates with parents, who want what is best for their children. Parents must be made aware of the fact that calculator use will in no way prevent Johnny or Jenny from learning mathematics; in fact, calculators make *learning* much easier.

## Benefits of Calculator Use

Rather than fearing potential damage that calculators might do, it is important to understand how calculators can contribute to the learning of mathematics. In this section, we focus on simple calculators, reserving discussion of graphing calculators for later.

### Calculators Can Be Used to Develop Concepts

The calculator can be much more than a device for calculation. Activities for teaching with the calculator have been suggested throughout the book, especially in the areas of numeration and computation. Here are a few more activities that illustrate this point.

---

**ACTIVITY**

### 24.1 And the Remainder Is . . .

Consider the fact that 796 ÷ 42 = 18.95238. The students' task is to find a method for determining the whole-number remainder with a simple four-function calculator. (Some calculators have an integer division key that provides the remainder.)

---

In Chapter 7, Activity 7.6 (p. 122) asked students to find the quotient without using the division key. A repeated subtraction or repeated addition method provides possible solutions to that task, and each will give the remainder. In Activity 24.1, the challenge is to use the result in some way to determine the remainder. One solution uses the whole-number part, 18. The other uses the decimal part (0.95238). In discussions where students invent and defend these solutions, a greater understanding of division will certainly result.

---

**ACTIVITY**

### 24.2 Too Hard for the Calculator?

Find a way to use the calculator to compute the product of two numbers such as 3456 and 88,888. When this product is entered on a simple calculator, the result is too large and results in an overload.

---

Solutions to Activity 24.2 require students to use place-value concepts and take numbers apart in creative ways. Not only does this help students explore numeration concepts, but the methods of taking numbers apart and recombining them are also fundamental to mental computation techniques.

---

**ACTIVITY**

### 24.3 Numbers in Between

Quickly review with students that a number can be multiplied by itself by pressing the number followed by ⊠ ⊟. For example, 4 ⊠ ⊟ produces 16. The task is to determine what number multiplied by itself will give 43. Students in about the third grade will quickly discover that 6 is too small and 7 is too large. What is needed is a number *between* 6 and 7. For students who have not yet experienced decimal numbers or are just learning about them, suggest numbers such as 6.1, 6.2, . . . , 6.9, explaining that these numbers are between 6 and 7.

---

Students exploring with "Numbers in Between" will begin to think of decimals in the same way they think of fractions. Further, the activity helps students understand that each successive decimal place is a subdivision of the preceding position value.

Algebraic reasoning involves searching for and describing patterns in all types of situations. The following activity provides an open-ended search for patterns. There are numerous interesting patterns to be found.

---

**ACTIVITY**

### 24.4 Keypad Partner Numbers

Define a *keypad partner number* (KPN) as a two-digit number than can be entered on a calculator by pressing two adjacent keys, either vertically, horizontally, or diagonally in any direction. Examples of KPNs are 63, 12, 21, and 48. The numbers 73 and 28 are not KPNs. The initial task is to find two different pairs of KPNs that have the same sum (for example, 32 + 65 = 62 + 35). After some pairs with the same sum are found, try to find some pattern or generalization about KPNs with like sums. Challenge students to explain why their patterns work. Instead of sums, look for common differences.

---

It is surprising how many different ideas students can discover with patterns on the calculator, especially if they work in groups. Ideas that rely on place value include looking at the sum of the digits and examination of the addition algorithm. Students sometimes draw pictures of the keypad and discover relationships involving the spatial configurations of the keys.

## Calculators Can Be Used to Practice Skills

The calculator is an excellent drill-and-practice device that requires no computer or software. For example, students who want to practice the multiples of 7 can press 7 ☒ 3 and delay pressing the ☐. The challenge is to answer the fact to themselves before pressing the ☐ key. Subsequent multiples of 7 can be checked by simply pressing the second factor and the ☐. In Chapter 11, activities with the calculator were suggested for developing mental computation and estimation skills.

A class can be split in half with one half required to use a calculator and the other required to do the computations mentally. For 3000 + 1765, the mental group wins every time. It will also win for simple facts and numerous problems that lend themselves to mental computation. Of course, there are many computations, such as 537 × 32, where the calculator is preferred and that side will win. Not only does this simple exercise provide practice with mental math, but it also demonstrates to students that it is not always appropriate to reach for the calculator.

## Calculators Enhance Problem Solving

As noted, the mechanics of computation can often distract students' attention from the meaning of the problem they are working on. As students come to understand the meanings of the operations, they should be exposed to realistic problems with realistic numbers. The numbers may be beyond their abilities to compute, but the calculator makes these realistic problems accessible.

## Calculators Help Improve Student Attitudes

The overwhelming conclusion of numerous research studies is that students' attitudes toward mathematics are better in classrooms where calculators are used than where they are not (Hembree & Dessart, 1986; Reys & Reys, 1987). Students using calculators tend to be confident and persistent in solving problems. Although these studies are old, there is no reason to believe they are less valid today.

## Calculators Save Time

By-hand computation is time-consuming, especially for young students who have not developed a high degree of mastery. Why should time be wasted having students add numbers to find the perimeter of a polygon? Why compute averages, find percents, convert fractions to decimals, or solve problems of any sort with pencil-and-paper methods when computation skills are not the objective of the lesson?

## Calculators Are Commonly Used in Society

Nowadays, almost everyone uses calculators in every facet of life that involves any sort of exact computation—everyone except schoolchildren. It is only logical that students be taught how to use this commonplace tool effectively. Many adults have not learned how to use the automatic constant feature of a calculator and are not practiced in recognizing gross errors that are often made on calculators. Effective use of calculators is an important skill that is best learned by using them regularly and meaningfully.

# Addressing Myths and Fears About Using Calculators

The lingering opposition to calculators is largely based on misinformation. Myths and fears about students not learning because of using calculators still persist, even in the face of evidence to the contrary.

## Myth: If Kids Use Calculators, They Won't Learn the "Basics"

Every advocate of calculator use must make it clear to parents that basic fact mastery and flexible computational skills, including mental computation, remain important goals of the curriculum. Research has demonstrated that the availability of calculators has no negative effect on traditional skills. Most important, the ability to perform tedious by-hand computations does not involve thinking or reasoning or solving problems. Employers want employees who can think and solve novel problems. They should know when it is appropriate to use technology and how to use it effectively.

## Myth: Calculators Make Students Lazy

Almost no mathematical thinking is involved in doing routine computations by hand. People who use calculators when solving problems are therefore using their intellect in more important ways—reasoning, conjecturing, testing ideas, and solving problems. When used appropriately, calculators enhance learning; they do not get in the way of learning.

## Myth: Students Should Learn the "Real Way" Before Using Calculators

Following rules for pencil-and-paper computation does little to help students understand the ideas behind them. A glaring example is the invert-and-multiply method for division of fractions. Few parents and not even all elementary teachers can explain why this method makes sense. And yet they all had extensive practice with that technique. The same is true of nearly all computational procedures, to one degree or another.

It is essential to point out that by-hand techniques are not to be totally abandoned and that introductory explorations are often best done without a calculator. The teacher must play a role in setting the necessary explorations in the classroom. The calculator should never replace understanding!

## Myth: Students Will Become Overly Dependent on Calculators

Calculators kept from students are like forbidden fruit. When finally allowed to use them, students often use them for the simplest of tasks. Teachers in the upper grades often complain that students are using their calculators all the time.

It is essential that mastery of basic facts, mental computation, and some attention to by-hand techniques continue to be requirements for all students. In lessons where these skills are the objective, the calculator should simply be off limits. When students learn these essential noncalculator skills, they rarely use the calculator inappropriately. Further, if the calculator is always available for appropriate uses, students learn when and how to use it wisely.

## Calculators for Every Student, Every Day

*Calculators should be in or on student's desks at all times from kindergarten through high school.* This position may seem radical to some people, but we should give it serious consideration. In addition to the benefits already described, here are a few arguments in favor of calculator access at all times:

- First and foremost, it does no harm. Any teacher can conduct an activity or pose tasks in which calculators are set off limits. Availability of calculators does not detract from the development of basic skills.

- Many excellent explorations that happen spontaneously in a problem-solving environment will be enhanced by the use of calculators. Students should not have to leave their desks or ask permission to use a calculator when solving a problem. Stopping the flow of a lesson to pass out calculators detracts from the learning process.

- When calculators are kept from students, they tend to be used for special "calculator lessons," promoting the student belief that calculators are not common tools for solving problems.

- Students must learn to make wise choices about when to use calculators—for tedious computations—and when to use mental math—for simple computations and estimations. They learn this only by making such choices independently and on a regular basis.

# GRAPHING CALCULATORS

The graphing calculator, once thought useful only in high school, is so important to middle school mathematics that it deserves some special attention. Today, a graphing calculator makes sense for all middle school students. Cost is still a possible deterrent. Several models are available for under $75, less than the cost of a pair of sneakers or a few CDs. A calculator purchased in the sixth grade may be the only one the student will need through high school. A school can purchase a classroom set for less than the price of a single computer.

## What the Graphing Calculator Offers

It is a mistake to think that graphing calculators are only for doing "high-powered" mathematics usually studied by honors students in high school. Here is a list of some features the graphing calculator offers, every one of which is useful within the standard middle school curriculum.

- The display window permits compound expressions such as $3 + 4(5 - 6/7)$ to be shown completely before being evaluated. Further, once evaluated, previous expressions can be recalled and modified. This promotes an understanding of notation and order of operations. The device is also a significant tool for exploring patterns and solving problems. Expressions can include exponents, absolute values, and negation signs, with no restrictions on the values used.

- Even without using function definition capability, students can insert values into expressions or formulas without having to enter the entire formula for each new value. The results can be entered into a list or table of values and stored directly on the calculator for further analysis.

- Variables can be used in expressions and then assigned different values to see the effect on expressions. This simple method helps with the idea of a variable as something that varies.

- The distinction between "negative" and "minus" is clear and very useful. A separate key is used to enter the negative of a quantity. The display shows the negative sign as a superscript. If $^-5$ is stored in the variable B, then the expression $^-2 - {}^-B$ will be evaluated correctly as $^-7$. This feature is a significant aid in the study of integers and variables.

- Points can be plotted on a coordinate screen either by entering coordinates and seeing the result or by moving the cursor to a particular coordinate on the screen.

- Very large and very small numbers are managed without error. The calculator will quickly compute factorials, even for large numbers, as well as permutations and combinations. Graphing calculators use scientific notation so that large and small numbers do not result in error statements. For example, $23! = 1.033314797 \times 10^{40}$.

- Built-in statistical functions allow students to examine the means, medians, and standard deviations of large sets of realistic data without a computer. Data are easily entered, ordered, added to, or changed almost as easily as on a spreadsheet.

- Graphs for data analysis are available, including box-and-whisker plots, histograms, and, on some calculators, pie charts, bar graphs, and pictographs.

- Random number generators allow for the simulation of a variety of probability experiments that would be difficult without such a device.

- Scatter plots for ordered pairs of real data can be entered, plotted, and examined for trends. The calculator will calculate the equations of best-fit linear, quadratic, cubic, or logarithmic functions.

- Functions can be explored in three of the five modes discussed in Chapter 20: equation, table, and graph. Because the calculator easily switches from one to the other and because of the trace feature, the connections between these modes become quite clear. Even seventh-grade students can explore a variety of types of functions along with their graphs and function tables. There is no need to wait until high school to let students explore how the $m$ and $b$ in $y = mx + b$ affect the graph.

- The graphing calculator is programmable. Programs are very easily written and understood. For example, a program involving the Pythagorean theorem can be used to find the length of sides of right triangles.

- Data, programs, and functions can be shared from one graphing calculator to another and thus to the display calculator for the overhead or TV monitor. This permits students to share and discuss work with the rest of the class. Calculators also connect to computers to store data and programs and to print out anything that can be seen on the calculator screen.

Most of the ideas on this list have been explored briefly in appropriate chapters in this book.

Arguments against graphing calculators are similar to those for other calculators—and are equally hollow and unsubstantiated. These amazing tools have the potential of significantly opening up real mathematics for students. It is time that graphing calculators became a regular tool in the middle grades.

## Electronic Data Collection

In addition to the capabilities of the graphing calculator alone, electronic data collection devices make them even more remarkable. Texas Instruments calls its version the CBL (for *computer-based laboratory*), and such calculators are often referred to by that acronym. The Casio version is called the EA-100 and is nearly identical in design. These devices accept a variety of data collection probes, such as temperature or light sensors and motion detectors, that can be used to gather real physical data. The data can be transferred to the graphing calculator, where it is stored in one or more lists. The calculator can then produce scatter plots or prepare other analyses.

A number of excellent resource books are available that describe experiments in detail. Most include disks with calculator programs that make the interface with the CBL quite easy. With a CBL, science and mathematics meet head-on.

The most popular probe for mathematics teachers is the motion detector. Texas Instruments has a special motion detector called a Ranger or CBR that connects directly to the calculator without requiring a CBL unit. Experiments with a motion detector include analysis of objects rolling down an incline, bouncing balls, or swinging pendulums. The motion actually determines the distance an object is from the sensor. When distance is plotted against time, the graph shows velocity. Students can plot their own motion walking toward or away from the detector. The concept of rate when interpreted as the slope of a distance-to-time curve can become quite dramatic.

Chapter 20 includes an example of a CBL activity. Further details on the use of these devices are beyond the scope of this text.

# THE COMPUTER AS A TOOL IN MATHEMATICS

*Tool software* is a generic term for software that performs a function that makes doing something easier. The most common tool software is the word processor. Other popular tools include spreadsheets, databases, and presentation software such as *PowerPoint*. A number of powerful tools have been created for use in the mathematics classroom. A mathematical software tool is somewhat like a physical manipulative; by itself, it does not teach. However, the user of a well-designed tool software package has an electronic "thinker toy" with which to explore mathematical ideas.

The sections that follow each describe, in general terms, types of tool software that now exist. No attempt is made to describe specific software titles in any detail. Representative programs are mentioned.

## Electronic Manipulatives for Numeration

Most tool software for grades K–4 falls in this category. In these programs, screen versions of popular manipulative models are available for students to work with freely without the computer posing problems, evaluating results, or telling the students what to do.

At the earliest level, there are programs that provide "counters" such as colored tiles, pictures of assorted objects, or in one specific case, Unifix cubes. Typically, students can drag counters to any place on the screen, change the colors, and put them in groupings. Some programs have options that turn on counters for the screen or subsets of the screen. In *Unifix Software* (Hickey, 1996), each bar of cubes can have a label indicating the number of cubes in the bar. Another option is for the screen or sections of the screen to indicate the total cubes in that section. Nonmathematical programs such as *Kid Pix* (Learning Company, 1999) can also be used to "stamp" discrete objects on the screen.

Base-ten blocks and assorted fraction pieces are available in some software packages. Usually these are not pure tool programs but have other components that would fall into the category of instructional software—programs that attempt to teach or tutor. Some fraction models are more flexible than physical models. For example, a circular region might be subdivided into many more fractional parts than is reasonable with physical models. When the models are connected with on-screen counters, it is possible with some programs to have fraction or decimal representations shown so that connections between fractions and decimals can be illustrated. So far, no tools for base-ten models or fraction models have been produced that are completely open to student use without some constraints. For example, in *MathKeys: Unlocking Whole Numbers, Grades 3–5* (MECC, 1995b), pieces can be combined or taken apart only by adding or subtracting two quantities. Other programs impose similar constraints.

Another numeration tool found combined with other features on some programs is a hundreds board. Students can color in squares with the click of a mouse and search for patterns.

The obvious question is, Why not simply use the actual physical models? When selecting these computer tools, there should always be some clear advantage to using the computer versions. The following are features or characteristics that may make these programs a worthwhile addition to your classroom. Not every program offers all of these features.

- *Freedom of manipulation.* Is it at least as easy to use the screen manipulative as it would be to use the physical version? Students should be allowed to use the models in their own way without undue guidance or feedback from the computer.
- *Connection with symbolism.* In what way are symbols attached to the models? Can the symbolism be turned on and off? Are there a variety of options?
- *Journal capability.* Many programs offer a space at the bottom of the screen where students can write about their work. Teachers may be able to use this same space to present problems that students then solve.
- *Print and save capabilities.* How easy is it for students to print a picture of their work? Can they easily save their work and return to it later? (This is unusual in most programs of this type.)

## Geometry Tools

Computer tools for geometric exploration are much closer to pure tools than those just described for numeration. That is, students can use most of these tools without any constraints.

They typically offer some significant advantages over physical models, although the computerized tools should never replace physical models in the classroom.

### Blocks and Tiles

Programs that allow students to "stamp" geometric tiles or blocks on the screen are quite common. Typically, there is a palette of blocks, often the same as pattern blocks or tangrams, from which students can choose by clicking the mouse. Often the blocks can be made "magnetic" so that when they are released close to another block, the two will snap together, matching like sides. Blocks can usually be rotated, either freely or in set increments. Different programs offer different variations and features. You may find the following:

- The ability to enlarge or reduce the size of blocks, usually by set increments
- The ability to "glue" blocks together to make new blocks
- The ability to reflect one or more blocks across a mirror line or to rotate them about a point
- Puzzle tasks built into the program
- The ability to measure area or perimeters
- The ability to select polygons with a variable number of sides
- The possibility of creating three-dimensional shapes and rotating them in space

In addition to these features, the presence of a journal or other space for writing is worth looking for, as with other tools. Print and save options are also important. With real blocks, the design is gone when the blocks are returned to the bucket. For students who have poor motor coordination or a physical disability that makes block manipulation difficult, the computer versions of blocks are a real plus. Colorful printouts can be displayed, discussed, and taken home.

### Drawing Programs

For younger students, drawing shapes on a grid is much easier and more useful for geometric exploration than free-form drawing. Several programs offer electronic geoboards on which lines can be drawn between points on a grid. When a shape such as a triangle is formed, it can typically be altered just as you would a rubber band on a geoboard. The electronic geoboard programs offer a larger grid on which to draw, ease of use, and the ability to save and print. Some include measuring capabilities as well as reflection and rotation of shapes, things that are difficult or impossible to do on a physical geoboard.

Although not restricted to drawing figures, Logo programs are a distinctly different way to draw shapes on the computer. Logo is essentially a computer programming language. Commands are used to direct a small "turtle" around the screen. The turtle can move only in straight lines, either forward or backward. It can turn to the left or right any number of degrees. As described in Chapter 17, Logo challenges students with a unique perspective on shape. Rather than having students think only about what a shape looks like, Logo demands that they think about the components of shapes and their orientation in the plane. This brief description of Logo is a gross oversimplification of an extremely powerful computer programming language.

### Dynamic Geometry Software

Dynamic geometry programs are much more than simple drawing packages. These exciting programs allow students to create shapes on the computer screen and then manipulate and measure them by dragging vertices. Relationships between lines and shapes once created are always preserved. Originally designed for the high school, there is now good reason for these programs to be a part of the classroom at least by grade 5. More detailed discussion of these programs can be found in Chapter 17. An example of a dynamic geometry exploration is shown in Figure 24.1. There the midpoints of a freely formed quadrilateral are joined. Subsequent drawings show the same figure after the vertices have been dragged to different positions. The midpoints remain as midpoints no matter how the shape is altered.

## Probability and Data Analysis Tools

These computer tools allow for the entry of data and a wide choice of graphs made from the data. In addition, most will produce typical statistics such as mean, median, and range. Some programs are designed for students in the primary grades. Others are more sophisticated and can be used through the middle grades. These programs make it possible to change the emphasis in data analysis from "how to construct graphs" to "which graph best tells the story."

It should be noted that the spreadsheet and the graphing calculator provide much the same capabilities as dedicated data graphing software. Generally, the data programs, described in Chapter 18, offer more graphing options and easier use than a spreadsheet since they are designed to assist in the development of data analysis concepts.

### Probability Tools

These programs, also described in Chapter 18, make it easy to conduct controlled probability experiments and see graphical representations of the results. The young student using these programs must accept that when the computer "flips a coin" or "spins a spinner," the results are just as random and have the same probabilities as if done with real coins or spinners. The value of these programs is found in the ease with which experiments can be designed and large numbers of trials conducted.

### Spreadsheets

*Spreadsheets* are programs that can manipulate rows and columns of numeric data. Values taken from one position in the spreadsheet can be used in formulas to determine entries

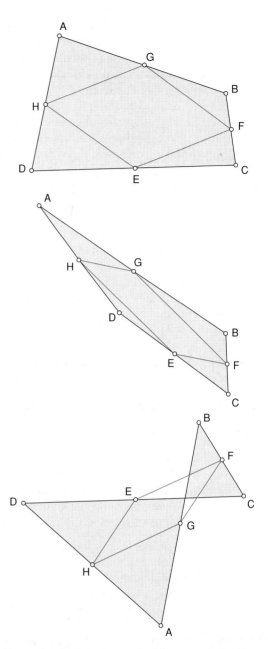

**Figure 24.1**   **The original quadrilateral with midpoints joined can be pulled and stretched into any configuration and the midpoints remain joined. Students can examine the results and form conjectures concerning observed relationships. What do you see in these screens produced by *The Geometer's Sketchpad*?**

elsewhere in the spreadsheet. When an entry is changed, the spreadsheet updates all values immediately. Words can also be written into spreadsheets as labels for columns or rows.

Because the spreadsheet is among the most popular pieces of standard tool software outside of schools, it is often available in integrated packages you may already have on your computer. There is a spreadsheet in *Microsoft Works*, *Claris Works*, and *Microsoft Office*. The program *Cruncher* (SRA/McGraw-Hill, 1996) is an example of a slightly simplified spreadsheet designed for use by students in grades 3 and up. It includes colorful graphing capability, a clip-art component, and a place in each file where students can add notes in text form. Standard spreadsheets also provide graphing capabilities. Figure 24.2 illustrates a standard spreadsheet used to explore functions in table form. Figure 24.3 (p. 474) was created with *Cruncher* and shows how the spreadsheet can be used as a data analysis tool.

| Polynomials and Rational Functions | | | | |
|---|---|---|---|---|
| Investigations | | | | |
| | | | | |
| First X value: | | −4 | | |
| Increment for X: | | 0.5 | | |
| | | | | |
| X | X ^ 2 | X ^ 3 | X ^ 3–X ^ 2 | (X ^ 3 + 2X)/(3+X) |
| −4.0 | 16 | −64 | −80 | 72 |
| −3.5 | 12.25 | −42.875 | −55.125 | 99.75 |
| −3.0 | 9 | −27 | −36 | #DIV/0! |
| −2.5 | 6.25 | −15.625 | −21.875 | −41.25 |
| −2.0 | 4 | −8 | −12 | −12 |
| −1.5 | 2.25 | −3.375 | −5.625 | −4.25 |
| −1.0 | 1 | −1 | −2 | −1.5 |
| −0.5 | 0.25 | −0.125 | −0.375 | −0.45 |
| 0.0 | 0 | 0 | 0 | 0 |
| 0.5 | 0.25 | 0.125 | −0.125 | 0.321428571 |
| 1.0 | 1 | 1 | 0 | 0.75 |
| 1.5 | 2.25 | 3.375 | 1.125 | 1.416666667 |
| 2.0 | 4 | 8 | 4 | 2.4 |
| 2.5 | 6.25 | 15.625 | 9.375 | 3.75 |
| 3.0 | 9 | 27 | 18 | 5.5 |
| 3.5 | 12.25 | 42.875 | 30.625 | 7.673076923 |
| 4.0 | 16 | 64 | 48 | 10.28571429 |
| 4.5 | 20.25 | 91.125 | 70.875 | 13.35 |
| 5.0 | 25 | 125 | 100 | 16.875 |

**Figure 24.2** **A typical spreadsheet program can be used to investigate functions in table form.**

## Function Graphers

Function graphing software permits the user to create the graph of almost any function very quickly. Multiple functions can be plotted on the same axis. It is usually possible to trace along the path of a curve and view the coordinates at any point. The dimensions of the viewing area can be changed easily so that it is just as easy to look at a graph for *x* and *y* between −10 and +10 as it is to look at a portion of the graph thousands of units away from the origin. By "zooming in" on the intersection of two graphs, it is possible to find points of intersection without algebraic manipulation. Similarly, the point where a graph crosses the axis can be found to as many decimal places as is desired.

All of the features just described are available on all graphing calculators. What computer programs add is speed, color, visual clarity, and a variety of other interesting features to help students analyze functions.

# INSTRUCTIONAL SOFTWARE

Instructional software, in contrast to tool software, is designed for student interaction in a manner similar to the textbook or a tutor. It is designed to teach. The distinction between tool and instructional software is not always clear since some packages include a tool-only component. Nor is it always clear how to categorize particular instructional programs. In the following discussion, the intent is to provide some perspective on the different kinds of input to your mathematics program that instructional software might offer.

## Concept Instruction

A growing number of programs make an effort to offer conceptual instruction. Some, like the *Fizz & Martina's Math Adventures* series of programs (Tom Snyder Productions, 1998) and the *Prime Time Math* series (Tom Snyder Productions, 1999), rely on real-world contexts to illustrate mathematical ideas. These are problem-solving situations in which specific concepts are developed in a guided manner to solve the problem.

More common in this category is the use of a visual model and much more directed instruction. MECC's *MathKeys* programs (MECC, 1995a, 1995b, 1995c, 1996a, 1996b), *CampOS Math* (Pierian Spring Software, 1996), and the Tenth Planet series (1998a, 1998b) use this approach. In *MathKeys*, the models are set up in a noncontextual manner. *CampOS Math* and the Tenth Planet packages embed models into a contextual format, but these stop short of being real-world.

CD-ROM technology gives authors the chance to create highly interactive models that are mathematically correct and inviting. What is most often missing is a way to make the mathematics problematic or to connect the conceptual activity with the symbolic techniques. Further, when students work on a computer, there is little opportunity for discourse, conjecture, or original ideas. In some instances, the programs might be best used with the teacher controlling the program on a large display screen with the class. In this way, the teacher can pose questions and entertain discussion that is simply not possible with one student on a computer.

## Problem Solving

With the current focus on problem solving, more software publishers purport to teach students to solve problems. The *Fizz & Martina* and *Prime Time Math* series can be included in the problem-solving category. Here the problems are not typical story problems awaiting a computation but more thoughtful stories set in real contexts. Another example is *The New Adventures of Jasper Woodbury* (Learning Company, 1996). Designed for students in middle school, these video episodes are on videodisk. Bar codes included with the print material make it easy to jump to appropriate sections of the extended problems. A single unit may take as many as 5 days to complete.

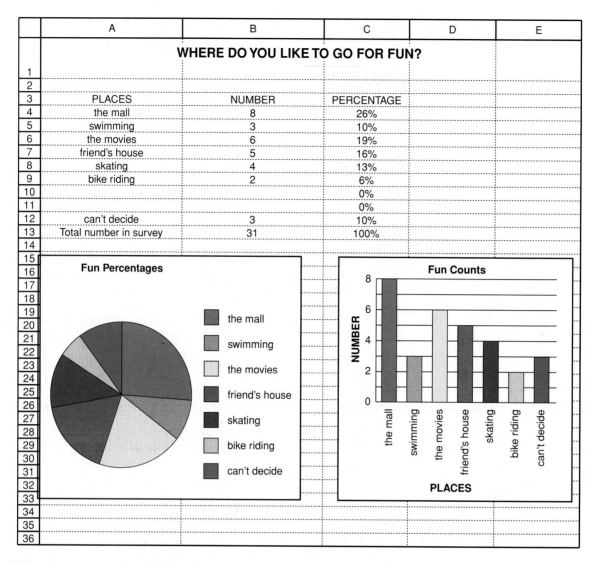

**Figure 24.3** A simple spreadsheet, *Cruncher,* can be used by elementary school students to investigate data and prepare appropriate graphs.

At the other end of the spectrum are programs that offer little more than a large library of typical story problems. Usually, the teacher can control for problem difficulty and the operations to be used. These programs would be more valuable if they offered some conceptual assistance if the student gets the problems incorrect, but that is rarely the case.

Logic problem solving is another variant of problem-solving software. This category includes attribute activities, as in *Logical Journey of the Zoombinis* (Brøderbund, 1996b), spatial reasoning, as in *Super Factory* (Sunburst Communications), and number patterns, as in *The King's Rule* (Sunburst Communications).

## Drill and Practice

Drill-and-practice programs give students practice with skills that are assumed to have been taught prior to using the pro-

grams. In general, a drill program poses questions that are answered directly or by selecting from a multiple-choice list. Many of these programs are set in arcade formats that make them exciting for students who like that sort of video game, but the format has nothing to do with the practice involved.

Drill programs evaluate responses immediately. How they respond to the first or second incorrect answer is one important distinguishing feature. At one extreme, the answer is simply recorded as wrong. There may be a second or third chance to correct it. At the other extreme, the program may branch to an explanation of the correct response. Others may provide a useful hint or supply a visual model to help with the task. Some programs offer record-keeping features for the teacher to keep track of individual students' progress.

Although computer drill is convenient, there is little evidence to suggest that it is any more effective than noncomputer drills. A major advantage is in the formats, which can add motivation to an otherwise boring drill. Drill programs are plentiful. They tend to be cheap, and their publishers promise results that are unlikely to be met. Some drill is important, but drill is not how students learn mathematics.

# GUIDELINES FOR SELECTING SOFTWARE

There is so much software for mathematics today, and it is so expensive, that it is important to make informed decisions when investing limited resources.

## Gathering Information

The most important thing to do before purchasing software is to be as well informed about the product as possible. One of the best sources of information is the review section of the NCTM journals or other journals that you respect. Typically, two or three pieces of software are reviewed each issue, or approximately 20 titles per year. Search through 2 or 3 years of back issues to find software that appeals. Also look for reviews on the Web.

Next, try to get a preview copy or at least a demonstration version. The latter may not let you actually interact with the software but rather view a form of commercial on your computer. Many distributors will send their software to you for 30-day approval. If this option is available, take advantage of it. Before purchasing, try the software with kids in the grade that will be using it.

Catalogs are useful for finding prices and titles. They are of limited value for understanding how the software works or even what the content is. A title that says it treats "addition and subtraction" does not tell you if this is basic facts, concepts, contextual problems, or multidigit computation. Drill-and-practice software is rarely distinguished from concept software. Remember, it is the content you are interested in, not the game the students will be playing.

## Criteria

Here are some things to think about as you review software before purchasing it or using it in your classroom:

- What does this do better than can be done without the computer? Don't select or use software just to put your students on the computer. Be sure to get past the clever graphics and the games. Focus on what students will be learning.

- How are students likely to be engaged with the *content* (not the bells and whistles)? Remember that student reflective thought is the most significant factor in effective instruction. Is the mathematics presented so that it is problematic for the student?

- How easy is the program to use? Students need not be able to learn the program on their own; you can teach them to use it. But there should not be so much tedium in using the program that attention is diverted from the content or students become frustrated.

- What sort of conceptual information is provided? In drill programs, how are wrong answers handled? Are the models or explanations going to aid in student understanding?

- What controls are provided to the teacher? Are there options that can be turned on and off (e.g., sound, types of feedback or help, levels of difficulty)? Is there a provision for record keeping so that you will know what progress individual students have made?

- What is the nature and quality of the print material and the manual? Minimally, the manual should make it clear how the program is to operate and provide assistance for troubleshooting. Many programs come with extensive off-computer activities, lesson plans, Blackline Masters, and suggestions for ways to use the program with your class.

- Is a site license or network license available? If you purchase a single-user package, it is not legal to install the software on multiple computers. Note also that many programs that come on a CD must have the CD in the computer in order to run the program. Does this constraint fit with your school situation?

# MATHEMATICS EDUCATION ON THE INTERNET

The World Wide Web is a wellspring of information and resources for both teachers and students interested in mathematics and teaching mathematics.

Instead of using a standard search engine to find mathematics-related information, it is better to have some places to begin. Several good Web sites in different categories will usually provide you with more links to other sites than you will have time to search. One place to get good Web sites is from the NCTM's *News Bulletin,* a newsletter sent free to all members nine times each year. For several years, the *Bulletin* has featured information about useful Web sites. Make it a habit to check these out in each issue.

## Professional Information

Most professional organizations have established Web sites on which they provide information about their organizations, conferences, current issues and events, publications, and other matters. Often these sites provide useful links to related resources or information. Periodic visits to these sites is a good way to stay current with what is going on. Here are some suggested sites.

### National Council of Teachers of Mathematics
http://www.nctm.org

NCTM's home page is growing and changing every month. There is up-to-date information about issues in mathematics education, including all NCTM position statements and a list of short papers that can be faxed to you free. There is conference information, including the ability to register for conferences and submit topics you may wish to present. Each of the journals has a separate page with information about the current issue. The full publications and materials catalog is available, and purchases can be made on line. Plus there are links to numerous organizations and sites of interest to the membership.

### Eisenhower National Clearinghouse
http://www.enc.org

This is a site of links. There are links to information about reform curriculum materials for K–12 mathematics and science, information and articles on reform issues, information about TIMSS, and ideas for classroom use.

### American Association for the Advancement of Science
http://www.aaas.org

This is the association for *Project 2061*, a national science standards document. Access to this and other information concerning science education is available.

### Association for Supervision and Curriculum Development
http://www.ascd.org

ASCD is an international nonprofit educational association that is committed to successful teaching and learning for all.

### EQUALS and Family Math
http://equals.lhs.berkeley.edu/Eqhome2htm

The EQUALS program is dedicated to equal opportunity for females in mathematics and science. It publishes *Family Math* and other valuable resources. For those interested in issues surrounding gender equity and parent involvement, this is a good place to begin.

# Teacher Resources

The Internet is a wonderful source of creative and useful lesson ideas. It is also a good way to find out about materials and software. The sites listed here were selected because of the quantity of information that is available on them and because the site addresses are not likely to change or disappear quickly. However, these few suggestions only scratch the surface. A large number of other resources are accessible through these sites.

### The Math Forum
http://forum.swarthmore.edu

Along with the NCTM site, this may be your most important source of information and links to useful sites. The Forum has resources for both teachers and students. There are suggestions for lessons, puzzles, and activities, plus links to other sites with similar information. There are forums where teachers can talk with other teachers. Two pages accept questions about mathematics from students or teachers (Ask Dr. Math) and about teaching mathematics from teachers (Teacher 2 Teacher). Problems are regularly posted, and solutions can be entered via the Internet. Information is available about software, and some can be downloaded free, including demo versions of *The Geometer's Sketchpad* and *Cabri Geometry II*.

### MegaMath!
http://www.c3.lanl.gov/mega-math/

This is a great site! A project of the Computer Research and Applications Group at Los Alamos National Laboratory, it is intended to bring unusual and important mathematical ideas to elementary classrooms.

### Mathematics Archives: K12 Internet Sites
http://archives.math.utk.edu/k12.html

This page contains a very large collection of links to lessons, software, information (both public domain and commercial), and curriculum materials. Each of the hundreds of sites has a brief description. If you are looking for an Internet address for a mathematics resource, this may be a good place to look.

### EdWeb Home Page
http://edweb.gsn.org

This site is sponsored by the Corporation for Public Broadcasting. It explores issues of educational reform and contains links to on-line resources around the world.

### Homepage for New Math Teachers
http://www.clarityconnect.com/webpages/terri/terri.html

A veteran teacher, Terri Santi offers advice on a list of subjects challenging the new teacher. In addition, she provides clever problems to pose to students, links to a huge number of useful sites, and much more.

### Annenberg/CPB Projects
http://www.learner.org

The site lists free on-line learning activities, including information about all sorts of interesting uses of mathematics and science in the real world, resources for free and inexpensive materials from Annenberg, and information about funding opportunities. It is a tremendous resource. Be sure to check the SAMI page.

## Data and Resources for Students

On many of the sites just listed, there is information designed for students as well as teachers. In addition to things such as games and activities, the Web is a bountiful source of data to be used in various projects, such as comparing your city to those in other parts of the world, or data related to economics or geography nationwide or around the world. Here are just a few sites that fall into this category of data resources.

### National Weather Information

http://www.ems.psu.edu/wx/usstats/uswsxtats.html

> All sorts of data related to the weather (including maps). Updated hourly.

### Stock Market Information

http://www.stockmaster.com

> A commercial page that provides up-to-the-minute stock reports and news items.

### U.S. Census Data

http://www.census.gov/

> Copious statistical information by state, county, or voting district.

### The World Fact Book

http://www.odci.gov/cia/publications/factbook/index.html

> This page provides demographic information for every nation in the world, including population, age distributions, death and birth rates, and information on the economy, government, transportation, and geography. Maps are included as well.

Not listed here but abundantly available are sites with activities just for students. Many links to sites for students can be found in the teacher sites listed earlier.

# REFLECTIONS ON CHAPTER 24

## Writing to Learn

1. Technology has affected the mathematics curriculum and how it is taught in three ways. Explain each, and give an example to support your explanation. Can you think of examples that are not included in this chapter?

2. Describe some of the benefits of using calculators regularly in the mathematics classroom. Which of these seem to you to be the most compelling? What are some of the arguments against using calculators? Answer each of the arguments against calculators as if you were giving a speech at your PTA meeting or arguing for regular use of calculators before your principal.

3. Aside from the special features of graphing calculators, what are some of the benefits that come simply from having a large display screen and the ability to recall prior statements?

4. What are at least three features of graphing calculators that truly improve the learning of mathematics in the middle grades?

5. Describe what is meant by tool software in mathematics. Describe several types.

6. Describe the three categories of computer instructional software. If you have seen or used examples from these categories, use those in your descriptions.

7. What are some criteria that seem most important to you when selecting software?

8. What kind of information can you expect to find on the Internet?

## For Discussion and Exploration

1. Talk with some teachers about their use or nonuse of calculators in the classroom. How do the teachers who use them go about doing so? What are the main reasons for not using them?

Read the Technology principle in *Principles and Standards for School Mathematics* and the NCTM position statement on calculators. How do the reasons the teachers you talked with compare to these positions?

2. Among the software kept at your school, find one example of drill-and-practice software and one of some other form of instructional software for mathematics. Try each, and decide how it would be used in your classroom (if at all). Be sure to check the documentation for suggested grade levels.

3. Check out at least three of the Web sites suggested for teacher resources. Be sure to follow some of the links to other sites. Share at least two good ideas with a friend. Get the friend to do the same.

## Recommendations for Further Reading

### Highly Recommended

Battista, M. T. (1994). Calculators and computers: Tools for mathematical exploration and empowerment. *Arithmetic Teacher, 41,* 412–417.

> In this article, Battista shares children's explorations with calculators, Logo, and a geometry tool, the forerunner of his later "shape Makers." The ideas remain timely and give a quick view of what can actually be done if we take advantage of the power of these tools.

Calvert, L. M. G. (1999). A dependence on technology and algorithms or a lack of number sense? *Teaching Children Mathematics, 6,* 6–7.

> Calvert offers simple but convincing answers to individuals, including teachers, who believe that calculators stop children from thinking. This two-page article is well worth looking up.

Clements, D. H. (1999). The effective use of computers with young children. In J. V. Copley (Ed.), *Mathematics in the early years* (pp. 119–128). Reston, VA: National Council of Teachers of Mathematics.

Clements is a well-known researcher in the area of computer use for young children. In this article, he offers guidance on the use of computers with young children, provides numerous examples of different types of programs for the young, and offers cautions about casually believing that all computer activities are good. There is an extensive bibliography.

Dockterman, D. A. (1991). *Great teaching in the one-computer classroom* (3rd ed.). Watertown, MA: Tom Snyder Productions.

Though not about teaching mathematics, this little book, written in a teacher-friendly style, is about practical uses of a single computer in the classroom. Topics include cooperative learning, interactive video, and using the computer to make classroom life easier.

## Other Suggestions

Barron, A. E., & Hynes, M. C. (1996). Using technology to enhance communication in mathematics. In P. C. Elliott (Ed.), *Communication in mathematics, K–12 and beyond* (pp. 126–136). Reston, VA: National Council of Teachers of Mathematics.

Battista, M. T. (1998). *Shape makers: Developing geometric reasoning with the Geometer's Sketchpad.* Emeryville, CA: Key Curriculum Press.

Bayliffe, J., Brie, R., & Oliver, B. (1994). Using technology to enhance "My travels with Gulliver." *Teaching Children Mathematics, 1,* 188–191.

Bitter, G. G., & Hatfield, M. M. (1998). The role of technology in the middle grades. In L. P. Leutzinger (Ed.), *Mathematics in the middle* (pp. 36–41). Reston, VA: National Council of Teachers of Mathematics.

Calculator-Enhanced Mathematics Instruction Steering Committee. (1992). *Calculators for classrooms* [Video and guidebook]. Reston, VA: National Council of Teachers of Mathematics.

Campbell, P. F., & Clements, D. H. (1990). Using microcomputers for mathematics learning. In J. N. Payne (Ed.), *Mathematics for the young child* (pp. 265–283). Reston, VA: National Council of Teachers of Mathematics.

Carlson, R. J., & Winter, M. J. (1998). *Transforming functions to fit data: Mathematical explorations using probes, electronic data-collection devices, and graphing calculators.* Emeryville, CA: Key Curriculum Press.

Charischak, I., & Berkman, R. (1995). Looking at random events with Logo software. *Mathematics Teaching in the Middle School, 1,* 318–322.

Doyle, A. (1999). A practitioner's guide to snaring the Net. *Educational Leadership, 56*(5), 12–15

Drier, H. S., Dawson, K. M., & Garofalo, J. (1999). Not your typical math class. *Educational Leadership, 56*(5), 21–25.

Drosdeck, C. C. (1995). Promoting calculator use in elementary classrooms. *Teaching Children Mathematics, 1,* 300–305.

Eisenhower National Clearinghouse for Mathematics and Science Education. (1999). Integrating technology in the classroom. [Theme issue]. *ENC Focus, 6*(3).

Fey, J. T. (Ed.). (1992). *Calculators in mathematics education.* Reston, VA: National Council of Teachers of Mathematics.

Jensen, R. J., & Williams, B. S. (1993). Technology: Implications for the middle grades. In D. T. Owens (Ed.), *Research ideas for the classroom: Middle grades mathematics* (pp. 225–243). Old Tappan, NJ: Macmillan.

Murray, M., Mokros, J., & Rubin, R. A. (1999). Mathematically rich, equitable game software. *Mathematics Teaching in the Middle School, 5,* 180–186.

Owens, J. E. (1995). Playing green globs on a TI-81. *Mathematics Teaching in the Middle School, 1,* 370–374.

Randall, J. (1998). *Sensor sensibility: Algebra explorations with a CBL, a TI-82 or TI-83, and Sensors.* Emeryville, CA: Key Curriculum Press.

Russell, J. C. (1998). *Spreadsheet activities in middle school mathematics* (2nd ed.). Reston, VA: National Council of Teachers of Mathematics.

Schielack, J. F., & Chancellor, D. (1995). *Uncovering mathematics with manipulatives and calculators: Level 1.* Dallas: Texas Instruments.

Schielack, J. F., & Chancellor, D. (1995). *Uncovering mathematics with manipulatives and calculators: Levels 2 and 3.* Dallas: Texas Instruments.

Taylor, L. J. C., & Nichols, J. A. (1994). Graphing calculators aren't just for high school students. *Mathematics Teaching in the Middle School, 1,* 190–196.

Zech, L., Vye, N. J., Bransford, J. D., Swink, J., Mayfield-Stewart, C., Goldman, S. R., & the Cognition and Technology Group at Vanderbilt. (1994). Bringing geometry into the classroom with videodisc technology. *Mathematics Teaching in the Middle School, 1,* 228–233.

# Appendix A

## Principles and Standards for School Mathematics

## Content Standards and Grade Level Expectations

*Source:* Reprinted with permission from *Principles and Standards for School Mathematics.* Copyright ©2000 by the National Council of Teachers of Mathematics. All rights reserved.

# Number and Operations

## STANDARD

*Instructional programs from prekindergarten through grade 12 should enable all students to—*

## Pre-K–2

### Expectations

In prekindergarten through grade 2 all students should—

## Grades 3–5

### Expectations

In grades 3–5 all students should—

| Standard | Pre-K–2 Expectations | Grades 3–5 Expectations |
|---|---|---|
| Understand numbers, ways of representing numbers, relationships among numbers, and number systems | • count with understanding and recognize "how many" in sets of objects;<br>• use multiple models to develop initial understandings of place value and the base-ten number system;<br>• develop understanding of the relative position and magnitude of whole numbers and of ordinal and cardinal numbers and their connections;<br>• develop a sense of whole numbers and represent and use them in flexible ways, including relating, composing, and decomposing numbers;<br>• connect number words and numerals to the quantities they represent, using various physical models and representations;<br>• understand and represent commonly used fractions, such as 1/4, 1/3, and 1/2. | • understand the place-value structure of the base-ten number system and be able to represent and compare whole numbers and decimals;<br>• recognize equivalent representations for the same number and generate them by decomposing and composing numbers;<br>• develop understanding of fractions as parts of unit wholes, as parts of a collection, as locations on number lines, and as divisions of whole numbers;<br>• use models, benchmarks, and equivalent forms to judge the size of fractions;<br>• recognize and generate equivalent forms of commonly used fractions, decimals, and percents;<br>• explore numbers less than 0 by extending the number line and through familiar applications;<br>• describe classes of numbers according to characteristics such as the nature of their factors. |
| Understand meanings of operations and how they relate to one another | • understand various meanings of addition and subtraction of whole numbers and the relationship between the two operations;<br>• understand the effects of adding and subtracting whole numbers;<br>• understand situations that entail multiplication and division, such as equal groupings of objects and sharing equally. | • understand various meanings of multiplication and division;<br>• understand the effects of multiplying and dividing whole numbers;<br>• identify and use relationships between operations, such as division as the inverse of multiplication, to solve problems;<br>• understand and use properties of operations, such as the distributivity of multiplication over addition. |
| Compute fluently and make reasonable estimates | • develop and use strategies for whole-number computations, with a focus on addition and subtraction;<br>• develop fluency with basic number combinations for addition and subtraction;<br>• use a variety of methods and tools to compute, including objects, mental computation, estimation, paper and pencil, and calculators. | • develop fluency with basic number combinations for multiplication and division and use these combinations to mentally compute related problems, such as $30 \times 50$;<br>• develop fluency in adding, subtracting, multiplying, and dividing whole numbers;<br>• develop and use strategies to estimate the results of whole-number computations and to judge the reasonableness of such results;<br>• develop and use strategies to estimate computations involving fractions and decimals in situations relevant to students' experience;<br>• use visual models, benchmarks, and equivalent forms to add and subtract commonly used fractions and decimals;<br>• select appropriate methods and tools for computing with whole numbers from among mental computation, estimation, calculators, and paper and pencil according to the context and nature of the computation and use the selected method or tool. |

# Number and Operations

## STANDARD

*Instructional programs from prekindergarten through grade 12 should enable all students to—*

| Standard | Grades 6–8 | Grades 9–12 |
|---|---|---|
| | **Expectations** | **Expectations** |
| | In grades 6–8 all students should— | In grades 9–12 all students should— |
| Understand numbers, ways of representing numbers, relationships among numbers, and number systems | • work flexibly with fractions, decimals, and percents to solve problems;<br><br>• compare and order fractions, decimals, and percents efficiently and find their approximate locations on a number line;<br><br>• develop meaning for percents greater than 100 and less than 1;<br><br>• understand and use ratios and proportions to represent quantitative relationships;<br><br>• develop an understanding of large numbers and recognize and appropriately use exponential, scientific, and calculator notation;<br><br>• use factors, multiples, prime factorization, and relatively prime numbers to solve problems;<br><br>• develop meaning for integers and represent and compare quantities with them. | • develop a deeper understanding of very large and very small numbers and of various representations of them;<br><br>• compare and contrast the properties of numbers and number systems, including the rational and real numbers, and understand complex numbers as solutions to quadratic equations that do not have real solutions;<br><br>• understand vectors and matrices as systems that have some of the properties of the real-number system;<br><br>• use number-theory arguments to justify relationships involving whole numbers. |
| Understand meanings of operations and how they relate to one another | • understand the meaning and effects of arithmetic operations with fractions, decimals, and integers;<br><br>• use the associative and commutative properties of addition and multiplication and the distributive property of multiplication over addition to simplify computations with integers, fractions, and decimals;<br><br>• understand and use the inverse relationships of addition and subtraction, multiplication and division, and squaring and finding square roots to simplify computations and solve problems. | • judge the effects of such operations as multiplication, division, and computing powers and roots on the magnitudes of quantities;<br><br>• develop an understanding of properties of, and representations for, the addition and multiplication of vectors and matrices;<br><br>• develop an understanding of permutations and combinations as counting techniques. |
| Compute fluently and make reasonable estimates | • select appropriate methods and tools for computing with fractions and decimals from among mental computation, estimation, calculators or computers, and paper and pencil, depending on the situation, and apply the selected methods;<br><br>• develop and analyze algorithms for computing with fractions, decimals, and integers and develop fluency in their use;<br><br>• develop and use strategies to estimate the results of rational-number computations and judge the reasonableness of the results;<br><br>• develop, analyze, and explain methods for solving problems involving proportions, such as scaling and finding equivalent ratios. | • develop fluency in operations with real numbers, vectors, and matrices, using mental computation or paper-and-pencil calculations for simple cases and technology for more-complicated cases;<br><br>• judge the reasonableness of numerical computations and their results. |

# Algebra
## STANDARD

*Instructional programs from prekindergarten through grade 12 should enable all students to—*

| | Pre-K–2 | Grades 3–5 |
|---|---|---|
| | Expectations | Expectations |
| | In prekindergarten through grade 2 all students should— | In grades 3–5 all students should— |
| Understand patterns, relations, and functions | • sort, classify, and order objects by size, number, and other properties;<br>• recognize, describe, and extend patterns such as sequences of sounds and shapes or simple numeric patterns and translate from one representation to another;<br>• analyze how both repeating and growing patterns are generated. | • describe, extend, and make generalizations about geometric and numeric patterns;<br>• represent and analyze patterns and functions, using words, tables, and graphs. |
| Represent and analyze mathematical situations and structures using algebraic symbols | • illustrate general principles and properties of operations, such as commutativity, using specific numbers;<br>• use concrete, pictorial, and verbal representations to develop an understanding of invented and conventional symbolic notations. | • identify such properties as commutativity, associativity, and distributivity and use them to compute with whole numbers;<br>• represent the idea of a variable as an unknown quantity using a letter or a symbol;<br>• express mathematical relationships using equations. |
| Use mathematical models to represent and understand quantitative relationships | • model situations that involve the addition and subtraction of whole numbers, using objects, pictures, and symbols. | • model problem situations with objects and use representations such as graphs, tables, and equations to draw conclusions. |
| Analyze change in various contexts | • describe qualitative change, such as a student's growing taller;<br>• describe quantitative change, such as a student's growing two inches in one year. | • investigate how a change in one variable relates to a change in a second variable;<br>• identify and describe situations with constant or varying rates of change and compare them. |

# Algebra
## STANDARD

*Instructional programs from prekindergarten through grade 12 should enable all students to—*

| | Grades 6–8 | Grades 9–12 |
|---|---|---|
| | Expectations | Expectations |
| | In grades 6–8 all students should— | In grades 9–12 all students should— |
| **Understand patterns, relations, and functions** | • represent, analyze, and generalize a variety of patterns with tables, graphs, words, and, when possible, symbolic rules;<br>• relate and compare different forms of representation for a relationship;<br>• identify functions as linear or nonlinear and contrast their properties from tables, graphs, or equations. | • generalize patterns using explicitly defined and recursively defined functions;<br>• understand relations and functions and select, convert flexibly among, and use various representations for them;<br>• analyze functions of one variable by investigating rates of change, intercepts, zeros, asymptotes, and local and global behavior;<br>• understand and perform transformations such as arithmetically combining, composing, and inverting commonly used functions, using technology to perform such operations on more-complicated symbolic expressions;<br>• understand and compare the properties of classes of functions, including exponential, polynomial, rational, logarithmic, and periodic functions;<br>• interpret representations of functions of two variables. |
| **Represent and analyze mathematical situations and structures using algebraic symbols** | • develop an initial conceptual understanding of different uses of variables;<br>• explore relationships between symbolic expressions and graphs of lines, paying particular attention to the meaning of intercept and slope;<br>• use symbolic algebra to represent situations and to solve problems, especially those that involve linear relationships;<br>• recognize and generate equivalent forms for simple algebraic expressions and solve linear equations. | • understand the meaning of equivalent forms of expressions, equations, inequalities, and relations;<br>• write equivalent forms of equations, inequalities, and systems of equations and solve them with fluency—mentally or with paper and pencil in simple cases and using technology in all cases;<br>• use symbolic algebra to represent and explain mathematical relationships;<br>• use a variety of symbolic representations, including recursive and parametric equations, for functions and relations;<br>• judge the meaning, utility, and reasonableness of the results of symbol manipulations, including those carried out by technology. |
| **Use mathematical models to represent and understand quantitative relationships** | • model and solve contextualized problems using various representations, such as graphs, tables, and equations. | • identify essential quantitative relationships in a situation and determine the class or classes of functions that might model the relationships;<br>• use symbolic expressions, including iterative and recursive forms, to represent relationships arising from various contexts;<br>• draw reasonable conclusions about a situation being modeled. |
| **Analyze change in various contexts** | • use graphs to analyze the nature of changes in quantities in linear relationships. | • approximate and interpret rates of change from graphical and numerical data. |

# Geometry

## STANDARD

*Instructional programs from prekindergarten through grade 12 should enable all students to—*

| Standard | Pre-K–2 Expectations | Grades 3–5 Expectations |
|---|---|---|
| | In prekindergarten through grade 2 all students should— | In grades 3–5 all students should— |
| Analyze characteristics and properties of two- and three-dimensional geometric shapes and develop mathematical arguments about geometric relationships | • recognize, name, build, draw, compare, and sort two- and three-dimensional shapes;<br>• describe attributes and parts of two- and three-dimensional shapes;<br>• investigate and predict the results of putting together and taking apart two- and three-dimensional shapes. | • identify, compare, and analyze attributes of two- and three-dimensional shapes and develop vocabulary to describe the attributes;<br>• classify two- and three-dimensional shapes according to their properties and develop definitions of classes of shapes such as triangles and pyramids;<br>• investigate, describe, and reason about the results of subdividing, combining, and transforming shapes;<br>• explore congruence and similarity;<br>• make and test conjectures about geometric properties and relationships and develop logical arguments to justify conclusions. |
| Specify locations and describe spatial relationships using coordinate geometry and other representational systems | • describe, name, and interpret relative positions in space and apply ideas about relative position;<br>• describe, name, and interpret direction and distance in navigating space and apply ideas about direction and distance;<br>• find and name locations with simple relationships such as "near to" and in coordinate systems such as maps. | • describe location and movement using common language and geometric vocabulary;<br>• make and use coordinate systems to specify locations and to describe paths;<br>• find the distance between points along horizontal and vertical lines of a coordinate system. |
| Apply transformations and use symmetry to analyze mathematical situations | • recognize and apply slides, flips, and turns;<br>• recognize and create shapes that have symmetry. | • predict and describe the results of sliding, flipping, and turning two-dimensional shapes;<br>• describe a motion or a series of motions that will show that two shapes are congruent;<br>• identify and describe line and rotational symmetry in two- and three-dimensional shapes and designs. |
| Use visualization, spatial reasoning, and geometric modeling to solve problems | • create mental images of geometric shapes using spatial memory and spatial visualization;<br>• recognize and represent shapes from different perspectives;<br>• relate ideas in geometry to ideas in number and measurement;<br>• recognize geometric shapes and structures in the environment and specify their location. | • build and draw geometric objects;<br>• create and describe mental images of objects, patterns, and paths;<br>• identify and build a three-dimensional object from two-dimensional representations of that object;<br>• identify and build a two-dimensional representation of a three-dimensional object;<br>• use geometric models to solve problems in other areas of mathematics, such as number and measurement;<br>• recognize geometric ideas and relationships and apply them to other disciplines and to problems that arise in the classroom or in everyday life. |

# Geometry

## STANDARD

*Instructional programs from prekindergarten through grade 12 should enable all students to—*

## Grades 6–8

### Expectations

In grades 6–8 all students should—

## Grades 9–12

### Expectations

In grades 9–12 all students should—

| STANDARD | Grades 6–8 Expectations | Grades 9–12 Expectations |
|---|---|---|
| **Analyze characteristics and properties of two- and three-dimensional geometric shapes and develop mathematical arguments about geometric relationships** | • precisely describe, classify, and understand relationships among types of two- and three-dimensional objects using their defining properties; <br>• understand relationships among the angles, side lengths, perimeters, areas, and volumes of similar objects; <br>• create and critique inductive and deductive arguments concerning geometric ideas and relationships, such as congruence, similarity, and the Pythagorean relationship. | • analyze properties and determine attributes of two- and three-dimensional objects; <br>• explore relationships (including congruence and similarity) among classes of two- and three-dimensional geometric objects, make and test conjectures about them, and solve problems involving them; <br>• establish the validity of geometric conjectures using deduction, prove theorems, and critique arguments made by others; <br>• use trigonometric relationships to determine lengths and angle measures. |
| **Specify locations and describe spatial relationships using coordinate geometry and other representational systems** | • use coordinate geometry to represent and examine the properties of geometric shapes; <br>• use coordinate geometry to examine special geometric shapes, such as regular polygons or those with pairs of parallel or perpendicular sides. | • use Cartesian coordinates and other coordinate systems, such as navigational, polar, or spherical systems, to analyze geometric situations; <br>• investigate conjectures and solve problems involving two- and three-dimensional objects represented with Cartesian coordinates. |
| **Apply transformations and use symmetry to analyze mathematical situations** | • describe sizes, positions, and orientations of shapes under informal transformations such as flips, turns, slides, and scaling; <br>• examine the congruence, similarity, and line or rotational symmetry of objects using transformations. | • understand and represent translations, reflections, rotations, and dilations of objects in the plane by using sketches, coordinates, vectors, function notation, and matrices; <br>• use various representations to help understand the effects of simple transformations and their compositions. |
| **Use visualization, spatial reasoning, and geometric modeling to solve problems** | • draw geometric objects with specified properties, such as side lengths or angle measures; <br>• use two-dimensional representations of three-dimensional objects to visualize and solve problems such as those involving surface area and volume; <br>• use visual tools such as networks to represent and solve problems; <br>• use geometric models to represent and explain numerical and algebraic relationships; <br>• recognize and apply geometric ideas and relationships in areas outside the mathematics classroom, such as art, science, and everyday life. | • draw and construct representations of two- and three-dimensional geometric objects using a variety of tools; <br>• visualize three-dimensional objects from different perspectives and analyze their cross sections; <br>• use vertex-edge graphs to model and solve problems; <br>• use geometric models to gain insights into, and answer questions in, other areas of mathematics; <br>• use geometric ideas to solve problems in, and gain insights into, other disciplines and other areas of interest such as art and architecture. |

# Measurement

## STANDARD

*Instructional programs from prekindergarten through grade 12 should enable all students to—*

| | Pre-K–2 | Grades 3–5 |
|---|---|---|
| | **Expectations** | **Expectations** |
| | In prekindergarten through grade 2 all students should— | In grades 3–5 all students should— |
| Understand measurable attributes of objects and the units, systems, and processes of measurement | • recognize the attributes of length, volume, weight, area, and time;<br>• compare and order objects according to these attributes;<br>• understand how to measure using nonstandard and standard units;<br>• select an appropriate unit and tool for the attribute being measured. | • understand such attributes as length, area, weight, volume, and size of angle and select the appropriate type of unit for measuring each attribute;<br>• understand the need for measuring with standard units and become familiar with standard units in the customary and metric systems;<br>• carry out simple unit conversions, such as from centimeters to meters, within a system of measurement;<br>• understand that measurements are approximations and understand how differences in units affect precision;<br>• explore what happens to measurements of a two-dimensional shape such as its perimeter and area when the shape is changed in some way. |
| Apply appropriate techniques, tools, and formulas to determine measurements | • measure with multiple copies of units of the same size, such as paper clips laid end to end;<br>• use repetition of a single unit to measure something larger than the unit, for instance, measuring the length of a room with a single meterstick;<br>• use tools to measure;<br>• develop common referents for measures to make comparisons and estimates. | • develop strategies for estimating the perimeters, areas, and volumes of irregular shapes;<br>• select and apply appropriate standard units and tools to measure length, area, volume, weight, time, temperature, and the size of angles;<br>• select and use benchmarks to estimate measurements;<br>• develop, understand, and use formulas to find the area of rectangles and related triangles and parallelograms;<br>• develop strategies to determine the surface areas and volumes of rectangular solids. |

# Measurement

## STANDARD

*Instructional programs from prekindergarten through grade 12 should enable all students to—*

| | Grades 6–8 | Grades 9–12 |
|---|---|---|
| | Expectations | Expectations |
| | In grades 6–8 all students should— | In grades 9–12 all students should— |
| Understand measurable attributes of objects and the units, systems, and processes of measurement | • understand both metric and customary systems of measurement;<br>• understand relationships among units and convert from one unit to another within the same system;<br>• understand, select, and use units of appropriate size and type to measure angles, perimeter, area, surface area, and volume. | • make decisions about units and scales that are appropriate for problem situations involving measurement. |
| Apply appropriate techniques, tools, and formulas to determine measurements | • use common benchmarks to select appropriate methods for estimating measurements;<br>• select and apply techniques and tools to accurately find length, area, volume, and angle measures to appropriate levels of precision;<br>• develop and use formulas to determine the circumference of circles and the area of triangles, parallelograms, trapezoids, and circles and develop strategies to find the area of more-complex shapes;<br>• develop strategies to determine the surface area and volume of selected prisms, pyramids, and cylinders;<br>• solve problems involving scale factors, using ratio and proportion;<br>• solve simple problems involving rates and derived measurements for such attributes as velocity and density. | • analyze precision, accuracy, and approximate error in measurement situations;<br>• understand and use formulas for the area, surface area, and volume of geometric figures, including cones, spheres, and cylinders;<br>• apply informal concepts of successive approximation, upper and lower bounds, and limit in measurement situations;<br>• use unit analysis to check measurement computations. |

# Data Analysis and Probability

## STANDARD

*Instructional programs from prekindergarten through grade 12 should enable all students to—*

| STANDARD | Pre-K–2 Expectations | Grades 3–5 Expectations |
|---|---|---|
| | In prekindergarten through grade 2 all students should— | In grades 3–5 all students should— |
| Formulate questions that can be addressed with data and collect, organize, and display relevant data to answer them | • pose questions and gather data about themselves and their surroundings;<br>• sort and classify objects according to their attributes and organize data about the objects;<br>• represent data using concrete objects, pictures, and graphs. | • design investigations to address a question and consider how data-collection methods affect the nature of the data set;<br>• collect data using observations, surveys, and experiments;<br>• represent data using tables and graphs such as line plots, bar graphs, and line graphs;<br>• recognize the differences in representing categorical and numerical data. |
| Select and use appropriate statistical methods to analyze data | • describe parts of the data and the set of data as a whole to determine what the data show. | • describe the shape and important features of a set of data and compare related data sets, with an emphasis on how the data are distributed;<br>• use measures of center, focusing on the median, and understand what each does and does not indicate about the data set;<br>• compare different representations of the same data and evaluate how well each representation shows important aspects of the data. |
| Develop and evaluate inferences and predictions that are based on data | • discuss events related to students' experiences as likely or unlikely. | • propose and justify conclusions and predictions that are based on data and design studies to further investigate the conclusions or predictions. |
| Understand and apply basic concepts of probability | | • describe events as likely or unlikely and discuss the degree of likelihood using such words as certain, equally likely, and impossible;<br>• predict the probability of outcomes of simple experiments and test the predictions;<br>• understand that the measure of the likelihood of an event can be represented by a number from 0 to 1. |

# Data Analysis and Probability

| STANDARD | Grades 6–8 | Grades 9–12 |
|---|---|---|
| *Instructional programs from prekindergarten through grade 12 should enable all students to—* | Expectations<br>In grades 6–8 all students should— | Expectations<br>In grades 9–12 all students should— |
| Formulate questions that can be addressed with data and collect, organize, and display relevant data to answer them | • formulate questions, design studies, and collect data about a characteristic shared by two populations or different characteristics within one population;<br>• select, create, and use appropriate graphical representations of data, including histograms, box plots, and scatterplots. | • understand the differences among various kinds of studies and which types of inferences can legitimately be drawn from each;<br>• know the characteristics of well-designed studies, including the role of randomization in surveys and experiments;<br>• understand the meaning of measurement data and categorical data, of univariate and bivariate data, and of the term variable;<br>• understand histograms, parallel box plots, and scatterplots and use them to display data;<br>• compute basic statistics and understand the distinction between a statistic and a parameter. |
| Select and use appropriate statistical methods to analyze data | • find, use, and interpret measures of center and spread, including mean and interquartile range;<br>• discuss and understand the correspondence between data sets and their graphical representations, especially histograms, stem-and-leaf plots, box plots, and scatterplots. | • for univariate measurement data, be able to display the distribution, describe its shape, and select and calculate summary statistics;<br>• for bivariate measurement data, be able to display a scatterplot, describe its shape, and determine regression coefficients, regression equations, and correlation coefficients using technological tools;<br>• display and discuss bivariate data where at least one variable is categorical;<br>• recognize how linear transformations of univariate data affect shape, center, and spread;<br>• identify trends in bivariate data and find functions that model the data or transform the data so that they can be modeled. |
| Develop and evaluate inferences and predictions that are based on data | • use observations about differences between two or more samples to make conjectures about the populations from which the samples were taken;<br>• make conjectures about possible relationships between two characteristics of a sample on the basis of scatterplots of the data and approximate lines of fit;<br>• use conjectures to formulate new questions and plan new studies to answer them. | • use simulations to explore the variability of sample statistics from a known population and to construct sampling distributions;<br>• understand how sample statistics reflect the values of population parameters and use sampling distributions as the basis for informal inference;<br>• evaluate published reports that are based on data by examining the design of the study, the appropriateness of the data analysis, and the validity of conclusions;<br>• understand how basic statistical techniques are used to monitor process characteristics in the workplace. |
| Understand and apply basic concepts of probability | • understand and use appropriate terminology to describe complementary and mutually exclusive events;<br>• use proportionality and a basic understanding of probability to make and test conjectures about the results of experiments and simulations;<br>• compute probabilities for simple compound events, using such methods as organized lists, tree diagrams, and area models. | • understand the concepts of sample space and probability distribution and construct sample spaces and distributions in simple cases;<br>• use simulations to construct empirical probability distributions;<br>• compute and interpret the expected value of random variables in simple cases;<br>• understand the concepts of conditional probability and independent events;<br>• understand how to compute the probability of a compound event. |

# Appendix B

## Professional Standards for Teaching Mathematics

## Teaching Standards

*Source:* From *Professional Standards for Teaching Mathematics*. Copyright ©1991 by the National Council of Teachers of Mathematics. Used by permission.

# Teaching Standards

## 1. Worthwhile Mathematical Tasks

The teacher of mathematics should pose tasks that are based on

- Sound and significant mathematics
- Knowledge of students' understandings, interests, and experiences
- Knowledge of the range of ways that diverse students learn mathematics

and that

- Engage students' intellect
- Develop students' mathematical understandings and skills
- Stimulate students to make connections and develop a coherent framework for mathematical ideas
- Call for problem formulation, problem solving, and mathematical reasoning
- Promote communication about mathematics
- Represent mathematics as an ongoing human activity
- Display sensitivity to, and draw on, students' diverse background experiences and dispositions
- Promote the development of all students' dispositions to do mathematics

## 2. Teacher's Role in Discourse

The teacher of mathematics should orchestrate discourse by

- Posing questions and tasks that elicit, engage, and challenge each student's thinking
- Listening carefully to students' ideas
- Asking students to clarify and justify their ideas orally and in writing
- Deciding what to pursue in depth from among the ideas that students bring up during a discussion
- Deciding when and how to attach mathematical notation and language to students' ideas
- Deciding when to provide information, when to clarify an issue, when to model, when to lead, and when to let a student struggle with a difficulty
- Monitoring students' participation in discussions and deciding when and how to encourage each student to participate

## 3. Students' Role in Discourse

The teacher of mathematics should promote classroom discourse in which students

- Listen to, respond to, and question the teacher and one another
- Use a variety of tools to reason, make connections, solve problems, and communicate
- Initiate problems and questions
- Make conjectures and present solutions
- Explore examples and counterexamples to investigate a conjecture
- Try to convince themselves and one another of the validity of particular representations, solutions, conjectures, and answers
- Rely on mathematical evidence and argument to determine validity

## 4. Tools for Enhancing Discourse

The teacher of mathematics, in order to enhance discourse, should encourage and accept the use of

- Computers, calculators, and other technology
- Concrete materials used as models
- Pictures, diagrams, tables, and graphs
- Invented and conventional terms and symbols
- Metaphors, analogies, and stories
- Written hypotheses, explanations, and arguments
- Oral presentations and dramatizations

## 5. Learning Environment

The teacher of mathematics should create a learning environment that fosters the development of each student's mathematical power by

- Providing and structuring the time necessary to explore sound mathematics and grapple with significant ideas and problems
- Using the physical space and materials in ways that facilitate students' learning of mathematics
- Providing a context that encourages the development of mathematical skill and proficiency
- Respecting and valuing students' ideas, ways of thinking, and mathematical dispositions

and by consistently expecting and encouraging students to

- Work independently or collaboratively to make sense of mathematics
- Take intellectual risks by raising questions and formulating conjectures
- Display a sense of mathematical competence by validating and supporting ideas with mathematical argument

## 6. Analysis of Teaching and Learning

The teacher of mathematics should engage in ongoing analysis of teaching and learning by

- Observing, listening to, and gathering other information about students to assess what they are learning
- Examining effects of the tasks, discourse, and learning environment on students' mathematical knowledge, skills, and dispositions

in order to

- Ensure that every student is learning sound and significant mathematics and is developing a positive disposition toward mathematics
- Challenge and extend students' ideas
- Adapt or change activities while teaching
- Make plans, both short- and long-range
- Describe and comment on each student's learning to parents and administrators, as well as to the students themselves

# REFERENCES

Ann Arbor Public Schools. (1993). *Alternative assessment: Evaluating student performance in elementary mathematics.* White Plains, NY: Cuisenaire–Dale Seymour.

Ashcraft, M. H., & Christy, K. S. (1995). The frequency of arithmetic facts in elementary texts: Addition and multiplication in grades 1–6. *Journal for Research in Mathematics Education, 26,* 396–421.

Austin, R., & Thompson, D. (1997). Exploring algebraic patterns through literature. *Mathematics Teaching in the Middle School, 2,* 274–281.

Babcock, J. E. (1998). *U.S. TIMSS Report No. 8.* East Lansing: TIMSS National Research Center, Michigan State University.

Backhouse, J., Haggarty, L., Pirie, S., & Stratton, J. (1992). *Improving the learning of mathematics.* Portsmouth, NH: Heinemann.

Baek, J. (1998). Children's invented algorithms for multidigit multiplication problems. In L. J. Morrow (Ed.), *The teaching and learning of algorithms in school mathematics* (pp. 151–160). Reston, VA: National Council of Teachers of Mathematics.

Baker, A., & Baker, J. (1991). *Maths in the mind: A process approach to mental strategies.* Portsmouth, NH: Heinemann.

Baker, J., & Baker, A. (1990). *Mathematics in process.* Portsmouth, NH: Heinemann.

Ball, D. L. (1992). Magical hopes: Manipulatives and the reform of math education. *American Educator, 16* (2), 14–18, 46–47.

Baratta-Lorton, M. (1976). *Mathematics their way.* Menlo Park, CA: AWL Supplemental.

Baroody, A. J. (1985). Mastery of the basic number combinations: Internalization of relationships or facts? *Journal for Research in Mathematics Education, 16,* 83–98.

Baroody, A. J. (1987). *Children's mathematical thinking: A developmental framework for preschool, primary, and special education teachers.* New York: Teachers College Press.

Baroody, A. J., & Hume, J. (1991). Meaningful mathematics instruction: The case of fractions. *Remedial and Special Education, 12,* 54–68.

Battista, M. T. (1998). *Shape makers: Developing geometric reasoning with the Geometer's Sketchpad.* Emeryville, CA: Key Curriculum Press.

Battista, M. T. (1999). The mathematical miseducation of America's youth: Ignoring research and scientific study in education. *Phi Delta Kappan, 80,* 424–433.

Becker, J. P., & Shimada, S. (Eds.). (1997). *The open-ended approach: A new proposal for teaching mathematics.* Reston, VA: National Council of Teachers of Mathematics.

Bell, M. (1998, Winter). Problems with implementing new curricula: The example of the K–6 Everyday Mathematics Curriculum. *UCSMP Newsletter, 24,* 1–2.

Bennett, D. (1992). *Exploring geometry with the Geometer's Sketchpad.* Emeryville, CA: Key Curriculum Press.

Bley, N. S. (1994). Accommodating special needs. In C. A. Thornton & N. S. Bley (Eds.), *Windows of opportunity: Mathematics for students with special needs* (pp. 137–163). Reston, VA: National Council of Teachers of Mathematics.

Bley, N. S., & Thornton, C. A. (1995). *Teaching mathematics to students with learning disabilities* (3rd ed.). Austin, TX: Pro-Ed.

Boaler, J. (1998). Open and closed mathematics: Student experiences and understandings. *Journal for Research in Mathematics Education, 29,* 41–62.

Booth, L. R. (1988). Children's difficulties in beginning algebra. In A. F. Coxford (Ed.), *The ideas of algebra, K–12* (pp. 20–32). Reston, VA: National Council of Teachers of Mathematics.

Borasi, R. (1994, April). *Implementing the NCTM Standards in "inclusive" mainstream classrooms.* Paper presented at the annual meeting of the National Council of Teachers of Mathematics, Indianapolis, IN.

Bresser, R. (1995). *Math and literature (grades 4–6).* Sausalito, CA: Math Solutions Publications.

Bright, G. W., Behr, M. J., Post, T. R., & Wachsmuth, I. (1988). Identifying fractions on number lines. *Journal for Research in Mathematics Education, 19,* 215–232.

Brooks, J. G., & Brooks, M. G. (1993). *In search of understanding: The case for the constructivist classroom.* Alexandria, VA: Association for Supervision and Curriculum Development.

Brownell, W. A., & Chazal, C. B. (1935). The effects of premature drill in third-grade arithmetic. *Journal of Educational Research, 29,* 17–28.

Brueningsen, C., Bower, B., Antinone, L., & Brueningsen, E. (1994). *Real-world math with the CBL system: 25 activities using the CBL and TI–82.* Dallas: Texas Instruments.

Burger, W. F. (1985). Geometry. *Arithmetic Teacher, 32*(6), 52–56.

Burger, W. F., & Shaughnessy, J. M. (1986). Characterizing the van Hiele levels of development in geometry. *Journal for Research in Mathematics Education, 17,* 13–48.

Burns, M. (1982). *Math for smarty pants.* New York: Little, Brown.

Burns, M. (1987). *A collection of math lessons from grades 3 through 6.* Sausalito, CA: Math Solutions Publications.

Burns, M. (1992a). *About teaching mathematics: A K–8 resource.* Sausalito, CA: Math Solutions Publications.

Burns, M. (1992b). *Math and literature (K–3).* Sausalito, CA: Math Solutions Publications.

Burns, M. (1995a). Timed tests. *Teaching Children Mathematics, 1,* 408–409.

Burns, M. (1995b). *Writing in math class.* Sausalito, CA: Math Solutions Publications.

Burns, M. (1996). *50 problem-solving lessons: Grades 1–6.* Sausalito, CA: Math Solutions Publications.

Burns, M. (1998). *Math: Facing an American phobia.* Sausalito, CA: Math Solutions Publications.

Burns, M. (1999, April). *Making sense of mathematics: A look toward the twenty-first century.* Paper presented at the annual meeting of the National Council of Teachers of Mathematics, San Francisco.

Burton, N. (1995). Trends in mathematics achievement for young men and women. In I. M. Carl (Ed.), *Prospects for school mathematics* (pp. 115–130). Reston, VA: National Council of Teachers of Mathematics.

Callahan, L. G., & MacMillan, D. L. (1981). Teaching mathematics to slow-learning and mentally retarded children. In V. J. Glennon (Ed.), *The mathematical education of exceptional children and youth: An interdisciplinary approach* (pp. 146–190). Reston, VA: National Council of Teachers of Mathematics.

Campbell, P. B. (1995). Redefining the "girl problem in mathematics." In W. G. Secada, E. Fennema, & L. B. Adajian (Eds.), *New directions for equity in mathematics education* (pp. 225–241). New York: Cambridge University Press.

Campbell, P. F. (1993). Making equity a reality in classrooms. *Arithmetic Teacher, 41,* 110–113.

Campbell, P. F. (1996). Empowering children and teachers in the elementary mathematics classrooms of urban schools. *Urban Education, 30,* 449–475.

Campbell, P. F. (1997, April). *Children's invented algorithms: Their meaning and place in instruction.* Paper presented at the annual meeting of the National Council of Teachers of Mathematics, Minneapolis, MN.

Campbell, P. F., & Johnson, M. L. (1995). How primary students think and learn. In I. M. Carl (Ed.), *Prospects for school mathematics* (pp. 21–42). Reston, VA: National Council of Teachers of Mathematics.

Campbell, P. F., Rowan, T. E., & Suarez, A. R. (1998). What criteria for student-invented algorithms? In L. J. Morrow (Ed.), *The teaching and learning of algorithms in school mathematics* (pp. 49–55). Reston, VA: National Council of Teachers of Mathematics.

Campione, J. C., Brown, A. L., & Connell, M. L. (1989). Metacognition: On the importance of understanding what you are doing. In R. I. Charles & E. A. Silver (Eds.), *The teaching and assessing of mathematical problem solving* (pp. 93–114). Reston, VA: National Council of Teachers of Mathematics.

Carey, D. A., Fennema, E., Carpenter, T. P., & Franke, M. L. (1995). Equity and mathematics education. In W. G. Secada, E. Fennema, & L. B. Adajian (Eds.), *New directions for equity in mathematics education* (pp. 93–125). New York: Cambridge University Press.

Carpenter, T. P., Ansell, E., Franke, M. L., Fennema, E., & Weisbeck, L. (1993). A study of kindergarten children's problem-solving processes. *Journal for Research in Mathematics Education, 24,* 428–441.

Carpenter, T. P., Carey, D. A., & Kouba, V. L. (1990). A problem-solving approach to the operations. In J. N. Payne (Ed.), *Mathematics for the young child* (pp. 111–131). Reston, VA: National Council of Teachers of Mathematics.

Carpenter, T. P., Franke, M. L., Jacobs, V. R., Fennema, E., & Empson, S. B. (1998). A longitudinal study of invention and understanding in children's multidigit addition and subtraction. *Journal for Research in Mathematics Education, 29,* 3–20.

Carpenter, T. P., & Moser, J. M. (1983). The acquisition of addition and subtraction concepts. In R. A. Lesh & M. Landau (Eds.), *Acquisition of mathematics concepts and processes* (pp. 7–44). Orlando, FL: Academic Press.

Carroll, W. M. (1988). Cross sections of clay solids. *Arithmetic Teacher, 35*(7), 6–11.

Carroll, W. M. (1996). Use of invented algorithms by second graders in a reform mathematics curriculum. *Journal of Mathematical Behavior, 15,* 137–150.

Carroll, W. M. (1997). Results of third-grade students in a reform curriculum on the Illinois State Mathematics Test. *Journal for Research in Mathematics Education, 28,* 237–242.

Carroll, W. M., & Porter, D. (1997). Invented strategies can develop meaningful mathematical procedures. *Teaching Children Mathematics, 3,* 370–374.

Chalouh, L., & Herscovics, N. (1988). Teaching algebraic expressions in a meaningful way. In A. F. Coxford (Ed.), *The ideas of algebra, K–12* (pp. 33–42). Reston, VA: National Council of Teachers of Mathematics.

Chambers, D. L. (1994). Cognitively guided instruction. *Teaching Children Mathematics, 1,* 116.

Chambers, D. L. (1996). Direct modeling and invented procedures: Building on students' informal strategies. *Teaching Children Mathematics, 3,* 92–95.

Charles, R. I., Chancellor, D., Harcourt, L., Moore, D., Schielack, J. F., Van de Walle, J. A., & Wortzman, R. (1998). *Scott Foresman-Addison Wesley MATH (Grades K to 5).* Glenview, IL: Scott Foresman–Addison Wesley.

Charles, R. I., Lester, F. K., Jr., & O'Daffer, P. (1987). *How to evaluate progress in problem solving.* Reston, VA: National Council of Teachers of Mathematics.

Clark, F. B., & Kamii, C. K. (1996). Identification of multiplicative thinking in children in grades 1–5. *Journal for Research in Mathematics Education, 27,* 41–51.

Clements, D. H., & Battista, M. T. (1990). Constructivist learning and teaching. *Arithmetic Teacher, 38*(1), 34–35.

Cobb, P. (1988). The tension between theories of learning and instruction in mathematics education. *Educational Psychologist, 23,* 87–103.

Cobb, P. (1995). Cultural tools and mathematical learning: A case study. *Journal for Research in Mathematics Education, 26,* 362–385.

Corwin, R. B. (1996). *Talking mathematics: Supporting children's voices.* Portsmouth, NH: Heinemann.

Countryman, J. (1992). *Writing to learn mathematics: Strategies that work, K–12.* Portsmouth, NH: Heinemann.

Cuisenaire–Dale Seymour Publications. (1995). *Investigations in number data and space.* White Plains, NY: Author.

Curcio, F. R., & Bezuk, N. S. (1994). *Understanding rational numbers and proportions: Addenda series, grades 5–8.* Reston, VA: National Council of Teachers of Mathematics.

Damarin, S. K. (1995). Gender and mathematics from a feminist standpoint. In W. G. Secada, E. Fennema, & L. B. Adajian (Eds.), *New directions for equity in mathematics education* (pp. 242–257). New York: Cambridge University Press.

Davidson, E., & Hammerman, J. (1993). Homogenized is only better for milk. In G. Cuevas & M. Driscol (Eds.), *Reaching all students with mathematics* (pp. 197–212). Reston, VA: National Council of Teachers of Mathematics.

Davis, R. B. (1986). *Learning mathematics: The cognitive science approach to mathematics education.* Norwood, NJ: Ablex.

de Villiers, M. D. (1999). *Rethinking proof with the Geometer's Sketchpad.* Emeryville, CA: Key Curriculum Press.

Downs, R. E., Mathew, J. L., & McKinney, M. L. (1994). Issues of identification. In C. A. Thornton & N. S. Bley (Eds.), *Windows of opportunity: Mathematics for students with special needs* (pp. 61–81). Reston, VA: National Council of Teachers of Mathematics.

Elliott, P. C., & Garnett, C. (1994). Mathematics power for all. In C. A. Thornton, & N. S. Bley (Eds.), *Windows of opportunity: Mathematics for students with special needs* (pp. 3–17). Reston, VA: National Council of Teachers of Mathematics.

Fennema, E., Carpenter, T. P., Franke, M. L., & Carey, D. A. (1993). Learning to use children's mathematics thinking: A case study. In R. B. Davis & C. A. Maher (Eds.), *School, mathematics, and the world of reality* (pp. 93–117). Needham Heights, MA: Allyn & Bacon.

Fennema, E., Carpenter, T. P., Levi, L, Franke, M. L., & Empson, S. (1997). *Cognitively guided instruction: Professional development in primary mathematics.* Madison: Wisconsin Center for Education Research.

Fennema, E., Peterson, P. L., Carpenter, T. P., & Lubinski, C. (1990). Teacher attributes and beliefs about girls, boys, and mathematics. *Educational Studies in Mathematics, 21,* 55–69.

Fey, J. T. (Ed.). (1992). *Calculators in mathematics education.* Reston, VA: National Council of Teachers of Mathematics.

Fischer, F. E. (1990). A part-part-whole curriculum for teaching number in the kindergarten. *Journal for Research in Mathematics Education, 21,* 207–215.

Fosnaugh, L. S., & Harrell, M. E. (1996). Covering the plane with rep-tiles. *Mathematics Teaching in the Middle School, 1,* 666–670.

Friel, S. N., Mokros, J. R., & Russell, S. J. (1992). *Statistics: Middles, means, and in-betweens. A unit of study for grades 5–6 from Used numbers: Real data in the classroom.* White Plains, NY: Cuisenaire–Dale Seymour.

Fuson, K. C. (1984). More complexities in subtraction. *Journal for Research in Mathematics Education, 15,* 214–225.

Fuson, K. C. (1992). Research on whole number addition and subtraction. In D. A. Grouws (Ed.), *Handbook of research on teaching and learning* (pp. 243–275). Old Tappan, NJ: Macmillan.

Fuson, K. C., & Hall, J. W. (1983). The acquisition of early number word meanings: A conceptual analysis and review. In H. P. Ginsburg (Ed.), *The development of mathematical thinking* (pp. 49–107). Orlando, FL: Academic Press.

Fuson, K. C., Wearne, D., Hiebert, J. C., Murray, H. G., Human, P. G., Olivier, A. I., Carpenter, T. P., & Fennema, E. (1997). Children's conceptual structures for multidigit numbers and methods of multidigit addition and subtraction. *Journal for Research in Mathematics Education, 28,* 130–162.

Fuys, D., Geddes, D., & Tischler, R. (1988). *The van Hiele model of thinking in geometry among adolescents (Journal for Research in Mathematics Education* Monograph No. 3). Reston, VA: National Council of Teachers of Mathematics.

Garland, T. H. (1987). *Fascinating Fibonaccis: Mystery and magic in numbers.* White Plains, NY: Cuisenaire–Dale Seymour.

Garofalo, J. (1987). Metacognition and school mathematics. *Arithmetic Teacher, 34*(9), 22–23.

Geddes, D., & Fortunato, I. (1993). Geometry: Research and classroom activities. In D. T. Owens (Ed.), *Research ideas for the classroom: Middle grades mathematics* (pp. 199–222). Old Tappan, NJ: Macmillan.

Gelman, R., & Gallistel, C. R. (1978). *The child's understanding of number.* Cambridge, MA: Harvard University Press.

Gelman, R., & Meck, E. (1986). The notion of principle: The case of counting. In J. C. Hiebert (Ed.), *Conceptual and procedural knowledge: The case of mathematics* (pp. 29–57). Mahwah, NJ: Erlbaum.

Ginsburg, H. P. (1977). *Children's arithmetic: The learning process.* New York: Van Nostrand.

Gnanadesikan, M., Schaeffer, R. L., & Swift, J. (1987). *The art and techniques of simulation: Quantitative literacy series.* White Plains, NY: Cuisenaire–Dale Seymour.

Greenes, C., Garfunkel, F., & De Bussey, M. (1994). Planning for instruction: The individualized education plan and the mathematics individualized learning plan. In C. A. Thornton & N. S. Bley (Eds.), *Windows of opportunity: Mathematics for students with special needs* (pp. 115–135). Reston, VA: National Council of Teachers of Mathematics.

Greer, B. (1992). Multiplication and division as models of situations. In D. A. Grouws (Ed.), *Handbook of research on mathematics teaching and learning* (pp. 276–295). Old Tappan, NJ: Macmillan.

Groff, P. (1996). It is time to question fraction teaching. *Mathematics Teaching in the Middle School, 1,* 604–607.

Gutstein, E., & Romberg, T. A. (1995). Teaching children to add and subtract. *Journal of Mathematical Behavior, 14,* 283–324.

Hankes, J. E. (1996). An alternative to basic-skills remediation. *Teaching Children Mathematics, 2,* 452–457.

Hashimoto, Y., & Becker, J. (1999). The open approach to teaching mathematics: Creating a culture of mathematics in the classroom: Japan. In L. J. Sheffield (Ed.), *Developing mathematically promising students* (pp. 101–119). Reston, VA: National Council of Teachers of Mathematics.

Hembree, R., & Dessart, D. D. (1986). Effects of hand-held calculators in precollege mathematics education: A meta-analysis. *Journal for Research in Mathematics Education, 17,* 83–99.

Hiebert, J. C. (1990). The role of routine procedures in the development of mathematical competence. In T. J. Cooney (Ed.), *Teaching and learning mathematics in the 1990s* (pp. 31–40). Reston, VA: National Council of Teachers of Mathematics.

Hiebert, J. C., & Carpenter, T. P. (1992). Learning and teaching with understanding. In D. A. Grouws (Ed.), *Handbook of research on mathematics teaching and learning* (pp. 65–97). Old Tappan, NJ: Macmillan.

Hiebert, J. C., Carpenter, T. P., Fennema, E., Fuson, K. C., Human, P. G., Murray, H. G., Olivier, A. I., & Wearne, D. (1996). Problem solving as a basis for reform in curriculum and instruction: The case of mathematics. *Educational Researcher, 25,* 12–21.

Hiebert, J. C., Carpenter, T. P., Fennema, E., Fuson, K. C., Wearne, D., Murray, H. G., Olivier, A. I., & Human, P. G. (1997). *Making sense: Teaching and learning mathematics with understanding.* Portsmouth, NH: Heinemann.

Hiebert, J. C., & Lindquist, M. M. (1990). Developing mathematical knowledge in the young child. In J. N. Payne (Ed.), *Mathematics for the young child* (pp. 17–36). Reston, VA: National Council of Teachers of Mathematics.

Hiebert, J. C., & Wearne, D. (1996). Instruction, understanding, and skill in multidigit addition and subtraction. *Cognition and Instruction, 14,* 251–283.

Hilliard, A. G., III. (1995). Mathematics excellence for cultural "minority" students: What is the problem? In I. M. Carl (Ed.), *Seventy-five years of progress: Prospects for school mathematics* (pp. 99–114). Reston, VA: National Council of Teachers of Mathematics.

Hoffer, A. R. (1983). Van Hiele-based research. In R. A. Lesh & M. Landau (Eds.), *Acquisition of mathematics concepts and processes* (pp. 205–227). Orlando, FL: Academic Press.

Hoffer, A. R., & Hoffer, S. A. K. (1992). Ratios and proportional thinking. In T. R. Post (Ed.), *Teaching mathematics in grades K–8: Research-based methods* (2nd ed., pp. 303–330). Needham Heights, MA: Allyn & Bacon.

Hope, J. A., Leutzinger, L. P., Reys, B. J., & Reys, R. E. (1988). *Mental math in the primary grades.* White Plains, NY: Cuisenaire–Dale Seymour.

Hope, J. A., Reys, B. J., & Reys, R. E. (1987). *Mental math in the middle grades.* White Plains, NY: Cuisenaire–Dale Seymour.

Hope, J. A., Reys, B. J., & Reys, R. E. (1988). *Mental math in the junior high school*. White Plains, NY: Cuisenaire–Dale Seymour.

House, P. A. (1999). Promises, promises, promises. In L. J. Sheffield (Ed.), *Developing mathematically promising students* (pp. 1–7). Reston, VA: National Council of Teachers of Mathematics.

Howden, H. (1989). Teaching number sense. *Arithmetic Teacher, 36*(6), 6–11.

Huinker, D. M. (1994, April). *Multistep word problems: A strategy for empowering students*. Paper presented at the annual meeting of the National Council of Teachers of Mathematics, Indianapolis, IN.

Huinker, D. M. (1998). Letting fraction algorithms emerge through problem solving. In L. J. Morrow (Ed.), *The teaching and learning of algorithms in school mathematics* (pp. 170–182). Reston, VA: National Council of Teachers of Mathematics.

Huinker, D. M., & Laughlin, C. (1996). Talk your way into writing. In P. C. Elliott (Ed.), *Communication in mathematics, K–12 and beyond* (pp. 81–88). Reston, VA: National Council of Teachers of Mathematics.

Irvine, R., & Walker, K. (1996a). *Smart arithmetic: A thinking approach to computation, grades 1–3*. Chicago: Creative Publications.

Irvine, R., & Walker, K. (1996b). *Smart arithmetic: A thinking approach to computation, grades 4–6*. Chicago: Creative Publications.

Janvier, C. (Ed.). (1987). *Problems of representation in the teaching and learning of mathematics*. Mahwah, NJ: Erlbaum.

Johnson, D. W., Johnson, R. T., & Holubec, E. J. (1993). *Circles of learning: Cooperation in the classroom* (4th ed.). Alexandria, VA: Association for Supervision and Curriculum Development.

Kamii, C. K. (1985). *Young children reinvent arithmetic*. New York: Teachers College Press.

Kamii, C. K. (1989). *Young children continue to reinvent arithmetic: 2nd grade*. New York: Teachers College Press.

Kamii, C. K., & Clark, F. B. (1995). Equivalent fractions: Their difficulty and educational implications. *Journal of Mathematical Behavior, 14*, 365–378.

Kamii, C. K., & Dominick, A. (1997). To teach or not to teach the algorithms. *Journal of Mathematical Behavior, 16*, 51–62.

Kamii, C. K., & Dominick, A. (1998). The harmful effects of algorithms in grades 1–4. In L. J. Morrow (Ed.), *The teaching and learning of algorithms in school mathematics* (pp. 130–140). Reston, VA: National Council of Teachers of Mathematics.

Kaput, J. J. (1998). Transforming algebra from an engine of inequity to an engine of mathematical power by "algebrafying" the K–12 curriculum. In *The nature and role of algebra in the K–14 curriculum: Proceedings of a national symposium* (pp. 25–26). Washington, DC: National Academy Press.

Karplus, R., Pulos, S., & Stage, E. K. (1983). Proportional reasoning of early adolescents. In R. A. Lesh & M. Landau (Eds.), *Acquisition of mathematics concepts and processes* (pp. 45–90). Orlando, FL: Academic Press.

Kenney, P. A., & Kouba, V. L. (1997). What do students know about measurement? In P. A. Kenney & E. A. Silver (Eds.), *Results from the sixth mathematics assessment of the National Assessment of Educational Progress* (pp. 141–163). Reston, VA: National Council of Teachers of Mathematics.

Kenney, P. A., & Silver, E. A. (Eds.) (1997). *Results from the sixth mathematics assessment of the National Assessment of Educational Progress*. Reston, VA: National Council of Teachers of Mathematics.

Kouba, V. L. (1989). Children's solution strategies for equivalent set multiplication and division word problems. *Journal for Research in Mathematics Education, 20*, 147–158.

Kouba, V. L., Brown, C. A., Carpenter, T. P., Lindquist, M. M., Silver, E. A., & Swafford, J. O. (1988a). Results of the fourth NAEP assessment of mathematics: Number, operations, and word problems. *Arithmetic Teacher, 35*(8), 14–19.

Kouba, V. L., Brown, C. A., Carpenter, T. P., Lindquist, M. M., Silver, E. A., & Swafford, J. O. (1988b). Results of the fourth NAEP assessment of mathematics: Measurement, geometry, data interpretation, attitudes, and other topics. *Arithmetic Teacher, 35*(9), 10–16.

Kouba, V. L., Zawojewski, J. S., & Strutchens, M. E. (1997). What do students know about numbers and operations? In P. A. Kenney & E. A. Silver (Eds.), *Results from the sixth mathematics assessment of the National Assessment of Educational Progress* (pp. 87–140). Reston, VA: National Council of Teachers of Mathematics.

Kroll, D. L., Masingila, J. O., & Mau, S. T. (1992). Cooperative problem solving: But what about grades? *Arithmetic Teacher, 39*(6), 17–23.

Kulm, G. (1994). *Mathematics assessment: What works in the classroom*. San Francisco: Jossey-Bass.

Labinowicz, E. (1985). *Learning from children: New beginnings for teaching numerical thinking*. Menlo Park, CA: AWL Supplemental.

Labinowicz, E. (1987). Assessing for learning: The interview method. *Arithmetic Teacher, 35*(3), 22–24.

Ladson-Billings, G. (1995). Making mathematics meaningful in multicultural contexts. In W. G. Secada, E. Fennema, & L. B. Adajian (Eds.), *New directions for equity in mathematics education* (pp. 126–145). New York: Cambridge University Press.

Lamon, S. J. (1993). Ratio and proportion: Connecting content and children's thinking. *Journal for Research in Mathematics Education, 24*, 41–61.

Lampert, M. (1990). When the problem is not the question and the solution is not the answer: Mathematical knowing and teaching. *American Educational Research Journal, 27*, 29–63.

Landwehr, J. M., & Watkins, A. E. (1987). *Exploring data: Quantitative literacy series*. White Plains, NY: Cuisenaire–Dale Seymour.

Lappan, G. (1998). Capturing patterns and functions: Variables and joint variation. In *The nature and role of algebra in the K–14 curriculum: Proceedings of a national symposium* (pp. 57–59). Washington, DC: National Academy Press.

Lappan, G., & Briars, D. (1995). How should mathematics be taught? In I. M. Carl (Ed.), *Seventy-five years of progress: Prospects for school mathematics* (pp. 115–156). Reston, VA: National Council of Teachers of Mathematics.

Lappan, G., & Even, R. (1989). *Learning to teach: Constructing meaningful understanding of mathematical content* (Craft Paper No. 89–3). East Lansing: Michigan State University.

Lappan, G., & Mouck, M. K. (1998). Developing algorithms for adding and subtracting fractions. In L. J. Morrow (Ed.), *The teaching and learning of algorithms in school mathematics* (pp. 183–197). Reston, VA: National Council of Teachers of Mathematics.

Leder, G. C. (1995). Equity inside the mathematics classroom: Fact or artifact? In W. G. Secada, E. Fennema, & L. B. Adajian (Eds.), *New directions for equity in mathematics education* (pp. 209–224). New York: Cambridge University Press.

Lesh, R. A., Post, T. R., & Behr, M. J. (1987). Representations and translations among representations in mathematics learning and problem solving. In C. Janvier (Ed.), *Problems of representation in the teaching and learning of mathematics* (pp. 33–40). Mahwah, NJ: Erlbaum.

Lesh, R. A., Post, T. R., & Behr, M. J. (1988). Proportional reasoning. In J. C. Hiebert & M. J. Behr (Eds.), *Number concepts and operation in the middle grades* (pp. 93–118). Reston, VA: National Council of Teachers of Mathematics.

Lester, F. K., Jr. (1989). Reflections about mathematical problem-solving research. In R. I. Charles & E. A. Silver (Eds.), *The teaching and assessing of mathematical problem solving* (pp. 115–124). Reston, VA: National Council of Teachers of Mathematics.

Lester, F. K., Jr. (1994). Musings about mathematical problem-solving research, 1970–1994. *Journal for Research in Mathematics Education, 25,* 660–675.

Lester, J. B. (1996). Establishing a community of mathematics learners. In D. Schifter (Ed.), *What's happening in math class? Envisioning new practices through teacher narratives* (pp. 88–102). New York: Teachers College Press.

Liedtke, W. W. (1988). Diagnosis in mathematics: The advantages of an interview. *Arithmetic Teacher, 36*(3), 26–29.

Lindquist, M. M. (1987a). Estimation and mental computation: Measurement. *Arithmetic Teacher, 34*(5), 16–17.

Lindquist, M. M. (1987b). Problem solving with five easy pieces. In J. M. Hill (Ed.), *Geometry for grades K–6: Readings from* The Arithmetic Teacher (pp. 152–156). Reston, VA: National Council of Teachers of Mathematics.

Lo, J., & Watanabe, T. (1997). Developing ratio and proportion schemes: A story of a fifth grader. *Journal for Research in Mathematics Education, 28,* 216–236.

Lodholz, R. D. (1990). The transition from arithmetic to algebra. In E. L. Edwards Jr. (Ed.), *Algebra for everyone* (pp. 24–33). Reston, VA: National Council of Teachers of Mathematics.

Lubinski, C. A., & Thiessen, D. (1996). Exploring measurement through literature. *Teaching Children Mathematics, 2,* 260–263.

Mack, N. K. (1995). Confounding whole-number and fraction concepts when building on informal knowledge. *Journal for Research in Mathematics Education, 26,* 422–441.

Madell, R. (1985). Children's natural processes. *Arithmetic Teacher, 32*(7), 20–22.

Marolda, M. R., & Davidson, P. S. (1994). Assessing mathematical abilities and learning approaches. In C. A. Thornton & N. S. Bley (Eds.), *Windows of opportunity: Mathematics for students with special needs* (pp. 83–113). Reston, VA: National Council of Teachers of Mathematics.

Mathematical Sciences Education Board, National Research Council. (1989). *Everybody counts: A report to the nation on the future of mathematics education.* Washington, DC: National Academy Press.

McCoy, L. P. (1997). Algebra: Real-life investigations in a lab setting. *Mathematics Teaching in the Middle School, 2,* 220–224.

Milauskas, G. A. (1987). Creative geometry problems can lead to creative problem solvers. In M. M. Lindquist (Ed.), *Learning and teaching geometry, K–12* (pp. 69–84). Reston, VA: National Council of Teachers of Mathematics.

Mokros, J., Russell, S. J., & Economopoulos, K. (1995). *Beyond arithmetic: Changing mathematics in the elementary classroom.* White Plains, NY: Cuisenaire–Dale Seymour.

Mulligan, J. T., & Mitchelmore, M. C. (1997). Young children's intuitive models of multiplication and division. *Journal for Research in Mathematics Education, 28,* 309–330.

National Council of Teachers of Mathematics. (1989). *Curriculum and evaluation standards for school mathematics.* Reston, VA: Author.

National Council of Teachers of Mathematics. (1991). *Professional standards for teaching mathematics.* Reston, VA: Author.

National Council of Teachers of Mathematics. (1995). *Assessment standards for school mathematics.* Reston, VA: Author.

National Council of Teachers of Mathematics. (1998). *1998–1999 NCTM member handbook: NCTM goals, leaders, and position statements.* Reston, VA: Author.

National Council of Teachers of Mathematics. (2000). *Principles and standards for school mathematics.* Reston, VA: Author.

Noddings, N. (1993). Constructivism and caring. In R. B. Davis & C. A. Maher (Eds.), *School, mathematics, and the world of reality* (pp. 35–50). Needham Heights, MA: Allyn & Bacon.

Noelting, G. (1980). The development of proportional reasoning and the ratio concept: 1. Differentiation of stages. *Educational Studies in Mathematics, 11,* 217–253.

Oakes, J. (1990). *Multiplying inequalities: The effects of race, social class, and tracking opportunities to learn mathematics and science.* Santa Monica, CA: Rand.

Oakes, J. (1995). Opportunity to learn: Can standards-based reform be equity-based reform? In I. M. Carl (Ed.), *Seventy-five years of progress: Prospects for school mathematics* (pp. 78–98). Reston, VA: National Council of Teachers of Mathematics.

O'Brien, T. C. (1999). Parrot math. *Phi Delta Kappan, 80,* 434–438.

Oppedal, D. C. (1995). Mathematics is something good. *Teaching Children Mathematics, 2,* 36–40.

Papert, S. (1980). *Mindstorms: Children, computers, and powerful ideas.* New York: Basic Books.

Poplin, M. S. (1988a). Holistic/constructivist principles of the teaching/learning process: Implications for the field of learning disabilities. *Journal of Learning Disabilities, 21,* 401–416.

Poplin, M. S. (1988b). The reductionistic fallacy in learning disabilities: Replicating the past by reducing the present. *Journal of Learning Disabilities, 21,* 389–398.

Post, T. R. (1981). Fractions: Results and implications from the National Assessment. *Arithmetic Teacher, 28*(9), 26–31.

Post, T. R., Behr, M. J., & Lesh, R. A. (1988). Proportionality and the development of prealgebra understandings. In A. F. Coxford (Ed.), *The ideas of algebra, K–12* (pp. 78–90). Reston, VA: National Council of Teachers of Mathematics.

Post, T. R., Wachsmuth, I., Lesh, R. A., & Behr, M. J. (1985). Order and equivalence of rational numbers: A cognitive analysis. *Journal for Research in Mathematics Education, 16,* 18–36.

Raimi, R. A., & Braden, L. S. (1998). *State mathematics: An appraisal of math standards in 46 states, the District of Columbia, and Japan.* Washington, DC: Thomas B. Fordham Foundation.

Rathmell, E. C. (1978). Using thinking strategies to teach the basic skills. In M. N. Suydam (Ed.), *Developing computational skills* (pp. 13–38). Reston, VA: National Council of Teachers of Mathematics.

Reese, C. M., Miller, K. E., Mazzeo, J., & Dossey, J. A. (1997). *NAEP 1996 mathematics report card for the nation and the states: Findings from the National Assessment of Educational Progress.* Washington, DC: National Center for Education Statistics.

Resnick, L. B. (1983). A developmental theory of number understanding. In H. P. Ginsburg (Ed.), *The development of mathematical thinking* (pp. 109–151). Orlando, FL: Academic Press.

Reys, B. J., & Reys, R. E. (1987). Calculators in the classroom: How can we make it happen? *Arithmetic Teacher, 34*(6), 12–14.

Reys, B. J., & Reys, R. E. (1995). Japanese mathematics education: What makes it work. *Teaching Children Mathematics, 1,* 474–475.

Reys, B. J., Robinson, E., Sconiers, S., & Mark, J. (1999). Mathematics curricula based on rigorous national standards: What, why, and how? *Phi Delta Kappan, 80,* 454–456.

Reys, R. E., & Reys, B. J. (1983). *Guide to using estimation skills and strategies (GUESS)* (Boxes I and II). White Plains, NY: Cuisenaire–Dale Seymour.

Ross, S. H. (1986). *The development of children's place-value numeration concepts in grades two through five.* Paper presented at the annual meeting of the American Educational Research Association, San Francisco. (ERIC Document Reproduction Service No. ED 2773 482)

Ross, S. H. (1989). Parts, wholes, and place value: A developmental perspective. *Arithmetic Teacher, 36*(6), 47–51.

Rowan, T. E. (1995, March). *Helping children construct mathematical understanding with IMPACT.* Paper presented at the regional meeting of the National Council of Teachers of Mathematics, Chicago.

Rowan, T. E., & Bourne, B. (1994). *Thinking like mathematicians: Putting the K–4 Standards into practice.* Portsmouth, NH: Heinemann.

Runion, G. E. (1990). *The golden section*. White Plains, NY: Cuisenaire–Dale Seymour.

Russell, S. J. (1997, April). *Using video to study students' strategies for whole-number operations*. Paper presented at the annual meeting of the National Council of Teachers of Mathematics, Minneapolis, MN.

Russell, S. J., & Corwin, R. B. (1990). *Sorting: Groups and graphs*. A unit of study for grades 2–3 from *Used numbers: Real data in the classroom*. White Plains, NY: Cuisenaire–Dale Seymour.

Scheer, J. K. (1980). The etiquette of diagnosis. *Arithmetic Teacher, 27*(9), 18–19.

Schifter, D., Bastable, V., & Russell, S. J. (1999a). *Developing mathematical ideas: Numbers and operations, Part 1: Building a system of tens* (Casebook). White Plains, NY: Cuisenaire–Dale Seymour.

Schifter, D., Bastable, V., & Russell, S. J. (1999b). *Developing mathematical ideas: Numbers and operations, Part 2: Making meaning for operations* (Casebook). White Plains, NY: Cuisenaire–Dale Seymour.

Schifter, D., Bastable, V., & Russell, S. J. (1999c). *Developing mathematical ideas: Numbers and operations, Part 2: Making meaning for operations* (Facilitator's guide). White Plains, NY: Cuisenaire–Dale Seymour.

Schifter, D., & Fosnot, C. T. (1993). *Reconstructing mathematics education: Stories of teachers meeting the challenge of reform*. New York: Teachers College Press.

Schmidt, W. H., McKnight, C. C., & Raizen, S. A. (1996). *Executive summary of a splintered vision: An investigation of U.S. science and mathematics education*. Boston: Kluwer.

Schoenfeld, A. H. (1988). What's all the fuss about metacognition? In A. H. Schoenfeld (Ed.), *Cognitive science and mathematics education* (pp. 189–215). Mahwah, NJ: Erlbaum.

Schoenfeld, A. H. (1992). Learning to think mathematically: Problem solving, metacognition, and sense making in mathematics. In D. A. Grouws (Ed.), *Handbook of research on teaching and learning* (pp. 334–370). Old Tappan, NJ: Macmillan.

Schoenfeld, A. H. (1994). Reflections on doing and teaching mathematics. In A. H. Schoenfeld (Ed.), *Mathematical thinking and problem solving* (pp. 53–70). Mahwah, NJ: Erlbaum.

Schroeder, T. L., & Lester, F. K., Jr. (1989). Developing understanding in mathematics via problem solving. In P. R. Trafton (Ed.), *New directions for elementary school mathematics* (pp. 31–42). Reston, VA: National Council of Teachers of Mathematics.

Schwartz, S. L. (1996). Hidden messages in teacher talk: Praise and empowerment. *Teaching Children Mathematics, 2*, 396–401.

Sconyers, J. M. (1995). Proof and the middle school mathematics student. *Mathematics Teaching in the Middle School, 1*, 516–518.

Seymour, D. (1971). *Tangramath*. Chicago: Creative Publications.

Sheffield, L. J. (1999). Serving the needs of the mathematically promising. In L. J. Sheffield (Ed.), *Developing mathematically promising students* (pp. 43–55). Reston, VA: National Council of Teachers of Mathematics.

Sheffield, S. (1995). *Math and literature, K–3* (Vol. 2). Sausalito, CA: Math Solutions Publications.

Silver, E. A., Smith, M. S., & Nelson, B. S. (1995). The QUASAR project: Equity concerns meet mathematics education reform in the middle school. In W. G. Secada, E. Fennema, & L. B. Adajian (Eds.), *New directions for equity in mathematics education* (pp. 9–56). New York: Cambridge University Press.

Silver, E. A., & Stein, M. K. (1996). The QUASAR project: The "revolution of the possible" in mathematics instructional reform in urban middle schools. *Urban Education, 30,* 476–521.

Simon, M. A. (1995). Reconstructing mathematics pedagogy from a constructivist perspective. *Journal for Research in School Mathematics, 26,* 114–145.

Skemp, R. (1978). Relational understanding and instrumental understanding. *Arithmetic Teacher, 26*(3), 9–15.

Smith, J. P., III. (1996). Efficacy and teaching mathematics by telling: A challenge for reform. *Journal for Research in Mathematics Education, 27,* 387–402.

Steffe, L. (1988). Children's construction of number sequences and multiplying schemes. In J. C. Hiebert & M. J. Behr (Eds.), *Number concepts and operations in the middle grades* (pp. 119–140). Mahwah, NJ: Erlbaum.

Stein, M. K., Grover, B. W., & Henningsen, M. (1996). Building student capacity for mathematical thinking and reasoning: An analysis of mathematical tasks used in reform classrooms. *American Educational Research Journal, 33,* 455–488.

Stein, M. K., & Lane, S. (1996). Instructional tasks and the development of student capacity to think and reason: An analysis of the relationship between teaching and learning in a reform mathematics project. *Educational Research and Evaluation, 2,* 50–58.

Steinberg, R. M. (1985). Instruction on derived facts strategies in addition and subtraction. *Journal for Research in Mathematics Education, 16,* 337–355.

Stenmark, J. K. (1989). *Assessment alternatives in mathematics: An overview of assessment techniques that promote learning*. Berkeley: EQUALS, University of California.

Stenmark, J. K. (Ed.). (1991). *Mathematics assessment: Myths, models, good questions, and practical suggestions*. Reston, VA: National Council of Teachers of Mathematics.

Stoessiger, R., & Edmunds, J. (1992). *Natural learning and mathematics*. Portsmouth, NH: Heinemann.

Strutchens, M. E., & Blume, G. W. (1997). What do students know about geometry? In P. A. Kenney & E. A. Silver (Eds.), *Results from the sixth mathematics assessment of the National Assessment of Educational Progress* (pp. 165–193). Reston, VA: National Council of Teachers of Mathematics.

Theissen, D., Matthias, M., & Smith, J. (1998). *The wonderful world of mathematics: A critically annotated list of childrens' books in mathematics* (2nd ed.). Reston, VA: National Council of Teachers of Mathematics.

Thompson, C. S. (1990). Place value and larger numbers. In J. N. Payne (Ed.), *Mathematics for the young child* (pp. 89–108). Reston, VA: National Council of Teachers of Mathematics.

Thompson, C. S., & Hendrickson, A. D. (1986). Verbal addition and subtraction problems: Some difficulties and some solutions. *Arithmetic Teacher, 33*(7), 21–25.

Thompson, C. S., & Van de Walle, J. A. (1984). The power of 10. *Arithmetic Teacher, 32*(3), 6–11.

Thompson, P. W. (1994). Concrete materials and teaching for mathematical understanding. *Arithmetic Teacher, 41,* 556–558.

Thompson, P. W., & Thompson, A. G. (1994). Talking about rates conceptually, Part 1: A teacher's struggle. *Journal for Research in Mathematics Education, 25,* 279–303.

Thornton, C. A. (1982). Doubles up—easy! *Arithmetic Teacher, 29*(8), 20.

Thornton, C. A. (1990). Strategies for the basic facts. In J. N. Payne (Ed.), *Mathematics for the young child* (pp. 133–151). Reston, VA: National Council of Teachers of Mathematics.

Thornton, C. A., & Bley, N. S. (Eds.). (1994). *Windows of opportunity: Mathematics for students with special needs*. Reston, VA: National Council of Teachers of Mathematics.

Thornton, C. A., & Noxon, C. (1977). *Look into the facts* (4 vols.). Chicago: Creative Publications.

Thornton, C. A., & Toohey, M. A. (1984). *A matter of facts* (4 vols.). Chicago: Creative Publications.

Trafton, P. R., & Claus, A. S. (1994). A changing curriculum for a changing age. In C. A. Thornton & N. S. Bley (Eds.), *Win-*

dows of opportunity: Mathematics for students with special needs (pp. 19–39). Reston, VA: National Council of Teachers of Mathematics.

Tsuruda, G. (1994). *Putting it together: Middle school math in transition.* Portsmouth, NH: Heinemann.

Tyrrell, J., Brown, C., Ellis, J., Fox, R., Kinley, R., & Reilly, B. (1994). Gender and mathematics: Equal access to successful learning. In J. Neyland (Ed.), *Mathematics education: A handbook for teachers* (Vol. 1, pp. 330–347). Wellington, New Zealand: Wellington College of Education.

Tzur, R. (1999). An integrated study of children's construction of improper fractions and the teacher's role in promoting learning. *Journal for Research in Mathematics Education, 30,* 390–416.

University of Chicago School Mathematics Project. (1999, Spring). Frequently asked questions about our materials. *UCSMP Newsletter, 25,* 2–3.

U.S. Department of Education, Office of Educational Research and Improvement. (1996). *Pursuing excellence: A study of U.S. eighth-grade mathematics and science teaching, learning, curriculum, and achievement in international context.* NCES 97–198. Washington, DC: U.S. Government Printing Office.

U.S. Department of Education, Office of Educational Research and Improvement. (1997a). *Introduction to TIMSS.* Washington, DC: U.S. Government Printing Office.

U.S. Department of Education, Office of Educational Research and Improvement. (1997b). *Moderator's guide to eighth-grade mathematics lessons: United States, Japan, and Germany.* Washington, DC: U.S. Government Printing Office.

U.S. Department of Education, Office of Educational Research and Improvement. (1997c). *Pursuing excellence: A study of U.S. fourth-grade mathematics and science achievement in international context.* NCES 97–255. Washington, DC: U.S. Government Printing Office.

Usiskin, Z. (1988). Conceptions of school algebra and uses of variables. In A. F. Coxford (Ed.), *The ideas of algebra, K–12* (pp. 8–19). Reston, VA: National Council of Teachers of Mathematics.

Usiskin, Z. (1993). If everybody counts, why do so few survive? In G. Cuevas & M. Driscol (Eds.), *Reaching all students with mathematics* (pp. 7–22). Reston, VA: National Council of Teachers of Mathematics.

Usiskin, Z. (1999). The mathematically promising and the mathematically gifted. In L. J. Sheffield (Ed.), *Developing mathematically promising students* (pp. 57–69). Reston, VA: National Council of Teachers of Mathematics.

von Glasersfeld, E., (1990). An exposition of constructivism: Why some like it radical. In R. B. Davis, C. A. Maher, & N. Noddings (Eds.), *Constructivist views on the teaching and learning of mathematics* (pp. 19–29). Reston, VA: National Council of Teachers of Mathematics.

Welchman-Tischler, R. (1992). *How to use children's literature to teach mathematics.* Reston, VA: National Council of Teachers of Mathematics.

Wheatley, G. H., & Hersberger, J. (1986). A calculator estimation activity. In H. Schoen (Ed.), *Estimation and mental computation* (pp. 182–185). Reston, VA: National Council of Teachers of Mathematics.

Whitin, D. J., & Whitin, P. E. (1998). The "write" way to mathematical understanding. In L. J. Morrow (Ed.), *The teaching and learning of algorithms in school mathematics* (pp. 161–169). Reston, VA: National Council of Teachers of Mathematics.

Whitin, D. J., & Wilde, S. (1992). *Read any good math lately? Children's books for mathematical learning, K–6.* Portsmouth, NH: Heinemann.

Whitin, D. J., & Wilde, S. (1995). *It's the story that counts: More children's books for mathematical learning, K–6.* Portsmouth, NH: Heinemann.

Willoughby, S. S. (1990). *Mathematics education in a changing world.* Alexandria, VA: Association for Supervision and Curriculum Development.

Winter, M. J., Lappan, G., Phillips, E., & Fitzgerald, W. (1986). *Middle grades mathematics project: Spatial visualization.* Menlo Park, CA: AWL Supplemental.

Wirtz, R. (1974). *Mathematics for everyone.* Washington, DC: Curriculum Development Associates.

Wood, T., Cobb, P., Yackel, E., & Dillon, D. (Eds.). (1993). *Rethinking elementary school mathematics: Insights and issues (Journal for Research in Mathematics Education* Monograph No. 6). Reston, VA: National Council of Teachers of Mathematics.

Wood, T., & Sellers, P. (1996). Assessment of a problem-centered mathematics program: Third grade. *Journal for Research in Mathematics Education, 27,* 337–353.

Wood, T., & Sellers, P. (1997). Deepening the analysis: Longitudinal assessment of a problem-centered mathematics program. *Journal for Research in Mathematics Education, 28,* 163–168.

Yackel, E., Cobb, P., Wood, T., Wheatley, G. H., & Merkel, G. (1990). The importance of social interaction in children's construction of mathematical knowledge. In T. J. Cooney (Ed.), *Teaching and learning mathematics in the 1990s* (pp. 12–21). Reston, VA: National Council of Teachers of Mathematics.

## Children's Literature

Anno, M. (1982). *Anno's counting house.* New York: Philomel Books.

Anno, M. (1994). *Anno's magic seeds.* New York: Philomel Books.

Anno, M., & Anno, M. (1983). *Anno's mysterious multiplying jar.* New York: Philomel Books.

Ash, R. (1996). *Incredible comparisons.* New York: Dorling Kindersley.

Briggs, R. (1970). *Jim and the beanstalk.* New York: Coward-McCann.

Carle, E. (1969). *The very hungry caterpillar.* New York: Putnam.

Chalmers, M. (1986). *Six dogs, twenty-three cats, forty-five mice, and one hundred sixteen spiders.* New York: HarperCollins.

Chwast, S. (1993). *The twelve circus rings.* San Diego, CA: Gulliver Books.

Clement, R. (1991). *Counting on Frank.* Milwaukee: Gareth Stevens.

Cushman, R. (1991). *Do you wanna bet? Your chance to find out about probability.* New York: Clarion Books.

Dee, R. (1988). *Two ways to count to ten.* New York: Holt.

Friedman, A. (1994). *The king's commissioners.* New York: Scholastic.

Gag, W. (1928). *Millions of cats.* New York: Coward-McCann.

Giganti, P. (1988). *How many snails? A counting book.* New York: Greenwillow.

Giganti, P. (1992). *Each orange had 8 slices.* New York: Greenwillow.

Hoban, T. (1981). *More than one.* New York: Greenwillow.

Hutchins, P. (1986). *The doorbell rang.* New York: Greenwillow.

Jaspersohn, W. (1993). *Cookies.* Old Tappan, NJ: Macmillan.

Juster, N. (1961). *The phantom tollbooth.* New York: Random House.

Lobal, A. (1970). *Frog and Toad are friends.* New York: HarperCollins.

Mathews, L. (1979). *Gator pie.* New York: Dodd, Mead.

McKissack, P. C. (1992). *A million fish . . . more or less.* New York: Knopf.

Munsch, R. (1987). *Moira's birthday.* Toronto: Annick Press.

Myller, R. (1990). *How big is a foot?* New York: Dell.

Norton, M. (1953). *The borrowers.* Orlando, FL: Harcourt Brace.

Parker, T. (1984). *In one day.* Boston: Houghton Mifflin.

Pluckrose, H. (1988). *Pattern.* New York: Franklin Watts.

St. John, G. (1975). *How to count like a Martian.* New York: Walck.

Schwartz, D. M. (1985). *How much is a million?* New York: Lothrop, Lee & Shepard.

Schwartz, D. M. (1989). *If you made a million.* New York: Lothrop, Lee & Shepard.

Schwartz, D. M. (1999). *If you hopped like a frog.* New York: Scholastic.

Scieszka, J., & Smith, L. (1995). *Math curse.* New York: Viking Penguin.

Sharmat, M. W. (1979). *The 329th friend.* New York: Four Winds Press.

Silverstein, S. (1974). One inch tall. In *Where the sidewalk ends* (p. 55). New York: HarperCollins.

Tahan, M. (1993). *The man who counted: A collection of mathematical adventures.* (Trans. L. Clark & A. Reid). New York: Norton.

Wells, R. E. (1993). *Is a blue whale the biggest thing there is?* Morton Grove, IL: Whitman.

Wolkstein, D. (1972). *8,000 stones.* New York: Doubleday.

# Computer Software

Brøderbund. (1995a). *James discovers math.* Novato, CA: Author.

Brøderbund. (1995b). *Tabletop, Jr.* Novato, CA: Author.

Brøderbund. (1996a). *Kid pix.* Novato, CA: Author.

Brøderbund. (1996b). *Logical journey of the Zoombinis.* Novato, CA: Author.

Clements, D. H., & Meredith, J. S. (1994). *Turtle math.* Highgate Springs, VT: Logo Computer Systems.

Clements, D. H., & Sarama, J. (1995). *Shapes: Mathematical thinking.* Highgate Springs, VT: Logo Computer Systems.

Davidson & Associates. (n.d.). *Math for the real world.* Torrence, CA: Author.

Davidson & Associates. (n.d.). *Mega math blaster.* Torrence, CA: Author.

Edmark Corp. (1993). *Millie's math house.* Redmond, WA: Author.

Edmark Corp. (1996). *GeoComputer.* Redmond, WA: Author.

Education Development Center. (1991). *My travels with Gulliver.* Scotts Valley, CA: Wings for Learning.

EduQuest. (1994). *Math and more 3: Patterns on lattices.* Atlanta: IBM Corp.

EdVenture Software. (1997). *Gold medal mathematics.* Norwalk, CT: Author.

Gamco Education Software. (1994). *Word problem square off.* Clayton, MO: Siboney Learning Group.

Hickey, A. (1996). *Unifix software.* Rowley, MA: Didax Educational Resources.

Jazz Interactive. (n.d.). *Performance math.* Glenview, IL: Scott Foresman–Addison Wesley.

Key Curriculum Press. (1995). *The geometer's sketchpad* (Version 3.0). Emeryville, CA: Author.

Learning Co. (1996). *The new adventures of Jasper Woodbury.* Mahwah, NJ: Author.

Learning Co. (1999). *Kid pix 2.* Mahwah, NJ: Author.

LOGAL Educational Software and Systems. (1994a). *Geometry inventor.* Cambridge, MA: Author.

LOGAL Educational Software and Systems. (1994b). *The probability constructor.* Cambridge, MA: Author.

MacWarehouse. (1996). *Power Rangers ZEO: Power active math.* Lakewood, NJ: Author.

MECC. (1994). *TesselMania!* Minneapolis, MN: Author.

MECC. (1995a). *MathKeys: Geometry, Vol. 1.* Minneapolis, MN: Author.

MECC. (1995b). *MathKeys: Unlocking whole numbers, grades 3–5.* Minneapolis, MN: Author.

MECC. (1995c). *MathKeys: Unlocking probability* (Vols. 1 & 2). Minneapolis, MN: Author.

MECC. (1995d). *Math munchers deluxe.* Minneapolis, MN: Author.

MECC. (1995e). *TesselMania! Deluxe.* Minneapolis, MN: Author.

MECC. (1996a). *MathKeys: Unlocking fractions and decimals, grades 3–5.* Minneapolis, MN: Author.

MECC. (1996b). *MathKeys: Unlocking whole numbers, grades K–2.* Minneapolis, MN: Author.

O'Brien, T. C. (n.d.). *Teasers by Tobbs: Numbers and operations.* Pleasantville, NY: Sunburst Communications.

Pierian Spring Software. (1996). *CampOS math.* Portland, OR: Author.

SkillsBank Corp. (1996). *CornerStone mathematics, grades 3–8.* Baltimore, MD: Author.

SRA/McGraw-Hill. (1996). *The SRA cruncher.* Columbus, OH: Author.

Sunburst Communications. (1995). *Shape up.* Pleasantville, NY: Author.

Sunburst Communications. (n.d.). *The king's rule.* Pleasantville, NY: Author.

Sunburst Communications. (n.d.). *Super factory.* Pleasantville, NY: Author.

Tenth Planet. (1997). *Grouping and place value.* Pleasantville, NY: Sunburst Communications.

Tenth Planet. (1998a). *Combining and breaking apart numbers.* Pleasantville, NY: Sunburst Communications.

Tenth Planet. (1998b). *Fraction operations.* Pleasantville, NY: Sunburst Communications.

Tenth Planet. (1998c). *Number meanings and counting.* Pleasantville, NY: Sunburst Communications.

Tenth Planet. (1998d). *Representing fractions.* Pleasantville, NY: Sunburst Communications.

Texas Instruments. (1994). *Cabri geometry II.* Dallas: Author.

Tom Snyder Productions. (1993). *The graph club.* Watertown, MA: Author.

Tom Snyder Productions. (1998). *Fizz & Martina's math adventures: Lights, camera, fractions.* Watertown, MA: Author.

Tom Snyder Productions. (1999). *Prime time math.* Watertown, MA: Author.

Note: Page numbers followed by an *f* refer to figures.

similar figures in, 336, 337*f*
software, 322–323
three-dimensional symmetry in, 334, 334*f*
*Shapes* (Clements and Sarama), 322
*Shape Up* (Sunburst), 322
Sharing, in fractions instruction, 211
Sheffield, L. J., 461
Sheffield, Stephanie, 167
Show-Me Center, 54
Silver, E. A., 22
Silverstein, Shel, 275
Similar figures, 336, 337*f*
Simplest terms, for fractions, 225, 225*f*
Simulations, 359–361, 359*f*
*Six Dogs, Twenty-Three Cats, Forty-Five Mice, and One Hundred Sixteen Spiders* (Chalmers), 167
Skemp, R., 30
Skills
  assessment of, 62, 64, 65
  basic, 11, 16, 43, 56
  calculators and, 468
  differing levels of, in classroom, 439–440, 451
  practice in, 445
Slow learners, 455
Smith, M. S., 22
Social equity, 456–457
Socioeconomic status, and math, 456–457
Software
  dynamic geometry software. *See* Dynamic geometry software
  graphing, 380, 473
  instructional, 473–475
  selection guidelines, 475
  tool, 470
    *vs.* instructional, 473
Solids, building, 318–319, 319*f*, 320*f*
Spatial relationships, 91, 92–93, 92*f*, 93*f*
  and LD children, 454
Spatial sense, 308–309
  assessment of, 348–349
  as geometry standard, 311
Special needs, 451–452
Spheres, 327*t*
Spreadsheets, 472–473, 473*f*
  for graphs, 380, 390
  for proportions, 267
  for statistics, 377, 380
  variables in, 396, 397*f*
Square roots, 431–432, 431*f*
Standard deviation, 374
Standards
  content, 7
  in *Principles and Standards for School Mathematics,* 7–9, 41
  process, 7–9, 8*t*, 41
  state, 11, 78–79
Statistics, 352–353
  assessment in, 380–381
  descriptive, 372–377
  functions and, 407
  literature for, 381
  technology for, 377
Stem-and-leaf plots, 369–370, 370*f*, 373*f*
Stenmark, J. K., 76, 80
Story problems
  assessment with, 125
  for invented strategies, 173
  in upper grades, 123–126
Strategies
  for addition facts, 131–136
  for division facts, 143–144
  drill and practice of, 144–146
  efficient, for basic facts, 129
    practice of, 129–130
  for estimation, 200–204
  invented, 171–173
    for addition and subtraction, 175–177
    benefits of, 172–173
    definition of, 172
    development of, 173–174
    for division, 184–186, 186*f*

literature for, 189–190
  for multiplication, 180–183
  *vs.* traditional algorithms, 172
mental, for addition and subtraction, 177
for multiplication facts, 140–143
for "near" facts, 143–144
paper, for addition and subtraction, 177
for problem solving, 57–58
  for large numbers, 123–124
  for multistep problems, 124–125
for subtraction facts, 136–139
for test taking, 79
Strategy retrieval, 130, 145
Strategy selection, 130
Structured attribute materials, 363–364
Students
  assessment of. *See* Assessment
  attitudes of, toward math, 57, 58–59, 65, 75, 77. *See also* Attitudes
  diversity among
    in ability, 439–440, 450–451
    multiethnic and social, 456–458
  gender inequity, 459–460
  goals for, 4–5, 57–59, 450
  groups of, in classroom, 37, 77, 439–442
  involvement of, 50–51
  with learning disabilities, 451–455
  mathematically promising, 451, 461–462
  with mental disabilities, 455–456
  multicultural and social equity and, 456–457
  portfolios for, 79–80, 81*t*
  rubrics, student involvement with, 71
  in traditional classroom, 15, 16, 40–41
Subtraction
  algorithms for, 177–180, 180*f*
  basic facts in, 128
  comparison models for, 114–115, 114*f*
  of decimals, 256, 256*f*
  estimation strategies for
    compatible numbers in, 202, 203*f*
    front-end, 201, 201*f*
    rounding, 201–202
  of fractions, 229–232
  with integers, 426–428, 427*f*
  invented strategies for, 175–177
  part-part-whole models for, 113–114, 113*f*
    think-addition in, 114
  strategies for
    back down through 10, 138, 138*f*
    build up through 10, 137–138, 138*f*
    for sums greater than 10, 137–139, 137*f*
    for sums to 10, 137
    think-addition in, 136–137, 136*f*, 138–139, 139*f*
  in traditional textbook, adaptation of, 51, 52*f*
  word problems for, 111–112
    types of, 109–111, 110*f*
Suggestions, in problem solving, 47–49
*Super Factory* (Sunburst Communications), 474
Symbolism
  and computers, 471
  for exponents, 419–420
  of fractional parts, 213*f*, 214–215
  models for, 35, 108–109
  for numbers, 89–90, 159–161, 160*f*, 162*f*
  for operations, 108–109, 109*f*, 118–119
  in *Principles and Standards,* 9
  in procedural knowledge, 32
  written, and relational understanding, 34, 34*f*
Symmetry
  line, 332–333, 332*f*, 333*f*, 349
  rotational, 333, 334, 334*f*, 335*f*
  in three-dimensional shapes, 334, 334*f*

**T**

Table representations, of functions, 404, 407, 408*f*
Tables of data
  to learn problem-solving strategies, 58
  and spreadsheets, for proportions, 267, 268*f*

# Blackline Masters and Materials Construction Tips

Permission is given to reproduce any of the Blackline Masters for classroom use. Pages are perforated.

## SUGGESTIONS FOR USE AND CONSTRUCTION OF MATERIALS

### Card Stock Materials

A good way to have many materials made quickly and easily for students is to have them duplicated on card stock at a photocopy store. Card stock is a heavy paper that comes in a variety of colors. It is also called *cover stock* or *index stock*. The price is about twice that of paper.

Card stock can be laminated and then cut into smaller pieces, if desired. The laminate adheres very well. Laminate first, and then cut into pieces afterward. Otherwise you will need to cut each piece twice.

Materials are best kept in plastic bags with zip-type closures. Freezer bags are recommended for durability. Punch a hole near the top of the bag so that you do not store air. Lots of small bags can be stuffed into the largest bags. You can always see what you have stored in the bags.

The following list is a suggestion for materials that can be made from card stock using the masters in this section. Quantity suggestions are also given.

**Dot Cards**

One complete set of cards will serve four to six children. Duplicate each set in a different color so that mixed sets can be separated easily. Laminate and then cut with a paper cutter.

**Five-Frames and Ten-Frames**

Five-frames and ten-frames are best duplicated on light-colored card stock. Do not laminate; if you do, the mats will curl and counters will slide around.

**10 × 10 Multiplication Array**

Make one per student in any color. Lamination is suggested. Provide each student with an L-shaped piece of tagboard.

**Base-Ten Pieces (Centimeter Grid)**

Use the grid (number 11) to make a master as directed. Run copies on white card stock. One sheet will make 4 hundreds and 10 tens or 4 hundreds and a lot of ones. Mount the printed card stock on white poster board using either a dry-mount press or permanent spray adhesive. (Spray adhesive can be purchased in art supply stores. It is very effective but messy to handle.) Cut into pieces with a paper cutter. For the tens and ones pieces, it is recommended that you mount the index stock onto *mount board* or *illustration board,* also available in art supply stores. This material is thicker and will make the pieces easier to handle. It is recommended that you *not* laminate the base-ten pieces. A kit consisting of 10 hundreds, 30 tens, and 30 ones is adequate for each student or pair of students.

### Bean Stick Base-Ten Pieces

Use dried beans (great northern, pinto, etc.) to make bean sticks. Craft sticks can be purchased in craft stores in boxes of 500. Use white glue (such as Elmer's) or a glue gun. Also dribble a row of glue over the beans to keep them from splitting off the sticks. (The white glue dries clear.) For hundreds, use the master mounted on poster board.

### Little Ten-Frames

There are two masters for these materials. One has full ten-frames and the other has 1 to 9 dots, including two with 5 dots. Copy the 1-to-9 master on one color of card stock and the full ten-frames on another. Cut off most of the excess stock (do not trim) and then laminate. Cut into little ten-frames. Each set consists of 20 pieces: 10 full ten-frames and 10 of the 1-to-9 pieces, including 2 fives. Make a set for each child.

### Place-Value Mat (with Ten-Frames)

Mats can be duplicated on any pastel card stock. It is recommended that you not laminate these because they tend to curl and counters slide around too much. Make one for every child.

One way to make a three-place place-value mat is simply to tape a half-sheet of blank card stock to the left edge of a two-place mat. Use strapping tape (filament tape used for packages). The tape will act as a hinge and permit the extra piece to be folded under for storage.

### Circular Fraction Pieces

First make three copies of each page of the master. Cut the disks apart and tape onto blank pages with three of the same type on a page. You will then have a separate master for each size with three full circles per master. Duplicate each master on a different color card stock. Laminate and then cut the circles out. A kit for one or two students should have two circles of each size piece.

### Hundredths Disk

These disks can be made on paper but are much more satisfying on card stock. Duplicate the master on two contrasting colors. Laminate and cut the circles and also the slot on the dotted line. The smiley face is used as a decimal point on the desktop. Make a set for each student. It's easy and worthwhile.

### Tangrams and Five Easy Pieces

Both tangrams and Five Easy Pieces should be copied on card stock and then laminated. Especially for younger children, the card stock should first be mounted on poster board to make the pieces a bit thicker and easier to put together in puzzles. You will want one set of each per student. Keep individual sets in plastic bags.

### Woozle Cards

Copy the Woozle Card master on white or off-white card stock. You need two copies per set. Before laminating, color one set one color and the other a different color. An easy way to color the cards is to make one pass around the inside of each Woozle, leaving the rest of the creature white. If you color the entire Woozle, the dots may not show up. Make one set for every four students.

# Transparencies and Overhead Models

A copy of any page can be made into a transparency with thermal transparency masters and a transparency machine. (Check with your media specialist.) Photocopiers can also be used to make transparencies.

Some masters make fine transparency mats to use for demonstration purposes on the overhead. The 10 × 10 array, the blank hundreds board, and the large geoboard are examples. The five-frame and ten-frame work well with counters. The place-value mat can be used with strips and squares or with counters and cups directly on the overhead. The missing-part blank and the record blanks for the four algorithms are pages that you may wish to use as write-on transparencies. Of course, you will want to copy these and many other pages on paper for your students to write on.

A transparency of the 10,000 grid is the easiest way there is to show 10,000 or to model four-place decimal numbers. You will need to be careful in making the transparency. If too dark, the squares run together, and if too light, you will find that some squares do not reproduce. It can be done! If you pull the overhead away from the screen until the square is as large as possible, each tiny square can be seen across the average room and individual squares or strips of squares can be colored with a pen.

All of the line and dot grids are useful to have available as transparencies. You may find it a good idea to make several copies of each and keep them in a folder where you can get to them easily.

For the Woozle Cards, dot cards, and little ten-frames, make a reduction of the master on a photocopy machine. Then make transparencies of the small cards, cut them apart, and use them on the overhead. The dot cards and little ten-frames are best on a colored transparency. Use two colors for the little ten-frames. The Woozle Cards are best on a clear transparency. Color them with a permanent transparency marker.

Dot cards—2

Dot cards—3

Dot cards—4

*Five-frame— 7*

Ten-frame—8

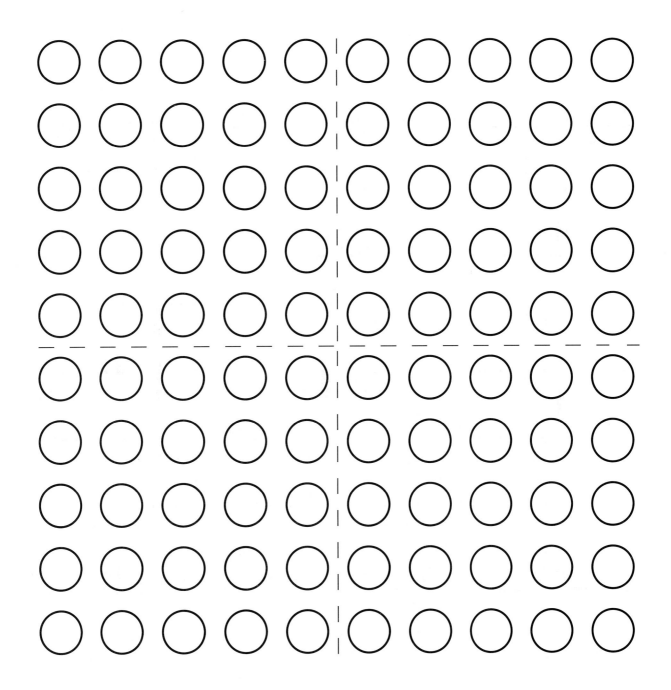

10 x 10 multiplication array—9

Copyright © 2001 by Addison Wesley Longman, Inc.

Missing-part blanks—10

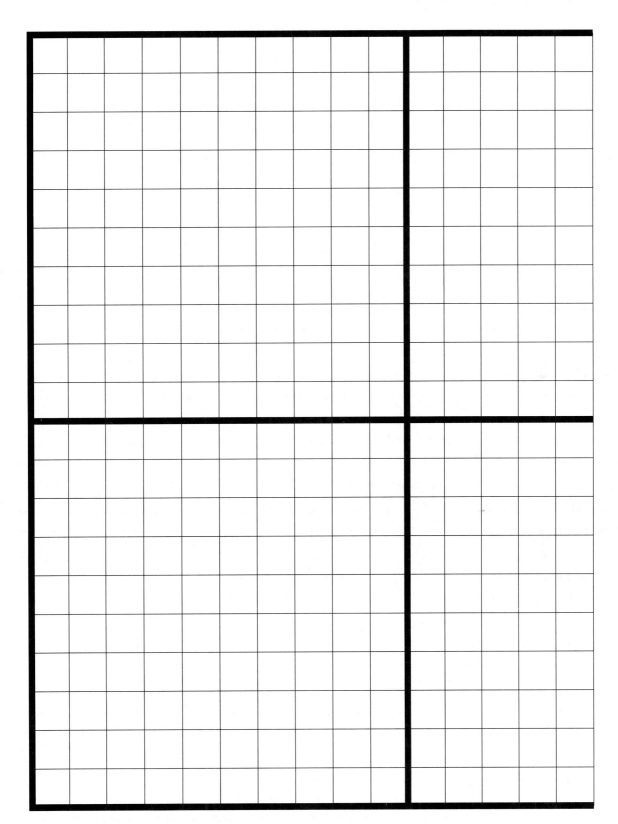

1. Make two copies of this page. Cut out the grid from each copy.
2. Overlap the two grids, and tape onto a blank sheet to form a 20-by-25-cm grid with 4 complete hundreds squares and 2 rows of 5 tens each.
3. Use this as a master to make copies on card stock.

*Base-ten materials grid—11*

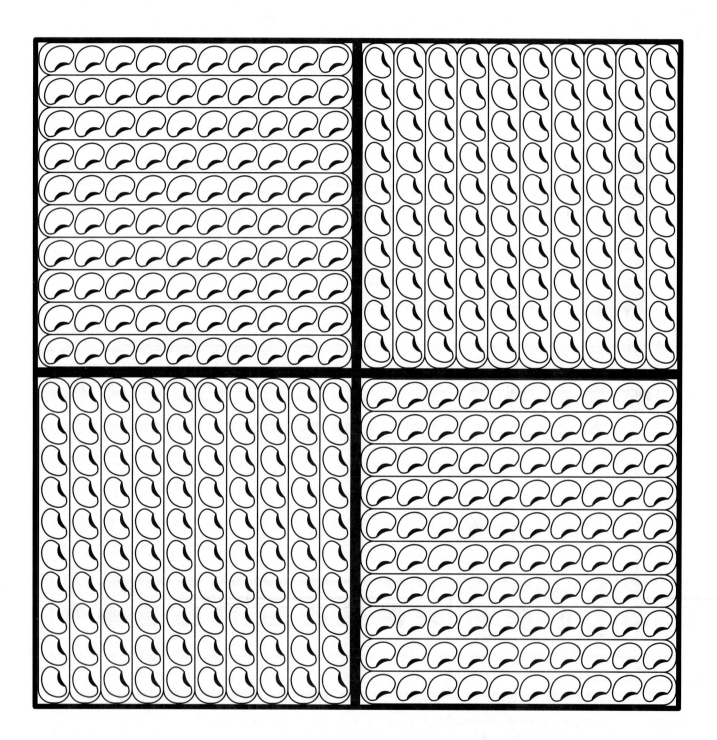

*Hundreds master for bean stick base-ten pieces—12*

Little ten-frames—14

Base-ten grid paper—16

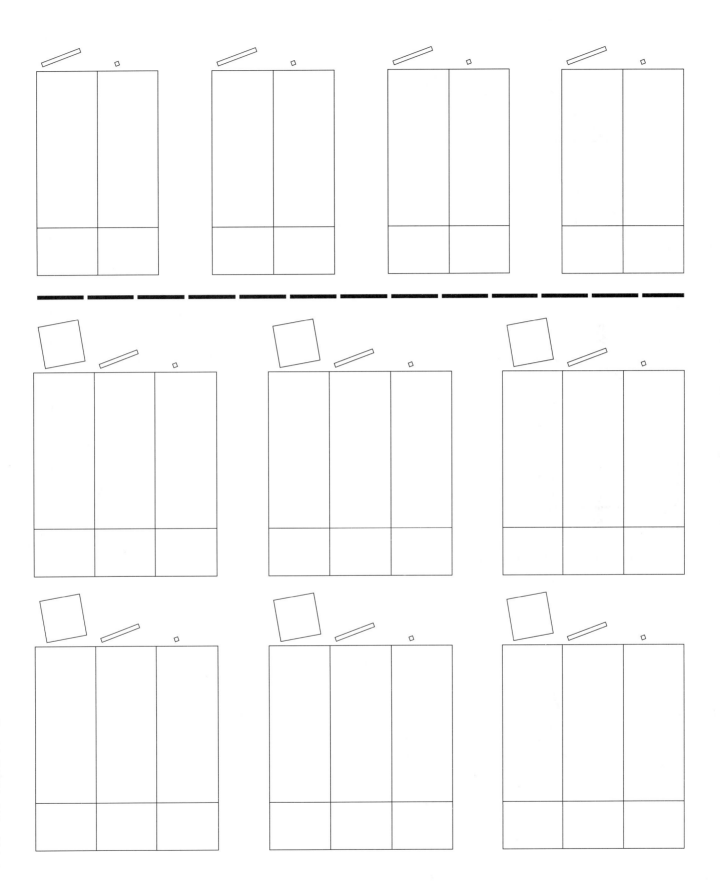

Addition and subtraction record blanks—17

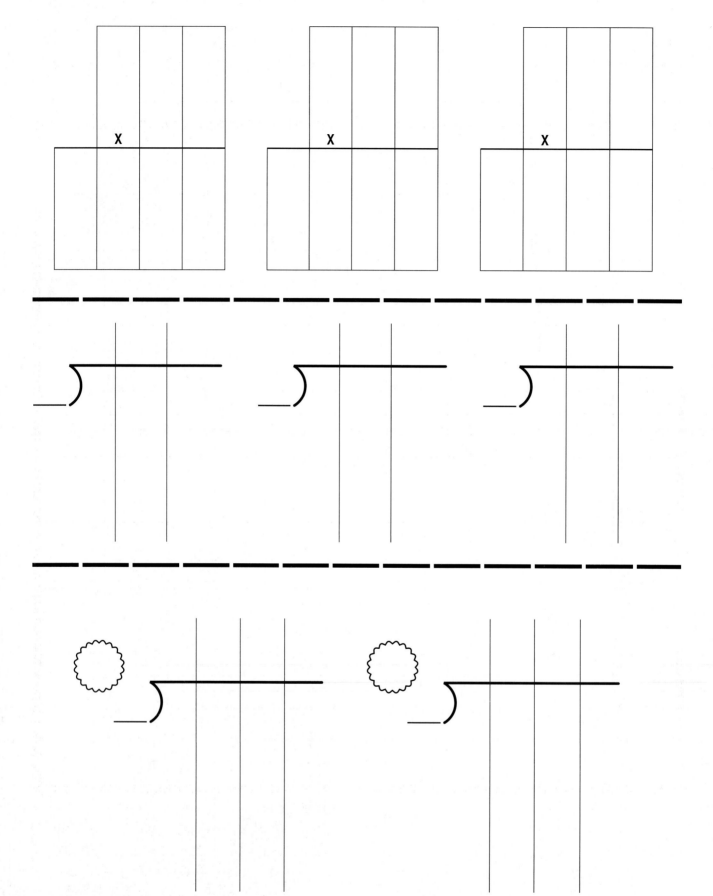

*Multiplication and division record blanks—18*

Blank hundreds or 0–99 chart (10 × 10 square)—19

| 0 | 1 | 2 | 3 | 4 | 5 | 6 | 7 | 8 | 9 |
|---|---|---|---|---|---|---|---|---|---|
| 10 | 11 | 12 | 13 | 14 | 15 | 16 | 17 | 18 | 19 |
| 20 | 21 | 22 | 23 | 24 | 25 | 26 | 27 | 28 | 29 |
| 30 | 31 | 32 | 33 | 34 | 35 | 36 | 37 | 38 | 39 |
| 40 | 41 | 42 | 43 | 44 | 45 | 46 | 47 | 48 | 49 |
| 50 | 51 | 52 | 53 | 54 | 55 | 56 | 57 | 58 | 59 |
| 60 | 61 | 62 | 63 | 64 | 65 | 66 | 67 | 68 | 69 |
| 70 | 71 | 72 | 73 | 74 | 75 | 76 | 77 | 78 | 79 |
| 80 | 81 | 82 | 83 | 84 | 85 | 86 | 87 | 88 | 89 |
| 90 | 91 | 92 | 93 | 94 | 95 | 96 | 97 | 98 | 99 |

| 0 | 1 | 2 | 3 | 4 | 5 | 6 | 7 | 8 | 9 |
|---|---|---|---|---|---|---|---|---|---|
| 10 | 11 | 12 | 13 | 14 | 15 | 16 | 17 | 18 | 19 |
| 20 | 21 | 22 | 23 | 24 | 25 | 26 | 27 | 28 | 29 |
| 30 | 31 | 32 | 33 | 34 | 35 | 36 | 37 | 38 | 39 |
| 40 | 41 | 42 | 43 | 44 | 45 | 46 | 47 | 48 | 49 |
| 50 | 51 | 52 | 53 | 54 | 55 | 56 | 57 | 58 | 59 |
| 60 | 61 | 62 | 63 | 64 | 65 | 66 | 67 | 68 | 69 |
| 70 | 71 | 72 | 73 | 74 | 75 | 76 | 77 | 78 | 79 |
| 80 | 81 | 82 | 83 | 84 | 85 | 86 | 87 | 88 | 89 |
| 90 | 91 | 92 | 93 | 94 | 95 | 96 | 97 | 98 | 99 |

| 0 | 1 | 2 | 3 | 4 | 5 | 6 | 7 | 8 | 9 |
|---|---|---|---|---|---|---|---|---|---|
| 10 | 11 | 12 | 13 | 14 | 15 | 16 | 17 | 18 | 19 |
| 20 | 21 | 22 | 23 | 24 | 25 | 26 | 27 | 28 | 29 |
| 30 | 31 | 32 | 33 | 34 | 35 | 36 | 37 | 38 | 39 |
| 40 | 41 | 42 | 43 | 44 | 45 | 46 | 47 | 48 | 49 |
| 50 | 51 | 52 | 53 | 54 | 55 | 56 | 57 | 58 | 59 |
| 60 | 61 | 62 | 63 | 64 | 65 | 66 | 67 | 68 | 69 |
| 70 | 71 | 72 | 73 | 74 | 75 | 76 | 77 | 78 | 79 |
| 80 | 81 | 82 | 83 | 84 | 85 | 86 | 87 | 88 | 89 |
| 90 | 91 | 92 | 93 | 94 | 95 | 96 | 97 | 98 | 99 |

| 0 | 1 | 2 | 3 | 4 | 5 | 6 | 7 | 8 | 9 |
|---|---|---|---|---|---|---|---|---|---|
| 10 | 11 | 12 | 13 | 14 | 15 | 16 | 17 | 18 | 19 |
| 20 | 21 | 22 | 23 | 24 | 25 | 26 | 27 | 28 | 29 |
| 30 | 31 | 32 | 33 | 34 | 35 | 36 | 37 | 38 | 39 |
| 40 | 41 | 42 | 43 | 44 | 45 | 46 | 47 | 48 | 49 |
| 50 | 51 | 52 | 53 | 54 | 55 | 56 | 57 | 58 | 59 |
| 60 | 61 | 62 | 63 | 64 | 65 | 66 | 67 | 68 | 69 |
| 70 | 71 | 72 | 73 | 74 | 75 | 76 | 77 | 78 | 79 |
| 80 | 81 | 82 | 83 | 84 | 85 | 86 | 87 | 88 | 89 |
| 90 | 91 | 92 | 93 | 94 | 95 | 96 | 97 | 98 | 99 |

| 0 | 1 | 2 | 3 | 4 | 5 | 6 | 7 | 8 | 9 |
|---|---|---|---|---|---|---|---|---|---|
| 10 | 11 | 12 | 13 | 14 | 15 | 16 | 17 | 18 | 19 |
| 20 | 21 | 22 | 23 | 24 | 25 | 26 | 27 | 28 | 29 |
| 30 | 31 | 32 | 33 | 34 | 35 | 36 | 37 | 38 | 39 |
| 40 | 41 | 42 | 43 | 44 | 45 | 46 | 47 | 48 | 49 |
| 50 | 51 | 52 | 53 | 54 | 55 | 56 | 57 | 58 | 59 |
| 60 | 61 | 62 | 63 | 64 | 65 | 66 | 67 | 68 | 69 |
| 70 | 71 | 72 | 73 | 74 | 75 | 76 | 77 | 78 | 79 |
| 80 | 81 | 82 | 83 | 84 | 85 | 86 | 87 | 88 | 89 |
| 90 | 91 | 92 | 93 | 94 | 95 | 96 | 97 | 98 | 99 |

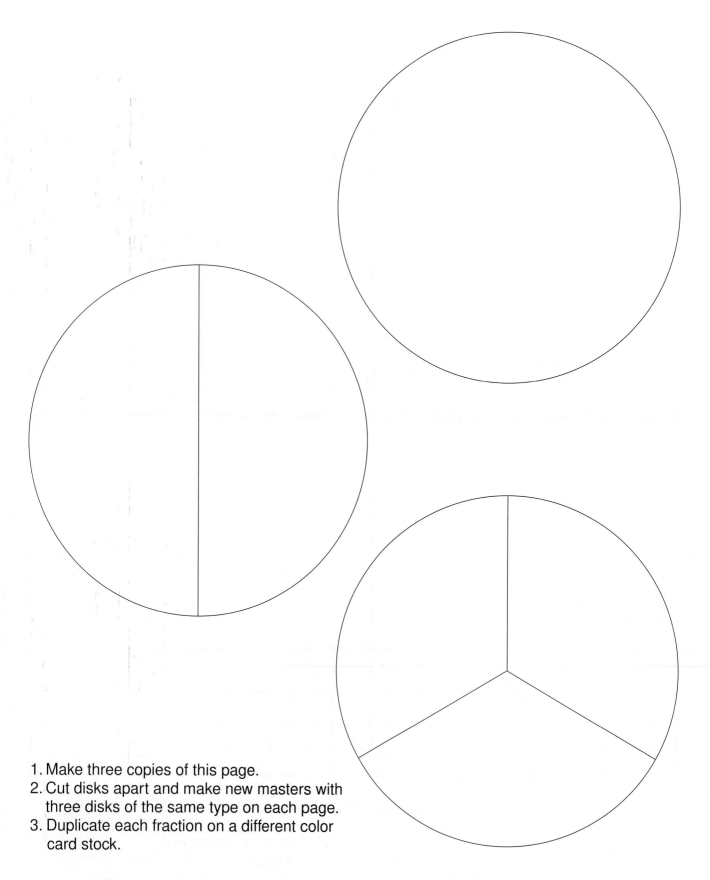

1. Make three copies of this page.
2. Cut disks apart and make new masters with three disks of the same type on each page.
3. Duplicate each fraction on a different color card stock.

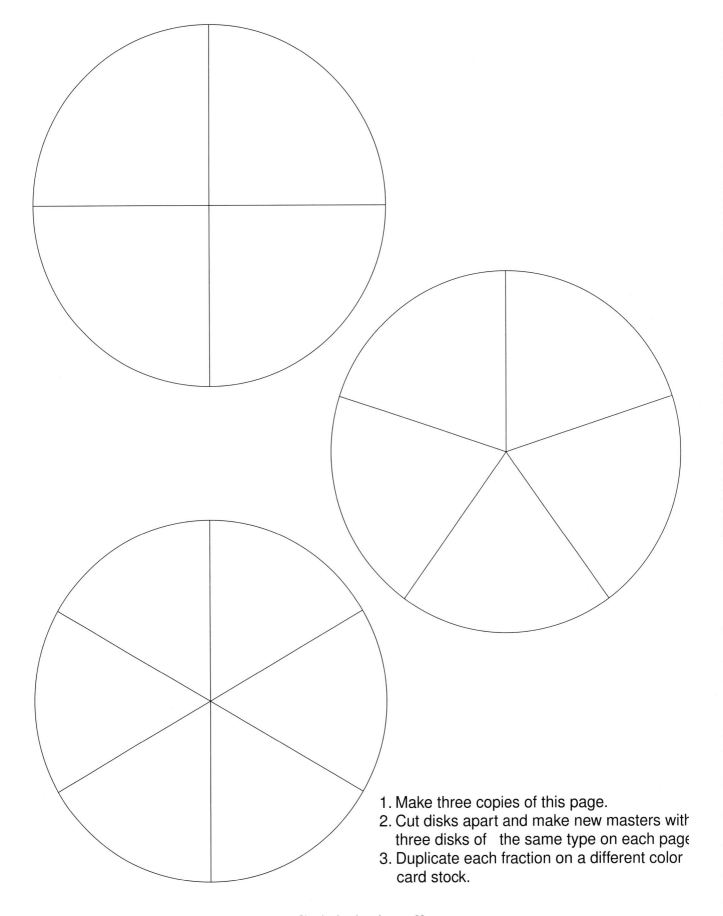

1. Make three copies of this page.
2. Cut disks apart and make new masters with three disks of  the same type on each page
3. Duplicate each fraction on a different color card stock.

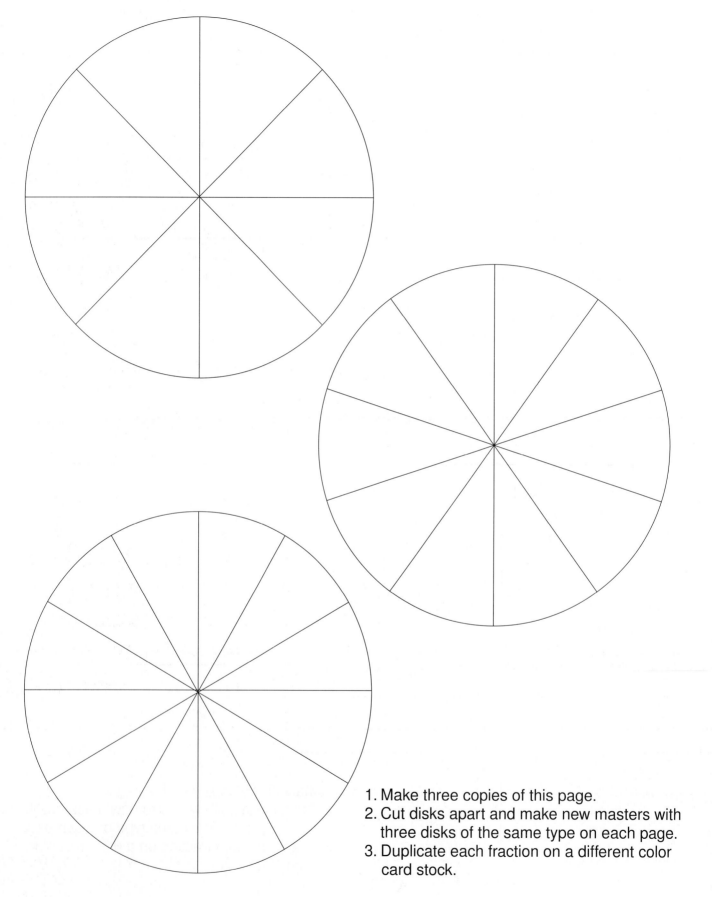

1. Make three copies of this page.
2. Cut disks apart and make new masters with three disks of the same type on each page.
3. Duplicate each fraction on a different color card stock.

*Circular fraction pieces—24*

Hundredths disk—26

2-cm square grid—28

1-cm square grid—29

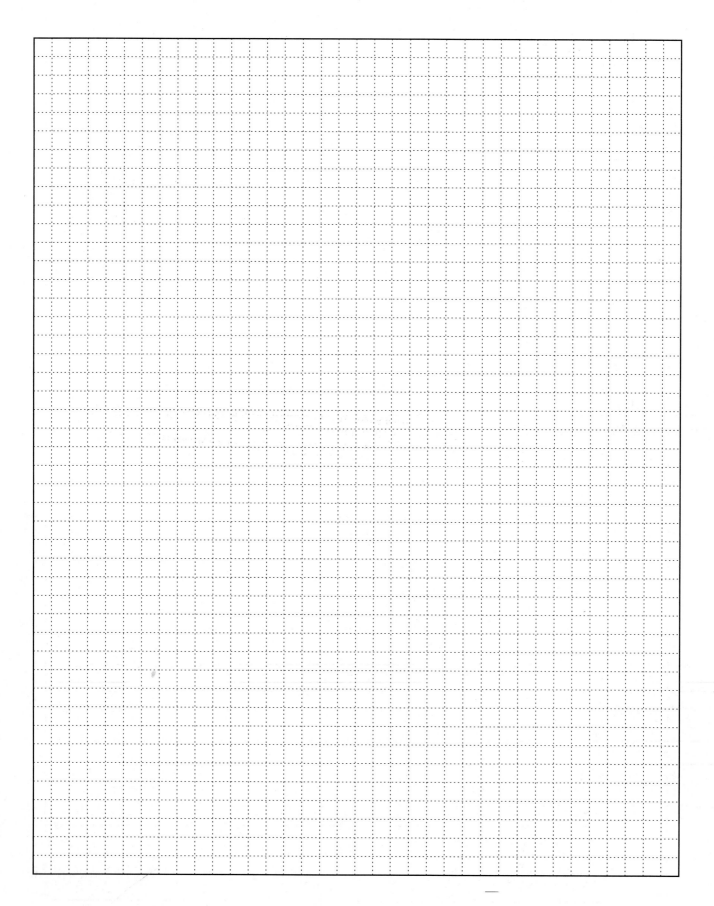

0.5-cm square grid—30